INTERNATIONAL HUMAN RIGHTS

LAW, POLICY, AND PROCESS

INTERNATIONAL HUMAN RIGHTS

FRANK NEWMAN

Justice, Supreme Court of California (retired)
Ralston Professor of International Law (emeritus)
University of California Law School, Berkeley

DAVID WEISSBRODT

Briggs & Morgan Professor of Law
University of Minnesota Law School

ANDERSON PUBLISHING CO./CINCINNATI

NEWMAN & WEISSBRODT, INTERNATIONAL HUMAN RIGHTS: LAW, POLICY, AND PROCESS

Library of Congress Cataloging-in-Publication Data

Newman, Frank C.
ternational human rights: law, policy, and process / Frank Newman, David Weissbrodt.
p. cm.
companied by Selected international human rights instruments.
cludes bibliographical references.
BN 0-87084-368-0
Human rights. I. Weissbrodt, David S. II. Title. III. Title: Selected international human
ts instruments.
.4.N39   1990   90-902
81—dc20   CIP

CONTENTS

PREFACE

This book provides an introduction to human rights law, policy, and process. At the outset readers may ask (1) why they should study international human rights and (2) whether international human rights law is really "law." This preface responds to those questions, commonly raised in the context of human rights studies.

This preface also will describe the book's organizational design and discuss the authors' rationale for choosing their approach.

Why study international human rights?

There are several reasons for pursuing that study. *First*, the course deals with many concerns that are the focus of civil liberties or civil rights law. People whose liberties and rights are violated (or threatened) need help. Often, part of the help they need is legal assistance. Readers of this book should expect to learn about laws, policies, and procedures designed to protect people against torture, inhuman treatment, arbitrary killing, discrimination, failure to take steps to provide adequate food and shelter, and countless other abuses — wherever they may occur.

Second, lawyers and law students who expect to practice civil liberties or civil rights law should know that if they do not prevail in a national forum — judicial, legislative, or administrative — there may be an international tribunal or other body to which they can take their case. Even the U.S. Supreme Court may not be the last resort for advocates working to protect important rights. Advocates should also be aware that there are arguments based on international law that ought to be raised in federal and state courts as well as in legislatures and administrative agencies. Civil liberties and civil rights attorneys arguably breach their professional responsibility if they practice without knowing about the international laws and procedures. At very least those attorneys would not accord their clients the most zealous representation possible.

The present status of international human rights law is comparable to earlier stages of civil liberties and civil rights law in the U.S. A century or more ago the impact of the Bill of Rights in the U.S. Constitution and similar clauses in state constitutions was minimal. It took a long time to develop protections for U.S. citizens and to train the legal profession to use those protections effectively. The process of legal development and education included adoption of the Bill of Rights of 1791 and post-war amendments to the Constitution from 1865 to 1970, including the Equal Protection Clause. It was not until the 20th Century that the U.S. Supreme Court decided the Bill of Rights applied to states as well as the federal government and that *Brown v. Board of Education*, 349 U.S. 483 (1954), finally declared segregated schools to be a violation of the Equal Protection Clause. That decision, followed by the Civil Rights Movement of the 1960's, the struggle for equal rights for women, and other pressures during the Vietnam era, demanded greater protection for liberties and rights.

By comparison, international human rights law has developed with more deliberate speed. The invigorated, worldwide, human rights movement was instituted in 1945 by the U.N. Charter, was articulated in 1948 by the Universal Declaration of Human Rights (the first segment of the International Bill of Human Rights), and was dramatically extended in succeeding years by scores of treaties and other instruments. In fact, there now exist more protections for human rights under international law in many cases than the protections found under U.S. law. Lawyers and others who practice in the area of civil liberties and civil rights should be trained to invoke those broader protections.

Third, this book should help train human rights professionals and assist readers to be more effective human rights advocates. Lawyers, law students, and others can help victims and work with international law in many ways. They can assist clients affected by human rights abuses. They can work also as government officials, members of human rights organizations, informal groups, and sometimes as individuals, working alone. They can litigate, advocate in non-adjudicative forums, negotiate, draft, write letters, advise, and participate in investigations throughout the world. As individuals they can petition, protest, speak, and write. This book considers those functions and helps evaluate their worth.

There are hundreds of international human rights jobs in international and national organizations, in intergovernmental organizations, and elsewhere. Many lawyers apply human rights law as part of their general practice in representing applicants for asylum or refugee status, for example, or in pursuing remedies for victims of human rights violations.

Readers should not, however, pursue this study with the expectation that paid employment will generally be available, after graduation, in the field of human rights. The work of volunteers is crucial and an increasing number of lawyers volunteer for *pro bono* work in human rights. Lawyers, students, and others can write letters to governments accused of rights violations, carry out research on rights abuses, and assist in publicizing violations. The work is invaluable, not only because volunteers are helping victims, but also because they are saying something about themselves. Writing letters, investigating wrongs, and speaking out are better indeed than remaining silent in the face of repression. As Elie Weisel said when he accepted the Nobel Peace Prize, it is sometimes necesary to speak truth to power. The study of human rights law provides a foundation for such activity. Similarly, learning to use international procedures provides mechanisms for action. While many volunteers may not need an understanding of the legal bases for their efforts, those familiar with law and procedure may help develop, improve, and even direct the work of others.

Fourth, as with any course about legal systems different from one's own, this book provides insights that often encourage a renewed understanding of one's own system. Human rights law, like international law generally, has much in common with other kinds of law, such as torts and constitutional law. The main focus is not, however, on appellate court opinions, as it is in many other courses. Instead, the course focuses on the U.N. Charter, the International Bill of Human Rights, the Charter of the Organization of American States, and many related instruments. The reader will learn to apply those sources to various fact situations and will learn how to advocate effectively for compliance with human rights norms.

Fifth, a course in international human rights law covers one aspect of international law and deals with several of the same issues: the nature of international law; drafting, ratification, and interpretation of treaties; customary international law; intergovernmental and nongovernmental organizations; the protection of aliens; and international factfinding.

Is international human rights law really law?

This book deals with a question that often arises in international law generally: whether international law is really law. The book permits readers to develop their own responses to that question. Yet it seems useful to provide an approach that readers can test against materials in the book: International law is law to the extent that governments are willing to conform their conduct to norms they accept or grudgingly acknowledge as prevailing rules among nations. Most international law is effective because it is in the reciprocal interests of governments to obey.

What good is a law if there are no police or other forms of coercion to enforce the rules? One can draw an analogy to national or local law. Most people in the U.S. drive on the right side of the road, not because they are afraid they will be arrested, but because they know that driving on the left side might cause an accident. They also perform their contracts, not because they fear being brought to court, but because they want to enjoy a reputation as trustworthy individuals with whom others can do ordinary business.

Similarly, international law appears to work best when governments make agreements as to which each believes that its interests are best served by fulfilling its obligations. International human rights law, however, regulates how a government treats its citizens and others. For some governments it seems harder to understand the idea of reciprocal international obligations in the human rights context.

Most governments care, though, about their image. Their human rights performance affects, among other things, their ability to engage in trade, to attract tourists, and to receive military or economic aid from other countries. Governments do not like to be shunned. One might think that the stronger the country militarily and economically, the less concerned the government need be about its human rights image. But even superpowers care deeply about their image and try to avoid criticism.

The remarkable success of international human rights law over recent decades is the extent to which governments have been willing to proclaim and help establish a large and complex body of norms they promise to obey. Beginning with the Universal Declaration of Human Rights the U.N. has presided over the promulgation of scores of instruments by which nations promise other nations they will not kill, torture, arbitrarily detain, or otherwise infringe on the prescribed rights of their own citizens. Including treaties and other instruments developed by the International Labor Organization, the Organization of American States, the Council of Europe, and other intergovernmental organizations, the total number of instruments has now reached into the hundreds. There is no more-codified domain of international law.

What about all the human rights abuses reported by the media almost every day? Even governments that helped develop the norms violate their promises. We should not expect too much of international law. Because there is a law does not mean there will be obedience. There have been laws against burglary for centuries. Have those laws eliminated burglary? Of course not.

So what about criminals and vicious governments that don't care about their reputation? They suffer. They do not go to prison because there exist no police strong enough or prisions big enough. Instead, we investigate their offenses; we attempt to persuade them to conform to international expectations; we embarrass them; we shun them in various ways; and we put economic or other pressure on them. The process takes time; the sanctions often are indirect; and we do not always succeed. This book explores techniques for enforcing international human rights laws and responding to violations.

How is the book organized?

The book begins with an introduction to the sources and structures of international human rights law. The rest of the book focuses on problems or factual situations that may inspire discussion and even opportunities for roleplaying. The problems have been selected to draw on five aspects of international human rights to provide a sampling of the subject: (1) procedural postures, (2) institutional settings, (3) a geographical spread of countries, (4) substantive human rights norms, and (5) changing approaches to learning.

The problems touch on the major channels for international human rights implementation: state reporting, individual complaints, emergency procedures, state v. state complaints, litigation in domestic courts, legislative hearings, factfinding, public discourse and decision in international forums, the work of nongovernmental organizations, advisory opinions, etc. The problems have been set in most major international institutions, including the U.N., the Human Rights Committee, the Inter-American Commission and Court on Human Rights, the European human rights system, the Helsinki process, nongovernmental organizations, and the International Court of Justice. The focus is on facts in such diverse places as Burma (Myanmar), Europe (including the U.S.S.R.), Kenya, Iran, the Israeli Occupied Territories, Palau, Peru, and the U.S. The problems deal with arbitrary arrest, rights of aliens, torture and mutilation, abortion and the right to life, indigenous rights, sex discrimination, arbitrary killings, disappearances, economic rights, etc. Finally there is a call for diversity in teaching style. Some overview lectures will be appropriate. Other sessions may involve advising a client, roleplaying, dialogue method, drafting, preparation of congressional testimony, advocacy in litigation, and many other skills.

All problems contain assigned readings and questions as a basis for discussion. Each chapter establishes the setting and suggests major questions for discussion. The chapters provide information needed to deal with the problems. Questions occasionally are posed to indicate the relevance of materials and to focus attention on particular issues.

Readers may also find the bibliography useful — particularly if research papers are assigned. A separate volume is published containing several international human rights instruments.

The materials for the book were used initially in a weekly seminar of two hours during a semester. The book has also been organized to be usable for courses meeting three hours per week during a semester. The chapters have been designed so that readers ordinarily would handle one chapter for each week of the course.

Some teachers may wish to assign chapters in an order different from their placement in the book. For example, teachers who have a civil liberties and civil rights orientation may want to start with chapter 12 on the use of U.S. federal and state courts. Chapter 12 is longer than most of the others and may require more class time. Chapters 12 and 13 also explore sources of international law including treaties, custom, and general principles.

While the book was designed primarily for use in law schools, parts of the draft have also been used in political science and international relations courses for both undergraduate and graduate students.

ACKNOWLEDGMENTS

We trace the origins of this book to the first seminar on international human rights offered at the University of California Law School, Berkeley, during the summer of 1968. Thomas Buergenthal, Frank Newman, Egon Schwelb, and Karel Vasak co-taught the course. Several of the participants became law teachers — including Dinah Shelton, Jon van Dyke, and David Weissbrodt.

Most materials in the book derive from the course in international human rights law offered for the past 15 years at the University of Minnesota. The idea of publishing arose from a discussion between Professors Shelton and Weissbrodt at a meeting of the American Society of International Law several years ago.

Parts of drafts of the book have been used by Philip Alston (then of Fletcher School of Law and Diplomacy, now of Australian National University), Robert Drinan (Georgetown), Joan Fitzpatrick (University of Washington), Hurst Hannum (then of American University, now of Fletcher School), Paul Hoffman (Loyola, L.A.), Bert Lockwood (Cincinnati), Steve Schnably (Miami), John Weeks (Hamline), and others. We are grateful for comments received from those and other colleagues.

We wish to thank Penny Bailey, Katherine Brennan, Carlos Figueroa, Sharla Flora, Mark Gardner, Ruth Gaube, Zara Kivi Kinnunen, Ramona Price, Rebecca Raliegh, Cynthia Reed, Sonia Rosen, Linda Sennholtz, Maria Treby, Deepika Udagama, and Jamie Wilson, as well as other students and staff at the Universities of California and Minnesota who assisted. Lyonette Louis-Jacques and Stan Riddle provided very helpful bibliographical assistance. We are specially indebted to Sandra Coliver (now lawyer for the human rights organization "Article 19" in London) for patient and constructive critique as well as for her significant contribution to chapter 12. Diane Gihl, Mary Jane Luedtke, Florence McKnight, and David Rayson did excellent secretarial work to make the book possible.

Frank Newman
David Weissbrodt

May 1990

CONTRIBUTIONS

The authors wish to express their thanks to copyright holders for graciously permitting us to include excerpts from their works (in alphabetical order by author):

Alston, *Out of the Abyss: The Challenges Confronting the New U.N. Committee on Economic, Social and Cultural Rights*, 9 Hum. Rts. Q. 332 (1987). Copyright by Johns Hopkins University Press. Reprinted by permission.

Alston and Quinn, *The Nature and Scope of States Parties' Obligations Under the International Covenant on Economic, Social and Cultural Rights*, 9 Hum. Rts. Q. 156 (1987). Copyright by Johns Hopkins University Press. Reprinted by permission.

Amnesty International, Iran: Violations of human rights: documents sent by Amnesty International to the government of the Islamic Republic of Iran, AI Index: MDE 13/09/87 (1987). Reprinted by permission.

Amnesty International, Report 1989 (1989) (several portions). Reprinted by permission.

Amnesty International, Summary of Selected International Procedures and Bodies Dealing with Human Rights Measures, AI Index: 30/01/89 (1989). Reprinted by permission.

Asia Watch & Minnesota Lawyers International Human Rights Committee, Human Rights in the Democratic Peoples Republic of Korea (1988). Reprinted by permission.

Atkins, R. & R. Pisani, The Hassle of Your Life: A Handbook for the Friends and Families of Americans Imprisoned Abroad (1985). Copyright 1985 by International Legal Defense Counsel, Philadelphia, Pa. Reprinted by permission.

Barsh, Russell, *Indigenous Peoples: An Emerging Object of International Law*, 80 Am. J. Int'l L. 369 (1986). Reprinted with the permission of the American Society of International Law and the author.

Bossuyt, Marc, *The Development of Special Procedures of the United Nations Commission on Human Rights*, 6 Hum. Rts. L. J. 179, 181-94, 202-03 (1985). Reprinted with permission from N.P. Engel, Publisher, and the author.

Buergenthal, Thomas, *The Advisory Practice of the Inter-American Human Rights Court*, 79 Am. J. Int'l L. 1 (1985). Reprinted by permission of the author and the American Society of International Law.

Buergenthal, Thomas, *The Inter-American Court of Human Rights*, 79 Am. J. Int'l L. 231 (1982). Reprinted by permission of the author and the American Society of International Law.

Buergenthal, T., R. Norris & D. Shelton, Protecting Human Rights in the Americas: Selected Problems 178-81 (1988). Reprinted with permission from N.P. Engel, Publisher.

Burke et al., *Application of International Human Rights Law in State and Federal Courts*, 1983 Tex. Int'l L.J. 291 (1983). Reprinted by permission.

Butler, W., G. Edwards & M. Kirby, Palau: A Challenge to the Rule of Law in Micronesia (1988). Reprinted by permission.

Carter, B., *International Economic Sanctions: Improving the Haphazard U.S. Legal Regime*, 75 Cal. L. Rev. 1163, 1170-74, 1177, 1179-82 (1982). © 1987 by California Law Review, Inc. Reprinted from California Law Review, Vol. 75, No. 4, July 1987 pp. 1159-1278, by permission. There is a longer book with the same title by Professor Carter (1988: Cambridge University Press).

Cohen, S., *Conditioning U.S. Security Assistance on Human Rights Practices*, 76 Am. J. Int'l L. 246 (1982). This article was researched and written for the International Human Rights Law Group under a grant from the Ford Foundation. Reprinted by permission of the International Human Rights Law Group.

Cole, D., J. Lobel, & H. Koh, Brief on Behalf of International Experts, in *Trajano v. Marcos*, 878 F.2d 1439 (9th Cir. 1989). Copyright 1989 Hastings College of the Law, reprinted from 12 Hastings Int'l L. Rev. 1 with permission.

Coliver, Sandra, *United Nations Machineries on Women's Rights: How Might They Better Help Women Whose Rights are Being Violated* in New Directions in Human Rights (Ellen Lutz, Hurst Hannum, & Kathryn J. Burke, eds.) Reprinted with permission from the University of Pennsylvania Press and the author.

Coliver & Newman, *Using International Human Rights Law to Influence United States Foreign Policy: Resort to Courts or Congress?*, 20 N.Y.U. J. Int'l L. & Pol. 1 (1987). Reprinted by permission of the New York University Journal of International Law and Politics.

D'Amato, Anthony, International Law: Process and Prospect 1-26 (1987). Reprinted by permission from *International Law: Process and Prospect* by Anthony D'Amato. Copyright 1987, Transnational Publishers, Inc.

Donnelly, Jack, *Cultural Relativism and Universal Human Rights*, 6 Hum. Rts. Q. 400 (1984). Copyright by Johns Hopkins University Press. Reprinted by permission.

Fitzpatrick, Joan, *UN Action with Respect to Disappearance and Summary or Arbitrary Execution*, 5 AIUSA Legal Support Network Newsletter 38-39 (Fall 1988). Reprinted with permission of the author.

Fraser, Donald, *Congress's Role in the Making of International Human Rights Policy*, in Human Rights and American Foreign Policy (D. Kommers & G. Loescher eds. 1979) 247, 247-54. From HUMAN RIGHTS AND AMERICAN FOREIGN POLICY edited by Donald P. Kommers and Gilburt D. Loescher. © 1979 by University of Notre Dame Press. Reprinted by permission.

Freeman, Alan, *Racism, Rights and the Quest for Equality of Opportunity: A Critical Legal Essay*, 23 Harv. C.R.-C.L. L. Rev. 295, 316-22, 324-28, 330-35 (1988). Copied with the permission of the Harvard C.R.-C.L. Law Review. Copyright © 1988 by the President and Fellows of Harvard College.

Gerstel & Segall, *Conference Report: Human Rights in American Courts*, 1 Am. U.J. Int'l L. & Pol'y 137 (1986). Reprinted by permission.

Hassan, Dr. S. Farooq, The Islamic Republic: Politics, Law & Economy (1984). Reprinted by permission.

Human Rights Watch, The Bush Administration's Record on Human Rights in 1989 (1990). Reprinted by permission.

Human Rights Watch & Lawyers Committee for Human Rights, Critique: Review of the Department of State's Country Reports on Human Rights Practices for 1988 (1989). Reprinted by permission.

International Committee of the Red Cross, *ICRC reacts to Israeli violations of Geneva Convention*, ICRC Bulletin No. 152, at 1 (September 1988). Reprinted by permission.

International Committee of the Red Cross, *Israel and the Occupied Territories*, Annual Report 80 (1988). Reprinted by permission.

Kamminga, M.T., *The Thematic Procedure of the UN Commission on Human Rights*,

34 Neth. Int'l L. Rev. 299 (1987). Reprinted with permission of the author and the Netherlands International Law Review.

Kampelman, Ambassador Max, Head, U.S. Delegation, Statement on Helsinki Monitors, May 12, 1981, *reprinted in* M. Kampelman, Three Years at the East-West Divide 39 (1983). Editor, Leonard R. Sussman. Publisher, Freedom House. Reprinted by permission.

Kirgis, Frederic L., Jr., *Agora: May the President Violate Customary International Law? (Cont'd)*, 81 Am. J. Int'l L. 371 (1987). Reprinted by permission of the author and the American Society of International Law.

Kramer & Weissbrodt, *The 1980 U.N. Commission on Human Rights and the Disappeared*, 3 Hum. Rts. Q. 18 (1981). Copyright by Johns Hopkins University Press. Reprinted by permission.

Lillich, R., *A United States Policy of Humanitarian Intervention and Intercession*, in Human Rights and American Foreign Policy (D. Kommers & G. Loescher eds. 1979) 278, 287-90. From HUMAN RIGHTS AND AMERICAN FOREIGN POLICY edited by Donald P. Kommers and Gilburt D. Loescher. © 1979 by University of Notre Dame Press. Reprinted by permission.

Linde, Hans A., *Comments*, 18 Int'l Lawyer 77 (1984). Reprinted by permission.

Marks, Stephen, *Emerging Human Rights: A New Generation for the 1980's*, 33 Rutgers L. Rev. 435 (1981). Reprinted by permission.

McDougal, Myres, Harold Lasswell, & Lung-Chu Chen, Human Rights and World Public Order: The Basic Policies of an International Law of Human Dignity 68-71, 73-75 (1980).

Morsink, Johannes, *The Philosophy of the Universal Declaration*, 6 Hum. Rts. Q. 309 (1984). Copyright by Johns Hopkins University Press. Reprinted by permission.

National Council on Crime & Delinquency, Council of Judges, Recommendations on Juvenile Detention, March 1, 1989. Reprinted by permission.

Nelson, Harold D. (ed.), *Kenya: A Country Study*, Washington, D.C.: Government Printing Office for The American University, 1984, pp. 218-20, 226-28. Reprinted by permission.

Newsom, David D., From chapter 1, "Introduction. The Diplomacy of Human Rights: A Diplomat's View," by David D. Newsom, in *The Diplomacy of Human Rights*, David D. Newsom, ed. (Washington: Institute for the Study of Diplomacy and University Press of America, 1986). Copyright by the Institute for the Study of Diplomacy, Georgetown University. Reprinted by permission.

Nickel, James, Making Sense of Human Rights: Philosophical Reflections on the Universal Declaration of Human Rights (1987). © 1987 The Regents of the University of California.

Note, *Recent Israeli Security Measures Under the Fourth Geneva Convention*, 3 Conn. J. Int'l. L. 485 (1988) (authored by Peter J. Morgan III). Reprinted by permission.

Pollis, Adamantia, "Liberal, Socialist, and Third World Perspective of Human Rights," in TOWARD A HUMAN RIGHTS FRAMEWORK, Adamantia Pollis and Peter Schwab, eds. (Praeger Publishers, New York, 1982), p. 10-11. Copyright © 1982 by Praeger Publishers. Reprinted with permission.

Quiroga, Cecilia Medina, The Battle of Human Rights: Gross Systematic Violations and the Inter-American System (1988). Reprinted by permission of Kluwer Academic Publishers.

Restatement, Third, Foreign Relations Law of the United States § 325(1) and (2); § 325 comments a, b, e, and g; § 702 (1987) § 711; § 711 comments b and c; § 713(1); § 713 comments a and b. Copyright 1987 by the American Law Institute. Reprinted with the permission of the American Law Institute.

Roberts, A., B. Joergensen, & F. Newman, Academic Freedom Under Military Occupation (1984). Reprinted by permission.

Rodley, Nigel, *On the Necessity of United States Ratification of the International Human Rights Convention*, in U.S. Ratification of Human Rights Treaties: With or Without Reservations? 3 (edited for the International Human Rights Law Group by R. Lillich, ed. 1981) Reprinted by permission of the International Human Rights Law Group.

Sesser, S., *A Reporter At Large: A Rich Country Gone Wrong*, The New Yorker, October 9, 1989. Reprinted by permission; © 1989 Stan Sesser. Originally in The New Yorker.

Shelton, Dinah, memorandum related to *Thompson v. Oklahoma*, 487 U.S. 815 (1988). Reprinted by permission.

Szabó, Imre, *The Theoretical Foundations of Human Rights*, in International Protection of Human Rights (Asbjorn Eide and August Schou eds. 1979) 39, 39-41. © The Nobel Foundation 1968 (Proceedings from Nobel Symposium no. 7 "International Protection of Human Rights").

Trubek, *Economic, Social and Cultural Rights in the Third World*, in Human Rights in International Law: Legal and Policy Issues (T. Meron ed. 1984) 205, 205-33. © Oxford University Press 1984. Reprinted from Human Rights in International Law: Legal and Policy Issues edited by Theodor Meron (1984) by permission of Oxford University Press.

Vargas, Edmundo, *Visions on the Spot, The Experience of the Inter-American Commission on Human Rights*, in International Law and Fact Finding in the Field of Human Rights (B. Ramcharen ed. 1982). Reprinted by permission of Kluwer Academic Publishers.

Weissbrodt, *Major Developments at the 1989 Session of the UN Commission on Human Rights*, 11 Hum. Rts. Q. 586 (1989). Copyright by Johns Hopkins University Press. Reprinted by permission.

Weissbrodt, *The Three "Theme" Special Rapporteurs of the UN Commission on Human Rights*, 80 Am. J. Int'l L. 685 (1986). Reprinted by permission.

Weissbrodt, *United States Ratification of the Human Rights Covenants*, 63 Minn. L. Rev. 35 (1978). Reprinted by permission.

Weston, Burns, *U.S. Ratification of the International Covenant on Economic, Social and Cultural Rights: With or Without Reservations*, in U.S. Ratification of the International Human Rights Convention: With or Without Reservations? 27 (edited for the International Human Rights Law Group by R. Lillich, ed. 1981) Reprinted by permission of the International Human Rights Law Group.

I *INTRODUCTION TO INTERNATIONAL HUMAN RIGHTS*

A. Developments During and After World War II
B. Multilateral Promotion and Protection of Human Rights
    1. U.N. Codification
    2. U.N. Machineries
C. Conclusion

This chapter explores institutional and legal contexts for factual situations and problems around which the remainder of the book is organized. It traces the development of human rights law — before, during, and after World War II — that led to the creation of the U.N. and its human rights machineries. It then describes the codification of human rights law largely through the U.N. Charter and related instruments. It also contains a summary of principal U.N. procedures and a note on nongovernmental organizations.

A. DEVELOPMENTS DURING AND AFTER WORLD WAR II

Modern international human rights law dates from the 1940's. To understand the new institutions it is necessary to recall events during which an estimated 50 million people were killed. The horror of Nazi atrocities during the war and also the Holocaust, in which 12 million are estimated to have died, made clear the need for codification of international standards to protect human rights.

World War II manifested an horrendous extension of principles of sovereignty that had come to dominate international relations during preceding years. Hitler and his colleagues sought to place Germany in a position of preeminence. In their military-political campaigns the individual ceased to be important. Though they failed the quest, their brutality demonstrated that earlier attempts to protect individuals from ravages of war were inadequate.

Germany carried out atrocities against millions of its citizens and nationals of neighboring countries during the 1930's and 1940's with little interference from other nations. It argued that treatment of citizens was not a matter of international concern, and other governments apparently were reluctant to intervene. The war and Holocaust demonstrated that unfettered sovereignty could not exist without untold suffering and ultimately the danger of destroying most human society.

Formulating plans for new international structures, political and juridical leaders looked to the promotion and protection of human rights as an end and a means of helping to ensure international peace and security. Governments responded by creating the United Nations, by establishing the Nuremberg and Tokyo tribunals, and by promulgating the Four Geneva Conventions of 1949. Soon thereafter, regional intergovernmental organizations in the Americas and Europe also established structures for promoting and protecting human rights.

B. MULTILATERAL PROMOTION AND PROTECTION OF HUMAN RIGHTS

1. U.N. Codification

The U.N. Charter sought "to reaffirm faith in fundamental human rights, in the dignity and worth of the human person, [and] in the equal rights of men and women and of nations large and small."[1] It was promulgated to help maintain peace and security, to develop friendly relations among nations based on respect for the principle of equal rights and self-determination, and to achieve international co-operation in solving international problems of an economic, social, cultural, or humanitarian character. Though it acknowledged the importance of noninterference in the internal affairs of states, it also established human rights as a matter of international concern. Joining the U.N., every government undertook to promote "universal respect for, and observance of, human rights and fundamental freedoms for all without distinction as to race, sex, language, or religion."[2]

In 1948 the U.N. General Assembly adopted the Universal Declaration of Human Rights, articulating rights as to which governments agreed to promote observance.[3] Following adoption of the Declaration the U.N. Commission on Human Rights drafted the remainder of the International Bill of Human Rights: the Covenant on Economic, Social and Cultural Rights;[4] the Covenant on Civil and Political Rights;[5] and the Optional Protocol to the Civil and Political Covenant.[6] The two Covenants interpret provisions

---

[1] U.N. Charter, Preamble, June 26, 1945, 59 Stat. 1031, T.S. 993, *entered into force* Oct. 24, 1945.

[2] *Id.* Arts. 55, 56.

[3] Universal Declaration of Human Rights, *adopted* Dec. 10, 1948, G.A. res. 217A (III), U.N. Doc. A/810, at 71 (1948).

[4] International Covenant on Economic, Social and Cultural Rights, Dec. 16, 1966, G.A. res. 2200A (XXI), 21 U.N. GAOR Supp. (No.16) at 49, U.N. Doc. A/6316 (1966), 993 U.N.T.S. 3, *entered into force* Jan. 3, 1976.

[5] International Covenant on Civil and Political Rights, Dec. 16, 1966, G.A. res. 2200A (XXI), 21 U.N. GAOR Supp. (No.16) at 52, U.N. Doc. A/6316 (1966), 999 U.N.T.S. 171, *entered into force* Mar. 23, 1976.

[6] Optional Protocol to the Covenant on Civil and Political Rights, Dec. 16, 1966, G.A. res. 2200A (XXI), 21 U.N. GAOR Supp. (No.16) at 59, U.N. Doc. A/6316 (1966), 999 U.N.T.S. 302, *entered into force* Mar. 23, 1976.

of the Universal Declaration in binding treaties and supply implementation procedures for states parties.

The Covenants separate civil and political rights from economic, social, and cultural rights. Civil and political rights such as the right to be free from torture and cruel, inhuman or degrading treatment are immediately applicable. Most economic, social, and cultural rights are to be implemented "to the maximum of available . . . resources, with a view to achieving progressively the full realization of the rights . . . by all appropriate means, including particularly the adoption of legislative measures."[7] In other words, governments that ratify the Covenants should immediately cease to torture their citizens, but are not immediately required to feed, clothe, and house them. Those latter obligations are to be accomplished only progressively as resources permit.

In addition to the International Bill of Human Rights the U.N. has drafted, promulgated, and now helps to implement scores of multilateral treaties and other human rights instruments dealing with problems such as *apartheid*, genocide, racial discrimination, discrimination against women, religious intolerance, the rights of disabled persons, torture, and rights of the child. The U.N. also has established procedures for protecting human rights. The efforts to codify and implement those measures have played a central role in internationalizing human rights and humanizing international law.

2. U.N. Machineries

Within the U.N., human rights activities are pursued under authority of the U.N. Charter or human rights treaties. The principal Charter-based bodies are the General Assembly, the Economic and Social Council, the Commission on Human Rights, the Sub-Commission on Prevention of Discrimination and Protection of Minorities, and the Commission on the Status of Women. On occasion the Security Council plays a role.

A number of treaties are implemented by expert bodies such as the Committee on the Elimination of All Forms of Racial Discrimination (CERD); the Human Rights Committee; the Committee on Economic, Social and Cultural Rights; the Committee for the Elimination of Discrimination against Women (CEDAW); the Committee against Torture; and the Group of Three under the *Apartheid* Convention.[8] The Centre for Human Rights, based in Geneva, staffs those bodies (except CEDAW and the Commission on the Status of Women, which get staff support from the Advancement of Women Branch of the Centre for Social Development and Humanitarian Affairs based in Vienna). The U.N. High Commissioner for Refugees and other specialized agencies undertake human rights work within their fields of

---

[7] Covenant on Economic, Social and Cultural Rights, *supra* note 4, Art. 2(1).

[8] "Convention" in this context means a multilateral treaty.

competence. Those agencies include the International Labor Organization (ILO); the U.N. Educational, Scientific and Cultural Organization (UNESCO); the Food and Agricultural Organization (FAO); and the World Health Organization (WHO).

The various bodies and procedures are discussed in the U.N. publication reproduced in large part below:[9]

[a.] *General Assembly and subsidiary bodies*

The General Assembly is the main representative body of the United Nations. It is made up of all Member States [numbering 160 in 1990] each of which has one vote. Its regular session begins each year on the third Tuesday of September and continues usually until mid-December.

Under Article 13 of the United Nations Charter, one of the functions of the General Assembly is to initiate studies and make recommendations for the purpose of ''promoting international co-operation in the economic, social, cultural, educational and health fields, and assisting in the realization of human rights and fundamental freedoms for all without distinction as to race, sex, language, or religion''.

For the most part, human rights items on the agenda of the General Assembly originate in sections of the report of the Economic and Social Council which relate to human rights, or in decisions taken by the Assembly at earlier sessions to consider particular matters. Items relating to human rights have also been proposed for inclusion in the Assembly's agenda by the other principal organs of the United Nations, by Member States, and by the Secretary-General.

Since the adoption of the Universal Declaration of Human Rights in 1948 the Assembly has adopted numerous declarations or conventions concentrating on human rights. They deal *inter alia* with genocide, racial discrimination, *apartheid*, refugees, stateless persons, the rights of women, slavery, marriage, children, youth, aliens, asylum, disabled and mentally retarded persons, torture, development and social progress. [The General Assembly also adopts several resolutions each year on human rights situations in particular countries and on such human rights concerns as disappearances, torture, summary or arbitrary executions, and the desirability of ratifying human rights treaties.]

Most items relating to human rights are referred by the General Assembly to its Third Committee, which deals with social, humanitarian and cultural matters. Some, however, are considered by the Assembly without reference to a Main Committee. Items which have a bearing on political, international security and disarmament issues are normally referred to the First Committee or to the Special Political Committee. Those of an essentially economic character are referred to the Second Committee, those relating to decolonization to the Fourth Committee, and those of a legal nature to the Sixth Committee. The Fifth Committee deals with administrative and budgetary questions, including those arising from the consideration of human rights items.

Subsidiary bodies of the General Assembly concerned with human rights and fundamental freedoms include: the Special Committee on the Situation with regard

---

[9] United Nations, *Human Rights Machinery*, Fact Sheet No. 1 (1987) (bracketed material added).

to the Implementation of the Declaration on the Granting of Independence to Colonial Countries and Peoples, known as the Special Committee on Decolonization; the United Nations Council for Namibia; the Special Committee against *Apartheid*; the Special Committee to Investigate Israeli Practices Affecting the Human Rights of the Population of the Occupied Territories; and the Committee on the Exercise of the Inalienable Rights of the Palestinian People.

[b.] *Economic and Social Council and subsidiary bodies*

Under Article 62 of the United Nations Charter, the Economic and Social Council [known as ECOSOC] may "make recommendations for the purpose of promoting respect for, and observance of, human rights and fundamental freedoms for all". It may also prepare draft conventions for submission to the General Assembly and call international conferences on human rights matters. Under Article 68, the Council "shall set up commissions in economic and social fields and for the protection of human rights".

[Under Article 64 ECOSOC may request reports from members of the United Nations regarding their efforts to comply with human rights obligations. ECOSOC may also request reports from the specialized agencies regarding their human rights activities.]

The Council, which is composed of 54 members, normally holds an organizational session and two regular sessions each year. In addition, it occasionally holds special sessions. Human rights items are usually referred to the first (spring) session of the Council's Second (Social) Committee, a "sessional" committee on which the 54 members of the Council are represented, although some items are dealt with in plenary meetings without reference to a committee. The reports of the Social Committee, which contain draft resolutions and draft decisions, are submitted to the Council for consideration and final action in plenary meetings.

To assist it in dealing with items relating to human rights, the Council has established the Commission on Human Rights and the Commission on the Status of Women. The Commission on Human Rights, in turn, has established the Sub-Commission on Prevention of Discrimination and Protection of Minorities. [ECOSOC must approve all measures recommended by the Human Rights and Women's commissions involving the expenditure of funds or requiring the attention of the General Assembly. In almost all cases ECOSOC approves recommendations from the commissions.]

From time to time the Council has set up *ad hoc* committees composed of representatives of Member States, experts nominated by their Governments, or outstanding personalities serving in their personal capacity. The Council has also, on occasion, appointed or authorized the Secretary-General to appoint special rapporteurs or committees of experts to prepare reports on technical subjects.

[c.] *Commission on Human Rights*

This Commission was set up by the Economic and Social Council in 1946, and has met annually since that time. It is the main body dealing with human rights issues, as it may deal with any matter relating to human rights.

The Commission makes studies, prepares recommendations and drafts international instruments relating to human rights. It also undertakes special tasks assigned to it by the General Assembly or the Economic and Social Council, including the investigation of allegations concerning violations of human rights and the handling of communications relating to such violations. It co-operates closely with all other United Nations bodies having competence in the field of human rights. In addition, it assists the Economic and Social Council in the co-ordination of activities concerning human rights in the United Nations system.

The Commission, originally made up of 18 members seized particularly with the task of drafting the International Bill of Human Rights, is now composed of the representatives of 43 Member States elected for three-year terms.[¹⁰] It meets each year for a period of six weeks [in February and the first half of March], and it operates under the Rules of Procedure of Functional Commissions of the Economic and Social Council. Only members of the Commission, or their alternates, have the right to vote. The Commission may, however, invite any State to participate in its deliberations on any matter of particular concern to that State, and may invite any national liberation movement recognized by, or in accordance with, resolutions of the General Assembly to participate in its deliberations on any matter of particular concern to that movement. Specialized agencies and certain other intergovernmental organizations may participate in the Commission's deliberations on questions of concern to them, and non-governmental organizations in consultative status with the Economic and Social Council may designate authorized representatives to sit as observers at public meetings of the Commission.

To assist in its work, the Commission has established a number of subsidiary bodies, including the Sub-Commission on Prevention of Discrimination and Protection of Minorities. In recent years, the Commission on Human Rights has set up organs to investigate human rights problems in specific countries and territories as well as on thematic situations. At present, the following Groups exist: the *Ad Hoc* Working Group of Experts on southern Africa; the Group of Three established under article IX of the International Convention on the Suppression and Punishment of the Crime of *Apartheid*; the Working Group to Examine Situations which Appear to Reveal a Consistent Pattern of Gross Violations of Human Rights; the Working Group on Enforced or Involuntary Disappearances; the Working Group of Governmental Experts on the Right to Development; and the Working Group to Continue the Overall Analysis on the Further Promotion and Encouragement of Human Rights and Fundamental Freedoms. In addition, the Commission has been actively employing a variety of methods for dealing with violations of human rights. These include fact-finding by experts consisting of special rapporteurs, representatives or other designees appointed by the Commission to study the situation of human rights either in specific countries such as Afghanistan, Chile, El Salvador, Guatemala, the Islamic Republic of Iran, [and Romania] or on thematic situations such as Summary or Arbitrary Executions, Religious Intolerance, [Torture,] and Mercenaries. The Commission has also established informal open-ended working groups to assist in the drafting of international declarations and conventions, namely a draft declaration on the rights of persons belonging to national, ethnic, religious and linguistic minorities ... and a draft declaration on the right and responsibility of individuals, groups and organs of society to promote and protect universally recognized human rights and fundamental freedoms.

[d.] *Sub-Commission on Prevention of Discrimination and Protection of Minorities*

At its first session, in 1947, the Commission on Human Rights established the

---

[¹⁰ In May 1990 ECOSOC decided to increase the size of the Commission to 53 members to be elected for the 1992 session.]

Sub-Commission on Prevention of Discrimination and Protection of Minorities "(*a*) to undertake studies, particularly in the light of the Universal Declaration of Human Rights, and to make recommendations to the Commission concerning the prevention of discrimination of any kind relating to human rights and fundamental freedoms and the protection of racial, religious and linguistic minorities; and (*b*) to perform any other functions entrusted to it by the Economic and Social Council or by the Commission".

The Sub-Commission is composed of 26 experts elected by the Commission on Human Rights to serve, as of 1988, for four-year periods. Although nominated by Governments, these experts act in their personal capacity and not as the representatives of States.

The Sub-Commission meets each year for a period of four weeks [usually during August]. Like the Commission on Human Rights it operates under the Rules of Procedure of Functional Commission of the Economic and Social Council. It is attended by its members or their alternates, by observers from Governments, United Nations bodies, specialized agencies, intergovernmental organizations, non-governmental organizations in consultative status with the Economic and Social Council, and national liberation movements concerned with questions on its agenda.

The Sub-Commission has established three working groups which meet regularly before each of its annual sessions to assist it with certain tasks: the Working Group on Communications, which examines communications containing allegations of violations of human rights and brings to the attention of the Sub-Commission those which appear to reveal a consistent pattern of gross and reliably attested violations of human rights; the Working Group on Slavery, which reviews developments in the field of slavery, slave trade practices similar to slavery, exploitation of child labour and exploitation of prostitutes; and the Working Group on Indigenous Populations, which reviews developments relating to the protection of the human rights of such populations.

In addition, the Sub-Commission may establish sessional working groups, which meet during its annual sessions to consider particular agenda items. Examples of these are the Working Group on the Encouragement of Universal Acceptance of Human Rights Instruments, the Working Group on the Rights of Persons Detained or Imprisoned, and the Working Group on the Question of Persons Detained on the Ground of Mental Ill-health.

Each of the working groups submits its reports to the Sub-Commission for consideration. On some questions, including those relating to the discharge of its functions, the Sub-Commission adopts its own resolutions and decisions. On others, it formulates draft resolutions and decisions for consideration by the Commission on Human Rights and the Economic and Social Council. The Sub-Commission submits a report on the work of each session to the Commission.

[e.] *Commission on the Status of Women*

This Commission was established by the Economic and Social Council in 1946. Its functions are (*a*) to prepare recommendations and reports to the Council on promoting women's rights in political, economic, civil, social and educational fields, and (*b*) to make recommendations to the Council on urgent problems requiring immediate attention in the field of women's rights, with the object of implementing the principle that men and women shall have equal rights, and to develop proposals to give effect to such recommendations.

The Commission is composed of the representatives of 32[11] United Nations Member States, elected by the Council for four-year terms. [Between 1972 and 1986 it met biennially for between one and two weeks; in 1988 it began to meet annually. Since 1978 its regular sessions have been held in Vienna.]

The Commission operates under the Rules of Procedure of Functional Commissions of the Economic and Social Council, and its arrangements for attendance and participation in its work are the same as those for the Commission on Human Rights. Its recent sessions have been attended by members and alternates, by observers from Member and non-member States of the United Nations, by representatives of various United Nations bodies and specialized agencies, by representatives of liberation movements and by observers from non-governmental organizations. The Inter-American Commission of Women and the Commission on the Status of Arab Women submit reports to each session of the Commission.

The Commission adopts its own resolutions and decisions and prepares draft resolutions and decisions for consideration by the Economic and Social Council.

[f.] *Bodies established in accordance with United Nations Human Rights instruments*

[i.] *Committee on the Elimination of Racial Discrimination*

This Committee, established in 1970 in accordance with article 8 of the International Convention on the Elimination of All Forms of Racial Discrimination, consists of 18 experts of high moral standing and acknowledged impartiality, elected by States parties to the Convention from among their nationals. Members are elected for a four-year term by secret ballot at a meeting of the States parties, and serve in their personal capacity.

The tasks of the Committee, as set out in part II of the Convention, are: to consider reports on the legislative, judicial, administrative or other measures States parties have adopted which give effect to the provisions of the Convention; to make suggestions and general recommendations based on the examination of those reports and other information; to assist in settling disputes among States parties concerning the application of the Convention; and to receive and consider communications from individuals or groups of individuals within the jurisdiction of States parties which have recognized the competence of the Committee to this effect. When necessary, it may establish an *ad hoc* conciliation commission to make available its good offices to States parties in a dispute concerning the application of the Convention, with a view to an amicable settlement on the basis of respect for the Convention. Such a commission would report to the Committee on all questions of fact relevant to the issue between the parties, and make recommendations for the amicable settlement of the dispute....

The Committee met for the first time on 19 January 1970. Since that time, it has normally held two [three-week] sessions each year (spring and summer), and has reported to the General Assembly annually.

At each session, the Committee examines the information placed at its disposal by States parties to the Convention and by the United Nations bodies concerned with dependent Territories. Representatives of States parties are usually present at the meetings of the Committee when their reports are examined, and may answer questions or submit additional information.

---

[11] As of 1989, the Commission membership was increased to 45.

The Committee may also comment on situations involving racial discrimination, or draw them to the attention of the General Assembly. It indicates matters on which it would like to receive detailed information from States parties. At the Assembly's request the Committee has also devoted particular attention in recent years to the situation of peoples struggling against the oppression of the colonialist and racist régimes in southern Africa.

By the end of [February 1990], there were [128] States parties to the International Convention on the Elimination of All Forms of Racial Discrimination, 12 of which had recognized the competence of the Committee to receive and consider communications from individuals or groups of individuals.

[ii.] *Human Rights Committee*

This Committee, established in 1977 in accordance with article 28 of the International Covenant on Civil and Political Rights, consists of 18 members of high moral character and recognized competence in the field of human rights, elected by States parties to the Covenant from among their nationals. Members are elected for a four-year term by secret ballot at a meeting of the States parties, and serve in their personal capacity.

The tasks of the Committee, as set out in articles 40 to 45 of the Covenant, are: to study reports on the measures States parties have adopted to give effect to the rights recognized in the Covenant, and on the progress made in the enjoyment of those rights; to transmit its reports, and such general comments as it may consider appropriate, to the States parties; to perform certain functions with a view to settling disputes among States parties concerning the application of the Covenant, provided that those parties have recognized the competence of the Committee to that effect; and when necessary to establish an *ad hoc* conciliation commission to make available its good offices to States parties involved in a dispute concerning the application of the Covenant, with a view to a friendly solution of the matter on the basis of respect for the Covenant. Such a commission must submit a report to the Committee Chairman, not later than 12 months after having been seized of the matter, for communication to the States parties concerned.

Under article 41 of the Covenant, a State party may at any time declare that it recognizes the competence of the Committee to receive and consider communications to the effect that a State party claims that another State party is not fulfilling its obligations under the Covenant. Communications received under this article are dealt with in accordance with a special procedure.

Under the Optional Protocol to the International Covenant on Civil and Political Rights, individuals who claim that any of their rights enumerated in the Covenant have been violated and who have exhausted all available domestic remedies may submit written communications to the Human Rights Committee for consideration. No communication can be received by the Committee if it concerns a State party to the Covenant which is not also a party to the Optional Protocol. The Committee considers communications in the light of all written information made available to it by the individual and by the State party concerned, and forwards its views to the State party concerned and to the individual.

As in the case of the Committee on the Elimination of Racial Discrimination, representatives of States parties to the International Covenant on Civil and Political Rights are present at the meetings of the Human Rights Committee when their reports are examined. The Committee may also inform a State party from which it decides to seek further information that it may authorize its representative to be present at a specified meeting. The representative should be able to answer questions put to him by the Committee and may make statements on reports already submitted by his State; he may also submit additional information from his State.

The Committee normally holds three [three-week] sessions each year, and reports annually to the General Assembly, through the Economic and Social Council.

At each session, the Committee examines reports from States parties to the Covenant on the measures taken by them to give effect to the rights recognized in the Covenant, on the progress made in the enjoyment of those rights and on any factors and difficulties affecting the implementation of the Covenant. It considers the reports in public meetings in the presence of representatives of the reporting States.

The Committee also considers communications received under the Optional Protocol, with the assistance of a working group established at every session on communications, consisting of not more than five of its members. All documents pertaining to the Committee's work under the Protocol are confidential, and they are examined in closed meetings. The texts of final decisions of the Committee, however, are made public. The Committee includes a summary of its activities under the Protocol in its annual report.

The Committee also regularly establishes a Working Group to assist it in the drafting of lists of issues in connection with the consideration of periodic States' reports and in the preparation of general comments. This Working Group is made up of not more than five members of the Committee.

By the end of [February 1990], there were [88] States parties to the International Covenant on Civil and Political Rights, [47] of which had also ratified or acceded to the Optional Protocol, and 21 States had made the declaration under article 41 of the Covenant recognizing the competence of the Human Rights Committee to consider communications relating to inter-State disputes.

[iii.] *Committee on Economic, Social and Cultural Rights*

This Committee, established in 1985 by the Economic and Social Council is composed of 18 experts with recognized competence in the field of human rights serving in their personal capacity. Its members are elected for a term of four years by the Council by secret ballot from a list of persons nominated by States parties to the International Covenant on Economic, Social and Cultural Rights.

The Committee carries out functions relating to the implementation of the Covenant. It examines reports submitted to it by States parties on the measures which they have adopted and the progress made in achieving the observance of the rights recognized in the Covenant, and assists the Economic and Social Council to fulfil its supervisory functions relating to the Covenant by making suggestions and recommendations of a general nature based on its consideration of reports submitted by States parties and the specialized agencies concerned.

As in the case of the Human Rights Committee, representatives of States parties to the International Covenant on Economic, Social and Cultural Rights may be present at the meetings of the Committee on Economic, Social and Cultural Rights when their reports are examined, may make statements on reports submitted by their States and reply to questions put to them by the members of the Committee.

The Committee holds one [three-week] session a year [usually in March] at the United Nations Office at Geneva.

By the end of [February 1990], there were [93] States parties to the International Covenant on Economic, Social and Cultural Rights.

[iv.] *Committee on the Elimination of Discrimination against Women*

This Committee, established in 1982 in accordance with article 17 of the Convention on the Elimination of All Forms of Discrimination against Women, consists of 23 experts of high moral standing and competence in the field covered by the Convention. Members are elected by secret ballot from a list of persons nominated by States parties, and serve for a term of four years. The Committee on the Elimination of Discrimination against Women meets once a year for a two-week period in Vienna (or New York).

The basic task of the Committee, as set out in article 17 of the Convention, is to consider the progress made in the implementation of the Convention. The Committee reports on its activities annually to the General Assembly through the Economic and Social Council. It may make suggestions and general recommendations based on its examination of reports and information received from States parties. By the end of [February 1990], [100] States had ratified or acceded to the Convention on the Elimination of [All Forms of] Discrimination against Women.

[v.] *Committee against Torture*

This Committee, established in 1987 in accordance with article 17 of the Convention against Torture and Other Cruel, Inhuman or Degrading Treatment or Punishment, consists of 10 experts of high moral standing and recognized competence in the field of human rights, elected by States parties to the Convention from among their nationals. Members are elected for a four-year term by secret ballot at a meeting of States parties, and serve in their personal capacity.

The tasks of the Committee, as set out in articles 19 to 24 of the Convention are: to study reports on the measures taken by States parties to give effect to their undertakings under the Convention; to make confidential inquiries, if it decides that this is warranted, concerning well-founded indications that torture is being systematically practised in the territory of a State party; to perform certain functions with a view to settling disputes among States parties concerning the application of the Convention, provided that those States parties have recognized the competence of the Committee against Torture to undertake such functions; to establish when necessary *ad hoc* conciliation commissions to make available its good offices to the States parties concerned with a view to a friendly solution of inter-State disputes; to consider communications from or on behalf of individuals subject to the jurisdiction of States parties concerned who claim to be victims of a violation of the provisions of the Convention, provided that those States parties have recognized the competence of the Committee to that effect; and to submit annual reports on its activities to the States parties and to the General Assembly of the United Nations.

The Committee [held] its first session at the United Nations Office at Geneva in April 1988 .... [The Committee has begun to meet in April-May and November each year.]

By the end of [February 1990], there were [51] States parties to the Convention against Torture and Other Cruel, Inhuman or Degrading Treatment or Punishment, [23] of which had accepted the competence of the Committee against Torture under articles 21 and 22 of the Convention to consider matters relating to inter-State disputes and communications from or on behalf of individuals.[¹²] [Eleven] of the States parties have declared that they do not recognize the competence of the Committee under article 20 of the Convention to undertake confidential inquiries or fact-finding missions on their territories.

[vi.] *Group of Three Established under the International Convention on the Suppression and Punishment of the Crime of Apartheid*

This group appointed annually by the Chairman of the Commission on Human Rights consists of three members of the Commission who are also representatives of States parties to the International Convention on the Suppression and Punishment of the Crime of *Apartheid*. It meets annually for a period of not more than five days before the session of the Commission on Human Rights to consider periodic reports submitted by States parties on the legislative, judicial, administrative, or other measures that they have adopted to give effect to the provisions of the Convention. The Group reports to the Commission on Human Rights on its activities and makes appropriate recommendations on the implementation of the Convention.

* * *

A number of United Nations bodies are concerned with human rights from time to time and in varying degrees. These include the Security Council, the Trusteeship Council, the International Law Commission, and the International Court of Justices.

[g.] *United Nations Secretariat*

[i.]   *Centre for Human Rights*

The Centre for Human Rights, located at the United Nations Office at Geneva, is the Secretariat Unit of the United Nations mostly concerned with human rights questions. The Centre, headed by the Under-Secretary-General for Human Rights who is also Director-General of the United Nations Office at Geneva, is made up of the office of the Under-Secretary-General and six main sections. The Centre maintains an office in New York at United Nations Headquarters.

[ii.] *Overview*

The Centre for Human Rights assists the General Assembly, the Economic and Social Council, the Commission on Human Rights and other organs of the United Nations in the promotion and protection of human rights and fundamental freedoms as envisaged in the Charter of the United Nations, the Universal Declaration of Human Rights, international conventions on human rights concluded under the auspices of the United Nations and various resolutions of the General Assembly. An organizational unit for providing such assistance has existed in the Secretariat since its inception. Formerly, it was known as the "Division of Human Rights". The Centre forms a part of the United Nations Office at Geneva. Its broad functions are as follows:

> Serves as the focal point of the United Nations in the field of human rights; provides secretariat and substantive services to United Nations organs concerned with human rights, including the General Assembly and its Third Committee, the Economic and Social Council and its Social Committee, the

---

[¹²] The United Kingdom has accepted only inter-state complaints.

Commission on Human Rights, the Sub-Commission on Prevention of Discrimination and Protection of Minorities and their subsidiary bodies, the Committee on the Elimination of Racial Discrimination, the Human Rights Committee, the Committee on Economic, Social and Cultural Rights and the Committee against Torture. Carries out research and studies on human rights at the request of the organs concerned; follows up and prepares reports on the implementation of human rights;

Administers the programme of advisory services and technical assistance on human rights; and co-ordinates liaison with non-governmental organizations, external institutions and the media on human rights. Collects and disseminates information, and prepares publications.

    [iii.] *Under-Secretary-General for Human Rights. . .*

    [iv.] *Office of the Under-Secretary-General*

        [(a)] *Administrative Support Unit. . .*

        [(b)] *New York Office. . .*

        [(c)] *Secretariat of the Working Group on Enforced or Involuntary Disappearances. . .*

        [(d)] *International Instruments Section. . .*

        [(e)] *Communications Section. . .*

        [(f)] *Special Procedures Section. . .*

        [(g)] *Research, Studies and Prevention of Discrimination Section. . .*

        [(h)] *Advisory Services Section. . .*

        [(i)] *External Relations, Publications and Documentation Section. . .*

[v. *Good Offices of the Secretary-General*

The successive Secretaries-General of the United Nations have developed a practice of receiving individual appeals for humanitarian assistance and of attempting to use diplomatic efforts to resolve the most compelling cases.[13] Because these efforts are usually made without publicity and the results are never published, authoritative information on the frequency and success of the use of the Secretary-General's good offices is not readily obtainable. Nevertheless, it appears that the Secretary-General has used good offices to seek clemency on behalf of prisoners who face summary or arbitrary execution, to encourage the reunification of families who have been separated by national frontiers, to appeal to a government whose policies have threatened an indigenous community, to request the release of prisoners of conscience (particularly if they are suffering from grave health problems), and in other circumstances requiring humanitarian assistance.]

----

[13] Ramcharan, *The Good Offices of the United Nations Secretary-General in the Field of Human Rights,* 76 Am. J. Int'l L. 130 (1982); *see also* Nayar, *Dag Hammarskjöld and U Thant: The Evolution of Their Office,* 7 Case W. Res. J. Int'l L. 36 (1974).

[vi. *United Nations Congress on the Prevention of Crime and the Treatment of Offenders*

Every five years the U.N. Congress on the Prevention of Crime and the Treatment of Offenders convenes to consider issues of criminal justice. Significant human rights issues, however, arise in connection with the Congress and the related Committee on Crime Prevention and Control. For example, the Fifth Congress in 1975 drafted the U.N. Declaration on the Protection of All Persons from Being Subjected to Torture and Other Cruel, Inhuman or Degrading Treatment or Punishment. In 1988 the Committee on Crime Prevention and Control at its 10th session adopted the Principles on the Effective Prevention and Investigation of Extra-legal, Arbitrary and Summary Executions, which was adopted by ECOSOC in 1989.]

[h.] *The UNHCR and Relevant Specialized Agencies*

The United Nations High Commissioner for Refugees and four specialized agencies of the United Nations system of organizations — the International Labour Organisation, the United Nations Educational, Scientific and Cultural Organization, the World Health Organization and the Food and Agriculture Organization of the United Nations (within their specific fields of competence) — have also a special interest in human rights matters.

[i].   *United Nations High Commissioner for Refugees*

The Office of the United Nations High Commissioner for Refugees (UNHCR), established by the General Assembly as of 1 January 1951, is entrusted with providing international protection, under United Nations auspices, to refugees falling within its competence by: (*a*) promoting the conclusion and ratification of international conventions for the protection of refugees, supervising their application, and proposing amendments thereto; (*b*) promoting, through special agreements with Governments, the execution of measures to improve the situation of refugees and to reduce the number requiring protection; (*c*) assisting governmental and private efforts to promote voluntary repatriation or assimilation within new national communities; (*d*) promoting the admission of refugees to the territories of States; (*e*) endeavouring to obtain permission for refugees to transfer their assets, especially those necessary for their resettlement; (*f*) obtaining from Governments information concerning the number and conditions of refugees in their territories and the laws and regulations concerning them; (*g*) keeping in close touch with the Governments and intergovernmental organizations concerned; (*h*) establishing contact with private organizations dealing with refugee questions; and (*i*) facilitating the co-ordination of efforts of private organizations concerned with the welfare of refugees. In addition, UNHCR may engage in repatriation and resettlement activities at the request of the General Assembly, and perform certain functions to assist stateless persons under the Convention on the Reduction of Statelessness.

[ii.] *International Labour Organisation*

The Constitution of the International Labour Organisation (ILO) recognizes that labour is not a commodity and affirms that all human beings, irrespective of race, creed or sex, have the right to pursue both their material well-being and their spiritual development in conditions of freedom and dignity, economic security and equal opportunity.

Since its establishment in 1919 as an autonomous institution associated with the League of Nations, ILO's main concern has been the formulation of international labour standards and their effective implementation. The International Labour Conference, which meets annually, has gradually build up a body of international labour conventions and recommendations, many of which deal with such human rights problems as the prohibition of forced labour, the protection of freedom of association, including trade union rights, the elimination of discrimination in employment and occupation, the application of the principle of equal remuneration for men and women workers for work of equal value, and the promotion of full employment, fair and safe conditions of employment, and social security.

[iii.] *United Nations Educational, Scientific and Cultural Organization*

The purpose of the United Nations Educational, Scientific and Cultural Organization (UNESCO) is, as laid down in its Constitution, "to contribute to peace and security by promoting collaboration among the nations through education, science and culture in order to further universal respect for justice, for the rule of law and for the human rights and fundamental freedoms which are affirmed for the peoples of the world, without distinction of race, sex, language or religion, by the Charter of the United Nations".

In addition to carrying out a programme involving many forms of direct action designed to deal with the complex problems encountered in the development of education, science and culture, UNESCO has prepared several conventions and recommendations relating to human rights. [The UNESCO Committee on Conventions and Recommendations considers communications alleging violations of the right to education, the right to participate freely in cultural life, freedom of conscience and expression, and other rights within UNESCO's competence.]

[iv.] *Food and Agriculture Organization*

A basic purpose of the Food and Agriculture Organization of the United Nations (FAO) is ". . . contributing towards an expanding world economy and ensuring humanity's freedom from hunger".

The agency is mainly concerned with raising levels of nutrition and standards of living, securing improvements in the efficiency of the production and distribution of food and agricultural products, bettering the condition of rural populations, and thus contributing towards an expanding world economy. Its activities are designed to help solve one of the fundamental problems of mankind, namely the overall provision of the world's food supply. The Freedom from Hunger Campaign, launched by FAO in 1960, spread public knowledge of development problems in the agency's fields of concern and mobilized public opinion for increased development efforts.

[v.] *World Health Organization*

The preamble to the Constitution of the World Health Organization (WHO) declares that the enjoyment of the highest attainable standard of health is a fundamental right of every human being and that Governments have a responsibility for the health of their peoples which can be fulfilled only by the provision of adequate health and social measures.

The agency serves as the co-ordinating authority on international health work. It maintains certain necessary international health services, promotes and conducts research in the field of health, and works to improve standards of teaching in the health, medical and related professions.

[i.] *Role of non-governmental organizations in consultative status*

Article 71 of the United Nations Charter authorizes the Economic and Social Council to make suitable arrangements for consultation with non-governmental organizations (NGOs) which are concerned with matters within its competence. The Council has accordingly made such arrangements with several hundred international and national organizations, which are contained in resolution 1296 (1968) of the Economic and Social Council.

These organizations are divided into three groups: Category I, which is made up of NGOs having a basic interest in most of the activities of the Council; Category II, which is made up of NGOs having a special competence but which are concerned with only a few of the Council's activities. Those NGOs which can make occasional and useful contributions to the Council's work are placed on a Roster for *ad hoc* consultations.

All these organizations may send observers to public meetings of the Council, its commissions, sub-commissions and other subsidiary bodies. They can submit written statements for circulation and present their views orally to the Council or to one of its subsidiary bodies. In addition, they may consult with the United Nations Secretariat on matters of mutual concern.

The Economic and Social Council, by its resolution 1987/5 of 26 May 1987, invited non-governmental organizations in consultative status to submit to it written statements which might contribute to full and universal recognition and realization of the rights contained in the International Covenant on Economic, Social and Cultural Rights, and requested the Secretary-General to make those statements available to the Committee on Economic, Social and Cultural Rights in a timely manner.

Under the procedures in effect for the handling of communications containing allegations of violations of human rights, NGOs may also play an important role by submitting written, reliable information to the United Nations. Those communications are considered admissible when they are based on direct and reliable knowledge of the violations involved. Admissible communications are then considered in private meetings by the Sub-Commission on Prevention of Discrimination and Protection of Minorities. If the Sub-Commission finds that they appear to reveal a consistent pattern of gross and reliably attested violations requiring attention by the Commission on Human Rights, the latter may examine the situation and decide whether it should be the subject of any investigation by an *ad hoc* committee. On the basis of such an investigation, the Commission must then decide whether to make recommendations to the Economic and Social Council for further action to be taken.

In studying or dealing with certain human rights problems, United Nations organs frequently call upon non-governmental organizations in consultative status to supply information, particularly on existing *de facto* situations. NGOs have responded generously and have supplied large amounts of useful information, thereby enhancing the role and facilitating the task, of the United Nations in the field of human rights.

[There are countless local, national, regional, and international NGOs concerned with various aspects of human rights; many but not all have attained consultative status with the U.N. or other intergovernmental organizations. NGOs contribute by providing information about specific cases, country situations, and particular kinds of violations, and help draft international standards. NGOs also undertake direct efforts to protect human rights by pursuing diplomatic initiatives, publishing reports, issuing public statements, mounting campaigns to mobilize public opinion, and assisting human rights victims. Many NGOs also attempt to influence the foreign policy of specific countries in their relations to states which are regularly responsible for human rights violations.]

C. CONCLUSION

The years since World War II have brought increased recognition of individual rights as an appropriate subject of international concern. The U.N. has responded by adopting the Charter and the International Bill of Human Rights, by promulgating scores of other multilateral human rights instruments, and by developing procedures for human rights implementation and enforcement.

In addition to the human rights machinery of the U.N., regional organizations have promulgated human rights treaties, incorporating many of the norms found in U.N. instruments, and have developed regional mechanisms to enforce the treaties. NGOs dedicated to protecting human rights have increased in number and sophistication. These organizations have contributed to the drafting of human rights standards, have assisted intergovernmental organizations with their investigations, and have intervened directly to protect the victims of human rights abuses.

The worldwide recognition of human rights law should lead to more widespread acceptance of human rights and, in turn, to increased protection of the rights.

II HOW CAN LAWYERS AND OTHERS ASSIST U.S. CITIZENS DETAINED IN FOREIGN COUNTRIES?

A Hypothetical Situation in Peru

A. **Introduction**

B. **Questions**

C. **The Situation in Peru**
1. **Background**
2. **Human Rights Situation in Peru**
3. **Constitution of Peru**
4. **United States-Peru Relations**
5. **Congressional Presentation for Security Assistance Programs**

D. **Sources of Aid**
1. **Introduction**
   Atkins & Pisani, The Hassle of Your Life: A Handbook for the Friends and
      Families of Americans Imprisoned Abroad
2. **Consular Services**
   Statement from a U.S. Passport
   Vienna Convention on Consular Relations
   Department of State, Providing Consular Services to the American Public
      Abroad
   Hearings before the Subcommittee on International Operations of the House
      Committee on Foreign Affairs
   Department of State, Travel Advisory
3. **Other U.S. Government Services**
   22 U.S.C. § 1732
   Redpath v. Kissinger
4. **Intergovernmental Procedures**
   The Inter-American Commission on Human Rights
   Ratification of Treaties by Peru and the United States
   International Trade Unions and Human Rights
   State Responsibility for Nonwealth Injuries to Aliens
   Restatement (Third) of the Foreign Relations Law of the United States
   Calvo, Derecho Internacional Teórico y Práctico de Europa y America
   Constitution of Peru
5. **Nongovernmental Organizations**
   Transnational Corporations and Human Rights
   Religious Organizations and Human Rights
   Universities and Human Rights
   The International Committee of the Red Cross

A. INTRODUCTION

This chapter familiarizes readers with traditional methods of protecting human rights — diplomatic concern of a government as to its own citizens — and reveals the inadequacy of the traditional method. To illustrate needs for international human rights law and organizations that help implement the law, the chapter begins with a hypothetical case involving a U.S. citizen who has been arrested in Peru for apparently political reasons. The questions ask readers to examine possible sources of help for obtaining the U.S. citizen's release, including legal action in the U.S. and in Peru, traditional diplomatic protection, and intergovernmental and nongovernmental human rights organizations.

To aid in determining available sources of help, the chapter provides background information on the human rights situation in Peru. The information arguably presents an accurate portrayal of the situation in Peru at the time of writing. Since, however, the human rights situation in a country can change quickly, readers should not view this material as a reflection of the current scene. Nonetheless, the situation is typical of that present and recurring in many countries at differing times and is a useful model for exploring the questions posed here.

The chapter presents an overview of international human rights organizations — intergovernmental and nongovernmental — that could be helpful in this situation, the types of aid organizations can provide, and procedures for obtaining that aid. Later chapters will examine many of the organizations and procedures in more detail.

In addition to the materials here, readers should acquaint themselves with the following human rights instruments found in the accompanying handbook, *Selected International Human Rights Instruments*: the United Nations Charter, the Universal Declaration of Human Rights, the International Covenant on Civil and Political Rights, and the American Convention on Human Rights. (Other instruments also may be relevant to the problem, but those four instruments will provide a sufficient basis for discussion.)

B. QUESTIONS

Kenneth Olson visited the office yesterday. He is concerned about his daughter Sara, who was expected to phone on her mother's birthday three weeks ago, but did not call. Sara is 28 years old, was born in Minneapolis, and attended Minneapolis Lutheran High School and St. Olaf College in Northfield (where she majored in Spanish); she went on to a Ph.D. program in Economics at the University of Minnesota. A year ago she began her dissertation on "Peru: The Role of the Mining Industry in a Developing Economy." Six months later, after several months of preparation and learning Quechua, she procured a U.S. passport and left for Peru. She normally is conscientious about writing her parents and phoning them on holidays.

Kenneth has been a client for some time and is the manager of the

Assembly Plant of the Ford Motor Company in St. Paul, Minnesota. He would like us to consider whether steps can be taken to find out what happened to Sara. He knows none of the people with whom she was working in Peru; telephone calls and letters to her residence have been unavailing.

Your research has revealed that the Associated Press reporter in Lima had heard that Sara was interviewing mining-union leaders in Lima when she was detained a month ago by military police and suspected of collaborating with the Shining Path armed opposition group. She is being held without charge and without being brought before a judicial official. We have been able to obtain the material set forth below about the general human rights situation in Peru.

1. What first step would you take to work for Sara's release were she imprisoned in another state of the United States? What are the problems with using that approach in Peru, based on the material set forth below?

2. What help might you expect from the U.S. State Department and its consulate in Peru?

    a. What duty does 22 U.S.C. § 1732 impose? How have U.S. courts interpreted the duty?

    b. What rights does the U.S. consul have as to citizens detained abroad under customary international law and Articles 5 and 36 of the Vienna Convention on Consular Relations?

3. Might the State Department be reluctant to pursue vigorously Sara's release? If so, why?

4. How might you put pressure on the State Department? What help might you obtain from Congress?

5. What arguments would you make for Sara's release if you were a U.S. consular official? How might a Peruvian official respond? What then would you argue?

6. May the U.S. government appropriately seek release of its nationals when Peruvians are detained and even tortured for similar ''offenses''?

7. What clauses of the U.N. Charter, the Universal Declaration of Human Rights, and the American Convention on Human Rights are relevant in this situation? (*See, e.g.*, Articles 1, 2(4), 2(7), 55, and 56 of the Charter, Articles 2, 9, 19, and 20 of the Universal Declaration, and Articles 5, 7, 8, 13, 16, 24, 27, and 41 of the American Convention.) Are there pertinent provisions other than those listed? How might the articles be used to assist Sara? Where could other instruments relevant to the situation be found?

8. Is it relevant that the Peruvian government has declared a state of emergency in the part of Peru where Sara was detained? Does the state of emergency change the arguments for Sara's release? For stopping the military police from torturing her?

9. What aid might be available from intergovernmental organizations? Which might help? Will the aid they could offer be quick enough?

10. Look at the factual situation. What are the personal/practical resources of the Olson family that might be available to aid in Sara's release? What organizations other than intergovernmental organizations might be helpful? Do you see any conflict of interest between the work of these organizations and your goal of freeing Sara?

C. THE SITUATION IN PERU

1. Background

Department of State, Background Notes: Peru 5-8 (1987):

GOVERNMENT

The president is popularly elected for a 5-year term and may not be reelected to a consecutive term. The first and second vice presidents also are popularly elected but have no constitutional functions unless the president is unable to discharge his duties. The principal executive body is the Council of Ministers, headed by a prime minister. Like other cabinet members, the prime minister is appointed by the president. All presidential decree laws or draft bills sent to Congress must be approved by the Council of Ministers.

The legislative branch consists of a bicameral Congress with a 60-member Senate and a 180-member Chamber of Deputies, both elected for 5-year terms. Constitutionally elected former presidents are also designated senators for life. Congress convenes from July 27 to December 15 and from April 1 to May 31, annually. In addition to passing laws, Congress is empowered to approve treaties, authorize government loans, and approve the government budget. Each congressional body has the power to initiate legislation, which is then submitted to the other body for revision. The president has the power to review legislation but may not veto laws passed by Congress.

The judicial branch of government is headed by a 16-member Supreme Court seated in Lima. The Tribunal of Constitutional Guarantees, a separate judicial body, interprets the constitution on matters of individual rights. An independent attorney general serves as a judicial ombudsman. Superior courts sit in departmental capitals and hear appeals from decisions by lower courts. Courts of first instance are located in provincial capitals and are divided into civil, penal, and special chambers.

Peru is divided into 24 departments and the constitutional province of Callao, the country's chief port, adjacent to Lima. The departments are subdivided into provinces, which are composed of districts. Local authorities below the departmental level are elected. . . .

ECONOMY

Peru's economy has moved somewhat erratically in recent years, the result of shifts in government orientation and policies, fluctuating international prices for the country's major exports, and, to a lesser extent, weather patterns that have had particularly negative effects on agriculture and fisheries. The government of former President Belaunde (1980-85) endeavored to rebuild a market economy, dismantling structural inefficiencies inherited from 12 years of military rule. Nonetheless, a swollen and corrupt bureaucracy, ill-chosen and often nonproductive investment projects, a heavy external debt burden, increasing budget deficits, and spiralling inflation inhibited the reformist government from meeting its goals. Popular dissatisfaction with the failures of the Belaunde presidency led to its replacement by the more interventionist García administration in 1985. . . .

Although industry is the country's dominant sector in terms of output, agriculture continues to provide a living for some 38% of all Peruvians. Large-scale, cooperatively owned irrigated farms located on the coast produce cotton, rice, and sugarcane, as well as fruit and vegetables for domestic and export sales. Most farmers, however, continue to work small subsistence plots in the highlands where they grow potatoes, corn, and fodder for their small herds. . . .

Peru has traditionally based its economy, in large part, on the nation's rich and varied mineral resources. Mining remains extremely important today, both as a source of badly needed foreign exchange as well as employment, particularly in the impoverished Andean highlands. Peru is one of the world's leading producers of silver, lead, zinc, copper, gold, and iron ore. . . . Labor unrest in the mines also took a toll on production, and several small and medium-sized mines have been closed. Peru has been a net petroleum exporter since 1978. Although the country's crude oil reserves are not great — only 500-550 million barrels — Occidental Petroleum has recently made several substantial discoveries both in the eastern jungle and on the northern part of the continental shelf. More importantly, Royal Dutch Shell has uncovered a major gas deposit near the Brazilian border; the initial estimate is that the find contains 7 trillion cubic feet of gas. . . .

FOREIGN TRADE

Foreign trade is critical to Peru's economic well-being. In the past, the country's diverse exports made the national economy less susceptible to the damaging effects of individual commodity price fluctuations than that of most other Latin American nations. . . .

U.S. INVESTMENT IN PERU

Much of the U.S. investment in Peru is concentrated in the mining and petroleum sectors; many other U.S. subsidiaries manufacture consumer products or provide services. Current book value of U.S. investment in the country is estimated at $3 billion. The largest single U.S. investors are the Southern Peru Copper Corporation — primarily owned by ASARCO — and Occidental Petroleum, which has important concessions and operations in the northern jungle areas.

The García administration is increasingly placing major importance on new investment as the only way to keep the economy growing in the absence of access to new external credits. It has, nonetheless, made it clear that investors must subordinate their interests to those of Peru. Potential investors are concerned about the government's price control policies, the continuing restriction on profit remittances, the uneasy situation resulting from the country's unorthodox debt service policies, and the lack of a clear set of rules of the game. Potential investors will also watch closely how the García administration follows through with its commitment to compensate the Enron Corporation for the assets of its Belco Oil subsidiary, which the state took over following the termination of its contract. Finally, investment is also hindered by restrictive Peruvian labor laws. Recently, the government has reinstated several tax and other financial incentives for new investors, with additional incentives for those willing to establish plants or projects outside metropolitan Lima. . . .

2. Human Rights Situation[1]

The past decade has marked a period of increased human rights abuses in Peru. Faced with a severe economic crisis, a high incidence of criminality related to drug trafficking, and a major armed opposition, the government has alternated between expressions of concern over human rights abuses and apparent indifference to them. There has been a steady rise in both the number and kinds of human rights violations. The decade began with the emergence of an armed opposition group known as *"Sendero Luminoso"* (Shining Path), centered in the Ayacucho region and employing violent means to overthrow the government. By 1982 the Army had declared a 13-province region an Emergency Zone under direct control of a politico-military command. The state of emergency was extended nationwide in 1984. During 1987 more people had disappeared or had been subjected to clandestine detention in Peru than in any other country. It has been estimated that 3,200 people have disappeared in Peru since 1982; more disappeared after 1982 than in any other country except Guatemala and El Salvador. The majority of the disappeared were peasants, students, and intellectuals — though victims came from many different occupations including businesspeople, lawyers, journalists, and justices of the peace. The government has estimated that 15,000 people have died in the continuing conflict between the military and armed opposition groups.

a. Respect for the Integrity of the Person

i. *Freedom from Arbitrary Executions, Detention, and Torture*

Despite legal protections, arbitrary executions, disappearances, detention, and torture continue in Peru. For example, on June 18, 1986, several hundred members of the Shining Path opposition group who were imprisoned in three compounds in the Lima area staged a coordinated rebellion. The Peruvian President Alan García ordered the Joint Command of the Armed Forces to regain control over the prisons. Within 24 hours, the armed forces resumed control by killing many of the prisoners who had taken part in

---

[1] The material in this section is derived principally from Department of State, Country Reports on Human Rights Practices for 1989, Report Submitted to the Senate Committee on Foreign Relations and the House Committee on Foreign Affairs, 101st Cong., 2nd Sess. 708 (1990), previous annual editions of the State Department Country Reports, reports from Americas Watch and Amnesty International, as well as other sources. For further references see the note at the end of the section.

the rebellion; a large number of prisoners were killed after they had surrendered to the authorities. In one prison, Lurigancho, all 124 prisoners died. Official accounts claimed that the deaths occurred during the army's effort to retake the facility. It was later ascertained, however, that over 100 had been summarily executed while they were lying on the ground; many were tortured before they were executed by a gunshot in the mouth. In the El Frontón island-prison, the government reported that one cell block had collapsed and buried many rebels. In fact, the military had razed the building after the prisoners had surrendered; 30-60 prisoners from that cell block were taken to a naval base and "disappeared." In the women's prison, inmates were subjected to the "dark alley" treatment ("callejón oscura") after the army regained control. These women were forced to march through a double-line of soldiers who beat and prodded them with rifle butts.

In May 1988 at least 29 residents of the Cayara district, Victor Fajardo province, Ayacucho, were reported killed by army troops in retaliation for the ambush by Shining Path of a military convoy the night before. These residents, however, were apparently not members of Shining Path and included several schoolchildren and the headmaster of the local school. They were beaten by clubs and hacked to death with machetes. Other people were killed as they returned to Cayara from tending their crops; they were similarly beaten and hacked to death with knives, machetes, axes, and agricultural tools. In September 1989 a 22-year-old nurse, who testified to officials investigating the 1988 slaughter in Cayara, was shot dead by men in army uniform, making her the ninth witness to the killings to fall victim to extrajudicial execution or disappearance.

Atrocities have also been committed by armed opposition groups — most notably Shining Path. Insurgent groups routinely torture, mutilate, and murder their captives — often after mock trials. In 1982 Shining Path began to carry out widespread execution-style killings in rural areas. Hundreds of public "executions" have occurred since then before assembled villagers in areas the Shining Path has sought to control. Agronomists, engineers, administrators, and other professionals working on government projects and cooperatives were a particular target for Shining Path attacks. For the first time in 1988 foreign development workers were killed by Shining Path. Prior to municipal elections in November 1989, the Shining Path assassinated over 100 mayors, local political leaders, and electoral candidates forcing many candidates to withdraw in fear. Shining Path was not, however, able to undermine the electoral process. Some analysts believe that the Shining Path opposition group is attempting to destabilize the political situation in order to provoke an army coup, leading to a popular uprising.

In response to the insurgency, it has become common practice for the Peruvian government to take large numbers of people from the streets or from their houses in rural areas under emergency law. They are brought to military barracks for interrogation. These round-ups are often arbitrary in nature. There are also reports that during the interrogations, torture has been commonly practiced and that many torture victims have died. The initiation of *habeas corpus* procedures, if declared admissible by the courts, usually produced no result, since the military authorities simply denied that the person concerned had been detained. It is also reported that torture was practiced at the Lima headquarters of the Division against Terrorism (DIRCOTE), a branch of the Investigatory Police (PIP).

ii. Public Trial

Only military courts have been able to assert jurisdiction over offenders in the military or police force. The last attempt to have a civilian court try a military officer occurred in 1986 and was thwarted when the officer fled to avoid trial. Because the military trials are not generally open to the public, little is known about specific cases. In 1989, however, public hearings under military jurisdiction were held in the cases of the 77 officers accused of assassinating prisoners in the Lurigancho prison during June 1986. Two of the 77 officers were sentenced to prison.

b. Respect for Political Rights

i. Freedom of Expression

Although the Peruvian Constitution guarantees freedom of the press, journalists have occasionally been subjected to violence and threats. Journalists are also barred from traveling in the rural areas which are under states of emergency.

ii. Freedom of Peaceful Assembly and Association

Freedom of peaceful assembly and association are expressly guaranteed in the Peruvian Constitution and are usually respected in areas not under a state of emergency. In recent years, however, peaceful public meetings often have ended in police use of tear gas and water cannons, arrests, and even death. The Peruvian Constitution provides for the right of workers to form labor unions without previous authorization. Government rules limit the formation of unions in the private sector to groups with 20 or more workers. Only one union is allowed for each enterprise or place of work and for each category of worker. In the public sector, 20 percent of the workers can request a union, thus allowing up to five unions to represent the workers in one workplace. The Constitution also provides for the right to strike "according to law," although most strikes are declared illegal. In order to show support for hospital staff strikes, even the doctors went on strike in Lima on one occasion in the late 1980's, effectively terminating all but emergency hospital care. In recent years, other sectors such as the mining industry and banks have nearly ceased functioning at various times due to large-scale strikes. In 1989 approximately one million Peruvians went on a three-day strike in the mining and farming areas in response to a demand by the Shining Path. The strike stopped all food shipments, electric power, and export minerals from three provinces.

iii. *Freedom of Religion*

The Constitution of Peru recognizes the Roman Catholic Church and establishes the separation of Church and State. It also assures freedom of religion and conscience. These rights are respected in practice by the government for Roman Catholics, members of minority religions, and missionary organizations. Several priests and Catholic lay workers, however, have been threatened by Shining Path and other armed opposition groups.

c. Government Responses to Alleged Violations of Human Rights

A highly publicized murder of eight Peruvian journalists in Uchuraccay in the early 1980's resulted in the appointment by President Fernando Belaunde Terry of an investigative commission headed by Peruvian writer Mario Vargas Llosa. His report, released in May 1983, characterized the event as an "aberration." The number of disappeared individuals continued to increase, however, and by the fall of that year a national consensus had emerged that the country was in the midst of a "dirty war" similar to that of Argentina during the period 1976-1982.

Dissatisfaction over the excesses of the "dirty war" increased through the early 1980's and at the same time Peru was faced with a mounting national debt. The Peruvian voters turned to a member of the American Popular Revolutionary Alliance, Alan García Pérez. García was elected President on April 14, 1985, receiving 53% of the vote. García sought to reverse national priorities, that is, to put Peruvian economic needs before the demands of international banks. García announced in his inaugural address a commitment to the restoration of control over those sectors responsible for human rights violations. By the end of 1985, however, human rights violations had increased to a total of 1,005 disappearances — 76 under the age of 18 years — as well as numerous reports of torture.

The suppression of the prison revolt in 1986 resulted in human rights violations committed by the armed forces which carried out the operation, but also demonstrated the indifference of the Peruvian government. President Alan García had previously issued many pronouncements in support of human rights, but eyewitness accounts of the prison massacre revealed the government's inadequate response to those atrocities. The government established a commission to investigate the Lurigancho incident, but when a prominent army general was identified as being responsible, jurisdiction was transferred to military courts, thus limiting public access to the commission's conclusions, until three years later in 1989. Relatives of the murdered prisoners appealed repeatedly to the government for complete lists of the victims, for copies of pertinent judicial records, and for custody of the victims' bodies. Those appeals went unanswered.

Despite the problems associated with the prison revolts, President García continued to pursue his social democratic policies. Both his political and economic agendas began suffering setbacks barely two years into his term, virtually immobilizing his already marginalized human rights agenda. According to the Andean Commission of Jurists, in 1988 the number of deaths caused by political violence reached 1,986; human rights violations have continued or worsened since then. A new President, Alberto Fujimori, was elected in 1990.

Local organizations remain active in the investigation and defense of human rights in Peru. There is a network of human rights groups in Peru called the National Coordinator for Human Rights. The network consists of several private human rights organizations, including: the Association for Human Rights (APRODEH), the Catholic Church's Episcopal Commission for Social Action (CEAS), the National Human Rights Commission (CONADEH), and the Institute for Legal Defense. Lima is also the headquarters for the Andean Commission of Jurists. Other human rights groups include the Committee for Disappeared-Detainees' Relatives who have Taken Refuge in Lima (COFADER), the National Association of Relatives of Abducted Persons and Disappeared-Detainees in the Zones under a State of Emergency in Peru (ANFASEP), La Red ("The Network"), and the Association of Democratic Lawyers, which has reported the short-term arrest of many of its human rights attorneys. These groups not only assist in providing legal defense for victims of human rights abuse, but also aid in informing the international community about conditions in Peru.

d. The Administration of Justice in Peru

The Constitution of Peru guarantees the inviolability of the home, freedom of movement, freedom of assembly, and freedom from arrest without a warrant. Under a state of emergency, however, the Constitution permits the government to suspend all these constitutional protections. In addition, the armed forces can assume control of any part of the country whenever the President of the Republic so directs.

The Attorney General and the judiciary do not lose their powers while a state of emergency is in force. The principal function of the Attorney General (Ministerio Público) is to defend the law, citizens' rights, and the public interest, as well as to prosecute crime. The Attorney General also has authority to initiate legal actions against civil servants and public employees.

In Peru the judiciary is an independent branch of government. Once criminal charges are filed, a judge determines if probable cause exists, in which case a public trial follows. The Constitution requires that civilians be tried in civilian courts. The Supreme Court has constitutional authority to decide if military or police offenders will be tried in civilian courts or in a separate military court system. Military courts, however, have taken jurisdiction of any such cases in the past several years. Military trials are usually not public.

The Constitution of Peru provides for *habeas corpus* proceedings to be instituted by the injured party or by any person acting on the party's behalf. *Habeas corpus* procedures are flexible and designed to provide immediate defense of the injured party. In cases of arbitrary detention, the judge must order the responsible authority to produce the detained person on the same day and explain the detention. The right of recourse to *habeas corpus* remains in force during a state of emergency, although the right of the courts to establish the legality of the detention is suspended. Unfortunately, the government often replies that it has no knowledge of a person who is alleged to have been detained. In addition, *amparo* (enforcement of constitutional rights) procedures also remain in force under emergency law for those rights which have not been suspended.

The Peruvian Code of Criminal Procedure authorizes detention *incommunicado* for a period not to exceed 10 days. This period has been extended to 15 days for persons suspected of terrorism. Their detention must be reported to the office of the Attorney General and to the judge within 24 hours of their arrest. The state of emergency, however, has suspended this requirement of notice within 24 hours. Under the 1987 Peruvian anti-terrorism law and its amendments, police must also notify the detainees' family and human rights groups of an arrest.

The Constitution prohibits torture and inhuman or humiliating treatment. *Habeas corpus* procedures apply in the case of torture as well. The 1987 anti-terrorism law and amendments require that persons detained for terrorism be interrogated only in the presence of a public prosecutor and a defense attorney. Recent changes in the law require that persons accused of crimes of terrorism be brought before a civil, rather than a military tribunal.

The judiciary lacks adequate finances and professional training. As a result, the courts are experiencing severe backlogs and slow progress in cases involving abuses of human rights. In July 1988 the Ministry of Justice reported a backlog of nearly 45,000 pending criminal cases. Many persons are detained without bail for up to four years while awaiting trial. It has been estimated that up to 95% of those accused of terrorism and brought before the courts are released. Consequently, the Peruvian public appears to have little respect for the judicial system, perceiving it as corrupt.

3. The Constitution of Peru (1979), Official Edition of the Ministry of Justice (1980) [translated from Spanish]:

Article 105

Principles contained in treaties relating to human rights are accorded constitutional priority. They cannot be modified except by the procedure of constitutional amendment. . . .

Article 231

The President of the Republic, with consent of the Council of Ministers, may decree for a determined period of time in all or part of the territory, and giving an account to Congress or to the Permanent Committee, states of exception [estados de excepción] which in this article are viewed as:

a. State of emergency, in the case of disturbance of the peace or of internal order, of catastrophe or of grave circumstances which affect the life of the Nation. In this eventuality, constitutional guarantees relative to personal liberty and security, the inviolability of the home, the freedom of assembly and movement in the territory, which are mentioned in paragraphs 7, 9, 10 and 20(g) of Article 2 can be suspended. Under no circumstance can the penalty of exile be imposed. The period for a state of emergency cannot exceed 60 (sixty) days. Its extension requires a new decree. In a state of emergency, the Armed Forces assume control of the internal order when the President of the Republic so decrees. . . .

Article 295

An act or omission on the part of any authority, official, or person who violates or threatens individual liberty, gives grounds for an action of *habeas corpus*.

An action of *amparo* protects the other rights recognized by the Constitution that may be violated or threatened by any authority, official or individual.

An action of *amparo* involves the same procedure as an action of *habeas corpus* to the extent that it is applicable. . . .

4. United States-Peru Relations

The U.S. government's attitude toward Peru may be characterized historically as one of mild indifference, as Peru does not command the strategic attention that the United States accords certain other Latin American countries. The rise of Shining Path in the 1980's, however, has led the State Department to send "anti-terrorist advisors" to meet with Peruvian military officers. At least one advisor has been linked in the past to human rights violations committed against indigenous peoples of Guatemala. Since 1980 the State Department has not seriously considered whether military assistance to Peru would violate Section 502B of the Foreign Assistance Act of 1961, which prohibits the U.S. from providing military assistance to countries engaging in a "consistent pattern of gross violations of internationally recognized human rights." 22 U.S.C. § 2304 (1986). Mechanisms within the government to ensure compliance with that provision are demonstrably weak and Congress has not insisted on enforcement.

In fiscal 1988, the U.S. government provided Peru nearly $52 million in aid of which $27 million was development assistance, $15 million was food aid under P.L. 480, $8.5 million was assistance to help Peru combat drugs, $0.4 million was for training military personnel, and $0.5 million was other economic support. In 1989 the Bush administration targeted over US$230 million to combat drug trafficking in, among other countries, Peru. The following excerpt summarizes U.S. foreign policy concerns in Peru:

5. United States, Congressional Presentation for Security Assistance Programs, Fiscal Year 1990, at 229-30 (1989):

POLICY CONSIDERATIONS

The fundamental U.S. interest in Peru is to support democracy in Peru and help the country meet the challenges of terrorism and narcotics trafficking. U.S. policy aims to support structural economic reform and responsible debt management while countering the substantial Soviet presence. Soviet military influence has complicated U.S. access and influence. U.S. narcotics policy focuses on law enforcement and crop eradication while drawing on scarce resources in a period of economic crisis and foreign exchange scarcity. The FY 1990 assistance package has economic and military components which will help promote the continuation of democracy in Peru, thereby contributing to regional stability. . . .

FY 1990 Request

Military financing will be used to acquire field equipment and spare parts and to maintain and overhaul existing equipment. The program will induce the military to combat the insurgency and narco-terrorism aggressively without committing human rights abuses. IMET [International Military Education and Training Program] permits a continued dialogue with the Peruvian military, whose support is critical to continued democratic government. ESF [Economic Support Fund] will support the anti-narcotics effort and improved administration of justice. Local currency generated by the program will be used for agricultural and community development activities, particularly in the Upper Huallaga Valley where most illegal coca is grown.

PERU

DOLLARS IN THOUSANDS

SUMMARY OF FY 1990 REQUEST

MILITARY:

Foreign Mil Sales Financing Prog	5,000
Military Assistance Program	0
Intl Mil Education & Trng Prog	525

ECONOMIC:

Economic Support Fund	5,000
Developmental Assistance	14,155
P.L. 480 [food assistance]	28,190
Peace Corps	0
International Narcotics Cntrl	10,000
TOTAL FOREIGN ASSISTANCE	62,870

. . . .

NOTE

For further reading, see material on Peru in chapter 5, *infra*; *see also*:

Americas Watch: Americas Watch, A Certain Passivity: Failure to Curb Human Rights Abuses in Peru (1987); Americas Watch, Tolerating Abuses: Violations of Human Rights in Peru (1988).

Amnesty International: Amnesty International, Peru: The Cayara Massacre, AI Index: AMR 46/56/89 (1989); Amnesty International, Peru: "Disappearances", Torture and Summary Executions by Government Forces After the Prison Revolts of June 1986, AI Index: AMR/46/03/87; Amnesty International, Peru: Human Rights in a State of Emergency, AI Index: AMR46/49/89 (1989); Amnesty International, Report 144-47 (1989).

Andean Commission: Andean Commission of Jurists, Andean Newsletter, Nos. 30-35 (1989); Andean Commission of Jurists, Peru y Chile: Poder Judicial y Derechos Humanos (1988).

Department of State: Department of State, Country Reports on Human Rights Practices for 1989, Report Submitted to the Senate Committee on Foreign Relations and the House Committee on Foreign Affairs, 101st Cong., 2nd Sess. 708 (1990).

United Nations: Report of the visit by two members of the Working Group on Enforced or Involuntary Disappearances (17-22 June 1985), U.N. Doc. E/CN.4/1986/18/Add.1 (1986); Report of the Special Rapporteur on Torture, U.N. Doc. E/CN.4/1989/15, at 33-38 (1989).

D. SOURCES OF AID

1. Introduction

R. Atkins & R. Pisani, The Hassle of Your Life: A Handbook For the Friends and Families of Americans Imprisoned Abroad 4-5, 10-12 (1982):

HIRING A FOREIGN ATTORNEY

Hiring a foreign attorney is one of the most important tasks for you or your representative. Although some embassies or consulates provide a list of local attorneys to their arrested nationals, there are no guarantees that the lawyers are competent in the required field of law, nor will the embassies make such guarantees. The local embassy will not assist you or your relative in any way in hiring a local attorney other than to provide him/her with a list. Often, the best attorneys are not on the lists.

It is not at all uncommon for foreign attorneys to require the payment of large retainers in exchange for vague promises, and then to ignore, abandon or otherwise victimize their clients. In addition, foreign counsel often fail to maintain adequate communication with the client and his or her family in the United States. . . .

Other sources that can be used to assist in the selection of the foreign attorney include the various Bar Associations and human rights organizations such as

Amnesty International. Checking on the experience of others who have been recently released from that country may also be helpful. . . .

It is important for you or your U.S. legal representative to have some understanding of the law and court procedures of the country so that you can make a realistic appraisal of what may happen to your relative. For example, the things you will need to know include:

1. The exact charges facing your relative;
2. The maximum penalties that can be imposed for that offense;
3. Whether any fines can be levied;
4. What has happened to other Americans who have been accused of similar charges;
5. Whether there are any provisions for bail or pretrial release and whether probation or parole is a possibility;
6. Whether credit is given for good time and/or work time;
7. Whether there is a right to a jury trial;
8. Whether plea bargaining is acceptable;
9. Whether the appeal process, if any, is mandatory or voluntary;
10. Whether the prosecutor has the right to appeal; and
11. How long the trial process will take.

In addition, you or your U.S. representative may want to investigate extra-legal procedures which your relative may be able to take advantage of. These include, but are not limited to, buying your relative out and arranging for his escape. However, these procedures are extremely dangerous, and while many individuals incarcerated abroad may seriously consider one or more of these alternatives, their use is fraught with danger for your relative, yourself, and any representatives participating in such a venture. . . .

Experienced attorneys, however, may be able to make use of more conventional means of having your relative released without going to trial. The most common method employed involves deportation from the country. However, request for deportation must be made to the proper authorities at the proper time, and it is usually only used in relatively minor offenses. . . .

BACK HOME

There are other duties and contacts which can be helpful to your relative in the United States. First, regular contact should be maintained with the case worker in the State Department's Arrest Division for recent developments. In addition, you may want to contact the Country Desk Officer in the respective political branch of the State Department dealing with that country. This person keeps a watch on political and economic activity in the country, which in turn may influence or have an effect on your relative's imprisonment. Should you discover that your relative was abused in a foreign country, it may prove worthwhile to contact the Human Rights and Humanitarian Affairs branch of the State Department and report this fact to them. . . .

OUTSIDE HELP

One of the people you should consider contacting immediately is your Congressman or Congresswoman. We have found that most are genuinely concerned about the welfare of their constituents. They will usually do whatever they can to assist constituents who are incarcerated abroad and their families. In addition, they maintain local offices in their home districts, making communication even easier. However, the ability of a Congressman to materially assist your relative in a foreign country is very limited due to the U.S. Constitution's requirement that the President be the sole authority in foreign affairs. However, they can put the pressure on the State Department to institute action on a particular matter, and they can send letters or cables directly to the consular officer to indicate that they are interested in their constituent's case. This has the effect of further sensitizing those contacted to the fact that there are people who are concerned about the outcome of the case. Thus, while a Congressman cannot perform any miracles, he can be helpful in a number of circumstances. . . .

TRANSFER TREATIES

One of the most effective methods for assisting Americans incarcerated in foreign jails that has been developed in the last few years is the promulgation of treaties on the transferability of penal sanctions, which are commonly known as prisoner transfer treaties. Although these treaties do very little to solve the problems of prisoners while they are in foreign countries, they do provide a viable long-term solution in that they allow Americans to return home to serve out their sentences once their trials and all appeals have been completed. . . .

NOTES AND QUESTIONS

1. The U.S. has prisoner transfer treaties with the following countries:

Bolivia, *entered into force* Aug. 17, 1978, 30 U.S.T. 796, T.I.A.S. No. 9219.

Canada, *entered into force* July 19, 1978, 30 U.S.T. 6263, T.I.A.S. No. 9552.

France, *entered into force* Feb. 1, 1985, T.I.A.S. No. 10823 (slip agreement).

Korea, Republic of, *entered into force* Feb. 12, 1982, T.I.A.S. No. 10406 (slip agreement).

Mexico, *entered into force* Nov. 30, 1977, 28 U.S.T. 7399, T.I.A.S. No. 8718.

Panama, *entered into force* July 21, 1980, 32 U.S.T. 1565, T.I.A.S. No. 9784.

Turkey, *entered into force* Jan. 1, 1981, 32 U.S.T. 3187, T.I.A.S. No. 9892.

Western Europe (multilateral treaty), *entered into force* July 1, 1985, T.I.A.S. No. 10824 (slip agreement).

2. Would you be able to use a prisoner-transfer treaty to obtain Sara's release from detention in Peru? Why or why not? Even if you were able to obtain her release through such a treaty, would you want to pursue that option if there were other possible avenues for obtaining her release? What are disadvantages of using the transfer-treaty option? Do you think those treaties were designed to help persons in Sara's situation?

3. For further reading, see Note, *Examination of the United States Prisoner Transfer Treaties*, 6 N.Y.L. Sch. J. Int'l & Comp. L. 709 (1986); Bassiouni, *Perspectives on the Transfer of Prisoners Between the United States and Other Countries*, in V. Nanda & M. Bassiouni, International Criminal Law 271-300 (1987).

2. Consular Services

U.S. passports issued from at least 1982-89 have contained the following statement:

"The Secretary of State of the United States of America hereby requests all whom it may concern to permit the citizen/national of the United States named herein to pass without delay or hindrance and in case of need to give all lawful aid and protection."

VIENNA CONVENTION ON CONSULAR RELATIONS, 21 U.S.T. 77, T.I.A.S. No. 6820, 596 U.N.T.S. 261, *entered into force* March 19, 1967:

Article 5
Consular functions

Consular functions consist in:

(a) protecting in the receiving state the interests of the sending state and its nationals, both individuals and bodies corporate, within the limits permitted by international law; . . .

(e) helping and assisting nationals, both individuals and bodies corporate, of the sending state; . . .

(i) subject to the practices and procedures obtaining in the receiving state representing or arranging appropriate representation for nationals of the sending state before the tribunals and other authorities of the receiving state, for the purpose of obtaining, in accordance with the laws and regulations of the receiving state, provisional measures for the preservation of the rights and interests of these nationals, where, because of absence or any other reason, such nationals are unable at the proper time to assume the defence of their rights and interests;

(j) transmitting judicial and extra-judicial documents or executing letters rogatory or commission to take evidence for the courts of the sending state in accordance with international agreements in force or, in the absence of such international agreements, in any other manner compatible with the laws and regulations of the receiving state; . . .

(m) performing any other functions entrusted to a consular post by the sending state which are not prohibited by the laws and regulations of the receiving state or to which no objection is taken by the receiving state or which are referred to in the international agreements in force between the sending state and the receiving state. . . .

Article 36
Communication and contact with nationals
of the sending state

1. With a view to facilitating the exercise of consular functions relating to nationals of the sending state:

(a) consular officers will be free to communicate with nationals of the sending state and to have access to them. Nationals of the sending state shall have the same freedom with respect to communication with and access to consular officers of the sending state;

(b) if he so requests, the competent authorities of the receiving state shall, without delay, inform the consular post of the sending state if, within its consular district, a national of that state is arrested or committed to prison or to custody pending trial or is detained in any other manner. Any communication addressed to the consular post by the person arrested, in prison, custody or detention shall also be forwarded by the said authorities without delay. The said authorities shall inform the person concerned without delay of his rights under this sub-paragraph;

(c) consular officers shall have the right to visit a national of the sending state who is in prison, custody or detention, to converse and correspond with him and to arrange for his legal representation. They shall also have the right to visit any national of the sending state who is in prison, custody or detention in their district in pursuance of a judgment. Nevertheless, consular officers shall refrain from taking action on behalf of a national who is in prison, custody or detention if he expressly opposes such action.

2. The rights referred to in paragraph 1 of this article shall be exercised in conformity with the laws and regulations of the receiving state, subject to the proviso, however, that the said laws and regulations must enable full effect to be given to the purposes for which the rights accorded under this article are intended. . . .

PROVIDING CONSULAR SERVICES

Department of State, Providing Consular Services to the American Public Abroad, July 14, 1977 (footnotes omitted):

Consular officials abroad do as much as possible to assist Americans placed under arrest, but they must work within the framework of foreign legal systems with standards of justice and detention that are often very different from those that prevail here at home. A citizen who travels abroad places himself under the laws and legal systems of the countries he visits. All the constitutional rights we sometimes take for granted do not go with him. Hardships endured by American prisoners abroad and charges of improper actions by foreign officials — including delays in due process and charges of physical abuse — are investigated promptly by American consular officials. Frequently, official protests are made to the foreign governments involved. Where possible and appropriate, embassies and consulates work with local officials to improve the conditions for American prisoners.

There is no question that some Americans incarcerated abroad are subject to penal and judicial systems that Americans would not tolerate at home. The Department is committed to helping these individuals in every way it can. However, some prisoners and their families, in their understandable anxiety, sometimes exaggerate the degree of leverage available to the U.S. mission or consulate to ameliorate penal and legal processes in foreign countries. Furthermore, the bottom line in the demands of many prisoners and their families is, quite understandably, "release." Obviously, we cannot demand from foreign governments a degree of immunity or "extraterritoriality" for American citizens that we are not prepared to grant foreign visitors to the United States. The watch word is reciprocity. What we must demand, however — unequivocally and unceasingly — is that American citizens not be discriminated against under local law and procedures and that their treatment meet generally accepted standards of human rights.

We have extended and expanded arrest services in an effort to meet the humanitarian needs of American prisoners. We require, with rare exceptions, that every American imprisoned abroad be visited by a consular officer at least once a month. We have increased consular monitoring of trials, pre-trial hearings, and other judicial proceedings. We have requested approval of, and received full support from, the Congress for a program to provide emergency medical and dietary assistance to prisoners.

Authorizing Appropriations for Fiscal Years 1984-85 for the Department of State, the U.S. Information Agency, the Board for International Broadcasting, the Inter-American Foundation to Establish the National Endowment for Democracy: Hearings Before the Subcomm. on International Operations of the House Comm. on Foreign Affairs, 98th Cong., 1st Sess. 333-54 (1983) (selected data and statement of Diego C. Asencio, Assistant Secretary of State for Consular Affairs):

AMERICANS ARRESTED ABROAD IN 1982: TOTALS AND SELECTED COUNTRIES

	Arrested calendar 1982	In custody 12/31/82
Total	3,042	1,729
Selected Countries		
Canada	364	222
Colombia	50	6
Cuba	15	22
Dominican Republic	141	62
Federal Republic of Germany	248	192
France	20	28
Israel	81	84
Italy	33	35
Jamaica	100	17
Japan	68	41
Mexico	841	365
Peru	16	23
Saudi Arabia	66	32
South Africa	6	2
Spain	46	42
Thailand	23	50
United Kingdom	105	69
U.S.S.R.	7	2
All Other Countries	812	435

OFFENSES MOST COMMONLY CHARGED AGAINST
AMERICANS ARRESTED ABROAD, 1982

Drug-related	35%
Immigration Violations	11%
Drunk and Disorderly	7%
Theft	6%
Fraud	5%
Assault	4%
Possession of Deadly Weapon	3%
Other	29%
Total	100%

DIALOGUE AMONG REP. DANTE FASCELL, SUBCOMMITTEE CHAIR, DIEGO ASENCIO, ASSISTANT SECRETARY FOR CONSULAR AFFAIRS, AND CARMEN DIPLACIDO, ACTING DEPUTY ASSISTANT SECRETARY FOR OVERSEAS CITIZENS SERVICES

MR. FASCELL. [Regarding Americans arrested abroad,] we had there for quite a while cases of harassment, maltreatment, mistreatment, frauds, abuse, stealing, starving, et cetera. Now, do we have anything like that pending?

MR. ASENCIO. I would say the major problem right now in some of the societies is the question of prompt notification and prompt access. The others, although we do have cases from time to time, I think we are generally able to make appropriate representations and get adequate treatment for our people — adequate within the context of what we are talking about.

MR. FASCELL. One of the problems that surfaced among others was just holding people without being charged or tried. Do we have any of those cases?

MR. DIPLACIDO. Recently, Mr. Chairman, we have not had such cases. . . .

MR. FASCELL. One of the problems that surfaced also was there was no way an individual who was arrested could get proper legal representation.

MR. ASENCIO. I think this is one of the traditional functions of the consular officer. . . . [F]or instance when I was a young vice consul in Mexico City, this was the first thing that was drilled into me, the fact that our ability to assist of course was limited by the conditions of the society — in effect you cannot represent the person yourself, although you can sometimes intercede for them. But you make certain that he is well and adequately represented. . . .

MR. FASCELL. Now, the other part of that problem was a regular visit by the consular officer. How are we doing today . . .?

MR. ASENCIO. We have stipulated, particularly in those societies where there are enormous difficulties, monthly visits minimum. Where perhaps — and I am not trying to be ludicrous, but where the jails are, you know, slightly more in keeping with our own standards — and there are no enormous problems — then it is at the discretion of the Ambassador. But always with the thought that consular officers should visit Americans in jail on a periodic basis. . . .

MR. FASCELL. Let me see. Would you restate? American nationals in jail in Cuba are 23?

MR. ASENCIO. Correct. . . .

MR. FASCELL. Could we make a good estimate as to the last time they were visited, for example? Somebody want to hazard a guess?

MR. DIPLACIDO. I would say every month, depending on the needs of each individual prisoner.

MR. FASCELL. The every month thing, is that a regulation or standard operating procedure? What is it? Guideline?

MR. DIPLACIDO. Guideline, that's correct.

MR. FASCELL. It is an unwritten guideline, once a month.

MR. DIPLACIDO. It is written.

MR. FASCELL. It is written.

MR. ASENCIO. In other words, we get reports, Mr. Chairman, on the prevailing conditions in the jails of a particular society and then we in fact negotiate out with our people what we think the regularity of their visits should be.

MR. FASCELL. You mean the Washington office and the field office get together and decide based on the circumstances what the visit rate ought to be?

MR. ASENCIO. That's correct. . . .

MR. FASCELL. Now, how do we who are not in the consular service get a report on the physical condition of these 23 inmates in the Cuban prisons?

MR. ASENCIO. Well, we, of course, get from the prisoner —

MR. FASCELL. Are they starving, have they been beaten to death, getting medicine?

MR. ASENCIO. We receive permission from the prisoners to whom we should convey information on that particular person and, of course, if he in fact says that he would like information on his condition conveyed to his Congressman, we would do that. And, of course, we do convey it to the family. Unless the prisoner tells us otherwise.

MR. FASCELL. Well it is up to the prisoner.

MR. ASENCIO. That's correct. . . .

MR. FASCELL. Just exactly what is your responsibility, if any, Mr. Secretary to insure the best possible treatment and the early release of American prisoners anywhere? But I am thinking now particularly of Cuba.

MR. ASENCIO. Well, if we believe that the individual is not receiving a fair shake, we have an obligation to make representations to the society, in all countries, particularly in the Cuban one. If we believe a prisoner is not being well treated, is being discriminated against in some way or is being made a particular target of whatever, we step in, we interpose ourselves.

MR. FASCELL. When you step in, interpose, you mean in the Cuban case somebody from the interests section would go where?

MR. ASENCIO. To the Foreign Ministry. . . .

MR. FASCELL. . . .I have been informed that you have implemented some new regulations with respect to a provision on food and other necessities for families. Do you want to tell me what is going on there? . . .

MR. DIPLACIDO. We have the two programs, one for incarcerated Americans and the other program for destitute Americans. . . . [T]he figures would show that we used more money last year than the year before that.

MR. FASCELL. All right. How much money?

MR. DIPLACIDO. Last year we used for both programs $62,000. For incarcerated Americans alone the dietary supplements were $14,000, medical loans for incarcerated Americans were $13,000, and funds for incarcerated Americans to buy food were $17,000.

Temporary subsistence for nonincarcerated Americans was $11,000.

It is working out fairly well.

MR. FASCELL. Well, at least one thing it has done, besides get necessities to the people who need various things, is the Foreign Service officers are not now having to dig into their pockets to make these payments.

MR. DIPLACIDO. Absolutely correct.

MR. ASENCIO. I can reiterate that, Mr. Chairman, in the sense that as I say when I started in this business we didn't have this available and I sunk quite a bit of my own cash in helping people. . . .

Department of State Bureau of Consular Affairs, Travel Advisory (1989):

PERU - WARNING

SUMMARY: THE DEPARTMENT OF STATE ADVISES U.S. CITIZENS THAT BOTH TERRORISM AND CRIME ARE SERIOUS PROBLEMS THROUGHOUT PERU. SINCE 1983 TWO TERRORIST GROUPS, SENDERO LUMINOSO (SHINING PATH) AND THE TUPAC AMARU REVOLUTIONARY MOVEMENT (MRTA), HAVE USED VIOLENT TACTICS IN AN ATTEMPT TO DESTABILIZE THE GOVERNMENT. OVER A PERIOD OF SEVERAL YEARS, THE PERUVIAN GOVERNMENT HAS DECLARED MOST OF THE CENTRAL ANDEAN REGION AS AN EMERGENCY ZONE UNDER MILITARY CONTROL. TRAVEL TO ALL EMERGENCY ZONES, HUARAZ, AND THE CORDILLERA BLANCA, THE HUAYHUASH AREA, THE UPPER HUALLAGA VALLEY, PUCALPA, AND ALONG THE INCA TRAIL SHOULD BE AVOIDED. IN ADDITION, A DIFFICULT ECONOMIC SITUATION HAS LED TO INCREASED CRIME IN TOURIST AREAS. WHILE CRIMINAL VIOLENCE IS RANDOM, AND POLITICAL VIOLENCE USUALLY IS TARGETED AT PERUVIAN CIVIC LEADERS AND INFRASTRUCTURE, VISITORS MUST EXERCISE CAUTION. OVER THE PAST SEVERAL YEARS, SEVERAL TOURISTS HAVE BEEN INJURED OR KILLED IN TERRORIST AND CRIMINAL INCIDENTS. TRAVEL BY PUBLIC BUS IS NOT RECOMMENDED BECAUSE OF TERRORISM, BANDITRY AND POOR ROAD CONDITIONS. VISITORS SHOULD BE AWARE THAT CONDITIONS IN PERU CAN CHANGE AT ANY TIME. ALTHOUGH THIS ADVISORY IDENTIFIES SPECIFIC AREAS TO AVOID AND SUGGESTS PRECAUTIONS TO TAKE, TRAVELERS ARE URGED TO SEEK THE LATEST TRAVEL INFORMATION UPON ARRIVAL IN PERU FROM THE EMBASSY'S CONSULAR SECTION.

LIMA: TERRORIST ATTACKS ARE UNPREDICTABLE. IN LIMA ATTACKS HAVE BEEN DIRECTED PRIMARILY AGAINST PERUVIAN GOVERNMENT PERSONNEL AND INSTALLATIONS, BANKS, BUSINESSES, AND FOREIGN DIPLOMATIC MISSIONS, INCLUDING U.S. GOVERNMENT BUILDINGS. LABOR STRIKES ARE FRE-

QUENT AND MAY GENERATE POLICE ACTION AND/OR MASK TERRORIST AC-
TIVITY. STREET CRIME IS ALSO PREVALENT. . . .

NOTES AND QUESTIONS

1. Two incidents illustrate U.S. government protest over abuse of U.S.
citizens' rights by other countries. In December 1988, Honduran authorities
detained a U.S. journalist entering the country, held her *incommunicado*
for 14 hours, withheld their knowledge of her arrival from U.S. Embassy
officials looking for her, and then placed her on a flight back to the U.S.
She had written an article describing human rights abuses in Honduras,
which apparently angered the Honduran government. U.S. Embassy officials
expressed concern over the denial of consular access to her and actively
sought an explanation from the Honduran government. *See* Adams, *U.S.
Protests Reporter's Ouster*, San Francisco Chron., Dec. 1, 1988, at A25.

In November 1988, three Panamanian policemen detained a U.S. naval
officer for parking in a no-parking zone. The policemen beat the officer,
put a gun to his head, and forced him to beg for his life. Pentagon officials
strongly protested the incident after a thorough investigation. *See* Sciolino,
Beating in Panama Protested by U.S., N.Y. Times, Jan. 12, 1989, at A5.

Are those incidents similar to Sara's? How do they differ? Are there
reasons why the U.S. government might be more or less willing to pursue
her case?

2. Another method the U.S. government can use in obtaining the release
of citizens imprisoned abroad is an armed rescue. A notable example is the
attempted rescue of the hostages held in Tehran in 1979. For further reading
on rescues and their legality under international law, see N. Ronzitti,
Rescuing Nationals Abroad Through Military Coercion and Intervention on
Grounds of Humanity (1985).

3. Other United States Government Services

22 U.S.C. § 1732. *Release of citizens imprisoned by foreign governments*

Whenever it is made known to the President that any citizen of the United
States has been unjustly deprived of his liberty by or under the authority of any
foreign government, it shall be the duty of the President forthwith to demand of
that government the reasons of such imprisonment; and if it appears to be wrongful
and in violation of the rights of American citizenship, the President shall forthwith
demand the release of such citizen, and if the release so demanded is unreasonably
delayed or refused, the President shall use such means, not amounting to acts of
war, as he may think necessary and proper to obtain or effectuate the release;
and all the facts and proceedings relative thereto shall as soon as practicable be
communicated by the President to Congress.

Redpath v. Kissinger, 415 F. Supp. 566 (W.D. Tex. 1976) (footnotes omitted):

SPEARS, Chief Judge

ORDER

On this date came on to be considered a Petition for a Writ of Mandamus filed by John Lee Redpath against Henry A. Kissinger, the Secretary of State of the United States, Joseph John Jova, Ambassador of the United States to the Republic of Mexico, Charles F. Brown, American Consul, and Mathias J. Orthwein, Consul General of the United States at Guadalajara, Mexico; and for the appointment of counsel. The substance of Petitioner's allegations are that he was incarcerated by Mexican officials, subjected to torture, and that the Defendants have negligently failed and refused to accord him the assistance which he as an American citizen was entitled to receive.

The government has filed a Motion to Dismiss, together with a Memorandum of Authorities in support thereof. Attached to the government's Motion is the affidavit of Alan W. Gise, Director of the Office of Special Consular Services, Bureau of Security and Consular Affairs, Department of State. This instrument sets out that Redpath was arrested in Morelia, Michoacan, Mexico on January 22, 1975 and charged with passing bad checks. The United States Consulate General was notified, a consular officer talked to Redpath the next day, and although Redpath at that time had no attorney, the affidavit shows he was in fact afforded a court appointed attorney, Public Defender Alicia Garcia Quintanos, who represented him during his trial which resulted in a sentence of five years in prison. Mr. Gise states that the sentence has been reduced, and that in due course upon good behavior the defendant will be released from imprisonment. The Gise report shows that he was a member of a panel of United States government officials which conducted an inquiry into allegations by American prisoners in Mexico about their treatment; that Redpath's allegations of torture were included in that inquiry; and that they were found to be unsubstantiated.

Attached to the government's reply is a copy of pertinent sections of the Special Consular Services Memorandum governing and directing the handling of foreign imprisoned American nationals. These rules and regulations appeared to have been followed wherever applicable. Although Redpath alleges that he has been "tortured", no specific instances of "torture" are found in his pleadings. In the main his allegations reflect incarceration in cold, dirty and inhospitable jail facilities.

There is no doubt that a District Court has no authority to grant the requested relief by Writ of Mandamus or otherwise, the applicable statute is 22 U.S.C. § 1732 . . . .

United States v. Dulles, 3 Cir., 222 F.2d 390, is dispositive of the instant petition for a Writ of Mandamus. In that case an American soldier had been tried for robbery by a French court and assessed a term of imprisonment. His wife filed a Petition for Habeas Corpus in the U.S. District Court for the District of Columbia, naming as Respondents the Secretary of State, the Secretary of Defense and the Secretary of the Army, alleging in substance that they had failed to perform their respective duties in protecting her husband from persecution. The Respondents' Motion to Dismiss was granted on the ground that the Petitioner was not in the custody of Respondents and that the court was without jurisdiction to grant the requested writ. Upon appeal, the appellate tribunal agreed with the trial court's disposition, but viewed and considered the case as one seeking a mandatory order requiring the Secretary of State to obtain Keith's release through diplomatic negotiations with France.... The Court of Appeals held:

"(The Secretary) was not under a legal duty to attempt through diplomatic processes to obtain Keith's release. Quite to the contrary, the commencement of diplomatic negotiations with a foreign power is completely in the discretion of the President and the head of the Department of State, who is his political agent. The Executive is not subject to judicial control or direction in such matters...."

The Supreme Court has defined the powers of the courts of the United States with respect to the disposition of matters such as the one under consideration. In *Oetjen v. Central Leather Company*, 246 U.S. 297, ...which involved a dispute over the seizure of certain property by Mexico and the interpretation of certain treaty rights claimed by the parties, it was held that the conduct of the foreign relations of the United States is committed by the Constitution to the Executive and Legislative Departments of the government, and the propriety of what may be done in the exercise of these powers is not subject to judicial inquiry or decision.

Now, as the government points out, the Petitioner received the services of American consular officers as set forth in the Consular Affairs memorandum attached to its Motion. Nothing is found from the Petitioner himself which reflects that his arrest and conviction were improper. The Director of Special Consular Services, who is the official apparently charged with the duty of investigating the imprisonment of American nationals abroad, made special inquiry into the torture allegations of Redpath and found no substantiation for that claim. The rights of Petitioner accruing under the statute concerning citizens in prison by foreign governments, 22 U.S.C. § 1732, to have his case examined into and a report made thereof have been accorded to him. The government's response shows that the claim of Petitioner has been followed up with appropriate inquiries by the officials charged with the protection of arrested American nationals, and any further action with respect to Redpath's situation will have to be taken by the executive through his agent, the Secretary of State. The general rule with respect to the use of mandamus which is an extraordinary writ is stated by the Court of Appeals for the Fifth Circuit as follows:

"Before the writ of mandamus may properly issue three elements must coexist: (1) A clear right in the plaintiff to the relief sought; (2) a clear duty on the part of defendant to do the act in question; and (3) no other adequate remedy available." *Carter v. Seamans*, 411 F.2d 767, cert. den. 397 U.S. 941...

Plaintiff's petition does not satisfy this requirement. The official actions sought are not ministerial, but are clearly of a diplomatic nature involving the exercise of discretion by the Executive, or under his direction.

In view of the disposition of this cause, no counsel will be appointed as requested by Plaintiff. It is accordingly,

ORDERED that the Petition for a Writ of Mandamus of John Lee Redpath be, and the same is hereby, DISMISSED.

NOTES

1. In *Dames & Moore v. Regan*, 453 U.S. 654 (1981), a corporation challenged the constitutionality of an executive order that nullified existing attachments on Iranian assets and established a separate tribunal for claims against Iran as part of the hostage settlement. Examining the legal bases of the order the court held that the Hostage Act (22 U.S.C. § 1732) did not grant authority for the executive order at issue in the case. *Id.* at 676-77. The court focused on the legislative history of the Act, which indicated congressional concern for the refusal of certain countries to recognize the citizenship of naturalized Americans when they traveled abroad. *Id.* at 676. Though the court did not hold that the Hostage Act applies only to such situations, it did hold that the broad language could not be taken at face value to support the executive order that was in question. *Id.* at 676-77.

2. In *Flynn v. Shultz*, 748 F.2d 1186 (7th Cir. 1984), the family of a U.S. citizen imprisoned in Mexico for criminal fraud sought the testimony of a State Department consular official under the Hostage Act, 22 U.S.C. § 1732. The Department refused to allow the official to testify, because of regulations requiring an official request from a Mexican court to waive consular immunity. The court held that in passing the Hostage Act "Congress placed a judicially enforceable duty on the Executive to inquire into the circumstances of an American citizen's extended detention abroad." *Id.* at 1195. The duty, however, is a limited one. "When the President is informed that a United States citizen is imprisoned abroad, the Hostage Act requires the Executive to undertake a meaningful inquiry into the circumstances of the detention in order to determine whether the citizen is unjustly deprived of liberty." *Id.* at 1196. The State Department had substantially assisted Mr. Flynn, including requesting and obtaining two independent legal reviews of his criminal conviction. The reviews concluded that the conviction was neither improper nor discriminatory. Relying on those reviews, the court found that the State Department had fulfilled its duty under the Hostage Act. As to compelling the testimony of the consular official, the court found that consular relations are committed to the political branches of government. Accordingly, a review of consular standards is a political question the courts are not empowered to consider.

3. In *Smith v. Reagan*, 844 F.2d 195 (4th Cir. 1988), plaintiffs, family members of U.S. servicemen listed as missing in action in Vietnam, sought mandamus ordering the U.S. government to pursue inquiries about the servicemen. In addition, they sought a declaratory judgment stating that such a class of people existed and could benefit from the protection of the Hostage Act. The district court held that the political question doctrine barred the court from ordering the inquiries, but that it could decide whether the class existed because that question was an "issue[] of fact arising out of rights derived from the United States Constitution and law . . . ."

Smith v. Reagan, 637 F. Supp. 964, 968 (E.D.N.C. 1986). The Fourth Circuit reversed, however, holding that the statute implied no private right of action and that the case presented a nonjusticiable political question.

4. In *Ramirez de Arellano v. Weinberger*, 745 F.2d 1500, 1512-15 (D.C. Cir. 1984) (en banc), a U.S. citizen complained that his ranch in Honduras had been occupied and effectively destroyed by U.S. military forces. The district court dismissed the suit on the ground that it presented a nonjusticiable political question. 568 F. Supp. 1236 (D.D.C. 1983). The D.C. Circuit reversed, holding that adjudicating plaintiff's claim would not "intolerably" impinge and intrude upon the Executive's conduct of foreign affairs. 745 F.2d at 1514. The court noted, "The Executive's power to conduct foreign relations free from unwarranted supervision of the Judiciary cannot give the Executive *carte blanche* to trample the most fundamental liberty and property rights of this country's citizenry." *Id.* at 1515. The Supreme Court vacated and remanded, 471 U.S. 1113 (1985), in light of the Foreign Assistance and Related Appropriations Act of 1985 and efforts by the Honduran government to provide restitution. On remand the D.C. Circuit affirmed the dismissal without prejudice to the suit's being reinstituted, 788 F.2d 762, 764 (D.C. Cir. 1986), in view of the withdrawal of U.S. military from the property and the resulting change of the balance of equities.

5. For thorough discussion of § 1732, see Mikva & Neuman, *The Hostage Crisis and the "Hostage Act"*, 49 U. Chi. L. Rev. 292 (1982); Note, *The United States-Iran Hostage Agreement: A Study in Presidential Powers*, 15 Cornell Int'l L.J. 149, 174-77 (1982).

---

4. Intergovernmental Procedures

THE INTER-AMERICAN COMMISSION ON HUMAN RIGHTS

The Inter-American Commission on Human Rights ("Inter-American Commission") is the body of the Organization of American States ("OAS") charged with promoting the observance of human rights in OAS member states, of which Peru is one. The Commission's functions include the examination of petitions alleging that a member state has violated the rights of an individual guaranteed in the American Declaration of the Rights and Duties of Man and, for states that have ratified it, the American Convention on Human Rights. Peru has ratified the Convention. Any individual or organization, including nongovernmental human rights organizations, may file a petition on behalf of individuals whose rights are being violated.

Chapter 7 of this book will examine in detail the Inter-American Commission's work on individual petitions. At this point it is sufficient to observe that, under the normal procedure, consideration of a petition takes several months at a minimum. The Commission does, however, have authority to take provisional measures in urgent cases to avoid irreparable harm to an individual. The measures include mandating medical attention for a prisoner and access to a prisoner held *incommunicado* whose life is endangered. In addition to the formal provisional measures, petitioners can request immediate intervention in urgent cases. Responding to those requests the Commission normally notifies the charged government immediately of the allegations and requests a prompt reply. If the reply is not satisfactory, the petition continues through the normal process. Nonetheless, an awareness that the Commission is monitoring the treatment of individuals may relieve immediate threats and prompt the government to treat individuals with greater care.

NOTE

For further discussion of the emergency procedures, see Farer & Rowles, *The Inter-American Commission on Human Rights*, in International Human Rights Law and Practice 47, 68 (J. Tuttle, ed. 1978); Norris, *The Individual Petition Procedure of the Inter-American System for the Protection of Human Rights*, in Guide to International Human Rights Practice 108, 119, 122 (H. Hannum ed. 1984).

RATIFICATION OF TREATIES BY PERU AND THE UNITED STATES

Peru and the U.S. are members of the United Nations, the International Labor Organization, and the Organization of American States. They have ratified the Vienna Convention on Consular Relations. Peru also has ratified several human rights treaties including: the ILO's Freedom of Association and Protection of the Right to Organize Convention; the American Convention on Human Rights; the International Covenant on Civil and Political Rights and the International Covenant on Economic, Social and Cultural Rights; the Optional Protocol to the International Covenant on Civil and Political Rights; and the Convention on the Elimination of All Forms of Discrimination Against Women. The U.S. has not ratified any of those six treaties.

Peru repeatedly has complied with Article 4 of the Covenant on Civil and Political Rights by notifying the U.N. of its intention to declare and maintain a state of emergency. Its first notification occurred on March 18, 1983, and suspended Articles 9, 12, 17, and 21 of the Covenant. These articles correspond to Paragraphs 7, 9, 10, and 20(g) of Article 2 of the Constitution of Peru and relate to the inviolability of the home, liberty of movement in the national territory, the right of peaceful assembly, and the right to liberty and security of person. As the state of emergency was extended to other departments and provinces Peru has continued to notify the U.N. Its attention to international norms indicates concern for its international image. The government is also aware of its unique relation with the U.N.; Secretary-General Javier Perez de Cuellar is a Peruvian. Peru also received visits from members of the U.N. Working Group on Enforced or Involuntary Disappearances in 1985 and 1986 and a visit by the U.N. Special Rapporteur on Torture in 1988.

INTERNATIONAL TRADE UNIONS AND HUMAN RIGHTS

International trade unions assist unions in developing countries by providing training for leaders; assistance in recruitment; and information useful for strike planning, collective bargaining, wages, and job evaluation. They also provide technical assistance, including medical supplies, office equipment, tools, and vocational training. In addition to advancing economic rights, international unions advance civil and political rights by lobbying governments for statutes and regulations favorable to the free exercise of union activities.

International unions have organized into three separate global organizations. The largest is the World Federation of Trade Unions (WFTU), with approximately 190 million members in 1980. It consists of trade unions largely from Eastern European countries and politically allied unions in other countries. Different craft and industrial unions within the WFTU, known as trade union internationals (TUIs), operate as departments controlled by the WFTU. Although the TUIs have their own structures, their policies and programs seem consistently aligned with those of the WFTU and official Communist Party views.

With membership of about 60 million in 1980, the second largest global labor organization is the International Confederation of Free Trade Unions (ICFTU). It generally includes trade unions from "Western" countries. The trade and craft unions affiliated with the ICFTU, known as international trade secretariats (ITSs), stand as autonomous entities collectively represented by the ICFTU.

The third umbrella organization, the World Confederation of Labour (WCL), is considerably smaller than the other two and recently lost the affiliation of several important unions.

It has been estimated that less than 20% of the work force in Peru is organized in unions. They do, however, affiliate freely with regional and international union organizations.

The International Labor Organization (ILO), like the international union associations, seeks to improve the rights and economic status of workers. First created in 1919 under the Treaty of Versailles, the ILO presently is a specialized agency associated with the United Nations whose members and sources of funding are individual governments. A principal function of the ILO is to author treaties and recommendations on international labor standards. Treaties ratified by ILO member states bind the states parties, but recommendations do not have the force of law. Both the U.S. and Peru are active members of the ILO Peru has ratified at least 66 of the total 169 treaties adopted by the ILO. The United States, however, has ratified only ten. In addition to drafting treaties and recommendations, the ILO through its permanent secretariat undertakes technical cooperation, research, and education programs around the world.

For discussion of the three international unions, see Industrial Research Unit, The Wharton School, Multinational Union Organizations in the Manufacturing Industries (1980); W. Feld, Nongovernmental Forces and World Politics: A Study of Business, Labor, and Political Groups 147-69 (1972).

For an interesting survey and appraisal of ILO projects in the Third World, see W. Galenson, The International Labour Organisation: An American View 284 (1981). For a summary of the structure and operations, see International Labour Office, International Labour Standards 197-99, 284 (1982).

STATE RESPONSIBILITY FOR NONWEALTH INJURIES TO ALIENS

While the Vienna Convention on Consular Relations, above, gives a government the right to visit its nationals detained in another state, to arrange for their legal representation, and to be informed of their arrest, the Convention does not specifically authorize further actions. The law of state responsibility for injuries to aliens, however, holds that one state is legally responsible to another state when the first treats the nationals of the second in a manner not allowed by international law. International treaties and customary law serve as minimum standards for the treatment of aliens. No responsibility arises, though, unless the national allegedly injured first exhausts local remedies for his or her claim. Local remedies need not be pursued if such pursuit would be futile.

The responsibility incurred by a state for injury to an alien gives the state of which the victim is a national the right to pursue remedies for the victim via diplomatic and other means. The victim does not have the right to pursue claims personally against the foreign state or to force the state of which he or she is a national to pursue the claim if that state chooses not to do so.

Many Latin American governments have insisted that no international standards apply to a state's treatment of aliens. Rather, it is insisted international law requires only that a state treat an alien no worse than it treats its own nationals and that an alien must be afforded only those remedies available to nationals. This doctrine, known as the "Calvo doctrine" (for the author of a treatise on the subject written in the 19th century), arose in response to the gunboat-style diplomacy accompanying 19th century capitalist expansion. Arguably, at least with respect to nonwealth injury to aliens, many Latin American governments implicitly repudiated the Calvo doctrine by ratifying human rights treaties that pronounce minimum standards for the treatment of all persons—nationals or aliens.

NOTES

For further reading, see R. Lillich, International Law of State Responsibility for Injuries to Aliens 1, 4-14 (1983); Carbonneau, *The Convergence of the Law of State Responsibility for Injury to Aliens and International Human Rights Norms in the Revised Restatement,* 25 Va. J. Int'l L. 99 (1984); G. von Glahn, Law Among Nations: An Introduction to Public International Law 229-31 (5th ed. 1986); I. Brownlie, System of the Law of Nations, State Responsibility (Part I) 1-10, 22-35 (1983).

Restatement (Third) of the Foreign Relations Law of the United States (1987):

§ 711. State Responsibility for Injury to Nationals of Other States

A state is responsible under international law for injury to a national of another state caused by an official act or omission that violates

(a) a human right that ... a state is obligated to respect for all persons subject to its authority;

(b) a personal right that, under international law, a state is obligated to respect for individuals of foreign nationality; or

(c) a right to property or another economic interest that, under international law, a state is obligated to respect for persons, natural or juridical, of foreign nationality . . . .

Comment: . . .

b. *International human rights as minimum standard.* Under international law, a state is responsible for injury to foreign nationals resulting from violations of their internationally recognized human rights, as well as for injury resulting from violation of other interests for which international law provides special protections to foreign nationals. Under clause (a), the state is responsible for injury due to violation of those rights which the state is obligated to respect for all persons subject to its authority, whether pursuant to international human rights agreements to which it is party or under the customary law of human rights . . . ; aliens enjoy these rights equally with the state's own nationals. Clause (b) declares that, in respect of foreign nationals, a state is responsible also for injury due to violation of those internationally recognized human rights that ... would not be protected by international law as regards the state's own nationals in the absence of international agreement. . . .

c. *Obligation to respect human rights of foreign nationals as customary law.* A state's responsibility to individuals of foreign nationality under customary law includes the obligation to respect the civil and political rights articulated in the principal international human rights instruments — the Universal Declaration and the International Covenant on Civil and Political Rights — as rights of human beings generally . . . , but not political rights . . . recognized as human rights only in relation to a person's country of citizenship, such as the right to vote and hold office, or the right to return to one's country. . . . Thus, a state party to the

Covenant on Civil and Political Rights is responsible for any violation of any of its provisions in relation to any human being subject to its jurisdiction, regardless of the individual's nationality; but every state, whether or not a party to the Covenant, is responsible for denying to nationals of another state any right specified in the Covenant that is guaranteed by rules of customary law relating to the protection of foreign nationals. Customary law also holds a state responsible for a "consistent pattern of gross violations" of human rights of any persons subject to its jurisdiction.... As regards foreign nationals, however, a state is responsible even for a single violation of many of the civil and political rights proclaimed in the Universal Declaration (other than those applicable only to citizens), even if it is not "gross."...

§ 713. Remedies for Injury to Nationals of Other States

(1) A state whose national has suffered injury under § 711... has, as against the state responsible for the injury, the remedies generally available between states for violation of customary law,... as well as any special remedies provided by any international agreement applicable between the two states....

Comments:

a.   *Remedies under international law.* A state whose national has suffered injury under § 711 ... may resort to any of the remedies usually available to a state that has been the victim of a breach of international law, including international claims procedures and other diplomatic measures or permissible international response.... The offended state may also invoke any special measures applicable by agreement between the two states, including arbitration or adjudication. Treaties of friendship, commerce, and navigation and other bilateral agreements commonly provide for resort to the International Court of Justice or to arbitration to resolve a claim that rights protected under the agreement have been violated....

In principle, the responsibility of a state under...§ 711...is to the state of the alien's nationality and gives that state a claim against the offending state. The claim derives from injury to an individual, but once espoused it is the state's claim, and can be waived by the state. However, the derivative character of the claim has practical consequences: for example, damages are often measured by the damage to the individual, not by the loss to the state or the affront to its honor. The derivative character of the claim is reflected also in the traditional rule that the accused state can reject an international claim if the individual victim has not exhausted domestic remedies ... or if the individual has reached a voluntary settlement with the respondent state....

b.   *Diplomatic protection.* A state has the right to afford its nationals diplomatic protection against violation by another state of obligations under...§ 711.... A state is entitled to communicate with a national arrested or charged with crime, to provide him assistance, and to have a representative present at his trial. A state may also intercede to assure other human rights of its nationals, their personal safety, or their property or other interests protected by...§ 711.... Formal diplomatic espousal usually awaits exhaustion of local remedies ..., but governments often intercede informally without regard to the person's domestic remedies....

C. Calvo, Derecho Internacional Teórico y Práctico de Europa y America §
294 (1st ed. 1868) [translated from Spanish]:

This question connects to the grave matter of the constant claims of the great
European powers with respect to the governments of the American states. All of
the claims have been founded on personal offenses, sometimes real, other times
exaggerated by the consuls, always painted by them with vivid colors. And the
rule that in more than one case the former [Europeans] have tried to impose on
the latter [Latin Americans] is, that foreigners deserve more consideration and
bigger privileges than the very nationals of the country in which they reside. This
principle, the application of which is notoriously unjust and in contravention of
the law of the equality of States, and the consequences of which are essentially
perturbing, does not constitute a rule of law applicable in the international relations
of the European countries, and always when one of them has demanded this right,
the answer of the other has been absolutely negative. And it should be this way,
because by the contrary rule the relatively weak peoples would be at the mercy
of the powerful, and the citizens of a country would have fewer rights and
guarantees than the foreign residents.

The Constitution of Peru (1979), Official Edition of the Ministry of Justice
(1980) [translated from Spanish]:

Article 126

Property is regulated exclusively by the laws of the Republic.

Regarding property, foreigners, natural or juridical persons have the same
status as Peruvians without, in any case, being able to invoke exceptional situations
or diplomatic immunity . . . .

5. Nongovernmental Organizations

There are many nongovernmental organizations (NGOs) engaged in the
protection of human rights. Working at international and national levels,
they safeguard human rights against governmental infringement, by techniques such as diplomatic initiatives, published reports, public statements,
efforts to influence the deliberations of human rights bodies established by
intergovernmental organizations, campaigns to mobilize public opinion, and
attempts to affect the foreign policy of countries with respect to their
relations with states that are regularly responsible for human rights violations.

NGOs share the same basic purpose; that is, to gather information that
can be effectively mustered — either directly or indirectly — to influence
the implementation and enforcement of human rights by governments.
Among international NGOs are Amnesty International, the Anti-Slavery
Society, the Commission of the Churches on International Affairs, Human
Rights Advocates, Human Rights Watch, the International Association of

Democratic Lawyers, the International Commission of Jurists, the International Committee of the Red Cross, the International Federation of Human Rights, the International Human Rights Law Group, the International League for Human Rights, the Lawyers Committee for Human Rights, the Minnesota Lawyers International Human Rights Committee, the Minority Rights Group, and Survival International.

One of the first questions an NGO must consider is whether it would be useful to intervene in a situation where human rights are being violated. Might intervention help or hurt victims? What sort of intervention would be most effective? Have interventions with the country or with respect to this type of problem been successful in the past? Are officials of the country receptive to initiatives from outsiders? Are the facts sufficiently well established to permit diplomatic intervention or publicity? Which NGO would be most effective in raising the issue?

NGOs have found that most governments are sensitive to criticism. For example, the U.S.S.R. has been very concerned about discussion as to the emigration of Armenians, Jews, and ethnic Germans or concerning the imprisonment of Soviet human rights leaders. Guatemala has been at times highly sensitive to criticism of torture, imprisonment, and killing of *campesinos*, Indians, journalists, lawyers, and unionists. The U.S. has considered its image in the world community to be very delicate regarding treatment of its minorities and indigenous peoples. Most countries are proud of humanitarian ideals that form one basis for the legitimacy of the state. Almost every country's constitution prominently sets forth the basic rights of its citizens. If a government — whether democratic or dictatorial — acts tyrannically toward its citizens, it violates the trust that permits it to continue ruling. Even dictators attempt to show at least a facade of respecting human rights.

Governments do not wish to be reminded that they are ignoring the rights of their citizens. They particularly do not like to be criticized in the openness of world debate. Further, the International Bill of Human Rights has attained such broad acceptance in the international community that a government cannot grossly violate human rights without some fear of exposure. The pointed finger of shame, particularly when directed by an organization with a reputation for impartiality and political independence, has caused executions to be stayed, death sentences to be commuted, torture to be stopped, prison conditions to be ameliorated, prisoners to be released, and more attention to be paid to the fundamental rights of many citizens.

In some ways NGOs are far freer to criticize where criticism is due than are governments or intergovernmental organizations. Most governments are concerned with keeping their bilateral relations on a friendly basis. Even where relations are quite close — or perhaps because they are quite close — governments hesitate to criticize one another.

a. Diplomatic Interventions and Visits by NGOs

Having investigated and selected a case, the NGO may decide to seek a visit with representatives of the government concerned. Unless there is need for immediate cessation of the human rights violations — as in the case of torture or an impending execution — the initial contact may only apprise the government that a violation has been noted and the NGO may propose inquiry by appropriate officials. Those contacts generally are made with no publicity. Often the NGO functions as a much-needed intermediary between highest officials in a government and human rights victims. In the absence of an effective right of *habeas corpus*, a free press, and an ombudsman, high officials may not know what is happening within their own prisons or may try to avoid knowing. Once an NGO brings a problem to the government's attention, however, it becomes more difficult to ignore violations. Interventions are generally made with diplomatic personnel who are familiar with the governing international standards of conduct. When made aware of the problem and the possible risk of embarrassment, those officials often take steps to help remedy the situation.

In addition, the NGO may offer or ask to send a delegation to the country, to interview alleged victims, lawyers, and government officials; to witness trials; to observe elections; or to attempt to mediate disputes. Some countries are sufficiently concerned about their image, or sufficiently confident that the accusations are unfounded, that they accept NGO visits.

b. Public Discussion of Human Rights Violations

Publicity is clearly an important weapon in the implementation of human rights law by NGOs. Consultative status with the U.N. permits NGOs to contribute to the work of the U.N. Commission on Human Rights, its Sub-Commission on Prevention of Discrimination and Protection of Minorities, and many other U.N. bodies identified in chapter 1. Representatives of NGOs often make written and oral presentations during discussions of human rights issues. Some of the NGO interventions add significantly to the debates and make important contributions to the drafting of international human rights standards.

c. The Contribution to International Procedures

NGOs also have used the developing procedures for individual communications about violations in the U.N. Commission on Human Rights, its Sub-Commission, other U.N. bodies, the International Labor Organization, the Inter-American Commission on Human Rights, and the European Commission of Human Rights. NGOs have had the right to, and often do, contribute to studies on various human rights issues and themes conducted by the United Nations. A large part of most U.N. human rights reports derive from the material the U.N. receives from NGOs.

d. Activities at Local Levels

There are many NGOs that work at local levels to gather information and publicize human rights violations. They also lobby for improvements in the legal protections afforded human rights; some have used courts and administrative agencies to pursue human rights objectives. The local human rights groups often obtain support from international nongovernmental organizations and supply information to the international organizations. For example, in many countries such as South Africa, Namibia, and Zimbabwe, certain Christian churches have performed invaluable work for human rights, while receiving vital encouragement and support from their sister churches abroad — particularly through the World Council of Churches, Lutheran World Federation, and Pontifical Commission Justice and Peace. Pressure may also be exerted by professional groups such as doctors, lawyers, trade unionists, teachers, and scientists expressing their concern about violation of the human rights of their fellow professionals or unionists. Amnesty International's success in recent years has been due considerably to its ability to mobilize the efforts of local groups who work for the human rights of named prisoners.

NOTES

1. The above topic is examined in more detail in Weissbrodt, *The Contribution of International Nongovernmental Organizations to the Protection of Human Rights*, in Human Rights in International Law: Legal and Policy Issues 403 (T. Meron ed. 1984) and Weissbrodt, *The Role of International Nongovernmental Organizations in the Implementation of Human Rights*, 12 Texas J. Int'l L.J. 293 (1977).

2. For further reading on the work of NGOs in protecting international human rights, see Chiang Pei-heng, Nongovernmental Organizations at the United Nations: Identity, Role and Function (1981);

L. Livezey, Nongovernmental Organizations and the Ideas of Human Rights (1988);

Kamminga & Rodley, *Direct Intervention at the UN: NGO Participation in the Commission on Human Rights and its Subcommission*, in Guide to International Human Rights Practice 186 (H. Hannum ed. 1984);

Leary, *A New Role for Non-governmental Organizations in Human Rights: A Case Study of Non-governmental Participation in the Development of International Norms on Torture*, in UN Law/Fundamental Rights: Two Topics in International Law 197 (A. Cassese ed. 1979);

Shestack, *Sisyphus Endures: The International Human Rights NGO*, 24 N.Y.L. Sch. L. Rev. 89 (1978);

Wiseberg & Scoble, *Monitoring Human Rights Violations: The Role of NGOs*, in Human Rights and American Foreign Policy 179 (D. Kommers & G. Loescher eds. 1979).

TRANSNATIONAL CORPORATIONS AND HUMAN RIGHTS

Transnational corporations, with their economic power, have a tremendous impact on the development of national economies, political life, and social policies. This impact can be positive when transnationals use their power to encourage the development of human rights. Transnationals can begin by providing their employees with fair wages, a safe work environment, and nondiscriminatory hiring policies. They can encourage economic development by providing jobs without stripping the host country of natural resources or channeling profits to the ruling class in repressive countries. When human rights violations in a country become numerous, transnationals can either leave the country to avoid supporting the government or work to improve the situation by supporting programs designed to effectuate social and economic changes.

The case of U.S. investment in South Africa provides a good example of the relationship between transnational corporations and human rights. Outrage over *apartheid* inspired the Reverend Leon Sullivan to set forth principles for U.S. companies to follow when doing business in South Africa. These principles included desegregating employment facilities, providing equal opportunities for employment and advancement, eliminating racial pay inequities, adhering to a minimum wage, taking affirmative steps to increase the number of nonwhites in managerial and other high-level jobs, taking steps to improve workers' lives outside the work environment with respect to housing, transportation, schooling, recreation, and health, and recognizing the right of all employees to organize into unions. Although the Reverend Sullivan no longer favors continued U.S. investment in South Africa, the companies that adopted the Sullivan principles continue to undergo an independent annual review of their progress toward achieving those principles.

In 1986 Congress passed a law requiring all U.S. companies with at least 25 employees doing business in South Africa that either were not signatories to the Sullivan Code or were not rated as making satisfactory progress under the Code, to adopt and follow a code of conduct essentially the same as the Sullivan Code. *See* Comprehensive Anti-Apartheid Act of 1986, Pub. L. No. 99-440, §§ 5001 to 5116. The Act requires the companies to submit to an annual review by the State Department to determine their compliance with the Code. Companies failing to achieve a satisfactory rating may not receive any export marketing assistance from any U.S. government agency.

In August 1988, a majority of the House of Representatives took the view that all United States companies should divest their holdings in South

Africa within 180 days. *See* H.R. 1580, 100th Cong., 2d Sess. (1988). The Senate did not pass the bill.

NOTES

1. For further reading, see McCarthy, *Transnational Corporations and Human Rights*, in U.N. Law/Fundamental Rights 175 (A. Cassese ed. 1979); Nagan, *Economic Sanctions, U.S. Foreign Policy, International Law and the Anti-Apartheid Act of 1986*, 4 Florida Int'l L. J. 85 (1988).

2. International organizations have also manifested a concern for the conduct of transnational enterprises. *See, e.g.*, United Nations Centre on Transnational Corporations, Policies and Practices of Transnational Corporations Regarding Their Activities in South Africa and Namibia 10-11 (1984); *Review of the United Nations Code of Conduct for Transnational Corporations, Hearings before the Subcomm. on Human Rights and International Organizations of the House Comm. on Foreign Affairs*, 100th Cong., 1st Sess. 22-52, 69-77 (1987).

3. For a discussion of the potential positive and negative effects transnational corporations might have on host country economies, see Moran, *Overview: The Future of Foreign Direct Investment in the Third World* in Investing in Development: New Roles for Private Capital? 3-17 (T. Moran ed. 1986). For contrasting case studies on these economic effects, *compare* T. Biersteker, Distortion of Development: Contending Perspectives on the Multinational Corporation (1978) (studying Nigeria) *with* D. Bennett and K. Sharpe, Transnational Corporations Versus the State: The Political Economy of the Mexican Auto Industry (1985).

4. With respect to the hypothetical situation of this chapter, Ford Motor Company does not have a production facility in Peru.

RELIGIOUS ORGANIZATIONS AND HUMAN RIGHTS

Religious organizations often are able to play an important role in defending human rights because of their large membership and extensive presence throughout the world. In Latin America, the Catholic Church since Vatican II has become increasingly involved in organizing poor communities to struggle for greater social and political rights and economic well-being. Religious "base communities" organized with the help of Catholic priests develop the sense of identity and confidence needed to take on self-improvement projects, such as building a village school, road, or well. They may act as catalysts for labor union activity or the formation of agrarian leagues; and sometimes church communities become a direct vehicle for mediating political demands to the state.

As in other Latin American countries, the Catholic Church in Peru has become increasingly divided in the years following Vatican II. On the one side, the traditional church hierarchy supports and is supported by the state-military structure. On the other, exists the Liberation Theology movement, one of whose primary exponents is Father Gustavo Gutiérrez, a priest who resides and works in the barrios of Lima. This politicization of the Church has led to extralegal actions against priests, nuns, and church lay workers perceived to be involved in organizing peasants in land reform, literacy campaigns, union organizing, and other social rights activities. Although Pope John Paul II has criticized ecclesiastic involvement in sociopolitical activities in Peru and elsewhere, the Liberation Theology trend continues, even as church grass-roots workers continue to become targets for vigilante groups operating under the orders of a few *caudillos*.

In Peru elements within the Catholic Church have advocated for families relocated onto agricultural colonization projects and have initiated a national dialogue among political and social sectors to facilitate a peaceful transition to a more open democratic system in Peru. The Church also publishes reports about human rights violations in its weekly paper.

Not only the Catholic Church is involved in human rights advocacy. The Fifth Assembly of the Lutheran World Federation (LWF) at Evian in 1970 adopted a resolution on human rights. The resolution recognized the continuing deprivation of both political and economic rights throughout the world and pledged that Lutheran churches would engage in corrective action in the areas of social justice, human rights, and world peace.

Many U.S. Protestant churches have taken an interest in Latin American social and political issues. Mainstream and fundamentalist congregations alike have organized visits to Central American countries, lobbied Congress against aid to the Nicaraguan ''contra'' rebels, and participated in the ''Sanctuary'' movement to assist refugees and asylum-seekers in the U.S. Although Protestant churches have steadily increased their presence in Peru, reports of their specific human rights activities are scarce.

In another context, the ability of religious organizations to affect human rights policy is demonstrated by the success of American Jewish organizations in making the plight of Soviet Jews a central concern of United States foreign policy.

NOTES

1. For further reading, see E. Cleary, Crisis and Change: The Church in Latin America Today (1986); *The Evian Assembly 1970: Resolution on Human Rights*, in A Lutheran Reader on Human Rights 1 (J. Lissner & A. Sovik eds. 1978); Foroohar, *Liberation Theology: The Response of Latin American Catholics to Socioeconomic Problems*, 13 Latin American Perspectives 37 (No. 3, 1986); Perkovich, *Soviet Jews and American Foreign*

Policy, 5 World Policy J. 435, 435-36 (1988); Ptacek, *U.S. Protestants and Liberation Theology*, 30 Orbis 433, 436-39 (1986).

2. For an extensive discussion of the human rights activities of various Protestant, Catholic, Jewish, and ecumenical U.S. religious organizations, see Livezey, *US Religious Organizations and the International Human Rights Movement*, 11 Hum. Rts. Q. 14 (1989).

UNIVERSITIES AND HUMAN RIGHTS

U.S. universities have significant foreign contacts due to their involvement in research abroad and academic exchanges with foreign universities and governments. Some commentators suggest that a university should end its relationship with institutions located in countries with serious human rights violations. Others suggest that where contacts involve research, universities should avoid a country only if the human rights situation affects the safety of university personnel in the country. Where the contact is to provide academic knowledge, however, some universities are careful not to give technical assistance or symbolic support to bolster repressive governments. Nonetheless, academic exchanges do provide a forum for protest and pressure by nationals against their government and may stimulate fresh thinking in a closed political system. *See, e.g.,* D. Bok, Beyond the Ivory Tower: Social Responsibilities of the Modern University 195-216 (1982); Hoffman, *Universities and Human Rights*, 6 Hum. Rts. Q. 5 (1984); Puryear, *Higher Education, Development Assistance and Repressive Regimes*, 17 Stud. Int'l Development 1 (1982).

THE INTERNATIONAL COMMITTEE OF THE RED CROSS

The International Committee of the Red Cross (ICRC) is a private organization formed in 1863. Its original and primary mission is to protect and assist victims of armed conflicts. One of its principal methods of protection traditionally has been to facilitate the development and implementation of international conventions on the humanitarian treatment of victims of armed conflict. The first of these "Geneva Conventions" was signed in 1864. The ICRC helped in 1949 to promulgate the four Geneva Conventions for the Protection of Victims of Armed Conflict and the two Additional Protocols of 1977. The ICRC encourages governments to ratify these instruments of international humanitarian law and reminds governments of their importance. In addition, ICRC delegates visit victims of armed conflict and provide them material assistance.

In recent years as noninternational armed conflicts have become less frequent and insurgencies more common, the ICRC has focused more attention on the refugees and innocent civilian victims of these conflicts. The ICRC delegates also have begun visiting political prisoners in countries not actually involved in any shooting war. The delegates inspect the material and psychological conditions of detention and the treatment accorded to prisoners. They provide material relief and ask the authorities to improve the conditions of detention. Reports after such visits remain confidential; the ICRC only publishes the names of the places visited and the number of people seen.

The ICRC works in coordination with the League of Red Cross Societies, a sister organization that orchestrates the activities of National Red Cross Societies. The National Societies principally handle disaster relief within their own countries. In times of acute need, the League helps channel extra assistance from other National Societies to the country facing a major disaster.

In 1987 the Peruvian Government withdrew permission for the International Committee of the Red Cross to visit important prison and detention centers. In 1989 the ICRC regained limited access to detainees in some emergency zones and police detention centers.

NOTE

For further reading, see International Committee of the Red Cross, Annual Report 1985, at 9-10, 45 (1986); P. Boissier, From Solferino to Tsushima: History of the International Committee of the Red Cross 297-384 (1985); A. Durand, From Sarajevo to Hiroshima: History of the International Committee of the Red Cross 247-74 (1984); G. Willemin and R. Heacock, The International Committee of the Red Cross 28-35, 136-42 (1984); International Committee of the Red Cross and League of Red Cross Societies, International Red Cross Handbook 19-317 (12th ed. 1983).

III *WHAT ARE THE SUBSTANTIVE AND PROCEDURAL FRAMEWORKS OF THE COVENANT ON CIVIL AND POLITICAL RIGHTS AND ITS OPTIONAL PROTOCOL?*

The Rights of Indigenous Peoples

A. INTRODUCTION

The preceding chapter contrasted (1) diplomatic protection of the rights of aliens with (2) establishment of international human rights standards. This chapter examines one method of implementing norms contained in international human rights instruments — a complaint by an individual against a government. Other instruments provide comparable procedures to help ensure government compliance with international obligations. Chapter 7 examines the petition process in the Inter-American system. Here the complaint procedure under the Optional Protocol to the Covenant on Civil and Political Rights is addressed.

One of the tasks of the Covenant's Human Rights Committee is that of deciding complaints submitted by individuals who allege violations of the Covenant. Chapter 8 discusses another Committee role, that of monitoring government reports on compliance with the Covenant. The right at issue in the Committee decisions described in this chapter is the right of indigenous peoples to self-determination. In addition to evaluating the Optional Protocol procedure, this chapter asks readers to consider whether the Covenant itself provides an adequate framework for resolving issues that arise in concertizing the right to self-determination.

The chapter requires examination of the content of the rights of indigenous peoples including the difficult issue of whether implementing the right to self-determination necessarily involves granting complete independence to indigenous peoples. Discussing implementation of the right, readers must also confront the problem of distinguishing between indigenous peoples and minorities, to whom different rights may apply. Further, the chapter introduces readers to the international protection of women's rights.

B. QUESTIONS

Assume the U.S. has ratified both the Covenant on Civil and Political Rights and its Optional Protocol (which in fact it has not). Ms. Martinez submits a communication to the Human Rights Committee based on the facts and decision in *Martinez v. Santa Clara Pueblo*. Assume that oral argument may be presented to the Committee, even though its procedures allow only written submissions. What contentions should counsel for Ms. Martinez present and how would counsel for the United States respond? While preparing arguments consider the following questions:

1. What facts in *Lovelace* appear relevant here?

2. What words in the Covenant on Civil and Political Rights did Ms. Lovelace use to support her position?

3. Which did Canada use to support its position?

4. What did the Human Rights Committee hold?

5. Did the Committee view this case as a matter of gender discrimination? If not, why not?

6. On what words in the Covenant did the Committee base its decision? Do you agree with the decision?

7. Do you think the Indians were happy with the decision?

8. What basis for decision might the Indians have preferred? Why?

9. What criteria determine whether a group constitutes a "people" with the right to self-determination? Do Indian tribes meet these criteria?

10. What is the meaning of self-determination for indigenous peoples? Does it imply control over matters such as foreign affairs and military forces?

11. If the Canadian Charter of Rights and Freedoms had been in force when Ms. Lovelace brought her case, would the Human Rights Committee have adjudicated her communication?

12. Do the Indian Act amendments solve Canada's problem as discussed in *Lovelace*? Do the amendments resolve the issue of self-determination?

13. What arguments pertain to allowing indigenous peoples the right to define their membership? Do sections 10(1) and (2) of the 1985 amendments to Canada's Indian Act, which give some control over tribal membership to the Indians, help the Indians achieve self-determination?

14. How can a body such as the Human Rights Committee get governments to adhere to its requirements and decisions?

15. Would Ms. Lovelace have been able to seek redress from the Inter-American Commission for her loss of Indian status under Article II of the American Declaration of the Rights and Duties of Man? Would she be able to bring a complaint under the American Convention on Human Rights? Assuming she could approach the Inter-American Commission, which decision-making body should she choose, the Inter-American Commission or the Covenant's Human Rights Committee?

16. How might delay and lack of factfinding mechanisms be avoided in the Human Rights Committee?

17. What is the major difference between the facts in *Lovelace* and those in *Martinez*? What is the significance of that difference?

18. As to *Martinez*:
a. What would you argue to show that the U.S. violated the Covenant on Civil and Political Rights?
b. What arguments would you expect in response?
c. How would *Lovelace* help or hinder your arguments?
d. Is Article 1 of the Covenant relevant in *Martinez*?
e. Is Article 27 of the Covenant relevant in *Martinez*?

19. Which decision is better from a human rights perspective, *Martinez* or *Lovelace*? Which right should have priority, self-determination or freedom from gender discrimination?

20. Consider the draft Universal Declaration on the Rights of Indigenous Peoples and the two sets of principles proposed by nongovernmental organizations (NGOs):
a. What are the implications for the right to self-determination from the varying sets of principles?
b. Do the draft principles offer any form of self-determination to indigenous communities?
c. How would the various principles help or hinder Ms. Martinez?

21. Compare the draft declaration on minorities with the draft Universal Declaration on the Rights of Indigenous Peoples. How do they differ? What distinguishes indigenous peoples from minorities?

22. What further arguments might you make on the basis of the Convention on the Elimination of Discrimination Against Women?

23. Does the Women's Convention help Ms. Lovelace or Ms. Martinez?

24. Could the Committee on the Elimination of Discrimination Against Women, the implementing body of the Convention, conclude that the facts found in *Lovelace* disclose a continuing violation of Articles 2, 9, and 16 of the Women's Convention?

25. Assuming that it would have been possible, do you think Ms. Lovelace should have brought her case under the Women's Convention instead of the Covenant on Civil and Political Rights?

C. THE *MARTINEZ* CASE

Martinez v. Santa Clara Pueblo, 540 F.2d 1039 (10th Cir. 1976) (footnotes omitted):

DOYLE, Circuit Judge.

This case draws into question the validity of a membership ordinance of the Santa Clara Pueblo in New Mexico. The challenge is by appellants, on behalf of themselves and others similarly situated. This appellant class is composed of female members of the Pueblo, who are married to non-members, together with their children. Appellees, on the other hand, are the Pueblo and Lucario Padilla, individually and as governor of the Pueblo. The ordinance grants membership in the Pueblo to "[a]ll children born of marriages between male members of the Santa Clara Pueblo and non-members. . . ." It precludes membership for "[c]hildren born of marriages between female members of the Santa Clara Pueblo and non-members. . . ." Appellants have alleged that the ordinance contravenes the equal protection and due process provisions of the Indian Civil Rights Act of 1968, 25 U.S.C. Section 1302(8). In a trial to the court the decision was in favor of defendants. *Martinez v. Santa Clara Pueblo*, 405 F.Supp. 5 (D.N.M. 1975). . . .

The trial court ruled for the Tribe, holding that the ordinance did not violate the Indian Civil Rights Act. Judge Mechem recognized the Pueblo's interest in membership policies generally and in the 1939 ordinance specifically and noted that if the Pueblo's ability to define who is a Santa Claran is limited or restricted, the Pueblo's culture would be changed. . . . In assessing the scope of the Indian Civil Rights Act, Judge Mechem found that the scope of the Act's equal protection provision was not coterminous with the constitutional guarantee of equal protection. ". . .[T]he Act and its equal protection guarantee must be read against the background of tribal sovereignty and interpreted within the context of tribal law and custom." *Id.* at 17. He concluded "that 25 U.S.C. Section 1302(8) should not be construed in a manner that would invalidate a tribal membership ordinance when the classification attacked is one based on criteria that have been traditionally employed by the tribe in considering membership questions.'' *Id.* at 18, and that, thus, the ordinance did not deny appellants equal protection within the meaning of the Indian Civil Rights Act. . . .

II.
THE MEANING TO BE GIVEN TO EQUAL PROTECTION OF THE LAWS AS PROVIDED IN THE INDIAN CIVIL RIGHTS ACT

A. *Legislative History.* . . .

The legislative history is not free of evidence that Congress considered that in an evaluation such as the present one the cultural autonomy and integrity of the tribes were entitled to be weighed. . . . At the same time nothing resembling a formula for determining which of these conflicting interests is to prevail has been furnished. . . .

About the only way to resolve this conflict is to recognize the necessity to evaluate and weigh both of these interests. Thus the scope, extent and importance of the tribal interest is to be taken into account. The individual right to fair treatment under the law is likewise to be weighed against the tribal interest by considering the clearness of the guarantee together with the magnitude of the interest generally and as applied to the particular facts. . . .

B. *Consideration of the Precedents.* . . .

There are cases which say that Congress did not intend in enacting the Indian Civil Rights Act to subject a tribe to identical compulsions as those which are exacted under the equal protection clauses of the Fourteenth and Fifth Amendments to the Constitution of the United States. That is not the same as saying that men can be preferred over women in a substantial way.

One example in which the equal protection standard comes into play but in which the discrimination is less pronounced is in the cases dealing with the quantum of Indian blood as a criterion for tribal membership. Under the Constitution this type of case would constitute a violation. *See for example Hirabayashi v. United States*, 320 U.S. 81. . .(1943). Courts have, however, had little trouble in upholding these requirements when they have been challenged under the Indian Civil Rights Act. . . .

The fact that the blood quantum requirement has been sustained furnishes little basis for upholding the discrimination in the case at bar because there is some semblance of basis for the classification. This is in terms of ancestral lines and in maintaining the integrity of the membership. Congress itself has employed these requirements in its definitions and other measures. . . .

The interest of the Tribe in maintaining its integrity and in retaining its tribal cultures is entitled due consideration. *See Means v. Wilson*, 522 F.2d 833 (8th Cir. 1975). And where the tribal tradition is deep-seated and the individual injury is relatively insignificant, courts should be and have been reluctant to order the tribal authority to give way. . . .

It is conceded that if the validity of the instant ordinance were to be measured by the Fourteenth Amendment alone, it would have to be held violative because it draws its classification lines solely on the basis of sex. . . .

The Fourteenth Amendment standards do not, however, apply with full force. They do, nevertheless, serve as a persuasive guide to the decision. The history and decisions teach us that the Indian Bill of Rights is modeled after the Constitution of the United States and is to be interpreted in the light of constitutional law decisions.

But we must still ask: is the Tribe justified in deviating from the Fourteenth Amendment standard on the basis that tribal, cultural and ethnic survival would suffer from full-scale enforcement of subsection (8) to these facts? We must hold that the facts do not support a decision that the Tribe's interest is compelling. The children of Julia and Myles Martinez are 100 percent Indian and 50 percent Santa Claran. They speak the language of the Santa Clara Pueblo, namely, Tewa. They practice the customs of the Tribe and are accepted into the Tribe's religion; nevertheless, they are denied membership and face exclusion with attendant loss of rights of inheritance, residency and voting, together with ability to pass tribal membership to their offspring, solely because their mother rather than their father is a Santa Claran. Compare this with the rights that are accorded the male member of the Santa Clara Pueblo. Even if he marries outside the Pueblo one who is not an Indian, and even though his family resides outside the territory of the Tribe, the offspring are entitled to tribal membership. The Tribe has not shown how such an incongruous and unreasonable result fosters and promotes cultural survival.

The contention is that the culture is patrilineal, patrilocal or patricultural. These, however, are conclusory characterizations. What is the history? The ordinance was passed in 1939 to deal with an unprecedented phenomenon, namely, mixed marriages on a relatively wide scale which resulted from Indians of different tribes meeting and encountering one another in Indian schools. An added element was Indians becoming acquainted while employed off the reservation. They met not only Indians from other tribes, but Anglos as well. Traditionally the Santa Clara female moved to the house of the Santa Clara husband and undoubtedly the Santa Clara male played a large role in educating the children in the Pueblo's traditions. This is the strongest argument in favor of the Tribe, but it falls short of justifying sex discrimination since there could have been a solution without discrimination. It is important to note also that prior to the adoption of this ordinance the mixed marriage problem was dealt with on an individual case basis. The evidence shows that under this policy there were situations in which the offspring of a Santa Clara woman were admitted to the Pueblo and so historically the 1939 ordinance cannot be said to represent the Santa Clara tradition.

There is evidence that the ordinance was the product of economics and pragmatics. It appeared to the governing body of the Tribe that the offspring of mixed marriages threatened to swell the population of the Pueblo and diminished individual shares of the property. If this were the pressing problem it could have been solved without resorting to discrimination—by simply excluding the offspring of both sexes where the parent, either male or female, married outside the Pueblo.

We do not deny that the power to control and define tribal membership is important in preserving the Tribe's culture and ethnic identity. 402 F.Supp. at 15. Also of great importance is the interest of the individual Indian in tribal membership. His interest extends to living in a particular cultural setting in close relationship with fellow members, inheriting tribal rights, and enjoying federal and other incidental benefits.... But if the equal protection clause of the ICRA is to have any consequence, it must operate to ban invidious discrimination of the kind present in this case....

The express terms and conditions of subsection (8) purport to guarantee equal justice. Congress could have couched this provision in different terms if it had not intended to enact an effective provision. It did not do so. It is not for us to say that the meaning is unclear or that some other effect was intended. We must conclude that subsection (8) means what it says and that the ordinance is out of harmony with it. The instant tribe policy is of relatively recent origin and so it does not merit the force that would be attributable to a venerable tradition. Also, inasmuch as it originates from practical economic considerations, it becomes an arbitrary and expedient solution to the problem which was then confronting the Tribe. In sum, if we were to approve their ordinance and in turn approve this plain discrimination, it would be tantamount to saying that the Indian Bill of Rights is merely an abstract statement of principle.

NOTES

1. In *Santa Clara Pueblo v. Martinez*, 436 U.S. 49 (1978), the Supreme Court reversed the 10th Circuit, holding that federal courts have no jurisdiction over complaints under the Indian Civil Rights Act (25 U.S.C. § 1302) and dismissing the case without discussing the merits. Though Congress has broad power over Indian tribes, the legislative history revealed a desire to protect tribal self-determination. The sole federal remedy prescribed is that of habeas corpus (25 U.S.C. § 1303). Since Congress failed to provide a remedy for suits based on the Indian Civil Rights Act, the Court reasoned that Congress intended that such suits be heard in tribal fora that are better equipped to evaluate questions of tribal tradition.

2. A spokesperson for United Pueblos explained why the Indians wanted to adjudicate their own cases:

> We have learned, through many centuries, what is best for us, and we hope that we may be allowed to follow the system which we have found best suited to our needs.... We believe we understand better than non-Indians, the background and traditions which shape Indian conduct and thinking, and we do not want so important a matter to be tried by those who are not familiar with them.... Pueblo officials are mindful of their people and careful consideration is given to the rights of the accused. Moreover, because we are not hedged about by the trappings of the white man's courts and the possibilities of the miscarriage of justice by lawyers who often succeed in defeating justice by forensic skill and adroitness, substantial justice is done and without resort to the delays characteristic of non-Indian courts.

Stetson, *Tribal Sovereignty: Santa Clara Pueblo v. Martinez: Tribal Sovereignty 146 Years Later*, 8 Amer. Indian L. Rev. 139, 147 (1980). Do you agree with that analysis?

3. Stetson also analyzes the tribe's attitude toward membership and concludes that Indians have been ''antagonistic'' to marriages outside the tribe because of its patrilineal tradition. Stetson asks: ''Would it not seem more realistic and desirable for Julia Martinez to conform to the norms of Santa Clara, the source of her existence, than for the norms of an alien society to which it owes no debts and which, from a Santa Clara perspective, has been the subject of much antagonism, and heartache over the years?" *Id.* at 155.

4. The Pueblo tribal culture dates back hundreds of years and has remained intact despite the influence of the Spanish and Anglo-Americans. Though the culture has been maintained, frictions within the tribe have arisen due to outside forces, among them the increased incidence of mixed marriages. The 1939 ordinance limiting tribal membership was designed to promote the survival of the Pueblo tribe by restricting membership in the case of mixed marriages. The tribe grants economic, cultural, and political rights through tribal membership and, because the Santa Clara Tribe has a patrilineal and patrilocal culture, membership status has been traced through the father. Hence, the 1939 ordinance granted membership status only to children whose fathers were members of the Santa Clara Pueblo.

Despite this rationale for the ordinance, the 10th Circuit dismissed the tribe's reason for the ordinance as "not compelling." Further, the language of the opinion suggested that the real reason for adoption of the ordinance was "economics and pragmatics." The court stated that there were alternative ways to restrict membership in the tribe that would not discriminate on the basis of sex. The tribe agreed there might be other ways but believed that its approach is the best solution for Pueblos. Is the Santa Clara tribe or the federal courts the proper body to resolve a conflict between rights purportedly granted to tribal members by Congress and the right of tribal self-determination?

5. One result of the Supreme Court's decision to grant exclusive jurisdiction to the tribe has been that children who are born to mixed marriages are granted tribal membership if their fathers are members. This policy discriminates against persons solely on the basis of gender, a result which runs counter to the equal protection doctrine of the U.S. Constitution and to several international human rights instruments which require equal treatment of men and women.

From the standpoint of the tribe's right to self-determination, however, there are advantages to the Supreme Court's decision in *Martinez*. The Court supplied a definitive ruling that the tribe had exclusive jurisdiction over the Indian Civil Rights Act. Prior to *Martinez*, the federal courts had reached inconsistent conclusions on this question. *See* Note, *Constitutional Law: Equal Protection: Martinez v. Santa Clara Pueblo - Sexual Equality Under the Indian Civil Rights Act*, 6 Am. Indian L. Rev. 187, 210-11 (1978).

A further advantage to American Indian tribes, in general, is the Court's acknowledgment of tribal sovereignty, an acknowledgment which the tribes have sought, often unsuccessfully, in federal courts. Stetson notes that "not only does this increase the authority of the tribal governments (which has been seriously eroded over the past few centuries), but it also renews tribal confidence in the workability of self-determination policies and gives an incentive to the younger members of the tribes to work within their own systems." Stetson, *supra*, at 158.

D. THE HUMAN RIGHTS COMMITTEE AND *LOVELACE*

1. Structure of the Committee

The Human Rights Committee was created by Article 28 of the Covenant on Civil and Political Rights to monitor implementation of the Covenant's provisions by governments. (See the accompanying handbook, *Selected International Human Rights Instruments*, for the text of documents referred to here.) The Committee consists of 18 members elected by the states parties. Each state may nominate two of its nationals, but Article 31 specifies that no more than one national can serve during the term set by the election. The Article also requires that states parties, electing Committee members, consider geographical distribution and representation of different legal systems and civilizations.

The Covenant structures the Committee as a body of experts by requiring in Article 28 that they "be persons of high moral character and recognized competence in the field of human rights." To preserve the integrity of the Committee as a neutral body the Article specifies that members serve in their personal capacities, not as government representatives. Provision of a four-year term of service in Article 32(1) and payment of expenses in Article 35 serve further to separate the Committee from political concerns. Yet it is important to note that governments must nominate members for election and that many members are employed by states parties, for example as diplomats, while they are not serving on the Committee, making it difficult for them to divorce themselves completely from political concerns.

The Covenant's only obligatory implementation mechanism — in Article 40 — is the submission of reports from states parties for examination by the Committee. Chapter 8 of this book examines this implementation mechanism in detail.

In addition to the report requirement the Covenant, in Article 41, provides an optional mechanism — an interstate complaint procedure — that is more adjudicative in nature. States may submit communications to the Committee regarding Covenant violations by other states parties. For the procedure to apply, however, both the complaining state and the alleged violator must have recognized the competence of the Committee to consider such communications. In addition, Article 41 allows the Committee only to "make available its good offices" in facilitating a friendly settlement, not to reach a decision on the communication. If the parties cannot reach a friendly settlement, Article 42 authorizes appointment by the Committee of a conciliation commission to resolve the dispute if the parties consent. To date no government has sought that procedure, making it impossible here to illustrate the procedure in action.

The Optional Protocol to the Covenant contains the final implementation mechanism — consideration of communications from individuals alleging Covenant violations by states parties. The Protocol grants authority to reach a decision on the merits, but the Committee does not issue judgments. Rather, it forwards its views to the individual and state party concerned. The Committee has, however, published views on some of the communications it has evaluated.

The next excerpt describes procedures of the Committee under the Optional Protocol. The *Lovelace* case, one of the Committee's published opinions, follows that description.

NOTES

1. For additional reading, see:

Nowak, *UN-Human Rights Committee: Survey of Decisions Given Up Till July 1986*, 7 Hum. Rts. L.J. 287 (1986);

de Zayas, Möller & Opsahl, *Application of the International Covenant on Civil and Political Rights under the Optional Protocol by the Human Rights Committee*, 28 German Y.B. Int'l L. 9 (1985);

Jhabvala, *The Practice of the Covenant's Human Rights Committee, 1976-82: Review of State Party Reports*, 6 Hum. Rts. Q. 81 (1984);

Fischer, *Reporting Under the Covenant on Civil and Political Rights: The First Five Years of the Human Rights Committee*, 76 Am. J. Int'l L. 142 (1982);

Opsahl & de Zayas, *The Uncertain Scope of Article 15(1) of the International Covenant on Civil and Political Rights*, 1983 Canadian Hum. Rts. Y.B. 237;

Robertson, *The Implementation System: International Measures*, in the International Bill of Rights: The Covenant on Civil and Political Rights 332 (L. Henkin ed. 1981);

Lippman, *Human Rights Revisited: The Protection of Human Rights under the International Covenant on Civil and Political Rights*, 10 Cal. W. Int'l L.J. 450 (1980);

Schwelb, *The International Measures of Implementation of the International Covenant on Civil and Political Rights and the Optional Protocol*, 12 Tex. Int'l L. J. 141 (1977).

2. The Convention on the Elimination of All Forms of Racial Discrimination contains a state-reporting requirement comparable to that contained in the Covenant. The Convention, like the Covenant, also establishes a Committee on the Elimination of Racial Discrimination. For discussion of experience with state-reporting under the treaty on racial discrimination, see Gomez del Prado, *United Nations Conventions on Human Rights: The Practice of the Human Rights Committee and the Committee on the Elimination of Racial Discrimination in Dealing with Reporting Obligations of States Parties*, 7 Hum. Rts. Q. 492 (1985); Buergenthal, *Implementing the UN Racial Convention*, 12 Tex. Int'l L.J. 187 (1977).

---

2. Procedure of the Committee

Report of the Human Rights Committee, 39 U.N. GAOR Supp. (No. 40) at 110-17, U.N. Doc. A/39/40 (1984):

III. CONSIDERATION OF COMMUNICATIONS UNDER THE OPTIONAL PROTOCOL

Introduction

558. Under the Optional Protocol to the International Covenant on Civil and Political Rights, individuals who claim that any of their rights enumerated in the Covenant have been violated and who have exhausted all available domestic remedies may submit written communications to the Human Rights Committee for consideration.... No communication can be received by the Committee if it concerns a State party to the Covenant which is not also a party to the Optional Protocol....

Procedure

559. Consideration of communications under the Optional Protocol takes place in closed meetings (art. 5(3) of the Optional Protocol). All documents pertaining to the work of the Committee under the Optional Protocol (submissions from the parties and other working documents of the Committee) are confidential. The texts of final decisions of the Committee, consisting of views adopted under article 5(4) of the Optional Protocol, are however made public. As regards decisions declaring a communication inadmissible, which are also final, the Committee has decided that it will normally make these decisions public, substituting initials for the names of the alleged victim(s) and the author(s).

560. In carrying out its work under the Optional Protocol, the Committee is assisted by Working Groups on Communications, consisting of not more than five of its members, which submit recommendations to the Committee on the action to be taken at the various stages in the consideration of each case. The Committee has also designated individual members to act as Special Rapporteurs in a number of cases. The Special Rapporteurs place their recommendations before the Committee for consideration.

561. The procedure for the consideration of communications received under the Optional Protocol consists of several main stages.

(a) *Registration of the communication*

Communications are received by the Secretariat and are registered....

(b) *Admissibility of communication*

Once a communication has been registered, the Committee must decide whether it is admissible under the Optional Protocol. The requirements for admissibility, which are contained in articles 1, 2, 3 and 5(2) of the Optional Protocol, are listed in rule 90 of the Committee's provisional rules of procedure. Under rule 91(1) the Committee or a Working Group may request the State party concerned or the author of the communication to submit, within a time-limit which is indicated in each such decision (normally between six weeks and two months), additional written information or observations relevant to the question of admissibility of the communication. Such a request does not imply that any decision has been taken on the question of admissibility (rule 91(3)). The decision to declare a communication admissible or inadmissible rests with the Committee. The Committee may also decide to terminate or suspend consideration of a communication if its author indicates that he wants to withdraw the case or if the Secretariat has lost contact with the author. A decision to declare a communication inadmissible or otherwise to terminate or suspend consideration of it may, in a clear case, be taken without referring the case to the State party for its observations.

(c) *Consideration on the merits*

If a communication is declared admissible, the Committee proceeds to consider the substance of the complaint. In accordance with article 4 of the Optional Protocol, it requests the State party concerned to submit to the Committee explanations or statements clarifying the matter. Under article 4(2), the State party has a time-limit of six months in which to submit its observations. When they are received, the author is given an opportunity to comment on the observations of the State party. The Committee then normally formulates its views and forwards them to the State party and to the author of the communication, in accordance with article 5(4) of the Optional Protocol. The State party may be requested to transmit a copy of the views to an imprisoned victim. In exceptional cases, further information may be sought from the State party or the author by means of an interim decision before the Committee finally adopts its views. A Committee member may also write an individual opinion, which is appended to the Committee's views.

Duration of procedure

562. Since the Committee, which meets three times a year, must allow both the author and the State party sufficient time to prepare their submissions, a decision on admissibility can only be taken between six months and a year after the initial submission; views under article 5(4) may follow one year later. The entire procedure normally may be completed within two to three years. The Committee tries to deal expeditiously with all communications. . . .

Issues considered by the Committee

569. The following summary illustrates the nature and results of the Committee's activities under the Optional Protocol. It does not constitute an exhaustive restatement. . . .

1. *Procedural issues*

570. A number of questions relating to the admissibility of communications have been dealt with in the Committee's earlier reports to the General Assembly or in the Committee's decisions on particular communications. These issues always depend, directly or indirectly, on the terms of the Optional Protocol, and concern, *inter alia*, the following matters.

(a) *The standing of the author*

571. Normally, a communication should be submitted by the individual himself or by his representative; the Committee may, however, accept to consider a communication submitted on behalf of an alleged victim when it appears that he is unable to submit the communication himself (rule 90(1)(b)). In practice, the Committee has accepted communications not only from a duly authorized legal representative, but also from a close family member acting on behalf of an alleged victim, but in other cases the Committee has found that the author of a communication lacked standing. In case No. 128/1982, the author was a member of a non-governmental organization and had taken interest in the alleged victim's situation. He claimed to have authority to act because he believed "that every prisoner treated unjustly would appreciate further investigation of his case by the Human Rights Committee". The Committee decided that the author lacked standing and declared the communication inadmissible. The Human Rights Committee has thus established through a number of decisions on admissibility that a communication submitted by a third party on behalf of an alleged victim can only be considered if the author justifies his authority to submit the communication.

572. The Committee has also held that an organization as such cannot submit a communication. In case No. 163/1984 . . . it stated: "According to article 1 of the Optional Protocol, only individuals have the right to submit a communication. To the extent, therefore, that the communication originates from the [organization], it has to be declared inadmissible because of lack of personal standing". . . .

(b) *The victim*

573. The Committee has clarified in case No. 35/1978 that "a person can only claim to be a victim in the sense of article 1 of the Optional Protocol if he or she is actually affected. It is a matter of degree how concretely this requirement should be taken. However, no individual can in the abstract, by way of an *actio popularis*, challenge a law or practice claimed to be contrary to the Covenant. If the law or practice has not already been concretely applied to the detriment of that individual, it must in any event be applicable in such a way that the alleged victim's risk of being affected is more than a theoretical possibility". That is, a person is not a victim unless he has personally suffered a violation of his rights. In case No. 61/1979 the Committee stressed "that it has only been entrusted with the mandate of examining whether an individual has suffered an actual violation of his rights. It cannot review in the abstract whether national legislation contravenes the Covenant, although such legislation may, in particular circumstances, produce adverse effects which directly affect the individual, making him thus a victim in the sense contemplated by articles 1 and 2 of the Optional Protocol".

(c) *Date of entry into force of the Covenant and the Optional Protocol*

574. The Committee has indicated frequently that it "can consider only an alleged violation of human rights occurring on or after 23 March 1976 (the date of entry into force of the Covenant and the Protocol for [the State party]) unless it is an alleged violation which, although occurring before that date, continues or has effects which themselves constitute a violation after that date". . . .

(e) *Preclusion under article 5(2)(a) of the Optional Protocol if the same matter is being examined under another procedure of international investigation or settlement*

577. The Optional Protocol precludes the competence of the Committee to consider

cases which are simultaneously being examined under other procedures of international investigation or settlement, such as the procedures of the Inter-American Commission on Human Rights (IACHR) and the European Commission of Human Rights. When this situation arises, the practice of the Committee has been to instruct the Secretariat to explain to the author that consideration by the Committee is precluded under article 5(2)(a) of the Optional Protocol. . . .

581. In the first case placed before it under the Optional Protocol, the Committee had occasion to determine that the examination of a particular human rights situation in a given country under Economic and Social Council resolution 1503 (XLVIII), which governs a procedure for the examination of situations which appear to reveal "a consistent pattern of gross and reliably attested violations of human rights and fundamental freedoms", does not within the meaning of article 5(2)(a) of the Optional Protocol constitute an examination of the "same matter" as a claim by an individual submitted to the Human Rights Committee under the Optional Protocol. The procedure governed by Economic and Social Council resolution 1503 (XLVIII) therefore does not bar the Human Rights Committee from considering an individual case. Also in one of the early cases considered, the Human Rights Committee determined that a procedure established by a non-governmental organization (such as the Inter-Parliamentary Council of the Inter-Parliamentary Union) does not constitute a procedure of international investigation or settlement within the meaning of article 5(2)(a) of the Optional Protocol.

582. At its twenty-first session, the Committee also observed, when declaring admissible a number of similar and related cases concerning the same country, "that a study by a intergovernmental organization either of the human rights situation in a given country (such as that by the IACHR) or a study of the trade union rights situation in a given country (such as the issues examined by the Committee on Freedom of Association of the ILO), or of a human rights problem of a more global character (such as that of the Special Rapporteur of the Commission on Human Rights on summary or arbitrary executions), although such studies might refer to or draw on information concerning individuals, cannot be seen as being the same matter as the examination of individual cases within the meaning of article 5(2)(a) of the Optional Protocol. . . .

(g) *Exhaustion of domestic remedies*

584. Under article 5(2)(a) of the Optional Protocol, the Committee shall not consider any communication unless it has ascertained that the author has exhausted all available domestic remedies. Numerous communications before the Committee have been declared inadmissible on this ground. In its decisions on admissibility, the Committee has clarified the meaning of article 5(2)(b) of the Optional Protocol, explaining, *inter alia*, that "exhaustion of domestic remedies can be required only to the extent that these remedies are effective and available" and further clarified that "an extraordinary remedy, such as seeking the annulment of decision(s) of the Ministry of Justice" does not constitute an effective remedy within the meaning of article 5(2)(b) of the Optional Protocol.

NOTES AND QUESTIONS

1. Do you think the Optional Protocol provides an adequate procedure for implementing rights prescribed in the Covenant?

2. By the end of February 1990, 88 states had ratified the Covenant on Civil and Political Rights but only 47 had also ratified the Optional Protocol.

---

3. The *Lovelace* Case

Human Rights Committee, Selected Decisions Under the Optional Protocol at 83, U.N. Doc. CCPR/C/OP/1, at 83-87 (1985); *Report of the Human Rights Committee*, 36 U.N. GAOR Supp. (No. 40) at 166, U.N. Doc. A/36/40 (1981) (footnotes omitted):

Communication No. 24/1977

Submitted by: Sandra Lovelace on 29 December 1977
Alleged victim: The author
State party: Canada
Date of adoption of views: 30 July 1981 (thirteenth session)

Views under article 5(4) of the Optional Protocol

1. The author of the communication dated 29 December 1977 and supplemented by letters of 17 April 1978, 28 November 1979 and 20 June 1980, is a 32-year-old woman, living in Canada. She was born and registered as "Maliseet Indian" but has lost her rights and status as an Indian in accordance with section 12(1)(b) of the Indian Act, after having married a non-Indian on 23 May 1970. Pointing out that an Indian man who marries a non-Indian woman does not lose his Indian status, she claims that the Act is discriminatory on the grounds of sex and contrary to articles 2(1), 3, 23(1) and (4), 26 and 27 of the Covenant. As to the admissibility of the communication, she contends that she was not required to exhaust local remedies since the Supreme Court of Canada, in *The Attorney-General of Canada v. Jeanette Lavell, Richard Isaac et al. v. Yvonne Bédard* [1974] S.C.R. 1349, held that decision 12(1)(b) was fully operative, irrespective of its inconsistency with the Canadian Bill of Rights on account of discrimination based on sex. . . .

5. In its submission under article 4(2) of the Optional Protocol concerning the merits of the case, dated 4 April 1980, the State party recognized that "many of the provisions of the . . . Indian Act, including section 12(1)(b), require serious reconsideration and reform". The Government further referred to an earlier public declaration to the effect that it intended to put a reform bill before the Canadian Parliament. It none the less stressed the necessity of the Indian Act as an instrument designed to protect the Indian minority in accordance with article 27 of the Covenant. A definition of the Indian was inevitable in view of the special privileges granted to the Indian communities, in particular their right to occupy reserve lands. Traditionally, patrilineal family relationships were taken into account for determining legal claims. Since, additionally, in the farming societies of the nineteenth century, reserve land was felt to be more threatened by non-Indian men than by non-Indian women, legal enactments as from 1869 provided that an Indian woman who married a non-Indian man would lose her status as an Indian. These reasons were still valid. A change in the law could only be sought in consultation with the Indians themselves who, however, were divided on the issue of equal rights. The Indian community should not be endangered by legislative changes. Therefore, although the Government was in principle committed to amending section 12(1)(b) of the Indian Act, no quick and immediate legislative action could be expected.

6. The author of the communication, in her submission of 20 June 1980,

disputes the contention that legal relationships within Indian families were traditionally patrilineal in nature. Her view is that the reasons put forward by the Canadian Government do not justify the discrimination against Indian women in section 12(1)(b) of the Indian Act. She concludes that the Human Rights Committee should recommend the State party to amend the provisions in question. . . .

9.2 It emerges from statistics provided by the State party that from 1965 to 1978, on an average, 510 Indian women married non-Indian men each year. Marriages between Indian women and Indian men of the same band during that period were 590 on the average each year; between Indian women and the Indian men of a different band 422 on the average each year; and between Indian men and non-Indian women 448 on the average each year.

9.3 As to the legal basis of a prohibition to live on a reserve, the State party offers the following explanations:

Section 14 of the Indian Act provides that "(an Indian) woman who is a member of a band ceases to be a member of that band if she marries a person who is not a member of that band". As such, she loses the right to the use and benefits, in common with other members of the band, of the land allotted to the band. It should, however, be noted that "when (an Indian woman) marries a member of another band, she thereupon becomes a member of the band of which her husband is a member". As such, she is entitled to the use and benefits of lands allotted to her husband's band.

An Indian (including a woman) who ceases to be a member of a band ceases to be entitled to reside by right on a reserve. None the less it is possible for an individual to reside on a reserve if his or her presence thereon is tolerated by a band or its members. It should be noted that under section 30 of the Indian Act, any person who trespasses on a reserve is guilty of an offence. In addition, section 31 of the Act provides that an Indian or a band (and of course its agent, the Band Council) may seek relief or remedy against any person, other than an Indian, who is or has been

"(a) unlawfully in occupation or possession of,

"(b) claiming adversely the right to occupation or possession of, or

"(c) trespassing upon a reserve or part thereof."

9.4 As to the reasons adduced to justify the denial of the right of abode on a reserve, the State party states that the provisions of the Indian Act which govern the right to reside on a reserve have been enacted to give effect to various treaty obligations reserving to the Indians exclusive use of certain lands. . . .

9.6 As to Mrs. Lovelace's place of abode prior to her marriage both parties confirm that she was at that time living on the Tobique Reserve with her parents. Sandra Lovelace adds that as a result of her marriage, she was denied the right to live on an Indian reserve. As to her abode since then the State party observes:

"Since her marriage and following her divorce, Mrs. Lovelace has, from time to time, lived on the reserve in the home of her parents, and the Band Council has made no move to prevent her from doing so. However, Mrs. Lovelace wishes to live permanently on the reserve and to obtain a new house. To do so, she has to apply to the Band Council. Housing on reserves is provided with money set aside by Parliament for the benefit of registered Indians. The Council has not agreed to provide Mrs. Lovelace with a new house. It considers that in the provision of such housing priority is to be given to registered Indians."

9.7 In this connection the following additional information has been submitted on behalf of Mrs. Lovelace:

"At the present time, Sandra Lovelace is living on the Tobique Indian Reserve, although she has no right to remain there. She has returned to the Reserve, with her children because her marriage has broken up and she has no other place to reside. She is able to remain on the reserve in violation of the law of the local Band Council because dissident members of the tribe who support her cause have threatened to resort to physical violence in her defence should the authorities attempt to remove her."

9.8 As to the other persisting effects of Mrs. Lovelace's loss of Indian status the State party submits the following:

"When Mrs. Lovelace lost her Indian status through marriage to a non-Indian, she also lost access to federal government programs for Indian people in areas such as education, housing, social assistance, etc. At the same time, however, she and her children became eligible to receive similar benefits from programs the provincial government provides for all residents of the province.

"Mrs. Lovelace is no longer a member of the Tobique band and no longer an Indian under the terms of the Indian Act. She however is enjoying all the rights recognized in the Covenant, in the same way as any other individual within the territory of Canada and subject to its jurisdiction."

9.9 On behalf of Sandra Lovelace the following is submitted in this connection:

"All the consequences of loss of status persist in that they are permanent and continue to deny the complainant rights she was born with.

"A person who ceases to be an Indian under the Indian Act suffers the following consequences:

"(1) Loss of the right to possess or reside on lands on a reserve (ss. 25 and 28(1)). This includes loss of the right to return to the reserve after leaving, the right to inherit possessory interest in land from parents or others, and the right to be buried on a reserve;

"(2) An Indian without status cannot receive loans from the Consolidated Revenue Fund . . . ;

"(3) An Indian without status cannot benefit from instruction in farming and cannot receive seed without charge from the Minister. . . ;

"(4) An Indian without status cannot benefit from medical treatment and health services . . . ;

"(5) An Indian without status cannot reside on tax exempt lands . . . ;

"(6) A person ceasing to be an Indian loses the right to borrow money for housing from the Band Council . . . ;

"(7) A person ceasing to be an Indian loses the right to cut timber free of dues on an Indian reserve . . . ;

"(8) A person ceasing to be an Indian loses traditional hunting and fishing rights that may exist;

"(9) The major loss to a person ceasing to be an Indian is the loss of the cultural benefits of living in an Indian community, the emotional ties to home, family, friends and neighbours, and the loss of identity."

10. *The Human Rights Committee,* in the examination of the communication before it, has to proceed from the basic fact that Sandra Lovelace married a non-Indian on 23 May 1970 and consequently lost her status as a Maliseet Indian under section 12(1)(b) of the Indian Act. This provision was — and still is — based on a

distinction *de jure* on the ground of sex. However, neither its application to her marriage as the cause of her loss of Indian status nor its effects could at that time amount to a violation of the Covenant, because this instrument did not come into force for Canada until 19 August 1976. Moreover, the Committee is not competent, as a rule, to examine allegations relating to events having taken place before the entry into force of the Covenant and the Optional Protocol. Therefore as regards Canada it can only consider alleged violations of human rights occurring on or after 19 August 1976. In the case of a particular individual claiming to be a victim of a violation, it cannot express its view on the law in the abstract, without regard to the date on which this law was applied to the alleged victim. In the case of Sandra Lovelace it follows that the Committee is not competent to express any view on the original cause of her loss of Indian status, i.e. the Indian Act as applied to her at the time of her marriage in 1970.

11. The Committee recognizes, however, that the situation may be different if the alleged violations, although relating to events occurring before 19 August 1976, continue, or have effects which themselves constitute violations, after that date. In examining the situation of Sandra Lovelace in this respect, the Committee must have regard to all relevant provisions of the Covenant. It has considered, in particular, the extent to which the general provisions in articles 2 and 3 as well as the rights in articles 12(1), 17(1), 23(1), 24, 26 and 27, may be applicable to the facts of her present situation.

12. The Committee first observes that from 19 August 1976 Canada had undertaken under article 2(1) and (2) of the Covenant to respect and ensure to all individuals within its territory and subject to its jurisdiction, the rights recognized in the Covenant without distinction of any kind such as sex, and to adopt the necessary measures to give effect to these rights. Further, under article 3, Canada undertook to ensure the equal right of men and women to the enjoyment of these rights. These undertakings apply also to the position of Sandra Lovelace. The Committee considers, however, that it is not necessary for the purposes of her communication to decide their extent in all respects. The full scope of the obligation of Canada to remove the effects or inequalities caused by the application of existing laws to past events, in particular as regards such matters as civil or personal status, does not have to be examined in the present case, for the reasons set out below.

13.1 The Committee considers that the essence of the present complaint concerns the continuing effect of the Indian Act, in denying Sandra Lovelace legal status as an Indian, in particular because she cannot for this reason claim a legal right to reside where she wishes to, on the Tobique Reserve. This fact persists after the entry into force of the Covenant, and its effects have to be examined, without regard to their original cause. Among the effects referred to on behalf of the author...the greater number...relate to the Indian Act and other Canadian rules in fields which do not necessarily adversely affect the enjoyment of rights protected by the Covenant. In this respect the significant matter is her last claim, that "the major loss to a person ceasing to be an Indian is the loss of the cultural benefits of living in an Indian community, the emotional ties to home, family, friends and neighbours, and the loss of identity".

13.2 Although a number of provisions of the Covenant have been invoked by Sandra Lovelace, the Committee considers that the one which is most directly applicable to this complaint is article 27, which reads as follows:

> "In those States in which ethnic, religious or linguistic minorities

exist, persons belonging to such minorities shall not be denied the right, in community with the other members of their group, to enjoy their own culture, to profess and practice their own religion, or to use their own language.''

It has to be considered whether Sandra Lovelace, because she is denied the legal right to reside on the Tobique Reserve, has by that fact been denied the right guaranteed by article 27 to persons belonging to minorities, to enjoy their own culture and to use their own language in community with other members of their group.

14. The rights under article 27 of the Covenant have to be secured to "persons belonging" to the minority. At present Sandra Lovelace does not qualify as an Indian under Canadian legislation. However, the Indian Act deals primarily with a number of privileges which, as stated above, do not as such come within the scope of the Covenant. Protection under the Indian Act and protection under article 27 of the Covenant therefore have to be distinguished. Persons who are born and brought up on a reserve, who have kept ties with their community and wish to maintain these ties must normally be considered as belonging to that minority within the meaning of the Covenant. Since Sandra Lovelace is ethnically a Maliseet Indian and has only been absent from her home reserve for a few years during the existence of her marriage, she is, in the opinion of the Committee, entitled to be regarded as "belonging" to this minority and to claim the benefits of article 27 of the Covenant. The question whether these benefits have been denied to her, depends on how far they extend.

15. The right to live on a reserve is not as such guaranteed by article 27 of the Covenant. Moreover, the Indian Act does not interfere directly with the functions which are expressly mentioned in that article. However, in the opinion of the Committee the right of Sandra Lovelace to access to her native culture and language "in community with the other members" of her group, has in fact been, and continues to be interfered with, because there is no place outside the Tobique Reserve where such a community exists. On the other hand, not every interference can be regarded as a denial of rights within the meaning of article 27. Restrictions on the right to residence, by way of national legislation, cannot be ruled out under article 27 of the Covenant. This also follows from the restrictions to article 12(1) of the Covenant set out in article 12(3). The Committee recognizes the need to define the category of persons entitled to live on a reserve, for such purposes as those explained by the Government regarding protection of its resources and preservation of the identity of its people. However, the obligations which the Government has since undertaken under the Covenant must also be taken into account.

16. In this respect, the Committee is of the view that statutory restrictions affecting the right to residence on a reserve of a person belonging to the minority concerned, must have both a reasonable and objective justification and be consistent with the other provisions of the Covenant, read as a whole. Article 27 must be construed and applied in the light of the other provisions mentioned above, such as articles 12, 17 and 23 in so far as they may be relevant to the particular case, and also the provisions against discrimination, such as articles 2, 3 and 26, as the case may be. It is not necessary, however, to determine in any general manner which restrictions may be justified under the Covenant, in particular as a result of marriage, because the circumstances are special in the present case.

17. The case of Sandra Lovelace should be considered in the light of the fact

that her marriage to a non-Indian has broken up. It is natural that in such a situation she wishes to return to the environment in which she was born, particularly as after the dissolution of her marriage her main cultural attachment again was to the Maliseet band. Whatever may be the merits of the Indian Act in other respects, it does not seem to the Committee that to deny Sandra Lovelace the right to reside on the reserve is reasonable, or necessary to preserve the identity of the tribe. The Committee therefore concludes that to prevent her recognition as belonging to the band is an unjustifiable denial of her rights under article 27 of the Covenant, read in the context of the other provisions referred to.

18. In view of this finding, the Committee does not consider it necessary to examine whether the same facts also show separate breaches of the other rights invoked. The specific rights most directly applicable to her situation are those under article 27 of the Covenant. The rights to choose one's residence (article 12), and the rights aimed at protecting family life and children (articles 17, 23 and 24) are only indirectly at stake in the present case. The facts of the case do not seem to require further examination under those articles. The Committee's finding of a lack of a reasonable justification for the interference with Sandra Lovelace's rights under article 27 of the Covenant also makes it unnecessary, as suggested above (paragraph 12), to examine the general provisions against discrimination (arts. 2, 3 and 26) in the context of the present case, and in particular to determine their bearing upon inequalities predating the coming into force of the Covenant for Canada.

19. Accordingly, the Human Rights Committee, acting under article 5(4) of the Optional Protocol to the International Covenant on Civil and Political Rights, is of the view that the facts of the present case, which establish that Sandra Lovelace has been denied the legal right to reside on the Tobique Reserve, disclose a breach by Canada of article 27 of the Covenant.

NOTES AND QUESTIONS

1. Did the Committee view this case as a matter of gender discrimination? If not, why not? On which words of the Covenant did the Committee base its decision? Do you agree with the decision? Do you think the majority of the Maliseet Band were happy with it? What basis for decision do you think they might have preferred?

2. The problem with classifying Indians as a "people" has to do with defining "people." The Permanent Court of International Justice suggested the following definition of a "community":

> a group of persons living in a given country or locality, having a race, religion, language and traditions of their own and united by the identity of race, religion, language and tradition in a sentiment of solidarity, with a view to preserving their traditions, maintaining their form of worship, ensuring the instruction and upbringing of their children in accordance with the spirit and traditions of their

race and rendering mutual assistance to each other. *Greco-Bulgarian "Communities" Case*, 1930 P.C.I.J. (ser. B) No. 17, at 21.

The International Commission of Jurists, The Events in East Pakistan 70 (1972), suggested criteria that include: "(1) a common history; (2) racial or ethnic ties; (3) cultural or linguistic ties; (4) religious or ideological ties; (5) a common territory or geographical location; (6) a common economic base; and (7) a sufficient number of people." *See* Clinebell and Thompson, *Sovereignty and Self-Determination: The Rights of Native Americans Under International Law*, 27 Buffalo L. Rev. 669, 707 (1978) (quoting criteria suggested by both the P.C.I.J. and the International Commission of Jurists).

How helpful are those guidelines? Could the principles apply also to "minorities"? Is there a distinction between "minority" and "people"? What criteria would you use in defining "people"?

For other definitions see Hannum, *The Limits of Sovereignty and Majority Rule: Minorities, Indigenous Peoples, and the Right to Autonomy*, E. Lutz, H. Hannum & K. Burke, New Directions in Human Rights 3, 7-14 (1989); Kiss, *The Peoples' Right to Self-Determination*, 7 Hum. Rts. L.J. 165, 173 (1986); Opekokew, *International Law, International Institutions, and Indigenous Issues*, in The Rights of Indigenous Peoples in International Law: Selected Essays on Self-Determination 1 (R. Thompson ed. 1987); *see also* J. Crawford, The Rights of Peoples (1988).

In *Lovelace* the Human Rights Committee classified Ms. Lovelace as a member of a minority and found a violation of her rights under Article 27 of the Covenant. Do you think the Committee classified her as a member of a minority rather than of a people in order to avoid the self-determination issue?

3. The importance of self-determination in relation to other rights has often been debated. One commentator suggests: "[Self-determination] is a prerequisite right for other human rights since there is no genuine exercise of individual human rights without realization of the rights of self-determination." Opekokew, *Self-Identification and Cultural Preservation: A Commentary On Recent Indian Act Amendments*, 2 Canadian Native L. Rep. 1, 8 (1986). Do you agree that self-determination is a prerequisite for other rights?

4. In June 1983 the Canadian government responded to the views of the Human Rights Committee expressed in *Lovelace*. The Committee printed the response in its 1983 report. *Report of the Human Rights Committee*, 38 U.N. GAOR Supp. (No. 40) at 249-53, U.N. Doc. A/38/40 (1983). The government outlined its efforts to amend the Indian Act (since amended, in 1985), which included forming a Parliamentary Sub-Committee to hear testimony from witnesses and issue recommendations. In addition, the response discussed enactment in 1982 of the Canadian Charter of Rights and Freedoms. The Charter states in Section 15.(1):

Every individual is equal before and under the law and has the right to the equal protection and equal benefit of the law without discrimination and, in particular, without discrimination based on race, national or ethnic origin, colour, religion, sex, age or mental or physical disability.

In addition to Section 15.(1), two other Charter clauses are Section 27 ("This Charter shall be interpreted in a manner consistent with the preservation and enhancement of the multicultural heritage of Canadians.") and Section 28 ("Notwithstanding anything in this Charter, the rights and freedoms referred to in it are guaranteed equally to male and female persons.")

Those three sections would provide Ms. Lovelace with a national remedy for violation of Section 12(1)(b) of the Indian Act. Had the sections been in force when she brought her case, would the Human Rights Committee have considered her communication?

5. On June 28, 1985, the *Indian Act* amendments (S.C. 1985, c. 27) came into force. The amended Act omits Sec. 12(1)(b), which provided that Indian women who marry non-Indians lose their Indian status. It allows registration of Indians who previously lost their Indian status under Sec. 12(1)(b). As a result of the amendments 24,000 persons regained status.

The Canadian government amended the Indian Act to avoid violating Sec. 15.(1) of the Charter of Rights and Freedoms. In addition, Canada sought to fulfill its obligations under the Covenant on Civil and Political Rights. Opekokew, *Self-Identification and Cultural Preservation: A Commentary on Recent Indian Act Amendments*, 2 Canadian Native L. Rep. 1, 2-5 (1986).

Do the amendments solve Canada's problem under the *Lovelace* decision? Do they resolve underlying issues of self-determination? Do they resolve the conflict between the Canadian government's desire "to protect the Indian minority" and its desire to treat men and women equally?

6. Some viewed the 1985 amendments as an aid to help the Indians achieve self-determination. The reasoning for that view stems from amendments that give some control over band membership to Indians. For example:

Section 10(1): "In order to assume control the band must:
(i) establish its membership rules or codes in writing;
(ii) give notice of its intention to assume control of its membership; and
(iii) obtain the consent of a majority of the electors to band control of its membership."

and

Section 10(2): "Once a majority of band electors have consented to the control over its own membership, it may:
(i) establish membership rules for itself; and
(ii) provide for a review mechanism." S.C. 1985, c. 27.

What arguments can you make for (and against) allowing indigenous communities the right to define their membership? Do the 1985 amendments help Indians achieve self-determination?

7. In a comment on *Lovelace*, William Pentney discusses criticisms of the Human Rights Committee and states: "The most obvious criticism of the process by which the Committee formulates its views is the delay involved. There is much truth in the maxim 'justice delayed is justice denied'." Pentney, *Lovelace v. Canada: A Case Comment*, 5 Canadian Legal Aid Bull. 259, 274 (1982). Note the delay of over three and a half years between the time Lovelace submitted her communication and the Committee's decision.

Pentney suggests three ways to speed up the Committee's work; first, expanding the role of the Secretariat; second, longer sessions to help reduce the delay; and third, establishing a permanent committee rather than the system of part-time members who, according to Pentney, have "only limited time and energy to devote to the work of this body." *Id.* at 274.

The second criticism he discusses is the failure to verify information the contestants submit, especially when a government denies the allegations. At present the contest involves only written submissions to the Committee. To help verify them Pentney suggests first, investigations conducted by the Committee, and second, allowing oral testimony by the contestants.

8. Other international bodies consider individual petitions. The petitioners in *Baby Boy* (chapter 7 of this book) filed with the Inter-American Commission on Human Rights. Article 26(1) of the Regulations of that Commission provides that:

> Any person or group of persons or nongovernmental entity legally recognized in one or more of the Member States of the Organization may submit petitions to the Commission, in accordance with these Regulations, on one's own behalf or on behalf of third persons, with regard to alleged violations of a human right recognized, as the case may be, in the American Convention on Human Rights or in the American Declaration of the Rights and Duties of Man.

Utilizing that clause had Canada been an OAS member, Lovelace would have been able to petition the Commission for her loss of Indian status under the American Declaration of the Rights and Duties of Man. Canada did not become a member of the Organization of American States until January 1, 1990.

If Canada had been an OAS member, are there reasons why Lovelace might have preferred to bring her case before the Inter-American Commission rather than the Human Rights Committee? Under the timetable for considering individual communications discussed in chapter 7, it may be possible to obtain a decision on a submission to the Inter-American Commission faster than on one submitted to the Human Rights Committee. Also, the Commission has authority to undertake on-site factfinding missions to investigate the facts independently of parties' submissions, though it uses this power only when it receives a large number of complaints about a particular country.

9. For further comment, see Bayefsky, *The Human Rights Committee and the Case of Sandra Lovelace*, 20 Canadian Y.B. Int'l L. Ann. 244 (1982).

10. The Human Rights Committee relied upon its *Lovelace* decision in *Kitok v. Sweden* (No. 197/1985), U.N. Doc. CCPR/C/33/D/197/1985 (1988). Kitok was removed from the rolls of his Sami village and was thus deprived of the right to breed reindeer, because he had engaged in another profession for three years. The Committee cited *Lovelace* for the view "that a restriction upon the right of an individual member of a minority must be shown to have a reasonable and objective justification and to be necessary for the continued viability and welfare of the whole." *Id.* at 12. The Committee found no violation of Article 27 in the *Kitok* case. *See also Lubicon Lake Band v. Canada* (No. 167/1984), U.N. Doc. CCPR/C/38/D/167/1984 (1990).

E. READINGS ON INDIGENOUS PEOPLES, MINORITIES, AND DISCRIMINATION AGAINST WOMEN

H. Gros Espiell, The Right to Self-Determination: Implementation of United Nations Resolutions at 8-16, U.N. Doc. E/CN.4/Sub.2/405/Rev.1 (1980) (footnotes omitted):

[Ed.: This is an excerpt from the final report of a rapporteur appointed by the U.N. Sub-Commission on Prevention of Discrimination and Protection of Minorities to study implementation of U.N. resolutions on the right of peoples under colonial and alien domination.]

Chapter 1

SOME QUESTIONS CONCERNING THE DEFINITION, SCOPE AND LEGAL NATURE OF THE RIGHT OF PEOPLES UNDER COLONIAL AND ALIEN DOMINATION TO SELF-DETERMINATION

46. [T]he modern concept of self-determination encompasses legal, political, economic, social and cultural aspects. Article 1 of the International Covenant on Civil and Political Rights states: "All peoples have the right of self-determination. By virtue of that right they freely determine their political status and freely pursue their economic, social and cultural development". In other words, as far as the International Covenants on Human Rights are concerned, the right to self-determination necessarily has political, legal, economic, social and cultural implications. . . .

47. The implementation of the right of peoples to self-determination involves not only the completion of the process of achieving independence or other appropriate legal status by the peoples under colonial and alien domination, but also the recognition of their right to maintain, assure and perfect their full legal, political, economic, social and cultural sovereignty. The right of peoples to self-

determination has lasting force, does not lapse upon first having been exercised to secure political self-determination and extends to all fields, including of course economic, social and cultural affairs. Many countries which no longer suffer from colonialism in the classic and traditional sense continue to suffer from neo-colonialism and imperialism in their various forms. . . .

56. Self-determination is essentially a right of peoples. The divergence of opinion among legal theorists which existed on this point until a few years ago has been overcome; the Declaration adopted in resolution 1514 (XV) and the International Covenants on Human Rights have provided the basis for unquestioned acceptance in international law of the fact that self-determination is a right of peoples under colonial and alien domination. To characterize self-determination as a collective right possessed by peoples raises awkward theoretical problems, because of the difficulty of defining the concept of a people and drawing a clear distinction between that and other similar concepts. Self-determination of peoples is a right of peoples, in other words of a specific type of human community sharing a common desire to establish an entity capable of functioning to ensure a common future. It is Peoples as such which are entitled to the right to self-determination. Under contemporary international law minorities do not have this right. People and Nation are two closely related concepts; they may be one and the same, but they are not synonymous. Modern international law has deliberately attributed the right to Peoples, and not to Nations and States. However, when the People and the Nation are one and the same, and when a People has established itself as a State, clearly that Nation and that State are, as forms or manifestations of the same People, implicitly entitled to the right to self-determination. . . .

57. To assert that self-determination constitutes a collective right of peoples does not mean that an individual right, to which all human beings are entitled, cannot exist at the same time. A right can be simultaneously an individual right and a collective right. The presumed incompatibility between the two types of rights is inadmissible. This conclusion, already recognized, for instance, with respect to the right to development, the right to form trade unions and the right to freedom of information, is perfectly applicable to the case of the right to self-determination.

58. In the Special Rapporteur's judgement, it is important likewise to try to conceptualize the right to self-determination as a right of the individual. The Commission on Human Rights has repeatedly invoked it as such, without giving a precise reason for that conception and without distinguishing self-determination as a right of the individual from self-determination as a condition or prerequisite for the effective exercise of the other rights and freedoms. In the Special Rapporteur's view, self-determination may be regarded also, as a consequence o[f] its initial recognition, as a right of peoples, as a right of the individual, in that it is every person's right that the people of which he is a member — if it is under colonial and alien domination — should be recognized as having the right to determine freely its own political, economic, social and cultural condition. The Special Rapporteur considers, moreover, that self-determination as a right of the human being is a consequence of the necessary recognition of the political rights of citizens and of the civil, economic, social and cultural rights of all individuals without any discrimination. The self-determination of citizens, individually, on the basis of the recognition of their political rights, is a prerequisite of the effective realization of self-determination as the people's collective right. . . .

59. In addition, however, the effective exercise of a people's right to self-determination is an essential condition or prerequisite, although not necessarily excluding other conditions, for the genuine existence of the other human rights and freedoms. Only when self-determination has been achieved can a people take the measures necessary to ensure human dignity, the full enjoyment of all rights, and the political, economic, social and cultural progress of all human beings, without any form of discrimination. Consequently, human rights and fundamental freedoms can only exist truly and fully when self-determination also exists. Such is the fundamental importance of self-determination as a human right and a prerequisite for the enjoyment of all the other rights and freedoms. . . .

60. The United Nations has established the right of self-determination as a right of peoples under colonial and alien domination. The right does not apply to peoples already organized in the form of a State which are not under colonial and alien domination, since resolution 1514 (XV) and other United Nations instruments condemn any attempt aimed at the partial or total disruption of the national unity and the territorial integrity of a country. If, however, beneath the guise of ostensible national unity, colonial and alien domination does in fact exist, whatever legal formula may be used in an attempt to conceal it, the right of the subject people concerned cannot be disregarded without international law being violated. . . .

61. This right of peoples gives rise to the corresponding duty of all States to recognize it and to promote it. The international community and all States not only have a legal duty to refrain from opposing and impeding the exercise of the right to self-determination, but also are under a positive obligation to help in securing its realization, by promoting its exercise and by co-operating in every possible way to ensure that peoples under colonial and alien domination achieve their independence and that those peoples which have already become independent as a result of exercising their right to self-determination achieve their complete sovereignty and full development. . . .

62. The right of peoples under colonial and alien domination to self-determination is not contingent on any kind of condition or requirement. In particular, resolution 1514 (XV) precludes any opposition to the exercise of the right to self-determination on the pretext that a people has not reached a sufficiently high level of development to lead an independent existence.

63. Peoples under colonial and alien domination accordingly have rights and obligations conferred by contemporary international law. They therefore possess an international personality and as regards the exercise of their rights and the performance of their duties can be regarded as subjects of international law. . . .

89. With regard to the preservation of the territorial integrity of the State in relation to implementation of the right of peoples to self-determination, both the Declaration on the Granting of Independence to Colonial Countries and Peoples and the Declaration on Principles of International Law concerning Friendly Relations and Co-operation among States assert in strong terms the need to respect and preserve that integrity. Where the territorial integrity of the State is involved, the right to self-determination does not in principle apply. This is an assertion of the greatest importance, which determines the attitude of the United Nations on the subject. But even the Declaration on Principles of International Law concerning Friendly Relations and Co-operation among States provides that sovereign and independent States, in order to be entitled to respect for their territorial integrity, should conduct themselves in compliance "with the principle of equal rights and self-determination" and should thus be "possessed of a government representing

the whole people belonging to the territory without distinction as to race, creed or colour''.

90. The express acceptance in those instruments of the principles of the national unity and the territorial integrity of the State implies non-recognition of the right of secession. The right of peoples to self-determination, as it emerges from the United Nations system, exists for peoples under colonial and alien domination, that is to say, who are not living under the legal form of a State. The right to secession from an existing State Member of the United Nations does not exist as such in the instruments or in the practice followed by the Organization, since to seek to invoke it in order to disrupt the national unity and the territorial integrity of a State would be a misapplication of the principle of self-determination contrary to the purposes of the United Nations Charter. However, to avoid any misunderstanding, it is necessary, in the Special Rapporteur's view, to specify that if the national unity claimed and the territorial integrity invoked are merely legal fictions which cloak real colonial and alien domination, resulting from actual disregard of the principle of self-determination, the subject people or peoples are entitled to exercise, with all the consequences thereof, their right to self-determination. . . .

108. The question of very small States has manifold implications. It is clear that it raises very serious and complex problems as regards the exercise of the right of peoples to self-determination. It is not the Special Rapporteur's intention to analyze this issue in depth, since it has been dealt with extensively in international theory and practice. There is no legal basis for denying the right to self-determination on the ground that the population of which a people is composed, or the territory which it inhabits, is small; consequently, the existence of the right to self-determination cannot be challenged by arguing that, if its exercise led to independence, a very small State might result. However, the matter requires serious thought because of the difficulties to which this could give rise; because in certain extreme cases very small States would not be in a position to form real free, independent and sovereign entities and would be unable to discharge the duties that inevitably flow from membership of the United Nations; and because the proliferation of very small States might have the effect of destroying or seriously undermining the very foundations of the existing community of nations, while at the same time giving rise to the problem that this type of very small State might be particularly suited to forms of intervention and/or influence which could well characterize dangerous manifestations of neo-colonialism. For the same reasons, it is necessary, without any course being taken which would affect the essence of the right of peoples to self-determination, to stress the desirability of the formation of unions, confederations or federations of States—provided that these result from the free expression of the sovereign will of the peoples composing them—which make it possible to overcome the major difficulties and more obvious dangers to which an uncontrolled and undefined proliferation of very small States would give rise.

* * *

DRAFTING A U.N. DECLARATION ON THE RIGHTS OF INDIGENOUS PEOPLES

The Working Group on Indigenous Populations meets during the week in late July or early August immediately before the session of its parent body, the U.N. Sub-Commission on Prevention of Discrimination and Protection of Minorities. The Group has a two-part mandate: (1) to review developments concerning the human rights of indigenous populations, and (2) to develop standards concerning indigenous rights. The Group has chosen to concentrate principally on the standard-setting task and has produced a draft Universal Declaration on the Rights of Indigenous Peoples for eventual adoption by the U.N. General Assembly.

The Group on Indigenous Populations was established in 1982 on the basis of a study which began a decade earlier in 1971. The following excerpt discusses efforts to establish the Group and its progress in drafting the Declaration.

Barsh, *Indigenous Peoples: An Emerging Object of International Law*, 80 Am. J. Int'l L. 369, 369-85 (1986) (footnotes omitted):

Development of the Indigenous Concept . . .

In 1971 the Sub-Commission appointed Mexican Ambassador José R. Martínez Cobo to conduct a thorough study of "discrimination against indigenous populations." The final part of the report, which contains its conclusions and recommendations, though only completed in 1983, has already been accepted as authoritative.

The Martínez Cobo report concludes that existing human rights standards "are not fully applied" to indigenous peoples and, moreover, are "not wholly adequate" to the task. Consequently, a declaration leading to a convention is required. Most important, the Special Rapporteur was persuaded that "self-determination, in its many forms, must be recognized as the basic pre-condition for the enjoyment by indigenous peoples of their fundamental rights and the determination of their own future." "In essence," the report states, self-determination

> constitutes the exercise of free choice by indigenous peoples, who must, to a large extent, create the specific content of this principle, in both its internal and external expressions, which do not necessarily include the right to secede from the State in which they may live and to set themselves up as sovereign entities. This right may in fact be expressed in various forms of autonomy within the State. . . .

Regional Scope and Definition . . .

Definition was the first substantive issue debated in the working group. India insisted on distinguishing between cases of recent immigration, such as the Americas, and situations in Asia involving historical coexistence and political integration. The Yugoslav member of the working group, Ivan Tosevski, agreed that definition must precede standard setting, a practice he had applied in his own Working Group on the Rights of Persons Belonging to Ethnic, Religious and Linguistic Minorities. Indigenous observers, however, argued that definition would be inappropriate without more broadly representative indigenous participation: a few groups from North America and Australia had no right to speak for Latin American or Asian peoples. While skeptical of the notion of "separate development," Australia and Canada supported the call for indigenous "self-definition."

The working group resolved to defer its consideration of definition, only noting the importance of both "objective" criteria such as "historical continuity" and "subjective" factors including self-identification. Yet at the second session in 1983, Asian and Latin governments again urged that attention be given to definition. So Chairman Eide asked the Secretariat to submit a discussion draft based on the Martínez Cobo study. The draft defines as "indigenous" groups "having a historical continuity with pre-invasion and pre-colonial societies, [which] consider themselves distinct from other sectors of the societies now prevailing in those territories." Culture, language, ancestry and occupation of the land all constitute evidence of continuity. "An indigenous person is one who belongs to these indigenous populations through self-identification as indigenous (group consciousness) and is recognized and accepted by these populations as one of [their] members (acceptance by the group)." . . .

The issue of regional scope nonetheless reemerged in 1985 at the working group's fourth session. The United States complained that "unfortunately large areas of the world remain unrepresented" because they are "either unable, or, more importantly, are not permitted to be present." Bangladesh countered that "indigenous" refers only to "those countries where racially distinct people coming from overseas established colonies and subjugated the indigenous populations." "The entire population" of Bangladesh was autochthonous, by comparison, and all had "coexisted" prior to the fomentation of ethnic divisions by British administrators. Indonesia described its own history similarly, and India maintained that "ethnically speaking, most of the existing tribes in India share their origins with the neighbouring non-tribal population." In Indian law, "tribal" referred to "underdeveloped," rather than colonized, groups and entitled them to a "system of positive discrimination."

The USSR, India and China have also maintained that there are no "indigenous" peoples in Asia, only minorities, and that, as Soviet Ambassador V. Sofinsky told the Sub-Commission in 1985, "indigenous" situations only arise in the Americas and Australasia where there are "imported" populations of Europeans. This attempt to reassociate indigenousness with classic colonialism was picked up, interestingly, by Mexico, which told the working group's fourth session that the marginalization of Indians "began with colonialism, and thereafter [continued] with internal colonialism and the expansion of a capitalist agricultural economy." It was virtually impossible, the Mexican observer concluded, to distinguish between indigenous populations and "peoples" entitled to self-determination.

Indigenous groups continue to oppose definition, contending that it is their concern, rather than that of states. They also understand that a superpower confrontation over classification of the Soviet Union's tribal peoples could neutralize the working group. Nevertheless, some have argued repeatedly that "indigenous" populations should be considered "peoples" in the sense of chapter XI of the Charter. "Those peoples we call indigenous are nothing more than colonized peoples who were missed by the great wave of global decolonization following the second world war," the Mikmaq delegation told the first session, "particularly where independence was granted, not to the original inhabitants of a territory, but to an intrusive and alien group newly arrived." The United States and Brazil countered that Indians participate in national institutions to an extent that constitutes "integrated." The United States emphasized its 1934 Indian Reorganization Act, under which tribes ratified charters of local self-government and elected local officers.

At the same time, indigenous groups have reacted vigorously to any suggestion that they are simply a special case of "minorities." In consequence, Jules Deschênes, the Sub-Commission's rapporteur on the definition of minorities, deferred to future deliberations of the Working Group on Indigenous Populations and suggested that "we should not attempt to deal with the question of indigenous populations" in discussing the rights or identity of minorities. . . .

Role of the United Nations

The problem of indigenous populations can be viewed as either discrimination or assimilation, i.e., as lack of equality or forced equality with the population of the administering state. The ILO took the first view in Convention No. 107 and encouraged states to remove all institutional obstacles to the complete integration of indigenous communities. Similarly, the Committee on the Elimination of Racial Discrimination has routinely sought to determine whether indigenous populations are accorded equal access to health, education and employment, and equal rights of land ownership. The Human Rights Committee established pursuant to the International Covenant for Civil and Political Rights has dealt with indigenous peoples as "minorities" under Article 27 of the Covenant; their "members have only been endowed with specific rights designed to secure the existence and survival of the community concerned," and not with any right of self-determination or autonomy.

At the working group's first session, Brazil continued in this vein by arguing forcefully for the "protection" and gradual "integration" of Indians. At the second session, Brazil suggested that indigenous autonomy was a form of racial discrimination that would invariably lead to oppression and injustice. At the heart of the Brazilian thesis was the belief that individual freedom can be realized only in multi-cultural states where different ethnic groups compete and counteract one another's prejudices through the majoritarian democratic process. "A group that was given an opportunity to participate in the life of [such] a State could not be said to have been denied the right to self-determination." The United States concurred that access to the electoral process in a multi-cultural democracy is all the self-determination that anyone needs.

Indigenous advocacy has gradually overcome this view. While "the just struggle of indigenous peoples is closely tied to the struggle of peasants for land and of workers for better living conditions" throughout the developing world, as Mexico explained at the working group's fourth session, most governments now agree with New Zealand that "policies and programmes which allow people to determine their place in society, and the place of their culture and traditions in that society," are preferable to assimilation. Some form of separate institutional existence for indigenous communities, albeit more or less within the framework of the territorial state, has become a relatively respectable concept. . . .

NOTES

1. For further reading, see L. Fritz, Native Law Bibliography (1984); B. Roy & D. Miller, The Rights of Indigenous Peoples in International Law:

An Annotated Bibliography (1985); Roy & Alfredsson, *Indigenous Rights: the Literature Explosion*, 13 Transnat'l Persp. 19 (1987); Sanders, *The UN Working Group on Indigenous Populations*, 11 Hum. Rts. Q. 406 (1989).

2. In 1989 the International Labour Conference adopted the Convention Concerning Indigenous and Tribal Peoples in Independent Countries (No. 169) to revise and replace the Indigenous and Tribal Peoples Convention, 1957 (No. 107). International Labour Conf. 76th Sess. Provisional Record 25 (1989). A representative of the ILO explained the purpose of the revised Convention to the U.N. Working Group on Indigenous Populations: "[O]ne of the main objectives of the drafting of the new Convention was to eliminate the paternalistic and integrationist approach of the former ILO Convention. He also highlighted certain significant issues in the new Convention, including the qualified use of the term 'peoples', the principle of consultation, collective land rights, the rights of ownership and possession of lands, the right to natural resources, and rights regarding the removal and relocation of indigenous people from land they traditionally occupy. . . ." *Report of the Working Group on Indigenous Populations on its seventh session*, U.N. Doc. E/CN.4/Sub.2/1989/36, at 10 (1989).

Representatives of indigenous organizations and communities "differed in their assessment of ILO Convention No. 169. Several of them expressed extreme dissatisfaction with the new Convention. They were of the view that the revision of Convention No. 107 had not been carried out as fully as it could have been done and that the standards agreed to in order to ensure the adoption of the new Convention were too low to effectively guarantee the rights of indigenous peoples. . . . There was a universal call from non-governmental observers for full or increased self-determination for indigenous peoples and for them to be accorded the political identity to which they feel entitled. This would avoid the present situation in which indigenous peoples were being marginalized and protect them from political oppression. There were numerous statements indicating that there was not adequate consultation between Governments and peoples regarding policies which directly affected the lives of indigenous peoples." *Id.* at 10-11. *See* Berman, *ILO and Indigenous Peoples: Revision of ILO Convention 107*, 41 Int'l Comm'n Jur. Rev. 48 (1988).

DRAFT PRINCIPLES FOR A U.N. DECLARATION ON THE RIGHTS OF INDIGENOUS PEOPLES

As preceding material indicates, the U.N. Working Group on Indigenous Populations is in the process of drafting a Universal Declaration on the Rights of Indigenous Peoples. The following excerpts contain principles proposed for inclusion in the declaration. The first two sets were proposed by NGOs representing indigenous peoples. The last set was prepared by the Chair of the Group as a basis for discussion. Contrast the sets of principles as you read them. In addition, consider the nature of self-determination they would give indigenous peoples.

Report of the Working Group on Indigenous Populations on its fourth session, Annex III, at 1-2, U.N. Doc. E/CN.4/Sub.2/1985/22 (1985) (footnote omitted):

Declaration of principles adopted at the Fourth General Assembly of the World Council of Indigenous Peoples in Panama, September 1984

Principle 1.   All indigenous peoples have the right of self-determination. By virtue of this right they may freely determine their political status and freely pursue their economic, social, religious and cultural development. . . .

Principle 5.   All indigenous peoples have the right to determine the person or group of persons who are included within its population.

Principle 6.   Each indigenous people has the right to determine the form, structure and authority of its institutions.

Principle 7.   The institutions of indigenous peoples and their decisions, like those of States, must be in conformity with internationally accepted human rights both collective and individual. . . .

Principle 9.   Indigenous people shall have exclusive rights to their traditional lands and its resources, where the lands and resources of the indigenous peoples have been taken away without their free and informed consent such lands and resources shall be returned. . . .

Principle 17.   Treaties between indigenous nations or peoples and representatives of States freely entered into, shall be given full effect under national and international law.

Report of the Working Group on Indigenous Populations on its fourth session, Annex IV, at 1-2, U.N. Doc. E/CN.4/Sub.2/1985/22 (1985) (footnote omitted):

Draft declaration of principles proposed by the Indian Law Resource Center, Four Directions Council, National Aboriginal and Islander Legal Service, National Indian Youth Council, Inuit Circumpolar Conference, and the International Indian Treaty Council

Declaration of principles

1. Indigenous nations and peoples have, in common with all humanity, the right to life, and to freedom from oppression, discrimination, and aggression.
2. All indigenous nations and peoples have the right to self-determination, by virtue of which they have the right to whatever degree of autonomy or self-government they choose. This includes the right to freely determine their political status, freely pursue their own economic, social, religious and cultural development,

and determine their own membership and/or citizenship, without external interference.

3. No State shall assert any jurisdiction over an indigenous nation or people, or its territory, except in accordance with the freely expressed wishes of the nation or people concerned.

4. Indigenous nations and peoples are entitled to the permanent control and enjoyment of their aboriginal ancestral-historical territories. This includes surface and subsurface rights, inland and coastal waters, renewable and non-renewable resources, and the economies based on these resources. . . .

9. The laws and customs of indigenous nations and peoples must be recognized by States' legislative, administrative and judicial institutions and, in case of conflicts with State laws, shall take precedence.

10. No State shall deny an indigenous nation, community, or people residing within its borders the right to participate in the life of the State in whatever manner and to whatever degree they may choose. This includes the right to participate in other forms of collective action and expression. . . .

15. Indigenous nations and peoples are subjects of international law.

16. Treaties and other agreements freely made with indigenous nations or peoples shall be recognized and applied in the same manner and according to the same international laws and principles as treaties and agreements entered into with other States.

17. Disputes regarding the jurisdiction, territories and institutions of an indigenous nation or people are a proper concern of international law, and must be resolved by mutual agreement or valid treaty.

18. Indigenous nations and peoples may engage in self-defence against State actions in conflict with their right to self-determination. . . .

20. In addition to these rights, indigenous nations and peoples are entitled to the enjoyment of all the human rights and fundamental freedoms enumerated in the International Bill of Human Rights and other United Nations instruments. In no circumstances shall they be subjected to adverse discrimination.

First revised text of the draft Universal Declaration on the Rights of Indigenous Peoples, as presented to the U.N. Working Group on Indigenous Populations by its Chairman/Rapporteur Ms. Erica-Irene Daes, U.N. Doc. E/CN.4/Sub.2/1989/36, at 31 (1989): . . .

The General Assembly, . . .

Solemnly proclaims the following declaration on rights of indigenous peoples and calls upon all States to take prompt and effective measures to implement the declaration in conjunction with the indigenous peoples.

1. The right to the full and effective enjoyment of all fundamental rights and freedoms, as well as the observance of the corresponding responsibilities which are universally recognized in the Charter of the United Nations and in existing international human rights instruments.

2. The right to be free and equal to all other human beings in dignity and rights and to be free from adverse distinction or discrimination of any kind. . . .

4. The [collective] right to maintain their ethnic and cultural characteristics and identity. . . .

5. The individual and collective right to protection against ethnocide. This protection shall include, in particular, prevention of any act which has the aim or effect of depriving them of their ethnic characteristics or cultural identity, of any form of forced assimilation or integration, of imposition of foreign life styles and of any propaganda derogating their dignity and diversity.

6. The right to preserve their cultural identity and traditions and to pursue their own cultural development. The rights to the manifestations of their cultures, including archeological sites, artifacts, designs, technology and works of art, lie with the indigenous peoples or their members. . . .

12. The right of collective and individual ownership, possession and use of the lands which they have traditionally occupied or used. The lands may only be taken away from them with their free and informed consent as witnessed by a treaty or agreement.

13. The right to recognition of their own land-tenure systems for the protection and promotion of the use, enjoyment and occupancy of the land.

14. The right to special measures to ensure their ownership and control over surface and substance of resources pertaining to the territories they have traditionally occupied or otherwise used including flora and fauna, waters and sea ice. . . .

18. The right to maintain and develop within their areas lands or territories their traditional economic structures and ways of life, to be secure in the traditional economic structures and ways of life, to be secure in the enjoyment of their own traditional means of subsistence, and to engage freely in their traditional and other economic activities, including hunting, fresh- and salt-water fishing, herding, gathering, lumbering and cultivation, without adverse discrimination. In no case may an indigenous people be deprived of its means of subsistence. The right to just and fair compensation if they have been so deprived. . . .

21. The right to participate on an equal footing with all the other citizens and without adverse discrimination in the political, economic and social life of their State and to have their specific character duly reflected in the legal system and in political and socio-economic institutions, including in particular proper regard to and recognition of indigenous laws and customs.

22. The right to participate fully at the State level, through representatives chosen by themselves, in decision-making about and implementation of all national and international matters which may affect their life and destiny.

23. The [collective] right to autonomy in matters relating to their own internal and local affairs, including education, information, culture, religion, health, housing, social welfare, traditional and other economic activities, land and resources administration and the environment, as well as internal taxation for financing these autonomous functions.

24. The right to decide upon the structures of their autonomous institutions, to select the membership of such institutions, and to determine the membership of the indigenous people concerned for these purposes.

25. The right to determine the responsibilities of individuals to their own community, consistent with universally recognized human rights and fundamental freedoms. . . .

28. The individual and collective right to access to and prompt decision by mutually acceptable and fair procedures for resolving conflicts or disputes

and any infringement, public or private, between States and indigenous peoples, groups or individuals. These procedures should include, as appropriate, negotiations, mediation, arbitration, national courts and international and regional human rights review and complaints mechanisms. . . .

NOTE

When a word or phrase appears in brackets [] in a U.N. draft standard, the brackets indicate that the language is tentative or not yet accepted.

Commission on Human Rights, *Report of the Working Group on the Rights of Persons Belonging to National, Ethnic, Religious and Linguistic Minorities*, U.N. Doc. E/CN.4/1990/41 at 11-14 (1990):

TEXT OF THE DRAFT DECLARATION AS ADOPTED IN ITS READING
*Draft declaration on the rights of persons belonging
to national or ethnic, religious or linguistic minorities*
The General Assembly, . . .
Proclaim this Declaration on the Rights of Persons Belonging to [National or] Ethnic, Religious or Linguistic Minorities:

Article 1
1. [Persons belonging to] [national or] ethnic, linguistic and religious minorities (hereinafter referred to as minorities) have the right to respect for, and the promotion of, their ethnic, cultural, linguistic and religious identity without any discrimination.
2. [Persons belonging to] minorities have the right to life, liberty and security of person and all other human rights and freedoms without discrimination.

Article 2
1. In accordance with the Charter of the United Nations and other relevant international instruments, [persons belonging to] minorities have the right to be protected against any activity, including propaganda, [directed against minorities] which:
  (i)   may threaten their existence [or identity];
  (ii) [interferes with their freedom of expression or association] [or the development of their own characteristics]; or
  (iii) otherwise prevents their full enjoyment and exercise of universally recognized human rights and fundamental freedoms.

2. In accordance with their respective constitutional processes [and in accordance with the relevant international treaties to which they are parties], all States shall undertake to adopt legislative or other appropriate measures to prevent and combat such activities, with due regard to the principles embodied in this Declaration and in the Universal Declaration of Human Rights.

Article 3

1. [Persons belonging to] minorities have the right, individually or in community with the other members of their group, to enjoy their own culture, to profess and practice their own religion, and to use their own language, freely and without interference or any form of discrimination.

2. All States [which have not yet done so] shall . . . [ensure that [persons belonging to] minorities are freely able to] express their characteristics, to develop their [education,] culture, language, religion, traditions and customs, and to participate on an equitable basis in the cultural, religious, social, economic and political life in the country where they live.

3. To the same ends, persons belonging to minorities shall enjoy, without any discrimination, the right to establish and maintain contacts with other members of their group [and with other minorities], especially by exercise residence within the borders of each State, and the right to leave any country, including their own, and to return to their countries. [This right shall be exercised in accordance with national legislation and relevant international human rights instruments.]

Article 4

1. All States shall take legislative or other appropriate and effective measures, especially in the fields of teaching, education, culture and information, to promote and protect the human rights and fundamental freedoms of [persons belonging to] minorities.

2. Such measures include facilitation of the enjoyment by [persons belonging to] minorities of their freedom to seek, receive and impart information and ideas of all kinds, regardless of frontiers, in particular through utilization of all forms of communication. [This freedom shall be exercised in accordance with national legislation and relevant international human rights instruments.]

3. Such measures should also include the exchange of information [and experience] among States in the aforementioned fields, with a view to strengthening mutual understanding, tolerance and friendship among all people, including [persons belonging to] minorities, [as well as to develop further friendly relations and co-operation among States in accordance with the Charter of the United Nations.] . . .

Article 5

1. Nothing in this Declaration shall prevent the fulfilment of international obligations of States in relation to [persons belonging to] minorities. In particular, States shall fulfil in good faith the obligations and commitments they have assumed under international treaties and agreements to which they are parties.

2. This Declaration shall not prejudice the enjoyment by all persons of universally recognized human rights and fundamental freedoms.

3. Nothing in the present Declaration may be construed as permitting any activity contrary to the purposes and principles of the United Nations and, in particular, contrary to the sovereignty, territorial integrity and political independence of States.

4. In exercising their rights [persons belonging to] minorities shall respect the universally recognized human rights and fundamental freedoms of others.

[Article 6

Member States of the United Nations shall endeavour, depending on their specific conditions, to create favourable political, educational, cultural and other conditions and to adopt adequate measures for the protection and promotion of the rights of minorities proclaimed in this Declaration.]

Article 7

(a) [Persons belonging to] [national,] ethnic, religious or linguistic minorities have the right to preserve their identity, and to participate effectively in the affairs of the State, and in decisions concerning the regions in which they live [through national institutions and, where possible, regional institutions].

(b) National policies and programmes, as well as programmes of international co-operation and assistance, shall be planned and implemented with due regard for their legitimate interests.

Article 8

The organs and specialized agencies of the United Nations system shall contribute to the full realization of the rights and principles set forth in this Declaration, within their respective fields of competence.

New article

This Declaration shall be carried out in a spirit of mutual understanding, tolerance, [good neighbourliness] and friendship among States and [all peoples]/[peoples] and [national], racial, ethnic, religious and linguistic groups in conformity with the purposes and principles of the United Nations. . . .

QUESTIONS

1. Consider the principles proposed by NGOs and the draft proposed by Ms. Daes:

a. What are the implications for the right of self-determination from each of the three sets?

b. How could the principles have helped or hindered Ms. Martinez?

2. Compare the draft declaration on minorities with the draft Universal Declaration on the Rights of Indigenous Peoples and the other drafts on indigenous peoples. How do they differ? What distinguishes indigenous peoples from minorities?

3. Might any of the drafts have helped in *Lovelace*?

Convention on the Elimination of All Forms of Discrimination against Women, *entered in force* Sept. 3, 1981, G.A. res. 34/180, U.N. GAOR Supp. (No. 46) at 193, U.N. Doc. A/34/46 (1980), *reprinted in* 19 I.L.M. 33 (1980):

Article 2

States Parties condemn discrimination against women in all its forms, agree to pursue by all appropriate means and without delay a policy of eliminating discrimination against women and, to this end, undertake:

(*a*) To embody the principle of the equality of men and women in their national constitutions or other appropriate legislation if not yet incorporated therein and to ensure, through law and other appropriate means, the practical realization of this principle;

(*b*) To adopt appropriate legislative and other measures, including sanctions where appropriate, prohibiting all discrimination against women;

(*c*) To establish legal protection of the rights of women on an equal basis with men and to ensure through competent national tribunals and other public institutions the effective protection of women against any act of discrimination;

(*d*) To refrain from engaging in any act or practice of discrimination against women and to ensure that public authorities and institutions shall act in conformity with this obligation;

(*e*) To take all appropriate measures to eliminate discrimination against women by any person, organization or enterprise;

(*f*) To take all appropriate measures, including legislation, to modify or abolish existing laws, regulations, customs and practices which constitute discrimination against women;

(*g*) To repeal all national penal provisions which constitute discrimination against women. . . .

Article 9

1. States Parties shall grant women equal rights with men to acquire, change or retain their nationality. They shall ensure in particular that neither marriage to an alien nor change of nationality by the husband during marriage shall automatically change the nationality of the wife, render her stateless or force upon her the nationality of the husband.

2. States Parties shall grant women equal rights with men with respect to the nationality of their children. . . .

Article 16

1. States Parties shall take all appropriate measures to eliminate discrimination against women in all matters relating to marriage and family relations and in particular shall ensure, on a basis of equality of men and women:

(*a*) The same right to enter into marriage;

(*b*) The same right freely to choose a spouse and to enter into marriage only with their free will and full consent;

(*c*) The same rights and responsibilities during marriage and at its dissolution;

(*d*) The same rights and responsibilities as parents, irrespective of their marital status, in matters relating to their children; in all cases the interests of the children shall be paramount. . . .

NOTES AND QUESTIONS

1. Canada ratified the Convention on the Elimination of All Forms of Discrimination Against Women on December 10, 1981. The Convention entered into force for Canada on January 9, 1982. The United States is not a party to the Convention.

2. The period 1976 to 1985 was proclaimed as the U.N. Decade for Women. *Report of the 1980 Conference of the U.N. Decade for Women,* U.N. Doc. A/Conf. 94/35 at 114 (1980). The Convention on the Elimination of All Forms of Discrimination Against Women was considered by many as a significant step toward achieving equality for women. The Convention set up a Committee that:

> consists of 23 experts of high moral standing and competence in the field covered by the Convention. Members are elected by secret ballot from a list of persons nominated by States parties, and serve for a term of four years. The Committee on the Elimination of Discrimination against Women meets once a year for a two-week period in Vienna (or New York).
>
> The basic task of the Committee, as set out in Article 17 of the Convention, is to consider the progress made in the implementation of the Convention. The Committee reports on its activities annually to the General Assembly through the Economic and Social Council. It may make suggestions and general recommendations based on its examination of reports and information received from States parties. . . .

United Nations Centre for Human Rights, Human Rights Machinery, Fact Sheet No. 1, at 15 (1988).

3. What is the significance of Articles 2, 9, and 16 of the Convention? Would they have helped Lovelace or Martinez? Could the Committee on the Elimination of Discrimination Against Women, the implementing body of the Convention, find that there was a continuing violation of the articles of the Convention in *Lovelace*? Assuming that it would have been possible, should Lovelace have brought her case under the Convention instead of the Covenant on Civil and Political Rights?

4. In addition to the Women's Convention and the Committee established under it, the U.N. Economic and Social Council established the Commission on the Status of Women (in 1946) to provide support for women's rights.

> Its functions are (*a*) to prepare recommendations and reports to the Council on promoting women's rights in political, economic, civil, social and educational fields, and (*b*) to make recommendations to the Council on urgent problems requiring immediate attention in the field of women's rights, with the object of implementing the principle that men and women shall have equal rights, and to develop proposals to give effect to such recommendations. . . .

United Nations Centre for Human Rights, Human Rights Machinery, Fact Sheet No. 1, at 9-10 (1988).

5. For further reading on protection of women's rights in the U.N., see Coliver, *United Nations Machineries on Women's Rights: How Might They Better Help Women Whose Rights are Being Violated?*, in New Directions in Human Rights 25 (E. Lutz, H. Hannum & K. Burke eds. 1989).

IV WHAT U.N. PROCEDURES ARE AVAILABLE WHEN VIOLATIONS OF HUMAN RIGHTS ARE ALLEGED?

ECOSOC Resolutions 1235 and 1503

A. INTRODUCTION

The preceding chapter introduced one technique for implementing human rights, that is, individuals' complaints against a government. That mechanism, however, is available only to residents of the 47 countries that as of February 1990, have ratified the Optional Protocol to the International Covenant on Civil and Political Rights. Most governments have not yet ratified the Optional Protocol. There are also situations in which violations are so widespread that individual complaints cannot provide an adequate international response.

This chapter deals with U.N. procedures which have been established to handle complaints of consistent patterns of gross human rights violations throughout the world. The procedures do not rely upon a specific treaty, but are based on resolutions of the Economic and Social Council (ECOSOC) — principally resolutions 1235 and 1503.

The chapter asks the reader to relate those procedures to human rights conditions in Myanmar (previously known as Burma).[1] The situation in that country has undergone much change and likely will continue changing. Hence, the material in the book must be taken as a snapshot of conditions in the country as of a particular moment; that is, late 1989.

This chapter gives the reader an opportunity to look at the facts and to identify the human rights norms that may have been violated. The reader must also determine how best to approach the U.N. since there are two basic alternatives: the public procedure established by ECOSOC resolution 1235 and the confidential procedure established by ECOSOC resolution 1503.

B. QUESTIONS

Citizens of Myanmar have requested your assistance in presenting their government's human rights abuses to the U.N. Consider the following questions. (This problem requires careful construction of U.N. resolutions. Be prepared to use operative language from the resolutions in answering the questions.)

1. The U.N. receives thousands of human rights communications each year. Before ECOSOC resolution 728F, the U.N. either discarded the letters (and sometimes, postcards) or filed them without response. In comparison to that initial process, what did 728F achieve?

2. What did ECOSOC resolution 1235 add? What does it require be done with communications mentioned in 728F?

3. What do materials here suggest about the evolution of practice under 1235?

4. How has ECOSOC resolution 1503 helped people's human rights?

5. What rights in the International Bill of Human Rights has Myanmar arguably violated?

6. Would those violations fall within the scope of resolution 1503? What is the basis for finding "a consistent pattern of gross and reliably attested violations of human rights"?

7. Which violations alleged under 1503 are most likely to produce a successful complaint? Why? What constitutes success?

  a. What violations are "gross" under resolutions 1235 or 1503?

---

[1] Although the country formerly known as the Socialist Republic of the Union of Burma changed its name to the Union of Burma and then to Myanmar, the chapter will use Burma and Myanmar interchangeably.

b. Does Article 4 of the Covenant on Civil and Political Rights, which permits the derogation of certain rights during periods of emergency, suggest which rights ought to be considered "gross"?

c. Is it more likely that a situation involving the violation of nonderogable rights will be considered "gross"?

d. should some violations of derogable rights be considered "gross"?

e. Does the International Bill of Human Rights indicate that certain rights ought to be considered more "fundamental" and, thus, their violation might be "gross"?

f. In construing what constitutes a "gross" violation should primary reference be made to the International Bill of Human Rights? (See also Sub-Commission resolution 1 in the accompanying handbook, *Selected International Human Rights Instruments.*)

8. Do any of the articles of the International Bill of Human Rights arguably provide a defense for Myanmar?

9. Are violations perpetrated by private individuals or armed opposition groups the responsibility of Myanmar under the International Bill of Human Rights? (See also chapter 13.)

10. What must be kept confidential under resolution 1503? (See also Sub-Commission resolution 1.) May a complainant issue a press release announcing submission of a claim under 1503? May the complainant publish the communication?

11. How may governments respond to complaints made under the 728F procedure? 1235 procedure? 1503 procedure?

12. What are the mechanisms available under the 1235 procedure for inducing a government to improve its human rights record? How do those differ from mechanisms available under 1503?

13. In what ways may nongovernmental organizations (NGOs) participate in the 1235 procedure? 1503 procedure?

14. If an NGO is presenting a human rights complaint against Myanmar to the U.N., should it choose 1235 or 1503? Why?

15. What is the significance of a "successful" 1503 complaint?

16. Why have there been so few "successful" 1503 complaints?

17. Does the 1503 process do more to protect the violating country than to exert pressure for improvement?

18. For U.S. complainants could 1503 be used with the Freedom of Information Act to pursue U.S. litigation and legislative efforts?

19. To what extent can 1235 and 1503 be used simultaneously or in sequence? Should an NGO mention its 1503 complaint when it presents an oral or written intervention in the Human Rights Commission or the Sub-Commission?

20. If an NGO wants to build the kind of consensus needed to achieve significant progress under 1235, are there other U.N. procedures that the NGO might use? (See chapter 5.)

C. BACKGROUND ON BURMA

Sesser, *A Reporter at Large: A Rich Country Gone Wrong*, New Yorker, Oct. 9, 1989, at 55 *et seq.* (1989):

Burma is a nation that does not have to worry about air pollution, because it has little industry. The country also avoids the plague of traffic congestion, because there are few cars. No one complains about urban overcrowding, because in Burma — a country the size of Texas, with forty million people — there are no jobs in the cities to attract migrants. No one needs to organize a historic-preservation movement, because hardly a new building has gone up since the British withdrew, in 1948. Rangoon and Mandalay, the only large cities, boast not a single skyscraper, and in the entire country there are just a handful of elevators and one escalator, which is boarded up. For twenty-seven years, Burma has stood isolated in the world, governed by a brutal and xenophobic military dictatorship, which, though it has maintained diplomatic relations with all major nations and has not refused foreign aid, is as suspicious of anything Russian or Chinese as of anything American. In the nineteen-sixties, the government, to guard against the taint of foreign ideas, limited visitors to a stay of one day. That limit gradually grew with the need for hard currency, jumping from seven days to fourteen in May of this year. But this liberalization came with a significant catch: all tourists must now hire an official government guide, whose duties include restricting contacts with the Burmese people.

For many years, the few visitors who have come have been fascinated by Burma — a nation that for three decades has shut itself off so tightly from the modern world it has all but faded from view. Then, during the summer of 1988, an uprising of unprecedented scale propelled Burma onto the front pages of American newspapers. A people's movement arose with what seemed like total spontaneity. Without any identifiable leadership, without a program or a platform beyond a demand for freedom, students and Buddhist monks took to the streets daily. They rallied their countrymen to the point where even government workers and policemen left their posts to join the demonstration. By September, the entire nation stood allied, opposed only by the government and the Army. America — a remote nation whose wealth and liberty people could only dream about — became a symbol of what the protesters wanted for Burma. Each day in Rangoon, the capital, crowds gathered downtown in front of a former bank building that houses the American Embassy. Hundreds of thousands of Burmese — many of whom did not understand English — marched under English-language banners calling for "DEMOCRACY."

But on September 19th, in an action that now seems almost a blueprint for what happened in China nine months later, soldiers took to the streets and the roofs and gunned down anyone in sight. At the American Embassy, frightened employees huddled on the floor as troops outside fired into groups of demonstrators. At Rangoon General Hospital, the bodies of the dead and the wounded piled up in corridors. The government decreed that from that day on outdoor political gatherings of more than four people would be fired upon. It kept its word. Life in Rangoon changed in many other ways as well, with the closing of all schools, a 10 P.M. curfew, and thousands of political arrests — arrests so numerous that in July the jails were emptied of most common criminals to make room for new political prisoners....

Amnesty International, Report 165-68 (1989):

BURMA (Myanmar)

Thousands of people were killed and thousands more arrested during widespread protests against military rule. Many detainees were freed but several hundred, including possible prisoners of conscience, were still held at the end of the year. Some detainees were reportedly tortured or ill-treated. More than 50 prisoners were killed when security personnel opened fire on rioting inmates at Insein Prison. Five executions were reported and at least 62 prisoners remained under sentence of death. There were reports of torture and extrajudicial killing of civilians belonging to Burma's ethnic minorities during army counter-insurgency operations.

In March, security forces violently broke up student demonstrations in Rangoon. The rest of the year was marked by widespread civil unrest, violent clashes between security forces and demonstrators, and frequent changes of heads of government. General Ne Win, the long-standing chairman of the Burmese Socialist Programme Party (BSPP), resigned his post in July as the head of what was then the country's only legal political party. He was replaced by Brigadier General Sein Lwin. However, he too resigned following renewed unrest and the imposition in August of a state of emergency and martial law — measures which permitted the authorities to "order the limitation as necessary of basic rights". He was replaced as head of government by a civilian, Dr. Maung Maung, who lifted the state of emergency and martial law but was himself deposed in September by the armed forces Chief-of-Staff, General Saw Maung. The new head of government banned all gatherings of more than four people, imposed a dusk-to-dawn curfew and abolished existing government and official bodies. He also introduced legislation to reform the courts and suspended some judicial functions until March 1989. The new government declared that it would "restore law, order, peace and tranquility" and began to establish multi-party democracy. Registration of political parties [was] permitted and the former single ruling party was dissolved.

There were thousands of arrests and deaths during demonstrations, allegedly a result of the actions of riot police and army personnel. In June protests in Rangoon resulted in a dusk-to-dawn curfew and an announcement by the government that anyone "gathering, making speeches, marching, instigating, encouraging, protesting, rioting and breaking the curfew" would face "serious action". The unrest spread to other cities, including Mandalay, Taunggyi and Pegu. By August it had become nationwide, with protesters demanding an end to military rule and the establishment of parliamentary democracy.

In early August, after the authorities had responded to small street demonstrations by imposing a state of emergency and martial law, hundreds of thousands of people demonstrated repeatedly and peacefully in Rangoon and other cities. Some 8,000 troops were dispatched to suppress the demonstrations; they included soldiers normally assigned to counter-insurgency operations and from units responsible for unlawful killings and torture of members of ethnic minorities.

The security forces repeatedly intervened in demonstrations which were overwhelmingly peaceful. During the March demonstration in Rangoon, many people were reportedly beaten unconscious by riot police and some of them allegedly drowned in Inya Lake. A further 41 died from suffocation in a police van — a fact acknowledged in June in a report by a government commission of inquiry into the events. After General Saw Maung seized power in September there was a new wave of demonstrations in protest against the reassertion of military control. Although leading opponents of the government had urged that the demonstrations be conducted peacefully, security forces again intervened violently.

Between March and July an estimated 200 protesters and prisoners were killed but the death toll increased dramatically following the demonstrations in August. Official reports stated that 12 people were killed and hundreds were wounded, but unofficial sources put the number of dead at up to 1,000. These sources alleged that most demonstrators were unarmed and had conducted themselves peacefully but that troops appeared to be under orders to shoot protesters. There were similar allegations after demonstrations in September when hundreds of peaceful protesters, including children, were reportedly shot. In Sagaing eyewitnesses said that troops had killed several dozen demonstrators. The authorities stated that 450 people had been killed between 18 September and mid-October, and the official radio station continued to report sporadic killings of "looters", "undisciplined elements" and "people bent on violence". Unofficial sources estimated that 1,000 people had been killed in the month after the coup and that the majority of victims had again been non-violent demonstrators.

In late September the government announced that it had suppressed "strike centres" in over 100 townships. In the process, it said, 180 demonstrators had been killed. The centres, which had been established throughout the country, had organized demonstrations and in some cases had functioned as a local administration.

The repeated waves of unrest resulted in thousands of arrests. In May, following the government-appointed commission of inquiry into the March protests, the authorities acknowledged the arrest of 625 Rangoon University students and announced that 484 of them had been released. In June a further 387 releases were announced. On 29 July retired Brigadier General Aung Gyi and nine of his associates were arrested in Rangoon, apparently in connection with several open letters he had written during the preceding months to former BSPP Chairman, General Ne Win. The letters had severely criticized the government's economic and human rights records. In August, during the period of Dr. Maung Maung's government, Amnesty International was informed of the release of these 10 prisoners. This was the first occasion on which the organization had received a response from the Burmese Government. The government also informed Amnesty International of the release of 2,750 prisoners arrested in connection with the August demonstrations.

At the end of September the government announced that 1,376 people had been arrested since the military resumed power earlier that month. Although it said that none of them were political prisoners, other sources claimed that the majority had been detained for their participation in the protest demonstrations. By December most detainees had been released after initial investigations had been conducted but a few remained in custody, including possible prisoners of conscience.

Between October and December the official radio station reported the arrest of at least 70 political activists, some of whom may have been prisoners of conscience. They included Za Gana, a dentistry student and humorist, who was arrested in October, apparently in connection with satirical performances given at mass rallies organized in August and September in favour of multi-party democracy. Like Za Gana, Nay Min — a lawyer accused of sending false information to the British Broadcasting Corporation (BBC) — was still in detention at the end of the year. Official reports also suggested that Aung Thet, Maung Maung Nyunt, Saw Phet Nyi Nyi and Ne Win were arrested while participating in a peaceful demonstration at Shwedagon Pagoda in Rangoon. They were also still in detention at the end of the year.

Ill-treatment in prisons and detention centres was said to be widespread. Some of those held after the March protests were allegedly beaten by prison staff. Victims included several dozen factory workers of Indian descent held in Tharawaddy. Several female students confirmed after their release that they had been raped and at least four detainees reportedly died from suffocation after several dozen of them were crammed into a small cell at Insein Prison.

Human rights violations were also committed by counter-insurgency troops deployed in remote and mountainous areas where armed opposition groups were active. Army units executed and tortured civilians suspected of supporting the opposition. Most of the victims were members of Burma's ethnic minorities. In April some 60 soldiers from the 77th Light Infantry Division allegedly surrounded and opened fire on villagers attending an ordination ceremony in Shan State, killing eight of them. The soldiers apparently suspected the Shan villagers of supporting insurgents. Soldiers also seized villagers to work as porters or guides and sometimes executed or tortured those whose work they considered unacceptable. In March members of the 49th Regiment beat to death three Shan porters they had seized who had collapsed while carrying heavy loads.

Riots at Insein Prison resulted in the alleged deaths of at least 73 inmates in two incidents. In April, 16 detainees were allegedly killed by security forces during disturbances. In August, when the prison may have held as many as 10,000 inmates, several hundred were reportedly killed when prison staff and army personnel opened fire on them. Sources said that during the incident some victims were shot in custody and others were prevented from leaving burning prison buildings. A few days later the government said that 57 prisoners had been killed, 106 had been wounded and 513 had escaped. According to foreign news reports, official sources privately admitted that the government had grossly under-estimated the number of deaths resulting from gunshots and from fire that engulfed the prison during the riot. Shortly afterwards the government announced the release of 4,806 prisoners, most of them criminal offenders, from the prison. Other prison disturbances in the towns of Sittwe and Bassein reported in the official press resulted in the deaths of seven inmates and the release or escape of 1,700 others.

In September military operations and house-to-house searches for political activists were followed by the flight of up to 7,000 dissidents who said they feared arrest and ill-treatment. The majority were students who fled to border areas controlled by opposition insurgents; some joined armed resistance groups. Government officials estimated that by late December 2,000 students had returned to their homes.

In February, in a letter addressed to the United Nations Special Rapporteur on summary or arbitrary executions, the government categorically rejected allegations of unlawful killings in frontier areas. It asserted that, "It is entirely inconceivable that summary or arbitrary executions have taken place in Burma." In May and August Amnesty International published two reports — *Burma: Extrajudicial execution and torture of members of ethnic minorities* and *Burma: Extrajudicial execution, torture and political imprisonment of members of the Shan and other ethnic minorities*. The reports described the long-term pattern of gross human rights violations against civilian members of ethnic minorities in Kachin, Karen, Kayah, Mon and Shan States. Based on over 150 interviews with victims of human rights violations and witnesses to abuses, the reports documented 106 cases of unlawful killings and 180 cases of torture or ill-treatment since 1984. In April Amnesty International submitted information about its concerns in Burma to the United Nations procedure (under Economic and Social Council Resolutions 728F/1503) for confidentially reviewing communications about human rights violations. In August the organization also raised its concerns in a statement delivered to the UN Working Group on Indigenous Populations.

Between August and December Amnesty International sent a series of urgent appeals to the Burmese authorities. The organization expressed concern that security forces assigned to quell protests appeared to have instructions allowing the use of lethal force even when such force was not permitted under international law. Amnesty International urged the government to implement substantive safeguards to protect detainees from execution by security forces and to prevent security forces deliberately shooting unarmed and peaceful demonstrators. It also urged the government to investigate all alleged killings of demonstrators by the security forces and sought assurances that all detainees arrested on political grounds would be either promptly charged with recognizable offences and fairly tried, or released. The organization sent several appeals to the government on behalf of Za Gana and Nay Min.

In August Amnesty International raised its concern about the killing of demonstrators with the UN Human Rights Sub-Commission.

In November Health Minister Pe Thein responded to an appeal by Amnesty International on behalf of nine detained doctors, saying that they had all been released after initial questioning. He denied allegations that they had been arrested for providing medical care to people shot by troops.

NOTES

1. For further reading, see: Amnesty International, Prisoners of Conscience in Myanmar (Burma): A Chronicle of Developments Since September 1988,

AI Index: ASA 16/23/89 (1989); Asia Watch, Burma (Myanmar): Worsening Repression (1990).

2. Readers should review the material in chapter 1 that introduces U.N. structures including ECOSOC, the Commission on Human Rights, and the Sub-Commission.

D. U.N. PROCEDURES FOR RESPONDING TO HUMAN RIGHTS VIOLATIONS

1. Development of Major U.N. Procedures

In articles 55 and 56 of the U.N. Charter, all member governments "pledge themselves to take joint and separate action" to "promote . . . higher standards of living . . . development . . . solutions of international economic . . . and related problems; and . . . universal respect for, and observance of, human rights and fundamental freedoms . . . ." Participants in the San Francisco Conference of 1945 proposed that the Charter should assure not only promotion and observance but also protection of human rights. That proposal was defeated because the United Kingdom and the United States believed that such language would inappropriately raise expectations of U.N. action on specific human rights problems. In 1947 the newly established U.N. Commission on Human Rights decided that it had "no power to take any action in regard to any complaints regarding human rights." ECOSOC confirmed that position but also requested the U.N. Secretariat to prepare an annual list of the complaints received.

Numerous efforts were made between 1947 and 1959 to alter the "no power" rule, but none was successful. In 1959 ECOSOC reaffirmed its "no power" rule in adopting resolution 728F, which consolidated the procedures for handling human rights communications. Resolution 728F does provide for the Secretary-General to prepare and distribute to the members of the Commission on Human Rights and its subsidiary body, the Sub-Commission on Prevention of Discrimination and Protection of Minorities, a "non-confidential list containing a brief indication of the substance of each communication . . . which deals with the principles involved in the pro-motion of . . . human rights," before their respective annual sessions. Resolution 728F also calls for the preparation of a "confidential list con-taining a brief indication of the substance of other communications con-cerning human rights, however addressed, and to furnish this list to members of the Commission [and Sub-Commission], in private, without divulging the identity of the authors of communications . . . ."

Economic and Social Council resolution 728F (XXVIII), 28 U.N. ESCOR Supp. (No. 1) at 19, U.N. Doc. E/3290 (1959):

COMMUNICATIONS CONCERNING HUMAN RIGHTS

The Economic and Social Council,

Having considered chapter V of the report of the Commission on Human Rights on its first session, concerning communications, and chapter IX of the report of the Commission on its fifteenth session,

1. *Approves* the statement that the Commission on Human Rights recognizes that it has no power to take any action in regard to any complaints concerning human rights;

2. *Requests* the Secretary-General:

(a) To compile and distribute to members of the Commission on Human Rights before each session a non-confidential list containing a brief indication of the substance of each communication, however addressed, which deals with the principles involved in the promotion of universal respect for, and observance of, human rights and to divulge the identity of the authors of such communications unless they indicate that they wish their names to remain confidential;

(b) To compile before each session of the Commission a confidential list containing a brief indication of the substance of other communications concerning human rights, however addressed, and to furnish this list to members of the Commission, in private meeting, without divulging the identity of the authors of communications except in cases where the authors state they have already divulged or intend to divulge their names or that they have no objection to their names being divulged;

(c) To enable the members of the Commission, upon request, to consult the originals of communications dealing with the principles involved in the promotion of universal respect for, and observance of, human rights;

(d) To inform the writers of all communications concerning human rights, however addressed, that their communications will be handled in accordance with this resolution, indicating that the Commission has no power to take any action in regard to any complaint concerning human rights;

(e) To furnish each Member State concerned with a copy of any communication concerning human rights which refers explicitly to that State or to territories under its jurisdiction, without divulging the identity of the author, except as provided for in sub-paragraph (b) above;

(f) To ask Governments sending replies to communications brought to their attention in accordance with sub-paragraph (e) whether they wish their replies to be presented to the Commission in summary form or in full;

3. *Resolves* to give members of the Sub-Commission on Prevention of Discrimination and Protection of Minorities, with respect to communications dealing with discrimination and minorities, the same facilities as are enjoyed by members of the Commission on Human Rights under the present resolution;

4. *Suggests* to the Commission on Human Rights that it should at each session appoint an *ad hoc* committee to meet shortly before its next session for the purpose of reviewing the list of communications prepared by the Secretary-General under paragraph 2(a) above and of recommending which of these communications, in original, should, in accordance with paragraph 2(c) above, be made available to members of the Commission on request.

In 1977 the Secretariat stopped issuing the non-confidential lists of communications. Resolution 728F further provides that any communications referring explicitly to a member state should be furnished to that state without divulging the identity of the author. The Government's reply, upon request, may be circulated to the Commission. In practice, authors of communications are sent a letter referring to the ''no power to take any action'' rule with a copy of resolution 728F. That letter remains the last information an author officially receives about the communication.

Instead of responding to communications alleging specific human rights violations, the Commission on Human Rights devoted its energies to establishing the principal norms of international human rights during its early years. Those norms included the Universal Declaration of Human Rights (1948), the Convention on the Prevention and Punishment of the Crime of Genocide (1948), the Covenant on Civil and Political Rights (1966), and the International Covenant on Economic, Social and Cultural Rights (1966).

In 1966, however, the Commission requested authority from ECOSOC to review its functions and to be empowered to make recommendations about specific violations brought to its attention. ECOSOC asked the General Assembly to let the Commission review the organization of its work and expanded the session of the Commission from four to six weeks. Shortly thereafter the General Assembly, in resolution 2144A of October 26, 1966, invited ECOSOC and the Commission to consider ways in which the U.N. could work to eliminate human rights violations. At its next session, in early 1967, the Commission adopted resolution 8 (XXIII), which requested authority to examine communications on the lists prepared pursuant to Council resolution 728F.[2]

a. Resolution 1235

The Economic and Social Council in resolution 1235 (XLII) of June 6, 1967,[3] approved the Commission's request. Accordingly, the Commission established an agenda item entitled '''Question of the violation of human rights and fundamental freedoms . . . and to examine information relevant to gross violations of human rights and fundamental freedoms . . .' . . . contained in the communications listed by the Secretary-General pursuant to Economic and Social Council resolution 728F. . . .'' Resolution 1235 also permitted the Sub-Commission to establish a similar agenda item. Further, resolution 1235 provided that the Commission undertake a ''thorough study of situations which reveal a consistent pattern of violations of human rights, as exemplified by the policy of *apartheid*. . . .''

---

[2] C.H.R. res. 8 (XXIII), U.N. Doc. E/CN.4/940, at 131 (1967). Also in 1967 the Commission sought ECOSOC authority for the establishment of the *Ad Hoc* Working Group of Experts to investigate and study policies and practices that violated human rights in South Africa and Namibia.

[3] E.S.C. res. 1235 (XLII), 42 U.N. ESCOR Supp. (No.1) at 17, U.N. Doc. E/4393 (1967).

Economic and Social Council resolution 1235 (XLII), 42 U.N. ESCOR Supp. (No. 1) at 17, U.N. Doc. E/4393 (1967):

The Economic and Social Council, . . .

1. *Welcomes* the decision of the Commission on Human Rights to give annual consideration to the item entitled "Question of the violation of human rights and fundamental freedoms, including policies of racial discrimination and segregation and of apartheid, in all countries, with particular reference to colonial and other dependent countries and territories," without prejudice to the functions and powers of organs already in existence or which may be established within the framework of measures of implementation included in international covenants and conventions on the protection of human rights and fundamental freedoms; and concurs with the requests for assistance addressed to the Sub-Commission on Prevention of Discrimination and Protection of Minorities and to the Secretary-General;

2. *Authorizes* the Commission on Human Rights and the Sub-Commission on Prevention of Discrimination and Protection of Minorities, in conformity with the provisions of paragraph 1 of the Commission's resolution 8 (XXIII), to examine information relevant to gross violations of human rights and fundamental freedoms, as exemplified by the policy of apartheid as practised in the Republic of South Africa and in the Territory of South West Africa under the direct responsibility of the United Nations and now illegally occupied by the Government of the Republic of South Africa, and to racial discrimination as practised notably in Southern Rhodesia, contained in the communications listed by the Secretary-General pursuant to Economic and Social Council resolution 728 F (XXVIII) of 30 July 1959;

3. *Decides* that the Commission on Human Rights may, in appropriate cases, and after careful consideration of the information thus made available to it, in conformity with the provisions of paragraph 1 above, make a thorough study of situations which reveal a consistent pattern of violations of human rights, as exemplified by the policy of apartheid as practised in the Republic of South Africa and in the Territory of South West Africa under the direct responsibility of the United Nations and now illegally occupied by the Government of the Republic of South Africa, and racial discrimination as practised notably in Southern Rhodesia, and report, with recommendations thereon, to the Economic and Social Council;

4. *Decides* to review the provisions of paragraphs 2 and 3 of the present resolution after the entry into force of the International Covenants on Human Rights;

5. *Takes note* of the fact that the Commission on Human Rights, in its resolution 6 (XXIII), has instructed an *ad hoc* study group to study in all its aspects the question of the ways and means by which the Commission might be enabled or assisted to discharge functions in relation to violations of human rights and fundamental freedoms, whilst maintaining and fulfilling its other functions;

6. *Requests* the Commission on Human Rights to report to it on the result of this study after having given consideration to the conclusions of the *ad hoc* study group referred to in paragraph 5 above.

* * *

In practice, resolution 1235 has served as the basis for annual debate during the sessions of the Commission and Sub-Commission on human rights violations around the world. These debates began as rather reserved discussions in which governments claimed that they could not be criticized by name. By the late 1970's, however, governments and nongovernmental organizations (NGOs) accepted this agenda item as the occasion for lively public discussion of violations committed by named governments. Based on those debates, the Commission and Sub-Commission began to adopt resolutions expressing concern about human rights violations in particular countries.

In addition, the Commission developed a practice under resolution 1235 of appointing special rapporteurs, special representatives, experts, and other envoys to monitor human rights violations in particular countries: Afghanistan (special rapporteur, 1984-present), Bolivia (special envoy, 1981-1984), Chile (working group, 1975-1979; special rapporteur, 1979-1990), Cuba (delegation of six members of the Commission, 1988; Secretary-General to maintain contacts, 1989-present), Democratic Kampuchea (member of the Sub-Commission to review materials, 1980-1983), El Salvador (special representative, 1981-present), Equatorial Guinea (special rapporteur, 1979; expert, 1980, 1984), Guatemala (special rapporteur, 1982-1985, special representative, 1986-1988), Iran (special representative, 1984-present), Poland (special rapporteur, 1982), and Romania (special rapporteur, 1989-present).

b. Resolution 1503

Although resolution 1235 refers to the communications listed pursuant to resolution 728F, the Commission may not refer to the substance of those communications directly because they remain confidential pursuant to resolution 728F. Moreover, resolution 1235 does not provide a mechanism for consideration or analysis of the communications themselves. Accordingly, in 1968 the Sub-Commission proposed that the 728F communications should be subjected to a three-stage screening process by a working group of the Sub-Commission, the whole Sub-Commission, and the Commission. In its resolution 17 (XXV) of 1969 the Commission essentially accepted the Sub-Commission's recommendation to the Economic and Social Council, but gave governments a year to consider the proposal. On May 27, 1970, ECOSOC adopted resolution 1503 (XLVIII).[4] The resolution established a procedure separate from the public debate conducted under resolution 1235 in the Commission and the Sub-Commission; the public discussion continued despite the adoption of resolution 1503.

Economic and Social Council resolution 1503 (XLVIII), 48 U.N. ESCOR (No. 1A) at 8, U.N. Doc. E/4832/Add.1 (1970):

---

[4] E.S.C. res. 1503 (XLVIII), 48 U.N. ESCOR Supp. (No.1A) at 17, U.N. Doc. E/4832/Add.1 (1970).

Procedure for dealing with communications relating to violations of human rights and fundamental freedoms

The Economic and Social Council,

Noting resolutions 7 (XXVI) and 17 (XXV) of the Commission on Human Rights and resolution 2 (XXI) of the Sub-Commission on Prevention of Discrimination and Protection of Minorities,

1. *Authorizes* the Sub-Commission on Prevention of Discrimination and Protection of Minorities to appoint a working group consisting of not more than five of its members, with due regard to geographical distribution, to meet once a year in private meetings for a period not exceeding ten days immediately before the sessions of the Sub-Commission to consider all communications, including replies of Governments thereon, received by the Secretary-General under Council resolution 728 F (XXVIII) of 30 July 1959 with a view to bringing to the attention of the Sub-Commission those communications, together with replies of Governments, if any, which appear to reveal a consistent pattern of gross and reliably attested violations of human rights and fundamental freedoms within the terms of reference of the Sub-Commission;

2. *Decides* that the Sub-Commission on Prevention of Discrimination and Protection of Minorities should, as the first stage in the implementation of the present resolution, devise at its twenty-third session appropriate procedures for dealing with the question of admissibility of communications received by the Secretary-General under Council resolution 728 F (XXVIII) and in accordance with Council resolution 1235 (XLII) of 6 June 1967;

3. *Requests* the Secretary-General to prepare a document on the question of admissibility of communications for the Sub-Commission's consideration at its twenty-third session;

4. *Further requests* the Secretary-General:

(a) To furnish to the members of the Sub-Commission every month a list of communications prepared by him in accordance with Council resolution 728 F (XXVIII) and a brief description of them together with the text of any replies received from Governments;

(b) To make available to the members of the working group at their meetings the originals of such communications listed as they may request, having due regard to the provisions of paragraph 2(b) of Council resolution 728 F (XXVIII) concerning the divulging of the identity of the authors of communications;

(c) To circulate to the members of the Sub-Commission, in the working languages, the originals of such communications as are referred to the Sub-Commission by the working group;

5. *Requests* the Sub-Commission on Prevention of Discrimination and Protection of Minorities to consider in private meetings, in accordance with paragraph 1 above, the communications brought before it in accordance with the decision of a majority of the members of the working group and any replies of Governments relating thereto and other relevant information, with a view to determining whether to refer to the Commission on Human Rights particular situations which appear to reveal a consistent pattern of gross and reliably attested violations of human rights requiring consideration by the Commission;

6. *Requests* the Commission on Human Rights after it has examined any situation referred to it by the Sub-Commission to determine:

(a) Whether it requires a thorough study by the Commission and a report and recommendations thereon to the Council in accordance with paragraph 3 of Council resolution 1235 (XLII);

(b) Whether it may be a subject of an investigation by an *ad hoc* committee to be appointed by the Commission which shall be undertaken only with the express consent of the State concerned and shall be conducted in constant co-operation with that State and under conditions determined by agreement with it. In any event, the investigation may be undertaken only if:

(i)   All available means at the national level have been resorted to and exhausted;

(ii) The situation does not relate to a matter which is being dealt with under other procedures prescribed in the constituent instruments of, or conventions adopted by, the United Nations and the specialized agencies, or in regional conventions, or which the State concerned wishes to submit to other procedures in accordance with general or special international agreements to which it is a party.

7. *Decides* that if the Commission on Human Rights appoints an *ad hoc* committee to carry on an investigation with the consent of the State concerned:

(a) The composition of the committee shall be determined by the Commission. The members of the committee shall be independent persons whose competence and impartiality is beyond question. Their appointment shall be subject to the consent of the Government concerned;

(b) The committee shall establish its own rules of procedure. It shall be subject to the quorum rule. It shall have authority to receive communications and hear witnesses, as necessary. The investigation shall be conducted in co-operation with the Government concerned;

(c) The committee's procedure shall be confidential, its proceedings shall be conducted in private meetings and its communications shall not be publicized in any way;

(d) The committee shall strive for friendly solutions before, during and even after the investigation;

(e) The committee shall report to the Commission on Human Rights with such observations and suggestions as it may deem appropriate;

8. *Decides* that all actions envisaged in the implementation of the present resolution by the Sub-Commission on Prevention of Discrimination and Protection of Minorities or the Commission on Human Rights shall remain confidential until such time as the Commission may decide to make recommendations to the Economic and Social Council;

9. *Decides* to authorize the Secretary-General to provide all facilities which may be required to carry out the present resolution, making use of the existing staff of the Division of Human Rights of the United Nations Secretariat;

10. *Decides* that the procedure set out in the present resolution for dealing with communications relating to violations of human rights and fundamental freedoms should be reviewed if any new organ entitled to deal with such communications should be established within the United Nations or by international agreement.

* * *

Resolution 1503 authorizes the Sub-Commission to appoint a working group consisting of not more than five of its members to meet in private for a period not exceeding 10 days immediately prior to the Sub-Commission's annual session to

> consider all communications, including replies of Governments thereon, received by the Secretary-General under Council resolution 728 F (XXVIII) of 30 July 1959 with a view to bringing to the attention of the Sub-Commission those communications, together with replies of Governments, if any, which appear to reveal a consistent pattern of gross and reliably attested violations of human rights and fundamental freedoms . . . .

The Sub-Commission in private meetings then considers whether the communications referred by the working group, together with any replies from governments and "other relevant information" should be referred to the Commission as "situations which appear to reveal a consistent pattern of gross and reliably attested violations of human rights . . . ."

At its 1971 session the Sub-Commission adopted standards and criteria for the admissibility of 1503 communications.[5] The Sub-Commission decided that communications "shall be admissible only if . . . there are reasonable grounds to believe that they may reveal a consistent pattern of gross and reliably attested violations of human rights and fundamental freedoms, including policies of racial discrimination and segregation and of *apartheid* in any country, including colonial and other dependent countries and peoples." Sub-Commission resolution 1 (XXIV) also stated that admissible

> communications may originate from a person or group of persons who . . . dare victims of the violations . . ., any person or group of persons who have direct and reliable knowledge of those violations, or non-governmental organizations acting in good faith in accordance with recognized principles of human rights, not resorting to politically motivated stands contrary to the provisions of the Charter of the United Nations and having direct and reliable knowledge of such violations.

Anonymous communications are not admissible, but the author of a communication may request that his or her name not be revealed to the government.

The communication must contain a "description of the facts and must indicate . . . the rights that have been violated." Second-hand information may be included, so long as accompanied by "clear evidence." "Communications shall be inadmissible if their language is essentially abusive and . . . if they contain insulting references to the State against which the complaint is directed." There is a provision for consideration of communications after the removal of abusive language. Communications are also

---

[5] Sub. Comm'n res. 1 (XXIV), U.N. Doc. E/CN.4/1070, at 50-51 (1971) (reproduced in the accompanying handbook).

inadmissible if they have "manifestly political motivations" or are "based exclusively on reports disseminated by mass media."

Communications shall be inadmissible if they would prejudice the functioning of U.N. specialized agencies (such as the International Labor Organization), if there exist domestic remedies which have not been exhausted and which are not "ineffective or unreasonably prolonged," if the matter has been satisfactorily settled, or if the communication is not submitted within "a reasonable time after the exhaustion of the domestic remedies . . . ."

The 1503 procedure has evolved since 1970. While the new practices may not be specifically authorized by resolution 1503, they appear to have become regular attributes of the procedure. For example, in 1974 the Commission decided to establish its own Working Group on Communications to meet just before the next annual session of the Commission and to consider the disposition of situations referred by the Sub-Commission to the Commission. The Commission's Working Group on Communications met for the first time in 1975 and has been established every year since then. In 1974 the Commission also decided to inform governments that they had been the subject of a situation referred by the Sub-Commission and to invite the governments to submit any observations.

In 1978 the Commission formalized a number of practices which had developed under the 1503 process. For example, the Commission decided to invite the Chair of the Sub-Commission's Working Group on Communications to participate in sessions of the Commission on 1503 matters. The Commission also gave accused governments the opportunity to respond during the confidential discussions of the Commission. Further, the Commission decided that the Sub-Commission and its Working Group should be given access to the confidential records of the Commission's meetings on 1503 matters.

For the first time, in 1978, the Chair of the Commission announced the names of the governments which had been the subject of discussion during the 1503 deliberations, but the Chair did not explain the substance of the complaints or the decisions reached. In 1984 the Commission's Chair announced not only the names of the countries discussed, but whether the Commission had decided to keep the matter under consideration or to terminate the consideration of particular countries.

The secrecy surrounding the 1503 procedure, which is one of its principal features, has been an obstacle to adequate knowledge about the functioning and effectiveness of the procedure. In 1985 and 1986 the new governments in Argentina, the Philippines, and Uruguay successfully requested that the records of the 1503 proceedings in their respective cases should be released to the public. The availability of this material has made it possible for a new evaluation of the 1503 procedures based on more comprehensive information. Also, human rights advocates can now be given some useful advice as to how they should present their 1503 communications.

2. Overview of the 1503 Procedure in Practice

There is a year-long 1503 process. The resolution provides that all communications alleging a consistent pattern of gross and reliably attested violations shall be considered initially by the Sub-Commission, and it has in turn delegated the first review of the thousands of communications received by the U.N. each year to a Working Group of five members of the Sub-Commission. The five members are selected for the following year by the Chair of the Sub-Commission at the end of each Sub-Commission session. The Chair consults with Sub-Commission members from each of the five regions represented in the U.N.: Africa, Asia, Eastern Europe, South America, and "Western Europe and Other."

The Working Group meets for two weeks before the commencement of the Sub-Commission session in August each year. The Working Group considers communications submitted during the previous year as well as any responses that the governments concerned may wish to provide. Until the late 1980's the Working Group usually received 20,000-25,000 communications per year.[6] Of the thousands of communications received by the U.N. only about two dozen may be sufficiently well prepared to be given serious consideration by the Group. Though there is authority within 1503 for consolidating individual communications, including postcards and letters, to assess whether there exists a consistent pattern of gross violations of human rights in a country, the Group only reviews with care those communications that muster sufficient facts to support a finding that a government is responsible for a consistent pattern of gross and reliably attested violations.

The Group meets in secret with only its members and the staff of the Communications Unit of the Centre for Human Rights present. Each member of the Group takes responsibility for identifying communications for referral to the Sub-Commission. The members ordinarily divide their responsibilities by categories of rights in the Universal Declaration. For example, the member from the "Western European and Other" group of nations may be responsible for raising cases involving torture, arbitrary killing, and other violations of personal integrity. The African member usually takes responsibility for communications regarding discrimination. The member from Eastern Europe may accept primary responsibility for communications raising violations of the right to leave and return. The assignments are not rigid, and any member may request consideration of any communication. The staff of the Centre assists the Group members in identifying communications appropriate for discussion.

---

[6] The U.N. Secretariat received some 350,000 complaints of human rights violations between 1972 and 1988, as well as several thousand replies from governments. U.N. Centre for Human Rights, Communications Procedures, Fact Sheet No. 7, at 6-7 (1989). In 1988 and 1989 the number of communications— principally postcards and duplicated appeals—rose to 200,000 and 350,000.

A majority of members of the Group, that is three out of five, must vote in favor of referring a communication to the Sub-Commission. On several occasions one or even two of the members of the Group have not arrived in Geneva in time for all or part of the Group sessions. The absences have made it more difficult to obtain the three votes required for action. The Group takes separate votes on the referral of each communication. Often several communications are referred to the Sub-Commission in regard to a particular country. In the past few years, the Group has ordinarily referred communications in regard to 8-10 countries each year. The Group has also developed a practice of holding a few additional cases for consideration during the following year. While not constituting a formal action under the 1503 process, this practice may indicate that the Working Group will seriously consider referral if the situation does not improve by the following year. As soon as the Group completes its deliberations, the Centre for Human Rights arranges for the translation of the communications referred by the Group, so that they can be considered by the Sub-Commission in the principal languages of the U.N. The Group reports its conclusions to the Sub-Commission in a confidential document.

The Sub-Commission meets in private session about three or four days in late August to consider communications referred by its Working Group. The Sub-Commission refers some communications to the Commission by a majority vote, refuses to refer other situations, and has developed a practice of keeping others under consideration until the following year's session.

The Sub-Commission decisions are confidential — at least vis-a-vis the authors of communications who do not officially know what happened to their communications. The Centre for Human Rights informs affected governments in October that communications have been transmitted to the Commission or have been kept under review by the Sub-Commission. The governments are invited to submit written observations on the situation in question.

The Commission has established a two-stage process like that of the Sub-Commission. A Working Group comprised of five members of the Commission meets in private session just before the Commission session each year in February-March to draft recommendations as to how each situation referred by the Sub-Commission should be handled by the Commission.

The Commission usually meets in private session for several days in late February or early March to consider situations brought to its attention by its Working Group. As to each situation the government concerned usually begins the Commission's discussion. After debate by Commission members, the Commission decides whether to accept its Group's recommended decision. The government concerned may be present during the vote and may comment afterwards.

Under resolution 1503 the Commission is authorized to recommend to ECOSOC the mounting of a "thorough study" or an even more intensive inquiry by an *ad hoc* factfinding body. The Commission recommended a "thorough study" only on one occasion[7] and has never recommended the use of an *ad hoc* factfinding body. Instead, the Group has proposed and the Commission has developed an expanding repertoire of approaches, including written questions to be posed to the governments concerned, the sending of a member of the Commission to make direct contacts with the government, the sending of a U.N. staff person to the country, keeping the case under consideration, dismissal, or some other approach.

When the Commission returns to public session, the Chair announces the list of countries that have been dropped or continued under the 1503 process and any other actions taken. Countries which are continued on the Commission agenda will be considered the following year whether or not they are the subject of new communications.

a. Deadline for Submission

Communications must be submitted prior to the annual meeting of the Sub-Commission's Working Group on Communications. Until 1989 the Working Group in theory considered all communications *dated* on or before June 30th of the year the Working Group met.

The Working Group preferred communications which were submitted sufficiently in advance of June 30th, so that governments could have a realistic opportunity to respond. Until 1989 most of the successful communications were ordinarily submitted during the period late March through late May.

In 1989 the Sub-Commission decided that governments should be given five months to respond. This view, if pursued, will require communications to be submitted by late February of the year in which they are to be considered by the Working Group. The difficulty with such a deadline is that a communication submitted in January 1989 will be over a year old when considered in February/March 1990 by the Commission on Human Rights. This difficulty may be mitigated to some extent if the Sub-Commission decides to request the Secretary-General to update year-old communications with more recent communications from the monthly lists prepared pursuant to resolution 728F.

b. Confidentiality of the 1503 Procedure

In order to use the 1503 process effectively, an advocate needs to know whether the government answered the communication, what the government responded, whether the Sub-Commission's Working Group referred the communication to the Sub-Commission, whether the Sub-Commission referred the matter to the Commission, what recommendation was made by the Commission's Working Group, the nature of the defense raised

---

[7] The subject of the "thorough study" was Equatorial Guinea. See the Bossuyt article, *infra*, for a report on the handling of Equatorial Guinea.

by the government at the Commission, and the Commission's resolution of the issue. At most stages of the process there are opportunities for advocacy with the Sub-Commission and Commission members who are responsible for decisions. Those opportunities are exploited by the concerned governments and can be used by the complainant if the requisite information can be gathered.

Despite the rather daunting language of ECOSOC 1503 and considerable effort by responsible U.N. officials to keep the process secret, most authors of communications who participate in the meetings of the Sub-Commission and Commission are able to obtain the relevant information. Some Sub-Commission members inform at least their own governments about the results of each step in the 1503 process — particularly if their government has been accused of violating human rights. Once the members disclose anything, it is not surprising that word travels fast.

Most of the successful 1503 communications are prepared by lawyers or researchers for NGOs that send representatives to the Sub-Commission. Most participants in the public sessions of the Sub-Commission who wish to know the 1503 decisions can discover them without effort. Indeed, the tentative list of countries developed by the Sub-Commission is often published in the International Herald Tribune or Le Monde.

Similarly, at the Commission on Human Rights, with dozens of government delegations privy to confidential information, those attending Commission sessions who wish to know what is happening under 1503 often are able to learn.

c. What Constitutes a Consistent Pattern of Gross and Reliably Attested Violations?

It is possible to infer from the names of the countries mentioned by the Chair of the Commission on Human Rights at the end of the Commission's 1503 deliberations and from publicly available information about those countries what sort of situation constitutes a "consistent pattern of gross and reliably attested violations." Through the 1988 session of the Commission, 44 nations had been considered under the 1503 process. The governments of those countries were responsible for a large number of cases involving torture, political detention, summary or arbitrary killing, and disappearance.[8]

d. Other Procedural Issues

There are several other issues which might be relevant to those individuals and organizations interested in using the procedures established

---

[8] *See* Tolley, *The Concealed Crack in the Citadel: The United Nations Commission on Human Rights' Response to Confidential Communications*, 6 Hum. Rts. Q. 420, 448 (1984).

by ECOSOC resolutions 728F, 1235, and 1503.[9] A more detailed analysis of these issues, however, is not required for the purposes of the present exposition.

3. Further Remarks on 1235 and 1503

In many cases human rights advocates must choose between the public procedures established by resolution 1235 and the confidential procedure established by resolution 1503. If an NGO files a complaint under 1503, the NGO may face objections from the government if the NGO also discusses the same situation in the public debate under resolution 1235. To mention the complaint in public discussion under 1235 risks an objection that the advocate has violated the confidentiality assured by 1503. Also, the U.N. Secretariat may refuse to circulate a written NGO intervention about a country, unless that country is already on the 1235 agenda for the Sub-Commission or Commission. A written intervention about violations in a country not already on the agenda will ordinarily be received as a complaint under resolutions 728F and 1503.

U.N. officials familiar with the 1503 process indicate that large numbers of individuals have petitioned the U.N. pursuant to resolution 728F and have obtained relief. The 728F process may be helpful to individual victims, even when individual complaints cannot establish a consistent pattern and thus are not referred to the Commission under 1503. For example, until the opening of the Berlin Wall in 1989, a large number of individual complaints were filed under 728F on behalf of residents of the German Democratic Republic who were detained for attempting to emigrate. The G.D.R. government reportedly responded to such complaints on a number of occasions by releasing the individuals. Also, those individuals were often the subject of buying-out arrangements with the Federal Republic of Germany such that they were able to leave the G.D.R. At minimum resolution 728F affords a mechanism for complaints to be received through official channels of the U.N. and for governments to be able to respond, if they so desire.

The 1503 process may encourage governments to engage in an exchange of views and possibly to improve the situation without the glare of substantial publicity. Many governments, including the U.S., regularly respond to 1503 communications. They may not provide a substantive answer to public criticism heard at the Commission or its Sub-Commission, because they have insufficient opportunity during the busy debate (under resolution 1235) to research and submit a good response. Also, unless there is a substantial consensus for action under 1235, governments may realize the

---

[9] For further reading, see Amnesty International, A Practical Guide to the United Nations '1503 Procedure': A Confidential Procedure for Complaints About Alleged Human Rights Violations, AI Index: IOR 30/02/89 (1989).

public criticism can safely be ignored. In addition, a few governments are so offended by public criticism that they stubbornly refuse to take action to improve the situation. Hence, the 1503 procedure may sometimes afford a better opportunity for constructive dialogue than the public 1235 process. Until 1989 Iran was an example of a country which was intransigent in the face of public actions under 1235. It is, though, doubtful whether Iran would have been more responsive under 1503.

While the 1503 process is painfully slow, complex, secret, and vulnerable to political influence at many junctures, it does afford an incremental technique for placing gradually increasing pressure on offending governments. Nevertheless, the confidentiality of the process can be used as a barrier to effective U.N. action in the case of governments that do not respond to incremental pressure and continue to engage, over several years in grave and widespread violations of human rights. If the objective is to obtain prompt publicity or public action for serious human rights violations, the 1503 process is inappropriate.

Resolution 1235 can be more often effective in situations wherein prompt publicity, public action, and continuous monitoring are required. The excerpts below illustrate how resolutions 1235 and 1503 have been used.

Bossuyt, *The Development of Special Procedures of the United Nations Commission on Human Rights*, 6 Hum. Rts. L.J. 179, 181-94, 202-03 (1985) (footnotes omitted):

I. THE CONFIDENTIAL PROCEDURE . . .

The confidential nature of the 1503 procedure is often criticized. It is, however, not without justification that the communications are kept confidential in the initial phase of the procedure, and that discussions of the Working Group and of the Sub-Commission on those communications are held in closed sessions. After all, the pre-trial enquiry and the deliberations of judges in a judicial trial are generally also confidential. Nevertheless, the emphasis on confidentiality in the 1503 procedure is grossly exaggerated. At least decisions of the Sub-Commission, taken with respect to communications forwarded by the Working Group, should be made public at the end of the closed meetings. If the Commission was able to establish such a practice beginning in 1978, there is absolutely no reason why the Sub-Commission should not be able to adopt exactly the same practice.

Being confidential, the 1503 procedure has all the advantages of established procedure, consisting of successive steps taken by the organs involved. A progressive adoption of these steps, which individually are considered to constitute sanctions, may induce the government concerned to accept a dialogue with the UN-organ involved. Before reaching the level of the Commission, the governments concerned are invited to present written replies; at the level of the Commission they are moreover invited to participate in the discussion of the human rights situation in their country. At every level of the procedure, it may be assumed that the cooperation shown by the government concerned in replying to these invitations, will generally dispose the organ involved favourably, and eventually increase the chances of the government of escaping further review. Whatever the organ may be, it is quite probable that cooperation will be appreciated and neglect resented.

Everything which induces a government to cooperate is particularly important because the efficacity of United Nations procedures in the field of human rights depends to a large extent, on the measure of dialogue which can be established between the United Nations and the government of the country concerned. The procedure is useful as long as it is a means of exercising pressure on the country concerned. By expressing regrets when communications are kept pending — particularly when this happens at the level of the Sub-Commission — instead of being forwarded to the superior organ, human rights friends overlook the point that there is no real solution to the problem at the end of the procedure. The succession of steps composing the procedure is more influential than the actual step itself. Keeping a communication pending at the level of the Sub-Commission can be more effective for inducing a government to start a dialogue with the United Nations than forwarding the communication to the Commission, where it can be rejected as soon as it gets there.

The possible effects of the 1503 procedure are often minimised because of its confidential nature. However, one should be aware of the limits of the confidentiality of the procedure. As a matter of fact, with the exception of the deliberations of the Sub-Commission's Working Group on communications which are really secret, not only the 26 independent experts of the Sub-Commission, but also the . . . Governments which compose the constantly renewed Commission, know exactly what happens under the confidential procedure. Consequently, all decision makers in the United Nations in the field of human rights are aware of the available information on the human rights situation in the countries concerned. This fact can be quite embarrassing to the governments concerned, particularly when they are invited to explain themselves before the Commission. There is no doubt that a continuous review of the human rights situation in a country progressively erodes its human rights reputation at the United Nations.

The main usefulness of the procedure is twofold:

a) confronting the human rights situation in a given country within the framework of the confidential procedure may facilitate the Commission's eventual decision to deal with it in public session. As will be demonstrated below, most "country oriented" (public) procedures have been preceded by a decision of the Sub-Commission to forward communications to the Commission within the framework of the confidential procedure;[10]

[10 In so far as it is possible to ascertain (from 1978 onward), Albania (first action in public 1988), Bolivia (1981), El Salvador (1981), Equatorial Guinea (1979), Guatemala (1981), and Haiti (1987 advisory services) were considered under the 1503 procedure before they were placed in the public agenda of the Human Rights Commission under ECOSOC res. 1235 or under the advisory services rubric. Chile (1975), Cuba (1988), Iran (1982), Israel (1970), Poland (1982), and Romania (1989) appeared on the public agenda without first being considered under 1503. Afghanistan was the subject of a public resolution in February 1980 under the self-determination agenda item; it was the subject of a 1503 complaint revealed in 1981; a special rapporteur under 1235 was appointed in 1984.]

b) situations in countries neglected by world public opinion can be brought to the attention of the Sub-Commission — and eventually the Commission — within the framework of the confidential procedure, although it is highly unlikely that these organs would ever address themselves to these situations if there was no such procedure.

However, since the adoption of ECOSOC resolution 1503 (XLVIII) of 27 May 1970, a tremendous development has taken place in the form of new public procedures. Particularly the "thematic" procedures, which grew out of the "country oriented" procedures — to which development the confidential procedure contributed substantially — could decrease somewhat the importance of the confidential procedure. The "thematic" working group and special rapporteurs can act much more swiftly than the organs involved in the confidential procedure. The confidential procedure probably suffers more from its inability to react immediately on urgent information and from the difficulty of breaking through the majority requirements of the Sub-Commission's Working Group on communications, than from its confidential nature.

II. THE PUBLIC PROCEDURE

Within the framework of the public procedure on "violation of human rights", which is based on ECOSOC resolution 1235 (XLII) of 6 June 1967, the members of the Commission and the Sub-Commission can, during a debate in public session, refer to violations of human rights in any part of the world. This procedure may lead to the adoption of resolutions and in exceptional cases to [the] establishment of special procedures. There has been a genuine breakthrough of those procedures since 1975. Before 1975, there was only the procedure concerning the Republic of Viet-Nam (in 1963) and the ongoing procedures concerning the "outcasts" of the United Nations in human rights: Southern Africa (since 1967) and the Israeli occupied territories (since 1969). . . .

[Since 1975] several additional procedures concerning a variety of countries came into existence. These procedures concern Chile (1975), Equatorial Guinea (1979), Bolivia, El Salvador and Guatemala (1981), Poland and Iran (1982), and Afghanistan (1984).[11] Along with this "country oriented" approach, a "thematic" approach came into existence and expanded with procedures regarding missing persons (1980), mass exoduses (1981), summary executions (1982) and torture (1985).

A. The "country oriented" approach

1. Chile

After the coup of 11 September 1973 against President Allende of Chile, the Sub-Commission, in its resolution 8 (XXVII) of 21 August 1974, addressed a recommendation to the Commission to study the situation in Chile. This recommendation was supported by the General Assembly in its resolution 3219 (XXIX) of 6 November 1974. In its resolution 8 (XXXI) of 27 February 1975 the Commission decided to establish an "Ad Hoc Working Group to inquire into the situation of human rights in Chile". . . . On its way to Santiago de Chile the Working Group

_____

[11 Similar procedures have been established in regard to Cuba (1988) and Romania (1989).]

received a message from President Pinochet stating that a visit would not be timely. The Working Group nevertheless continued its activities, and each year reported to the Commission and the General Assembly on the basis of information from all relevant sources. Finally, three members of the Working Group visited Chile from 12 to 27 July 1978. . . .

After its visit to Chile, the General Assembly, in its resolution 33/174 of 20 December 1978, established a United Nations Trust Fund for Chile. In its resolution 11 (XXXV) of 6 March 1979 the Commission replaced the Working Group by a) a special rapporteur on the situation of human rights in Chile: Justice A. Diéyé (Senegal); and b) two experts to study the fate of missing persons in Chile: Professor F. Ermacora (Austria) and Mr. W. Sadi (Jordanié). Justice A. Diéyé carried out this function until his untimely death on 17 March 1983. . . . The successive special rapporteurs on Chile report each year to the Commission and to the General Assembly.

As far as missing persons in Chile are concerned, Mr. W. Sadi withdrew soon after and Professor F. Ermacora reported alone to the General Assembly and to the Commission. In its resolution 20 (XXXVI) of 29 February 1980 the Commission established a "Working Group on missing persons", the mandate of which has been extended every year since. It marked the beginning of what is called a "thematic" approach in contrast to the classic "country oriented" approach.[12]

2. Equatorial Guinea

In 1975, the situation of human rights in Equatorial Guinea had already been forwarded by the Sub-Commission to the Commission, within the framework of the confidential procedure. However, in 1976, the Commission decided that there was insufficient data to determine the existence of gross and systematic violations of human rights. In 1977, on the basis of new complaints, the Commission requested the Secretary-General, still within the framework of the confidential procedure, to establish direct contacts with the Government of Equatorial Guinea. When the Government did not cooperate, the Commission renewed its request in March 1978 adding that, in the absence of new elements, the situation in Equatorial Guinea would be dealt with in public procedure. Although the Secretary-General had contact in May 1978 with the representative of the Government of Equatorial Guinea, in September 1978, it refused contact on the basis of the above mentioned request from the Commission.

On 8 March 1979 the Commission decided to deal with the situation in Equatorial Guinea in public procedure, and requested the Chairman of the Commission in its resolution 15 (XXXV) of 13 March to appoint a special rapporteur. Thus Professor F. Volio Jiménez (Costa Rica) was appointed. On 3 August 1979 a coup took place in Equatorial Guinea and deposed President Macías, who was executed on 29 September 1979. The Special Rapporteur confirmed in his report to the Commission regarding his visit to Equatorial Guinea from 1 to 15 November 1979 the veracity of the complaints about the dictatorial regime of Macías. He also expressed concern about the absence of a date for the restoration of political rights, and regret about the lack of cooperation and interest from the Government for his mission.

[12 See discussion of thematic approach in this chapter, *infra*, and in chapter 5, *infra*.]

In its resolution 33 (XXXVI) of 11 March 1980 the Commission asked the Secretary-General, at the request of the Government of Equatorial Guinea, to appoint an expert with a view to assisting the Government for taking the necessary action for the full restoration of human rights. Professor F. Volio Jiménez (Costa Rica) was appointed as the expert. In his report — after visiting Equatorial Guinea from 27 November to 4 December 1980 — the expert formulated a series of recommendations for the restoration of human rights in Equatorial Guinea. The Commission adopted, on 11 March 1981, its resolution 31 (XXXVII) requesting the Secretary-General to draw up a draft plan of action. On the basis of resolutions 1982/34 of 11 March 1982 and 1983/32 of 8 March 1983, the Secretary-General reported to the Commission on the progress made in implementing the plan of action. In this matter, the Secretary-General called upon the cooperation of two experts in constitutional law, who proposed 37 modifications in the draft constitution, 25 of which were accepted by the Government.

After having noted in its resolution 1984/51 of 14 March 1984 that there had been no major change in the situation of human rights since 3 August 1979, the Commission requested the Secretary-General to appoint an expert to study the best way of implementing the plan of action. Professor F. Volio Jiménez (Costa Rica), who was again appointed, paid a visit to Equatorial Guinea from 13 to 20 November 1984. In his report on this mission, the expert recognizes that the Government has made efforts in the legislative field, but he continues to insist on other measures including modifications in the constitution. The Commission took note in its resolution 1985/30 of 11 March 1985 of the improvement in the observance of human rights in Equatorial Guinea and requested the Secretary-General to appoint an expert to cooperate with the Government in the full implementation of the plan of action proposed by the United Nations and accepted by the Government.

3. Bolivia . . .

4. El Salvador . . .

5. Guatemala . . .

6. Poland . . .

7. Iran

With respect to Iran, the Sub-Commission played a stimulating role. The Sub-Commission adopted successively on 9 September 1981 its resolution 8 (XXXIV) concerning the situation of Baha'is in Iran; on 8 September 1982 a more general resolution 1982/25 with special attention for summary executions and religious intolerance; on 5 September 1983 resolution 1983/14 and on 29 August 1984 resolution 1984/14.

In the meanwhile, the Commission had in its resolution 1982/27 — adopted on 11 March 1982 — requested the Secretary-General to establish direct contacts with Iran. This request was renewed in resolution 1983/34 adopted on 8 March 1983. From the annual announcement of the Chairman of the Commission, it appears that in 1984, the Commission — within the framework of the confidential procedure — had to take a decision concerning Iran for the first time. On 14 March 1984 the Commission requested in its resolution 1984/54 the appointment of a special representative. On 19 October 1984 Mr. A. Aguilar (Venezuela) was appointed, who in February 1985 presented a preliminary report without having obtained cooperation from the Iranian Government. His mandate was extended for one year by resolution 1985/39 of 13 March 1985, which moreover requested him to present an interim report to the General Assembly. [Since then a new special rapporteur, Mr. Galindo Pohl (Guatemala) has been appointed and his mandate has been renewed from year to year. In 1989 he was permitted to visit Iran for the first time.]

8. Afghanistan

Hardly six weeks after the take-over in Afghanistan by Babrak Karmal on 27 December 1979 the Commission already condemned on 14 February 1980, the Soviet military aggression against the Afghan people in its resolution 3 (XXXVI). Since then, the Commission has adopted every year resolutions concerning the situation in Afghanistan. From the annual announcement of the Chairman of the Commission, it appears that the Sub-Commission forwarded the situation on human rights in Afghanistan in 1980 to the Commission within the framework of the confidential procedure, and since then, it has been dealt with every year by the Commission.

As in 1981 [resolution 11 (XXXIV)] and in 1982 (resolution 1982/21) the Sub-Commission adopted on 5 September 1983 a resolution (1983/20) concerning Afghanistan, but requesting that the Commission appoint a special rapporteur to study the situation of human rights in Afghanistan. In 1984, the Commission adopted two resolutions concerning Afghanistan. Within the framework of the agenda item on self-determination, the Commission adopted resolution 1984/10 of 29 February 1984. Within the framework of the agenda item "violation of human rights", the Commission requested the Chairman of the Commission in its resolution 1984/55 adopted on 15 March 1984 to appoint a special rapporteur on Afghanistan. On the other hand, the Chairman of the Commission announced the following day that the Commission had decided to put an end to its review of the situation in Afghanistan within the framework of the confidential procedure.

Professor F. Ermacora (Austria) was appointed special rapporteur on Afghanistan on 13 August 1984 by the Chairman of the Commission. He did not receive cooperation from the Afghan authorities, reported to the Commission after a visit to Pakistan from 14 to 22 December 1984. His mandate [has been] extended for [each year since then and he has visited Afghanistan several times.] . . .

9. Haiti

A request for the Secretary-General's "advisory services" for Haiti resulted from consideration of this country within the framework of the confidential procedure. From the annual announcement of the Chairman of the Commission, it appears that the situation of human rights in Haiti has been under review by the Commission since 1981. The Commission made public a decision (1984/109) adopted on 1 March 1984 requesting the Secretary-General to continue his consultations with the Government of Haiti, with a view to further exploring ways and means of providing assistance to facilitate the realization of full enjoyment of human rights for the people of Haiti.

It appears from the report of the Secretary-General that Mr. J. Foli (Ghana), the expert appointed by the Secretary-General, had already fulfilled several missions to Haiti within the framework of the confidential procedure. In October 1984 he paid a new visit to Haiti for consultations with the National Commission on human rights regarding the establishment of a center of documentation, the granting of scholarships, and the organisation of a national seminar on human rights. [Two other experts have since been appointed to provide advisory services and to monitor the human rights situation.] . . .

III. ANALYTICAL ASSESSMENT . . .

2. Interaction with the confidential procedure

There are also interactions between the confidential and the public procedure. Confidential procedure being confidential, it is not always possible to demonstrate these interactions. In exceptional cases it is nevertheless possible to give indications, particularly since the Chairman of the Commission started in 1978, to announce which countries are dealt with by the Commission within the framework of this procedure.

The interaction between the confidential and the public procedure is obvious in the case of Equatorial Guinea, since the [ECOSOC] has, on the recommendation of the Commission, decided on 10 May 1979 (decision 1979/35) to make the relevant material public. The forwarding in 1975 of communications by the Sub-Commission to the Commission was not successful in 1976, but it was in 1977. When the government concerned refused to establish direct contacts with the Secretary-General on the matter, the Commission requested its Chairman in March 1979 to appoint a special rapporteur, as announced within the framework of the confidential procedure in 1978.

The situation of human rights in Bolivia, El Salvador and Guatemala had already been submitted to the Commission by the Sub-Commission within the framework of the confidential procedure when the Commission decided in 1981 to start with a public procedure. The Sub-Commission had decided thus in 1977 for Bolivia, and in 1980 for El Salvador and Guatemala.

The Commission's review of the situation in Afghanistan under the confidential procedure from 1981 onward, did not prevent the Commission — nor the Sub-Commission — from adopting public resolutions with respect to the human rights situation in that country. When the Commission decided in its resolution 1984/55 of 15 March 1984 to request its Chairman to appoint a special rapporteur, its Chairman announced the following day that the Commission had decided to discontinue its review of the situation in Afghanistan within the framework of the confidential procedure.

The situation of human rights in Haiti, which was also under review by the Commission within the framework of the confidential procedure since 1981, led in March 1984 to a public request by the Commission to the Secretary-General to hold consultations with the Government of Haiti. It appears from the report of the expert appointed by the Secretary-General on his visit to Haiti, that previously he had already accomplished several missions to Haiti within the framework of the confidential procedure. . . .

Coliver, *United Nations Machineries on Women's Rights: How Might They Better Help Women Whose Rights are Being Violated?* in New Directions in Human Rights 25, 30-31 (E. Lutz, H. Hannum, & K. Burke eds. 1989) (footnotes omitted):

The 1235 and 1503 procedures derive their effectiveness from the Commission's ability to "mobilize shame." They are most likely to have an impact when the investigated government is sensitive to international scrutiny and condemnation, when publicity or the threat of publicity is substantial, and when the Commission identifies concrete steps that must be taken if the government is to escape further scrutiny. A few countries appear impervious to U.N. condemnation but most are not. On several occasions governments have announced planned reforms during Commission or Sub-Commission meetings as concessions to escape further criticism. Most governments respond to requests from rapporteurs concerning specific cases; even when they deny allegations, their treatment of victims often improves.

NOTES

1. The Amnesty International report excerpted above notes that violence against women in detention is one of the violations committed by Myanmar. Coliver's article above indicates that the U.N. Commission on the Status of Women in 1984 established a procedure analogous to resolution 1503 for communications that appeared to reveal "a consistent pattern of reliably attested injustice and discriminatory practice against women." ECOSOC res. 1983/27. Coliver concluded, however, "The Commission's handling of communications in 1984, 1986, and 1988 provides scant encouragement for predicting that the procedure will contribute significantly to protection of women's rights, at least not without concerted NGO and government effort."

2. Resolution 1503 calls for a review of its procedure "if any new organ entitled to deal with such communications should be established within the United Nations or by international agreement." On March 23, 1976, the Optional Protocol to the International Covenant on Civil and Political Rights entered into force authorizing the Human Rights Committee to consider communications from individuals who claim to be victims of violations by governments party to the Optional Protocol. In 1977 the Human Rights Committee began considering such communications. In 1979 the Secretary-General prepared an analysis comparing resolution 1503 procedures with the Optional Protocol and concluding that the two procedures were quite different. U.N. Doc. E/CN.4/1317, at 8-12 (1979). Resolution 1503 communications must reveal a consistent pattern of gross and reliably attested violations of human rights. Communications under the Optional Protocol can relate simply to a single individual. Also, 1503 communications may be filed against any government, but the Optional Protocol applies only to the 47 countries that are party to it. *See* U.N. Centre for Human Rights, *How do the procedures differ?*, Communications Procedures, Fact Sheet No. 7, at 12-13 (1989); *see also* chapter 3, *supra*.

Brody & Weissbrodt, Country-Related and Thematic Developments at the 1989 Session of the U.N. Commission on Human Rights:[13]

On March 10, 1989, the United Nations Commission on Human Rights concluded its six week session in Geneva with a number of significant decisions as to country situations in which human rights violations have occurred, including the establishment of a Special Rapporteur on Romania. The Commission also continued monitoring disappearances, torture, executions, religious intolerance, and mercenaries. The Commission refused to seek greater scrutiny of the human rights situation in Cuba, despite strenuous lobbying by the United States delegation.

Country Situations

The Commission on Human Rights took action on a variety of country situations and received significant information about human rights abuses in an even wider group of nations, but experienced increasing difficulty in taking action on some countries which received political support from strengthened regional blocs. The Commission adopted resolutions — principally under the authority of ECOSOC resolution 1235 — on Afghanistan, Albania, Burma, Chile, Cuba, El Salvador, Guatemala, Haiti, Iran, Israeli-Occupied Territories, Southern Lebanon, Romania, and South Africa. The Commission also adopted resolutions on Equatorial Guinea, Kampuchea, Namibia, and Western Sahara. In addition, the Commission continued its scrutiny of Brunei, Haiti, Paraguay, and Somalia, under the confidential procedure authorized by Economic and Social Council resolution 1503. The Commission failed to take action on Iraq either in public session or under the confidential 1503 procedure and also discontinued its consideration under 1503 of Honduras, Syria, and Zaire. Once again the Commission postponed any decision on the situation in a divided Cyprus. A far broader group of countries were the subject of scrutiny by the Commission under the thematic procedures discussed below.

Action on country situations at the Commission has become increasingly difficult with the strengthening of regional blocs which are able to prevent or control measures sought to be taken against one of the region's governments. This problem has long undermined Commission initiatives in Africa (outside of Southern Africa) and has recently become evident in Latin America where the "Group of 8"[14] now effectively determines the limits of resolutions on Chile, El Salvador, and Guatemala. According to several Latin diplomats, this trend towards regionalization was accelerated by the U.S. campaign against Cuba which, in the words of one, "made us realize that this is a political forum, not a human rights forum, and we had to develop a political response." The Asian group in the Commission had long been divided by a great diversity of economic systems, cultures, languages, and forms of government represented in that continent. Nevertheless, the Asian group coalesced at the 1989 session of the Commission to limit substantially a French initiative on Burma. In contrast, the Commission's resolution on Romania was made

---

[13] This topic is examined in more detail in Brody & Weissbrodt, *Major Developments at the 1989 Session of the UN Commission on Human Rights*, 11 Hum. Rts. Q. 586 (1989).

[14] The "Group of 8" comprise Argentina, Brazil, Colombia, Mexico, Panama, Peru, Uruguay, and Venezuela.

possible because Bulgaria, the German Democratic Republic, the Ukrainian S.S.R., and the U.S.S.R. decided not to participate in that vote.

Afghanistan

The Commission received a brief report on the human rights situation in Afghanistan from its Special Rapporteur, who had received cooperation from the Afghan authorities and had been permitted to visit the country. The Commission, without a vote, adopted a resolution welcoming the cooperation of the Afghan authorities and urging all parties concerned to work for a comprehensive political solution based on the right of self-determination. Following its approach at the 1988 General Assembly, the U.S.S.R. joined the consensus on the resolution rather than forcing a vote which would have been overwhelming. The Commission urged all parties to the conflict to release all prisoners of war in accordance with humanitarian law and to do everything possible to facilitate the safe return of refugees and displaced persons. It called again upon the Afghan authorities to investigate the fate of disappeared persons.

Albania

Last year the Commission decided to transfer its consideration of Albania from the confidential 1503 procedure to a public consideration under agenda item 12 (the "Question of the violation of human rights and fundamental freedoms in any part of the world . . ." authorized by ECOSOC res. 1235). In 1988 the Commission also recommended that ECOSOC release all records about Albania which accumulated under the 1503 procedure over a five year period during which that government had refused to respond. By a close vote ECOSOC, however, rejected the recommendation to make public the 1503 materials on Albania. Hence, despite last year's decision, there was no reference to Albania in the agenda of the 1989 session. The Commission did receive a resolution on Albania from its Sub-Commission on Prevention of Discrimination and Protection of Minorities. On a Portuguese initiative, the Commission adopted (by a vote of thirty-three in favor, three against, and thirteen abstentions) a resolution regretting that the exhaustive efforts to solicit the cooperation of Albania under the 1503 procedure had been in vain and also that the government had failed for the second consecutive year to respond to allegations submitted by the Special Rapporteur on Religious Intolerance. The Commission called upon the government to provide information on the concrete manner in which its constitutional and legal measures complied with the provisions of the Universal Declaration of Human Rights and to respond to the allegations transmitted by the Special Rapporteur. The Commission's consideration of the situation in Albania was handicapped by the lack of timely and adequate information about conditions in the country.

Burma

The Commission also was handicapped by insufficient information about the current human rights situation in Burma. The French delegation proposed a draft resolution which sought the appointment of a Special Rapporteur to assess the situation. The French proposal met with strong resistance from the Asian delegates. After long negotiations, the Commission, without a vote, adopted a compromise decision, submitted by the Chair, expressing "concern . . . at the reports and allegations of violations of human rights in Burma in 1988" and encouraged the Burmese authorities to fulfill their promises of holding elections.

Chile

Once again the Commission expressed its concern at the persistence of serious violations of human rights in Chile, as described in the comprehensive report of the Special Rapporteur, which referred to cases of murder, abduction, disappearances, torture, arbitrary arrest, prolonged periods of *incommunicado* detention, political prisoners, death threats, and the intimidation of opponents of the government. Despite the abstention of Japan, the United States, and eight developing countries, the Commission again urged the government to put an end to those human rights abuses and to continue adopting measures to permit the restoration of the rule of law in Chile and the full enjoyment of human rights.

Cuba

The most politically-charged debate at the 1989 session arose over the attempt by the United States to continue the Commission's intensive scrutiny of the human rights situation in Cuba. At its 1988 session the Commission had accepted an invitation from the Government of Cuba for a delegation of six Commission members to visit that country and "prepare a report to be submitted for consideration by the Commission, which would decide on the manner in which the report was to be examined."

The Commission's delegation visited Cuba for ten days in September 1988 and met with government officials, NGOs, and private individuals. The group also visited prisons (and met in private with prisoners), schools, hospitals, and other facilities. The Cuban government publicized the trip and published the telephone numbers at which the group could be contacted, with the result that the group received over 1,600 complaints alleging human rights violations.

When the Commission began its 1989 session, the U.S. made clear, as it had last year, that it wanted the discussion to take place under agenda item 12 (violation of human rights and fundamental freedoms under ECOSOC res. 1235). The Cuban delegation and their Latin American allies were equally insistent that Cuba could not be compared to other countries on the Commission's agenda under item 12, such as Afghanistan, El Salvador, and Iran; they proposed discussing the report under item 11 (further promotion and encouragement of human rights and fundamental freedoms). The compromise solution was to deal with the report under a separate, special item 11 *bis*, sparing Cuba from item 12 treatment, but permitting a full debate by Commission members and observers.

The report itself, finally released at the end of the Commission's third week, provided a revealing picture of conditions in Cuba. The document issued by the group which visited Cuba ran 400 pages and was apparently the largest human rights report ever produced under U.N. auspices. The document, however, contained only fifty-five pages of actual text in which the group summarized the allegations of human rights violations received by the group and the government's responses. The remainder of the document comprised a series of annexes mostly containing allegations of human rights violations. One annex listed by category 1,600 complaints received by the group of which 1,183 concerned the right to leave the country or to return. Another annex reproduced the questions on the Cuban constitutional and legal system prepared by Ambassador Lillis (Ireland) on behalf of the group. Several annexes reproduced articles and allegations by opponents of the Cuban government. The document also included tables showing the gains in the enjoyment of economic, social, and cultural rights that have occurred since the Cuban revolution of 1961.

The report was remarkable in that it was adopted by consensus of all six Commission members from different parts of the world, including the Bulgarian member representing the Eastern European countries. Evidently, the consensus nature of the report made it impossible for the group to reach any conclusions, because the report lacked both factual findings and recommendations. A careful reading of the allegations of human rights violations and the government's responses did indicate recent improvements in that a number of prisoners had been released, prison conditions had improved, and complaints of ill-treatment of prisoners had diminished. The principal remaining problems dealt with the right of Cubans to leave their country or return. Cuba did not respond to many of the individual allegations mentioned in the document and the group was not able to study these cases.

The United States in 1988 had contended that there were 10-15,000 political prisoners in Cuba, extrajudicial executions, and disappearances. The report did not substantiate these allegations, although they were repeated less stridently by the U.S. delegation to the 1989 Commission session. Most disturbing, however, were reports that the Cuban government had retaliated against some individuals who gave evidence to the group or sought to do so. The U.S. delegation left no doubt that its highest, if not sole, priority for the 1989 Commission was achieving a condemnation of Cuba, but the delegation did not repeatedly present public statements throughout the session, as occurred in 1988. U.S. lobbying, while reportedly as intense as in 1988 in the capitals of the voting members of the Commission, was somewhat less visible in the Commission and its corridors. While Cuba remained largely a U.S. concern as in 1987 and 1988, this year several other countries joined the U.S. initiative, including Morocco, Netherlands, and the United Kingdom.

The United States had four concrete objectives regarding Cuba at the 1989 Commission:

(1) To continue the mandate of the group of six who visited Cuba;

(2) To ask the group of six to continue to observe the human rights situation in Cuba pursuant to agenda item 12 (violation of human rights);

(3) To ask the group to investigate the individual allegations that had been presented to the group and the allegations of retaliation against some witnesses or prospective witnesses; and

(4) to encourage the Cuban government to accept a second visit.

These objectives were embodied in a draft which the U.S. delegation circulated informally.

The Latin American group, however, sought a text that did not keep Cuba on the agenda of the Commission, maintain the existence of the group, nor meet any of the other objectives of the United States. Instead, the Latin American draft essentially terminated consideration by the Commission of the issue. The European Community negotiators sought some follow-up related to the report on Cuba.

Finally, at a few minutes before 11:00 p.m. on Thursday, March 9, 1989, the negotiators entered the Commission's room and called for the Commission to come into public session.[15] Neither the Chair of the Commission nor most delegations

---

[15] The negotiators had evidently been informed that the interpreters had only been hired until 11:00 p.m. that night.

were apparently informed as to what would happen next. The head of the United Kingdom delegation first asked the Commission to consider resolution L.90 (the Latin American draft) before the U.S. resolution in L.89 (which had by then been co-sponsored in revised form by Canada, Morocco, the Netherlands, and the United Kingdom). That request was accepted by the Commission without a vote.

The Latin draft resolution in L.90 was then amended orally by its sponsors to state that the U.N. Secretary-General would continue to maintain direct contacts with the Government of Cuba. The U.K. Ambassador sought the floor once again to introduce a proposal for an additional amendment to L.90 which added two concepts: first, that the Secretary-General would maintain contact not only with the government, but also with the "people of Cuba"; and second, the Secretary-General would report to the Commission "as appropriate." The U.K. ambassador explained that these two elements were the only remaining issues of dispute between the negotiators, but that no agreement could be achieved.

The proposed U.K. amendment to L.90, which would have strengthened it slightly and would have kept Cuba on the agenda of the Commission for 1990, was then put to a vote. The vote was far closer than anyone had anticipated: seventeen in favor, seventeen against, and eight abstentions. The proposed U.K. amendment thus failed. In the end, L.90 was adopted by a vote of thirty-two in favor, one (Morocco) against, and ten abstaining.

Then the U.K. head of delegation stated that he wished to seek a vote on the U.S. resolution in L.89. In view of the failure to obtain a majority even on the very modest British amendment to L.90, it was very difficult to understand why the U.K. head of delegation would pursue a vote on the far more ambitious resolution in L.89. It was even harder to understand why the U.S. delegation, which was sitting right next to the U.K. delegation, did not suggest that L.89 be withdrawn. Instead, the vote was taken and the draft resolution in L.89 lost badly on a procedural motion by the Cuban delegation to take no action: sixteen in favor of taking no action; seven against the motion; and nineteen abstaining. The U.S.-U.K. position was not even supported by Belgium, France, Italy, Japan, Portugal, or Sweden, which had generally supported the U.S.-U.K. efforts up to that point. Several of those delegates and even such countries as Bangladesh and Gambia (which had voted with the United States on every issue) complained after the session that they had been told that L.89 would never be brought to a vote; that they had not been advised adequately of the tactics to be followed; and that they could not understand why L.89 had been brought to a vote. Neither the U.S. nor the U.K. delegates could explain why they pursued a series of votes which demonstrated deepening disarray and ultimately made the U.S. position look like an abject failure, when in fact, the Commission was quite evenly divided on the critical vote.

[At its 1990 session the Commission adopted a resolution, by a vote of nineteen in favor, twelve against, and twelve abstaining, requesting the Secretary-General to maintain contacts with Cuba, to report on those contacts at the 1991 session, to safeguard witnesses against reprisals, and to discuss Cuba under agenda item 12 in 1991.]

El Salvador

The Special Representative on El Salvador, Pastor Ridruejo of Spain, reported that the situation of human rights in that country had seriously deteriorated. In particular, he noted, "An alarming number of politically motivated summary executions, including mass executions, have been carried out by members of the

State apparatus, particularly members of the armed forces . . ." and that this number had increased over that of recent years. Nevertheless, the resolution on El Salvador, written by Colombia, Mexico, and Peru but negotiated with the government of El Salvador, was considerably weaker than in previous years, failing to mention, for instance, the "death squads" who, according to the Special Representative, had "increased their criminal activities" in the past year.

Guatemala

Hector Gros Espiell of Uruguay, the Expert appointed in 1987 under the Advisory Services program, pointed in his report to serious human rights violations in Guatemala. Once again, however, he seemed to treat the government as a victim of circumstance: "these [violations] are the outcome not of government orders or policy but of factors, of acts committed by power circles and a persistent climate of violence that are still beyond effective government control . . . ." He thus failed to identify the major cause of the continuing violations, that is, the government's "dirty war" counter-insurgency policy which is in the hands of the military and not the civilian authorities. Guatemalan opposition groups pointed out that the Expert's evaluation of the situation was more positive than those of the Inter-American Commission on Human Rights, independent human rights monitors, and the Commission's own reports on disappearances and executions.

Several Commission participants, including the Swedish delegation, still believe that the decision in 1987 to remove Guatemala from agenda item 12 (violations) and place it under agenda item 22 (advisory services) was "premature." The weak Commission resolution in 1989 "recognized," however, the government's commitment to human rights while expressing the Commission's concern "at the harmful conditions that still exist."

Haiti

The excellent report by the Expert appointed under the Advisory Services program, Philippe Texier of France, concluded that under the government of General Prosper Avril, "the political will to take specific measures aimed at ensuring everyday observance of [human] rights has not so far been convincingly demonstrated . . . ." Consequently, he wondered "whether minimum standards of respect for international norms should not be required in order for a country to benefit from United Nations advisory services," and asked the Commission to consider the possibility of appointing a Special Rapporteur (under ECOSOC res. 1235). If Advisory Services were to be continued, he recommended that the program's focus should be on organizing elections and promoting an independent judiciary, and that local human rights groups be associated with the program. The French delegation promoted and the Commission adopted a resolution to continue the mandate of the Expert, adopting his suggestions and also requesting him "to provide information . . . on the development of the human rights situation in Haiti."

Iran

Since July 1988, Special Rapporteur Galindo Pohl of El Salvador, recorded reliable reports of arbitrary arrests, ill-treatment of political prisoners, torture, and unfair trials. A western-sponsored resolution, which was adopted twenty in favor, six against, with twelve abstentions, urged Iran to grant access to the Special

Rapporteur and expressed deep concern over the wave of executions as well as the numerous and detailed allegations of other human rights violations.

As has been the practice for the last couple of years, no delegation introduced a resolution against Iran because of concern that that government or its citizens might be singled out for retaliation. Nevertheless, several Western European and Other governments jointly tabled the resolution. The vote against Iran was much stronger than at the Commission in 1988 or in the General Assembly in 1988, apparently because of the death threats against Salman Rushdie. While at the General Assembly, there had been efforts to negotiate with the Iranian government for a moderate resolution in exchange for assurances by Iran of cooperation with the Special Rapporteur. The Rushdie affair ended, at least for the 1989 session, any efforts at negotiation with the Iranian delegation. [In early 1990 the Special Rapporteur was permitted to visit Iran for the first time.]

Iraq

The Commission's most dismal failure was its refusal to take action on Iraq which, according to Amnesty International, "clearly and incontrovertibly presents a situation of the most flagrant and massive violations of human rights." With the Special Rapporteur on Executions recording thousands of alleged deaths by chemical weapons and mass executions and the Working Group on Disappearances listing over 2,600 unresolved cases and reports of routine torture even against the children of political opponents, both the International Commission of Jurists and Amnesty International said in their oral interventions that the "credibility of the Commission" depended on its taking action against Iraq. After consideration of Iraq was discontinued under the confidential 1503 procedure, the twelve European Community countries (minus France), Australia, Canada, and Sweden tabled a resolution to appoint a Special Rapporteur. Only Japan, Peru, and Togo joined the western countries in opposing a motion by Iraq (17-13-9) to take no action on the draft. The successful plurality included the six Moslem and Arab countries as well as Botswana, Brazil (a principal source of arms to Iraq), China (which also sells missiles to Iraq), Cuba, Cyprus, Ethiopia, India, the Philippines, Sao Tome, Sri Lanka, and Yugoslavia.

Israeli-Occupied Territories

The Commission reaffirmed the inalienable right of the Palestinian people to self-determination and the establishment of an independent sovereign state on their national soil, welcomed the declaration of the State of Palestine, and considered the decisions of the Palestine National Council of November 15, 1988, a prerequisite for the establishment of a just and lasting peace in the Middle East.

Southern Lebanon

The Commission, by thirty in favor, one (U.S.) against, and twelve (mostly Western European countries) abstaining, strongly condemned Israel for its continued violations of human rights in southern Lebanon and called upon Israel to put an immediate end to such practices, to liberate Lebanese prisoners, to return all those expelled to their homes, to stop expelling Palestinians arbitrarily to southern Lebanon, and to implement the resolutions of the Security Council which require the immediate, and unconditional withdrawal of Israel from all Lebanese territory.

Romania

For the first time in five years, the Commission on Human Rights in 1989 recommended to the Economic and Social Council that a new Special Rapporteur be appointed on a country situation. The human rights situation has been deteriorating in Romania. At the 1989 session, the proposed rural "systematization," the treatment of the Hungarian and German minorities, and the declining enjoyment of economic, social, and cultural rights were the subject of numerous governmental and NGO interventions. A Swedish resolution to appoint a Special Rapporteur to study the human rights situation in Romania received an enormous boost when the Deputy Foreign Minister of Hungary came to the Commission to announce his country's co-sponsorship for the measure. This gesture prevented the issue from becoming an East-West matter and made passage of the resolution likely. Two days before the vote, and reportedly at the insistence of the Soviet Union, Romania informally offered to invite the Commission's Bureau to visit Romania. When the co-sponsors of the resolution insisted that the offer be made in writing and contain at least the guarantees provided to the mission which visited Cuba, however, the Romanians withdrew their offer. With the countries of Eastern Europe not participating in the vote, the Swedish resolution passed easily, twenty-one in favor, seven against, and ten abstentions. The Romanian delegate responded that his country considered the vote "null and void" and made it understood that the Special Rapporteur was not likely to be permitted into his country.

The Commission also adopted a resolution by a vote of twenty-six in favor, five against, and twelve abstentions, calling for an advisory opinion by the International Court of Justice about applicability of the U.N. Convention on Privileges and Immunities to the detention by the Romanian government of a Romanian citizen, Dumitru Mazilu, who had been prevented from completing his work as an expert on youth matters for the U.N. Sub-Commission on Prevention of Discrimination and Protection of Minorities.

South Africa (and Namibia)

The Commission heard the report of the "Group of Three" created within the framework of the International Convention on the Suppression and Punishment of the Crime of *Apartheid* and the report of the *ad hoc* Working Group of Experts on South Africa. This latter report is essentially based on first hand information which the experts collected, in cooperation with the Special Rapporteur on Summary and Arbitrary Executions, in Europe and in front-line states. For twenty years, access to South Africa has been continually refused to the *ad hoc* Working Group. The Commission again adopted resolutions demanding that South Africa abolish the system of *Apartheid* in all its forms, reaffirming the inalienable right of the people of South Africa and Namibia to self-determination and independence, and condemning the continuing collaboration of certain Western states which obstruct efforts to eliminate *Apartheid*. The Commission called once again upon all governments to take measures at a national level with a view to putting a stop to their commercial activities in the territory of South Africa as well as of Namibia.

The ECOSOC Resolution 1503 Procedure

Under the confidential procedure established pursuant to ECOSOC resolution 1503, the Commission continued consideration of the cases of Brunei, Haiti, Paraguay, and Somalia while discontinuing consideration of Honduras, Iraq, Syria, and Zaire. The viability of this procedure is increasingly being questioned. First, it is unclear what positive effect "confidential" actions have. Second, delegations appear even less likely to criticize their counterparts in confidential voting than when those votes are publicly recorded. Hence, while the confidential voting on Iraq was reported to be twenty-four in favor, twelve against, and seven abstentions in that government's favor, the no-action motion on the public resolution was passed by only seventeen in favor, thirteen against, and nine abstentions.

Theme Procedures

Since 1980 the Commission on Human Rights has been slowly developing an approach to human rights violations which focuses on the kind of abuse and not solely on countries where serious problems arise. Accordingly, the Commission established the Working Group on Enforced or Involuntary Disappearances in 1980, the Special Rapporteur on Summary or Arbitrary Executions in 1982, the Special Rapporteur on Torture in 1985, and the Special Rapporteur on Religious Intolerance in 1986. Each of these mechanisms has the authority to receive information on human rights problems within its area of concern and to take "effective action" in trying to urge governments to resolve the problems. In 1987 the Commission also established a Special Rapporteur on Mercenaries, who is authorized to visit countries where mercenaries have committed abuses, but who has not yet been given authority to take "effective action." Nevertheless, in 1988 the Commission characterized the Special Rapporteur on Mercenaries as a theme procedure and extended its mandate for two years at the same time as it extended the mandate of other theme mechanisms. Together, the theme procedures do the most important concrete work of the Commission in protecting human rights in specific cases by saving lives, stopping torture, resolving disappearances, etc. Nevertheless, the theme procedures are still evolving and being improved....

Working Group on Enforced or Involuntary Disappearances

In its best report yet, the Working Group on Enforced or Involuntary Disappearances reported transmitting 392 cases alleged to have taken place in 1988 in fifteen countries. The largest number of outstanding cases are found in Argentina (3,387, all from before 1983), Guatemala (2,851), Iraq (2,728) and El Salvador (2,141). The group expressed its "concern over the total lack of cooperation from ... Governments which have never provided substantive replies to the allegations transmitted to them, such as Afghanistan, Angola, Chile, Guinea, the Islamic Republic of Iran, Nepal and Seychelles."

Special Rapporteur on Torture

In his fourth annual report, the Special Rapporteur on Torture, Professor Peter Kooijmans of the Netherlands concluded that "torture is still rampant in various parts of the world," most often accompanying civil strife and civil war. During the year, he accepted invitations for consultative visits to South Korea, Peru, and Turkey and in each case made evaluations and recommendations which are included in his report. During the year he transmitted allegations to thirty-seven countries for clarification and sent forty-two urgent appeals for immediate government attention. Some twenty states did not reply in any form. All in all, the fourth report was a considerable improvement over the third report in providing more detail about the information received by the Special Rapporteur and what he did in response.

Special Rapporteur on Summary or Arbitrary Executions

In his seventh report to the Commission, the Special Rapporteur on Summary or Arbitrary Executions, Amos Wako of Kenya, reported addressing urgent cables to twenty-three governments (of whom only eight responded) and letters concerning alleged executions to thirty-six governments (of whom only fifteen responded). Mr. Wako's report provided detailed summaries of the situations giving rise to his concerns with particularly gruesome details on Iran and Iraq.

Special Rapporteur on Religious Intolerance

The Commission received the report of its Special Rapporteur on Religious Intolerance, Angelo Vidal D'Almeida Ribeiro of Portugal, whose report followed the same approach as the other theme rapporteurs.

Special Rapporteur on Mercenaries

In the second year of his mandate, the Special Rapporteur on Mercenaries, Enrique Bernales Ballesteros of Peru, responded to invitations from Angola and Nicaragua to examine reports of mercenary aggression against those countries. . . .

NOTES

For further reading on ECOSOC resolutions 728F, 1235, and 1503, see Bossuyt, *The Development of Special Procedures of the United Nations Commission on Human Rights*, 6 Hum. Rts. L.J. 179 (1985);

Möller, *Petitioning the United Nations*, Universal Hum. Rts. 57 (No.4, 1979);

Newman, *The New United Nations Procedure for Hum. Rts. Complaints: Reform, Status Quo, or Chamber of Horrors?*, 34 Annales des Droit 129 (1974);

B. Ramcharan, The Concept and Present Status of the International Protection of Human Rights 104-09 (public debate principally under 1235), 113-14 (written NGO statements), 136-41 (1503), 151-57 ("thorough study") (1989);

M. Tardu, *The "Gross Violations" Procedure under Council Resolution 1503 (XLVIII)* in 1 Human Rights: International Petition System 25 (1985);

Tardu, *United Nations Response to Gross Violations of Human Rights: The 1503 Procedure*, 20 Santa Clara L. Rev. 567 (1980);

H. Tolley, The U.N. Commission on Human Rights 111-33 (1987);

Tolley, *The Concealed Crack in the Citadel: The United Nations Commission on Human Rights' Response to Confidential Communications*, 6 Hum. Rts. Q. 420 (1984);

United Nations Action in the Field of Human Rights, U.N. Doc. ST/HR/2/Rev.3, at 314-26 (1988);

U.N. Centre for Human Rights, Communications Procedures, Fact Sheet No. 7 (1989);

van Boven, *Creative and Dynamic Strategies for Using United Nations Institutions and Procedures: The Frank Newman File* in New Directions in Human Rights 215 (E. Lutz, H. Hannum, & K. Burke eds. 1989);

T. Zuidwijk, Petitioning the United Nations (1982).

---

4. Role of Nongovernmental Organizations

Amnesty International, Summary of Selected International Procedures and Bodies Dealing with Human Rights Measures, AI Index: IOR 30/01/89, at 11-12 (1989):

Direct intervention at the UN Commission and Sub-Commission (through oral and written statements) is possible only for representatives of NGOs that have been granted consultative status with ECOSOC. Around 600 NGOs presently have consultative status with ECOSOC, under the following three categories:

Category I: organizations concerned with most of the activities of ECOSOC

Category II: organizations concerned with only a few of the fields of activity covered by ECOSOC

Roster: more specialized organizations which can make occasional and useful contributions to the work of ECOSOC

Only a small portion of these 600 NGOs attend the sessions of the UN human rights bodies.

The conditions and procedures for granting consultative status are set out in ECOSOC Resolution 1296 (XLIV) (1968). Among the requirements of this resolution are that the organization be international in structure, and be of representative character and recognized international standing, although a broad interpretation of these requirements is often accepted. . . .

ECOSOC res. 1296 (XLIV), 44 U.N. ESCOR (Supp. No. 1) at 22, U.N. Doc. E/4548 (1968):

The Economic and Social Council, . . .

ARRANGEMENTS FOR CONSULTATION
WITH NON-GOVERNMENTAL
ORGANIZATIONS . . .

Attendance at meetings

22. Organizations in categories I and II may designate authorized representatives to sit as observers at public meetings of the Council and its subsidiary bodies [including the Commission on Human Rights and its Sub-Commission]. Those on the Roster may have representatives present at such meetings concerned with matters within their field of competence.

Written statements

23. Written statements relevant to the work of the Council [and its subsidiary bodies — the Human Rights Commission and its Sub-Commission —] may be submitted by organizations in categories I and II on subjects in which these organizations have a special competence. Such statements shall be circulated by the Secretary-General of the United Nations to the members of the Council, except those statements which have become obsolete, for example, those dealing with matters already disposed of and those which had already been circulated in some other form.

24. The following conditions shall be observed regarding the submission and circulation of such statements:

(a) The written statement shall be submitted in one of the official languages [Arabic, Chinese, English, French, Russian, or Spanish].

(b) It shall be submitted in sufficient time for appropriate consultation to take place between the Secretary-General and the organization before circulation.

(c) The organization shall give due consideration to any comments which the Secretary-General may make in the course of such consultation before transmitting the statement in final form.

(d) A written statement submitted by an organization in category I will be circulated in full if it does not exceed 2,000 words. Where a statement is in excess of 2,000 words, the organizations shall submit a summary which will be circulated or shall supply sufficient copies of the full text in the working languages for distribution. A statement will also be circulated in full, however, upon a specific request of the Council or its Committee on Non-Governmental Organizations.

(e) A written statement submitted by an organization in category II or on the Roster will be circulated in full if it does not exceed 500 words. Where a statement is in excess of 500 words, the organization shall submit a summary which will be circulated; such statements will be circulated in full, however, upon a specific request of the Council or its Committee on Non-Governmental Organizations. . . .

(g) A written statement or summary, as the case may be, will be circulated by the Secretary-General in the working languages, and, upon the request of a member of the Council, in any of the official languages. . . .

FREEDOM OF INFORMATION ACT AND CONFIDENTIALITY UNDER THE 1503 PROCEDURE

The Freedom of Information Act (FOIA) requires the U.S. government to make public documents with certain specified exceptions. Complainants under ECOSOC resolution 1503 have used the statute to obtain copies of the U.S. response to their complaints. In June 1981 the President of the Black Law Student Association at the University of Minnesota filed a communication under ECOSOC resolution 1503 against the U.S. The communication alleged multiple violations of the rights of black people in the U.S. The Working Group on Communications considered the communication but did not recommend it to the Sub-Commission. In October 1981 another student at the University of Minnesota requested, under the FOIA, a copy of the U.S. response to the 1503 communication. The U.S. sent the material requested without protest.

Similarly, the Indian Law Resource Center submitted a 1503 communication in 1980 relating to human rights violations against the Six Nations Iroquois Confederacy. The communication was held for a year by the Sub-Commission and was then referred to the U.N. Working Group on Indigenous Populations. The Working Group on Indigenous Populations never considered the communication. The Indian Law Resource Center filed an FOIA request for the U.S. response to the 1503 communication. At first the State Department refused because the U.N. process was not clearly completed. After it became obvious that the Six Nations communication was no longer under consideration, the State Department released the U.S. response to the communication.

Freedom of Information Act, 5 U.S.C. § 552(a)(3):

... (3) ... [E]ach agency upon any request for records which (A) reasonably describes such records and (B) is made in accordance with published rules stating the time, place, fees (if any), and procedures to be followed, shall make the records promptly available to any person....

(b) This section does not apply to matters that are—

(1)(A) specifically authorized under criteria established by an Executive order to be kept secret in the interest of national defense or foreign policy and (B) are in fact properly classified pursuant to such Executive order....

V WHAT HUMAN RIGHTS "THEME PROCEDURES" ARE AVAILABLE AT THE U.N.?

The Working Group on Enforced or Involuntary Disappearances

A. INTRODUCTION

Two preceding chapters have focused on complaints about individual violations and about country situations. This chapter introduces a new format for pursuing human rights violations — one that concentrates on types of violations occurring in any country rather than on specific countries allegedly committing human rights violations. Commentators label the procedures "thematic" to distinguish them from country-specific procedures.

The U.N. Human Rights Commission has created four thematic procedures — the Working Group on Enforced or Involuntary Disappearances
("Group") established in 1980, the Special Rapporteur on summary or
arbitrary executions established in 1982, the Special Rapporteur on torture
established in 1985, and the Special Rapporteur on religious intolerance
established in 1986. This chapter introduces those procedures and asks
readers to recommend ways to improve their effectiveness. It also illustrates
how U.N. procedures originate, how they evolve, and how their effectiveness
can improve as they are implemented.

B. QUESTIONS

In light of the materials in this chapter, recommend changes the Working
Group on Enforced or Involuntary Disappearances could make in its methods
of work that would allow it, within its mandate, to give optimum help to
disappeared individuals. In order to formulate these recommendations,
consider the issues raised by the questions below. Consider further whether
the theme rapporteurs, with their differing mandates, should adopt the
Group's current methods of work or your proposed changes.

1. What observations can be drawn about the process by which the U.N.
creates a new human rights mechanism, based on your reading of the
Kramer & Weissbrodt article?

2. What was the initial purpose of the Working Group? Did the Commission
decide to change that purpose? Has the Group, in fact, changed its purpose?

3. What is the Group trying to achieve when it acts on specific cases?
Have theme rapporteurs followed the Group's nonjudgmental approach? Do
the mandates of the theme procedures require that approach?

4. Do you think the Commission wisely assigned the task of defining a
disappearance to the Group? Exactly how has the Group defined a disappearance? Do you think the rapporteurs should follow the Group's approach
in defining matters within their mandates?

5. From what sources should the Group and the theme rapporteurs accept
information?

6. What information should be required before action is taken?

7. How fast should the Group and theme rapporteurs respond to reports
of violations?

8. Should the Group and rapporteurs require that complainants exhaust
domestic remedies or at least submit complaints to the government before
invoking a theme procedure?

9. What should the Group and rapporteurs do when a government does
not respond or responds inadequately to transmitted information?

10. Should theme procedures allow complainants to respond to government replies? What are advantages and disadvantages of that process?

11. Should the Group and rapporteurs remind governments of unclarified cases? How often should reminders be issued?

12. How long should an individual's case be pursued through the theme procedures? Should the Group and rapporteurs prescribe a "statute of limitations" for complaints?

13. What information should the Group and the rapporteurs include in their reports?

14. What measures besides diplomatic correspondence can the Group and rapporteurs take in fulfilling their mandates?

15. How can the Commission and General Assembly reinforce the efforts of the Group and the rapporteurs?

16. Since the theme procedures deal with disappearances, arbitrary or summary executions, torture, and religious intolerance, is there a continued need for ECOSOC resolution 1503 concerning gross violations of human rights?

17. What other human rights issues should be the subject of these procedures?

C. THEME PROCEDURES

Kramer & Weissbrodt, *The 1980 U.N. Commission on Human Rights and the Disappeared*, 3 Hum. Rts. Q. 18, 18-31 (1981) (footnotes omitted):

On a United Nations time scale, the phenomenon of disappearances was a relatively new issue. The General Assembly had first considered it on 20 December 1978 by expressing its concern and recognizing the urgency of the problem. The next year, in March 1979, the issue of disappearances was included on the agenda of the Human Rights Commission, but was given such low priority that time expired before it could be debated. It was simply postponed until the 1980 session. In the year's interim, international nongovernmental organizations (NGOs) performed an immense job of publicizing the issue and creating international pressure for meaningful action by the Human Rights Commission. . . .

By the time of the 1980 session of the Human Rights Commission, disappearances had emerged from the netherworld of nonrecognition, but had not yet become crusted over with political or ideological affiliations that would make passage of a resolution impossible. The issue of disappearances was ripe for action by the Commission.

The overwhelming concern of the family members of the disappeared as well as the NGOs was not whether the Commission would act, but what the nature of that action would be. The experience of the most active NGOs — Amnesty International, the International Commission of Jurists, and the International League for Human Rights — strongly indicated that the first several days after the initial arrest of a person were the most crucial. In cases in which NGOs had been successful in directing international attention immediately toward the government concerned, they had had significant success in protecting the disappeared person from torture or other mistreatment, and even in causing persons to "reappear." The debate was expected to center around the question of whether the Commission should set up a mechanism that could deal with individual cases of disappearances on an emergency basis.

PREPARATIONS FOR THE PUBLIC DEBATE

Long before the public debate on disappearances began, the Commission delegates present had been conducting intense, private negotiations. The issue seemed too new, uncertain, and potentially explosive to be handled entirely within the cumbersome procedures of formal debate....

This strong interest in the issue of disappearances among all the Western delegates caused difficulties as the delegates squabbled among themselves to determine who would take a leadership role in formulating and sponsoring a resolution on disappearances. France, having come to the Commission with a prepared draft resolution, took the initiative. The French proposed that a group of three experts acting in their individual capacities would examine all reports of disappearances in any part of the world. The experts would be empowered to seek information from the governments and families concerned, and to take appropriate action, in consultation with the governments concerned....

Western Bloc Reservations

The Western bloc reached agreement on all the provisions contained in the draft except for paragraph 6(a), which defined disappeared persons. To several of the Western countries — the United States, Canada, Australia, and the Netherlands — broadly defining disappeared persons as those who cannot be located immediately or following a brief investigation once an abduction was reported to the government was an open invitation to other countries to find the resolution imprecise and unworkable. The definition seemed to cover all *missing* persons, instead of all *disappeared* persons. It did not exclude a voluntary disappearance by someone who, for personal reasons, might wish to hide from the authorities or perhaps from their family. Nor did it exclude those cases in which it was thought that a person had voluntarily left the country. Yet the French insisted on their language....

The Western bloc had decided that it was necessary for them to take the initiative in proposing a resolution on disappearances. They were unable, however, to draft a suitable resolution. They argued among themselves late into the night, and because no agreement was reached, there was no text with which to approach nonaligned nations in an effort to get their support. This disagreement continued late into the third week....

The indecision of the Western bloc created a vacuum which Argentina tried to fill with a resolution of its own. That country — continually accused by the NGOs of being the worst perpetrator of disappearances — was the country most vehemently against the creation of any new U.N. mechanism for dealing with disappearances. Argentina's resolution urged governments to inform the Secretary-General of the measures they were adopting to cope with the problem of disappearances. It called upon governments to express their opinion as to what procedures might be appropriate to deal with disappeared persons without encroaching upon the sovereignty of any nation. A working group of five persons would then meet a week before the 1981 session of the Human Rights Commission to evaluate the submissions of the government and to make appropriate recommendations to the Commission. The Argentine proposal, essentially postponing any action for at least a year, was circulated just before the beginning of public debate.

THE PUBLIC DEBATE

On 22 February 1980 at the end of the third week of the Commission session, the public debate on disappearances began. The Western nations had still not agreed among themselves on the text of a resolution. The nonaligned nations were still reacting to the Argentine proposal. The socialist bloc was waiting to see what the nonaligned countries would do. As a consequence, no nation was prepared to speak.

The floor then unexpectedly went to the NGOs. The representative of Amnesty International (AI) spoke first. He defined the nature of the problem and described AI's efforts in collecting and submitting to the United Nations thousands of names of disappeared persons in Argentina, Afghanistan, Democratic Kampuchea, Ethiopia, Nicaragua, and Uganda. He then proceeded to discuss the case of two Argentines, who had been disappeared, tortured, and imprisoned in a secret camp, but who had escaped to tell of their experiences. Argentina harshly interrupted the speech and demanded to know from the Chairman what right an NGO had to attack a government in front of the Commission. The representative from Uruguay supported Argentina and denounced AI for attacking a government during the Commission session. Ethiopia also spoke against AI, accusing it of making false representations against Argentina, based solely on Western media reports. Canada and the United States came to the defense of AI in particular and NGOs in general, arguing that NGOs could not separate a discussion of particular instances of disappearances in various countries from a discussion of disappearances in general. The United States pointed out that NGOs had been allowed to mention specific countries during the discussion of previous items on the agenda and that the contribution of NGOs to the understanding of the phenomenon of disappearances had been particularly valuable. The Chair, Waleed M. Sadi of Jordan, ruled that although NGOs may not attack particular countries, they may provide the Commission with information about particular countries. This ruling allowed AI and the other NGOs to continue presenting their "information" to the Commission. . . .

This initial public debate of 22 February 1980 revealed several things about how the issue of disappearance was to fare before the Human Rights Commission. First, the debate exemplified just how critical the issue was for countries — such as Argentina — accused of disappearing persons. Second, the public debate disclosed a strategy that might defeat any action to establish a U.N. mechanism for handling disappearances. It was clear that the NGOs, which seemed to be primarily Western in orientation, advocated an effective resolution. It was also clear that they had the full support of the Western nations. If the initiative surrounding the issue of disappearances was viewed as Western, there was a significant danger that, for that reason alone, Third World countries might not support it. Clearly, no resolution could pass the Commission without the support of a good number of Third World nations.

The Role of Nonaligned Nations . . .

Monday, February 25, the beginning of the fourth week of the Commission session, was the deadline for the introduction of all proposed resolutions concerning the issue of disappearances. Therefore, France briefly took the floor and introduced its draft resolution, although that resolution lacked the support of even the Western nations. No other resolutions were introduced.

Responding to the needs of the Third World, the Western nations finally ended their isolation. Later that day, Australia, Canada, and the Netherlands met with Iraq, Cuba, and Yugoslavia to ask for help. They had come to believe that it was necessary to encourage the drafting of a text by nonaligned nations, even if it might seem weak in comparison to the text drafted by Western nations. A text that would be sponsored by the nonaligned nations would have the immense advantage of assuring an overwhelming majority, or possibly even creating a consensus. The USSR and the other socialist bloc countries would not vote against a resolution that had the support of the Third World. Argentina would risk further isolating itself by voting against such a proposal. Consensus would be important in assuring that the decision of the Commission would win the approval and funding of the Economic and Social Council. A relatively weak proposal passed by consensus might have a better chance of being implemented successfully than a relatively strong text passed by a bare majority. Overall, it seemed easier and more effective for the West to try to upgrade a nonaligned proposal than to attempt to find enough votes for a Western proposal....

The Iraqi Proposal

Iraq, with the help of Cuba, drew up a proposal which became the focus of the discussion among countries throughout the fourth week. After making some changes that Iraq accepted, the United States, and finally the other Western countries, accepted the draft. It provided for a working group of five of the Commission members in their own capacities (instead of three independent experts) to be appointed for just one year (instead of an indefinite time period). The working group was to examine the question of enforced or involuntary disappearances of persons. The United States succeeded in persuading Iraq to agree to extend the working group's mandate to examine the question of "cases of" enforced or involuntary disappearances. This would ensure that the working group could respond to individual cases and not just the problem of disappearances in general. The United States also added a provision allowing "humanitarian organizations and others" to provide information to the working group which would not only allow NGOs to provide information but other organizations and individuals as well. No attempt was made to define what a disappeared person was; presumably, that would be left to the working group to decide.

On Wednesday, February 27, Iraq took the resolution, as amended, back to the other nonaligned countries. Several countries were in favor of it. Other countries reacted neutrally or even unfavorably, but were interested in avoiding a situation in which the nonaligned bloc would be split down the middle.... The result was that the amendment suggested by the United States — that the working group was to consider cases or individual persons — was deleted. The language now read that the working group was to respond effectively to urgent situations, not cases.

Intense Negotiations...

The United States, seeing that "cases" was not acceptable, decided to lobby for a different set of words. It now proposed that instead of providing that the working group "examine the question of enforced or involuntary disappearances of persons" which could be interpreted as a mandate to study the question in abstract terms only, the language should provide that the working group "examine *questions relating to* enforced or involuntary disappearances of persons [emphasis added]." The change was slight — only three words — and therefore acceptable to nearly all delegations, yet it seemed to tip the balance in favor of letting the working group respond to individual cases. At least, if the working group chose to do so, no one could dispute that it was not functioning within its mandate. . . .

Return to Public Debate

On 29 February 1980 after one week of tense negotiations, the public debate resumed. The galleries were again packed with the relatives of the disappeared who had come to make sure that the plight of their family members was not ignored.

The countries that had agreed on the proposal on disappearances had also agreed on a plan of debate. According to Commission procedure, the only proposal that could be the subject of debate was the French proposal, as it was the only one that had been submitted in time. Therefore, France would agree to accept any amendments proposed by Iraq. Iraq would essentially introduce a new proposal as an amendment to the French resolution. Algeria would propose the three words, "questions relevant to," and Nigeria would give its support to this U.S. wording. Finally, Iraq would move that the resolution be adopted without a vote, in order to preserve an appearance of unanimity; those countries who might abstain or vote "no" in a roll call vote would not have their position recorded if the measure was passed without a vote. The only uncertain factor was how effective Argentina would be in introducing and passing its amendments.

The representative of Iraq spoke first, introducing his proposal. The delegate pleaded that politics should not be involved in the question of disappearances. His concern was to carry out the duty of the Human Rights Commission in regard to human rights and to avoid emotional attacks on any countries. He expressed the view that his proposal — co-sponsored by Iraq, Cyprus, Yugoslavia, and Senegal (later Iran and Costa Rica were added) — was the best possible compromise between the various versions other countries had put forward. Not all countries agreed with it, but he hoped there would not be "a problem to deal with it." He moved to adopt the resolution without a vote.

Algeria spoke next. The delegate underlined the objective character of the mechanism being created and introduced the U.S. amendment, adding the words "questions relevant to" enforced or involuntary disappearances. Nigeria spoke simply to give its support to the amendment. France enthusiastically endorsed the Iraqi proposal and the amendment.

The Argentine forces then made their move. Brazil agreed with the proposal and the amendment, but wanted to make one small modification. It proposed an amendment that limited the Sub-Commission.[1] to making only general recommen-

---

[1] Ed.: The Sub-Commission on Prevention of Discrimination and Protection of Minorities is a subsidiary body of the Commission on Human Rights. *See* chapter 1, *supra*. The Commission was considering a proposal that would have established the Group, but would also have requested the Sub-Commission to "continue studying the most effective means for eliminating enforced or involuntary disappearances of persons with a view to making recommendations to the Commission. . . ."

dations to the Human Rights Commission. The unamended text did not specify whether the recommendations by the Sub-Commission were to be general or specific thereby allowing the Sub-Commission to make specific recommendations concerning individual cases. The Brazilian amendment would bar the Sub-Commission from making recommendations on individual cases.

Uruguay spoke after Brazil, and although stating it was in favor of a consensus, proposed another amendment. It pointed out that there was no provision by which a government under investigation by the proposed working group might present its own case to the Human Rights Commission. It insisted that the working group on disappearances should not be able to present its conclusions to the Commission if the government being investigated had no chance to make its own presentation to the Commission. At the least, there should be a provision providing for simultaneous presentations by both the working group and the government. It had no specific language prepared but asked that the debate be delayed until it had a chance to consult with other nations on the issue.

Iraq then asked for the floor again. The delegate spoke in favor of the Brazilian amendment, but asked Uruguay to withdraw its proposed amendment. Agreement had been reached among all the countries, the time was late, and all countries had been consulted. The Chairman strongly supported Iraq's request to Uruguay. He pointed out that there had been many days of negotiations and he pleaded with everyone to cooperate. Uruguay could, of course, insist on the amendment if that is what it wanted to do, but Uruguay was strenuously urged to withdraw it. Had Uruguay pressed forward, the consensus might very well have broken down. Instead, Uruguay, although complaining that it had not been consulted regarding Iraq's proposal, withdrew its amendment.

THE ADOPTED PROPOSAL

The proposal, as amended, was then adopted without a vote. [The operative paragraphs of the resolution — the original mandate of the Working Group — are reproduced in part D of this chapter, *infra.*]

The battle over the meaning of the proposal immediately began. In explaining their position after the adoption of the resolution, the USSR, Argentina, and Ethiopia urged a restrictive reading of the resolution. The USSR, for instance, pointedly referred to the fact that the working group had been created for one year only. It presumed that the group would work by strict consensus and that the duration of any meetings would be limited. It saw no need for the group to meet at all until two to three weeks before the 1981 session of the Human Rights Commission.

A reading that would allow the working group to consider individual cases of disappearance was urged by the U.S., Australia, Cyprus, Netherlands, and Canada. The United States specifically pointed out that the mandate of the working group of experts would allow it to consider the thousands of individual cases in existence. The general feeling of the Commission was that the working group would establish its own working methods and would be able, if it so chose, to investigate individual cases.

NOTES AND QUESTIONS

1. What have you learned from the preceding excerpt about how the

Commission on Human Rights creates a new process? About the role of NGOs in influencing Commission actions?

2. NGOs may participate in the work of the Commission and other bodies of the Economic and Social Council if they have consultative status with the Council. The different categories of status and procedures for obtaining it are set out in E.S.C. res. 1296 (XLIV), 44 U.N. ESCOR Supp. (No. 1) 21, U.N. Doc. E/4548 (1968) (reproduced in part in the previous chapter (part D), *supra*).

The preceding excerpt described one role NGOs with consultative status play in the Commission — participation in public debate at meetings. Another way NGOs with consultative status may participate in work of the Commission is by submitting written statements regarding items on the agenda. The following excerpt is a portion of a statement that several NGOs, including the International Commission of Jurists, the International League for Human Rights, and the Minority Rights Group, submitted as to disappearances. The statement was circulated as an official U.N. document at the 1980 session of the Commission on Human Rights, U.N. Doc. E/CN.4/NGO/283 (1980) (footnotes omitted):

DISAPPEARED PERSONS AND SOME INTERNATIONAL EMERGENCY MEASURES TO COPE WITH THIS PHENOMENON ...

The Phenomenon of Disappearances ...

People ordinarily disappear as a result of well planned procedures, either directly executed by governmental authorities, or with their tacit approval. The victims are then taken, usually blindfolded, to some location where, in virtually all cases, they are seriously mistreated — beaten, tortured, and humiliated. Families have no recourse. The government denies all knowledge and responsibility. *Habeas corpus* procedures, where available, are ignored. Families are left with no financial means of support and the fear that any protest may lead to their own disappearance or the death of their loved one. The family does not know whether to mourn or hope, but is left in horrible uncertainty.

A Few International Measures for Disappeared Persons

The experience of several organizations has shown that the phenomenon of disappearances necessitates emergency action.

Amnesty International has established an Urgent Action Network for such cases. When specific information is received regarding a disappeared person, thousands of notices are sent to Amnesty International members all over the world, who in turn send telegrams and letters to specific government officials who may have influence over the fate of the prisoner. Though it is not feasible in most cases to establish a direct correlation between the

Urgent Action Network and the fate of prisoners, Amnesty's records indicate that in 47% of the cases treated by the Network, the situation improved — either the treatment of the prisoners improved or the prisoners were released. Amnesty International also reports continuous encouragement and requests for urgent action from released prisoners, their relatives, and lawyers.

The National Council of Churches in the United States has a less formal procedure to respond to the problem of disappearances on an emergency basis. The experience of this organization is that the crucial period for a disappeared person is the first 48 hours after capture. If sufficient details can be presented — through telegrams to the proper officials — as to whom the disappeared person is, where the arrest occurred, and the identity of the persons performing the arrest, the individual can often be helped. Great efforts are made in cases where a country has no general problem of disappearances, and where the person involved has symbolic importance such as being the head of an opposition party or a labor union.

The Inter-American Commission on Human Rights, one of the principal organs of the Organization of American States, also has established emergency procedures to deal with cases where it is "feared that a detained person is being subjected to torture or is threatened with execution or is in urgent need of medical attention." Such an emergency procedure is normally invoked by telegrams to the Commission detailing violations of human rights that have just occurred. In urgent cases which are sufficiently documented, the Chair of the Commission sends a cable to the government expressing concern about the disappearance.

The International Committee of the Red Cross carries out its humanitarian work in countries where there are a large number of missing or disappeared persons. It maintains lists of missing persons, which it presents to the governments concerned; but its main work in countries where there are large numbers of political detainees, is to visit the places of detention in order to improve conditions. In 1979 alone thousands of detainees were visited by representatives of the International Committee of the Red Cross.

It is the general experience of those working directly on the problem of disappearances that the first few days after the initial arrest are most crucial; if international attention in any form can be directed to the government concerned within this time, there is some chance that a disappeared person might "reappear." In order to act promptly, it is impossible to undertake the painstaking verification of the facts which human rights organizations normally pursue in regard to other sorts of violations. At the same time the emergency procedures are not accompanied by substantial publicity, because the facts are rarely so clear as to justify such broad dissemination.

The Need For Emergency Measures

A disappearance is only successful when cloaked in anonymity. As soon as the disappearance becomes the subject of international attention, the chances increase that the government will acknowledge its responsibility for the disappearance, if the individual is still alive. Acknowledgement by the government that a person is in custody can be very important. The laws of the country, such as *habeas corpus*, can be utilized; the arrested person will have a greater chance to receive aid from relatives and friends; the likelihood of torture diminishes.

Whatever the reasons a government may have to carry out a disappearance, fear of international attention about the arrest of the person and the desire to deprive the person of the help of family and friends must be among them. Once the arrest becomes known internationally, these purposes are frustrated. Immediate international attention can contribute greatly to turning the disappearance into an illegal arrest or a kidnapping, to be handled according to the legal procedures of the country.

Conclusion

The wall of secrecy surrounding the "disappeared" can best be breached, perhaps can *only* be breached, by immediate international response.

Further study is needed as to the phenomenon of disappearances, its causes, its characteristics, and what emergency and longer term measures should be taken to safeguard human rights in the face of this redoubled threat.

This statement merely endeavors to inform the Commission about the kinds of emergency action on the "disappeared" which have been undertaken by other organizations. It is impossible to anticipate the exact nature of any emergency response United Nations bodies may be able to implement. The experience of the organizations discussed in this statement indicates that whatever form an international emergency response may take, it should focus on precisely what occurred in each particular case and what measures are required.

At a minimum it is hoped that the Commission will endorse the proposal from the Sub-Commission to establish a working group of experts to consider appropriate measures in regard to the phenomenon of disappearances.

3. As Kramer and Weissbrodt point out, the U.N. first addressed the issue of disappearances in a 1978 resolution of the General Assembly. That resolution, G.A. Res. 33/173, 33 U.N. GAOR Supp. (No. 45) at 158, U.N. Doc. A/33/45 (1979), called on governments to take certain measures to reduce disappearances, urged the Secretary-General to continue to use his good offices in cases of disappearance, and requested the Commission on Human Rights to "consider the question of disappeared persons with a view to making appropriate recommendations." The resolution set in motion the process that resulted in formation of the Working Group.

Weissbrodt, *The Three "Theme" Special Rapporteurs of the UN Commission on Human Rights*, 80 Am. J. Int'l L. 685, 685-95 (1986) (footnotes omitted):

In March 1982, the United Nations Commission on Human Rights initiated the appointment of a Special Rapporteur on summary or arbitrary executions. The Special Rapporteur on summary or arbitrary executions has done far more than merely study that grave human rights problem; he has received complaints about impending and past executions, issued appeals to governments about threatened executions and the need to investigate past killings, and reported publicly on much of his activity. The Commission on Human Rights not only has renewed the Special Rapporteur on summary or arbitrary executions in its subsequent annual sessions, but has followed this precedent by appointing in 1985 a similar Special Rapporteur on torture and in 1986 a Special Rapporteur on intolerance and discrimination based on religion or belief.

The development of the "theme" special rapporteur is a relatively new and remarkably flexible approach to implementing international human rights norms. Although the concept grew out of the practice of the Working Group on Enforced or Involuntary Disappearances, the special rapporteur, as a single individual of recognized international standing, is ordinarily less expensive and less visible, as well as more efficient, than the five-member working group in achieving similar objectives.

The Working Group on Enforced or Involuntary Disappearances

The Working Group on Enforced or Involuntary Disappearances, which was initiated by the Commission on Human Rights in 1980, has developed an effective approach to coping with the human rights violations within its narrow mandate. The evolution of the Working Group not only has given guidance to the special rapporteurs, but has presaged how their activities will develop.

The resolution that established the Working Group on Enforced or Involuntary Disappearances gave that body of five members authority (1) to "examine questions relevant to enforced or involuntary disappearances"; (2) to "seek and receive information from governments, intergovernmental organizations, humanitarian organizations and other reliable sources"; and (3) "to bear in mind the need to be able to respond effectively to information that comes before it and to carry out its work with discretion." It was directed to report to the Commission's next session. While the mandate of the working group to "examine questions" might at first glance appear to suggest an academic study of the issue, the working group relied principally upon its authority to "respond effectively" in raising specific cases of disappearances and in requesting responses from governments without seeking any publicity about the cases.

After receiving the Working Group's first report, the Commission extended the group's tenure for another year, but made several significant changes in its mandate to reflect both approval of and some limitations on its activities. The Commission noted that governments had not always given the working group the full cooperation "warranted by its strictly humanitarian objectives and its working methods based on discretion." The working group had embarrassed the Argentine government by reprinting its reply in full, and thus the group was reminded "to discharge its mandate with discretion"; on the one hand, it should "protect persons providing information," and on the other, "limit the dissemination of information provided by Governments."

While the Commission simply extended the working group's mandate in 1982 and 1983 without making significant changes, it did express "complete confidence" in the group. In 1984 the Commission for the first time requested that the working group "help eliminate the practice of enforced or involuntary disappearances" and encouraged governments to permit the group to make site visits to fulfill "its mandate more effectively." The Commission continued this approach in 1985....

The Working Group on Enforced or Involuntary Disappearances has developed incrementally into an effective human rights implementation mechanism on no broader a consensual basis than a consensus of the Commission on Human Rights and without the authority of any human rights treaty beyond the United Nations Charter. The special rapporteurs are gradually following in the footsteps of the Working Group.

The Special Rapporteur on Summary or Arbitrary Executions

The Special Rapporteur on summary or arbitrary executions was the first special rapporteur on a theme or particular kind of human rights violation. The 1982 mandate of the special rapporteur was styled to some extent upon the 1980 resolution that established the Working Group, that is, to "examine the questions related to summary or arbitrary executions" and to report annually to the Commission on the rapporteur's activities....

Although his position was initiated in March 1982 and his authority confirmed by the Economic and Social Council in May 1982, the first Special Rapporteur on summary or arbitrary executions, Amos Wako of Kenya, was not actually appointed by the Chairman of the Human Rights Commission until August of that year. Rather than take the incremental approach handed down by the Working Group on Enforced or Involuntary Disappearances, Mr. Wako's first report attempted to begin at the level of activity that the working group had achieved after several years. He evidently failed to note that the authorizing resolution did not instruct him to "respond effectively" but only to gather information, examine the question and report to the Commission. Instead, he had ambitiously identified 37 governments that had allegedly been responsible for summary or arbitrary executions; he had then sent the allegations to those governments, and the responses of 16 of them were summarized forthrightly in his report.

This first report was roundly criticized by members of the Commission — particularly by representatives of the governments that had been discussed. Consequently, Mr. Wako was again in 1983 not given authority to "respond effectively" to summary or arbitrary killings. His second and third reports omitted most references to countries, except for reprinting the telexes he had continued to send, without clear authority, in an attempt to avert specific summary or arbitrary executions. Accordingly, the special rapporteur's reports became less controversial; his mandate was more easily renewed in 1984 and 1985, and he was finally given authority to "respond effectively to information that comes before him."

The fourth report largely returned to the practice of identifying the governments that had allegedly engaged in summary or arbitrary executions. Indeed, the greatest part of the report contained the substance of the special rapporteur's appeals against summary or arbitrary executions during the previous year, the requests made by the special rapporteur for information about past executions and the responses of governments. This laudable record demonstrated that the special rapporteur had finally achieved the credibility he had sought at first and that his initially weak authority had been enhanced by the Commission. The report indicates that the special rapporteur has been quite active in pursuing his mandate and in attempting to prevent summary or arbitrary executions. The report makes no effort, however, to resolve the issues raised by the allegations and the replies of governments, and it makes only a rudimentary effort to synthesize the material presented and to draw useful conclusions and recommendations.

The Special Rapporteur on summary or arbitrary executions has not been as careful and successful in developing his mandate as the Working Group on Enforced or Involuntary Disappearances. Nevertheless, he has generally followed the approach of the Working Group and has been given the additional responsibility of helping to develop standards on such important subjects as international norms for the investigation of summary or arbitrary killings. As will be seen below, the Special Rapporteur on torture has benefited both from the mistakes of the Special Rapporteur on summary or arbitrary executions and from the guidance afforded by the Working Group on Enforced and Involuntary Disappearances.

The Special Rapporteur on Torture

During its session in 1985, the Commission on Human Rights established a Special Rapporteur on torture with the authority to "respond effectively to credible and reliable information" on torture. It was understood at the time that the Chairman of the Human Rights Commission would appoint Professor P. H. Kooijmans of the Netherlands. . . .

In many ways, the special rapporteur's report is a model first step in what promises to be a very effective United Nations approach to a serious human rights problem. Professor Kooijmans describes the nature of the problem, his mandate, international legal norms against torture and his activities, including the material he received from governments, the Organization of American States and nongovernmental organizations such as Amnesty International. He established his authority to transmit allegations of torture to national authorities by sending such information to 33 governments. The special rapporteur avoids angering these governments unnecessarily in his initial report by identifying only those nations which were already on the Commission's agenda, that is, Afghanistan, Chile, El Salvador, Guatemala and Iran.

Professor Kooijmans also records that he engaged in consultations with governments, nongovernmental organizations and individuals; without identifying those involved, he thus established his authority to undertake such consultations. In addition, he reports his decision to make eight urgent appeals to governments to prevent the occurrence of torture in Chile, the Comoros, Ecuador, Honduras, Indonesia, South Africa, Uganda and the USSR. The special rapporteur identifies some of these urgent situations very briefly and is careful to describe the governmental response, if any. For example, the report states, "The Special Rapporteur was informed that the USSR rejected the allegation sent to it as baseless and false and pointed out that the action of the Special Rapporteur violated the provisions of the Commission resolution 1985/33." While the report does not contain even a vague description of the problem that prompted this brusque reply, it appears to have been reports of psychiatric abuse in the USSR.

The remainder of the report largely deals with national legislative provisions forbidding torture; the barring of statements induced by torture as evidence in proceedings; the provision of remedies, such as *amparo* or habeas corpus, for torture allegations; and legislative provisions on matters creating a risk of torture, such as incommunicado detention, states of emergency and trade in implements of torture. Although countries are very rarely identified, except in a positive light, the United States is mentioned because of the export regulations regarding "specially designed implements of torture." The report concludes by listing the kinds of torture that have been identified, analyzing briefly the relationship between torture and other sorts of human rights violations (such as disappearances, arbitrary killings) and submitting a set of recommendations.

In general, the special rapporteur's work was well received by the Commission in March 1986....

When the Commission debated the agenda item entitled "Question of the human rights of all persons subjected to any form of detention or imprisonment," which includes a review of the work of the Special Rapporteur on torture, the Australian delegation introduced an idea borrowed from the Special Rapporteur on summary or arbitrary executions: that international standards be set for investigations into "cases of suspicious death, and that these investigations should include an adequate autopsy." Australia pointed to "the general need for accurate information to determine the cause of death where there is suspicion of torture" and reiterated the advantages international standards would confer on practitioners that were mentioned in the debate on summary and arbitrary executions.

Although these sentiments were not reflected in the Belgian resolution to prolong the special rapporteur's mandate for another year, the Commission is definitely beginning to see the theme special rapporteurs as a mechanism not only for implementing human rights norms but also for developing standards....

The Special Rapporteur on Intolerance and Discrimination Based on Religion or Belief

The most significant single development at the 42nd session of the Human Rights Commission was its decision in March 1986 to establish a Special Rapporteur on intolerance and discrimination based on religion or belief. The newest special rapporteur will presumably follow the same approach as his predecessors, that is, to study the phenomenon of intolerance and discrimination based on religion or belief; to "respond effectively to credible and reliable information that comes before him and to carry out his work with discretion and independence"; and to report to the Commission at its next session in 1987 about his activities.

The decision to establish a Special Rapporteur on intolerance and discrimination based on religion or belief arose from a long history of United Nations activity on this issue culminating in the proclamation by the General Assembly in 1981 of the Declaration on the Elimination of All Forms of Intolerance and of Discrimination Based on Religion or Belief. The Declaration was the product of 20 years of drafting work in the Commission on Human Rights and the very thorough Study on Discrimination in the Matter of Religious Rights and Practices, released in 1960. The new special rapporteur has been asked to "examine" "incidents and governmental actions in all parts of the world which are inconsistent with the provisions of the Declaration."

NOTES

1. The article excerpted above mentions the need for standards on the investigation of summary or arbitrary killings and torture. The Committee on Crime Prevention and Control drafted Principles on the Effective Prevention and Investigation of Extra-Legal, Arbitrary and Summary Executions. Those principles were adopted by ECOSOC in May 1989. E.S.C. res. 1989/65, U.N. Doc. E/1989/INF/7, at 129 (1989) and were endorsed by the General Assembly in G.A. res. 44/159 of Dec. 15, 1989 and in G.A. res. 44/162 of Dec. 15, 1989.

2. For further reading on theme procedures, see:

Bossuyt, *The Development of Special Procedures of the United Nations Commission on Human Rights*, 6 Hum. Rts. L.J. 179, 194-99 (1985);

Rodley, *United Nations Action Procedures Against "Disappearances," Summary or Arbitrary Executions, and Torture*, 8 Hum. Rts. Q. 700 (1986);

Kamminga, *The Thematic Procedures of the U.N. Commission on Human Rights*, 34 Netherlands Int'l L. Rev. 299 (1987);

N. Rodley, The Treatment of Prisoners Under International Law 191-218 (1987);

Fitzpatrick, *UN Action With Respect to "Disappearances" and Summary or Arbitrary Executions*, 5 AIUSA Legal Support Network Newsletter 35 (Fall 1988).

SPECIAL RAPPORTEUR ON MERCENARIES

In 1987 the Commission decided to appoint a rapporteur "to examine the question of the use of mercenaries as a means of violating human rights and of impeding the exercise of the right of peoples to self-determination." The Commission did not authorize the rapporteur to respond effectively to information received, a right that other theme procedures have used to justify transmittal of complaints to governments. *See* C.H.R. res. 1987/16, U.N. Doc. E/CN.4/1987/60, at 60 (1987).

In a 1988 report, his first, the Special Rapporteur (Enrique Bernales Ballesteros of Peru) examined international law relating to mercenaries and summarized information received from governments, IGOs, and NGOs. In addition, he examined the issue of how to define the word mercenary and outlined three broad types of mercenaries. He concluded that mercenary practices still are present in the world and recommended further study. *See* U.N. Doc. E/CN.4/1988/14 (1988).

In his 1989 report, he once again summarized information received; the bulk of the report is devoted to his visit to Nicaragua. The aim was to conduct an on-site study of effects the use of mercenaries has on human rights, especially the right to self-determination. He also visited Angola and sent letters to governments involved in an apparent use of mercenary aggression against the government of Maldives. The report contained several recommendations, including a proposal that states should adopt penal legislation prohibiting and punishing mercenary activities. *See* U.N. Doc. E/CN.4/1989/14 (1989).

NOTES AND QUESTIONS

1. How does the Special Rapporteur on mercenaries differ from the other theme procedures? Compare the mandate of the Special Rapporteur on mercenaries with the mandates of the other theme procedures excerpted in the next section for help in outlining differences. Are the differences important? Is the Special Rapporteur on mercenaries really a theme procedure? What makes a procedure "thematic"?

2. Does the subject matter of the Special Rapporteur on mercenaries require a different approach than the other theme procedures? Should all new theme procedures necessarily be modeled after the Working Group?

3. The Commission on Human Rights at its forty-fourth session in 1988 referred to the Special Rapporteur on mercenaries as a "thematic" procedure in its decision to extend the mandates of all the "rapporteurs on thematic issues" for two years. *See* Commission on Human Rights, Report on the Forty-Fourth Session, U.N. Doc. E/CN.4/1988/88, at 11 (1988). In 1990 the Commission on Human Rights extended for another two years the mandates of the Working Group on Enforced or Involuntary Disappearances, the Special Rapporteur on Mercenaries, and the three theme rapporteurs.

4. In addition to appointing country-specific and thematic rapporteurs, the Commission on Human Rights appoints study rapporteurs. The mandates of study rapporteurs typically require them to study a given human rights problem or the implementation of U.N. resolutions relating to specific human rights. You have already seen the work of one such rapporteur in chapter 3 where you read an excerpt from the report of Special Rapporteur H. Gros Espiell. Mr. Gros Espiell's mandate required him to study the implementation of U.N. resolutions relating to the right of self-determination. Despite the Commission's apparent view that the Special Rapporteur on mercenaries is a thematic position, do you think it might more properly be classified as a study rapporteur? Why or why not?

D. MANDATES AND METHODS OF WORK

MANDATES OF THEME RAPPORTEURS

The operative parts of the Commission on Human Rights resolutions establishing the thematic procedures are reproduced below:

Enforced or Involuntary Disappearances
　　C.H.R. res. 20 (XXXVI), U.N. Doc. E/CN.4/1408, at 180 (1980):

1. *Decides* to establish for a period of one year a working group consisting of five of its members, to serve as experts in their individual capacities, to examine questions relevant to enforced or involuntary disappearances of persons;

2. *Requests* the Chairman of the Commission to appoint the members of the group;

3. *Decides* that the working group, in carrying out its mandate, shall seek and receive information from Governments, intergovernmental organizations, humanitarian organizations and other reliable sources;

4. *Requests* the Secretary-General to appeal to all Governments to co-operate with and assist the working group in the performance of its tasks and to furnish all information required;

5. *Further requests* the Secretary-General to provide the working group with all necessary assistance, in particular staff and resources they require in order to perform their functions in an effective and expeditious manner;

6. *Invites* the working group, in establishing its working methods, to bear in mind the need to be able to respond effectively to information that comes before it and to carry out its work with discretion;

7. *Requests* the working group to submit to the Commission at its thirty-seventh session a report on its activities, together with its conclusions and recommendations; . . . .

　　C.H.R. res. 1990/30, U.N. Doc. E/CN.4/1990/L.11/Add.2, at 9 (1990):

3. *Decides* to extend for two years the term of the mandate of the Working Group as defined in Commission resolution 20 (XXXVI) so as to enable the Working Group to take into consideration all the information that may be transmitted to it concerning the cases brought to its attention, while maintaining the principle of annual reporting by the Working Group;

4. *Requests* the Working Group to report on its work to the Commission at its forty-seventh session and reminds the Working Group of the obligation to discharge its mandate in a discreet and conscientious manner;

5. *Also requests* the Working Group, in its efforts to help eliminate the practice of enforced or involuntary disappearances, to present to the Commission all

appropriate information it deems necessary and all concrete suggestions and recommendations regarding the fulfillment of its task;

6. *Reminds* the Working Group of the need to observe, in its humanitarian task, United Nations standards and practices regarding the receipt of communications, their consideration, their evaluation, the transmittal to Governments of all communications received and the consideration of Government replies;

7. *Expresses its appreciation* to the Working Group on Detention of the Sub-Commission for the progress made in 1989 in preparing the first draft of a declaration on enforced or involuntary disappearances and invites the Sub-Commission to finalize the draft as soon as possible with a view to submitting it to the Commission;

8. *Notes with concern* that, as the Working Group points out in its report, some Governments have never provided substantive replies concerning disappearances alleged to have occurred in their country;

9. *Reminds* Governments of the need to ensure that their competent authorities conduct prompt and impartial inquiries when there is reason to believe that an enforced or involuntary disappearance has occurred in a territory under their jurisdiction;

10. *Urges* the Governments concerned, particularly those which have not yet responded to communications transmitted to them by the Working Group, to co-operate with and assist the Working Group so that it may carry out its mandate effectively, and in particular to answer expeditiously requests for information addressed to them by the Working Group;

11. *Also urges* the Governments concerned to intensify their co-operation with the Working Group in regard to any measure taken in pursuance of recommendations addressed to them by the Group;

12. *Once again urges* the Governments concerned to take steps to protect the families of disappeared persons against any intimidation or ill-treatment to which they might be subject;

13. *Encourages* the Governments concerned to give serious consideration to inviting the Working Group to visit their country, so as to enable the Group to fulfill its mandate even more effectively; . . .

17. *Requests* the Secretary-General to ensure that the Working Group receives all necessary assistance, in particular the staff and resources it requires to perform its functions, especially in carrying out missions or holding sessions in countries which would be prepared to receive it. . . .''

Summary or Arbitrary Executions

C.H.R. res. 1982/29, U.N. Doc. E/CN.4/1982/30, at 147 (1982):

1. *Strongly deplores* the increasing number of summary or arbitrary executions taking place in various parts of the world;

2. *Decides therefore* to appoint for one year a special rapporteur to examine the questions related to summary or arbitrary executions;

3. *Requests* the Chairman of the Commission, after consultations within the Bureau, to appoint an individual of recognized international standing as special rapporteur;

4. *Considers* that the special rapporteur in carrying out his mandate may seek and receive information from Governments as well as specialized agencies, intergovernmental organizations and non-governmental organizations in consultative status with the Economic and Social Council;

5. *Requests* the special rapporteur to submit a comprehensive report to the Commission at its thirty-ninth session on the occurrence and extent of the practice of such executions together with his conclusions and recommendations;

6. *Urges* all Governments to co-operate with and assist the special rapporteur in the preparation of his report;

7. *Requests* the Secretary-General to provide all necessary assistance to the special rapporteur. . . .

C.H.R. res. 1984/50, U.N. Doc. E/CN.4/1984/77, at 86 (1984):

5. *Requests* the Special Rapporteur in carrying out his mandate to continue to examine situations of summary or arbitrary executions and to pay special attention to cases in which a summary or arbitrary execution is imminent or threatened;

6. *Requests* the Special Rapporteur in carrying out his mandate to respond effectively to information that comes before him;

7. *Considers* that the Special Rapporteur in carrying out his mandate should continue to seek and receive information from Governments, United Nations bodies, specialized agencies, regional intergovernmental organizations and non-governmental organizations in consultative status with the Economic and Social Council;

8. *Requests* The Secretary-General to continue to provide all necessary assistance to the Special Rapporteur so that he may carry out his mandate effectively. . . .

C.H.R. res. 1985/37, U.N. Doc. E/CN.4/1985/66, at 80 (1985):

6. *Requests* the Special Rapporteur in carrying out his mandate to respond effectively to information that comes before him, in particular when a summary or arbitrary execution is imminent or threatened. . . .

C.H.R. res. 1986/42, U.N. Doc. E/CN.4/1986/65, at 110 (1986):

7. *Takes note* of the need to develop international standards designed to ensure effective legislation and other domestic measures so that proper investigations are conducted by appropriate authorities into all cases of suspicious death, including provisions for adequate autopsy;

8. *Invites* the Special Rapporteur to receive information from appropriate United Nations agencies and other international organizations and to examine the elements to be included in such standards and to report to the Commission on Human Rights on progress made in this respect. . . .

C.H.R. res. 1987/57, U.N. Doc. E/CN.4/1987/60, at 125 (1987):

3. *Takes note with appreciation* of the report (E.CN.4/1987/20) of Mr. S. *Amos Wako*, Special Rapporteur, and welcomes his recommendations with a view to eliminating summary or arbitrary executions. . . .

C.H.R. res. 1988/66, U.N. Doc. E/CN.4/1988/88, at 145 (1988):

4. *Decides* to renew the mandate of the Special Rapporteur for two years, while keeping the annual reporting cycle, in order to enable him to submit further conclusions and recommendations to the Commission at its forty-fifth and forty-sixth sessions. . . .

C.H.R. res. 1990/51, U.N. Doc. E/CN.4/1990/L.11/Add.3, at 9 (1990):

4. *Decides* to continue the mandate of the Special Rapporteur for two years in

order to enable him to submit further conclusions and recommendations to the Commission. . . .

Torture

C.H.R. res. 1985/33, U.N. Doc. E/CN.4/1985/66, at 71 (1985):

1. *Decides* to appoint for one year a special rapporteur to examine questions relevant to torture;

2. *Requests* the Chairman of the Commission to appoint, after consultation with the other members of the Bureau, an individual of recognized international standing as special rapporteur;

3. *Decides further* that the special rapporteur, in carrying out his mandate, shall seek and receive credible and reliable information from Governments, as well as specialized agencies, intergovernmental organizations and non-governmental organizations;

4. *Requests* the Secretary-General to appeal to all Governments to co-operate with and assist the special rapporteur in the performance of his tasks and to furnish all information requested;

5. *Further requests* the Secretary-General to provide all necessary assistance to the special rapporteur;

6. *Invites* the special rapporteur, in carrying out his mandate, to bear in mind the need to be able to respond effectively to credible and reliable information that comes before him and to carry out his work with discretion;

7. *Requests* the special rapporteur to submit a comprehensive report to the Commission at its forty-second session on his activities regarding the question of torture, including the occurrence and extent of its practice, together with his conclusions and recommendations. . . .

C.H.R. res. 1990/34, U.N. Doc. E/CN.4/1990/L.11/Add.2, at 17 (1990):

13. *Decides* to continue the mandate of the Special Rapporteur for another two years, while maintaining the annual reporting cycle in order to enable him to submit further conclusions and recommendations to the Commission;

14. *Decides* that the Special Rapporteur, in carrying out his mandate, shall continue to seek and receive credible and reliable information from Governments, as well as specialized agencies, intergovernmental organizations and non-governmental organizations; . . .

17. *Appeals* to appeal to all Governments to co-operate with and assist the Special Rapporteur in the performance of his tasks and to furnish all information requested. . . .

Intolerance and Discrimination Based on Religion or Belief

C.H.R. res. 1986/20, U.N. Doc. E/CN.4/1986/65, at 67 (1986):

1. *Expresses its deep concern* about reports of incidents and governmental actions in all parts of the world which are inconsistent with the provisions of the Declaration on the Elimination of All Forms of Intolerance and of Discrimination Based on Religion or Belief;

2. *Decides* therefore to appoint for one year a special rapporteur to examine such incidents and actions and to recommend remedial measures, including, as appropriate, the promotion of a dialogue between communities of religion or belief and their Governments;

3. *Requests* the Chairman of the Commission, after consultations within the Bureau, to appoint an individual of recognized international standing as special rapporteur;

4. *Decides further* that the Special Rapporteur in carrying out his mandate shall seek credible and reliable information from Governments, as well as specialized agencies, intergovernmental organizations and non-governmental organizations, including communities of religion or belief;

5. *Requests* the Secretary-General to appeal to all Governments to co-operate with and assist the Special Rapporteur in the performance of his duties and to furnish all information requested;

6. *Further requests* the Secretary-General to provide all necessary assistance to the Special Rapporteur;

7. *Invites* the Special Rapporteur, in carrying out his mandate, to bear in mind the need to be able to respond effectively to credible and reliable information that comes before him and to carry out his work with discretion and independence;

8. *Requests* the Special Rapporteur to submit a report to the Commission at its forty-third session on his activities regarding questions involving implementation of the Declaration, including the occurrence and extent of incidents and actions inconsistent with the provisions of the Declaration, together with his conclusions and recommendations. . . .

C.H.R. res. 1990/27, U.N. Doc. E/CN.4/1990/L.11/Add.2, at 1 (1990):

11. *Decides* to extend for two years the mandate of the Special Rapporteur appointed to examine incidents and governmental actions in all parts of the world which are inconsistent with the provisions of the Declaration on the Elimination of All Forms of Intolerance and of Discrimination Based on Religion or Belief and to recommend remedial measures, as appropriate. . . .

Mercenaries

C.H.R. res. 1987/16, U.N. Doc. E/CN.4/1987/60, at 60 (1987):

1. *Decides* to appoint for one year a special rapporteur to examine the question of the use of mercenaries as a means of violating human rights and of impeding the exercise of the right of peoples to self-determination;

2. *Requests* the Chairman of the Commission, after consultations with the other members of the Bureau, to appoint an individual of recognized international standing as special rapporteur;

3. *Decides further* that the Special Rapporteur in carrying out his mandate shall seek and receive credible and reliable information from Governments, as well as specialized agencies, intergovernmental organizations and non-governmental organizations;

4. *Requests* the Secretary-General to appeal to all Governments to co-operate with and assist the Special Rapporteur in the performance of his duties and to furnish all information requested;

5. *Further requests* the Secretary-General to provide all necessary assistance to the Special Rapporteur;

6. *Requests* the Special Rapporteur to submit to the Commission at its forty-fourth session a report on his activities regarding this question. . . .

C.H.R. res. 1990/7, U.N. Doc. E/CN.4/1990/L.11, at 4 (1990):

8. *Decides* to extend the mandate of the Special Rapporteur for two years to enable him to submit further conclusions and recommendations to the Commission. . .

14. *Further requests* the Special Rapporteur, in carrying out his mandate, to study credible and reliable reports of mercenary activity in developing countries, in particular smaller States, to determine the scope and implications of such activities and the possible responsibility of third parties by means, *inter alia*, of on-site visits where appropriate. . . .

QUESTIONS

1. Compare the mandates of the Working Group and the rapporteurs. How do they differ? How do the differences affect the methods of work?

2. Compare the original mandates with the more recent versions. Have the changes broadened or restricted the powers conferred by the procedures? What implications are there as to methods of work?

3. Note that the Commission at its 1988 and 1990 sessions extended all the mandates for two years. Does that suggest a view as to the procedures' effectiveness?

METHODS OF WORK

U.N. Working Group on Enforced or Involuntary Disappearances, *Methods of Work*, U.N. Doc. E/CN.4/1988/19, at 5-7 (1988):

16. The Working Group's methods of work are based on its mandate as stipulated in Commission on Human Rights resolution 20 (XXXVI) and are specifically geared to its main objective. That objective is to assist families in determining the fate and whereabouts of their missing relatives who, having disappeared, are placed outside the protective precinct of the law. To this end, the Working Group endeavours to establish a channel of communication between the families and the Governments concerned, with a view to ensuring that sufficiently documented and clearly identified individual cases which the families, directly or indirectly, have brought to the Group's attention, are investigated and the whereabouts of the missing person clarified. The Group's role ends when the fate and whereabouts of the missing person have been clearly established as a result of investigations by the Government or the search by the family, irrespective of whether that person is alive or dead. The Group's approach is strictly non-accusatory. It does not concern itself with the question of determining responsibility for specific cases of disappearance or for other human rights violations which may have occurred in the course of disappearances. In sum, the Group's activity is humanitarian in nature.

17. A typical example of enforced or involuntary disappearance may be described in general terms as follows: a clearly identified person is detained against his will by officials of any branch or level of government or by organized groups or private individuals allegedly acting on behalf or with the support, permission or acquiescence of the Government. These forces then conceal the whereabouts of that person or refuse to disclose his fate or to acknowledge that the person was detained.

18. The Working Group does not deal with situations of international armed conflict, in view of the competence of the International Committee of the Red Cross (ICRC) in such situations, as established by the Geneva Conventions of 12 August 1949 and the Protocols additional thereto.

19. In transmitting cases of disappearances, the Working Group deals exclusively with Governments, basing itself on the principle that Governments must assume responsibility for any violation of human rights on their territory. If, however, disappearances are attributed to terrorist or insurgent movements fighting the Government on its own territory, the Working Group has refrained from processing them. The Group considers that, as a matter of principle, such groups may not be approached with a view to investigating or clarifying disappearances for which they are held responsible.

20. Reports on disappearances are considered admissible by the Working Group when they originate from the family or friends of the missing person. Such reports may, however, be channelled to the Working Group through representatives of the family, Governments, intergovernmental organizations, humanitarian organizations and other reliable sources. They must be submitted in writing with a clear indication of the identity of the sender.

21. In order to enable Governments to carry out meaningful investigations, the Working Group provides them with information containing at least a minimum of basic data. In addition, the Working Group constantly urges the sources of reports to furnish as many details as possible on the identity of the missing person (if available, identity card numbers) and the circumstances of the disappearance. The Group requires the following minimum elements:

    (a)   Full name of the missing person;

    (b)   Date of disappearance, i.e., day, month and year of arrest or abduction or day, month and year when the missing person was last seen. When the missing person was last seen in a detention centre, an approximate indication is sufficient (i.e. March or spring 1980);

    (c)   Place of arrest or abduction or where the missing person was last seen (at least indication of town or village);

    (d)   Parties presumed to have carried out the arrest or abduction or to hold the missing person in unacknowledged detention;

    (e)   Steps taken to determine the fate or whereabouts of the missing person or at least an indication that efforts to resort to domestic remedies were frustrated or have otherwise been inconclusive.

22. Reported cases of disappearances are placed before the Working Group for detailed examination during its sessions. Those which fulfil the requirements as outlined above are transmitted, upon the Group's specific authorization, to the Governments concerned requesting them to carry out investigations and to inform

the Group about their results. The reported cases are communicated by letter from the Group's Chairman to the Government concerned through the Permanent Representative to the United Nations.

23. Cases that occurred within the three months preceding receipt of the report by the Group are transmitted directly to the Ministers for Foreign Affairs by means of a cable. Their transmission can be authorized by the Chairman on the basis of a specific delegation of power given to him by the Group. Cases which occurred prior to the three-month limit but not more than one year before the date of their receipt by the Secretariat, provided that they had some connection with a case which occurred within the three-month period, can be transmitted between sessions by letter upon authorization by the Chairman.

24. At least once a year the Working Group reminds every Government concerned of the cases which have not yet been clarified. Furthermore, at any time during the year, any Government may request the summaries of the outstanding and/or clarified cases which the Working Group has transmitted to it.

25. All replies received from Governments on reports of disappearances are examined by the Working Group and summarized in the Group's annual report to the Commission on Human Rights. The number of cases on which a Government has provided one or several specific replies are listed in the statistical summary concerning each country in the annual report. Any information given on specific cases is forwarded to the sources of those reports who are invited to make observations thereon or to provide additional details on the cases.

26. If the reply clearly indicates where the missing person is (whether alive or dead) and if that information is sufficiently definite for the family to be reasonably expected to accept it, the Working Group considers the case clarified at the session following the receipt of that information. The case is accordingly listed under the heading ''Cases clarified by the Government's responses'' in the statistical summary of the annual report.

27. If the reply provides definite information on the missing person's fate after the reported date of disappearance, but does not unambiguously specify the person's present whereabouts (for instance that the person was released from prison some time ago or that he is free without stating where), a reply from the source has to be awaited. If the source does not respond within six months of the date on which the Government's reply was communicated to it, the case is considered clarified. If the source contests the Government's information on reasonable grounds, the Government is so informed and invited to comment.

28. If the sources provide well-documented information that a case has erroneously been considered clarified, because the Government's reply referred to a different person, does not correspond to the reported situation or has not reached the source within the six-month period described above, the Working Group transmits the case to the Government anew requesting it to comment. In such instances the respective case is again listed among the outstanding cases and a specific explanation is given in the Group's report to the Commission on Human Rights, describing the above-mentioned errors or discrepancies.

29. Any substantive additional information which the sources submit on an outstanding case is placed before the Working Group and, following its approval, transmitted to the Government concerned. If the additional information received

amounts to a clarification of the case, the Government is informed immediately without awaiting the Group's next session. Clarifications by the sources are summarized in the Group's annual report and listed in the statistical summary under the heading "Cases clarified by non-governmental sources".

30. The Working Group retains cases on its files as long as the exact whereabouts of the missing persons have not been determined, in accordance with the criteria outlined in paras. 16, 26 and 27. This principle is not affected by changes of Government in a given country. However, the Working Group accepts the closure of a case on its files when the competent authority specified in the relevant national law pronounces, with the concurrence of the relatives and other interested parties, on the presumption of death of a person reported missing.

NOTES AND QUESTIONS

1. Do you think the Working Group's refusal to investigate disappearances caused by nongovernmental entities (for example, terrorist groups) is wise? Does the Group's mandate require refusal? What are advantages and disadvantages of the policy? Should rapporteurs follow the Working Group's approach?

2. Note the sources from which the Group will accept information on disappeared persons. Recalling the international complaint procedures discussed in chapters 3 and 4, do you think the Group's approach is broader or narrower? Why do you think the Group chose its approach? Are there differences in the mandates or work of rapporteurs that might require a broader or narrower approach to sources of information?

3. Note the Group's description of a case it considers clarified. Do you think the description is adequate? What should a government reply include for the Group to consider it sufficient to clarify a case? What information should rapporteurs consider sufficient to clarify a case?

4. What should the Working Group and rapporteurs do when a government does not respond or responds inadequately to transmitted information? Should they presume the allegations to be true, as do other international bodies, for example, the Inter-American Commission? Are there differences in the power of the Group and rapporteurs when compared with the Inter-American Commission's powers that might render such an approach problematic?

5. Should theme procedures allow complainants to respond to government replies?

The General Assembly apparently approves theme procedures that encourage such a practice. In a 1988 resolution concerning the Special Rapporteur on summary or arbitrary executions, the G.A. requested the rapporteur "to promote exchanges of views between Governments and those who provide reliable information to the Special Rapporteur, where the Special Rapporteur considers that such exchange of information might be useful." G.A. res. 43/151, 43 U.N. GAOR (Supp. No. 49), U.N. Doc. A/43/49 (1989).

Fitzpatrick, *UN Action With Respect to "Disappearances" and Summary or Arbitrary Executions*, 5 AIUSA Legal Support Network Newsl. 35, 38-39 (Fall 1988) (footnotes omitted):

Two attitudes have framed the Working Group's approach: *humanitarianism* and *discretion*. By a "humanitarian" approach, the Working Group means that its sole interest is learning the fate of the "disappeared" and informing relatives of that fate, and not in fixing blame upon particular governments or individuals. While the Working Group believes that this non-judgmental attitude has gradually increased the willingness of governments to cooperate, it may also have led to increased frustration on the part of relatives, especially those who have provided highly detailed accounts, sometimes even naming the arresting officers, and have received nothing but generalized denials or silence from governments. The Working Group has rejected the suggestion from some NGOs and relatives that it publish lists of well-documented "disappearances" after prolonged government unresponsiveness. It also rejected the approach of the Inter-American Commission on Human Rights (IACHR) and the UN Human Rights Committee which take as true allegations to which the accused government fails to respond adequately. Instead, the Working Group simply continues to list cases as unclarified and its reports retain a studied anonymity and generality (although the sections on individual countries will roughly categorize the cases, by summarizing the professions of the reported "disappeared" and the common mode of their abduction). . . .

The second approach, *discretion*, presents central issues concerning the character of the Working Group and its place in the general scheme of international mechanisms for the protection of human rights. By "discretion," the Working Group means both confidentiality and causation. The original mandate of Commission on Human Rights res. 20 (XXXVI) permitted the Working Group to establish its working methods but "to bear in mind the need to be able to respond effectively to information that comes before it and to carry out its work with discretion. . . ."

Kamminga, *The Thematic Procedures of the UN Commission on Human Rights*, 34 Netherlands Int'l L. Rev. 299, 305-07 (1987) (footnotes omitted):

Each of the procedures has been requested by the Commission on Human Rights to operate 'with discretion'. The meaning of these words may not be immediately obvious, but the intention of the drafters was probably to admonish those administering the procedures not to be too harsh on governments — at least not publicly.

The 1981 resolution renewing the mandate of the Working Group on Disappearances somewhat clarified the Commission's intention. It reminded the Working Group 'to bear in mind the obligation to discharge its mandate with discretion, so as, *inter alia*, to protect persons providing information or to limit the dissemination of information provided by governments'. In other words, two reasons were being given for being 'discreet'. First, because the people providing information might be subjected to governmental reprisals if their identity became known. Second, because governments should not be embarrassed by the Working Group. Surely a curious mix of arguments! ...

Another line of criticism — exemplified by the USSR — has attempted to curb the input side of the procedures by emphasizing strict admissibility requirements. This approach was reflected in a preambular paragraph introduced for the first time in the 1981 Commission resolution renewing the mandate of the Working Group on Disappearances. In it the Commission reminded the Working Group of 'the need to observe United Nations standards and practice regarding the receipt of communications, their transmittal to the Governments concerned and their evaluation'.

Again, it is not immediately clear what was intended by this [exhortation]. Most likely, the paragraph referred to the handling of communications under the 1503-procedure. If so, it may have meant that the Working Group should not act on the basis of information received from biased or politically motivated sources. This argument has been convincingly refuted by the Special Rapporteur on Torture. He has pointed out that victims of torture are often opponents of the government in power. First-hand information about torture therefore tends to come from opposition groups. It would be quite wrong to reject such information out of hand merely because it derives from an opposition source. Another possible interpretation is that the Working Group was told not to be concerned with individual cases but only with 'consistent patterns'. If this was the intention, it did not affect the practice of the Working Group. Both the Working Group and the other thematic procedures have taken action and reported on single cases. There has been no 'threshold' policy.

A more recent type of criticism of the working methods of the Working Group has been made by Colombia. It has suggested that the Working Group should apply the admissibility criteria established under the Optional Protocol to the International Covenant on Civil and Political Rights. The Working Group has correctly replied that 'its procedure was in no way linked to the criteria of admissibility under the Optional Protocol and that the Group's purely humanitarian efforts ... differed considerably from the objectives, scope and applicability of the Optional Protocol and thus necessitated a much less formal approach'....

NOTES

Article 5 of the Optional Protocol to the International Covenant on Civil and Political Rights requires a complainant to exhaust all available domestic remedies, but specifies that the individual need not exhaust remedies if they are "unreasonably prolonged." *See* the accompanying handbook. The Kamminga article excerpted above refers to the Colombian government's suggestion that the Working Group on Enforced or Involuntary Disappearances apply the exhaustion requirement. Was the Group's reply adequate to answer the Colombian government? What is the meaning of "unreasonably prolonged" in the context of disappearances? Should the Group at least require that the complainant notify the government of the disappearance before seeking the assistance of the Group?

HUMAN RIGHTS VIOLATED BY DISAPPEARANCES

In previous chapters this book has focused on violations of rights prescribed in a variety of international human rights instruments. Those rights, which governments have promised in treaties to respect, serve as the basis for challenge to a government's actions against its own citizens. The specific rights which are threatened by government practices under investigation in the theme procedures are generally apparent. For example, individuals are expressly protected against torture or arbitrary deprivation of life. Because there is no explicit prohibition against enforced or involuntary disappearances in existing U.N. human rights instruments, however, the human rights at issue need explication. In its first report, the Group examined this question. Below are excerpts from its conclusions in *Report of the Working Group on Enforced or Involuntary Disappearances*, U.N. Doc. E/CN.4/1435, at 79-80 (1981) (footnotes omitted):

184. The information reflected in the present report shows that in instances of enforced or involuntary disappearance a wide range of human rights of the victim himself and of his family may be denied or infringed. These include civil and political rights as well as economic, social and cultural rights. With regard to the person who is subjected to enforced or involuntary disappearance, the following may be identified as the principal human rights which he is denied.

   (a)   The right to liberty and security of person. This is the principal human right denied by the very fact of enforced or involuntary disappearance. Connected rights, such as the right to freedom from arbitrary arrest, the right to a fair trial in criminal matters and the right to recognition as a person before the law, are all involved;

   (b)   Right to humane conditions of detention and freedom from torture, cruel or degrading treatment or punishment. Some of the information before the Group deals with the conditions of detention, including ill-treatment, suffered by the missing or disappeared persons;

   (c)   Right to life. Portions of the information received by the Group indicate that during detention the missing or disappeared person may be killed.

185. Disappearances of the sort under consideration by the Group also involve infringements of certain of the "Standard Minimum Rules for the Treatment of Prisoners" approved by the Economic and Social Council in its resolution 663 C (XXIV) of 31 July 1957. Relevant to enforced or involuntary disappearances are the following rules of a general nature which, under rule 4, are applicable to all categories of prisoners, criminal or civil, untried or convicted, including prisoners subject to "security measures": rule 7, which requires that detailed records shall be kept for each prisoner; rule 37, which ensures that prisoners shall be able to communicate with their family; and rule 44, which requires the authorities to inform a prisoner's spouse or nearest relative in the case of his death, or serious illness, and affords the prisoner the right to inform at once his family of his imprisonment or his transfer to another institution. Rule 92, which applies to untried prisoners also recognizes the prisoner's right to communicate with his family and to inform his family immediately of his detention.

186. If these may be said to be the principal human rights of the missing person who suffers enforced or involuntary disappearance, a reading of the Universal Declaration and the International Covenants on Human Rights shows that to a greater or lesser degree practically all basic human rights of such a person are infringed. Particular concern has been expressed to the Group about the right to a family life of the persons who suffer enforced or involuntary disappearance and of their relatives. In the case of pregnant women, children and refugees who suffer enforced or involuntary disappearance, their specific rights, as contained in the international human rights instruments, are infringed; for example the right of every child to measures of protection. A review of the economic, social and cultural rights guaranteed by the various international human rights instruments shows that most of them are denied to greater or lesser extent by enforced or involuntary disappearances.

187. The information before the Group shows that various human rights of the members of the family of a missing or disappeared person may also be infringed by that person's enforced absence. Their right to a family life may be seen as the principal right involved but other rights of an economic, social and cultural nature can also be directly affected; for example, the family's standard of living, health care and education may all be adversely affected by the absence of a parent. The adverse impact of the disappearance of a parent on the mental health of children has been pointed out elsewhere. Finally, the Additional Protocol I to the Geneva Convention of 12 August 1949 has recognized "the rights of families to know the fate of their relatives" and this right of relatives to be informed of the whereabouts and fate of missing or disappeared family members has been reflected in resolutions of United Nations bodies.

NOTES

1. For further discussion of human rights law that other international bodies, including the Human Rights Committee, Inter-American Commission on Human Rights, and the European Commission on Human Rights, have deemed to be violated by disappearances, see N. Rodley, The Treatment of Prisoners Under International Law 198-205 (1987).

2. For further reading on international norms violated by disappearances and possible methods of dealing with the problem, see Disappeared: Technique of Terror (1986) (a report for the Independent Commission on International Humanitarian Issues); Berman & Clark, *State Terrorism: Disappearances*, 13 Rutgers L.J. 531 (1982); Reoch, *"Disappearances" and the International Protection of Human Rights*, 36 Y.B. World Aff. 166 (1982); U.N. Centre for Human Rights, Enforced or Involuntary Disappearances, Fact Sheet No. 6, at 5-6 (1989).

3. Existing U.N. treaties and other instruments do not explicitly refer to disappearances as a violation of human rights. In 1988, however, the U.N. Sub-Commission on Prevention of Discrimination and Protection of Minorities and its Working Group on Detention began to prepare a Declaration on the

Protection of All Persons from Enforced or Involuntary Disappearances. The draft Declaration is intended for eventual adoption by the General Assembly after acceptance by the Commission on Human Rights and ECO-SOC. *See Report of the Working Group on Detention*, U.N. Doc. E/CN.4/ Sub.2/1988/28, Annex I, at 15 (1988); *see also* U.N. Doc. E/CN.4/Sub.2/1989/ 29/Rev.1, at 14 (1989). Some human rights activists look to the declaration as the first step in the creation of a worldwide treaty against disappearances. A regional treaty against disappearances is also being pursued in the Americas.

URGENT ACTION PROCEDURES

In its 1985 report the Working Group explained its urgent action procedure and described the results as follows in *Report of the Working Group on Enforced or Involuntary Disappearances*, U.N. Doc. E/CN.4/1985/ 15, at 23-24 (1985):

80. At its first session, in 1980, the Working Group gave careful consideration to the manner in which it should approach its task and to the methods of work it should adopt. In accordance with the terms of Commission resolution 20 (XXXVI), the Group adopted methods of work designed to enable it to respond as effectively as possible to the information it received and to perform its functions in the most expeditious manner. The Group also considered it essential, in the pursuit of its humanitarian function, not to interrupt contacts with Governments in the periods between sessions. It, therefore, authorized its Chairman to transmit any urgent reports of enforced or involuntary disappearances received between sessions immediately by means of a cable to the Government of the country concerned.

81. This urgent action procedure has proved in many cases to be effective in clarifying cases of disappearances. It has enabled the Group to be continuously available to the families of missing persons and to act with the sense of urgency which is required to save human lives. Furthermore, the urgent action procedure has in many cases facilitated the investigations carried out by Governments and may have helped to prevent the occurrence of other cases.

82. The application of this procedure has been improved over the years and the Group has accepted the principle that all reports received between sessions and which provide reliable information on disappearances that occurred within the three months preceding receipt by the Group, should be transmitted to the Government by means of a cable from the Chairman of the Working Group. Under the discretionary power conferred upon him, the Chairman, in approving such urgent action cables, keeps in mind that the reports thus transmitted must contain sufficient elements for meaningful investigations . . . .

84. Since its creation, the Working Group has transmitted to the Governments concerned 1,121 cases under the urgent action procedure (68 in 1981; 504 in 1982; 354 in 1983; 195 in 1984). It was possible to clarify 216 of those cases - a considerably higher percentage than the clarifications obtained on transmissions under the ordinary procedure. In many instances several cases were transmitted in a single cable.

NOTES AND QUESTIONS

1. What reasons does the Group give for adopting an urgent action procedure? Are there other reasons why an immediate response to a recent disappearance might be necessary?

2. How fast should the Group respond to information regarding recent disappearances? Are there advantages and disadvantages of setting a deadline for response by the Group? What about a deadline for the government to answer?

3. What do data regarding clarification of urgent actions compared with ordinary transmittals suggest about the effectiveness of the urgent action procedure? Should rapporteurs adopt similar procedures? Might differences in the work of rapporteurs make an urgent procedure less effective than it appears to be for disappearances?

4. The Special Rapporteur on summary and arbitrary executions responds to communications "containing allegations of imminent or threatened summary executions which appear[] *prima facie* relevant to his mandate" by sending a message via cable to the government involved, reporting information concerning the allegations. For a summary of messages sent in 1988 and government replies, see *Report of the Special Rapporteur on Summary and Arbitrary Executions*, U.N. Doc. E/CN.4/1990/22, at 3 (1990).

5. The Special Rapporteur on torture also has an urgent action procedure. *See Report of the Special Rapporteur on Torture*, U.N. Doc. E/CN.4/1990/ 17, at 5 (1989).

ANNUAL REPORTS OF THE WORKING GROUP

The mandate of the Working Group, like the mandates of theme rapporteurs, requires submission of annual reports to the Commission on Human Rights. The Group's recent reports begin with a brief description of its activities during the year, followed by a summary of information regarding the Group's actions as to each country regarding which it has received information of disappearances, and finishing with conclusions and recommendations on the problems. This excerpt on Peru from the Group's 1989 report illustrates the type of information the reports include on specific countries:

Report of the Working Group on Enforced or Involuntary Disappearances, U.N. Doc. E/CN.4/1989/18, at 61-64 (1989) (footnotes omitted):

Peru
Information reviewed and transmitted to the Government

225. The Working Group has recorded its activities in relation to disappearances in Peru in its last four reports to the Commission.

226. During 1988, the Working Group transmitted to the Government of Peru 226 newly reported cases of disappearance, 170 of them alleged to have occurred in 1988. Forty-four cases were transmitted by a letter dated 20 June 1988, seven by a letter of 30 September 1988, 55 by a letter dated 9 December 1988 and 120 by various cables under the urgent action procedure. By the same letters, the Group retransmitted to the Government a total of 72 cases containing additional information received from the sources. As regards the 61 cases transmitted by the Working Group in December 1988, in accordance with its methods of work, it must be understood that the Government could not respond prior to the adoption of the present report.

227. By a letter of 20 June 1988, the Government was reminded of the outstanding cases and, by letters of 14 April, 7 July, 30 August, 30 September and 9 December 1988, the Working Group advised the Government that 66 cases had been considered clarified on the basis of replies received from the sources.

228. By its letter of 30 September 1988, the Working Group also expressed concern regarding the protection and security of members of relatives' organizations who had allegedly been subjected to harassment and death threats.

229. The files of the Working Group were revised and it was found that four cases had been duplicated. The statistics were adjusted and the Government was informed accordingly.

Information and views received from relatives of missing persons or non-governmental organizations

230. The cases transmitted during 1988 were submitted by Amnesty International, the Andean Commission of Jurists (CAJ), the Episcopal Social Action Commission (CEAS), the Human Rights Association (APRODEH), the Human Rights Commission (COMISEDH) and the Federation of Yanesha Indigenous Communities of Peru (FECONAYA). The reported disappearances occurred between June 1987 and October 1988 in the departments of Ayacucho (104), Apurimac (42), Huancavelica (17), Lima (3), Loreto (4), San Martin (51) and Huanuco (5). For the great majority of the cases, army personnel in uniform were reportedly responsible for the disappearance; in a few cases, members of the Peruvian Investigatory Police (PIP) or the navy were allegedly identified. In many cases, the relatives indicated the barracks where the missing person had been taken after the arrest, but officials in those barracks had denied the detention. In fact, detentions leading to disappearances were generally carried out openly by uniformed members of the armed forces, sometimes acting with the Civil Defence Groups, in the presence of witnesses; sometimes several persons had been detained and later disappeared, despite the fact that entire peasant communities had been present during such military operations.

231. The above-mentioned organizations also provided a number of general reports on human rights in Peru, including their evaluation of the situation in relation to disappearances. In those reports it was recalled, *inter alia*, that for more than eight years Peru had been ravaged by a conflict between the Government and the terrorist movement Sendero Luminoso (Shining Path), which had claimed more than 11,000 lives. The task of ending that violence had been made even more

difficult by the emergence of another guerrilla movement — Movimiento Revolucionario Tupac Amaru (MRTA). The Sendero Luminoso strategy was to wage a protracted guerrilla war against the cities from Peru's mountainous rural areas. It seemed to be strongest in the southern Andean Departments of Ayacucho, Apurimac and Huancavelica. MRTA had grown chiefly in the urban centres as an alternative to Sendero Luminoso. However, in November 1987, MRTA had significantly broadened the scope of its operations when it had successfully occupied a town in the rural Department of San Martin. The Government's main response to the guerrilla challenges had been to declare a state of emergency in approximately 30 of Peru's 180 provinces to be administered by the armed forces. Disappearances and extrajudicial executions continued to be reported on an almost daily basis in those areas. It was a matter of great concern that the number of disappearances had again sharply increased during 1988.

232. Non-governmental organizations stated that, although many detainees who had been missing for weeks or months were subsequently released without charges, former victims of prolonged secret detention had described being tortured and threatened with death; other missing persons had been found dead.

233. The reports received by the Working Group stated that the testimonies of the persons who had reappeared highlighted and confirmed the ways in which enforced disappearances were carried out by members of the security, military and police forces: they concealed their identity, used false names, covered their faces, wore field uniforms and drove army vehicles. According to the sources, clandestine detention centres existed in military barracks and posts such as "Los Cabitos" BIM-51 Barracks, the Political-Military Command Headquarters in the city of Ayacucho, the Castropampa Barracks in Huanta and "La Oroya" BIM-34 Barracks in Pampa Cangallo, where torture was a common practice and it had been reported that doctors took part in torture sessions. If any questions were asked by relatives, the presence of detainees at those places was denied. The same testimonies had helped to ascertain the whereabouts of other missing detainees and indicated their appalling physical condition.

234. According to non-governmental organizations, a special commission of public prosecutors (fiscales), sent by the Office of the Attorney-General (Ministerio Público) to rural areas of Ayacucho to investigate reports of grave violations of human rights committed by the armed forces, had actively investigated cases of disappearance and succeeded in locating a number of missing persons. Public prosecutors reported that many of those released from military custody had visible signs of having been tortured; several police doctors who had failed to register the physical condition of such prisoners when they were received into police custody from the military had been charged with obstructing justice. Furthermore, the public prosecutors had complained of the obstruction and lack of co-operation and respect that they had experienced when dealing with the military authorities during their investigations in the Ayacucho emergency zone.

235. Despite the fact that a large number of persons had reappeared and made lengthy statements to the special commission of public prosecutors in Ayacucho, it had only been possible to institute criminal proceedings in one case of disappearance. That was because, for the purpose of a criminal trial, Peruvian law required full identification of the person presumed to be guilty, something that was extremely difficult to prove because such acts were generally carried out by persons who

remained completely anonymous. As far as legal protection against disappearances is concerned, writs of *habeas corpus* on behalf of persons detained or missing had little effect; although the formalities were observed, the results were by and large negative and the cases were not effectively investigated.

236. The information received by the Working Group included a number of demands made by relatives of missing persons and human rights organizations to the President of the Republic and other authorities, such as the establishment of a special commission of inquiry into disappearances, which would include among its members representatives of the Catholic Church, the relatives, parliament, human rights organizations and eminent figures known for their work in protecting human rights and human life; explicit arrangements for trials for human rights violations committed by the military and the police in the course of their duties to be held in the ordinary courts so as to ensure impartiality; the repeal of Act No. 24.150, which grants unlawful and anti-constitutional powers to the political-military commands in the zones under a state of emergency, favouring conditions that are propitious for disappearances and other attacks against the lives of individuals; the adoption and ratification by parliament of the United Nations Convention against Torture and other Cruel, Inhuman or Degrading Treatment or Punishment; the creation of a central register containing information on detainees to be reported within a maximum of 24 hours of arrest; an immediate end to the enforced disappearance of detainees, which should be condemned as a crime against humanity.

237. The above-mentioned organizations also reported that the National Association of Relatives of Abducted Persons and Disappeared Detainees in the Zones under a State of Emergency in Peru (ANFASEP) was subjected to constant harassment and intimidation and that death threats against its Executive Committee had been conveyed personally to the President and one of the members of the Committee by an officer of the intelligence service at the headquarters in Ayacucho.

238. Finally, human rights organizations informed the Working Group promptly of their own findings in relation to cases of disappearance, thereby clarifying 67 cases.

Information and views received from the Government

239. By letters dated 6 and 17 October and 1 November 1988, the Government provided replies on 12 cases of disappearance. Regarding 11 of those cases the Government indicated that, according to the information provided by the Ministry of Defence, it had not been possible to establish where the persons concerned [were] or that they had not been arrested or detained by forces answerable to the Ministry of Defence. In the remaining case, the Government indicated that the person had been arrested, held in PIP custody and later released in accordance with a judge's decision.

240. The Permanent Mission of Peru to the United Nations Office at Geneva also sent the Working Group a request from the Ministry of Defence that cases transmitted to the Government should contain, in addition to the information required by the Working Group, further identity data, the precise domicile of the missing person and a clear identification of the source, including identity data and domicile of the latter. In that connection, the Working Group replied that efforts would be made to obtain as much information as possible, but that cases containing

the basic elements required would continue to be transmitted to the Government, as indicated in the Working Group's methods of work (see E/CN.4/1988/19, paras. 16-30) and as endorsed by the Commission on Human Rights.

Statistical summary

I. Cases reported to have occurred in 1988	170
II. Outstanding cases	1,361
III. Total number of cases transmitted to the Government by the Working Group	1,621
IV. Government responses	
(a) Number of cases on which the Government has provided one or more specific responses	179
(b) Cases clarified by the Government's responses[a]	78
V. Cases clarified by non-governmental sources[b]	182

[a] Persons detained: 7

Persons arrested and released: 41

Persons who obtained a voter's card after the date of their alleged
   disappearance: 29

Person found dead: 1

[b] Persons whose bodies were found and identified: 35

Persons released from detention: 117

Persons in prison: 25

Person wounded in a summary execution and subsequently able to return
   home: 1

Persons taken to a hospital after detention: 2

Person at liberty: 1

Person in military service: 1

NOTES AND QUESTIONS

1. The Working Group visited Peru in 1985 and 1986. Excerpts from reports on those visits are reprinted later in this chapter. Compare the tone of the Group's reports on those visits with the 1988 report, excerpted above.

2. Commentators have criticized the generality and statistical approach of the Working Group's reports because it "tends to dehumanize the problem of disappearances." *See* Fitzpatrick, *U.N. Action with Respect to "Disappearances" and Summary or Arbitrary Executions,* 5 AIUSA Legal Support Network Newsletter 35, 39 (Fall 1988).

Do you think the Group's approach dehumanizes the problem? Would reports be more valuable if the Group reprinted allegations and government responses in full? What are advantages and disadvantages of that approach? Would the approach conflict with the Group's goals of discretion and clarification without judgment?

Professor Fitzpatrick comments that the "Working Group has now struck a rough balance between a statistical and narrative approach in its reports and the statistical presentation is actually quite helpful for ascertaining and comparing the rate of governmental responses." *Id.*

Do you agree? Can you think of other reasons the statistical summaries might be useful? While maintaining its nonjudgmental stance, what could the Group do to make reports more helpful for human rights advocates?

3. The 1989 report of the Rapporteur on summary or arbitrary executions, like the Group's report, lists situations he has addressed by country. *See* U.N. Doc. E/CN.4/1989/25 (1989). Unlike the Group's report, however, he provides no statistical summary for each country. He summarizes the contents of allegations transmitted to governments and their replies, if any, rather than taking the more general approach of the Working Group. In earlier years he did not organize the information in his reports by country. Commentators have criticized those earlier reports as being difficult to use in evaluating the situation in individual countries. *See* Kamminga, *The Thematic Procedures of the UN Commission on Human Rights*, 33 Netherlands Int'l L. Rev. 299, 315 (1987).

THE ROLE OF THE INTERNATIONAL COMMITTEE OF THE RED CROSS

The Working Group has refused to investigate disappearances that take place in a situation of armed conflict. That refusal has been based in part on a desire to avoid overlapping with the work of the International Committee of the Red Cross ("ICRC"). The ICRC is a nongovernmental organization that works for disinterested implementation of humanitarian law.

The four 1949 Geneva Conventions and their two Protocols constitute the main treaties of humanitarian law. The full protection of the Conventions applies only to armed conflicts between or among states and occupations by one state of another's territory. Protocol I extends protection to armed conflicts "in which peoples are fighting against colonial domination and alien occupation and against racist regimes in the exercise of their right of self-determination." Protocol II extends lesser protections to civil wars in which each side controls part of the state's territory. Other non-international armed conflict, however, is governed by only common article 3 of the Conventions, which prescribes protections for persons not taking part in the hostilities.

Jan Egeland has evaluated ICRC action on disappearances in his Humanitarian Initiatives Against Political "Disappearances" (1982). The Geneva Conventions, when their full protection applies, authorize the ICRC to search for victims and to maintain a Central Tracing Agency that collects information on prisoners of war and civilians in occupied territories and searches for missing persons. In internal armed conflict, common article 3 allows the ICRC to offer its services to the parties to the conflict. As Egeland points out, however, disappearances occur most frequently in situations of internal disturbances — situations that involve the use of force to maintain order without reaching the level of non-international conflict protected by common article 3. *Id.* at 27. Though the protections of the Geneva Conventions do not apply to such situations, he argues that the ICRC's right to take action under its own statute protecting victims of armed conflicts provides it with authority to investigate disappearances even where no "armed conflict" exists. *Id.* at 27-34. The ICRC expressed concern about disappearances in its Resolution II (XXIV) of 1981, *id.* at 57, which recommends that "the ICRC take any appropriate action which might reveal the fate of missing persons." *Id.* at 58.

NOTES AND QUESTIONS

1. Do you think the Working Group's refusal to investigate disappearances in situations of armed conflicts makes sense?

2. Might ICRC work overlap that of the Group, assuming the ICRC follows the initiative toward investigating disappearances outlined in Mr. Egeland's study? Would overlap necessarily be bad? Are there other situations in which jurisdictions of human rights machineries overlap?

3. For a suggestion that human rights groups should utilize humanitarian law as well as human rights law when investigating violations, see Weiss-brodt, *The Role of International Organizations in the Implementation of Human Rights and Humanitarian Law in Situations of Armed Conflict,* 21 Vand. J. Transnat'l L. 313 (1988).

4. Overlaps occur also between and among the jurisdictions of theme procedures. An individual may be the victim of different violations; for example, a disappeared person may also be tortured and then summarily executed. Should theme procedures apportion responsibility for overlapping cases?

5. Chapter 13 examines humanitarian law and the ICRC's work to implement that law in more detail. Readers should consult that chapter.

Report of the Working Group on Enforced or Involuntary Disappearances, Addendum at 1-2, 30-32, U.N. Doc. E/CN.4/1986/18/Add.1 (1986) (footnotes omitted):

Report on the visit to Peru by two members of the Working Group on Enforced or Involuntary Disappearances (17-22 June 1985)

I. INTRODUCTION

1. Upon the invitation of the Government of Peru, two members of the Working Group on Enforced or Involuntary Disappearances, Mr. Toine van Dongen and Mr. Luis Varela Quirós, visited Peru from 17 to 22 June 1985 on the Group's behalf. The purpose of the present report on their mission should be understood as an effort to provide the Commission on Human Rights, as the Working Group's parent body, with an analysis of the situation of disappearances in Peru. It must be emphasized that the report relates primarily to the situation as the mission's members found it in June 1985. It therefore only covers facts and developments until that point in time.

2. In the conduct of the visit the two members of the Working Group were received by the President of the Republic, the Prime Minister and Minister for Foreign Affairs, the Ministers of the Interior and Justice, the President of the Supreme Court, the Attorney-General (*Fiscal de la Nación*), the Joint Command of the Armed Forces, the Political-Military Commander of National Security Sub-Zone Nr. 5 and other high officials of the Government as well as by local authorities in Ayacucho and Huanta. The members also met a great number of witnesses, relatives of missing persons and representatives of their associations as well as organizations dealing with human rights in general. Dignitaries of the Roman Catholic Church and its Episcopal Social Action Committee (CEAS), representatives of universities, educational and national development institutions, academicians and members of the Peruvian Parliament, the bar and the media were also heard. During the short time available, every effort was made to obtain from different segments of Peruvian political, legal, religious and intellectual life a maximum of views on the complex socio-political environment in which enforced or involuntary disappearances developed. The meetings both with officials and non-governmental sources were not only limited to the capital of Lima, but further expanded during the Group's visit to the cities of Ayacucho and Huanta on 20 and 21 June. The mission's members wish to stress that they received every co-operation and assistance from the Peruvian Government in the organization of their meetings with officials and did not encounter any obstacles in receiving private informants, witnesses, or relatives of missing persons. They were, however, not allowed to visit military compounds.

3. As the Working Group's mandate is limited to the examination of questions relevant to enforced or involuntary disappearances, the present report focuses on that phenomenon. Thus, allegations of summary or arbitrary executions and torture, that were brought to the attention of the two members of the Working Group could not be dealt with on their merits in the framework of this report.

4. Chapter II discusses the context of violence in which disappearances have occurred. Chapter III briefly explains the nation's legal and institutional framework in which the problem has to be considered. Chapter IV describes the main characteristics of individual cases of disappearances which were brought to the Group's attention, the mechanics involved as reported by relatives and witnesses, and the steps taken by them before the authorities; it further gives an appreciation of the quality of the evidence by quoting some typical testimonies and provides a detailed statistical summary; the chapter also contains a graph showing the development of the phenomenon, based on the date of the cases of disappearances which the Group has transmitted to the Government of Peru. In chapter V the position of the Government of Peru and of other official sources, such as the Office

of the Attorney-General, is reflected; chapter VI describes the different non-governmental sources from which the Working Group has received information; chapter VII contains observations on social and economic consequences. Finally, concluding observations are presented in chapter VIII of the report.

5. It should be born in mind that, as a matter of principle, the Working Group on Enforced or Involuntary Disappearances discharges its mandate in a humanitarian spirit, taking a non-accusatory approach. The mission two of its members have undertaken in Peru should be viewed in the same light. . . .

VIII. CONCLUDING OBSERVATIONS

101. The Working Group thanks the Government of Peru and appreciates its invitation to come and visit the country, during what are, no doubt, trying times, and the measure of co-operation that the members of the mission received.

102. The Working Group is not a court of law and hence is not called upon to establish the guilt or innocence of individuals in relation to specific allegations. Instead, in addition to clarifying cases, it is called upon, at a higher level of abstraction, to establish what the mechanics are and who is involved in a given question of enforced or involuntary disappearances, with a view to informing the Commission accordingly. Therefore, the standards of evidence to be met by prosecutors and to be applied by judges in criminal cases do not come into play. Nonetheless, the Group is bound to evaluate any situation of disappearances in the light of all material and testimonies available to it after carefully weighing their veracity.

103. The situation of Peru is not an enviable one. In addition to climatic disasters and a heavily mortgaged economy, the country has been beset by a brutal guerrilla organization [(*Sendero Luminoso*)]. Under the circumstances, the country requires extraordinary leadership, deeply committed to human rights, to wage an effective fight against Sendero Luminoso's terror without resorting to counter-terror. That task is in any event a formidable one.

104. Ironically, Sendero Luminoso resorted to actual use of violence for the first time on the eve of democratic government following 12 years of military rule over the country. There can be no doubt that since then a great many disappearances have taken place in Peru. Indeed, the vast majority of cases denounced to the Attorney-General in the course of the ensuing five years would seem to be genuine cases of missing persons, even if one deducts the number of cases where people listed as missing evidently registered on the Peruvian electoral roll after the alleged date of disappearance.

105. There is considerable evidence that Sendero Luminoso has abducted people, although mainly with a view to forcing them to join its ranks and less as a method of reprisal. Generally, disappearances do not seem to figure prominently among the methods of elimination Sendero has applied. However, [given] the attraction the movement is shown to have, particularly for the young, it seems likely that a number of people listed as missing may in reality have enrolled with Sendero Luminoso voluntarily.

106. It appears from the overwhelming number of testimonies and statements from a wide variety of sources that the largest proportion of disappearances occurred in the course of the counter-insurgency campaign undertaken by the various branches of the armed forces and the police since the end of 1982. . . .

107. A state of emergency has been declared in Peru, formally suspending

four rights and freedoms from which derogation may indeed be made under the terms of the International Covenant on Civil and Political Rights, to which Peru is a party. The area, to which the state of emergency applies in particular, centers on Ayacucho City and encompasses all provinces where Senderistas have spread their subversive activities. Under the law, the Political-Military Command in the area has taken full control not only over all armed forces and the entire police, but also over all civil authorities as well. From there only a slim line of authority runs to the Government in Lima. Thus, as of 1982 the armed forces were granted a great deal of latitude in fighting Sendero Luminoso and in restoring public order as they saw fit, while their actions were no longer subject to ordinary democratic controls. As a result the stage was set for a situation where disappearances and concomitant violations of human rights were almost bound to take place sooner or later.

108. Relatives of missing persons have in most cases turned to the authorities and denounced the disappearance; yet to little avail. Indeed, some sort of institutional paralysis in matters pertaining to the protection of human rights seems to have settled on the emergency zone. Prosecutors are being criticized for not carrying out proper investigations to identify the responsible parties or ensure the release of persons believed to be detained. Prosecutors, for their part, maintain that their efforts are frustrated by the military and police authorities and that they lack proper resources. They further point to the fact that the Investigatory Police (PIP), which is supposed to assist them in their work, is placed under military command. The military authorities contend that they are not responsible for disappearances and remain silent about their actions under the state of emergency. The judiciary refers all cases involving military personnel to military courts. It appears, therefore, that theoretically a solid system of law, which when strictly applied ought to ensure protection of human rights, is not made to function properly. As a result, few of those who have disappeared are actually acknowledged to have been arrested and there are no known cases of those thought responsible having been convicted.

109. Human rights organizations and family associations left a favourable impression, generally having provided the mission and the Working Group with solid and well-documented information. Despite the climate of fear that is said to have permeated the Ayacucho area, hundreds of witnesses openly came to see the mission's members, invariably under the eyes of the military. Amazing too was the unbridled freedom of the media, which reported extensively on the mission's activities. . . .

110. The question of violence in Peru reflects a serious and complex interrelationship of socio-economic and political factors which are a legacy from centuries ago. In Ayacucho, the severe underdevelopment of the area has been a major contributing factor. It would appear, therefore, that only through a comprehensive development strategy can one hope to render the social fabric of the affected population more resilient in the long run. Then perhaps people would better withstand the perverting influence of violent movements and lead a normal life at last.

111. In the short term, it would occur to the members of the mission that a number of measures could be considered that might alleviate some of the aspects of the problem of disappearances. First of all, security and personal safety seem of the essence, so that the people in the towns and countryside will no longer feel

threatened by violence from all sides. Secondly, members of the police and the armed forces operating in the area should be taught the basic concepts of the Peruvian legal system and be trained in human rights matters. Thirdly, both the judiciary and the Office of the Attorney-General need to be effectively guaranteed the co-operation of all branches of the executive, notably the armed forces, as well as the resources to carry out their functions properly. Lastly, in the light of the acute hardship of the many relatives of disappeared people, it would appear that some form of relief programme is called for in order to ease their sorry lot.

Report of the Working Group on Enforced or Involuntary Disappearances, Addendum at 1, 13-14, U.N. Doc. E/CN.4/1987/15/Add.1 (1986);

Report on a second visit to Peru by two members of the Working Group on Enforced or Involuntary Disappearances (3-10 October 1986):

I. INTRODUCTION

1. In June 1985, two members of the Working Group, Mr. Toine van Dongen and Mr. Luis Varela Quirós, visited Peru in response to an invitation addressed to the Group by the Government of President Fernando Belaúnde Terry to send a mission to Peru. The Government of President Alan García Pérez, which assumed power on 28 July 1985, extended a further invitation to the Working Group for a second visit to the country. Mr. van Dongen and Mr. Varela Quirós again represented the Working Group on that visit, which took place from 3 to 10 October 1986.

2. The two members of the Working Group again received ample co-operation from the Government of Peru in the conduct of the visit and were able freely to meet all witnesses, relatives of missing persons and other private sources they wished to hear. They were received on behalf of the Government by the Ministers for Foreign Affairs, Justice and the Interior, the President of the Senate and members of the human rights commissions of both houses of the Peruvian parliament, the Attorney-General (Fiscal de la Nación), the Joint Command of the Armed Forces, the Acting Political-Military Commander in Ayacucho and members of parliament and officials of the Executive and the Judiciary, in both Lima and Ayacucho. The members of the mission heard many relatives of missing persons, as well as representatives of organizations dealing with human rights in general. They also met dignitaries of the Roman Catholic Church and its Episcopal Social Action Committee (CEAS), academic staff of the University of Huamanga (Ayacucho) and representatives of the bar and the media. The members again paid a one-day visit to Ayacucho. They were not permitted to visit military compounds.

3. The present report updates the report on the Group's first visit to Peru (E/CN.4/ 1986/18/Add.1) and should be read in conjunction with it. The present report relates the developments which have occurred since President García Pérez took office as they were conveyed to the members of the mission. . . .

V. CONCLUDING OBSERVATIONS

42. The Working Group is grateful to the Peruvian Government for providing an opportunity to review the progress made in combating the phenomenon of disappearances in Peru, following its first visit in June of 1985.

43. As already stated in last year's report, in assessing the situation of missing persons in Peru, the Working Group has to pay due regard to the overall context

of violence in which disappearances have been reported to it. For, in both intellectual and practical terms, it is not feasible to divorce the issue of disappearances completely from related violations of human rights or from the socio-political processes that have engendered them. If it did so, the Group would not be exercising its mandate properly in the manner consistently supported over the years by the Commission on Human Rights.

44. Being faced with a terrorist movement such as Sendero Luminoso amidst a variety of urgent economic and social problems is not an enviable position for any government to be in. Terrorist violence rages unabated, without the least respect for life, limb or property. Worse still, although for a long time it was confined to some provinces of Ayacucho and neighbouring departments, insurgence has now spread to the Departments of Cerro de Pasco (north of Ayacucho) and of Cuzco and Puno (to the south) and the capital itself has become affected. In consequence, the area covered by the state of emergency has been extended.

45. Clearly, in its contacts with the Working Group, the previous Government was loath to admit that disappearances had indeed occurred in significant numbers and avoided apportioning responsibility for any excesses to the armed forces or the police. It was heartening, therefore, to note that the new President declared upon taking office that his administration would not fight ''barbarism with barbarism''. Indeed, that promise as well as concrete action bear witness to a firm resolve to call a halt to disappearances and other violations of human rights by government forces. Civil participation has been sought in finding long-term solutions for internal strife and in promoting the cause of human rights. Establishing the National Council for Human Rights is but one example. The present Government has also resolutely opened its doors to international scrutiny of Peru's human rights record. It has taken a much more co-operative attitude towards the Group, swiftly responding to cases transmitted to it and making immediate efforts to clarify them.

46. In parliament, interest for human rights seems to have increased markedly and this had led to the introduction of legislation designed to remedy lacunae in Peruvian human rights law.

47. One of the major concerns expressed in the previous report concerned the wide latitude granted by the central Government to the armed forces and the police to fight Sendero Luminoso and restore public order in the manner they saw fit. At the same time it was argued that such latitude would almost inevitably lead sooner or later to disappearances and concomitant violations of human rights. It would seem that the present administration has made great strides towards regaining control over the counter-insurgency strategy followed by the armed forces. Consequently, the incidence of disappearances has decreased considerably, particularly since the end of 1985. . . .

48. However, disappearances still continue to occur in Peru on an appreciable scale, and other forms of violence at the hands of government forces appear to have increased, particularly since the middle of 1986. The Working Group has transmitted to the Government some 160 cases that occurred in the emergency zone between August 1985 and November 1986. About half of these cases have subsequently been clarified: detention was acknowledged or subjects were turned over to the police by the armed forces or released. While this shows a welcome increase in the measure of responsiveness of the armed forces, it is also indicative of the

practice of short-term disappearances as a method of counter-insurgency in breach of Peruvian law.

49. In last year's report attention was drawn to what was described as some sort of institutional paralysis pertaining to the protection of human rights in the emergency zone. Little progress can be reported in that regard. In the majority of cases prosecutors are still obstructed in their efforts to follow up on denunciations of disappearances. The Judiciary seems ill at ease with *habeas corpus* proceedings, which in any case meet with lack of co-operation from the respondents. Almost without exception civilian courts refer cases involving military and police personnel to military courts, despite the fact that the Code of Military Justice does not cover homicide, maltreatment and the like. The broad powers concentrated in the hands of the military in the emergency zone further diminish the role which civil institutions might otherwise play in applying the rule of law.

50. Establishing a Human Rights Office under the auspices of the Attorney-General has admirably expedited the processing of cases of missing persons. Yet that fact in itself has not substantially enhanced the measure of protection extended to citizens at large. Undoubtedly, adequate access to registers of arrests maintained by the armed forces would have not only a curative but also a preventive effect. At any rate, the armed forces must be prevailed upon to co-operate more closely in the emergency zone with prosecutors and judicial authorities. Moreover, the latter are in dire need of material and human resources, as was pointed out in last year's report.

51. The situation of the victims among the indigenous population in the affected areas remains dismal. Humanitarian aid from national and international sources is an increasingly vital necessity. A long-term development strategy, designed to eliminate the poverty and neglect which are among the root causes of the Ayacuchan drama, is slowly getting under way, even though efforts have been set back by terrorist onslaughts.

52. Violence cannot be countered with violence alone. Only when the structural factors that contributed to the spiral of terror and counter-terror are properly dealt with, can there be any hope of preventing a recurrence of the excesses of the past. The Peruvian Government seems keenly aware of that fact. Its task remains a formidable one.

NOTES AND QUESTIONS

1. The Working Group's first report contained this statement:

> The Working Group at its first session came to the conclusion that one of the means by which it might deal with allegations of enforced or involuntary disappearances, and gain an understanding of the circumstances surrounding such allegations would be for it, through one or two of its members, to establish direct contact with those immediately concerned in such matters. The Group wrote to the Governments of those countries about which it had received expressions of concern relating to enforced or involuntary disappearances, asking if the Government would in principle be

disposed to invite the Group to visit the country in order to establish such direct contacts.

U.N. Doc. E.CN.4/1435, at 16 (1981).

Do you think that statement is consistent with the Working Group's original mandate? Is it a broad or narrow interpretation of the mandate? Do later versions of the mandate support the Group's interpretation?

2. In the next chapter there will be discussion of the on-site visit of the Inter-American Commission on Human Rights to Argentina. After having read chapter 6 on factfinding, consider ways in which the Group's visit to Peru is similar to the Inter-American Commission's visit to Argentina. In what ways is it different? What might explain the differences?

3. The Group conducted three on-site visits prior to the visits to Peru. On the first visit to Mexico in 1982 one commentator observed:

The Working Group's first mission to *Mexico* in 1982, was an embarrassing failure. Although the delegates met both senior government representatives and domestic human rights groups, in reality it appears that they were 'taken for a ride' by the Government. The Working Group was apparently so much taken by the 'co-operation' shown by the Mexican Government that it agreed not to further pursue 'disappearance' cases in Mexico. In return, the Government promised to inform the families of the 'disappeared' of the results of any investigations. Not surprisingly, no such information has been forthcoming and for several years the 'Mexican deal' remained one of the most serious blots on the record of the Working Group. By 1986, the Working Group's patience had finally run out and it transmitted 177 newly reported cases, much to the annoyance of the Mexican Government.

Kamminga, *The Thematic Procedures of the U.N. Commission on Human Rights*, 34 Netherlands Int'l L. Rev. 299, 312 (1987).

Do you think undue concern with obtaining governmental cooperation biased the Working Group's conclusions on its visits to Peru?

Kamminga was less critical of the Group's reports on the visits to Peru. In his view "the reader is left in little doubt that the delegates hold the Peruvian Government responsible for the large majority of 'disappearances' that have occurred." He goes so far as to conclude that the Working Group "came tantalizingly close to abandoning its traditional nonjudgmental style." *Id.* at 313. *See also* N. Rodley, The Treatment of Prisoners Under International Law 211-14 (1987) (discussing the Group's on-site visits and concluding that the Group in its Peruvian visit reports dropped its traditional agnosticism, unmistakably implying that the government was responsible for many disappearances).

Do you agree with that analysis of the Peru reports? Must the Working Group's nonjudgmental posture necessarily hinder its on-site visits? Which purposes do the Working Group's visits seek to achieve?

4. Kamminga also commented on the Group's visits to Cyprus in 1982 and Bolivia in 1984. *See* Kamminga, *supra*, at 312-13. The Group has conducted at least two on-site visits after the visits to Peru — to Guatemala in 1987 and to Colombia in 1988. *See Report of the Working Group on Enforced or Involuntary Disappearances*, U.N. Doc. E/CN.4/1989/18/Add.1 (1989) (Colombia); *Report of the Working Group on Enforced or Involuntary Disappearances*, U.N. Doc. E/CN.4/1988/19/Add.1 (1988) (Guatemala).

5. Note that the Group's "Methods of Work" contain no reference to on-site visits. Do you think it should adopt procedures for identifying situations that merit on-site visits and rules to govern the conduct of visits? Why might it be reluctant to prepare such procedures?

6. The rapporteurs have begun following the Group's lead in conducting on-site visits. The Special Rapporteur on summary or arbitrary executions has conducted several: three to Suriname (1984, 1987, 1989), one to Uganda in 1986, and one to Colombia in 1989. *See Report of the Special Rapporteur on Summary or Arbitrary Executions*, U.N. Doc. E/CN.4/1985/17, at Annex V (1985) (Suriname); *Report of the Special Rapporteur on Summary or Arbitrary Executions*, U.N. Doc. E/CN.4/1988/22, at Annex I (1988) (Suriname); *Report of the Special Rapporteur on Summary or Arbitrary Executions*, U.N. Doc. E/CN.4/1987/20, at Annex II (1987) (Uganda). *Report of the Special Rapporteur on Summary or Arbitrary Executions*, U.N. Doc. E/CN.4/1990/22, at 4 (1990). For Kamminga's comments on the first visit to Suriname and the visit to Uganda, see Kamminga, *supra*, at 313-14.

The Special Rapporteur on religious intolerance visited Bulgaria in 1987 and the Soviet Union in 1988. *See Report on Religious Intolerance*, U.N. Doc. E/CN.4/1988/45 (1988) (Bulgaria); *Report of the Special Rapporteur on Religious Intolerance*, U.N. Doc. E/CN.4/1989/44, at 49 (1989) (Soviet Union).

The Special Rapporteur on torture visited Argentina, Colombia, and Uruguay in 1987. *See Report of the Special Rapporteur on Torture, Addendum, Visit by the Special Rapporteur to Argentina, Colombia, and Uruguay*, U.N. Doc. E/CN.4/1988/17/Add.1 (1988). In 1988 he visited Peru, the Republic of Korea, and Turkey. *See Report of the Special Rapporteur on Torture*, U.N. Doc. E/CN.4/1989/15, at 32-48 (1989). In 1989 he visited Zaire. *Report of the Special Rapporteur, Visit of the Special Rapporteur to Zaire*, U.N. Doc. E/CN.4/1990/17/Add.1 (1990).

7. When this book was written, many of the problems identified in the Working Group's report on Peru remained unresolved. For further reading, see Americas Watch, Tolerating Abuses: Violations of Human Rights in Peru (1988); Amnesty International, Peru: 'Disappearances,' Torture and Summary Executions by Government Forces After the Prison Revolts of June 1986, AI Index: AMR/46/03/87 (1987); Nowak, *The Strained Human Rights Situation in Peru: Interview with Francisco Soberon Garrido, Coordinator of the Peruvian Human Rights Association APRODEH*, 6 Netherlands Q. Hum. Rts. 28 (No. 3, 1988); see also chapter 2, *supra*.

VI *WHAT ARE THE STANDARDS AND METHODS FOR FACTFINDING IN INTERNATIONAL HUMAN RIGHTS?*

A Hypothetical Factfinding Visit to Palau

A. INTRODUCTION

This chapter deals with an issue implicit in many of the previous
chapters — how human rights organizations can determine the veracity of

allegations that governments are violating international human rights norms. When human rights bodies — such as the Human Rights Committee and the Inter-American Commission — examine individual communications, they must reach a decision as to the truth of the facts alleged in the petition. Likewise, examination of state reports — such as the Human Rights Committee process discussed previously — involve an element of factfinding. The present chapter, however, examines the factfinding issues that arise when an organization — whether intergovernmental or nongovernmental — decides to investigate the human rights situation in a particular country.

In order to put those issues into perspective, readers will act as members of a nongovernmental organization (NGO) planning a factfinding visit to Palau. Readers will determine the appropriate procedures for the visit based on the scholarly commentary and illustrations of factfinding investigations contained in this chapter.

The first factfinding illustration involves the on-site factfinding experience of the Inter-American Commission. Although the situation of the Inter-American Commission, as an intergovernmental organization (IGO), may differ in some respects from that of an NGO conducting an on-site visit, much of the Commission's experience is applicable to NGOs. The second illustration involves an NGO undertaking a factfinding investigation in a situation where an on-site visit is not possible.

The chapter closes with material on the impact of factfinding. That material will require readers to consider what effect their investigation can have on the human rights situation in Palau and how to tailor their procedures in order to have the maximum positive impact.

B. QUESTIONS

You will act as members of an NGO undertaking an investigation of human rights violations in Palau. You should prepare rules of procedure for the investigation, including procedures for both an on-site visit and the collection of information outside Palau. The procedures should cover all the stages of the investigation, from the decision to undertake the investigation to the preparation and dissemination of a report on the results of the investigation. Before preparing the rules of procedure, read the materials in the chapter and consider the following questions.

1. Under what circumstances should an organization decide to conduct a factfinding visit? What is the goal sought in conducting such a visit?

2. Should permission to conduct a visit be obtained? What assurances should be requested from the government before the visit commences? Does it make a difference whether the sending organization is an IGO (intergovernmental organization) or an NGO (nongovernmental organization)?

3. Why would a government accept factfinding visits? Can a government misuse its willingness to receive a factfinding visit as a public relations measure? What can the sending organization do to prevent misuse by the government of the fact that a visit has occurred?

4. What should an organization do if a government refuses to grant permission to enter its territory and conduct the study? Can a study be done without a fact finding visit? What factfinding techniques can be utilized without a visit?

5. What are potential advantages and disadvantages of conducting a fact-finding visit? Is the information obtained on a visit necessarily more reliable than that available from sources outside the country?

6. What factors should be considered when selecting members for a fact-finding visit?

7. What research should be done before a factfinding delegation enters a country? How detailed should the terms of reference be?

8. What factors should be considered in deciding whom to interview and what to see?

9. What can be done to protect witnesses who provide information?

10. When evaluating the statements of witnesses, what can be done to help ensure that the information is reliable?

11. How can a factfinding delegation avoid being misled by government-staged testimony, model prisons, and other deceptive measures?

12. What are potential advantages or disadvantages of developing procedural rules for the use of factfinding delegations?

13. At what points in its visit to Argentina did the Inter-American Commission meet with the Argentine government? When should discussions with the government in Palau be scheduled?

14. What are potential advantages or disadvantages of issuing preliminary recommendations to the government at the end of a visit? Should those recommendations, if made, be released to the media?

15. Should factfinders attempt to improve directly the human rights situation in a country during a visit or should they remain dispassionate observers? After the visit is completed, should factfinders develop recommendations to the government or should they leave that to the organization which sponsored the visit?

16. What are potential advantages and disadvantages of publishing accounts such as "Discovering Disappeared Persons: A Staff Member's Notes" or writing factfinding guidelines on such issues?

17. What standards of proof should a factfinding delegation use while preparing its report?

18. Should a delegation submit its report to the government for comment before publication? What are advantages and disadvantages of such an approach?

19. What impact can a factfinding visit have on the human rights situation of a country?

20. Are there other effective techniques for using information gathered during a visit other than publishing a report?

C. BACKGROUND ON PALAU

W. Butler, G. Edwards, & M. Kirby, Palau: A Challenge to the Rule of Law in Micronesia 4, 9-10, 13-14, 17-18, 23-38 (1988) (footnotes omitted):

Palau (earlier Pellew or Belau) is part of the cluster of the Pacific Islands known geographically and ethnically as Micronesia. . . .

On 18 July 1947, a Trusteeship Agreement for the Trust Territory of the Pacific Islands, entered into by the United States of America and the Security Council of the United Nations on 2 April 1947 was approved by the United States Congress. Under the terms of the agreement, "full powers of administration, legislation and jurisdiction" were "granted" to the United States. . . .

The Trusteeship Agreement authorizing United States administration of that part of the Trust Territory of the Pacific Islands which includes Palau is still in force. . . .

[T]he United States of America in 1947, as the Administering Power under the Trusteeship Agreement with the United Nations and pursuant to Article 76 of the U.N. Charter, owed a duty as Trustee to:

". . . promote the political, economic, social and educational advancement of the inhabitants of the trust territories, and their progressive development towards self government or independence as may be appropriate to the particular circumstances of each territory and its peoples and the freely expressed wishes of the peoples concerned . . ." . . .

After many years there evolved a pattern in 1975 to the effect that the Northern Marianas were moving towards "commonwealth" status and the Marshalls, Federated States of Micronesia and Palau were tending towards "independent" republics.

The general plan was to allow these three states through processes of self-determination, to establish their own constitution and governmental institutions after which they would each enter into "Compacts of Free Association with the United States."

The Compacts of Free Association with the United States and the Federated States and the Marshall Islands were accepted in referendum in these States in 1983 and came into effect by a Proclamation of President Reagan on Nov. 3, 1986.

The Compacts generally allow for local independence and autonomy but delegate ultimate foreign affairs powers and some financial controls to the United States with a commitment by the United States to defend these countries against foreign intrusion. These Compacts all give the United States the right to use the territory for military purposes. These new political entities would also receive substantial financial support and subsidies from the U.S. conditional upon U.S. approval of development and spending plans.

[As part of the plan for obtaining independence, in April 1979 the Palauan Constitutional Convention adopted a proposed constitution for Palau. The constitution, much to the dismay of the U.S., contained provisions which prohibited the use, testing, storage, or disposal of nuclear materials in Palau without the express approval of seventy-five percent of Palauans voting in a referendum on that question. The constitution also required seventy-percent voter approval for international agreements that would authorize such uses of nuclear materials in Palau.

Under pressure from the U.S., the Palauan legislature in July 1979 nullified the proposed constitution. Supporters of the constitution filed a lawsuit challenging the nullification and a referendum on the constitution was held. Ninety-two percent of those voting in the referendum approved the constitution. In August 1979, however, the Palauan High Court upheld the nullification, action that invalidated the referendum. The legislature established a Drafting Commission, boycotted by supporters of the original constitution. The Drafting Commission produced a constitution acceptable to the U.S. which, in October 1979, seventy-percent of Palauan voters rejected. In July 1980, seventy-eight percent of Palauans voting approved the original constitution.

The Compact of Free Association with Palau, which has been submitted to the voters of Palau in various forms six times since 1983, contains a provision allowing the U.S. to operate nuclear capable or nuclear propelled vessels or aircraft within the jurisdiction of Palau. This provision, under the Palauan Constitution, requires approval by three-quarters of the votes cast in the referendum on the Compact. The Compact has failed to receive the required approval in each referendum. The events surrounding the referendum in August 1987 and subsequent developments will be the focus of the proposed factfinding inquiry.]

A.   *Palau — January 1-July 1, 1987*

Any examination of the tragic events which occurred on Palau in September of 1987 requires some comment concerning the social and economic climate leading up to the decision of the legislature to provide for the August referendum.

[Palau has limited economic resources and virtually no industry. The government employs over sixty percent of the total workforce and relies heavily on subsidies from the U.S. government to meet its budget. The U.S., however, has not substantially increased its aid to Palau since the controversy over the nuclear-free constitution began. In addition to its refusal to increase aid, the U.S. encouraged foreign investors to lend a large amount of money to Palau in the early 1980's to build a power plant, stating that Palau would be able to repay the loans with the increased aid it would receive from the U.S. under the Compact. Repayment of those obligations contributed to Palau's insolvency. Those U.S. actions have led some Palauan citizens to accuse the U.S. of attempting to coerce Palau into accepting the Compact. The U.S. denies such accusations, but there is no doubt that Palau's location is strategic in terms of U.S. control over the Pacific region. The U.S., however, justifies its insistence on the right to use nuclear materials in Palau on Palau's request for military defense.]

It is well known in both Palau and the United States that Palau, in recent years, has not been fiscally solvent and that it is now constantly threatened with public bankruptcy.

Early in 1987 it became abundantly clear that appropriations for the fiscal years 1986 and 1987 would exceed the revenue of the National Government by approximately 5 million dollars. . . .

Faced with economic insolvency of this magnitude the government proceeded to take surgical action. Among other measures it . . . furlough[ed] the majority of the national government employees for lack of funds. About 900 out of 1331 employees were furloughed from July 8, 1987-October 1, 1987. . . .

B.   *The Legislative Sessions of July 1987*

It is hard for one not present on Palau during these times to imagine the climate of fear engendered as a consequence of the foregoing events. Heads of families and others were out of work. The thought of not being able to feed one's family or to make payments on a mortgage, or an auto loan or even to pay for the basic necessities of life gradually, during the months of June, July and August, developed into a state of hysteria which in turn resulted in violence, threats of violence, and intimidation described below.

As the pressure crescendoed, leaders of the government including President Salii, repeatedly assured the unemployed that the solution to all their problems was to be found in the ratification of the Compact of Free Association.

The reasoning was that if the Compact were ratified, subsidies from the United States would increase and the solvency of the government would return.

Many workers formed a "Furlough Committee". . . and the leadership began a concentrated effort to force the Palauan National Congress to adopt enabling legislation which would authorize two referenda:

1.   To amend the Constitution in order to allow adoption of a compact by a simple majority of those voting, and
2.   Submitting to the People of Palau, for the sixth time, the Compact of Free Association, this time requiring only a simple majority instead of the 75% vote required by the present constitution.

[In pursuance of these goals, the following events took place:]

1.   The Furlough Committee had surrounded the Legislative buildings and had pitched tents. It informed the Congress that they intended to remain there until the appropriate legislation was adopted.
2.   Many of the workers wore red bands on their heads which in Palau society is a well accepted symbol constituting a threat to those opposed to the committee.
3.   There was evidence that many were under the influence of alcohol and/or drugs.
4.   At times there was evidence of mob hysteria and a corresponding failure or inability of Palau's law enforcement agencies to curb the intimidation of the legislators. . . .

C.   *The Amendment Referendum and the Compact Vote of August 4, 1987 and August 21, 1987.*

In the foregoing climate and circumstances Republic of Palau Public Law #2-30 was passed by the legislature and was signed into law by President Salii on July 19, 1987. Pursuant to its provisions the referendum on the Amendment to the Constitution, which purported to amend the constitution so as to allow the Compact to be adopted by a 50% vote of those voting (thereby altering the constitutional requirement of 75%) was to be held on August 4, 1987.

The sixth vote on the Compact was to be held on August 21, 1987, in the event the proposed amendment was adopted on August 4th by a majority vote in three-quarters of the States.

These two events took place as scheduled. [The voters of Palau approved both these measures by a 73% majority.]

D.   *Legal Challenges to the Validity of the Legislation Authorizing the Amendment Referendum and the 5th Compact Referendum.*

Prior to the August 4th referendum and on July 29, 1987, in a case known as *Merep et al. vs. Salii et al.* (Civil Action 139-87) a complaint was filed in the Supreme Court of Palau requesting:

1.   A Declaratory Judgment that RPPL-2-30 authorizing the amendment referendum was null and void and unconstitutional; and
2.   A preliminary and permanent injunction enjoining the government from carrying out its August 4th votes [and 21st]. . . .

A hearing was held on August 18, 1987, on the plaintiff's motion for a temporary injunction to restrain the carrying out of the referendum of August 21, 1987. The hearing was heard before Chief Justice Nakamura, who refused to enjoin the plebescite itself. However, he enjoined the tabulation of the voting until the Full Court could consider the constitutional issues involved in the plaintiffs' challenge.

This decision angered not only the Palauan administration, but also some of the legislators, representatives of a number of States, and more importantly the Furloughed Workers Committee which immediately launched an organized attack against the Chief Justice.

1.   On August 19, 1987, the next day, at noon, a letter signed by members of the Legislature was hand-delivered at his residence accusing him of being:
     a.   "politically whitewashed,"
     b.   "involved in conflicts of interest,"
     c.   "biased,"
     d.   the letter also called into question the Chief Justice's integrity, and demanded his disqualification.
2.   On the same day, August 19, 1987, the Furloughed Government Employees Committee presented a petition signed by its members urging the Chief Justice:
     a.   to reverse himself,
     b.   threatening him with removal, and
     c.   accusing him of unethical conduct, etc.
3.   Also on the same day, August 19, 1987, prominent members of the Palau National Congress sent another letter to Lazarus E. Salii, President of the Republic, urging him to become actively involved in reversing a decision rendered by the Supreme Court enjoining the tabulation of votes.

This letter, among other things, accused the Chief Justice of being "highly politically motivated"; it accused the Chief Justice of a conflict of interest, stating that the "Chief Justice's brothers were over-zealous opponents of the Compact of Free Association"; and accused the Chief Justice of impropriety because a relationship "exists between the Chief Justice's spouse and her uncle the Ibedul, who has continuously stood in the way of a Compact of Free Association." The letter also stated that the Chief Justice should divorce himself from the case and allow his associates to hear the same. Furthermore, it accused the Chief Justice of having "knowingly and willingly plunged the judiciary branch into the political arena.". . .

> In August, 1987 the Chief Justice reversed himself and denied the motion for a preliminary injunction in full, and

> On August 25, 1987, the Chief Justice recused himself from the case and appointed Judge Hefner, an Associate Judge of the Supreme Court of Palau, a resident of Saipan, to sit in his place.

A hearing of this suit never took place for on August 28, 1987, the case was "settled" and, at that time, all constitutional objections to the August Referendum were, for a moment, put to rest.

On August 29, 1987, the Ibedul (Paramount Chief) informed the nation that he had made a satisfactory arrangement with President Salii whereby President Salii agreed to designate the Council of Chiefs of Palau, headed by the Ibedul, to be charged with "the responsibility of considering all requests by the United States government for land use rights within the Republic of Palau pursuant to the Compact of Free Association."

In return for this arrangement, the Ibedul agreed to cause the *Merep* case to be dismissed (although he was not a formal party in the lawsuit) thereby agreeing to withdraw all pending constitutional challenges to the August referenda.

E.   *Palauan Citizens Are Denied Access To Their Legal Institutions*

. . . When the news broke that the Ibedul had settled his action an important segment of Palauan Society took great exception. The women of Palau regarded the settlement as a "sellout." Palau traditionally is a matrilineal society. The women elders elect the chiefs and these processes have worked for the Palauans for centuries. The women, through their leaders, notably Gabriela Ngirmang, Tosie Keldermans, Rafaela Sumang and others immediately filed a similar challenge to the constitutionality of the August referendum.

Their case, known as *Ngirmang, et al. vs. Salii* (Civil Action #161-87) was filed on August 31, 1988, just two days after the settlement of *Merep*.

The pleadings in the action essentially repeated, almost word for word, the allegations of *Merep*.

All of the plaintiffs signed the complaint in person and because of their inability to retain counsel, they acted "pro se," i.e., on their own behalf.

On September 1st at 5:00 p.m., the government filed a Motion to Dismiss the suit alleging *res judicata* (citing *Merep* and other points). A hearing was set for September 8th at 2:00 p.m. before Judge Hefner.

[The following events occurred before the hearing:]

1. On September 3, 1987, Mr. Joel Toribiong issued a statement on behalf of the Government of Palau warning the plaintiffs that the Government would take every action to support the Compact.

2. On September 4, 1987, a Government employee named Nazario Tellames, driving a government vehicle arrived at the home of Roman Bedor, a prominent lawyer who had represented the Plaintiffs in *Merep*, and proceeded to cut his power lines. When intercepted, Tellames said that he had been given a list of homes to cut lines.

3. One hour later, on September 4, 1987, the same Tellames went to the home of Tosie Keldermans, a plaintiff in the last mentioned case (*Ngirmang, et al. vs. Salii*), and cut her power lines while she was cooking dinner.
4. On September 5, 1987, the Speaker of the House of Delegates returned from Guam where he had fled for a month as a result of threats to himself and his family. At 11:00 p.m. that evening a "red sedan" passed his house in which a person was indiscriminately firing shots in the air. One hour later, the same car returned and more shots were fired in a passby.
5. On September 6, 1987, a "red sedan," apparently the same, passed by the house of plaintiff Rafaela Sumang and several shots were fired in the air over her house.
6. On September 7, 1987, the day before the scheduled hearing before Judge Hefner, Rafaela Sumang and Gabriela Ngirmang requested police protection from Thomas O. Remengesau, Minister of Justice and Vice President of Palau. The request was refused.

    Later that night the electric power on Koror was cut off and a fire bomb exploded outside the home of plaintiff Gabriela Ngirmang and the Abai Ra Metal night club was bombed.
7. The murder of the father of plaintiff Tosie Keldermans occurred on the same evening. The father had gone to the law office of his son, Roman Bedor, for a flashlight. When he came to the door he was shot twice by a man described as having a white mask over his head. Roman Bedor told us he saw a "red sedan" leaving and that his father told him there were two people involved in the shooting. The elder Bedor died later at the local hospital.
8. [Interviews with eight of the plaintiffs revealed the following:]
    a. Threats began immediately after the suit was filed on August 30, 1988.
    b. All plaintiffs were approached by people who asked them to withdraw the suit, threatening "bombings," "shootings," "bloodshed" to those who go to court on September 8, 1987.
    c. The government-controlled radio station referred constantly to those who were destroying the country by going to the courts.
    d. One of the plaintiffs described a visit by a Mr. Orak, who several times told her, "If you don't withdraw your name on Monday there will be shooting and bloodshed all over Koror." He continued, "You will get hurt if you do not withdraw. The women in the lawsuit will be first killed. I am not lying because I am there at the Furlough Committee office and I hear them talking."
    e. Gabriela Ngirmang described a visit to her home by the Ibedul himself, pleading with her to withdraw the suit "because it was dangerous."

And so the stage was set for the hearing before Judge Hefner at 2:30 p.m. on September 8, 1987. . . .
—   The power lines had been cut, putting Koror Island in total darkness.
—   The government radio was continually airing warnings of a national disaster.
—   The Furlough Committee had surrounded the Court wearing red head bands and demanding that the Court dismiss the case.

Only Rafaela Sumang appeared in court to file a petition for an adjournment to obtain counsel. She was given a Stipulation of Dismissal to sign. She thought it was for a postponement.

Judge Hefner became concerned. He said in court that he would not allow the dismissal to be filed unless it was signed by all plaintiffs in person.

Several persons, including policemen in police cars were then dispatched to the homes of the plaintiffs to obtain the necessary signatures. The plaintiffs told us they were given the alternative to "sign or else."

All twenty-two plaintiffs signed the stipulation and submitted it to Judge Hefner for approval. However, Judge Hefner refused to sign the customary "so ordered" at the foot of the stipulation.

Instead he wrote [an] opinion stating that there was evidence that the case had been withdrawn as a result of threats of violence. . . .

[W]hen Judge Hefner left for the airport to return to Saipan on September 9, 1987, he was accompanied by a cadre of twelve policemen apparently because of the government's concern for his personal safety in light of what he had felt obliged to do and say.

NOTES

For further reading on the situation in Palau, see Minority Rights Group, Micronesia: the Problems of Palau (1983); *Palau: Islands' Quest for Autonomy Making Headway on Hill*, Congressional Quarterly, August 19, 1989, at 2184; *Trusteeship Council told 'overwhelming majority' in Palau wants 'free association' status*, U.N. Chronicle, September 1989, at 28-30.

D. METHODS OF FACTFINDING

The following two readings deal with the methods organizations can use when undertaking a human rights investigation. The first reading below discusses the different purposes for which an organization might conduct an on-site visit, including investigation of human rights abuses. Readers should note that while this chapter deals primarily with the on-site visit as a factfinding tool, such visits can be used to accomplish other human rights goals as well. The second reading examines the procedural issues organizations must face when planning and implementing an investigation. Both readings focus on the on-site investigation as a human rights observation and factfinding tool. As the readings explain, however, many organizations engage in factfinding without such investigations. Readers should keep the distinction between on-site and other investigations in mind as they read the following materials, observing how the procedural issues differ depending on the type of investigation the organization decides to conduct. Readers should also note the advantages and disadvantages — discussed in the second reading — of conducting on-site investigations.

TYPES OF ON-SITE VISITS

Human rights visits generally pursue one or more related purposes:

factfinding, trial observation, contacts with government officials, election observation, or other objectives. At times these purposes overlap.

1. Research and Factfinding

Research visits are undertaken without the expectation that the information gathered will necessarily result in a formal or published report. The research might, instead, be used to develop contacts, gather information about possible prisoners of conscience, or investigate an extrajudicial killing. Some research visits involve factfinding, that is, they are expected to result in a report for consideration by the government and usually for publication as a memorandum or report.

In order to inspire corrective efforts by governments, human rights organizations must develop reliable factual conclusions from information gathered through generally accepted procedures. A reputation for fairness and impartiality lends credibility to the organization's observations on the human rights conditions in the countries investigated, recommendations, and other work.

Most factfinding actually occurs within the central offices of human rights organizations and through the efforts of volunteers who monitor public sources of information. Some countries, however, impede the flow of information and make passive fact-gathering techniques less effective.

On-site visits supplement the information available from passive fact-gathering. Delegates who participate in factfinding visits will want to interview as many knowledgeable persons as possible, including government officials; victims and their families; witnesses; human rights, religious, and social activists; scholars; and community leaders. Documentary evidence, such as newspaper accounts, trial records, relevant laws, and government documents are also collected. Finally, careful observation of the general human rights conditions in the country supplies the context in which to interpret the information gathered. In all investigations, the delegate should keep careful notes to support the facts and statements gathered. In order to ensure the safety of contacts and members of the delegation, the delegates must also preserve the confidentiality of all sensitive information.

2. Trial Observation

The presence of international observers at a trial involving human rights issues can have a substantial impact on the fair treatment of the defendant. A visit for the purpose of trial observation makes known to the court, the government officials, and the public the international interest and concern for the trial in question. The delegate influences the court by maintaining an authoritative, impartial, and visible presence during the trial. At the same time, the observer can collect information on the nature of the charges, the law pertaining to the trial, and the manner in which the court conducts the trial. The observation may induce a fairer trial for the accused. Previous experience and comments of defense advocates in many parts of the world attest to the change in atmosphere in the court and facilities available to the defense resulting from observation.

The delegate cannot function as a party to or mediator of the dispute. The trial observer seeks primarily to assess the extent to which the trial accords with international norms and national legal standards. A trial observer should discover what substantive law the court applies to the accused; whether duress, intimidation, or torture have influenced evidence or the court's decision; and how the political and legal environment in the country affected the trial.

3. Election Observation, Contacts with Government Officials, and Other Purposes.

Increasingly, human rights organizations have sent observers to monitor elections and other important national events. Visiting delegations for the purpose of observing elections function much as in trial observation, maintaining a neutral presence and gathering as much information as possible on the conduct of the elections.

Human rights delegations visiting government officials seek either to discuss the human rights situation with the government of the country visited or to present a report on the findings of a previous inquiry. Presenting a report can be the first step in improving human rights through recommendations from previous factfinding or it can be part of ongoing monitoring of compliance with human rights standards. As a part of factfinding, trial observation, or other visits the delegate will want to interview relevant officials to learn the government position on the matter in question. Government contacts visits are least likely to result in a visit report, unless combined with an element of factfinding.

The range of purposes for other visits may vary with the human rights concern addressed. Previous visits have observed political demonstrations, interviewed refugees and visitors from other nations, visited prisons to inspect allegations of abuse, or provided technical assistance in implementing recommendations for improving human rights conditions. On some recent visits, medical personnel have accompanied human rights lawyers to examine victims of torture for evidence.

Weissbrodt & McCarthy, *Fact-Finding by International Nongovernmental Human Rights Organizations*, 22 Va. J. Int'l L. 7, 42-84 (1981) (text partially updated; footnotes omitted):

[Ed. Note: The following excerpt deals specifically with the procedure followed by NGOs in conducting a factfinding inquiry rather than the procedures utilized by IGOs. One of the main differences between an IGO and an NGO investigation is that states have often consented in advance to cooperate with an IGO investigation, either by becoming a party to a human rights treaty or simply by being a member of the organization, while

NGOs must rely on other factors to gain the cooperation of a government and sometimes must operate without such cooperation. An additional difference is that IGOs often have permanent bodies with fixed procedural rules to conduct factfinding investigations while NGOs frequently utilize *ad hoc* visits and procedures. Nevertheless, as the authors note, IGOs face many of the same procedural issues as NGOs when conducting investigations. While reading the following excerpt, note the main issues that organizations face when conducting factfinding visits. Keep those issues in mind while reading the remaining material in this chapter, identifying how the various factfinding visits which this chapter examines dealt with these issues.]

A. *Composition and Nature of the Factfinding Body*

1. *Terms of Reference*

In bilateral and multilateral forms of inquiry, [for example an inquiry by an IGO such as the International Labor Organization (ILO)] the terms of reference governing the competence of the commission are established by negotiation between two or more States. The sovereignty of the State under investigation is either relinquished by its own agreement or is encroached upon by the authority of a multilateral instrument. The authority for NGO factfinding, however, is usually self-created. NGOs define the scope of their study and legitimize their efforts after the fact by the reliability of their findings. . . .

Terms of reference serve several useful purposes and should be used by NGOs. First, written terms of reference may induce governments to cooperate and may be subject to negotiation with the governments. Although most NGO visits are not established by formal agreement between the NGO and the State, there is often some contact with the government prior to the establishment of a visit. Second, formal terms of reference act as a factfinding commission's letter of introduction to the government. This is helpful not only for on-site visits, but also for commissions making contact through the mail or with embassies and consulates. . . . Third, terms of reference serve as an aid to commission members in resolving disputes over the scope of a commission's activities. . . .

The factors discussed above tend to call for narrowly stated terms of reference. However, as with the formulation of other procedures, there is a danger in making the terms too specific. Narrow terms of reference may hamper a visit's operation or, if the visit exceeds its terms, give the government a pretext for attacking its findings.

2. *Members*

Like IGOs, NGOs face the problem of finding qualified and impartial factfinders who can add the weight of personal prestige to their findings. The bulk of NGO factfinding is done by permanent employees of NGO Secretariats and by distinguished individuals who participate at the request of the NGO. No NGO or group of NGOs has established a panel of experts for inquiry visits such as has been recommended for the U.N. and established by the ILO. Such a panel is not really necessary nor is it particularly feasible.

There is no simple method for ensuring the expertise of the members of a visit. Since service on visits is voluntary and can involve some hardship, members characteristically have a strong interest in and are very knowledgeable about human rights. NGOs that regularly engage in factfinding make use of the previous factfinding experience of individuals.... Given the amount of evidence concerning physical abuse, [NGOs have] recognized that a visit can be assisted in its factfinding by a doctor and thus have included physicians on several visits.... Some NGO visits have included foreign scholars who possess expertise on the country studied.

In addition to the expertise needed to facilitate factfinding, another factor considered by NGOs in selecting commission members is the prestige associated with the names of experts in various fields.... Personal prestige is more important for ad hoc commissions of inquiry than for permanent NGOs that have established their own respectability....

B. *Methods of Inquiry*

1. *Background Factfinding by Secretariats*

[T]he bulk of NGO factfinding is performed by the national and international offices of the organizations. There are no limitations on the types of information gathered. At their international centers, NGOs collect information about human rights problems from newspapers, magazines, professional journals, U.N. publications, government reports, letters, telegrams, phone calls, and visits. Sources of information include church officials, relatives of prisoners, former prisoners or refugees, visitors, labor unions, opposition groups, expatriate groups, concerned public officials, lawyers, journalists, and other NGOs. Church-sponsored human rights organizations often obtain a wealth of information through a web of personal contacts. Older organizations have clipping files and dossiers on human rights violations dating back ten or twenty years....

2. *Sources of Information for Inquiry Visits*

IGOs and NGOs also gather background information before undertaking factfinding by visits of inquiry. Both NGO and IGO commissions take an active role in gathering the evidence required to fulfill their terms of reference. For example, the first action of the U.N. *Ad Hoc* Working Group of Experts on South Africa was to ask all U.N. member States for information — particularly for the names of possible witnesses — and to issue a communique through the U.N. Office of Public Information inviting contact from "all the persons who believe that they could provide specific and relevant information on this matter, in particular those who have been 'imprisoned or detained for opposing or violating the policies of apartheid.'" In inquiries about South Africa, the *Ad Hoc* Group of Experts has solicited names of witnesses and information not only from member States and the general public, but from the Organization of African Unity and various private organizations, including some African liberation movements....

Almost all NGOs follow the practice of actively seeking information. Since there are no "parties" to NGO investigations, the NGOs make use of information gathered by their Secretariats and by persons who come forward with evidence on their own initiative or in response to publicity about the inquiry. The NGOs also direct specific requests for information to the concerned government, church groups, political parties, and national humanitarian organizations....

NGOs...for the most part, actively solicit governmental cooperation. Governments are approached concerning the establishment of an inquiry commission, they are regularly asked to submit documents and names of witnesses, and are invited to comment on information received by the commissions. NGOs have not been totally without success in achieving a degree of cooperation with concerned governments.

a. *On-Site Observation*

. . . On-site visits both provide useful information and lend credibility to the conclusions of factfinding visits. Occasionally, they afford some temporary relief in individual cases through the mere presence of outside observers. On-the-spot investigations can also provide the sort of fresh information that may be necessary for prompt remedial action. . . .

Despite the emphasis in this and other discussions of NGOs with respect to on-site investigations, most human rights factfinding is done without such visits. Factfinding visits are too expensive to be used very widely and may require at least the acquiescence, if not the assistance, of the government subject to scrutiny. Such cooperation is not always forthcoming. Because of these difficulties, the great bulk of human rights factfinding by both IGOs and NGOs is accomplished without on-site visits.

It should not be presumed, however, that on-site visits are always necessary for effective factfinding. First-hand evidence is frequently available outside the country being investigated; refugees may provide their testimony; legal documents are usually available; complaints are often smuggled out of the subject country; the government may be asked to respond to accusations in writing or through diplomats; the long distance telephone is a very effective investigative tool; and testimony may be taken from other visitors to the country. While these factfinding approaches may not all be as reliable as direct observation, human rights organizations can and do achieve reliable results without on-site visits. . . .

Furthermore, on-site investigation may actually be less reliable than other methods of inquiry in some cases. Governments often shift prisoners, cordon off potential witnesses, prevent access to prisons, and otherwise prevent delegates from access to accurate information during the necessarily short period of their visits. Governments cannot as easily control the availability of information when the factfinders are gathering evidence over a long period outside the subject territories. . . .

b. *Oral Evidence*

All factfinding visits rely on both oral and written evidence. Oral testimony is the backbone of both inquiry and adjudication. It has traditionally been considered of utmost reliability because it allows a finder of fact to listen to and immediately question a witness, and to evaluate demeanor and credibility. . . .

There are various procedures governing the conduct of witnesses and commission members during the giving of testimony. In IGO factfinding, an oath or affirmation is usually required, and the witness establishes his or her credentials. The U.N. Draft Model Rules call for the commission's terms of reference to be explained and for preliminary questions to be put to the witness. The witness is allowed to make a statement before submitting to questioning at the direction of the Chair. The witness may be excluded from the proceedings after giving testimony. The Hague Convention of 1907 provides several other helpful rules. Under the Convention, the witness is not allowed to read a statement or answer from a written draft in presenting evidence, except to consult notes and documents. Also, the witness is asked to sign the transcript of his or her testimony. . . .

A difficult problem for all human rights investigation is providing protection for persons who come forward and give oral testimony, especially in hearings within the country under investigation. In some instances, the public nature of hearings renders futile any attempt to preserve the anonymity of witnesses or the confidentiality of testimony. Both NGO and IGO factfinding visits have routinely found it necessary, however, to receive testimony privately and for witnesses to remain anonymous. While these measures have helped, they have not prevented governments from surrounding commissions' temporary headquarters, arresting prospective witnesses, roughing up people as they enter or leave the site of a commission, and detaining, torturing, or killing witnesses after their testimony. NGOs are helpless in the face of such tactics except to complain publicly or to cancel hearings in the event that witnesses are subjected to danger. In such situations it may be better to rely on written testimony or to interview witnesses only outside the country.

Another approach to the problem of witness protection is reflected in the Belgrade Rules [developed by the International Law Association in 1980], which would require that an NGO receive from a government assurances of non-retaliation before a factfinding visit could proceed. Unfortunately, NGOs have experienced great difficulty in obtaining and enforcing assurances that governments will not retaliate. To require such assurances as a condition precedent to NGO factfinding would make it extremely difficult to establish a factfinding visit. Governments would simply refuse to make promises concerning non-retaliation. Even were such promises made, an NGO has no guarantee that they will be fulfilled. . . .

C. *Admission of Evidence*

International fact-finding bodies and arbitral tribunals have traditionally avoided the sort of restrictions on the admissibility of evidence that are recognized by common law courts. . . .

D. *Ensuring the Reliability of Evidence*

The broad approach to admissibility necessitates the use of procedures to ensure the reliability of the factual conclusions drawn by the fact-finding body from the evidence gathered. Such methods for achieving reliability include both procedures for the taking of evidence and considerations used in weighing the evidence.

1. *Procedures for the Taking of Evidence*

a. *Testimony Under Oath or Affirmation*

The U.N. Draft Model Rules and the rules for the U.N. *Ad Hoc* Working Group on Chile provide that all nongovernmental witnesses shall be sworn before testifying. Although U.N. and nongovernmental bodies lack contempt and perjury prosecution power, it is believed that the taking of an oath at least impresses upon witnesses the seriousness of oral testimony. . . .

NGO factfinding commissions rarely take sworn testimony from those whom they interview and generally do not attempt to reproduce the style of court proceedings. The formality of oath-taking might have a chilling effect on human rights victims and other potential informants, who fear reprisal and often demand that their testimony not be attributed. NGO factfinding commissions thus generally rely upon polite probing, questioning, and cross-checking to assure the reliability of oral testimony.

b. *Careful Questioning of Witnesses* . . .

Intergovernmental factfinding proceedings are generally far more formal than similar efforts by NGOs, whose inquiries resemble interviews more than adjudicative hearings. In some ways, NGO factfinders conduct themselves like *juges d'instruction* in a civil law country. The NGO questioner need not demonstrate facts to some independent body, such as a judge or jury, but both poses the inquiries and analyzes the responses. Hence, the interviewer can get meaningful information through polite, and sometimes indirect questioning. Mildly suggestive or leading questions are used by IGOs to elicit information from witnesses and could be employed by NGOs. Nevertheless, on some occasions, such as examination of governmental representatives, NGO fact-finders have needed to use more forceful questioning. . .

2. *Methods of Assessing the Reliability of Evidence*

a. *Corroboration*

For international NGOs, corroboration is the most significant and commonly-used method for determining the reliability of human rights information. Faced with unreliable or politically motivated informants and frequently with circumstantial evidence, the NGO attempts to sift its information for common patterns and corroborative data deriving from independent sources. . . .

Sometimes a commission receives corroborative physical evidence such as bruises, scars, and other physical evidence of torture, although the passage of time often makes this type of evidence very difficult to acquire. On-site visitation can provide an opportunity to verify witnesses' descriptions of buildings and rooms. . . .

b. *Use of Direct Evidence* . . .

Every visit tries, whenever possible, to base its findings on direct evidence. Most NGOs do not, however, exclude all findings based on hearsay testimony, especially where the testimony is consistent with other evidence available to the visit. . . .

In the absence of direct evidence, NGO visits rely on the number of allegations of torture and the similarity of alleged circumstances to establish a prima facie case of mistreatment. Where 50 complaints of mistreatment are received, and all describe similar types of torture at the same locations, there is a substantial likelihood that some form of torture is being conducted. Findings of fact based on such evidence have proven reliable in the past. . . .

d. *Witness Conduct*

The demeanor of a witness may indicate confidence or nervousness, from which a finder of fact may infer the veracity of statements made or merely that the individual has a certain disposition. The fact-finding reports of IGOs and NGOs do not usually make reference to the importance of a witness' conduct in assessing reliability, even though on-site visits are motivated to some extent by a desire to see and hear witnesses. . . .

e. *Burden of Proof and Production of Evidence*

The concepts of burden of proof and burden of production of evidence play a very significant role in assuring the reliability of factual findings by placing responsibility for the production of evidence on the party who either ought to possess the evidence or has the greatest interest in presenting it, and by establishing a burden of persuasion for the proponent of a position. It may well be that an NGO, which is both the investigator and the decision-maker, bears the burden of producing all evidence necessary to support its findings. The accused government, however, has both an interest in the proceeding and is most able to locate and present relevant material. The Inter-American Commission on Human Rights appears to place a burden of production upon governments under investigation. Similarly, if an NGO can at least establish a prima facie case that human rights violations have occurred, it may then insist that the government discharge a burden of presenting contradictory evidence. This "rule" probably best describes the working of public opinion when an NGO has reported that human rights have been violated and the government has failed to rebut the findings presented in the report. . . .

The degree of proof employed by an NGO may vary, depending upon the impact of the action that follows a fact-finding effort. For example, if an NGO proposes only to send a diplomatic letter of inquiry to a government, the NGO may merely need credible second-hand reports of human rights violations. If an NGO is publishing a major report, it ought to require more substantial evidence of wrongdoing. . . .

E. *Dissemination of Reports*

The major question concerning dissemination of factfinding reports is whether reports should be submitted to the concerned government for comment or rebuttal before release to the public. [One reason for following this procedure is that] given the less than conclusive evidence upon which some findings are based, fairness requires that governments be given a chance to rebut the conclusions. . . .

NGOs regularly submit their findings to and/or solicit evidence from concerned States. Often, an agreement to submit findings and receive government comment is a precondition to permission for on-site visitation. The major problem with this procedure has been the refusal of governments to respond. . . .

An NGO should never make a commitment to withhold publication of a report until it receives a government's comment. A time limit for response should be set at the time the report is submitted to the government, with the proviso that the full report will be published immediately upon any public release or public comment by the government. . . .

MODEL RULES FOR FACTFINDING

The previous excerpt referred to various sets of model rules of procedure which exist to guide factfinders. The first international codification of factfinding procedure was the Hague Convention of 1907. Hague Convention for the Pacific Settlement of Disputes of 1907, 36 Stat. 2199, T.S. No. 536. The Hague Convention provided for a commission of inquiry that would be constituted by agreement between two disputing states and set out rules of procedure to govern the inquiry. Although the Hague Convention's inquiry mechanism received little use, the procedural rules continue to serve as a model for factfinding.

Many IGOs, as noted earlier, have formulated their own factfinding procedures. This chapter discusses one such procedure, that of the Inter-American Commission on Human Rights, in greater detail in the next section.

Another set of influential IGO factfinding standards can be found in the Model Rules of Procedure for United Nations Bodies Dealing with Violations of Human Rights. U.N. Doc. E/CN.4/1021/Rev.1 (1970). Although the U.N. has yet to adopt the rules in their full form, at least one U.N. factfinding visit has used them as the basis for rules of procedure and they will probably serve as a model for future visits. *See also* Committee Against Torture, Rules of Procedure, U.N. Doc. CAT/C/3/Rev.1, at 23-27 (1989) (rules for an inquiry).

A final set of factfinding rules that deserves mention is the Belgrade Rules adopted by the International Law Association in 1980. *The Belgrade Minimum Rules of Procedure for International Human Rights Fact-finding Visits*, 75 Am. J. Int'l L. 163 (1981).

STATE DEPARTMENT COUNTRY REPORTS

Each year the State Department issues Country Reports on Human Rights Practices. These reports are the result of an extensive factfinding process within the U.S. Government concerning human rights in all countries which receive aid from the U.S. or which are members of the U.N.

The State Department Country Reports were initiated by a 1976 amendment to Section 502B of the Foreign Assistance Act of 1961 that required the State Department to prepare a "full and complete report . . . with respect to practices regarding the observance of and respect for internationally recognized human rights in each country proposed as a recipient of security assistance." 22 U.S.C. § 2304(b). The first State Department Human Rights Report was made available to the public in March 1977. *Department of State, Country Reports on Human Rights Practices for 1977, Report Submitted to the Senate Committee on Foreign Relations*, 95th Cong., 1st Sess. (1977). The initial report dealt with only 82 countries receiving military assistance and not the 139 countries which had been the subject of arms exports from the United States. The initial report was criticized as being "vague, extremely general, and 'tactfully' drafted to protect the countries discussed." *See* Weissbrodt, *Human Rights Legislation and United States Foreign Policy*, 7 Ga. J. Int'l L.J. 231, 264 n.11 (1977). The first report stressed general historical, structural, and legalistic descriptions rather than discussing specific human rights "practices."

The reports have improved over the years in both quantity and quality. The Congress broadened the reporting requirements in 22 U.S.C. § 2151n to include countries receiving economic assistance and members of the United Nations. The State Department in its 1989 report covered 169 nations including several countries which neither receive aid nor are members of the U.N. *Department of State, Country Reports on Human Rights Practices for 1989, Report Submitted to the Senate Committee on Foreign Relations and the House Committee on Foreign Affairs*, 101st Cong., 2nd Sess. (1990). While some of the individual reports may be criticized for hewing too close to U.S. foreign policy objectives, the State Department has over the years "become decidedly better informed on and sensitized to human rights violations as they occur around the globe." *Country Reports for 1989* at 1.

In recent years the State Department has explained its factfinding process. For example, in the State Department Country Reports for 1989, at 1549-50, there is the following explanation:

Notes on Preparation of the Reports

The annual Country Reports on Human Rights Practices are based upon all information available to the United States Government. Sources include American officials, officials of foreign governments, private citizens, victims of human rights abuse, congressional studies, intelligence information, press reports, international organizations, and nongovernmental organizations concerned with human rights. We are particularly appreciative of, and make reference in most reports to, the role of nongovernmental human rights organizations, ranging from groups in a single country to major organizations that concern themselves with human rights matters in larger geographic regions or over the entire world. While much of the information we use is already public, information on particular abuses frequently cannot be attributed, for obvious reasons, to specific sources.

The reports by law must be submitted to Congress by January 31 [of each year]. To comply, United States diplomatic missions are given guidance in September for submission of draft reports during October and November; contributions are received from appropriate offices in the Department of State; and a final draft is prepared under the coordination of the Bureau of Human Rights and Humanitarian Affairs. Because of the preparation time required, it is possible that developments in the latter part of the year may not be fully reflected; moreover, reports from some of the nongovernmental organizations are for periods ending well before the end of the year. We make every effort to include reference to major events or significant changes in trends.

We have attempted to make these country reports as comprehensive as space will allow, while taking care to make them objective and as uniform as possible in both scope and quality of coverage. We have given particular attention to attaining a high standard of consistency despite the multiplicity of sources and the obvious problems related to varying degrees of access to information, structural differences in political and social systems, and trends in world opinion regarding human rights practices in specific countries. There is a conceptual difficulty in applying a single standard of evaluation to societies with differing cultural and legal traditions. There is also a problem of perspective in discussing countries that face differing political realities, which must be taken into account in describing the human rights environment. Rather than viewing a country in isolation, these reports take as their point of departure the world as it is and then seek to apply a consistent approach in assessing each country's human rights situation. While we have tried to make each report self-contained by including enough background information to place the human rights situation in context, readers who need to delve more deeply may wish to consult other sources, including previous country reports.

To improve the uniformity of the reports, the introductory section of each report contains a brief setting, indicating how the country is governed and providing the context for examining the country's human rights performance. A description of the political framework and a discussion of the security and law enforcement situation are followed by an economic background statement. The setting concludes with an overview of human rights developments in the year under review . . . .

The Lawyers Committee for Human Rights and Human Rights Watch have regularly issued reviews of the State Department reports. *See, e.g.,* Human Rights Watch & Lawyers Committee for Human Rights, Critique: Review of the Department of State's Country Reports on Human Rights Practices for 1987 (1988); Watch Committees & Lawyers Committee for Human Rights, Critique: Review of the Department of State's Country Reports on Human Rights Practices for 1985 (1986). *See* chapter 11, *infra,* for more discussion of the State Department Country Reports in the context of U.S. foreign policy relating to human rights.

E. EXPERIENCE OF THE INTER-AMERICAN COMMISSION ON HUMAN RIGHTS WITH ON-SITE OBSERVATIONS

The Inter-American Commission has one of the most well developed and frequently utilized procedures for on-site factfinding. The Commission has conducted numerous on-site observations in conjunction with the investigation of human rights in member states. The U.N. Commission on Human Rights, through its special rapporteurs and working groups, has also been active in on-site factfinding. In contrast, many other human rights bodies, such as the Human Rights Committee discussed in chapters 3 and 8, and the European Commission on Human Rights discussed in chapter 10, rely for factual information on materials collected from governments and other interested persons and organizations. Even the Inter-American Commission often engages in this type of passive factfinding when investigating individual petitions, as illustrated in the readings from chapter 7.

The first two readings in this section illustrate the Inter-American Commission's procedures for on-site factfinding in connection with the commission's visit to Argentina in 1980. The first reading is an excerpt from the report the Commission prepared based on the information it gathered during its visit. The second reading is a description of an incident which occurred during the visit. As you read the materials, you should think about how the Commission dealt with the procedural issues identified in the Weissbrodt & McCarthy article, *supra.*

Inter-American Commission on Human Rights (IACHR), Report on the Situation of Human Rights in Argentina at 1-12, 219-31, O.A.S. Doc. OEA/Ser.L/V/II.49, doc. 19 corr. 1 (1980) (footnotes omitted):

Introduction

A. *Background*

1. In recent years, both before and after the March 1976 military takeover, the IACHR has received denunciations of serious violations of human rights in

Argentina, which it has processed according to its regulations. In addition on a number of occasions, it has informed representatives of the Argentine Government of its concern about the increase in the number of denunciations, and about information received from various sources that comprises a pattern of serious, generalized and systematic violations of basic human rights and freedoms.

2. In light of this situation, the IACHR decided to prepare the present report, and when it informed the Argentine Government of this decision, the Commission also advised it of its interest in conduct[ing] an on-site observation in Argentina, in the belief that this is the most suitable method of determining precisely and objectively the status of human rights in a particular country at a particular time in history.

3. In a Note dated December 18, 1978, the Argentine Government extended an invitation to the IACHR to conduct an on-site observation, pursuant to its regulations, . . .

B. *Activities of the Commission during its on-site observation . . .*

2. The on-site observation began on September 6, and was completed on September 20, 1979. The Commission's first step upon arrival in Buenos Aires was to [issue] a press release. . . .

a. *Interviews with public authorities*:

From September 7 through September 20, the Commission met with [various government authorities, including: the President, the members of the military junta, several government ministers, the President of the Supreme Court of Justice, the members of the Federal Chamber of Appeals, a federal judge, and selected governors and military officials.] . . .

The members of the Commission explained the objectives of the mission to all these officials, and received offers of full cooperation from the authorities.

b. *Former Presidents of the Republic*

The Commission felt it advisable to visit all the former presidents of Argentina to discuss the status of human rights in the country. . . .

c. *Interviews with major religious figures . . .*

The Commission. . . had the opportunity to talk with representatives of various religious groups.

d. *Human rights organizations*

In the afternoon of Friday, September 7, the Commission held separate meetings with Argentine human rights organizations, including: the Permanent Assembly for Human Rights; the Argentine League for Human Rights; the Ecumenical Movement for Human Rights; the Mothers of the Plaza de Mayo, and the leaders of the group called Families of "the Disappeared" and Persons Detained for Political Reasons (*Familiares de Desaparecidos y Detenidos por Razones Políticas*).

In the days following, the Commission received other groups and delegations from a number of cities in the interior of the country, who had traveled to meet it. . . .

e. *Representatives of political organizations*

[The Commission met with various representatives of political organizations.]

f. *Professional associations*

The Commission exchanged views with the Argentine Federation of Bar Associations, and with the Buenos Aires Bar Association. These institutions received the Commission in their headquarters on September 8 and September 13, respectively.

The Commission discussed a number of aspects of the legal profession during a visit at its offices from a group of defense lawyers and trade union lawyers.

Meetings were also held with [professional associations of architects, physi050914 engineers, and psychologists.]

g. *Trade-union organization[s] and syndicates*

[The Commission met with various trade organizations and syndicates.]

h. *Commercial, industrial and business entities*

[The Commission met with representatives of various commercial, industrial, and business entities.]

i. *Other meetings held . . .*

[T]he Commission met with a number of other individuals whose testimony it was particularly interested in hearing. These included meetings with the author Ernesto Sábato; the trade union leader Lorenzo Miguel; the journalist Jacobo Timerman, and the trade union leader Professor Alfredo Brazo.

Lastly, on Tuesday September 18, the Commission met with the director or representatives of the mass communications media to discuss the topic of freedom of the press.

j. *Investigation of certain cases*

In the cities of Buenos Aires, Córdoba, La Plata and Rosario, the Commission did some investigative work inherent in the on-site observation, and received individuals and groups interested in stating problems or filing denunciations about human rights violations.

k. *Detention centers*

[The Commission visited various prisons and police stations.]

l. *Denunciations received*

In its initial press release, the Commission invited all persons who considered that any of their rights, as defined in the American Declaration, had been violated, to submit the corresponding denunciation.

Members of the public were received in Buenos Aires (in the offices on Avenida de Mayo 760) from Friday, September 7, to Saturday, September 15. In Córdoba, denunciations were received in the Hotel Crillón from September 10 through September 14, and in the city of Tucumán, in the Hotel Versailles, on April 14 and 15. . . .

4. The Argentine Government cooperated with the Commission at all times, provided it with all the facilities it needed for its work, and repeated its commitment to take no reprisals against persons or institutions who provided the Commission with information, testimony, or evidence of whatever nature. . . .

5. On Thursday, September 20, the full Commission met for the second and last time with the President, Lieutenant General (Retired) Jorge Rafael Videla, who was accompanied by the Ministers of the Interior and of Foreign Affairs. In light

of its importance, the Commission at that time delivered to the President a document containing preliminary recommendations, the text of which appears below:

RECOMMENDATIONS OF THE INTER-AMERICAN COMMISSION ON HUMAN RIGHTS TO THE GOVERNMENT OF ARGENTINA

The Inter-American Commission on Human Rights, on the occasion of its on-site observation to the Republic of Argentina, takes the liberty of making the following preliminary recommendations to the Government of Argentina:

I. *The Disappeared*:

The Commission believes that the problem of the disappeared is one of the most serious human rights problems that Argentina faces. The Commission thus recommends the following:

a)   That detailed information be provided on the status [of] the disappeared persons, understood to mean those persons who have been apprehended in operations in which, because of the conditions in which they took place and because of their characteristics, it is presumed that the state authorities participated.

b)   That the necessary instructions be given to the proper authorities that minors who have disappeared as a result of the detention of their parents and other relatives, and children born in detention centers, whose whereabouts are unknown, be handed over to their natural parents or other close family members.

c)   That the relevant measures be adopted to discontinue the procedures that have led to the disappearance of persons. In this regard, the Commission notes that cases of this nature have occurred recently, and should be clarified as soon as possible, as should all the other cases.

II. *Persons detained under orders of the Executive ("PEN"), and the right to exercise one's option to leave the country*:

The Commission learned of the status of persons detained under orders of the Executive, and of the procedures for exercising the right of option to leave the country. The Commission recommends the following in this regard:

a)   That the power granted to the Head of State under Article 23 of the Constitution, which authorizes the detention of persons during a State of Siege, be made subject to a test of reasonable cause, and that such detentions not be extended indefinitely.

b)   That, as a result, the following persons, detained at the disposal of the Executive (PEN) be released:

   i.   Those who have been detained without reasonable cause for a prolonged period, in order that the preventive detention itself not become the punishment, which may only be imposed by the Judiciary;

   ii.   Those who have been acquitted or who have already completed their sentences;

   iii. Those who are eligible for parole, provided they have been sentenced.

c)   That the exercise of the right of option to leave the country be completely restored, so that the processing of applications not be delayed in any way that might hinder the actual exercise of this right.

III. *Methods of Investigation*:

The Commission recommends the following with regard to methods of investigation:

That there be an in-depth investigation of denunciations concerning the use of torture and other illegal uses of force in the interrogation procedures used on detainees, that those responsible for such acts be punished with the full force of the law, and that the necessary measures be taken to prevent the use of such measures.

IV. *Prison System*:

The Commission recommends the following with respect to the prison system:

That the relevant measures be taken to ensure that detainees in some penitentiaries no longer be deprived of the conditions for their physical and mental health, such as sunlight, reading and physical exercise, that excessive time spent in cells be reduced, and that punishment not be imposed for trivial infractions.

V. *Military Jurisdiction*:

The Commission recommends the following with respect to persons who are in the process of being tried and sentenced by military tribunals:

a)   That persons brought to trial before military tribunals be assured of due process guarantees particularly the right to a defense by an attorney of the defendant's choosing.

b)   That a Commission of qualified jurists be appointed to study the trials conducted by military tribunals during the state of siege, and which would be authorized to make pertinent recommendations in those cases where due process guarantees were lacking.

VI. *Guarantees of due process and fair trials*:

The Commission recommends the following with regard to the due process guarantees and fair trials:

a)   That guarantees and facilities be provided to judges so that they may effectively investigate cases of persons detained under the security laws.

b)   That the guarantees essential for an effective defense by attorneys providing legal services to defendants be granted.

Buenos Aires, Federal Capital
September 20, 1979

6. On September 20, the Commission concluded its on-site observation in Argentina and issued its final press release.

C. *Methodology*

1. In preparing this report, the IACHR used information obtained through its own resources, both before, during, and after the on-site observation. Special consideration was given to denunciations, testimonies and information received by

the IACHR or by the Special Commission that visited Argentina, which were used in preparing the present document, although the report is not merely an aggregate of these denunciations, testimonies and information.

Careful study also was given to the Argentine legal system, the body of laws handed down by domestic courts and the applicable international human rights instruments. The IACHR consulted various documents that directly or indirectly deal with the status of human rights in Argentina or in some way enable the Commission to increase its understanding of the recent history of that country, which included documents prepared by the Argentine Government and by various Argentine organizations.

2. The IACHR also wishes to record that during its on-site observation, in addition to the information provided by governmental authorities, it received information and heard from officials of institutions representing all sectors of Argentine society, and also heard from all the individuals who wished to submit complaints or testimony on the Argentine human rights situation.

3. The present report takes into consideration the Argentine Government's observations dated February 29, 1980, on the preliminary report, which had been approved by the Commission, and delivered to the Argentine Government, on December 14, 1979.

The Commission considers it appropriate to make some general comments about those observations, particularly in relation to the individual case histories included in the present report.

In the judgment of the Commission, these case histories are used to illustrate various topics and situations discussed in the report, and an attempt was made to use them in order to present with greater objectivity the situation of human rights in Argentina.

The Commission wishes to point out that its presentation of these case histories does not necessarily entail any prejudgment of them, in those instances where the Commission has not yet taken a resolution. Each individual case mentioned in the present report has been or will be processed according to the Commission's Regulations. The end of the process in each case is a statement or resolution on the merits.

The IACHR has already adopted a resolution on some individual cases included in the present report. In cases where the Argentine Government has requested a reconsideration, careful study has been made of the cases in the light of new information supplied by the Government; if they are still included, it is because, in the opinion of the Commission, reconsideration of the case was not justified.

In cases where the Commission has decided to include a denunciation which has not yet been completely processed, it is because the Commission has decided, on the basis of the available evidence, that the charges are *prima facie* true, particularly in cases where the observations of the Argentine Government do not permit the denunciation to be refuted.

Moreover, the report contains not only individual cases, but also refers to information and documents received during the on-site observation, which was conducted precisely in order to collect such information.

With respect to the information collected during the on-site observation, the IACHR considered that the proper procedural moment to make it known to the Government, was, of course, in the preliminary report itself; this gave the

Government the opportunity to make whatever observations it considered appropriate.

It should also be noted that in each of the case histories recorded — which are identified in this report by number — the IACHR informed the Argentine Government of the case prior to the Commission's approval of the report, and that in each case, the Government has had an opportunity to make such comments and observations as it considered appropriate.

4. Finally, the Commission wishes to note that in transcribing the pertinent parts of the denunciations contained in the report, it was decided to omit the names of those public officials or security agents who were accused of human rights violations, in cases where the Commission had no direct information. However, the Commission is confident that such an omission will not prevent the Argentine Government from taking the necessary measures, in accordance with its domestic laws, to investigate these denunciations, and in the event abuses or crimes are proven, to punish those responsible with the full force of the law.

[The following excerpt from a chapter of the report illustrates the way the Commission outlined the human rights violations it investigated.]

CHAPTER VI

THE RIGHT TO A FAIR TRIAL AND DUE PROCESS

A. *General Considerations*

1. According to the Argentine Constitution, the administration of justice is vested in the Judiciary, whose organizational structure and operations are set forth in Section Three, Chapters 1 and 2, entitled: ''The Judiciary''. These articles read as follows:

Article 94. The judicial Power of the nation shall be vested in one supreme Court and in such inferior Courts as the Congress may establish in the territory of the Nation.

Article 95. In no case may the President exercise judicial functions, assume jurisdiction over pending cases, or reopen those decided.

For its part, Article 100 provides that the Supreme Court and the lower courts of the Nation have jurisdiction to resolve all causes submitted to them for decision.

2. In furtherance of these constitutional provisions, Law No. 27 of October 16, 1862, which regulates the nature and general operations of the judicial Power in Argentina, provides in Article 1, ''National justice shall always proceed in application of the Constitution and national laws....''; Article 3, states, ''One of its purposes is to enforce the Constitution and to disregard, when it decides cases, any provision applicable to any of the national branches which may be contrary to the Constitution.'' Article 21 of this law states: ''The national Courts and Judges, in the exercise of their functions, shall proceed to apply the Constitution as the Supreme Law of the Land, the laws that the Congress has passed or will pass, treaties with foreign nations, individual laws of the provinces, general laws that prevailed prior to the establishment of the Nation and the principles of International Law, as required, respectively, in cases submitted to it in the order of priority that is established.''

3. The highest organ of the judicial Power is the Supreme Court. This Court

is composed of five members and the Attorney General is the Chief prosecutor. The Attorney General is in charge of all public prosecutors.

To apply the federal Law, which derives from Article 100 of the Constitution, the provinces of Argentina currently have approximately fifty federal trial courts and eight appeals courts. Buenos Aires has a more complicated judicial organization divided into different jurisdictions that hear cases according to subject matter. This organization consists of several hundred single judge trial courts and appeals chambers.

Besides the federal judicial system, each province—which according to Article 5 of the Constitution must ensure its own administration of justice—has its own judicial organization and procedural laws....

B. *Organization of the Judicial System under the Present Government*

1. Pursuant to the Act for the National Reorganization Process, issued on the date of the military takeover, March 24, 1976, changes were made in the Argentine judicial system, the Supreme Court, the Office of the Attorney General, and in the membership of the Superior Provincial Courts. This act signified that the new authorities assumed the power to remove any sitting judge without prior judgment or complaint of misconduct....

3. The removal and replacements mentioned above, allowed the military authorities to appoint a new Supreme Court and Attorney General, new superior courts and district attorneys general and to replace a large number of judges.

All of these new magistrates were obliged to swear allegiance to and respect for the Acts and Objectives of the institutional process decreed by the Military Junta.

4. In an interview with the President of the Supreme Court, Dr. Adolfo Grabielli, the Commission raised this issue. The President of the Supreme Court confirmed to the Commission the source of these judicial appointments. He added, however, that most of these appointments involved persons with proven moral and professional background and were generally individuals with several years of experience as judges.

Dr. Grabielli also maintained that in seeking to enforce the Constitution and the laws, the Supreme Court had shown its independence of the Executive Branch in many cases....

5. However, the Commission has also received information on many cases involving persons who have been detained for a long time without any charges having been brought against them, or who have been released by courts or have completed their sentences. In these cases, the Courts have not sought their release due to the fact some authority in the Executive Branch has so ordered or requested....

C. *Military Tribunals*

1.... The very day of the military takeover, Law 21.264 was promulgated. This law creates Special Standing Military Tribunals throughout all of Argentina .... [T]hese special tribunals have the power to pass judgment on crimes covered in this law....

On the same date, March 24, 1976, the Military Junta stated that as of 1:00 p.m. of that day, personnel of the security forces, police and penitentiary forces, both national and provincial, were under military jurisdiction....

2. During its on-site observation, the Commission confirmed the complaints submitted to it to the effect that a large number of persons detained for subversive activity had been judged and sentenced by military courts. The sentences were as high as 25 years in prison.

The alleged criminals were not allowed to choose their own defense attorneys but were assigned official military defenders who are not licensed lawyers. These circumstances and the fact that civilians were made subject to military jurisdiction under the prevailing legislation were serious infringements of the right to defense inherent in due process.

The Commission flagged its concern about this matter with the national authorities. It also heard the ideas of experts in this field. These experts all agreed that both the military courts and trials for which they assumed responsibility were unconstitutional; they said they did not know of any cases in which civil attorneys had been allowed to participate. These situations violate basic provisions of the Constitution. . . .

D. *Guarantees of Administration of Justice*

1. . . . As will be explained further on, . . . fundamental guarantees of the administration of justice have been seriously violated in Argentina. Protection of these guarantees is taken up in the American Declaration of the Rights and Duties of Man and in the Argentine Constitution itself. Among these guarantees the following should be mentioned:

2. a. *Nullum crimen, nulla pena, sine lege* (no crime, no penalty, without law) is provided in Article No. XXV of the American Declaration and Article 18 of the Argentine Constitution. The latter reads as follows: "No inhabitant of the Nation may be punished without a prior judgment pursuant to a law which antedates the trial. . . ".

Despite the express norms implementing this juridical principle, the Military Government, in the Act of Institutional Responsibility, expressly abrogated this principle, establishing explicit[l]y the retroactivity of these norms in referring to prior actions, and in establishing in Article 1, that: "The Military Junta assumes the function and responsibility of considering the conduct of those persons who have prejudiced the national interest by having committed . . . ".

3. b. *Declaration of Presumption of Innocence*, is provided for in Article XXVI of the American Declaration. This principle was eliminated as a judicial guarantee by Law 21.460 which gave the Armed Forces and security personnel the power to detain persons suspected of crimes of subversion against which they have "half proof" of their guilt, and to institute against them the corresponding proceedings, whenever they have knowledge of that "half proof:". . .

4. c. *Right to an impartial trial*. This elementary and basic principle, expressly recognized by Article XXVI of the American Declaration of the Rights and Duties of Man, has been the subject of much testimony and information received by the Commission. According to this information, the Military Courts composed of officers involved in the repression of the same crimes they are judging, do not offer guarantees of sufficient impartiality. This is aggravated by the fact that in a military court, the defense is in the hands of a military officer, meaning, that the defense is taken over by a person who is also part of, and has strong disciplinary ties to, the same force responsible for investigation and repressing the acts with which the accused is charged.

5. d. *Right to be brought to trial within a reasonable time.* This guarantee, as stipulated in Article XVIII of the American Declaration of the Rights and Duties of Man, is not enforced in Argentina, because, as the great majority of the complaints involving detainees show, the corresponding appeals generally are not resolved opportunely. . . .

E. *The Writ of Habeas Corpus* . . .

2. The writ of *Habeas Corpus* in Argentina is an institution that is not expressly set forth in the Constitution; it is found instead in the Code of Criminal Procedure, although it is understood to be implicitly guaranteed by the Constitution, and applies to both the administration of justice in Buenos Aires and throughout all the federal territory. In the Provinces, similar legal provisions exist and even permit the writ to be processed without formality. . . .

4. First, the Commission will analyze the situation and processing of a writ of *Habeas Corpus* of the type involving an individual who ultimately is added to the growing list of the disappeared.

Within 48 hours of receiving a *Habeas Corpus*, a judge generally will request a report on the situation covered in the writ by means of telegrams to the Ministry of the Interior, the Federal Police or to Armed Forces Command Units. These telegrams are also addressed in some cases to police authorities in the place where the detention occurred. The various authorities generally reply to the effect that they have no information about the detention of such person. With that reply in hand, the Court forwards the information to the attorney and the parties, and then proceeds to hand down a ruling which states that the person is not in detention; that there are no grounds for the writ and that it is, therefore, rejected. Before placing the file in the archives, the federal judges submit a copy of the proceedings to the criminal court of the locality where it is alleged that the disappearance of the person, [on] whose behalf the *Habeas Corpus* was filed, took place, so that the disappearance of that person is investigated. . . .

6. The Supreme Court sought to remedy these inefficient investigations of the disappeared. The Court decided that the judges should expand the investigations and take the necessary measures to clarify the situations of disappeared persons. . . .

The accumulated evidence subsequently led the Supreme Court, upon the third presentation of the case *Pérez de Smith, et al.* to reiterate in its judgment of December 21, 1978, that there reigns a situation of actual loss of jurisdiction which the judges are unable to remedy.

7. It is appropriate to recognize that the main responsibility for this situation of loss of jurisdiction is with organizations which effectively monopolize the exercise of state force. Even so, it must be pointed out in this Chapter that the judges have not taken exceptional steps to clarify the instances of loss of jurisdiction which they have had to face. In none of the recorded cases have the judges come to the headquarters of the security forces in order to establish, *in situ*, the truth of the reports that have been submitted to them. Neither have special investigatory measures been provided for, despite the awareness of the magnitude of the cases at hand, nor has any public official ever been tried who may have participated in the operations involving the disappearance of individuals. It is not acceptable — and in particular it should not be acceptable to the judges — that so many

thousands of cases of disappeared persons remain unsolved, and that no official has to answer for them, no official among all those who have assumed the exercise of the authority of the state, which involves, among other obligations, the obligation of guaranteeing the safety of the community.

8. In cases in which petitions for *Habeas Corpus* are entered, with regard to persons detained on instructions of the Executive branch, the results thus far have been equally ineffective. In these cases, the judge requests information from the Executive branch, which, through the Ministry of the Interior, submits a copy of the arrest warrant signed by the President to the judge. This warrant states that the measure has been pursuant to the authority granted by Art. 23 of the Constitution....

Having seen the arrest warrant, the judge rejects the petition for *Habeas Corpus*, stating that the Executive is authorized to detain anyone pursuant to the aforementioned constitutional article.

In most instances, the Courts of Appeal have followed the same reasoning, limiting themselves to confirming that the arrest has been ordered by the Executive branch and withdrawing from exercising any review over the constitutionality of the arrest.

9. This pattern was broken in April 1977, with the judgment handed down by the federal Court of Appeals in Criminal and Correctional Matters of Buenos Aires, which accepted a petition for *Habeas Corpus* presented on behalf of the lawyer, Carlos Mariano Zamorano. The Court, applying the theory of reasonableness in determining the justification for his prolonged detention under the Executive branch, stated, among other things, as follows: ...

> In view of the need to choose between individual freedom and the hypothetical and undemonstrated dangerous nature (of the detainee), we choose the former, running the risks that it involves, safeguarding a value which no Argentine has renounced.

The federal Court ordered the Executive to release the person detained, but the judgment was not executed. In view of the appeal of the government attorney, the Supreme Court, in August 1977, demanded a more detailed response from the Executive branch, and accepting the arguments presented by the government, decided that the detention by the Executive could continue, since the aforementioned report was now accurate and specific with regard to the connection between the reasons for the State of Siege and the detention of Dr. Zamorano.

10. In all the subsequent instances in which the courts applied the doctrine of the *Zamorano* case, in accordance with the terms of the federal Court of Appeals judgment handed down on April 23, 1977, the Supreme Court, upon taking up the petition for *Habeas Corpus* on motion by the Government Attorney, has revoked the order for release....

11. In the light of this background, the conclusion that can be drawn is that the petition of *Habeas Corpus* has been frustrated. It is not a matter of the Commission's recommending an improvement — which might be possible — in the nature of the *Habeas Corpus*, but rather its seeking an end to the procedure followed in detentions or kidnappings, which is the basis for the frustration of the jurisdictional guarantee of the right to life, liberty and the physical integrity of all the inhabitants of Argentina....

NOTES

The Argentine government challenged the report, claiming that it exaggerated the overall problem and gave a false impression of human rights conditions in Argentina. Nonetheless, Argentina reported actions taken in improving its human rights situation to an OAS meeting in November 1980. *See* Department of State, Country Reports on Human Rights Practices for 1980, Report Submitted to the Senate Committee on Foreign Relations and the House Committee on Foreign Affairs, 97th Cong., 1st Sess. 337-38 (1981).

T. Buergenthal, R. Norris, & D. Shelton, Protecting Human Rights in the Americas: Selected Problems 179-81 (1986):

> Discovering Disappeared Persons: A Staff Member's Notes [Ed.: written by a staff member of the Inter-American Commission]

According to the Executive Secretary of the [Inter-American] Commission, the government of Argentina had declared that there were no political prisoners in Córdoba. Therefore, during the course of the [Commission's] visit, I was not to visit the Cárcel Penitenciaria in that city; however, I had requested my liaison with the Ministry of Foreign Affairs to provide me with a list of all the prisoners held in the provinces of Córdoba and Tucumán.

Upon arriving in Córdoba on September 7, I arranged to speak with the Minister of Government of that Province with regard to my mission and to the plans I would make for the visit of two Members of the Inter-American Commission scheduled to arrive several days later. I explained that we had no plans to visit the penitentiary, but that Commissioners often changed their minds and we should be aware of that possibility. On the basis of previous experience, I described very briefly our normal procedure for visiting jails and other detention centers. The Members would meet with the prison authorities for a briefing, prior to a tour of the locale. They would be interested in interviewing any prisoners who might have a case before the Commission, and they would probably select several prisoners at random for personal interviews with regard to prison conditions. Those interviews would take place in private, and the Members of the Commission might require a temporary office for the purpose. I reminded him that I had requested an alphabetized list of the prisoners in the Province of Córdoba and would need it as soon as possible.

As I conducted interviews with petitioners during the next few days, I was informed of the names of several persons who were allegedly being held in the Cárcel Penitenciaria for political reasons. Without mentioning this information, I called the Minister of Government to advise him that the Members would visit the prison and would need the list previously requested.

When the list finally arrived, I carefully went over the names, searching for the "political" cases reportedly detained at the penitentiary. One fact stood out; not one of those names was on the list! I then called a private individual who I knew could make contact with one of the prisoners and asked him to try to obtain a list of all the persons held in the same cellblock. He was only partially successful; he could not get all the names, but he did bring back several, along with the exact number of men and women being held there. Again I checked the list and none of those names were on it. It was an exciting moment; I had a "gut feeling" that some of those people were "disappeared," and the mission had yet to uncover any of the thousands of people who had been abducted and literally dropped from sight. I was afraid at the same time that someone might tip the authorities off and the prisoners would be moved before the visit of the Commissioners.

The prisoners sent word through my contact that they were worried about the confidentiality of the interviews. They were afraid of being overheard, and they were also afraid that the government might take advantage of the announced visit to send a "fake party," as it had allegedly done in that prison some months before under the guise of a Red Cross visit.

I replied, again through the contact, that I would bring plenty of paper and pens in my briefcase so they would not have to talk. They would be sure that it was an official visit by the Commission by asking "Are you Dr....?" My only reply would be to take out my official OAS passport and show them. Any verbal reply should put them on guard.

When the Members of the Commission did arrive, I briefed them on the situation and provided them with a memorandum on how we should proceed if they wished to visit the penitentiary. They accepted and asked me to finalize the arrangements.

On September 13, I accompanied Professor Carlos Dunshee de Abranches (Brazil) and Dr. Luis Tinoco Castro (Costa Rica) to the penitentiary. In our preliminary briefing by the Director of the prison, Professor Abranches asked for a general explanation of prison rules affecting the inmates. When the Director had finished speaking about visiting rights, Professor Abranches inquired whether all prisoners had the same rights. The reply was affirmative. He then noted that, "according to Dr....[the staff member] there is a sign in one part of the prison which refers to "special prisoners." "We have a complete list of the names of those prisoners, eleven women and thirty-one men, but it is an unofficial list, and we would like to have an official list before we visit that cellblock."

We had no such list, of course, but the fact we knew the exact number must have convinced them that we did. The Director turned to one of his assistants and asked: "Didn't you give them a list of the special prisoners?" "No sir." "Oh, I see. You didn't give them a list of the special prisoners!"

There followed a long moment of silence. Professor Abranches interrupted: "Since there are only a few names involved, we will simply wait here while the list is prepared." The Director then asked an assistant to bring a list. It only required a few minutes as a list was apparently brought from a file in another room. I could hardly believe my eyes. It was a bonanza, containing not only the names, but under whose disposition. Only seven had been presented before a court of law. Many of the others were at the orders of special councils of war, meaning they were being held indefinitely. Most were held by executive decree, but three were at the orders of the local military commandant. Those three had "disappeared" in the typical fashion just a month before!

When we reached the women's section, we asked to be allowed behind the bars into a large area which served as a dining hall. On the other side of the dining area was a long corridor with tiny cells on either side. We asked that the prisoners be released from their cells, and the Director complied. Not all of the women were accounted for. Professor Abranches shouted down the corridor: "Is anyone else there"? We heard a scream "We're here, we're here" and a hand emerged from a small opening in the door of the very last cell on the right. We had "found" two disappeared persons—Irma Cristina Guillen de Palazzesi and Stella Maria Palazzesi de Cavigliasso. The other women later told us that they had been warned not to mention the presence of the two prisoners being held incommunicado. They were not allowed to talk to them at all.

We left Dr. Tinoco to talk to the women and we continued with the Director to the men's section upstairs. There was another surprise in store. Professor Abranches told the prison officials, "Now that we are here, we'll just stay in the cellblock and interview the prisoners here." "But you can use my office; it's all prepared," blurted the Director. "Tell us who you want to see, and we'll take him to the office where you'll have all the facilities necessary." "No, thank you very much," said Professor Abranches, "we'll stop and see you on the way out!"

Again, we had the prisoners released from their cells, into the dining area, which was also behind bars. The guards withdrew, I brought out the paper and pens and explained what type of information we wanted. When everyone had finished, I took a small tape recorder from my briefcase, chose a cell at random, and interviewed a group of prisoners on general prison conditions. . . .

QUESTIONS

What lessons can be drawn from this account? Was it a good idea for the Commission members to reveal this incident to the public? What potential advantages and disadvantages could the revelation create for future fact-finding missions?

Inter-American Commission on Human Rights, Case 9265 Inter-Am. C.H.R. 113, OEA/Ser.L/V/II.66, doc. 10 rev. 1 (1985):

[Ed.: As noted earlier, the Inter-American Commission ordinarily engages in passive factfinding when it examines individual petitions. As the following case illustrates, however, the Commission occasionally undertakes an on-site factfinding visit in connection with its decision on an individual petition.]

BACKGROUND

1. On December 6, 1983 the Inter-American Commission on Human Rights received the following complaint and forwarded it to the Government of the Republic of Suriname for its observations:

We have received the names of the following people reportedly arrested during the past two weeks and detained at Fort Zeelandia Military Police headquarters:

Iwan Rajwinderpersad Gobardhan, aged 27.

Omprakash (Oemperkash) Gobardhan, aged 24, Dutch citizen.

Krishnapersad Gobardhan, aged 21, reportedly badly beaten; present at the arrest of his brother-in-law (below).

Ramlall Bekaroe, aged 27, brother-in-law of above brothers.

Harden Kasi, aged 21.

Mrs. Ch. Doerga, aged 40 arrested on 27 November at Nickerie.

K.P. Doerga, aged 24, arrested on 27 November at Nickerie.

Parents of Mrs. Doerga, above; mother reported to suffer from diabetes and may die if she does not receive medication.

Mr. Alibux (not Prime Minister).

Radiksjoen (spelling uncertain).

Austen, businessman.

Linveld.

On 29 November 1983 the Suriname authorities announced that they had arrested ten people during the previous week on suspicion of plotting a coup against the Government. They are reportedly being held for questioning at Fort Zeelandia Military headquarters. Other reports alleged that up to 69 people, mainly from the Indian (Hindustani) community have been arrested during this period. We have received reports that some of those arrested have been beaten while in custody.

A further report was received from a refugee arriving in Holland that for the past 2-3 weeks four bodies were kept under military guard in the Paramaribo mortuary. Bodies rumoured to include Imro Themen and Henk Essed (leader of People's Militia, dismissed three weeks ago).

Two of those arrested—Omprakash Gobardhan and Linveld above—appeared on Suriname television on 29 November at a press conference given by the Deputy Commander of the Military Police, Sergeant Major Zeeuw. The two men 'confessed' to their involvement in the attempted coup. The Government has accused those involved of having distributed anti-government leaflets and of setting fire to Government buildings, reportedly in preparation for an invasion by mercenaries.

We are concerned for the safety of those in custody, in view of the past treatment of people arrested on suspicion of plotting coups in Suriname. We urge the Government to grant those detained protection of right to life and humane treatment.

2. On March 20, 1984 the Commission received the following response from the Government of Suriname and forwarded it to the complainant for his observations:

According to information from the Attorney-General to the Court of Justice in Suriname, the accused persons referred to in the appendix were brought up before the Chief-Prosecutor, Mr. A.I. Ramnewash LI.D., by the Military Police on 10 December 1983. In respect of the accused I. Bissumbar and H. Kasie, an order for their release was issued when they were brought in for the second hearing on 20 December 1983. On January 3, 1984 the case was referred to the examining magistrate for a preliminary judicial examination.

In regard to the rumour that there would be bodies placed under military guard, in respect of which the names of Mssrs. Imro Themen and Henk Essed have been mentioned, we wish to comment as follows: Mr. Imro Themen is at present a civil servant employed at the Ministry of General Affairs, while Mr. Henk Essed was recently on vacation in the United States of America.

The Government of Suriname deplores the fact that your Commission is being supplied with incomplete and incorrect information, and cannot resist the impression that insinuations in this respect are made on purpose, evidently with the intention to discredit our country with your organization. We take the most definite exception to this. . . .

3. Subsequently the following additional information was received and transmitted by the Government for its comments:

Arrest of Political Opponents on 24 November 1983:

Names:

1. Gobardhan, Iwan Rajinderpersad
Born on 22 November 1956.
2. Gobardhan, Omprakash
Born on 5 August 1960
3. Gobardhan, Krishnapersad
Born on 22 April 1962
4. Bekaroe, Ramlall
Born on 16 December 1950
5. Kasi, Harden
Born on 12 October 1962
6. Doerga, Lila
7. Doerga, Krishna
8. Lindveld, Karel
9. Oudsten

On 24 November 1983 these Surinamese citizens were arrested and transported to Fort Zeelandia by armed men in civilian clothes. This was kept secret. Even when relatives went to the military police they denied having arrested the above-mentioned people.

In December 1983 Omprakash Gobardhan and Lindveld were interrogated on TV in the presence of the press including the Dutch media.

Only military Police Commander Liew Yen Tair put a few questions to the prisoners, who had to answer with a yes or no. The press was not allowed to ask questions. On the film the expression of fear and terror could be seen clearly on their faces. In this 'show' the Council was accused of destabilizing activities in Suriname and sending mercenaries to Suriname. However, all persons who had been arrested had Surinamese nationality.

Mrs. Lila Doerga is a diabetic but she could not take any medicine.

In February, the prisoners were put under custody of the civil police. It is reported that in the meantime Karsi, Lila Doerga and Krishna Doerga have been released.

The other prisoners are still held. Most probably they will appear before the court on June 14, 1984.

4. On July 27, 1984 the Commission received the further observations of the Government of Suriname. The pertinent parts of the observations read as follows:

Referring to Your letter of July 5, 1984, Case 9265, I have the honour to inform You as follows: . . .

Mr. Harden Kasi, Mrs. Lila Doerga, Mr. Krishna Doerga, and Mr. R. Oudsten were not prosecuted and have been released.

Mr. Iwan R. Gobardhan was sentenced to 1 year and 6 months, with reduction of the time of his pre-trial detention.

Mr. O. Gobardhan was sentenced to 2 years with reduction of the time of his pre-trial detention.

Mr. Ramlall Bekaroe was sentenced to 1 year with reduction of the time of his pre-trial detention.

Mr. Karel Lindveld was sentenced by the judge in the first circuit (kanton) to 1 year and by the judge in the third circuit (kanton) to 2 years. In both cases his time was reduced with the time of his pre-trial detention.

In case Your Secretariat would like to receive a copy of the above-mentioned judiciary decisions, please feel free to notify us.

5. Subsequently, on November 5, 1984 the Government of Suriname sent photostatic copies of the sentences handed down by the Court on Mssrs. Krishna-persad Gobardhan, Iwan Gobardhan, and Karel Lindveld.

6. On January 9, 1985 a special commission of the IACHR interviewed certain eyewitnesses to the detention of the subjects of this case and heard testimony to the effect that they were tortured at the outset of their incarceration, in some cases lasting several months, and effectively denied legal counsel until the day before their trials in July of 1984, more than seven months after their arrest. The tortures included severe beatings over their entire bodies including their sex organs. These usually took place at night either in Fort Zeelandia or Membre Boekoe Kazerne. Specific mistreatment also included the placing of a chair leg on the victims's outstretched hand while the torturer jumped on the chair. Another technique consisted of forcing the prisoner to drink a liquid that burned the drinker's throat. The torture also included punches, kicks and beatings with clubs and rifle butts. The Commission saw evidence on a number of the victims of broken teeth, noses, legs, collarbones and assorted scars. One had been tied to a car and dragged. Several had been forced to sign confessions.

Psychological torture included the firing of machine guns at the victims' feet. Threats were also made against the wives, mothers and other relatives of the victims. On one occasion several of the victims were forced to lie in freshly dug graves in a local cemetery and threatened with summary execution. One of the victims was subject to an attempted homosexual rape by a military policeman.

7. On January 16, 1985 the special commission of the IACHR visited Santo Boma Penitentiary outside of Paramaribo. There it interviewed a number of prisoners including four who are the subjects of this case.

8. The Commission has verified that most of the subjects of this case have been released.

9. From independent eyewitnesses the Commission received testimony that the torturers included [certain] Surinamese military personnel . . . .

10. The special commission of the IACHR met with certain military authorities

during its on-site visit in Suriname and discussed these accusations of torture and denial of due process. Colonel Liew Yen Tair and Sgt. Major Zeeuw denied the allegations of torture and stated that the decree laws in force under the state of siege permit prolonged detention without judicial warrant and without benefit of counsel by the military police. As to the injuries reported by the victims, the officers indicated that these occurred because the subjects had resisted arrest.

CONSIDERING:

1. That the Government of Suriname has made no response to the Commission regarding the alleged beatings and torture of the subjects of this case.

2. That the decree laws currently in force in Suriname that deal with due process of law *prima facie* violate this non-derogable right.

3. That the American Declaration of the Rights and Duties of Man to which the Government of Suriname is bound as a member state of the Organization of American States, *inter alia*, provides:

Article I. Every human being has the right to life, liberty and the security of his person.

Article XVIII. Every person may resort to the courts to ensure respect for his legal rights. There should likewise be available to him a simple, brief procedure whereby the courts will protect him from acts of authority that, to his prejudice, violate any fundamental constitutional rights.

Article XXV. No person may be deprived of his liberty except in the cases and according to the procedures established by pre-existing law.

Every individual who has been deprived of his liberty has the right to have the legality of his detention ascertained without delay by a court, and the right to be tried without undue delay, or otherwise to be released. He also has the right to humane treatment during the time he is in custody.

Article XXVI. Every accused person is presumed to be innocent until proved guilty.

Every person accused of an offense has the right to be given an impartial and public hearing, and to be tried by courts previously established in accordance with pre-existing laws, and not to receive cruel, infamous or unusual punishment.

4. That the oral testimony of the various non-military eye-witnesses interviewed by the Commission regarding the torture of the subjects of this case and the denial of due process coincide in their essential aspects and corroborate the original complaint and are deemed to be credible by the Commission.

5. That the physical evidence viewed by the Commission in Suriname and abroad bearing on the allegations under consideration tend to corroborate the original complaint insofar as torture and denial of due process are concerned.

6. That the denial of said allegations by the military authorities cited above is deemed by the Commission to be unpersuasive.

THE INTER-AMERICAN COMMISSION ON HUMAN RIGHTS,

RESOLVES:

1. To declare that the Government of Suriname violated the human rights of

the subjects of this case notwithstanding the fact that some were ultimately released from custody.

2. To observe that the violations in question consist in the practice of torture and the denial of due process as provided for in Articles I, XVIII, XXV and XXVI of the American Declaration of the Rights and Duties of Man.

3. To recommend to the Government of Suriname that it immediately commence an exhaustive investigation into the circumstances of this case and duly prosecute and punish those persons responsible for the human rights violations cited herein.

4. To recommend that the Government of Suriname send said report to the IACHR within 60 days of the date of this Resolution.

5. To publish this Resolution in its next Annual Report to the General Assembly of the Organization of American States in the event that the recommendations cited in this Resolution are not satisfactorily implemented.

NOTES

1. The government of Suriname requested reconsideration of Case 9265 on September 11, 1985, approximately two months after the Inter-American Commission decided the case. *See* Case 9265 (Decision on a Request for Reconsideration), Inter-Am. C.H.R. 119, OEA/Ser.L/V/II.66, doc. 10 rev. 1 (1985). The government requested that since it had cooperated with the Commission, had only learned of the allegations of torture when it received the Commission's decision on the case, and was currently investigating the allegations, the Commission reconsider its decision as premature. *Id.* at 120. The Commission denied the request, noting that the original petition had contained allegations of beatings, which should have put the government on notice that the case involved allegations of torture, and the government had failed to provide proof that the torture allegations overwhelmingly corroborated by evidence collected during the Commission's visit were false. *Id.* at 121.

2. For further reading, see: Amnesty International, Suriname: Violations of Human Rights, AI Index: AMR 48/02/87 (1987); International Alert, Suriname (1988); Human Rights Advisory Committee, Human Rights in Suriname (1984).

Vargas, *Visits on the Spot: The Experience of the Inter-American Commission on Human Rights*, in International Law and Fact-Finding in the Field of Human Rights 137-50 (B. Ramcharan ed. 1982):

The Decision to Undertake an On-Site Observation

A visit of the Commission may arise from a spontaneous gesture from the government, inviting the Commission to carry out a visit, or, it may be the result of an express request on the part of the Commission for that government's consent. The latter situation generally arises when, in the judgement of the Commission, there is reason to believe that the situation of human rights in that country warrants investigation.

There is also an intermediate "diplomatic" situation, by which the Commission initiates negotiations with a government, affording it the opportunity to invite the Commission, before its consent is formally requested. This generally happens when the Commission takes the initiative by planning a study of human rights in a particular country. Upon communicating this decision to the government, the Commission suggests that, since a report is in preparation, its understanding would be enhanced if the Commission had the opportunity to visit that country. . . .

If the government does not decide to invite the Commission, the Commission makes a public request for consent to carry out an investigation. If there are still objections, the Commission notes the government's denial of consent in its country report as it did in the cases of Uruguay and Paraguay. . . .

On the other hand, in the cases of Panama, El Salvador, Haiti, Colombia and the second mission to Nicaragua, the initiative for the invitation came from the Governments themselves. These Governments were interested in having the Commission report on the human rights situation in their respective countries which they felt would constitute a reply to what they considered had been unjust criticism levelled against them. . . .

Regulations Governing On-Site Observations

. . . The present Statute of the Commission, approved at the General Assembly in La Paz, Bolivia in 1977, leaves without doubt the Commission's authority to conduct on-site observations even in States not party to the American Convention. The source for this authority is Article 18(g), which states that the Commission shall have powers with respect to all member states of the OAS:

g) to conduct on-site observations in a state, with the consent or at the invitation of the government in question. . . .

Chapter IV (Article 51 to 55) of the Commission's Regulations govern on-site observations.

These articles prescribe the creation of a Special Commission. If a member is a national or a resident of the State in question he is to be disqualified from participation in this Special Commission. In extending its invitation, or in the act of granting its consent to a visit, the government offers to furnish the Special Commission with all the facilities necessary for carrying out an on-site observation. And under the provision of "all necessary facilities" is understood that the government undertakes not to engage in any reprisals against those persons or organizations that provide information or testimony to the Commission. This guarantee is so crucial that it is set forth twice in the Regulations. . . .

Under "all the necessary facilities" which the government undertakes to furnish the Commission during its on-site observation, the following are specifically singled out:

— freedom to interview anyone the Commission chooses in private, without fear of reprisal against the informant;

— freedom to travel freely throughout the national territory in available local means of transportation;

— access to prisons and other centers of detention in order to interview prisoners and detainees, in private;

— access to governmental documents required for the writing of the report;

— freedom to use whatever recording or reproducing devices the Commission chooses in collecting information;

— access to adequate security measures to ensure the safety of the Commission; and

— access to appropriate lodging.

Except for the provision of adequate security measures, the expenses of the Commission and support staff during the visit are borne by the Commission.

Activities During a Visit

Until now, the average duration of an on-site visit by the Commission has been between 6 and 16 days.

Upon arrival, the Special Commission meets to schedule its program of activities using as a working paper the provisional program prepared by the Secretariat.

Next, the Special Commission usually holds a press conference to publicize its program and to call upon the representative sectors of society to present their points of view. This communiqué also alerts persons, who feel that their human rights have been violated, to present their complaints at the local offices of the Commission, which are usually set up in the hotel where the Commission is staying.

The program undertaken by the Commission basically consists of interviews with government officials and with representatives of the different sectors of the national life . . . .

Immediate Importance and Results of the Visit

Whereas the principal objective of an on-site observation is to investigate the situation of human rights in a country in order to prepare a report, the very presence of the Commission in a country, in addition to facilitating the verification of certain facts, also brings about a certain improvement in the observance of human rights. The fact that a government invites or consents to a Commission visit, reveals, at a minimum, a desire to improve the observance of human rights.

The case of the Colombia visit in 1980 evidenced the Commission's utility in the resolution of a specific problem which the Government (as well as the militants) wished to see resolved.

When the Commission arrived in Bogotá on April 21, 1980, it was invited by the Colombian Government to participate in the negotiation process then being carried out between the Government and the captors of the Embassy of the Dominican Republic in that capital. The latter were members of an urban guerrilla organization known as M-19.

The Commission, in keeping with its humanitarian mandate, decided to intervene in that process but refused to act as either mediator or a formal negotiator. Rather, it limited its role to offering its good offices to both sides.

Based on an understanding between the M-19 guerrillas and the Government, the IACHR, by means of an exchange of letters between its President and the Minister of Foreign Relations, agreed to assure the guerrillas' safe-conduct out of the country by physically accompanying the captors and their hostages to the airport.

In addition the Commission committed itself to monitoring certain ongoing military trials in which members of M-19 and another guerrilla organization, known as the Fuerzas Armadas Revolucionarias Colombianas (FARC), were tried on charges of having committed crimes against the state. The Commission's task in this regard consists in assuring the fairness of the trials and respect for the human rights of the accused.

Even the most skeptical observers of the Commission acknowledge that its visits have an impact. A politician, known for his criticism of the OAS, expressed the following when the Commission arrived in his country: "I think that this visit will only serve to obtain the release of certain political prisoners and to have the walls of the jails painted." Certainly, this statement is an over-simplification, for the results of the visits have been much more important; but, even if such were the case, the judge of the utility of a Commission visit ought to be that of released political prisoners.

[Some] governments have responded to the Commission's recommendations [by] permitt[ing] gradual improvements. Moreover, as in the case of Panama, suggestions made by the Commission towards the end of its visit to the Head of State, General Omar Torrijos, brought about some changes in legislation. Three decrees, restrictive of freedom of assembly, freedom of expression, and the right to due process, were revoked just prior to the Special Commission's departure. In the course of the second visit to Nicaragua, the Minister of Interior, Commander Tomas Borge, during his visit with the members of the Commission, ordered the release of all the women prisoners (with the exception of two).

But the most important result obtained from an on-site observation is the confirmation of certain violations of which the government has been accused. In El Salvador, for example, the Special Commission was able to confirm the existence of secret cells by means of marks left by the former detainees who had subsequently disappeared, and in Nicaragua in 1978, it collected evidence of the acts of violence attributed to the National Guard, in particular, during September, 1978.

Drafting, Approval and Publication of the Report

Once the visit is completed, the staff of the Commission, in addition to processing the complaints received, compiles all available documentation and in some cases prepares a draft report on the on-site observation. . . .

The structure of each [report] must follow that used in all of the country reports prepared by the IACHR. A report begins with an introduction, a description of the background history of the visit and a summary of the program of activities carried out by the Special Commission. In Chapter One, there follows a study of the legal system of the country with respect to human rights, and in successive chapters, an analysis, the observance of each of the rights set forth in the American Declaration of the Rights and Duties of Man or the American Convention on Human Rights, when appropriate — the right to life, integrity of the person, physical liberty, justice, and due process, including *habeas corpus* and *amparo*,[1] the

[1 Ed.: *Amparo* is a writ in Latin American law whereby the claimant can seek protection from any governmental infringement of rights and duties. Like *habeas corpus*, *amparo* can be used to challenge illegal detention, but it can also be used against other illegal conduct.]

freedom of expression, of religion and conscience, and of assembly and association. Finally, in the last chapter, the Commission summarizes its conclusions and makes its recommendations. . . .

[A]fter [the report] is approved [by the Commission] it is sent to the government in question which is requested to present its observations and comments.

Usually the Commission requests the government to submit its reply within six weeks, but in special circumstances, that period is adjusted. In Nicaragua, because of the urgency of the human rights situation, the fact that the 17th Meeting of Consultation of Foreign Ministers had requested the Commission to accelerate the date for its trip, and the fact that the Commission was not scheduled to meet until some months later, motivated the Commission to request that the Government of Nicaragua respond within eight days, without prejudice to presenting further observations to the Meeting of Consultation at a later date.

The government's observations and comments are considered in a plenary session of the Commission, which may decide to modify the report as regards evident inaccuracies in the light of the reply. If the government makes no observations, but only comments, as was the case with Panama, the Commission does not change the original text but publishes the report together with the government's comments.

F. FACTFINDING WITHOUT ON-SITE OBSERVATION

As discussed earlier, on-site observations are not always practical or even possible. The following reading is an excerpt from a study prepared by two NGOs — Asia Watch and the Minnesota Lawyers International Human Rights Committee — on the human rights situation in the Democratic People's Republic of Korea. The study was prepared without a visit, for reasons described in the report. In reading the report, examine the reasons the NGOs decided to undertake the study and consider how the NGOs dealt with the issues identified in the Weissbrodt & McCarthy article. In addition, note the factfinding techniques the NGOs were able to utilize without visiting the country and question how an on-site visit, assuming one was possible, would have aided or hindered the investigation. Finally, consider the value of investigating a country like the Democratic People's Republic of Korea, about which the sources of reliable information are extremely limited, and the problems associated with such an investigation.

Asia Watch & Minnesota Lawyers International Human Rights Committee, Human Rights in the Democratic People's Republic of Korea (North Korea) 1-11 (1988) (footnotes omitted):

INTRODUCTION

A. **Objectives**

We undertook this study out of a desire to examine a society that had largely evaded international scrutiny of its human rights practices. Many human rights organizations, including our own, have devoted scant attention to the Democratic People's Republic of Korea because of the tremendous difficulty of acquiring information. We found this inattention troubling. Because the credibility of human rights organizations depends in large measure on their willingness to apply human rights standards to all countries of the world, we feared that the failure to address human rights conditions in countries like the DPRK, albeit for practical reasons, might call that credibility into question.

We began this study with an optimism that, even as to the DPRK, a sustained effort could overcome the many obstacles to human rights monitoring. Now that the study has been completed, we must concede that we have succeeded only in part. Although we believe that we have unearthed substantial evidence of a pattern of gross human rights violations in the DPRK, we at times have been required to state our conclusions in relatively tentative terms. For example, as explained more fully in the next section on methodology, we were denied access to the DPRK, and thus were forced to rely on accounts by former residents now outside the DPRK and foreign travelers. As a result, the information we managed to acquire was often less comprehensive, or more dated, than we would have liked, limiting our ability to make unequivocal assertions of fact.

We believe, nonetheless, that the conclusions we do reach are sound. There remains the possibility, however, that further research will require modification or updating of our findings. We welcome such research, and, indeed, hope that this study will serve as a springboard to further monitoring efforts. Only ongoing attention will reveal the full dimensions of the serious human rights violations plaguing the DPRK. In the meantime, we feel justified in assigning responsibility to the DPRK Government for any inaccuracies that its policies of enforced secrecy might have caused.

B. Methodology

1. Obstacles

We faced several obstacles in our research. The first, which we did not really expect, was a widespread indifference to human rights in the DPRK based on a sense that the problem was so overwhelming that efforts at change were futile. One very visible human rights leader told us that he was initially uninterested in our study because, he believed, everyone knows that "there are no human rights in North Korea; the people are so repressed that there is no dissent and no one in prison." But while human rights in the DPRK are, indeed, severely repressed, we believe that there is a distinct value in documenting that repression in order to illustrate the emptiness of the DPRK's professed respect for human rights, with the aim of encouraging greater respect for international human rights norms.

A second, and rather similar, unexpected obstacle came from some Asian scholars who believe the DPRK is so unique that comparing its human rights situation to that of any other country is useless. This study, like the rest of our work, does not engage in such comparisons, but assesses the record of the DPRK against established international standards to which the Government of the DPRK has agreed to be bound. On 14 September 1981 the DPRK acceded to the International Covenant on Civil and Political Rights and the International Covenant on Economic, Social and Cultural Rights. By this action, the Government indicated its willingness to be bound by the fundamental human rights guarantees protected by those two multilateral treaties and related international human rights instruments.

We also anticipated a number of barriers to our research which often plague human rights monitoring efforts. These included:

a. A climate of fear that would prevent individuals from reporting violations because of an inordinate risk of reprisal.... [T]he DPRK Penal Code contains a number of provisions which effectively forbid the transmission of information about human rights violations abroad. The Penal Code and the policies of the DPRK Government have created a climate of fear which makes it almost impossible to obtain information directly from North Korean citizens currently living in the DPRK. Diplomats and many who have visited Pyongyang report being isolated from ordinary residents of the DPRK because of their extreme reluctance to talk to foreigners. At best, many DPRK residents simply repeat their Government's line that they live in the ideal society, even when faced with direct evidence to the contrary.

b. A lack of popular awareness of human rights norms or expectation that basic rights should be respected. The DPRK Government has taken many measures ... to prevent North Koreans from learning about their international human rights or receiving any information that the Government does not wish them to hear. Article 53 of the DPRK Constitution provides: "Citizens have freedom of speech, the press, assembly, association and of demonstration." In reality, however, these constitutional rights are not known to most North Koreans and are practiced only with specific permission of the DPRK authorities.

c. The lack of an independent judiciary which could respond to reports of human rights violations from an independent bar. [T]here is very little evidence of an independent judiciary or an independent legal profession in the DPRK. Lawyers and judges are, in any case, too frightened to provide information to international human rights organizations or to challenge the Government in any way.

d. The lack of domestic organizations which concern themselves with human rights. Because no such human rights organizations exist in the DPRK, there is no natural source of human rights information or publicity of human rights violations....

e. The inability of the local media to report human rights matters. We have monitored DPRK newspapers and radio for several years and have found no reporting on human rights matters, even though the media does provide some indirect information that gives an indication of human rights problems. The newspapers, radio, and all other forms of media are controlled completely by the Government. No foreign journalists are known to be accredited to Pyongyang, although a few have traveled to the DPRK for very brief and closely monitored visits....

f. The unreliability of human rights information that does become available. Because the Government is nearly the only source of information from within the DPRK, it emits a steady stream of self-congratulatory statements which almost certainly are unreliable. Indeed, visitors are frequently presented with obviously fraudulent statements, materials, and demonstrations. For example, a Latin American visitor to the 1987 meeting of the Non-aligned Movement in Pyongyang told of being taken past stores with fully stocked windows. When the meeting adjourned at an unscheduled hour, the delegate passed the same stores to find that the food had been removed before any North Korean shopper could have had access. Another visitor was shown a "typical" apartment with many electrical appliances. The visitor noted, however, that the apartment lacked electrical outlets to accommodate the appliances. A tall Scandinavian visitor was surprised to find that a Pyongyang newspaper photograph of Kim Il Sung and him had been cropped and altered to make it appear that the visitor was not much taller than Kim Il Sung. Many visitors have indicated that their guides made statements which the visitors thought to be absurd and unbelievable; the guides were apparently unwilling to retract these statements even if shown obvious evidence to the contrary.

The Republic of Korea (South Korea) has also engaged in a systematic pattern of issuing misinformation and inaccurate information about the DPRK, often providing inaccurate data to outsiders and then quoting their reports as if they were independent. As a result, any material which derives directly or indirectly from South Korean sources must be checked and rechecked against independent data.

g. A language with which human rights researchers tend not to be familiar. Many human rights organizations do not employ Korean-speaking researchers to investigate abuses in the Korean peninsula. The language barrier has been overcome in the case of South Korea because the country is relatively open to foreign travel, journalists, and to human rights investigators. But since the flow of information from the DPRK is so limited, the lack of Korean-speaking human rights investigators can severely hamper research capacity.

h. The lack of communication links (e.g., telephone, letters, business travel, etc.) with the outside world. . . . [T]he DPRK is almost completely isolated from the Western countries where most international human rights organizations and international media are located. The diplomats stationed in Pyongyang represent mainly socialist and Third World countries. Other visitors are often confined to highly regulated show tours which prevent them from seeing more than the Government wishes them to see. Some business travel into North Korea has begun to occur in recent years, but most business visitors are afraid to talk lest their business relations be severed by the Government. And it appears that correspondence with the DPRK is monitored by government censors.

i. The difficulty of relying on a refugee or expatriate community. Much of the information about the DPRK comes from refugees who, because they must continually justify their decision to flee, may not always be the most trustworthy source of information. Since the end of the Korean Conflict in 1953, there have been somewhat less than 1,000 people who have escaped from North to South Korea. The Government of the Republic of Korea (South Korea) has developed a practice of isolating escaped North Koreans for a period varying from a few weeks to two years so as to debrief them thoroughly and ensure that they are not spies. Because these escaped North Koreans are often indoctrinated during this period, evidence gleaned from them must be carefully scrutinized and cross-checked. Some North Koreans, however, have escaped via Japan, Singapore, and other countries, so that they can provide somewhat more reliable information.

j. The impossibility of sending a fact-finding mission to the country. As discussed above, no international human rights organization has been able to send a fact-finding mission to the DPRK. Asia Watch and the Minnesota Lawyers International Human Rights Committee sought on several occasions during the past two years to obtain permission to visit the DPRK. The DPRK did not answer any of the letters requesting visits and failed to respond substantively to oral requests tendered to DPRK diplomats at the United Nations. The DPRK Government has been willing to receive various visitors — many of whom we interviewed — including selected scholars, journalists, church leaders, and Korean-Americans. But these visits are strictly controlled, and visitors are encouraged to write adulatory comments about what they see. Scholars and others know that strongly negative portrayals of life in North Korea will jeopardize their future access to the country.

Some visitors and Asian scholars also have political leanings which may limit the trustworthiness of their reports on the DPRK.

2. *Research Steps*

These considerable obstacles make understandable the failure of international human rights organizations to undertake more fact-finding and reporting about the DPRK. We hoped to overcome these obstacles through a concentrated effort by a group of scholars who, unlike many human rights researchers, would work only on this single country.

First, the most important step in conducting this study was to recruit a Korean-speaking researcher. We were very fortunate to have a Korean-speaking lawyer who had no previous involvement or apparent bias on issues relating to the DPRK or the Republic of Korea.

Second, we undertook a very thorough survey of the available secondary information on the DPRK, of which we found a tremendous quantity. Although much of this information is in the English language, the most valuable material was in Korean and Japanese. There was additional material in German, Russian, Swedish, and other languages.

Third, we subscribed to the Foreign Broadcast Information Service (FBIS) and other journals that allowed some monitoring of recent information about events in the DPRK.

Fourth, we notified over one hundred scholars and other potential sources of information that we were undertaking the research. We received written responses and obtained documentary information from a large number of these scholars, and we interviewed many of them as well as other secondary informants.

Fifth, we gathered the reports which the DPRK Government has issued about its own human rights performance. For example, the Government has submitted reports to the Human Rights Committee and the Committee on Economic, Social and Cultural Rights, pursuant to the International Covenant on Civil and Political Rights and the International Covenant on Economic, Social and Cultural Rights.

Sixth, we traveled to and/or gathered relevant information from the People's Republic of China, Denmark, France, Japan, the Republic of Korea, Sweden, the Union of Soviet Socialist Republics, and other countries. For example, there are several thousand Koreans in Japan who have visited relatives in the DPRK. These Korean-Japanese are a substantial resource for information on the DPRK. Very few scholars and human rights organizations have systematically interviewed these visitors. We visited Japan several times to gather information. There also exists a rather insular community of Koreans in Dong-bei, which is the region of the People's Republic of China adjoining the DPRK. We undertook some research in that area, but additional resources and time would yield far more information than we were able to obtain.

Seventh, we interviewed a number of North Koreans who had escaped from their country, as well as foreigners who had previously lived in North Korea but have now left. It would have been best primarily to have interviewed persons whose first place of residence outside the DPRK was not South Korea, as such persons might provide somewhat more reliable information. Unfortunately, we had only limited sources in this regard, as most of the ex-residents of North Korea whom we interviewed came first to live in the South. Nonetheless, we took measures to attempt to guard against bias. Rather than solicit generalities, the interviews concentrated on personal experiences and observations, daily life, and other concrete matters. Informants were politely cross-examined and the information provided was cross-checked with other sources. We undertook these interviews without the presence of any translator or other person who might have made the interviewed individual reluctant to speak freely. We have summarized several of the interviews ... but we have omitted the names of the persons interviewed to protect them and their families from reprisals. The individuals were assured that their identities would be held in confidence....

Eighth, we organized our analysis around the internationally accepted definition of human rights provided by the Universal Declaration of Human Rights. The Universal Declaration furnishes a simpler format for presenting the report than do the more detailed and complex provisions of the two International Covenants. The basic rights in the Universal Declaration are amplified by the provisions of the International Covenant on Civil and Political Rights and the International Covenant on Economic, Social and Cultural Rights, which have been ratified by the DPRK and which are cited where their provisions add substantially to the norms quoted from the Universal Declaration.

Ninth, we have generally begun each chapter of this report with pertinent provisions from the DPRK Constitution and other laws, as well as official statements of the rights that are afforded in the DPRK. These citations allow the reader to assess the degree to which these official pronouncements reflect the facts we present.

Tenth, we have followed the format of most international human rights fact-finding reports in omitting most footnotes and references to individuals who provided information — particularly if there is fear of retaliation against family members. We also have not disclosed the identity of other sources (such as academics, businesspeople, and diplomats) because their access to the DPRK might be jeopardized. In some contexts we have cited secondary sources because they provided significant supporting material. The bibliography provides a list of the most significant primary and secondary sources of published information. By providing only some references, however, the text may give the impression that we lacked sources for the other findings in the report. On the contrary, the findings in the report are supported by interviews, primary materials, or the secondary materials listed in the bibliography, as well as our analysis of the accuracy and consistency of the information that we gathered.

Eleventh, this report does not claim to give a completely up-to-date record of human rights violations in the DPRK, but rather represents a pattern of such violations documented over several years. This report reflects research which was completed up to January 1988, but some more recent information has been added up through October 1988. In some cases we have only been able to illustrate recent violations by reference to occurrences of the past. We believe these gaps reflect our lack of access to contemporary information rather than a fundamental change in current practices. Before incorporating such cases in our reports, we made certain that corroborative information suggested that the practices continued into the recent period. Such corroborative information has come from more recent documents, as well as from diplomats, visiting scholars, businesspeople, and other travelers. Indeed, as a general matter, we have reason to believe that the human rights situation in the DPRK has not changed significantly over the past fifteen years. For example, the information that we collected from multiple sources about the ill-treatment of prisoners shows a very consistent pattern over a wide span of years, through at least the mid-1980s. There is no information suggesting that prisoners at any time through the present have been treated humanely. Contributing to this continuity is the fact that, throughout its history, the Government of the DPRK has had one leader, whose role has been steadily consolidated. For all these reasons, we believe that we have painted an accurate picture despite the obvious difficulties we encountered in gathering information. Nonetheless, with respect to specific reports of abuses, the reader should take seriously the qualifying language that we use, as it has not been possible to confirm each and every report that we believe merited inclusion in this study. If errors emerge, we believe they will be due principally to the DPRK Government, which has sought to shroud its actions under a veil of secrecy. Within these constraints, however, we take responsibility for the conclusions drawn in this report.

Twelfth, we sent a draft of this study to the DPRK Government for its response and comments before publication.... The response charged that the draft report was "full of lies and falsifications," asserted that human rights violations in the DPRK are "unthinkable" because the country "is a most advanced one which places the highest value on the sovereignty and dignity of man," and threatened that if we printed the report, we would be "held fully responsible for all the consequences arising therefrom." The response failed, however, to address any of the specific concerns detailed in the report. A short time later, an assistant to the DPRK Ambassador telephoned to inquire whether his letter had been received and whether the report would be published. We told the assistant that the Ambassador's letter was inadequate because of its lack of specificity. The Ambassador then sent a second letter..., which repeated the general denials, again without reference to any specific point in the report....

NOTES

For further reading on factfinding, see:

Cohn, *International Fact-Finding Processes*, 18 Rev. Int'l Commiss'n Jurists 40 (1977);

Franck & Fairley, *Procedural Due Process in Human Rights Fact-Finding by International Agencies*, 74 Am. J. Int'l L. 308 (1980);

L. Garber, Guidelines for International Election Observing (1984);

Norris, *Observations In Loco: Practice and Procedure of the Inter-American Commission on Human Rights, 1979-1983*, 19 Tex. Int'l L.J. 285 (1984);

International Law and Fact-Finding in the Field of Human Rights (B. Ramcharan ed. 1982);

Orentlicher, *Bearing Witness: The Art and Science of Human Rights Fact-Finding*, 3 Harv. Hum. Rts. J. 83 (1990);

H. Thoolen & B. Verstappen, Human Rights Missions: A study of the fact-finding practice of non-governmental organizations (1986);

B. Verstappen, *Human Rights Reports: An annotated bibliography of fact-finding missions* (1987);

von Potobsky, *On-the-Spot Visits: An Important Cog in the ILO's Supervisory Machinery*, 120 Int'l Labour Rev. 581 (1981);

Weissbrodt, *International Trial Observers*, 18 Stan. J. Int'l L. 27 (1982);

Weissbrodt, *International Factfinding in Regard to Torture*, 57 Nordic J. Int'l L. 151 (1988).

G. IMPACT OF FACTFINDING INVESTIGATIONS

Americas Watch, Asia Watch, & Helsinki Watch, Four Failures: A Report on the U.N. Special Rapporteurs on Human Rights in Chile, Guatemala, Iran and Poland 15-21 (1986) (footnotes omitted):

[Ed. Note: The following reading is an excerpt from an NGO report criticizing the work of four U.N. special rapporteurs. Chapter 5 introduced the Special Rapporteur process. Reader may want to review the material in chapter 5 describing that process before reading the following excerpt.]

The Colville Report on Guatemala

Since 1979, at its annual sessions, the Commission on Human Rights has repeatedly expressed its concern about the human rights situation in *Guatemala*. In March 1982, in resolution 1982/31 the Commission requested its Chairman to appoint a Special Rapporteur to prepare a study of the situation of human rights in Guatemala to be presented to the Commission at its next session.

The government of Guatemala declared its willingness to cooperate with the Special Rapporteur, a fact acknowledged in resolution 37/184 of the General Assembly on December 17, 1982. As of that date, a Rapporteur had not yet been appointed. On December 31, 1982, the Chairman of the Commission appointed Mrs. Elizabeth Odio Benito [Costa Rica] to the post. The government of Guatemala, however, objected to this choice and requested that another candidate should be proposed before the next session of the Commission. . . .

In March 1983 the Chairman appointed Viscount Colville of Culross, former member of the Conservative government in Britain, as Special Rapporteur on human rights in Guatemala. Sources close to the Human Rights Commission have told Americas Watch that before Lord Colville was appointed, the Guatemalan government had made it clear that it would cooperate if he was designated.

A. Methodology

Over the past three years, Lord Colville's reports have drawn criticism of methodology and substance from many quarters. The major concern over methodology is Colville's use of military escort and transportation during his site visits. Lord Colville continues to assert, however, that a stranger, flying by Army helicopter to remote Indian villages, accompanied by a member of a Guatemalan Army intelligence unit and a member of the Foreign Ministry, will receive candid accounts from victims in cases where it is alleged that the Army has been implicated in gross abuses of human rights. Lord Colville addressed these criticisms in his 1985 report, saying that it was the Guatemalan government's concern for his safety that required him to travel with a military escort.

In contrast to his previous reports, Lord Colville's 1985 report described cases where informants appeared frightened or unwilling to cooperate. In one case, Lord Colville indicated that one of his informants had been murdered. These difficulties in his fact-finding are not mentioned in the section of his report in which Lord Colville addresses criticisms of his methodology.

B. Reinterpretation of the Mandate

The 1985 Colville report differs from his previous reports in another respect. According to paragraph 15 of U.N. Human Rights Commission resolution 1985/36, the Special Rapporteur for Guatemala is asked "to assess in particular allegations of politically motivated killings, disappearances, acts of torture, extrajudicial executions and confinement in clandestine prisons." In his 1985 report, however, Colville asserted that the issue of disappearances fell under the purview of the U.N. Working Group on Enforced or Involuntary Disappearances. Having thus redefined his task, Lord Colville eliminated from his mandate one of the major aspects of human rights abuse in Guatemala. The problem of disappearances has been an ongoing tragedy there for the past 20 years. Of some 90,000 disappearances reported throughout Latin America, an estimated 35,000 occurred in Guatemala where the practice originated in 1966. Colville did not decline to consider disappearances in 1983 and 1984. But, in 1985, the Special Rapporteur on Human Rights for Guatemala unilaterally altered the mandate given him by resolution of the U.N. Human Rights Commission.

C. Civil Patrols

There are other problems of continuity in Colville's reports. The 1985 report allots three paragraphs for discussion of civil patrols in which some 900,000 males perform onerous unpaid service. The Special Rapporteur fails to address the compulsory nature of service, although in a previous report he acknowledged that an army circular required all men between 18 and 50 to join, with refusal regarded as an indication of subversive tendencies. He also failed to address the complaint that service in civil patrols turns villagers into combatants, and therefore under the international laws of war, legitimate targets for the insurgents. Though Colville has compared service in the civil patrols to military service, he neglects any mention that patrollers are unpaid, while soldiers are paid. Instead, Colville indirectly justifies this distinction by noting that, though the patrols may disrupt a man's work, they are considered worthwhile for the sense of security they bring.

Guatemala's new Constitution includes a provision guaranteeing that no one may be required to join an organization for the purpose of self-defense. While not directly acknowledging the compulsory nature of civilian patrols, Colville does recognize that this provision would have to be amended for their continued operation.

D. Evidence of Official Responsibility for Abuses

Colville has consistently played down any evidence of official responsibility for killings and disappearances. He has done this by omission, denial, or by understated acknowledgment of evidence pointing to government culpability.

In 1985, for the first time, Colville took note of the statistics on politically-motivated killings provided by the Guatemalan Human Rights Commission, a group that is based in Mexico. Based on these statistics, Colville focused on seven incidents of allegations of major human rights abuses. In two cases, he found evidence that abuses did take place. In three cases, he did not have time to visit the site involved. In one case, he found no evidence of government involvement and chose not to make a site visit.

The final case involved a report published in the Guatemalan press that the bodies of two finca administrators were thrown from a helicopter into Mazate Stadium. Both bodies were recovered revealing evidence of torture including amputation of genital organs, stab wounds, and bullet holes.

Colville reported that the National Police knew of the case, but that they disputed the press account. According to the police, "The two men were not dead but wounded; they were picked up by a helicopter and lowered onto the football stadium at Mazatenango with ropes. It was the only site to ensure their transfer to hospital. Police records will be provided and the Special Rapporteur will report further." . . .

In another case, one in which the Special Rapporteur visited Saquiya, he reports that he spoke with villagers who confirmed the disappearances of eleven people. He took this information to the *comandante* in Chimaltenango who reported that indeed, eleven people had been captured in army operations against a guerrilla band. Colville transmitted the list of eleven names to the Working Group on Enforced or Involuntary Disappearances. In the next paragraph, Colville reached the conclusion that "there was no easy answer available to the question of who was responsible," despite the admission of army involvement by the *comandante* himself.

As the Special Rapporteur's findings sharply contradict virtually every other report from international human rights organizations — such as the OAS Inter-American Commission on Human Rights, Amnesty International and Americas Watch — one is led to ask what accounts for such a drastic divergence. Lord Avebury, chairman of the British Parliamentary Human Rights Group and co-author of its report on Guatemala, *Bitter and Cruel*, who has discussed the differences in his findings with the Special Rapporteur, suggests a possible explanation. Colville takes the view, according to Avebury, that it is important to take all steps possible to further Guatemala's movement toward democracy. This goal is widely shared. However, is the furtherance of this goal intended by the United Nations to justify efforts to influence reporting on the level of human rights abuse?

In an interview with the *Wall Street Journal*, Colville made it clear that he does consider that his particular agenda — which may be laudable in and of itself — should affect his reporting:

> The question is, unless you're in favor of a communist victory, how do you persuade a military government to give up its power and go back to the barracks. You don't do that by writing a 100-page report of pure condemnation.

The Special Rapporteur has apparently taken on a political role that involves him at the center of current internal developments in Guatemala.

Lord Colville has stated that he has tried to produce a balanced report, in which the good can be weighed against the bad. Yet, how can political murder and disappearances be "weighed" against progress in electoral reform? Wedding the publication of a balanced report to an assessment of the actual human rights situation seriously compromises the mission of the Special Rapporteur and his findings must be evaluated accordingly.

QUESTIONS

What effects did the perceived flaws in the Special Rapporteur's methodology have on the impact of his factfinding activities? Are the Special Rapporteur's justifications for his procedures valid? What procedures could he have followed to avoid the criticisms and yet still protect his safety and expedite the factfinding process? Did the circumstances surrounding the Commission's appointment of the Special Rapporteur affect the impact of the factfinding process? You should consider the lessons learned regarding the need for fair and unbiased procedures as you formulate procedures for your mission to Palau.

ASSESSING THE IMPACT OF FACTFINDING INVESTIGATIONS

It is often difficult to assess the impact of factfinding. As the material on Argentina reprinted in the chapter suggests, the focus of international attention on human rights violations in a country may lead to a substantial improvement. Human rights abuses often decrease after factfinding inquiries due to the government's embarrassment at disclosure of abuses and desire to improve its image in the world community. At the very least, confirming the allegations of human rights violations makes denial difficult and forces governments to account for their wrongdoing in an international forum.

In addition to public embarrassment, establishing human rights violations through factfinding can lead to sanctions directed at the violating country. The U.S., for example, hinges a certain amount of its foreign aid on the human rights record of recipient countries. Although sanctions are usually bilateral, in certain egregious cases — such as South Africa — countries participate in multilateral sanctions. The use of sanctions to promote compliance with human rights norms is beyond the scope of this chapter and will be addressed in chapter 11. Nevertheless, readers should be aware that governments may use the results of factfinding investigations as a basis for imposing sanctions on the violating country. The common pairing of sanctions with factfinding makes it difficult to assess the impact of factfinding without considering the impact of the sanctions on human rights violators pursued as a result of that factfinding.

In studying the excerpt below, readers might consider whether the article demonstrates a causal connection between human rights factfinding and other international pressures, on the one hand, and improvements in the human rights situation, on the other.

M. Bartolomei & D. Weissbrodt, The Impact of Factfinding and International Pressures on the Human Rights Situation in Argentina, 1976-1983:[2]

It is remarkable that there are almost no academics or activists who have even attempted to assess the effectiveness of human rights measures. It is, of course, very difficult to demonstrate effectiveness in many areas of human endeavor and particularly in international human rights work. Human rights activists investigate abuses and write letters to governments because they believe that speaking out is better than remaining silent in the face of repression. When challenged they can point to anecdotal evidence of prisoners released, torture stopped, and executions prevented. More formal proof of results is harder to find.

The case of Argentina during the period 1976-83 provides an opportunity to consider the effectiveness of human rights factfinding and pressure. There are at least two reasons for selecting the case for study: First, an historical record has been developed on what happened during the relevant period. The Argentine government made considerable efforts after 1983 to investigate what happened. A lot of evidence was adduced at the trials of some of the leaders who were responsible. Many victims have written accounts of their experiences. There is also an extensive scholarly literature about the period, even though this article is apparently the first to correlate human rights efforts with results. Second, there exist relatively reliable statistics about the most prevalent form of human rights abuse, that is, disappearances. Such statistics permit an analyst to track the prevalence of abuses against the human rights measures attempted.

The difficulties in this analysis are impressive. Unfortunately, no one has systematically interviewed high government officials or the less well-known perpetrators of human rights abuses to learn why they started killing people and why they stopped. There are also so many different influences which may affect a government's conduct. External pressures are often far less significant than internal events. In the case of Argentina, Ronald Dworkin has written, "The junta's power was finally broken, not by any domestic or international concern about human rights, but by its own economic and, in the end, military ineptitude."[3] Dworkin in some ways reflects the popular view that it was the 1982 war in the South Atlantic which brought down the Argentine military government. But he realized that the disappearances had ended far earlier, that is, in 1979. The question is why did they end? There is no simple answer.

1. *The Human Rights Situation in Argentina*

On March 24, 1976, a military coup overthrew the government of "Isabella" Peron to stabilize the economy and to get rid of "leftist threats" to public order. In a matter of days, the new Argentine military government dissolved the Congress

---

[2] This article is a substantially edited version of a more detailed study with the same title. The article took as a point of departure: M. Bartolomei, Gross and Massive Violations of Human Rights in Argentina, 1976-1983, draft LL.D. thesis in International Law, University of Lund, Sweden (1990).

[3] Dworkin, *Introduction*, in Argentine National Commission on the Disappeared, Nunca Más xv (1986).

and other legislative bodies; dismissed judges, including judges of the Supreme Court with life tenure; appointed new judges; authorized the military to arrest "subversives"; and suspended constitutional rights. At first, the military government focused their repressive measures against the members of "guerilla groups" and militant workers in factories. The "dirty war," as it was called even by the military, soon extended much further: During 1976 and 1977 thousands were arrested, were subjected to disappearance, were tortured, and were killed. The military government focused principally on younger people in that over 80% of those affected were aged 21 to 40. In addition to the disappeared, thousands of Argentine nationals were acknowledged by the government to be in detention. Many of those prisoners were tortured and/or killed. During the period 1976 through 1983 approximately 12-15,000 persons disappeared in Argentina.

2. *Human Rights Factfinding and Pressure*

There were at least five kinds of international human rights factfinding and pressure brought to bear in the case of Argentina. The world got its *first* warning of the horrors of the "dirty war" when families of victims were alerted. A *second* wave of information came from Argentine organizations — like the Mothers of the Plaza de Mayo. *Third*, international human rights organizations investigated and publicized the abuses. *Fourth*, the Inter-American Commission on Human Rights of the Organization of American States, together with the U.S. Government, played an important role. And *fifth*, the assistance of the United Nations was sought.

a. *Early Warning: Foreigners Caught in the Net*

The first warning of the government's "dirty war" came to the families of the many young people who were abducted. The families tried to discover what had happened to their relatives who had disappeared. The families sought explanations from the Argentine government and the authorities refused to acknowledge that they had custody of the disappeared individuals. For the outside world, the first indication of what was occurring in Argentina came when foreigners were abducted. For example, Gwen Loken Lopez — a Minnesota native who had married a young Argentine lawyer — was abducted in April 1976, tortured, and then released in September 1976 after Representative Donald Fraser of Minneapolis obtained the intercession of Alejandro Orfila, the Argentine Secretary-General of the Organization of American States. Father Patrick Rice, an Irish priest working in Argentina, was detained in October 1976 and was later released due to the efforts of the Irish government. Dagmar Hagelin, a seventeen year-old with joint Swedish and Argentine nationality, was shot, stuffed in the trunk of an automobile, and abducted by a group of men outside the home of one of her friends in January 1977. The Swedish government took up the case, but she was never found. The deteriorating situation was further publicized by the disappearance of two French nuns. The Argentine government's refusal to acknowledge their detention prompted the French government and the French media to seek information about the whereabouts of the two French nationals. While their fate is still unknown, there is some indication that they were killed by being thrown from an airplane into the sea.

After March 1976 a considerable number of refugees from other countries in Latin America, who had previously sought refuge in Argentina, were abducted; some were returned forcibly to their countries of origin where they suffered persecution; others were threatened with abduction or *refoulement*. The United

Nations High Commissioner for Refugees sought to protect the refugees in Argentina, to seek their release, and/or to find new homes for them in other countries.

b.   *The Role of Argentine Nongovernmental Organizations*

In addition to the publicity caused by the abduction of foreigners, a number of organizations in Argentina drew national and international attention to the human rights violations. For example, a number of women whose children had been abducted, began in April-May 1977 to hold vigils in the Plaza de Mayo directly across from the President's residence. The women received considerable attention from the international media and were called the Mothers of the Plaza de Mayo. In October-November 1977 another group of women organized themselves as the Grandmothers of the Plaza de Mayo. The two organizations became known for their continuing courageous vigils which provided a public witness to the plight of the thousands of disappeared and their families.

The Permanent Assembly for Human Rights was established in 1976 prior to the military coup. The Argentine League for the Rights of Man had been in existence since the 1930's. The Ecumenical Movement for Human Rights was composed of representatives of the various religious denominations. A number of other human rights organizations, including the Center of Legal and Social Studies (CELS), which was formed in 1979, and the Servicio Paz y Justicia also worked against the repression in Argentina. The Permanent Assembly for Human Rights, in cooperation with several other organizations, produced several lists of the thousands of individuals who had disappeared after 1975. The lists were submitted to the Argentine authorities, but the lists were confiscated. The offices of the organizations and their bank accounts were seized by the Argentine authorities.

Some Argentinians were also able to leave the country and attempted to inform world opinion about the situation in their homeland. For example, the Argentine Commission for Human Rights presented testimony during hearings in September 1976 before the House Subcommittee on International Organizations, chaired by Donald Fraser, and before the Senate Subcommittee on Foreign Assistance in April 1977. The Argentine Commission successfully sought the cut-off of U.S. military aid to the Argentine government, as discussed below.

c.   *The Role of International Nongovernmental Organizations*

In addition to the efforts of Argentine groups, several international nongovernmental organizations received information about the abuses in Argentina. Some sent factfinding missions to the country and issued significant reports that drew the attention of the Inter-American Commission on Human Rights of the Organization of American States and the United Nations, as well as alerting the international media. The most visible nongovernmental organization was Amnesty International (AI).

Amnesty sent a factfinding mission to Argentina in November 1976. Amnesty selected prominent delegates who gave visibility to the mission. They included Lord Avebury, a member of the British House of Lords, and Father Robert Drinan, a member of the U.S. House of Representatives. They met with a number of high ranking officials but not with President Videla. They were followed by 20 plain-clothed police officers wherever they went, who then questioned, intimidated, and even detained individuals with whom the delegates met. The mission received testimony from prisoners who were tortured. In addition, the AI delegates received personal testimony from the relatives of more than 100 individuals who had been abducted by government agents.

Amnesty International published its report based on the November 1976 mission in March 1977 describing the new repressive legislation and estimating that there were between 5,000 and 6,000 political prisoners. Amnesty also reported that the most commonly quoted figure for disappearances in Argentina at that time was 15,000.

Amnesty kept up the pressure with thousands of letters from AI members — principally from Europe, but also from other countries — to the Argentine government as well as appeals to the Inter-American Commission of Human Rights and to the United Nations. Somewhat less visible, but similar missions to Argentina were undertaken by the International Federation of Human Rights in January 1978 and by the Lawyers Committee for Human Rights in April 1979. Other human rights organizations, including the International Commission of Jurists and Pax Christi, also publicized the abuses in Argentina and lobbied in the United Nations and the Inter-American Commission on Human Rights.

d.   *Inter-American Commission on Human Rights*

Beginning in 1975 before the coup, the Inter-American Commission on Human Rights of the Organization of American States received an increasing number of complaints about human rights violations in Argentina. The Organization of American States is an intergovernmental organization comprised of almost all of the governments in the Western Hemisphere. The OAS is centered in Washington, D.C., and its principal human rights institution is comprised of seven independent experts who are elected to the Inter-American Commission on Human Rights. As early as 1977 the Commission asked for permission to conduct an on-site visit to Argentina to resolve the many complaints it was receiving as to human rights violations in Argentina. When the Commission did not receive permission to enter, the Commission informed the Argentine government of its decision to prepare a report anyway. In early 1978 the Argentine Government accepted a visit for the limited purpose of reviewing the legal situation. The Commission refused that limitation on their on-site visit. Finally, in late 1978 the Argentine government notified the Commission that it would accept a visit according to the standard conditions of the Commission which permitted the Commission to choose its own itinerary.

There is some question as to why the Argentine government accepted the visit of the Commission. It may have been that the government believed that it had completed the killing of its principal opposition. Another possibility was that the United States placed pressure on Argentina that led to the visit by the Commission. After the coup, the State Department began to make appeals on behalf of the U.S. citizens who were arrested or abducted. Soon after President Carter took office in January 1977 Secretary of State Vance announced that U.S. military aid to Argentina would be reduced from $48.4 million to $15 million. In July 1977 Congress cut off all military aid and sales to Argentina, effective as of September 1978. During 1977 and 1978 there were several visits to Argentina by State Department officials to discuss the human rights situation, culminating in the visit of Secretary Vance in November 1977 during which he submitted a list of thousands of disappeared to the Argentine government.

In July 1978 the State Department indicated that it could not recommend

Export-Import (EXIM) Bank financing for the export of Allis Chalmers generators for the Yaciretá a hydroelectric power project. During the same period the U.S. began to abstain when votes were taken on loans to Argentina in the Inter-American Development Bank. In September 1978, however, the State Department gave approval for the EXIM Bank financing — apparently in exchange for the agreement of the Argentine government to accept the Inter-American Commission visit.

Before the Inter-American Commission visited Argentina it received briefings from representatives of the Mothers of the Disappeared in Argentina, other Argentine human rights organizations, Amnesty International, and similar groups. These preliminary interviews provided the Commission with information and ideas for the agenda of their visit. Six members of the Commission (from Brazil, Colombia, Costa Rica, El Salvador, the United States, and Venezuela) and a staff of five visited Argentina September 6-20, 1979. They met with President Videla, other government officials, political figures, representatives of Argentine human rights organizations, trade union officials, lawyers, victims, and their families. The Commission received over 5,500 complaints of which over 4,000 were new.

The most dramatic illustration of the immediate impact of a factfinding visit occurred when the Commission announced that it would receive testimonies in person from victims and their families. In Buenos Aires thousands of individuals filled a street in front of the building where the Commission was hearing testimonies. That single outpouring of people who had suffered has been credited with giving confidence to many people to seek information concerning the whereabouts of their relatives, thus taking an important step toward the end of repression.

The report of the Commission was broadly disseminated outside of Argentina and was very influential in focusing world public opinion on the human rights abuses in Argentina. The report made it difficult for people outside Argentina to say they did not know what was happening in Argentina. When the report was initially released, newspapers in Argentina published the conclusions and recommendations together with a reply by the government. The report was not officially available in Argentina, but 500 copies were informally distributed and 2,000 photocopies of a clandestine edition were disseminated to journalists, judges, bishops, and others. Human rights organizations in Argentina were able to use the report as proof of the disappearances and other rights violations.

After the Commission's visit it appears that the disappearances in Argentina diminished. Indeed, the Commission was told that the government "had won the war" against subversion as of the time the Commission visited Argentina. The Commission noted that "compared with 1975, 1976, 1977, and 1978, there was a smaller number of disappeared detainees in 1979, and that since October 1979 [just after the Commission's visit of September 1979], the Commission has received no new claims of disappearances." Information submitted to the Argentine National Commission on the Disappeared and to the U.N. Working Group on Enforced or Involuntary Disappearances indicates that relatively few disappearances did occur after the visit. For example, the U.N. Working Group published a chart of the frequency of disappearances since 1971, based on the date of occurrence and based on information received by the Working Group. The data show that disappearances virtually ceased after the Inter-American Commission's visit in September 1979 and declined precipitously in September 1978 — that is, a year before the Commission's visit and just when the Argentine government agreed under pressure from the U.S. government to accept the Commission's visit. That agreement apparently occurred when Vice President Mondale met with President Videla, the leader of the Argentine junta, while they were both in Rome attending the funeral of Pope John Paul I.

e.   *United Nations*

While arrangements for the visit of the Inter-American Commission and the actual visit played a very important role in the Argentine case, the same cannot generally be said of the United Nations activities. The U.N. Sub-Commission on Prevention of Discrimination and Protection of Minorities adopted a resolution in August 1976 — only a few months after the coup — expressing deep concern about reports that basic human rights "are in jeopardy in Argentina" and referring particularly to the plight of refugees. During the period 1977-79 several nongovernmental organizations as well as the Austrian, French, Swedish, and U.S. delegates to the Commission on Human Rights also mentioned violations of human rights in Argentina. Despite those speeches and the prompt Sub-Commission resolution, the Commission neither established a working group to investigate the situation, as had been done in regard to Chile (1975-1979) and South Africa (1967-present), nor took any other action authorized by Economic and Social Council resolution 1235.

Instead of using the more expeditious and thus usually more effective approach available under resolution 1235, nongovernmental organizations and the U.N. generally pursued the more elaborate, slower, and confidential procedure delineated by ECOSOC resolution 1503. The first communications on Argentina under the 1503 procedure were submitted during 1976 and 1977. Those communications were not, however, found by the Sub-Commission's Working Group on Communications to merit transmission to higher U.N. bodies.

During 1978 more 1503 communications were submitted by nongovernmental organizations. The Working Group on Communications, meeting in July 1978, decided that three communications did present a consistent pattern of gross and reliably attested violations of internationally recognized human rights. The Sub-Commission, however, under the influence of its Argentine member, Mario Amadeo, decided in August 1978 *not* to transmit them to the Commission on Human Rights.

After the Sub-Commission refused to act, three more communications were submitted by nongovernmental organizations. The Working Group on Communications again found a consistent pattern of gross and reliably attested violations in the three communications from 1979, plus the three held from 1978, and transmitted all six to the Sub-Commission. On September 5, 1979, during a closed session, the Sub-Commission voted — 18 in favor, 1 (Argentina) against, and 4 abstaining —to refer the situation of Argentina to the Commission.

The Commission during confidential sessions in February 1980 discussed the situation on the basis of the communications referred by the Sub-Commission and the government's replies to the communications. The Commission decided to ask several searching questions of the government, in order to place some pressure on Argentina to improve the situation. It was at that same 1980 session that the Commission authorized the establishment of the Working Group on Enforced or Involuntary Disappearances. The Working Group was designed to consider the problem of disappearances in all parts of the world, but there was no doubt that the presence of Mothers of the Disappeared from Argentina in the meeting room gave the Commission a sense of the urgent need for action on the problem of the disappeared.[4]

There were several more 1503 communications on Argentina during the period 1980-1983 with the most important coming from Amnesty International and the Lawyers Committee for Human Rights. Each year from 1980 through 1983 the Working Group on Communications transmitted the communications to the Sub-Commission; the Sub-Commission by consensus found a situation warranting Commission attention; and the Commission kept the situation under consideration.

For several reasons, the U.N. encountered difficulty in achieving a consensus for action in the case of Argentina. *First*, the U.N. normally requires a substantial factual showing in order to pursue action. Hence, action by the U.N. was stalled until the Inter-American Commission, Amnesty International, and other human rights organizations had published persuasive reports. *Second*, under the 1503 procedure the U.N. needs to establish that there is a consistent pattern of reliably attested gross violations of human rights, which requires the sort of factual showing that was not available until about 1979. *Third*, Argentina was represented by an ambassador, Gabriel Martínez, who was an experienced and effective advocate in using U.N. procedures to block action by the Commission on Human Rights. *Fourth*, his work was reinforced by the influential role of Argentina in its own region and in the world. Governments were reluctant to take a stand against a Third World country which, unlike Chile, had important friends. Also, Argentina cared about its image in the world and worked hard to present a favorable case against U.N. action. Accordingly, it always answered complaints against it, so that no government could say Argentina was not cooperating. It realized that failure to cooperate would constitute an important reason for coercive U.N. action under the authority of ECOSOC resolution 1235. Another example can be found in Argentina's decision to retain an expensive public relations firm to present a good image in the world. *Fifth*, consensus for U.N. action was made more difficult by an unusual alliance of Argentina and the U.S.S.R. Trade relations between them grew substantially as early as 1974. Those relations significantly increased after the U.S. imposed a grain embargo in 1979 against the U.S.S.R. The U.S.S.R. and its allies thus also supported Argentina in resisting U.N. action.

3. *Conclusion*

a. *War in the South Atlantic*

The war in the South Atlantic between Argentina and the United Kingdom occurred in April-June 1982. As a consequence of their defeat, the Argentine military were forced to resign. Indeed, even before the war the military government was criticized and weakened by strikes and demonstrations — particularly related to human rights abuses under the military. Despite significant changes in the government of Argentina, the U.N. Commission on Human Rights in February 1983 kept Argentina under consideration in the 1503 process. Only after President Alfonsín was installed in office in December 1983 did the U.N. Commission on Human Rights end the consideration of the situation under the 1503 process.

b. *What factfinding and pressures were effective?*

The Inter-American Commission was much more effective in responding to

---

[4] See Chapter 5, *supra*, for a discussion of the activities of the Working Group.

the situation in Argentina than were U.N. bodies. The Commission was able to respond promptly in 1976-77 because its staff was able to collect information and initiate efforts to obtain an on-site visit. The Commission has a small membership of seven individuals who meet two or three times a year and thus can respond quickly to evolving human rights problems. It has developed a practice of visiting countries with human rights problems that may be unmatched in the human rights world. It need not seek a consistent pattern of gross violations in order to undertake a visit; it need find only that a visit might be useful to help resolve complaints it has received. Arranging the visit and then the visit itself played a crucial role in changing the climate for protection of rights in Argentina. The Commission's work also was facilitated by the pro-human rights policies of the U.S. Congress and the Carter Administration.

The Inter-American Commission has a relatively simple, staff-motivated, flexible and, in important ways, independent process for responding to alleged violations. In contrast, several U.N. procedures, particularly under ECOSOC resolution 1503, are complex and require many steps vulnerable to political influence. U.N. discussions and decisions were almost entirely secret under ECOSOC resolution 1503; whereas the Inter-American Commission published a full, detailed, and influential report. Indeed, that report formed the factual foundation for later U.N. action under ECOSOC resolution 1503.

In the U.N. the process is controlled by the Commission on Human Rights and its Sub-Commission, which had at that time 43 and 26 members respectively. The two bodies meet separately, but only once per year; both require considerable efforts to obtain a consensus before action is possible. Visits to countries on behalf of U.N. bodies are exceptional. Ironically, it was the Argentine situation that prompted the establishment of the Working Group on Enforced or Involuntary Disappearances — one of the first U.N. bodies that has begun to develop a practice of visiting countries where there are problems, but too late to help stop disappearances in Argentina.

In the Argentine case the U.N. was slow to respond; but, once the Commission decided to consider the case under 1503, the consideration continued well beyond the point at which the worst violations were occurring. Indeed, most disappearances, arrests, and killings had ended before the 1503 procedure began. By 1982 and 1983 the principal issue was the need to account for what had happened to the disappeared from the 1976-79 period. So one can say that the Commission was slow to act, but also was slow to respond to improvements. And though the 1503 procedure ended in 1984 after the election that brought President Alfonsín to power, the Working Group on Enforced or Involuntary Disappearances is still pursuing Argentina for explanations about the disappeared.

In conclusion, the present account demonstrates how difficult it is to sort out actions that may cause improvements in a human rights situation. Despite the difficulties, the Argentine case provides one of the best opportunities to consider causation issues. One can state that a complex combination of multilateral and bilateral pressures on the Argentine government, combined with internal pressures, did have an effect in diminishing and ultimately ending the grave violations of human rights that were prevalent during the period 1976-79. Indeed, one can compare the frequency of disappearances during that period with the activities of nongovernmental organizations, governments, the Inter-American Commission on Human Rights, and U.N. bodies. Such a comparison suggests that the final cut-off of U.S. military aid at the end of September 1978 and the Mondale-Videla deal in the same month, which led to the Argentine acceptance of the Inter-American Commission on Human Rights visit, coincide with a significant decrease in the frequency of disappearances. Having accepted the Inter-American Commission's visit, the Argentine government apparently recognized that it had to end the most virulent of its human rights abuses.

If human rights factfinding and pressure apparently did work in the case of Argentina, the question arises as to why they have not yet succeeded in several other countries of the Western Hemisphere or in other places. That question requires further study.

Postscript

For five months in 1985 nine military leaders were tried for specific offenses during the "dirty war." On December 9, 1985, the court issued its verdict. Jorge Videla and Emilio Massera, who commanded the army and the navy, were sentenced to life in prison. Two were sentenced to a term of years, and the remaining defendants were acquitted. Although hundreds of other prosecutions were initiated, almost all of the junior officers and perpetrators of the most heinous abuses were ultimately exempted from prosecution by the Punto Final Legislation and the Law of Due Obedience during the Presidency of Raul Alfonsín. Human rights organizations have continued to seek information about thousands of disappeared whose cases have not been resolved.

After President Alfonsín had served nearly six years, Carlos Menem, a candidate allied with the Peronist Party, was elected President on May 14, 1989. Carlos Menem took office as President in July 1989 — several months ahead of schedule. On October 6, 1989, he pardoned nearly all the remaining military officers and civilians who were subject to prosecution for their role in violating human rights and undermining democracy during the "dirty war," except for Guillermo Suarez-Mason and the high military officers who had already been convicted.

NOTES

1. For more information on the situation in Argentina, see Americas Watch, Truth and Partial Justice in Argentina (1987); Amnesty International, Argentina: The Military Juntas and Human Rights, Report of the Trial of the Former Junta Members, 1985, AI Index: AMR: 13/04/87, at 7 (1987); Argentine National Commission on the Disappeared, Nunca Más (1986); I. Guest, Behind the Disappearances, Argentina's Dirty War against Human Rights and the United Nations (1990); D. Poneman, Argentina: Democracy on Trial (1987); J. Simpson & J. Bennett, The Disappeared and the Mothers of the Plaza (1985).

2. The situation in Argentina after 1983 raised the very difficult issue of how successor governments should deal with the human rights violations of the previous government. *See* Zalaquett, *Confronting Human Rights Violations Committed by Former Governments: Principles Applicable and*

Political Constraints, in State Crimes: Punishment or Pardon 23 (A. Henkin ed. 1989).

3. A few scholars have begun to explore the impact of factfinding and pressures on human rights abuses, with varying success:

E. Landy, The Effectiveness of International Supervision: Thirty Years of ILO Experience (1966);

V. Leary, International Labor Conventions and National Law: The Effectiveness of the Automatic Incorporation of Treaties in National Legal Systems (1982);

Sanders, *The UN Working Group on Indigenous Populations*, 11 Hum. Rts. Q. 406, 422-27 (1989) (concerning Bangladesh);

A. Schmid, Research on Gross Human Rights Violations (1989);

Shelton, *Utilization of Fact-Finding Missions to Promote and Protect Human Rights: The Chile Case*, 2 Hum. Rts. L.J. 1 (1981);

K. Sikkink, The Influence of U.S. Human Rights Policy on Argentina and Guatemala (draft memorandum, July 1989);

Weissbrodt, *International Trial Observers*, 18 Stan. J. Int'l L. 1, 110-14 (1982).

4. The effectiveness of international sanctions has been explored in many other contexts. *See, e.g.*, MacDonald, *Economic Sanctions in the International System*, [1969] Can. Y.B. Int'l L. 61, 80; Taubenfield & Taubenfield, *The Economic Weapon: the League and the United Nations*, 58 Am. Soc. Int'l L. Proc. 183, 184-86 (1964); L. Kapunga, The United Nations and Economic Sanctions against Rhodesia (1971). *See also* chapter 11, *infra*, on U.S. foreign policy in regard to human rights.

FACTFINDING FOR ALLEGED HUMAN RIGHTS VIOLATIONS OF THE UNITED STATES

Most of the factfinding efforts discussed in this chapter involved large-scale violations of rights with a physical element, such as torture, arbitrary arrests and detention, and summary executions. Those types of violations can be confirmed by factfinding methods like visits to prisons and examination of alleged victims.

In contrast, factfinding investigations in the U.S. and other similar countries usually involve more subtle violations such as racial discrimination. To establish government-sanctioned racial discrimination in a country like the U.S. requires compiling data on numerous situations involving both minorities and nonminorities in order to show that nonminorities receive better treatment. The ease of access to public records in the U.S. makes such an endeavor possible, but also increases the bulk of materials through which a factfinder must search in order to make the compilation accurate. That problem makes it necessary to rely on data collection by national NGOs, which constantly monitor U.S. actions in certain fields. As the Inter-American Commission's visit to Argentina illustrates, fact finders often consult with local human rights organizations. In situations like the Argentina visit, however, the factfinders have an opportunity to verify some of the information they receive from NGOs while factfinders in the U.S. might find verification impractical.

NOTES

1. A number of complaints alleging racial discrimination have been filed against the U.S. in the U.N. Commission on Human Rights under the 1503 procedure which this book examined in chapter 4. To establish the consistent pattern of gross and reliably attested violations required by the procedure those petitions have relied on both sample cases and statistical data. *See, e.g.,* Communication to the United Nations Commission on Human Rights and Sub-Commission on Prevention of Discrimination and Protection of Minorities: Human Rights Violations by the Police Against Blacks in the U.S.A., submitted by A. Ray McCoy, Black American Law Student Association, University of Minnesota Chapter, June 10, 1982 (detailing two situations of organized police brutality against blacks and alleging a pattern of police officers depriving blacks of life without minimum procedural guarantees coupled with exoneration of the officers by the criminal justice system); Communication to the United Nations Commission on Human Rights and Sub-Commission on Prevention of Discrimination and Protection of Minorities: Human Rights Violations of Black People in the United States, submitted by Theophous Reagans, President, Black American Law School Association, University of Minnesota Law School Chapter, June 22, 1981 (alleging violation of numerous economic social rights of blacks); Petition to the United Nations Commission on Human Rights and Sub-Commission on Prevention of Discrimination and Protection of Minorities: Human Rights Violations in the United States, submitted by The National Conference of Black Lawyers, The National Alliance Against Racist and Political Repression, & United Church of Christ Commission for Racial Justice, Dec. 13, 1978 (presenting case histories of racial minority prisoners allegedly targeted and convicted for political beliefs). The attorney for the petitioners in the last petition has published an adaptation of the petition. L. Hinds, Illusions of Justice: Human Rights Violations in the United States (1978).

It is interesting to note that the petitioners in the last communication organized their own factfinding investigation to confirm that their allegations presented a prima facie case sufficient to trigger an in-depth study of the petition by the U.N. The members of the factfinding mission were independent international jurists, invited by the petitioners to participate. The jurists' visit took place from August 3 to 20, 1979, and consisted mainly of visiting prisons and interviewing the various prisoners whose cases were detailed in the petition. The jurists published a report explaining their findings and recommending that the U.N. investigate the allegations. *See* Report of International Jurists Visit with Human Rights Petitioners in the United States, August 3-20, 1979.

2. Amnesty International has also conducted several factfinding investigations in the U.S. These investigations have been based on both individual cases and statistical compilations. *See, e.g.,* Amnesty International, United States of America: The Death Penalty, AI Index: AMR 51/01/87 (1987); Amnesty International, Proposal for a Commission of Inquiry into the Effect of Domestic Intelligence Activities on Criminal Trials in the United States of America, AI Index: AMR 51/05/81 (1981).

3. Helsinki Watch, an NGO that monitors U.S. compliance with the human rights provisions of the Helsinki Final Act (discussed in chapter 10 of this book), has published a series of factfinding reports. *See, e.g.,* Helsinki Watch, A Helsinki Record: Racial Discrimination in the United States (1980).

4. *See also* Lawyers Committee for Human Rights, The Detention of Asylum Seekers in the United States: A Cruel and Questionable Policy (1990); Minnesota Lawyers International Human Rights Committee, Oakdale Detention Center: The First Year of Operation (1987).

VII HOW ARE PRONOUNCEMENTS OF HUMAN RIGHTS IN INTERNATIONAL INSTRUMENTS INTERPRETED?

The "Baby Boy" Case in the Inter-American Commission

A. INTRODUCTION

The previous chapters have principally examined U.N. human rights instruments and procedures for implementing the rights therein. Future chapters will discuss other U.N. instruments and procedures. The U.N. is not, however, the only international organization that promulgates human rights instruments and works to protect human rights. Regional systems in Africa, the Americas, and Europe function similarly for governments in their regions. The present chapter examines one of those regional systems — that of the Organization of American States ("OAS").

The second chapter briefly introduced the individual petition process of the Inter-American Commission on Human Rights — the chief OAS organ charged with promoting human rights in OAS member states. In chapter 6 the reader also learned about factfinding visits undertaken by the Inter-American Commission on Human Rights. This chapter re-examines the petition process in the context of a complaint filed with the Commission on behalf of an aborted fetus ("Baby Boy"). The petition alleged that the United States, by allowing abortion, violated Baby Boy's right to life guaranteed by Article I of the American Declaration of the Rights and Duties of Man ("American Declaration"). The Commission's analysis and decision in *Baby Boy* illustrate both its procedure in dealing with individual petitions and the possible limitations of its decision-making power when it is confronted with a case requiring sophisticated interpretation of words in human rights instruments.

This chapter will introduce readers to the principal aid used for interpreting treaties, the basic canons of interpretation codified in the Vienna Convention on the Law of Treaties (the "Treaty on Treaties"). The questions require readers to consider whether the canons found in that treaty ought to apply to the American Declaration and whether the Commission correctly applied those canons in *Baby Boy*. The chapter also examines the Vienna Convention's provisions on treaty reservations in the context of a proposed reservation by the United States to the right-to-life provision (Article 4) of the American Convention on Human Rights ("American Convention"). In addition, the chapter raises the question as to whether the American Declaration, with its relatively vague language, can be applied as a legally binding instrument.

Finally, the chapter discusses the advisory jurisdiction of the Inter-American Court of Human Rights and asks readers to consider whether the Commission — a body more accustomed to dealing with factual issues than with analysis of the scope of prescribed rights — should consider requesting an advisory opinion from the Court when it confronts difficult legal issues comparable to those raised in *Baby Boy*.

B. QUESTIONS

1. In regard to the "Baby Boy" case, what are the final legal conclusions (holdings) of the Commission?

2. Does the Commission consider whether there is a jurisdictional problem in this case?

3. Can you see a jurisdictional problem under Article 26 of the Commission's Regulations?

4. Why, do you think, does the Commission not discuss the jurisdictional problem?

5. Does the Commission follow the canons of interpretation set forth in the Treaty on Treaties?

6. Do the dissenting and concurring opinions respect those rules?

7. Since the United States has not ratified the Treaty on Treaties, are its rules relevant in this case?

8. Is it significant that the American Declaration was not promulgated as a treaty? Should it be applied as a legally binding instrument?
QQB,

9. What is the Commission's conclusion from the *travaux préparatoires* (the drafting history similar to legislative history) of the American Declaration?

10. Is that conclusion correct?

   a. What difference do you see between the initial and the final versions?

   b. If the Commission is correct about the removal of the ''moment of conception'' language, what should be inferred from the removal of the other words from that same sentence?

   c. Are there other significant changes in the final version?

11. What do you think of the Commission's observation that many member states permitted abortion at the time the Declaration was adopted? Is it appropriate to interpret a right by reference to state practice at the time of its adoption?

12. Is the difference between the wording of Article I and of all the other articles of the American Declaration (See Handbook) significant?

13. What do you think of the way the Commission interpreted the wording of Article 4 of the American Convention on Human Rights? Do you think that the Commission will follow this approach consistently?

14. Considering United Nations instruments, is there reason to interpret the Universal Declaration of Human Rights in the light of the two Covenants? Focus on Article 29 of the Universal Declaration (See Handbook) and Article 4 of the Civil and Political Covenant (See Handbook) in formulating your answer.

15. Since the U.S. has signed but not ratified the American Convention, would Article 18 of the Treaty on Treaties suggest how the American Convention ought to be viewed in the *Baby Boy* case? Should the American Convention have been applied in the *Baby Boy* case?

16. What about the proposed U.S. reservation to Article 4? Is that reservation acceptable under American Convention Article 75 (See Handbook) and Article 19 of the Treaty on Treaties?

17. Suppose the American Convention does apply to the U.S. Would the U.S. be in violation of Article 4?

18. Is Article 32 of the American Convention (See Handbook) relevant?

19. Based on materials in this chapter, do you think the Commission is a reliable decision-making body when it considers cases involving complex legal issues? When it considers cases involving primarily factual issues? Should advocates advance creative legal arguments for expanding the meaning of the American Declaration? What sort of case would you bring before the Commission?

20. Would it have been possible in 1981 for the Commission to seek an advisory opinion from the Court on the legal issues posed by the *Baby Boy* case? Could the Commission seek such an advisory opinion now?

21. In view of the inadequate reasoning of the Commission's opinion, do you think it would be wise for the Commission to ask for an advisory opinion from the Court? If so, on which issues should the Commission seek advice?

22. Would there be legal objections to the Court's acceptance of advisory opinion jurisdiction over some of the issues raised in the *Baby Boy* case?

23. Do you believe the *Baby Boy* case will make it more or less likely that the United States will eventually ratify the American Convention?

C. JURISPRUDENCE OF THE INTER-AMERICAN COMMISSION

The *"Baby Boy"* Opinion, Case 2141, Inter-Am. C.H.R. 25, OEA.Ser.L/V/II.54, doc. 9 rev. 1 (1981) (citations omitted):

SUMMARY OF THE CASE:

1. On January 19, 1977, Christian S. White and Gary K. Potter, filed with the Inter-American Commission on Human Rights a petition against the United States of America and the Commonwealth of Massachusetts for the purposes established in the Statute and Regulations of the Commission. . . .

2. The pertinent parts of the petition are the following:

Name of the person whose human rights have been violated: *"Baby Boy"*. . . .

Description of the violation: *Victim was killed by abortion process (hysterectomy), by Dr. Kenneth Edelin, M.D., in violation of the right to life granted by the American Declaration of the Rights and Duties of Man, as clarified by the definition and description of "right to life" contained in the American Convention on Human Rights.* . . .

Final decision of the authority (if any) that acted in the matter: *The Supreme Judicial Court of Massachusetts, Boston, Massachusetts, acquitted Edelin [of manslaughter] on appeal, on December 17, 1976.* . . .

3. In the "Amplificatory Document" attached to the petition, the petitioners add, *inter alia*, the following information and arguments: ...

b) This violation of the following rights granted by the American Declaration of the Rights and Duties of Man,[1] Chapter 1, Article I ("... right to life ..."), Article II ("All persons are equal before the law ... without distinction as to race, sex, language, creed, or any other factor," here, age), Article VII ("All children have the right to special protection, care, and aid") and Article XI ("Every person has the right to the preservation of his health...") began on January 22, 1973, when the Supreme Court of the United States handed down its decisions in the cases of *Roe v. Wade*, 410 U.S. 113 and *Doe v. Bolton*, 410 U.S. 179.

c) The effect of the *Wade* and *Bolton* decisions, *supra*, in ending the legal protection of unborn children set the stage for the deprivation of "Baby Boy's" right to life. These decisions in and of themselves constitute a violation of his right to life, and the United States of America therefore stands accused of a violation of Chapter 1, Article I of the American Declaration of the Rights and Duties of Man.

The United States Government, through its Supreme Court, is guilty of that violation.

d) At trial, the jury found Dr. Edelin guilty of manslaughter, necessarily finding as fact that the child was such as to fit within a "protectable exception" (over six months past conception and/or alive outside the womb) to the Supreme Court of the United States' rubric in the *Wade* and *Bolton* cases. On appeal, the Supreme Judicial Court of Massachusetts reversed, on these grounds:

1) Insufficient evidence of "recklessness" and "belief in" [or concern about] "the viability of the fetus" (paraphrased)....

2) Insufficient evidence of life outside the womb....

3) Procedural error....

e) This decision came down on December 17, 1976, and, by preventing Dr. Edelin from being punished for his acts, put the State of Massachusetts in the posture of violating "Baby Boy's" right to life under the Declaration....

WHEREAS:

1. The basic facts described in the petition as alleged violations of Articles I, II, VII and IX of the American Declaration occurred on January 22, 1973 (date of the decisions of cases *Roe v. Wade* and *Doe v. Bolton* by U.S. Supreme Court), October 3, 1973 (date of abortion of Baby Boy performed at the Boston City Hospital) and December 17, 1976 (date of final decision of the Supreme Judicial Court of Massachusetts that acquitted Dr. Edelin, the performer of the abortion). The defendant, the U.S. Government[,] is not a state party to the American Convention on Human Rights. The petition was filed on January 19, 1977, before the Convention entered into force on July 18, 1978.

2. Consequently, the procedure applicable to this case is that established in Articles 53 to 57 of Regulations of the Commission, approved in 1960 as amended, in accordance with Article 24 of the present Statute and Article 49 of the new Regulations....

15. The international obligation of the United States of America, as a member

---

[1 Ed.: The American Declaration can be found in the accompanying handbook, *Selected International Human Rights Instruments*.]

of the Organization of American States (OAS), under the jurisdiction of the Inter-American Commission on Human Rights (IACHR) is governed by the Charter of OAS (Bogotá, 1948) as amended by the Protocol of Buenos Aires on February 27, 1967, ratified by United States on April 23, 1968.

16. As a consequence of Articles 3 *j*, 16, 51 *e*, 112 and 150 of [the OAS Charter], the provisions of other instruments and resolutions of the OAS on human rights, acquired binding force. Those instruments and resolutions approved with the vote of U.S. Government, are the following:

— American Declaration of the Rights and Duties of Man (Bogotá, 1948)
— Statute and Regulations of the IACHR 1960, as amended by resolution XXII of the Second Special Inter-American Conference (Rio de Janeiro, 1965)
— Statute and Regulations of IACHR of 1979-1980.

17. Both Statutes provide that, for the purpose of such instruments, the IACHR is the organ of the OAS entrusted with the competence to promote the observance and respect of human rights. For the purpose of the Statutes, human rights are understood to be the rights set forth in the American Declaration in relation to States not parties to the American Convention on Human Rights (San José, 1969). (Articles 1 and 2 of 1960 Statute and Article 1 of 1979 Statute).

18. The first violation denounced in the petition concerns Article I of the American Declaration of Rights and Duties of Man: "Every human being has the right to life...". The petitioners admitted that the Declaration does not [answer] "when life begins," "when a pregnancy product becomes a human being," or other such questions. However, they try to answer these fundamental questions with two different arguments:

a) The *travaux préparatoires* [Ed.: drafting history similar to legislative history], the discussion of the draft Declaration during the IX International Conference of American States at Bogotá in 1948 and the final vote, demonstrate that the intention of the Conference was to protect the right to life "from the moment of conception."

b) The American Convention on Human Rights, promulgated to advance the Declaration's high purposes and to be read as a corollary document, gives a definition of the right to life in Article 4.1: "This right shall be protected by law from the moment of conception."

19. A brief legislative history of the Declaration does not support the petitioner's argument, as may be concluded from the following information and documents:

a) Pursuant to Resolution XL of the Inter-American Conference on Problems of War and Peace (Mexico, 1945), the Inter-American Juridical Committee of Rio de Janeiro formulated a preliminary draft of an International Declaration of the Rights and Duties of Man to be considered by the Ninth International Conference of American States (Bogotá, 1948)....

b) Article I - Right to Life - of the draft submitted by the Juridical Committee reads: "Every person has the right to life. This right extends to the right to life from the moment of conception; to the right to life of incurables, imbeciles and the insane. Capital punishment may only be applied in cases in which it has been prescribed by pre-existing law for crimes of exceptional gravity."

c) A Working Group was organized to consider the observations and amendments introduced by the Delegates and to prepare an acceptable document. As a result of its work, the Group submitted to the Sixth Committee a new draft entitled *American Declaration of the Fundamental Rights and Duties of Man*, Article I of which reads: "Every human being has the right to life, liberty, security and integrity of his person."

d) This completely new Article I and some substantial changes introduced by the Working Group in other articles have been explained, in its Report of the Working Group to the Committee, as a compromise to resolve the problems raised by the Delegations of Argentina, Brazil, Cuba, United States of America, Mexico, Peru, Uruguay, and Venezuela, mainly as consequence of the conflict existing between the laws of those States and the draft of the Juridical Committee.

e) In connection with the right to life, the definition given in the Juridical Committee's draft was incompatible with the laws governing the death penalty and abortion in the majority of the American States. In effect, the acceptance of this absolute concept — the right to life from the moment of conception — would imply the obligation to derogate the articles of the Penal Codes in force in 1948 in many countries because such articles excluded the penal sanction for the crime of abortion if performed in one or more of the following cases: A - when necessary to save the life of the mother; B - to interrupt the pregnancy of the victim of a rape; C - to protect the honor of an honest woman; D - to prevent the transmission to the fetus of a hereditary or contagious disease; E - for economic reasons (angustia económica).

f) In 1948, the American States that permitted abortion in one of such cases and, consequently, would be affected by the adoption of article I of the Juridical Committee, were: Argentina ...; Brazil ...; Costa Rica ...; Cuba ...; Ecuador ...; Mexico (Distrito y Territorios Federales) ...; Nicaragua ...; Paraguay ...; Peru ...; Uruguay ...; Venezuela ...; United States of America ...; Puerto Rico....

h) Consequently, the defendant is correct in challenging the petitioners' assumption that Article I of the Declaration has incorporated the notion that the right to life exists from the moment of conception. Indeed, the conference faced this question but chose not to adopt language which would clearly have stated that principle.

20. The second argument of the petitioners, related to the possible use of the Convention as an element for the interpretation of the Declaration, requires also a study of the motives that prevailed at the San José Diplomatic Conference with the adoption of the definition of the right to life....

25. To accommodate the views that insisted on the concept "from the moment of conception," with the objection raised, since the Bogotá conference, based on the legislation of American States that permitted abortion, *inter alia*, to save the

mother's life, and in case of rape, the IACHR, redrafting Article 2 [of the Convention] (Right to life), decided, by majority vote, to introduce the words "in general." This compromise was the origin of the new text of Article 2: "1. Every person has the right to have his life respected. This right shall be protected by law, *in general*, from the moment of conception."

26. The rapporteur of the *Opinion* proposed, at this second opportunity for discussion of the definition of the right [to] life, to delete the entire final phrase "...in general, from the moment of conception." He repeated the reasoning of his dissenting opinion in the Commission; based on the abortion laws in force in the majority of the American States, with an addition: "to avoid any possibility of conflict with article 6, paragraph 1, of the United Nations Covenant on Civil and Political Rights, which states this right in a general way only."...

27. However, the majority of the Commission believed that, for reasons of principle, it was fundamental to state the provision on the protection of the right to life in the form recommended to the Council of the OAS in its *Opinion* (Part One). It was accordingly decided to keep the text of paragraph 1 without change....

30. In the light of this [drafting] history, it is clear that the petitioners' interpretation of the definition given by the American Convention on the right to life is incorrect. The addition of the phrase "in general, from the moment of conception" does not mean that the drafters of the Convention intended to modify the concept of the right to life that prevailed in Bogotá, when they approved the American Declaration. The legal implications of the clause "in general, from the moment of conception" are substantially different from the shorter clause "from the moment of conception" as appears repeatedly in the petitioners' briefs.

31. However, accepting *gratia argumentandi* [for the sake of argument], that the American Convention had established the absolute concept of the right to life from the moment of conception - it would be impossible to impose upon the United States Government or that of any other Member State of the OAS, by means of "interpretation," an international obligation based upon a treaty that such State has not duly accepted or ratified.

32. The question of what reservation to Article I of the Convention should be admissible, as suggested by President Jimmy Carter in his Letter of Transmittal to the Senate on February 23, 1978, has no direct link with the objective of the petition. *This is not the appropriate place or opportunity for the consideration of this matter.* [Emphasis added.]

33. The other rights which the petitioners contend were violated — Articles II, VII, and XI of the American Declaration — have no direct relation to the facts set forth in the petition, including the decision[s] of the U.S. Supreme Court and the Supreme Judicial Court of Massachusetts which were challenged in this case.

THE INTER-AMERICAN COMMISSION ON HUMAN RIGHTS

RESOLVES:

1. The decision[s] of the U.S. Supreme Court and the Supreme Judicial Court of Massachusetts and other facts stated in the petition do not constitute a violation of Articles I, II, VII and XI of the American Declaration of Rights and Duties of Man....

CONCURRING DECISION OF DR. ANDRES AGUILAR M....

5. In my view, the opinion of the majority comes to the correct conclusion,

that none of the rights set forth in said Declaration had been violated. In effect, it is clear from the *travaux préparatoires* that Article I of the Declaration, which is the fundamental legal provision in this case, sidesteps the very controversial question of determining at what moment human life begins.

The legislative history of this article permits one to conclude that the draft which was finally approved is a compromise formula, which even if it obviously protects life from the moment of birth, leaves to each State the power to determine, in its domestic law, whether life begins and warrants protection from the moment of conception or at any other point in time prior to birth. . . .

7. The decision of the majority does not begin, and could not begin, to judge whether abortion is reprehensible from a religious, ethical, or scientific point of view, and it correctly limits itself to deciding that the United States of America has not assumed the international obligation to protect the right to life from conception or from some other moment prior to birth and that, consequently, it could not be correctly affirmed that it had violated the right to life set forth in Article I of the American Declaration of the Rights and Duties of Man.

8. For the reasons expressed, I dissent on this point, from the opinion of my distinguished colleagues Dr. Luis Demetrio Tinoco and Dr. Marco Gerardo Monroy Cabra. On the other hand, I completely share their judgment, based in the opinions of well-known men of science, that human life begins at the very moment of conception and ought to warrant complete protection from that moment, both in domestic law as well as international law. . . .

DISSENT OF DR. MARCO GERARDO MONROY CABRA

I dissent from the majority opinion of the Inter-American Commission on Human Rights in Case 2141 for the following reasons:

1. Article I of the American Declaration of the Rights and Duties of Man reads: "Every human being has the right to life, liberty, and the security of his person." Since the text is not explicit, I think that the interpretation most in accord with the genuine protection of the right to life is that this protection begins at conception rather than at birth.

2. The historical argument, upon which the majority opinion of the Commission is based, is unclear. Indeed, a review of the report and the minutes of the Working Group of the Sixth Committee shows that no conclusion was reached to permit the unequivocal inference that the intention of the drafters of the Declaration was to protect the right to life from the time of birth—much less to allow abortion, since this topic was not approached. . . .

5. Since Article I does not define when life begins, one can resort to medical science which has concluded that life has its beginning in the union of two series of chromosomes. Most scientists agree that the fetus is a human being and is genetically complete.

6. If international agreements are to be faithfully and literally interpreted, in keeping with the meaning that should be attributed to the terms of a treaty and read in context, taking into account the objective and purpose of that treaty, there is no doubt that the protection of the right to life should begin at the moment of conception. Since Article I is general, the protection should begin when life begins, and we have already seen that life begins at the time fertilization is completed in the union of two series of chromosomes. . . .

8. The intentional and illegal interruption of the physiological process of

pregnancy, resulting in the destruction of the embryo or death of the fetus, is unquestionably an offense against life and, consequently, a violation of Article I of the American Declaration of the Rights and Duties of Man. The maternal womb in which the flame of life is lighted is sacred and may not be profaned to extinguish what God has created in his image and in his likeness. It has been said repeatedly, that, from the biological standpoint, human life exists from the moment that the ovum is fertilized by the sperm and, more specifically, from the time the egg travels to the uterus. . . .

9. Life is the primary right of every individual. It is the fundamental right and the condition for the existence of all other rights. If human existence is not recognized, there is no subject upon which to predicate the other rights. It is a right that antecedes other rights and exists by the mere fact of being, with no need for the state to recognize it as such. It is not up to the state to decide whether that right shall be recognized in one case and not in another, since that would mean discrimination. The life of the unborn child, the infant, the young, the old, the mentally ill, the handicapped, and that of all human beings in general, must be recognized.

The foregoing means that if conception produces a human life, and this right is the primary and fundamental one, abortion is an attack on the right to life and, therefore, runs counter to Article I of the American Declaration of the Rights and Duties of Man. . . .

DISSENT OF DR. LUIS DEMETRIO TINOCO CASTRO. . .

I depart from the opinion of the majority when it affirms, in paragraph 19 of the Preamble of the Resolution, that "a brief legislative history of the Declaration does not support the petitioners' argument" and that may be concluded from the report presented by the Working Group that studied the draft wording of Article I of the Declaration, as well as from the fact that in that Group the concept contained in the draft of the Inter-American Juridical Committee had been eliminated, where it said, after stating every person has the right to life, "This right extends to the right to life from the moment of conception; to the right to life of incurables, imbeciles, and the insane." . . .

Study of the Minutes and Documents of the Working Group concerned, and of the Sixth Committee, which was responsible for consideration of these articles of the Draft Declaration, leads me to conclusions contrary to those established in the vote of the majority. . . .

The American Declaration of the Rights and Duties of Man, for its part, plainly and clearly states: "Every human being has the right to life."

Leaving aside the legal background that led to this simple wording of Article I of the Declaration, to decide this Case it is necessary first to answer the transcendental question of the nature of the unborn, the topic of most significant legal and moral consequences of stipulating whether what has been formed in the womb of a woman and is still therein is a "human being" with the right to life. Or whether it should be understood that the "right to life" that every human being has in accordance with the above-mentioned Article I of the Declaration of Bogotá should be understood to protect only those already living their own lives, outside the womb. In other words: at what moment in his long process of formation, development, decadence, and death is it considered that there exists a "human being" with the "right to life" and to the protection given him by the basic legal instruments of the new discipline of Human Rights. More specifically, as it affects the problem raised by Case 2141, to which I refer: when the woman's ovum is fertilized by action of the man, has a human being been constituted and does it have the right to life?

The question was put barely three years ago to the eminent Dean of the Teaching and Research Unit of the University of Paris, holder of the Chair of Fundamental Genetics, there, Professor Jerome Lejeune. . . . "Of course," he replied, adding, "it has been shown that all the genetic qualities of the individual are already present in that first cell, that the embryo, seven days after fertilization. . . emits a chemical message that stops the menstruation of his mother. . .that at twenty days after fertilization. . .his heart (as large as a grain of wheat) begins to beat. . .at two months. . .he already has human form completely: he has a head, he has arms, he has his fingers and toes. . .and even the lines on his hands drawn. . .and between the second and third months. . .the fingerprints are already indicated. . .and will not change to the end of his life. . .at three months he is already able to close his eyes, to clench his fists, and if at that moment his upper lip were caressed with a thread, he would make a face. . . . A human being exists. . .there is no doubt about that." And the same Professor, in a magazine article, stated: "The fetus is a human being. Genetically he is complete. This is not an appearance; it is a fact."

The opinion of the vast majority of scientists, not to say all of them, is the same as that of Professor Lejeune. . . . Dr. Ingelman-Sundberg and Dr. Cears Wirsen in their work *The Drama of Life before Birth*, published in 1965. Dr. Bart Hefferman, in a book entitled *The Early Biography of Every Man*, published in 1972. . . .

The reasons stated leave no doubt in my mind that the American Declaration of the Rights and Duties of Man refers to the complete period of human life—from conception to death — when it states that "every human being has the right to life"; that, for that valuable instrument of international law, life does not begin at birth — the final phase of the process of gestation — but at the moment of conception, which is the moment at which a new human being, distinct from the father and from the mother, is formed; and that, in recognizing the right of the unborn to life, the Declaration rejects the legitimacy of any act that authorizes or considers acceptable acts or practices that will lead to its death.

NOTES

1. The O.A.S. Charter provisions mentioned in paragraphs 15-16 of the *Baby Boy* opinion are reproduced in the accompanying handbook, *Selected International Human Rights Instruments*.

2. For commentary on *Baby Boy*, see Shelton, *Abortion and the Right to Life in the Inter-American System: The Case of "Baby Boy"*, 2 Hum. Rts. L.J. 309 (1981); Weissbrodt, *Ethical Problems of an International Human Rights Law Practice*, 7 Mich. Y.B. Int'l Legal Stud. 217, 245-48 (1985).

3. The United States Supreme Court in 1989 restricted abortion rights in *Webster v. Reproductive Health Services*, 492 U.S. ____, 109 S.Ct. 3040 (1989). In *Webster*, the Court upheld provisions of a Missouri statute prohibiting the use of state employees and facilities in nontherapeutic abortions. Writing for the Court, Chief Justice Rehnquist reasoned that the Due Process Clause generally does not confer affirmative rights to governmental aid. The Chief Justice further asserted that the statute leaves the pregnant woman ". . . with the same choices as if the State had chosen not to operate any public hospitals at all." *Id.* at ___, 109 S.Ct. at 3052. The Chief Justice, along with Justices White and Kennedy, next concluded that the provisions of the statute requiring physicians to perform viability tests for any fetus of at least twenty weeks gestational age did not violate the Constitution. According to Chief Justice Rehnquist, the *Roe v. Wade* trimester framework should no longer be used as a standard for evaluating the interests of the mother and the state. Justice O'Connor, in her concurring opinion, also found the *Roe* trimester framework problematic. She, however, asserted that viability testing did not conflict with past decisions and thus did not necessitate a reexamination of *Roe.* Justice Scalia argued that the entire *Roe* decision should be overruled in order to avoid the court's further involvement in an area where ". . . the answers to most of the cruel questions posed are political and not juridical. . . ." *Id.* at ___, 109 S.Ct. at 3064. Justice Blackmun, joined by Justices Brennan and Marshall, dissented, arguing that the public facility ban leaves the pregnant woman with fewer choices. The dissent also maintained that the plurality had unnecessarily set up a conflict between the Missouri statute and the *Roe* framework while failing to address the true jurisprudential issue: the right to privacy. Justice Stevens also dissented and focused on the statute's preamble which declares that life begins at conception. Whereas the plurality did not pass on the constitutionality of the preamble, Justice Stevens concluded that the preamble violates the Constitution because it impairs the freedom to use contraceptive procedures and violates the Establishment Clause of the First Amendment.

REGULATIONS OF THE INTER-AMERICAN COMMISSION ON HUMAN RIGHTS, in Basic Documents Pertaining to Human Rights in the Inter-American System, OAS Doc. OEA/Ser.L/V/II.71, at 75, 84 (1988):

ARTICLE 26

Presentation of Petitions

1. Any person or group of persons or nongovernmental entity legally recognized in one or more of the Member States of the Organization may submit petitions to the Commission, in accordance with these Regulations, on one's own behalf or on behalf of third persons, with regard to alleged violations of a human right recognized, as the case may be, in the American Convention on Human Rights or in the American Declaration of the Rights and Duties of Man.

2. The Commission may also, *motu proprio* [Ed.: on its own motion], take into consideration any available information that it considers pertinent and which

might include the necessary factors to begin processing a case which in its opinion fulfills the requirements for the purpose.

QUESTIONS

1. Can you see a jurisdictional problem for the Commission's consideration of the *Baby Boy* case under Article 26 of the Commission's Regulations?

2. Why, do you think, does the Commission not discuss the jurisdictional problem?

ADDITIONAL INTER-AMERICAN CASES RAISING DIFFICULT LEGAL ISSUES

Three other petitions filed with the Commission against the United States raise questions of interpretation comparable to those in *Baby Boy*.

In Case 9647 (*Roach*), U.S. lawyers brought a petition on behalf of James Roach and Jay Pinkerton, juveniles sentenced to death for separate crimes committed when they were 17 years old. Case 9647, Inter-Am. C.H.R. 147, OEA/Ser.L/V/II.71, doc. 9 rev. 1 (1987). The petition alleged that U.S. execution of juveniles violated not only the right to life prescribed in Article I of the American Declaration, construed by the Commission in *Baby Boy*, but also the Article VII protection for children and the Article XXVI prohibition of cruel, infamous or unusual punishments. Petitioners urged the Commission to find that customary international law proscribes execution of juveniles, pointing to the prohibition of juvenile executions in several treaties, including the American Convention, and widespread practice of governments in abolishing juvenile execution. Petitioners asked the Commission to use that customary norm in interpreting the American Declaration as prescribed by Article 31 of the Treaty on Treaties (Vienna Convention on the Law of Treaties, *supra*).

The U.S. denied the existence of a customary norm proscribing juvenile executions. In addition, the U.S. claimed that, even if such a norm existed, the U.S. had dissented from it and thus was not bound. Moreover, the U.S. argued, capital punishment for juveniles did not constitute cruel, infamous or unusual punishment because many states allowed such punishment at the time of the American Declaration's adoption. Finally, the U.S. disagreed with petitioners' interpretation of children in Article VII to mean those under 18.

The Commission reaffirmed its holding in *Baby Boy* that the American Declaration is binding on the U.S. as a member of the OAS. *Id.* para. 48. It refused to find a customary norm prohibiting execution of juveniles under 18, although it did find that such a norm was emerging. *Id.* para. 60.

Moreover, the Commission commented that the U.S. had protested the emerging norm by proposing a reservation to Article 4 of the American Convention designed to preserve current U.S. practice of capital punishment, including execution of juveniles. The Commission stated that due to this protest the U.S. could not be bound by the norm. *Id.* paras. 53-54. The Commission noted that if a norm attains the status of *jus cogens*,[2] the norm binds all states, even protesters. *Id.* para. 54. The Commission did find that a *jus cogens* norm prescribing the execution of children exists among the OAS member states; yet, the Commission could not agree on the age limit for the norm. *Id.* para. 56.

Instead, the Commission based its decision that the United States had violated the American Declaration by allowing its states to execute Roach and Pinkerton on the Article II right to equality before the law. *Id.* para. 63. The Commission reasoned that the United States violated this right by not mandating a uniform minimum age for imposition of the death penalty in all states. *Id.* In so holding, the Commission avoided the issue of whether the American Declaration prohibits juvenile execution. Commentators have criticized the Commission for refusing to find prohibition against juvenile executions within customary international law, while finding a *jus cogens* norm against the execution of children. The Commission's position appears anomalous because the existence of a *jus cogens* norm is much more difficult to establish than a rule of customary law. The Commission has also been criticized for finding that the U.S. is a persistent objector to the customary norm without sufficient evidence, for partially basing its decision on the different laws authorizing the execution of juveniles in the various states of the U.S. federal system, and for basing its decision on an article of the American Declaration which neither of the parties had raised or argued before the Commission.

Another case requiring a legally sophisticated interpretation of the right to life in Article I of the American Declaration is still pending before the Commission. Case 9213, Inter-Am. C.H.R., OAS Doc. OEA/Ser.L./V/II.67, doc. 6 (1986) (decision on admissibility). In Case 9213, Disabled Peoples' International ("DPI") filed a petition on behalf of patients in a Grenadan mental institution who were either killed or injured when the United States bombed the institution. Although some controversy as to the factual circumstances surrounding the bombing exists, the chief issue in the case is the applicability of Article I's right to life guarantee in armed conflict. In resolving this issue, DPI asked the Commission to construe Article I in conformity with international humanitarian law principles. (International

---

[2] A *"jus cogens"* norm is a peremptory rule of international law that prevails over any conflicting rule or agreement. A *jus cogens* norm permits no derogation and can be modified only by a subsequent international law norm of the same character. 1 Restatement (Third) of the Foreign Relations Law of the United States § 102 comment k (1987).

humanitarian law governs armed conflicts. This book will examine humanitarian law in chapter 13.) Since Article I of the American Declaration does not indicate how states are to observe the right to life in armed conflict, Article 31 of the Vienna Convention on the Law of Treaties allows the Commission to consider the humanitarian law obligations of the United States when interpreting the right to life.

The third case (Case No. 10,031) involved the application of the death penalty. Unlike the petitioner in *Roach*, however, the petitioner in the third case — Willie Celestine — was not a juvenile. Celestine was a black man who was sentenced to death in a Louisiana court for raping and murdering an elderly white woman. Celestine sought review of his sentence in state and federal court, claiming violation of the eighth and fourteenth amendments to the U.S. Constitution. Celestine based his claim on the racial prejudice admitted by one of the jurors before trial, the elimination from the jury of any jurors who revealed reluctance to impose the death penalty, and statistical studies which demonstrated that Louisiana applied the death penalty in a racially discriminatory manner. All his appeals were defeated, however, and a petition was filed on his behalf with the Commission. Unfortunately, despite urgent appeals from the Commission to the Secretary of State and the governor of Louisiana, Louisiana executed Celestine before the Commission could decide his case.

The petitioners alleged that the U.S. violated three provisions of the American Declaration. First, the petitioners claimed that the U.S. arbitrarily deprived Celestine of his right to life guaranteed by Article I because Louisiana applies the death penalty in a racially discriminatory manner, a practice which would also violate Article II's guarantee of equal treatment before the law. The second basis for the petition was that the U.S. denied Celestine an impartial hearing as guaranteed by Article XXVI because his jurors were selected based on their willingness to impose the death penalty and that this denial violated Article II's guarantee of equal treatment before the law. Third, the petitioners argued that imposition of the death penalty on Celestine violated Article XXVI's prohibition against cruel, infamous or unusual punishment because it was imposed in the absence of an impartial hearing and equality before the law. In 1989 the Commission decided against Celestine, finding that the petitioners failed to establish an adequate factual basis for their claim of discrimination. Case 10,031, Inter-Am. C.H.R. res. 23/89, OEA/Ser.L./V/II.76, doc. 44 (1989). The Commission was apparently convinced of the fairness of the proceedings by the fact that blacks were seated as jurors in the case.

NOTES

1. For commentary on *Roach*, see Cerna & Young, *The Inter-American Commission on Human Rights and the Death Penalty*, 34 Fed. B. News &

J. 398 (1987); *Inter-American Commission on Human Rights (IACHR), Washington: Application of Death Penalty on Juveniles in the U.S./Violation of Human Rights Obligation Within the Inter-American System*, 8 Hum. Rts. L.J. 345 (1987) (including commentary by Dinah Shelton); Weissbrodt, *Execution of Juvenile Offenders by the United States Violates International Human Rights Law*, 3 Am. U. J. Int'l L. & Pol'y 339 (1987).

2. For suggestions on how the Commission could interpret the American Declaration in light of international humanitarian law, see Weissbrodt & Andrus, *The Right to Life During Armed Conflict: Disabled Peoples' International v. United States*, 29 Harv. Int'l L.J. 59 (1988).

3. In chapter 10 the reader will become acquainted with the *Soering Case*, 161 Eur. Ct. Hum. Rts. (series A) (1989), 28 I.L.M. 1063 (1989). At that point the reader may consider whether the Inter-American Commission's decision in *Baby Boy* and *Roach* were as well-reasoned as *Soering*.

TYPICAL CASES IN THE INTER-AMERICAN COMMISSION

Cases requiring sophisticated interpretation of rights in human rights instruments, such as *Baby Boy*, are not typical of the work pursued by the Inter-American Commission. Generally the Commission has focused its expertise on studying the human rights situation in member countries, often utilizing factfinding missions, rather than on individual petitions. This book in chapter 6 examines the Commission's experience with country studies.

Furthermore, most individual petitions filed with the Commission allege conduct that applicable instruments clearly prohibit such as torture or arbitrary arrest and imprisonment. In the typical case the main issue for the Commission to decide is whether the alleged ill-treatment actually took place. If the Commission establishes the truth of the allegations, it can easily find violations of human rights provisions. That approach contrasts with the situation in *Baby Boy* where the parties did not dispute the facts, but rather contested whether the facts constituted a violation of human rights norms.

The following cases provide examples of typical individual petitions filed with the Commission. The first case involves the common situation where the government fails to respond to the Commission's request for information regarding the alleged violation. The second case involves a governmental response which, in light of the evidence presented by the petitioner, the Commission finds inadequate to rebut the allegations.

Case 2646, Inter-Am. C.H.R. 67, OEA/Ser.L/V/II.61, doc. 22 rev. 1 (1983):

1. In a communication dated November 24, 1977, the Inter-American Commission on Human Rights received the following petition:

Mr. Anous Pierre, a Haitian citizen, resident of l'Arcahaie (Robert rural section) was arrested in September, 1976. His age is 35 years and he is being held in the Fort Dimanche prison in cell No. 2.

Anous Pierre is still being held after more than one year in flagrant violation of the Haitian Constitution which provides:

No one may be kept under arrest more than forty-eight (48) hours, unless he has appeared before a judge who is assigned to rule on the legality of the arrest and the judge has confirmed the arrest by a decision giving reasons therefore. (Article 17)

Anous Pierre should be released or, if some charges have been placed against him, he should be tried immediately by a jury of his peers.

2. On March 16, 1978, the Commission addressed the Government of Haiti and transmitted to it pertinent parts of the petition and requested it to furnish the information it considered appropriate in connection with the facts charged.

3. On April 17, 1978, the Commission received from the Haitian Government a communication dated April 5 in which the government acknowledged receipt of the letter of March 16 and stated the following:

The Chancellery hastens to reiterate once again that there are no political prisoners in Haiti. It also requests you to not take into consideration any more petitions and accusations of this type that are lodged against the Haitian Government. Moreover, all persons having such petitions may always address the Department of Justice which is required to provide them with all necessary information.

4. Since the reply of the Haitian Government confines itself to denying in a general fashion the existence of political prisoners in Haiti and does not refer specifically to the status of Mr. Anous Pierre, whose personal identification and place of detention were made known to the government when the pertinent parts of the petition were transmitted to it, the Commission decided to request the Government of Haiti once again to furnish information on the case in question, which it did in a communication dated January 3, 1979. The pertinent parts of this communication read:

We request the Haitian Government to forward to us specific information in connection with the following:

1. Has Mr. Anous Pierre been arrested or imprisoned and what was the date of his arrest or imprisonment?

2. If the aforementioned person has been arrested or imprisoned, what is the date of his release and what legal provisions have been invoked?

3. In the event that this person has been arrested or imprisoned, what has he been accused of and what was the decision handed down in the case?

4. According to the allegations received by the Commission, Mr. Pierre has died during the course of his detention and, should that be the case, what were the date and the cause of his death?

5. The Government of Haiti did not reply to this new request for information even though the same request was made in another note dated October 19, 1981, which also warned of eventual application of Article 39 of the Regulations of the

Commission if the information requested was not received within a reasonable time.

WHEREAS:

1. In its note dated April 5, 1978, the Government of Haiti confined itself to denying in a general fashion the existence of political prisoners in the country, and did not refer specifically to the status of Mr. Anous Pierre.

2. That the term stipulated in Article 31 of the Regulations of the Commission has lapsed and the Government of Haiti has not replied to repeated requests for information made by the IACHR in connection with the status of Mr. Anous Pierre, and this leads to the presumption that there are no further remedies under domestic law that must be exhausted (Article 46 of the American Convention) in accordance with the procedures established in that Convention.

3. Article 39 of the Regulations of the Commission reads:

Article 39

The facts reported in the petition whose pertinent parts have been transmitted to the government of the state in reference shall be presumed to be true if, during the maximum term set by the Commission under the provisions of Article 31 paragraph 5, the government has not provided the pertinent information, as long as the other evidence does not lead to a different conclusion.

4. Article 1 of the American Convention on Human Rights reads:

Article 1. Obligation to Respect Rights

1. The States Parties to the Convention undertake to respect the rights and freedoms recognized herein and to ensure to all persons subject to their jurisdiction the free and full exercise of those rights and freedoms, without any discrimination for reasons of race, color, sex, language, religion, political or other opinion, national or social origin, economic status, birth or any other social condition.

5. The Republic of Haiti is a State Party to the American Convention on Human Rights.

Therefore, in view of the foregoing information and the considerations made, and since the Commission does not have other information that would lead it to conclude otherwise, on the grounds of Article 39 of its Regulations,

THE INTER-AMERICAN COMMISSION ON HUMAN RIGHTS

RESOLVES:

1. To presume to be true the facts denounced in the communication of November 24, 1977, relating to the status of Mr. Anous Pierre, arrested in September, 1976, and located, at the time of the denunciation, in cell No. 2 of the Fort Dimanche prison, considering that no information has been received as to his release or having been placed under the orders of a competent authority, or, in the event that he has died in prison, what were the date and the cause of his death.

2. To declare that these facts constitute a grave violation of the following rights protected in the American Convention on Human Rights: right to personal

liberty (Article 7); right to humane treatment (Article 5); right to a fair trial (Article 8).

3. To recommend to the Government of Haiti: a) that it provide for the immediate release of Mr. Anous Pierre; b) that in the event that Mr. Pierre has died in prison, to report the date on which his death occurred and the causes of it.

Furthermore, to recommend to the Government of Haiti: a) that it make a full and impartial investigation to determine who is responsible for the facts denounced; b) that, in accordance with Haitian law, it punish those responsible for the facts denounced; c) that it report to the Commission within a term of ninety days on the measures that it has taken to put the aforementioned recommendations into practice.

4. To communicate this resolution to the Government of Haiti and to the petitioner.

5. To include this resolution in its Annual Report of the General Assembly of the Organization of American States.

* * *

Case 9426, Inter-Am. C.H.R. 119, OEA/Ser.L/V/II.71, doc. 9 rev. 1 (1987):

HAVING SEEN the background information on this case, viz:

1. In a communication dated September 4, 1984 the Inter-American Commission on Human Rights received the following complaint:

On July 24, 1984 eighteen-year old JUAN DARIO CUYA LAINE was arrested at his home, in the Province of Ayacucho, by members of the army and the police. His mother has stated that she saw him on July 30, 1984 when visiting him at the Quiscapata barracks. At that time he presented visible signs of torture. Since then his whereabouts are unknown. The officials at Quiscapata, where he had been detained, now deny his arrest. According to information received the facilities at Quiscapata used to be a school. We fear for the life and integrity of Juan Darío in view of the recent well known events in Ayacucho. All internal remedies have been exhausted. We urgently request the IACHR to press the Government of Peru to acknowledge the arrest of Mr. Cuya, determine his whereabouts and guarantee his safety.

2. In a cablegram dated September 5, 1984 the Commission transmitted the pertinent parts of the claim to the Government of Peru requesting it to provide information, in accordance with Article 34 (formerly 31) of the Regulations. This request was repeated in a note on September 10, 1984.

3. In a note dated December 10, 1984 . . . , the Government of Peru replied to the Commission as follows:

Acting on the instructions of its Government, the Permanent Mission of Peru informs the Honorable Executive Secretariat that the Ministry of the Interior has reported that the Peruvian citizen, Mr. Juan Darío Cuya Laine, has not been intervened nor arrested by the forces of Law and Order in the Emergency Zone. Moreover, it is noted that this citizen has no social-political record in the registers of the Peruvian police; and that his present whereabouts are unknown, in spite of efforts to locate him made according to the request of the Inter-American Commission on Human Rights.

4. In a letter dated January 30, 1985, the Commission made known the pertinent parts of the above-mentioned information to the petitioner, requesting that he send his observations within a period of 45 days; this request was reiterated in a letter dated May 1st, 1986 pointing out that should it not receive any information within a period of 60 days, the Commission would discontinue processing the case.

5. In his communication of May 14, 1986, the petitioner sent additional information and observations on the case, as follows:

In its note of December 10, 1984 the Peruvian Government states that JUAN DARIO CUYA LAINE was not arrested by the security forces operating in the state of emergency zone and that he does not have a police record. The Government adds that, in spite of all efforts to locate him, his whereabouts are still unknown.

We consider there to be an important discrepancy between the information provided by the Government and the two declarations sworn to before the District Attorney at Ayacucho, copies of which we are sending to the Commission.

On June 25, 1984 the witness stated in a sworn statement that on June 24, 1984, and after having searched his home around 6 a.m., Juan Darío was arrested by a group of 15 Army officials. Also the witness stated he believed Juan Darío had been taken to the "Los Cabitos" barracks and requested that he be released or transferred to the Investigations Police of Peru (PIP).

On August 31, 1984 the witness stated in a new affidavit that he had learned that Juan Darío had been in police custody in a building known as "Casa Rosada" and that later he had been transferred to the army barracks at Quiscapata. The witness said he visited him at that facility on July 30, 1984 and verified that the prisoner was vomiting blood. The witness also stated that at Quiscapata he was promised Juan Darío would be released 15 days later but in fact he was never seen again. He said he later heard that Juan Darío was at the "Casa Rosada", then at "Los Cabitos" and he asked the District Attorney to look into said facilities.

6. In its communications of May 22 and 28, 1986 the Commission transmitted the pertinent parts of the observations and new information sent by the petitioner to the Government of Peru and set a period of 30 days for this Government to furnish information on the case.

7. In its communication of May 22, the Commission informed the petitioner of the above-mentioned procedure.

CONSIDERING:

1. That this case meets all the admissibility requirements set forth in the Commission's Regulations.

2. That the Government of Peru has not replied to the last request for information by the Commission, dated May 22, 1986.

3. That the information provided by the Government of Peru in its note of December 10, 1984, denying the arrest of Mr. Juan Darío Cuya Laine by security forces, contradicts the testimony given under oath by Mr. Cuya Laine's mother before the ad-hoc District Attorney of Ayacucho, on June 25, 1984, which is on file. . . .

6. That in view of the facts on file, those provided by the petitioner as well as those presented by the afore-mentioned Government, it is affirmed that the facts claimed are considered to be true and that, consequently, Mr. Juan Darío Cuya Laine was arbitrarily arrested by agents of the Government of Peru and kept in illegal detention facilities, that is, in military barracks or facilities, until his disappearance which, by his own mother's testimony, must have occurred between the end of July and the beginning of August, 1984.

7. That in this case the petitioners exhausted the internal remedies available to them upon requesting the Ayacucho District Attorney to verify the presence and status of Mr. Juan Darío Cuya Laine, and that the judicial authorities, not having complied with the requested action nor initiated preliminary proceedings to clarify the facts, constituted an act of denial of justice, and whereby the Commission shall not apply the provisions established in Article 37, paragraph 1 of its Regulations.

8. That, furthermore, in the case that is the subject matter of this resolution, the Commission has not been able, by reason of the nature of the petition, that is, the forced disappearance of Mr. Juan Darío Cuya Laine, to apply the friendly settlement procedure provided for in Article 48, paragraph 1, *f* of the American Convention on Human Rights and in Article 45 of its Regulations.

9. That in accordance with the provisions set forth in Article 42 (formerly 39) of the Regulations the Commission will presume to be true the facts stated in the petition, as long as other evidence does not lead to a different conclusion.

THE INTER-AMERICAN COMMISSION ON HUMAN RIGHTS

RESOLVES:

1. To presume true the facts claimed in the communication dated September 5, 1984 regarding the arbitrary arrest and disappearance of Mr. Juan Darío Cuya Laine, in Ayacucho, on June 24, 1984.

2. To point out to the Government of Peru that such events constitute very serious violations of the right to life (Art. 4); to personal integrity (Art. 5) and to personal liberty (Art. 7) set forth in the American Convention on Human Rights.

3. To recommend to the Government of Peru that, in the shortest time possible, it order a complete investigation of the facts denounced so as to clarify events, determine the agents responsible for Mr. Cuya Laine's disappearance and to punish them.

4. To state that the relatives of Mr. Juan Darío Cuya Laine deserve a just compensation, according to law, and that, therefore, it is the responsibility of the Government of Peru to provide such compensation.

5. To request the Government of Peru to inform the Commission, within 60 days, on measures taken to implement the recommendations set forth in this resolution; and if after that period the Government of Peru has not submitted any observations, the Commission will include this Resolution in its Annual Report to the General Assembly of the OAS, in accordance with Article 63 *g*, of the Commission's Regulations.

6. To transmit the text of this Resolution to the Government of Peru and the petitioner.

NOTES

As indicated by the material in chapters 2 and 5, the government of Peru has not investigated or adequately responded to disappearances such as occurred in the case of Juan Darío Cuya Laine. Many of these cases have remained unresolved.

D. THE INTER-AMERICAN COMMISSION ON HUMAN RIGHTS

C. Medina Quiroga, The Battle of Human Rights: Gross, Systematic Violations and the Inter-American System 69-72, 76-79, 85, 87, 113, 116-21, 144-51 (1988) (footnotes omitted):

The functions and powers of the original [Inter-American] Commission [on Human Rights] . . .

Legal basis; Resolution VIII and the Statute

Resolution VIII, paragraph II, of the Fifth Meeting of Consultation [of Ministers of Foreign Affairs of the Organization of American States] had created the [Inter-American] Commission [on Human Rights] to further respect for human rights [in 1959]. Article 9 of the Commission's Statute vested it with the following functions and powers:

a) To develop an awareness of human rights among the peoples of America;

b) To make recommendations to the Governments of the Member States in general, if it considers such action advisable, for the adoption of progressive measures in favor of human rights within the framework of their domestic legislation and, in accordance with their constitutional precepts, appropriate measures to further the faithful observance of those rights;

c) To prepare such studies or reports as it considers advisable in the performance of its duties;

d) To urge the Governments of the Member States to supply it with information on the measures adopted by them in matters of human rights;

e) To serve the Organization of American States as an advisory body in respect of human rights.

Article 2 of the Statute clarified that "For the purpose of this Statute, human rights are understood to be those set forth in the American Declaration of the Rights and Duties of Man." . . .

Of the five paragraphs of article 9, its section (b) was the object of a thorough discussion, which culminated in a broad interpretation of the provision. It did not seem clear to the Commission members whether the Commission could only make recommendations to the governments of the member states in general or whether it was empowered to make general recommendations to individual member states. "After carefully considering each aspect of the question, the Commission at its seventh meeting, held on October 12, [1961,] agreed to establish that 'paragraph b) of article 9 of the Statute of the Commission should permit this body, if it considers such action advisable, to make general recommendations to each individual Member State, as well as to all of them' ''. . . .

The original Commission and individual communications; the starting point for the broadening of the Commission's powers.

[I]ndividual communications concerning violations of human rights had begun to reach the Commission as soon as it started to function. At its First Session, the Commission stated that "it was not empowered to make any individual decision with regard to written communications or claims that it might receive, although it would take cognizance of them for the purpose of using them in fulfillment of paragraphs b) and c) [of article 9 of the Statute]''. . . .

When its Second Session started (April 10 to 26, 1961), the Commission had in hand 45 communications concerning violations of human rights in Cuba, and it "carefully examined the question as to whether or not it was empowered to make some recommendations to the Government of Cuba with respect to the cases submitted to it, and its conclusion was that it could do so. For its competence included not only the power to recommend the adoption of general measures in favor of human rights in the domestic legislation of each State, but also to recommend to the Member States that they take . . . the appropriate measures to further the faithful observance of those rights''. The statutory basis of this decision was, thus, article 9, section (b). "Furthermore, the Commission felt that it was justified in requesting a report from the Government of Cuba on the measures it was taking in respect to human rights in the circumstances the country was going through'' under the authority of article 9, section (d) of the same statute. The Commission also decided that "upon acknowledging the communications regarding the Cuban situation, [it] should send their authors a verbatim copy of the message cabled to the Government of Cuba.'' Finally, at that same Session, the Commission resolved "to release publicly the aforementioned cable . . .'', thereby starting to make use of publicity to bring pressure to bear on the governments that did not comply with human rights standards as set forth in the American Declaration of the Rights and Duties of Man.

During its Third Session, the Commission decided to ask the Dominican Republic for permission to visit that country. . . .

The Dominican Republic acceded to the request, and this visit constituted the first step towards setting up the most powerful instrument the Commission has in order to investigate the situation of human rights in a particular country: observations *in loco* or on-the-spot analysis of facts. During that first visit, the Commission performed investigatory work as a fact-finding group: interviews with the authorities, with groups and private individuals, with leaders of political parties and trade unions. Furthermore, the Commission pleaded and bargained to obtain the release of prisoners, the improvement of conditions in jails, and so forth, thus becoming a true "action body''. . . .

THE BROADENING OF THE POWERS OF THE COMMISSION AT THE SECOND SPECIAL INTER-AMERICAN CONFERENCE OF 1965. . .

A belated acknowledgment of the Commission's competence to protect human rights was provided by Resolution XXII of the Second Special Conference. . . .

[T]he provisions of Resolution XXII had to be incorporated into the Statute, and this was done by the Commission itself. An article 9(bis) was added to the Statute which read:

The Commission shall have the following additional functions and powers:

a. To give particular attention to observance of the human rights referred to in Articles I, II, III, IV, XVIII, XXV, and XXVI of the American Declaration of the Rights and Duties of Man;

b. To examine communications submitted to it and any other available information; to address to the government of any American State a request for information deemed pertinent by the Commission; and to make recommendations, when it deems this appropriate, with the objective of bringing about more effective observance of fundamental human rights;

c. To submit a report annually to the Inter-American Conference or to the Meeting of Consultation of Ministers of Foreign Affairs, which should include: (i) a statement of progress achieved in realization of the goals set forth in the American Declaration; (ii) a statement of areas in which further steps are needed to give effect to the human rights set forth in the American Declaration; and (iii) such observations as the Commission may deem appropriate on matters covered in the communications submitted to it and in other information available to the Commission.

d. To ascertain, as a condition precedent to the exercise of the powers set forth in paragraphs b) and c) of the present Article, whether the internal legal procedure and remedies of a Member State have been duly pursued and exhausted. . . .

THE COMMISSION BECOMES AN ORGAN OF THE OAS; THE AMENDMENT OF THE OAS CHARTER. . .

Until the Protocol of Buenos Aires amending the OAS Charter entered into force [in 1970], the status of the existing Inter-American Commission on Human Rights was rather difficult to specify. According to its Statute the Commission was an autonomous entity of the Organization, but the meaning of that expression had never been discussed or explained. . . .

The Protocol of Buenos Aires modified article 51 of the Charter by including an Inter-American Commission on Human Rights in the list of organs by means of which the Organization was to accomplish its purposes. . . .

The Inter-American Commission on Human Rights, which was described up to now in its role of promotor and protector of human rights, first as an autonomous entity of the Organization of American States and later as an organ of the OAS, saw its powers legitimized and enlarged by means of the American Convention of Human Rights. . . .

THE INTER-AMERICAN COMMISSION ON HUMAN RIGHTS AND THE LEGAL BASIS OF ITS POWERS AFTER THE ENTRY INTO FORCE OF THE AMERICAN CONVENTION

The Commission presently has three categories of powers. One with respect to all member states of the Organization of American States; another vis-á-vis the states parties to the American Convention on Human Rights; and a third with regard to the OAS member states not parties to the American Convention. This fact not-withstanding, it is only one organ, whether it exercises its powers vis-à-vis states parties or states not parties to the Convention....

A different question is whether this one organ, the Commission, derives different powers from different sources. It should first be noted that the general functions of the Commission, viz. to promote the observance and protection of human rights and to serve as a consultative organ of the Organization in these matters, are set forth in Article 112 of the OAS Charter, which is binding for all OAS member states. These general functions have been given more concrete expression in Article 41 of the Convention, which states:

The main function of the Commission shall be to promote respect for and defense of human rights. In the exercise of its mandate, it shall have the following functions and powers:

a. to develop an awareness of human rights among the peoples of the Americas;

b. to make recommendations to the governments of the member states, when it considers such action advisable, for the adoption of progressive measures in favor of human rights within the framework of their domestic law and constitutional provisions as well as appropriate measures to further the observance of those rights;

c. to prepare such studies or reports as it considers advisable in the performance of its duties;

d. to request the governments of the member states to supply it with information on the measures adopted by them in matters of human rights;

e. to respond, through the General Secretariat of the Organization of American States, to inquiries made by the member states on matters related to human rights and, within the limits of its possibilities, to provide those states with the advisory services they request...;

f. to take action on petitions and other communications pursuant to its authority under the provisions of Articles 44 through 51 of this Convention; and

g. to submit an annual report to the General Assembly of the Organization of American States.

Aside from Article 41, the Commission's Statute contains in Chapter IV, under the heading "Functions and powers," three articles. Article 18 sets forth the powers of the Commission with respect to all OAS member states - both parties and non-parties to the Convention - by reproducing almost verbatim sections a) through e) of Article 41 quoted above, and by adding three new powers, namely, to conduct on-site observations in a state, and to submit (i) annual reports, and (ii) the program-budget to the General Assembly of the Organization. Article 19 establishes the powers of the Commission with respect to the states parties to the Convention by reproducing several provisions of the Convention clearly dealing only with those states. Article 20 sets forth the functions and powers with respect to states not parties to the Convention by reproducing almost verbatim article 9 (bis), (a), (b), and (d) of the old Commission's Statute. These provisions establish the duty of the Commission to pay particular attention to certain human rights, and confer the power to examine communications, after the domestic legal remedies have been exhausted....

COMPOSITION AND FUNCTIONING

According to article 34 of the Convention, the Commission "shall be composed of seven members, who shall be persons of high moral character and recognized competence in the field of human rights".

The Commission's members are elected in a personal capacity by the General Assembly of the OAS from a list of candidates proposed by the governments of all OAS member states. Each Government may propose up to three candidates who may be nationals of any member state of the OAS. In this slate of three, at least one candidate must be a national of a state other than the one proposing it. The election system is changed in the case of vacancies occurring for reasons other than the normal expiration of a term. In that case, the vacancies are filled by the Permanent Council. No two nationals of the same state may be members of the Commission at the same time. The Commission's members are elected for a term of four years and may be reelected only once.

The Statute of the Commission declares incompatible with membership of the Commission "other activities that might affect the independence or impartiality of the member or the dignity or prestige of his post on the Commission." It is the Commission's competence to consider possible cases of incompatibility and decide on it by an affirmative vote of at least five of its members. Once the decision is reached, the Commission submits the case to the General Assembly for a final decision. The General Assembly's declaration of incompatibility must be taken by a majority of two-thirds of the member states of the OAS and shall result in the removal of the member of the Commission from his post.

A member can also be removed by the General Assembly - again at the request of the Commission - for committing a serious violation of any of the duties specified in article 9 of the Statute. . . .

The Commission elects every year a Chairman, a First Vice-Chairman and a Second Vice-Chairman, which constitute the officers of the Commission. The Chairman, among other duties, represents the Commission before all other organs of the Organization and other institutions; presides over the meetings; must promote the work of the Commission; sees to the compliance with the decisions of the Commission; and may designate special committees, ad hoc committees and sub-committees to carry out any mandate within his area of competence.

The Commission is helped in its work by a Secretariat, composed of an Executive Secretary, an Assistant Executive Secretary and the professional, technical, and administrative staff needed to carry out its activities.

The Commission meets for a period not to exceed a total of eight weeks a year, divided into however many regular meetings the Commission may decide. It may also meet in special sessions. Sessions are held in Washington, at its headquarters, but the Commission may decide to meet elsewhere, with the consent or at the invitation of the government concerned. The Commission may decide to establish a working group to deal with petitions or communications, prior to their being handled by the Commission in full. It may also decide to establish other working groups to consider specific subjects. . . .

The handling of communications under articles 44 through 51 of the American Convention and article 20 of the Commission's Statute

The Commission has in principle two sets of rules to handle communications. One set is to be applied to states parties to the American Convention; the other set regulates the procedure to be followed with communications lodged against OAS member states not parties to the Convention.

The scope and nature of the states' obligations in the field of human rights vary depending on whether the state is a party to the American Convention. The obligations of parties are set forth in the American Convention. If a state is not a party, the human rights standards against which its conduct will be measured are those set forth in the American Declaration of the Rights and Duties of Man. Differences between parties and non-parties are also found in the manner in which the states relate to the Commission. As a general rule, however, most of the Convention provisions for communications regarding states parties to the American Convention are made applicable to communications concerning states not parties to the Convention by means of article 52 of the Regulations. The differences are thus minor and do not justify a separate treatment. Consequently, the exercise of the Commission's powers to handle communications will be studied without making this distinction, and the differences will be pointed out whenever that is called for.

Active and passive legitimation

The Convention allows private individuals and states to lodge communications alleging violations of human rights committed by states parties. By the mere fact of ratifying the Convention, the states allow "any person, or group of persons or any nongovernmental entity legally recognized in one or more member states of the Organization" to "lodge petitions with the Commission containing denunciations or complaints of violations of this Convention by a State Party". Article 19 of the Commission's Statute vests the Commission with the power "to act on petitions and other communications, pursuant to the provisions of articles 44 to 51 of the Convention."

Both articles, as is plain to see, do not limit the contents of a petition except by stating that they have to allege a violation of the Convention. Article 26 of the Commission's Regulations, on the contrary, specifies this by setting forth that:

> Any person or group of persons or a nongovernmental entity legally recognized in one or more of the member states of the Organization may submit petitions to the Commission, in accordance with these Regulations, on his own behalf or on behalf of third persons, with regard to alleged violations of a human right recognized, as the case may be, in the American Convention on Human Rights or in the American Declaration of the Rights and Duties of Man.

The Regulations, thus, limit the possibility of complaining against a violation of the Convention to allegations of violation of a human right set forth therein. At the same time, this provision clarifies that the Commission may also process communications against states not parties to the Convention, in which case the human rights standards to be applied are those of the American Declaration....

The Commission itself may start procedures on its own motion since it may "take into consideration any available information that it considers pertinent and which might include the necessary factors to begin processing a case which in its opinion fulfills the requirements for that purpose [under article 26(2) of the Regulations]."...

Admissibility

A communication...must fulfill several requirements in order to be admitted for consideration. There are, first, requirements concerning certain information that the communication must contain, such as identification of the person lodging the complaint, an account of the act or situation leading to the alleged violation, identification of the state which the petitioner considers responsible, mention of the human rights allegedly being violated, and information on whether the remedies under domestic law have been exhausted or whether it has been impossible to do so. The omission of any of these requirements will usually result in the Commission asking the petitioner to supply the information, and not in declaring the petition inadmissible for that reason alone.

The Convention sets forth several conditions of admissibility in articles 46 and 47.... The first is the exhaustion of domestic legal remedies in accordance with generally recognized principles of international law. A second is the existence of a six-month deadline to present the petition, counted from "the date on which the party alleging violation of his rights was notified of the final judgment." These requirements are not applied when:

> a. the domestic legislation of the state concerned does not afford due process of law for the protection of the right or rights that have allegedly been violated;
>
> b. the party alleging violation of his rights has been denied access to the remedies under domestic law or has been prevented from exhausting them; or
>
> c. there has been unwarranted delay in rendering a final judgment under the aforementioned remedies.

Article 37 of the Regulations places the burden of proof with regard to the exhaustion of domestic remedies upon the government concerned, when the petitioner contends that he is unable to prove that fact, unless it is clearly evident from the background information contained in the petition that the remedies under domestic law have not been exhausted.

A third admissibility requirement is that the subject of the petition or communication must not be "pending in another international proceeding for settlement", and the petition or communication must not be "substantially the same as one previously studied by the Commission or by another international organization". The Commission's Regulations have further specified these rules in article 39 by setting forth that:...

2. The Commission shall not refrain from taking up and examining a petition in cases provided for in paragraph 1 when:

> a. The procedure followed before the other organization or agency is one limited to an examination of the general situation of human rights in the state in question and there has been no decision on specific facts that are the subject of the petition submitted to the Commission, or is one that will not lead to an effective settlement of the violation denounced;
>
> b. The petitioner before the Commission or a family member is the alleged victim of the violation denounced and the petitioner before the organization

in reference is a third party or a nongovernmental entity having no mandate from the former.

A fourth admissibility requirement underscores the fact that only the rights set forth in the Convention can serve as grounds for an individual communication. It declares inadmissible communications that do not state facts that tend to establish a violation of the rights guaranteed by the Convention.

A fifth admissibility requirement is that the communication must not be manifestly groundless or obviously out of order. It has to be remembered that it is not required that the individual applicant be the victim of the violation.

For communications against states not parties to the Convention, similar requirements apply.

All these requirements are examined at first by the Secretariat of the Commission, where communications are registered. The Secretariat also acknowledges receipt of the communication to the petitioner.

Further consideration of the case

If the Secretariat accepts, in principle, the admissibility of the communication, the contentious procedure begins. The Secretariat may then request information from the government of the state against which the complaint was lodged, including in the request the pertinent parts of the petition.

The government must provide the information "as quickly as possible, within 90 days after the date on which the request is sent". An extension may be granted but not for more than 180 days after the date on which the first communication is sent to the government concerned. The pertinent parts of the reply and the documents provided by the government shall be made known to the petitioner, who may submit observations and any available evidence within thirty days. Finally, these observations are transmitted to the government, which may submit final observations within thirty days.

This procedure may be altered under special circumstances. In "serious or urgent cases or when it is believed that the life, personal integrity or health of a person is in imminent danger, the Commission shall request the promptest reply from the government, using for this purpose the means it considers most expeditious". This means in practice that requests for information are made by telegram or even by telephone.

At this initial stage the Commission may also find its powers increased when the petition concerns a serious and urgent case. Article 48(2) of the Convention provides that with "only the presentation of a petition or communication that fulfills all the formal requirements of admissibility" the Commission may "conduct an investigation with the prior consent of the state in whose territory a violation has allegedly been committed".

The Regulations of the Commission also envisage the possibility of urgent measures to be taken at this stage when carrying out its protective function. Article 29, a general provision applicable to states parties and not parties to the Convention and to the Commission's procedures in general, sets forth that:

> 2. In urgent cases when it becomes necessary to avoid irreparable damage to persons, the Commission may request that provisional measures be taken to avoid irreparable damage in cases where the denounced facts are true.

The expression "where the denounced facts are true" can only be described as highly unfortunate, especially if read together with section 4 of the same provision which sets forth that:

> 4. The request for such measures and their adoption shall not prejudice the final decision.

Perhaps the most suitable interpretation is that the provision in section 2 refers to the Commission's opinion that the communication is prima facie well-founded, while section 4 refers to the final decision which will include a well-founded opinion on the veracity of the facts of the case, on the existence of a violation and on the identity of the individual or individuals responsible for it. The decision to take provisional measures may be adopted by the Commission's Chairman or one of the Vice-Chairmen, when the Commission is not in session.

The procedure may also be altered in serious and urgent cases of human rights violations involving states parties to the American Convention. Article 69 of the Commission's Regulations sets forth that:

> 1. In cases of extreme gravity and urgency, and when it becomes necessary to avoid irreparable damage to persons in a matter that has not yet been submitted to the Court for consideration, the Commission may request it to adopt any provisional measures it deems pertinent. . . .

Examination of the merits; friendly settlement

Once the first stage of the procedure is completed, the Commission examines whether the communication is admissible and whether the grounds for the communication still exist. If this is the case, the Commission examines the merits of the case, for which purpose different means among those discussed above may be used. Article 42 of the Regulations establishes a presumption of veracity of the facts reported in the petition if the state does not provide pertinent information during the maximum period it has to make observations to the petitioner's allegations, and as long as other evidence in the case does not lead to a different conclusion. This may lead to the Commission's conclusion that the government has violated the Convention, even though the evidence rendered in the case may be insufficient by itself to support it. This provision, which may not appeal to the legal mind, is the consequence of the de facto situation obtaining in so many countries of the Americas. The great majority of individual cases handled by the Commission occur in countries where the rule of law does not prevail and where it is evident that there is a deliberate governmental policy of human rights violations, while, at the same time, the governments of these countries are not likely to cooperate with the Commission in its investigation. It should be noted that article 42 is applied in most of the individual cases handled by the Commission so far.

According to article 48(1)(f) of the Convention, at any stage of the examination of a communication against a state party to the Convention, "the Commission shall place itself at the disposal of the parties concerned with a view to reaching a friendly settlement of the matter on the basis of respect for human rights" laid down in the American Convention on Human Rights. . . .

There is no provision equivalent to article 48(1)(f) of the Convention for cases concerning states not parties to the Convention. However, since "the Commission may, at its own initiative, or at the request of a party, take any action it considers necessary for the discharge of its functions'', nothing prevents the Commission from attempting a friendly settlement in any case in which it is engaged. Article 49 of the Convention sets forth that if a settlement is reached, a report shall be drawn up, transmitted to the petitioner and to the states parties to the Convention and then communicated to the Secretary General of the OAS for publication. The report shall contain a brief statement of the facts and the solution reached.

The decision

At the point when the merits of the case have been examined, the procedure for states not parties to the Convention departs from the one for states parties thereto. In the case of the former, once the investigatory stage ends, the Commission adopts a final decision which includes any recommendations the Commission deems advisable and a deadline for their implementation. The decision is transmitted to the state in question. The latter may request reconsideration of the Commission's conclusions or recommendations on the basis of new facts or arguments. When this occurs, the Commission may request the petitioner to present observations on the request. The Commission may change its decision or stand by it. If necessary, a new deadline for implementation of recommendations is set. If the state does not adopt the measures recommended by the Commission within the deadline imposed, the Commission may publish its decision in the annual report or in any other way it sees fit....

In contrast with this simple procedure, the steps to be taken in cases involving states parties to the Convention are much more cumbersome. Once the investigatory stage is over, and no friendly settlement has been reached, the Commission prepares a first report "stating the facts and conclusions regarding the case submitted to it for its study". This report is transmitted to the states concerned, which are not at liberty to publish it. The Commission may make such proposals and recommendations as it sees fit in transmitting the report.

A three month period follows this transmittal during which the matter may be (i) settled, either because a friendly settlement has been reached or because the state has complied with the proposals and recommendations of the Commission contained in the first report, or (ii) submitted by the Commission or the state concerned to the Court, when the requirements for the Court to have jurisdiction in the case have been met.

When neither has occurred, the Commission "may, by the vote of an absolute majority of its members, set forth its opinion and conclusions concerning the question submitted for its consideration", and where appropriate may "make pertinent recommendations" and "prescribe a period within which the state is to take the measures that are incumbent upon it to remedy the situation examined". This is, thus, a second report, the adoption of which needs a majority vote of the members present. Any Commission member may attach a separate opinion to the report. Also attached to it are the written and oral statements by the parties. This second report is transmitted to the parties concerned and must be kept unpublished. When the prescribed period has expired, the Commission decides by an absolute majority of its members whether the state has taken adequate measures to remedy the situation. At that moment, it also decides whether to publish the report, either in the Commission's annual report to be presented to the OAS General Assembly or in any other form the Commission considers suitable.

In practice, however, the Commission does not usually write two reports in the cases against states parties. These cases, in imitation of the procedure established for states not parties to the Convention, usually end by a resolution which begins with a description of the facts of the case and the different phases of the procedure (allegations of the petitioner, observations of the government, mention of evidence collected). This is followed by legal considerations and then by the resolution proper, in which the Commission declares whether or not the facts have been proven true, and whether or not they constitute a violation of one of the human rights set forth in the Convention ascribable to the government of the country concerned. The resolution then proceeds, when the Commission deems it pertinent, to recommend that the government concerned take certain measures with regard to the violation committed, and to set a deadline for this. At its end the resolution frequently reads approximately as follows: "If after the period established in paragraph... of this resolution [the period given to the government to take certain measures recommended], the ... government has not set forth its observations, the Commission shall include this resolution in its annual report to the General Assembly pursuant to article 59 [current article 63] section (g) of the Commission's Regulations".

NOTES

1. For further reading on the Inter-American Commission on Human Rights, see:

Grossman, *Proposals to Strengthen the Inter-American System of Protection of Human Rights*, 32 German Y.B. Int'l L. 264 (1990);

D. O'Donnell, Protección Internacional de los Derechos Humanos (1989);

Sepulveda, *The Inter-American Commission on Human Rights of the Organization of American States*, 28 German Y.B. Int'l L. 65 (1985);

Inter-American Commission on Human Rights, 25 Years of Struggle for Human Rights in the Americas (1984);

Norris, *The Individual Petition Procedure of the Inter-American System for the Protection of Human Rights*, in Guide to International Human Rights Practice 108 (H. Hannum ed. 1984);

Sepulveda, *The Inter-American Commission on Human Rights (1960-1981)*, 12 Israel Y.B. Hum. Rts. 46 (1982);

Farer, *The Inter-American Commission on Human Rights: Operations and Doctrine*, 9 Int'l J.L. Libr. 251 (1981);

L. LeBlanc, The OAS and the Promotion and Protection of Human Rights (1977).

2. Professor Dinah Shelton of the University of Santa Clara Law School has recommended measures the Commission could take to improve its effectiveness. They include decreasing response-time for urgent cases, emphasizing prevention, improving legal analysis, adopting a policy in favor of publishing decisions and making them available to the public, and appointing counsel for victims unable to afford counsel. Shelton, *Improving Human Rights Protections: Recommendations for Enhancing the Effectiveness of the Inter-American Commission and Inter-American Court of Human Rights*, 3 Am. U.J. Int'l L. & Pol'y 323 (1988).

E. TREATY INTERPRETATION AND RESERVATIONS

Vienna Convention on the Law of Treaties, 1155 U.N.T.S. 331, T.S. No. 58 (1980), 8 I.L.M. 679 (1969), *entered into force* Jan. 27, 1980:

Article 18

Obligation not to defeat the object and purpose
of a treaty prior to its entry into force

A State is obliged to refrain from acts which would defeat the object and purpose of a treaty when:

(a)   it has signed the treaty or has exchanged instruments constituting the treaty subject to ratification, acceptance or approval, until it shall have made its intention clear not to become a party to the treaty; or

(b)   it has expressed its consent to be bound by the treaty, pending the entry into force of the treaty and provided that such entry into force is not unduly delayed.

SECTION 2. RESERVATIONS

Article 19

Formulation of reservations

A State may, when signing, ratifying, accepting, approving or acceding to a treaty, formulate a reservation unless:

(a)   the reservation is prohibited by the treaty;

(b)   the treaty provides that only specified reservations, which do not include the reservation in question, may be made; or

(c)   in cases not falling under sub-paragraphs (a. and b.), the reservation is incompatible with the object and purpose of the treaty.

SECTION 3. INTERPRETATION OF TREATIES

Article 31

General rule of interpretation

1. A treaty shall be interpreted in good faith in accordance with the ordinary meaning to be given to the terms of the treaty in their context and in the light of its object and purpose.

2. The context for the purpose of the interpretation of a treaty shall comprise, in addition to the text, including its preamble and annexes:

(a)   any agreement relating to the treaty which was made between all the parties in connection with the conclusion of the treaty;

(b)   any instrument which was made by one or more parties in connexion with the conclusion of the treaty and accepted by the other parties as an instrument related to the treaty.

3. There shall be taken into account, together with the context:

(a)   any subsequent agreement between the parties regarding the interpretation of the treaty or the application of its provisions;

(b)   any subsequent practice in the application of the treaty which establishes the agreement of the parties regarding its interpretation;

(c)   any relevant rules of international law applicable in the relations between the parties. . . .

4. A special meaning shall be given to a term if it is established that the parties so intended.

Article 32

Supplementary means of interpretation

Recourse may be had to supplementary means of interpretation, including the preparatory work of the treaty and the circumstances of its conclusion, in order to confirm the meaning resulting from the application of Article 31, or to determine the meaning when the interpretation according to Article 31:

(a)   leaves the meaning ambiguous or obscure; or

(b)   leads to a result which is manifestly absurd or unreasonable.

NOTES AND QUESTIONS

1. The Vienna Convention on the Law of Treaties represents a worldwide consensus on how international instruments should be construed. The Convention entered into force on January 27, 1980, but has not yet been ratified by the United States. In its Letter of Submittal to the President, however, the Department of State said that "the Convention is already generally recognized as the authoritative guide to current treaty law and practice." S. Exec. Doc., 92nd Cong., 1st Sess. 1 (1971). The Legal Advisor of the Department of State wrote:

> While the United States has not yet ratified the Vienna Convention on the Law of Treaties, [the United States has] consistently applied those of its terms which constitute a codification of customary international law. Most provisions of the Vienna Convention, including Articles 31 and 32 on matters of treaty interpretation, are declaratory of customary international law.

Nash, *Contemporary Practice of the United States Relating to International Law*, 75 Am. J. Int'l L. 142, 147 (1981).

For possible differences between treaty interpretation in the U.S. and treaty interpretation under the Vienna Convention, see the Restatement (Third) of the Foreign Relations Law of the United States § 325 and comments following this note.

2. The Inter-American Court of Human Rights in several of its opinions has used the rules of interpretation in the Vienna Convention as its sole guide for construing the American Convention on Human Rights. In its opinions the court has acknowledged that the Vienna Convention contains the principles of international law relevant to the interpretation of treaties.

Although the American Declaration on the Rights and Duties of Man was not initially promulgated as a treaty, it has arguably become incorporated by reference within the Charter of the Organization of American States by the Protocol of Buenos Aires which revised the Charter and came into force in 1970. Even if the American Declaration is not considered to be incorporated within the OAS Charter, the Inter-American Commission arguably should still use the Vienna Convention approach to interpretation because it constitutes the best conceived technique for construing international instruments such as the Declaration. *See* R. Wetzel, *Introduction*, The Vienna Convention of the Law of Treaties, Travaux Préparatoires 12-14 (1978).

3. Professor Shelton in an unpublished memorandum related to *Thompson v. Oklahoma*, 487 U.S. 815 (1988), has interpreted Article 18 of the Vienna Convention that forbids a government "from acts which would defeat the object and purpose of a treaty" it has signed:

The Inter-American Court of Human Rights has emphasized that

"modern human rights treaties in general, and the American Convention in particular, are not multilateral treaties of the traditional type concluded to accomplish the reciprocal exchange of rights for the mutual benefit of the contracting States. Their object and purpose is the protection of the basic rights of individual human beings, irrespective of their nationality, both against the State of their nationality and all other contracting States." [The Effect of Reservations on the Entry into Force of the American Convention (Arts. 74 and 75), Advisory Opinion OC-2/82, Inter-Am. Ct. H.R. (Ser. A) (1982).]

Similarly, the character of human rights treaties has been recognized by the European Commission of Human Rights. It has said that the obligations of the European Convention are

"designed rather to protect the fundamental rights of individual human beings from infringements by any of the High Contracting Parties than to create subjective and reciprocal rights for the High Contracting Parties themselves." [Austria v. Italy, 4 European Y.B. Hum. Rts. 116, at 140 (1961).]

Similar views about the purpose of human rights treaties were voiced by the International Court of Justice in its *Advisory Opinion on Reservations to the Convention on the Prevention and Punishment of the Crime of Genocide*, 1951 I.C.J. 15, where the Court also noted that "the [human rights] principles underlying the Convention are principles which are recognized by civilized nations as binding on States, even without any conventional obligation."

Thus, the object and purpose of human rights treaties is manifestly humanitarian entailing a commitment not to violate the human rights of individuals.

4. The acceptability of reservations that tend to defeat the object and purpose of human rights treaties is also discussed in chapters 9 and 12, *infra*.

5. Should the American Convention have been applied in the *Baby Boy* case since the U.S. has signed but not ratified that treaty? What legal effect, if any, should the Commission have given to the Convention? Should the Commission have discussed the proposed U.S. reservation to Article 4 of the American Convention, reproduced below?

Four Treaties Pertaining to Human Rights: Message From the President of the United States, 95th Cong., 2nd Sess. at xvii-xviii (1978):

[Ed.: After President Carter signed the American Convention on Human Rights and three other treaties on June 1, 1977, the State Department proposed a number of reservations, understandings, and declarations for the advice and consent of the Senate as to the ratification of the American Convention.]

The following is a summary of the provisions of the Convention, with the reservations, understandings and declarations to them recommended to the Senate by the Department of State [and transmitted to the Senate by President Carter]. . . .

. . . . Article 4 deals with the right to life generally, and includes provisions on capital punishment. Many of the provisions of Article 4 are not in accord with United States law and policy, or deal with matters in which the law is unsettled. The Senate may wish to enter a reservation as follows:

"United States adherence to Article 4 is subject to the Constitution and other law of the United States."

* * *

1 Restatement (Third) of the Foreign Relations Law of the U.S. § 325 (1987):

§ 325. Interpretation of International Agreement

(1) An international agreement is to be interpreted in good faith in accordance with the ordinary meaning to be given to its terms in their context and in the light of its object and purpose.

(2) Any subsequent agreement between the parties regarding the interpretation of the agreement, and subsequent practice between the parties in the application of the agreement, are to be taken into account in its interpretation. . . .

Comment . . .

e. Recourse to travaux préparatoires. The Vienna Convention, in Article 32, requires the interpreting body to conclude that the "ordinary meaning" of the text is either obscure or unreasonable before it can look to "supplementary means."

Some interpreting bodies are more willing to come to that conclusion than others. (Compare, for example, the experience in the United States with the parol evidence rule in interpreting contracts.) Article 32 of the Vienna Convention reflects reluctance to permit the use of materials constituting the development and nego- tiation of an agreement (*travaux préparatoires*) as a guide to the interpretation of the agreement. The Convention's inhospitality to *travaux* is not wholly consistent with the attitude of the International Court of Justice and not at all with that of United States courts. See Comment *g*.

g. Interpretation by United States courts. This section suggests a mode of interpretation of international agreements somewhat different from that ordinarily applied by courts in the United States. Courts in the United States are generally more willing than those of other states to look outside the instrument to determine its meaning. In most cases, the United States approach would lead to the same result, but an international tribunal using the approach called for by this section might find the United States interpretation erroneous and United States action pursuant to that interpretation a violation of the agreement.

NOTES AND QUESTIONS

1. How does the Restatement approach to treaty interpretation compare to the approach taken by the Vienna Convention? What appears to be the principal difference between the two approaches? What are advantages and disadvantages of each approach?

2. In the *Baby Boy* case, did the Inter-American Commission follow the rules for interpretation set forth in the Vienna Convention?

3. F. Newman & S. Surrey, Legislation: Cases and Materials 645-59 (1955) discusses basic methods of statutory interpretation under U.S. law. There are many other scholarly discussions of statutory interpretation. *See gen- erally* W. Eskridge & P. Frickey, Cases and Materials on Legislation: Statutes and the Creation of Public Policy 569-828 (1988). What are the similarities and differences between statutory interpretation and treaty interpretation? Are there differences between the two contexts that would justify different rules of interpretation?

4. The method of treaty interpretation in the Vienna Convention represents the majority view. Different approaches to treaty interpretation do exist, however. One example is an approach suggested by Myres McDougal, Howard Lasswell, and James Miller. This approach emphasizes giving effect to the shared expectations of the parties to the fullest extent possible, using interpretive methods such as those found in the Vienna Convention to determine the shared expectations. When traditional methods are unable to clarify the parties' expectations, this approach supplements the more explicit expressions of the parties with the basic constitutive policies of the larger community. Finally, the interpreter must consider the parties' expec- tations in light of fundamental community policy, including policies of the world community, in order to determine whether the parties' goals conflict with community policy. Where such a conflict exists, community policy overrides the expectations of the parties. *See* M. McDougal, H. Lasswell, & J. Miller, The Interpretation of Agreements and World Public Order: Principles of Content and Procedure 35-118 (1967).

Frank Newman has suggested another approach to treaty interpretation, at least with regards to interpreting the human rights clauses of the U.N. Charter. Rather than utilizing the contemporaneous discussions of the Charter clauses in interpretation, Newman argues that the primary source of interpretation should be first the actual language of the Charter followed by the subsequent U.N. human rights declarations and treaties — especially the International Bill of Human Rights. *See* Newman, *Interpreting the Human Rights Clauses of the U.N. Charter*, 1972 Revue des Droits de l'Homme 283.

For an overview of further approaches to treaty interpretation — including civil law and socialist law approaches, see E. Yambrusic, Treaty Interpretation: Theory and Reality 9-54 (1987).

For an illustration of interpreting treaties (the two International Covenants on Human Rights) in the light of natural justice and due process see Newman, *Natural Justice, Due Process, and the New International Covenants on Human Rights: Prospectus*, 1967 Pub. L. 274.

Treaty interpretation also is discussed in chapter 12, *infra*.

F. THE ADVISORY JURISDICTION OF THE INTER-AMERICAN COURT OF HUMAN RIGHTS

Buergenthal, *The Inter-American Court of Human Rights*, 76 Am. J. Int'l L. 231, 231-36, 239-40 (1982) (footnotes omitted):

The Court was established by the American Convention on Human Rights, which entered into force in 1978; . . . . The Court consists of seven judges, nominated and elected by the states parties to the Convention. The judges must be nationals of an OAS member state, but they need not have the nationality of the states parties to the Convention. The regular term of the judges is 6 years; they may be reelected for one additional term. The judges constituting the first Court were elected in May 1979. . . .

The Convention provides that "the Court shall have its seat at the place determined by the States Parties to the Convention in the General Assembly of the Organization." A resolution adopted by the Assembly in 1978 located the permanent seat of the Court in Costa Rica. A two-thirds vote of the states parties would be required to change the permanent seat. But the Court is not required to meet only in Costa Rica, for "it may convene in the territory of any member state . . . when a majority of the Court consider it desirable, and with the prior consent of the state concerned." . . .

II. THE COURT AND ITS INSTITUTIONAL CONTEXT

The draft Statute presented to the OAS General Assembly by the Court in

1979 envisaged a permanent tribunal consisting of full-time judges. This proposal was motivated by the Court's concern that a part-time tribunal might give that body an ad hoc image, likely to diminish the prestige and legitimacy it might need to obtain compliance with and respect for its decisions in the Americas. But the General Assembly found this proposal unacceptable, ostensibly at least on the ground that a full-time court would be too expensive and was unjustified until the Court had a substantial case load. The Assembly opted instead for a tribunal composed of part-time judges. It adopted a Statute that leaves the judges free to exercise their respective professions and stipulates merely that certain types of employment, particularly active government service, are incompatible with their judicial functions. As a result, the judges are not on the OAS payroll; they are not required to live in Costa Rica; and they are free to practice law, to teach, and to engage in whatever other occupations they may have in their native countries. . . .

All judicial decisions of the Court must be adopted by the Plenary Court. It does not sit in smaller panels or chambers as does the European Court of Human Rights, for example. Both its small size and the requirement under Article 56 of the Convention that "five judges shall constitute a quorum for the transaction of business by the Court" would seem to rule out the use of chambers. . . .

The Inter-American Court of Human Rights has adjudicatory or so-called contentious jurisdiction, that is, jurisdiction to decide disputes involving charges that a state party has violated the human rights guaranteed by the Convention. It also has advisory jurisdiction, which empowers the Court to interpret the Convention and other human rights instruments at the request of OAS member states and various OAS organs.

Adjudicatory Jurisdiction

The Submission of Cases. The Court's power to decide a case referred to it for adjudication is conditioned on the acceptance of its jurisdiction by the states parties to the dispute. A state is not deemed to have accepted the jurisdiction of the Court merely by ratifying the Convention. Acceptance of its jurisdiction is optional under the Convention and requires a separate declaration or a special agreement. That "declaration may be made unconditionally, on condition of reciprocity, for a specific period, or for specific cases." . . . In addition, of course, all states parties to the Convention may permit the Court at any time, on an *ad hoc* basis, to adjudicate a specific dispute relating to the application of the Convention. Article 62(3) of the Convention reads as follows:

> The jurisdiction of the Court shall comprise all cases concerning the interpretation and application of the provisions of this Convention that are submitted to it, provided that the States Parties to the case recognize or have recognized such jurisdiction, whether by special declaration pursuant to the preceding paragraphs, or by a special agreement.

This provision needs to be read together with Article 61(1), which declares that "only the States Parties and the Commission shall have the right to submit a case to the Court." Individuals have no standing to do so. Moreover, the states suing and those being sued have to have accepted the jurisdiction of the Court before it may hear the case. Of course, the Commission is free to invite a state that has not accepted the Court's jurisdiction to do so for a specific case, but the state is free to reject the request.

Before the Court may "hear a case,...the procedures set forth in Articles 48 to 50 shall have been completed." The procedures referred to are those that govern the disposition by the Commission of cases submitted to it by states or individuals charging violations of the Convention....

Judgments and Preliminary Decisions. The proceedings before the Court in a contentious case terminate with a judgment. By ratifying the Convention, the states parties assumed the obligation "to comply with the judgment of the Court in any case to which they are parties." The Court has the power to enter a declaratory judgment and to award damages. The basic provision on the subject is Article 63(1), which reads as follows:

> If the Court finds that there has been a violation of a right or freedom protected by this Convention, the Court shall rule that the injured party be ensured the enjoyment of his right or freedom that was violated. It shall also rule, if appropriate, that the consequences of the measure or situation that constituted the breach of such right or freedom be remedied and that fair compensation be paid to the injured party.

This provision requires the Court to determine not only whether in the specific case before it there has been a violation of the Convention and what rights the injured party is entitled to enjoy, but also what steps may have to be taken to remedy the violation. As for the power of the Court to award damages, Article 68(2) provides that that part of a "judgment that stipulates compensatory damages may be executed in the country concerned in accordance with domestic procedure governing the execution of judgments against the state."...

In addition, the Court has the power to grant an extraordinary remedy in the nature of a temporary injunction. This power is spelled out in Article 63(2) of the Convention, which reads as follows:

> In cases of extreme gravity and urgency, and when necessary to avoid irreparable damage to persons, the Court shall adopt such provisional measures as it deems pertinent in matters it has under consideration. With respect to a case not yet submitted to the Court, it may act at the request of the Commission.

As this provision indicates, the temporary injunction is available in two distinct circumstances: for cases already pending before the Court and for cases being dealt with by the Commission that have not yet been referred to the Court for adjudication....

Enforcement of Judgments. The Convention does not establish a formal procedure to enforce the rulings of the Court against recalcitrant states. One provision, however — Article 65 — does bear on this subject. It reads:

> To each regular session of the General Assembly of the Organization of American States the Court shall submit, for the Assembly's consideration, a report on its work during the previous year. It shall specify, in particular, the cases in which a state has not complied with its judgments, making any pertinent recommendations.

This provision enables the Court to inform the OAS General Assembly of situations involving noncompliance with its decisions, and it permits the Assembly to discuss the matter and to adopt whatever political measures it deems appropriate....

NOTES

As the preceding excerpt points out, individuals do not have the right to bring cases before the Inter-American Court of Human Rights. Rather, the proper forum for individual petitions is the Inter-American Commission on Human Rights. Nevertheless, an individual's case might come before the Court, for example, where the Commission refers to the Court a case involving a state that has accepted the Court's adjudicatory jurisdiction. For further suggestions as to how individuals can obtain access to the Court, see Vargas, *Individual Access to the Inter-American Court of Human Rights*, 1 Int'l L. & Pol. 601, 604-16 (1984).

Buergenthal, *The Advisory Practice of the Inter-American Human Rights Court*, 79 Am. J. Int'l L. 1, 3-12 (1985) (footnotes omitted):

II. ADVISORY JURISDICTION: ITS ROLE AND SCOPE

The advisory power of the Court is spelled out in Article 64 of the Convention, which reads as follows:

1. The member states of the Organization may consult the Court regarding the interpretation of this Convention or of other treaties concerning the protection of human rights in the American states. Within their spheres of competence, the organs listed in Chapter X of the Charter of the Organization of American States, as amended by the Protocol of Buenos Aires, may in like manner consult the Court.

2. The Court, at the request of a member state of the Organization, may provide that state with opinions regarding the compatibility of any of its domestic laws with the aforesaid international instruments. . . .

Treaties Subject to Interpretation. Article 64(1) extends the Court's advisory jurisdiction to the interpretation of the "Convention or. . .other treaties concerning the protection of human rights in the American states." While the reference to the "Convention" needs no explanation, the same is not true of the meaning of "other treaties." Some of the issues it raises were dealt with by the Court in its first advisory opinion. In that case, the Government of Peru asked the Court to decide "how. . .the phrase 'or of other treaties concerning the protection of human rights in the American states' [should] be interpreted." Without taking a position on the meaning of the phrase, Peru suggested that it might be interpreted to refer either to treaties adopted within the framework of the inter-American system, to treaties concluded solely among American states, or to treaties that included one or more American states as parties. The Court ruled that, in principle, the provision conferred on it "the power to interpret any treaty as long as it is directly related to the protection of human rights in a Member State of the inter-American system." In short, the treaty need not be one that was adopted within the inter-American system or a treaty to which only American states may be parties. It may be bilateral or multilateral, and it need not be a human rights treaty as such, provided the provisions to be interpreted relate to the protection of human rights.

This holding is probably narrower than it appears at first glance. After concluding that there was no valid reason, in principle, to distinguish between regional and international human rights treaties, the Court emphasized that its power to comply with a request to interpret these instruments was discretionary. Whether it would exercise the power depended upon various factors related to the purposes of its advisory jurisdiction. "This jurisdiction," the Court declared, "is intended to assist the American States in fulfilling their international human rights obligations and to assist the different organs of the inter-American system to carry out the functions assigned to them in this field." Consequently, "any request for an advisory opinion which has another purpose would weaken the system established by the Convention and would distort the advisory jurisdiction of the Court." . . .

Two other questions bearing on the meaning of the phrase "other treaties concerning the protection of human rights in the American states" suggest themselves. They have not as yet been dealt with by the Court. One has to do with the definition of "human rights." It has already been noted that the reference is not only to human rights treaties as such, and that it permits the Court to interpret the human rights provisions of bilateral or multilateral treaties, whether or not such treaties deal exclusively with human rights. Examples here might be the human rights provisions of an extradition treaty or of a bilateral commercial agreement. But, and this is a question that remains to be answered, what is a "human rights" provision? In dealing with this problem, the Court might look to the catalog of rights found in the principal international and regional human rights instruments and in the constitutions of the states constituting the inter-American system. The OAS Charter and the American Convention, it should be noted, refer expressly not only to civil and political rights, but also to economic, social and cultural ones. The same is true of many international human rights instruments, which suggests the pervasive scope of the Court's advisory jurisdiction.

The second question is more difficult. It concerns the Court's jurisdiction to interpret the American Declaration of the Rights and Duties of Man. The Declaration was adopted in 1948 in the form of an inter-American conference resolution. As such, it is clearly not a "treaty" within the meaning of Article 64(1) of the American Convention. It is generally recognized, however, that the Protocol of Buenos Aires, which amended the OAS Charter, changed the legal status of the Declaration to an instrument that, at the very least, constitutes an authoritative interpretation and definition of the human rights obligations binding on OAS member states under the Charter of the Organization. This view is reflected in the Statute of the Inter-American Commission on Human Rights, which was adopted by the OAS General Assembly in 1979 pursuant to Article 112 of the OAS Charter and Article 39 of the American Convention. Article 1 of the Statute, after declaring in paragraph 1 that the Commission is an OAS organ "created to promote the observance and defense of human rights and to serve as consultative organ of the Organization in this matter," reads as follows:

2. For the purposes of the present Statute, human rights are understood to be:

a. The rights set forth in the American Convention on Human Rights, in relation to the States Parties thereto;

b. The rights set forth in the American Declaration of the Rights and Duties of Man, in relation to the other member states.

The Statute also relies on the Declaration in defining the powers of the Commission in relation to all OAS member states as well as with respect to states that have not ratified the Convention. Since the Commission's powers with regard to the latter states are derived from the OAS Charter, it can be argued that the General Assembly, in approving the Commission's Statute and the references to the Declaration, confirmed the normative status of the Declaration as an instrument giving specific meaning to the vague human rights provisions of the Charter. If these considerations justify the conclusion that the Charter incorporates the Declaration by reference or that the Declaration constitutes an authoritative interpretation of the human rights provisions of the Charter, the Court's power under Article 64(1) to interpret the Charter would embrace the power to interpret the Declaration as well. It remains to be seen whether the Court will adopt the approach just indicated or opt for a strict textual construction, concluding that since the Declaration is not a "treaty," it does not fall within the Court's jurisdiction under Article 64(1).

A related question concerning the status of the Universal Declaration of Human Rights, which raises similar issues, might be presented to the Court in the context of a request for an advisory opinion seeking an interpretation of the human rights provisions of the UN Charter. Here it is relevant to note that the Convention makes specific reference to the American Declaration and to the Universal Declaration of Human Rights. The reference to the American Declaration in Article 29(d) of the Convention is particularly significant, for it declares that no provision of the Convention shall be interpreted as "excluding or limiting the effect that the American Declaration of the Rights and Duties of Man and other international acts of the same nature may have." To the extent that the Court, in applying Article 29, may be called upon to interpret the American Declaration, it has the power to do so under Article 64(1); it would merely be interpreting the Convention.

Restrictions to the Death Penalty, Advisory Opinion OC-8/83, 3 Inter-Am. Ct. H.R. (ser. A) 54-56, 65-75 (1983) (citations omitted):

STATEMENT OF THE ISSUES

8. Invoking Article 64(1) of the [American] Convention [on Human Rights], the Commission requested the Court, in communications of April 15 and 25, 1983, to render an advisory opinion on the following questions relating to the interpretation of Article 4 of the Convention:

> 1) May a government apply the death penalty for crimes for which the domestic legislation did not provide such punishment at the time the American Convention on Human Rights entered into force for said state?
> 2) May a government, on the basis of a reservation to Article 4(4) of the Convention made at the time of ratification, adopt subsequent to the entry into force of the Convention a law imposing the death penalty for crimes not subject to this sanction at the moment of ratification?...

10. In its explanation of the considerations giving rise to the request, the Commission informed the Court of the existence of certain differences of opinion between it and the Government of Guatemala concerning the interpretation of the last sentence of Article 4(2) of the Convention as well as on the effect and scope of Guatemala's reservation to the fourth paragraph of that article....

OBJECTIONS TO THE JURISDICTION OF THE COURT

30. The Court can now turn to the jurisdictional objections advanced by the Government of Guatemala. It contends that, although Article 64(1) of the Convention and Article 19(d) of the Statute of the Commission authorize the latter to seek an advisory opinion from the Court regarding the interpretation of any article of the Convention, if that opinion were to concern a given State directly, as it does Guatemala in the present case, the Court could not render the opinion unless the State in question has accepted the tribunal's jurisdiction pursuant to Article 62(1) of the Convention [which Guatemala has not done]. The Government of Guatemala argues accordingly that because of the form in which the Commission submitted the present advisory opinion request, linking it to an existing dispute between Guatemala and the Commission regarding the meaning of certain provisions of Article 4 of the Convention, the Court should decline to exercise its jurisdiction.

31. The Convention distinguishes very clearly between two types of proceedings: so-called adjudicatory or contentious cases and advisory opinions. The former are governed by the provisions of Articles 61, 62 and 63 of the Convention; the latter by Article 64. . . .

32. In contentious proceedings, the Court must not only interpret the applicable norms, determine the truth of the acts denounced and decide whether they are a violation of the Convention imputable to a State Party; it may also rule "that the injured party be ensured the enjoyment of his right or freedom that was violated." [Convention, Art. 63(1).] The States Parties to such proceeding are, moreover, legally bound to comply with the decisions of the Court in contentious cases. [Convention, Art. 68(1).] On the other hand, in advisory opinion proceedings the Court does not exercise any fact-finding functions; instead, it is called upon to render opinions interpreting legal norms. Here the Court fulfills a consultative function through opinions that "lack the same binding force that attaches to decisions in contentious cases.". . .

33. The provisions applicable to contentious cases differ very significantly from those of Article 64, which govern advisory opinions. Thus, for example, Article 61(2) speaks of "case" and declares that "in order for the Court to hear a *case*, it is necessary that the procedures set forth in Articles 48 to 50 shall have been completed (emphasis added)." These procedures apply exclusively to "a petition or communication alleging violation of any of the rights protected by this Convention." [Convention, Art. 48(1).] Here the word "case" is used in its technical sense to describe a contentious case within the meaning of the Convention, that is, a dispute arising as a result of a claim initiated by an individual (Art. 44) or State Party (Art. 45), charging that a State Party has violated the human rights guaranteed by the Convention.

34. One encounters the same technical use of the word "case" in connection with the question as to who may initiate a contentious case before the Court, which contrasts with those provisions of the Convention that deal with the same issue in the consultative area. Article 61(1) provides that "only States Parties and the Commission shall have a right to submit a case to the Court." On the other hand, not only "States Parties and the Commission," but also all of the "Member States of the Organization" and the "organs listed in Chapter X of the Charter of the Organization of American States" may request advisory opinions from the Court. [Convention, Art. 64(1).] There is yet another difference with respect to the subject matter that the Court might consider. While Article 62(1) refers to "all matters

relating to the interpretation and application of this Convention," Article 64 authorizes advisory opinions relating not only to the interpretation of the Convention but also to "other treaties concerning the protection of human rights in the American states." It is obvious, therefore, that what is involved here are very different matters, and that there is no reason in principle to apply the requirements contained in Articles 61, 62 and 63 to the consultative function of the Court, which is spelled out in Article 64.

35. Article 62(3) of the Convention — the provision Guatemala claims governs the application of Article 64 — reads as follows:

> The jurisdiction of the Court shall comprise all *cases* concerning the interpretation and application of the provisions of this Convention that are submitted to it, provided that the States Parties to the *case* recognize or have recognized such jurisdiction, whether by special declaration pursuant to the preceding paragraphs, or by a special agreement (emphasis added).

It is impossible to read this provision without concluding that it, as does Article 61, uses the words "case" and "cases" in their technical sense. . . .

38. The powers conferred on the Commission require it to apply the Convention or other human rights treaties. In order to discharge fully its obligations, the Commission may find it necessary or appropriate to consult the Court regarding the meaning of certain provisions whether or not at the given moment in time there exists a difference between a government and the Commission concerning an interpretation, which might justify the request for an advisory opinion. If the Commission were to be barred from seeking an advisory opinion merely because one or more governments are involved in a controversy with the Commission over the interpretation of a disputed provision, the Commission would seldom, if ever, be able to avail itself of the Court's advisory jurisdiction. . . .

39. The right to seek advisory opinions under Article 64 was conferred on OAS organs for requests falling "within their spheres of competence." This suggests that the right was also conferred to assist with the resolution of disputed legal issues arising in the context of the activities of an organ, be it the Assembly, the Commission, or any of the others referred to in Chapter X of the OAS Charter. It is clear, therefore, that the mere fact that there exists a dispute between the Commission and the Government of Guatemala regarding the meaning of Article 4 of the Convention does not justify the Court to decline to exercise its advisory jurisdiction in the instant proceeding. . . .

41. The Commission, as an organ charged with the responsibility of recommending measures designed to promote the observance and protection of human rights. . . , has a legitimate institutional interest in the interpretation of Article 4 of the Convention. The mere fact that this provision may also have been invoked before the Commission in petitions and communications filed under Articles 44 and 45 of the Convention does not affect this conclusion. Given the nature of advisory opinions, the opinion of the Court in interpreting Article 4 cannot be deemed to be an adjudication of those petitions and communications.

42. In The Effect of Reservations on the Entry into Force of the American Convention (Arts. 74 and 75) (I/A Court H.R., Advisory Opinion OC-2/82 of September 24, 1982. Series A No. 2), this Court examined in considerable detail

the requirements applicable to OAS organs requesting advisory opinions under Article 64. The Court there explained that Article 64, in limiting the right of OAS organs to advisory opinions falling "within their spheres of competence," meant to restrict the opinions "to issues in which such entities have a legitimate institutional interest." (*Ibid.*, para. 14.) After examining Article 112 and Chapter X of the OAS Charter, as well as the relevant provisions of the Statute of the Commission and the Convention itself, the Court concluded that the Commission enjoys, in general, a pervasive legitimate institutional interest in questions bearing on the promotion and protection of human rights in the inter-American system, which could be deemed to confer on it, as a practical matter, "an absolute right to request advisory opinions within the framework of Article 64(1) of the Convention." (*Ibid.*, para. 16.) Viewed in this light, the instant request certainly concerns an issue in which the Commission has a legitimate institutional interest. . . .

44. Article 49(2)(b) of the Rules of Procedure requires that each request for an advisory opinion by an OAS organ "shall indicate the provisions to be interpreted, how the consultation relates to its sphere of competence, the considerations giving rise to the consultation, and the name and address of its delegates." The requirement of a description of "the considerations giving rise to the consultation" is designed to provide the Court with an understanding of the factual and legal context which prompted the presentation of the question. Compliance with this requirement is of vital importance as a rule in enabling the Court to respond in a meaningful manner to the request. . . .

Thus, merely because the Commission, under the heading of "Considerations giving rise to the consultation," has described for the Court a set of circumstances indicating that there exist differences concerning the interpretation of some provisions of Article 4 of the Convention, it certainly does not follow that the Commission has violated the Rules of Procedure or that it has abused the powers conferred on it as an organ authorized to request advisory opinions. The same conclusion is even more valid when the issue presented calls for the interpretation of a reservation, considering how difficult it is to respond with precision to a question that relates to a reservation and which is formulated in the abstract.

45. The fact that this legal dispute bears on the scope of a reservation made by a State Party in no way detracts from the preceding conclusions. Under the Vienna Convention on the Law of Treaties (hereinafter cited as Vienna Convention), incorporated by reference into the Convention by its Article 75, a reservation is defined as any "unilateral statement, however phrased or named, made by a State when signing, ratifying, accepting, approving or acceding to a treaty, whereby it purports to exclude or to modify the legal effect of certain provisions of the treaty in their application to that State." [Art. 2(d).] The effect of a reservation, according to the Vienna Convention, is to modify with regard to the State making it the provisions of the treaty to which the reservation refers to the extent of the reservation. [Art. 21(1)(a).] Although the provisions concerning reciprocity with respect to reservations are not fully applicable to a human rights treaty such as the Convention, it is clear that reservations become a part of the treaty itself. It is consequently impossible to interpret the treaty correctly, with respect to the reserving State, without interpreting the reservation itself. . . .

NOTES

1. In its Restrictions to the Death Penalty Advisory Opinion, *supra*, the Inter-American Court of Human Rights held that "a reservation which was designed to enable a State to suspend any of the non-derogable fundamental rights must be deemed to be incompatible with the object and purpose of the Convention" and, consequently, not permitted by it.

2. In 1989 the Inter-American Court of Human Rights issued an advisory opinion on the legal effect to be given to the American Declaration of the Rights and Duties of Man. The government of Colombia had requested an advisory opinion as to whether the Inter-American Court of Human Rights has authority under the Inter-American Convention on Human Rights to render advisory opinions interpreting the American Declaration. The Inter-American Court decided that it possessed authority to interpret the American Declaration. The Court also stated that a government which has ratified the Convention is not thereby freed from its obligations deriving from the Declaration because the government continues to be a member of the Organization of American States. The Court concluded, "The fact that the Declaration is not a treaty does not thus import the conclusion that it lacks legal effect, nor is the Court prevented from interpreting it. . . ." Interpretation of the American Declaration of the Rights and Duties of Man in the Context of Article 64 of the American Convention on Human Rights, Advisory Opinion OC-10/89, Inter-Am. Ct. H.R. (1989)(translated from Spanish).

G. OTHER REGIONAL SYSTEMS

As mentioned previously, regional systems for the protection of human rights also exist in Africa and Europe. In addition to those systems, a more rudimentary process of discussion on human rights problems and of opportunities for bilateral contacts has been initiated for the European and Atlantic nations which are parties to the Helsinki Accord, a process this book examines in chapter 10. Chapter 10 also deals with the European system. Relatively little has been done to establish a regional human rights system in Asia.[3] This failure may be due in part to the variety of government

---

[3] *See* van Dyke, *Prospects for the Development of Intergovernmental Human Rights Bodies in Asia and the Pacific*, in New Directions in Human Rights 51 (E. Lutz, H. Hannum, & K. Burke eds. 1989); Yamane, *Approaches to Human Rights in Asia*, in International Enforcement of Human Rights 99 (R. Bernhardt & J. Jolowicz eds. 1987).

systems, religions, philosophies, and cultural traditions found in Asian countries. Governments in the Asian region apparently lack a sense of regional identity and cohesiveness necessary for the establishment of inclusive regional organizations or human rights machineries. Additionally, though the League of Arab States established a Commission on Human Rights in 1968, this Commission has not been active.

The Organization of African Unity and Human Rights

The Organization of African Unity (OAU) is a regional intergovernmental organization that brings together governments of the African continent and its surrounding islands. The Charter of the OAU was adopted in 1963 and reaffirms adherence to the principles of the U.N. Charter and the Universal Declaration of Human Rights. Charter of the Organization of African Unity, 479 U.N.T.S. 39, *came into force* Sept. 13, 1963. The OAU adopted its human rights treaty, the African Charter on Human and Peoples' Rights in 1981. African [Banjul] Charter on Human and Peoples' Rights, OAU Doc. CAB/LEG/67/3 rev. 5, 21 I.L.M. 58 (1982), *entered into force* Oct. 21, 1986.

The African Charter contains roughly the same basic provisions as other human rights instruments, covering economic, social, and cultural rights as well as civil and political rights. Some of its distinctive features are the right to development and particular state duties, such as the duty to strengthen national independence and contribute to the defense of one's country. Unlike the International Covenant on Civil and Political Rights and other regional instruments, the African Charter does not contain a clause permitting derogation in times of emergencies.

The African Charter creates the African Commission on Human and Peoples' Rights, the body charged with supervising implementation of the African Charter. The Commission can review complaints both from states and other sources. When communications reveal a series of serious violations, the OAU Assembly may request an in-depth study and report from the Commission. The Commission has broad investigative powers, including the right to carry out on-site investigations. In addition, the African Charter requires states to submit reports on human rights implementation to the Commission every two years. Finally, the African Charter, in contrast to the European and American systems, establishes no form of judicial review for decisions of the Commission.

NOTES

For further reading, see: M. Hamalengwa, C. Flinterman, & E. Dankwa, The International Law of Human Rights in Africa: Basic Documents and Annotated Bibliography (1988); Amnesty International, The Organization of African Unity and Human Rights, AI Index: IOR 03/04/87 (1987); Weston,

Lukes & Hnatt, *Regional Human Rights Regimes: A Comparison and Appraisal*, 20 Vanderbilt J. Transnat'l L. 585 (1987); International Commission of Jurists, Human and Peoples' Rights in Africa and the African Charter (1986); Gittleman, *The African Charter on Human and Peoples' Rights: A legal analysis*, 22 Virginia J. Int'l L. 667 (1982); Mbaye, *Human Rights in Africa*, in The International Dimensions of Human Rights 583 (K. Vasak & P. Alston eds. 1982); Buergenthal, *The American and European Conventions on Human Rights: Similarities and Differences*, 30 Am. U.L. Rev. 155 (1981).

VIII   WHAT ARE THE ORIGINS OF HUMAN RIGHTS PRONOUNCED IN INTERNATIONAL INSTRUMENTS, AND IS THERE ROOM FOR CULTURAL RELATIVITY IN HUMAN RIGHTS LAW?

The Islamic Penal Code in Iran

A. INTRODUCTION

Preceding chapters have examined the need for international human rights law and the application of norms contained in several human rights instruments. Some commentators have questioned whether it is possible to create human rights norms that apply universally to all cultures. The debate between universality of rights, on the one hand, and cultural relativism, on the other, derives from conflicting views about the source of authority for human rights.

This chapter examines the juridical basis of international human rights law, using one particular right — to be free from torture or other cruel, inhuman, or degrading treatment or punishment — as a focus of discussion. That right appears in many human rights instruments, but this chapter focuses principally on its presence in Article 5 of the Universal Declaration of Human Rights and Article 7 of the Covenant on Civil and Political Rights.

The chapter begins with a description of several punishments prescribed by the Islamic Penal Code of Iran adopted after the Islamic revolution of 1979. The questions ask readers to consider whether those punishments violate international human rights law. In order to provide an institutional and procedural context for discussion readers are asked to engage in a role playing exercise in which they serve either as members of the Human Rights Committee or as representatives of Iran. A majority of Committee members will argue that the punishments violate Article 7 of the Covenant and will seek to persuade the government to comply with its obligations. The government's representatives will argue that the punishments, as part of Islamic law that Iranians view as the source of human rights in their culture, do not constitute torture or other cruel, inhuman or degrading treatment or punishment. This conflict requires that readers examine the origins of the rights prescribed in international instruments as well as current interpretations of those rights.

To aid analysis, the chapter provides examples of how the Human Rights Committee and other bodies have interpreted the prohibition against torture or other cruel, inhuman, or degrading treatment or punishment. Using those interpretations forces readers to confront the issue of whether international human rights norms are valid for people in all cultures or whether rights can only apply when interpreted within particular cultural contexts. Readers also must discuss whether international human rights law is law that sovereign states must obey or simply sets forth norms that states may choose to follow or disregard as they wish.

B. QUESTIONS

This chapter provides an opportunity for a roleplaying exercise. Members of the group should be assigned roles as either members of the Human Rights Committee or representatives of Iran. A wide range of countries should be represented in the membership of the committee, with at least one member espousing each of the theories of rights identified in question seven. (The following questions are written from the point of view of the members of the Human Rights Committee. Students should also consider these issues from the perspective of the representatives of Iran.)

1. As a member of the Human Rights Committee, what questions would you ask the Iranian representative?

2. How would you argue to the Iranian government that it should refrain from crucifying its citizens, amputating their fingers, or whipping them?

3. How would you try to convince the government to comply with the Covenant on Civil and Political Rights?

[In preparing questions and responses, consider the following:]

4. Would you cite Shari'a provisions that appear to be consistent with international norms?

5. What are the precise norms Iran arguably has violated? Is there a specific norm against chopping off fingers? Might precision or lack thereof in the international norms affect your success in convincing Iran to comply?

6. When did Iran ratify the Covenant on Civil and Political Rights? Is that date significant? Do you think the incumbent government wants to comply? Could they get out of it? (See Article 40 reproduced in the accompanying handbook.) Have they tried?

7. Assume that these are the leading human rights theories: the natural law view, the positivist view, the Marxist view, the cultural relativist position, and the critical-legal view. Which might be most helpful in convincing Iran?

8. Is there anything distinctive about the source of authority upon which rights theories are based that will assist or hinder you in persuading Iran to comply with international norms?

9. What generally is the source of rights in U.N. human rights instruments, and what influence might that source have on Iran?

10. What in fact is the benefit of calling something a right?
Is there no right without a remedy? What sort of remedy does international human rights law provide?

11. Why do governments obey or disobey laws? Why do individuals obey or disobey laws?

12. Is it reasonable to anticipate universal compliance with international human rights law? Is there universal respect for ordinary legal norms, such as the prohibition of burglary?

13. Should the international community expect countries with varying civil, political, economic, social, and cultural traditions to respect human rights standards in the same ways? Is there room for diversity?

C. THE SITUATION IN IRAN

CREATION OF THE ISLAMIC REPUBLIC OF IRAN

In January 1979, the Shah of Iran was compelled to abdicate under pressure of violent resistance to his continued rule. In place of the Shah's westernized government the resistance instituted a republic founded on tenets of Islam. To implement the transformation the new government created a system of revolutionary courts, military police, and provisional laws. Readers should keep that history in mind when reading the material on Iran that follows. One of the major projects of the new government was to adopt an Islamic penal code, which forms the basis of discussion in this chapter. The following excerpt examines three parts of the Islamic Penal Code of Iran: *Ta'azirat, Hodoud,* and *Qesas.*

Amnesty International, Iran: Violations of Human Rights: Documents Sent by Amnesty International to the Government of the Islamic Republic of Iran 57-60, 45-48 (1987) (footnotes omitted and the order of the text slightly changed for clarity):

The Universal Declaration of Human Rights (Article 5), the International Covenant on Civil and Political Rights (Article 7) and several other international human rights instruments forbid torture or cruel, inhuman or degrading treatment or punishment.
Article 38 of the Constitution of the Islamic Republic of Iran is consistent with these international norms in specifying:

"Any form of torture for the purpose of extracting confessions or gaining information is forbidden. It is not permissible to compel individuals to give testimony, make confessions, or swear oaths, and any testimony, confession, or oath obtained in this fashion is worthless and invalid. Punishments for the infringement of these principles will be determined by law."

There are a few provisions in the Islamic Penal Code of Iran which would appear to forbid torture: for example, Article 58 of the *Ta'azirat* forbids physical ill-treatment in order to obtain a confession, thus rendering the infliction or ordering of such acts punishable offences. Similarly, Article 49 of the Law of *Hodoud* and

Qesas states, "Retribution by a blunt and unsharp instrument causing torment to the criminal is not permitted."

The Islamic Penal Code of Iran, however, contains several provisions which impose punishments constituting torture or cruel, inhuman, or degrading treatment or punishment. The punishments include stoning, crucifixion, mutilation and flogging.

A. *Stoning*

Article 119 of the Law of *Hodoud* and *Qesas* makes clear that the purpose of the punishment of stoning is the intentional infliction of grievous pain leading to death. Article 119 states with respect to the penalty for adultery:

"In the punishment of stoning to death, the stones should not be too large so that the person dies on being hit by one or two of them; they should not be so small either that they could not be defined as stones."

B. *Crucifixion*

Article 207 of the Law of *Hodoud* and *Qesas* also makes clear that the purpose of crucifixion is the intentional infliction of severe pain or suffering which may lead to death. Article 207 states:

"The crucifixion of a *mohareb* [at enmity with God] and *mofsed fil arz* [corrupt on earth] shall be carried out by observing the following conditions:

a)   The manner of tying does not cause his death;

b)   He does not remain on the cross for more than three days; but if he dies during the period of three days, he may be brought down after his death;

c)   If he remains alive after three days, he must not be killed."

C. *Mutilation*

The Law of *Hodoud* and *Qesas* contains provisions calling for amputation of limbs and mutilation of other parts of the body for such offences as being *mohareb* and *mofsed fil arz* under Article 208, theft under Article 218, and intentional mayhem or inflicting injury to a limb under Articles 55-80. . . .

The Islamic Penal Code of Iran, in stipulating a number of offences that are punishable by amputation, also prescribes the manner in which this should be inflicted. Article 218 (*Hodoud* and *Qesas*) states:

"Punishment of *hadd* for theft for the first time is the dismembering of four fingers of the right hand of the thief from the fingers' extremity so that only the thumb and palm of the thief remain; for the second time the dismembering of the left foot of the thief from the lower part of the protrusion so that half his foot and part of the place of anointment remain; for the third time the thief is condemned to life imprisonment; for the fourth time, if he commits theft in the prison, he shall be condemned to death.

"Note 1: A number of thefts, so long as the *hadd* is not inflicted, shall be regarded as one theft.

"Note 2: Where the fingers of the thief's hand are dismembered and after the infliction of this punishment another theft committed by him prior to the infliction of the punishment is proved, his left foot shall be dismembered.''

Amnesty International does not have a complete record of the number of amputations carried out. However, during 1985 and the first half of 1986, it recorded 11 cases (all of which were reported in Iranian newspapers) involving individuals convicted of repeated theft.

In an interview published by *Keyhan International* on 16 February 1986, Hojatoleslam Moqtadaie, spokesman of the Supreme Judicial Council, stated that there had been ''numerous cases of severing of hands in Tehran and other provincial cities''.

Amputations are believed at the moment to be inflicted by the Judicial Police. According to an interview reported in *Keyhan* on 21 November 1984, the head of the Judicial Police, Abbas Hashemi Ishaqpour, said:

> ''The Judicial Police have already prepared a device which very speedily severs the hand of the thief . . . To facilitate the enactment of Islamic law on severance of thieves' hands, help has been sought from relevant competent authorities, such as the Coroner's Office, the Ministry of Health, and the Medical Faculties of Tehran and Beheshti Universities.''

The machine was reportedly installed in February 1985 in Qasr Prison and, Amnesty International believes, is still being used to amputate fingers. . . .

D. *Flogging*

The Law of *Hodoud* and *Qesas* contains a number of provisions imposing the punishment of flogging on those who commit such offences as adultery (Articles 100-104), taking alcohol (Articles 123-136), sodomy (Article 152), lesbianism (Articles 159, 164), pimping (Article 168), and *qazf* (malicious accusation) (Articles 176, 178, 187). Article 102, for example, provides, ''Punishment for fornication by a man or woman who is not qualified as married is one hundred (100) lashes.'' Article 178 prescribes flogging for a ''discerning'' minor who maliciously accuses someone. Article 131 provides, ''Punishment for drinking liquor is eighty (80) lashes, whether it is a man or woman.'' Article 132 provides, ''A man is whipped while standing and his body naked except a cover on his privy parts but a woman is whipped while sitting with her dress tied to her body.'' (See the similar provisions in Article 115 for adultery). While Article 187 slightly ameliorates the kind of flogging imposed for malicious accusation, that provision gives some indication of the intention to inflict severe pain and suffering by flogging: ''Lashes are inflicted over the normal clothes and with average force, not with the force used in the punishment for fornication.''. . .

The reports of flogging received by Amnesty International have not mentioned any medical examination either before or after the infliction of the prescribed number of lashes, and it has received reports of women who, having been flogged when pregnant, have subsequently had miscarriages. This is evidently a breach of Article 107 of the Islamic Penal Code of Iran (*Hodoud* and *Qesas*) which states:

> ''If the infliction of whipping is likely to harm the foetus or suckling baby, the whipping of a pregnant or nursing woman should be delayed.''. . .

Amnesty International has interviewed both a number of former prisoners who were themselves flogged as a judicial punishment and many others apparently flogged in order to extract information or confessions. . . . From these interviews the organization has concluded that flogging methods have been harsher than those prescribed by law. Although some victims have claimed that the lashes were delivered with minimal force, others have told Amnesty International that they were lashed very hard by several officers in turn, and that the pain was so intense that they lost consciousness. Indeed, Amnesty International knows of cases in which the physical results of such lashings lasted for many months; in some cases prolonged medical treatment has been necessary because of damage to internal organs. . . .

The *Ta'azirat* provisions of the Islamic Penal Code contain more than 50 articles prescribing lashing of up to 74 strokes. The provisions include Article 29 (forgery), . . . 40 (negligent failure of an officer to arrest an accused), . . . 72 (impersonating a government official), . . . 82 (destruction of officially held documents), 87 (insulting high government officials), 88 (collusion to commit crimes against foreign or internal security), 89 (destruction of evidence or obstruction of justice), 97, 98 (refusal to return a child), 99 (abandonment of a child), 100 (tampering with a grave), 102 (failure of women to wear veils and other offences in public places), 103 (encouraging prostitution), 105 (failure to support wife), 106 (medical personnel revealing patient's secrets), . . . 115 (fraudulent bankruptcy), 116 (fraud), 117 (defrauding a minor), 118 (misuse of an official seal), 119 (failure to return property), 120-122 (other business fraud and deception including trade mark infringement), . . . 140, 141 and 143 (defamation), 145 (transactions involving alcohol), 146, 147 (establishment of and keeping a place for gambling or alcohol), 156 (driving without a licence), and 158 (tampering with a speedometer). There are a few other *Ta'azirat* provisions which carry the penalty of lashing: Article 86 (up to 30 lashes for vulgar insults) and Article 101 (up to 99 strokes for kissing by an unmarried couple).

* * *

HUMAN RIGHTS COMMITTEE

Chapters 1, 2, and 3 introduced the Human Rights Committee — the body responsible for monitoring compliance with the Covenant on Civil and Political Rights — and discussed its power to examine individuals' communications under the Optional Protocol to the Covenant. This chapter examines the Covenant's only obligatory implementation mechanism — the submission of reports from states parties for examination — and the Committee's practice of issuing general comments on the reports. Article 40 of the Covenant requires states parties to submit reports within one year after the Covenant enters into force for a party and, thereafter, whenever the Committee requests. In practice, the Committee has generally requested reports every five years after the initial report. At its second session the Committee formulated guidelines for reports specifying that states are to provide a description of protections and limitations for each right, any difficulties affecting implementation of rights, and progress on implementation.

The Committee reviews reports at public meetings, preferably with a representative of the government present to answer questions and provide supplementary reports when necessary. In order to illustrate this process this section includes an excerpt from Iran's 1982 report and the Committee's discussion of that report. The practice of having government representatives at meetings, though not required, reflects the Committee's understanding of its relationship with governments. Rather than acting as an adjudicative body evaluating reports, Committee members raise issues and offer governments assistance and cooperation.

The Committee's interpretations of its role in commenting on reports further illustrate the goal of cooperation and assistance. Article 40 instructs the Committee to transmit "its reports, and such general comments as it may consider appropriate, to the States Parties." The Covenant does not define the scope of general comments, an omission that resulted in disputes. Some states maintained that the Committee should prepare separate comments on each report evaluated, in addition to the annual report for the General Assembly and general comments on matters of interest to all states parties. Others viewed Article 40 as authorizing only general comments to all states, not comments directed at specific states. The Committee appeared to settle the controversy in favor of the latter view by reaching consensus on guidelines for general comments that do not authorize specific comments. The guidelines specify that the aim is to summarize experience the Committee gained in reviewing reports as a means to improve the reporting procedure and stimulate the promotion and protection of human rights. Under the guidelines the content of general comments can relate to reporting procedures, implementing substantive rights in the Covenant, interpreting articles of the Covenant, and promoting cooperation among governments.

The Committee has issued a number of general comments. They are considered especially authoritative because the Committee has adopted them by consensus based on its considerable experience as a body of experts reviewing reports. This chapter contains the Committee's general comments on Article 7 of the Covenant — the article prohibiting torture and other cruel, inhuman, or degrading treatment or punishment — as an example of the Committee's comments on provisions of the Covenant and to provide aid in evaluating the actions of Iran at issue here.

The following two readings illustrate the reporting mechanism under the Covenant. The first is an excerpt from Iran's report to the Committee in 1982. The second is an excerpt from the comments of an Iranian representative during the Committee's examination of the report.

Human Rights Committee, Consideration of Reports Submitted by States Parties Under Article 40 of the Covenant: Iran, at 2-5, U.N. Doc. CCPR/C/1/Add.58 (1982):

In implementation of article 40 of the International Covenant which reads: "The States Parties to this Covenant undertake to submit reports on the measures they have adopted which give effect to the rights recognized herein and on the progress made in the enjoyment of those rights . . .", and with a view to submitting a report on the law and regulations approved to guarantee the individual's rights and liberties, I have the honour to inform you as follows: . . .

The Islamic Revolution of Iran is based on the belief that so long as man is not liberated from ideological, cultural, political and economic enslavement and dependence, freedom and independence will not be possible and without freedom and independence respect for human rights will not have any correct and proper applicability. Accordingly, the intention of the Islamic Revolution is to liberate man from slavery and servitude to another "slave", and to bestow upon him human growth and grandeur ("In order to liberate man from servitude of man and direct him to servitude of God"). It is on the basis of this belief that the third principle of the Constitution of the Islamic Republic of Iran reads as follows:

> Principle 3: The Government of the Islamic Republic of Iran is bound to take into consideration all its possibilities to achieve the objectives referred to under Principle 2 above for:
>
> 1. Creation of a favourable atmosphere for furtherance of moral virtues based on the faith and righteousness and struggle against all manifestations of corruption and ruin; . . .
>
> 6. Putting an end to any despotism, autocracy and oligarchy;
>
> 7. Ensuring political and social freedom within the domain of the law . . . .

[All] the laws which for long years governed the deprived people of this country, were enacted in such a way as to bring about the domination of a small group over the rest of the people while disregarding the equality, liberties and rights of human beings. Since the Revolution therefore, the Ministry of Justice of the Islamic Republic of Iran has set out to review and amend these laws or to rewrite or change them in a rational and reasonable manner so as to guarantee the individual's rights and liberties. . . .

[Bills] and laws have been approved and enacted to determine and ensure the rights and liberties of the people. The measures taken in this regard may be summarized as follows: . . .

> *Laws and regulations approved to ensure rights and liberties*
>
> 1.   *The Constitution of the Islamic Republic of Iran*

The Constitution of the Islamic Republic of Iran, every word, or better, every letter of which is the crystallization of the drops of the pure blood of the martyrs who have freely and consciously chosen martyrdom, is persuasive evidence of respect for and guarantee of human rights and liberties. . . .

> 2.   *State General Inspection Act*

This Act, which, on the basis of Principle 174 of the Constitution of the Islamic Republic of Iran, was passed, in 14 articles and several notes, by the Islamic Consultative Assembly, enables the Judiciary to investigate, in its continuous and extraordinary inspections, any discord or offence committed by civil and military organs and all the Revolutionary Institutions, and to pursue the matter through legal channels until the attainment of the final results. . . .

> 3.   *Administrative Court of Justice Act*

. . .Principle 173 of the Constitution of the Islamic Republic of Iran. . . provides:

> To investigate litigations, complaints and protests of the public against

Government officials, units or regulations and to administer justice in such cases a tribunal known as the 'Administrative Court of Justice' shall be formed under the control of the Supreme Judicial Council. The jurisdiction and procedure for the functioning of this tribunal shall be established by law.

Enactment of a law in such a manner is unprecedented in the history of the Iranian Ministry of Justice. If ever such a law has been enacted under other titles it has never been put into practice. The approval of the Administrative Court of Justice Act permits and enables any individual of the nation to lodge a complaint with one of the benches of the Administrative Court of Justice against any injustice or oppression committed by Government employees or units, through regulations or decrees, against people and cause justice [to] be administered. . . .

It must be acknowledged that in a Revolutionary society in which all former criteria and rules are reversed, much time is needed to establish a new order. This is natural and ordinary in any revolution. For this very reason and in order to see us through this critical period, the Leader of the Revolution declared the year 1360 (1981) as the Year of the Law and, in his orders and edicts, instructed all to comply with laws and protect the rights of individuals.

* * *

Report of the Human Rights Committee, 37 U.N. GAOR Supp. (No. 40) at 66-72, U.N. Doc. A/37/40 (1982):

Iran

298. The Committee considered the report of Iran (CCPR/C/1/Add.58) at its 364th, 365th, 366th and 368th meetings held on 15, 16 and 19 July 1982 (CCPR/C/SR.364, 365, 366 and 368).

299. The report was introduced by the representative of the State party who explained the ideological foundation of the Islamic Revolution in Iran. . . .

300. The representative stated that, although many of the articles of the Covenant corresponded to the teachings of Islam, in the case of differences between the two sets of laws, the tenets of Islam would prevail. . . .

324. [The Iranian representative] stressed that the criteria for determining the validity of any law would be the values given by God and transmitted to earth, that since human traits were considered to be in harmony with revealed values, values derived from human civilization and from reason were held to be close to Islamic values, and that whenever divine law conflicted with man-made law, divine law would prevail. He explained that the Koran contained guidance on a comprehensive range of matters involving morals, historical analysis, a criminal code and precepts regarding the distribution of wealth, teachings on community growth and spiritual values, and when a nation recognized and accepted the principles of Islam, as the basis for its existence, Islamic precepts would be followed in resolving problems. However, in Shi'ite canon law the basic requirements governing the continuity of community life could be viewed in historical terms, and the divine laws could be interpreted and implemented accordingly. Unfortunately, the conspiracies that had occurred in Iran since the revolution had prevented the Government from having sufficient time to develop new laws along those lines. Never-

theless, an attempt was being made to establish, at an early date, the three separate powers of the judiciary, the executive and the legislative in conformity with Islamic law. After the legislative power had been established, the relative conformity of each law with Islamic precepts would be determined. In this connexion, he explained his Government's position on the incorporation of international instruments on human rights in Islamic law and stated that if the intention was that such instruments should complement and add to the Islamic laws with a view to harmonizing them in a single legal system, then his Government would have to respond negatively, since it considered that the Islamic laws were universal and Shi'ite canon law would take any new needs of society into account. If, however, it was intended that international instruments on human rights and Islamic laws should be taken together in an effort to achieve mutual understanding and to explore what they had in common, then such an endeavour would be accepted with pleasure. He pointed out that laws of non-religious inspiration were not necessarily contrary to the Moslem faith; however, any laws contrary to the tenets of Islam would not be acceptable.

* * *

Report of the Human Rights Committee, General Comments on Article 7 of the Covenant, 37 U.N. GAOR Supp. (No. 40) at 94-95, U.N. Doc. A/37/40 (1982):

[Ed.: The following selection consists of general comments on Article 7 of the International Covenant on Civil and Political Rights issued by the Human Rights Committee pursuant to Article 40 of the Covenant.]

1. In examining the reports of States parties, members of the Committee have often asked for further information under article 7 which prohibits, in the first place, torture or cruel, inhuman or degrading treatment or punishment. The Committee recalls that even in situations of public emergency such as are envisaged by article 4 (1) this provision is non-derogable under article 4 (2). Its purpose is to protect the integrity and dignity of the individual. The Committee notes that it is not sufficient for the implementation of this article to prohibit such treatment or punishment or to make it a crime. Most States have penal provisions which are applicable to cases of torture or similar practices. Because such cases nevertheless occur, it follows from article 7, read together with article 2 of the Covenant, that States must ensure an effective protection through some machinery of control. Complaints about ill-treatment must be investigated effectively by competent authorities. Those found guilty must be held responsible, and the alleged victims must themselves have effective remedies at their disposal, including the right to obtain compensation. Among the safeguards which may make control effective are provisions against detention incommunicado, granting, without prejudice to the investigation, persons such as doctors, lawyers and family members access to the detainees; provisions requiring that detainees should be held in places that are publicly recognized and that their names and places of detention should be entered in a central register available to persons concerned, such as relatives; provisions making confessions or other evidence obtained through torture or other treatment contrary to article 7 inadmissible in court; and measures of training and instruction of law enforcement officials not to apply such treatment.

2. As appears from the terms of this article, the scope of protection required goes far beyond torture as normally understood. It may not be necessary to draw sharp distinctions between the various prohibited forms of treatment or punishment. These distinctions depend on the kind, purpose and severity of the particular treatment. In the view of the Committee the prohibition must extend to corporal punishment, including excessive chastisement as an educational or disciplinary measure. Even such a measure as solitary confinement may, according to the circumstances, and especially when the person is kept incommunicado, be contrary to this article. Moreover, the article clearly protects not only persons arrested or imprisoned, but also pupils and patients in educational and medical institutions. Finally, it is also the duty of public authorities to ensure protection by the law against such treatment even when committed by persons acting outside or without any official authority. For all persons deprived of their liberty, the prohibition of treatment contrary to article 7 is supplemented by the positive requirement of article 10 (1) of the Covenant that they shall be treated with humanity and with respect for the inherent dignity of the human person.

* * *

NOTES

For further reading, see:

Human Rights Committee, *General Comments*, U.N. Doc. CCPR/C/21/Rev.1 & Add.1 (1990);

Gomez del Prado, *United Nations Conventions on Human Rights: The Practice of the Human Rights Committee and the Committee on the Elimination of Racial Discrimination in Dealing with Reporting Obligations of States Parties*, 7 Hum. Rts. Q. 492 (1985);

Jhabvala, *The Practice of the Covenant's Human Rights Committee, 1976–82: Review of State Party Reports*, 6 Hum. Rts. Q. 81 (1984);

Fischer, *Reporting Under the Covenant on Civil and Political Rights: The First Five Years of the Human Rights Committee*, 76 Am. J. Int'l L. 142 (1982).

COUNTRY RAPPORTEUR PROCESS OF THE U.N. COMMISSION ON HUMAN RIGHTS

Following this note is an excerpt from the preliminary report of the U.N. Commission on Human Rights' ("Commission") Special Representative on Iran. The Commission has developed the process of appointing rapporteurs and representatives as part of its broader efforts to monitor the human rights situation in specific countries. The Commission has appointed these country rapporteurs and representatives pursuant to ECOSOC resolution 1235 which grants it authority to "make a thorough study of situations which reveal a consistent pattern of violations of human rights.'' The Commission has established several approaches to implementing ECOSOC resolution 1235 that are examined in chapter 4 of this book. At this point, however, it is only important to note that the Special Representative to Iran acts under the Commission's authority, while the Human Rights Committee acts under authority granted by the Covenant on Civil and Political Rights. Consequently, the Special Representative's report relies on a broad range of U.N. instruments in evaluating the human rights situation in Iran; whereas the Human Rights Committee only has authority to monitor implementation of the Covenant.

The Commission has not developed specific guidelines for its rapporteurs and representatives to follow in carrying out their investigative duties. Rather, the resolution establishing each rapporteur specifies the rapporteur's mandate in broad terms, usually involving a direction to study the human rights situation in the country at issue and prepare a report to the Commission, including conclusions and recommendations. The mandate of the Special Representative to Iran, described in this excerpt from his report, is typical. As part of their factfinding, several rapporteurs and representatives have conducted on-site missions in the countries which they were assigned to investigate. Such factfinding efforts are discussed in chapter 6 of this book. Though the Special Representative on Iran was authorized in 1984, Iran did not permit an on-site visit until January 1990.

Resolutions establishing special rapporteurs and representatives generally authorize the Chair of the Commission, after consultation with regional representatives, to appoint a recognized international human rights expert. Often the Chair will consult with the country under consideration as well, to enhance the likelihood of that country's cooperating with the special rapporteur. Most mandates are of only a year's duration, but the Commission usually will renew the mandate on a yearly basis until the country resolves the situation or the Commission decides to drop the case. Several countries have been the subject of rapporteur investigations, including: Afghanistan, Bolivia, Chile, Guatemala, El Salvador, Iran, and Romania. For particularly egregious human rights violations — such as those existing in South Africa — the Commission has appointed a working group of experts rather than a single rapporteur to study the human rights situation. For additional information on the country-specific rapporteur process and practice, see H. Tolley, The U.N. Commission on Human Rights 111-24 (1987); Bossuyt, *The Development of Special Procedures of the United Nations Commission on Human Rights*, 6 Hum. Rts. L.J. 179 (1985).

* * *

Preliminary Report by the Special Representative of the Commission on Human Rights on the Human Rights Situation in the Islamic Republic of Iran, U.N. Doc. E/CN.4/1985/20, at 3–9 (1985) (footnotes omitted):

1. At its fortieth session, on 14 March 1984, the Commission on Human Rights adopted resolution 1984/54 on the human rights situation in the Islamic Republic

of Iran. By that resolution the Commission requested the Chairman to appoint, after consultation within the Bureau, a special representative of the Commission whose mandate would be to establish contacts with the Government of the Islamic Republic of Iran and to make a thorough study of the human rights situation in that country based on such information as he might deem relevant, including comments and materials provided by the Government, containing conclusions and appropriate suggestions, to be presented to the Commission at its forty-first session. The Commission further requested the Government of the Islamic Republic of Iran to extend its co-operation to the Special Representative of the Commission and decided to continue its consideration of the situation of human rights and fundamental freedoms in the Islamic Republic of Iran at its forty-first session.

2. Pursuant to resolution 1984/54, the Chairman of the Commission on Human Rights, on 19 October 1984 designated Mr. Andrés Aguilar as Special Representative of the Commission. . . .

10. The Special Representative has received from various sources, including non-governmental organizations in consultative status with the Economic and Social Council, communications and documents containing information on alleged violations of human rights in the Islamic Republic of Iran. The Special Representative, due to his recent designation and to the lack of direct contact with the authorities of the Islamic Republic of Iran, has not yet been in a position to evaluate the information received from these sources and the allegations contained therein. . . .

11. It may be recalled in this context that Iran, on 4 April 1968, signed the International Covenant on Civil and Political Rights and the International Covenant on Economic, Social and Cultural Rights. It ratified both Covenants on 24 June 1975. . . .

12. In its resolution 1984/54 which established the mandate of the Special Representative, the Commission on Human Rights was expressly guided by the principles embodied in the Charter of the United Nations, the Universal Declaration of Human Rights and the International Covenants on Human Rights. The Commission further reaffirmed that all Member States had an obligation to promote and protect human rights and fundamental freedoms and to fulfill the obligations they had undertaken under the various international instruments in that field.

13. This position of principle, as expressed in the above-mentioned resolution, is in line with the Charter of the United Nations of which Iran is an original member. The purposes of the United Nations as spelled out in Article 1, paragraph 3, of the Charter expressly include the achievement of international co-operation in solving international problems of an economic, social, cultural, or humanitarian character, and in promoting and encouraging respect for human rights and for fundamental freedoms for all without distinction as to race, sex, language, or religion. Moreover, under Article 56 of the Charter all Member States pledge themselves to take joint and separate action in co-operation with the Organization for the achievement of the purposes set forth in Article 55 which in turn includes the promotion of universal respect for, and observance of, human rights and fundamental freedoms for all without distinction as to race, sex, language, or religion.

14. The Universal Declaration of Human Rights gave expression to the human rights principles contained in the Charter of the United Nations. The Universal Declaration is thus an emanation of the Charter providing as it does common standards of

achievement for *all* peoples and *all* nations. Through practice over the years, the basic provisions of the Universal Declaration of Human Rights can be regarded as having attained the status of international customary law and in many instances they have the character of *jus cogens*. This is, for example, the case with the right to life, freedom from torture, freedom of thought, conscience and religion and the right to a fair trial.

15. Such fundamental guarantees of the Universal Declaration of Human Rights cannot be open to challenge by any State as they are indispensable for the functioning of an international community based on the rule of law and respect for human rights and fundamental freedoms.

16. States of all political, economic, social, cultural and religious persuasions participated in the drafting of the Charter, the Universal Declaration of Human Rights and the International Covenants on Human Rights. The Universal Declaration of Human Rights and the International Covenants thus contain norms which, distilled from the collective experience and the common heritage of the world's peoples, represent universal standards of conduct for all peoples and all nations.

17. Within the framework of the International Covenants on Human Rights, States of all religious, cultural or ideological persuasions co-operate in the implementation of universal standards of human rights in their respective countries. The General Assembly has repeatedly emphasized the importance of the strictest compliance by States parties with their obligations under the International Covenants and has further stressed the importance of uniform standards of implementation of the International Covenants.

18. Therefore it must be concluded that no State can claim to be allowed to disrespect basic, entrenched rights such as the right to life, freedom from torture, freedom of thought, conscience and religion, and the right to a fair trial which are provided for under the Universal Declaration and the International Covenants on Human Rights, on the ground that departure from these standards might be permitted under national or religious law.

19. It is the firm conviction of the Special Representative that the following fundamental principles are applicable to the situation in the Islamic Republic of Iran as indeed to the situation, present or future, in any other country:

(a) States members of the United Nations are bound to abide by universally accepted standards of conduct in so far as the treatment of their population is concerned, particularly as regards the protection of human life, freedom from torture and other cruel, inhuman or degrading treatment or punishment, freedom of thought, conscience and religion and the right to a fair trial;

(b) In so far as the basic rights and freedoms of the individual are concerned, the Universal Declaration of Human Rights gives expression to the human rights principles of the Charter of the United Nations and essential provisions such as those referred to above represent not only rules of international customary law but rules which also have the character of *jus cogens*;

(c) The International Covenants on Human Rights give added conventional force to those provisions of the Universal Declaration of Human Rights which already reflect international customary law. Since the Islamic Republic of Iran is a party to the International Covenants on Human Rights, the latter's provisions in their entirety are legally binding upon the Government of the Islamic Republic of Iran. They must be complied with in good faith.

NOTES

1. Following Mr. Aguilar's submission of the preliminary report, the Commission on Human Rights extended his mandate for one year and requested a final report to be presented at the Commission's forty-second session in 1986. *See* C.H.R. Res. 1985/39, U.N. Doc. E/CN.4/1985/66, at 81 (1985). Mr. Aguilar resigned in January 1986, however, and was not able to complete the final report. *See* U.N. Doc. E/CN.4/1986/25 (1986). At its forty-second session, the Commission extended the Special Representative's mandate for another year. *See* C.H.R. Res. 1986/41, U.N. Doc. E/CN.4/1986/65, at 108 (1986).

In July 1986 the Commission appointed Mr. Reynaldo Galindo Pohl, a lawyer from El Salvador, as Special Representative on Iran and he subsequently submitted a report to the Commission at its forty-third session in January 1987. *See Commission on Human Rights, Report on the Human Rights Situation in the Islamic Republic of Iran by the Special Representative of the Commission, Mr. Reynaldo Galindo Pohl*, U.N. Doc. E/CN.4/ 1987/23 (1987). His report details allegations of human rights violations, but does not reach any significant conclusions regarding either those allegations or the overall situation in Iran because the Iranian government refused to allow an on-site visit or even reply to Mr. Pohl's requests for information.

In January 1989 Mr. Pohl submitted a further report to the Commission at its forty-fifth session. That report discussed several meetings that had taken place between Mr. Pohl and representatives of the Iranian government. In addition, the report reaches some general conclusions regarding Iranian human rights violations. *See Report on the Human Rights Situation in the Islamic Republic of Iran by the Special Representative of the Commission on Human Rights, Mr. Reynaldo Galindo Pohl*, U.N. Doc. E/CN.4/1989/26 (1989). As of 1990 the Commission has continued to extend the Special Representative's mandate on a yearly basis.

2. The Special Representative on Iran, in the preceding excerpt, stresses the legal obligation of Iran to observe the provisions of the Covenant on Civil and Political Rights in good faith. The concept that states have an obligation to observe treaties to which they are parties is based on the doctrine of *pacta sunt servanda* (treaties are to be observed). The doctrine is a norm of customary international law that developed as the growing intercourse among nations necessitated respect for international agreements.

Modern formulations of the doctrine add the element of good faith. One· example can be found in Article· 26 of the Vienna Convention on the Law of Treaties. "Every treaty in force is binding upon the parties to it and must be performed by them in good faith." Vienna Convention on the Law of Treaties, Art. 26, 1155 U.N.T.S. 331, T.S. No. 58, 8 I.L.M. 679 (1969), *entered into force* Jan. 27, 1980. The Restatement (Third) of the Foreign Relations Law of the United States follows the language of the Vienna

Convention, substituting the phrase "international agreement" for the word "treaty." 1 Restatement (Third) of the Foreign Relations Law of the United States § 321 (1987). The U.N. Charter imposes a similar obligation of good faith in Article 2(2). "All members . . . shall fulfil in good faith the obligations assumed by them in accordance with the present Charter." For further reading, see Meron, *Iran's Challenge to the International Law of Human Rights*, 13 Human Rts. Internet Rep. 8 (Spring 1989).

In January 1990 Mr. Pohl was allowed to visit Iran. *See Report on the Human Rights Situation in the Islamic Republic of Iran by the Special Representative of the Commission on Human Rights, Mr. Reynaldo Galindo Pohl*, U.N. Doc. E/CN.4/1990/24, at 20-51 (1990).

IRANIAN VIOLATIONS OF INTERNATIONAL LAW

The Iranian penal sanctions discussed in this chapter provide a useful basis for an exploration of relativism in the application of human rights norms. Yet by presenting this material the authors do not wish to imply that these penal sanctions represent the most significant aspect of Iran's violations of human rights law during the period from the institution of the Islamic Republic of Iran to the publication of this book.

Reynaldo Galindo Pohl's report of January 1987, for example, contains allegations of numerous violations, including summary executions; torture and other ill-treatment; warrantless arrests; lengthy detentions without formal charge or trial; expedited trials with no access to counsel or right to call witnesses, to testify, or to appeal; and harassment, discrimination, and persecution of religious minorities, especially members of the Baha'i faith. *Commission on Human Rights, Report on the human rights situation in the Islamic Republic of Iran by the Special Representative of the Commission, Mr. Reynaldo Galindo Pohl*, U.N. Doc. E/CN.4/1987/23 (1987); *see also* U.N. Doc. E/CN.4/1990/24 (1990).

Iran has also been accused of perpetrating numerous human rights violations in connection with its war against Iraq. *See, e.g., Armed Conflict and Iran*, U.N. Doc. E/CN.4/1987/NGO/51 (1987) (written Statement submitted to the Commission on Human Rights by Human Rights Advocates, an NGO in consultative status); *Report of the Mission Dispatched by the Secretary-General on the Situation of Prisoners of War in the Islamic Republic of Iran and Iraq*, U.N. Doc. S/20147 (1988).

D. THE INTERNATIONAL LAW PROHIBITION OF TORTURE AND OTHER CRUEL, INHUMAN OR DEGRADING TREATMENT OR PUNISHMENT

The following readings concern the prohibition of torture and other cruel, inhuman or degrading treatment or punishment. The selections should be useful in interpreting the prohibition, ascertaining whether a consensus exists as to its scope, and determining whether Iran's actions have violated the prohibition.

Standard Minimum Rules for the Treatment of Prisoners, *adopted* Aug. 30, 1955, by the First U.N. Congress on Prevention of Crime and Treatment of Offenders, U.N. Doc. A/CONF/6/1, Annex I, A (1956); *adopted* July 31, 1957, by Economic and Social Council res. 663C, 24 U.N. ESCOR Supp. (No. 1) at 11, U.N. Doc. E/3048 (1957), *amended* E.S.C. res. 2076, 62 U.N. ESCOR Supp. (No. 1) at 35, U.N. Doc. E/5988 (1977) (adding Article 95):

31. Corporal punishment, punishment by placing in a dark cell, and all cruel, inhuman or degrading punishments shall be completely prohibited as punishments for disciplinary offences.

32. (1) Punishment by close confinement or reduction of diet shall never be inflicted unless the medical officer has examined the prisoner and certified in writing that he is fit to sustain it.

(2) The same shall apply to any other punishment that may be prejudicial to the physical or mental health of a prisoner. In no case may such punishment be contrary to or depart from the principle stated in rule 31.

(3) The medical officer shall visit daily prisoners undergoing such punishments and shall advise the director if he considers the termination or alteration of the punishment necessary on grounds of physical or mental health.

NOTES

The Standard Minimum Rules also contain specific protections for insane and mentally abnormal prisoners (Rule 82), prisoners under arrest or awaiting trial (Rules 84-93), civil prisoners (Rule 94), and persons arrested or detained without charge (Rule 95). Some of these provisions are discussed further in chapter 12.

Declaration on the Protection of All Persons from Being Subjected to Torture and Other Cruel, Inhuman or Degrading Treatment or Punishment, G.A. res. 3452, 30 U.N. GAOR Supp. (No. 34) at 91, U.N. Doc. A/10034 (1976):

Article 1

1. For the purpose of this Declaration, torture means any act by which severe pain or suffering, whether physical or mental, is intentionally inflicted by or at the instigation of a public official on a person for such purposes as obtaining from him or a third person information or confession, punishing him for an act he has committed or is suspected of having committed, or intimidating him or other persons. It does not include pain or suffering arising only from, inherent in or incidental to, lawful sanctions to the extent consistent with the Standard Minimum Rules for the Treatment of Prisoners.

2. Torture constitutes an aggravated and deliberate form of cruel, inhuman or degrading treatment or punishment.

Convention Against Torture and Other Cruel, Inhuman or Degrading Treatment or Punishment, G.A. res. 39/46, 39 U.N. GAOR Supp. (No. 51) at 197, U.N. Doc. A/39/51 (1985), *entered into force* June 26, 1987:

Article 1

1. For the purposes of this Convention, the term "torture" means any act by which severe pain or suffering, whether physical or mental, is intentionally inflicted on a person for such purposes as obtaining from him or a third person information or a confession, punishing him for an act he or a third person has committed or is suspected of having committed, or intimidating or coercing him or a third person, or for any reason based on discrimination of any kind, when such pain or suffering is inflicted by or at the instigation of or with the consent or acquiescence of a public official or other person acting in an official capacity. It does not include pain or suffering arising only from, inherent in or incidental to lawful sanctions.

2. This article is without prejudice to any international instrument or national legislation which does or may contain provisions of wider application. . . .

Article 16

1. Each State Party shall undertake to prevent in any territory under its jurisdiction other acts of cruel, inhuman or degrading treatment or punishment which do not amount to torture as defined in article 1, when such acts are committed by or at the instigation of or with the consent or acquiescence of a public official or other person acting in an official capacity. . . .

NOTES

The Torture Convention created the Committee Against Torture to help implement the Convention's provisions. Established in 1987, the Committee

consists of 10 experts of high moral standing and recognized competence in the field of human rights, elected by States parties to the Convention from among their nationals. Members are elected for a four-year term by secret ballot at a meeting of States parties, and serve in their personal capacity.

The tasks of the Committee, as set out in articles 19 to 24 of the Convention, are: to study reports on the measures taken by States parties to give effect to their undertakings under the Convention; to make confidential inquiries, if it decides that this is warranted, concerning well-founded indications that torture is being systematically practised in the territory of a State party; to perform certain functions with a view to settling disputes among States parties concerning the application of the Convention, providing that those States parties have recognized the competence of the Committee against Torture to undertake such functions; to establish when necessary *ad hoc* conciliation commissions to make available its good offices to the States parties concerned with a view to a friendly solution of inter-State disputes; to consider communications from or on behalf of individuals subject to the jurisdiction of States parties concerned who claim to be victims of a violation of the provisions of the Convention, provided that those States parties have recognized the competence of the Committee to that effect; and to submit annual reports on its activities to the States parties and to the General Assembly of the United Nations. . . .

By [the end of February 1990], there were [51] States parties to the Convention against Torture and Other Cruel, Inhuman or Degrading Treatment or Punishment, [23] of which had accepted the competence of the Committee against Torture under articles 21 and 22 of the Convention to consider matters relating to inter-State disputes and communications from or on behalf of individuals. [Eleven] of the States parties have declared that they do not recognize the competence of the Committee under article 20 of the Convention to undertake confidential inquiries or fact-finding missions on their territories.

United Nations Centre for Human Rights, Human Rights Machinery, Fact Sheet No. 1, at 15-16 (1988) (updated to February 1990), *reprinted in* chapter 1 above.

Body of Principles for the Protection of All Persons under Any Form of Detention or Imprisonment, G.A. res. 43/173, 43 U.N. GAOR Supp. (No. 49), U.N. Doc. A/43/49, at 297 (1988):

Principle 1

All persons under any form of detention or imprisonment shall be treated in a humane manner and with respect for the inherent dignity of the human person. . .

Principle 6

No person under any form of detention or imprisonment shall be subjected to torture or to cruel, inhuman or degrading treatment or punishment.* No circumstance whatever may be invoked as a justification for torture or other cruel, inhuman or degrading treatment or punishment.

---

* The term "cruel, inhuman or degrading treatment or punishment" should be interpreted so as to extend the widest possible protection against abuses, whether physical or mental, including the holding of a detained or imprisoned person in conditions which deprive him, temporarily or permanently, of the use of any of his natural senses, such as sight or hearing, or of his awareness of place and the passing of time.

EUROPEAN SYSTEM

The first three readings below are excerpts of European decisions. The first is from a decision of the European Commission of Human Rights; the other two are from decisions of the European Court of Human Rights. All three interpret Article 3 of the European Convention on Human Rights, which states that "[n]o one shall be subjected to torture or to inhuman or degrading treatment or punishment." Chapter 10, *infra*, discusses the structure and jurisprudence of the European system in a bit more detail; at this point it is necessary only to note that the decisions are official interpretations of Article 3. For further reading, see Duffy, *Article 3 of the European Convention on Human Rights*, 32 Int'l & Comp. L.Q. 316 (1983); N. Rodley, The Treatment of Prisoners under International Law 71-95 (1987).

Ireland v. United Kingdom, 1976 Y.B. Eur. Conv. on Hum. Rts. 512, 748, 792-94 (Eur. Comm'n of Hum. Rts.) (extracts from Commission's report; citations omitted):

[Ed.: This case involved the detention and interrogation of persons in Northern Ireland by British authorities. The authorities used a combination of five techniques including: forcing detainees to stand for periods of several hours leaning against a wall, keeping black hoods over detainees' heads at all times except during interrogation, holding detainees pending interrogation in a room where there was a continuous loud hissing noise, depriving detainees of sleep pending interrogation, and depriving detainees of adequate food and drink during the period of detention. The government of Ireland lodged an application with the European Commission, alleging that these interrogation practices violated Article 3 of the European Convention.]

2. *The interpretation of Art. 3*

The ordinary meaning and purpose of Art. 3 of the Convention which provides that "no one shall be subjected to torture or to inhuman or degrading treatment or punishment" does not seem difficult to assess.

Difficulties arise, however, when it comes to defining the scope of the terms concerned and to applying them to the circumstances of particular acts purported to be in breach of that provision.

In the First Greek Case the Commission considered the notions of "torture," "inhuman treatment" and "degrading treatment" first in relation to each other and found that "all torture must be inhuman and degrading treatment and inhuman treatment also degrading." Describing each notion separately, it started from the notion of "inhuman treatment" which covered "at least such treatment as deliberately causes severe suffering, mental or physical, which, in the particular situation, is unjustifiable." As regards "torture" the Commission considered that it was "often used to describe inhuman treatment, which has a purpose, such as the obtaining of information or confessions, or the infliction of punishment, and it is generally an aggravated form of inhuman treatment." Finally, "[t]reatment or punishment of an individual may be said to be degrading if it grossly humiliates him before others or drives him to act against his will or conscience."

The Commission also explained further what constituted non-physical torture, namely "the infliction of mental suffering by creating a state of anguish and stress by means other than bodily assault."

Finally, the Commission distinguished in the Greek Case between acts prohibited by Art. 3 and what it called "a certain roughness of treatment." The Commission considered that such roughness was tolerated by most detainees and even taken for granted. It "may take the form of slaps or blows of the hand on the head or face. This underlines the fact that the point up to which prisoners and the public may accept physical violence as being neither cruel nor excessive varies between different societies and even between different sections of them."

Concerning the five techniques in the present case, the Commission considers that it should express an opinion only as to whether or not the way in which they were applied here, namely in combination with each other, was in breach of Art. 3. It observes that, if they were considered separately, deprivation of sleep or restrictions on diet might not as such be regarded as constituting treatment prohibited by Art. 3. It would rather depend on the circumstances and the purpose and would largely be a question of degree.

In the present case, the five techniques applied together were designed to put severe mental and physical stress, causing severe suffering, on a person in order to obtain information from him. It is true that all methods of interrogation which go beyond the mere asking of questions may bring some pressure on the person concerned, but they cannot, by that very fact, be called inhuman. The five techniques are to be distinguished from those methods.

Compared with inhuman treatment [as defined in the Greek case] the stress caused by the application of the five techniques is not only different in degree. The combined application of methods which prevent the use of the senses, especially the eyes and the ears, directly affects the personality physically and mentally. The will to resist or to give in cannot, under such conditions, be formed with any degree of independence. Those most firmly resistant might give in at an early stage when subjected to this sophisticated method to break or even eliminate the will.

It is this character of the combined use of the five techniques which, in the opinion of the Commission, renders them in breach of Art. 3 of the Convention in the form not only of inhuman and degrading treatment, but also of torture within the meaning of that provision. . . .

Ireland v. United Kingdom, 25 Eur. Ct. H.R. (ser. A) 65-67 (1978):

[Ed. Note: After the Commission filed its report in *Ireland v. United Kingdom,* the Irish government referred the case to the European Court of Human Rights. The following is an excerpt from the Court's decision.]

162. As was emphasised by the Commission, ill-treatment must attain a minimum level of severity if it is to fall within the scope of Article 3. The assessment of this minimum is, in the nature of things, relative; it depends on all the circumstances of the case, such as the duration of the treatment, its physical or mental effects and, in some cases, the sex, age and state of health of the victim, etc. . . .

164. In the instant case, the only relevant concepts are "torture" and "inhuman or degrading treatment", to the exclusion of "inhuman or degrading punishment". . . .

167. The five techniques were applied in combination, with premeditation and for hours at a stretch; they caused, if not actual bodily injury, at least intense physical and mental suffering to the persons subjected thereto and also led to acute psychiatric disturbances during interrogation. They accordingly fell into the category of inhuman treatment within the meaning of Article 3. The techniques were also degrading since they were such as to arouse in their victims feelings of fear, anguish and inferiority capable of humiliating and debasing them and possibly breaking their physical or moral resistance.

On these two points, the Court is of the same view as the Commission.

In order to determine whether the five techniques should also be qualified as torture, the Court must have regard to the distinction, embodied in Article 3, between this notion and that of inhuman or degrading treatment.

In the Court's view, this distinction derives principally from a difference in the intensity of the suffering inflicted.

The Court considers in fact that, whilst there exists on the one hand violence which is to be condemned both on moral grounds and also in most cases under the domestic law of the Contracting States but which does not fall within Article 3 of the Convention, it appears on the other hand that it was the intention that the Convention, with its distinction between "torture" and "inhuman or degrading treatment", should by the first of these terms to attach a special stigma to deliberate inhuman treatment causing very serious and cruel suffering.

Moreover, this seems to be the thinking lying behind Article I *in fine* of Resolution 3452 (XXX) adopted by the General Assembly of the United Nations on 9 December 1975, which declares: "Torture constitutes an *aggravated* and deliberate form of cruel, inhuman or degrading treatment or punishment".

Although the five techniques, as applied in combination, undoubtedly amounted to inhuman and degrading treatment, although their object was the extraction of confessions, the naming of others and/or information and although they were used systematically, they did not occasion suffering of the particular intensity and cruelty implied by the word torture as so understood.

168. The Court concludes that recourse to the five techniques amounted to a practice of inhuman and degrading treatment, which practice was in breach of Article 3.

* * *

Tyrer Case, 26 Eur. Ct. H.R. (ser. A) 14-17 (1978) (citations omitted):

[Ed. Note: This case involved a 15-year-old citizen of the United Kingdom and a resident of the Isle of Man. He assaulted a schoolmate and was sentenced to three strokes of a birch in accordance with Manx law. He appealed, but the appeal was dismissed. Subsequently police officers birched him at a police station in accordance with his sentence. They forced him to take down his trousers and underwear and bend over a table in preparation for the birching. Two held him while another officer administered the punishment. The birching raised his skin but did not cut it. He was sore for approximately 10 days after the birching.

He then lodged an application with the European Commission, claiming a violation of Article 3 and other articles of the European Convention. The Commission concluded that the corporal punishment inflicted was degrading and violated Article 3. The Commission then referred the case to the Court of Human Rights.]

29. The Court shares the Commission's view that Mr. Tyrer's punishment did not amount to "torture" within the meaning of Article 3. The Court does not consider that the facts of this particular case reveal that the applicant underwent suffering of the level inherent in this notion as it was interpreted and applied by the Court in its judgment of 18 January 1978 (Ireland v. the United Kingdom, Series A no. 25, pp. 66-67 and 68, §§ 167 and 174).

That judgment also contains various indications concerning the notions of "inhuman treatment" and "degrading treatment" but it deliberately left aside the notions of "inhuman punishment" and "degrading punishment" which alone are relevant in the present case (ibid., p. 65, § 164). Those indications accordingly cannot as such, serve here. Nevertheless, it remains true that the suffering occasioned must attain a particular level before a punishment can be classified as "inhuman" within the meaning of Article 3. Here again, the Court does not consider on the facts of the case that that level was attained and it therefore concurs with the Commission that the penalty imposed on Mr. Tyrer was not "inhuman punishment" within the meaning of Article 3. Accordingly, the only question for decision is whether he was subjected to a "degrading punishment" contrary to that Article.

30. The Court notes first of all that a person may be humiliated by the mere fact of being criminally convicted. However, what is relevant for the purposes of Article 3 is that he should be humiliated not simply by his conviction but by the execution of the punishment which is imposed on him. In fact, in most if not all cases this may be one of the effects of judicial punishment, involving as it does unwilling subjection to the demands of the penal system.

. . .It would be absurd to hold that judicial punishment generally, by reason of its usual and perhaps almost inevitable element of humiliation, is "degrading" within the meaning of Article 3. Some further criterion must be read into the text. Indeed, Article 3, by expressly prohibiting "inhuman" and "degrading" punishment, implies that there is a distinction between such punishment and punishment in general.

In the Court's view, in order for a punishment to be "degrading" and in breach of Article 3, the humiliation or debasement involved must attain a particular level and must in any event be other than that usual element of humiliation referred to in the preceding subparagraph. The assessment is, in the nature of things, relative: it depends on all the circumstances of the case and, in particular, on the nature and context of the punishment itself and the manner and method of its execution.

31. The Attorney-General for the Isle of Man argued that the judicial corporal punishment at issue in this case was not in breach of the Convention since it did not outrage public opinion in the Island. However, even assuming that local public opinion can have an incidence on the interpretation of the concept of "degrading punishment" appearing in Article 3, the Court does not regard it as established that judicial corporal punishment is not considered degrading by those members of the Manx population who favour its retention: it might well be that one of the

reasons why they view the penalty as an effective deterrent is precisely the element of degradation which it involves. As regards their belief that judicial corporal punishment deters criminals, it must be pointed out that a punishment does not lose its degrading character just because it is believed to be, or actually is, an effective deterrent or aid to crime control. Above all, as the Court must emphasize, it is never permissible to have recourse to punishments which are contrary to Article 3, whatever their deterrent effect may be.

The Court must also recall that the Convention is a living instrument which, as the Commission rightly stressed, must be interpreted in the light of present-day conditions. In the case now before it the Court cannot but be influenced by the developments and commonly accepted standards in the penal policy of the member States of the Council of Europe in [abolishing corporal punishment]. Indeed, the Attorney-General for the Isle of Man mentioned that, for many years, the provisions of Manx legislation concerning judicial corporal punishment had been under review.

32. As regards the manner and method of execution of the birching inflicted on Mr. Tyrer, the Attorney-General for the Isle of Man drew particular attention to the fact that the punishment was carried out in private and without publication of the name of the offender.

Publicity may be a relevant factor in assessing whether a punishment is "degrading" within the meaning of Article 3, but the Court does not consider that absence of publicity will necessarily prevent a given punishment from falling into that category: it may well suffice that the victim is humiliated in his own eyes, even if not in the eyes of others. . . .

33. Nevertheless, the Court must consider whether the other circumstances of the applicant's punishment were such as to make it "degrading" within the meaning of Article 3.

The very nature of judicial corporal punishment is that it involves one human being inflicting physical violence on another human being. Furthermore, it is institutionalized violence, that is in the present case violence permitted by the law, ordered by the judicial authorities of the State and carried out by the police authorities of the State. Thus, although the applicant did not suffer any severe or long-lasting physical effects, his punishment — whereby he was treated as an object in the power of the authorities — constituted an assault on precisely that which it is one of the main purposes of Article 3 to protect, namely a person's dignity and physical integrity. Neither can it be excluded that the punishment may have had adverse psychological effects.

The institutionalized character of this violence is further compounded by the whole aura of official procedure attending the punishment and by the fact that those inflicting it were total strangers to the offender.

Admittedly, the relevant legislation provides that in any event birching shall not take place later than six months after the passing of sentence. However, this does not alter the fact that there had been an interval of several weeks since the applicant's conviction by the juvenile court and a considerable delay in the police station where the punishment was carried out. Accordingly, in addition to the physical pain he experienced, Mr. Tyrer was subjected to the mental anguish of anticipating the violence he was to have inflicted on him. . . .

35. Accordingly, viewing these circumstances as a whole, the Court finds that the applicant was subjected to a punishment in which the element of humiliation attained the level inherent in the notion of "degrading punishment" as explained

at paragraph 30 above. The indignity of having the punishment administered over the bare posterior aggravated to some extent the degrading character of the applicant's punishment but it was not the only or determining factor.

The Court therefore concludes that the judicial corporal punishment inflicted on the applicant amounted to degrading punishment within the meaning of Article 3 of the Convention.

Geneva Conventions for the Protection of Victims of Armed Conflict, 75 U.N.T.S. 31, 85, 135, 287, Common Article 3, *entered into force* Oct. 21, 1950:

In the case of armed conflict not of an international character occurring in the territory of one of the High Contracting Parties, each Party to the conflict shall be bound to apply, as a minimum, the following provisions:

(1) Persons taking no active part in the hostilities, including members of forces who have laid down their arms and those placed *hors de combat* by sickness, wounds, detention, or any other cause, shall in all circumstances be treated humanely, without any adverse distinction founded on race, colour, religion or faith, sex, birth or wealth, or any other similar criteria.

To this end, the following acts are and shall remain prohibited at any time and in any place whatsoever with respect to the above-mentioned persons:

(a) violence to life and person, in particular murder of all kinds, mutilation, cruel treatment and torture;

(b) taking of hostages;

(c) outrages upon personal dignity, in particular humiliating and degrading treatment . . . .

Restatement (Third) of the Foreign Relations Law of the United States (1987):

§ 702. Customary International Law of Human Rights

A state violates international law if, as a matter of state policy, it practices, encourages, or condones

(a) genocide,

(b) slavery or slave trade,

(c) the murder or causing the disappearance of individuals,

(d) torture or other cruel, inhuman, or degrading treatment or punishment,

(e) prolonged arbitrary detention,

(f) systematic racial discrimination, or

(g) a consistent pattern of gross violations of internationally recognized human rights.

U.N. RESPONSE TO AMPUTATIONS UNDER THE ISLAMIC PENAL CODE OF SUDAN

The penal code of Sudan has prescribed the amputation (right hand or right hand and left foot) for offenses of theft and persistent or armed robbery. The penal sanctions are based on Islamic law (Shari'a). Over 120 amputations were carried out in a two-year period by the government that was overthrown in 1985. The code was not changed by the new government and offenders continued to be sentenced to amputation although the sentences were not carried out. Amnesty International, Amputation Sentences, AI Index: AFR 54/01/87 (1987); International Comm'n Jurists, The Return of Democracy in Sudan 72-73 (1986).

In response to this situation, the U.N. Sub-Commission on Prevention of Discrimination and Protection of Minorities adopted a resolution in 1984 which recommended that the Commission on Human Rights urge governments to abolish amputation as a penal sanction. The Sub-Commission recalled Article 5 of the Universal Declaration of Human Rights as the basis for the resolution. Report of the Sub-Commission on Prevention of Discrimination and Protection of Minorities, 37th Session, U.N. Doc. E/CN.4/1985/ 3; E/CN.4/Sub.2/1984/43, at 95 (1985).

The original draft of the resolution called directly on Sudan to abolish the infliction of amputation as a penalty. A number of Sub-Commission members, however, questioned the appropriateness of challenging Islamic law, judging internal penal policies, or singling out Sudan for condemnation. The revised text omitted references to Islamic law and Sudan and was readily adopted. N. Rodley, The Treatment of Prisoners Under International Law 246 (1987). The Sub-Commission's parent body, the Commission on Human Rights, took no action in response to this resolution, however.

E. THEORETICAL FOUNDATIONS OF HUMAN RIGHTS

M. McDougal, H. Lasswell, & L. Chen, Human Rights and World Public Order: The Basic Policies of an International Law of Human Dignity 68-71, 73-75 (1980) (footnotes omitted):

The Natural Law Approach

The natural law approach begins with the assumption that there are natural laws, both theological and metaphysical, which confer certain particular rights upon individual human beings. These rights find their authority either in divine will or in specified metaphysical absolutes. The natural law constitutes a "higher law" which is "the ultimate standard of fitness of all . . . national or international [law];" decisions by state elites which are taken contrary to this law are regarded as mere exercises of naked power.

The great historic contribution of the natural law emphasis has been in the affording of this appeal from the realities of naked power to a higher authority which is asserted to require the protection of individual rights. The observational standpoint assumed by those who take this approach has commonly been that of identification with the whole of humanity. A principal emphasis has been upon a common human nature that implies comparable rights and equality for all. For many centuries this approach has been an unfailing source of articulated demand and of theoretical justification for human rights. . . .

The principal inadequacies of the natural law approach stem from its conception of authority. When authority is conceived in terms of divine will or metaphysical absolutes, little encouragement is given to that comprehensive and selective inquiry about empirical processes which is indispensable to the management of the variables that in fact affect decision. It is not to be expected, further, that scholars and decision makers, whose primary concern is to put into effect on earth either divine will or the import of transcendental essences, will devote much attention to the formulation of human rights problems in terms of the shaping and sharing of values or to the location of such problems in the larger community processes which affect their solution. Similarly, the establishment of the most basic, overriding, and abstract goals of the community by the use of exercises in faith, rather than by the empirical exploration of common interest, can only provoke the assertion of different, and perhaps opposing, goals by those who profess a different faith.

The intellectual task most relied upon in the natural law approach is syntactic derivation. Though appropriate concern is exhibited for the establishment and clarification of goals, the method by which clarification is sought for decision in particular instances is not by the disciplined, systematic employment of a variety of relevant intellectual skills, but rather by derivation from postulated norms achieved by techniques such as the revelation of divine will, messages obtained by consultation of oracles or entrails, transcendental cognition of absolutes, and participation in natural reason.... The abiding difficulty with the natural law approach is that its assumptions, intellectual procedures, and modalities of justification can be employed equally by the proponents of human dignity and the proponents of human indignity in support of diametrically opposed empirical specifications of rights, and neither set of proponents has at its disposal any means of confirming the one claim or of disconfirming the other....

The Positivist Approach

The positivist approach assumes that the most important measure of human rights is to be found in the authoritative enactment of a system of law sustained by organized community coercion. Within this approach authority is found in the perspectives of established officials, and any appeal to a "higher law" for the protection of individual rights is regarded as utopian or at least as a meta-legal aspiration....

The great contribution of the positivists has been in recognizing the importance of bringing organized community coercion, the state's established processes of authoritative decision, to bear upon the protection of human rights. By focusing upon deprivations in concrete situations and by stressing the importance of structures and procedures, as well as prescriptions, at phases of implementation, the positivists have enhanced the protection of many particular rights and strengthened explicit concern for more comprehensive means of fulfillment.

The fatal weakness of the positivist approach is in its location of authority in the perspective of established officials. The rules of law expressing these perspectives are commonly assumed to have a largely autonomous reference, different from community policy in context.... Actually, in the positivist approach the task of specifying the detailed content of the human rights protected in a community goes forward very much as in the natural law approach — by logical, syntactic derivation. The difference is that, while the natural lawyer takes off from theological or metaphysical absolutes, the positivist takes off from assumptions about the empirical reference of traditional legal concepts.

The difficulties inherent in clarifying the content of human rights, either as a whole or in particular, by relying on logical derivation from highly abstract and traditional legal concepts are multiple. The most obvious difficulty is that the inherited concepts may embody not the values of human dignity, but those of human indignity.

* * *

S. Hassan, The Islamic Republic: Politics, Law and Economy 106-21 (1984) (footnotes and citations omitted):

Shariah: Basic Constitutional Concepts

Prophet Mohammed showed a path to mankind, the path of a universal law, i.e., the Shariah. Contrary to the rigid limitations of race, national frontiers, language, and geographical configuration, it contains many commandments about the political setup of an ideal Islamic community. . . .

The Shariah contains many principles for public, private, social, national, and international conduct; these principles govern all human action for life in this world and also for life hereafter. . . . Shariah is . . . a complete science which is not specialized for a particular period of time, but is meant for all periods and times. It cannot be amended or modified . . . for it is given by God, who is Perfect and Creator of the universe and all things. The principles laid down by the Shariah are above every man-made society and, being perennial, are adoptable for every new situation. . . .

The system of the Shariah is based upon divine principles and its institutions are sacred. The infringement of the moral rules of the system, as opposed to secular rules, includes unlawful conduct, and it is also a sin against religion and God. There is a double protection of human rights. The rules of law work not only for the prevention of injurious conduct towards others, but they also go deeper than other systems through internal conscience. It is not only an offense but is also a sin to injure or damage the rights of other individuals.

The basic and most fundamental right is the protection of life. (Article 3 of the Universal Declaration of Human Rights, 1948). The Quran declares: "If anyone slew a person unless it be for murder or for preventing mischief in the land, it would be as if he slew the whole people; and if anyone saved a life, it would be as if he saved the life of the whole people". Moreover, the Quran declares: "And slay not the life which Allah hath forbidden save with right". Apart from this right, constitutional laws and various international documents attempt to guarantee other rights, like that of property, reputation or family. The provisions of the Quran are more clear on this subject. Thus, dishonoring others, hoarding, smuggling, defamation, back biting, and destroying others' property are declared offenses and sins.

The conception of freedom recognized by the Shariah is much wider than is commonly perceived. The rules of Shariah provide for the freedom of religion, conscience, expression, speech, avocation, movement, education, assembly, etc. . . . The freedom given to man is related to the establishment of right and justice. The Quran makes it the duty of every individual to speak the truth without any fear. . . . This freedom is given through limitations set up in public interest, and anything which disturbs the public in general is not permitted. All possible methods of demonstration against evil by expression are possible, but they must be under the limits of the rules of morality. Freedom of speech must observe the constitutional means for expression. It should not be violent and injurious and should not give rise to other evils or wrongs. Nevertheless, the Shariah makes provision for rising against authority when there is a violation of the sacred principles on its part. The traditions of the Prophet make it clear that orders or directions to do what is sinful are not to be obeyed. . . .

The conception of pacta sunt servanda [treaties are to be observed] has a special place in any law, so the Muslims are bound by their stipulations. . . . The social and economic rights of the community are safeguarded by the particular guarantee of freedom of contract. In addition to the secular operation of contracts between the parties, it is a divine institution. . . . The moral sanctity in Islam of contracts makes redundant the modern international law recourse to the doctrine of pacta sunt servanda. Thus treaties, like contracts, are binding because Providence has commanded in His law to make all agreements binding.

The contemporary declarations on human rights especially provide and preach for the right to equality and equal protection of the law. In addition to Article 1 of the Universal Declaration (also Article 2), similar elements are contained in most modern constitutions. To what extent these declarations are implemented is another question. The principles of justice in the Shariah incorporate perfect observation of equality before law and equal protection thereof without any kind of discrimination whatsoever. . . . The exercise of justice and its principles is a vital rule of religion, and it is a duty of every Muslim to abide by these principles. The Quran further says that there is to be no discrimination between the sexes; that man is one nation and no discrimination is allowed on the basis of race, region, caste, color, religion, etc. The traditions of the Prophet contain many principles of justice and equality in treatment of men and women. The notion of justice in the Shariah binds a Muslim not only to God but also to his fellow men including the non-Muslims. This principle is applied not only to private matters but also in public transactions and even in international relations. There is a sacred duty to administer justice without any fear or prejudice, and the history of Islam has many remarkable examples in the dispensation of justice.

The modern approaches, in protecting human rights, operate upon the principles of rights of the people. The concept of democracy which establishes a State by the people, must work for the betterment of human life. The Shariah's conception of Umma is a system which has the same goals for an Islamic State. But it was centuries before the modern notions came to be established. . . . The principles of the Shariah lay down the limitations of any ruler. When the ruler violates the rules of the Shariah, particularly those dealing with human rights, it is a person's duty to disobey such ruler's authority. The concepts of imamate and caliphate are based upon the theory of the trust of the public. The moment the ruler or the government violates the mandate of God and His book, the change of government is essential. . . . It leads to the natural result that the Shariah principles imply the protection of human rights in a most comprehensive manner. Only some of them have been reproduced in the above pages. They are enough to show the vast field covered by the list of human rights of the Shariah.

NOTES

1. Dr. S. Farooq Hassan, author of *The Islamic Republic: Politics, Law and Economy*, is a professor of law, a member of the International Institute of Strategic Studies in London, and a member of the bar of the United Kingdom, Pakistan, and the United States. In his preface, the author states that he prepared the text in part to respond to interest in the concept of an ideal Islamic state generated by the emergence of the Islamic Republic of Iran. He bases his work in the primary sources for Islamic jurisprudence — the Qur'an and the Sunnah — and avoids citing post-tenth-century authors. Yet, he states that his interpretations fall in the Sunni school of Islamic law. The Islamic Republic of Iran, however, is founded on the views of the Shi'a school.

2. For further reading on the theoretical basis of human rights in Islam, see P. Ali, Human Rights in Islam (1980); Conferences on Moslem Doctrine and Human Rights in Islam (1974); Farraq, Human Rights in a Pluralist World (J. Berting et al. eds. 1990); Hassan, *On Human Rights and the Qur'anic Perspective*, 19 J. of Ecumenical Studies 51 (Summer 1982); Human Rights in Islam: Report of a Seminar Held in Kuwait, December 1980 (1982) (Islamic scholars from various countries, including at least one Iranian, participated in the seminar.); Nasr, *The Concept and Reality of Freedom in Islam and Islamic Civilization*, in The Philosophy of Human Rights: International Perspectives 95 (Rosenbaum ed. 1980) (The author is a former director of the Iranian Academy of Philosophy.); Said, *Human Rights in Islamic Perspectives*, in Human Rights: Culture and Ideological Perspectives 86 (A. Pollis & P. Schwab eds. 1979) (The author was Professor of International Relations at the American University, Washington, D.C. at the time the book was published.); *see also* Note, *Human Rights Practices in the Arab States: The Modern Impact of Shari'a Values*, 12 Ga. J. Int'l & Comp. L. 55 (1982); *La Commission arabe des droits de l'homme*, 3 Hum. Rts. J. 101 (1970); International Institute of Higher Studies in Criminal Sciences, Draft Charter of Human and People's Rights in the Arab World (1987); International Institute of Human Rights, Pour une Commission d'etude sur la protection des droits de l'homme dans le context musulman (1971); International Institute of Human Rights, Sélection bibliographique des ouvrages concernant de droit en général et les droits de l'homme dans les pays islamiques (1971).

I. Szabó, *The Theoretical Foundations of Human Rights*, in International Protection of Human Rights 35, 39-41 (A. Eide & A. Schou eds. 1967):

[The socialist concept of human rights based on Marxism] is alternately branded as being of the natural-law or the positivist type, although in fact it is neither. A few analogous elements may be found in it, but basically it is a radically new, different theory. Its starting point is criticism, which is applied partly against the aforesaid trends and partly — more emphatically — against the duality which can be found in the constitutions of the states differentiating between human rights and citizens' rights, respectively. The declared reason for such a division is to separate those rights which — allegedly — derive from man's quality as such, and those deriving from man's quality as citizen. In fact, however, these are not the real reasons. Differentiation is based on the social conditions upon which the given types of rights are built up. Let us take a closer look at them.

The said standpoint — as is known — uses the term "human rights" to denote those rights which, allegedly, are due to mankind even in the absence of the state, yea even preceding the existence of the state. These should be regarded as inalienable rights, born with man. As against this: citizens' rights derive from the state and their character is essentially political. While human rights were supposed to be unconditional (i.e. guaranteed in any case), citizens' rights were dependent on the type of the state, its political system and other conditions. As against this, the socialist standpoint declares that there is no difference between the origins of the said two types of rights, because all right is derived from the state; — at most their social preconditions may differ. Those fighting for bourgeois society under the slogan of "enlightenment" called human or eternal and inalienable rights those rights which expressed or protected the fundamental institutions of the social system based on capitalistic private ownership: private property, the freedom of enterprise. These, then, were conceived of as human rights because they were of fundamental importance for the said social system. Therefore they tried to lay down such basic social institutions and conditions under the shape of rights which — supposedly — did not originate from the state, but had existed previously. On the other hand the rights connected with the *political* system of the bourgeois society — equality before law, the political freedoms — were regarded as citizens' rights; in other words: such rights which the political power *may* grant to man in his quality as a citizen but which are not necessarily granted under every state structure. One of these twofold categories, i.e. the human rights — which were "inalienable" — required to be explained by natural law. In the case of the other type — citizens' rights — a strictly positivist interpretation seemed appropriate. Subsequently these two types of rights and two kinds of explanations were to be mixed up, and both types were uniformly accompanied by either a natural-law motivation, or a positivist one.

The socialist theory denies the double origin of human rights both in respect of the social systems based on private ownership and in respect of those based on social ownership of the means of production. It recognizes *the priority* of the property relations in both systems (in fact in any system); it recognizes their existence "preceding" that of the state, even the social pretensions that these be regulated. However, it does not "project" such claims or pretensions into rights, much less human rights. The less so, because the property relations — being the fundamental institution of the society — ultimately determine even the rights called human rights. The socialist concept will speak in a uniform manner of citizens' rights, because it considers every positive right as being created by the state. This is why some of its critics accuse the socialist concept of making the citizens' rights directly dependent on the will of the state-power, in other words they accuse it of unbridled positivism. The fact is, however, that the socialist concept does not regard the constitutional expression of the citizens' rights as being dependent on the arbitrariness of the state. Why? Because it considers this will itself to be determined by objective circumstances, and therefore it makes efforts to reveal the factors determining and influencing the state will.

Pollis, *Liberal, Socialist, and Third World Perspectives of Human Rights*, in Toward a Human Rights Framework 1, 10-11 (P. Schwab & A. Pollis eds. 1982) (footnotes omitted):

Since man is not and should not be a competitive, atomized being, but a social being, his rights are inextricably interwoven and interdependent with his duties. In fact, the mutuality between rights and obligations is central for attaining freedom. Marxist theory, however, has not elaborated with sufficient precision how individual self-fulfillment and freedom, supportive of creativity, can be reconciled and meshed with the notion of social harmony and unity. Since there is no fixed human nature, but a human nature determined by the material conditions of existence, communism will overcome man's alienation in bourgeois society and create the requisite conditions for self-fulfillment. But the parameters of this individuality within a socially integrated whole have not been clearly explicated. This theoretical lacuna has made it easier for socialist states to emphasize conformity at the expense of individual expression and dissent without appearing to grossly distort Marx.

In the transitional stage of socialism . . . the state is still in existence and is the mechanism for bringing about the necessary material and social conditions that will lead to communism. The state is now a proletarian state — a dictatorship of the proletariat — which has overthrown and replaced the bourgeois state. Gradually the state itself will wither away as communism unfolds. During the transitional period the state is the social collectivity and the vehicle for the transformation of society. Such a conceptualization of the nature of society precludes the existence of individual rights with a prior philosophic standing. Only legal rights exist, rights that are granted by the state and whose exercise is contingent on the fulfillment of obligations to society and to the Soviet state. Furthermore, since capitalism is exploitative and individual rights, including the right to private property, are bourgeois rights, social rights, rights which satisfy the basic needs of survival and security, are the substance of human rights. The relations of production in bourgeois society are such that little possibility exists for fulfilling the basic economic and social needs of the workers; with socialism, it becomes the responsibility of the state to satisfy them. Just as in recent decades liberal states espouse economic and social rights but view them as secondary and contingent on economic factors outside the purview of the state, socialist states espouse civil and political rights but view them as secondary to the fulfillment of basic needs and subject to the prior claims of society and to the building of communism by the Soviet state.

NOTES

1. Modern human rights theorists attempt to address the tension between liberty and equality and create an entire system of rights. Their theories are eclectic, borrowing concepts from earlier theories to achieve a synthesis. For further reading in modern human rights jurisprudence, see R. Dworkin, Taking Rights Seriously (1977); R. Nozick, Anarchy, State and Utopia (1974); J. Rawls, A Theory of Justice (1971); M. Winston, The Philosophy of Human Rights (1989). For a brief overview of both traditional and modern human rights theories, see: Shestack, *The Jurisprudence of Human Rights*, in Human Rights in International Law: Legal and Policy Issues 70 (T. Meron ed. 1984); G. Haarscher, Philosophie des Droits de L'homme (1989); L. Henkin, The Age of Rights 1-10, 31-41, 191-93 (1990). For a discussion of the traditional theories of human rights from a socialist point of view, see Szabó, *Historical Foundations of Human Rights and Subsequent Developments*, in The International Dimensions of Human Rights 11 (K. Vasak & P. Alston eds. 1982).

2. One jurisprudential theorist — Hans Kelsen — developed a theory of law based on a hierarchy of legal norms. According to Kelsen, legal systems are founded on one basic norm from which further norms are created and validated. For further reading on Kelsen's theory of hierarchical norms, see A. Ehrenzweig, Law: A Personal View 27-67 (1977); H. Kelsen, General Theory of Law and State 3-161 (A. Wedberg trans. 1945).

3. One of the leading jurisprudential theorists in the area of positivism — H.L.A. Hart — developed a theory based on primary and secondary rules. Primary rules are rules that create obligations. Secondary rules are rules that govern recognition of primary rules and create the power to modify, adjudge, create, or destroy primary rules. The combination of those two types of rules creates a legal system. For further reading on Hart's theory of law, see H. Hart, The Concept of Law (1961).

4. With changes in the Soviet Union and Central Europe human rights theories may also be changing. *C.f.* Mullerson, *Sources of International Law: New Tendencies in Soviet Thinking*, 83 Am. J. Int'l L. 494 (1989); Juvelier, *Guaranteeing Human Rights in the Soviet Context*, 28 Colum J. Transnat'l L. 133 (1990); Gusev, *The international instruments on the protection of human rights in the USSR and their interpretation in USSR judicial practice*, 89/1 Bull. Hum. Rts. 48 (1990).

Freeman, *Racism, Rights and the Quest for Equality of Opportunity: A Critical Legal Essay*, 23 Harv. C.R.-C.L. L. Rev. 295, 316-22, 324-28, 330-35 (1988) (footnotes omitted):

As a practical matter, there is no CLS [Critical Legal Studies] party line, no "movement," if that requires consensus on content, and no official position on "rights" (or on anything else for that matter). Nevertheless, two recurring forms of argument have been identified with CLS often enough to merit some commentary and response. These two are the "indeterminacy critique" and the "contradiction critique."

That legal argument is as a logical matter indeterminate is hardly a recent discovery, having been known by many people for some time now. . . .

In context, indeterminacy arguments are useful. Many lawyers still believe in formalism, or some version of it, despite the realists. When formality is invoked as compelling a (bad) result, it is helpful to be able to respond, "No, there is no result which is compelled." Similarly, the project Mari Matsuda calls "critical legalism" may be better served if people are willing to make imaginative arguments that are sure losers today but nevertheless logically and formally appropriate. Students are especially empowered by learning that they can always fashion counter-arguments, and the law school classroom may be one of the best settings for employing indeterminacy in a progressive way. . . .

The second form of critique that has been regularly associated with CLS and its position on rights is that of "contradiction." The usual approach is to take a seemingly coherent or progressively reformist body of legal doctrine and show that in fact it can be easily (though the job is often quite tedious) collapsed into some pair of "fundamental" contradictions. Once again, neither the method nor the problem of contradiction can be touted as a CLS discovery. . . .

Despite criticism to the contrary, CLS makes efforts to expose ostensible coherence as contradiction have made valuable political contributions. The "method" has gone by many names: decoding, structuralism, demystification, deconstruction, trashing. . . .

The careful demonstration of contradiction in particular substantive settings remains politically useful, especially in view of the rising hegemony of right-wing legal thought that claims to offer unity and coherence. When, as happened recently at a public academic gathering, I am told that contract law is coherent because it promotes allocative efficiency by protecting security of expectations, I like being able to respond by pointing out the contradictory and incoherent nature of the claim. The very same "efficiency" promoted by a decision for "security" is ill-served by the concomitant restraint on "market-freedom." In fact, the contradiction between freedom and security pervades and undercuts any claim of coherence for contract doctrine. Moreover, by exposing the contradictions of law and economics generally, one can bring back to light the political and moral issues masked by its false claim of positive science.

The same sort of issue arises when I teach antidiscrimination law. More and more students (armed with more cases each year) announce that the key principles are "rationality" and "color blindness" and that affirmative action programs utilizing racial criteria are clear violations of settled norms. In the face of such complacency, my painstaking response is to demonstrate that the development of antidiscrimination law is an ongoing dialogue (I mean "dialectical engagement" but that's too heavy for most classes) between the concrete historical reality of oppression and the principles generated by that experience. The abstract principles may end up contradicting reality and history when they are permitted or encouraged to take on lives of their own. Thus, to claim that the affirmative use of "blackness" as a criterion violates "principle" stands in tragic contradiction to the fact that for over 350 years blacks in America have been categorically oppressed by whites on account of the very same "blackness."

Contradiction methodology, then, seems most helpful when it speaks to the otherwise troubled experience of real people and provides weapons of argument to employ against those who would rationalize oppression with words. . . .

When employed as no more than an exercise in logic, contradiction critique may well be fairly characterized as nihilistic, apolitical and remote from the experience of people, particularly oppressed people. Here again, for me, ideology, not indeterminacy or contradiction, is the central notion that gives power to critiques of rights. To reach the real experiences of people in the world, one must expose the difference between the world as it is imagined within the structures of thought that we are somehow led to believe in (or ones that at least serve to rationalize existing power relationships) and the world as experienced by people unencumbered by those particular structures of thought. . . .

Trying to free oneself from the straitjacket of prevailing ideology is not easy. From within a culture, it seems difficult if not impossible to acquire a consciousness so cynical of prevailing norms as to reject their pull altogether. . . .

The ideological character of rights should hardly be surprising. The paradigmatic right in Anglo-American legal history and culture has been that of property. Property rights still serve to legitimate our "freedom" to own, acquire, trade, and accumulate property, to withhold, exclude, and otherwise exploit one's propertyless fellow citizens. . . .

The Civil War Amendments promised for a time that rights might mean more than just protection of property. Those texts, however, were quickly interpreted to limit the public's accountability for its acts of racism by making rights protection inapplicable in the private context. The rights themselves, such as the provisions concerning voting or equal treatment, were reduced to formal, empty shells with no substantive content.

One can tell a similar story about the "Second Reconstruction," a period when rights were sought, struggled for, obtained and manipulated to provide much, much less than equality. I do not intend to imply by these examples that no progress resulted from these changes in the law. Real changes have occurred. Slavery was abolished, and formal apartheid has been dismantled. These changes are most evident in public accommodations and voting. Repression through terror, in the form of lynchings and the like, has been largely curbed as well.

As a white, I am unable to minimize the importance of these changes. Yet, although these changes were secured by the granting of "rights," the promise of the changes in law have been contained and undercut by the very same rights rhetoric. One must also note well what has not changed, or has gotten worse. The statistics on poverty and powerlessness are worse than ever for nonwhite Americans. The future looks bleak for far too many children of poverty, especially given a national government that insanely diverts our resources into stockpiling weapons for Armageddon. . . .

Does the persistence of grossly racist behavior lead, however, to a conclusion that more and better formal rights are a solution or even an appropriate goal? Like the basic choice between formality and informality in dispute resolution, answers must be contextual. It is clear that informal alternative dispute resolution can easily be controlled by the powerful to distort results at lower costs to themselves. However, such distortion is not likely in all imaginable settings, and the price of preferring formality must be recognized as well. . . .

Rights are granted to, or bestowed upon, the powerless by the powerful. They are ultimately within the control of those with authority to interpret or rewrite the sacred texts from which they derive. To enjoy them, one must respect the forms and norms laid down by those in power. One must especially avoid excesses in behavior or demands. Rights are never "owned," merely loaned, and all too easily manipulated away or neutralized by the dismissal of their potentially transformative promise as fantasy. It is easy to catalog the false promises and harsh realities associated with regimes of rights.

Yet there may be a sense in which these rights "realities" just do not matter. Despite Mari Matsuda's argument to the contrary, experience may be just as contradictory as logic. There is a power associated with some forms of rights experience that may well be indifferent to cynical pessimism. One of the most powerful stories in our mythic tradition is that of St. Paul, who, about to be tortured with some barbaric technique called "scourging," rendered the local inquisitors powerless by invoking his Roman citizenship (you could scourge others but not Romans).

Membership rights thus seem especially powerful. The traditional mode of categorical domination employed by oppressors is to define and treat the oppressed as "other": beast not human; heathen not Christian; child not grown-up; barbarian not civilized; outsider not allowed in. The *Dred Scott* case not only treated black Americans as property secured by the due process rights of their owners, but went further to deny them, even when free, the membership right of U.S. citizenship.

In that context, and for a people so solemnly ruled "other," the first sentence of the fourteenth amendment declaring that "All persons born or naturalized in the United States...are citizens of the United States, and of the state in which they reside" is obviously much more than a merely formal legalism. However unrealized in practice, it remains a statement of liberation that gives sustenance and aspiration to the culture and struggles of the oppressed....

That I have flipped back and forth on rights and rights critiques in this section is not a tribute to my indecision or incoherence about the issue. Rather, I believe simultaneously in the truth of rights critique and the authenticity of rights experiences. The truth of both conceptions is...another testament to the contradictory and dialectical nature of our political experience. I believe that the manipulability of rights, and their consequent ideological character, does matter and may endanger, rather than sustain, the quest for substantive social justice. I also recognize the unique power of rights rhetoric and belief as a source of imagery and inspiration, especially when experienced in communal and spiritual settings. Rights consciousness seems, accordingly, to play a continuing role in what I would call a dialectic of image and power. There is, however, a discernable difference between the felt authenticity of communal struggle for rights, and defensive complacency about the functional utility of rights.

NOTES

1. The Critical Legal Studies ("CLS") movement came into existence with the first conference on Critical Legal Studies in 1977. As with any new movement, the jurisprudence associated with it has yet to be codified, and there is no unified CLS theory of rights. Nonetheless, the thrust of CLS rights analysis is criticizing the legitimacy of labeling concepts as rights. One tenet underlying the critique, alluded to by Freeman, is that rights are bestowed by the ruling powers to disguise and legitimate their control without providing substantive entitlements. *Cf.* Stone, *The Post-War Paradigm in American Labor Law*, 90 Yale L.J. 1509 (1981) (critiquing the ideology which underlies the current structure of collective bargaining).

Freeman mentions two critiques directed at the concept of rights by CLS scholars — the indeterminacy critique and the contradiction critique. Another common CLS critique is that calling a concept a right divorces that concept from human experience and "reifies" it into an abstract legal concept. One CLS scholar has argued, building on the reification and indeterminacy critiques, that a system of rights leads to individual alienation by substituting the passive possibility of possessing rights for the active exercise of those rights in concert with others for a common good. Gabel, *The Phenomenology of Rights-Consciousness and the Pact of the Withdrawn Selves*, 62 Tex. L. Rev. 1563 (1984).

2. For further reading on the CLS rights critique, see Sparer, *Fundamental Human Rights, Legal Entitlements, and the Social Struggle: A Friendly Critique of the Critical Legal Studies Movement*, 36 Stan. L. Rev. 509 (1984); Tushnet, *An Essay on Rights*, 62 Tex. L. Rev. 1363 (1984).

3. Thus far there does not seem to be a serious CLS critique of international human rights law. One CLS scholar, however, has described a human rights mission in which he participated from a CLS perspective. *See* Kennedy, *Spring Break*, 63 Tex. L. Rev. 1377 (1985).

Morsink, *The Philosophy of the Universal Declaration*, 6 Human Rts. Q. 309, 310-20 (1984) (footnotes omitted):

NATURAL RIGHTS IN THE UNIVERSAL DECLARATION

The initial presumption is that the Universal Declaration reflects some sort of natural rights view of human rights. Of the thirty articles of the Declaration, the first twenty-one are devoted to the classical eighteenth-century civil and political rights. The social and economic rights seem, to a casual reader at least, to be tacked on at the end, like nineteenth- and twentieth-century grafts on what is basically an eighteenth-century tree. And that same casual reader cannot help but notice certain key eighteenth-century fighting words. The preamble speaks of "inherent dignity" and of "equal and inalienable rights." Article 1 asserts that "[a]ll human beings are born free and equal in dignity and rights." It further claims that all are "endowed with reason and conscience." The "spirit of brotherhood" to which it refers has the familiar ring of eighteenth-century *fraternité*.

There is a remarkable similarity between these 1948 phrases and many eighteenth-century declarations of rights. . . .

The delegates to the [U.N. General Assembly's] Third Committee [the body responsible for drafting much of the Declaration] agreed that Article 1 was to be a basic statement of principle from which the rest of the Declaration was to be more or less deducible. Given the initial presumption of a natural rights philosophy for the Universal Declaration, one would therefore expect Article 1 to contain a reference to either Nature or God as the transcendent normative source of the rights listed in the document. Yet, there is no such appeal to either God or Nature. A slight surprise.

The draft prepared by the Human Rights Commission did refer to nature, stating that all human beings were "endowed by nature with reason and conscience." The insertion of the phrase "by nature" had been meant as an explicit reference to a natural rights model of human rights but it was deleted in the Third Committee for rather pragmatic reasons. The Brazilian delegation made an amendment that grounded the rights of the Declaration in man's divine origin. A number of other delegations strongly objected to this proposal, however, because, as the Uruguayan delegate said, "no reference to a godhead should be made in a United Nations document, for the philosophy on which the United Nations was based should be universal." As a result of the numerous objections the Brazilian delegation withdrew its proposal. Unlike their Enlightenment counterparts, some delegates saw possible opposition between the concepts of God and nature. Accordingly they urged that in deference to the Brazilian withdrawal of the reference to God, the reference to nature should be deleted. . . .

The text, without any reference to nature, does not represent the real thinking of the Third Committee. Notwithstanding the tradeoff between the references to God and nature, the statements of many delegates show that they did think human rights were grounded in nature, understood in some nontranscendent sense. There was a clear desire to derive human rights from the nature of man, rather than from some social, civil, or political source. This was, of course, in keeping with the philosophy behind the eighteenth-century declarations. . . .

[Nevertheless,] Article 29 [the Declaration's limitations clause] admits that rights are balanced by and are correlative with duties. Thus, human rights, even when conceived of as natural rights, are not unlimited. Two votes connected with the adoption of Article 29 have special significance in relation to limits on the exercise of rights. The first vote supported a natural rights interpretation of the Declaration, while the second one introduced a corrective measure against the excessive individualism so often associated with natural rights.

The second paragraph of Article 29 states that the exercise of a person's rights and freedoms may be limited for the purpose "of meeting the just requirements of morality, public order and the general welfare in a democratic society." The Soviet delegation proposed to add the words "and also [for the purpose of] the corresponding requirements of the democratic state." Soviet delegate Alexei Pavlov defended the addition on the grounds that:

> The proper coordination of the interests of the individual and society was only possible under a socialist regime. All rights laid down in the declaration would be implemented in democratic societies by the democratic States. The law was nothing without the machinery to implement it and, at the present time, that machinery was the State. It was impossible, therefore, to ignore the requirements of the democratic State.

This proposal was not well received. New Zealand delegate Mrs. A.M. Newlands objected because "an escape clause . . . should be as narrow as possible if the statement of rights and freedoms was to have any real meaning." Melchar P. Aquino of the Philippines felt that

> [t]he U.S.S.R. amendment, by raising the State above . . . society, would destroy the intent and meaning of the article. Since the definition of the "corresponding requirements" of a State would lie with that State,

it could under the terms of the U.S.S.R. amendment annul all individual rights and freedoms contained in the declaration.

The U.S.S.R. amendment was rejected by a vote of 23 to 8, with 9 abstentions. This vote and the discussion that preceded it are indicative of a preference for the philosophy of natural rights, that is, of rights held by individuals over and against the state.

After defining rights to be held against the state and not to be limited by the needs or laws of the state, the Committee, in its discussion of the first paragraph of Article 29, was quick to step back from an excessive individualistic interpretation of the Declaration. The text of paragraph one of Article 29 as adopted by the Commission on Human Rights said that "[e]veryone has duties to the community which enables him freely to develop his personality." Watt of Australia suggested substituting the phrase "in which alone the free and full development of his personality is possible." The key word is, of course, "alone." Its insertion amounts to a rejection of eighteenth-century individualism because it asserts an organic connection between the individual and either the state or society.

Fernand Dehousse of Belgium objected to the Australian amendment on the grounds that "while there was no doubt that society contributed to the development of the individual's personality, it was no less true that that development was conditioned by other factors." Explaining his reservation about the word "alone," Dehousse said he wanted to avoid the erroneous interpretation that "the individual could only develop his personality within the framework of society; it was, however, only necessary to recall the famous book by Daniel DeFoe, *Robinson Crusoe*, to find proof of the contrary."

The Australian amendment was supported by Soviet delegate Alexei Pavlov who thought that the amendment was:

> important in that it stressed the harmonious relations which should exist between the individual and the society in which he lived. The word "alone," which had been criticized by some delegations, seemed to him excellent. It rightly stressed the fact that the individual could not fully develop his personality outside society. The example of *Robinson Crusoe*, far from being convincing, had on the contrary, shown that man could not live and develop his personality without the aid of society. Robinson had, in fact, had at his disposal the products of human industry and culture, namely, the tools and books he had found on the wreck of his ship.

Since the Australian delegation did not wish to insist upon its amendment, the U.S.S.R. delegation took it up at this point. The amendment containing the word "alone" was adopted by a vote of 23 to 5, with 14 abstentions.

These two votes on Article 29 constitute a refinement of the classical natural rights philosophy. On the one hand, by excluding the U.S.S.R. amendment which made reference to the rights of the state from the second paragraph, the Universal Declaration, like its classical predecessors, took the position that human rights were not to be limited by the state and thus were held over against the state, except insofar as limitations are necessary to preserve morality, public order, and the general welfare. On the other hand, by asserting that it is only in the context of society that an individual can fully develop his personality, as it does in paragraph one of Article 29, the Universal Declaration avoids the extreme individualism often associated with a natural rights philosophy of human rights.

NOTES

As the preceding excerpt illustrates, rights articulated in the Universal Declaration of Human Rights arose from a complex process of drafting, discussion, and consensus among representatives of United Nations member states. The rights in the two International Covenants, as well as those in many other human rights instruments, were developed in a similar fashion. States had already developed many of the rights at a national level; and the international drafting process codified those rights on which states could reach a consensus at least as to their broad outlines if not their specific meaning.

A. D'Amato, International Law: Process and Prospect 1-4, 8, 13-14, 14, 21-25 (1987) (footnotes omitted):

IS INTERNATIONAL LAW REALLY "LAW"?

Many serious students of the law react with a sort of indulgence when they encounter the term "international law," as if to say, "well, we know it isn't *really* law, but we know that international lawyers and scholars have a vested professional interest in calling it 'law.'" Or they may agree to talk about international law as *if* it were law, a sort of quasi-law or near-law. But it cannot be true law, they maintain, because it cannot be enforced: How do you enforce a rule of law against an entire nation, especially a superpower such as the United States or the Soviet Union?...

One intriguing answer to these serious students of the law is to attempt to persuade them that enforcement is not, after all, the hallmark of what is meant, or what should be meant, by the term "law." As Roger Fisher observed, much of what we call "law" in the domestic context is also unenforceable. For example, where the defendant is the United States, such as in a case involving constitutional law, how would the winning private party enforce his or her judgment against the United States? Upon reflection, we see that the United States, whenever it loses a case (and these cases are very frequent — the myriad cases involving income taxes, social security benefits, welfare, and the like), only complies with the court's judgment because it wants to.... In terms of power, there is nothing to stop the United States from disregarding adverse judgments of its own courts. In this sense, therefore, a great deal of what we normally call "law" in the United States is unenforceable by private parties arrayed against the state....

Let us then consider a second line of reasoning against the proposition that enforcement is the hallmark of law. This argument is not associated with any particular writer, because it relies on early conceptions of law and also on the philosophy of law itself. If we consider what law is *not*, we soon realize that it is *not* a rationale for the application of force. It is not a system of "might makes right'' in the sense that the state constantly has to compel people, at gunpoint, to behave in a certain way. . . . Most of "law" concerns itself with the interpretation and enforcement of private contracts, the redress of intentional and negligent harms, rules regarding sales of goods and sales of securities, rules relating to the family and the rights of members thereof, and other such rules, norms, and cases. The rules are obeyed not out of fear of the state's power, but because the rules by and large are perceived to be right, just, or appropriate. . . .

Yet the serious student of law may not be satisfied with the preceding argument in its entirety. We want to ask what happens if the need for physical coercion should arise. In the international system, at least, we have states which occasionally break the rules of international law and which seem not to be deterred by expressions of social disapproval from the other states. This is a reality of international life. . . .

I believe that a conclusive argument can be fashioned that international law is really law, by showing that international law is enforceable in the same way that domestic law is enforceable. . . .

[National law] typically provides for deprivations, for disabilities. When a person disobeys the law, the law "punishes" him in some way. The possibility of punishment, in turn, is supposed to deter a rational person from violating the law in the first place. . . .

. . . As a construct of international law, a nation is nothing more nor less than a bundle of entitlements, of which the most important ones define and secure its boundaries on a map, while others define its jurisdictional competency and the rights of its citizens when they travel outside its borders. . . .

[A]s a matter of its very identity, a state should act in such a manner as to preserve its entitlements. Yet, its identity as a state, its "bundle of entitlements," is dependent upon the acquiescence of all the other states in the system. Since every state has the same bundle of entitlements — otherwise there would be legal inequality among states, a proposition that has never seriously been advocated — the other states in the system have an obvious interest in acquiescing in the entitlements of any given state. In this manner, a new state starts out . . . with its full complement of entitlements.

But just as all the states in the international legal system have a collective interest in acquiescing to all the entitlements for any given state in the system, they also have an interest in preserving the entitlements per se. For ease of illustration, let us consider the . . . entitlement of diplomatic immunity. . . .

To preserve this entitlement, the states in the system collectively will allow certain actions to be taken against any given state which violates the entitlement of diplomatic immunity. Prior to 1979, it would have been difficult to come up with a single example of a state which directly violated that entitlement. . . . But in 1979, after some radical students occupied the American Embassy in Teheran, the government of Iran took the unprecedented step of ratifying the action and holding the American diplomatic personnel hostage. This was a case of a deliberate violation of international law, the violation of the entitlement of diplomatic immunity. To allow it to go unremedied would constitute a threat to the existence of that entitlement in the international legal system.

What legal recourse did states have to prevent the erosion of such an entitlement? An obvious move would be to allow the United States to violate Iran's similar entitlement by arresting diplomatic and consular officials of Iran who were physically present in the United States at the time of the takeover of the American embassy in Iran. While this tit-for-tat strategy is generally regarded as legal under international law, . . . it nevertheless could operate to erode rather than to preserve the entitlement in question. For instance, if the United States had jailed all Iranian diplomatic and consular officials, such an action at least in theory could be interpreted not as an attempt to punish Iran for its initial act but rather as a recognition that Iran's act was correct and that in fact diplomats are not entitled to immunity. . . .

The United States, in fact, did not retaliate by jailing Iranian consular and diplomatic officials . . . . Instead, the United States took steps that were also justified under international law and which constitute a more sophisticated . . . method of enforcement. The United States "froze" approximately thirteen billion dollars of Iranian deposits in American banks and in various European banks where the United States, through American corporations, had the power to act. If it were not for the initial Iranian act of holding the American diplomats hostage, the United States would be unjustified under international law in violating the Iranian entitlement to the use of its own bank deposits abroad. Indeed by freezing the Iranian assets, the United States was effectively confiscating the interest those assets would have earned. This was a direct deprivation of Iranian property by the United States. Yet there was no condemnation of the American action by the international community; instead, the American action in violating a different Iranian entitlement from the one that Iran violated in the first place (diplomatic immunity) was tolerated by general silence, whereas governments from all over the world expressly condemned Iran's seizure of the American embassy. The workings of international law are rarely as explicit as scholars might like them to be, but I believe we are entitled to infer from the reaction of the community of nations that they did not perceive a threat to the shared entitlement of keeping state-owned deposits in foreign banks as a result of the American action, but rather regarded the U.S. action as a temporary infringement of an Iranian entitlement for the limited purpose of enforcing the original entitlement of diplomatic immunity. . . .

Of course, I am not attempting here to support my theory of a reciprocal-violation-of-a-different-entitlement by the single case of the American hostages in Teheran. The pattern is a general one and can be substantiated by numerous examples. Moreover, the tit-for-a-different-tat pattern "makes sense" in a legal system that does not have a central court of compulsory jurisdiction, a world legislature, and a world police force. The absence of these institutions does not mean that international law isn't really law; rather, it simply means that international law is enforced in a different way.

There is a danger in relying on the enforcement of international law by allowing a retaliatory deprivation of the offending nation's entitlement. The danger is the potential escalation of entitlement violations, ultimately leading to international anarchy. . . . But the fact that law can become ineffective doesn't mean that it isn't law in the first place. . . . [W]hile international law could destroy itself through a runaway series of violations of entitlements, until then it polices itself by the meta-rule I have described: that it is legal to deter the violation of an entitlement by threatening a counter-violation of the same or a different entitlement. This latter enforcement action is the "physical sanction" provided by the international legal system, just as the rules regulating police, prison officials, sheriffs, etc., are its domestic legal equivalents.

NOTES

1. One commentator, J. Shand Watson, has taken a different view on the binding nature of international human rights norms. He argues that under the current system international law is not superior to national law. Rather, states create international norms through interaction with each other and must consent to either treaties or customary law before being bound. States will not, the argument continues, consent to be bound by norms with which they do not agree. Moreover, the principal enforcement mechanisms of international law constitute sanctions by other states or compliance in order to receive the benefit of reciprocal compliance by other states. Neither of these enforcement mechanisms work well in the context of human rights law, argues Professor Watson; states will be unwilling to sanction other states for human rights violations because future situations may arise in which they will want to invoke their own sovereignty against criticism of behavior that arguably violates their citizens' rights. In addition, states receive no reciprocal benefit from protecting their citizens' rights under international human rights law. Hence, Watson concludes that international human rights norms are valuable only as goals towards which states may strive, not as binding law. *See* Watson, *Normativity and Reality in International Human Rights Law*, 13 Stetson L. Rev. 221 (1984).

2. For a further discussion of the binding character of international law, addressing and challenging the validity of arguments made by skeptics such as Professor Watson, see Schachter, *International Law in Theory and Practice: General Course in Public International Law*, 178 Collected Courses of the Hague Academy of International Law 1, 21-39 (1982).

F. CULTURAL RELATIVISM AND INTERNATIONAL HUMAN RIGHTS LAW

Donnelly, *Cultural Relativism and Universal Hum. Rights*, 6 Hum. Rts. Q. 400, 410-19 (1984) (footnotes omitted):

CULTURE AND RELATIVISM...

Standard arguments for cultural relativism rely on examples such as the precolonial African village, Native American tribes, and traditional Islamic social systems. Elsewhere I have argued that human rights — rights/titles held against society equally by all persons simply because they are human beings — are foreign to such communities, which instead employed other, often quite sophisticated, mechanisms for protecting and realizing defensible conceptions of human dignity. The claims of communal self-determination are particularly strong here, especially if we allow a certain moral autonomy to such communities and recognize the cultural variability of the social side of human nature. It is important, however, to recognize the limits of such arguments....

In the Third World today, more often than not we see dual societies and patchwork practices that seek to accommodate seemingly irreconcilable old and new ways. Rather than the persistence of traditional culture in the face of modern intrusions, or even the development of syncretic cultures and values, we usually see instead a disruptive and incomplete westernization, cultural confusion, or the enthusiastic embrace of "modern" practices and values. In other words, the traditional culture advanced to justify cultural relativism far too often no longer exists.

Therefore, while recognizing the legitimate claims of self-determination and cultural relativism, we must be alert to cynical manipulations of a dying, lost, or even mythical cultural past. We must not be misled by complaints of the inappropriateness of "western" human rights made by repressive regimes whose practices have at best only the most tenuous connection to the indigenous culture....

In traditional cultures — at least the sorts of traditional cultures that would readily justify cultural deviations from international human rights standards — people are not victims of the arbitrary decisions of rulers whose principal claim to power is their control of modern instruments of force and administration. In traditional cultures, communal customs and practices usually provide each person with a place in society and a certain amount of dignity and protection. Furthermore, there usually are well-established reciprocal bonds between rulers and ruled, and between rich and poor....

[In addition,] there are substantive human rights limits on even well-established cultural practices, however difficult it may be to specify and defend a particular account of what those practices are. For example, while slavery has been customary in numerous societies, today it is a practice that no custom can justify. Likewise, sexual, racial, ethnic, and religious discrimination have been widely practiced, but are indefensible today; the depth of the tradition of anti-Semitism in the West, for example, simply is no defense for the maintenance of the practice....

RESOLVING THE CLAIMS OF RELATIVISM AND UNIVERSALISM

Despite striking and profound international differences in ideology, levels and styles of economic development, and patterns of political evolution, virtually all states today have embraced — in speech if not in deed — the human rights standards enunciated in the Universal Declaration of Human Rights and the International Human Rights Covenants....

While human rights — inalienable entitlements of individuals held in relation to state and society — have not been a part of most cultural traditions, or even the western tradition until rather recently, there is a striking similarity in many of the basic values that today we seek to protect through human rights. This is particularly true when these values are expressed in relatively general terms. Life, social order, protection from arbitrary rule, prohibition of inhuman and degrading treatment, the guarantee of a place in the life of the community, and access to an equitable share of the means of subsistence are central moral aspirations in nearly all cultures.

This fundamental unity in the midst of otherwise bewildering diversity suggests a certain core of "human nature" — for all its undeniable variability, and despite our inability to express that core in the language of science. And if human nature is relatively universal, then basic human rights must at least initially be assumed to be similarly universal....

ASSESSING CLAIMS OF CULTURAL RELATIVISM

Rights are formulated with certain basic violations, or threats to human dignity, in mind. Therefore, the easiest way to overcome the presumption of universality for a widely recognized human right is to demonstrate either that the anticipated violation is not standard in that society, that the value is (justifiably) not considered basic in that society, or that it is protected by an alternative mechanism. . . . I would argue that such a test can be met only rarely today, and that permissible exceptions usually are relatively minor and generally consistent with the basic thrust of the Universal Declaration.

For example, it is hard to imagine cultural arguments against recognition of the basic personal rights of Articles 3 through 11. Rights to life, liberty, and security of the person; the guarantee of legal personality; and protections against slavery, arbitrary arrest, detention, or exile, and inhuman or degrading treatment are so clearly connected to basic requirements of human dignity, and are stated in sufficiently general terms, that any morally defensible contemporary form of social organization must recognize them (although perhaps not necessarily as inalienable rights). In fact, I am tempted to say that conceptions of human nature or society incompatible with such rights would be almost by definition indefensible; at the very least, such rights come very close to being fully universal.

Civil rights such as freedom of conscience, speech, and association would be a bit more relative; as they assume the existence and a positive evaluation of relatively autonomous individuals, they are of questionable applicability in strong traditional communities. In such communities, however, they would rarely be at issue. If traditional practices truly are based on and protect culturally accepted conceptions of human dignity, then members of such a community simply will not have the desire or need to claim such civil rights. But in the more typical contemporary case, in which the relatively autonomous individual faces the modern state, they would seem to be close to universal rights; it is hard to imagine a defensible modern conception of human dignity that did not include at least most of these rights. A similar argument can easily be made for the basic economic and social rights of the Declaration.

The Declaration does list some rights that are best viewed as "interpretations," subject to much greater cultural relativity. For example, the already mentioned right of free and full consent of intending spouses not only reflects a specific cultural interpretation of marriage, but an interpretation that is of relatively recent origin and by no means universal today even in the West. Notice, however, that the right, as Section 2 of Article 16, is subordinate to the basic right to marry and found a family. Furthermore, some traditional customs, such as bride price, provide alternative protections for women, and a sort of indirect conditionality to marriage that addresses at least some of the underlying concerns of Article 16(2). Such factors make it much easier to accept cultural relativity with regard to this right.

When we consider the much more detailed International Human Rights Covenants, a number of listed rights approach specifications at the level of form. For example, Article 10(2)(b) of the International Covenant on Civil and Political Rights requires the segregation of juvenile defendants. In many cultures, the very notion of a juvenile criminal defendant does not exist. Similarly, penitentiary systems, mentioned in Article 10(3), are culturally specific institutions. . . .

Such cases, however, are the exception rather than the rule. And if my arguments above are correct, we can justifiably insist on some form of weak cultural relativism; that is, on a fundamental universality of basic human rights, tempered by a recognition of the possible need for limited cultural variations. Basic human rights are, to use an appropriately paradoxical phrase, relatively universal.

NOTES AND QUESTIONS

1. Do you agree with Donnelly's conclusion that the content of some human rights may vary depending on the cultural context?

Compare Donnelly's conclusion to the early interpretation of the four-teenth amendment to the U.S. Constitution. Under that interpretation the content of the right to racial equality varied from state to state, an interpretation that allowed substantial racial discrimination in some states. Do you think that allowing cultural relativism in international human rights law will necessarily achieve the same result?

2. Does Donnelly suggest any methods for incorporating cultural relativism into human rights law? Should certain rights not be enforceable in some countries? Who should make such a determination?

J. Nickel, Making Sense of Human Rights: Philosophical Reflections on the Universal Declaration of Human Rights 74-79 (1987) (footnotes omitted):

Prescriptive Relativism

Prescriptive relativism is a moral position that endorses normative diversity and tolerance among groups. The prescriptive relativist denies that there are any (or at least that there are many) universal and exceptionless norms, except for a norm requiring tolerance of other people's mores and practices. This position is the antithesis of the view that there are numerous universal and absolute moral standards that admit of no exceptions. The strongest form of prescriptive relativism holds that the only valid universal norm is one requiring tolerance. The prescriptive relativist need not be a moral skeptic: he or she may hold that it is possible for the standards of a particular group to be objectively justified, but to bind only the members of that group.

In its more modest forms, prescriptive relativism holds that universal norms should be few and broad so that most local standards and practices will be compatible with them. This modest version seems to have much to recommend it from a moral point of view. The enormous differences among groups in traditions, social arrangements, world views, levels of economic and political development, and problems faced make it unlikely that we can defend the existence and universal applicability of numerous detailed and exceptionless norms. A norm setting out a father's obligations in European societies may be inappropriate in a society where many responsibilities for children are assigned to their maternal uncles. Standards of blasphemy appropriate to a highly religious society might be inappropriate in a secular one. The relaxed legal standards appropriate to a homogeneous, stable, and peaceful society may be insufficient to provide order in a troubled, ethnically divided new state.

Prescriptive Relativism and Human Rights

Prescriptive relativists often dislike the idea of human rights, particularly in cross-cultural contexts. We saw that high priority and definiteness were distinctive features of rights, allowing them to express moral and legal requirements that leave relatively little room for discretion and interpretation. Prescriptive relativists are likely to be suspicious of such inflexible norms. Even modest prescriptive relativists who endorse minimal standards of international political morality may not wish to see these standards stated in the language of rights; they may prefer the more flexible language of high-priority goals.

But rights can be modified by abstract language and exceptions to make them more flexible. The human rights movement has often modified its norms in this way, and I suspect that these norms are sufficiently limited in scope, broad in terms, and liberal in exceptions to permit a reasonable amount of diversity among social systems, legal practices, and forms of government. . . .

Human rights standards have a number of characteristics that allow diversity. Perhaps the most obvious and important is that they provide only minimal standards in a limited number of areas. For example, the rights one has as a parent, home owner, teacher, or union member depend not on human rights but on the morality, laws, and customs of one's country. It is possible, of course, that some of the rights found in the Universal Declaration and other human rights documents are insufficiently basic and that one who wanted to preserve local flexibility against international human rights would set the criterion for a "minimal standard" or "basic right" rather high.

Second, the terms used in formulating human rights are often broad or abstract enough to allow some latitude to local interpretation. For example, article 9 of the International Covenant on Civil and Political Rights includes the provision: "No one shall be subjected to arbitrary arrest or detention. No one shall be deprived of his liberty except on such grounds and in accordance with such procedures as are established by law." Here the vague word "arbitrary" allows considerable room for interpretation in judging arrests, and the reference to "procedures as established by law" requires only formal legality. Another example, article 10 of the same covenant, requires that people in prison be "treated with humanity and with respect for the inherent dignity of the human person." This permits the operation of varying conceptions of human dignity. What counts as an indignity usually depends on how most people live and are treated and on what the local culture finds repulsive. If many people work in the fields pulling plows because there are no tractors or beasts of burden, then a punishment involving such work would be no indignity. But if such work is normally done by tractors, and only prisoners are required to pull plows, this may amount to a substantial indignity.

Those who formulate human rights may be pulled both ways in regard to precision and detail. Standards that are definite in requiring, for example, particular kinds of institutions, are easier to interpret and make it more difficult for repressive regimes to pretend that they are complying when they are not. But institution-specific requirements may condemn perfectly adequate alternatives; for this reason and others the modest prescriptive relativist is likely to be uncomfortable with them. Except in the area of fair criminal procedures, the human rights movement has leaned toward broad and flexible standards that allow for a variety of implementations. . . .

Strong Prescriptive Relativism: Pros and Cons

The standards of the international human rights movement are for the most part compatible with a modest prescriptive relativism, but some people desire even greater diversity in norms and practices than is permitted by these standards. I now turn to some arguments for and against greater relativism.

The appeal of indigenous standards. One might try to defend strong prescriptive relativism by arguing that indigenous moral and political norms and practices, flowing from long experience, are likely to be well suited to a group's needs and thus advantageous to its welfare. Imported standards, it might be argued, are likely for the same reasons to function poorly or not at all. One might try, for example, to defend the practice in some Arab states of cutting off the hands of thieves on the grounds that it is deep-rooted, indigenous, and has survived because it is well suited to local needs.

But the superiority of indigenous standards, on which this kind of argument rests, is often exaggerated. We know from our own culture that indigenous institutions often work badly and become outdated. Social and technological changes often make older norms and practices ill suited to a group's needs. For example, when education and wide availability of radio and television make people more knowledgeable about politics and less willing to have no influence on important political decisions, the absence of even rudimentary democratic institutions becomes a problem. Further, one cannot assume that the existing norms and practices that violate human rights are in fact indigenous. Techniques of repression are often imported (sometimes with the help of the great powers) and thus a cessation of torture or the release of political prisoners may be more in accord with traditional norms and values than continued torture and imprisonment.

The second part of this claim, namely, that imported standards generally function poorly or not at all, is also an exaggeration. Many transplanted institutions are successful, especially if a transition period is planned. The parliamentary institutions created in Japan after World War II are one striking example of successful transplantation. Borrowing between countries occurs constantly and ranges from political institutions (civil service systems, judicial review, ombudsmen, income tax) to technology and economics (assembly line production, worker self-management). . . .

The value of cultural diversity. This argument asserts the great value of preserving the diverse cultures and ways of life that now exist. Because distinctive values and practices are essential parts of culture, the argument concludes that we must refrain from encouraging countries to adopt the Western norms and practices that are commended by the documents of the human rights movement.

Cultural diversity is an important value, I think, but it is not absolute nor does it rule out many of the changes involved in complying with human rights. One may see the value of preserving, say, the cultural and religious traditions of India without concluding that the Indian caste system should be preserved. Cultures and value systems typically have many parts, and it is sometimes possible to preserve the best and most distinctive features while jettisoning the most repugnant — particularly when making the changes required for compliance with human rights. These rights have the behavior of governments as their central focus, and government practices are seldom central to the identity and persistence of a culture. A group's culture is not likely to be destroyed if torture and cruel punishments are eliminated, political prisoners are released, political dissent is permitted, and programs to combat hunger and illiteracy instituted. Although the human rights movement is part of the general trend toward Westernization in cultures around the world, it is a relatively small part, and terminating it would do little or nothing to terminate Westernization. The question for our era is not whether rapid cultural change should occur — it is occurring — but rather what direction such change should take.

NOTES AND QUESTIONS

1. What do you think of Nickels' argument that the Civil and Political Covenant's requirement that states respect the inherent human dignity of prisoners permits cultural variations in determining what constitutes treatment with dignity? Is an activity dignified simply because many people in a given culture perform that activity? For example, many people enjoy running for long distances. Does that necessarily mean that forcing a person to run for long distances in a prison yard is dignified?

2. Nickels contends that "[e]xcept in the area of fair criminal procedures, the human rights movement has leaned toward broad and flexible standards that allow for a variety of implementations." Based on what you have learned so far and on a reading of the Universal Declaration of Human Rights and the two Covenants, do you think that statement is true?

3. In 1989 the Ayatollah Khomeini, leader of Iran, issued an order for faithful followers to kill a British author, Salman Rushdie, for writing a book called *The Satanic Verses*. Rushdie was raised in the Islamic faith. Khomeini found certain parts of the book to be heretical, inspiring the death threat. In the Moslem faith, as it is practiced in Iran, the killing of heretics is apparently acceptable. Should the argument for cultural relativism in human rights law extend to allowing the killing of heretics? If not, where would you draw the line? What kind of standard would you propose to keep cultural variations within limits?

4. For further reading on cultural relativism and human rights, see:

Brennan, *The Influence of Cultural Relativism on International Human Rights Law: Female Circumcision as a Case Study*, 7 J. Law & Inequality 367 (1989);

Eide, *Making Human Rights Universal: Unfinished Business*, 6 Nordic J. Hum. Rts. 51 (No. 4, 1988);

Cobbah, *African Values and the Human Rights Debate: An African Perspective*, 9 Hum. Rts. Q. 309 (1987);

J. Donnelly, Universal Human Rights in Theory and Practice (1989);

Renteln, *The Unanswered Challenge of Relativism and the Consequences for Hum. Rights*, 7 Hum. Rts. Q. 514 (1985);

Tesón, *International Human Rights and Cultural Relativism*, 25 Va. J. Int'l L. 869 (1985);

International Commission of Jurists, Human Rights in Islam (1982).

5. For a discussion of cultural relativism in the context of the Islamic view of freedom of religion, see An-Na'im, *Religious Minorities Under Islamic Law and the Limits of Cultural Relativism*, 9 Hum. Rts. Q. 1 (1987). For a comparison of Western and Islamic views on freedom of religion, see D. Little, J. Kelsay, & A. Sachedina, Human Rights and the Conflict of Cultures: Western and Islamic Perspectives on Religious Liberty (1988); Merenbach, *Religious Law and Religious Freedom in Saudi Arabia and Israel: A Comparative Study*, 12 Hastings Int'l L.J. 235 (1988). *See also* Amjad, *Shi'ism and Revolution in Iran*, 31 J. Church & State 35 (1989).

IX HOW SHOULD THE COVENANT ON ECONOMIC, SOCIAL AND CULTURAL RIGHTS BE IMPLEMENTED, AND WHAT ARE U.S. VIEWS AS TO THAT COVENANT?

A. INTRODUCTION

Previous chapters have focused primarily on civil and political rights. This chapter examines a different kind of rights with which many U.S. readers may not be familiar — economic, social, and cultural rights. Many instruments articulate those rights, but this chapter concerns the rights set forth in the Covenant on Economic, Social and Cultural Rights. That treaty is the companion to the Covenant on Civil and Political Rights discussed in previous chapters. Together with the Universal Declaration of Human Rights, which itself proclaims economic, social, and cultural rights, the two Covenants make up the International Bill of Human Rights.

This chapter examines the nature of economic, social, and cultural rights as well as their implementation and enforcement. Readers should consider how economic, social, and cultural rights differ from civil and political rights. To highlight the issues the chapter asks whether the U.S. should ratify the Covenant.

The readings also discuss the work of the Committee on Economic, Social and Cultural Rights, which is the body established to monitor implementation of the Covenant. The analysis compares the government reporting procedures of this Committee with the government reporting procedures of the Human Rights Committee, which were the subject of chapter 8.

The chapter also briefly examines the recognition of new rights, such as the right to development and the right to peace. Those rights are often discussed in conjunction with economic, social, and cultural rights.

B. QUESTIONS

1. Exactly what are economic, social, and cultural rights? In answering this question, consider:

   a. Articles 55 and 56 of the U.N. Charter.

   b. Articles 1, 2, 7, 17, and 22-30 of the Universal Declaration of Human Rights.

   c. Covenant on Economic, Social and Cultural Rights.

   d. Preamble and Article 22 of the Covenant on Civil and Political Rights.

   e. Articles 16, 29-31, 34-35, 40, 42-45, 47-48, and 52(d) of the O.A.S. Charter.

   f. Preamble, Articles XI-XVI, XXIII, XXVIII, and XXXV-XXXVII of the American Declaration of the Rights and Duties of Man.

   g. Articles 21 and 26 of the American Convention on Human Rights.

2. How, if at all, do the above provisions relate to the "Four Freedoms" speech President Franklin D. Roosevelt delivered in 1941? Or Roosevelt's State of the Union message in 1944?

3. This chapter provides an opportunity for a roleplaying exercise. The group will act as the Senate Committee on Foreign Relations, conducting a hearing on whether the U.S. should ratify the Covenant on Economic, Social and Cultural Rights. Some will testify in favor of ratification; others against. Still others will question the "witnesses" and debate the issues. In deciding whether to vote for U.S. ratification, consider these questions:

a. What is the significance of President Carter's signature of the Covenant?

b. Has the U.S. already accepted economic, social, and cultural rights articulated in other international instruments?

c. What advantages might the U.S. government gain by ratifying? What advantages might U.S. citizens gain through ratification? Are there disadvantages in not ratifying?

d. Are there disadvantages in ratifying?

e. What are the differences between civil and political rights and economic, social, and cultural rights? In what ways do implementation and enforcement of the two sets of rights differ?

f. Are there conflicts between achievement of civil and political rights and achievement of economic, social, and cultural rights?

g. What obligations would the U.S. assume by ratifying the Covenant? Do you think it likely that the U.S. would ever be found in violation? If so, by whom?

h. How is a government's compliance monitored? Could the monitoring be improved?

i. Are there differences between economic, social, and cultural *rights* and economic, social, and cultural *goals*?

j. If the U.S. were to ratify the Covenant should there be reservations, declarations, and understandings? Should the Senate accept all of President Carter's 1978 proposals? Should it propose some of its own?

4. Should a right to development be recognized as a legal construct combining all the economic, social, and cultural rights? Does it make sense to articulate the right to development when many of its constituent economic, social, and cultural rights are not yet adequately defined?

C. WHAT ARE ECONOMIC, SOCIAL, AND CULTURAL RIGHTS?

Many international instruments articulate economic, social, and cultural rights. Several of the most significant instruments are reproduced in the accompanying handbook, *Selected International Human Rights Instruments.* Readers should review the relevant provisions of the U.N. Charter, the Universal Declaration of Human Rights, the Covenant on Economic, Social and Cultural Rights, the OAS Charter, the American Declaration of the Rights and Duties of Man, and the American Convention on Human Rights.

Franklin D. Roosevelt, "Four Freedoms" Speech (1941) and State of the Union (1944):

On January 6, 1941, while German bombers continued their nightly blitz of British cities and Hitler planned the conquest of the Soviet Union which would ultimately leave 20 million people dead, President Roosevelt, in his annual State of the Nation address to Congress, outlined his vision of the future based upon "four essential human freedoms." Roosevelt declared,

In the future days, which we seek to make secure, we look forward to a world founded upon four essential human freedoms.

The first is the freedom of speech and expression everywhere in the world.

The second is the freedom of every person to worship God in his own way everywhere in the world.

The third is the freedom from want, which, translated into world terms, means economic understandings which will secure to every nation a healthy peacetime life for its inhabitants everywhere in the world.

The fourth is freedom from fear — which, translated into world terms, means a world-wide reduction of armaments to such a point and in such a thorough fashion that no nation will be in a position to commit an act of physical aggression against any neighbor — anywhere in the world. 87-I Cong. Rec. 44, 46-47 (1941).

Later in World War II, President Roosevelt's State of the Union message of January 11, 1944, returned to this theme:

It is our duty now to begin to lay the plans and determine the strategy for the winning of a lasting peace and the establishment of an American standard of living higher than ever before known. We cannot be content, no matter how high that general standard of living may be, if some fraction of our people — whether it be one-third or one-fifth or one-tenth — is ill-fed, ill-clothed, ill-housed, and insecure.

This Republic had its beginning and grew to its present strength, under the protection of certain inalienable political rights — among them the right of free speech, free press, free worship, trial by jury, freedom from unreasonable searches and seizures. They were our rights to life and liberty.

As our Nation has grown in size and stature, however — as our industrial economy expanded — these political rights proved inadequate to assure us equality in the pursuit of happiness.

We have come to a clear realization of the fact that true individual freedom cannot exist without economic security and independence. "Necessitous men are not free men." People who are hungry and out of a job are the stuff of which dictatorships are made.

In our day these economic truths have become accepted as self-evident. We have accepted, so to speak, a second Bill of Rights under which a new basis of security and prosperity can be established for all — regardless of station, race or creed.

Among these are:

The right to a useful and remunerative job in the industries or shops or farms or mines of the Nation;

The right to earn enough to provide adequate food and clothing and recreation;

The right of every farmer to raise and sell his products at a return which will give him and his family a decent living;

The right of every businessman, large and small, to trade in an atmosphere of freedom from unfair competition and domination by monopolies at home or abroad;

The right of every family to a decent home;

The right to adequate medical care and the opportunity to achieve and enjoy good health;

The right to adequate protection from the economic fears of old age, sickness, accident, and unemployment;

The right to a good education.

All of these rights spell security. And after this war is won, we must be prepared to move forward, in the implementation of these rights, to new goals of human happiness and well-being.

America's own rightful place in the world depends in large part upon how fully these and similar rights have been carried into practice for our citizens. For unless there is security here at home there cannot be lasting peace in the world. . . . 90-I Cong. Rec. 55, 57 (1944).

Trubek, *Economic, Social, and Cultural Rights in The Third World: Human Rights Law and Human Needs Programs*, in Human Rights in International Law: Legal and Policy Issues 205, 205-33 (T. Meron ed. 1984):

A. INTRODUCTION

International human rights law recognizes a distinction between political and civil rights, on the one hand, and economic, social, and cultural rights, on the other. This essay deals with rights classified as economic, social, and cultural. . . .

I shall refer to this set of rights collectively, as 'social welfare rights'. This label is my own, and is not widely used in the literature. I adopt it not merely to avoid constant repetition of the phrase 'economic, social, and cultural rights', or the use of such barbarisms as 'ESC rights'. Rather, I employ this term because I think it evokes what is most basic and universal about this sphere of international law. Behind all the specific rights enshrined in international documents and supported by international activity lies a social view of individual welfare. That is, the idea of protecting these rights rests on the belief that individual welfare results in part from the economic, social, and cultural conditions in which all of us live, and the view that government has an obligation to ensure the adequacy of such conditions for all citizens. . . .

B. THE CORE LEGAL DOCUMENTS AND THEIR MEANING

International social welfare law embraces a wide variety of materials ranging from U.N. General Assembly resolutions to programmatic documents issued by international conferences and specialized agencies. To understand the assertion that there is an international law of social welfare, the student must be aware of the entire gamut of relevant materials and see how resolutions, covenants, declarations, and programs relate to one another. In addition, the student must grasp the overall social, economic, and political system within which these normative sources are embedded and through which they take on meaning.

1. *The Charter and the Universal Declaration*

...The U.N. Charter, the Universal Declaration of Human Rights, and the International Covenant on Economic, Social and Cultural Rights are the fundamental sources of international social welfare law and the basis for the concept of programmatic obligations under international law. . . .

The earliest and most basic of these documents is the U.N. Charter, specifically articles 55 and 56. Article 55 commits the United Nations to promote:

> higher standards of living, employment, and development; solutions to international economic, social, and health problems; international cultural and educational cooperation; and respect for human rights.

Article 56 constitutes a pledge by all members to achieve these purposes separately and jointly in cooperation with the United Nations.

These very general purposes and obligations were given more specificity in the Universal Declaration of Human Rights, approved without dissent by the U.N. General Assembly in 1948. Article 22 of the Universal Declaration states that '[e]veryone . . . is entitled to realization, through national effort and international co-operation and in accordance with the organization and resources of each State, of the economic, social and cultural rights indispensable for his dignity and the free development of his personality'. Furthermore, the Universal Declaration states that everyone has rights to social security, to work and to join trade unions, to rest, to an adequate standard of living (including medical care), to education, and to participate freely in cultural life.

2. *The International Covenant on Economic, Social and Cultural Rights*

The most detailed and specific document that deals with the entire field of international social welfare law is the Economic Covenant, which was adopted by the U.N. General Assembly in 1966 and came into effect in 1976. It is a principal source of international social welfare obligations for those states which have ratified it. For those which have yet to do so, it has value as a detailed interpretation of the Charter's obligations. . . .

(i) *Background.* The Universal Declaration sets forth a wide range of rights, including rights relating to political participation, individual liberty, and social welfare. In order to give greater specificity to the principles established by the Universal Declaration and to provide an instrument which individual states could ratify, the United Nations proceeded to develop a Covenant on Human Rights. The original concept was a single covenant covering all the rights set forth in the Universal Declaration. However, in the course of drafting the decision was made to divide the Human Rights Covenant into two separate instruments: one covering political and civil rights — the Political Covenant; and one dealing with economic, social, and cultural rights — the Economic Covenant.

The reasons for this important decision were complex and have been little researched. However, several factors seem to have been influential, among which was a belief that it was impossible to develop a single system of implementation for both the political-civil and the social welfare rights. This problem itself had two aspects. It was obvious to some states that some rights, *e.g.*, the right to a fair trial, could be enacted into law immediately, while other rights, *e.g.*, the right to health, would require programs of action over time before they could be realized. Appropriate national responses would vary with the 'nature' of the right. Protecting political and civil rights meant passing laws and revising constitutions, while guaranteeing social rights meant the establishment of programs as well. The second aspect of the objections to a single human rights implementation system was that the distinction between civil-political and social welfare rights suggested substantial differences in possible international measures to implement these rights. It seemed that some form of international tribunal could and should be created to deal with alleged violations of political and civil rights, but that no court-like structure could be created at the international level to supervise the rights to work, health, etc. Whether these views are objectively correct or not, they seem to have influenced the decisions of the delegates considering a Human Rights Covenant.

The other factor which was influential in the division of the proposed Covenant was more political. There was substantial disagreement over the desirability of a covenant which dealt with social welfare at all. Some states which were prepared to support a covenant guaranteeing political and civil rights were not willing to agree to a document that would commit them to social welfare rights and thus to specific social welfare programs. This led some states to suggest that the proposed covenant be limited to political and civil rights. However, this option was blocked by a General Assembly resolution which directed the drafters to include both political-civil and social rights.

Thus the decision to have two covenants avoided the dilemmas facing the drafters. It allowed them to comply with the General Assembly resolution and still establish different approaches for the implementation of the two categories of rights. At the same time, a state would now be able to ratify a covenant protecting one set of rights even if it was unwilling to specifically guarantee all the rights set forth in the Universal Declaration. This, it was thought, would increase the chances that the overall program would be accepted by the world community.

(ii) *Rights Specific to the Economic Covenant.* The decision to divide the Human Rights Covenant into two documents was not a decision to have two totally independent documents. There is substantial overlap between the substantive provisions of the two. Both proclaim the right of self-determination, prohibit discrimination, and protect the right to join trade unions. However, . . . [t]he social welfare rights which are the subject of this chapter are included only in the Economic Covenant. Those rights are stated in a specific form of language, and are subject only to the Economic Covenant's unique system of implementation.

There is a linguistic convention in the Economic and Political Covenants that warrants mention. . . . Most of the rights in the Political Covenant are declared. For instance, article 14 of the Political Covenant states, 'All persons shall be equal before the courts and tribunals. . . .' A few political and civil rights, *e.g.*, the right to non-discrimination, are 'ensured' by the parties. On the other hand, most of the rights in the Economic Covenant are 'recognized'. When this language is used, the Economic Covenant then lists steps that will be taken 'to achieve full realization'. . . .

Alston & Quinn, *The Nature and Scope of States Parties' Obligations Under the International Covenant on Economic, Social and Cultural Rights*, 9 Hum. Rts. Q. 156, 157-60, 164-74, 177-81, 183-92 (1987) (footnotes omitted):

I. INTRODUCTION

The concept of economic, social, and cultural rights has long generated controversy among philosophers, as indeed has the very notion of human rights itself. From a legal perspective, however, this controversy should have been laid to rest by the adoption of the International Covenant on Economic, Social and Cultural Rights by the United Nations General Assembly.... Nevertheless, the debate remains at least as polarized today as it ever was in the days when the international community had yet to recognize formally the legitimacy of economic, social, and cultural rights. . . .

The purpose of this article is to examine the nature and scope of the obligations of states parties under Parts I, II, and III of the Covenant. While the paper purports neither to present a general theory of economic, social, and cultural rights, nor to respond systematically to the many criticisms that have been levelled against those rights, it is hoped that a clearer understanding of the obligations contained in the Covenant will serve to destroy some of the fallacies and misperceptions which in the past have too often served to distort and obfuscate the debate. . . .

A.   *An Overview of Common Perceptions of Economic, Social and Cultural Rights*

Before embarking on a textual analysis of the Covenant it is appropriate first of all to take note of some of the ways in which economic, social, and cultural rights are commonly perceived. For the most part the relevant characterizations are put forward in the context of comparisons between civil and political rights on the one hand and economic, social, and cultural rights on the other.

The first and most commonly drawn distinction is between positive and negative rights. Thus civil and political rights are characterized as negative in that they require only that governments should abstain from activities that would violate them. Economic, social, and cultural rights require active intervention on the part of governments and cannot be realized without such intervention. Closely linked to this is a distinction between resource-intensive and cost-free rights. Thus it is said that civil and political rights can be realized without significant costs being incurred, whereas the enjoyment of economic, social, and cultural rights requires a major commitment of resources. Largely for that reason the former are considered to be capable of immediate and full realization whereas the latter constitute no more than long term aspirational goals.

A further distinction arises from the fact that in direct contrast to the obligations attaching to economic, social, and cultural rights those relating to civil and political rights are considered to be capable of relatively precise definition, to be readily justiciable, and to be susceptible of enforcement. Similarly civil and political rights relate to widely shared values to which governments are genuinely committed and raise issues that are manageable and within reach. By contrast, economic, social, and cultural rights have attracted no real governmental commitment, and concern issues that are considered to be inherently intractable and unmanageable and are thus much too complex to be dealt with under the rubric of rights.

Finally, civil and political rights are seen as essentially non-ideological in nature and are potentially compatible with most systems of government. By contrast, economic, social, and cultural rights are often perceived to be of a deeply ideological nature, to necessitate an unacceptable degree of intervention in the domestic affairs of states, and to be inherently incompatible with a free market economy.

Although it is not specifically designed to resolve any of these issues, the following analysis demonstrates the validity, or at least partial validity, of some of the above mentioned perceptions and the invalidity or partial invalidity of others. Whatever conclusions may be drawn, the examination and evaluation of such perceptions at least serves to sharpen our understanding of the critical issues involved. In the final analysis the central underlying question concerns the extent to which the concept of economic, social, and cultural rights can or should be artificially moulded so as to fit a predetermined conception of rights which by definition has been tailored to reflect the perceived characteristics of civil and political rights. . . .

II. THE NATURE OF STATES PARTIES' DOMESTIC OBLIGATIONS UNDER THE COVENANT

The focus of this analysis is twofold. Attention is given first to the wording of the general obligation contained in Article 2(1) and then to the specific words or phrases used to describe states' obligations with respect to particular rights dealt with in Part III of the Covenant.

Article 2(1) reads as follows:

> Each State Party to the present Covenant undertakes to take steps, individually and through international assistance and co-operation, especially economic and technical, to the maximum of its available resources, with a view to achieving progressively the full realization of the rights recognized in the present Covenant by all appropriate means, including particularly the adoption of legislative measures.

A. *An Analysis of the Words and Phrases Used in Article 2(1)*

(i) *"undertakes to take steps"*

The original proposal under which states parties would have undertaken "to promote" the rights recognized was replaced almost immediately by this phrase. Its use reflects in part the view held by some of the drafters of the Covenant that each Article should specify in detail the particular steps to be undertaken in order to implement the relevant right. On that basis it would be appropriate for states to undertake the steps thus identified. In practice, however, the approach finally adopted in the Covenant is uneven so that, for example, Article 11 contains a long list of steps relevant to the right to be free from hunger whereas Article 9 simply recognizes the right to social security and makes no mention whatsoever of any steps relevant to its implementation.

During the preparatory work most states' representatives indicated a preference for the phrase "to take steps" rather than "to guarantee." The former had the "virtue" of avoiding a formal undertaking to guarantee the rights, a commitment that would have been too "onerous in the circumstances." It was a more "guarded" expression and more realistically reflected what could be expected of states. Proposals to use the terms "to ensure" and "to pledge themselves" were unacceptable to the majority of the members of the Commission on Human Rights.

In essence the undertaking is akin to assuming an obligation of conduct, the implications of which are examined below. While the resulting obligation is clearly to be distinguished from, and is less demanding than a guarantee, it nonetheless represents a clear legal undertaking. The key point is that the undertaking to take steps is of immediate application. Thus, at least in this respect, the Covenant imposes an immediate and readily identifiable obligation upon states parties. While the full realization of the relevant rights may be achieved progressively, steps towards that goal must be taken either before or within a reasonably short time after ratification.

(ii) *"by all appropriate means, including particularly the adoption of legislative measures"*

As a general rule, the ratification of a treaty need not necessarily entail domestic legal consequences provided, of course, that the treaty itself does not explicitly call upon states parties to take legal measures. In the case of the International Covenant on Civil and Political Rights the nature of the obligation imposed upon states parties by Article 2 makes it abundantly clear that legal measures are required. However, in the case of the International Covenant on Economic, Social and Cultural Rights it is unclear whether states parties are required to take such action. . . .

Incorporation into National Law. It has been suggested . . . that incorporation of the Covenant into national law can be considered to be "an essential first step in fulfilling the aims and provisions of the Covenant." Some states parties have in fact adopted such an approach so that, for example, under the Portuguese Constitution the Covenant is directly applicable in domestic law. But an obligation to incorporate cannot be deduced from the text of Article 2 and no such proposal was even considered during the drafting of the Covenant. . . .

Is Legislation Essential? The next issue is whether states parties must adopt legislation in order to give effect to their obligations under Article 2(1). The draft proposed by the Commission on Human Rights would have required them "to take steps . . . by legislative as well as by other means." But an obligation to legislate was considered inappropriate by some states whose representatives argued that treaty ratification entailed "no more than the fulfillment of the obligations expressed in the treaty, whether by legislation, administrative action, common law, custom or otherwise. The international community could not ask more and had no concern with the question whether legislation was the method adopted.". . .

It is clear therefore that legislation is not mandatory under the terms of the Covenant and that it is a matter for each state party to determine whether or not it is needed. . . .

Is Legislation Sufficient? A related issue, perhaps of greater practical significance, is whether the enactment of legislation is sufficient to fulfill a state party's obligation to use "all appropriate means." Analysis of the reports submitted by some states parties could give the impression that legislation *per se* is indeed sufficient. Accordingly, those reports confine themselves to a recitation, sometimes chapter and verse, sometimes in the barest outline, of the relevant constitutional and legislative texts. Such an approach, however, is not in line with the intent of the drafters of the Covenant. . . .

The view that legislation alone is sufficient is also refuted by the suggestions contained in the guidelines governing the form and content of states' reports under the Covenant. The guidelines clearly indicate that states should provide details not only of relevant laws but also of relevant agreements, court decisions, policies, programs, techniques, measures, etc. Having received reports that patently do not conform to the guidelines, the [Working Group of Governmental Experts on the Implementation of the International Covenant on Economic, Social and Cultural Rights (hereinafter referred to as the ECOSOC Working Group)] has consistently requested states parties in recent years "to submit balanced reports, which should be more than a mere transcription of legislative or administrative measures. . . ."

. . . [T]he mere enactment of legislation does not *ipso facto* constitute a discharge of the relevant obligations. What is required is "to make the provisions of the Convention effective in law and in fact . . . . Full conformity of the law . . . is therefore essential, but taken alone is not enough." . . .

Judicial Remedies. A requirement that judicial remedies for violations be provided in national law is a characteristic of the great majority of international human rights treaties. . . .

For some commentators, the formal justiciability of a right is an indispensable element. Thus for Kelsen "the essential element [of a right] is the legal power bestowed upon the [individual] by the legal order to bring about, by a law suit, the execution of a sanction as a reaction against the nonfulfillment of the obligation." While some other writers do not go so far, it is frequently contended that a claim must be *enforceable* if it is to qualify as a human right. The issue then is how enforceability differs from justiciability. . . .

When the Covenant on Civil and Political Rights was being drafted it was contended that the provision of effective remedies was implicit in the general obligation imposed upon states parties and that an explicit statement to this effect was unnecessary. That view was rejected, however, and Article 2(3) is both explicit and detailed. No counterpart to it was proposed during the drafting of the Economic and Social Covenant although the issue was touched upon on occasion. . . . It is clear from the preparatory work therefore that the provision of judicial remedies cannot be considered to be an indispensable element of the obligation contained in Article 2(1). . . .

Even where the provisions of the Covenant are not justiciable they may play a significant role in influencing the interpretation of domestic legislation on relevant issues. It is generally accepted that when doubt arises as to the meaning or implications of domestic law it should be interpreted in such a way as to be consistent with any relevant international obligation assumed by the state. . . .

Other Appropriate Means. In addition to the various possible means of implementation referred to above, mention should also be made of what have traditionally been termed promotional measures. These might include measures to disseminate the text of the Covenant, to translate it into local languages, to promote teaching and discussion, to provide training courses for judges and lawyers, etc. . . .

      (iii) *"achieve progressively"*

The concept of progressive achievement is in many ways the linchpin of the whole Covenant. Upon its meaning turns the nature of state obligations. Most of the rights granted depend in varying degrees on the availability of resources and this fact is recognized and reflected in the concept of "progressive achievement." The concept thus mirrors the inevitably contingent nature of state obligations. The question that arises is whether the nature of the obligation is so contingent as to deprive it of any normative significance. Does the word "progressive" enable the obligations of states parties "to be postponed to an indefinite time in the distant future" as argued by Hungary during the preparatory work on the Covenant?

A preliminary issue, which can only be raised in passing in the present context, relates to the characterization of the obligation incumbent upon states parties to the Covenant on Civil and Political Rights. Commentators invariably contrast the concept of progressive achievement with that of immediate implementation which is said to be required by Article 2 of the Civil and Political Rights Covenant. During the drafting of that Article it was generally agreed that "the notion of implementation at the earliest possible moment was implicit in article 2 as a whole." Nevertheless, the reality is that the full realization of civil and political rights is heavily dependent both on the availability of resources and the development of the necessary societal structures. The suggestion that realization of civil and political rights requires only abstention on the part of the state and can be achieved without significant expenditure is patently at odds with reality.

This point was argued most cogently in the context of the preparatory work on the Covenants by the Israeli representative, Mr. Najar. For example, he noted with respect to the justiciability of civil and political rights that "the effective implementation of those rights called for a highly developed judiciary organization, which could not be achieved at short notice." In a memorandum submitted to the Third Committee by Israel in 1952, the assumption that the distinction between immediate and progressive realization was synonymous with the distinction between economic, social, and cultural rights and civil and political rights was strongly contested. . . .

While this proposal was rejected it is important in the present context because it serves to demonstrate the artificiality of the idealized way in which the immediate/ progressive distinction is often portrayed. In practice it can be strongly argued that, in at least some states parties to the Covenant on Civil and Political Rights, certain of those rights are by no means susceptible of immediate realization. . . .

In the context of the preparatory work for Article 2 the need to reflect economic circumstances in determining the nature of state obligations was recognized by most as legitimate. As one representative put it, the "Covenant would recognize rights whose content would differ greatly from country to country, depending on available resources, and it therefore could not impose absolute obligations on the states parties to it." The commitment "was conditional and depended upon factors outside [state] control, such as international co-operation, available resources and progressive action." . . .

(iv) *"to the maximum of its available resources"*

It is the state of a country's economy that most vitally determines the level of its obligations as they relate to any of the enumerated rights under the Covenant. From an evaluation of these circumstances flows a picture of a state's abilities and from this may be determined the thresholds it must meet in discharging its obligations. In ascertaining the quantum of resources to be set aside to promote realization of the rights, the state is of course entitled to a wide measure of discretion. Nevertheless such discretion cannot be entirely open-ended or it would have the *de facto* effect of nullifying the existence of any real obligation.

The main dilemma that arises in connection with the use of this phrase is clearly posed by the following analysis contained in the commentary on the tentative draft of the Restatement of the Foreign Relations Law of the United States:

> By adhering to this Covenant the United States would be obligated to take legislative, executive and other measures, federal or State, generally of the kind which are already common in the United States, "to the maximum of its available resources," "with a view to achieving progressively the full realization" of those rights. Since there is no definition or standard in the Covenant, the United States would largely determine for itself the meaning of "full realization" and the speed of realization,

and whether it is using "the maximum of its available resources" for this purpose.

The word "largely" is used in a controlling sense so as to convey the impression that the United States would determine entirely for itself whether it had satisfied the obligation contained in Article 2(1). It would, in other words, be the sole judge of its own compliance.

This interpretation, however, raises the fundamental question as to why it is necessary, or even appropriate, to have an international treaty if each state party is only to be held accountable, with respect to the central element in the obligation, to itself. An open-ended, self-evaluated obligation of this type would seem more characteristic of a declaration or recommendation than of a convention or covenant.

It is therefore not surprising that the interpretation offered by the drafters of the Restatement is not supported by the *traveaux préparatoires*. To the contrary, a number of delegations indicated that they did not consider that a state party's subjective determination as to what constitutes an adequate resource allocation is entitled to complete deference. Thus, for example, the Lebanese representative noted that "it must be made clear that the reference [to resources] was to the real resources of the country and not to budgetary appropriations." Implicit in this formulation is the assumption that governmental allocations, as reflected in the national budget, are not automatically to be taken as authoritative in determining whether the maximum of available resources has been devoted to the satisfaction of the requisite rights. Rather, it may be appropriate to probe beyond those allocations and take account of the country's "real" resources. . . .

States must therefore, as the French representative put it, "without exceeding the possibilities open to them . . . do their utmost in implementing the rights." In avoiding excessive idealism and in accommodating the text to the changing realities of economic circumstances the framers did not thereby intend to let states arbitrarily and artificially determine for themselves the level of commitment required by the Covenant. Moreover the reference to resources was deemed by many to include whatever international as well as national resources were available. . . .

By the same token it is clear from the *traveaux* that states parties are presumed to have considerable discretion in determining what resources are in fact available for use in economic, social, and cultural rights-related concerns. . . .

The discretion to which a state is entitled is, however, not unlimited, and its position is clearly not immune from scrutiny by the international body charged with responsibility for supervising states parties' compliance with their treaty obligations. While the Covenant itself is, inevitably, devoid of specific allocational benchmarks, there is presumably a process requirement by which states might be requested to show that adequate consideration has been given to the possible resources available to satisfy each of the Covenant's requirements, even if the effort was ultimately unsuccessful. If a state is unable to do so then it fails to meet its obligation of conduct to ensure a principled policy-making process — one reflecting a sense of the importance of the relevant rights. . . .

C.   *The Nature of State Obligations Implied by the Use of Specific Words and Phrases in Part III of the Covenant*

As noted above the main difference between the rights recognized in the two Covenants consists of the fact that economic and social rights require relatively greater state action for their realization than do civil and political rights. This difference separates the two sets of rights more in terms of degree than in kind and the relevant question to pose is not *whether* any particular kind requires positive state action but rather the *extent* to which it can subsist as a meaningful right without such active state support. Given that the chief difference is one of degree it may be said in general terms that economic and social rights are, on average, somewhat more dependent for their full realization on positive state action than are civil and political rights.

This conclusion is recognized both implicitly and explicitly in the text of both Covenants. Some civil and political rights, for example, require more state involvement than do others. An obvious example is the civil right to a fair trial which requires a fully functioning judicial system to be operational. Conversely not all economic and social rights require the expenditure of the same amount of resources as others and some will require a lesser element of state intrusiveness through supervision than others. This suggests that the degree of state involvement required is not dependent on which Covenant is involved but on the nature of the specific right in question.

The above observations are important to bear in mind when evaluating the legal significance of the various words and phrases used in Part III of the Covenant to describe particular state obligations with reference to the various rights contained in that Part. At one end of the spectrum are words and phrases that create state obligations roughly akin to those minimalist ones created by classic civil rights. An example of such an undertaking is the one created by the word simply to "respect" certain of the rights. At the other end of the spectrum are various words and phrases that trigger positive and continuous programs designed to ensure the realization of certain rights. An example of a word creating such maximalist state duties is the undertaking to "guarantee" certain of the rights. In between these two poles are some shades of grey.

(i)   *The undertaking to "respect" certain of the rights*

The minimalist undertaking to merely "respect" certain rights is found in Articles 13(3) (undertaking to respect the liberty of parents regarding certain aspects of their children's education) and 15(3) (undertaking to respect the freedom indispensable to scientific research and creative activity). Though the word "respect" ordinarily connotes obligations of a generally negative character it must be remembered that the European Court of Human Rights has interpreted it in the context of family rights as sometimes giving rise to positive state duties. Taken at its face value, however, the word "respect" probably represents the lowest rung of state obligations under the Covenant.

(ii)   *Progressive achievement of rights "recognized" in Part III*

Next to the minimalist undertaking merely to "respect" certain of the rights is the general obligation imposed under Article 2(1) to progressively achieve the rights "recognized" in Part III of the Covenant. The obligation to "take steps" to "progressively achieve" thus created under Article 2(1) links up with the various rights "recognized" by states in Part III. Mere "recognition" of a right in Part III does not mean the absence of any real state obligations. Rather recognition triggers the application of general state obligations under Article 2(1).

Where the texts of the various rights are silent on the concrete steps to be taken by states in fulfillment of their obligations with regard to the rights "recognized" the relevant obligations can best be understood as hybrids between obligations of result and obligations of conduct. They are obligations of result in the sense that states must match their performance with their objective capabilities. They are loose obligations of conduct in the sense that states are obliged to take active, though largely unspecified, steps toward their satisfaction. This hybrid mixture of obligation types is due to the fact that the concept of "progressive achievement" mandates the existence of an ongoing process of development the adequacy of which is loosely controlled by norms deduced from a state's objective capabilities. The existence of such a process or course of conduct is, in other words, a necessary but not a sufficient element of the full satisfaction of state obligations under the Covenant.

Where the text of the various "recognized" rights specify the "steps" to be taken for their achievement then the obligations so created can truly be said to be obligations of conduct. This gives rise to state obligations of a more tangible and conventional nature.

(iii) *Undertakings to "ensure" and "guarantee"*

The phrase "undertakes to ensure" connotes obligations of a stronger variety relative to those created by the mere "recognition" of rights taken in conjunction with Article 2(1). The use of this phrase signifies that though the right in question is appropriate for inclusion in the Covenant it is not subject to the flexibility inherent in the notion of "progressive achievement." The examples of the use of this clause in the Covenant occur in Articles 3 (equal rights of men and women) and 8 (trade union rights). Such rights must be implemented immediately.

The word "guarantee" appears twice in the Covenant and likewise signifies that the rights to which it relates are to be implemented at once. It occurs in Articles 2(2) (general nondiscrimination clause) and 7(a)(1) (prohibition of gender discrimination with respect to remuneration for employment, etc.). Together the words "respect" and "guarantee" represent the highest rung of state obligation under the Covenant.

(iv) *Concluding observations on Part III of the Covenant*

Two further observations are in order. The first is that some of the provisions contained in the Covenant were not intended to impose any specific and binding obligations on states. A clear example of such a provision is the statement in Article 15 of the Covenant in which states "recognize the benefits to be derived from the encouragement and development of international contacts and co-operation in the scientific and cultural fields." The absence of any obligation flowing from that provision was specifically noted during the preparatory work on the Covenant.

The final observation relates to the obligation contained in Article 13(2) which enumerates obligations regarding educational systems. Article 13(2) is often cited as an exception to the general principle of progressive achievement. Several commentators have suggested that the obligation flowing from that provision is of an immediate nature. This suggestion, however, is refuted by the report of the Third Committee which indicates general agreement that the introductory clause in the paragraph should make it clear that "the measures enumerated thereunder were to be taken progressively, in accordance with Article 2 of the Covenant."...

III. THE NATURE OF STATES PARTIES' INTERNATIONAL OBLIGATIONS; THE MEANING OF THE PHRASE: "INDIVIDUALLY AND THROUGH INTERNATIONAL ASSISTANCE AND CO-OPERATION, ESPECIALLY ECONOMIC AND TECHNICAL"

The Covenant contains three provisions that could be interpreted as giving rise to an obligation on the part of the richer states parties to provide assistance to poorer states parties in situations in which the latter are prevented by a lack of resources from fulfilling their obligations under the Covenant to their citizens. The first is the phrase quoted above, which appears in Article 2(1). The second is the provision in Article 11(1) according to which states parties agree to "take appropriate steps to ensure the realization of this right [to an adequate standard of living], recognizing to this effect the essential importance of international co-operation based on free consent." Similarly in Article 11(2) states parties agree to take, "individually and through international co-operation," relevant measures concerning the right to be free from hunger.

Almost inevitably, dramatically diverging interpretations of the significance of these provisions have been put forward. On the one hand they have been said to give rise to quite specific international obligations on the part of industrialized countries and to provide the foundations for the existence of a right to development. On the other hand, the Carter administration, in seeking the advice and consent of the U.S. Senate to U.S. ratification of the Covenant, proposed a reservation to the effect that: "It is also understood that paragraph 1 of article 2, as well as article 11 . . . import no legally binding obligation to provide aid to foreign countries."

. . . [T]he phrase under consideration is of direct and immediate relevance to the nature of the obligations implicit in the phrase "to the maximum of its available resources." As noted above, it was made clear during the preparatory work that the word "its" is to be interpreted as including both the resources available to a country internally as well as externally, i.e., from international sources. . . .

During the preparatory work it was conceded by virtually all delegations that the developing states would require some forms of international assistance if they were to be able to promote effectively the realization of economic and social rights. . . .

Those arguing in favor of imposing a strong obligation on the developed countries invoked a wide range of justifications. Perhaps the least controversial was the argument based on interdependence. . . .

On occasion, however, this argument was closely linked to the view that international cooperation was owed to the formerly colonized states in reparation for "the systematic plundering of their wealth under colonialism." As another representative put it, "nations that were or had been colonized did not go begging, but called for the restoration of their rights and property." . . . It was also argued that the absence of a provision relating to international cooperation would render the undertakings of developing countries "purely academic" because they would be unable to afford to implement them.

The only formal suggestion of the existence of a binding obligation came from the Chilean representative who observed "that international assistance to under-developed countries had in a sense become mandatory as a result of commitments assumed by States in the United Nations."

The arguments against that proposition took a variety of forms and came from a significant range of states. France argued simply that "multilateral assistance could not be mandatory" and an almost identical argument was made by the Soviet Union. In the view of the representative of Greece "developing countries like her own had no right to demand financial assistance through such an instrument; they could ask for it, but not claim it." . . .

[O]n the basis of the preparatory work it is difficult, if not impossible, to sustain the argument that the commitment to international cooperation contained in the Covenant can accurately be characterized as a legally binding obligation upon any particular state to provide any particular form of assistance. It would, however, be unjustified to go further and suggest that the relevant commitment is meaningless. In the context of a given right it may, according to the circumstances, be possible to identify obligations to cooperate internationally that would appear to be mandatory on the basis of the undertaking contained in Article 2(1) of the Covenant....

In conclusion, it seems appropriate to assume that states are likely to accept a far greater level of international obligation *in practice* than they will ever formally accept *in writing*.

NOTES

For further reading, see Kartashkin, *Economic, Social and Cultural Rights*, in International Dimensions of Human Rights 111 (K. Vasak & P. Alston eds. 1982); Realization of Economic, Social and Cultural Rights, U.N. Doc. E/CN.4/Sub.2/1989/19 (1989) (preliminary report of a study for the Sub-Commission on Prevention of Discrimination and Protection of Minorities); United Nations Action in the Field of Human Rights, U.N. Doc. ST/HR/2/Rev.3, at 163-83 (1988).

D. PROBLEMS OF IMPLEMENTATION AND ENFORCEMENT

Alston, *Out of the Abyss: The Challenges Confronting the New U.N. Committee on Economic, Social and Cultural Rights*, 9 Hum. Rts. Q. 332 (1987) (footnotes omitted):

I.   INTRODUCTION

In May 1986, the United Nations created a new expert Committee on Economic, Social and Cultural Rights. Its task is to assist the Economic and Social Council in monitoring states parties' compliance with their obligations under the International Covenant on Economic, Social and Cultural Rights....

II.   AN OVERVIEW OF THE COVENANT'S IMPLEMENTATION PROCEDURES

Before embarking on an analysis of the background to the establishment of the new Committee it is necessary to provide at least a broad overview of the relevant implementation provisions contained in Part IV of the Covenant. Articles 16-22 may be summarized as follows: The states parties are required to report, in accordance with a program to be determined by the Economic and Social Council after consultation with the specialized agencies concerned and the states parties, on the measures they have adopted and the progress made in achieving the observance of the rights recognized in the Covenant. The reports may indicate factors and difficulties affecting the degree of fulfillment of the obligations. They are to be submitted to the Secretary-General, who is required to transmit copies to the Council and copies of all the relevant parts to the agencies. Where information has already been furnished to an agency, it is sufficient for the report to refer thereto. Provision is made for arrangements between the Council and agencies whereby the latter will report on progress achieved in the observance of the Covenant. The Commission on Human Rights may receive from the Council copies of both the state and agency reports and may make "general" recommendations thereon. The agencies and states parties are entitled to submit comments on any such recommendations to the Council. The Council, in turn, may submit reports to the General Assembly with recommendations of a general nature and a summary of the information received. It may also bring to the attention of the agencies matters that might warrant the provision of technical assistance or the taking of other international measures. The role of the new Committee is to assist the Council in fulfilling all of its responsibilities and, in particular, those provided for in Articles 21 and 22 of the Covenant.

III.   BACKGROUND TO THE ESTABLISHMENT OF THE COMMITTEE

The context in which the decision to establish the Committee was taken is, in several respects, without precedent in the UN system. In the first place, the creation of such a committee had been debated at length when the Covenant was being drafted but two specific proposals, championed by the United States and Italy respectively, conspicuously failed to win support. As a result, the Covenant makes no provision for the establishment of any specialist supervisory body.

Secondly, the decision to establish an expert committee was taken after relatively limited and somewhat inconclusive consultations with states parties and with surprisingly few objections having been raised in advance. Thirdly, and perhaps most significantly, the decision can be seen, in a sense, as a last ditch effort to establish a meaningful international implementation system for the Covenant in the wake of the failure of earlier approaches. . . .

B.   *The Process of Evolution from a Working Group to a Committee of Independent Experts*

(i)   *The Working Group and Its Shortcomings*

Shortly after the Covenant entered into force on 3 January 1976, the Economic and Social Council met to consider the best means of operationalizing the implementation procedures laid down in Part IV (Articles 16-23). It decided from the outset to establish a "Sessional Working Group" of the Council to assist it in the consideration of reports due under the Covenant, thereby exercising the discretion it retained to determine for itself the most appropriate arrangements for ensuring effective supervision. Members of the Group were appointed by the President of the Council after due consultation with the regional groups. After a review of the experience of that Group's first four sessions (1979-1982), the Council concluded that specialist expertise was required in the Group's membership. It therefore renamed the Group the Sessional Working Group of Governmental Experts and decided that its members were to be elected by the Council for three-year terms from among nominees put forward by the states parties to the Covenant.

A detailed review of the performance of the Working Group in each of its two incarnations is beyond the scope of this article. . . . A survey by the International Commission of Jurists of the work of the Sessional Working Group at its first three sessions identified a large number of shortcomings, many of which continued to characterize the work of the expert group between 1983 and 1986. Among the criticisms most commonly cited, mention may be made of the following:

a. "[t]he examination of reports has been cursory, superficial, and politicized";

b. the Group has failed to establish standards for the evaluation of reports;

c. the Group's reports to the Council have contained very few substantive conclusions, have been largely procedural, and have failed to indicate whether reporting states are complying with their obligations under the Covenant. . . .

However, the most significant shortcomings of the Group's work relate to its output. The Group has failed to include any summary of states' reports, or its deliberations thereon, in its own reports to the Council and has for the most part abstained from making recommendations on other than procedural matters. It has, as a result, not provided the Council with anything of substance on the basis of which the latter could, if it wished, have exercised its right under Article 21 of the Covenant to "submit from time to time to the General Assembly reports with recommendations of a general nature and a summary of the information received from the States Parties . . . and the specialized agencies. . . ." Accordingly, even after eight years the Council has not been able to make any such report to the General Assembly.

(ii)   *Rejecting the Option Involving the Commission*

As of February 1987 the majority of the Covenant's Articles dealing with implementation remained inoperative. In other words, the Council has failed to exercise any of the options available to it under Articles 19-22. Two of those provisions (Articles 19 and 20) concern the role the Commission on Human Rights might play if the Council chose to transmit the various reports to it "for study and general recommendation or, as appropriate, for information." . . .

(iii)   *Reemergence of Proposals for a Committee of Independent Experts*

In 1980, at the Council's request, the Secretary-General consulted all states parties to the Covenant as well as members of the Council as to the type of arrangements under which the Working Group should operate in the future. Only eighteen states replied but those that had bothered to do so clearly took the matter seriously. Almost half of them indicated a lack of satisfaction with existing arrangements and suggested the desirability of establishing a new committee along the lines of the Human Rights Committee. By contrast the other half were more or less satisfied with the existing arrangements. In the event, the Council opted in 1982 for a compromise, but one that had very little impact. . . .

IV.   THE COMPOSITION AND TERMS OF REFERENCE OF THE COMMITTEE

The new Committee resembles in several respects the Committee on Human Rights established under the Covenant on Civil and Political Rights. Thus, for example, its members are designated as "experts with recognized competence in the field of human rights, serving in their personal capacity." In contrast to the members of the old Working Group, they are therefore not acting as representatives of governments. Also like its counterpart, the Committee will have eighteen members with "due consideration" being given in their election to "equitable geographical distribution and to the representation of different forms of social and legal systems." However, this general principle has been translated into a relatively inflexible formula whereby each of the five geopolitical regional groupings has three members and an additional three seats are allocated "in accordance with the increase in the total number of States parties per regional group." At the 1986 elections this formula resulted in one extra seat each going to the Latin American, African, and Western European and Others groups.

Only states parties to the Covenant can nominate persons for election to the Committee. Although there appears to be nothing to prevent the nomination of an individual who is not a national of a state party, there have been no precedents and the chances of election would probably be slight. Unlike elections for the Human Rights Committee, in which only states parties can vote, all members of the Economic and Social Council, whether or not they are parties to the Covenant, are entitled to take part in the secret ballot by which the members of the Committee are elected.

Members of the Committee are elected for four years with elections for half the membership being held every two years. Members are eligible for reelection. These provisions are of particular importance in view of the detrimental consequences flowing from the unduly high rate of turnover in membership of the old Working Group. It may be hoped that a significant degree of continuity will thus be ensured.

The Committee is scheduled to meet annually in Geneva for up to three weeks and its members' expenses will be paid by the United Nations, thus underlining their independence from the governments that nominated them.

The principal differences between the new Committee and the Human Rights Committee relate to their status and independence as committees. Whereas the latter is a treaty-based organ whose mandate is laid down in the Covenant on Civil and Political Rights and which is responsible directly only to the states parties to that Covenant, the former exists entirely at the pleasure of ECOSOC. Its terms of reference, its composition, and its working arrangements can thus be altered at any stage by the Council. Moreover, its mandate is in a sense only an indirect one in that its task is "to assist the Council" in fulfilling the Council's role under the Covenant rather than to be directly responsible, in its own right, for supervisory activities. . . .

V.   THE PRINCIPAL CHALLENGES CONFRONTING THE COMMITTEE. . .

A.   *Norm Clarification*

One of the most striking features of the Covenant is the vagueness of the normative implications of the various rights it recognizes. While some of the formulations are no more vague or ill-defined than some of those in the other Covenant, the difference in the extent of elaboration of their normative content undertaken both before and after the adoption of the Covenant is immense. Several factors account for this discrepancy. In the first place, the content of the Covenant on Economic, Social and Cultural Rights was not based upon any significant bodies of domestic jurisprudence as was the case with civil and political rights. Thus, phrases like "cruel, inhuman or degrading treatment or punishment" had been the subject of in-depth judicial and academic analysis long before their inclusion in the Covenant on Civil and Political Rights. By contrast, the range of rights recognized in the other Covenant was, with the exception of labor-related rights, considerably in advance of most national legislation. Indeed, this is still the case today so that international lawyers seeking enlightenment as to the meaning of rights such as those pertaining to food, education, health care, clothing, and shelter will find little direct guidance in national law.

The second reason for the discrepancy lies in the failure of the international community to develop jurisprudence of any significance on many of the principal economic rights since the Covenant's adoption in 1966. By contrast, the meaning and precise policy implications of specific civil and political rights have been the subject of detailed legal analysis and of carefully-honed judicial and quasi-judicial interpretation, as well as being spelled out in much greater detail in specialized instruments such as the Standard Minimum Rules for the Treatment of Prisoners and the Convention Against Torture. Economic, social, and cultural rights have been the beneficiaries of remarkably few such endeavors and those that have been undertaken have not been very revealing. . . .

As a result, even a state that is deeply committed to achieving the fullest possible implementation of the Covenant will be hard pressed to determine for itself exactly what the Covenant requires of it with respect to a given right. For the same reason, the Committee itself will face equally intractable dilemmas until such time as it consciously and systematically addresses itself to the normative issue.

In its endeavors to clarify the normative content of the rights the challenge facing the Committee will be to strike a balance between an expansive, literal interpretation of the Covenant's provisions according to which governments are obligated to take a comprehensive set of measures with respect to each right and a highly flexible, subjective interpretation which accords to each state party a virtually unlimited degree of discretion. . . . [T]he Committee should seek to identify some minimum core content of each right that cannot be diminished under the pretext of permitted "reasonable differences." . . . In other words, there would be no justification for elevating a "claim" to the status of a right (with all the connotations that concept is generally assumed to have) if its normative content could be so indeterminate as to allow for the possibility that the rightholders possess no particular entitlement to anything. Each right must therefore give rise to an absolute minimum entitlement, in the absence of which a state party is to be considered to be in violation of its obligations.

The question for the Committee is how to go about identifying the core entitlement flowing from each right recognized in the Covenant. In the first instance, of course, the responsibility rests with the states parties themselves. . . .

In this regard the role of the Committee will be to encourage governments to undertake such efforts as an integral part of the obligations they have under-taken. . . . Thus, government representatives might systematically be asked what effort has been made to define rights such as the rights to food or education, and to indicate the form that the process has taken and the results achieved. In the event that no such effort has been made, an undertaking to engage in some form of future reflection could be sought.

The second approach is for the Committee to develop a more systematic manner of examining reports by which specific issues would be emphasized with a view to eliciting from states parties information on the basis of which the Committee could piece together an interpretative analysis of particular rights that would in turn provide guidance to all states parties. . . . [T]he second approach is unlikely to be productive unless pursued in tandem with the third.

The third approach is for the Committee itself, or other groups acting in its behest, to undertake a detailed study of the normative implications of the various rights. The Working Group came close to such an approach in its 1986 report when it recommended that the Council should urge the specialized agencies, on the basis of the experience gained in other bodies and of the reports so far submitted and considered by the Group, to provide their views on the implementation of the Covenant within their special fields of competence. . . .

. . . Past experience, however, would seem to indicate that vague, open-ended invitations issued with no specific goal in mind are likely to generate about as much serious reflection as went into making them in the first place. Thus, the most effective strategy might be for the Committee, or one of its rapporteurs or working groups, to prepare draft issue outlines speculating as to the possible core content of each right. . . . Such outlines would reflect all available input and would be designed to stimulate, and act as a focus for, further discussion and debate at both the national and international levels. The exercise would not be designed to lead to the adoption of hard and fast rules, but to enable the Committee itself, as well as states parties, to develop a better understanding of the nature of the rights recognized in the Covenant and of the duties that attach to them.

B.   *Encouraging More Meaningful Reporting by States Parties . . .*

. . . [T]he credibility of the Covenant's implementation procedures is a function of the effectiveness of the reporting system which, in turn, is largely dependent upon the quality of states' reports and upon the information that can be elicited from other sources in response to those reports. . . . [T]he quality of reports to date has been strongly criticized. But the task of improving the quality by revitalizing the overall reporting procedure will be particularly difficult for the Committee at a time of increasing skepticism as to the viability of reporting systems in general. Such skepticism is a function of the strains resulting from a considerable expansion in the number of states involved, a proliferation of new instruments bringing additional and usually uncoordinated reporting obligations along with new supervisory bodies, and the increasingly obvious disparity between states' own version of the situation and that reflected in usually reliable alternative sources.

The Covenant contains two provisions dealing with the nature of the reports that states parties are required to submit. Under Article 16(1) they are to report "on the measures which they have adopted and the progress made in achieving the observance of the rights recognized" in the Covenant. This provision is supplemented by Article 17(2), which states that "[r]eports may indicate factors and difficulties affecting the degree of fulfillment of obligations. . . ." The exact nature of the reports required is thus not spelled out with any great clarity, although the general thrust is apparent.

Experience to date confirms the view that states parties have been given enormous, if not quite total, discretion to determine for themselves the type of reports they will submit. This has been the case notwithstanding the existence of relatively detailed guidelines (to be examined below) and admonitions by the Working Group to states "to submit balanced reports, which should be more than a mere transcription of legislative or administrative measures or a reproduction of detailed statistical data in narrative form."

The approach to be adopted by the new Committee will depend to a large extent upon its perception of the functions of reporting and the objectives of the process of "supervision" or monitoring of compliance. In general terms, the preparation and submission of reports by states parties can serve the following functions:

1. to raise the consciousness of government officials (preferably in ministries dealing with domestic policy rather than just foreign ministries) by obliging them

to undertake regularly a careful comparison of treaty obligations with domestic laws and practices;

2. to facilitate "principled decision-making" by requiring the preparation of integrated statements of government policy in a given social or economic sector;

3. to provide the basis for, and to stimulate the holding of, public debates as to the appropriateness of existing policies, by providing an opportunity for diverse sectors of society to make an input into, and perhaps to comment upon, the government's assessment of the situation;

4. to provide the basis on which the relevant international supervisory organs can effectively monitor the extent of a state's compliance with its obligations;

5. to provide a mechanism by which to develop a better understanding of the common problems faced by states and to identify the most appropriate means by which the international community might assist states to fulfill their obligations; and

6. to reaffirm the credibility of the international implementation system by demonstrating that states cannot ignore their treaty obligations with impunity....

...Leaving aside measures the reporting states themselves might take, four issues should be of particular concern to the Committee.

In the first place it must find a way of conveying to states the fact that priority must be accorded to the satisfaction of minimum subsistence levels of enjoyment of the relevant rights by *all* individuals. Their reports should therefore concentrate initially on that issue with particular emphasis being placed on the situation of vulnerable and disadvantaged groups. Descriptions of macro- or even microeconomic policies, such as those that have tended to predominate in states' reports to date, are in fact of *no intrinsic* value. They are relevant only insofar as they shed light on the extent to which individuals are enjoying, or will enjoy, the rights in question.

The second issue concerns the implications of the phrase "factors and difficulties affecting the degree of fulfillment of obligations" contained in Article 17(2) of the Covenant. Because that phrase is preceded by the permissive "may" rather than the mandatory "shall" it is sometimes argued that reference by states to any difficulties is entirely optional. But in practice it must be assumed that no state will consistently be in full compliance with the whole range of Covenant obligations. Moreover, even where compliance does appear to have been achieved, potentially adverse factors and difficulties will still exist. The Article 16 reports on "progress made" must by implication deal also with progress not made. They should thus acknowledge relevant difficulties and refer to remedial measures that have been, or are proposed to be, taken. If states continue to submit reports that omit all reference to difficulties or shortcomings the Committee will be forced either to adopt an adversarial posture or to become a rubber stamp that simply acknowledges the extraordinarily positive achievements of all governments. The way to avoid either of these extremes is for reporting states to be more forthcoming about their problems, an approach that is likely only if the Committee develops satisfactory access to alternative sources of information.

A third means of improving the quality of reporting is to improve the reporting guidelines so that officials responsible for the preparation of the reports are given a relatively precise indication as to the types of information required....

The final issue, to which only passing reference can be made, is the complex one of periodicity, or, in other words, how often states parties should be required to submit reports.... The principal options open to the new Committee would be to seek to reduce the overall length of the complete reporting cycle (nine years currently) or, perhaps more realistically, to devise a method by which it could call upon all states to submit reports on specific issues (e.g., the right to housing) at the same time thereby enabling a thorough review of the global situation.

C.   *The Possibilities of Cooperation Between the Committee and UN Agencies*

The future prospects for cooperation between the Committee on the one hand and the principal UN specialized agencies (notably the ILO, the United Nations Educational, Scientific and Cultural Organization (UNESCO), the World Health Organization (WHO), and the Food and Agricultural Organization (FAO)) on the other can only be understood against the background of the historical evolution of the relationship between those agencies and the UN's human rights organs. In a number of respects that relationship has been competitive and, on occasion, antagonistic....

In general, however, it must be concluded that FAO and WHO, and to a lesser extent UNESCO, have demonstrated an almost total lack of interest in contributing to the Covenant's implementation procedures. Whether this can be attributed to a lack of appreciation of the importance of the Covenant, a fear that involvement in human rights matters will bring unwanted politicization, an inability to understand the concept of economic rights, concern to protect agency jurisdiction, or some other reason, it seems unlikely that their positions will change significantly in the foreseeable future.

D.   *The Role of Nongovernmental Organizations*...

...Experience in all the various UN human rights organs clearly demonstrates the critical need for supervisory bodies to have access to alternative sources of information when examining and evaluating the reports received from governments. There is nothing inherently subversive in this conclusion. Governments cannot generally be expected to act as their own critics, particularly vis-á-vis the international community. The importance of providing NGOs with direct access to international fora has been recognized in the context of procedures for the examination of complaints of violations of human rights such as that established under Council Resolution 1503. Similarly, in the context of reporting procedures, it is widely recognized that the success of the system established by the ILO is due in large part to the fact that information from workers' and employers' organizations is always used to supplement that provided by governments.

The Covenant is in fact no different in this regard from its counterpart, the Covenant on Civil and Political Rights or from instruments such as the Convention on the Elimination of All Forms of Racial Discrimination. Neither of those two treaties provides for the submission of information by NGOs to the relevant committees. In practice, this lack of formal standing has not prevented the evolution of an informal relationship on the basis of which several prominent NGOs regularly supply members of the committees (as opposed to the committees themselves) with information pertinent to their examination of states' reports.

... There is a tendency in dealing with international human rights treaty obligations to neglect, or at least downplay, the contribution that can be made by groups at the national level. This is especially unfortunate when it comes to assessing the progress made and the difficulties encountered in realizing economic, social, and cultural rights. Because of the complexity and pervasiveness of the issues involved there can be no more effective stimulus to implementation than meaningful, focused, and extended national debate.

For that reason the Committee should encourage states to foster greater involvement of domestic NGO groups in the preparation or critique of reports submitted in accordance with the Covenant. . . .

E. *More Streamlined Working Methods*

The working methods followed by each of the various UN human rights supervisory committees tend, perhaps inevitably, to follow a remarkably similar pattern. . . .

[An] example of an area in which the Committee should seek to develop its own specially tailored working methods is the need to develop specialist expertise, perhaps by moving towards a functional division of labor according to which different Committee members would assume primary, but not exclusive, competence for making observations and posing questions with respect to particular rights. Thus, for example, on the basis of existing professional expertise or interests a given member could concentrate much of his or her attention on the right to social security or the right to housing.

Another matter of working methods to which the Committee will inevitably have to address itself is the desirable length of its sessions. At present the Council has provided for a single annual three-week session. It is clear, however, that such a short time will not be sufficient to enable the Committee to evaluate reports from a large number of states parties in a sufficiently conscientious fashion. But while the need for an extended session or sessions seems inevitable, the Council should make the favorable consideration of any such request dependent upon a clear demonstration by the Committee that it has already done everything possible to ensure the optimal use of available time. This goal could be promoted by eliminating unnecessary duplication of questions posed by members, restricting the amount of time available to states representatives to introduce their reports and to respond to questions, developing effective guidelines for reporting, and moving towards a system of preliminary processing of reports by a working group.

The final aspect of the Committee's working methods concerns the means by which it will make decisions. In the absence of any specific provisions in the relevant Council resolutions, the principal options are to do so by consensus or by simply majority vote. Consensus decisionmaking has much to recommend it. . . . Nevertheless, while it is in one sense the most democratic of procedures and has the greatest potential, in theory, to encourage the adoption of compromise solutions in contentious cases, it also offers the opportunity to a single member (or a consistently small minority) to obstruct or frustrate the work of the entire Committee. While the pros and cons of applying consensus decisionmaking to the work of the new Committee are too complex to explore in this article, it may nevertheless be observed that the principle of consensus should never be treated as an unbreakable rule.

F. *Effective Follow-Up to the Examination of States' Reports*

On the basis of the approach adopted by the Working Group and of the provisions of the resolutions by which the Committee was established, there will be at least three possible types of follow-up to the examination of states' reports by the Committee. Two are country-specific and the third is of general relevance.

The first follow-up consists of the responses (if any) provided by the representative of the state party to the various questions posed by members of the Committee. Over time, the Committee will need to develop a procedure whereby an indication is given as to the adequacy or otherwise of the responses given and under which further information can be sought on issues not adequately dealt with. The second follow-up consists of a "summary" of the consideration of each state party's report which is to be included in the Committee's annual report. The principal virtue of these summaries is to bring to the attention of a broader public the details of the Committee's deliberations. . . .

The third follow-up mechanism consists of the adoption of general observations such as those contained in the 1986 report of the Working Group. . . . It would clearly be desirable for the new Committee to move in the direction of adopting "general comments" along the lines of those regularly drawn up by the Human Rights Committee. Such comments can deal with both procedural and substantive issues arising out of the Covenant. . . . The nature of the challenges confronting the Committee on Economic, Social and Cultural Rights would seem to make it particularly appropriate for it to begin at an early stage to work on the formulation of general comments that would help to throw light on the many unresolved issues relating to the nature and scope of states parties' obligations under the Covenant.

NOTES

1. In 1986 a group of experts in international law, convened by the International Commission of Jurists, the Faculty of Law of the University of Limburg (Netherlands), and the Morgan Institute for Human Rights, University of Cincinnati, met to consider the nature and scope of the obligations of states parties to the Covenant on Economic, Social and Cultural Rights. They also discussed the consideration of states parties' reports by the newly constituted Committee on Economic, Social and Cultural Rights and the achievement of international co-operation under the Covenant. The experts drafted the Limburg Principles on the Implementation of the International Covenant on Economic, Social and Cultural Rights. U.N. Doc. E/CN.4/1987/17 (1987). The principles closely followed the views of Professor Alston in the two articles reproduced above and have been influential in guiding the Committee on Economic, Social and Cultural Rights, of which Professor Alston is a member.

2. The Economic and Social Council decided in 1987 that nongovernmental organizations in consultative status may submit written statements to the Committee on Economic, Social and Cultural Rights. E.S.C. res. 1987/5, U.N. Doc. E/C.12/1987/4, at 27, 28 (1988). Several NGOs have submitted written statements. The Committee has also invited experts, including a representative of an NGO, to make presentations on specific topics. NGOs are generally not permitted to make oral statements during Committee proceedings as they are in the Commission on Human Rights and its Sub-Commission.

3. For further reading on the work of the Committee on Economic, Social and Cultural Rights, see Alston, *Implementing economic, social and cultural rights: the functions of reporting obligations,* 89/1 Bull. Hum. Rts. 5 (1990); Alston & Simma, *First Session of the U.N. Committee on Economic, Social and Cultural Rights,* 81 Am. J. Int'l L. 747 (1987); Report of the Committee on Economic, Social and Cultural Rights on its first session, U.N. Doc. E/C.12/1987/5 (1987); Report . . . on its second session, U.N. Doc. E/C.12/1988/4 (1988); Comment, *Monitoring Mechanisms for International Agreements Respecting Economic and Social Human Rights,* 12 Yale J. Int'l L. 390, 410-19 (1987).

E. SHOULD THE U.S. RATIFY THE COVENANT ON ECONOMIC, SOCIAL AND CULTURAL RIGHTS?

Dobriansky,[1] U.S. Human Rights Policy: An Overview, U.S. Dept. of State, Bureau of Public Affairs, Current Policy No. 1091, at 2-3 (1988):

Myths and Realities

Myth #1: "Economic and social rights" constitute human rights. While the pursuit of human rights is a generally popular undertaking, considerable confusion still permeates discussions of this subject. Let's consider the very definition of human rights. There have been efforts to obfuscate traditional civil and political rights with "economic and social rights." We believe that traditional political rights provide a vital foundation for any democratic society. As noted in our human rights bureau's annual *Country Reports on Human Rights Practices:*

> . . . the right of self-government is a basic political right, that government is legitimate only when grounded on the consent of the governed, and that government thus grounded should not be used to deny life, liberty, and the pursuit of happiness. Individuals in a society have the inalienable right to be free from governmental violations of the integrity of the person; to enjoy civil liberties such as freedom of expression, assembly, religion, and movement, without discrimination based on race, ancestry, or sex; and to change their government by peaceful means.

We believe that under present conditions "economic and social rights" are really more in the nature of aspirations and goals than "rights." This semantic distinction is highly important. It does not make sense to claim that a particular level of economic and social entitlements are rights if most governments are not able to provide them. In contrast, any government can guarantee political and civil rights to its citizens. Obfuscating a goal with fundamental rights promotes not only conceptual confusion but often is used to justify actual human rights violations. Not surprisingly, we have usually found that political rights are often denigrated by repressive governments claiming that, in order to promote "economic and social rights," they must deny their citizens political and civil rights.

---

[1] When she wrote this "overview" Paula Dobriansky was Deputy Assistant Secretary of State for Human Rights and Humanitarian Affairs.

In fact, there exists a symbiotic relationship between human rights and economic development. Experience demonstrates that it is individual freedom that fosters economic and social development; it is repression that stifles it. Those who try to justify subordinating political and civil rights on the grounds that they are concentrating on economic aspirations invariably deliver on neither.

Myth #2: Economic deprivation is a valid rationale for denial of civil/ political rights. This does not mean that we seek to disparage the sincere desire of those well-meaning people who genuinely promote improved economic and social standards. It is true that poverty and deprivation plague many parts of the world. And, even in developed Western countries, poverty still has not been eradicated. This is a very real problem which merits a sustained effort to resolve it. We believe that democracy and free enterprise offer the best solution to improving the economic well-being of people.

Unfortunately, this point seems to be often overlooked or ignored by those who seek to justify their own egregious violations of political and civil rights by asserting that, after all, even in the United States, poverty has not been fully conquered, and a number of Americans have been unable to secure shelter or stable income. This, of course, is a flawed argument. The fact that economic deprivation has not yet been fully eradicated provides absolutely no justification for denying people their political rights or torturing one's political opponents. Sadly, the whole subject has become so heavily laden with hypocrisy that dictators who often torture and maim their subjects see fit to lecture the United States on human rights.

* * *

Department of State, Country Reports on Human Rights Practices for 1989, Report Submitted to the Senate Committee on Foreign Relations and the House Committee on Foreign Affairs, 101st Cong., 2nd Sess. 1 (1990): [Ed.: Emphasis added. Readers may find some paragraphs in this introduction to be irrelevant to economic, social, and cultural rights. The full introduction has been reproduced here because readers will need to consult this intro- duction again in connection with chapter 11 on U.S. human rights policy.]

1989 Human Rights Report

This report is submitted to the Congress by the Department of State in compliance with Sections 116(d)(l) and 502B(b) of the Foreign Assistance Act of 1961, as amended. The legislation requires human rights reports on all countries that receive aid from the United States and all countries that are members of the United Nations. In the belief that the information would be useful to the Congress and other readers, we have also included reports on the few countries which do not fall into either of these categories and which are thus not covered by the Congressional requirement.

Congress amended the Foreign Assistance Act with the foregoing sections of law so as to be able to consult these reports when considering assistance programs for specific foreign countries. One of the very important consequences — perhaps unintended — of these legislative provisions is that they have made human rights concerns an integral part of the State Department's daily reporting and daily decisionmaking. A human rights officer in an Embassy overseas who wants to write a good annual human rights report on the country in which he or she works must carefully monitor and observe human rights developments throughout the year on a daily basis. As a consequence he or she will report on such developments whenever something of human rights significance happens in the country of assignment. In the past 12 years, the State Department has become decidedly better informed on and sensitized to human rights violations as they occur around the globe. . . .

This year, as last, there are 169 separate reports. The guidelines followed in preparing the reports are explained in detail in Appendix A [Ed.: reproduced in chapter 6]. In Appendix B is a discussion of reporting on worker rights, as required by Section 505(c) of the Trade Act of 1974, as amended by Title V of the Trade and Tariff Act of 1984 (Generalized System of Preferences Renewal Act of 1984). Although the legislation requires reports on worker rights only in developing countries that have been beneficiaries under the Generalized System of Preferences, in the interest of uniformity, and to provide a ready basis for comparison, we have here applied the same reporting standards that we have applied to all countries on which we prepare reports. Appendix C contains a list of 12 international human rights covenants and agreements and indicates which countries have ratified them. Appendix D contains explanatory notes on the statistical table in Appendix E, which shows the amounts obligated for U.S. economic and military assistance for fiscal 1989.

Definition of Human Rights

Human rights as defined in Section 116(a) of the Foreign Assistance Act, include freedom from torture or other cruel, inhuman, or degrading treatment or punishment; prolonged detention without charges; disappearance due to abduction or clandestine detention; and other flagrant denial of the rights to life, liberty, and the security of the person. Internationally recognized worker rights, as defined in Section 502(a) of the Trade Act, include (A) the right of association; (B) the right to organize and bargain collectively; (C) prohibition on the use of any form of forced or compulsory labor; (D) a minimum age for the employment of children; and (E) acceptable conditions of work with respect to minimum wages, hours of work, and occupational safety and health.

In addition to discussing the topics specified in the legislation, *our reports, as in previous years, cover other internationally recognized political rights and civil liberties and describe the political system of each country.*

In applying these internationally recognized standards, we seek to be objective. But the reports unashamedly reflect the U.S. view that the right of self-government is a basic political right, that government is legitimate only when grounded on the consent of the governed, and that government thus grounded should not be used to deny life, liberty, and the pursuit of happiness. Individuals in a society have the inalienable right to be free from governmental violations of the integrity of the person; to enjoy civil liberties such as freedom of expression, assembly, religion, and movement, without discrimination based on race, ancestry, or sex; and to change their government by peaceful means. The reports also take into account the fact that terrorists and guerrilla groups often kill, torture, or maim citizens or deprive them of their liberties; such violations are no less reprehensible if committed by violent opponents of the government than if committed by the government itself.

We have found that the concept of economic, social, and cultural rights is often confused, sometimes willfully, by repressive governments claiming that, in order to promote these "rights," they may deny their citizens the right to integrity of the person as well as political and civil rights. There exists a profound connection between human rights and economic development. Experience demonstrates that it is individual freedom that sets the stage for economic and social development; it is repression that stifles it. Those who try to justify subordinating political and civil rights on the ground that they are concentrating on economic aspirations invariably deliver neither. *That is why we consider it imperative to focus urgent attention on violations of basic political and civil rights. If these basic rights are not secured, experience has shown the goals of economic development are not reached either.* This is a point which the Soviet Union's reformers seem to have recognized.

United States Human Rights Policy

From this premise, that basic human rights may not be abridged or denied, it follows that our human rights policy is concerned with the limitations on the powers of government that are required to protect the integrity and dignity of the individual. Further, it is in our national interest to promote democratic processes in order to help build a world environment more favorable to respect for human rights and hence more conducive to stability and peace. We have developed, therefore, a dual policy, reactive in the sense that we continue to oppose specific human rights violations wherever they occur, but at the same time active in working over the long term to strengthen democracy.

In much of the world, the United States has a variety of means at its disposal to respond to human rights violations. We engage in traditional diplomacy, particularly with friendly governments, where frank diplomatic exchanges are possible and productive. Where we find limited opportunities for the United States to exert significant influence through bilateral relations, we resort to public statements of our concerns, calling attention to countries where respect for human rights is lacking. In a number of instances, we employ a mixture of traditional diplomacy and public affirmation of American interest in the issue.

The United States also employs a variety of means to encourage greater respect for human rights over the long term. Since 1983 the National Endowment for Democracy has been carrying out programs designed to promote democratic practices abroad, involving the two major United States political parties, labor unions, business groups, and many private institutions. Also, through Section 116(e) of the Foreign Assistance Act, funds are disbursed by the Agency for International Development for *programs designed to promote civil and political rights abroad.* We also seek greater international commitment to the protection of human rights and respect for democracy through our efforts in the United Nations and other international organizations, and in the process devised by the Conference on Security and Cooperation in Europe. . . .

* * *

Schifter,[2] U.S.-Soviet Quality of Life: A Comparison, U.S. Dept. of State, Bureau of Public Affairs, Current Policy No. 713, at 1 (1985).

---

[2] During the period 1980-90, Richard Schifter served variously as U.S. Ambassador to the U.N. Commission on Human Rights, a U.S. delegate in the various meetings following the (Helsinki) Conference on Security and Cooperation in Europe, and also Assistant Secretary of State for Human Rights and Humanitarian Affairs.

When we use the term "right," we think of a claim which can be enforced in the courts. The rights guaranteed in the U.S. Constitution, which . . . are referred to as political and civil rights, are rights which every citizen can call upon the courts to protect.

We view what are . . . referred to as economic and social rights as belonging in an essentially different category. They are, as we see it, the goals of government policy in domestic affairs. Government, as we see it, should foster policies which will have the effect of encouraging economic development so as to provide jobs under decent working conditions for all those who want to work at income levels which allow for an adequate standard of living. These goals should be attained in a setting which allows freedom of choice of his work to everyone. For those who are unable to find jobs we provide unemployment compensation and, if that is unavailable, other forms of social assistance. The economic system which is now in place in our country is fully in keeping with the relevant articles of the Universal Declaration of Human Rights.

NOTES AND QUESTIONS

1. Do you agree that economic, social, and cultural concerns are goals, not rights? Would the recognition of rights encourage governments to conform their practice accordingly? Do methods of implementing rights under the Economic, Social and Cultural Covenant fully address the Reagan/Bush administration's argument that capability for immediate implementation is necessary for these claims to be defined as rights?

2. The U.S. view of economic, social, and cultural rights has not always been negative. President Carter signed the Covenant on Economic, Social and Cultural Rights and submitted it to the Senate for advice and consent to ratification. The Carter administration viewed human rights as falling into three broad categories: rights that protect the integrity of the person; rights that guarantee fulfillment of basic economic and social needs; and rights that protect civil and political liberties. The administration promoted protection of all the categories of rights as being complementary and mutually reinforcing. *See* Vance, *Human Rights and Foreign Policy*, 7 Ga. J. Int'l & Comp. L.J. 223 (1977).

3. For further reading, see A. Mower, Human Rights and American Foreign Policy: The Carter and Reagan Experience 37-40 (1987). For criticism of the inclusion of economic, social, and cultural rights, see J. Muravchik, The Uncertain Crusade: Jimmy Carter and the Dilemmas of Human Rights Policy 88-105 (1986).

4. Do you agree with the statement of Assistant Secretary of State Schifter, "The economic system which is now in place in our country is fully in keeping with the relevant articles of the Universal Declaration of Human Rights"?

5. If the U.S. were a party to the Covenant on Economic, Social and Cultural Rights, would the U.S. violate its obligations by (a) failing to provide adequate housing for the homeless, (b) reducing the distribution of food stamps, (c) reducing Medicare benefits for the elderly, or by (d) spending more on national defense and less on aid for families with dependent children?

6. The Reagan/Bush administration argued that viewing economic, social, and cultural goals as rights leads governments to deny civil and political rights in the search for economic stability. Were were that assertion true, is it a valid objection to recognizing economic, social, and cultural rights; or does it merely reflect the view that civil and political guarantees are more important than economic stability? Should all governments strive to provide civil and political rights and also economic, social, and cultural rights? *See* Howard, *The Full Belly Thesis: Should Economic Rights Take Priority Over Civil and Political Rights*, 5 Hum. Rts. Q. 467 (1983).

F. RESERVATIONS, UNDERSTANDINGS, DECLARATIONS, ETC.

Four Treaties Pertaining to Human Rights: Message From the President of the United States, 95th Cong., 2nd Sess. at VIII-XI (1978):

[Ed.: Submitting the Economic, Social and Cultural Rights Covenant to the Senate for advice and consent to ratification, the Carter administration suggested these reservations, understandings, and declarations.]

The International Covenant on Economic, Social and Cultural Rights sets forth a number of rights which, while for the most part in accord with United States law and practice, are nevertheless formulated as statements of goals to be achieved progressively rather than implemented immediately. . . .

Article 1 affirms in general terms the right of all peoples to self-determination, and the right to freely dispose of their natural wealth and resources without prejudice to any obligations arising out of international economic cooperation, based upon the principle of mutual benefit, and international law. This is consonant with United States policy.

Paragraph (1) of Article 2 sets forth the basic obligation of States Parties "to take steps," individually and through international assistance and cooperation, "to the maximum of its available resources, with a view to achieving progressively the full realization of the rights recognized" by the Covenant "by all appropriate means, including legislative measures." In view of the terms of paragraph (1) of Article 2, and the nature of the rights set forth in Articles 1 through 15 of the Covenant, the following statement is recommended:

"The United States understands paragraph (1) of Article 2 as establishing that the provisions of Articles 1 through 15 of this Covenant describe goals to be achieved progressively rather than through immediate implementation."

It is also understood that paragraph (1) of Article 2, as well as Article 11, which calls for States Parties to take steps individually and through international cooperation to guard against hunger, import no legally binding obligation to provide aid to foreign countries.

Paragraph (2) of Article 2 forbids discrimination of any sort based on race, color, sex, language, religion, political or other opinion, national or social origin, property, birth or other status. United States and international law permit certain limited discrimination against non-nationals in appropriate cases (*e.g.*, ownership of land or of means of communication). It is understood that this paragraph also permits reasonable distinctions based on citizenship. Paragraph (3) of Article 2 provides that developing countries, with due regard to human rights and their national economy, may determine to what extent they will guarantee the economic rights recognized in the Covenant to non-nationals. Of related significance is Article 25, which provides that nothing in the Covenant is to be interpreted as impairing the "inherent right of all peoples to enjoy and utilize fully and freely their natural wealth and resources." With respect to paragraph (3) of Article 2 and to Article 25, the following declaration is recommended:

"The United States declares that nothing in the Covenant derogates from the equal obligation of all States to fulfill their responsibilities under international law. The United States understands that under the Covenant everyone has the right to own property alone as well as in association with others, and that no one shall be arbitrarily deprived of his property."

This declaration and understanding will make clear the United States position regarding property rights, and expresses the view of the United States that discrimination by developing countries against non-nationals or actions affecting their property or contractual rights may only be carried out in accordance with the governing rules of international law. Under international law, any taking of private property must be nondiscriminatory and for a public purpose, and must be accompanied by prompt, adequate, and effective compensation.

Article 3 provides that the Parties undertake to ensure the equal rights of men and women with respect to the rights set forth in the Covenant. Article 4 permits derogation from the rights enumerated in the Covenant only by law for the general welfare and only insofar as such limitations may be compatible with the nature of the rights.

Paragraph (1) of Article 5 provides that nothing in the Covenant may be interpreted as implying for any State, group or person any right to engage in any activity or to perform any act aimed at the destruction of any of the rights or freedoms recognized in the Covenant, or at their limitation to a greater extent than provided for in the Covenant. This clause raises in indirect fashion the problem of freedom of speech, and accordingly, the following statement is recommended:

"The Constitution of the United States and Article 19 of the International Covenant on Civil and Political Rights contain provisions for the protection of individual rights, including the right to free speech, and nothing in this Covenant shall be deemed to require or to authorize legislation or other action by the United States which would restrict the right of free speech protected by the Constitution, laws, and practice of the United States.". . .

Articles 6 through 9 of the Covenant list certain economic rights, including the right to work (Article 6), to favorable working conditions (Article 7), to organize unions (Article 8), and to social security (Article 9). Some of the standards established under these articles may not readily be translated into legally enforceable rights, while others are in accord with United States policy, but have not yet been fully achieved. It is accordingly important to make clear that these provisions are understood to be goals whose realization will be sought rather than obligations requiring immediate implementation.

Similarly, Articles 10 through 14 detail certain social rights, among them the right to protection of the family, including standards for maternity leave (Article 10), the right of freedom from hunger (Article 11), the right to physical and mental health (Article 12), and the right to education (Articles 13 and 14). Article 15 provides for certain cultural rights, all of which are appropriately protected by United States law and policy. . . .

Articles 26 through 31 are the final clauses. Article 28 states that "The provisions of the present Covenant shall extend to all parts of federal States without any limitations or exceptions." In view of the nature of the United States federal system, this Article is not acceptable as formulated. With respect to Article 28, the following reservation is recommended:

"The United States shall progressively implement all the provisions of the Covenant over whose subject matter the Federal Government exercises legislative and judicial jurisdiction; with respect to the provisions over whose subject matter constituent units exercise jurisdiction, the Federal Government shall take appropriate measures, to the end that the competent authorities of the constituent units may take appropriate measures for the fulfillment of this Covenant."

In addition, it is further recommended that a declaration indicate the non-self-executing nature of Articles 1 through 15 of the Covenant.

QUESTIONS

Is the first paragraph of the above excerpt accurate in stating that the Covenant on Economic, Social and Cultural Rights is "for the most part in accord with United States law and practice"? What about the final sentence of the second paragraph?

Weston, *U.S. Ratification of the International Covenant on Economic, Social and Cultural Rights: With or Without Qualifications*, in U.S. Ratification of the Human Rights Treaties: With or Without Reservations? 27, 30-38 (R. Lillich ed. 1981) (footnotes omitted):

I. *The Two Reservations*

A. *Free Speech*

The first proposed reservation pertains to Article 5(1) of the [Economic, Social and Cultural Rights] covenant, which provides that "[n]othing in the present Covenant may be interpreted as implying for any State, group or person, any right to engage in any activity or to perform any act aimed at the destruction of any of the rights or freedoms recognized herein, or at their limitation to a greater extent than is provided for in the present Covenant." Correctly, the Carter Administration has perceived a potential conflict with the First Amendment free-speech guarantees of our Constitution. Accordingly, because a treaty cannot be ratified by the Senate if it conflicts with the Constitution, the administration has recommended the following reservation: "[T]hat nothing in this Covenant shall be deemed to require or to authorize legislation or other action by the United States which would restrict the right of free speech protected by the Constitution, laws, and practice of the United States." The trouble with this reservation is that, while appropriate in referring to the Constitution, it goes too far in referring also to the "laws and practice of the United States."

In the first place, this additional reference is unnecessary. Free speech laws and practices in the U.S. are constitutionally protected; therefore, they would be protected by a reservation limited in reference to the U.S. Constitution only. Secondly, as our colleague David Weissbrodt from the University of Minnesota has recently pointed out, this additional reference could be used perversely to authorize U.S. "laws and practice" that would be *less* protective of free speech than Article 19 of the International Covenant on Civil and Political Rights. Because Article 19 could be interpreted to prohibit "laws and practice" that heretofore have been sanctioned by our Supreme Court — for example, authorization of police surveillance of peaceful demonstrations — the proposed reservation actually may offer less free-speech protection than is afforded by the covenants. Accordingly, the reservation could be used to prevent any treaty-based improvement in U.S. laws and practice.

In sum, insofar as the free speech reservation refers to "laws and practice of the United States," it is superfluous and probably very shortsighted. Furthermore, because it signals to the world that we will abide by the covenant so long as such adherence does not require any improvement in our own free speech practices, it encourages other countries to make similar status quo reservations—reservations that, in turn, would seriously jeopardize the protection of free speech as envisioned in the Civil and Political Covenant. Therefore, the proposed reservation should be revised so as to exclude reference to the "laws and practice of the United States."

B. *States' Rights*

The second reservation pertains to Article 28 of the ECOSOC covenant, which stipulates that "the provisions of the present Covenant shall extend to all parts of federal States without any limitation or exceptions." According to the Carter Administration, which seems to fear some violation of states' rights or some inconsistency with our federal system, this provision requires the following reservation:

> The United States shall progressively implement all the provisions of the Covenant over whose subject matter the Federal Government exercises legislative and judicial jurisdiction; with respect to the provisions over whose subject matter constituent units exercise jurisdiction, the Federal Government shall take appropriate measures, to the end that the competent authorities of the constituent units may take appropriate measures for the fulfillment of this Covenant.

In short, the Carter Administration would limit the impact of the covenant on state governments within the U.S.

In thus proceeding, however, the Carter Administration has forgotten our constitutional history and consequently has reopened old wounds. In a phrase, this proposed states' rights reservation constitutes a legal/historical anachronism. In addition to the fact that the U.S. Supreme Court has unequivocally upheld the power of the federal government to make treaties in respect of matters that otherwise would be the sole prerogative of the separate states, the recent trend of constitutional decision, at least since the early 1950s, has been to resolve virtually all states' rights doubts in favor of federal power — via the commerce clause and via the thirteenth, fourteenth, and fifteenth amendments. Moreover, there is absolutely no question that the U.S. government has the authority to enter into human rights treaties per se.

But the real objection to the proposed states' rights reservation is that it could be not just a silly anachronism but a *costly* one, both domestically and internationally. Domestically, there is the possibility that it would refuel politically retrogressive (perhaps even racist) divisions that, in turn, could call into question even the limited international human rights commitments that have so far been made by the U.S. And internationally, because the reservation is so explicitly contrary to the language and intent of Article 28, it could vitiate the covenant in major part . . . .

As I see it, then, the proposed states' rights reservation should be ruled out entirely. So also should any equivalent alternatives, since the matter of federalism, especially in the human rights field, is best left up to our courts on a case-by-case basis.

II. *The Three [Understandings]*

A. *Progressive Implementation*

In contrast to the Civil and Political Covenant, which speaks in less futuristic terms, Article 2(1) of the [Economic, Social and Cultural Rights] covenant provides that "[e]ach State Party ... undertakes to take steps, individually and [collectively] ... with a view to achieving progressively the full realization of the rights recognized" by the covenant. The Carter Administration's stipulated understanding of this provision is that Articles 1 through 15 of the covenant "describe goals to be achieved progressively rather than through immediate implementation." In the end, this proposed understanding might prove only redundant, and therefore harmless for being superfluous. However, by adding the language of nonimmediacy — *i.e.*, "rather than through immediate implementation" — it is possible that it could be interpreted to justify unwarranted delays, much too deliberate speed, in taking immediate steps toward the progressive achievement of the goals enumerated. Also, at the very least, it communicates an embarrassing foot-dragging that scarcely is in keeping with a full and constructive commitment to the human rights cause. Accordingly, the understanding should be dropped entirely.

B. *Foreign Aid*

Again with reference to Article 2(1) of the [Economic, Social and Cultural Rights] covenant, the Carter Administration asserts an understanding that the covenant does not require foreign economic aid when it obligates each State Party "to take steps, individually and through international assistance and cooperation . . . to the maximum of its available resources, . . . [and] by all appropriate means" toward the progressive realization of the rights enumerated. Because Article 2(1) does not actually impose a duty to give foreign economic aid, this understanding surel y would instill or reinforce an impression of Scrooge-like churlishness on the part of the U.S. in relation to the meeting of basic human needs, and it provides unfortunate grist for the anti-American propaganda mill. This proposed understanding, too, should be stricken from the record.

C. *Citizenship Discrimination*

The third and final understanding proposed by the Carter Administration relates to Article 2(2) of the [Economic, Social and Cultural Rights] covenant forbidding discrimination in implementation of the covenant on the basis of "race, colour, sex, language, religion, political or other opinion, national or social origin, property, birth or other status." The proposed understanding is that this language "permits reasonable distinctions based on citizenship" — for instance, in ownership of land or of means of communication (two examples expressly mentioned in the Carter transmittal message). Presumably, this proposed understanding is designed to protect domestically based U.S. industries and assets from foreign control. This seems clear. Not so clear, however, is how one should respond to it — bearing in mind that, if retained, it would invite equivalent and probably even more far-reaching understandings from other States Parties to the Covenant. The answer, I believe, must necessarily depend on one's views about the global economic system. If one believes that it is desirable to foster conditions conducive to direct U.S. capital investment abroad, particularly in the developing world where anti-U.S. and anticapitalist sentiment may be strong, then probably the understanding should be discarded — because, as we say, what is sauce for the goose is sauce for the gander. If, on the other hand, one believes that the export of U.S. capitalism is not always or even usually in the best interests of the host countries involved, then probably it should be retained. The decision here is more ideological than legal.

III. *The Two Declarations*

A. *Private Property Rights*

Article 2(3) of the [Economic, Social and Cultural Rights] covenant provides that "[D]eveloping countries, with due regard to human rights and their national economy, may determine to what extent they would guarantee the economic rights recognized in the present Covenant to non-nationals." In addition, Article 25 provides that nothing in the covenant "shall be interpreted as impairing the inherent right of all peoples to enjoy and utilize fully and freely their natural wealth and resources."

In response to these two provisions, the Carter Administration proposes the following combined declaration and understanding: "The United States declares that nothing in the Covenant derogates from the equal obligation of all States to fulfill their responsibilities under international law. The United States understands that under the Covenant everyone has the right to own property alone as well as in association with others, and that no one shall be arbitrarily deprived of his property." In other words the right to own private property, one of the fundamental — and often stridently espoused — tenets of U.S. law and policy, is given special protection.

Of course, there can be no objection to requiring all states to fulfill their responsibilities under international law. However, considering the dangers of ethnocentrism, I have serious misgivings when it comes to insisting that "everyone has the right to own property," particularly in an increasingly ideologically divided world. Also, for similar reasons, I have misgivings about the Department of State's express gloss on the declaration, namely, that "under international law, any taking of private property . . . must be accompanied by prompt, adequate, and effective compensation." My point is that the international law of state responsibility, early fashioned by a Western capital-exporting world and now subject to the pressures of a Third World movement for a "new international economic order," is changing rapidly. It is by no means clear that the Department's views of international law in this realm are today either accurate or justified.

On the other hand, given the exemption extended to the "developing countries" under Article 2(3) of the covenant, some safeguards do seem justified. The ultimate purpose of international legal decision — and so, international human rights decision — is and should be the reconciliation and accommodation of competing points of view and interests. Accordingly, I would revise the Carter Administration's property rights declaration and understanding to read as follows: "The United States declares that nothing in the Covenant derogates from the equal obligation of all States to fulfill their responsibilities under international law relative to foreign private wealth ownership, including the duty to ensure that no one shall be arbitrarily deprived of his property." Such a declaration, I believe, would be judiciously appropriate.

B. *Non-Self-Executing Treaty*

Finally, despite a constitutional supremacy clause tradition that says that treaties, as part of the supreme law of our land, may sometimes be considered applicable by the courts without special implementing legislation, the Carter Administration proposes to declare that "the provisions of Articles 1 through 15 of the...Covenant are not self-executing." More than any other qualifying statement, this one, in my view, does the most harm. In effect, it emasculates the covenant (the more so when it is seen in conjunction with the non-immediate-implementation understanding mentioned earlier). Contrary to the language of the covenant that conveys a clear self-executing intent, in particular as regards the obligation to take steps toward the progressive realization of the rights enumerated, the proposed declaration would require intermediate legislative action to implement the covenant's provisions, and, accordingly, the covenant would have little or no effect beyond that of a lofty policy pronouncement. No one could sue in court to enforce its provisions; no one could use the covenant as a source of genuinely binding law. For these and related reasons, therefore, this declaration should be stricken — assuming, that is, that it is not already too late. By attempting to remove the issue of the self-executing nature of the covenant from the courts, where traditionally this issue ultimately has resided, President Carter may have given away too much too soon and thereby have dealt a severe blow to the human rights movement with which he has become so closely identified.

NOTES

1. Hurst Hannum commented on Weston's views in U.S. Ratification of the Human Rights Treaties: With or Without Reservation? 39-40 (R. Lillich ed. 1981).

2. Other views of interest are those of Louis Henkin in U.S. Ratification of the Human Rights Treaties: With or Without Reservation? 20 (R. Lillich ed. 1981); Clyde Ferguson, *id.*, at 41; Thomas Buergenthal, *id.*, at 47; the general discussion, *id.*, at 68-81; and especially Arthur Rovine and Jack Goldklang, *id.*, at 54 (defending the reservations, understandings, and declarations).

3. As to the acceptability of reservations to multilateral human rights treaties, the International Court of Justice has held that reservations that undermine the object and purpose of a multilateral treaty may vitiate any attempted ratification of the treaty. *Advisory Opinion on Reservations to the Convention on the Prevention of Genocide*, 1951 I.C.J. 16, 24; *see* Vienna Convention on the Law of Treaties, 1155 U.N.T.S. 331, art. 20, *entered into force* Jan. 27, 1980; *Belilos Case*, 132 Eur. Ct. H.R. (ser. A)(1988); Bourguignon, *The Belilos Case: New Light on Reservations to Multilateral Treaties*, 29 Virginia J. Int'l L. 347 (1989).

4. Readers should consult the discussion of reservations in chapter 7, *supra*, and chapter 12, *infra*.

G. U.S. RATIFICATION OF HUMAN RIGHTS TREATIES

Rodley, *On the Necessity of United States Ratification of the International Human Rights Conventions*, in U.S. Ratification of the Human Rights Treaties: With or Without Reservations? 3, 4-13 (R. Lillich ed. 1981):

One of the most important activities of the UN has been the elaboration of the International Bill of Rights consisting of the Universal Declaration of Human Rights, the International Covenant on Economic, Social and Cultural Rights, the International Covenant on Civil and Political Rights, and the Optional Protocol to the latter covenant. The withdrawal in 1953 of the U.S. from the process of drafting these instruments and its continuing aloofness from participating in their operation demonstrate a degree of inconsistency that it is fair to say the U.S. must rectify if it is to maximize its declared commitment in favor of human rights, a commitment that we are assured is being sustained and is "the soul" of American foreign policy. . . .

I. *Disadvantages of Nonparticipation*

One of the disadvantages of nonparticipation in the promotion of human rights through the development of international standards became apparent when the U.S. opted out of the process of negotiating the texts of the international covenants on human rights. But even where the U.S. has participated in the development of such standards, as for example in the conclusion of the Convention on the Elimination of All Forms of Racial Discrimination or, more recently, in the development of international standards (including a convention) against torture, the impact of that participation may well have been weakened by the possible perception on the part of representatives of other states that for the U.S. such activity is, in terms of future legal obligations, more academic than real.

Similarly, U.S. credibility is at stake in efforts to develop mechanisms to monitor compliance at the international level. The U.S. has taken strong and positive positions on the strengthening of the existing UN mechanisms providing for thorough studies or investigations of situations appearing to reveal consistent patterns of gross and reliably attested violations of human rights pursuant to Economic and Social Council Resolution 1503 (XLVIII). It has similarly sought to promote the establishment within the UN of a High Commissioner for Human

Rights. Both of these efforts are designed to advance UN involvement in the protection of human rights by developing fact-finding techniques that would function on an objective basis. The development of such mechanisms would inhibit manipulation according to the preferences of fluctuating government majorities. Indeed, no delegation at the UN has been more vocal in the last few years than that of the U.S. in denouncing the apparent double standard with which the UN assesses various allegations of violations of human rights. Yet it is precisely the mechanisms established under the various international human rights instruments that are designed to institutionalize a more objective, consistent, and depoliticized approach to assessing such allegations. By standing aloof from participation in such UN human rights mechanisms, the credibility of the U.S. position is impaired when it eloquently complains about alleged double standards in actual UN investigations.

What is also damaging about the failure of the U.S. government to integrate itself into the standard-setting and compliance-assessment systems provided by the international instruments is that the U.S. opens itself to the charge that, despite concern for the protection of human rights in other countries, it is not willing to enter into an international obligation to protect human rights at home. You may not consider it a particularly fair argument or even a particularly cogent one, but as far as arguments go in the field of international politics it is an extremely telling one. Every time representatives of other countries introduce that argument in the UN or other international forums — and they often do so — they "score," and they would not continue this practice if they did not think they were scoring.

Of course, the damaging effect of noninvolvement in the international treaty protection systems is not just evident at the multilateral level; it also must inevitably limit the amount of influence the U.S. government can bring to bear bilaterally. This would be particularly true in the case of governments with which the U.S. does not already have a tradition of influence, especially of governments that have themselves ratified the instruments. When the Soviet Union, which has ratified, accuses the U.S. of exercising a double standard as a result of its nonratification, it is simply not a sufficient answer for the U.S. to retort that it only undertakes obligations that it intends to meet. For nonratification indicates either inability or unwillingness to comply with the obligation.

Indeed, the double-standard charge against the U.S. takes on particular significance in the context of some of the interesting legislation that has over the past few years been adopted by the Congress whereby U.S. aid policy is made subject to the taking into account of and compliance with "internationally recognized human rights." There are a number of places one might go to look for internationally recognized human rights, but the International Bill of Rights, and not just the Declaration, would certainly be one such place. It can hardly enhance the integrity of the U.S. posture when it is prepared to incorporate into its own legislation standards for application against others that it is not prepared to apply juridically to itself . . . .

II. *The Advantages of Participation*

So far, I have concentrated on the disadvantages that flow from the U.S.'s nonratification of the major international human rights conventions. I shall now turn to the advantages that I see would flow from its ratification of the same conventions. Perhaps it goes without saying that the principal advantage would be avoidance of the disadvantages that I have already described. The major reproaches of inconsistency, hypocrisy, and the exercise of a double standard would lose their force. . . .

More particularly, the U.S. may feel it has something to contribute to the work of the [Human Rights] Committee. It could not have a governmental delegate on the Committee; that, indeed, is the Committee's strength. However, it would be one of the electors of the Committee, and it could nominate an expert who might be able to bring something of the rich tradition of American jurisprudence and legal creativity to bear upon the work of the Committee.

Meanwhile, there would be far greater opportunities for U.S. participation in the appropriate forums of the UN in discussion of the annual reports of the Human Rights Committee. At the moment, any such participation by the U.S., or any other country that has not become a party to the covenant, is hardly likely to carry much weight, and when all is said and done it may well be that the long-term efficacy of the Committee will depend on how the General Assembly, to which the Committee reports through ECOSOC, will react to the work of the Committee.

I do not hesitate to deal with what some would perceive to be the disadvantages of the U.S. being subjected to criticism by others in an international forum. This should indeed be listed amongst the manifest advantages of the U.S. being a party to the covenants and subject to the substantive and procedural obligations of those instruments. In my view, it is good for any and every country to be subjected to criticism. It is healthy and constructive, and this is so even if the criticism itself is not. For, in the final analysis, a forum for rational discussion of criticism, well- or ill-founded, is precisely the value that is afforded by the work of the Human Rights Committee. As I indicated earlier, there are no doubt areas of human rights where the U.S. would think it had reason to be fairly satisfied with its performance. I think there are other areas where that may not so easily be the case, and obviously here I have in mind to some extent the field of economic, social, and cultural rights. Of course, the examination of reports on these subjects under the appropriate covenant is subject to a different procedure. I am also mindful that, in various areas of civil and political rights, the history of the U.S., as of other countries, does not demonstrate continuous and uniform commitment to certain very fundamental civil and political rights. President Carter has recently acknowledged that "the struggle for full human rights for all Americans — black, brown and white, male and female, rich and poor — is far from over." Not only is there further to go, it is necessary to build safeguards against retrogression. Systematic international scrutiny is one such safeguard. . . .

It may also be cause for some satisfaction that what the U.S. does or does not do is frequently influential on the behavior of other countries. In the final analysis there can surely be no more desirable way to influence the behavior of others than by the example of one's own behavior. This is not mere rhetoric. I can assure you that in at least one Third World country it has been a matter of deep disappointment to those who are seeking to persuade their government of the importance of ratifying the covenants that the U.S. has itself not done so. It has been a partial answer that an administration of the U.S. has at least declared an intention to secure ratification. A complete answer would have been better. . . .

* * *

HUMAN RIGHTS TREATIES RATIFIED BY THE UNITED STATES

The U.S. generally becomes party to a treaty by ratification (when it signs a treaty within the time specified by the treaty) or by accession (when it does not). The President commences the ratification process by signing a treaty and submitting it, along with any recommended reservations, understandings, and declarations drafted by the State Department in consultation with the Justice Department and interested other departments or agencies, to the Senate for advice and consent. If two-thirds of the Senate vote to consent, the treaty is returned to the President, who then completes the process by signing the instrument of ratifiction. If the treaty is administered by an organization such as the U.N., the O.A.S., or the I.C.R.C., ratification is complete only when the President deposits the signed ratification instrument with the organization. The accession process is similar but is commenced with the President's transmittal of the treaty to the Senate rather than with signing the treaty.

Because the U.S. almost always has played a signficant role in the drafting of human rights treaties, it generally has signed them. Hence, throughout this chapter, the term "ratification" is used as a shorthand for the various ways by which a government may become a party to a treaty, recognizing that the U.S. will adhere to some treaties through the process of accession rather than ratification. The term "signatory" is not, however, used as a shorthand reference for a country that has become party to a treaty since many countries that sign treaties are not parties and some countries that have not signed may be parties through accession.

International agreements include not only treaties but also executive agreements which differ from treaties in that they may be concluded by the President without the Senate's consent. Agreements may be accorded the same status as treaties for most purposes in international as well as U.S. law, although their status is open to interpretation and generally depends on the extent of the agreements' acceptance. For instance, the London Charter, also called the Nuremberg Charter, is an executive agreement among the four Western allied powers which generally has been accorded the status of a treaty in both U.S. and international law. The Nuremberg Charter is discussed in chapter 13, *infra*.

The U.S. has become a party to a number of treaties protecting human rights: (The number of states parties are generally indicated as of February 1990 or as of the most recent available information.)

(a) U.N. Charter, 59 Stat. 1031, *entered into force including for the U.S.* Oct. 24, 1945 (160 states parties);

(b) Slavery Convention, 46 Stat. 2183, *entered into force* Dec. 7, 1927, *entered into force for the U.S.* Mar. 21, 1929 (68 states parties);

(c) Protocol Amending the Slavery Convention, 182 U.N.T.S. 51, *entered into force* Dec. 7, 1953, *entered into force for the U.S.* Mar. 7, 1956 (86 states parties);

(d) Supplementary Convention on the Abolition of Slavery, the Slave Trade and Institutions and Practices Similar to Slavery, 226 U.N.T.S. 3, *entered into force* April 30, 1957, *entered into force for the U.S.* Dec. 6, 1967 (104 states parties);

(e) Convention on the Political Rights of Women, 193 U.N.T.S. 135, *entered into force* July 7, 1954, *entered into force for the U.S.* July 7, 1976 (96 states parties);

(f) Protocol Relating to the Status of Refugees, 606 U.N.T.S. 267, *entered into force* Oct. 4, 1967, *entered into force for the U.S.* Nov. 1, 1968 (103 states parties);

(g) Convention on the Prevention and Punishment of the Crime of Genocide, 78 U.N.T.S. 277, *entered into force* Jan. 12, 1951, *entered into force for the U.S.* Feb. 23, 1989 (102 states parties);

(h) Four Geneva Conventions for the Protection of Victims of Armed Conflict, 75 U.N.T.S. 31, 85, 135, 287, *entered into force* Oct. 21, 1950, *entered into force for the U.S.* Feb. 2, 1956 (166 states parties);

(i) O.A.S. Charter, 119 U.N.T.S. 3, *entered into force including for the U.S.* Dec. 13, 1951, *amended* 721 U.N.T.S. 324, *entered into force including for the U.S.* Feb. 27, 1970 (33 states parties);

(j) Inter-American Convention on the Granting of Political Rights to Women, 27 U.S.T. 3301, *entered into force* Apr. 22, 1949, *entered into force for the U.S.* May 24, 1976 (21 states parties).

The U.S. has signed ten other human rights treaties, but has not yet become a party to them:

(a) International Covenant on Economic, Social and Cultural Rights, G.A. res. 2200A (XXI), 21 U.N. GAOR Supp. (No. 16) at 49, U.N. Doc. A/6316 (1966), *entered into force* Jan. 3, 1976 (93 states parties);

(b) International Covenant on Civil and Political Rights, G.A. res. 2200A (XXI), 21 U.N. GAOR Supp. (No. 16) at 52, U.N. Doc. A/6316 (1966), *entered into force* Mar. 23, 1976 (88 states parties);

(c) International Convention on the Elimination of All Forms of Racial Discrimination, 660 U.N.T.S. 195, *entered into force* Jan. 4, 1969 (133 states parties);

(d) Convention on the Elimination of All Forms of Discrimination Against Women, G.A. res. 34/180, 34 U.N. GAOR Supp. (No. 46) at 193, U.N. Doc. A/RES/34/180, *entered into force* Sept. 3, 1981 (100 states parties);

(e) Convention Against Torture and Other Cruel, Inhuman and Degrading Treatment or Punishment, G.A. res. 39/46, 39 U.N. GAOR Supp. (No. 51) at 197, U.N. Doc. A/39/51 (1984), *entered into force* June 26, 1987 (51 states parties);

(f) Convention on the Consent to Marriage, Minimum Age for Marriage and Registration of Marriages, 521 U.N.T.S. 231, *entered into force* Dec. 9, 1964 (35 states parties);

(g) Convention on the Abolition of Forced Labour (ILO No. 105), 320

U.N.T.S. 291, *entered into force* Jan. 17, 1959 (111 states parties);
(h) American Convention on Human Rights, O.A.S. Off. Rec. OEA/Ser.L/V/II.23, doc. 21, rev. 6 (1979), *entered into force* July 18, 1978 (21 states parties);
(i) Additional Protocols I and II to the Geneva Conventions of 1949, 16 I.L.M. 1391, 1442 (1977), *entered into force* Dec. 7, 1978 (Protocol I — 92 states parties, Protocol II — 82 states parties).

There are 21 additional human rights treaties, identified in an authoritative U.N. collection of human rights instruments, which the U.S. has neither signed nor ratified. U.N., A Compilation of International Instruments, U.N. Doc. ST/HR/1/Rev.3 (1988). Of the 169 International Labour Conventions, the U.S. has ratified only 10. Chart of Ratications of International Labour Conventions, Jan. 1, 1990 (updated).

NOTES

1. For arguments in favor and against U.S. ratification, see Alston, *U.S. Ratification of the Covenant on Economic, Social and Cultural Rights: The Need for an Entirely New Strategy*, 84 Am. J. Int'l L. 365 (1990); Kaufman & Whiteman, *Opposition to Human Rights Treaties in the United States Senate: The Legacy of the Bricker Amendment*, 10 Hum. Rts. Q. 309, 321-37 (1988);
Weissbrodt, *United States Ratification of the Human Rights Covenants*, 63 Minn. L. Rev. 35 (1978).

2. The Convention on the Prevention and Punishment of the Crime of Genocide was adopted unanimously by the U.N. General Assembly on December 9, 1948, and was signed by President Truman on December 11, 1948. The Genocide treaty was transmitted to the Senate in 1949. The Senate Foreign Relations Committee reported favorably to the Senate in 1970, 1971, 1973, and 1976. As of the end of July 1988, there were 98 states parties to the Genocide Convention — not including the U.S. It was not until 1986, however, that the U.S. Senate adopted a resolution giving its advice and consent to ratification of the Convention. 132 Cong. Rec. S1377 (daily ed. Feb. 19, 1986). Ratification was qualified by two reservations, five understandings, and one declaration. One reservation requires specific consent to submitting a dispute about the treaty to the International Court of Justice. The Senate also asserted a reservation indicating the supremacy of the U.S. Constitution over any treaty obligation. The five understandings limited the meaning of several provisions. The Senate declared that implementing legislation would be required before the administration would deposit the formal ratification of the treaty. The implementing legislation was finally adopted in 1988. Genocide Convention Implementation Act of 1987, P.L. 100-606; 102 Stat. 3045 (Nov. 5, 1988).

The U.S. deposited its notice of ratification with the U.N. on November 25, 1988. Nine European nations have objected to the U.S. reservation which indicated the supremacy of the U.S. Constitution over the treaty. *See also* Leblanc, *The Intent to Destroy Groups in the Genocide Convention: the Proposed U.S. Understanding*, 78 Am. J. Int'l L. 369, 369-70 (1984); Leblanc *The ICJ, the Genocide Convention, and the United States*, Wisc. I.L.J. 43, 43-45 (1987); R. Lillich ed., International Human Rights Instruments 130.1- .16 (1986); Comment, *International Convention on the Prevention and Punishment of the Crime of Genocide: United States Senate Grant of Advice and Consent to Ratification*, 1 Harv. Hum. Rts. Y.B. 227 (1988).

3. On December 10, 1984, the U.N. General Assembly adopted the Convention against Torture and Other Cruel, Inhuman or Degrading Treatment or Punishment (Treaty against Torture). As of February 1990, 51 governments have become parties to the Treaty against Torture, including all the members of the U.N. Security Council except the U.S. The Treaty against Torture came into force on June 26, 1987. Status of the Convention against Torture and Other Cruel, Inhuman or Degrading Treatment or Punishment. . . , U.N. Doc. CAT/C/Add.1 (1989).

On April 18, 1988, the U.S. signed the Treaty against Torture. On May 20, 1988, President Reagan submitted the Convention for the advice and consent of the Senate as to ratification. He attached to his submission a letter from Secretary of State Shultz suggesting a number of reservations, understandings, and declarations that might be attached to the treaty at the time of ratification. Letter from Secretary of State George Shultz to President Reagan (May 10, 1988), Message from the President of the United States transmitting the Convention against Torture and Other Cruel, Inhuman or Degrading Treatment or Punishment, 100th Cong., 2nd Sess. (1988).

The Shultz letter proposed 3 reservations, 8 understandings, and 4 declarations. The overall aim evidently was to assure that the Convention would have little or no impact in the U.S., because U.S. law is regularly asserted as the source of reservations or interpretations of the treaty.

For example, the Shultz letter proposed that the treaty would not be self-executing, that is, it would have no effect in U.S. courts in the absence of separate legislation. The letter proposed a limitation upon the impact of the treaty on state governments, as distinguished from the federal government.

The letter proposed several understandings to limit the meaning of "torture" under the treaty: In order to constitute torture, an act must be a deliberate and calculated act of an extremely cruel and inhuman nature, specifically intended to inflict excruciating and agonizing physical or mental pain or suffering. Torture could only be committed against persons in the offender's custody or physical control. The U.S. understood that it could still impose "sanctions" including enforcement actions authorized by U.S. law or by judicial interpretation of such law. Torture could only be the subject of acquiescence if the public official, prior to the activity constituting torture, had knowledge of such activity and thereafter breached a legal responsibility to intervene to prevent such activity. Further, noncompliance with applicable legal procedural standards would not *per se* constitute torture.

The letter proposed an understanding that would permit the use of such common law defenses as self-defense or sovereign immunity against a charge of torture, even though the treaty would admit of no defense.

The letter proposed a reservation as to the treaty requirement of extraditing torturers, "insofar as it conflicts with the obligations of the United States toward States not party to the Convention under bilateral extradition treaties with such States." The Shultz letter also stated the view that the Treaty against Torture was not a sufficient basis for extradition in the absence of a separate treaty.

The letter proposed a severe limitation on the treaty's prohibition against "cruel, inhuman or degrading treatment or punishment," restricting that prohibition to treatment already proscribed by the U.S. Constitution.

The letter recommended that the U.S. not accept the competence of the Committee against Torture for complaints initiated by one state against another state, individual complaints, or for *sua sponte* visits. The State Department proposed a reservation, pursuant to Article 30(1), that it will decide on a case-by-case basis whether to refer a dispute under the treaty between two governments to the International Court of Justice.

In addition, the Shultz letter proposed a few other limitations. None of the reservations, understandings, or declarations proposed in the Shultz letter were required by the U.S. Constitution. In 1989 the Bush administration made it clear that the Treaty against Torture had the highest priority for ratification of any human rights treaty. The Civil and Political Covenant and the Covenant on Economic, Social and Cultural Rights were not accorded any priority, but remained under consideration by the State Department. In December 1989 the Bush administration withdrew several of the Reagan/ Shultz proposed reservations, understandings, and declarations, but proposed its own package of 3 reservations, 8 understandings, and 2 declarations.

The Bush administration proposed a new reservation limiting the treaty's prohibition against "cruel, inhuman or degrading treatment or punishment" to the narrower protections afforded by the Fifth, Eighth, and/or Fourteenth Amendments to the U.S. Constitution; and reasserted the Shultz reservations on the application of the treaty to state governments and on the use of the Intenational Court of Justice to resolve disputes under the treaty.

The Bush package withdraws the proposed reservation as to U.S. participation in the Committee against Torture in regard to State v. State complaints, but does not suggest that the U.S. would permit individual complaints to the Committee.

The Bush administration withdrew some of the most intrusive restrictions on the meaning of torture in the Shultz package and proposed several of its own understandings on the meaning of torture. Other Bush understandings were maintained from the Shultz letter.

The Bush package also kept the Shultz proposal that the treaty not be considered self-executing. Just prior to hearings on the Treaty against Torture in the Senate Foreign Relations Committee on January 30, 1990, the Bush administration proposed another declaration stating that the treaty would not restrict U.S. use of the death penalty.

Senator Helms has also proposed a reservation similar to the reservation he attached to the Genocide Convention, stating:

> Nothing in the Convention requires or authorizes legislation or other action by the United States of America prohibited by the Constitution of the United States, as interpreted by the United States.

The State Department has opposed this proposed reservation because it might lead other governments to make similar reservations inappropriately indicating that national law should be invoked as a justification for failure to perform a treaty.

H. THE RECOGNITION OF NEW RIGHTS

Marks, *Emerging Human Rights: A New Generation for the 1980s?*, 33 Rutgers L. Rev. 435 (1981) (footnotes omitted):

[Ed.: The author outlines three generations of human rights. The first generation of civil and political rights derives from the 18th century. The second generation of economic, social, and cultural rights came into prominence at the end of the 19th century and the beginning of the 20th century. The author then advocates:]

... A NEW GENERATION OF HUMAN RIGHTS ...

The distinguishing characteristics of the new generation of human rights have been expressed by the person who in fact forged the notion of a "third generation of human rights," Karel Vasak. In his inaugural lecture ... in July 1979, he said that the new human rights of the third generation

> are new in the aspirations they express, are new from the point of view of human rights in that they seek to infuse the human dimension into areas where it has all too often been missing, having been left to the State, or States.... [T]hey are new in that they may both be *invoked against* the State and *demanded* of it; but above all (and herein lies their essential characteristic) they can be realized only through the concerted efforts of all the actors on the social scene: the individual, the State, public and private bodies and the international community.

Vasak has further distinguished the three generations of human rights as corresponding successively to each of the elements of the motto of the French revolution: *liberté, egalité, fraternité*. The third generation is the generation of human rights predicated on brotherhood (*fraternité*), in the sense of solidarity. Vasak has, in fact, called these rights "solidarity rights" or "rights of solidarity.". . .

Six areas are currently under consideration: environment, development, peace, the common heritage, communication, and humanitarian assistance.

The case of *environment* is perhaps the most "classical" case of a set of claims which have been given a holistic formulation in terms of human rights. All the features of a right of the new generation are there: elaboration of a specialized body of law, an easily identifiable international legislative process, incorporation of the right as a human right within municipal legal systems, and need for concerted efforts of all social actors. . . .

At the international level the first formulation in human rights terms was in the Stockholm Declaration, adopted by the U.N. Conference on the Environment in 1972. Principle I of the Declaration reads as follows: "Man has the fundamental right to freedom, equality and adequate conditions of life, in an environment of a quality that permits a life of dignity and well-being, and he bears a solemn responsibility to protect and improve the environment for present and future generations.". . . In 1972 the Consultative Assembly of the Council of Europe adopted a recommendation proposing to study whether or not the right to a decent environment should be raised to the status of a human right to be recognized in an appropriate legal instrument, and the second conference of ministers of the environment made a similar recommendation the following year, endorsed by the Assembly. In the meantime the government of the Federal Republic of Germany proposed that the right to a healthy and balanced environment be incorporated into an additional protocol to the European Convention on Human Rights. That a protocol or other instrument has not been adopted does not mean that this right has been rejected. On the contrary, the constitutions of numerous nations and states . . . have already affirmed it expressly. Other less explicit formulations exist . . . and other constitutions . . . stipulate that the government shall protect the environment. These examples and the conclusions of numerous scientific or non-governmental meetings on the subject justify including this right among the new generation of human rights emerging in the 1980s.

Like other solidarity rights, this one has both an individual and a collective dimension. The individual right is the right of any victim or potential victim of an environmentally damaging activity to obtain the cessation of the activity and reparation for the damage suffered. The collective dimension implies the duty of the state to contribute through international cooperation to resolving environmental problems at a global level. As with all solidarity rights, the collective aspect means, in the last analysis, that the state and all other appropriate social actors have the duty to place the human interest before the national or individual interest.

The right to *development* as a human right has been the subject of extensive reflection and proposed formulations for nearly a decade and is well advanced in acquiring the status of an internationally recognized human right. . . .

. . .SOME OBJECTIONS AND A TENTATIVE CONCLUSION

Much hostility has been voiced against the idea of a new generation of human rights. Not only is proliferation of rights considered to be dangerous, but also the use of the term "generation" implies, the detractors say, that the rights belonging to earlier generations are outdated. It is also frequently said that the rights of the new generation are too vague to be justiciable and are no more than slogans, at best useful for advancing laudable goals of the U.N., at worst useful for the propaganda of certain countries.

Indeed, it would weaken the idea of human rights in general if numerous claims or values were indiscriminately proclaimed as human rights. It is also true that the essential normative task in the field of human rights was accomplished during the first three decades after the founding of the U.N., and that the more urgent task now is implementation. Nevertheless, I have tried to stress the dynamic nature of the process by which these rights are recognized and the consequent emergence of new human rights. . . .

. . . [T]he human rights specialist is, to a certain extent, faced with the choice of resisting the rights which, whether he likes it or not, are emerging, or understanding and contributing to the process by which a limited number of new rights will succeed in attaining international recognition because (a) the need for them is sufficiently great and (b) the international community is ready to recognize them as human rights. He should seek to apply rigorous standards to the definition of new rights, and in particular, . . . see that they have a clearly defined object and an identifiable subject and can be reasonably expected to be enforced. Many human rights already recognized for several decades fall short of these standards. The proclamation of these rights nevertheless increased the likelihood that they would be translated into law and practice. As long as emerging rights are not so unrealistic or trivial as to be treated with mockery, their recognition does serve the advancement of the cause of human rights without endangering the rights of earlier generations.

NOTES AND QUESTIONS

1. Is the concept of generations of rights useful? Some commentators are critical of the concept. Using "generation" to refer to different categories of rights, they say, might mislead people into thinking that the new generation of rights gradually will replace the old. Nor is the concept historically correct. Civil and political rights and economic, social, and cultural rights were often developed together, rather than one set neatly following the other as the generational concept may suggest. *See* Alston, *A Third Generation of Solidarity Rights: Progressive Development or Obfuscation of International Human Rights Law?*, 29 Neth. Int'l L. Rev. 367 (1982).

Professor Alston has expressed concern that proliferation of new rights urged by Marks and other commentators might undermine the normative force of labeling a concept a right. He bases his concern on the recent lack of deliberation or meaningful consultation with governments and intergovernmental bodies before proclaiming new rights. He acknowledges the need for a dynamic approach to new rights in response to changing views. But he proposes guidelines for international organizations to follow when proclaiming new rights, so as to protect the legitimacy of those proclaimed.

Alston's proposal, in general terms, calls for the preparation of studies on the content of proposed new rights and their relation to existing rights, solicitation of comments from governments and concerned intergovernmental and nongovernmental organizations, revision of the studies on the proposed rights (reflecting comments received), appointment of a committee to report on proposals, and finally proclamation by the appropriate body. *See* Alston, *Conjuring Up New Human Rights: A Proposal for Quality Control*, 78 Am. J. Int'l L. 607 (1984).

The U.N. General Assembly has adopted a resolution that provides guidelines for governments and U.N. bodies when they articulate new rights. Proposed new human rights instruments should:

(a)   Be consistent with the existing body of international human rights law;

(b)   Be of fundamental character and derive from the inherent dignity and worth of the human person;

(c)   Be sufficiently precise to give rise to identifiable and practicable rights and obligations;

(d)   Provide, where appropriate, realistic and effective implementation machinery, including reporting systems;

(e)   Attract broad international support.

G.A. res. 41/120, 41 U.N. GAOR Supp. (No. 53) at 178, U.N. Doc. A/41/53 (1987).

2.   Another method of dealing with proliferation of new rights is to establish a hierarchy. Some rights would be deemed "fundamental" or "peremptory," and governments could not violate them. The hierarchical concept is founded in part on the existence of certain nonderogable rights in human rights instruments which governments cannot restrict, even in emergencies. Another basis for a hierarchical concept is the principle of *jus cogens* (peremptory norms) in international law. Under customary international law as codified in Article 53 of the Vienna Convention on the Law of Treaties, agreements that conflict with those peremptory norms are void.

For discussion of the hierarchical concept, including an examination of possible legal bases, see Meron, *On a Hierarchy of International Human Rights*, 80 Am. J. Int'l L. 1 (1986).

Do you find the hierarchical concept useful? Can you foresee problems with implementing the concept?

3.   Some commentators have criticized international organizations for expending limited time and resources proclaiming new rights while many existing rights remain vague. The actions governments must take in order to fulfill many rights discussed in this chapter (rights to food and health, for example) are just beginning to be defined. *See, e.g.,* K. Tomasevski, The Right to Food (1987). Many new rights discussed by Marks are even broader and less-well defined. *See, e.g.,* Interrelationship between human rights and international peace, U.N. Doc. E/CN.4/Sub.2/1988/2 (1988); *Agora: What Obligation Does Our Generation Owe to the Next? An Approach to Global Environmental Responsibility*, 84 Am. J. Int'l L. 190 (1990) (articles by

D'Amato, Weiss, Gundling); W. Gormley, Human Rights and Environment: The Need for International Cooperation (1976). The right to peace is discussed briefly in chapter 13 of this book.

Yet at least one of the new rights — the right to development — has served as a potent symbol in inspiring some governments to improve the human rights of their citizens. Though contours of the right to development are vague, it encompasses many of the economic, social, and cultural rights discussed in this chapter that themselves are ill-defined. *See* Alston, *Making Space for New Human Rights: The Case of the Right to Development*, 1 Harv. Hum. Rts. Y.B. 3 (1988); The regional and national dimensions of the right to development as a human right, U.N. Doc. E/CN.4/1488 (1981); The international dimensions of the right to development..., U.N. Doc. E/CN.4/1334 (1979).

Do you think a declaration on the right to development might be helpful?

Below are selected paragraphs from the Declaration on the Right to Development, adopted by the U.N. General Assembly. G.A. res. 41/128, 41 U.N. GAOR Supp. (No. 53) at 186, U.N. Doc. A/41/53 (1986):

Article 1

1. The right to development is an inalienable human right by virtue of which every human person and all peoples are entitled to participate in, contribute to and enjoy economic, social, cultural and political development, in which all human rights and fundamental freedoms can be fully realized....

Article 2

1. The human person is the central subject of development and should be the active participant and beneficiary of the right to development.

2. All human beings have a responsibility for development, individually and collectively, taking into account the need for full respect of their human rights and fundamental freedoms as well as their duties to the community, which alone can ensure the free and complete fulfilment of the human being, and they should therefore promote and protect an appropriate political, social and economic order for development.

3. States have the right and the duty to formulate appropriate national development policies that aim at the constant improvement of the well-being of the entire population and of all individuals, on the basis of their active, free and meaningful participation in development and in the fair distribution of the benefits resulting therefrom.

Article 3

1. States have the primary responsibility for the creation of national and international conditions favourable to the realization of the right to development.

2. The realization of the right to development requires full respect for the principles of international law concerning friendly relations and co-operation among

States in accordance with the Charter of the United Nations.

3. States have the duty to co-operate with each other in ensuring development and eliminating obstacles to development. States should fulfil their rights and duties in such a manner as to promote a new international economic order based on sovereign equality, interdependence, mutual interest and co-operation among all States, as well as to encourage the observance and realization of human rights.

Article 4

1. States have the duty to take steps, individually and collectively, to formulate international development policies with a view to facilitating the full realization of the right to development.

2. Sustained action is required to promote more rapid development of developing countries. As a complement to the efforts of developing countries effective international co-operation is essential in providing these countries with appropriate means and facilities to foster their comprehensive development. . . .

Article 6

1. All States should co-operate with a view to promoting, encouraging and strengthening universal respect for and observance of all human rights and fundamental freedoms for all without any distinction as to race, sex, language and religion.

2. All human rights and fundamental freedoms are indivisible and interdependent; equal attention and urgent consideration should be given to the implementation, promotion and protection of civil, political, economic, social and cultural rights.

3. States should take steps to eliminate obstacles to development resulting from failure to observe civil and political rights as well as economic, social and cultural rights. . . .

Article 8

1. States should undertake, at the national level, all necessary measures for the realization of the right to development and shall ensure, *inter alia*, equality of opportunity for all in their access to basic resources, education, health services, food, housing, employment and the fair distribution of income. Effective measures should be undertaken to ensure that women have an active role in the development process. Appropriate economic and social reforms should be made with a view to eradicating all social injustices.

2. States should encourage popular participation in all spheres as an important factor in development and in the full realization of all human rights.

Article 9

1. All the aspects of the right to development set forth in this Declaration are indivisible and interdependent and each of them should be considered in the context of the whole. . . .

Article 10

Steps should be taken to ensure the full exercise and progressive enhancement of the right to development, including the formulation, adoption and implementation of policy, legislative and other measures at the national and international levels.

X *THE HELSINKI HUMAN RIGHTS PROCESS: WHO BENEFIT?*

A. INTRODUCTION

The face of Europe changed in 1989 and 1990. Since the end of World War II, the continent had been divided between East and West, Warsaw Pact and NATO,[1] COMECON[2] and other economic/political groupings including the European Community and the European Free Trade Association, and between governments which had ratified the European Convention on Human Rights and those which had not. The division of Europe was symbolized by the wall which divided the city of Berlin. In 1989 the Berlin

---

[1] The North Atlantic Treaty Organization is the military and political alliance of Western Europe, Canada, and the United States.

[2] The Council for Mutual Economic Assistance, known as COMECON, is an economic alliance of Eastern European governments. For ease of reference "Eastern European governments" is used here to include the U.S.S.R., although much of the Soviet Union lies in Asia.

Wall fell; the governments of Bulgaria, Czechoslovakia, the German Democratic Republic, Hungary, Poland, and Romania followed the lead of the U.S.S.R. in permitting themselves to be substantially restructured with a new orientation toward democracy and human rights. This chapter poses the question: Should the Eastern European governments rely for their human rights norms and procedures upon the process which began at Helsinki, Finland, in 1975 with the Final Act of the Conference on Security and Cooperation in Europe, or should they join the Council of Europe, based in Strasbourg, France, so that they can ratify the European Convention on Human Rights? When should activists seeking to promote human rights protections in Europe use the Helsinki procedures and when the procedures of the Council of Europe? In other words, the chapter asks the question: Whither Europe: Helsinki or Strasbourg?

Most of the previous chapters have discussed U.N. human rights instruments and procedures. This chapter deals with two overlapping regional human rights systems centered in Europe. The Conference on Security and Cooperation in Europe involves 35 nations from Turkey and the U.S.S.R. on the East to Canada and the United States on the West. The European Convention on Human Rights applies to all 23 member states of the Council of Europe. Which of these contexts afford a stronger basis for European efforts to protect human rights? For U.S. readers the chapter also raises the question: To what extent can or should the U.S. be involved in the future of human rights processes centered in Europe?

Since the situation in Europe is evolving quite rapidly, it is likely that this chapter will, more than other chapters, need to be supplemented by current material.

B. QUESTIONS

This chapter provides another opportunity for a roleplaying exercise. The group will act as an advisory committee assembled by the Secretary of State to consider U.S. policy in regard to the future of human rights processes centered in Europe. One or more participants in the discussion might be asked to advocate that the U.S. withdraw from the Helsinki process and the advisory committee is considering this proposal. Other participants might represent the perspectives of the U.S. Ambassador to the Helsinki Follow-up meetings (who hypothetically wants to continue her work) and such State Department bureaus and officials as the Bureau of International Organization Affairs (supporting reliance on U.N. mechanisms), the Bureau of Human Rights and Humanitarian Affairs (urging whatever approach will assist human rights and democracy in Eastern Europe), the Bureau of European Affairs (supporting reliance on the Strasbourg system), the Bureau of Economic and Business Affairs, the Bureau of Political and Military Affairs, and the Legal Adviser. Others might represent the Commission on Security and Cooperation in Europe and scholars with different views. In preparing for the discussion, consider these questions:

1. Why did the Helsinki Conference on Security and Cooperation in Europe (CSCE) occur? Why did the East participate? Why did the West participate? Are those original intentions relevant to the present situation or to the future of the process?

2. What are the follow-up and implementation procedures of the Final Act? How successful have those procedures been?

3. What differences do you see between the ways the Helsinki and Strasbourg processes have developed or are likely to change in the future?

4. The Strasbourg process relies upon the European Convention on Human Rights as it has been applied and interpreted by the European Commission and Court of Human Rights, together with a few adjustments by way of protocols the states parties may accept. *See* European Convention in accompanying handbook. The Helsinki process has been dominated by large multilateral meetings at which participants make speeches, undertake some bilateral and diplomatic initiatives, and ultimately accept by consensus a series of agreements. Which approach is more conducive to achieving human rights improvements in the short or longer term?

5. What is the legal status of the Helsinki Final Act? What obligations did the signatories assume? Is it significant that the Helsinki Accords do not constitute a treaty, but the European Convention does?

6. Why are the Helsinki Accords far better known in both Eastern Europe and the U.S. than the Covenants or other human rights instruments? How is that popular awareness relevant to the effective implementation of the human rights instruments? Why has the Helsinki process been so important even though the Final Act is not a legally binding treaty?

7. Are the highly structured adjudicative procedures of the Strasbourg system more effective for implementing human rights than the more political and consensus-oriented approach of the Helsinki process? Is there a difference between the usefulness of those two approaches in Eastern and Western Europe? How well will the two approaches respond to discrimination against minorities, ethnic strife, or other difficulties arising in Hungary, Romania, Yugoslavia, and other countries?

8. What benefit can be achieved from speeches in the Helsinki conference sessions criticizing the human rights performance of other governments? What do you think of the accuracy and adequacy of the statements included in the chapter? How should the U.S. respond, if at all, to Soviet charges of human rights violations in the U.S.? What is the significance of the decision to open to the public at least some of the future meetings in the Helsinki process?

9. Do bilateral diplomatic contacts between governments, parallel to the plenary meetings of the Helsinki process, provide a more useful implementation technique than public criticism?

10. Is case-by-case adjudication — the principal approach of the Strasbourg system — an appropriate technique for pursuing human rights improvements in Eastern Europe?

11. What, if anything, could be done to improve the Helsinki follow-up? Should the Helsinki process develop implementation procedures along the lines of the Strasbourg system? Or the Inter-American system?

12. Is the open-ended and very flexible nature of the Helsinki process better than the relatively rigid Strasbourg system?

13. Is it likely that Eastern European governments could ratify the European Convention on Human Rights in the near future? What changes would be required before ratification?

14. Most of the Eastern European governments are already parties to the Covenant on Civil and Political Rights and the Covenant on Economic, Social and Cultural Rights; but none have accepted the Optional Protocol to the Civil and Political Covenant. Would ratification of the European Convention represent a significant increase in their international obligations?

15. If the Eastern European governments fail to make a declaration under Article 25 of the European Convention to accept individual petitions, is there much left of the European human rights machinery? Is it likely that Council of Europe members will not permit Eastern European governments to become Council members unless they give assurances of ratifying the European Convention and accepting individual petitions?

16. Are the provisions of the Helsinki Accords of 1975 or the Vienna concluding document of 1989 more or less protective of human rights than either the European Convention or the Covenants? In what respects?

17. What relevance do (a) the European Convention, (b) the Helsinki Accords of 1975, or (c) the Vienna document of 1989 have for the implementation and legal effect of the International Bill of Human Rights, including the Universal Declaration of Human Rights and the Covenants? For example, do those three instruments and their interpretation limit the capacity of governments to take advantage of limitations clauses in the International Bill of Human Rights?

18. What is the significance of the reference in Principle VII (Basket I) of the Helsinki Accords to the Covenants?

19. Can any government ratify the European Convention on Human Rights? According to the Convention, how does a government qualify?

20. Should joining the Council of Europe and ratifying the European Convention on Human Rights be seen as necessary steps for Eastern European governments towards ultimately gaining a close association with, if not membership in, the European Community? Hence, are there as many, if not more, economic and political advantages to the Strasbourg approach than to the Helsinki process?

21. What are the advantages or defects of including within the Helsinki process issues such as the environment, confidence building measures, arms control, trade, tourism, etc., as well as economic, social, cultural, civil, and political rights?

22. What advantages or defects are there to the almost exclusive focus of the Strasbourg system on civil and political rights? Would the European Social Charter and related instruments change that focus?

23. Can the Helsinki process be viewed as the means to integrating Eastern Europe eventually into the Council of Europe and other European institutions? In other words, does the road to Brussels (the center of the European Community) start at Helsinki and go through Strasbourg?

24. Would a human rights system in Europe be more protective of human rights if the U.S. did or did not participate?

25. Would human rights in the U.S. be improved if the Helsinki process is continued and becomes the focus of European economic, political, and human rights cooperation?

C. HELSINKI PROCESS

Department of State, Office of Public Affairs, *The Conference on Security and Cooperation in Europe* 1-3 (1986):

The Soviet Union first proposed a conference on security in Europe at the Berlin Foreign Ministers meeting in February 1954. This and subsequent Warsaw Pact proposals during the later 1950s failed to win approval from the United States and its Western European Allies. In the mid-1960s, the Warsaw Pact renewed calls for a European security conference. The relaxation of East-West tensions, the Federal Republic of Germany's *Ostpolitik*, and the Great Powers' 1971 Quadripartite Agreement on Berlin set the stage for NATO participation in a European security conference. . . .

The Conference on Security and Cooperation in Europe (CSCE), July 3, 1973-July 25, 1975

On November 22, 1972, representatives from all the European countries (except Albania), the United States, and Canada gathered at Helsinki for preliminary discussions. Delegations submitted proposals for a conference agenda, literally putting them into baskets. These proposals, which eventually fell into three areas, political (including military security), economic, and cultural-humanitarian (the three "baskets"), were studied by working groups as they developed a provisional agenda.

In June 1973, the delegates, who had organized themselves into major groupings — NATO, Warsaw Pact, and the neutral and nonaligned countries (NNAs) — agreed upon an agenda and submitted it to their governments as a final recommendation for a conference. The first phase of the meeting began the next month; the delegates ratified the agenda and the conference sites, then returned home to prepare for negotiations.

The second, or working, phase of CSCE began in Geneva the following September. For the next 2 years, delegates discussed and drafted the Final Act. The NATO nations agreed they must avoid any implication of legal recognition of the territorial status quo in Eastern Europe. The Soviet Union sought the legitimization of the European territorial and ideological status quo. Soviet negotiating efforts centered on that goal, which was obtained on April 23, 1974, when the 35 states agreed to the principle of inviolability of frontiers.

"Human contacts" remained an item of unfinished business on the agenda. The Soviet Union, long intransigent in this area, was now anxious to conclude the conference. Seeing potential gains, the NATO nations utilized Soviet desire for a summit to bargain for progress on human contacts. By December 1974, the Soviet Union had promised freer movement of people and information, including family reunification. Western officials felt that such progress merited planning for a final summit.

The Helsinki Final Act, August 1, 1975

Negotiations concluded in July 1975. The Final Act was signed on August 1, 1975, by the leaders of 35 nations at a Summit lauded as the largest assemblage of Heads of State and Government since the Congress of Vienna.[3] Also known as the Helsinki Accords, the Final Act is not a treaty, but rather a statement of principles of behavior for states toward their own citizens as well as other states. It includes four baskets. Basket I outlines 10 principles on interstate behavior including sovereign equality, respect for human rights, and refraining from the threat or use of force. While referring to the inviolability of frontiers and the territorial integrity of states, Basket I allows that "frontiers can be changed in accordance with international law, by peaceful means and by agreement." It also includes confidence-building measures to promote European security.

Basket II addresses cooperation in the fields of economics and technology with provisions to improve and expand commercial relations between East and West. Further, Basket II provides for scientific and technical cooperation, including scholarly exchanges. Basket III applies to cooperation in humanitarian fields to promote the freer flow of information, ideas, and people among the participating states. It contains specific measures to foster human contacts and cultural exchanges, including family reunification. A final and less well-known Basket IV provides for the continuation of the CSCE process in the form of follow-up meetings and conferences.

The Belgrade Follow-up Meeting, October 4, 1977-March 9, 1978

As part of his emphasis on human rights, President Jimmy Carter stressed the provisions contained in Principle VII and Basket III of the Helsinki Final Act. The Administration's tone and actions at the first Follow-up Meeting, held at Belgrade, reflected President Carter's belief that human rights belonged in the first rank of U.S. foreign policy concerns.

[3 The Congress of Vienna was convened in 1814-15 to redraw the map of Europe after the fall of Napoleon.]

At the Follow-up Meeting, the United States cited Soviet human rights violations, particularly persecution of Helsinki monitoring groups in Warsaw Pact countries. The United States charged the Soviet Union with violations of Principle VII, which called for respect for human rights and fundamental freedoms, including the freedom of thought, conscience, and religion. The Warsaw Pact responded by citing Principle VI, prohibiting intervention in the internal affairs of states.

The Belgrade Concluding Document was brief, containing a schedule for future meetings, and admitting disagreement among the delegations. The Concluding Document recognized "that the exchange of views constitutes in itself a valuable contribution towards the achievement of the aims set by CSCE, although different views were expressed as to the degree of implementation of the Final Act reached so far."

The Road to Madrid, 1978-1980

Between the Belgrade and Madrid follow-up meetings, experts' meetings spawned from the Concluding Document were held at various European cities. The Montreux Conference of October 31 to December 9, 1978, defined procedures for the peaceful settlements of disputes. From February 13 to March 26, 1979, delegates met in Valletta to discuss economic, cultural, and scientific cooperation among the Mediterranean states.

A Scientific Forum at Hamburg, February 18-March 3, 1980, allowed scholars and scientists from East and West to meet and discuss problems related to their academic disciplines. Western scientists, sharply critical of Soviet repression, sent a message of solidarity to dissident physicist Andrei Sakharov. In the final communiqué, Eastern delegations acknowledged that human rights and freedom were a necessary foundation for successful scholarly cooperation. These experts' meetings, along with preparations for the Madrid Follow-up Meeting, ensured the continuity of the CSCE process.

The Madrid Follow-up Meeting, November 11, 1980-September 9, 1983

Throughout the Madrid meeting, which would last nearly 3 years, the NATO nations and several NNAs stressed Soviet and Eastern European human rights violations, particularly the Soviet invasion of Afghanistan and the imposition of martial law in Poland. In response, the Warsaw Pact nations charged the West with interference in their internal affairs in violation of Principle VI of the Final Act. The Warsaw Pact insisted that discussions of a Soviet proposal for a conference on European disarmament could be far more productive than discussions on human rights.

The Madrid Follow-up Meeting ended on September 9, 1983, with the signing of a concluding document by the Foreign Ministers of the participating states that stressed security and genuine detente, while deploring the deterioration of the international situation since the 1977 Belgrade meeting. In a statement before the participants, Secretary of State George Shultz praised the addition of "important new commitments with respect to human rights, trade union freedoms, religious liberties, reunification of families, free flow of information and measures against terrorism" as accomplishments of Madrid.

Supplementary Meetings: 1984-1986

The Concluding Document of the Madrid Follow-up Meeting ensured the continuation of the Helsinki process by providing for several more experts' meetings.

A CSCE experts' meeting on Peaceful Settlement of Disputes held at Athens March 21-April 30, 1984, continued the work begun at the Montreux Conference 6 years earlier. A seminar on Mediterranean cooperation was held at Venice on October 16-26, 1984, where the delegations reviewed initiatives taken after the 1979 Malta meeting.

An experts' meeting to review human rights progress convened at Ottawa on May 7, 1985. For 6 weeks, until June 17, 1985, delegates from East and West discussed human rights, trading charges on violations and proposing specific language for a concluding document. The United States and its NATO Allies introduced a comprehensive proposal setting forth a series of highly-specific steps in human rights conduct. But the Soviet Union and its allies refused to accept the Allied proposal or the shorter one introduced by the NNAs. . . .

A meeting of experts on human contacts convened in Bern, Switzerland, on April 15, 1986. At that meeting, the United States and its Allies addressed issues of divided families, separated spouses, and Soviet emigration figures, which had plummeted since the late 1970s. The Soviet Union charged that the United States ignored the possibilities for contacts between "mass" organizations such as peace groups. The NATO Allies tabled a draft concluding document. Subsequently, the United States declined to consent to an NNA compromise draft since it backtracked from several Final Act commitments on human contacts. Although the meeting ended without a concluding document, it provided an opportunity for East-West bilateral discussions on human contacts. Moreover, before the meeting adjourned, the Soviet Union agreed to allow 119 Soviet citizens to join their families in the United States.

The Conference on Confidence- and Security-Building Measures and Disarmament in Europe (CDE) began on January 17, 1984, in Stockholm to negotiate militarily significant, politically binding, verifiable confidence- and security-building measures applicable to the whole of Europe, including the entire European portion of the Soviet Union. On September 19, 1986, CDE adopted a final document which created verifiable mechanisms for the notification and observation of all significant military activities in Europe, in an effort to provide for a more open European military environment and increase the political cost of using military force for political intimidation. The verification measure of the accord provides, for the first time, for inspection of military activities in Soviet territory upon request of a participating state. . . .

NOTES

For further reading, see:

N. Andren & K. Birnbaum eds., Belgrade and Beyond: The CSCE Process in Perspective (1980);

Belgrade Meeting Following Conference on Security and Co-operation in Europe: Selection of Documents Illustrating the Negotiations of the Belgrade Meeting, 17 I.L.M. 1206 (1987);

A. Bloed & P. van Dijk eds., Essays on Human Rights in the Helsinki Process (1985);

Dimitrijevic, *The Place of Helsinki on the Long Road to Human Rights*, 13 Vanderbilt J. Trans. L. 270 (1980);

M. Dominick ed., Human Rights and the Helsinki Accord: A Five-Year Road to Madrid (1981);

Granier, *Human Rights and the Helsinki Conference on Security: an Annotated Bibliography of U.S. Government Documents*, 13 Vanderbilt J. Trans. L. 529 (1980);

K. Kavass, J. Granier, & M. Dominick eds., Conference on Security and Cooperation in Europe, 1973-75 (1981);

L. Louis-Jacques & S. Nevin, Human Rights in the Soviet Union and Eastern Europe, A Research Guide and Bibliography (1990);

J. Maresca, To Helsinki: The Conference on Security and Cooperation in Europe, 1973-1978 (1987);

V. Mastny, Helsinki, Human Rights and European Security: Analysis and Documentation (1986);

R. Spencer ed., Canada and the Conference on Security and Co-operation in Europe (1984).

Conference on Security and Co-operation in Europe, Final Act, Helsinki 1975, 73 State Dept. Bull. 323 (Sept. 1975); 14 I.L.M. 1292-1325 (1975):

The Conference on Security and Co-operation in Europe, which opened at Helsinki on 3 July 1973 and continued at Geneva from 18 September 1973 to 21 July 1975, was concluded at Helsinki on 1 August 1975....

[Basket I:]

QUESTIONS RELATING TO SECURITY IN EUROPE

The States participating in the Conference on Security and Co-operation in Europe ...

Have adopted the following:

1.

(a) Declaration on Principles Guiding Relations between Participating States

The participating States,

Reaffirming their commitment to peace, security and justice and the continuing development of friendly relations and co-operation; ...

Reaffirming, in conformity with their membership in the United Nations and in accordance with the purposes and principles of the United Nations, their full and active support for the United Nations and for the enhancement of its role and effectiveness in strengthening international peace, security and justice, and in promoting the solution of international problems, as well as the development of friendly relations and co-operation among States; ...

I. *Sovereign equality, respect for the rights inherent in sovereignty*

The participating States will respect each other's sovereign equality and individuality as well as all the rights inherent in and encompassed by its sovereignty, including in particular the right of every State to juridical equality, to territorial integrity and to freedom and political independence. They will also respect each other's right freely to choose and develop its political, social, economic and cultural systems as well as its right to determine its laws and regulations.

Within the framework of international law, all the participating States have equal rights and duties. They will respect each other's right to define and conduct as it wishes its relations with other States in accordance with international law and in the spirit of the present Declaration. They consider that their frontiers can be changed, in accordance with international law, by peaceful means and by agreement. They also have the right to belong or not to belong to international organizations, to be or not to be a party to bilateral or multilateral treaties including the right to be or not to be a party to treaties of alliance; they also have the right to neutrality.

II. *Refraining from the threat or use of force . . .*

III. *Inviolability of frontiers . . .*

IV. *Territorial integrity of States . . .*

V. *Peaceful settlement of disputes*

The participating States will settle disputes among them by peaceful means in such a manner as not to endanger international peace and security, and justice . . . .

VI. *Non-intervention in internal affairs*

The participating States will refrain from any intervention, direct or indirect, individual or collective, in the internal or external affairs falling within the domestic jurisdiction of another participating State, regardless of their mutual relations.

They will accordingly refrain from any form of armed intervention or threat of such intervention against another participating State.

They will likewise in all circumstances refrain from any other act of military, or of political, economic or other coercion designed to subordinate to their own interest the exercise by another participating State of the rights inherent in its sovereignty and thus to secure advantages of any kind.

Accordingly, they will, *inter alia*, refrain from direct or indirect assistance to terrorist activities, or to subversive or other activities directed towards the violent overthrow of the regime of another participating State.

VII. *Respect for human rights and fundamental freedoms, including the freedom of thought, conscience, religion or belief*

The participating States will respect human rights and fundamental freedoms, including the freedom of thought, conscience, religion or belief, for all without distinction as to race, sex, language or religion.

They will promote and encourage the effective exercise of civil, political, economic, social, cultural and other rights and freedoms all of which derive from the inherent dignity of the human person and are essential for his free and full development.

Within this framework the participating States will recognize and respect the freedom of the individual to profess and practise, alone or in community with others, religion or belief acting in accordance with the dictates of his own conscience.

The participating States on whose territory national minorities exist will respect the right of persons belonging to such minorities to equality before the law, will afford them the full opportunity for the actual enjoyment of human rights and fundamental freedoms and will, in this manner, protect their legitimate interests in this sphere.

The participating States recognize the universal significance of human rights and fundamental freedoms, respect for which is an essential factor for the peace, justice and well-being necessary to ensure the development of friendly relations and co-operation among themselves as among all States.

They will constantly respect these rights and freedoms in their mutual relations and will endeavour jointly and separately, including in co-operation with the United Nations, to promote universal and effective respect for them.

They confirm the right of the individual to know and act upon his rights and duties in this field.

In the field of human rights and fundamental freedoms, the participating States will act in conformity with the purposes and principles of the Charter of the United Nations and with the Universal Declaration of Human Rights. They will also fulfil their obligations as set forth in the international declarations and agreements in this field, including *inter alia*, the International Covenants on Human Rights, by which they may be bound.

VIII. *Equal rights and self-determination of peoples*

The participating States will respect the equal rights of peoples and their right to self-determination, acting at all times in conformity with the purposes and principles of the Charter of the United Nations and with the relevant norms of international law, including those relating to territorial integrity of States.

By virtue of the principle of equal rights and self-determination of peoples, all peoples always have the right, in full freedom, to determine, when and as they wish, their internal and external political status, without external interference, and to pursue as they wish their political, economic, social and cultural development. . . .

IX. *Co-operation among States*

The participating States will develop their co-operation with one another and with all States in all fields in accordance with the purposes and principles of the Charter of the United Nations. In developing their co-operation the participating States will place special emphasis on the fields as set forth within the framework of the Conference on Security and Co-operation in Europe, with each of them making its contribution in conditions of full equality.

They will endeavour, in developing their co-operation as equals, to promote mutual understanding and confidence, friendly and good-neighbourly relations among themselves, international peace, security and justice. They will equally endeavour, in developing their co-operation, to improve the well-being of peoples and contribute to the fulfilment of their aspirations through, *inter alia*, the benefits resulting from increased mutual knowledge and from progress and achievement in the economic, scientific, technological, social, cultural and humanitarian fields. They will take steps to promote conditions favourable to making these benefits available to all; they will take into account the interest of all in the narrowing of differences in the levels of economic development, and in particular the interest of developing countries throughout the world. . . .

X.   *Fulfilment in good faith of obligations under international law*

The participating States will fulfil in good faith their obligations under international law, both those obligations arising from the generally recognized principles and rules of international law and those obligations arising from treaties or other agreements, in conformity with international law, to which they are parties.

In exercising their sovereign rights, including the right to determine their laws and regulations, they will conform with their legal obligations under international law; they will furthermore pay due regard to and implement the provisions in the Final Act of the Conference on Security and Co-operation in Europe. . . .

All the principles set forth above are of primary significance and, accordingly, they will be equally and unreservedly applied, each of them being interpreted taking into account the others.

The participating States express their determination fully to respect and apply these principles, as set forth in the present Declaration, in all respects, to their mutual relations and co-operation in order to ensure to each participating State the benefits resulting from the respect and application of these principles by all. . . .

(b)   Matters related to giving effect to certain of the above principles

(i)   *The participating States. . .*

Declare that they are resolved to respect and carry out, in their relations with one another, *inter alia*, the following provisions which are in conformity with the Declaration on Principles Guiding Relations between Participating States:

—   To give effect and expression, by all the ways and forms which they consider appropriate, to the duty to refrain from the threat or use of force in their relations with one another.

—   To refrain from any use of armed forces inconsistent with the purposes and principles of the Charter of the United Nations and the provisions of the Declaration on Principles Guiding Relations between Participating States, against another participating State, in particular from invasion of or attack on its territory.

—   To refrain from any manifestation of force for the purpose of inducing another participating State to renounce the full exercise of its sovereign rights.

—   To refrain from any act of economic coercion designed to subordinate to their own interest the exercise by another participating State of the rights inherent in its sovereignty and thus to secure advantages of any kind.

—   To take effective measures which by their scope and by their nature constitute steps towards the ultimate achievement of general and complete disarmament under strict and effective international control.

—   To promote, by all means which each of them considers appropriate, a climate of confidence and respect among peoples consonant with their duty to refrain from propaganda for wars of aggression or for any threat or use of force inconsistent with the purposes of the United Nations and with the Declaration on Principles Guiding Relations between Participating States, against another participating State.

— To make every effort to settle exclusively by peaceful means any dispute between them, the continuance of which is likely to endanger the maintenance of international peace and security in Europe, and to seek, first of all, a solution through the peaceful means set forth in Article 33 of the United Nations Charter.

To refrain from any action which could hinder the peaceful settlement of disputes between the participating States. . . .

2.

Document on confidence-building measures
and certain aspects of security and disarmament...

I.   *Prior notification of major military manoeuvres...*

Prior notification of other military manoeuvres...

The participating States recognize that they can contribute further to strengthening confidence and increasing security and stability, and to this end may also notify smaller-scale military manoeuvres to other participating States, with special regard for those near the area of such manoeuvres. . . .

Exchange of observers...

Prior notification of major military movements...

Other confidence-building measures...

II. *Questions relating to disarmament...*

III. *General considerations...*

— The complementary nature of the political and military aspects of security. . . .

[Basket II.]

CO-OPERATION IN THE FIELD OF ECONOMICS, OF SCIENCE AND TECHNOLOGY AND OF THE ENVIRONMENT

The participating States...

Aware of the diversity of their economic and social systems,

Reaffirming their will to intensify such co-operation between one another, irrespective of their systems, . . .

Have adopted the following:

1.   *Commercial Exchanges...*

2.   *Industrial co-operation and projects of common interest...*

3.   *Provisions concerning trade and industrial co-operation...*

4.   *Science and technology...*

Forms and methods of co-operation

Express their view that scientific and technological co-operation should, in particular, employ the following forms and methods:

— exchange and circulation of books, periodicals and other scientific and technological publications and papers among interested organizations, scientific and technological institutions, enterprises and scientists and technologists, as well as participation in international programmes for the abstracting and indexing of publications;

—   exchanges and visits as well as other direct contacts and communications among scientists and technologists, on the basis of mutual agreement and other arrangements, for such purposes as consultations, lecturing and conducting research, including the use of laboratories, scientific libraries, and other documentation centres in connexion therewith . . . .

5.   *Environment*

The participating States,

Affirming that the protection and improvement of the environment, as well as the protection of nature and the rational utilization of its resources in the interests of present and future generations, is one of the tasks of major importance to the well-being of peoples and the economic development of all countries and that many environmental problems, particularly in Europe, can be solved effectively only through close international co-operation. . . .

Affirming that experience has shown that economic development and technological progress must be compatible with the protection of the environment and the preservation of historical and cultural values; that damage to the environment is best avoided by preventive measures; and that the ecological balance must be preserved in the exploitation and management of natural resources.

Aims of co-operation

Agree to the following aims of co-operation, in particular: . . .
—   to take the necessary measures to bring environmental policies closer together and, where appropriate and possible, to harmonize them;
—   to encourage, where possible and appropriate, national and international efforts by their interested organizations, enterprises and firms in the development, production and improvement of equipment designed for monitoring, protecting and enhancing the environment.

Fields of co-operation

To attain these aims, the participating States will make use of every suitable opportunity to co-operate in the field of environment and, in particular, within the areas described below as examples:

Control of air pollution

Desulphurization of fossil fuels and exhaust gases; pollution control of heavy metals, particles, aerosols, nitrogen oxides, in particular those emitted by transport, power stations, and other industrial plants; systems and methods of observation and control of air pollution and its effects, including long-range transport of air pollutants;

Water pollution control and fresh water utilization . . .

Protection of the marine environment . . .

Land utilization and soils . . .

Nature conservation and nature reserves . . .

Improvement of environmental conditions in areas of human settlement . . .

Fundamental research, monitoring, forecasting and assessment of environmental changes...

Legal and administrative measures...

Forms and methods of co-operation...

6. *Co-operation in other areas*

Development of transport...

Promotion of tourism...

Economic and social aspects of migrant labour...

Training of personnel...

QUESTIONS RELATING TO SECURITY AND CO-OPERATION IN THE MEDITER-RANEAN...

[Basket III:]

CO-OPERATION IN HUMANITARIAN AND OTHER FIELDS...

1. *Human Contacts*

The participating States...

Express their intention now to proceed to the implementation of the following:

(a) *Contacts and Regular Meetings on the Basis of Family Ties*

In order to promote further development of contacts on the basis of family ties the participating States will favourably consider applications for travel with the purpose of allowing persons to enter or leave their territory temporarily, and on a regular basis if desired, in order to visit members of their families....

(b) *Reunification of Families*

The participating States will deal in a positive and humanitarian spirit with the applications of persons who wish to be reunited with members of their family, with special attention being given to requests of an urgent character — such as requests submitted by persons who are ill or old....

They confirm that the presentation of an application concerning family reunification will not modify the rights and obligations of the applicant or of members of his family....

(c) *Marriage between Citizens of Different States*

The participating States will examine favourably and on the basis of humanitarian considerations requests for exit or entry permits from persons who have decided to marry a citizen from another participating State....

(d) *Travel for Personal or Professional Reasons*

The participating States intend to facilitate wider travel by their citizens for personal or professional reasons and to this end they intend in particular:...

They confirm that religious faiths, institutions and organizations, practising within the constitutional framework of the participating States, and their representatives can, in the field of their activities, have contacts and meetings among themselves and exchange information....

(e) *Improvement of Conditions for Tourism on an Individual or Collective Basis...*

(f)   *Meetings among Young People...*

(g)   *Sport...*

(h)   *Expansion of Contacts*

By way of further developing contacts among governmental institutions and non-governmental organizations and associations, including women's organizations, the participating States will facilitate the convening of meetings as well as travel by delegations, groups and individuals.

2.   *Information*

The participating States...

Express their intention in particular:

(a)   *Improvement of the Circulation of, Access to, and Exchange of Information*

    (i)   *Oral Information...*

    (ii)   *Printed Information...*

    (iii)   *Filmed and Broadcast Information...*

(b)   *Co-operation in the Field of Information...*

(c)   *Improvement of Working Conditions for Journalists*

The participating States, desiring to improve the conditions under which journalists from one participating State exercise their profession in another participating State, intend in particular to:

—   examine in a favourable spirit and within a suitable and reasonable time scale requests from journalists for visas; ...

—   grant to journalists of the participating States the right to import, subject only to its being taken out again, the technical equipment (photographic, cinematographic, tape recorder, radio and television) necessary for the exercise of their profession; ...

3.   *Co-operation and Exchanges in the Field of Culture...*

    Access

To promote fuller mutual access by all to the achievements — works, experiences and performing arts — in the various fields of culture of their countries, and to that end to make the best possible efforts, in accordance with their competence, more particularly:

—   to promote wider dissemination of books and artistic works, in particular by such means as:

    facilitating, while taking full account of the international copyright conventions to which they are party, international contacts and communications between authors and publishing houses as well as other cultural institutions, with a view to a more complete mutual access to cultural achievements; ...

4.   *Co-operation and Exchanges in the Field of Education...*

    (b)   *Access and Exchanges*

To improve access, under mutually acceptable conditions, for students, teachers and scholars of the participating States to each other's educational, cultural and scientific institutions, and to intensify exchanges among these institutions in all areas of common interest, in particular by:

increasing the exchange of information on facilities for study and courses open to foreign participants, as well as on the conditions under which they will be admitted and received;

facilitating travel between the participating States by scholars, teachers and students for purposes of study, teaching and research as well as for improving knowledge of each other's educational, cultural and scientific achievements . . .

(c) *Science* . . .

To develop in the field of scientific research, on a bilateral or multilateral basis, the co-ordination of programmes carried out in the participating States and the organization of joint programmes, especially in the areas mentioned below, which may involve the combined efforts of scientists and in certain cases the use of costly or unique equipment. . . .

(d) *Foreign Languages and Civilizations*

To encourage the study of foreign languages and civilizations as an important means of expanding communication among peoples for their better acquaintance with the culture of each country, as well as for the strengthening of international co-operation; to this end to stimulate, within their competence, the further development and improvement of foreign language teaching and the diversification of choice of languages taught at various levels, paying due attention to less widely-spread or studied languages . . . .

(e) *Teaching Methods*

To promote the exchange of experience, on a bilateral or multilateral basis, in teaching methods at all levels of education, including those used in permanent and adult education, as well as the exchange of teaching materials . . .

FOLLOW-UP TO THE CONFERENCE

The participating States,

1. *Declare their resolve,* in the period following the Conference, to pay due regard to and implement the provisions of the Final Act of the Conference.

(a) unilaterally, in all cases which lend themselves to such action;

(b) bilaterally, by negotiations with other participating States;

(c) multilaterally, by meetings of experts of the participating States, and also within the framework of existing international organizations, such as the United Nations Economic Commission for Europe and UNESCO, with regard to educational, scientific and cultural co-operation;

2. *Declare furthermore their resolve* to continue the multilateral process initiated by the Conference:

(a) by proceeding to a thorough exchange of views both on the implementation of the provisions of the Final Act and of the tasks defined by the Conference, as well as, in the context of the questions dealt with by the latter, on the deepening of their mutual relations, the improvement of security and the development of co-operation in Europe, and the development of the process of détente in the future;

(b) by organizing to these ends meetings among their representatives, beginning with a meeting at the level of representatives appointed by the Ministers of Foreign Affairs. This meeting will define the appropriate modalities for the holding of other meetings which could include further similar meetings and the possibility of a new Conference . . . .

NOTES

1. The International Court of Justice has discussed the effect to be given to the Helsinki Accords in its judgment in the Case Concerning Military and Paramilitary Activities in and against Nicaragua (Nicaragua v. United States), 1986 I.C.J. 14, 97, 123: . . .

> 204. . . . In a different context, the United States expressly accepted the principles . . . appearing in the Final Act of the Conference on Security and Co-operation in Europe (Helsinki, 1 August 1975), including an elaborate statement of the principle of non-intervention; while these principles were presented as applying to the mutual relations among the participating States, it can be inferred that the text testifies to the existence, and the acceptance by the United States, of a customary principle which has universal application . . . .

> 264. The Court has also emphasized the importance to be attached, in other respects, to a text such as the Helsinki Final Act. . . . Texts like these, in relation to which the Court has pointed to the customary content of certain provisions such as the principles of non-use of force and non-intervention, envisage the relations among States having different political, economic and social systems on the basis of coexistence among their various ideologies; the United States not only voiced no objection to their adoption, but took an active part in bringing it about . . . .

2. For further reading, see:

Arrangio-Ruiz, *Human Rights and Non-Intervention in the Helsinki Final Act*, 157 Recueil des Cours 195 (1977);

Bossuyt, *Human Rights and Non-Intervention in Domestic Matters*, 35 Rev. Int'l. Comm. Jurists 45 (1985);

Chalidze, *The Humanitarian Provisions of the Helsinki Accord: A Critique of their Significance*, 13 Vanderbilt J. Trans. L. 429 (1980);

Dean, *Beyond Helsinki: the Soviet View of Human Rights in International Law*, 21 Virginia J. Int'l L. 55 (1980);

Jhabvala, *The Soviet-bloc's View of the Implementation of Human Rights Accords*, 7 Human Rights Q. 461 (1985);

Jonathon & Jacqué, *Obligations Assumed by the Helsinki Signatories*, in Human Rights, International Law and the Helsinki Accord 43 (T. Buergenthal, ed. 1977);

V. Kudriatsev ed., International Covenants on Human Rights and Soviet Legislation (1986);

Meissner, *Right of Self-Determination After Helsinki and its Significance for the Baltic Nations*, 13 Case Western Reserve J. Int'l L. 375 (1981);

Paust, *Transnational Freedom of Speech: Legal Aspects of the Helsinki Final Act*, 45 Law & Contemporary Prob. 53 (1982);

Reinke, *Treaty and Non-Treaty Human Rights Agreements: A Case Study of Freedom of Movement in East Germany*, 24 Columbia J. Trans. L. 647 (1986);

Schachter, *The Human Rights Provisions of the Helsinki Final Act: A Report on a Conference Convened by the Committee on International Human Rights*, 33 The Record 105 (1978).

RATIFICATIONS OF HUMAN RIGHTS INSTRUMENTS BY HELSINKI COUNTRIES

All 35 nations that participated in the Conference on Security and Cooperation in Europe (CSCE) are members of the U.N. except the Holy See and Switzerland. The majority are parties to both the Covenant on Economic, Social and Cultural Rights and the Covenant on Civil and Political Rights, except Greece (which ratified only the Economic, Social, and Cultural Covenant) and the Holy See, Liechtenstein, Malta, Monaco, Switzerland, Turkey, and the U.S. (which ratified neither). Fewer than half of the nations have accepted the Optional Protocol to the Covenant on Civil and Political Rights — mostly Council of Europe countries: Austria, Canada, Denmark, Finland, France, Iceland, Italy, Luxembourg, Netherlands, Norway, Portugal, San Marino, Spain, and Sweden. None of the Eastern European countries has ratified the Optional Protocol which permits individuals to complain that their rights have been violated.

All 23 of the Council of Europe nations participated in the CSCE process and are parties to the European Convention on Human Rights. The CSCE countries that are not members of the Council of Europe include eight Eastern European nations, Canada, the U.S., Finland, and the Holy See.

Hungary and Poland have applied for membership in the Council of Europe and indicated that they intend to ratify the European Convention on Human Rights. Czechoslovakia has expressed an interest in joining the Council of Europe. Hungary has stated that it intends to make a declaration under Article 25 of the European Convention to permit individuals to file petitions in regard to violations. As to applicant nations, Council of Europe members will inquire whether they will protect the rule of law, will assure free and fair elections, and will be able to meet the relatively modest financial obligations of a Council member. Should Hungary and Poland be admitted? Will Czechoslovakia, Yugoslavia, or other countries follow?

Albania has not been a participant in the CSCE process, but in 1990 it indicated its intention to participate in the future. Albania is a member of the U.N. It is not, however, a party to the two Covenants or the European Convention on Human Rights.

NOTES

1. For further reading, see:

E. Chossudovsky, The Helsinki Final Act Viewed in the United Nations Perspective (1980);

Frowein, *The Interrelationship between the Helsinki Final Act, the International Covenants on Human Rights, and the European Convention on Human Rights*, in Human Rights, International Law and the Helsinki Accord 71 (T. Buergenthal ed. 1977);

Ioffe, *Soviet Attitudes Toward International Human Rights Law*, 2 Conn. J. Int'l. L. 361 (1986).

2. The Helsinki Final Act provided for its publication and wide dissemination within signatory countries. The Final Act was published in the Soviet Union and Eastern European countries. This publication generated enthusiasm for human rights activity and led to the creation of Helsinki watch groups. The groups attempted to monitor compliance with the human rights provisions of the Final Act; but many group members were arrested, exiled, sentenced to forced labor, or committed to psychiatric hospitals. The Helsinki watch groups continue to exist and to publish reports on state compliance with the Final Act. The groups and their members have also formed the basis for political parties in several Eastern European countries and have begun to assume leadership roles.

The excerpt below provides more information about the Helsinki watch groups. It was delivered at several of the follow-up meetings in the Helsinki process.

Ambassador Max Kampelman, Head, U.S. Delegation, Statement on Helsinki Monitors, May 12, 1981, *reprinted in* M. Kampelman, Three Years at the East-West Divide 39 (1983):

On May 12, 1976, five years ago today, in Moscow, nine citizens of the Soviet Union met to organize the Moscow Group to Promote Observance of the Helsinki Accords. Their intent was to express their strong support for the decisions made by their government and thirty-four other governments the previous year in Helsinki. They committed themselves to strengthen the Helsinki process by monitoring its observance.

Other men and women of courage soon joined this group. They and countless others in their country, in my country, and in all the countries of Europe looked upon the Helsinki Final Act as a new impulse in man's evolution toward a higher form of civilized international behavior. The CSCE offered a means to encourage peaceful, gradual evolution away from the roots of East-West confrontation.

These men and women in Moscow were not the only ones who saw it as their duty, as well as their right, to form Helsinki monitoring groups in their own country. Similar groups were formed in other parts of the Soviet Union, in the United States, and in many other countries. Americans were particularly pleased because of the early indications that the Soviet Union would at least tolerate the formation of those groups within its borders. This seemed to us to be a sign of maturity, a concrete indication that the "détente" which the Final Act set as a goal could, in fact, be achieved. We looked with favor upon the formation of these groups in the United States. I remind the delegates to this body that members of the Helsinki monitoring groups in the United States served as public members of the American delegation during the first phase of our Madrid meeting.

But this was not to be. This delegation and others have already expressed their deep and profound regret that the Helsinki monitors in the Soviet Union were not at all tolerated. Instead, they faced repression, exile, arrest, imprisonment and ostracism in their pursuit of that which they had a right to pursue under the Final Act. The power of the Soviet state has, in these past five years, been used to oppress these men and women of compassion rather than to protect their rights.

The Moscow group was not the only Helsinki monitoring group to be formed and then forcibly harassed and persecuted in the Soviet Union. A Ukrainian group, a Lithuanian group, a Georgian group, an Armenian group, the Christian Committee for the Defense of Believers, the Working Commission on Psychiatric Abuse, the Group for the Legal Struggle of the Faithful and Free Seventh Day Adventists, the Catholic Committee for the Defense of Believers — were all formed. And those who joined them found themselves punished for their conviction that the commitments of the Helsinki Final Act were to be taken seriously. They have been told that their activities, in behalf of the observance by their government of the Helsinki Final Act, are considered by the authorities to be "anti-Soviet." There are now forty-seven Soviet Helsinki monitors from this group either in prison or in internal exile, a number of them tried and sentenced during our Madrid meeting.

Moscow monitor group members imprisoned today are Vladimir Slepak, Yuri Orlov, Anatoly Shcharansky, Viktor Nekipelov, Tatyana Osipova, Leonard Ternovsky, Malva Landa, and Feliks Serebrov; and they are serving a total of fifty-seven years of labor camp and exile sentences. Many other names have here been mentioned by us and by other delegations. And they are representative of endless numbers of other nameless men and women whose rights are being violated and whom our delegation today remembers as we mark the anniversary of the founding of the Helsinki monitoring group.

In Czechoslovakia, too, a group of individuals formed what became known as the Charter 77 Human Rights Movement to engage their government in peaceful dialogue about the fulfillment of its pledges to its people and to all of us under the Helsinki Final Act. During the convening of the Belgrade CSCE meeting in the fall of 1977, the world learned to its dismay that mass arrests of this Charter 77 group had taken place. We know that these arrests in no small measure adversely affected the atmosphere of that Belgrade meeting.

Now again we note with deep regret the arrest of former Foreign Minister

Jiri Hajek and about thirty other Czechoslovakian supporters of the Charter 77 human rights movement in that country, persons of distinction and courage, now charged, we understand, with "subversion." We condemn with the utmost seriousness the arrests of these Helsinki monitors by Czechoslovakian authorities....

NOTES

1. A Commission on Security and Cooperation in Europe was established by the U.S. Congress in 1976 as an independent agency to monitor and encourage compliance with the 1975 Helsinki Final Act. It includes six Senators, six Representatives, and a representative from the Departments of Commerce, Defense, and State. Members of the Commission have attended various Helsinki sessions, have gathered material from the Helsinki watch groups from the 34 other countries participating in the CSCE process, have held public hearings on the progress of follow-up meetings, and have published reports on human rights and other issues involving the implementation of the Helsinki Accords.

2. In 1979 a U.S. Helsinki Watch Committee was established as an NGO in New York to monitor the compliance of the U.S. and other countries with the Helsinki Accords. The Committee has since become part of the larger NGO — Human Rights Watch including Africa Watch, Americas Watch, Asia Watch, and Middle East Watch.

3. For further reading, see:

Amnesty International, Czechoslovak Human Rights Activists under Protective Surveillance, AI Index: EUR 16/13/85 (1985);

Galey, *Congress, Foreign Policy and Human Rights Ten Years After Helsinki,* 7 Hum. Rts. Q. 334 (1985);

Helsinki Watch, An Open Letter to the Secretary General of the United Nations from the Helsinki Committee in Poland on the U.N. Report on the Situation in Poland (1984);

Human Rights Internet, Directory: Eastern Europe and the USSR (1987);

I. Kavass & J. Granier eds., Human Rights, the Helsinki Accords, and the United States: Selected Executive and Congressional Documents (1982);

Laber, *Ten Years Later, the Legacy of the Moscow Helsinki Group,* N.Y. Times, May 11, 1987, at 21, col. 1;

Pechota, *East European Perceptions of the Helsinki Final Act and the Role of Citizen Initiatives,* 13 Vanderbilt J. Trans. L. 467 (1980);

L. Polakiewicz & N. Davies, Solidarity Lives (1990);

Scharansky, Bonner, & Alekseyeva, *The Tenth Year of the Watch,* N.Y. Rev. Books, June 26, 1986, at 5;

U.S. Helsinki Watch Committee, The Moscow Helsinki Monitors: Their Vision, Their Achievement, the Price They Paid (1986).

4. The excerpt below provides an example of the sort of activities watch committees pursued under the inspiration of the Helsinki Accords.

Commission on Security and Cooperation in Europe, A Thematic Survey of the Documents of the Moscow Helsinki Group, May 12, 1981, at 19: . . .

. . . *Socio-Economic Rights*

The Moscow Helsinki Group is the first Soviet human rights group to focus on socio-economic problems. In a supplement to Moscow Helsinki Group Document 7, the Group described arrests of workers in the aftermath of strikes in the Riga, Latvian port in May 1976. In December 1976, the Moscow Helsinki Group issued Document 13, "Workers' Requests to Emigrate for Political and Economic Reasons," which is based on workers' statements to the Moscow Helsinki Group requesting assistance in emigrating to any capitalist country, since in the USSR they cannot earn enough to feed their families. This document also stresses that Soviet labor unions are not effective defenders of workers' interests.

The Moscow Helsinki Group returned to this theme in Document 85, a survey of "Violations of Socio-Economic Rights in the USSR: The Right to Work:"

> "The most serious violation of the rights of blue and white collar workers is their actual inability to defend their own interests. Soviet law does not give people the right to strike; any attempt at collective action is cruelly repressed. Soviet trade unions are essentially Party-State agencies rather than workers' organizations to secure better living standards and improved working conditions . . . In the USSR, trade unions deal with problems of production, plan fulfillment, labor discipline, and ideological indoctrination . . . Their defense of workers' interests is marginal at best."

Since early 1978, socio-economic issues have played an important role in Moscow Helsinki Group documents. Moscow Helsinki Group Document 36 comments on the creation of independent labor unions in the USSR, affirming the absolute legality of such organizations. Document 37 discusses social benefits according to categories, revealing that pensions can be meager, especially for those who become incapacitated for work at an early age. Document 85 notes: the USSR makes no provisions for the unemployed, including unemployment compensation; the low wages of the vast majority of the population; the exploitation of women to perform heavy labor; the existence of various forms of forced and semi-forced unpaid labor, including overtime work to fulfill the plan, "voluntary" work on holidays, people being sent from the cities to work on collective farms, etc., and the very limited choice of a place of employment due to the system of workbooks and residence permits.

Other Moscow Helsinki Group documents note discrimination in the work sphere against various categories of citizens: invalids (Documents 6 and 46), applicants for emigration (Document 47), and members of unofficial citizens' groups (Documents 47, 75, 76, 77 and 96).

Moscow Helsinki Group documents also present information on the widespread use of forced labor in the USSR. In addition to the system of forced labor for most workers (described in Document 85) there is also a system of forced labor legalized in articles on "parasitism" in the criminal codes of the Soviet republics (Document

47). "Anyone can be accused of parasitism who lives off the proceeds of income derived from unofficial jobs."

In legal practice, the issue of "income derived from unofficial jobs" is not actually investigated. This law is often used against dissidents who earlier are expelled from their jobs and not given the chance to find other work. . . .

NOTES

For further reading, see G. Urban, Social and Economic Rights in the Soviet Bloc: A Documentary Review Seventy Years after the Bolshevik Revolution (1988).

Implementation of the Helsinki Accords, Hearings Before Commission on Security and Cooperation in Europe, 99th Cong., 1st Sess. 5-9 (1985) (testimony of Ambassador Richard Schifter):

[The following excerpt provides an insight into the nature of the plenary and informal discussions during one part of the Helsinki process, that is, the experts' meeting on human rights in Ottawa.]

Mr. Chairman, members of the Commission, the Ottawa Human Rights Experts' Meeting was an international conference quite different from the kind of conference to which we have become accustomed.

Most international conferences convene for the purpose of negotiating and resolving disputes or for the purpose of discussing a problem of common concern and reaching agreement on a cooperative solution to that problem.

The kind of dispute which traditionally was the subject of international negotiations and agreements was a dispute that involved conflicting national interests. The issue of human rights, which involves, essentially, the treatment by the Government of a country of its own citizens has, until the recent past, not been viewed as an appropriate subject for discussion at international conferences.

When the issue of human rights was first put on the agenda of the negotiations that led up to the Helsinki accords, it was dealt with as one of a series of problems of common concern to all the participants in the negotiation. Yet anyone who even cursorily examined the text of Principle VII, the human rights provisions of the accords, would have noted that some of the signatory states had merely recodified their own practices in dealing with their citizenry, while others had, in effect, pledged themselves to make significant changes in the relationship between individual citizens and their Government.

The question of what the Soviet representatives had in mind when they agreed to the inclusion of human rights provisions in the Helsinki accords can, for some time to come, be an interesting topic of speculation. What we can safely assume, though, is that they did not give a great deal of thought at that time to the possibility of their being held accountable at international gatherings for shortfalls in their performance under the Helsinki accords.

Nevertheless, accountability in the area of human rights has been introduced into the Helsinki follow-up process and has been a topic of discussion at Belgrade, at Madrid and, once again, at Ottawa.

The ideal result of a follow-up meeting would be an agreement under which a country which is not now in compliance with the human rights provisions of the Helsinki accords would obligate itself to comply henceforth. However, such a result cannot realistically be expected from the Soviet Union or from other countries in the Soviet sphere.

In that case, what good can be accomplished by a meeting such as that which had been scheduled to take place in Ottawa? That was indeed the critical question which we pondered as we prepared ourselves for Ottawa.

We reached the conclusion that we faced two possibilities. As we saw it, the Soviet Union could use the occasion of the Ottawa Human Rights Experts' Meeting as an occasion in anticipation of which it might review some of its policies which are deemed human rights violations and might agree to alterations therein.

With that possibility in mind, we engaged in the months preceding the Ottawa meeting in informal conversations with Soviet representatives. We emphasized the contribution which the resolution of human rights problems could make to the relaxation of international tension.

We also suggested that if some of these matters could be resolved in informal discussion, such resolution could have beneficial effects on the meeting. To our regret, though not to our surprise, the Soviet response to our inquiries was not positive.

We, therefore, had to fall back on our plan for the second possibility, namely, that the Soviet Union would decide to tough it out at Ottawa.

In that case, we decided, we would speak plainly and clearly of human rights violations in the Soviet Union and other states whose governments violate the human rights of their citizens. Recognizing the framework provided by the Helsinki accords, we decided that we would concentrate on human rights violations which we deemed could be corrected with relative ease, without effecting systemic change within the Soviet Union or the other states in the Soviet sphere. . . .

We decided to take the latter course. And when I say "we," I refer to the 16 participants who belong to the North Atlantic Treaty Organization and who caucused every working day of the Ottawa conference. Representatives of the 16 NATO countries met regularly, sifted through a series of suggestions made by the various member states, and then formulated specific recommendations.

As the Helsinki Final Act and the Madrid Concluding Document were couched in rather general terms, the thrust of our proposal at Ottawa was toward specificity. We recommended arrangements for the monitoring of criminal trials, reductions in the time period of incommunicado detention, freedom of movement, free contacts between representatives of free labor unions, et cetera.

Any fairminded observer would have characterized our proposals as moderate both in tone and in substance. Yet not one of them was acceptable to the Soviet delegation. . . .

As the meeting progressed and the circumstances under which we would be concluding our session came more clearly into focus, the members of the alliance came increasingly to the conclusion that no document at all would be preferable to a concluding document that would do nothing other than mislead the public as to the nature of the conference.

The neutrals and nonaligned made a final effort at the end of the conference to obtain agreement on a short document, an important element of which was a recommendation for future meetings of this kind. When, after acceptance of this proposal by the Western countries, the Soviet bloc rejected it, even the neutrals and nonaligned gave up. The result was no document at all.

As there has been quite a bit of comment on the fact that the Ottawa meeting did not end with the adoption of any final text, let me therefore state again, in summary form, the conclusions that I would draw from that fact.

First, we should note that the reason why there was no final document was, in its essence, that the Soviet Union was not prepared at this meeting to commit itself to changes in its human rights policies that would have given real meaning to a final text.

Second, the participants in the Ottawa conference faced up to the absence of an agreement on questions of substance by letting the world see that fact plainly, without the varnish of a final text.

If there never was a chance of reaching a meaningful agreement, was there any purpose to the Ottawa conference? I would say there was, and would now like to set forth the reasons that lead me to that conclusion:

First, I share the view of a good many participants in the conference that we made a significant impact on the smaller Warsaw Pact countries. We were left with the impression that these countries are interested in improving their standing in and relations with the West. From the messages they received at Ottawa from a great many Western countries, they seemed to have recognized that improvement in their human rights performance could play a significant role in improving their standing in the West. There is reason to believe that this is the message that they have taken home.

Second, the fact that international meetings take place at which attention is paid to their plight encourages the brave men and women behind the Iron Curtain who stand up for their rights to continue their struggle.

As news about the Ottawa meeting was broadcast to Eastern Europe, the meeting made a valuable contribution to keeping up the spirit of those who have sacrificed a great deal for the cause of freedom.

Third, though the Soviet leadership is not likely to respond directly to complaints presented to them by diplomats in conferences closed to the outside world, the Soviet leadership does seem to be sensitive to adverse publicity. To the extent to which the Ottawa meeting has received and may continue to receive publicity which the Soviet Union deems adverse to its interests, it might have contributed to the forces at work that might, over time, change Soviet human rights policy.

Fourth, the chances of improving human rights performance in the Warsaw Pact countries are significantly enhanced by an appeal from the West which is delivered in unison. At Ottawa, we were able to hammer out, as I mentioned before, a series of proposals for specific improvements in human rights conditions.

These proposals were at the end of the session, combined into a single document, designated OME 47, which was tabled in the name of 17 countries. These were the 10 countries which make up the European Community as well as the 7 countries which belong to NATO but not to the EC.

Operating under the pressure cooker of a conference, we composed this document in the space of about 2 weeks. In the absence of a conference, it might have taken years of crossing t's and dotting i's before such a document could have been completed. It is now on the record and can serve as the basis of a unified Western human rights campaign in the years to come.

Fifth, the fact that the neutrals in the West saw, basically, eye to eye at the Ottawa Conference underlined the fact that the issue of human rights is not one that is tied to purely military alignments, but is one which truly concerns the conscience of the civilized world.

There is one final point which I would like to make. We must keep in mind that a meeting such as that which was held at Ottawa was unthinkable as recently as 15 years ago. The concept of limited government, the ideas of the rights of the individual which originated with the thinkers and writers of the 18th century and which were enshrined in our own Declaration of Independence were ideas advanced first by individuals, then by groups and movements, and were then adopted by countries, but only for domestic application.

The notion that governments might monitor the behavior of other governments toward their own citizens. That there would be international conferences at which the domestic practices of participating countries would be subjected to scrutiny is one of very recent origin.

While the results might be meager in their beginning stage, they might be more plentiful in the future. What this means is that we ought to give the CSCE process further time to evolve before passing judgment on whether it has accomplished anything and whether the results justify our investment of effort. . . .

NOTES

1. The European Community has 12 members: Belgium, Denmark, France, the Federal Republic of Germany, Greece, Ireland, Italy, Luxembourg, Netherlands, Portugal, Spain, and the United Kingdom. It was established in 1967 as a combination of the European Economic Community and other alliances dating back as early as 1951. The center of the European Community is in Brussels.

The European Court of Justice has observed that "human rights are enshrined in the general principles of Community law and protected by the Court." *Stauder v. City of Ulm*, (1969) ECR 419, at 425. The Court of Justice has considered on several occasions whether specific Community measures are consistent with the basic principles of human rights incorporated within Community law and has referred to the European Convention on Human Rights for guidance in discerning general principles of human rights.

The European Community has issued directives and developed policies relevant to human rights, particularly concerning employment discrimination, other equality issues, migrant workers, freedom of association, education, fair application of the law, and other social concerns. The European Community is in the process of preparing a European Charter of Fundamental Social Rights which is expected to have considerable prominence in developing Community policies. *See* Preliminary Draft Community Charter of Fundamental Social Rights, 5-1989 Bull. EC 9 (1989).

The European Parliament has also monitored human rights problems in many parts of the world. The European Parliament has adopted a number of resolutions on human rights issues. *See, e.g.*, Declaration of Fundamental Rights and Freedoms. European Communities, Official Journal, C 120/52, Doc. A 2-3/89 (May 16, 1989). For further reading, see:

A. Byre, Leading Cases and Materials on the Social Policy of the EEC (1989);

Foster, *The European Court of Justice and the European Convention for the Protection of Human Rights*, 8 Hum. Rts. L.J. 245 (1987);

P. Kapteyn & P. van Themaat, Introduction to the Law of the European Communities (2d ed. L. Gormley ed. 1989);

Mendelson, *The European Court of Justice and Human Rights*, 1981 Y.B. European Law 125 (1982);

B. Rudden, Basic Community Cases (1987);

H. Schermers, Judicial Protection in the European Communities (3d ed. 1983).

2. The North Atlantic Treaty Organization (NATO) was established in 1949 as a military and political alliance under Article 51 of the U.N. Charter, which affirms the right of collective self-defense. 34 U.N.T.S. 243, *entered into force* August 24, 1949. There are 16 NATO countries: Belgium, Canada, Denmark, France, the Federal Republic of Germany, Greece, Iceland, Italy, Luxembourg, Netherlands, Norway, Portugal, Spain, Turkey, the United Kingdom, and the United States. The headquarters is in Brussels. The North Atlantic Assembly is the interparliamentary assembly of NATO member countries. In light of the events in Eastern Europe, the U.S. has advocated a larger political role for NATO and the North Atlantic Assembly. Can or should NATO pursue human rights issues? For further reading, see *NATO At 40*, Senate Comm. on Foreign Relations, 101st Cong., 1st Sess. (1989).

3. The Warsaw Pact was established in 1955 as a military and political alliance. The Pact countries are Bulgaria, Czechoslovakia, German Democratic Republic, Hungary (with drawing), Poland, Romania, and the U.S.S.R. The headquarters is in Moscow. Albania and Yugoslavia are not Warsaw Pact countries. In late 1989 and 1990 the Warsaw Pact was weakened as a military alliance, but continues to some extent as a political alliance.

4. The European Free Trade Association (EFTA) was established in 1960 and includes Austria, Iceland, Norway, Portugal, Sweden, and Switzerland, with Finland as an associate member. EFTA has removed trade barriers with the European Community but has not sought to harmonize financial and other governmental policies with the European Community. EFTA has weakened as the European Community has grown stronger.

5. The Western European Union (WEU) has seven members: Belgium, France, Federal Republic of Germany, Italy, Luxembourg, Netherlands, and the United Kingdom. It was established in 1955 and helps coordinate the political and security affairs of members. The WEU became somewhat more active after 1984, but plays a relatively minor role in European affairs.

6. The following two excerpts provide examples of the public discussions during the sessions which lead to the Vienna Concluding Document of 1989. The first excerpt shows the interplay between the Helsinki monitoring groups and the follow-up meetings. The second illustrates that human rights violations in the U.S. and other Western countries may also be the subject of criticism in the Helsinki process.

Ambassador Samuel Wise, Deputy Head, U.S. Delegation, Statement on the Detention of Vaclav Havel, February 17, 1987:

I had not planned today to return to issues introduced by my distinguished Czechoslovak colleague yesterday, because I am aware that a member of my delegation has already provided an adequate response. Unfortunately, however, events in Prague of this morning compel me to speak on this matter.

This morning, the delegation of U.S. Congressmen, led by the Chairman Steny Hoyer of the U.S. Commission on Security and Cooperation in Europe, which visited this body last week, had arranged to meet with Czechoslovak private citizens including human rights activists and government officials. Congressman Hoyer has informed us a short while ago that one of the most prominent of those activists, Vaclav Havel, a playwright, founding member of Charter 77, and recent recipient of the prestigious Erasmus Prize, was forcibly prevented from attending the meeting and was taken into police custody a block away. His current fate is unknown.

I wish to stress that this action against Mr. Havel is directly contrary to the assurances we all heard yesterday in this meeting and on Friday in the plenary, that all delegations, including Congressman Hoyer's delegation, are free to meet with those Czechoslovak citizens with whom they choose. It is sadly ironic that only yesterday the Czechoslovak delegate alleged that "so-called human rights activists" in his country reside in "villas", and only today one of the most prominent of them is in police custody merely for wishing to meet with foreign dignitaries.

We would welcome an explanation and immediate action from the Czechoslovak delegation and authorities in this deplorable and incomprehensible situation.

Thank you. . . .

NOTES

In December 1989 Vaclav Havel was elected President of Czechoslovakia. For further reading, see Comm'n. on Security and Cooperation in Europe, Human Rights in Czechoslovakia: The Documents of Charter 77, 1977-1982 (1982) & Human Rights in Czechoslovakia: The Documents of Charter 77, 1982-1987 (1988).

Statement of Ambassador Samuel Wise, Deputy Head, U.S. Delegation, Allegations on U.S. Political Prisoners, March 31, 1987:

Mr. Chairman:

We have repeatedly stated our desire to promote a constructive dialogue at this conference. By constructive, we mean a dialogue leading to fuller implementation of our commitments under the Final Act. On occasion, we have expressed our concern about specific cases in some participating states. We will continue to do so — but not to place other states before a "tribunal", as one of our distinguished colleagues has suggested. Rather, we strive to expose violations of Helsinki commitments from whatever quarter in order to call for the restoration of the rights of our people, and in order to identify the general areas where we must redouble our efforts.

With this goal in mind, I raised a number of cases of prisoners of conscience in the Soviet Union and Czechoslovakia on March 16 in order to illustrate the need for the Vienna Conference to adopt WT.39. In response, the Soviet delegate named several cases of alleged political prisoners in the United States.

I understand that the Soviet delegation raised some of these same cases in the plenary today, noting the lack of a U.S. response. I welcome this renewed expression of Soviet interest in WT.39 which we have already heard from the Soviet delegate in this group. I would like to respond to the allegations of the Soviet delegation today. But let me establish clearly that I do so not with the intention to provoke, but to share information of concern to our work here. I trust that my Soviet colleague will do likewise with the many cases we have raised, much as the Czechoslovak Ambassador provided information relevant to the concerns of many states about the trial of the Jazz Section members. If the Soviet representative has forgotten the cases I raised, I will be pleased to remind him and to provide him with many more.

Allow me to begin with a response to our Soviet colleague on the cases he raised of so-called political prisoners in the United States.

1) Leonard Peltier — Mr. Peltier was convicted by a jury in the United States District Court of South Dakota on June 25, 1975 for the brutal murders of two FBI agents. In 1978, he appealed his conviction to the Eighth Circuit Court of Appeals, and the court affirmed it on September 14, 1978. The court denied a motion for rehearing on October 27, 1978 and again in May, 1986. Mr. Peltier, having been recaptured after an escape attempt, is serving two life sentences.

2) Dennis Banks — Mr. Banks was convicted in South Dakota courts in 1975 on charges of arson, riot and assault stemming from a 1973 incident in Custer, South Dakota. In 1976, Mr. Banks fled to California while released on bail. In 1978, the Supreme Court of California held that the California Governor's refusal to extradite Banks to South Dakota was constitutional. Today Mr. Banks is free.

3) Elmer "Geronimo" Pratt — Mr. Pratt was convicted of conspiracy and possession of illegal weapons following a four-hour shoot-out between Los Angeles police and Black Panther activists in 1969.

In 1972, Pratt was convicted of murdering and robbing a woman from Santa Monica and was sentenced to life in prison. Mr. Pratt's appeal to the California Supreme Court was unsuccessful. The case is still pending due to a request for a new trial.

4) Johnny Harris — Mr. Harris was sentenced in 1971 to five consecutive life sentences after pleading guilty to one count of rape and four counts of robbery. While serving this sentence, Mr. Harris was sentenced to death for murdering a prison guard.

5) Helen Woodson, Paul Kabot, Carl Kabot and Larry Cloud-Morgan — These four individuals were convicted on charges of "damaging government property" after they attempted to break into an inter-continental ballistic missile site near Kansas City with a jackhammer. Carl Kabot is serving a sentence of 18 years, Helen Woodson 12 years, Paul Kabot 10 years, and Larry Cloud-Morgan 8 years.

We have reviewed the other names that, upon our request, the Soviet delegation provided, but we have been unable to identify them. If our Soviet colleagues can provide more information, perhaps we can explain the other cases as well. We hope that the Soviet delegation will respond in kind to the cases we have raised. But I will emphasize again that we intend this to be a constructive exercise, not a finger-pointing session. Nevertheless, I must underscore the obvious difference in the cases raised by my delegation and those brought up by the Soviet delegation.

In my speech on March 16, I spoke of cases of Soviet citizens convicted on charges such as anti-Soviet agitation and propaganda, spreading anti-Soviet slander, and resisting military draft. In contrast, the distinguished Soviet representative has inquired about American citizens who have been convicted on charges such as murder, rape, forcible assault and armed robbery. In responding to his inquiry, I want to point out that there is a world of difference in the two sets of cases. Suffice it to say that, in the view of my delegation and in the context of the Helsinki Final Act, the cases of persecuted individuals in the Soviet Union are political prisoners and as such represent glaring violations of our Helsinki commitments. The Soviet Union has tacitly, if not openly, admitted this fact by initiating the release of some of these prisoners. Since this is the case, we merely ask now at this Vienna review meeting why the Soviet leadership does not take the next logical step and release all such political and psychiatric prisoners. Such a move would not only move the Soviet Union forward in its commitment to the Helsinki Accords but would greatly simplify our common task of drafting a concluding document at Vienna.

Thank you, Mr. Chairman.

NOTES

The Concluding Document of the Vienna Follow-Up Meeting is excerpted below. It represents conclusions and doctrinal developments during the nearly 14 years after the Helsinki Final Act of 1975.

Concluding Document of the Vienna Meeting, State Department, CSCE Vienna Follow-Up Meeting, A Framework for Europe's Future 5 (1989):

An open and frank discussion was held about the application of and respect for the principles of the Final Act. Concern was expressed about serious violations of a number of these principles. In particular, questions relating to respect for human rights and fundamental freedoms were the focus of intensive and controversial discussion. The participating States agreed that full respect for the principles, in all their aspects, is essential for the improvement of their mutual relations.

. . . It was considered that the numerous possibilities offered by the Final Act had not been sufficiently utilized.

The participating States also expressed concern about the spread of terrorism and condemned it unreservedly. . . .

In their deliberations the representatives of the participating States took into account the results of

— the Stockholm Conference on Confidence- and Security-Building Measures and Disarmament in Europe;

— the Athens meeting of Experts in order to pursue the examination and elaboration of a generally acceptable method for the peaceful settlement of disputes aimed at complementing existing methods;

— the Venice Seminar on Economic, Scientific and Cultural Co-operation in the Mediterranean, the Ottawa Meeting of Experts on Questions concerning Respect, in their States, for Human Rights and Fundamental Freedoms, in all their Aspects, as embodied in the Final Act;

— the Budapest "Cultural Forum";

— the Bern Meeting of Experts on Human Contacts. . . .

The participating States express their determination

— to build on the current positive developments in their relations in order to make detente a viable, comprehensive and genuine process, universal in scope;

— to assume their responsibility fully to implement the commitments contained in the Final Act and other CSCE documents;

— to intensify their efforts to seek solutions to problems burdening their relations and to strengthen safeguards for international peace and security;

— to promote cooperation and dialogue among them, to ensure the effective exercise of human rights and fundamental freedoms and to facilitate contacts and communication between people;

— to exert new efforts to make further progress to strengthen confidence and security and to promote disarmament.

Principles

1. The participating States reaffirm their commitment to all ten principles of the Final Act's Declaration on Principles Guiding Relations between Participating States and their determination to respect them and put them into practice. The participating States reaffirm that all these Principles are of primary significance and, accordingly, will be equally and unreservedly applied, each of them being interpreted taking into account the others.

2. They stress that respect for and full application of these principles as well as strict compliance with all CSCE commitments deriving from them, are of great political importance and essential for building confidence and security as well as for the development of their friendly relations and of their cooperation in all fields.

3. In this context, they confirm that they will respect each other's right freely to choose and develop their political, social, economic and cultural systems as well as their right to determine their laws, regulations, practices and policies. In exercising these rights, they will ensure that their laws, regulations, practices and policies conform with their obligations under international law and are brought into harmony with the provisions of the Declaration on Principles and other CSCE commitments.

4. They also confirm that, by virtue of the principle of equal rights and self-determination of peoples and in conformity with the relevant provisions of the Final Act, all peoples always have the right, in full freedom, to determine, when and as they wish, their internal and external political status, without external interference, and to pursue as they wish their political, economic, social and cultural development.

5. They confirm their commitment strictly and effectively to observe the principle of the territorial integrity of States. They will refrain from any violation of this principle and thus from any action aimed by direct or indirect means, in contravention of the purposes and principles of the Charter of the United Nations, other obligations under international law or the provisions of the Final Act, at violating the territorial integrity, political independence or the unity of a State. No actions or situations in contravention of this principle will be recognized as legal by the participating States.

6. The participating States confirm their commitment to the principle of peaceful settlement of disputes, convinced that it is an essential complement to the duty of States to refrain from the threat or use of force, both being essential factors for the maintenance and consolidation of peace and security. . . .

8. The participating States unreservedly condemn, as criminal, all acts, methods and practices of terrorism, wherever and by whomever committed, including those which jeopardize friendly relations among States and their security, and agree that terrorism cannot be justified under any circumstances. . . .

11. They confirm that they will respect human rights and fundamental freedoms, including the freedom of thought, conscience, religion or belief, for all without distinction as to race, sex, language or religion. They also confirm the universal significance of human rights and fundamental freedoms, respect for which is an essential factor for the peace, justice and security necessary to ensure the development of friendly relations and co-operation among themselves, as among all States.

12. They express their determination to guarantee the effective exercise of human rights and fundamental freedoms, all of which derive from the inherent dignity of the human person and are essential for his free and full development. They recognize that civil, political, economic, social, cultural and other rights and freedoms are all of paramount importance and must be fully realized by all appropriate means.

13. In this context they will

13a. — develop their laws, regulations and policies in the field of civil, political, economic, social, cultural and other human rights and fundamental freedoms and put them into practice in order to guarantee the effective exercise of these rights and freedoms;

13b. — consider acceding to the International Covenant on Civil and Political Rights, the International Covenant on Economic, Social and Cultural Rights, the Optional Protocol to the Covenant on Civil and Political Rights and other relevant international instruments, if they have not yet done so; . . .

13d. — ensure effectively the right of the individual to know and act upon his rights and duties in this field, and to that end publish and make accessible all laws, regulations and procedures relating to human rights and fundamental freedoms;

13e. — respect the right of their citizens to contribute actively, individually or in association with others, to the promotion and protection of human rights and fundamental freedoms;

13f. — encourage in schools and other educational institutions consideration of the promotion and protection of human rights and fundamental freedoms;

13g. — ensure human rights and fundamental freedoms to everyone within their territory and subject to their jurisdiction, without distinction of any kind such as race, colour, sex, language, religion, political or other opinion, national or social origin, property, birth or other status;

13h. — ensure that no individual exercising, expressing the intention to exercise or seeking to exercise these rights and freedoms, or any member of his family, will as a consequence be discriminated against in any manner;

13i. — ensure that effective remedies as well as full information about them are available to those who claim that their human rights and fundamental freedoms have been violated; they will, *inter alia*, effectively apply the following remedies:

   — the right of the individual to appeal to executive, legislative, judicial or administrative organs;

   — the right to a fair and public hearing within a reasonable time before an independent and impartial tribunal, including the right to present legal arguments and to be represented by legal counsel of one's choice;

— the right to be promptly and officially informed of the decision taken on any appeal, including the legal grounds on which this decision was based. This information will be provided as a rule in writing and, in any event, in a way that will enable the individual to make effective use of further available remedies.

14. The participating States recognize that the promotion of economic, social, and cultural rights as well as of civil and political rights is of paramount importance for human dignity and for the attainment of the legitimate aspirations of every individual. They will therefore continue their efforts with a view to achieving progressively the full realization of economic, social and cultural rights by all appropriate means, including in particular by the adoption of legislative measures.

In this context they will pay special attention to problems in the areas of employment, housing, social security, health, education and culture. They will promote constant progress in the realization of all rights and freedoms within their countries, as well as in the development of their relations among themselves and with other States, so that everyone will actually enjoy to the full his economic, social and cultural rights as well as his civil and political rights.

15. The participating States confirm their determination to ensure equal rights of men and women. Accordingly, they will take all measures necessary, including legislative measures, to promote equally effective participation of men and women in political, economic, social and cultural life. They will consider the possibility of acceding, if they have not yet done so, to the Convention on the Elimination of All Forms of Discrimination Against Women.

16. In order to ensure the freedom of the individual to profess and practice religion or belief the participating States will, *inter alia,*

16a. — take effective measures to prevent and eliminate discrimination against individuals or communities, on the grounds of religion or belief in the recognition, exercise and enjoyment of human rights and fundamental freedoms in all fields of civil, political, economic, social and cultural life, and ensure the effective equality between believers and non-believers;

16b. — foster a climate of mutual tolerance and respect between believers of different communities as well as between believers and non-believers;

16c. — grant upon their request to communities of believers, practising or prepared to practise their faith within the constitutional framework of their States, recognition of the status provided for them in their respective countries;

16d. — respect the right of religious communities to

— establish and maintain freely accessible places of worship or assembly,

— organize themselves according to their own hierarchical and institutional structure,

— select, appoint and replace their personnel in accordance with their respective requirements and standards as well as with any freely accepted arrangement between them and their State,

— solicit and receive voluntary financial and other contributions;

16e. — engage in consultations with religious faiths, institutions and organizations in order to achieve a better understanding of the requirements of religious freedom;

16f. — respect the right of everyone to give and receive religious education in the language of his choice, individually or in association with others;

16g. — in this context respect, *inter alia*, the liberty of parents to ensure the religious and moral education of their children in conformity with their own convictions;

16h. — allow the training of religious personnel in appropriate institutions;

16i. — respect the right of individual believers and communities of believers to acquire, possess, and use sacred books, religious publications in the language of their choice and other articles and materials related to the practice of religion or belief;

16j. — allow religious faiths, institutions and organizations to produce and import and disseminate religious publications and materials;

16k. — favorably consider the interest of religious communities in participating in public dialogue, *inter alia*, through mass media;

17. The participating States recognize that the exercise of the above-mentioned rights relating to the freedom of religion or belief may be subject only to such limitations as are provided by law and consistent with their obligations under international law and with their international commitments. They will ensure in their laws and regulations and in their application the full and effective implementation of the freedom of thought, conscience, religion or belief;

18. The participating States will exert sustained efforts to implement the provisions of the Final Act and of the Madrid Concluding Document pertaining to national minorities. They will take all the necessary legislative, administrative, judicial and other measures and apply the relevant international instruments by which they may be bound, to ensure the protection of human rights and fundamental freedoms of persons belonging to national minorities within their territory. They will refrain from any discrimination against such persons and contribute to the realization of their legitimate interests and aspirations in the field of human rights and fundamental freedoms.

19. They will protect and create conditions for the promotion of the ethnic, cultural, linguistic and religious identity of national minorities on their territory. They will respect the free exercise of rights by persons belonging to such minorities and ensure their full equality with others.

20. The participating States will respect fully, the right of everyone

   — to freedom of movement and residence within the borders of each State, and

   — to leave any country, including his own, and to return to his country.

21. The participating States will ensure that the exercise of the above-mentioned rights shall not be subject to any restrictions except to those which are provided by law and consistent with their obligations under international law, in particular the International Covenant on Civil and Political Rights and their international commitments, in particular the Universal Declaration of Human Rights. These restrictions have the character of exceptions. The participating States will ensure that these restrictions are not abused and are not applied in an arbitrary manner, but in such a way that the effective exercise of these rights is ensured.

22. In this context they will allow all refugees who so desire to return in safety to their homes.

23. The participating states will

23a. — ensure that no one shall be subjected to arbitrary arrest, detention or exile;

23b. — ensure that all individuals in detention or incarceration will be treated with humanity and with respect for the inherent dignity of the human person;

23c. — observe the UN Standard Minimum Rules for the Treatment of Prisoners as well as the UN Code of Conduct for Law Enforcement Officials;

23d. — prohibit torture and other cruel, inhuman or degrading treatment or punishment and take effective legislative, administrative, judicial and other measures to prevent and punish such practices;

23e. — consider acceding to the Convention against Torture and other Cruel, Inhuman or Degrading Treatment or Punishment, if they have not yet done so;

23f. — protect individuals from any psychiatric or other medical practices that violate human rights and fundamental freedoms and take effective measures to prevent and punish such practices.

24. With regard to the question of capital punishment, the participating States note that capital punishment has been abolished in a number of them. In participating States where capital punishment has not been abolished, sentence of death may be imposed only for the most serious crimes in accordance with the law in force at the time of the commission of the crime and not contrary to their international commitments. This question will be kept under consideration. In this context, the participating States will cooperate within relevant international organizations. . . .

27. The participating States heard accounts of the Meeting of Experts on questions concerning respect, in their States, for Human Rights and Fundamental Freedoms, in all their aspects, as embodied in the Final Act, held in Ottawa from 7 May to 17 June 1985. They welcomed the fact that frank discussions had taken place on matters of key concern. Noting that these discussions had not led to agreed conclusions, they agreed that such thorough exchanges of views themselves constitute a valuable contribution to the CSCE process. In this respect it was noted in particular that proposals made at the meeting had received further consideration at the Vienna Follow-Up Meeting. They also welcomed the decision to allow public access to part of the meeting and noted that this principle was further developed at later meetings.

CONFIDENCE- AND SECURITY-BUILDING MEASURES AND CERTAIN ASPECTS OF SECURITY AND DISARMAMENT IN EUROPE. . .

Stockholm Conference: Assessment of Progress Achieved

The participating States,

In accordance with the relevant provisions of the Madrid Concluding Document, assessed progress achieved during the Conference on Confidence- and Security-Building Measures and Disarmament in Europe, which met in Stockholm from 17 January 1984 to 19 September 1986.

They welcomed the adoption at Stockholm of a set of mutually complementary confidence- and security-building measures. . . .

New Efforts for Security and Disarmament in Europe

The participating States,

Recalling the relevant provisions of the Final Act and of the Madrid Concluding

Document according to which they recognize the interest of all of them in efforts aimed at lessening military confrontation and promoting disarmament,

Reaffirming their determination expressed in the Final Act to strengthen confidence among them and thus to contribute to increasing stability and security in Europe....

Negotiations on Confidence- and Security-Building Measures...

Negotiation on Conventional Armed Forces in Europe...

Meetings in Order to Exchange Views and Information Concerning the Course of the Negotiation on Conventional Armed Forces in Europe...

CO-OPERATION IN THE FIELD OF ECONOMICS, OF SCIENCE AND TECHNOLOGY AND OF THE ENVIRONMENT...

Trade and Industrial Cooperation...

Science and Technology...

Environment...

Co-operation in Other Areas...

40. The participating States emphasize the need for effective implementation of the provisions of the Final Act and the Madrid Concluding Document relating to migrant workers and their families in Europe. They invite host countries and countries of origin to make efforts to improve further the economic, social, cultural and other conditions of life for migrant workers and their families legally residing in the host countries. They recommend that host countries and countries of origin should promote their bilateral co-operation in relevant fields with a view to facilitating the reintegration of migrant workers and their families returning to their country of origin.

41. The participating States will, in accordance with their relevant commitments undertaken in the Helsinki Final Act and the Madrid Concluding Document, consider favourably applications for family reunification as well as family contacts and visits involving migrant workers from other participating States legally residing in the host countries.

42. The participating States will ensure that migrant workers from other participating States and their families can freely enjoy and maintain their national culture and have access to the culture of the host country....

QUESTIONS RELATING TO SECURITY AND CO-OPERATION IN THE MEDITERRANEAN...

CO-OPERATION IN HUMANITARIAN AND OTHER FIELDS...

Human Contacts

1. In implementing the human contacts provisions of the Final Act, the Madrid Concluding Document and the present Document, they will fully respect their obligations under international law as referred to in the subchapter of the present Document devoted to principles, in particular that everyone shall be free to leave any country, including his own, and to return to his country, as well as their international commitments in this field....

6. ... [T]hey will decide upon applications relating to family reunification or

marriage between citizens of different States, in normal practice within three months. . . .

8. In dealing favourably with applications relating to family meetings, they will also allow visits to and from more distant relatives. . . .

— They will decide as expeditiously as possible upon applications relating to travel by those who are seriously ill or by the elderly, and other travel of an urgent humanitarian nature. . . .

18. Within one year of the conclusion of the Vienna Follow-up Meeting they will publish and make easily accessible, where this has not already been done, all their laws and statutory regulations concerning movement by individuals within their territory and travel between States. . . .

20. They will deal favourably with applications for travel abroad without distinction of any kind, such as race, colour, sex, language, religion, political or other opinion, national or social origin, property, birth, age or other status. They will ensure that any refusal does not affect applications submitted by other persons. . . .

29. In accordance with the Universal Postal Convention and the International Telecommunication Convention, they will

— guarantee the freedom of transit of postal communication;

— ensure the rapid and unhindered delivery of correspondence, including personal mail and parcels;

— respect the privacy and integrity of postal and telephone communications; and

— ensure the conditions necessary for rapid and uninterrupted telephone calls, including the use of international direct dialing systems, where they exist, and their development.

30. They will encourage direct contacts between the citizens of their States, *inter alia,* by facilitating individual travel within their countries and by allowing foreigners to meet their citizens as well as, when invited to do so, to stay in private homes.

31. They will ensure that the status of persons belonging to national minorities or regional cultures on their territories is equal to that of other citizens with regard to human contacts under the Final Act. . . .

32. They will allow believers, religious faiths and their representatives, in groups or on an individual basis, to establish and maintain direct personal contacts and communication with each other, in their own and other countries, *inter alia,* through travel, pilgrimages and participation in assemblies and other religious events. In this context and commensurate with such contacts and events, those concerned will be allowed to acquire, receive and carry with them religious publications and objects related to the practice of their religion or belief. . . .

Information

34. They will continue efforts to contribute to an ever wider knowledge and understanding of life in their States, thus promoting confidence between peoples.

They will make further efforts to facilitate the freer and wider dissemination of information of all kinds, to encourage co-operation in the field of information and to improve the working conditions for journalists.

In this connection and in accordance with the International Covenant on Civil and Political Rights, the Universal Declaration of Human Rights and their relevant international commitments concerning seeking, receiving and imparting information of all kinds, they will ensure that individuals can freely choose their sources of information. . . .

Co-operation and Exchanges in the Field of Culture. . .

Co-operation and Exchanges in the Field of Education

63. They will ensure access by all to the various types and levels of education without discrimination as to race, colour, sex, language, religion, political or other opinion, national or social origin, property, birth or other status.

64. In order to encourage wider co-operation in science and education, they will facilitate unimpeded communication between universities and other institutions of higher education and research. They will also facilitate direct personal contacts, including contacts through travel, between scholars, scientists and other persons active in these fields. . . .

HUMAN DIMENSION OF THE CSCE. . .

The participating States decide further to convene a Conference on the Human Dimension of the CSCE in order to achieve further progress concerning respect for all human rights and fundamental freedoms, human contacts and other issues of a related humanitarian character. The Conference will hold three meetings before the next CSCE Follow-up meeting.

The Conference will:

— review developments in the human dimension of the CSCE including the implementation of the relevant CSCE commitments; . . .

— consider practical proposals for new measures aimed at improving the implementation of the commitments relating to the human dimension of the CSCE and enhancing the effectiveness of the procedures. . . .

On the basis of these proposals, the Conference will consider adopting new measures.

The first Meeting of the Conference will be held in Paris from 30 May to 23 June 1989.

The second Meeting of the Conference will be held in Copenhagen from 5 June to 29 June 1990.

The third Meeting of the Conference will be held in Moscow from 10 September to 4 October 1991. . . .

FOLLOW-UP TO THE CONFERENCE. . .

The fourth main Follow-Up meeting will be held in Helsinki commencing on 24 March 1992. . . .

The participating States examined the scope for rationalising the modalities for future CSCE follow-up meetings, for enhancing their effectiveness and for ensuring the best possible use of resources. In the light of their examination and in connection with the steps taken at the main Vienna Meeting, including the drawing up of mandates annexed to this document, they decided:

— to dispense with preparatory meetings unless otherwise agreed;

— bearing in mind the purpose of the meeting, to limit the number of subsidiary working bodies meeting simultaneously to the lowest possible;

— to limit the duration of meetings, unless otherwise agreed, to a period not exceeding four weeks;

— in the case of meetings to which non-governmental participants are invited to contribute, to make maximum use of the possibility of having informal meetings in order to allow for a more spontaneous discussion . . . .

The main Helsinki Meeting will review these arrangements and other modalities in the light of experience, with a view to making any improvements which may be necessary . . . .

NOTES

1. The June 1990 meeting of the CSCE in Copenhagen was marked by an increased role for nongovernmental organizations in lobbying government delegations, attending plenary sessions of the conference, and participating in active parallel meetings of interested NGOs.
2. Though there have been significant improvements in the human rights situation in Eastern Europe, the changes have not been uniform, and problems still exist. The excerpts below describe some changes in the U.S.S.R.

Statement by Ambassador Warren Zimmerman, Chairman of the U.S. Delegation to the Vienna CSCE Follow-Up Meeting, May 5, 1987, Vienna, Austria:

We return to Vienna for a long and intensive stage of our meeting. Ahead of us is a schedule that provides the flexibility for the painstaking and detailed work of negotiating and drafting a final document. That document is critically important. It should highlight and strengthen the obligations of the Helsinki Final Act, particularly those obligations — as in the human dimension — where implementation has been weak. It should give impetus to both the security and the cooperative aspects of the Helsinki process. It should set the date and place for the successor meeting to Vienna, and should provide for a limited number of intersessional meetings on key topics. It should be a substantive document and a balanced one.

As we turn to detailed work on our final document, however, we must not lose sight of an element of the Helsinki process that is even more important than words on paper — performance on the ground. As we don our eyeshades, pick up our pencils, and adjust our spectacles, let us not forget that there is one aspect of the CSCE house that is worth more than its lease or its furniture — its inhabitants. Whether the people who live in the CSCE house do better or worse in their lives is the ultimate test of the value of the Helsinki process. For that reason it is important from time to time in these plenary meetings to make an evaluation. Today I want to look once more at the remarkable and dynamic phenomena of "glasnost" and "perestroika" in the Soviet Union, and to examine their effect so far on people.

In the short time since we last assembled in Vienna, much has happened in the bilateral relationship between the United States and the Soviet Union. Secretary of State Shultz led a large American delegation to Moscow for probing discussions with General Secretary Gorbachev, Prime Minister Ryzkhov, and Foreign Minister Shevardnadze. Difficult but productive talks were held on the issue of intermediate range nuclear forces; and we are now engaged in thorough consultations with our allies on the implications of those talks. The Secretary received a comprehensive account of "perestroika" from the Soviet leaders, and was able to describe American priorities, including human rights, in turn. Also during our recess, a major delegation of American Congressmen, including the Vice Chairman of the U.S. Vienna Delegation, Steny Hoyer, visited Moscow and conferred with Mr. Gorbachev and four of his Politburo colleagues.

It is clear that changes continue to affect major areas of Soviet life. A new historical play touches the heretofore taboo figures of Trotsky and Bukharin, two major Soviet revolutionaries about whom more is known by Westerners than by the Soviet people themselves. And as of last Friday, May 1, thousands of Soviet citizens will be able by a new law to sell their services privately. While it is too much to hope that this development will lead to large-scale private enterprise in the Soviet Union, it can certainly demonstrate that, as many have discovered since the days of Adam Smith, incentives enhance productivity.

There has also been some progress in the human dimension of the Helsinki Final Act. Here I would like to examine as specifically as possible the major categories, with the objective of welcoming what has been accomplished but also recognizing how much still remains to be done. A reasonable perspective, based on facts as we know them, can only assist our work here in Vienna.

First, over 100 Soviet political prisoners have been released. The American human rights organization Helsinki Watch has been able to document 131 releases since the first Supreme Soviet decree was signed at the beginning of February. Yet this figure does not compare favorably to the 280 prisoners who Foreign Ministry spokesman Gerasimov said on February 10 were either released or under review. By contrast, the Polish government released nearly all its 200 political prisoners in two days last September. And the number of those released pales beside the 550 who are specifically known to remain in prison, or the estimate of 1000 still jailed made by ex-prisoners, or the many more who are undocumented, uncounted, and nameless. Whatever the real number of prisoners of conscience, those released form only a small percentage of it. All of these prisoners are incarcerated for offenses which would not cost them an hour's freedom in the vast majority of the countries represented here. That is a measure of how far the Soviet Union still has to go.

Moreover, as new data become available, so too do disturbing trends become apparent. Prisoner releases have not been unconditional. Prisoners have been required to sign statements regarding their future conduct. At least 12 have been returned to labor camps for refusing to sign. In addition, in the largest category of political prisoners — the 242 believers who have been imprisoned for seeking to exercise their religious rights — there have been no releases at all. And of the 119 who are being held in psychiatric institutions, only a handful have been freed. Twelve Helsinki Monitors have been released by Supreme Soviet decree, but 26 remain in prison or labor camp. And in the dreaded Perm Labor Camp No. 36-1 — where 20 prisoners of conscience, including eight Helsinki Monitors, are being subjected to conditions as severe as anywhere in the Soviet Union — there have been no known releases. Six of those eight are members of the Ukrainian Helsinki Monitoring Group; the Ukrainian group is thus being subjected to harsher conditions than any other Helsinki group. Ten political prisoners have died in the Perm camp in the last three years, a measure of the danger for those being held there.

Lest there be any question about the criminality of the prisoners of conscience condemned to the Perm camp, let me recall the story of one of them. Mart Niklus is a 52-year-old Estonian, by profession an ornithologist, who was sentenced to ten years of special regimen camp and five years of exile for circulating samizdat and listening to the Voice of America. His lawyer asked for dismissal of these and other charges on the grounds that Niklus's actions were fully consistent with the Soviet Constitution and the Helsinki Final Act. Andrei Sakharov, who has expressed to the representatives of several CSCE participants his fears for the fate of the Perm prisoners said of Niklus that one has only to meet him, "an ornithologist and a true scientist, an absolutely honest and sensitive person, to appreciate the full cruelty and injustice of his sentence."

We can be thankful that there have been no recent political arrests. But the continuing travail of Mart Niklus and of the hundreds — perhaps thousands — like him reminds us that "glasnost" has so far had little overall effect on most Soviet citizens who have been brave enough to speak out for their rights and those of others.

Second, the picture on Soviet emigration is improving but mixed. Jewish, German, and Armenian emigration all rose sharply in March. The Jewish figures for April were even better, marking a rise from 98 in January to 146 in February to 470 in March to 717 in April. Here too perspective is necessary. Even if Jewish emigration for the rest of 1987 continued at the March-April rate, the yearly total would be only 7,000, less than one-seventh of the peak year of 1979. Moreover, almost all Jews who are emigrating seem to be drawn from the approximately 11,000 documented refuseniks, and even some of those have been turned down again. Very few new applications are being approved or even processed; and virtually none who lack first-degree relatives abroad can even get their applications accepted. In light of this growing data base, I am compelled to revise the statement I made April 10 that Soviet authorities did not seem to be taking a rigid view of their new legislation on entry and exit. In fact, as far as new applicants are concerned, the law is being applied with no discernible flexibility at all. Is it the intention of the Soviet authorities to close the door on emigration, except for close relatives, once the backlog of current refuseniks has been dealt with? If so, then any claims of liberalized emigration will be revealed to be a sham.

Behind the statistics it helps, as always, to look at the people. There is no sign that the shameful official intimidation of all who apply to emigrate has lessened. Prospective emigrants continue to face job dismissals, social ostracism, and official harassment. In addition, the secrecy disqualification for emigration continues to be used and abused. . . .

Third, there has been some progress, though not enough, in reunifying Soviet citizens with their families in the United States. Eighty of 135 family reunification cases have been resolved since President Reagan and General Secretary Gorbachev first met in Geneva. But since then the list has continued to grow with new cases until it is about the same size as at the time of the Geneva summit. In the same period, twenty-two Soviets have been allowed to join their spouses in the United States, but 11 are inexplicably prevented. And negative action continues even in this time of "glasnost." In January, officials gave Svetlana Braun hope that she could join her husband Keith, but ever since this young couple has been kept in limbo. Yuriy Balovlenkov, whose "secret" work was no more mysterious than computer programming, is entering his tenth year of separation from his American wife and two children. Soviet officials in Vienna and Moscow have been willing to discuss with Andrea Wine her work as representative of a coalition of divided spouses, but they did not prevent her husband Viktor Faermark from again being refused an exit visa in March.

Fourth, if a society is to be "open," then surely it should be open to the free flow of communication with foreign countries. Yet the continued jamming of Western radios, including the Voice of America, Radio Liberty, and Radio Free Europe, continues. Many of us had hoped that the unjamming of the BBC's Russian language service would be the harbinger of a genuine opening to information transmitted by foreign media. Instead, it seems to be a lonely exception to a rule which stands as a stunning contradiction of "glasnost." Indeed, the jammers taken off the BBC are now being directed against Radio Liberty. Moreover, restrictions on mail and telephone communication have continued throughout this period of "glasnost." Parcels disappear, letters are lost, phone calls are blocked or interfered with, and registered materials disappear. The only openness practiced in this area is the continued openness of private and personal correspondence to the censor's scrutiny and disposal.

Fifth, religion in the Soviet Union remains unfree. Believers are not allowed to organize bible study groups, conduct religious classes for children, perform charitable or social activities, or make contact with foreign believers of the same faith. Government regulation of religion means that many religious groups fail to be registered and thus cannot practice legally. The sphere of authorized activity remains limited to ritual functions. During Secretary Shultz's visit, Soviet authorities assured American officials that at least recognized denominations will be allowed to open more places of worship, import bibles and prayer books, and maintain contact with co-religionists abroad. Such steps would unfortunately not affect unregistered faiths nor establish the independence of religious activity in general. Nevertheless, they would be significant and welcome. We will watch with interest to see if they are actually taken.

In all these categories, therefore, there are significant remnants of a closed society. They continue to resist the impulses toward greater openness which have marked Mr. Gorbachev's stewardship. Indeed, they have so far shown themselves stronger than those impulses. Whether they will yield, or whether still stronger impulses are necessary, is a matter of conjecture. But objective examination of the evidence available at this moment leads to the conclusion that, when measured by the standard of the Helsinki and Madrid documents, the Soviet Union remains in substantial violation. For that reason the Western countries have put forward a comprehensive set of proposals that cover every area of the human dimension to which I have referred today.

I hope, however, that the Soviet Union will not wait for the completion of a Vienna Final Document before it takes substantial steps toward compliance with its obligations. Waiting would only condemn this Vienna meeting to a long and sterile existence. The time to step up the pace of performance is now.

Performance is one test of a country's seriousness in meeting its obligations. Institutionalization of performance is another. Performance can be ephemeral when the incentives which produced it fade. Prisoners can be rearrested. Emigration rates can be driven down as well as up. Jamming can be re-imposed just as fast as it can be lifted. Mechanisms to institutionalize performance would therefore increase trust. An illustrative list, by no means exhaustive, could include the following:

— Declaration of amnesty for all political prisoners as called for by Academician Sakharov and many others. It has been done without danger in other countries of Eastern Europe and would eliminate an entire class of Helsinki violations in a single sweep.

— Abolition of the articles of the Criminal Code which are used for political arrests and trials, and assurance that other articles — such as drug possession — will not be substituted. The infamous Articles 70 and 190 have not been used in Moscow, Leningrad, or Kiev since late November. Why not abolish them altogether?

— High-level assurances that emigration will not be restricted to the former refuseniks and first-degree relatives who today appear to be the only beneficiaries of the rising rate. Emigration for all should be permitted to rise to and to remain at, significant levels.

— A secrecy rule for emigration which, if it must exist at all, should be reasonable and fair. Mr. Gorbachev told his U.S. Congressional visitors two weeks ago that he stood by his statement in Paris in 1985 that a five-to-ten year waiting period was sufficient, though he left a loophole for "exceptional cases."

— A commitment to resolve all, not just some, divided family cases. As noted, the Soviet Union has recently taken steps to reunite some divided families, but new refusals continue, so that the number of unresolved cases at any moment remains high. The best solution is to resolve issues on the spot so that families are not separated in the first place.

— Abolition of the psychiatric hospitals run by the Ministry of the Interior or at least their transfer to competent medical authorities. Even the criminally insane have a right not to be treated with drugs that are obsolete or dangerous. The fact that such drugs are used on perfectly sane political dissenters makes the existence of such hospitals an outrage.

— A high-level declaration or decree that "glasnost" extends to openness of communication, including each citizen's unhindered access to information from foreign media. An end to radio jamming and to the exclusion of the foreign press would be the logical accompaniment.

— Freedom of travel for medical reasons. A patient's right to seek medical treatment and second opinions wherever he chooses is well-established in the West. In fact, while serving in the American Embassy in Moscow, I helped to administer a program by which visiting American patients could avail themselves of the first-rate eye surgery available in Moscow.

— Legislation to ensure that, if religious activity must come under government regulation, at least all believers must be given the broadest scope for free observance and perpetuation of their faiths.

The perspective here presented remains an unclear one. The Gorbachev leadership has undoubtedly made the Soviet Union a different and more hospitable place than it was two years ago. Yet there is an understandable tendency to exaggerate progress. Promises are not performance; objectives are not achievements. "Glasnost" and "perestroika" represent an encouraging process; but they do not — at least not yet — describe considerable accomplishments. . . .

Department of State, Country Reports on Human Rights Practices for 1988, Report Submitted to the Senate Committee on Foreign Relations and the House Committee on Foreign Affairs, 101st Cong., 2nd. Sess. 1274-75 (1990):

The Union of Soviet Socialist Republics (U.S.S.R.) has been a one-party state, dominated by the leadership of the Communist Party of the Soviet Union (CPSU). That leadership has been a self-perpetuating elite which, with the assistance of a powerful secret police apparatus, attempted to direct all aspects of public life. Although the Soviet Union is a multinational state, political power has always been highly centralized in Moscow.

The past year witnessed a remarkable opening up of the political process and improvements in human rights practices, although the Soviet Union has a considerable distance to go before it will meet the standards set forth in the Helsinki Final Act. In March, elections of deputies to the newly created Congress of People's Deputies were the freest since November 1917. Many old-line regional party bosses and machine candidates lost to reformers, some of whom were not party members. The Congress elected a legislature, the U.S.S.R. Supreme Soviet, that has shown some independence in confirming ministerial appointments and drafting legislation.

Though the Communist Party remains the sole recognized political party (with a few local exceptions), the leadership no longer rigidly controls all party members' expressions and actions. Clear differences between conservative and reformist party members have emerged in public. Party members in the Congress of People's Deputies and the Supreme Soviet have not voted a party line. Article 6 of the U.S.S.R. Constitution, which enshrines the Party's leading role in society, has come under fierce public attack.

Some important reforms have been institutionalized, including the creation of new legislative bodies and an election process that in many, if not all, cases allows a genuine choice between candidates. Local elections, scheduled for 1990, may contribute significantly to political decentralization. Legal reform, on the other hand, has proceeded slowly (although major steps are promised for 1990). The widely held view that President Mikhail Gorbachev's continued presence at the helm is critical to the success of reform suggests that the human rights improvements effected in recent years can still be reversed.

The Committee for State Security (KGB), police authorities, and prosecutors' offices are charged by the party leadership with enforcing the population's compliance with policy decisions, directives, and legislation. In some parts of the country, they have sought to intimidate dissenters and potential dissenters through short-term detention and administrative sentencing of demonstrators, summoning persons selectively for warning conversations, and harsh press attacks on dissidents. Unlike other government agencies, the KGB has been subjected to only a modicum of glasnost (openness) and perestroika (restructuring), although a media campaign has attempted to clean up its image and portray it as an agency that observes the law and protects citizens' rights.

In response to growing socioeconomic problems and in conjunction with a broader effort at reform, Soviet authorities have initiated the gradual decentralization of economic decisionmaking and authority. In October 1989, the Supreme Soviet took up a range of laws expanding earlier reforms and significantly revamping notions of property, land, and enterprise. This was aimed at introducing market elements into the economy. While private enterprise remains highly circumscribed, new scope was provided under perestroika for quasi-private activity by independent farmers and cooperatives.

In 1989, though the top leadership's approach to the exercise of power changed significantly, old authoritarian habits continued to pervade the governmental system at lower levels. There were frequent instances of the use of arbitrary authority, including the attempted intimidation of dissidents by the local police, particularly the KGB. The inability of these local officials to follow through with the ruthlessness that was once possible made their arbitrary actions increasingly ineffective.

Subject to the foregoing limitations, there is now general respect for freedom of expression, freedom of association, some freedom of the press and of assembly, and freedom of religion. The Ukrainian Catholic Church, the last denomination to suffer severe repression, was permitted to register its congregations in December. Government interference in religion has now been substantially reduced, and the Government's official sponsorship of atheism is now on the decline.

This generally positive picture, reflecting the intentions of the reform leadership, is marred, however, by the inability or unwillingness of lower ranks of the bureaucracy to adhere to the new standards. Thus, while severe punishment for dissent is now a matter of the past, petty harassment of citizens who offend the sensibilities of local bureaucrats continues.

Emigration from the Soviet Union increased dramatically during 1989. Ethnic Germans, Jews, Armenians, and other Soviet emigrants totaled about 200,000 during 1989, more than any other year in recent memory. More liberal bills on freedom of conscience and the press are expected to be introduced.... Of the new laws adopted so far, one specifically allows strikes, although it forbids them in such key areas as transportation and energy....

NOTES

1. For further reading, see:

L. Alekseeva, Soviet Dissent: Contemporary Movements for National, Religious, and Human Rights (1985);

Amnesty International, Report 1989, at 237-39 (1989);

Dimitrijevic, *Human Rights in the Constitutional Systems of Socialist States*, 8 Netherlands Q. Hum. Rts. 5 (No. 1, 1990)

V. Kuritsyn, The Development of the Rights and Freedoms in the Soviet State (1987);

Skryba, *The Human Rights Literature of the Soviet Union*, 4 Hum. Rts. Q. 124 (1982);

A. Szymanski, Human Rights in the Soviet Union (1984);

R. Toscano, Soviet Human Rights Policy and Perestroika (1989);

U.S. Helsinki Watch Committee, Soviet Abuse of Psychiatry for Political Purposes: A Helsinki Watch Report Update (1988);

U.S. Helsinki Watch Committee, Ten Years Later: Violations of the Helsinki Accords (1985).

2. Amnesty International has recorded the release of over 300 prisoners of conscience in the U.S.S.R. since 1987. Nevertheless, in April 1990 AI was continuing to work for the release of 50 known or suspected prisoners of conscience from prisons and psychiatric hospitals. AI, USSR: Four Long-Term Prisoners Still Awaiting a Review, AI Index: 46/10/90 (1990).

3. For a discussion of changes in U.S. human rights policies vis-à-vis the U.S.S.R., see the excerpts from Human Rights Watch, The Bush Administration's Record in Human Rights in 1989 (1990), reproduced in chapter 11, *infra*.

EVENTS IN EUROPE

Since Mikhail Gorbachev became the Soviet head of state in March 1985, the *U.S.S.R.* has sought to initiate economic and political reforms. The U.S.S.R. has also been plagued by ethnic tension and economic crisis. In March 1989 the freest elections in Soviet history resulted in many Communist Party candidates being defeated. The governments of Eastern Europe began to emulate and exceed the reforms in the Soviet Union. In July 1989 the Warsaw Pact agreed that its forces would not be used to interfere in the affairs of the Eastern European countries which are members. (A similar undertaking had been made in the Vienna Concluding Document of January 1989.) When it became clear that the Soviet military would not impede political change, the governments of Eastern Europe began to fall and the Communist parties in those countries lost power.

In May 1988 the prime minister of *Hungary*, who had been in office since the Soviet military stopped the uprising of 1956, was replaced and reformers were given power. In November 1988 the office of prime minister changed hands again with the new prime minister pledging to establish a market-based economy. In January 1989 Hungary took its first steps toward democracy by adopting a law to permit the establishment of independent political parties. Hungary ratified the Protocol on the Status of Refugees and dismantled its barrier to travel to Austria. Hungary began to receive refugees from the Hungarian minority in Romania. On October 7, 1989, the Communist Party renamed itself the Hungarian Socialist Party with an indication that Hungary would pursue a multiparty democracy, the protection of human rights, and a market economy. Later in October 1989 the Hungarian People's Republic was renamed the Hungarian Republic. In November 1989 there was a binding referendum as to when and how to select the president of the new republic.

In April 1989 Solidarity was permitted to function openly in *Poland* after being illegal for seven years. The Communist Party was no longer assured a leading role in the government. After elections in June 1989 a parliamentary coalition was formed and the first non-communist prime minister was selected in Poland since World War II. Poland began to undertake reforms to develop a market economy.

In August 1989 thousands of East Germans entered West German embassies in Czechoslovakia, Hungary, and Poland attempting to obtain permission to emigrate. From Hungary some East Germans were then able to enter Austria and ultimately West Germany. On September 10, 1989, Hungary dropped the requirement that East Germans needed to have exit permission to enter Hungary and opened its border with Austria so that the East Germans could leave. On September 30, 1989, East and West Germany agreed to allow the East Germans waiting in West German embassies to enter West Germany. From August through mid-October over 45,000 East Germans had entered West Germany. There were mounting demonstrations in the *German Democratic Republic* — particularly in Leipzig. On October 18, 1989, the G.D.R. head of state resigned and was replaced by the former head of security. On October 27, 1989, the State Council decreed an amnesty for all persons who had committed such offenses as illegally crossing the border or violating public order in connection with demonstrations. On November 9, 1989, the G.D.R. removed restrictions for its citizens to travel; the Berlin Wall was opened, after 28 years. On December 1, 1989, the Parliament of the German Democratic Republic voted that the Communist Party would no longer be guaranteed a preeminent role in the government. On December 9, 1989, new reformist leadership was selected to replace leaders who had been in office for less than two months. Several of the prominent ministers from previous governments were imprisoned for economic offenses. Leaders allied with the Federal Republic of Germany won elections in the G.D.R. and German reunification appeared to be inevitable; it was unclear, however, how a unified Germany would fit within NATO.

On November 14, 1989, *Czechoslovakia* announced that it will no longer require permission for citizens wishing to travel abroad. On November 17, 1989, the government brutally suppressed a student demonstration in Prague. On November 24, 1989, the entire Communist Party leadership resigned. After increasing demonstrations every day and a two-hour general strike, the Czech Parliament voted on November 28, 1989, to remove the constitutional provision which had previously assured the Communist Party a preeminent role in governing the country. The governments of Czechoslovakia and the U.S.S.R. admitted on December 4, 1989, that the Warsaw Pact committed an error in invading Czechoslovakia to suppress the 1968 Prague Spring. A new government was formed with non-communists in the Cabinet. On December 10, 1989, the President resigned. Vaclev Havel, a leading human rights activist, was elected President in December 1989.

During October 1989 the government of *Yugoslavia* indicated that it may begin to permit a multiparty democracy. Regional conflict, however, increased. The Communist Party lost power in several parts of Yugoslavia.

On November 10, 1989, the long-serving government of *Bulgaria* fell and was replaced with a younger, more liberal head of the Communist Party. A political opposition is for the first time in 40 years beginning in Bulgaria. Thousands demonstrated to celebrate the end of the previous government and for further reforms. On December 15, 1989, the Communist Party gave up its guarantee of power.

In mid-December demonstrations against the government in *Romania* were brutally suppressed. On December 22, 1989, Nicholae Ceausescu was forced to resign from office and then summarily executed. He had been the only signatory of the 1975 Helsinki Accords who remained in power. The National Salvation Front won elections in May 1990, but Romania continued to face political instability, economic difficulties, ethnic tensions, and uncertain efforts to achieve democracy.

Albania appeared as of 1990 largely to have resisted the winds of change which are altering the face of Eastern Europe. First Secretary Enver Hoxha ruled Albania from 1946 until his death in 1985. Hoxha's designated successor, First Secretary Ramiz Alia has begun to liberalize and to diminish human rights violations. In November 1989 Alia decreed an amnesty for political prisoners. Alia has also made some efforts to end the country's isolation from the rest of the world. Albania has been the only government in Europe that has not participated in the Helsinki process, but in 1990 Albania announced that it would like to participate in future CSCE meetings.

As the Soviet domination over Eastern Europe has diminished, developments in Eastern Europe have had consequences in the Soviet Union. The government has committed itself to a multiparty system in which the Communist Party would no longer have guaranteed leadership. The U.S.S.R. is faced with ethnic/nationalist tensions, economic dislocation, and the failure to fulfill consumer expectations. In October 1989 the Latvian Popular

Front began to pursue independence for *Latvia*. In December 1989 the Lithuanian Parliament removed the constitutional provision which had guaranteed the Communist Party a "leading role" in the government of *Lithuania*. The Lithuanian Communist Party also declared itself independent from the Communist Party in Moscow. In 1990 Lithuania declared itself independent, but met with economic sanctions and political resistance from the Soviet leadership in Moscow. Similar changes are occurring in *Estonia* and in other parts of the U.S.S.R.

It is unclear whether the end of Soviet domination will result in viable democratic governments in the U.S.S.R. and Eastern Europe. Few countries in the region have any experience with democracy. Ethnic/national minorities are encountering intolerance and are the cause of tensions within as well as among the countries of the region. Every country in the region, except Poland, has a significant ethnic/national minority. For example, there are a large number of Hungarians in Czechoslovakia, Romania, and Yugoslavia. If Hungarians are subjected to discrimination or intolerance in other countries, tensions rise between Hungary and its neighbors. Also, there continue to be border disputes among several countries in the region. Accordingly, it is not clear whether the end of Soviet domination will be accompanied by a peaceful transition to democracy.

In the West the 12 governments of the *European Community* are taking steps to achieve travel, financial, and other forms of integration by 1992. While Western European countries have established democratic structures, they are not free from human rights problems. In November 1989 Amnesty International expressed human rights concerns in a number of Western European countries. For example, A.I. found evidence of ill-treatment of people in police custody in Austria, France, Italy, Portugal, and Spain. A.I. also published information about the isolation of prisoners detained under anti-terrorist laws in the Federal Republic of Germany, killings in Gibraltar, alleged forced admissions during *incommunicado* detention in the United Kingdom, and the imprisonment of conscientious objectors in Cyprus, Finland, Greece, and Switzerland. *See* Amnesty International, Concerns in Western Europe, AI Index: EUR 03/02/89 (1989).

NOTES AND QUESTIONS

1. For further reading, see:

Amnesty International, Albania: Political Imprisonment & the Law (1984);

Amnesty International, Bulgaria: Imprisonment of Ethnic Turks and Human Rights Activists (1989);

Amnesty International, Romania: Human Rights Violations in the Eighties (1987);

Amnesty International, Yugoslavia: Prisoners of Conscience (1985);

Baker, *U.S.-Soviet Relations: A Discussion of Perestroika and Economic*

Reform, State Dept. Bureau of Public Affairs, Current Policy No. 1209 (1989);

Eagleburger, *The Challenge of the European Landscape in the 1990s*, 89 State Dept. Bull. 37 (1989);

O. Gruenwald, & K. Rosenblum-Cale eds., Human Rights in Yugoslavia (1986);

H. Hannum, Autonomy, Sovereignty, and Self-Determination 358-69 (1990);

International League for Human Rights, Human Rights in Poland (1987);

International League for Human Rights, Romania's Human Rights Record: Comments on the Government of Romania's Official Report to the Human Rights Committee (1987);

Koshy, *Perestroika*, 1988/1 Background Information, Comm. Churches Int'l Affairs 5 (1988);

Legal Reform in the Soviet Union, 28 Colum. J. Transnat'l L. 1 (1990);

G. Lundestad, The Relationship Between Justice and Stability in Eastern Europe, Feb. 16, 1990;

Minnesota Lawyers International Human Rights Committee, Human Rights in the People's Socialist Republic of Albania (1989);

R. Schifter, The Helsinki Process: Then and Now, January 29, 1990;

Seitz, *Europe: A Climate of Dramatic Change*, State Dept. Bureau of Public Affairs, Current Policy No. 1220 (1989);

U.S. Helsinki Watch Committee, Violations of the Helsinki Accords, Romania: A Report Prepared for the Helsinki Review Conference (1986).

2. How will developments in Europe affect the nature of the discussions in the CSCE meetings?

D. STRASBOURG PROCESS

1. The European System

a. Codification

The European system is the most fully developed of the regional human rights structures in existence. The European Convention for the Protection of Human Rights and Fundamental Freedoms entered into force in 1953.[4] The Convention created two bodies for human rights implementation: the European Commission of Human Rights and the European Court of Human Rights.

The European Convention protects civil and political rights. The Convention guarantees the rights to life, liberty, and the security of the person

---

[4] [European] Convention for the Protection of Human Rights and Fundamental Freedoms, 213 U.N.T.S. 222 (1950), *entered into force* Sept. 3, 1953.

as well as the rights to privacy, freedom of conscience and religion, peaceful assembly, association, and due process of law. The European Convention also prohibits discrimination based on race, gender, national origin, and language; torture; inhuman or degrading treatment or punishment; slavery; servitude; and forced or compulsory labor.[5] The separate European Social Charter of the Council of Europe proclaims economic and social rights, and contains an implementation procedure calling for state reporting on the application of the provisions of the Charter.[6]

b. Implementation

The European Convention established the European Commission of Human Rights as the principal body to determine whether a state has violated the European Convention. Each state party to the European Convention appoints one member to the Commission. Parties to the Convention may refer alleged violations by other states under article 24 to the Commission. In addition, article 25 allows parties voluntarily, by a separate decision, to accept the competence of the Commission to hear applications brought by individuals. The Commission therefore can receive applications brought by one state against another and applications brought against a state by or on behalf of an individual or group. The Commission, if unable to promote a friendly settlement between the parties, determines the facts of the case and issues an opinion to the parties and to the Committee of Ministers of the Council of Europe as to whether the Commission finds a breach of the Convention.

Within three months of the issuance of the Commission's report, the Commission, the state against which the complaint was brought, or the state of the individual who lodged the complaint may take the case before the European Court of Human Rights. If after three months the case has not been referred to the Court, the Committee of Ministers of the Council of Europe makes the final decision whether the state has violated the European Convention. A decision by the Committee of Ministers requires a two-thirds majority, rather than the simple majority required for a decision by the Court.

---

[5] Council of Europe member states also have adopted and ratified eight Protocols to the European Convention. See European Convention on Human Rights, Collected Texts 23-62 (1987). The first Protocol guarantees rights to property, education, and free elections. *Id.* at 24. Subsequent Protocols give the European Court competence to issue advisory opinions and guarantee the rights of aliens and the right of freedom to travel. *See id.* at 28 (Protocol No. 2); 37 (Protocol No. 4); 52 (Protocol No. 7). Protocol No. 6 abolishes the death penalty. *Id.* at 47.

[6] European Social Charter, E.T.S. 35, *entered into force* Feb. 26, 1965. In addition, the European Convention for the Prevention of Torture and Inhuman or Degrading Treatment or Punishment, Doc. No. H(87)4 (1987), *entered into force* Feb. 1, 1989, established a committee of experts with unlimited access to places of detention and detainees, although the committee must notify governments of their intention to undertake a visit.

The Commission usually will refer to the Court cases that Commission members believe raise important questions for interpretation under the European Convention. Respondent states, however, are likely to prefer disposition of cases through the Committee of Ministers. This preference arises out of the Committee's composition. The Committee of Ministers is composed of the Foreign Ministers of Council of Europe member-states or their representatives, who, unlike members of the Commission or the Court, serve as governmental representatives rather than in their individual capacities. The decisions of the Committee of Ministers tend to be motivated by political considerations rather than human rights or legal principles. In addition, because the Committee of Ministers must decide cases by a two-thirds majority, the Committee may close cases without decisive action if the requisite majority is not reached. Because of these difficulties, the European Commission would rather refer most cases in which it has found a violation of the Convention to the European Court of Human Rights.[7]

The Court consists of 21 judges elected by the Consultative Assembly of the Council of Europe. If a case is referred to the Court, the Committee of Ministers relinquishes its jurisdiction. The Court's decision is final and binding, although the Court lacks the capacity to execute judgment. Instead, the Committee of Ministers supervises execution of the Court's judgment. Although the Committee of Ministers' supervision of compliance with the Court's judgment has been criticized as perfunctory, states adjudged as being in violation of the Convention generally have been prepared to take the action necessary to correct their violations.

The European system for the protection of human rights has compiled its body of jurisprudence slowly. Although the Commission received more than 2,700 applications in its first thirteen years of operation, the Commission referred only three cases to the Court. During the same period, the Committee of Ministers considered only an additional ten cases. These figures reflect the narrow interpretation that the Commission initially gave to the European Convention, finding admissible less than one half of one percent of the first 2,700 applications it received. The Commission's narrow reading of the Convention has increased state confidence in the Convention over its more than thirty-five year existence. In 1966, only eleven Council of Europe member-states had recognized the compulsory jurisdiction of the Court and the competence of the Commission to receive individual petitions. By 1990, however, twenty-one of the twenty-three Council of Europe member-states had recognized the Court's jurisdiction and twenty-two states had ratified the European Convention. By January 1, 1989, the Commission had received 14,466 applications and decided 12,903 cases. The Commission found admissible 575, or about 4% of the applications filed. The Commission

---

[7] The Council of Europe, European Commission, and European Court have been considering the possible unification of the functions of the Commission and Court. *See* Council of Europe, *Committee of Experts for the Improvement of Procedures for the Protection of Human Rights*, 11 Eur. Hum. Rts. Rep. 421 (1989).

had rendered decisions on 286 cases.[8]

The European Court gradually has compiled a substantial body of jurisprudence, having decided 151 cases by September 1989.[9] The court decided its first case, the *Lawless Case*,[10] in 1961. The Court's opinion described the kind of public emergency that would permit derogations from the European Convention under article 15. The Court subsequently has addressed applications invoking the European Convention's guarantees of a fair public trial, the presumption of innocence, and the right to counsel. Other claimants have alleged violations of the Convention's prohibition of torture or inhuman or degrading treatment or punishment. In its 1978 decision in the *Tyrer Case*,[11] for example, the Court found that a school's punishment of a student by caning constituted degrading treatment in violation of Article 3 of the Convention. The Court also has had several occasions to examine allegations that state criminal procedures have unreasonably deprived persons of liberty. Of particular interest to the U.S. is the *Soering Case*, in which the European Court of Human Rights concluded that a national of the Federal Republic of Germany could not be extradited to Virginia, because he might face the degrading prospect of a long wait on Death Row.[12]

The increasing awareness by Europeans of the existence of the European Convention on Human Rights has produced a steady rise in the number of applications the Commission receives each year. The European system has clearly been successful in implementing the human rights codified in the European Convention.

---

[8] Of those cases, 180 were referred to the European Court of Human Rights and the remainder were referred to the Committee of Ministers.

[9] While the Commission has referred 180 cases, one case was split into two decisions. The Court had 31 cases pending as of September 1989.

[10] *Lawless Case*, 1961 Y.B. Eur. Conv. on Human Rights 430 (Eur. Ct. of Human Rights).

[11] *Tyrer Case*, 1978 Y.B. Eur. Conv. on Human Rights 612 (Eur. Ct. of Human Rights).

[12] *Soering Case*, 161 Eur. Ct. Hum. Rts. (series A) (1989), 28 I.L.M. 1063 (1989).

NOTES

1. For further reading, see:

R. Beddard, Human Rights and Europe: A Study of the Machinery of Human Rights Protection of the Council of Europe (1980);

Berenstein, *Economic and Social Rights: Their Inclusion in the European Convention on Human Rights. Problems of Formulation and Interpretation,* 2 Human Rights L.J. 257 (1981);

Boyle, *Practice and Procedure on Individual Applications Under the European Convention on Human Rights*, in Guide to International Human Rights Practice 133 (H. Hannum ed. 1984);

Drzemczewski, *The Role of NGOs in Human Rights Matters in the Council of Europe*, 8 Hum. Rts. L.J. 273 (1987);

S. Ercman, European Convention on Human Rights: Guide to Case Law (1981);

European Comm'n Hum. Rts., Organization, procedure and activities (1990);

Higgins, *The European Convention on Human Rights*, in Human Rights in International Law: Legal and Policy Issues 495 (T. Meron ed. 1985);

P. Leuprecht & P. van Dijk, ed., Digest of Strasbourg Case-Law Relating to the European Convention on Human Rights (1984);

J. Merrills, The Development of International Law by the European Court of Human Rights (1988);

P. van Dijk & G. van Hoof, Theory and Practice of the European Convention of Human Rights (1984).

2. For comparisons of the three major regional systems — the European, Inter-American, and African systems — see Buergenthal, *The American and European Conventions on Human Rights: Similarities and Differences*, 30 Am. U.L. Rev. 155 (1981); Weston, Lukes, & Hnatt, *Regional Human Rights Regimes: A Comparison and Appraisal*, 20 Vand. J. Transnat'l L. 585 (1987).

---

2. Soering Case

Soering Case, 161 Eur. Ct. Hum. Rts. (series A) (1989), 11 Eur. Hum. Rts. Rep. 439 (1989), 28 I.L.M. 1063 (1989) (citations and footnotes omitted):

The European Court of Human Rights . . .

Delivers the following judgment . . .

PROCEDURE

1. The case was brought before the Court . . . by the European Commission of Human Rights ("the Commission"), . . . by the Government of the United Kingdom . . . and . . . by the Government of the Federal Republic of Germany, within . . . the Convention for the Protection of Human Rights and Fundamental Freedoms ("the Convention"). It originated in an application . . . against the United Kingdom lodged with the Commission under Article 25 by a German national, Mr. Jens Soering. . . .

. . . The object of the request and of the two governmental applications was to obtain a decision from the Court as to whether or not the facts of the case disclosed a breach by the respondent State of its obligations under Articles 3, 6 and 13 of the Convention. . . .

4. [F]ollowing requests for an interim measure made by the Commission and the

applicant, the Court indicated to the United Kingdom Government that it would be advisable not to extradite the applicant to the United States of America pending the outcome of the proceedings before the Court. . . .

11. The applicant, Mr. Jens Soering, was born on 1 August 1966 and is a German national. He is currently detained in prison in England pending extradition to the United States of America to face charges of murder in the Commonwealth of Virginia.

12. The homicides in question were committed in Bedford County, Virginia, in March 1985. The victims, William Reginald Haysom (aged 72) and Nancy Astor Haysom (aged 53), were the parents of the applicant's girlfriend, . . . a Canadian national. . . . At the time the applicant. . . , aged 18. . . , [was a student] at the University of Virginia. [He] disappeared. . . from Virginia in October 1985, but [was] arrested in England in April 1986 in connection with cheque fraud.

13. The applicant was interviewed in England between 5 and 8 June 1986 by a police investigator from the Sheriff's Department of Bedford County. In a sworn affidavit dated 24 July 1986 the investigator recorded the applicant as having admitted the killings. . . .

14. [T]he Government of the United States of America requested the applicant's . . . extradition under the terms of the Extradition Treaty of 1972 between the United States and the United Kingdom. . . .

15. [T]he British Embassy in Washington addressed a request to the United States' authorities in the following terms:

> "Because the death penalty has been abolished in Great Britain, the Embassy has been instructed to seek an assurance, in accordance with the terms of . . . the Extradition Treaty, that, in the event of Mr. Soering being surrendered and being convicted of the crimes for which he has been indicted. . . , the death penalty, if imposed, will not be carried out.
>
> Should it not be possible on constitutional grounds for the United States Government to give such an assurance, the United Kingdom authorities ask that the United States Government undertake to recommend to the appropriate authorities that the death penalty should not be imposed or, if imposed, should not be executed."

16. [T]he applicant was interviewed in prison by a German prosecutor (*Staatsanwalt*) from Bonn. . . .

[T]he local court in Bonn issued a warrant for the applicant's arrest in respect of the alleged murders. . . . [T]he Government of the Federal Republic of Germany requested his extradition to the Federal Republic under the Extradition Treaty of 1872 between the Federal Republic and the United Kingdom. . . .

19. [T]he Government of the United Kingdom informed the Federal Republic of Germany that the United States had earlier "submitted a request, supported by *prima facie* evidence, for the extradition of Mr. Soering." The United Kingdom Government notified the Federal Republic that they had "concluded that, having regard to all the circumstances of the case, the court should continue to consider in the normal way the United States' request". . . .

20. Mr. Updike swore an affidavit in his capacity as Attorney for Bedford County, in which he certified as follows:

"I hereby certify that should Jens Soering be convicted of the offence of capital murder as charged in Bedford County, Virginia . . . a representation will be made in the name of the United Kingdom to the judge at the time of sentencing that it is the wish of the United Kingdom that the death penalty should not be imposed or carried out." . . .

During the course of the present proceedings the Virginia authorities have informed the United Kingdom Government that Mr. Updike was not planning to provide any further assurances and intended to seek the death penalty in Mr. Soering's case because the evidence, in his determination, supported such action. . . .

24. . . . [T]he Secretary of State signed a warrant ordering the applicant's surrender to the United States' authorities. However, the applicant has not been transferred to the United States by virtue of the interim measures indicated in the present proceedings firstly by the European Commission and then by the European Court. . . .

25. On 5 August 1988 the applicant was transferred to a prison hospital where he remained until early November 1988 under the special regime applied to suicide-risk prisoners.

According to psychiatric evidence adduced on behalf of the applicant . . . , the applicant's dread of extreme physical violence and homosexual abuse from other inmates in death row in Virginia is in particular having a profound psychiatric effect on him. The psychiatrist's report records a mounting desperation in the applicant, together with objective fears that he may seek to take his own life.

26. . . . [T]he applicant stated that should the United Kingdom Government require that he be deported to the Federal Republic of Germany he would consent to such requirement and would present no factual or legal opposition against the making or execution of an order to that effect. . . .

36. There is no provision in the Extradition Acts relating to the death penalty, but Article IV of the United Kingdom-United States Treaty provides:

"If the offence for which extradition is requested is punishable by death under the relevant law of the requesting Party, but the relevant law of the requested Party does not provide for the death penalty in a similar case, extradition may be refused unless the requesting Party gives assurances satisfactory to the requested Party that the death penalty will not be carried out."

37. In the case of a fugitive requested by the United States who faces a charge carrying the death penalty, it is the Secretary of State's practice, pursuant to Article IV of the United Kingdom-United States Extradition Treaty, to accept an assurance from the prosecuting authorities of the relevant State that a representation will be made to the judge at the time of sentencing that it is the wish of the United Kingdom that the death penalty should be neither imposed nor carried out. . . .

There has, however, never been a case in which the effectiveness of such an undertaking has been tested.

38. Concurrent requests for extradition in respect of the same crime from two different States are not a common occurrence. If both requests are received at the same time, the Secretary of State decides which request is to be proceeded with, having regard to all the facts of the case, including the nationality of the fugitive and the place of commission of the offence. . . .

42. The sentencing procedure in a capital murder case in Virginia is a separate proceeding from the determination of guilt. Following a determination of guilt of capital murder, the same jury, or judge sitting without a jury, will forthwith proceed to hear evidence regarding punishment. All relevant evidence concerning the offence and the defendant is admissible. Evidence in mitigation is subject to almost no limitation, while evidence of aggravation is restricted by statute . . . .

44. The imposition of the death penalty on a young person who has reached the age of majority — which is 18 years . . . — is not precluded under Virginia law. Age is a fact to be weighed by the jury. . . .

49. The law of Virginia generally does not recognise a defence of diminished capacity. . . .

50. A plea of insanity at the time of the offence is recognised as a defence in Virginia and, if successful, is a bar to conviction. Such a plea will apply where the defendant knows that the act is wrong but is driven by an irresistible impulse, induced by some mental disease affecting the volitive powers, to commit it. . . .

51. In a capital murder trial, the defendant's mental condition at the time of the offence, including any level of mental illness, may be pleaded as a mitigating factor at the sentencing stage. . . .

56. . . . The average time between trial and execution in Virginia, calculated on the basis of the seven executions which have taken place since 1977, is six to eight years. The delays are primarily due to a strategy by convicted prisoners to prolong the appeal proceedings as much as possible. The United States Supreme Court has not as yet considered or ruled on the "death row phenomenon" and in particular whether it falls foul of the prohibition of "cruel and unusual punishment" under the Eighth Amendment to the Constitution of the United States. . . .

61. There are currently 40 people under sentence of death in Virginia. The majority are detained in Mecklenburg Correctional Center, which is a modern maximum security institution with a total capacity of 335 inmates. . . .

63. The size of a death row inmate's cell is 3m by 2.2m. Prisoners have an opportunity for approximately 7½ hours' recreation per week in summer and approximately 6 hours' per week, weather permitting, in winter. The death row area has two recreation yards, both of which are equipped with basketball courts and one of which is equipped with weights and weight benches. Inmates are also permitted to leave their cells on other occasions, such as to receive visits, to visit the law library or to attend the prison infirmary. In addition, death row inmates are given one hour out-of-cell time in the morning in a common area. Each death row inmate is eligible for work assignments, such as cleaning duties. When prisoners move around the prison they are handcuffed with special shackles around the waist.

   When not in their cells, death row inmates are housed in a common area called "the pod." The guards are not within this area and remain in a box outside. In the event of disturbance or inter-inmate assault, the guards are not allowed to intervene until instructed to do so by the ranking officer present.

64. The applicant adduced much evidence of extreme stress, psychological deterioration and risk of homosexual abuse and physical attack undergone by prisoners on death row, including Mecklenburg Correctional Center. This evidence was strongly contested by the United Kingdom Government on the basis of affidavits sworn by administrators from the Virginia Department of Corrections. . . .

68. A death row prisoner is moved to the death house 15 days before he is due to be executed. The death house is next to the death chamber where the electric chair is situated. Whilst a prisoner is in the death house he is watched 24 hours a day. He is isolated and has no light in his cell. The lights outside are permanently lit. A prisoner who utilises the appeals process can be placed in the death house several times. . . .

69. Relations between the United Kingdom and the United States of America on matters concerning extradition are conducted by and with the Federal and not the State authorities. However, in respect of offences against State laws the Federal authorities have no legally binding power to provide, in an appropriate extradition case, an assurance that the death penalty will not be imposed or carried out. In such cases the power rests with the State. If a State does decide to give a promise in relation to the death penalty, the United States Government would have the power to give an assurance to the extraditing Government that the State's promise will be honoured. . . .

PROCEEDINGS BEFORE THE COMMISSION

76. Mr. Soering's application . . . was lodged with the Commission on 8 July 1988. In his application Mr. Soering stated his belief that, notwithstanding the assurance given to the United Kingdom Government, there was a serious likelihood that he would be sentenced to death if extradited to the United States of America. He maintained that in the circumstances and, in particular, having regard to the "death row phenomenon" he would thereby be subjected to inhuman and degrading treatment and punishment contrary to Article 3 of the Convention. In his further submission his extradition to the United States would constitute a violation of Article 6 § 3 (c) because of the absence of legal aid in the State of Virginia to pursue various appeals. Finally, he claimed that, in breach of Article 13, he had no effective remedy under United Kingdom law in respect of his complaint under Article 3. . . .

78. The Commission declared the application admissible on 10 November 1988.

In its report adopted on 19 January 1989 (Article 31) the Commission expressed the opinion that there had been a breach of Article 13 (seven votes to four) but no breach of either Article 3 (six votes to five) or Article 6 § 3 (c) (unanimously). . . .

AS TO THE LAW

I.   ALLEGED BREACH OF ARTICLE 3

80. The applicant alleged that the decision by the Secretary of State for the Home Department to surrender him to the authorities of the United States of America would, if implemented, give rise to a breach by the United Kingdom of Article 3 of the Convention, which provides:

> "No one shall be subjected to torture or to inhuman or degrading treatment or punishment."

A.   *Applicability of Article 3 in cases of extradition*

81. The alleged breach derives from the applicant's exposure to the so-called "death row phenomenon." This phenomenon may be described as consisting in a combination of circumstances to which the applicant would be exposed if, after having been extradited to Virginia to face a capital murder charge, he were sentenced to death. . . .

88. . . . The question remains whether the extradition of a fugitive to another State where he would be subjected or be likely to be subjected to torture or to inhuman or degrading treatment or punishment would itself engage the responsibility of a Contracting State under Article 3. That the abhorrence of torture has such implications is recognised in Article 3 of the United Nations Convention Against Torture and Other Cruel, Inhuman or Degrading Treatment or Punishment, which provides that "no State Party shall . . . extradite a person where there are substantial grounds for believing that he would be in danger of being subjected to torture". The fact that a specialised treaty should spell out in detail a specific obligation attaching to the prohibition of torture does not mean that an essentially similar obligation is not already inherent in the general terms of Article 3 of the European Convention. It would hardly be compatible with the underlying values of the Convention, that "common heritage of political traditions, ideals, freedoms and the rule of law" to which the Preamble refers, were a Contracting State knowingly to surrender a fugitive to another State where there were substantial grounds for believing that he would be in danger of being subjected to torture, however heinous the crime allegedly committed. Extradition in such circumstances, while not explicitly referred to in the brief and general wording of Article 3, would plainly be contrary to the spirit and intendment of the Article, and in the Court's view this inherent obligation not to extradite also extends to cases in which the fugitive would be faced in the receiving State by a real risk of exposure to inhuman or degrading treatment or punishment proscribed by that Article. . . .

91. In sum, the decision by a Contracting State to extradite a fugitive may give rise to an issue under Article 3, and hence engage the responsibility of that State under the Convention, where substantial grounds have been shown for believing that the person concerned, if extradited, faces a real risk of being subjected to torture or to inhuman or degrading treatment or punishment in the requesting country. The establishment of such responsibility inevitably involves an assessment of conditions in the requesting country against the standards of Article 3 of the Convention. Nonetheless, there is no question of adjudicating on or establishing the responsibility of the receiving country, whether under general international law, under the Convention or otherwise. In so far as any liability under the Convention is or may be incurred, it is liability incurred by the extraditing Contracting State by reason of its having taken action which has as a direct consequence the exposure of an individual to proscribed ill-treatment. . . .

92. . . . It therefore has to be determined on the above principles whether the foreseeable consequences of Mr. Soering's return to the United States are such as to attract the application of Article 3. This inquiry must concentrate firstly on whether Mr. Soering runs a real risk of being sentenced to death in Virginia, since the source of the alleged inhuman and degrading treatment or punishment, namely the "death row phenomenon," lies in the imposition of the death penalty. Only in the event of an affirmative answer to this question need the Court examine whether exposure to the "death row phenomenon" in the circumstances of the applicant's case would involve treatment or punishment incompatible with Article 3.

    1.   *Whether the applicant runs a real risk of a death sentence and hence of exposure to the "death row phenomenon"*

94. . . . The United Kingdom Government [is] justified in their assertion that no assumption can be made that Mr. Soering would certainly or even probably be

convicted of capital murder as charged.... Nevertheless, as the Attorney General conceded on their behalf at the public hearing, there is "a significant risk" that the applicant would be so convicted.

95. Under Virginia law, before a death sentence can be returned the prosecution must prove beyond reasonable doubt the existence of at least one of the two statutory aggravating circumstances, namely future dangerousness or vileness.... In this connection, the horrible and brutal circumstances of the killings ... would presumably tell against the applicant, regard being had to the case-law on the grounds for establishing the "vileness" of the crime....

Admittedly, taken on their own the mitigating factors do reduce the likelihood of the death sentence being imposed. No less than four of the five facts in mitigation expressly mentioned in the Code of Virginia could arguably apply to Mr. Soering's case. These are a defendant's lack of any previous criminal history, the fact that the offence was committed while a defendant was under extreme mental or emotional disturbance, the fact that at the time of commission of the offence the capacity of a defendant to appreciate the criminality of his conduct or to conform his conduct to the requirements of the law was significantly diminished, and a defendant's age....

98. ... Whatever the position under Virginia law and practice..., and notwithstanding the diplomatic context of the extradition relations between the United Kingdom and the United States, objectively it cannot be said that the undertaking to inform the judge at the sentencing stage of the wishes of the United Kingdom eliminates the risk of the death penalty being imposed. In the independent exercise of his discretion the Commonwealth's Attorney has himself decided to seek and to persist in seeking the death penalty because the evidence, in his determination, supports such action.... If the national authority with responsibility for prosecuting the offence takes such a firm stance, it is hardly open to the Court to hold that there are no substantial grounds for believing that the applicant faces a real risk of being sentenced to death and hence experiencing the "death row phenomenon".

99. The Court's conclusion is therefore that the likelihood of the feared exposure to the applicant to the "death row phenomenon" has been shown to be such as to bring Article 3 into play.

2.   *Whether in the circumstances the risk of exposure to the "death row phenomenon" would make extradition a breach of Article 3*

(a)   *General considerations*

100. As is established in the Court's case-law, ill-treatment, including punishment, must attain a minimum level of severity if it is to fall within the scope of Article 3. The assessment of this minimum is, in the nature of things, relative; it depends on all the circumstances of the case, such as the nature and context of the treatment or punishment, the manner and method of its execution, its duration, its physical or mental effects and, in some instances, the sex, age and state of health of the victim ....

Treatment has been held by the Court to be both "inhuman" because it was premeditated, was applied for hours at a stretch and "caused, if not actual bodily injury, at least intense physical and mental suffering", and also "degrading" because it was "such as to arouse in [its] victims feelings of fear, anguish and inferiority capable of humiliating and debasing them and possibly breaking their physical or moral resistance".... In order for a punishment or treatment associated with it to be "inhuman" or "degrading", the suffering or humiliation involved must in any event go beyond that inevitable element of suffering or humiliation connected with a given form of legitimate punishment. . . . In this connection, account is to be taken not only of the physical pain experienced but also, where there is a considerable delay before execution of the punishment, of the sentenced person's mental anguish of anticipating the violence he is to have inflicted on him.

101. Capital punishment is permitted under certain conditions by Article 2 § 1 of the Convention, which reads:

> "Everyone's right to life shall be protected by law. No one shall be deprived of his life intentionally save in the execution of a sentence of a court following his conviction of a crime for which this penalty is provided by law."

In view of this wording, the applicant did not suggest that the death penalty *per se* violated Article 3. He, like the two Government Parties, agreed with the Commission that the extradition of a person to a country where he risks the death penalty does not in itself raise an issue under either Article 2 or Article 3. On the other hand, Amnesty International in their written comments . . . argued that the evolving standards in Western Europe regarding the existence and use of the death penalty required that the death penalty should now be considered as an inhuman and degrading punishment within the meaning of Article 3.

102. Certainly, "the Convention is a living instrument which . . . must be interpreted in the light of present-day conditions"; and, in assessing whether a given treatment or punishment is to be regarded as inhuman or degrading for the purposes of Article 3, "the Court cannot but be influenced by the developments and commonly accepted standards in the penal policy of the member States of the Council of Europe in this field". . . . *De facto* the death penalty no longer exists in time of peace in the Contracting States to the Convention. In the few Contracting States which retain the death penalty in law for some peacetime offences, death sentences, if ever imposed, are nowadays not carried out. This "virtual consensus in Western European legal systems that the death penalty is, under current circumstances, no longer consistent with regional standards of justice", to use the words of Amnesty International, is reflected in Protocol No. 6 to the Convention, which provides for the abolition of the death penalty in time of peace. Protocol No. 6 was opened for signature in April 1983, which in the practice of the Council of Europe indicates the absence of objection on the part of any of the Member States of the Organisation; it came into force in March 1985 and to date has been ratified by thirteen Contracting States to the Convention, not however including the United Kingdom.

Whether these marked changes have the effect of bringing the death penalty *per se* within the prohibition of ill-treatment under Article 3 must be determined on the principles governing the interpretation of the Convention.

103. . . . Article 3 evidently cannot have been intended by the drafters of the Convention to include a general prohibition of the death penalty since that would nullify the clear wording of Article 2 § 1.

Subsequent practice in national penal policy, in the form of a generalised abolition of capital punishment, could be taken as establishing the agreement of the Contracting States to abrogate the exception provided for under Article 2 § 1 and hence to remove a textual limit on the scope for evolutive interpretation of Article 3. However, Protocol No. 6, as a subsequent written agreement, shows that the intention of the Contracting Parties as recently as 1983 was to adopt the normal method of amendment of the text in order to introduce a new obligation to abolish capital punishment in time of peace and, what is more, to do so by an optional instrument allowing each State to choose the moment when to undertake such an engagement. In these conditions, notwithstanding the special character of the Convention..., Article 3 cannot be interpreted as generally prohibiting the death penalty.

104. That does not mean however that circumstances relating to a death sentence can never give rise to an issue under Article 3. The manner in which it is imposed or executed, the personal circumstances of the condemned person and a disproportionality to the gravity of the crime committed, as well as the conditions of detention awaiting execution, are examples of factors capable of bringing the treatment or punishment received by the condemned person within the proscription under Article 3. Present-day attitudes in the Contracting States to capital punishment are relevant for the assessment whether the acceptable threshold of suffering or degradation has been exceeded.

(b) *The particular circumstances...*

i. *Length of detention prior to execution*

106. The period that a condemned prisoner can expect to spend on death row in Virginia before being executed is on average six to eight years.... This length of time awaiting death is, as the Commission and the United Kingdom noted, in a sense largely of the prisoner's own making in that he takes advantage of all avenues of appeal which are offered to him by Virginia law....

Nevertheless, just as some lapse of time between sentence and execution is inevitable if appeal safeguards are to be provided to the condemned person, so it is equally part of human nature that the person will cling to life by exploiting those safeguards to the full. However well-intentioned and even potentially beneficial is the provision of the complex of post-sentence procedures in Virginia, the consequence is that the condemned prisoner has to endure for many years the conditions on death row and the anguish and mounting tension of living in the ever-present shadow of death.

ii. *Conditions on death row*

107. As to conditions in Mecklenburg Correctional Center, where the applicant could expect to be held if sentenced to death, the Court bases itself on the facts which were uncontested by the United Kingdom Government, without finding it necessary to determine the reliability of the additional evidence adduced by the applicant, notably as to the risk of homosexual abuse and physical attack undergone by prisoners on death row....

... In this connection, the United Kingdom Government drew attention to the necessary requirement of extra security for the safe custody of prisoners condemned to death for murder. Whilst it might thus well be justifiable in principle, the severity of a special regime such as that operated on death row in Mecklenburg is compounded by the fact of inmates being subject to it for a protracted period lasting on average six to eight years.

iii. *The applicant's age and mental state*

108. At the time of the killings, the applicant was only 18 years old and there is some psychiatric evidence, which was not contested as such, that he "was suffering

from [such] an abnormality of mind . . . as substantially impaired his mental responsibility for his acts''. . . .

Unlike Article 2 of the Convention, Article 6 of the 1966 International Covenant on Civil and Political Rights and Article 4 of the 1969 American Convention on Human Rights expressly prohibit the death penalty from being imposed on persons aged less than 18 at the time of commission of the offence. Whether or not such a prohibition be inherent in the brief and general language of Article 2 of the European Convention, its explicit enunciation in other, later international instruments, the former of which has been ratified by a large number of States Parties to the European Convention, at the very least indicates that as a general principle the youth of the person concerned is a circumstance which is liable, with others, to put in question the compatibility with Article 3 of measures connected with a death sentence.

It is in line with the Court's case-law . . . to treat disturbed mental health as having the same effect for the application of Article 3. . . .

iv. *Possibility of extradition to the Federal Republic of Germany*

110. For the United Kingdom Government and the majority of the Commission, the possibility of extraditing or deporting the applicant to face trial in the Federal Republic of Germany . . ., where the death penalty has been abolished under the Constitution . . ., is not material for the present purposes. Any other approach, the United Kingdom Government submitted, would lead to a ''dual standard'' affording the protection of the Convention to extraditable persons fortunate enough to have such an alternative destination available but refusing it to others not so fortunate.

. . . It is therefore a circumstance of relevance for the overall assessment under Article 3 in that it goes to the search for the requisite fair balance of interests and to the proportionality of the contested extradition decision in the particular case. . . .

(c) *Conclusion*

111. For any prisoner condemned to death, some element of delay between imposition and execution of the sentence and the experience of severe stress in conditions necessary for strict incarceration are inevitable. The democratic character of the Virginia legal system in general and the positive features of Virginia trial, sentencing and appeal procedures in particular are beyond doubt. The Court agrees with the Commission that the machinery of justice to which the applicant would be subject in the United States is in itself neither arbitrary nor unreasonable, but, rather, respects the rule of law and affords not inconsiderable procedural safeguards to the defendant in a capital trial. Facilities are available on death row for the assistance of inmates, notably through provision of psychological and psychiatric services . . . .

However, in the Court's view, having regard to the very long period of time spent on death row in such extreme conditions, with the ever present and mounting anguish of awaiting execution of the death penalty, and to the personal circumstances of the applicant, especially his age and mental state at the time of the offence, the applicant's extradition to the United States would expose him to a real risk of treatment going beyond the threshold set by Article 3. A further consideration of relevance is that in the particular instance the legitimate purpose of extradition could be achieved by another means which would not involve suffering of such exceptional intensity or duration.

Accordingly, the Secretary of State's decision to extradite the applicant to the United States would, if implemented, give rise to a breach of Article 3.

This finding in no way puts in question the good faith of the United Kingdom Government, who have from the outset of the present proceedings demonstrated their desire to abide by their Convention obligations, firstly by staying the applicant's surrender to the United States authorities in accord with the interim measures indicated by the Convention institutions and secondly by themselves referring the case to the Court for a judicial ruling. . . .

[The Court rejected the other substantive claims of the applicant.]

IV.   *APPLICATION OF ARTICLE 50*

125. Under the terms of Article 50,

"If the Court finds that a decision or a measure taken by a legal authority or any other authority of a High Contracting Party is completely or partially in conflict with the obligations arising from the . . . Convention, and if the internal law of the said Party allows only partial reparation to be made for the consequences of this decision or measure, the decision of the Court shall, if necessary, afford just satisfaction to the injured party." . . .

126. No breach of Article 3 has as yet occurred. Nevertheless, the Court having found that the Secretary of State's decision to extradite to the United States of America would, if implemented, give rise to a breach of Article 3, Article 50 must be taken as applying to the facts of the present case. . . .

The applicant's essential concern, and the bulk of the argument on all sides, focused on the complaint under Article 3, and on that issue the applicant has been successful. The Court therefore considers that in equity the applicant should recover his costs and expenses in full.

FOR THESE REASONS, THE COURT UNANIMOUSLY

1. *Holds* that, in the event of the Secretary of State's decision to extradite the applicant to the United States of America being implemented, there would be a violation of Article 3;

2. *Holds* that, in the same event, there would be no violation of Article 6 § 3 (c);

3. *Holds* that it has no jurisdiction to entertain the complaint under Article 6 §§ 1 and 3 (d);

4. *Holds* that there is no violation of Article 13;

5. *Holds* that the United Kingdom is to pay to the applicant, in respect of legal costs and expenses, the sum of a £26,752.80 (twenty-six thousand seven hundred and fifty-two pounds sterling and eighty pence) and 5,030.60 FF (five thousand and thirty French francs and sixty centimes), together with a value added tax that may be chargeable;

6. *Rejects* the remainder of the claim for just satisfaction.

CONCURRING OPINION OF JUDGE DE MEYER. . .

The second sentence of Article 2 § 1 of the Convention was adopted nearly forty years ago, in particular historical circumstances, shortly after the Second World War. In so far as it still may seem to permit, under certain conditions, capital punishment in time of peace, it does not reflect the contemporary situation and is now overriden by the development of legal conscience and practice.

Such punishment is not consistent with the present state of European civilisation. . . .

No State Party to the Convention can in that context, even if it has not yet ratified the Sixth Protocol, be allowed to extradite any person if that person thereby incurs the risk of being put to death in the requesting State. . . .

NOTES

1. Would Central European countries be able to participate in a human rights system using the adjudicative approach and the norms exemplified by the *Soering* decision? Is it relevant that most Central European governments (except the German Democratic Republic, Hungary, and possibly Romania) have the death penalty? What are the other difficulties or advantages of Central European participation in the European Convention?

2. Would the United States be able to participate in a human rights system centered in Europe? The U.S. government did not make a formal appearance in the *Soering* case. The U.S. government considered making an appearance, but instead decided that the U.K. was adequately representing the U.S. interests in the case.

3. In *Forti v. Suarez-Mason*, 672 F. Supp. 1531 (N.D. Cal. 1988), the district court held that the prohibition against torture is a customary norm enforceable in U.S. courts, but the prohibition against cruel, inhuman or degrading treatment or punishment is not. Is *Forti* consistent with the *Soering* decision?

4. Compare the quality of the reasoning in *Soering*, on the one hand, with the *Baby Boy* and *Roach* cases discussed in chapter 7, on the other. Should the U.S. be more confident of the decision-making process in the European Court or in the Inter-American Commission on Human Rights?

5. For further reading, see Coliver, *European Court of Human Rights Condemns Conditions on Virginia's Death Row*, 13 Hum. Rts. Advocates Newsl. 23 (November 1989); Henkin, *Rights: Here and There*, 81 Colorado L. Rev. 1582 (1981).

6. After the *Soering* decision the prosecutor in Bedford County, Virginia, amended the charges to remove the offense of capital murder. The United Kingdom then extradicted Mr. Soering for trial in Virginia.

---

3. Interstate Cases in the European System

While the individual petition procedure of Article 25 of the European Convention is optional, all states parties to the European Convention have agreed in Article 24 to interstate complaints of human rights violations by other states parties. Nevertheless, the interstate procedures of the European Convention have rarely been invoked. There have been 18 interstate applications under the European Convention, relating to six situations:

(a) *Greece v. United Kingdom*, 2 Y.B. Eur. Conv. Hum. Rts. 182-99 (1958-59); 18 Y.B. Eur. Conv. Hum. Rts. 94 (1975)(two applications by Greece against the United Kingdom relating to Cyprus during the period 1956-57);

(b) *Austria v. Italy*, 4 Y.B. Eur. Conv. Hum. Rts. 116-82 (1961); 6 Y.B. Eur. Conv. Hum. Rts. 740-800 (1963)(six youths alleged that they had not received a fair trial for murder of a customs officer);

(c) *Denmark, Netherlands, Norway, & Sweden v. Greece*; *Denmark, Norway, & Sweden v. Greece*, 12 Y.B. Eur. Conv. Hum. Rts. (1969)(four applications relating to torture by the Greek colonels)(see note below);

(d) *Cyprus v. Turkey*, 18 Y.B. European Conv. Hum. Rts. 82-126 (1975), 21 Y.B. Eur. Conv. Hum. Rts. 100-246 (1978); 22 Y.B. Eur. Conv. Hum. Rts. 440 (1979)(two applications by Cyprus relating to violations of the rights of Greek Cypriots after Turkey invaded Cyprus);

(e) *Ireland v. United Kingdom*, 19 Y.B. Eur. Conv. Hum. Rts. 516 (1976); 20 Y.B. Eur. Conv. Hum. Rts. 602 (1978)(12 suspected I.R.A. members were subjected to five interrogation techniques that constituted inhuman or degrading treatment);

(f) *Denmark, France, Netherlands, Norway, & Sweden v. Turkey*, 35 Eur. Comm. Hum. Rts. 143-70 (1984)(five applications concerning torture, resolved by a friendly settlement in 1985, including Turkey's agreement to accept individual petitions under Article 25).

4. Greek Case

The Greek case is probably the most dramatic example of state versus state complaints under the European Convention. The case arose out of the April 21, 1967, military coup in Greece. Immediately upon taking power, the new government imposed martial law and announced the suspension of certain rights under martial law and under Article 15 of the Convention. Reports of mass arrests, torture, and other violations filtered out of Greece. These reports prompted four countries — Norway, Sweden, Denmark, and the Netherlands — to file applications to the Commission charging multiple violations of human rights.

The Commission spent two years considering the case. It received submissions from the parties to determine admissibility and then held hearings on the merits of the case. The Greek government protested the case and directed economic sanctions against the complainant countries, but they participated fully in the proceedings. The turning point came when the Subcommission (formed to examine the merits of the case) visited Greece. The Greek government allowed some witnesses to appear, but refused access to many others and refused to allow visits to certain notorious prisons. After the visit, the Subcommission refused to grant the Greek government any more extensions and began negotiations on a friendly settlement. No such settlement was reached, however, because the Greek government refused to establish a timetable for elections. On November 5, 1969, the Commission adopted its report. The Commission sent the report to the Committee of Ministers. On December 11, 1969, the Committee was preparing to vote on a proposed suspension of Greece from the Council of Europe. The Committee had to wait three months before officially considering reports, but the contents of the report were doubtless influential at the December meeting. The Greek government walked out of the Committee meeting when it became clear the vote would go against them. Greece then withdrew from both the Council of Europe and the European Convention. For further reading, see Becket, *The Greek Case Before the European Human Rights Commission*, 1 Hum. Rts. J. 91 (1970); The Greek Case, 12 Y.B. Eur. Conv. on Hum. Rts. (1969) (Eur. Comm'n on Hum. Rts.); The Greek Case, Council of Europe (Committee of Ministers) (1970).

The U.N. Commission on Human Rights and Sub-Commission on Prevention of Discrimination and Protection of Minorities also considered the issue of violations of human rights in Greece under ECOSOC resolution 1503. For further reading on the treatment of Greece at the U.N., see R. Lillich & F. Newman, International Human Rights: Problems of Law and Policy 340-71 (1979).

After Greece left the Council of Europe, European banks withdrew financing from Greece. The military government continued, however, bolstered by the support of the U.S. In late 1973 a coup established new leadership, but the military government remained in power until it invaded Cyprus. The U.S. supported Turkey in the ensuing struggle and a new coup overthrew the government in July 1974. The new Greek government tried the accused torturers under Greek law. For more information on the trial, see Amnesty International, Torture in Greece: The First Torturers' Trial 1975 (1977).

NOTES AND QUESTIONS

1. In view of the paucity of interstate complaints, can interstate complaints be considered to be an effective implementation approach for the European Convention?

2. Why have there been so few such complaints? Will the same considerations apply to any Central European governments that ratify the European Convention?

3. For further reading, see:

Cameron, *Turkey and Article 25 of the European Convention on Human Rights*, 37 Int'l & Comp. L. Q. 887 (1988);

Council of Europe, Stock-Taking on the European Convention on Human Rights (1954-1984) (1984);

Leckie, *The Inter-State Complaint Procedure in International Human Rights Law: Hopeful Prospects or Wishful Thinking?*, 10 Hum. Rts. Q. 249 (1988).

---

5. Interrelationship of International Human Rights Institutions

Multiple instruments and systems for human rights protection exist in the modern world. There is both overlap and the potential for conflict among these systems. In order to avoid multiple institutions considering the same complaint, most instruments exclude from admissibility complaints that are pending under different systems or different procedures in the same system. This distinction, however, is complicated by the difficulty of defining what constitutes the same complaint. Must the complainants, for example, always be the same if the broad allegations against a certain country are the same? There are also differences between the substantive rights protected and the procedural systems created by various instruments. The U.N. and Helsinki systems protect a broader range of rights than the European Convention. The European system, however, provides respected adjudicative institutions and legally binding decisions. Within the European Convention, states have agreed to use the European institutions for procedures against other parties to the European system. Nevertheless, the choice of forums can lead to conflicting interpretations of the application of rights and their allowable limitations. On the positive side, however, the systems developed by regional organizations often contain greater protections for human rights than are politically achievable on a global scale. In addition, the expertise found in specialized agencies provides more detailed protections for certain rights than is possible in general U.N. instruments.

The potential for conflict and duplication of effort present in the current variety of institutions has prompted some international lawyers to call for coordination. Other international lawyers have cautioned against a rigid approach to coordination. For one view of the problem and proposals for coordination, see Meron, *Norm Making and Supervision in International Human Rights: Reflections on Institutional Order*, 76 Am. J. Int'l L. 754 (1982). For another view, see *Report of the Human Rights Committee*, 39 U.N. GAOR Supp. (No. 40) at 116-17, U.N. Doc. A/39/40 (1984); Weissbrodt, *The Three "Theme" Rapporteurs of the U.N. Commission on Human Rights*, 80 Am. J. Int'l L. 685, 698-99 (1986).

XI HOW CAN THE UNITED STATES INFLUENCE SITUATIONS IN OTHER NATIONS?

Human Rights in Kenya and U.S. Foreign Policy

A. INTRODUCTION

Previous chapters examined methods of protecting human rights in international forums including the U.N., the O.A.S., and the Helsinki process. This chapter explores how the U.S. government uses "bilateral" dealings with governments to affect human rights. Differing views on the role of human rights in foreign policy are set forth; and readers should consider how the U.S. government should balance the aim to protect human rights against economic, security, and other perceived interests.

Several U.S. statutes and regulations link the granting of certain types of foreign assistance to the human rights record of the country seeking assistance. Readers should think about the role of Congress in setting standards for assistance and also the varying methods Executive officials use to help protect human rights in other countries through foreign policy.

The chapter focuses on two relatively intrusive methods of protecting human rights in foreign countries — physical and economic coercion — and discusses the propriety of those methods under international law.

The illustrative case is the situation in Kenya — a close ally of the U.S. Using information on Kenya, readers should consider methods of influencing the Kenyan government's human rights policies and also should confront the difficult issue of the extent to which protecting human rights should take precedence over other interests when dealing with an ally.

B. QUESTIONS

Assume you are staff assistant to a member of the Subcommittee on Africa of the House Committee on Foreign Affairs, which is holding a hearing on Kenya's human rights violations. What actions should the U.S. take to help improve the situation? In formulating a list of actions consider the following questions:

1. Should U.S. foreign policy promote international human rights? What is the legal foundation for U.S. policy? Do Sections 116 and 502B suggest an answer?

2. Should human rights receive priority over other national interests in foreign policy? (Commercial interests? Security interests? Others?)

3. What tools are available to an administration that wants to promote international human rights? Which seem most effective?

   a. When should an administration use quiet diplomacy?

   b. What are the legal limits, national or international, on action against human rights violators?

   c. Have the State Department annual reports on the human rights situation in other countries been constructive?

4. How should the U.S. develop its foreign policy to favor human rights?

   a. Compare the Carter, Reagan, and Bush administrations' approaches.

   b. What is the appropriate role of Congress? Can legislation create greater consistency in the policies of administrations?

   c. Is it feasible to treat all countries equally in regard to their human rights performance? Is it possible to avoid charges of a double standard? How should the U.S. treat human rights violations by its closest allies?

d. What should the standards be for action against human rights violators? Which does Section 502(b) suggest?

5. How can one measure the success or failure of an international human rights policy? What are the benefits? What are the costs?

6. In the U.S. has there been compliance with international human rights law, as to the treatment of aliens, "minorities," women, detainees, the sick, homeless, hungry, etc.?

7. Outside its territorial boundaries has the U.S. government complied with international human rights law?

8. Is it hypocritical for the U.S. government to criticize human rights violations of other governments?

9. Is it appropriate for the U.S. government to criticize human rights violations of governments that have ratified human rights treaties which the U.S. has not ratified?

10. In the decade of the 1990's will the U.S. government contribute notably to the work of intergovernmental bodies that help promote and protect human rights: in the U.N., the OAS, NATO, the Helsinki process, etc.?

11. Have U.S. policies and actions regarding economic, military, and other aid, "sanctions," and comparable peaceful "encroachments" on other nations' affairs been commendable?

C. BACKGROUND ON KENYA

The following materials on Kenya represent a snapshot in its history and are for use in analyzing potential U.S. action to influence the human rights situation there. The circumstances in Kenya undoubtedly will change after publication of these materials. They are not presented as an exhaustive description of the human rights situation in that country. Instead, they serve as a factual context in which to evaluate human rights considerations in U.S. foreign policy at a particular time.

The first reading in this section reflects the U.S. government view of human rights in Kenya. Sections 116(d)(1) and 502B(b) of the Foreign Assistance Act require the State Department to prepare a report on the human rights situation in each country proposed as a recipient of U.S. assistance and on each country that is a member of the U.N. The legislation originally required reports only on countries proposed as recipients of U.S. assistance. The State Department decided to expand its coverage to almost all countries (169 in 1990) in order to provide a comparative basis for evaluation.

The annual State Department Country Reports have been praised as singly the most extensive and detailed compilation of human rights conditions around the world. Nevertheless the Department has been criticized for omissions and inaccuracies in reports on countries strategically important to the U.S. In recent years, however, the accuracy of reports has improved owing to congressional oversight and criticisms from independent human rights groups.

Two active nongovernmental organizations — the Lawyers Committee for Human Rights and/or Human Rights Watch — have for several years published a critique of the reports. The Critique — the second reading in this section of the chapter — represents an independent evaluation of the human rights situation in Kenya and the official U.S. attitude towards violations in Kenya.

The final excerpt in this section is taken from the U.S. government's Area Handbook on Kenya. The handbook is part of a series prepared by Foreign Area Studies at the American University on a variety of countries. Each handbook deals with a particular country, describing and analyzing economic, political, cultural and social conditions. The excerpt shows the security and commercial interests the U.S. must consider in developing a policy to influence the human rights situation in Kenya.

Department of State, Country Reports on Human Rights Practices for 1988, Report Submitted to the Senate Committee on Foreign Relations and the House Committee on Foreign Affairs, 101st Cong., 1st Sess., 155-68 (1989):

KENYA

Although Kenya has had an elected civilian government since independence in 1963, it has been a de facto one-party state almost since independence and a de jure one-party state since 1982. President Daniel T. arap Moi maintains firm control over both the Government and the party, the Kenyan African National Union (KANU). KANU membership is a prerequisite for participation in national political affairs. The popularly elected National Assembly of 202 members (including 12 appointed by the President and 2 ex officio members) has little genuine power in national political affairs. Its role is generally limited to local and regional issues and in affirming the President's initiatives. President Moi was reelected unopposed to a third 5-year term in 1988.

The Kenyan armed forces constitute a small professional establishment with a total strength of 22,500 members. Kenya has an internal security apparatus that includes the police Criminal Investigation Division (CID), the paramilitary General Services Unit (GSU), and the Directorate of Security and Intelligence (DSI or Special Branch). The CID and Special Branch are used to monitor and control people whom the State considers subversive. The Preservation of Public Security Act sanctions indefinite detention without charge or trial in security cases, and the courts have upheld the constitutionality of properly executed actions taken under the authority of that Act.

Kenya's modern, market-oriented economy includes a well-developed private sector for trade and light manufacturing as well as an agricultural sector that provides food for local consumption and substantial exports of coffee, tea, and other commodities. In 1988 a continued decline in world coffee prices exacerbated a balance of payments problem. Economic growth continued, but a persistently high population growth rate contributed to a serious and growing problem of unemployment. Kenyans are free to engage in private economic activity and own property without government interference.

In 1988 there were several important developments adversely affecting the human rights situation. In the spring, two-stage parliamentary elections took place amid much controversy over the public queuing system (voters must publicly line up behind photographs of their candidate) used in the key primary (party) election and charges of fraud in some races. The electoral outcome further strengthened executive branch and central party control over the legislature. In August the new National Assembly unanimously and speedily passed two presidentially supported constitutional amendments which further increased the President's power by giving him authority to fire senior judges and members of the Public Service Commission and expanded police authority to detain without charge suspects in capital crimes up to 14 days (previously 24 hours). The President and his advisers staunchly defended these changes as necessary to maintain a ''rule of law.'' Critics charged that they seriously undermined the independence of the judiciary and invited increased police mistreatment of detainees. In a more positive vein, by contrast with 1986-1987 when more than 70 persons suspected of belonging to the illegal dissident group, Mwakenya, were convicted and sentenced amid reports of police abuse, there were 9 publicly confirmed security convictions in 1988. As of December 1988, 7 Kenyans were being detained without charge under the Preservation of Public Security Act, as compared with 12 Kenyans in detention in December 1987.

RESPECT FOR HUMAN RIGHTS

Section 1 Respect for Integrity of the Person, Including Freedom from:

a.   Political Killing

Violence among supporters of rival candidates in several areas of Kenya during the 1988 election campaigns resulted in approximately 5 deaths nationwide.

By the end of 1988, no officials had been held responsible for the 1986-1987 deaths in custody of two Mwakenya suspects. In a January ruling, a magistrate stated he believed Peter Karanja had been tortured and referred the matter to the Attorney General's office for further investigation. A similar case involving the death of Stephen Wanjema in 1986 had not been heard by the end of 1988.

b.   Disappearance

Kenyan authorities frequently detain people, in some cases for prolonged periods, without allowing notification of families, friends, or lawyers as to their whereabouts and have even failed to acknowledge the detention when inquiries were made. For example, when Raila Odinga, a former detainee, was rearrested on August 30, his family inquired at Nairobi police stations as to his whereabouts but were given no information. On September 8, in response to a habeas corpus petition filed by Odinga's wife, authorities announced that he had been detained under the Preservation of Public Security Act, but they did not bring him to the habeas corpus hearing or inform his family where he was being held. As of the end of the year, neither his family nor his lawyer had been allowed to see him.

The 1987 habeas corpus case brought by the wife of a missing Kiambu farmer was dismissed in 1988. Police claimed they had shot the man, a robbery suspect, while he was trying to escape, but they never produced the body for examination.

    c.   Torture and Other Cruel, Inhuman, and Degrading Treatment or Punishment

Although torture is proscribed under the Constitution, reports of torture and police brutality continued in 1988. Mistreatment of suspects is common and occasionally results in death. A number of Kenyans told the press they had been physically abused by the police, and in several 1988 cases, citizens presented evidence in court to that effect. Maina wa Kinyatti, a historian and university lecturer who completed a 6-year term for possession of seditious documents in October, held a press conference upon his release. Speaking with difficulty, a condition he attributed to more than 1 year in solitary confinement, he denied that he had ever been associated with Mwakenya, and described his mistreatment, including beatings, inadequate diet and medical care, confinement with prisoners who were insane, and being forced to perform exhausting and degrading exercises. In November Harris O. Arara testified in court that during his interrogation at CID headquarters he was starved for 5 days and threatened with harsher treatment if he did not plead guilty to possession of seditious documents.

Although some police officers have been charged in connection with abuse of prisoners, no policeman has been convicted of such abuse in political/security cases. Apparently, no policemen were convicted of abuse in other types of cases during 1988. In Mombasa, two robbery suspects — a Kenyan and a Zairian — died while in police custody. Five police officers were arrested in connection with the case, and two of these officers mysteriously died in the custody of their colleagues. A Mombasa magistrate ruled that "no particular police officer" was responsible for the death of the Kenyan suspect, but police officers were charged with the death of the Zairian suspect, and their trial was under way at the end of the year. In July two policemen in Kisumu were charged with murder, and in August two policemen in Eldoret were ordered to stand trial for allegedly murdering a farmer during interrogation. A closed hearing was held in January into allegations of torture of Wanyiri Kihoro, one of three detainees who remained in detention throughout 1988. Family members and the press were denied entry into the hearing. The court ruled that Kihoro had not been ill-treated. Two other cases involving similar allegations had not been heard by the end of the year. President Moi appointed a new police commissioner early in 1988 and charged him with cleaning up the police force, stating that police officers who committed illegal acts would be punished.

Prison conditions in Kenya are poor. Detainees and prisoners have complained of beatings, poor food, and inadequate facilities and medical care. Prisoners often must sleep on cold cement floors. The Preservation of Public Security Act allows for solitary confinement, with no contact with family or legal counsel, although in some cases lawyers and families have been permitted to visit detainees. Other prisoners (not detainees under the Preservation of Public Security Act) are allowed one brief visit per month by family members. Prison or security officers are usually present during visits by family members or lawyers. Correspondence with prisoners is monitored and occasionally not delivered.

d. Arbitrary Arrest, Detention or Exile

The Constitution provides that most arrested or detained persons shall be brought before a court "as soon as is reasonably practicable," and that if such person is not brought within 24 hours of his arrest or from the commencement of his detention the burden of explanation is on the authorities. The Constitution was amended in August to allow the police to hold people suspected of capital offenses for 14 days before being brought before a court. The Attorney General argued that this additional detention time was required to complete investigations, but many legal experts in Kenya and abroad denounced this change as an invitation to police mistreatment. Capital offenses include such crimes as murder and treason. In practice, suspects of all types are often held incommunicado for long periods before being brought before a court. In all nine of the security case convictions in 1988, the suspects were held incommunicado, some for up to 28 days before being brought to court.

The Preservation of Public Security Act allows the State to detain an individual indefinitely without charges or trial. A formal detention order must be signed and published in the gazette. There is no judicial review of the legality of detention. Detention cases are reviewed by a board appointed by the President which meets in camera. The Government is not bound by this board's recommendations.

In February the President released 9 of 12 detainees held under the Preservation of Public Security Act, including Raila Odinga, who had been jailed in 1982 and was the longest-serving of the 9, and Israel Otiena Agina. The three who remained in detention — lawyers Mirugi Kariuki and Wanyiri Kihoro and university lecturer Mukaru Ng'ang'a, held since December, October, and July 1986 respectively — had earlier challenged the legality of their detention, hired legal counsel, and complained of torture and abuse. Subsequently, in August and September, the Government again detained Raila Odinga and Israel Otieno Agina on security grounds. In September Samuel Okumu Okwany and Richard Obuon Guya, two alleged members of the Kenya Patriotic Front (KPF), were detained under the Preservation of Public Security Act. As of December 1988, these 7 Kenyans remained in detention under the Act.

Neither exile nor threat of exile is used by the Government as a means of intimidation or punishment. Self-exile is a course of action sometimes chosen by Kenyan dissidents. In some cases, the Government states that these exiles are wanted for questioning for possible criminal charges in Kenya, although in most cases the exiles have not been formally charged with crimes. The Government has invited some of the exiles to return and publicly announced they would be safe in Kenya. One such exile returned in December 1987. . . .

e. Denial of Fair Public Trial

Kenya's legal system, as defined in the Judicature Act of 1967, is based on the Kenyan Constitution, laws passed by Parliament, and common law or court precedent. Customary law is used as a guide in civil matters affecting people of the same ethnic groups so long as it does not conflict with statutory law. Kenya does not have the jury system. The court system consists of a Court of Appeals, a High Court, and two levels of magistrates' courts where most criminal and civil cases originate. Civilians are tried in civilian courts, and verdicts may be appealed to the Kenyan High court and ultimately to the Court of Appeals. Military personnel are tried by military courts, and verdicts may be appealed within the military system. Attorneys for military personnel are appointed on a case by case basis by the Chief Justice.

The President appoints the Chief Justice of the High Court, and he appoints other High Court judges with the advice of the Judicial Service Commission. The President also appoints the Attorney General. His power over the judicial system has steadily increased through constitutional amendments adopted in 1986 and 1988. Inter alia, these changes give the President a free hand in firing the Attorney General, the Auditor General, and High Court judges. Critics charged that these amendments further undermined the independence of the judiciary and the "rule of law." One High Court judge has already been removed since enactment of the new provision.

In cases involving the Preservation of Public Security Act, judicial authority is limited to ensuring compliance with procedural provisions. In cases without political implications the right to a fair public trial is normally observed, although long delays and postponements are common.

The constitutional right to a fair public trial has been circumscribed in some instances, notably in political/security cases such as those involving alleged Mwakenya or KPF members. In 1987 at least 39 persons allegedly belonging to Mwakenya were brought to court and convicted. In 1988 there were nine convictions involving charges of membership in subversive organizations. In the first public prosecution in 1988 involving charges of membership in a subversive organization, Andrew K. Muigai was convicted in 20 minutes based on his confession and sentenced to 6 years' imprisonment. He was held for 21 days before being charged, was allowed no visitors before being brought to court, and had no legal counsel.

In September four persons were sentenced to 7 years' imprisonment for sedition in connection with membership in the KPF, an organization allegedly founded by self-exile Koigi wa Wamwere. All pleaded guilty to KPF membership and all were held over 2 weeks before being brought to trial, apparently without legal representation. In October one person was jailed for 5 years for possession of seditious documents and membership in Mwakenya. . . . All but one of these cases followed a pattern that has raised serious questions about the fairness of most security trials: a long period of incommunicado detention, followed by a short unannounced trial in which the defendant, without legal representation, pleads guilty (thus precluding any appeal of the conviction, even if the guilty plea were coerced). Only the sentence may be appealed. Human rights organizations, such as Amnesty International and Human Rights Watch Committees, have criticized these trials as unfair. They have pointed to the fact that the defendants did not have advance notice of the trials and did not have legal representation. The large number of "confessions" in these trials is also cited as suspicious.

Members of the press usually attended and reported on courtroom proceedings. Some trials involving allegations of torture, however, were not public. In one instance, two American human rights observers were forced to leave a public inquest into the death in custody of Peter Karanja (see Section 1.a.). The men were held and questioned for 8 hours before release.

Kenyans do not have a right to legal counsel except in certain capital cases. In those cases, most persons tried for capital offenses are provided counsel free of charge if they cannot afford it. Recent instances in which the Government detained lawyers involved in sensitive cases and attacked the Law Society of Kenya, which criticized the constitutional amendments, could discourage vigorous legal represen-tation in security cases. When the Chairman of the Law Society of Kenya asked the Attorney General to clarify press reports that a Kenyan had been convicted for failure to give a ride to a local official (which is not a crime under Kenya's Penal Code), the President suggested publicly that the Attorney General should seek the arrest of the Chairman for "contempt of court." The conviction for failure to give a ride was later dismissed on appeal. An announcement by the Government in 1988 of its intention to require lawyers and other professionals to have licenses has raised fears that the system could be used to intimidate the legal community, as has the announcement that the Government would establish a commission to probe into the conduct of lawyers. Human rights groups have charged that Government intimidation may also have discouraged family members of detainees from pursuing habeas corpus actions.

The harassment of Kenyan attorney Gibson Kamau Kuria, who served as legal counsel for several Mwakenya suspects, continued to attract wide international attention in 1988. He had been detained without charge in 1987, shortly after filing notices to sue the Government for illegal detention and torture on behalf of several clients, and was held for 9 months under the Preservation of Public Security Act.

f.   Arbitrary Interference with Privacy, Family, Home, or Correspondence

Searches without warrants are allowed under the Constitution in certain instances "to promote the public benefit," including security cases. Security officials also conduct searches without warrants to apprehend suspected criminals or to seize property suspected to be stolen. Homes of suspected dissidents have been searched without warrants, as have the residences of foreign missionaries. Security forces reportedly employ a variety of surveillance techniques, including electronic sur-veillance and a network of informers.

Section 2 Respect for Civil Liberties, Including:

a.   Freedom of Speech and Press

Although the Constitution provides for freedom of speech and press, the exercise of these rights is restricted. No criticism of the President is tolerated in any form. Human rights groups have criticized Kenya's sedition laws for failing to distinguish between violent and nonviolent opposition to the Government. They have charged that security detentions and prosecutions have sometimes been used to restrict the expression of peaceful dissenting views.

Parliament rarely debates national issues such as foreign policy. Even when the Government introduced important constitutional amendments in Parliament in mid-1988, there was no parliamentary debate, and the amendments were adopted without any opposing votes after less than 2 hours of discussion.

Government and KANU action against outspoken politicians, clergymen, and law-yers, as well as the detention provisions of the Preservation of Public Security Act, discourage public exchange of views on some political topics. Some churchmen who opposed government policies, including queuing and the recent constitutional amendments, were sharply criticized and subjected to investigations. In this con-nection, the magazine Beyond, published by the National Council of Churches of Kenya (NCCK), was banned in 1988 after publishing an issue that was critical of queue voting and the overall conduct of the KANU nomination elections. The editor of the magazine, Bedan Mbugua, was convicted of improper financial management of the publication and given an unusual 9 month custodial sentence in August. As of December 1988 Mbugua was free on bail pending his appeal. The authorities also arrested several persons for possessing copies of Beyond, and two were given 2-year sentences. Other persons were convicted of possession of literature defined as seditious, including possession of a Mwakenya publication.

Privately owned newspapers and journals contribute importantly to the lively tradition of the press in Kenya. There is no systematic official censorship of the press, but officials of the newly created Ministry of National Guidance and Political Affairs (whose duties include censorship) have attacked publications they find objectionable. In March the Ministry condemned the Financial Review for an article criticizing the replacement of the Vice President and suggested the magazine might be banned. In December the editor of the Financial Review was held at CID headquarters for several hours of questioning regarding articles which had appeared in his magazine. Journalists practice self-censorship and keep commentary within usually understood but legally undefined limits. The press criticizes government policies and occasionally government officials, but it never criticizes the President. The Kenyan media gave good coverage of the 1988 elections, including the controversial queue voting issue.

At times the Government intervenes to tell editors how to handle sensitive stories. In separate instances during 1988, a cabinet minister ordered reporters to read back their notes for his approval, and a district officer in Kakamega warned journalists they would be arrested and beaten for publishing any stories about his district without his permission. (The latter was rebuked by higher officials.)

Newspapers, magazines, and books from abroad are readily available, although in 1988 several issues of international publications which contained articles critical of Kenya were not allowed normal distribution within Kenya. More than 100 foreign journalists representing western news organizations are based in Kenya. In 1988 the Government continued its attacks on this group for its coverage of Kenyan issues, e.g., the queue voting. It warned the public about speaking to foreign reporters. In one incident foreign journalists were briefly detained in Kisumu for attempting to film a burial service. In August a Kenya-based stringer for the British Broadcasting Corporation had her work permit canceled on leaving Kenya, but was later permitted to return to Kenya. The Kenyan authorities also require certification of union membership for foreign press accreditation in Kenya. In at least one instance in 1988, the lack of such union membership led to the denial of press credentials for an Associated Press reporter.

The single television and all radio stations are owned and controlled by the Government and reflect government policies in coverage of national and international events and issues. A 10-member television censorship board has established guidelines for what can be shown. A 10- to 12-member film censorship board under the Ministry of National Guidance and Political Affairs must approve all films shown in Kenya. A variety of foreign films is available, though in August the Government banned nearly 200 foreign films (most, if not all, X-rated) on ''protection of public morals'' grounds. The films were not political.

There are no formal limits to academic freedom. While numerous books critical of the Government, such as the works by dissident self-exile Ngugi wa Thiongo, are available in Kenya, some writings on recent Kenyan history and politics have been considered sensitive, and the academic climate does not encourage writing on these topics. Eighteen publications that were prohibited in 1986 remain blacklisted. University professors were among those detained on security grounds.

b.   Freedom of Peaceful Assembly and Association

The Constitution provides for freedom of assembly, but it is limited by the Public Order and Police Act, which gives authorities power to control public gatherings, defined as meetings of three or more persons. It is illegal to convene an unlicensed meeting, and politicians have been arrested for violations of this Act. Although licenses to hold public meetings are rarely denied, in the preliminaries to the 1988 elections some politicians complained that they were not able to obtain a license, while government-favored candidates held rallies without licenses.

Freedom of association is generally allowed. With the important exception of civil servants, who are required to join KANU, Kenyans are not legally bound to join any political organization. Party membership, however, has become a form of loyalty test, even though the party and the Government emphasize that it is voluntary. For a discussion of freedom of association as it applies to labor unions, see Section 6.a.

c.   Freedom of Religion

Kenya has no state religion. Freedom of worship is acknowledged in the Constitution and allowed in most cases. Foreign missionaries of many denominations are permitted to work in Kenya, although on occasion the President and other officials have publicly questioned the motives of certain missionaries and periodically warned foreign missionaries not to engage in politics. Several American missionaries, including the leader of the Church of Jesus Christ of Latter-day Saints, were questioned about their activities and illegal meetings. Although no foreign mission-ary was known to have been deported in 1988, some who had been targets of government criticism had to leave when their work permits were not renewed.

Churches new to Kenya must obtain government approval to be registered. The Church of Jesus Christ of Latter-day Saints is one group which has tried without success for 7 years to obtain registration. In 1987 another group, the Jehovah's Witnesses, were deregistered but continued in 1988 to hold services under a stay order from the high court. In March 73 Jehovah's Witnesses were picked up for holding an "unlawful assembly," detained briefly, and released. In 1988 the Associated Christian Churches of Kenya, an American-based missionary organiza-tion, was also deregistered.

There is no religious requirement for voting or holding office. Clergymen in Kenya have spoken out on political as well as religious issues from their pulpits. In 1988 senior officials sharply criticized certain clergymen, including Anglican bishops Alexander Muge and Henry Okullu, for making political statements. Twice in July, after charging that the administration had shown political favoritism in distributing relief supplies in West Pokot, worshipers were reportedly prevented from attending services where Muge was to preach. As noted, government officials also criticized the National Council of Churches of Kenya (NCCK), which comprises most of the Protestant denominations, and banned the monthly NCCK magazine Beyond after it ran an edition on election irregularities.

d.   Freedom of Movement Within the Country, Foreign Travel, Emigration, and Repatriation

In general, Kenyans can travel freely within the country restricted only by provisions of the Preservation of Public Security Act, which limit the movement of persons considered dangerous to the public security. These provisions are rarely invoked. In one instance in July, Bishop Muge was reportedly prevented by local police from traveling to preach at a church.

Kenya does not prohibit emigration of its citizens, but on occasion does prevent citizens from traveling abroad. The Government sometimes refuses to return passports or issue new passports to people previously detained under the Preservation of Public Security Act. The Government does not regard the issuance of passports to citizens as a constitutional right and reserves the right to issue or deny passports at its discretion. In 1988 lawyer and former detainee Gibson Kamau Kuria was unable to get his passport back to visit the United States to receive a humanitarian award. The American Bar Association, the Lawyers' Committee for Human Rights, Human Rights Watch, and the Robert F. Kennedy Memorial had invited him to the United States to honor him for his legal representation of victims of human rights abuse. Kuria's wife and children also were unable to obtain passports to travel to the United States. One of Kuria's colleagues had his passport taken when he returned to Kenya after accepting the Robert F. Kennedy Memorial award on Kuria's behalf. Also in 1988, Nairobi businessman John Harun Mwau lost his court battle to regain his passport which was withdrawn in 1983. Charles Njonjo, a former Minister for Constitutional Affairs who lost his position and his passport in 1983, had his passport restored in 1988, and he traveled to the United Kingdom.

During 1988 there was no known instance in which citizenship was revoked for political reasons.

Kenya continues to accept refugees, despite its own high population growth rate and severe unemployment problems. The United Nations High Commissioner for Refugees estimates that in 1988 Kenya provided refuge to approximately 12,000 refugees, with more than 5,500 coming from Uganda. There are perhaps another 5,000 displaced persons not officially registered as refugees.

Section 3 Respect for Political Rights: The Right of Citizens to Change Their Government

The Kenyan Constitution prohibits formation of any political party other than KANU, and President Moi and a small group of advisers control all major policy decisions within the Government and the party. Citizens cannot, therefore, change the system of government or replace the party in power through the electoral process. Since 1964, when Kenya adopted a presidential system, the party's candidate for president has been unopposed. Moi was reelected in 1988 to a third 5-year term. Numerous candidates compete for party and parliamentary elections — also held every 5 years — but all candidates must be KANU members, and the national party headquarters must clear all candidates for political office.

In the 1988 national elections, 17 candidates failed to win KANU approval to stand for elections. Several others were informed that they could not run because they participated in a commission to redraw electoral boundaries. Some candidates claimed that they were physically prevented from filing their papers. Few of the parliamentarians who had questioned executive policy were returned to the Assembly. Ministers and other deputies who are expelled from KANU automatically relinquish their seats in Parliament. In July two members of Parliament from the

West Pokot district who expressed support for Bishop Muge's criticisms of local administrators were expelled from KANU for engaging in activities which "disturbed peace and security." A government official who resigned his portfolio in December (to protest a KANU sub-branch election which he claimed was rigged) subsequently was expelled from the party and thus from his seat in Parliament.

For the 1988 elections, the party adopted a queuing system for electing KANU nominees, requiring voters to line up in public behind photographs of the candidates. Only those who had KANU membership cards were allowed to participate in the nomination process. Candidates who received 70 percent of the KANU vote were automatically elected without having to contest the general election. Over 60 candidates (out of a total of 188) were elected this way. KANU party members comprise at most two-thirds of the registered voter population. There was a low turnout in some areas.

The public nature of the queuing process caused some concern about voter intimidation, but others argued that secret ballots were also subject to abuse. Numerous claims of irregularities were made during the party primary. These included charges that vote counts were altered by the administrative authorities carrying out the elections and that supporters of some candidates were intimidated by beatings, kidnappings, and police detentions. In response to an appeal against the queuing process, a High Court judge ruled that the Court could not hear cases involving alleged fraud in the KANU elections as this would amount to interference with the internal affairs of KANU. Other appeals were directed to KANU President Moi, who allowed one queuing vote to be repeated.

Allegations of irregularities in the general election (by secret ballot) included unannounced early poll closings, misplaced ballot boxes, and failure to allow observation of ballot box closings. General election results may be appealed to the courts, and 25 losers formally did so. Such appeals are expensive, a fact which may have deterred some other losers. As of December 1988, none of the election appeals had been heard.

Members of all ethnic groups may run for office, and ethnic representation at the minister and assistant minister level is broad. Twelve of Kenya's ethnic groups are represented in the Cabinet. Seventeen ethnic groups, including one Caucasian, are represented at the assistant minister level. There is one female assistant minister, and two women hold seats in the National Assembly.

Section 4 Governmental Attitude Regarding International and Nongovernmental Investigation of Alleged Violations of Human Rights

The Government rejects criticism of its human rights record and discourages Kenyans from providing outside human rights groups with information. In 1988 President Moi repeatedly attacked Amnesty International and other groups for meddling in Kenya's internal affairs. The President has accused certain groups, including lawyers, of being "agents of enemies of the country, such as Amnesty International."

In January 1988 the authorities took action against two American citizens who had come to Kenya to observe an inquest into the death of a Mwakenya suspect (see section 1.e. above). The two were ordered to leave the courtroom and were taken into police custody where they were held and questioned for 8 hours. One of these was a representative of the Lawyers' Committee for Human Rights. Neither was allowed to call the U.S. Embassy. They were told by security officers that Kenya did not recognize the right of foreigners arrested in Kenya to contact their embassies. (Kenya is a signatory to the 1963 Vienna Convention on Consular Relations.)

Several Kenyan organizations, such as the Law Society of Kenya, address issues related to human rights, but none focuses exclusively on human rights concerns. Kenya has not ratified the Organization of African Unity's Human and Peoples' Rights Charter, adopted in 1981 in Nairobi.

Section 5 Discrimination Based on Race, Sex, Religion, Language, or Social Status

Kenya is a diverse country that does not practice legal discrimination on the basis of race, sex, religion, language or social status. Several intertribal clashes occurred in northern Kenya as in previous years. Women may own property and businesses but remain underrepresented in educational institutions, government, and business, despite the emergence of influential women in all these areas. Statistics on enrollment in Kenyan universities for the 1987/88 school year showed that female students represented 28 percent of the total enrollment. Traditional culture, rather than government policy, has long prescribed limited roles for women.

Women are a crucial element in the Kenyan labor force, especially in agriculture where they account for 75 percent of the total. Women are likely to retain this dominant role in agriculture for the near future, as there is a continuing migration of men to the cities in search of higher paying jobs. Women make up approximately 21 percent of the wage labor work force. They hold some 10 percent of the jobs in the traditionally male-dominated manufacturing sector, and 22 percent of the jobs in the finance and insurance sectors. Thirty percent of Kenya's education workers are women. In the modern sector, women frequently earn less than men for comparable work. There are women's groups in Kenya which attempt to educate and help women attain their full rights.

Polygamy is not legal for people married under the Christian Marriage Act, but it is permitted for those who marry under African customary law. Kenya's Law of Succession, which governs inheritance rights, provides for equal treatment of male and female children (in contrast to much customary law which favors the eldest male child). Some Kenyan ethnic groups still practice female circumcision, although the Government has mounted a campaign against the practice and prohibits such operations in government hospitals.

The Asian community, numbering about 65,000, accounts for a disproportionate share of the nation's economic wealth and output. The Government's policy of Africanization of the economy has resulted in some Asian emigration. Kenya amended its citizenship law in 1984, depriving some Asians and Europeans of citizenship. Under present law, persons born in Kenya of non-Kenyan parents can no longer claim citizenship.

Section 6 Worker Rights

  a.   The Right of Association

Workers in Kenya, with one significant exception, enjoy the right of association as defined by the International Labor Organization (ILO). The Government, however, has a decisive role on some important labor issues. The one group which cannot organize is civil servants, whose union was disbanded by the authorities in the early 1980's. Since 1985 all civil servants have moreover been required to be members of the ruling KANU party. Other workers, according to law, can establish and join organizations of their choosing, make their own rules, elect their own leaders, join with other unions, and affiliate with international organizations. Union registration is controlled by a registrar in the Attorney General's office. In 1987, at the suggestion of a committee made up of representatives of the Ministry of Labor, the Central Organization of Trade Unions (COTU), and the Federation of Kenyan Employers (FKE), several unions were proposed for deregistration. In June 1988, the Government deregistered the Kenya Timber and Furniture Workers' Union. The stated purpose of these amalgamations was to eliminate unions which were too small to be financially viable and to avoid conflicts of jurisdiction.

COTU, which is Kenya's legally mandated trade union federation, is affiliated with the Organization of African Trade Union Unity and maintains relations, though not affiliation, with the International Confederation of Free Trade Unions (ICFTU). It sends observers to ICFTU and World Federation of Trade Unions meetings. Both COTU and the FKE participate in the ILO.

There are approximately 1.3 million wage earners in Kenya, out of an estimated 8-million-person work force. COTU has about 360,000 members and another 100,000 workers belong to the Kenya National Union of Teachers which is not part of COTU. COTU is strong in such areas as the docks, railroads, banking, and telecommunications, but weak in agriculture, by far Kenya's largest employment sector.

Though unions enjoy relative autonomy from the Government and the ruling party, there are limits. In July-August, when the head of the dockworkers' union was involved in an apparent conflict of interest between his union job and his private business interests, the Government and party called for his resignation. He resigned and was replaced in new union elections. In September President Moi suggested that KANU study ways of affiliating COTU with the party.

Kenyan unions have the right to strike, but the nation's industrial relations machinery makes it almost impossible to do so legally. Unions are required to give notice of intent, register their grievances with the industrial court, and exhaust all possible avenues of resolution before striking. Consequently, most strikes are illegal, short-lived, and local. In 1987 there were 109 strikes with 93,749 workdays lost. Kenya's industrial court has a reputation for objectivity and is strongly supported by unions as well as employers.

  b.   The Right to Organize and Bargain Collectively...

  c.   Prohibition of Forced or Compulsory Labor...

  d.   Minimum Age for Employment of Children...

  e.   Acceptable Conditions of Work...

* * *

Human Rights Watch & Lawyers Committee for Human Rights, Critique: Review of the Department of State's Country Reports on Human Rights Practices for 1988, at 99-104 (1989):

KENYA

Although the report on Kenya touches on some important developments in 1988, it fails to capture the accelerating trend toward autocracy and seriously underestimates the effect of certain government measures on human rights. The report thus falls short of focusing necessary international attention on the worsening human rights situation in Kenya.

A serious failure of the report is its superficial treatment of two constitutional amendments passed by Parliament in August 1988 without debate. The first extends from 24 hours to 14 days the period during which the police may hold those suspected of committing capital offenses in incommunicado detention without recourse to judicial scrutiny. This change is particularly troubling given that at least eight people are reported to have died in police custody over the last year. The report fails to note that this constitutional amendment increases the likelihood of continued mistreatment and death of prisoners and detainees. The report also minimizes Kenya's harsh prison conditions — which have also played a role in prison deaths — by referring to them simply as "poor."

In similar fashion, the report fails to point out that the second constitutional amendment — which gives the president the authority to fire senior judges and members of the Public Service Commission — further concentrates power in the executive at the expense of the judiciary. In addition, by referring to those opposed to these two amendments as mere "critics," the report fails to convey the opposition of broad sectors of Kenyan society. The report's assertion that the amendments were "unanimously and speedily" passed by the National Assembly implies their popularity; instead, the State Department should have pointed out that the National Assembly is packed with loyalists of the Kenya African National Union (KANU) — the single authorized party — and is a rubber-stamp for all presidential initiatives.

In discussing arbitrary detentions and detention conditions, the report fails to note that:

— Wanyiri Kihoro and Mirugi Kariuki, two lawyers detained without charge or trial, are in very poor health and were denied access to doctors of their choice;

— These two and a university lecturer, Mukaru Ng'ang'a, who was also detained without charge or trial,* continue to be held simply because they have sued the government for allegedly torturing them;

— The courts have never voided detention orders or acts taken under the Preservation of the Public Security Act, a reflection of the subordination of the judiciary to the executive;

— There have been no vigorous and publicly announced investigations into mistreatment and deaths in custody of prisoners or detainees; and

— Following the detention of Gibson Kamau Kuria and John Khaminwa for representing individuals critical of the government, lawyers are afraid to appear for detainees; instead, the report simply notes that detention of lawyers involved in sensitive cases "could" discourage vigorous legal representation when in fact such discouragement is common.

Conspicuously absent from the report is any mention of widely reported cases of the use of excessive and deadly force by the police in apprehending suspects. Over the last several years, numerous suspects have been fatally shot by the police, allegedly while fleeing. A recent example is Francis Okute, an elderly carpenter

---

* The detainees mentioned here were among seven who had been held without charges who were released in June 1989.

at the College of Veterinary Science and Agriculture, who was shot by a senior police officer from Kabete Police Station on August 11, 1988. There has been no vigorous effort to investigate or curb these acts of police violence.

The report correctly notes that in cases without political implications the right to a fair trial is normally observed, although long delays are common. While the report correctly points out that in trials involving Mwakenya/Kenya Patriotic Front suspects and sympathizers questions of unfairness have arisen, it minimizes the seriousness of concerns over the large number of "confessions" obtained for such trials by implying that only human rights organizations have doubted their reliability. In fact, broad sectors of Kenyan society and the international community have charged that most of these "confessions" were obtained through intimidation, torture or both.

The report's treatment of the two-stage 1988 parliamentary elections under the "queuing" system — which ended the secret ballot — is superficial and insufficient. The report neglects to mention the intimidation inherent in requiring voters to line up publicly behind candidates. The election results — in which none of the candidates critical of KANU or government policies was elected — illustrates that the elections were not free or fair. The report notes that queuing engendered "controversy"; more accurate language would have described the broad-based opposition from the clergy, the media, lawyers and voters in general.

The report asserts that President Daniel arap Moi was re-elected unopposed for a third five-year term. This statement is misleading in its failure to mention that Kenya is a *de jure* one-party state and that the ruling party, KANU, nominates only one presidential candidate; President Moi could not therefore have been opposed.

The report correctly describes government control of broadcast journalism and restrictions on foreign journalists. In an attempt to appear evenhanded, however, the State Department downplays restrictions on the press and ultimately contradicts itself. The report thus goes out of its way to refer to the "lively tradition" of the press in Kenya, even as it catalogues government attacks on publications found "objectionable," government censorship of editorials, self-censorship by intimidated journalists and denials of work permits to foreign correspondents. The report also fails to note that the prosecution and conviction of Bedan Mbugua, editor of *Beyond*, on charges of "improper financial management" appears to have been prompted by his publication of an article that criticized queue voting and questioned KANU's conduct during the 1988 elections.

The report omits mention of government harassment and prosecution of Gitobu Imanyara, editor of the popular *Nairobi Law Monthly*, an independent legal journal with a human rights component. In addition to pressuring his corporate sponsors and harassing his printers, the government brought charges against Imanyara in 1988 alleging that the publication was improperly registered. These moves appear to be part of a governmental attempt to close down the journal.

The report correctly observes that there are no "formal" limits to academic freedom. But it fails to mention that over the years, and particularly since 1982 when student leaders were alleged to have met with the organizers of a failed coup attempt, the government has taken numerous steps that have had the effect of restricting academic freedom. For example, the state has enlisted the services of loyal students and professors who, together with plainclothes security forces, monitor the content of classroom exchanges and report on the activities of the university community. University students and academics have been detained or prosecuted and imprisoned for allegedly seditious activities, and numerous professors and academics who were detained in 1982 have been denied re-employment at the university once they have been released. Clashes with the police and the General Service Unit (GSU), a paramilitary force which has been used in the past to coerce students, have become common at the Universities of Nairobi and Kenyatta; hardly a year passes without police action against students and the attendant closure of the universities. Many students have been injured during these confrontations and at least several deaths have been reported. In the aftermath of the 1982 coup attempt, an unspecified but reportedly large number of students were killed. Due to these pressures, leading Kenyan intellectuals, including the celebrated writer Professor Ngugi wa Thiong'o, have been forced to flee the country. Other previously detained academics, such as Al-Amin Mazrui, have had their passports confiscated, preventing them from travelling abroad. Mazrui was prevented from assuming a teaching position at Ohio State University.

The report refers to the rule requiring lawyers to register with the state but does not examine or give due weight to this troubling development. The requirement, which is unnecessary since lawyers traditionally have been regulated by the local law association, the Kenya Law Society, provides the government with the opportunity to weed out "undesirable" lawyers, especially lawyers disposed to handle human rights and other politically sensitive cases. In addition, although the report mentions the removal of the passports of Gibson Kamau Kuria and Paul Muite, it fails to note that these are not isolated incidents but part of a pattern of intimidation directed against the legal community.

The report fails to capture the magnitude of the problem of exile. By stating simply that "self-exile is a course of action sometimes chosen by Kenyan dissidents," the report misses the point that since 1982, particularly in light of the government's response to Mwakenya suspects and their alleged sympathizers, a climate of fear has grown. Widespread arbitrary arrests, detention, unfair trials and reports of torture created that climate, particularly among lawyers, academics and opposition politicians. As a result, a sizeable number of Kenyans have sought refuge abroad. The government has repeatedly attacked these exiles and accused them of plotting to overthrow it. In light of these attacks, many exiles regard skeptically the government's invitations for them to return, fearing that detention or persecution awaits them.

The report paints a rosy but inaccurate picture of worker rights. It should have pointed out the seriousness of the prohibition against civil servants organizing unions since most Kenyan workers are in the government's employ. The legally mandated trade union, the Central Organization of Trade Unions, caters only to workers in certain branches of the private sector, and its ability to represent workers vigorously is suspect because of heavy government interference and the close relationship between its leadership and the Ministry of Labor. The report should also have noted that the right of workers to strike, organize and bargain collectively is severely curbed by government regulations that require state approval at almost every turn.

Although the report briefly touches on conflicts between the clergy and the state, it does not clearly describe the strained relationship between these two institutions that existed throughout 1988. The church has consistently spoken out against human rights abuses and other restrictions of basic freedoms. Senior government officials, in turn, have attacked it sharply for its advocacy. The banning of *Beyond* — published by the National Council of Churches of Kenya — and the prosecution of its editor, Bedan Mbugua, was symptomatic of these strains. A number of church leaders, include the Reverend Daniel Gitari of Mount Kenya East, voiced their opposition to the electoral changes of 1988. In September, Reverend Gitari condemned the fall elections as "fraudulent." His remarks prompted the Secretary-General of KANU to threaten that the government was considering abolishing the constitutional right of worship.

The report also fails to mention that the right to travel is restricted in the northeastern part of the country, where emergency regulations remain in effect. Nor does the report refer to the tension that continues in that part of the country, where security forces continue to engage in violations of individual freedoms, including killings.

NOTES AND QUESTIONS

1. Are the above criticisms of the State Department report on Kenya correct?

2. In December 1986, Amnesty International sent a delegate to Kenya to investigate human rights violations. During Amnesty's investigation the Kenyan government denied allegations of unlawful detention, refusal of legal representation, and torture. Amnesty published its report after the government failed to respond to its findings and recommendations. For a report of the visit with findings and recommendations, see Amnesty International, Kenya: Torture, Political Detention and Unfair Trials (1987).

Kenya's President Moi and the U.S. State Department both criticized Amnesty's report. In July 1987, President Moi said, "Amnesty International should stop spreading premeditated and malicious propaganda about Kenya and instead pay attention to human rights violations in South Africa and other countries where people are suffering untold sufferings." The State Department said that Amnesty International failed to consider improvements in Kenya: "[T]he government of Kenya has addressed human rights concerns forthrightly by arresting several police officials accused of police brutality and by reaffirming its commitment to a society based on law." The Washington Post, July 28, 1987, at A-27.

After President Moi had been sent a copy of Amnesty International's 1987 report, he threatened to detain any A.I. delegate who might visit the country. In January 1988 the American Association for the Advancement of Science and the Lawyers Committee for Human Rights sent the chief coroner of Chicago and a former federal judge to an inquest in Nairobi. The inquest related to the death of Peter Njenga Karanja, who had been arrested for a suspected political offense. The two U.S. observers were detained for several hours and interrogated by police. They were released after pressure from the U.S. Embassy in Nairobi. In the furor caused by that detention the Kenyan President demoted the Minister of State in the

Office of the President for Internal Security, who had been responsible not only for the detention of the U.S. observers but also for most of the other political detentions in Kenya. Several political detainees were then released.

3. In May 1989 the government ordered the closing of the *Financial Review* — apparently because it had published several stories about the grain trade that were embarrassing to the government. The government had previously closed a magazine of the National Council of Churches because of its criticisms of irregularities in parliamentary elections. *See* Africa Watch, Kenya: Suppression of Press Freedom, Banning of Critical Papers and Intolerance of Dissent, December 6, 1989; Africa Watch, Once Again, a Critical Magazine Faces Threat of a Banning Order, April 5, 1990; Perlez, *Nairobi Orders Closing of 2d Magazine in a Year*, N.Y. Times, May 10, 1989, at A7, cols. 2-7.

4. Beginning in November 1989 the government forced several thousand Somali asylum-seekers in northeastern Kenya to return to Somalia, where they faced repression. Africa Watch, Forcible Return of Somali Refugees, Government Repression of Kenyan Somalis, November 17, 1989; Amnesty International, Kenya: 2,500 Somali asylum-seekers in northeastern Kenya, AI Index: AFR 32/07/89 (1989); *see also* Africa Watch, Kenya: Harassment of Ethnic Somalis, December 6, 1989.

5. For views of Kenyans in London who oppose the government, see United Movement for Democracy in Kenya, Moi's Reign of Terror (1989). For further reading, see Amnesty International, Report 58-60 (1989); Human Rights Watch & Lawyers Committee for Human Rights, Critique: A Review of the Department of State's Country Reports on Human Rights Practices for 1987, at 88-93 (1988).

Kenya: A Country Study 218-20, 226-28 (H. Nelson ed. 1983):

Foreign Relations

Kenya's foreign policy since independence has been characterized by moderation, pragmatism, and continuing reliance on the Western world as the source of needed capital and technical collaboration in developing the modern sectors of its economy. . . .

Kenya's nonalignment policy has not inhibited it from taking an unambiguous position against aggressive behavior by the Soviet Union. It condemned the Soviet invasion of Afghanistan in late 1979 and withdrew from the Moscow Olympics in the summer of 1980, in spite of the fact that its athletes were among the most talented in Africa. Although Kenya backed proposals to declare the Indian Ocean a zone of peace and resisted the establishment of foreign military bases there, the growing Soviet presence impelled the Moi government to authorize United States access to naval facilities at Mombasa and to certain Kenyan air bases.

Nairobi's status as a major African capital and the site of many international conferences contributed to the decision to locate two international agencies there, the United Nations Environmental Program (UNEP) and the United Nations Commission for Human Settlements (Habitat). Kenya has aligned itself with other member states of the OAU [Organization of African Unity] that have insisted on the elimination of white majority rule in South Africa and Namibia (South West Africa), as it had for Southern Rhodesia before that colony became independent Zimbabwe. . . .

Kenyan leaders have remarked on the fact that all of the country's neighbors are committed to a socialist approach, contrasting with Kenya's free-ranging private and state enterprise system. They have asserted that this has not been a cause of anxiety, noting the good relations that have long prevailed with Ethiopia in spite of its revolutionary, pro-Soviet leanings. Cordial relations have also been maintained with Sudan, whose socialism has largely been abandoned in practice and whose political outlook since the mid-1970s has been more compatible with that of Kenya. In the early 1980s it was expected that the two nations would develop closer mutual interests when an improved road linking southern Sudan with Nairobi was completed. A direct telecommunications link between the two countries was also to become operational in 1983. . . .

United States

Kenya and the United States have enjoyed close and cooperative relations at both official and private levels. A hospitable business climate has induced many American firms to invest in the country. Kenya has become one of the largest recipients of American aid in Africa. Pleasant living conditions and excellent international communications have persuaded many American organizations to select Nairobi as a regional center for banking, administrative, and marketing operations. The resident American population of over 6,000 includes about 1,400 missionaries and their families.

Kenya's moderate, conciliatory approach to the major problems of the African continent has accorded broadly with the policies being pursued by the United States on African issues. Kenya, along with the other African countries most concerned, has been consulted by the five Western nations (the United States, Britain, France, West Germany, and Canada) negotiating with South Africa over Namibian independence. . . .

After Kenyan independence the United States became an important source of development assistance. With its Western-oriented, open society and free market economic system, the East African country was regarded as an important growth model justifying American support. In recent years the United States aid program has been concentrated on rural production and employment, health services, and reduction of population growth. A Peace Corps contingent of 240 volunteers in 1982 was the largest in Africa and second in scope in the entire world. . . .

Until 1976 United States-Kenyan cooperation did not have a military component. But that year rising Soviet military assistance to Kenya's volatile neighbors, Somalia and Uganda, caused Nairobi to embark on a program to modernize and expand Kenyan defensive capabilities. A squadron of F-5 aircraft and helicopters mounted with antitank missiles were the principal items of equipment procured from the United States. . . .

Growing Soviet naval activity in the Indian Ocean, the Soviet invasion of Afghanistan, and the establishment of a radical Muslim regime in Iran by early 1980 intensified American concerns over security in the strategic Persian Gulf and the Indian Ocean supply lines for Middle East oil. The United States felt impelled to expand its naval presence in the Indian Ocean and to create a domestically based rapid deployment force capable of being dispatched to trouble spots world-wide. In addition to the buildup centered on the British-owned island base of Diego Garcia, negotiations were opened with Oman, Somalia, and Kenya for access to certain support facilities.

The Facilities Access Agreement reached with Kenya on June 26, 1980, provided for overflights, landing rights at three airfields, and port of call rights at Mombasa, although the full terms of the agreement were not disclosed. At the same time, United States military assistance to Kenya increased . . . . The Moi government insisted that the agreement be implemented in an inconspicuous manner with a minimum number of United States personnel permanently stationed in the country and no plans for major new installations.

One objective of the new agreement was to permit increased calls at Mombasa by United States naval vessels stationed in the Indian Ocean to provide relaxation for crews and to replenish supplies. In event of an emergency, airfield landing rights would facilitate the movement of rapid deployment forces based in the United States. An American-financed dredging project enabled United States aircraft carriers to dock at the port of Mombasa in all seasons. It was estimated that the crews of the 31 ships calling at Mombasa in 1982 gave a boost to the local economy amounting to more than US$9 million.

By 1981 the value of investments in Kenya made by the 200 private American firms amounted to more than US$315 million. Industrial production, food canning, hotel management, banking, insurance, and transportation were among the sectors represented. Major American companies operating in Kenya included Firestone, Colgate-Palmolive, Crown Cork, Del Monte, Union Carbide, General Motors, and Coca-Cola. A consortium of United States oil companies conducted drilling offshore in 1981-82 with inconclusive results. . . .

NOTES

1. After recounting the "puzzling and disturbing . . . infringements of human rights in Kenya," Kenneth Brown (Deputy Assistant Secretary of State for African Affairs) testified in February 1989 that "our policy challenge is to make clear our concerns on these issues while maintaining the special friendship with a country which remains one of Africa's success stories in terms of economic growth and political stability. We believe we should remain engaged and continue our forthright dialogue on human rights issues with senior Kenyan officials." Department of State, Bureau of Public Affairs, *Human Rights Issues in Africa*, Current Policy No. 1148 (1989).

2. For further reading, see Department of State, Background Notes: Kenya (1988); Department of Commerce, Foreign Economic Trends and Their Implications for the United States: Kenya (1988).

D. INCORPORATING HUMAN RIGHTS CONSIDERATIONS INTO U.S. FOREIGN POLICY

A study of the human rights policies of recent U.S. administrations illustrates differing views of foreign policy and the position of human rights considerations in that policy. Excerpts have been selected to reflect the Carter, Reagan, and Bush administrations. The first is an excerpt from a speech by Warren Christopher, Deputy Secretary of State in the Carter administration. The second is the introduction to the annual State Department Country Report for 1988 which reflects views of the Reagan administration and which was reproduced in chapter 9, *supra*. The third is an excerpt from a speech by James Baker, Secretary of State in the Bush administration. Contrast the administrations' position on (1) the place of moral and ethical concerns in United States foreign policy; (2) the definition of human rights; (3) the extent to which protection of human rights is in the national interest of the United States; and (4) the best policy to protect human rights.

Warren Christopher, *Human Rights and the National Interest*, Department of State, Bureau of Public Affairs, Current Policy No. 206 (1980):

Three and a half years ago, President Carter introduced into our foreign policy a theme both old and new: old, because it arose from our most basic national values; new in the sharp emphasis the President gave it. I am referring, of course, to human rights. "Because we are free," the President said in his inaugural address, "we can never be indifferent to the fate of freedom elsewhere."

From the beginning, the President was determined that American foreign policy should give active, explicit support to three categories of human rights:

— The right to be free from violations of personal integrity — torture, arbitrary arrest or imprisonment, and violations of due process;

— The right to fulfill vital economic needs, such as food, shelter, health care, and education; and

— Civil and political rights — freedom of thought, expression, assembly, travel, and participation in government. . . .

[O]ur commitment to human rights rests upon a large and growing body of law. Domestically, human rights legislation enacted by our Congress makes clear that our commitment is truly a national commitment — and that it is here to stay. Internationally, the human rights conventions, the Universal Declaration of Human Rights, and other basic documents make clear that the values we are seeking to advance are truly global values. . . .

In the 3½ years since President Carter proclaimed his policy, we have made real progress. We have effectively institutionalized human rights as a major element of U.S. foreign policy. A Bureau of Human Rights and Humanitarian Affairs has been established by statute, headed by an Assistant Secretary of State. Every American Ambassador has been instructed to report regularly on human rights conditions in the country to which he or she is posted. And the State Department's annual country reports on human rights have become one of the most important and objective sources of information on human rights conditions around the world. . . .

[H]uman rights has been placed squarely on the diplomatic table. The subject has become an item of serious discussion between us and the nations with which we deal — a dramatic change from past diplomatic practice. We have worked to strengthen the human rights effort of international bodies like the United Nations and the Inter-American Human Rights Commission. And human rights performance has become one of the key criteria we use in apportioning American aid to other nations.

This new emphasis in our foreign policy has not come without controversy. There has been vigorous criticism of our human rights policy on the ground that it smacks of fuzzy-headed idealism, that it is unrelated to the pursuit of our basic national interests. Some critics have suggested that human rights are a millstone around the neck of U.S. foreign policy; that it has injected into our diplomacy an interventionist element that can only weaken our position in the world and even destabilize other governments.

. . . To abandon the pursuit of human rights would gravely damage not only the hopes of millions abroad but also the foreign policy and long-term security of the United States.

A firm emphasis on human rights is not an alternative to "realpolitik," nor is it simply a side issue in our foreign policy. It is, instead, a central part of a pragmatic, tough-minded policy. Our human rights policy serves not just the ideals but the interests of the United States.

Let me support that assertion by discussing four of the ways in which our stress on human rights serves important interests of our nation.

Peace and Stability

First, our human rights policy directly serves our long-term interest in peace and stability.

There is, perhaps, a natural temptation to equate stability with status quo. Yet experience has demonstrated that the opposite is often true. The silence of official repression may appear to be "stability" — but it is often far more fragile than it appears. The misleading quiet of repression has too often turned out to be the calm before a violent, revolutionary storm. In such storms of violence, American interests are often damaged — and targets of opportunity are created for the Soviet Union or other forces hostile to the United States.

Governments that respect the rights of their people, and which reflect the will of their people, are far less vulnerable to such disruptions. . . .

By advancing human rights, we help to alleviate the sources of tension and instability before they erupt into violence, before our interests are harmed.

Our human rights policy is, thus, a vital element of our effort to align the United States with support for peaceful, constructive change. We are not so naive as to equate all change with progress — for that equation makes no more sense than equating stability and the status quo. But we recognize that the suppression of peaceful change often makes violence and terror inevitable. . . .

All should recognize the American support for democratic change in struggling Third World countries is complex and risky and involves difficult judgments. But the alternatives are riskier still, both for our values and for our security interests. . . .

There is, as I have said, an economic dimension to our support for human rights. Some of the most dangerous sources of instability in the world are economic. Such instability is bad for our security interests, and it is bad for American business, too. Respect for human rights creates an atmosphere of stability in which business and investment can flourish.

Foreign assistance is one of the most effective tools for coping with these economic sources of instability. Today, unfortunately, our foreign assistance is too meager to serve adequately our own humanitarian, economic, or security interests. But we try to target such aid as we can provide to narrow income disparities, to help people directly, and thus to ease social tensions in developing countries. We also channel our aid increasingly to countries that respect human rights, to countries that are trying to preserve representative government or to move from dictatorship to democracy.

This channeling of our aid is sometimes attacked as "intervention." We are admonished that other governments have a right to choose their own practices and forms of governments. Of course they do. But we have the right, and the obligation, to choose which governments and practices we will support with our scarce dollars.

Our resources and our powers are limited. But by working to ease grinding poverty, by supporting peaceful, constructive change, we believe we serve the cause of real peace and stability in the world. And this is very much in our national interest.

U.S. Security

The second point I wish to emphasize is that the United States will be more secure in a world where more governments respect the rights of their people — because countries that respect human rights make stronger allies and better friends.

This reality is illustrated by the democracies in Western Europe, in the Andean Pact in South America, in Japan and in the ASEAN [Association of South East Asian Nations] group in Southeast Asia. Their commitment to human rights gives them an inner strength and stability that enables them to stand steadfastly with us on the most difficult security issues of our time. By seeking to widen the circle of such countries, our human rights policy directly enhances our security interests.

Unfortunately, of course, not all our friends and allies can meet this high standard. One of the greatest challenges we will face in future years is the challenge of meshing our security assistance with human rights persuasion: combining military assistance to those who need it with strong encouragement to undertake the kind of internal reform necessary for long-term stability.

We face this challenge in our dealing with allies like South Korea and the Philippines — nations whose friendship is important to our security, nations whose governments we are trying to influence on human rights issues. Our security assistance to such countries supports a basic human right — the right of their people to live in safety from external attack. At the same time, by encouraging their governments to undertake internal reforms that will improve life for their people, we serve their long-term security interests and our own.

U.S. Influence

Third, support for human rights enhances the influence of the United States in important world arenas.

Too often in the past, the United States has allowed itself to be portrayed as a complacent, status quo power, insensitive to the quest of others for the freedoms we enjoy. And the result has often weakened the influence of the United States.

Our human rights policy counters that tendency. It identifies the United States with leaders around the world who are trying to improve the lot of their people.

We stand at a moment in history when widening literacy, mass communications, and urbanization have produced a global political awakening. This is a fundamental event in human history that expresses itself, above all, in the intensified demand for human rights. And our response to that demand has meant a new influence and good will for our country . . . .

In essence, our support for human rights gives us a way of emphasizing what we are for, not simply what we oppose. It gives us a way of taking the ideological initiative, instead of merely reacting. It gives us a rubric under which to organize our support for due process, economic progress, and democratic principles.

In the competition between the Soviet Union and ourselves, we benefit enormously from the comparison between our values and political methods and those of the Soviets. We pursue human rights for their own sake and would do so even if there were no Soviet Union. But there can be no doubt that our human rights policy does confound our adversaries.

The Soviets fear our human rights policy because their own human rights record is so abysmal and because they sense the power that the ideas of freedom and human dignity exert. Georgi Vladimov, a Soviet author and dissident, recently commented on U.S. human rights policy. "I don't know if President Carter will enter American history," he said, "but he has already entered Russian history with this policy." . . .

The influence and goodwill we gain by standing up for human rights cannot always be tangibly measured, but it is real. Our Embassy reports, our conversations with foreign diplomats, and the foreign press show that U.S. foreign policy is widely perceived as clearly and courageously supporting human rights. We need more, not less, of this positive policy.

Refugee Problem

Fourth, our support for human rights may offer the only long-term solution to one of the most pressing problems on the international agenda — the problem of refugees. . . .

[T]he solution lies not simply in arrangements to ease the plight of refugees; it lies in efforts to end the misery and repression that caused them to flee in the first place.

When a government respects the human rights of its citizens, refugees are a rare phenomenon. And we know that refugees are more likely to return home when the human rights situation has improved at home. . . .

Global Progress

As we look over the past 3½ years, we can see that the United States is identified more clearly than ever as a beacon of support for human rights. Worldwide publicity and concern for human rights have increased dramatically. . . .

Our efforts to express our deepest values through our human rights policy are working. They give us a glimpse of something we see all too seldom in the world: a happy situation in which American interests and American ideals converge.

Department of State, Country Reports on Human Rights Practices for 1988, Report Submitted to the Senate Committee on Foreign Relations and the House Committee on Foreign Affairs, 101st Cong., 1st Sess. 1 (1989).

Chapter 9 reproduces the introduction to the State Department Country Reports for 1989, which provides an insight to the approach of the Bush and Reagan administrations to U.S. foreign policy concerning human rights. The reader should review that introduction in connection with chapter 11.

Indeed, a review of each successive introduction to the annual State Department Country Reports provides a fascinating and significant perspective on the changing orientation of the U.S. human rights policies. The introductions to the 1988 and 1989 Country Reports, however, are nearly identical.

The following reading provides an indication of the approach of the Bush administration to human rights:

James Baker, Secretary of State, *The International Agenda and FY 1990 Budget Request*, Department of State Bureau of Public Affairs, Current Policy No. 1147 (1989):

I am honored to appear before you as Secretary of State to discuss the main lines of our foreign policy. . . .

In my confirmation hearing, I noted that America is vastly different from the country we knew even as recently as the beginning of this decade. Then American values and institutions were being questioned. Eight years of the Reagan era, however, have reaffirmed them. As a consequence, America today is a more vibrant and stronger nation. We have demonstrated once again that our form of government works, and that progress is possible in a setting which encourages the creativity of the individual and respects his or her rights.

Some of that vibrancy is reflected in international developments of our time. Our most powerful foe, the Soviet Union, so aggressive a decade ago, is undergoing a soul-searching of historic proportions. Democracy is continuing to take root and grow around the world on an impressive scale. Regional conflicts long thought to be intractable have begun moving toward resolution with the help of creative American diplomacy. And the international economy, driven by the longest American peacetime economic expansion on record, has provided new hope for progress. . . .

We could advance toward an increasingly democratic world, or, if fragile democracies fail, the cause of freedom could be set back. . . .

How should we approach this rapidly changing world? As a conservative and a realist, I believe our policy must always be guided by the basic American principles to which I adhere — freedom, democracy, equal rights, respect for human dignity, fair play. And I am convinced that we can advance these values if we are resolved on two issues.

The first is the necessity for American leadership. As the most powerful democracy, the largest economy, the wealthiest society with the greatest concentration of scientific talent, we are going to substantially affect the course of human events whether we do so consciously or not. We can be a force for freedom and peaceful change unlike any other in this world. But if we fail to do so, we will not be able to run or to hide from the consequences.

Second, the executive and the Congress must approach foreign policy in the spirit of bipartisanship. This does not mean that we will not have our differences. Airing those differences in a manner that respects the right of others to disagree is a strong affirmation of the democratic process. But eventually we must proceed, and when we do it is best that we do so together if we are to achieve the national interest. . . .

A unified bipartisan approach in this country is essential to achieve our objectives. Such an approach will certainly increase our leverage. . . .

Thanks to our policy of pursuing peace through strength, our dealings with the Soviet Union are less tense. We have made progress in arms control — especially the INF Treaty — human rights, bilateral ties, including a dramatic expansion in academic and cultural exchanges, and regional conflicts. We are pleased that Soviet troops have left Afghanistan on schedule. . . .

In light of both the change and continuity in the Soviet Union, realistic policy for America and its allies should be guided by these principles.

First, we should continue to welcome and encourage reform in the Soviet Union that promises more freedom. But we should never measure the progress of Mr. Gorbachev's [Soviet President Mikhail Gorbachev] reforms by how many credits, concessions, or accommodations we might make ostensibly to help him succeed with his domestic plans. *Perestroika* depends not on help from outside but on changes in the Soviet Union itself. That's a lesson Gorbachev learned from Brezhnev's failures. We should learn it as well. . . .

Third, we must continue to probe, even challenge, Moscow along every aspect of our agenda — arms control, human rights, regional conflicts, bilateral relations, and transnational or global issues. We are interested in cooperating and negotiating to make progress wherever it can be made. We are also interested in seeing the "new thinking" applied in practice, not just in slogans. . . .

NOTES AND QUESTIONS

1. President Carter emphasized international human rights as a central concern of his administration's foreign policy. Though the Carter administration was not always able to put human rights above other national interests in carrying out its foreign policy, the rhetoric of human rights and morality at the core of U.S. foreign policy proved popular with the U.S. and world public.

As the above excerpts demonstrate, the popularity of that rhetoric eventually forced the Reagan administration to include the protection of human rights as one of its foreign policy goals. At the beginning of Reagan's first term, however, the administration appeared to reject the idea that human rights had any place in foreign policy except as a weapon against communism. Indeed, Ernest Lefever, President Reagan's first nominee for head of the Human Rights Bureau, publicly opposed attempts by the U.S. to change the domestic policies of other countries by making human rights a foreign policy consideration. He stated that "[w]e have no moral mandate to remake the world in our own image." American Association for the International Commission of Jurists, Human Rights and American Foreign Policy: The First Decade 1973-1983, at 32 (1984) (quoting Morality and Foreign Policy, Ethics and Public Policy Center, Georgetown University, 1977). In Lefever's view, giving too much significance to human rights in U.S. foreign policy could endanger the primary goals of that policy — U.S. economic and security interests. The Senate rebuffed the Lefever nomination, forcing President Reagan to rethink his position on the place of human rights in U.S. foreign policy.

Do you think U.S. foreign policy should include protection of human rights in other countries? What do you think of Lefever's contention that the U.S. has no moral mandate to promote freedom in the world but should instead look out for its own interests? Can the U.S. use promotion of human rights as an ideology or organizing principle for its foreign policy to justify its conduct in the world arena? In this context, would protection of human rights advance U.S. interests?

If you believe that human rights should play a role in foreign policy decisions, do you think human rights goals should take precedence over U.S. economic and security goals when those goals clash? As you read the rest of the materials in this chapter consider whether it is ever possible or desirable for a country to place promotion of human rights ahead of other foreign policy goals.

2. In her article, *Dictatorships and Double Standards*, Commentary, Nov. 1979, at 34-45, Jeanne Kirkpatrick sharply criticized the Carter administration's human rights policy, arguing that a distinction should be made between authoritarian dictators friendly to the United States and totalitarian Marxist states. She argued that human rights violations by dictators should be viewed with less hostility because their governments are more subject to liberalization and friendly relations are necessary for American security interests. Totalitarian Marxist states, the argument continues, create the situations in which human rights violations occur. What do you think of that analysis? Do you think that human rights violations occur more frequently in totalitarian Marxist states than in states governed by right-wing dictatorships? Are states governed by friendly dictators more subject to liberalization, perhaps even democratization, than Marxist states? Does history confirm or contradict Kirkpatrick's arguments? In what ways?

Cyrus Vance, Secretary of State under the Carter administration, criticized the Reagan administration's adoption of Kirkpatrick's distinction between right- and left-wing dictatorships. According to Vance, the idea that the U.S. should turn a blind eye to, perhaps even support, serious human rights abuses committed by any country makes U.S. foreign policy morally bankrupt. Individual victims, as Vance observes, suffer regardless of the abuser's political orientation. Moreover, the Reagan administration's position undermines the longstanding U.S. image as a protector of human rights and freedom, the precise image that distinguishes the U.S. from the Soviet Union. *See* Vance, *The Human Rights Imperative*, 63 Foreign Policy 3, 9-12 (1986).

3. Supporting Deputy Secretary Christopher's assertion that promoting human rights is in the United States' security interest, Charles Brockett argues that the United States should pursue a foreign policy in Central America based on humanitarian concerns. Brockett, *The Right to Food and International Obligations: The Impact of U.S. Policy in Central America* in Human Rights and Third World Development (G. Shepherd, Jr., & V. Nanda eds. 1985).

4. For criticism of the Reagan administration's concentration on "democracy" over humanitarian concerns, see Minear, *The Forgotten Human Agenda*, 73 Foreign Policy 76 (1988-89). For a discussion of methods the U.S. could use in promoting democracy and the legality of those methods under international law, *see* Farer, *The United States as Guarantor of Democracy in the Caribbean Basin: Is There a Legal Way?*, 10 Hum. Rts. Q. 157 (1988). *See also* Steiner, *Political Participation as a Human Right*, 1 Harv. Hum. Rts. Y.B. 77 (1988).

5. For analyses of the Carter and Reagan administrations' human rights policies, see: American Association for the International Commission of Jurists, Human Rights and U.S. Foreign Policy: The First Decade 1973-1983, at 15-44 (1984); Carleton & Stahl, *The Foreign Policy of Human Rights: Rhetoric and Reality From Jimmy Carter to Ronald Reagan*, 7 Hum. Rts. Q. 205 (1985); D. Forsythe, Human Rights and World Politics 88-124 (1983); G. Mower, Human Rights and American Foreign Policy: The Carter and Reagan Experiences (1987); J. Murvachik, The Uncertain Crusade: Jimmy Carter and the Dilemma of Human Rights Policy (1986); Jacoby, *The Reagan Turnaround on Human Rights*, 64 Foreign Affairs 1066 (1986); Rossiter & Smith, *Human Rights: The Carter Record, The Reagan Reaction*, Int'l Pol'y Rep., Sept. 1984; Schifter, *Building Firm Foundations: The Institutionalization of United States Human Rights Policy in the Reagan Years*, 2 Harv. Hum. Rts. Y.B. 3 (1989); Shestack, *An Unsteady Focus: The Vulnerabilities of the Reagan Administration's Human Rights Policy*, 2 Harv. Hum. Rts. Y.B. 25 (1989).

6. Other countries have considered the role of human rights in their foreign policies. *See, e.g.,* Bossuyt, *Human rights as an element of foreign policy*, 89/1 Bull. Hum. Rts. 27 (1990).

E. THE ROLE OF CONGRESS IN U.S. HUMAN RIGHTS POLICY

In the 1970's, before the Carter administration, the Congress passed legislation that has permitted or required linking human rights considerations to security assistance, economic assistance, and participation in international financial institutions. The amendments in the 1970's to the 1961 Foreign Assistance Act culminated in Sections 116 (the Harkin Amendment) and 502B.

Section 502B (22 U.S.C. § 2304), consists of four major provisions. *First*, section 502B(a)(1) mandates that the promotion of international human rights be a principal goal of United States foreign policy. *Second*, section 502B(a)(3) directs the President to administer security assistance in a manner which promotes human rights and avoids identifying the United States with repressive foreign governments. *Third*, section 502B(a)(2) forbids security assistance to countries which engage "in a consistent pattern of gross violations of internationally recognized human rights." Notwithstanding that provision, security assistance may be provided under section 502B(a)(2) if the President certifies that extraordinary circumstances exist, or under section 502B(e) if the President finds that the human rights situation in a proposed recipient country has significantly improved. *Fourth*, section 502B(b) requires the State Department to prepare a report on the human rights practices of each proposed recipient of security assistance. The report on Kenya, reprinted earlier in this chapter, is an example of such a report. In addition Congress may demand further information on human rights practices of countries receiving security assistance.

In language similar to Section 502B, Section 116 (the Harkin Amendment) clearly prohibits granting economic aid to countries engaged "in a consistent pattern of gross violations of internationally recognized rights." The Harkin Amendment, however, exempts situations in which the assistance will directly benefit the "needy people" in the country.

Section 701 of the International Financial Institutions Act requires the U.S. government, in connection with its voice and vote in certain international financial institutions, to advance human rights "by seeking to channel assistance toward countries other than those whose governments engage in...a consistent pattern of gross violations of internationally recognized human rights." (Reprinted in the accompanying handbook, *Selected International Human Rights Instruments*).

The principal legislation just discussed, Sections 116 and 502B of the Foreign Assistance Act, are reproduced below:

Prohibition Against Foreign Assistance to Gross Violators of Human Rights (Harkin Amendment), 22 U.S.C.A. § 2151n (1990):

Foreign Assistance Act of 1961, Section 116, as amended

(a) No assistance may be provided under subchapter I of this chapter to the government of any country which engages in a consistent pattern of gross violations of internationally recognized human rights, including torture or cruel, inhuman, or degrading treatment or punishment, prolonged detention without charges, causing the disappearance of persons by the abduction and clandestine detention of those persons, or other flagrant denial of the right to life, liberty, and the security of person, unless such assistance will directly benefit the needy people in such country.

(b) In determining whether this standard is being met with regard to funds allocated under subchapter I of this chapter, the Committee on Foreign Relations of the Senate or the Committee on Foreign Affairs of the House of Representatives may require the Administrator primarily responsible for administering subchapter I of this chapter to submit in writing information demonstrating that such assistance will directly benefit the needy people in such country, together with a detailed explanation of the assistance to be provided (including the dollar amounts of such assistance) and an explanation of how such assistance will directly benefit the needy people in such country. If either committee or either House of Congress disagrees with the Administrator's justification it may initiate action to terminate assistance to any country by a concurrent resolution under section 2367 of this title.

(c) In determining whether or not a government falls within the provisions of subsection (a) of this section and in formulating development assistance programs under subchapter I of this chapter, the Administrator shall consider, in consultation with the Assistant Secretary for Human Rights and Humanitarian Affairs —

(1) the extent of cooperation of such government in permitting an unimpeded investigation of alleged violations of internationally recognized human rights by appropriate international organizations, including the International Committee of the Red Cross, or groups or persons acting under the authority of the United Nations or of the Organization of American States; and

(2) specific actions which have been taken by the President or the Congress relating to multilateral or security assistance to a less developed country because of the human rights practices or policies of such country.

(d) The Secretary of State shall transmit to the Speaker of the House of Representatives and the Committee on Foreign Relations of the Senate, by January 31 of each year, a full and complete report regarding —

(1) the status of internationally recognized human rights, within the meaning of subsection (a) of this section —

(A) in countries that receive assistance under subchapter I of this chapter, and

(B) in all other foreign countries which are members of the United Nations and which are not otherwise the subject of a human rights report under this chapter;

(2) wherever applicable, practices regarding coercion in population control, including coerced abortion and involuntary sterilization; and

(3) the steps the Administrator has taken to alter United States programs under subchapter I of this chapter in any country because of human rights considerations.

(e) The President is authorized and encouraged to use not less than $3,000,000 of the funds made available under this part and part IV of subchapter II of this chapter for each of the fiscal years ... for studies to identify, and for openly carrying out, programs and activities which will encourage or promote increased adherence to civil and political rights, as set forth in the Universal Declaration of Human Rights, in countries eligible for assistance under this part. None of these funds may be used, directly or indirectly, to influence the outcome of any election in any country....

Prohibition Against Security Assistance to Gross Violators of Human Rights, 22 U.S.C.A. § 2304 (1990):

Foreign Assistance Act of 1961, Section 502B, as amended

(a)(1) The United States shall, in accordance with its international obligations as set forth in the Charter of the United Nations and in keeping with the constitutional heritage and traditions of the United States, promote and encourage increased respect for human rights and fundamental freedoms throughout the world without distinction as to race, sex, language, or religion. Accordingly, a principal goal of the foreign policy of the United States shall be to promote the increased observance of internationally recognized human rights by all countries.

(2) Except under circumstances specified in this section, no security assistance may be provided to any country the government of which engages in a consistent pattern of gross violations of internationally recognized human rights. Security assistance may not be provided to the police, domestic intelligence, or similar law enforcement forces of a country, and licenses may not be issued under the Export Administration Act of 1979 [50 App. U.S.C.A. § 2401 et seq.] for the export of crime control and detection instruments and equipment to a country, the government of which engages in a consistent pattern of gross violations of internationally recognized human rights unless the President certifies in writing to the Speaker of the House of Representatives and the chairman of the Committee on Foreign Relations of the Senate and the chairman of the Committee on Banking, Housing, and Urban Affairs of the Senate (when licenses are to be issued pursuant to the Export Administration Act of 1979 . . .) that extraordinary circumstances exist warranting provision of such assistance and issuance of such licenses. Assistance may not be provided under part V of this subchapter to a country the government of which engages in a consistent pattern of gross violations of internationally recognized human rights unless the President certifies in writing to the Speaker of the House of Representatives and the chairman of the Committee on Foreign Relations of the Senate that extraordinary circumstances exist warranting provision of such assistance.

(3) In furtherance of paragraphs (1) and (2), the President is directed to formulate and conduct international security assistance programs of the United States in a manner which will promote and advance human rights and avoid identification of the United States, through such programs, with governments which deny to their people internationally recognized human rights and fundamental freedoms, in violation of international law or in contravention of the policy of the United States as expressed in this section or otherwise.

(b) The Secretary of State shall transmit to the Congress, as part of the presentation materials for security assistance programs proposed for each fiscal year, a full and complete report, prepared with the assistance of the Assistant Secretary of State for Human Rights and Humanitarian Affairs, with respect to practices regarding the observance of and respect for internationally recognized human rights in each country proposed as a recipient of security assistance. Whenever applicable, such report shall include information on practices regarding coercion in population control, including coerced abortion and involuntary sterilization. In determining whether a government falls within the provisions of subsection (a)(3) of this section and in the preparation of any report or statement required under this section, consideration shall be given to —

    (1) the relevant findings of appropriate international organizations, including nongovernmental organizations, such as the International Committee of the Red Cross; and

    (2) the extent of cooperation by such government in permitting an unimpeded investigation by any such organization of alleged violations of internationally recognized human rights.

(c) (1) Upon the request of the Senate or the House of Representatives by resolution of either such House, or upon the request of the Committee on Foreign Relations of the Senate or the Committee on Foreign Affairs of the House of Representatives, the Secretary of State shall, within thirty days after receipt of such request, transmit to both such committees a statement, prepared with the assistance of the Assistant Secretary of State for Human Rights and Humanitarian Affairs, with respect to the country designated in such request, setting forth —

(A) all the available information about observance of and respect for human rights and fundamental freedom in that country, and a detailed description of practices by the recipient government with respect thereto;

(B) the steps the United States has taken to —

(i) promote respect for and observance of human rights in that country and discourage any practices which are inimical to internationally recognized human rights, and

(ii) publicly or privately call attention to, and disassociate the United States and any security assistance provided for such country from, such practices;

(C) whether, in the opinion of the Secretary of State, notwithstanding any such practices —

(i) extraordinary circumstances exist which necessitate a continuation of security assistance for such country, and, if so, a description of such circumstances and the extent to which such assistance should be continued (subject to such conditions as Congress may impose under this section), and

(ii) on all the facts it is in the national interest of the United States to provide such assistance; and

(D) such other information as such committee or such House may request.

(2) (A) A resolution of request under paragraph (1) of this subsection shall be considered in the Senate in accordance with the provisions of section 601(b) of the International Security Assistance and Arms Export Control Act of 1976.

(B) The term ''certification'', as used in section 601 of such Act, means, for the purposes of this subsection, a resolution of request of the Senate under paragraph (1) of this subsection.

(3) In the event a statement with respect to a country is requested pursuant to paragraph (1) of this subsection but is not transmitted in accordance therewith within thirty days after receipt of such request, no security assistance shall be delivered to such country except as may thereafter be specifically authorized by law from such country unless and until such statement is transmitted.

(4) (A) In the event a statement with respect to a country is transmitted under paragraph (1) of this subsection, the Congress may at any time thereafter adopt a joint resolution terminating, restricting, or continuing security assistance for such country. In the event such a joint resolution is adopted, such assistance shall be so terminated, so restricted, or so continued, as the case may be.

(B) Any such resolution shall be considered in the Senate in accordance with the provisions of section 601(b) of the International Security Assistance and Arms Export Control Act of 1976.

(C) The term "certification", as used in section 601 of such Act, means, for the purposes of this paragraph, a statement transmitted under paragraph (1) of this subsection.

(d) For the purposes of this section —

(1) the term "gross violations of internationally recognized human rights" includes torture or cruel, inhuman, or degrading treatment or punishment, prolonged detention without charges and trial, causing the disappearance of persons by the abduction and clandestine detention of those persons, and other flagrant denial of the right to life, liberty, or the security of person; and

(2) the term "security assistance" means —

(A) assistance under part II (military assistance) or part IV (economic support fund) or part V (military education and training) or part VI (peacekeeping operations) or part VIII (antiterrorism assistance) of this subchapter;

(B) sales of defense articles or services, extensions of credits (including participations in credits, and guaranties of loans under the Arms Export Control Act [22 U.S.C.A. § 2751 et seq.]; or

(C) any license in effect with respect to the export of defense articles or defense services to or for the armed forces, police, intelligence, or other internal security forces of a foreign country under section 38 of the Arms Export Control Act [22 U.S.C.A. § 2778].

(e) Notwithstanding any other provision of law, funds authorized to be appropriated under subchapter I of this chapter may be made available for the furnishing of assistance to any country with respect to which the President finds that such a significant improvement in its human rights record has occurred as to warrant lifting the prohibition on furnishing such assistance in the national interest of the United States.

(f) In allocating the funds authorized to be appropriated by this chapter and the Arms Export Control Act [22 U.S.C.A. § 2751 et seq.], the President shall take into account significant improvements in the human rights records of recipient countries, except that such allocations may not contravene any other provision of law. . . .

NOTES AND QUESTIONS

1. The legislation just excerpted is often termed "general" because it applies generally to all countries. General legislation often grants significant discretion to the Executive in carrying out the legislation, and the discretion has made it possible for the Executive to avoid the spirit of the legislation when granting assistance. For a discussion of situations in which both the Carter and Reagan administrations avoided the intent of general human rights legislation, see Forsythe, *Congress and Human Rights in U.S. Foreign*

Policy: The Fate of General Legislation, 9 Hum. Rts. Q. 382, 382-95 (1987).

2. Decisions at multilateral development banks and the World Bank, in particular, are supposed to be made solely on the basis of economic factors without taking into account any political considerations. That policy has led some commentators to argue that Section 701's requirement that the U.S. use its vote in the multilateral development banks to channel assistance toward countries with good human rights records violates the apolitical nature of the banks. *See, e.g.*, Kneller, *Human Rights, Politics, and the Multilateral Development Banks*, 6 Yale Stud. World Pub. Ord. 361 (1980) (arguing that bank directors can only consider human rights in voting on loans to the extent that such considerations have economic implications relevant to the banks' purposes).

Other commentators, however, have argued that though the banks' original purposes were apolitical, bank decisions have become politicized in certain areas. Consequently it would not harm the banks to recognize human rights as a relevant consideration in making loan decisions. *See, e.g.*, Spiro, *Front Door or Back Stairs: U.S. Human Rights Policy in the International Financial Institution*, in Human Rights and U.S. Foreign Policy 133 (B. Rubin & E. Spiro eds. 1979).

The International Monetary Fund (IMF) provides short-term credit to countries experiencing balance of payment difficulties and recommends social and economic measures to assist governments in improving their economic balance with the rest of the world. The IMF recommendations often require austerity measures that may result in widespread suffering, including violations of economic, social, and cultural rights. Some governments have resorted to repression in order to sustain the austerity measures. Hence, the IMF may find it difficult to contend that its decisions are entirely apolitical and that it need not consider the human rights implications of its recommendations.

3. Congress has enacted other legislation with provisions designed to promote human rights, although the primary purposes of the statutes may not have been principally related to human rights. For example, the 1988 Omnibus Trade and Competitiveness Act authorizes the President to impose trade sanctions against countries that violate workers' rights. It authorizes presidential action when a country's labor practices constitute "a persistent pattern of conduct that: (I) denies workers the right of association, (II) denies workers the right to organize and bargain collectively, (III) permits any form of forced or compulsory labor, (IV) fails to provide a minimum age for the employment of children, or (V) fails to provide standards for minimum wages, hours of work, and occupational safety and health of workers." 19 U.S.C.A. § 2411(d)(3)(B)(iii) (West Supp. 1989). For further reading, see Lawyers Committee for Human Rights, Worker Rights under the U.S. Trade Laws (1989).

4. For an uncomplimentary assessment of the U.S. human rights legislation and other approaches, see K. Tomashevski, Development Aid and Human

Rights 50-59 (1989); *see also* K. Tomashevski, Foreign Aid and Human Rights: Case Studies of Bangladesh and Kenya (1988).

Fraser, *Congress's Role in the Making of International Human Rights Policy*, in Human Rights and American Foreign Policy 247, 247-54 (D. Kommers & G. Loescher eds. 1979):

This paper attempts to answer four questions. *First, what is Congress's role in monitoring the impact of American foreign policy on human rights abroad and developing legislative guidelines for such a policy?*

Congress has an important role to play in this matter. First, through public discussion of issues, particularly through hearings as well as on the floor of the House, Congress can very effectively draw attention to human rights problems abroad and thereby increase public concern and the receptivity of foreign governments to ameliorate their practices. Second, it establishes through law the standards upon which the Executive Branch uses the various assistance programs for leverage in the promotion of human rights.

Hearings have been a principal means by which the Congress has monitored foreign policy and sought to influence its direction. An important example of such a forum is the Fascell Commission — a joint Congressional-Executive Branch commission specifically designed to monitor compliance with the final act of the Helsinki Agreement. Over the last few years my own subcommittee has held more than 80 hearings on the subject of human rights and foreign policy. Nongovernmental witnesses have proved an invaluable resource in providing us with information with which to compare Department of State testimony. By listening to and questioning departmental testimony, we believe we have influenced the conduct of policy at least a little. If nothing else, the hearings have required the Department of State to place matters on the record that otherwise might not have been disclosed publicly. Also, from my own personal experience with respect to our subcommittee's hearings, I am certain that the hearings are taken very seriously by most foreign governments. They make every effort to indicate that their performance conforms with international human rights standards.

Congress also has enacted legislation in the field of human rights and foreign policy. Specific examples include Sections 502B (human rights and security assistance) and 116 (human rights and development assistance) of the Foreign Assistance Act as well as the human rights amendments aimed at the multilateral banks.

Both Sections 502B and 116 provide the Executive with a general framework within which the Administration is expected to shape its security and development assistance programs. However, neither law dictates specific decisions; rather, each allows flexibility for action in individual circumstances. For example, Section 502B prohibits, except under extraordinary circumstances, military aid or sale of military equipment to governments with a consistent pattern of gross violations of internationally recognized human rights. Congress has placed especially stringent standards on military aid because of the symbolic and sometimes practical importance of such assistance in carrying out repressive policy in numerous countries.

The relationship between human rights and development aid poses a more complicated question. Because we do not want to penalize the poor, Section 116 prohibits bilateral development aid to a repressive government only if that aid is not directly beneficial to needy people. Congress enacted this legislation under the Nixon and Ford administrations because of our belief that in certain nations, particularly Chile and South Korea, the Administration was using economic aid to prolong the staying power of regimes more than to provide help for needy people. . . .

Congress also has enacted legislation concerning specific countries. Such legislation was enacted during the Ford Administration and has continued during the Carter Administration. . . .

Ironically, during the Carter Administration, an even greater number of specific country legislative prohibitions or limitations on military aid were enacted as compared with the Ford Administration. Many members of Congress are not as patient as the Administration in terms of encouraging repressive regimes to change their practices. They believe that many of these regimes have had a long enough time to mend their practices. They do not favor compromising the legislative principle that repressive regimes, except in extraordinary circumstances, should be disqualified from receiving military assistance. They favor a policy of frankness, of public opprobrium, and of a straightforward disassociation of the United States with the repressive regime through termination of military aid. . . .

The second question is what tensions exist between Congress and the Executive? As the conflict over specific country legislation and legislation affecting the international institutions indicates, Congress has not accepted as fully bona fide the Administration's commitment to human rights. Tensions do exist; perhaps they are inevitable and desirable — even when the same party controls both the White House and Congress. Even if Congress had complete faith in the Administration's commitment, disagreement might remain over its implementation. There are many forces militating against a strong human rights element in foreign policy. The Executive Branch needs Congressional support, and in some instances this may mean that the Congress will take the lead on human rights initiatives or principles in human rights policy. Particularly since the Carter Administration took office, my preference has been for a "low-profile" Congressional policy giving the Executive an opportunity to work out a human rights policy and a reasonable period of time in which to achieve results. . . .

The promotion of human rights is a complicated and difficult task. National pride makes other governments extremely sensitive to foreign criticism. The Executive Branch, as compared with Congress, has more tools and instruments at its disposal for bringing its concern regarding human rights to the attention of other governments. It can act with greater subtlety. It can take firm measures, including sanctions, without introducing these sanctions into the public arena. Consequently, an Administration willing to exert itself can have more effectiveness in this field than can Congress. . . .

The third question is how effective is the Congressional role? Despite the confrontational relationship that has existed between the executive and legislative branches in recent years, the Congress has achieved some positive results. In effect, Congress has laid a basis for the new Administration's human rights policy. Congressional initiatives have included the following:

1.   The establishment of the human rights performance of the recipient government as a basic factor in decisions regarding military and economic assistance.

2.   The creation of the Office of Coordinator for Human Rights and Human-

itarian Affairs in the State Department and the suggestion that human rights officers in the regional bureaus be appointed. This suggestion has been accepted, and the coordinator has been elevated to the rank of assistant secretary.

3. The establishment of human rights reporting as a regular function of the embassies and of public reporting on proposed recipients of security and development assistance.

4. Pressure on the State Department to make human rights representations to foreign governments.

5. Pressure on the State Department in public hearings to take positions on human rights situations in individual countries.

All these activities have had the effect of raising the consciousness of foreign service officers regarding the relevance of human rights to foreign policy. . . .

The fourth question is how can Congress play a more effective role? The Congressional role as a partner, rather than as an adversary, in the formulation of foreign policy will be enhanced if the Executive maintains a steady dialogue with the Congress. The new Administration has made constructive efforts in this regard.

Congress needs to think creatively rather than to merely react belatedly to situations. Congress has often been reactive because it has lacked the resources — particularly information — upon which to foretell developments. Perhaps Congress needs its own independent source of information apart from the services already provided by the Congressional Research Service. . . .

Clearly, not enough is known of the initiatives taken by the foreign governments, parliaments, and political parties around the world with respect to human rights issues. Congress can encourage international parliamentary efforts in defense of human rights. Concerting international responses to human rights violations may be one of the effective means open to outsiders seeking to influence another government's actions. . . .

Congress, of course, must ratify more of the human rights conventions. The United States lags badly behind most countries in the numbers of such conventions it has ratified. . . .

NOTES AND QUESTIONS

1. Note that the author, former Representative Donald Fraser, wrote the preceding piece during the Carter administration. Despite Carter's announced goal of making human rights promotion an important part of U.S. foreign policy, Fraser opined that many members of Congress viewed the administration's progress on that goal as too slow. Do you think that Congress and the Executive will inevitably hold different views on the place of human rights promotion in foreign policy? Why do you think this might be so? For one suggestion, see Cohen, *Conditioning U.S. Security Assistance on Human Rights Practices*, reprinted in section F of this chapter.

2. In a speech titled, "Human Rights and the Moral Dimension of U.S. Foreign Policy," then Secretary of State George Shultz observed,

The role of Congress is another question. There is no doubt that congressional concerns and pressures have played a very positive role in giving impetus and backing to our efforts to influence other governments' behavior. This congressional pressure can strengthen the hand of the executive branch in its efforts of diplomacy. At the same time, there can be complications if the legislative instrument is too inflexible or heavy-handed, or, even more, if Congress attempts to take on the administrative responsibility for executing policy. Legislation requires that we withhold aid in extreme circumstances. If narrowly interpreted, this can lead us rapidly to a "stop-go" policy of fits and starts, all or nothing — making it very difficult to structure incentives in a way that will really fulfill the law's own wider mandate: to "promote and encourage increased respect for human rights and fundamental freedoms. . . ." Department of State, Bureau of Public Affairs, Current Policy No. 551 (1984).

Contrast Fraser's view on the importance of congressional initiative and Shultz's remarks on legislation reprinted in the previous section. Who do you think is right?

3. What are advantages and disadvantages of a strong congressional role in the promotion of human rights and U.S. foreign policy?

4. In addition to the legislation discussed previously, Fraser notes that Congress can pass country-specific legislation placing conditions on the Executive's discretion in awarding assistance to a given country. Congress exercises that power when it is displeased with the Executive's decisions regarding a certain country under the general legislation. The general legislation gives the Executive a fairly broad range of discretion in granting assistance; country-specific legislation narrows that discretion for the target country. Past country-specific legislation has taken several forms, including prohibiting the grant of certain types of assistance to the target country or establishing conditions that the country must satisfy in order to receive assistance in the future. The latter attempts to improve the human rights situation in the target country through the promise of increased assistance. For a discussion of country-specific legislation and its use with respect to El Salvador, see Comment, *Human Rights and United States Security Assistance: El Salvador and the Case for Country-Specific Legislation*, 24 Harv. Int'l L.J. 75 (1983).

One problem with the type of legislation used in the case of El Salvador, as opposed to legislation which prohibits assistance, is that the former gives the Executive more discretion. That discretion arises as a result of the Executive's role in certifying whether the target country has or has not met the legislative conditions for increased assistance. For discussion of the first two presidential certifications under the El Salvador legislation and congressional criticism of those certifications, see Horton & Sellier, *The Utility of Presidential Certifications of Compliance with United States*

Human Rights Policy: The Case of El Salvador, 1982 Wis. L. Rev. 825.

5. U.S. military assistance to Kenya grew from $16.02 million in fiscal year 1988 to $26.6 million in fiscal 1989. The State Department requested $31.4 million for fiscal 1990. The U.S. Navy's access to facilities in Mombasa is subject to a five-year renewal in 1990. Hence, the proposed increase for 1990 may be related to that renewal. Economic and development aid for Kenya remained relatively constant during the 1988-90 period: $41.1 million (1988), $40 million (1989), and $39 million (request for 1990). P.L. 480 (food assistance) was $11.1 million for fiscal 1988; $6.7 million for fiscal 1989; and $12.3 million was requested for fiscal 1990.

6. In 1989 the House of Representatives passed H.R. 2658 including the following provision: (The Senate did not act on this bill.)

Sec. 1025. ASSISTANCE FOR KENYA.

(a) STATEMENT OF POLICY.—The provision to Kenya of economic support assistance and foreign military financing under the Foreign Assistance Act of 1961 for fiscal years 1990 and 1991 shall bear a relation to signficant steps by the Government of Kenya to increase respect for internationally recognized human rights in Kenya. Such steps should include—

(1) an end to intimidation and harassment of elements of Kenyan society that are critical of the Government's policies, especially the church, the press, and the legal community; and

(2) effective safeguards to ensure the independence of the judiciary and to guarantee due process and other rights for individuals imprisoned or otherwise detained by the Government.

(b) REPORT TO CONGRESS.—The Secretary of State shall, not later than February 1, 1990, and not later than February 1, 1991, report to the Committee on Foreign Affairs and the Committee on Appropriations of the House of Representatives and the Committee on Foreign Relations and the Committee on Appropriations of the Senate on the actions the United States Government has taken to carry out subsection (a).

7. For further reading on U.S. human rights legislation and the role of Congress in promoting human rights, see Bedau, *Human Rights and Foreign Assistance Programs*, in Human Rights and U.S. Foreign Policy 29 (P. Brown & D. MacLean eds. 1979); D. Forsythe, Human Rights and Foreign Policy: Congress Reconsidered (1988); Galey, *Congress, Foreign Policy and Human Rights Ten Years After Helsinki*, 7 Hum. Rts. Q. 334, 343-67 (1985). Harkin, *Human Rights and Foreign Aid: Forging an Unbreakable Link*, in Human Rights and U.S. Foreign Policy 15 (P. Brown & D. MacLean eds. 1979); Weissbrodt, *Human Rights Legislation and U.S. Foreign Policy*, 7 Ga. J. Int'l & Comp. L. 231 (1977).

8. What political forces might be interested in the formulation of U.S. foreign policy vis-a-vis Kenya? Would those forces be more effective in pressing the Executive or the Congress? For example, would the tourist industry be sufficiently interested in Kenya to urge that Kenya's human rights violations be ignored in favor of continued tourism? Or would the tourist industry have no particular stake in Kenya and simply shift tours to Tanzania or other countries? What position would members of the Congressional Black Caucus take in regard to human rights violations in Kenya? Would the Caucus be influential in the formulation of foreign policy in regard to Kenya? *Cf.* McGee, *Rep. Dymally's Contacts Raise Issue of Public Trust, Private Interests*, Washington Post, Jan. 2, 1990, at A15, cols. 1-6.

9. In a symposium on human rights in the administration which was to take office in 1989, two commentators recommended that Congress strengthen its role in promoting human rights by enacting more country-specific legislation, conducting closer review of diplomatic initiatives, cutting off aid to countries with serious and ongoing human rights violations, and forcing the Executive to report more frequently on particular countries' human rights situations and U.S. assistance and trade policies toward those countries. Posner & Zavis, *Human Rights Priorities for a New Administration and Congress*, 28 Va. J. Int'l L. 893, 897-98 (1988).

F. THE ROLE OF THE ADMINISTRATION

A commitment to human rights by the administration is necessary for the effective implementation of human rights policy. The U.S. Constitution grants the President significant authority in the area of foreign policy. Though Congress may pass legislation dealing with human rights concerns, wield power through the appropriations process, and influence policy through its oversight power, the dynamic nature of foreign affairs and international human rights conditions require that the President and the State Department conduct the day-to-day management of human rights policy.

The following materials by Human Rights Watch and the Lawyers Committee for Human Rights analyze the Reagan administration's preparation of the Country Reports on Human Rights Practices and the Administration's general record on human rights policy. As stated in the introduction to the materials on Kenya, Human Rights Watch and/or the Lawyers Committee annually prepare a critique of the State Department's Country Reports. In addition, each year Human Rights Watch and/or the Lawyers Committee critique the Administration's human rights policy as a whole.

In reading these excerpts, consider what impact a single administration or Congress can have on the development of a long range U.S. human rights policy.

Human Rights Watch & Lawyers Committee for Human Rights, Critique: Review of the Department of State's Country Reports on Human Rights Practices for 1988, at 1-8 (1989):

INTRODUCTION

The biases in the State Department's reporting shifted over the course of the Reagan Administration. In the initial years, the reports reflected East-West conflicts. Reports on human rights abuses in the Soviet Union, Eastern Europe and some other Communist-ruled countries, such as Cuba and Vietnam, were thorough and complete and in some cases exaggerated. Meanwhile, the reports on certain allies, Guatemala, Honduras, El Salvador, the Philippines, Chile and Pakistan, for example, often understated the extent of abuses or attempted to shift the blame from the governments of those countries.

As time passed, however, a more complex pattern emerged which reflected both the Reagan Administration's changing approach to the human rights cause and the evolution of East-West relations.

After an initial repudiation, the Reagan Administration publicly embraced the human rights cause. The Administration's new human rights policy soon focused on electoral democracy as the way to promote respect for human rights. A perceived transition from dictatorship to democracy through elections ensured favorable reporting on the human rights situation, as exemplified in reports on Turkey, Guatemala and the Philippines. Elsewhere, as in Chile, where a democratic transition has not yet occurred, the Reagan Administration shifted over time from outspoken friendship and support for the Pinochet dictatorship to criticism, and then to outright support for its replacement by a democratic government during the Administration's last year. This shift is reflected in the *Country Reports* by the welcome fact that the reporting on Chile and Paraguay is currently as comprehensive and as critical as the reporting on Bulgaria and Czechoslovakia.

Yet the emphasis on elections and "transitions to democracy" has led the State Department to overlook the influence of the military and paramilitary groups in numerous nominally democratic countries and to understate the extent of human rights abuses in these nations. The reports on El Salvador, Guatemala, Colombia and the Philippines illustrate the State Department's equating the emergence of elected civilian governments with the existence of civilian rule and respect for human rights. Though these countries have had elected civilian presidents who are not suspected by anyone of personal complicity in political violence, those presidents have not prevented their armed forces from committing many gross abuses of human rights. The State Department's reporting on these countries presents a misleading picture in which the extent of violence is understated and the government's responsibility for curbing the violence and punishing those responsible is almost entirely ignored.

...State Department reports...such as those on Chile, South Africa, the Sudan and Czechoslovakia are comprehensive and balanced and the methods of analysis employed in these reports should be used in all. These reports should serve as models for future reports, in part because they:

— include detailed accounts of specific cases;
— cite information and statistics from a variety of sources, especially from non-governmental groups and court records, where applicable;

— describe comprehensively the context surrounding an event or issue;
— assert the State Department's own views and conclusions unambiguously;
— distinguish between rights and freedoms theoretically guaranteed by law and the actual observance of such rights and freedoms.

In particular, close and sustained contact between an embassy and local human rights monitors and other groups spanning the political spectrum is a common characteristic of the better reports.

The roster of weak reports is depressingly familiar. The reports on Haiti, El Salvador, Guatemala, the Philippines, Indonesia, Singapore and Malaysia, for example, fail to convey the causes, extent and frequency of human rights violations. In addition to political and geopolitical considerations this weakness stems from the State Department's use of certain methods common to many of the poorer reports:

— Accepting a government's statements of intent, the passage of legislation or the launching of investigations as proof of improvement in human rights observance: in the Zimbabwe report the situation of detainees is described as though the legal standards were actually applied in practice without exception; Turkey's ratification of the European Convention and United Nations Convention Against Torture did not end torture; in Pakistan, the "lifting" of martial law did not end many of its features which remain in force; in Israel, the report implies that the government's declaration that a controversial "beatings" policy was illegal ended such beatings . . . ;
— Excusing violations because of a lack of resources rather than stating that in many cases violations stem from a failure of will: in the Philippines, the report states that the justice system works slowly, but the State Department does not analyze why; the report on Turkey ascribes poor prison conditions to poverty yet many conditions could be improved with minimal expenditures; the report on Haiti asserts that weaknesses in the judicial system explain lengthy pre-trial detention yet sometimes the government refuses to present prisoners to a judge;
— Failure to offer an independent analysis and a conclusion in the State Department's own voice: the Israel report fails to offer its own assessment concerning allegations of torture and beatings by security forces; the reports on China and Pakistan cite governmental statistics on deaths in detention that are widely known as inaccurate, do not cite statistics gathered by independent groups, and therefore make no judgment on what constitutes accurate figures . . . ;
— Excusing human rights violations because of poor training of soldiers and police or ascribing violations to "irregular" forces: this rationale appears in the reports on Pakistan and Liberia; the Somalia report attributes violations by the police to poor pay and lack of discipline while ignoring the political aspect of the abuses and superior officers' tolerance of extortion as a means to persecute and intimidate critics;
— Failing to see connections between facts: the Kenya report describes a constitutional amendment extending the time a person may be held in incommunicado detention yet does not explain how this change affects the incidence of mistreatment and deaths in prison or harsh prison conditions in general;

— Misleading use of words: in Kenya the report notes that Parliament voted "unanimously" for certain constitutional amendments, yet Kenya is a *de jure* one-party state and one party dominates Parliament; the Yugoslavia report states that Yugoslavia "extends temporary asylum to refugees" yet fails to explain that "asylum" often means a jail cell for Romanian refugees;

— Creating a misleading impression of the human rights situation by describing events or violations in one section while such events or violations should have been included in a different or additional section: in China, the prohibition on advocating Tibetan independence is described in the section on discrimination and should also have been described in the section on freedom of speech; . . . in Tanzania, the report includes the killings at a Muslim demonstration in the section on citizens' rights to change the government but the section on political killings omits any mention of these killings;

— Criticizing human rights groups for failing to fulfill certain tasks: the reports on El Salvador and the Philippines criticize certain human rights groups for failing to provide enough evidence to convict violators or to assist authorities to prosecute human rights violations, yet human rights groups are not prosecutors: their job is to monitor and report on human rights violations; the effect of these criticisms is to appear to excuse the governments that have actually demonstrated an unwillingness to prosecute military and paramilitary personnel for gross abuses even when overwhelming evidence of culpability is readily available;

— Omitting important background information thereby creating a partial and often misleading context: the Singapore and Somalia reports state that no non-governmental organizations monitor human rights abuses, but the State Department fails to note that each government deters and suppresses the formation of any such groups; . . . in Kenya, the report observes that only civil servants are forbidden to organize while omitting that most wage earners in Kenya are civil servants.

In addition, the State Department sometimes treats the same issue differently depending on the country. The China report does not discuss the effects of the population transfers of ethnic Chinese to Tibet. The report on Vietnam, however, details the government's program to resettle ethnic Vietnamese in the central highlands and assimilate minorities. The Vietnam report also describes carefully circumscribed visits by outside delegations while remaining silent on similarly orchestrated visits to East Timor in the Indonesian report.

The El Salvador report notes that accounts of a resurgence of death squads "have not been substantiated." The Liberia report states there are "unconfirmed allegations" of deaths in prisons. In these cases independent and reliable information confirms increased death squad activity in El Salvador and deaths in Liberian prisons. Yet in the China report, the State Department relies without qualification on official estimates of deaths during demonstrations. This pattern of applying different standards to substantiate evidence appears in many reports.

The State Department adopts a passive and non-judgmental position regarding the accuracy of accounts of torture and beatings in the Israeli occupied territories, noting, "reports of beatings of suspects and detainees continue, as do reports of harsh and demeaning treatment of prisoners and detainees." The State Department sheds this passivity when discussing torture in Syria ("there have been numerous credible reports of torture") and Iraq ("reliable reports make clear that both physical and psychological torture are used by the authorities"). . . .

One foreign service officer's account of his experiences in Guatemala as a human rights officer appeared in the May 1989 *Foreign Service Journal*. In that article, Thomas Shannon identifies a number of chronic problems that contribute to the uneven quality of the reports and permit the injection of political concerns into the analysis. Some of these problems are of a managerial nature. Shannon notes that human rights officers "are usually chosen at random and receive no training for their jobs" and they do not debrief their predecessors. More important, we believe, is the lack of bureaucratic clout of the Bureau of Human Rights and Humanitarian Affairs within the State Department, resulting in the Bureau's inability to provide consistent support to human rights officers. Thus, according to Shannon, "the quality of human rights reporting depends on the demands made of the officer by his geographic bureau and his ambassador." This lends support to our view that the demands of the geographic bureaus at the State Department, and of particular ambassadors, have undermined the objectivity of certain reports.

Despite the criticisms set forth here, we believe that the *Country Reports* have continued to improve and that they serve as an ever more useful compendium of information on human rights practices worldwide. The Bush Administration could make the *Country Reports* even more useful by following some of the managerial suggestions offered in the Shannon article. As he points out, "The State Department offers courses in political tradecraft, economic reporting and labor affairs, but it offers nothing to prepare human rights officers for their jobs."

Yet just as well-trained police officers will not produce respect for human rights when the political leadership of a country is intent on repression, so well-trained foreign service officers will not produce a reliable volume of *Country Reports* unless the political leadership of the Department of State is committed to fair, objective and comprehensive reporting. We call on the Bush Administration in general, and on Secretary of State James Baker in particular, to send out the message that, regardless of political and geopolitical considerations, each of the reports should be a reliable record of human rights developments; that the United States should speak in its own voice in condemning abuses; and that efforts to excuse or cover up abuses by understating them, exculpating those responsible, or pretending that culpability has not been established, have no place in the reports. . . .

NOTES AND QUESTIONS

1. For an analysis of the State Department's Country Reports, including discussion of their history and examination of their impact, see de Neufville, *Human Rights Reporting as a Policy Tool: An Examination of the State Department Country Reports*, 8 Hum. Rts. Q. 681 (1986).

The de Neufville article recommended that "the participation of NGOs and academic experts in evaluating and improving the methods of gathering and analyzing the data should be formalized and regularized through task forces, advisory groups, or user groups.'' *Id.* at 699. Do you think providing an official role for NGOs in the compilation of the country reports would be useful? Would it help to alleviate the administration's biases that influence some of the reports?

Despite her recommendation de Neufville concludes that the professional staff who prepare the reports are "increasingly willing and able to resist pressures to slant the *Reports* for political purposes." *Id.* at 690. Do you think the NGO authors of the preceding critiques on the Country Reports would agree? Is it ever possible for a branch of the Executive to resist all political pressures? *See* Lawyers Committee for Human Rights, Bureaucracy and Diplomacy (1989).

2. In a 1988 symposium, W. Michael Reisman proposed another way of insulating human rights reporting from political pressures. Under his proposal a statutory human rights agency would be established. The agency would monitor all the human rights information obtained by the government and release information about possible human rights violations as soon as it was available. The agency would be independent, and thus relatively insulated from political pressures that might influence the Executive to withhold information when publication conflicted with other national interests. Reisman, *American Human Rights Diplomacy: The Next Phase*, 28 Va. J. Int'l L. 899, 901-02 (1988).

What do you think of Professor Reisman's proposal? Would it solve the problem of biased information? Is it realistic?

3. For a discussion of the difficulties inherent in collecting and interpreting human rights data for different countries, see Heginbotham & Bite, *Issues in Interpretation and Evaluation of Country Studies*, in Human Rights and U.S. Foreign Policy 195 (B. Rubin & E. Spiro eds. 1979); Howard, *Monitoring Human Rights: Problems of Consistency*, 4 Ethics & Int'l Affairs 33 (1990). The State Department Country Reports are also discussed briefly in chapter 6 as a kind of factfinding.

Human Rights Watch, The Bush Administration's Record on Human Rights in 1989, at 1-15 (1990):

INTRODUCTION

With the extraordinary changes in Eastern Europe and the Soviet Union in 1989, human rights should have emerged as a central element of U.S. foreign policy. Easing East-West tensions created an unprecedented opportunity for the Bush administration to work for a post-cold war order founded on respect for the rights of the individual.

Unfortunately, our review of the public positions taken by the Bush administration during its first year reveals a widespread disregard for human rights. While the administration supported change in Eastern Europe and occasionally elsewhere — most notably in South Africa and Burma — it failed to seize the opportunity to embrace human rights throughout the world. Its insistence on seeing the world in geopolitical terms, and other priorities, gave rise to a striking silence on abuses in many countries, and a frequent refusal to adjust U.S. policy in light of those abuses. The result has been a failure to take the lead in making respect for human rights the basis of the world order of the 1990's.

The administration's policy toward China is perhaps the most visible example of this failure. Although China's importance as a strategic asset diminished as U.S. relations with the Soviet Union improved, the administration consistently opposed taking a stand on human rights that might offend China's leaders. In February, when uniformed Chinese police barred one of China's leading human rights advocates, Fang Lizhi, from attending a dinner hosted by visiting President Bush, the President acquiesced and the administration blamed its embassy for inviting Fang. In May, when Chinese authorities met mass demonstrations for democracy with a declaration of martial law, the administration said nothing. And in June, when Chinese authorities crushed the democracy movement and killed hundreds, the administration imposed the minimum sanctions that an outraged U.S. public would tolerate, and lobbied hard against legislation to impose further sanctions. It also stopped short of announcing the steps that Chinese authorities would have to take for sanctions to be lifted — crucial for making sanctions meaningful — such as, at minimum, freeing all members of the democracy movement who did not use or advocate violence.

Instead, within a month and without receiving any human rights concessions, the administration breached the sanctions restricting loans (by renewing processing of Export-Import Bank loans), the sanctions halting military sales (by delivering three Boeing jets with sensitive navigational systems), and the sanctions barring high-level contacts (by secretly sending National Security Advisor Brent Scowcroft and Deputy Secretary of State Lawrence Eagleburger to Beijing). The administration thus made clear that the killing and imprisonment of pro-democracy demonstrators would have no material impact on its dealings with the Chinese leadership.

The administration's policy toward El Salvador has shown a similar disregard for human rights. Despite reduced fears that leftists advances in Central America would provide a beachhead for Soviet expansionism, the administration persisted in acting as apologist for abuses committed by the Salvadoran military in its war with leftist rebels. Shortly after the Salvadoran guerrillas began a November offensive, six Jesuit priests and two of their employees were murdered under circumstances implicating the Salvadoran army. The murder gave rise to pressure in Congress to reduce military aid to El Salvador until those responsible for this atrocity were brought to justice. The administration, instead of using this pressure to insist that the Salvadoran armed forces respect human rights, sought actively to discredit evidence of army responsibility. When a witness stepped forward to testify that she had seen soldiers at the crime scene, U.S. embassy officials and FBI investigators in Miami put her through a grueling four-day interrogation — in an unfamiliar environment, without a lawyer, in the presence of a Salvadoran officer, and under reported threats of deportation to El Salvador and almost certain death — in an effort that could not plausibly have been designed to get at the truth. This attempt to discredit an inconvenient witness made a mockery of U.S. demands that the Salvadoran government identify the murderers, as well as of the U.S. commitment to promote due process and the rule of law.

With regard to the Soviet Union, the Bush administration has all but stopped public comment on human rights issues. President Reagan gave human rights a prominent place on the agenda of every U.S.-Soviet summit, but President Bush barely mentioned human rights at Malta. The administration's silence seems to be based in large part on new geopolitical considerations — the fear that pressing for human rights might weaken Gorbachev. But the failure to take any public notice of continuing abuses has deprived Soviet liberals of pressure they might have harnessed to promote reforms.

The State Department's principal human rights officer has argued that public statements on human rights are unnecessary because Soviet reformers "recognize their problems" and thus the U.S. need not "lord it over them" but should "work with" the Soviets in refashioning repressive institutions. While the changed circumstances in the Soviet Union certainly warrant a change in tone, they do not justify the abandonment of public human rights commentary. Such abandonment might be appropriate for a nation that had ceased violating the rights of its citizens and needed only to dismantle a few anachronistic institutions of repression. But rights violations continue in the Soviet Union, in the form of psychiatric abuse, widespread disrespect for due process, restrictions on freedom of assembly and travel, new arrests and short-term detentions on political grounds, a refusal to tolerate a multi-party system, and continued imprisonment for some previously convicted of treason for attempting to contact U.S. diplomats in an effort to emigrate or send manuscripts abroad. Silence in the face of these abuses can only slow their end.

The Bush administration made little change in U.S. support of abusive rebel troops in regional conflicts, despite the withdrawal of Soviet troops from Afghanistan and Vietnamese troops from Cambodia, and the continuing phased withdrawal of Cuban troops from Angola.

- In Afghanistan, the administration firmly protested abuses by the Soviet-backed government but was sparing in its criticism of the U.S.-funded resistance, even when those forces committed summary executions and indiscriminately shelled civilian areas. The administration may have taken a positive step by reportedly cutting off aid to the most abusive resistance force, Hezb-e Islami headed by Gulbuddin Hokmatyar, but then undercut the gesture by refusing to state that a serious effort to curb abuses was a precondition for receiving U.S. aid, or to call on Saudi Arabia, the largest resistance funder, to stop financing Hekmatyar's group.

- In Cambodia, despite increased public recognition toward the end of the Reagan administration of the importance of preventing the return to power of Pol Pot's Khmer Rouge, the Bush administration refused to break with China and the administration's Southeast Asian friends by opposing a coalition government that would include the Khmer Rouge.

- And in Angola, the Bush administration continued to deliver funds to UNITA despite widespread reports that UNITA has kidnapped civilians, burned opponents at the stake, and used mines indiscriminately. . . .

Like the Reagan administration, the Bush administration generally closed its eyes to — and often defended — abuses committed by militaries under the nominal control of elected civilian governments. The administration's apologies for military abuses in El Salvador, referred to earlier, are an example of this policy. Other examples included:

- The Bush administration strengthened ties with the Guatemalan military although political killings increased dramatically and President Vinicio Cerezo showed less inclination than ever to control the armed and security forces, let alone to investigate and prosecute their abuses. The administration deplored the mounting political violence but refused to assign responsibility, despite substantial evidence implicating the military.
- In the Philippines, the presidency of Corazon Aquino — as well as a strong leftist insurgency and the U.S. interest in continued use of the Subic naval base and Clark air force base — yielded a hands-off approach to ongoing abuses. While the administration intervened militarily to help foil a coup attempt by right-wing army factions, it refrained from criticizing widespread killings, including beheadings, by paramilitary and vigilante groups tied to the military.

The Bush administration continued the Reagan administration's refusal to press for prosecution of those responsible for past military abuses after transitions to elected governments. In Argentina, the Bush administration said nothing when President Menem pardoned most of the military officers responsible for torture and disappearances during the "dirty war." And in Uruguay, administration officials quietly opposed an effort by referendum to repeal an amnesty for such abuses.

The Bush administration also continued its predecessor's policy of largely ignoring abuses in areas of the world that do not attract much public attention in the United States:

- In Sudan, where government forces have been responsible for executing civilians and using starvation as a weapon in the southern part of the country, the administration sought a waiver of a U.S. law requiring the cutoff of aid after a coup overthrew the elected civilian government in June. The stated purpose of the waiver was to provide C-130 transport planes for relief efforts, but Sudan had never used the planes for relief, only to transport troops.
- In Mauritania, the administration made no public comment on the mass expulsion, often after severe beating, of tens of thousands of black Mauritanians, following a border dispute with Senegal. Nor did it address the massacre of hundreds of blacks by government-organized bands.
- In Malawi, the administration said nothing publicly in the face of a purge of government opponents that included the widespread use of detention without trial, reports of torture, and the death of two in custody.
- In Kenya, the administration issued no public comment on severe mistreatment and forced expulsion of ethnic Somalis in the northern part of the country.

In the case of several countries, the strongest U.S. criticisms of their human rights practices made in 1989 were contained in the *Country Reports on Human Rights Practices in 1988*. While issued in February 1989, during the first days of the Bush administration, the *Country Reports* were prepared entirely by the Reagan administration. The *Country Reports* on Israel, Morocco and Turkey, for example, described serious abuses, but the Bush administration generally refused to repeat these criticisms publicly, while continuing to pump aid to those responsible for the abuses. With regard to Israel despite a report of unprecedented candor, the administration used its efforts for a regional peace settlement as a pretext to avoid speaking out further on abuses in the occupied territories, where approximately 300 Palestinians were killed by Israeli forces and thousands more were detained for months without charge or trial during the second year of the intifada.

In similar fashion in Somalia, a specially commissioned State Department report described large-scale atrocities committed by government troops against the Isaak clan in the northern part of the country. But the administration sought $21 million in emergency aid for the Somali government, at a moment when abuses by government troops were at their height. Congress, to its credit, rejected the request, but the State Department's chief human rights officer, while acknowledging the abuses, publicly defended the appeal for emergency aid.

The administration's declared war on drug-trafficking has been waged with virtual indifference to human rights. In Colombia, the administration funneled millions of dollars to the military without making any visible attempt to undo the alliance between drug traffickers and military elements which has led to the killing of thousands of leftist politicians, union leaders, grass-roots organizers, journalists and human rights monitors. In Peru, the administration's drug interdiction program in the Upper Huallaga valley led to increasing U.S. involvement in a counterinsurgency effort that has been marked by massacres and other violent abuses. In both countries as well as Bolivia, the administration successfully sought reversal of a ban in place since the 1970's against aiding police forces — a ban which had worked well in keeping the United States from supporting police practices of torture, disappearance and execution.

There have been bright spots in the Bush administration's human rights policy. In Eastern Europe, the Bush administration modified the Reagan administration's policy of "differentiation" among Eastern Europe states according to which trade benefits were awarded primarily on the basis of foreign-policy distance from the Soviet Union rather than respect for human rights. The Reagan administration's policy toward Romania exemplified this approach: the Ceausescu government's maverick foreign policy earned it Most Favored Nation ("MFN") trade benefits while its ruthless human rights practices continued largely without interruption. That situation prevailed until 1988, when Romania renounced MFN benefits under Congressional human rights pressure. The Bush administration articulated a new policy of "differentiation" according to which economic and trade incentives are allocated not on the basis of foreign-policy differences with the Soviet Union but on the basis of political and economic reforms. Hungary and Poland are now major recipients of U.S. economic aid, and by the time of the overthrow of the Ceausescu regime in late December, Romania had become a virtual pariah state. The new "differentiation" thus provided an important incentive to reform in Eastern Europe.

Our main difference with this vastly improved approach toward Eastern Europe is that the Bush administration has been so preoccupied with promoting the emergence of elected governments that it has neglected the legal developments needed to secure and institutionalize basic freedoms. In an area of the world with little democratic tradition and often serious ethnic tensions, it is far from clear that the emergence of elected governments will in itself secure fundamental rights. The Bush administration should remain vigilant to the need for legislation to secure rights that today are still exercised only as a matter of governmental grace.

In South Africa, the Bush administration has begun a welcome break from the policies of its predecessor. It has called for an end to the state of emergency, the freeing of political prisoners and the abolition of various legislative pillars of apartheid. It has then backed these demands with a specific timetable for change. It has also been a less strident advocate of "constructive engagement" and a less vocal opponent of anti-apartheid sanctions. And in an important symbolic act of support for the anti-apartheid movement, President Bush met with Albertina Sisulu, co-president of the restricted United Democratic Front.

In Burma, in the aftermath of the September 1988 crackdown on a pro-democracy movement, the administration played a constructive role in maintaining strong public pressure on the government. It protested the house arrest of leading opposition figures and noted that elections without their participation cannot be free and fair. It confirmed reports of torture and resulting deaths, as well as the practice of forced portering of arms and ammunition for Burmese troops. And it suspended trade benefits under the Generalized System of Preferences and cautioned Japan not to renew aid.

Vice President Quayle contributed to human rights at the beginning of the term, although his support soon foundered. In a February visit to El Salvador, he urged top military commanders to bring to justice those responsible for the highly publicized army massacre of ten peasants in San Sebastian in September 1988 — a move which led to a breakthrough in the case, the revelation of a prior cover-up, and the arrest of several soldiers, including two officers, for the murders. The visit called to mind the December 1983 visit to El Salvador by then Vice President Bush, in which he demanded that the Salvadoran armed forces put an end to the death squads.

That the Salvador visit did not signal a broad commitment by the Vice President to uphold human rights became clear during his Asia tour in May. In Indonesia, he praised the human rights practices of the repressive Suharto government. In South Korea, he vowed support for human rights in general terms without even mentioning the serious deterioration of Korean rights practices at the time of his visit. In Singapore, he left unrebutted the government's charge that he had no right to raise human rights violations. Even in El Salvador, on a return trip in June, the Vice President broke long-standing U.S. policy to meet with Roberto D'Aubuisson, the death-squad leader and mastermind of the 1980 murder of Archbishop Oscar Romero.

One notable and unfortunate development in 1989 was the Bush administration's downgrading of the State Department's Bureau of Human Rights and Humanitarian Affairs. Apart from its production of the generally more accurate *Country Reports*, the Bureau has increasingly assumed a role of public irrelevance. Richard Schifter, the Assistant Secretary of State for Human Rights and Humanitarian Affairs held over from the Reagan administration, appears to have directed most of his energies toward the Soviet Union. Through January 1989 he had some important success in securing the release of political prisoners. Since then, however, with the concluding of the Vienna phase of the Helsinki review process, Assistant Secretary Schifter has adopted the policy of accommodation cited above, with the result that public commentary on rights violations in the Soviet Union has been drastically cut back and watered down. The Bureau made occasional public forays — an attack on the obvious target of Cuba, the above-noted acknowledgment of abuses and defense of military aid in Somalia — but in most of the world, it played no public role at all. While the Bureau may be more significant behind the scenes, it is unfortunate that the Bush administration has allowed this important post for publicly criticizing abusive governments to fall into such disuse.

The Bush administration's use of the United Nations to promote human rights has been as selective as that of the Reagan administration. The current administration continued its predecessor's single-minded preoccupation with Cuba before the U.N. Commission on Human Rights. In contrast to these efforts on Cuba, the

Bush administration refused to join its European allies in sponsoring a critical resolution on Iraq, even though the *Country Reports* described Iraq's use of chemical weapons during 1988 against its civilian Kurdish population, as well as the government's practice of murder, extra-legal detention, torture and disappearance of political opponents. The administration ultimately voted against an Iraqi move to block the resolution, but the administration's failure to sponsor the resolution or support it actively helped contribute to its defeat. Nor did the administration give needed support to efforts to secure more rigorous U.N. scrutiny of Guatemala, despite serious abuses. . . .

In addition to the [Convention Against Torture and Other Cruel, Inhuman or Degrading Treatment or Punishment], five other key international human rights treaties have been signed by previous presidents and are awaiting consent to ratification by the Senate. These are: the International Covenant on Civil and Political Rights; the International Covenant on Economic, Social and Cultural Rights; the American Convention on Human Rights; the Convention on the Elimination of All Forms of Discrimination Against Women; and the International Convention on the Elimination of All Forms of Racial Discrimination. Reservations attached to several of these are as damaging as those placed on the Torture Convention. We urge the Bush administration to reexamine these reservations as well and to urge the Senate to consider these important human rights instruments expeditiously and without qualification. . . .

PRACTICALITY OF IMPLEMENTING A HUMAN RIGHTS POLICY

Section 502B of the Foreign Assistance Act declares the significance of human rights in United States foreign policy:

It is the policy of the United States, in accordance with its international obligations as set forth in the Charter of the United Nations and in keeping with the constitutional heritage and traditions of the United States to promote and encourage increased respect for human rights and fundamental freedoms for all without distinction as to race, sex, language, or religion. To this end, a principal goal of the United States is to promote the increased observance of internationally recognized human rights by all countries. 22 U.S.C. § 2304(a)(1).

Despite the provisions regarding security assistance, economic assistance, international financial institutions, and trade, discussed previously, the experiences of the Carter, Reagan, and Bush administrations demonstrate the practical obstacles to implementing a human rights policy. The following reading discusses implementation of Section 502B under the Carter administration, an administration often criticized for placing too much emphasis on promoting human rights in its foreign policy.

Cohen, *Conditioning U.S. Security Assistance on Human Rights Practices*, 76 Am. J. Int'l L. 246, 246, 256-74 (1982) (footnotes omitted):

In the United States, with its government of separated powers and functions, it is the executive branch, and in particular the Department of State, that bears responsibility for implementing legislation on foreign relations. The success of implementation will depend on political decisions, involving competing national interests, as well as on institutional and personal considerations of the officials concerned. Inevitably, there is a gap between legislation and execution, especially when the Executive is not wholly sympathetic to the law. The gap may even devour legislated policies as the Executive refuses "to take Care that the Laws be faithfully executed," and bureaucratic and personal considerations distort judgments, exploit the generality and uncertainty of language, and lead to abuse of discretion. A notable instance of this problem has been executive implementation of legislation on international human rights. . . .

II. RESISTANCE OF THE CAREER BUREAUCRACY UNDER CARTER

The installation of the Carter administration in January 1977 produced a dramatic shift in attitudes of high political officials on the human rights issue. As a presidential candidate, Jimmy Carter had strongly advocated increased emphasis on human rights in American foreign policy and he reaffirmed this position in his inaugural address. Although he did not mention the specific issue of human rights and military ties or indicate his position on implementation of section 502B, his personal call for a human rights oriented foreign policy implied a promise to do considerably more than his predecessors to follow the legislation.

The executive branch, however, did not attempt to conform to the statute's requirements without a fierce internal struggle. Despite the change in attitudes at the highest political level (from opposition to section 502B to endorsement of its underlying principle), the Department of State's career bureaucracy remained implacably hostile and continued to resist implementation. The result was intense bureaucratic warfare between career officials, who resisted implementation, and the office of the newly established Assistant Secretary for Human Rights, which sought adherence to the law.

The Attitude of the Career Bureaucracy

The career bureaucracy of the Department of State is the Foreign Service, and the core of the Foreign Service serves in the five regional bureaus for Africa, East Asia, Europe, Latin America, and the Near East. Each bureau has responsibility for managing relations with countries within its region, including issues of military aid and arms sales.

The opposition of the Foreign Service to section 502B was a logical consequence of its conception of its special role or of (what one student of the bureaucracy has labeled) its "organizational essence." The Foreign Service views its primary role or essence as the maintenance of smooth and cordial relations with other governments. It believes that military aid and arms sales are an indispensable means to achieving this goal. When provided, the other government is grateful and more inclined to get along with the United States. When refused, a cordial relationship may be harder to maintain, especially if the other government suspects that the reason for refusal is a judgment that it has mistreated its own citizens.

Keeping other governments happy becomes an end in itself. This phenomenon is often referred to as "clientism" because the Foreign Service views other governments as "clients" with whose interests it identifies, rather than as parties to be dealt with at arm's length according to the national interest of the United States. . . .

The phenomenon of "clientism" has a number of causes. A Foreign Service officer is typically required to develop personal relations and spend substantial periods of time with high officials of other governments. He tends, therefore, to sympathize and identify with their point of view. If the other government is accused of human rights abuses, he deals with officials who either deny the accusations or explain the excesses as regrettable, but necessary to stem "terrorism" and avoid social chaos. He is much less likely to encounter the victims of repression and hear their point of view.

In addition, the tour of duty in the Foreign Service is usually of 2 to 3 years' duration, after which the officer is rotated to another post. An officer is likely to work on country A for 3 years, then switch to country B, then to country C, and so on. Thus, the short duration reduces the incentive to consider the longer run consequences of decisions.

. . . [T]he regional bureaus have continually opposed implementation of legislation conditioning security assistance on human rights concerns. They have virtually never initiated a proposal that military aid or arms sales be cut off or reduced on account of a government's human rights performance. Even after the Carter administration entered office in 1977, the regional bureaus vigorously fought nearly all attempts to apply section 502B to specific cases. This resistance took a number of different forms. First, they tried to minimize the relevance of section 502B. During the first 2 years, they argued that it could be ignored because it was merely a statement of policy and not legally binding. After it was made legally binding, they argued that the statutory rule was only one of several factors to be weighed in decisions on security assistance.

Second, the career bureaucracy attempted to distort information about human rights conditions in particular countries. The extent of abusive practices was consistently underreported. . . . In the case of Argentina, the Latin American Bureau argued that, at most, hundreds of individuals had been summarily executed by security forces. As the evidence became incontrovertible that the number was actually 6,500 or more, the bureau shifted gears and argued that only Marxist terrorists were the victims. When it was documented that most of the victims were neither Marxists nor terrorists, the bureau maintained that the abuses were the work of local military commanders whom the ruling junta was struggling to control.

As it minimized or concealed negative aspects of a "client's" human rights practices, the career bureaucracy exaggerated positive signs. Improvements were said to have occurred on the basis of insubstantial evidence or self-serving declarations of the government power. . . .

Third, the regional bureaus overstated the extent of U.S. interests at stake in particular cases and the damage that could possibly result from failure to approve proposed security assistance. . . .

The Human Rights Bureau

Given the resistance of the career bureaucracy, concentrated in the regional bureaus, implementation of section 502B during the Carter administration depended on the newly created Bureau of Human Rights, headed by an outsider who was personally committed to the policy of the statute and staffed, to a significant degree, by persons from outside the career bureaucracy. The new bureau began to serve as a counterweight to the "clientism" of the regional bureaus. It took the initiative in insisting that section 502B had to be satisfied before security assistance could be provided, notwithstanding the argument of the career bureaucracy that the statute could be ignored or treated merely as one of several factors. The bureau also developed independent sources of information about human rights conditions in particular countries, which enabled it to challenge the factual reporting of the career bureaucracy. Finally, it attempted to question the national security reasons offered to justify security assistance when the recipient appeared to "engage in gross [human rights] violations." . . .

This newly strengthened human rights office inserted itself into the established Department of State procedures with vigor. By virtue of section 502B, it was able to claim a right to participate in all decisions on security assistance. When it disagreed with the regional bureaus, which was quite frequent, it insisted that a decision paper — known formally as an action memorandum — be prepared and sent to the Secretary of State for resolution of the issue.

During the first 18 months of the Carter administration, individual proposals for both military aid and arms sales were continually at issue between the regional bureaus and the Bureau of Human Rights and therefore "litigated" through the action memorandum procedure. In some ways, this resembled a judicial process, for it was adversarial in nature, and the action memorandum can be viewed as containing briefs for the position of each side. The action memorandum described each bureau's view of human rights conditions in the country concerned and of U.S. interests said to require approval of the proposed security assistance. The Human Rights Bureau argued its position in the context of section 502B. The bureau cited the statute and emphasized that there were two basic issues for decision: first, whether the proposed recipient was engaged in gross abuses, and second, whether extraordinary circumstances nevertheless required such assistance. The Human Rights Bureau challenged security assistance proposals when it believed the intended recipient was engaged in serious human rights abuses. The concerned regional bureau virtually always disagreed. The action memorandum process thus provided a formal mechanism by which the Human Rights Bureau could attempt to apply section 502B to specific cases.

The Significance of Bureaucratic Resistance

A recurring theme in modern studies of American government is the unresponsiveness of the bureaucracy to presidential decisions and directives. Presidents Roosevelt, Truman, Eisenhower, Kennedy, and Nixon all remarked on the persistent resistance of career bureaucrats to presidential policies they viewed as misguided. . . .

The history of section 502B illustrates that the same basic point can be made about congressional directives. . . .

The bureaucracy is most likely to succeed in resisting legislation when high political officials are hostile to the congressional effort, as Kissinger was during the Nixon and Ford administrations. With the approval of its superiors, the bureaucracy can simply ignore the statute. . . .

III. INTERPRETATION AND APPLICATION OF THE STATUTE UNDER CARTER

The public generally identifies the Carter administration with aggressive pursuit of a human rights oriented foreign policy. Some foreign affairs specialists have charged that its "single-minded" approach seriously overemphasized human rights objectives and failed to consider or pursue other important foreign policy goals, to the detriment of U.S. interests. The general public's impression and the specialists' criticism are attributable, in large measure, to the rhetoric of high administration officials, particularly President Carter himself, who even 2 years into his term declared, "Human rights is the soul of our foreign policy."...

Yet a careful examination of actual decisions under section 502B leads to a very different conclusion: that the Carter administration exhibited a remarkable degree of tentativeness and caution, so that its pursuit of human rights goals was anything but "single-minded." Relatively few governments were considered to be "engaged in a consistent pattern of gross [human rights] violations." Security assistance was actually cut off to even fewer, because other U.S. interests were often found to outweigh human rights concerns under the exception for "extraordinary circumstances." Moreover, in some instances, the Carter administration adopted a highly strained reading of the statute which, although not contrary to its literal terms, produced a result contrary to congressional intent. In other cases, the language was simply disregarded, so that decisions violated even the letter of the law.

Fear of Finding

Perhaps the most remarkable evidence of the administration's conservative approach to section 502B was its policy never to determine formally, even in a classified decision, that a particular government was engaged in gross abuses. The primary reason for this policy was the belief that such a determination, even if classified, would inevitably be leaked to the press and become generally known. It was feared that each country named would then consider itself publicly insulted, with consequent damage to our bilateral relationship. In addition, there was concern that once such a finding was revealed, the freedom to alter it might be severely constrained by public political pressures....

The Development of a Body of Precedents

Because of the administration's policy of not making explicit findings under section 502B, the legal basis for particular outcomes was rarely made clear to the contesting bureaus. It was often difficult to say in a particular case exactly why the Secretary of State believed that section 502B did or did not apply....

Owing to this lack of clear direction and the persistence with which both the Human Rights Bureau and the regional bureaus pursued their respective objectives, a considerable volume of action memorandums on security assistance issues were produced during the first half of the Carter administration. After the initial period, however, when a body of precedents was created, the amount of "litigation" began to decrease as contesting bureaus inferred by the pattern of outcomes how the Secretary of State was interpreting section 502B. The major issues of interpretation are discussed below. The three key questions were:

(1) When was a foreign government considered to be engaged "in a consistent pattern of gross violations of internationally recognized human rights"?

(2) What U.S. interests constituted "extraordinary circumstances"?

(3) What was encompassed by the category "security assistance"?

1. Gross Violations. The threshold issue under section 502B is whether a particular government "engages in a consistent pattern of gross violations of internationally recognized human rights."...

A definition of internationally recognized human rights is contained in section 502B itself. According to subsection (d)(1), this term "*includes* torture or cruel, inhuman, or degrading treatment or punishment, prolonged detention without charges and trial, and other flagrant denial of the right to life, liberty, or the security of the person'' (emphasis added). The use of the word ''includes'' suggests that the list of abusive practices in the statute is not meant to be all-encompassing. The formulation is open-ended and holds out the distinct possibility that violations other than those listed might trigger the termination of security assistance. However, the statute's sponsor, Representative Fraser, opposed this view, and the legislative history contains strong evidence that Congress wanted the quoted language to be interpreted narrowly rather than expansively. . . .

The Carter administration followed Fraser's interpretation. In its decisions on security assistance, it was careful to go no further than required by the abuses specifically listed in subsection (d)(1). . . .

The second element, that the violations must be ''gross,'' was read to mean that they must be significant in their impact. For example, although arbitrary imprisonment is one of the listed violations, detention without charges for several days was not considered ''gross'' because of the relatively brief period of confinement.

Third, the element of a ''consistent pattern'' was held to mean that abuses had to be significant in number and recurrent. Isolated instances of torture or summary execution, while certainly gross abuses, would not trigger termination of security assistance under section 502B. . . .

Even when gross abuses were significant in number and recurrent, the ''pattern'' was occasionally held not to be ''consistent,'' if steps were taken to stop some abuses. . . .

Ordinarily, the fourth element, that the government itself engage in or be responsible for the violations, was not an issue if the other criteria were already met. In most instances, governments did not deny responsibility but sought to justify the abuses to U.S. officials on grounds of national security, fighting terrorism, anticommunism, and the like. Absent such an admission, however, the word ''engages'' was read to require ''approval'' by the highest ranking officials of the government in question, even if they lacked effective control over the military forces committing the abuses. . . .

2. Extraordinary Circumstances. The Carter administration always gave considerable weight to arguments that other U.S. interests might require continuation of security assistance, even when the government in question was thought to be a ''gross violator.'' Thus, the charge that its pursuit of human rights was ''single-minded'' and to the exclusion of other interests was far wide of the mark. If anything, the administration gave excessive credence to claims that some specific foreign policy objective would and could be promoted only if security assistance were provided, and often failed to subject such claims to rigorous analysis.

The administration did require some showing of a substantial and specific interest before the exception for extraordinary circumstances was available. A mere desire for cordial relations, without more, was never held sufficient to constitute ''extraordinary circumstances.'' However, once a specific interest of some substantiality was cited, the exception was usually invoked. Because of the liberal use made of the exception for ''extraordinary circumstances,'' the number of countries subject to a section 502B cutoff was quite modest. In the end, human rights concerns resulted in the termination of security assistance to only eight countries, all in Latin America: Argentina, Bolivia, El Salvador, Guatemala, Haiti, Nicaragua, Paraguay, and Uruguay. . . .

3. Security Assistance. Even when a government was considered to be a "gross violator" and there were no "extraordinary circumstances," the termination of security assistance by the Carter administration was at times less than complete. Special exceptions to the general rule of subsection (a)(2) were created, most notably for the sale of certain military items to "gross violators" when it was believed that approval might induce human rights progress. These exceptions were not set out in the statute and therefore went beyond the letter of the law. . . .

The Carter administration did not automatically terminate all sales of defense items when a government was considered to be engaged in "gross violations" and "extraordinary circumstances" were not found. It adopted instead a "flexible" approach and broke up the panoply of defense items subject to the Arms Export Control Act (and therefore section 502B) into a number of subcategories:

(1) New weapons: tanks, artillery, fighters and bombers, and naval warships;
(2) Spare parts for previously acquired weapons;
(3) Support equipment: trucks, unarmed aircraft and ships, radios, and radars; and
(4) Safety-related items: ambulance aircraft and air-sea rescue equipment.

New weapons were consistently withheld, whenever requested. On the other hand, safety-related items were almost never denied, and spare parts and support equipment were approved for sale on numerous occasions. These exceptions, of course, are contrary to the literal language of section 502B, and the regional bureaus advocating approval felt it necessary to construct a legal rationale for this position. The exception for safety-related items was justified in terms of the underlying purpose of the statute, that is, the protection of basic human rights. To disapprove the sale of equipment devoted to rescuing lives, it was argued, would defeat the basic goals of the statute. Items in the two middle categories (spare parts for weapons and support equipment) were approved on the basis of a different, but related, consideration: that a sale of defense items was on occasion needed to encourage another government to improve human rights conditions, and that spare parts and support equipment (as contrasted with new weapons) were an acceptable means of providing an inducement. In effect, section 502B was read to mean that Congress was concerned most about actual weapons and would be willing to permit the sale of other items when it was reasonable to suppose that it would lead to human rights improvements.

While the exception for safety-related items appears reasonable because of the direct connection with saving lives, that for spare parts and support items is fraught with danger. Such items are as critical to military performance as weapons themselves. Moreover, spare parts and support equipment typically make up a large part of a military's total acquisitions. Thus, to continue to approve such items is to continue a significant military supply relationship between the United States and the recipient. This danger may be acceptable if there are definite advantages to be gained in terms of human rights improvements. The risk, however, is that exceptions will be granted on the basis of unrealistic hopes that improvements will follow. If that turns out to be the case, then making these exceptions could undermine the purposes of section 502B.

NOTES AND QUESTIONS

1. According to one study, in neither the Carter administration nor the early years of the Reagan administration was the relation between foreign assistance and human rights statistically significant. Carleton & Stohl, *The Foreign Policy of Human Rights: Rhetoric and Reality from Jimmy Carter to Ronald Reagan*, 7 Hum. Rts. Q. 205, 211-227 (1985). That study suggests, as did the Cohen article excerpted just above, that even an Executive committed to promoting human rights on a moral level may have difficulty putting that commitment into practice. Why might it be difficult to implement a commitment to human rights in U.S. foreign policy? Must competing interests always win out over human rights?

2. The Reagan and Bush administrations did not continue to implement Sections 116 and 502B in the ways described above by Professor Cohen. In a 1988 symposium several commentators suggested ways the Executive could carry out a commitment to human rights in foreign policy. *See Symposium on Human Rights: An Agenda For the New Administration*, 28 Va. J. Int'l L. 827 (1988) (various authors).

3. This chapter, partially because of congressionally initiated laws, tends to emphasize U.S. foreign aid, sanctions, and other country-specific concerns. Yet even as to those concerns which affect governments charged with human rights violations, U.S. officials indeed are aware that action by the U.N., the OAS, European entities, and other intergovernmental organizations can have significant impact. Nonetheless, the bulk of attention (in the media and by scholars and other observers) seems to have involved relatively little critique of the U.S. stance in the multilateral sphere.

To mention Afghanistan, Angola, Cuba, Iran, Iraq, Lebanon, Libya, Nicaragua, and the West Bank merely introduces a list of dozens of countries as to which the State Department annual reports disclose serious violations of human rights. For many reasons — including, *e.g.*, the avoidance of apparent double standards — the U.S. government might wisely seek more cooperation from other governments and allot fewer resources to questions such as: "Unilaterally shall we cut off military and/or economic aid and impose other sanctions?"

An outstanding survey of many matters highlighted in this chapter is the paper titled "Bureaucracy and Diplomacy" published by the Lawyers Committee on Human Rights as part of its 1988 project to prepare for the advent of a new administration in 1989. The preface explains the project as follows:

Lawyers Committee for Human Rights, *Human Rights and U.S. Foreign Policy: Bureaucracy and Diplomacy*, 1988 Project Series No. 4, at iv (1989):

> This is one of a series of papers drawn from memoranda prepared as part of the 1988 Project, a review of human rights

and U.S. foreign policy issues undertaken in 1988 by the Lawyers Committee for Human Rights. The Committee is an 11-year-old non-governmental human rights organization. The ultimate purpose of the project was to identify specific and practical recommendations for executive and congressional policymakers in each of fourteen topic areas. The first and in many respects most important phase of the review process was the preparation of detailed memoranda by some of the most respected law firms in the United States.

The conclusion of Lawyers Committee for Human Rights, Bureaucracy and Diplomacy 96 (1989) reads:

> This study presents a critique of the administration of human rights policy by the U.S. government, focusing upon five areas of concern: 1) the bureaucracy of the State Department; 2) the Inter-Agency Group on Human Rights and Foreign Assistance; 3) the preparation of the annual country reports; 4) human rights training for foreign service officers; and 5) the bureaucracy of other federal departments as it relates to human rights. This study shows that there are weaknesses in the way the U.S. human rights policy is administered. Fortunately, the steps that must be taken to make necessary improvements are well within reach.

Readers of this book will be enlightened immensely by the reports the Lawyers Committee 1988 project inspired: Lawyers Committee for Human Rights, Human Rights and U.S. Foreign Policy: Report and Recommendations (1988); Linking Security Assistance and Human Rights (1989); United States Policy Toward South Africa (1989); Worker Rights under the U.S. Trade Laws (1989). The report quoted above was also published in Maynard, *The Bureaucracy and Implementation of US Human Rights Policy*, 11 Hum. Rts. Q. 175 (1989).

Newsom, *The Diplomacy of Human Rights: A Diplomat's View*, in The Diplomacy of Human Rights 3, 5-9 (D. Newsom ed. 1986) (footnotes omitted):

The effectiveness of U.S. diplomacy in the field of human rights has been aided by the fact that most nations are sensitive to how the outside world looks at their internal practices. Idi Amin and Bokassa were exceptions to this rule. Most nations respond to charges of mistreatment of their citizens either with genuine efforts to correct abuses or cosmetic actions to divert attention, or by defending what they are doing. International pressure helps focus attention on the abuses. Governments, however, will not readily submit to changes that may threaten their political power. Where improvements are possible without running this risk, the chances are likely that improvements can be made. Where the abuses are deemed essential for the retention of power, changes are less likely. . . .

Effective diplomatic action in support of human rights in another country involves both the individual actions of the diplomat and those policies and measures of the diplomat's country that can provide leverage and inducements for change.

In an ideal world, the diplomat would like to see change result from such efforts. In many regimes, as will be discussed below, change may not be possible, at least in the short term. The diplomat must then consider whether it is in the interest of his or her country to recommend "distance" from the regime. Public statements and policy actions can lessen the degree to which the diplomat's country is publicly identified, both at home and abroad, with the policies of the offending regime. Distancing is not necessarily "walking away" from an issue. It may serve to make our polices and principles more credible with others. The pressure of the resulting isolation can sometimes influence an internal situation.

"Distancing" can also give a signal of the seriousness of U.S. intentions to other countries where similar violations exist.

Where a U.S. diplomat determines that influence is possible, there are a number of tools available:

1. *Access.* A diplomat cannot effectively influence the actions or decisions of another country without access to that country's leaders, decision makers and opinion molders. The diplomat of the United States often has the advantage that, even if the host country is not sympathetic with the efforts being made, high officials are available because relations with the United States are important for other reasons. The ability to meet with human rights organizations and the political opposition is also important, both to gain information on the circumstances in the country and to give a signal that the United States is not wholly committed to the position of the government in power.

The diplomat must weigh carefully the degree to which he presses for access either to government officials or private organizations. There are limits in both cases. There may be only limited time or opportunities for discussions with senior leaders; the agenda must be carefully constructed. Contacts with human rights organizations or opposition groups in authoritarian countries may be firmly opposed by the government — or, if carried out, can create serious barriers in relations with the authorities on other matters.

2. *Public Statements.* Depending on the objective of the diplomatic efforts, the diplomat abroad may wish to speak out on the human rights situation in the host country or encourage the home government back in the capital to do so. Herein lies the heart of the debate over "quiet diplomacy." The diplomat must weigh whether a statement will move a government to take action or will increase its sensitivity to outside pressures and make other diplomatic efforts more difficult. Generally, public statements are used in the diplomacy of human rights when it appears that quiet efforts may not bear fruit or when the objective is more to "distance" the United States from a foreign regime than it is to influence that regime. The impact of such statements is of course enhanced if they are made at the presidential level or cabinet level. Official statements can be given further strength by special efforts to make them known internationally through the Voice of America and the other media of USIA.

3. *Legislation.* For the United States diplomat the existence of legislation requiring annual reports on the human rights situations in individual countries and requiring a consideration of human rights and emigration in questions of foreign assistance and trade provides both a problem and an opportunity. The problem arises when foreign governments consider that the application of U.S. legislative sanctions or requirements (such as the annual reports to the Congress) constitutes an unacceptable intrusion into their internal affairs. U.S. laws may represent a genuine political problem for foreign leaders if actions are taken in the face of

such pressures. It is possible, however, for the diplomat to use the existence of legislation as an indication of the general feeling of the American people on an issue. If this is presented without the suggestion of a threat, it can assist in supporting diplomatic efforts to make progress on a human rights problem . . . .

U.S. laws can be more effective in abeyance than in application. It is difficult to find cases where the actual application of the laws has led to changes in another country's human rights practices. Knowledge of a U.S. law, however, can sometimes help a faction within a foreign government arguing for more liberal practices. . . .

4. *U.S. Programs.* The legislation enacted during the 1970s provided U.S. administrations with the authority and, in some cases, with a mandate to apply human rights criteria to programs of military assistance, military sales, police assistance, export credits, trade, and economic assistance programs that did not fall in the category of "basic human needs." These were obvious tools of pressure on foreign governments. The legislation in many instances, however, left the interpretation of given situations to the discretion of the administration. During the Carter administration, major interagency machinery was established to monitor and manage the application of human rights legislation and executive policies. Much of the diplomacy of the period was devoted to explaining the rationale for U.S. actions to affected countries and to other nations that had an interest in the U.S. programs. . . .

5. *Consultation with Like-minded Governments.* Many Western European democracies share the concern of the United States over human rights violations both in Eastern Europe and in the Third World. They are less inclined to use economic and military programs for pressure, but they are often prepared to support the United States with diplomatic efforts. Human rights issues have become in recent years an important part of our agenda of diplomatic consultation with allies, including Japan. Diplomats from such countries have often been helpful to United States diplomats in reinforcing the international concern in specific situations. . . .

6. *Multilateral Banks.* Another area of pressure created by the legislation in support of U.S. diplomacy relates to actions in the multilateral lending agencies — the World Bank, the Inter-American Development Bank, the Asian Development Bank, and the African Development Bank. It was the clear sense of Congress that the United States should not support any loans by these agencies to countries that were violators of human rights principles, except where it could clearly be shown that the loans would support projects related to "basic human needs." In practice, the only activity of these agencies over which the United States has a veto is the "soft loan" window of the Inter-American Bank. Actions in the other banks are limited to voting or abstaining. The United States has not ever been able to get sufficient support from other members of the banks to stop any loans. In some cases, the threat of U.S. opposition has led countries to withhold or withdraw applications.

To U.S. diplomats in developing countries, this "tool" has been, in many ways, the least effective. The use of the banks as instruments of pressure has been seen as "politicizing" the banks. Such actions are often resented particularly by those technocrats and managers in offending countries who are potential allies on many human rights issues. The task of bilateral diplomacy in this phase of the human rights policy has been to seek to explain and defend the action of the United States in taking action against a loan. . . .

[Ed.: The author proceeded to discuss diplomatic efforts through international organizations, such as the U.N., and the work of nongovernmental organizations, such as the International Commission of Jurists and Amnesty International.]

NOTES AND QUESTIONS

1. As the preceding excerpt suggests, quiet diplomacy is usually the first tool used by the Executive in addressing human rights violations in another country. If quiet diplomacy fails to achieve results, the Executive must decide whether or not to undertake open diplomacy by publicly denouncing a country for its violations. The Reagan administration criticized the Carter administration for using too much public pressure — open diplomacy — rather than first pursuing quiet diplomacy. The Reagan administration, however, has in turn been criticized for relying too heavily on quiet diplomacy with "friendly" governments, refusing to publicly denounce U.S. allies for human rights violations. Most, though not all, of the Reagan administration's open diplomacy on human rights issues was directed at communist countries. For further reading, see A.G. Mower, Human Rights and American Foreign Policy 89-100 (1987); Christopher, *The Diplomacy of Human Rights: The First Year*, in Human Rights and U.S. Foreign Policy 257 (B. Rubin & E. Spiro eds. 1979); Salzberg, *The Carter Administration and Human Rights*, in The Diplomacy of Human Rights 61 (D. Newsom ed. 1986).

2. What are advantages and disadvantages of both quiet and open diplomacy? Should the Executive always attempt quiet diplomacy before making public denouncements, assuming the U.S. has diplomatic relations with the country at issue? Should the Executive always make public denunciations when quiet diplomacy fails?

3. James Thyden of the State Department's Office of Human Rights under the Reagan Administration defended that administration's use of diplomacy to effectuate improvements in human rights, observing that the State Department has been fairly outspoken on human rights issues. Nevertheless, he pointed out that the essence of quiet diplomacy is keeping quiet not only about the diplomatic efforts but also any resulting improvements. Thyden, *An Inside View of United States Foreign Policy Under the Reagan Administration*, 7 Whittier L. Rev. 705, 711-12 (1985).

4. For illustrations of human rights diplomacy as it has operated in eight countries — Argentina, Brazil, Indonesia, Iran, Korea, Romania, South Africa, and the Soviet Union — see The Diplomacy of Human Rights, 69-200 (D. Newsom ed. 1986).

5. As the Newsom book excerpted just above observes, the U.S. does not have veto power in most of the banks; its vote is only one among many. Consequently, even when the U.S. has complied with the directive of Section 701 and voted against loans to countries with serious human rights violations, the banks have nonetheless approved the loans. To carry out Section 701's intent more effectively, a recent study prepared by the Lawyers Committee for Human Rights recommends that the U.S. "should launch diplomatic efforts both within the [banks] and bilaterally to secure negative votes on loans to or investments in countries with [egregious] violations" of human rights. Lawyers Committee for Human Rights, Human Rights and U.S. Foreign Policy: Report and Recommendations 24-25 (1988). *See also* Sanford, *U.S. Policy Toward the Multilateral Development Banks: The Role of Congress*, 22 George Washington J. Int'l L. & Econ. 1 (1988).

G. METHODS OF IMPLEMENTING A HUMAN RIGHTS POLICY

Thus far this chapter has focused on protecting human rights through U.S. foreign policy. The remaining materials examine two methods governments, including the U.S., can use to encourage other governments to respect human rights. The first is humanitarian intervention. Essentially, it involves a government's using physical force to stop another government from engaging in human rights violations. The following excerpt discusses the legality of humanitarian intervention in light of the U.N. Charter.

Lillich, *A United States Policy of Humanitarian Intervention and Intercession*, in Human Rights and American Foreign Policy 278, 287-90 (D. Kommers & G. Loescher eds. 1979) (footnotes omitted): . . .

As far as humanitarian intervention's legality is concerned, the present writer concluded some years ago that "the doctrine appears to have been so clearly established under customary international law that only its limits and not its existence is subject to debate." However, what has been the impact of the U.N. Charter upon this customary international law doctrine? Here two problems arise. The first is whether such interventions still are lawful or whether they now are precluded by the U.N. Charter. The second, assuming that such interventions remain lawful, is what criteria should be used to judge a particular intervention's legality.

Although Article 1(7) of the U.N. Charter enjoins the United Nations itself not "to intervene in matters which are essentially within the domestic jurisdiction of any state," Article 2(4), which applies to member states, contains no mention of intervention. Rather, it requires states to refrain from "the threat or use of force against the territorial integrity or political independence of any state." Although many commentators have concluded that this provision prohibits humanitarian intervention, among those international lawyers who believe such intervention still is legal, at least four different legal theories have been advanced.

The first approach is that of the Australian jurist Julius Stone, who advocates a literal reading of the language of Article 2(4). It "does *not* forbid 'the threat or use of force' *simpliciter*," he contends; "it forbids it only when directed 'against the territorial integrity or political independence of any State, or in any other manner inconsistent with the Purposes of the United Nations.'" In his opinion a humanitarian intervention would not be so directed and, hence, would not fall within the prohibition of Article 2(4). . . .

The second approach employed to justify the claim that humanitarian intervention has survived the adoption of the U.N. Charter is that of Reisman. Adopting what some critics have labeled a "teleological" interpretation, Reisman views Article 2(4) as an important part of the document, but still only a part. Looking at the Preamble, Article 1, and Articles 55 and 56, all of which evidence great concern for the advancement of human rights, he concludes that

> [T]he cumulative effect of the Charter in regard to the customary institution of humanitarian intervention is to create a coordinate responsibility for the active protection of human rights: members may act jointly with the organization in what might be termed a new organized, explicitly statutory humanitarian intervention or singly or collectively in the customary or international common law humanitarian intervention. In the contemporary world there is no other way the most fundamental purposes of the Charter in relation to human rights can be made effective.

Reisman's approach is distinguished from Stone's in that humanitarian intervention is not unaffected by the Charter as Stone thinks but, rather, is a logical extension of concern for norms that are rooted firmly in the Charter. One must look to the dominant purposes of the Charter as a whole and not blindly allow a single general principle like Article 2(4) — admirable though that principle may be — to impede other major goals of the Charter.

There is a third approach that stands apart from the first and perhaps from the second in that it does not necessarily accord a permanent status in international law to humanitarian intervention. Rather, this approach permits its substitution for the procedure contemplated by the Charter, an emergency mechanism to be deactivated should the normal U.N. machinery in the Security Council ever begin to function smoothly. The problem with — and the virtue of — this approach is that it requires a rather sophisticated reinterpretation of the Charter in light of events since 1945. Because the enforcement machinery of the Security Council has not worked out as planned or hoped, the argument goes, one is left with the undesirable choice of applying stopgap measures or doing nothing at all. Of these two choices, certainly the former requires adoption. As Richard Baxter, who has suggested this approach, puts it:

> Given the fact that we do live in an imperfect world, in which the United Nations is not operating as it should, it seems to me inevitable that there will be [humanitarian interventions]. It is almost as if we were thrown back on customary international law by a breakdown of the Charter system.

The present writer, who has associated himself with this view in the past, hereby reaffirms his support of it.

A fourth approach by which humanitarian intervention might be condoned, if not actually justified, has been developed by Richard Falk and, to a lesser extent, by Ian Brownlie. Both scholars view the U.N. Charter as prohibiting humanitarian intervention yet consider this broad prohibition potentially counterproductive. Thus, while not approving such interventions, Falk, by using a "second-order level of legal inquiry" which involves criteria similar to ones suggested by advocates of humanitarian intervention, nevertheless would not condemn them all. Brownlie, in a less sophisticated but nevertheless interesting analysis of the problem, compares humanitarian intervention to euthanasia. Both actions, he contends, are unlawful, but at the same time they are both moral actions which may find justification in higher considerations of public policy and moral choice. Brownlie's variant of the fourth approach has been criticized by John Norton Moore and the present writer for its failure "to perform the...intellectual task of trying to develop a set of criteria. You can't end it by saying it is illegal but also moral. We have to go beyond that and develop criteria for appraisal of the kinds of situations that we would recommend *ought to be* legal."

...In 1966 Ved Nanda advanced five criteria for judging the legality of humanitarian interventions. The following year the present writer recommended five of his own. Subsequently Moore synthesized the Nanda-Lillich criteria, with some additions and modifications. Moore's synthesis in turn has been summarized most recently by Tom Farer:

That there be an immediate and extensive threat to fundamental human rights.

That all other remedies for the protection of those rights have been exhausted to the extent possible within the time constraints posed by the threat.

That an attempt has been made to secure the approval of appropriate authorities in the target state.

That there is a minimal effect on the extant structure of authority (e.g., that the intervention not be used to impose or preserve a preferred regime).

That the minimal requisite force b[e] employed and/or that the intervention is not likely to cause greater injury to innocent persons and their property than would result if the threatened violation actually occurred.

That the intervention be of limited duration.

That a report of the intervention be filed immediately with the Security Council and, where relevant, regional organizations.

NOTES

1. In 1988 Fernando Tesón published a book that analyzes humanitarian intervention and concludes that it is consistent with international law. He defines humanitarian intervention as "the proportionate transboundary help, including forcible help, provided by governments to individuals in another state who are being denied basic human rights and who themselves would be rationally willing to revolt against their oppressive government." F. Tesón, Humanitarian Intervention: An Inquiry into Law and Morality 5 (1988). He first establishes a moral and philosophical framework (*Id.* at 3-123) and then discusses legality under the U.N. Charter. *Id.* at 127-244. For another view, see F. Boyle, The Future of International Law and American Foreign Policy (1989).

For another examination of humanitarian intervention's lawfulness and use in a slightly different context, see N. Ronzitti, Rescuing Nationals Abroad Through Military Coercion and Intervention on Grounds of Humanity (1985).

2. When U.S. troops invaded Panama in December 1989, the U.S. Government notified the U.N. that it was exercising its inherent right of self-defense under Article 51 of the U.N. Charter, because of attacks upon U.S. military personnel. The U.S. did not refer to humanitarian intervention, but President Bush explained the invasion as necessary to restore democracy to Panama. The OAS General Assembly and the U.N. General Assembly did not apparently accept the U.S. explanation for its military action.

ECONOMIC SANCTIONS

Economic sanctions against a state which violates the human rights of its own citizens are a more frequently used method of persuading, possibly even coercing, the violating state to improve its record. Indeed, the concept of economic sanctions lies at the heart of much U.S. legislation on human rights. In considering the following excerpt on the effectiveness of such sanctions, readers should think about the advisability of imposing sanctions for human rights objectives.

Carter, *International Economic Sanctions: Improving the Haphazard U.S. Legal Regime*, 75 Cal. L. Rev. 1162 (1987) (footnotes omitted):

THE PURPOSES AND EFFECTIVENESS OF
ECONOMIC SANCTIONS. . .

A.   *The Purposes of Sanctions*

There are three broad rationales for imposing sanctions:

— seeking to influence a country to change its policies or even its government;
— punishing a country for its policies; and
— symbolically demonstrating opposition against the target country's policies to many possible audiences, including constituencies in the sender country as well as audiences in the target country, other potential target countries, or allied countries.

More than one rationale can be involved in the decision to employ a sanction or set of sanctions in a particular situation. For example, the widening U.S. sanctions against South Africa stem from a mix of all the above considerations. The sanctions involve an effort to influence South Africa to change its apartheid policy, a dose of punishment, and a symbolic statement of U.S. opposition to apartheid.

Besides these broad rationales, a sender country generally has more specific foreign policy motives for imposing sanctions. Hufbauer and Schott characterized these objectives as follows:

(1) "Change target country policies in a relatively modest way (modest in the scale of national goals, but often of burning importance to participants in the episode)." These goals include slowing nuclear

proliferation, promoting human rights, fighting terrorism, and resolving expropriation claims;

(2) "Destabilize the target government," and thus change its policies;

(3) "Disrupt a minor military adventure," as illustrated by the United Kingdom's sanctions against Argentina over the Falkland Islands dispute;

(4) "Impair the military potential of the target country," as illustrated by sanctions against the Warsaw Pact by the United States and its allies; and

(5) "Change target country policies in a major way," as illustrated by U.S. efforts and those of other countries against South Africa's system of apartheid. . . .

B.   *Effectiveness of Sanctions*

It is difficult to measure the success of sanctions because of the frequent ambiguity of the rationales and objectives behind their use. Even if the real goal is discernible, it still may be difficult to determine the extent to which the sanctions contributed to the desired outcome.

. . . Target countries are perhaps becoming more immune to sanctions because of two factors. First, the recent targets have been less dependent on trade with the United States. Second, other countries, such as the Soviet Union, have stepped forward more often to assist the target states.

1.   *Effectiveness as a Function of Purpose*

The success rate varies according to the foreign policy objective being pursued. Sanctions designed to *destabilize* a government (objective 2) have been especially effective. Examples include the toppling of Haiti's Duvalier in February 1986, Uganda's Idi Amin in 1979, Chile's Allende in 1973, and the Dominican Republic's Trujillo in 1961. Indeed, it would appear that in the study's fourteen cases since 1954 where the United States applied economic sanctions for destabilization purposes, it was successful in ten episodes and unsuccessful in two. The outcome of two cases is still uncertain, as U.S. sanctions continue against Libya and Nicaragua. [Ed.: In 1990 a U.S.-backed coalition won elections and took power in Nicaragua.]

U.S. sanctions designed to achieve *more narrow policy goals* — such as dealing with expropriation of U.S. corporations, nuclear proliferation, terrorism, or human rights abuses (objective 1) — have been effective about 40% of the time, though the rate varies according to the particular goal. . . .

In the area of human rights, sanctions such as cutting back on U.S. military and economic assistance usually have not been successful in stopping the target countries' gross violations of internationally recognized rights.

The United States has also used economic sanctions — such as restricting various financial assistance programs and imposing export controls — against countries designated as supporting terrorism. It does not appear, however, that these selective sanctions had much effect in the 1980's on the policies of two of the principal target countries — Syria and Libya. . . .

2.   *Effectiveness of Sanctions by Type*

An analysis of the effectiveness of sanctions must also consider whether certain *types* of sanctions are more effective than others, in achieving their objectives. Relative effectiveness may, of course, also depend on the circumstances of particular situations.

For example, if the United States were to impose sanctions against South Korea for human rights violations, import controls might be more effective economically than export controls, given the importance of U.S. purchases to South Korean trade. The United States imports about 39% of all of South Korea's foreign sales. In contrast, U.S. exports total about 21% of South Korea's foreign purchases. Product breakdowns reveal more subtle differences. The amount and type of the principal U.S. imports from South Korea (manufactured articles and clothes) suggest that South Korea cannot easily change long-established business relationships and find willing buyers in other countries. At the same time, South Korea would probably have less trouble and incur fewer additional costs finding other suppliers for present U.S. exports to it, such as machinery, crude materials, and chemical products. These are generally available in world markets.

Even for countries where the United States plays about the same role in percentage terms as an exporter and as an importer, import controls might, for similar reasons, still be more effective than export controls. For example, the United States imports about 40% of Guatemala's foreign sales and exports about 40% of its purchases. Guatemala, however, might have serious difficulty selling elsewhere, at comparable prices, the coffee, sugar, bananas, and other vegetables and fruits that constitute its principal U.S. sales, because trade barriers against agricultural products are widespread.

Similarly, the United States imports a large amount of Chile's copper production, an important revenue earner for that country. Chile would probably find it more difficult to change its long-established relationships with U.S. copper purchasers than to find new suppliers for the goods it buys from the United States. Thus, U.S. import controls would likely be more effective than export restrictions.

An analysis of the relative effectiveness of sanctions should also assess the possible contribution of controls on private financial transactions. For example, . . . U.S. banks now make a large share of the foreign loans to borrowers in certain countries, such as South Korea (26%), Guatemala (33%), and Chile (47%). Controls on financial transactions might be effective, but there are many potential problems that are discussed below.

History provides several concrete examples of the effectiveness of controls on imports and private financial transactions. Increased U.S. duties on the Dominican Republic's sugar imports in 1961-62 helped topple the Trujillo regime . . . As for financial controls, the freeze on $12 billion in Iranian deposits in 1979-81 probably had the greatest impact among all the comprehensive sanctions. Similarly, the private decisions by several U.S. banks not to roll over South Africa's short-term loans helped create a financial crisis there in August-September 1985. The official U.S. sanctions later included a ban on new loans to that government, and then on new investment in that country. These financial controls have probably created more problems for South Africa than any of the other recently imposed sanctions.

In short, each use of sanctions should be rooted in a careful analysis of the vulnerabilities of the target country. In terms of effectiveness, export controls do not have any natural advantage over import controls or financial controls. Indeed, one of the most interesting conclusions of the Hufbauer and Schott study was that ''[t]he multiple regression analysis suggests that financial controls are marginally more successful than export controls, but that import controls are the most successful of all types.'' . . .

3.   *Costs to the Sender Country*

It is also important to recognize that economic sanctions usually involve some costs to the sender country. The type and amount of these costs depend, of course, on the particular situation and on the type of sanctions imposed. Many costs stem from the indirect effects of sanctions, such as the loss of sales by a supplier when the manufacturer is prevented from making an export sale to a target country. Other costs result from long-term changes in business patterns, which often occur when the target country seeks to minimize the financial effects of future sanctions.

These myriad domestic costs are rarely calculated in any detail or with much reliability. Cost calculations might not be important to U.S. policymakers, particularly when the United States is imposing sanctions against a country with a much smaller economy, like Nicaragua. Moreover, there may be considerable incentives for the government *not* to calculate domestic costs. Careful estimates might highlight those costs and exacerbate political problems with domestic constituencies hurt by the sanctions.

Despite the complexities, a few general observations about U.S. costs are worth mentioning. First, terminating or reducing bilateral programs, such as foreign assistance can initially *save* money. Such measures may, however, involve indirect costs, as in lost sales for U.S. companies. Foreign recipients of U.S. programs often spend much of their aid on U.S. goods and services, sometimes because U.S. laws require them to do so.

Second, restrictions on imports and private financial transactions often cost less than export controls, though all these sanctions have domestic costs. Export sanctions directly cause lost sales and lost jobs. The immediate impact might be reduced by finding other customers, but complete substitutability is not assured, and such alternative sales would presumably be on less favorable terms (or they would have occurred before the controls were imposed). Export restrictions also create long-term problems for U.S. sales abroad, as they jeopardize the reputation of U.S. businesses as reliable suppliers.

Import controls generally involve smaller costs. Since new foreign policy sanctions are usually applied against only one country or a few countries, alternative foreign suppliers frequently exist. As a result, the U.S. purchaser does not have to do without a good, but faces only the increased costs that must be paid to a higher-priced supplier. While this increased cost might mean that the U.S. purchaser has to raise its prices and thus lose some sales of its own product, the cost differences are often so small that the resulting losses are marginal.

Moreover, the initial U.S. purchaser should be able to pass on much of the added costs to its customers by raising its own prices. While these customers will then bear some of the costs, their individual burden will probably be a small share of the total domestic costs of import sanctions, because the costs may be spread among many purchasers at different levels of the distribution process.

NOTES AND QUESTIONS

1. Jurists and governments have used the considerations discussed by Lillich as to article 2(4) of the U.N. Charter regarding humanitarian intervention to allege that economic sanctions violate article 2(4). U.N. documents such as the Charter of Economic Rights and Duties of States, G.A. res. 3171, 29 U.N. GAOR Supp. (No. 31) at 50, 55, U.N. Doc. A/9631 (1974), which prohibits states from using economic sanctions to subordinate a state's sovereign rights, support this view. For further reading, see Bowett, *International Law and Economic Coercion*, 16 Va. J. Int'l L. 245 (1976); Comment, *The Use of Nonviolent Coercion: A Study in Legality Under Article 2(4) of the Charter of the United Nations*, 122 Univ. Pa. L. Rev. 983 (1974).

2. Professor Carter, who authored the excerpt reproduced above, has expanded upon his article in B. Carter, International Economic Sanctions (1988).

3. Does the fact that the U.S. is not party to most human rights treaties affect the legality of U.S intervention, economic or otherwise, based on human rights conditions in other countries? *See* Szasz, *The International Legal Aspects of the Human Rights Program of the United States*, 12 Cornell Int'l L. J. 161, 164-67 (1979).

4. For further reading, see Abbott, *Linking Trade to Political Goals: Foreign Policy Export Controls in the 1970s and 1980s*, 65 Minn. L. Rev. 739 (1981).

5. The U.S. has imposed trade and financial sanctions against South Africa. Comprehensive Anti-Apartheid Act of 1986, 22 U.S.C. §§ 5001-16 (Supp. IV 1986). For further reading on the use of sanctions and other policy options in regard to South Africa, see: Lawyers Committee for Human Rights, United States Policy Toward South Africa (1989); *reprinted in* Clarizio, Clements, & Geetter, *United States Policy Toward South Africa*, 11 Hum. Rts. Q. 249 (1989); Nagan, *Economic Sanctions, U.S. Foreign Policy, International Law and the Anti-Apartheid Act of 1986*, 4 Florida Int'l L.J. 85 (1988); Rothberg, *Sections 402 and 403 of the Comprehensive Anti-Apartheid Act of 1986*, 22 George Washington J. Int'l L. & Econ. 117 (1988); Weissbrodt, *International Legal Action Against Apartheid*, 4 Law & Inequality J. 485 (1986); Note, *Economic Sanctions Against South Africa: Problems and Prospects for Enforcement of Human Rights Norms*, 22 Va. J. Int'l L. 345 (1982).

XII HOW EFFECTIVE MAY INTERNATIONAL LAW BE IN U.S. COURTS AND LEGISLATURES TO HELP PROTECT HUMAN RIGHTS?

A. INTRODUCTION

International law and U.S. law reflect different and partially overlapping systems. The overlap has been increasing particularly with respect to human rights. Some commentators have characterized U.S. law as evidencing elements of both "dualist" and "monist" approaches.[1] Countries that adopt the monist view, *e.g.*, Austria and Belgium, treat international law as an integral part of national law with status equal to or supreme over national law. A few countries, such as the Netherlands, view international law as supreme even over its national constitution. Dualist countries, *e.g.*, the

---

[1] *See Committee of U.S. Citizens Living in Nicaragua v. Reagan*, 859 F.2d 927, 937 (D.C. Cir. 1988) excerpted in part J, *infra*; *cf. Introductory Note*, 1 Restatement (Third) of the Foreign Relations Law of the United States 40-42 (1987); I. Brownlie, Principles of Public International Law 33-36 (2d ed. 1973); H. Kelsen, Pure Theory of Law 333-44 (1967).

United Kingdom, do not consider international law to be judicially enforceable unless there is implementing legislation.[2]

A century ago the U.S. Supreme Court opined, regarding treaties but in words applicable also to other sources of international law, that a treaty

> depends for the enforcement of its provisions on the interest and the honor of the governments which are parties to it. If these fail, its infraction becomes the subject of international negotiations and reclamations . . . [but] with all this the judicial courts have nothing to do and can give no redress. *Head Money Cases*, 112 U.S. 580, 598 (1884).

When a U.S. court refuses to enforce an international obligation, its refusal says nothing about the existence or importance of the obligation. Rather the U.S. (1) remains bound, (2) may in fact be in default, and (3) may be subject to international sanctions including diplomatic, political, economic, and even military measures. For discussion of sanctions, see chapter 11, *supra*.

While courts often seem reluctant to compel the U.S. government to comply with international obligations, they have done so on many occasions. They also have required federal and state agencies to comply with international obligations assumed by the U.S. government.

This chapter discusses the use of treaties and customary law in courts, legislatures, and administrative agencies. Part J of the chapter discusses hurdles to application of that law. Part K addresses the use of international law as an interpretive aid in construing U.S. federal, state, and local laws. Part L considers the incorporation of international law in statutes and regulations. In part M strategy issues are raised concerning the choice of courts, legislatures, and agencies for raising human rights concerns.

The chapter illustrates the application of international law in the context of a situation that might benefit from use of human rights norms. The situation concerns the detention of youths awaiting trial in the same cell with youths who have been found to be violators of criminal laws.

B. QUESTIONS

Fourteen-year-old Richard Smith and his thirteen-year-old friend, Andy Olson, hot wired their neighbor's car and ran away from their Arkansas homes. Two days later, in Rolling Green, Ohio, a police officer arrested Richard for unauthorized use of an automobile and detained Andy for running away from home.

The detention intake worker for Wool County placed the boys in Rolling Green's juvenile detention center. The intake worker believed that detention was needed to prevent the boys from running away again.

---

[2] A. Drzemczewski, The European Convention in Domestic Law 177-87 (1983).

The Wool County Detention Center[3] was designed over 80 years ago for short-term, pre-trial custody. The county, however, has increasingly used it as a place to commit youths who have been found by the juvenile court to have violated criminal laws. Because of the growing number of commitments to the Center, 100 youths have been confined to facilities designed for 50. Moreover, conditions in the facility have deteriorated, and post-adjudicated youths often commingle with youths awaiting trial. Consequently, boys in the Center are often subjected to violence and encouraged by other youths to pursue further criminal behavior. The purpose of their detention is undermined. Poor staff control compounds the problems. Only a few staff members have received the training necessary to supervise and care for juveniles.

When Richard and Andy arrived at the Center, the staff placed them together in a cell designed to hold one. It was filthy, and water covered much of the floor. They laid out their jackets over the dirty cots and spent the night in the cell.

At their hearings the next day the court ordered that they remain in the Center until they could be transported to Arkansas. That night the staff separated the boys. Richard was placed in a single cell. Andy, however, had to share a single cell with a seventeen year old who was also waiting for transportation to a more secure detention facility. During the night the seventeen-year-old pulled Andy from his bed, broke his arm, and raped him. The juvenile court had committed the seventeen-year-old to the Center for sexual assault.

The boys' parents have brought a civil rights action pursuant to 42 U.S.C. § 1983 to challenge the legality of the boys' detention and to obtain the release of Richard and Andy. The senior partner of your law firm has asked you to prepare arguments for the § 1983 action. She would like you to use arguments based on Ohio, federal, and international human rights law.

1. Does Ohio law permit the boys to challenge their detention in a facility with youths who have been held to be law violators?

2. Is there basis for challenging the conditions of their confinement under the Due Process Clause of the Fourteenth Amendment or the Eighth Amendment rules incorporated within that clause?

3. Does *Tewksbury* hold that the Due Process Clause forbids detention of youths awaiting trial with youths who have violated criminal laws?

4. What position do the Institute of Judicial Administration - American Bar

---

[3] Though the facts of this case are hypothetical, the conditions are typical of several juvenile detention centers in the U.S. *See* Council of Judges, National Council on Crime & Delinquency, Recommendations on Juvenile Detention (March 1, 1989).

Association Joint Commission and the National Council on Crime and Delinquency suggest as to the detention of pre-adjudicated and post-adjudicated youths? Do the standards suggest how the Due Process Clause should be interpreted?

5. Does the Covenant on Civil and Political Rights forbid detention of youths awaiting trial with youths who have violated criminal laws?

6. What do the U.N. Standard Minimum Rules for the Treatment of Prisoners say about the detention of accused with post-adjudicated youths? The U.N. Body of Principles for the Protection of All Persons under Any Form of Detention or Imprisonment? The Minimum Rules for the Administration of Juvenile Justice (the Beijing Rules)?

7. Do standards against mixing sentenced and non-sentenced adult prisoners apply to adjudicated and non-adjudicated children?

8. How might international standards be invoked in this case?

9. Which would you consider most effective: advocacy based on (1) treaties, (2) customary law, or (3) the use of international law to interpret due process or other relevant federal, state, or local laws? Why?

10. Are there applicable treaties?

11. What are the problems with seeking to enforce relevant provisions of the U.N. Charter?

12. What about the 1989 Convention on the Rights of the Child?

13. If the U.S. were to ratify the Covenant on Civil and Political Rights, what arguments might you make for its application to this case? What responses would you anticipate?

14. What if the U.S. in ratifying the Covenant attaches one or both of the following limitations proposed by the Carter administration?

  a. The United States shall implement all provisions of the Covenant over whose subject matter the Federal Government exercises legislative and judicial jurisdiction; with respect to the provisions over whose subject matter constituent units exercise jurisdiction, the Federal Goverment shall take appropriate measures, to the end that the competent authorities of the constituent units may take appropriate measures for the fulfillment of this Covenant.

  b. The United States declares that the provisions of Articles 1 through 27 of the Covenant are not self-executing.

15. Given that the U.S. has signed but not ratified the Covenant, can it be used to support the youths' position? What is the relevance of Article 18 of the Vienna Treaty on Treaties?

16. How most effectively might you make arguments based on customary international law?

17. Would you make those arguments even if the U.S. had ratified the Covenant?

18. What arguments would you make to support the existence of a relevant customary norm in this case?

19. Assuming there is a customary norm how would you argue for its application in a federal court?

20. Would you argue that the norm should be applied as federal law? On what basis?

21. What is the test for determining whether a norm may be invoked by an individual in federal court? Does the norm meet that test?

22. What is the impact of a federal statute or regulation on a customary norm concerning the same subject? What did *The Paquete Habana* say about that issue?

23. Are there federal statutes, for example 42 U.S.C. § 1983, that might bar application of the customary norm? Is 42 U.S.C. § 1983 inconsistent with the customary norm?

24. How would you argue for application of the customary norm in a state court?

25. Could a state court of general jurisdiction refuse to apply customary international law? What does the second paragraph of Article VI of the U.S. Constitution require?

26. What would be the effect of a state statute inconsistent with the customary norm?

27. Would you choose to bring an action based on the customary norm in state or in federal court? In which do you think defendant(s) would prefer to have the case heard?

28. What is a third way of using international law, in addition to or instead of invocation of treaty or customary law?

29. Which federal and state laws might appropriately be construed in light of international instruments to support the youths? For example, could international instruments help interpret the Due Process Clause of the Fourteenth Amendment and 42 U.S.C. § 1983?

30. How likely would judges be to use international instruments to inform the interpretation of clauses such as Due Process and Equal Protection clauses?

31. What arguments would you use to convince judges that they ought to construe those clauses in light of international instruments? (Particularly as to detention of youths?)

32. Having identified three ways of using international law (treaties, custom, or internatonal law used to help interpret state or federal law), would you use all three or select one or two? Why?

33. Would you argue that the two youths are entitled to the best law — local, state, national, or international — to protect their rights? What authority might you cite for that idea?

34. Would you use the arguments with the Director of the Wool County Detention Center, the Ohio Youth Commission, the Ohio Department of Youth Services, the Ohio Attorney General, or other Ohio authorities responsible for the detention and care of juveniles?

35. Could international law be used to challenge the execution of juvenile offenders? Could detention of the mentally ill or retarded be challenged on the basis of international law?

36. What are the advantages and disadvantages of using U.S. courts and legislatures as compared with the use of international procedures?

   a. for getting relief to the victims?

   b. for factfinding?

   c. for publicity about human rights violations?

   d. for access to the procedures?

   e. for building international human rights structures possessing legitimacy?

C. OHIO LAW

Opinion of the Ohio Attorney General, 1977 Opinion No. 77-006 (1977):

To: William K. Willis, Director, Ohio Youth Commission, Columbus, Ohio
By: William J. Brown, Attorney General, February 23, 1977...

Your first two questions ask, in effect, whether anything in Am. H.B. No. 1196, effective 8/9/76, may be construed as authority for, or a prohibition against, the co-mingling of pre-adjudicated youth and post-adjudicated youth. Your final question is whether R.C. 5139.281, which was enacted by Am. H.B. No. 1196, authorizes the Ohio Youth Commission to prohibit such co-mingling.

Am. H.B. No. 1196 was enacted by the General Assembly for the stated purpose of authorizing "state assistance for the operation of regional detention facilities and *to permit approved facilities to provide both detention and post-adjudication rehabilitation services.*" (Emphasis added.) To this end the General Assembly amended R.C. 2151.34 *et seq.* to authorize detention homes to receive children for both pre-adjudication and post-adjudication confinement and to apply for state assistance. With respect to your questions, R.C. 2151.34 may be set out in pertinent part as follows:

> "No child under eighteen years of age shall be placed in or committed to any prison, jail, or lockup, nor shall such child be brought into any police station, vehicle, or other place where the child can come in contact or communication with any adult convicted of crime or under

arrest and charged with crime. A child may be confined in a place of juvenile detention for a period not to exceed ninety days, during which time a social history may be prepared to include court record, family history, personal history, school and attendance records, and such other pertinent studies and material as will be of assistance to the juvenile court in its disposition of the charges against such juvenile offenders. . . .

"The county or district detention home shall be maintained as provided in sections 2151.01 to 2151.54 of the Revised Code. . . .

R.C. 2151.355 provides in part as follows for the disposition of a child found to be delinquent:

"If a child is found to be a delinquent child, the court may make any of the following orders of disposition:

"(A) Any order which is authorized by section 2151.353 of the Revised Code. . . .

"(C) Commit the child to the temporary custody of any school, camp, institution or other facility for delinquent children operated for the care of such children by the county by a district organized under section 2151.34 or 2151.65 of the Revised Code, or by a private agency or organization, within or without the state, which is authorized and qualified to provide the care, treatment, or placement required;

"(D) Commit the child to the legal custody of the Ohio youth commission. . . ."

It may initially be noted that nothing in the above sections mandates the separation of pre-adjudicated youth and post-adjudicated youth when both are confined pursuant to the statutes in the same detention home. Nor does there appear to be a basis for infering such a requirement. To the contrary it appears that the co-mingling of pre-adjudicated and post-adjudicated youth, if not expressly contemplated, is at least implicitly sanctioned by the statutes in point. . . .

The specific needs of an individual youth, who has been adjudged delinquent, may, however, require special consideration and treatment. In such cases the Youth Commission may, pursuant to R.C. 5139.281, require the separation of such youth for purposes of care, treatment or training or to insure the safety of either that youth or any other youth in the detention home. . . .

NOTES AND QUESTIONS

1. In *Matter of: Gary Hale, Alleged Delinquent Child*, Court of Appeals, Sixth District of Ohio, April 25, 1986. C.A. No. WD-85-74, slip opinion (LEXIS, States library, Ohio file), the court of appeals found that under the Ohio Revised Code, a juvenile court may order a delinquent child to a detention home provided that the Department of Youth Services had approved the detention home as being in compliance with the necessary rules for the care, treatment, and training of delinquent children.

2. *Doe v. McFaul*, 599 F. Supp. 1421 (D. Ohio, 1984), involved a civil rights action brought by juveniles who were incarcerated in an adult correction center in Cuyahoga County, Ohio, where they were attacked by other juveniles. The district court in *McFaul* stated that the Eighth and Fourteenth Amendments to the U.S. Constitution provided the juveniles with a right to be free from attacks by other inmates. The court noted, however, that in order to sustain a §1983 claim against state officials for failing to prevent an attack by inmates, the plaintiffs would have to "show more than mere inadvertence or negligence" by the officials. *Id.* at 1435. The court also stated that the Juvenile Justice and Delinquency Act of 1974, 42 U.S.C. §§ 5601-40 (1982 & Supp. IV 1986) did not provide for a private cause of action. *But see Hendrickson v. Griggs*, 672 F. Supp. 1126 (N.D. Iowa 1987) *appeal dismissed*, 856 F.2d 1041 (8th Cir. 1988), and discussion of the Juvenile Justice and Delinquency Act of 1974, *infra* in this part.

3. Do those cases provide a basis for a challenge under Ohio law of the detention of Smith and Olson in a facility with youths who have been found in violation of criminal laws?

D. FEDERAL STANDARDS

U.S. Constitution:

Article VI, Clause 2. This Constitution, and the Laws of the United States which shall be made in Pursuance thereof; and all Treaties made, or which shall be made, under the Authority of the United States, shall be the supreme Law of the Land; and the Judges in every State shall be bound thereby, any Thing in the Constitution or Laws of any State to the Contrary notwithstanding.

Amendment VIII. Excessive bail shall not be required, nor excessive fines imposed, nor cruel and unusual punishments inflicted.

Amendment XIV, Section 1. All persons born or naturalized in the United States and subject to the jurisdiction thereof, are citizens of the United States and of the State wherein they reside. No State shall make or enforce any law which shall abridge the privileges or immunities of citizens of the United States; nor shall any State deprive any person of life, liberty, or property, without due process of law; nor deny to any person within its jurisdiction the equal protection of the laws.

D.B. v. Tewksbury, 545 F. Supp. 896 (D. Or. 1982):

This is a civil rights action brought pursuant to 42 U.S.C. § 1983. Plaintiffs and members of plaintiffs' class are all children who are presently confined, or who are subject to confinement in the Columbia County Correctional Facility (CCCF), an adult jail, in St. Helens, Oregon. Plaintiffs challenge the constitutionality of defendants' actions in confining plaintiffs and members of their class in CCCF. Plaintiffs seek declaratory and injunctive relief. . . .

CONFINEMENT IN CCCF AS PUNISHMENT

Oregon statutory law allows a child to be detained in local correctional facilities such as CCCF so long as the portion of the facility holding the child is screened from the sight and sound of adult prisoners. ORS 419.575, ORS 169.079 (1979) (amended 1981; renumbered ORS 169.740). Under Oregon law, then, plaintiffs may legitimately be incarcerated in CCCF prior to an adjudication of their status or guilt. It is the scope of their federal constitutional rights during this period of confinement before a hearing that is the focus of this case.

The Due Process Clause of the Fourteenth Amendment to the United States Constitution requires that a pretrial detainee not be punished. *Bell v. Wolfish*, 441 U.S. 520...(1979). A state does not acquire the power to punish a person — adult or child (assuming a child is convicted of committing a crime) — until after it has secured a formal adjudication of guilt in accordance with due process of law. Not every disability imposed in preadjudication detention amounts to "punishment," however. The very fact of detention implies a measure of restriction of movement, choice, privacy, and comfort.

This court must determine whether the conditions imposed upon plaintiffs are imposed for the purpose of punishment or whether they are incidents of some other legitimate governmental purpose. In this case the determination is simple. Defendant Tewksbury has stated publicly and expressly that he intends to punish children detained in CCCF. It is the express intent of defendants that plaintiffs' confinements in CCCF be punishments. The intent to punish is carried out in the extraordinary conditions of confinement imposed on plaintiffs while confined in CCCF. Confinement of child pretrial detainees in CCCF as it now exists is punishment prior to an adjudication of guilt.

Defendants have violated plaintiffs' due process rights under the Fourteenth Amendment to be free from pretrial punishments by confining plaintiffs in CCCF. Those extraordinary conditions which alone and in combination constitute punishment are:

1. Failure to provide any form of work, exercise, education, recreation, or recreational materials.

2. Failure to provide minimal privacy when showering, using toilets, or maintaining feminine hygiene.

3. Placement of intoxicated or drugged children in isolation cells without supervision or medical attention.

4. Placement of younger children in isolation cells as a means of protecting them from older children.

5. Failure to provide adequate staff supervision to protect children from harming themselves and/or other children.

6. Failure to allow contact between children and their families.

7. Failure to provide an adequate diet.

8. Failure to train staff to be able to meet the psychological needs of confined children.

9. Failure to provide written institutional rules, sanctions for violation of those rules, and a grievance procedure.

10. Failure to provide adequate medical care.

CONFINEMENT IN JAILS AS PUNISHMENT FOR STATUS OFFENDERS

Plaintiffs also contend and ask the court to rule that even if the conditions of confinement at CCCF are corrected, plaintiffs and plaintiffs' class may not be detained in CCCF because the confinement of plaintiffs and plaintiffs' class in *any* adult jail constitutes punishment *per se* and is therefore unconstitutional. The court will address this contention first as it relates to status offenders, i.e., runaway children or children who are out of parental control. . . .

A child who has run away from home or is out of parental control is clearly a child in distress, a child in conflict with his family and his society. But nobody contends he is a criminal. A runaway child or a child out of control, as an addict or an insane person, may be confined for treatment or for the protection of society, but to put such a child in a jail — any jail — with its criminal stigma — constitutes punishment and is a violation of that child's due process rights under the Fourteenth Amendment to the United States Constitution. No child who is a *status* offender may be lodged constitutionally in an adult jail.

CONFINEMENT IN JAILS FOR CHILDREN ACCUSED OF COMMITTING CRIMES

The Court must now turn to the issue of whether it is constitutionally permissible to lodge children who have been accused of committing crimes in adult jails pending adjudication of the charges against them. The court has above ruled that confining children in CCCF pending adjudication of crimes or status constitutes punishment, and the court has further ruled that detaining children in *any* jails on the basis of their status or condition constitutes punishment and is an unconstitutional deprivation of due process. The court must now deal with children charged with committing crimes and must suppose that the jails in which these children are lodged are modern, "enlightened" kinds of jails — ones which provide different methods of discipline, care, and treatment appropriate for individual children according to age, personality, and mental and physical condition. The court must further suppose that these jails are adequately staffed and provide reasonable measures of comfort, privacy, medical care, food, and recreation. Would it be constitutionally permissible to lodge children accused of committing crimes in these jails?

In deciding this issue, the court declines to rule on the "punishment" aspect of the due process clause of the 14th Amendment. Instead the court will rely on the "fundamental fairness" doctrine enunciated in *In Re Gault*, 387 U.S. 1 . . . (1967) and juvenile cases decided after the *Gault* decision. . . .

Juvenile proceedings, in the State of Oregon as elsewhere, are in the nature of a guardianship imposed by the state as *parens patriae* to provide the care and guidance that under normal circumstances would be furnished by the natural parents. It is, then, fundamentally fair — constitutional — to deny children charged with crimes rights available to adults charged with crimes if that denial is offset by a special solicitude designed for children.

But when the denial of constitutional rights for children is not offset by a "special solicitude" but by lodging them in adult jails, it is fundamentally unfair. When children who are found *guilty* of committing criminal acts cannot be placed in adult jails, it is fundamentally unfair to lodge children *accused* of committing criminal acts in adult jails. . . .

The supervisors at jails are guards — not guardians. Jails hold convicted criminals and adults charged with crimes. Jails are prisons, with social stigmas. Children identify with their surroundings. They may readily perceive themselves as criminals, for who goes to jail except for criminals? A jail is not a place where a truly concerned natural parent would lodge his or her child for care and guidance. A jail is not a place where the state can constitutionally lodge its children under the guise of *parens patriae*.

To lodge a child in an adult jail pending adjudication of criminal charges against that child is a violation of that child's due process rights under the Fourteenth Amendment to the United States Constitution. . . .

NOTES

1. *Tewksbury* represents a high water mark of successful litigation brought on behalf of children held in jails. *See* Soler, *Litigation on Behalf of Children in Adult Jails*, 34 Crime & Delinquency 190, 196-97 (1988). *Tewksbury* has not been followed everywhere, however.

2. *Tewksbury* was initiated under 42 U.S.C. § 1983 (1982) which provides:

> Every person who, under color of any statute, ordinance, regulation, custom, or usage, of any State or Territory or the District of Columbia, subjects, or causes to be subjected, any citizen of the United States or other person within the jurisdiction thereof to the deprivation of any rights, privileges, or immunities secured by the Constitution and laws, shall be liable to the party injured in an action at law, suit in equity, or other proper proceeding for redress.

3. In response to a rise in juvenile crime and resulting problems in the juvenile justice system, Congress enacted the Juvenile Justice and Delinquency Prevention Act (JJDPA) in 1974. 42 U.S.C. §§ 5601-40 (1982 & Supp. IV 1986); *see* Congressional Statement of Findings, JJDPA, 42 U.S.C. § 5601. The Act compels states which receive JJDPA funds to remove status offenders from secure facilities, separate juveniles from adult offenders, remove all juveniles from jails, and provide due process protections to children.

Many states have accepted JJDPA funds without substantially complying with the JJDPA mandates. *See* Costello and Worthington, *Incarcerating Status Offenders: Attempts to Circumvent the Juvenile Justice & Delinquency Prevention Act*, 16 Harv. C.R.-C.L. L. Rev. 40, 58 (1981); Swanger, *Hendrickson v. Griggs: A Review of Legal and Policy Implications for Juvenile Justice Policymakers*, 34 Crime & Delinquency 209, 211 (1988). States that have accepted funds without complying with the requirements may be in trouble if the ruling in *Hendrickson v. Griggs*, 672 F. Supp. 1126 (N.D. Iowa 1987) is followed elsewhere.

Hendrickson ruled that, under JJDPA, juveniles have rights actionable under 42 U.S.C. § 1983. *Id.* at 1136. The court concluded that Iowa had failed to comply with the JJDPA requirement of removing juveniles from adult jails. The court thus ordered the state to submit to the court a plan to bring Iowa into JJDPA compliance by the end of 1987. 672 F. Supp. at 1144-45; *but see Doe v. McFaul*, 599 F. Supp. 1421, 1430 (D. Ohio 1984).

On appeal the Eighth Circuit questioned the trial court's reasoning, but ultimately dismissed the appeal because the trial ruling was not yet reviewable. *Hendrickson v. Griggs*, 856 F.2d 1041, 1045 (8th Cir. 1988).

4. Because the Eighth Amendment forbids cruel and unusual *punishment*, the principle as applied through the Due Process Clause of the Fourteenth Amendment has been held inapplicable to individuals who have not been convicted. *See City of Revere v. Massachusetts General Hospital*, 463 U.S. 239, 244 (1983); *Bell v. Wolfish*, 441 U.S. 520, 535 n.16 (1979).

E. U.S. JUVENILE JUSTICE STANDARDS

Institute of Judicial Administration - American Bar Association Joint Commission on Juvenile Justice Standards, Interim Status: The Release, Control, and Detention of Accused Juvenile Offenders Between Arrest and Disposition (1980): . . .

2.10 Secure detention facility [is defined as a] facility characterized by physically restrictive construction and procedures that are intended to prevent an accused juvenile who is placed there from departing at will. . . .

2.11 Nonsecure detention facility [is defined as a] detention facility that is open in nature and designed to allow maximum participation by the accused juvenile in the community and its resources. It is intended primarily to minimize psychological hardships on an accused juvenile offender who is held out-of-home, rather than to restrict the freedom of the juvenile. These facilities include, but are not limited to:

    A. single family foster homes or temporary boarding homes;

    B. group homes with a resident staff, which may or may not specialize in a particular problem area, such as drug abuse, alcohol abuse, etc.; and

    C. facilities used for the housing of neglected or abused juveniles. . . .

10.4 Mixing accused juvenile offenders with other juveniles.

    A. In nonsecure facilities. The simultaneous housing in a nonsecure detention facility of juveniles charged with criminal offenses and juveniles held for other reasons should not be prohibited.

    B. In secure facilities. Juveniles not charged with crime should not be held in any secure detention facility for accused juvenile offenders.

Commentary

    In order to avoid unnecessarily secure detention, this standard permits the alternative of *nonsecure* detention facilities that normally house juveniles not charged with crimes to be used also as interim facilities for criminal cases. For example, a house for runaways or a foster home for neglected children could be designated as the nonsecure detention facility for a particular juvenile charged with criminal conduct. . . .

Recommendations on Juvenile Detention, National Council on Crime and Delinquency, Council of Judges (March 1, 1989): . . .

6. Minors detained before trial should be held in a facility that meets accepted standards for juvenile detention. This precludes secure, pre-trial detention in an

adult jail or lockup. Minors in juvenile detention facilities are entitled to humane and safe care, including attention to special physical, medical and emotional needs of each young person who is detained. The staff of the juvenile facility should be adequately trained in the care of minors and should have special training in suicide prevention.

7. Many of the nation's juvenile detention centers are older facilities that need to be improved or remodeled to meet current code and safety standards. . . .

8. In most cases, juvenile detention centers should not be used for the commitment of minors after adjudication. Increasingly, the nation's detention centers have been used as places for secure, post-trial commitments lasting as long as six or nine months. The rationale for such dispositions is that they may be in lieu of commitments to a more restrictive secure facility, such as the state training school. Nevertheless, the vast majority of juvenile detention centers were built for short-term, pre-trial custody. They are not designed or staffed to provide the level of schooling, counseling and personal care necessary for longer stays. Moreover, post-adjudicated youth are often co-mingled with pre-trial youth in these detention centers. Use of the detention center for commitment of youth cannot be justified where this use causes the detention center to become overcrowded, or where the commitment program is used solely for punishment or other avoidance of the goals of the juvenile court law. Jurisdictions needing short-term or medium-term alternatives to state training schools should focus resources on the development of alternatives outside the detention center, where the need to restrain the minor can be balanced by an ability to provide meaningful programs serving the rehabilitative goals of the juvenile court law. . . .

F. INTERNATIONAL STANDARDS

Standard Minimum Rules for the Treatment of Prisoners, *adopted* Aug. 30, 1955, by the First United Nations Congress on the Prevention of Crime and the Treatment of Offenders, U.N. Doc. A/CONF/611, ANNEX I *adopted* July 31, 1957, E.S.C. res. 663C, 24 U.N. ESCOR Supp. (No. 1) at 11, U.N. Doc. E/3048 (1957), *amended* E.S.C. res. 2076, 62 U.N. ESCOR Supp. (No. 1) at 35, U.N. Doc. E/5988 (1977) (adding Article 95):

PRELIMINARY OBSERVATIONS . . .

5.   (1) The rules do not seek to regulate the management of institutions set aside for young persons such as Borstal institutions or correctional schools, but in general part I would be equally applicable in such institutions.

(2) The category of young prisoners should include at least all young persons who come within the jurisdiction of juvenile courts. As a rule, such young persons should not be sentenced to imprisonment. . . .

PART I

RULES OF GENERAL APPLICATION . . .

Separation of categories

8. The different categories of prisoners shall be kept in separate institutions

or parts of institutions taking account of their sex, age, criminal record, the legal reason for their detention and the necessities of their treatment. Thus,

(a) Men and women shall so far as possible be detained in separate institutions; in an institution which receives both men and women the whole of the premises allocated to women shall be entirely separate;

(b) Untried prisoners shall be kept separate from convicted prisoners;

(c) Persons imprisoned for debt and other civil prisoners shall be kept separate from persons imprisoned by reason of a criminal offence;

(d) Young prisoners shall be kept separate from adults. . . .

PART II

RULES APPLICABLE TO SPECIAL CATEGORIES. . .

C. Prisoners Under Arrest or Awaiting Trial

84. (1) Persons arrested or imprisoned by reason of a criminal charge against them, who are detained either in police custody or in prison custody (jail) but have not yet been tried and sentenced, will be referred to as "untried prisoners" hereinafter in these rules.

(2) Unconvicted prisoners are presumed to be innocent and shall be treated as such.

(3) Without prejudice to legal rules for the protection of individual liberty or prescribing the procedure to be observed in respect of untried prisoners, these prisoners shall benefit by a special régime which is described in the following rules in its essential requirements only.

85. (1) Untried prisoners shall be kept separate from convicted prisoners.

(2) Young untried prisoners shall be kept separate from adults and shall in principle be detained in separate institutions.

86. Untried prisoners shall sleep singly in separate rooms, with the reservation of different local custom in respect of the climate.

87. Within the limits compatible with the good order of the institution, untried prisoners may, if they so desire, have their food procured at their own expense from the outside, either through the administration or through their family or friends. Otherwise, the administration shall provide their food.

88. (1) An untried prisoner shall be allowed to wear his own clothing if it is clean and suitable.

(2) If he wears prison dress, it shall be different from that supplied to convicted prisoners.

89. An untried prisoner shall always be offered opportunity to work, but shall not be required to work. If he chooses to work, he shall be paid for it.

90. An untried prisoner shall be allowed to procure at his own expense or at the expense of a third party such books, newspapers, writing materials and other means of occupation as are compatible with the interests of the administration of justice and the security and good order of the institution.

91. An untried prisoner shall be allowed to be visited and treated by his own doctor or dentist if there is reasonable ground for his application and he is able to pay any expenses incurred.

92. An untried prisoner shall be allowed to inform immediately his family of his detention and shall be given all reasonable facilities for communicating with

his family and friends, and for receiving visits from them, subject only to such restrictions and supervision as are necessary in the interests of the administration of justice and of the security and good order of the institution. . . .

Covenant on Civil and Political Rights, G.A. res. 2200A, 21 U.N. GAOR Supp. (No. 16) at 49, U.N. Doc. A/6316 (1966), 999 U.N.T.S. 171, 6 I.L.M. 360 (1967), *entered into force* March 23, 1976: . . .

Article 10

1. All persons deprived of their liberty shall be treated with humanity and with respect for the inherent dignity of the human person.

2.   (*a*) Accused persons shall, save in exceptional circumstances, be segregated from convicted persons and shall be subject to separate treatment appropriate to their status as unconvicted persons;

(*b*) Accused juvenile persons shall be separated from adults and brought as speedily as possible for adjudication.

3. The penitentiary system shall comprise treatment of prisoners the essential aim of which shall be their reformation and social rehabilitation. Juvenile offenders shall be segregated from adults and be accorded treatment appropriate to their age and legal status. . . .

Article 24

1. Every child shall have, without discrimination as to race, colour, sex, language, religion, national or social origin, property or birth, the right to such measures of protection as are required by his status as a minor, on the part of his family, society and the State. . . .

NOTES

1. Eighty-eight governments as of February 1990 have ratified or acceded to the Covenant on Civil and Political Rights. The U.S. has signed but not ratified. The Covenant is reproduced in the accompanying handbook and contains several other provisions potentially relevant to this case.

2. On April 5, 1989, the Human Rights Committee adopted general comments on Article 24 of the Covenant. *Report of the Human Rights Committee,* U.N. Doc A/44/40, at 173 (1989). The Committee stated that "if lawfully deprived of their liberty, accused juvenile persons shall be separated from adults and are entitled to be brought as speedily as possible for adjudication; in turn, convicted juvenile offenders shall be subject to a penitentiary system that involves segregation from adults and is appropriate to their age and legal status, the aim being to foster reformation and social rehabilitation."

A note in chapter 8, *supra*, discussed the purpose and procedure governing general comments issued by the Human Rights Committee.

3. The U.N. General Assembly unanimously adopted Minimum Rules for the Administration of Juvenile Justice on November 29, 1985 (the Beijing Rules). *See* Instruments and Resolutions Relating to the Administration of Justice and the Human Rights of Detainees at 3, U.N. Doc. E/CN.4/Sub.2/1987/CRP.1 (1987). Because of the danger to juveniles of "criminal contamination" while in detention pending trial, rule 13.1 states that detention pending trial should "be used only as a measure of last resort and for the shortest possible period of time." Rule 13.3 declares that "[j]uveniles under detention pending trial shall be entitled to all rights and guarantees of the Standard Minimum Rules for the Treatment of Prisoners." The commentary to rule 13.3 noted that juveniles are also entitled to the rights and guarantees of the Covenant on Civil and Political Rights.

4. On December 8, 1988, the General Assembly adopted the Body of Principles for the Protection of All Persons under Any Form of Detention or Imprisonment. G.A. res. 43/173. Principle 8 provides that "[p]ersons in detention shall be subject to treatment appropriate to their unconvicted status. Accordingly, they shall, whenever possible, be kept separate from imprisoned persons."

5. On November 20, 1989, the General Assembly adopted the Convention on the Rights of the Child and opened it for ratification by all governments. G.A. res. 44/25, 28 I.L.M. 1448 (1989). Article 37 of the treaty provides, "No child shall be subjected to torture or other cruel, inhuman or degrading treatment or punishment. . . . Every child deprived of liberty shall be treated with humanity and respect for the inherent dignity of the human person, and in a manner which takes into account the needs of persons of his or her age." Article 41 states, "Nothing in the present Convention shall affect any provisions which are more conducive to the realization of the rights of the child and which may be contained in: (*a*) The law of a State Party; or (*b*) International law in force for that State."

G. APPROACHES TO USING INTERNATIONAL HUMAN RIGHTS LAW

U.S. federal and state courts as well as administrative agencies have applied international law pursuant to three theories. *First*, if the right sought to be advanced is guaranteed by a self-executing treaty clause, courts and agencies may apply the clause directly. *Second*, if the right is protected by a customary norm, adjudicators may enforce it. *Third*, courts and agencies may find clauses of international instruments, whether or not they have attained the status of customary law, persuasive in construing open-ended provisions of national law.

"Direct incorporation" of international law pursuant to the first two of those theories results in law that binds courts. For that reason direct incorporation may appear more powerful than the third theory — "indirect incorporation" — which leaves application of international law to the discretion of judges. But various rules of interpretation and application create obstacles to direct incorporation. Moreover, direct incorporation — a bolder step — gives rise to decisions that often seem more likely to be reversed on appeal. Also, litigators in state courts may have a special interest in urging indirect incorporation of international law into state law in order to develop independent state grounds and thus avoid creation of federal issues.[4] In most cases lawyers are better advised to pursue indirect incorporation, though many courts are likely to be leery even of that "softer" use of international law.

Efforts to persuade courts and agencies to apply international law pursuant to any of the three theories are assisted by incorporation of, or at least reference to, international standards in federal and state statutes and regulations. For that reason, activists committed to advancing internationally recognized rights are well-advised to consider legislative as well as judicial and administrative strategies.

In the following comments Judge Linde[5] of the Oregon Supreme Court offers advice to lawyers on how most effectively to use international human rights law in federal and state courts, concluding with a reminder to work with the legislative and executive branches as well.

Linde, *Comments*, 18 Int'l Lawyer 77 (1984) (footnotes omitted):

I am here today not because I am an expert in international human rights law, but because I am a judge who has written an opinion which refers to that source of law. I suppose I am here more in the nature of an exhibit than as a person who is going to teach you any law. You can take what I say as illustrative of what you may face in actually talking to a domestic court about international human rights law. . . .

Out there in the world of people who have not had the good fortune to attend conferences on international human rights law, it is largely taken as an article of faith that the United States provides the best protection for human rights in the world. If there are any rights recognized in international law that are not recognized in U.S. law, people may assume that there is a good reason for that nonrecognition. On the other hand, whether or not our protection of human rights is the best, there is a strong urge to agree that it *should* be the best. These ingrained perspectives give you both an opportunity and a challenge.

---

[4] *See* Hoffman, *The Application of International Human Rights in State Courts: A View From California*, 18 Int'l Lawyer 61, 63 (1984).

[5] Judge Linde authored the majority opinion in *Sterling v. Cupp*, 290 Or. 611, 625 P.2d 123 (1981) (construing state constitutional provision prohibiting "unnecessarily rigorous treatment" of inmates in light of the International Bill of Human Rights and other international instruments).

You may as well assume, simply as a matter of probability, that these views also are likely to prevail among the judges you will face. If we judges have not yet decided to recognize a certain right under one of the numerous, elastic clauses that are available to courts in this country, we probably believe that there is a good reason why we haven't. A lawyer who comes to tell us that we should follow some principle because it is part of an evolving body of international human rights law has a lot of explaining to do. But we also take pride in American law as being in the lead on individual human rights. These attitudes, I think, are important in understanding what role international human rights materials can play in domestic courts.

It is potentially a powerful argument to say to a court that a right which is guaranteed by an American constitutional provision, state or federal, surely does not fall short of a standard adopted by other civilized nations.

It is a much more difficult, and riskier, argument to tell a court that it must displace some law of a state, or of the United States, with an external international standard.

A lawyer considering the use of international human rights law in a national court, state or federal, must consider carefully whether he or she means to claim the international document as a source of standards for the proper application of the nation's own law, or as a source of legally binding obligations. A lawyer must tell a court clearly whether he or she is asserting a claim under international law, or presenting an international norm in support of a desired interpretation of our domestic law.

To point to the international standard as a goal or an achievement to be matched may prove very successful. To point to it as an external law to be obeyed may backfire. It may backfire because, unless the legally binding nature of the international source is clear and strong, opposing counsel and the court may give more time and attention to refuting the claim that the international source has binding force than to looking at the substance of the human rights in question.

The use of human rights norms as customary international law . . . is undeniably appealing. Here we have documents full of more or less eloquent and powerful language, adopted in many cases by unanimous vote in the United Nations, the Organization of American States, or the European Commission on Human Rights. Eminent authorities, including Frank Newman, Louis Sohn, Louis Henkin, and Anthony D'Amato, have devoted a great deal of very able effort to showing (1) that the "pledge" made by U.N. members under article 56 of the charter to take separate as well as joint action in cooperation with the organization to promote human rights created an obligation binding on the United States, and (2) that the aggregate international bill of human rights offers an authoritative, or at least persuasive, interpretation of the article 56 obligation.

I have little problem with those separate conclusions. Assuming they are correct, nevertheless, they are insufficient to establish the direct applicability of international documents in domestic courts. Incantation of the classic formula that the law of nations is part of the law of the United States, . . . by itself is not enough to establish that even the most widely accepted norms of human rights law displace American law in American courts.

The U.N. Charter, of course, is a treaty and part of the "supreme law of the land." But the Universal Declaration on Human Rights was deliberately drafted not to be a treaty. Other human rights documents that were drafted to be treaties or covenants have not been ratified by the United States. These have been deliberate governmental decisions not to undertake certain legal obligations, made with full attention to the choices among instruments that are designed to create one or the other legal effect.

The problem in establishing that a provision of an international document binds our courts as domestic law is that you must show a decision on the part of our government to be so bound. And you cannot show such an intention regarding any instrument other than treaties or similar formal agreements. Other declarations and draft conventions are entered into simply by presidential instructions to ambassadors. They reflect no more than a presidential decision that a certain stance in one of the international forums, or a particular speech, or a vote for a specific declaration advances the foreign policy interests of the United States. Presidents generally do not mean to make domestic law by these means. Ordinarily they take great care to reassure everyone, including the Congress, that they are not making any law binding on this country by voting for or even signing international human rights documents. Even when a President has signed a draft convention that is intended to be a proposed treaty, he or his successor often has decided not to submit the convention for the advice and consent of the Senate, or perhaps to submit it with the explicit reservation that the ratified treaty would have no domestic effect.

For instance, Dean Rusk, who worked with Eleanor Roosevelt in her efforts to have the Universal Declaration of Human Rights unanimously adopted, wrote in a recent article that it was perfectly well understood at the time that the declaration would have no legal consequences within the United States. . . .

Human rights enthusiasts understandably welcome any theory that promises to promote human rights without too much scrutiny of its implications. But the trouble with theory is that it always extends beyond the immediate case. We have learned to be cautious about unilateral executive power to act in domestic affairs, say, to settle a labor dispute by seizing the steel industry. Why should the executive have more domestic power by agreeing with other governments, say, to assure equal employment rights in the steel industry? If the president can make human rights law for the United States by having an ambassador make a speech, negotiate a declaration, or cast a vote in the General Assembly, can he make other kinds of American law by the same means? Could he, for instance, act on his own to override the property law of the states and transfer property from one claimant to another?

. . . I have no doubt that the United States could commit itself to expend money by ratification of a treaty. But this is far from empowering a court to mandate a state to spend money in order to help the United States achieve some general treaty goal, even at the wish of the national executive. . . .

In short, if you are to succeed with your argument that a provision of human rights law is law in a domestic court, you must be able to show that the national lawmakers, by treaty or otherwise, intended this effect. This, at least, is the kind of skeptical reaction that a lawyer is likely to meet if he or she tries to convince a court to apply purely declaratory international human rights documents as legally binding on the court. But often there is no need to take on that burden.

If instead, you argue that a court should look to international instruments to assist it in interpreting a domestic statute or constitution, then you are asking the court to do what it is empowered to do and using international law in the process.

Moreover, an advocate wishing to invoke international human rights norms reasonably could argue that an applicable domestic law already contains the protections that the claimant contends, but that, if the court were not to accept this view, then the court might well find itself running afoul of national policy as expressed by the United States government through its participation in international human rights activities and declarations.

... So if the court is persuaded of the merits of a particular human rights claim, the court almost certainly can recognize that claim under a clause of a state constitution or of the federal constitution without venturing onto the thin ice of making doubtful precedents about the domestic effect of executive declarations in international forums.

I venture a guess that arguments invoking international human rights standards would have the greatest chance of success in matters where the claim invokes an issue of international interest, or where other countries and international agencies have had greater experience than has the United States. Examples may include the treatment of aliens, the legal status and rights of diverse racial, ethnic, linguistic, religious and nationality groups, and the treatment of detained persons.

In conclusion, I want to leave you with a theme that for twenty years has been a favorite of Frank Newman's and mine and that Paul Hoffman also mentioned, namely, that it is a grave mistake to think that courts are the only forums in which human rights law is made or developed. The harder, less immediately rewarding, but more important pursuit of international human rights, as of other policies, occurs not in the courts, but in persuading those responsible for policy-making, in the Congress, the State Department, and the White House that Americans care about human rights abroad as well as at home. . . .

NOTES

For discussion of theories of incorporation of international law in U.S. law, see:

Bilder, *Integrating International Human Rights Law into Domestic Law — U.S. Experience*, 4 Hous. J. Int'l L. (1981);

Burke, Coliver, de la Vega, & Rosenbaum, *Application of International Human Rights Law in State and Federal Courts*, 18 Tex. Int'l L.J. 291 (1983) [hereafter Burke];

Christenson, *The Uses of Human Rights Norms to Inform Constitutional Interpretation*, 4 Hous. J. Int'l L. 39 (1981);

Hartman, *"Unusual" Punishment: The Domestic Effects of International Norms Restricting the Application of the Death Penalty*, 52 Cin. L. Rev. 655 (1983);

Lillich, *Invoking International Human Rights Law in Domestic Courts*, 54 Cin. L. Rev. 367 (1985);

Lillich, *The United States Constitution and International Human Rights Law*, 3 Harv. Hum. Rts. J. 53 (1990);

Oliver, *Problems of Cognition and Interpretation in Applying Norms of*

Customary International Law of Human Rights in United States Courts, 4 Hous. J. Int'l L. 59 (1981);

Paust, *Litigating Human Rights: A Commentary on the Comments*, 4 Hous. J. Int'l L. 81 (1981);

Schneebaum, *International Law as a Guarantor of Judicially-Enforceable Rights: A Reply to Professor Oliver*, 4 Hous. J. Int'l L. 65 (1981).

H. TREATIES

Article 38(1) of the Statute of the International Court of Justice identifies the sources of international law: (a) treaties, (b) international custom, as evidence of a general practice accepted as law, (c) general principles of law, and (d) judicial decisions and the teachings of the most highly qualified publicists.[6]

Most treaties to which the U.S. is party are bilateral or involve a small number of states. They generally are interpreted pursuant to rules similar to canons for interpreting contracts; that is, the intent of the parties is paramount.

In contrast, the major human rights treaties are multilateral, drafted not by the parties but by governments acting under the auspices of an intergovernmental organization (*e.g.*, the U.N., O.A.S., Council of Europe, and Organization of African Unity) or a nongovernmental organization (such as the International Committee of the Red Cross). Once drafted the treaties are adopted by general assemblies or other plenary bodies of the organizations and then are opened for ratification or other form of acceptance by governments, often including those not involved in the drafting process.[7]

Treaties so drafted are interpreted pursuant to rules similar to those used in construing legislation. The most authoritative collection of rules concerning the interpretation of treaties is the Vienna Convention on the Law of Treaties, 1155 U.N.T.S. 331, T.S. No. 58 (1980), 8 I.L.M. 679 (1979), *entered into force* January 27, 1980. The Vienna Treaty on Treaties has not been ratified by the U.S., but the State Department has acknowledged that "the Convention is already generally recognized as the authoritative guide to current treaty law and practice." Vienna Convention on the Law of Treaties S. Exec. Doc., 92nd Cong., 1st Sess. 1 (1971); *see* Treaty on Treaties excerpts and discussion in chapter 7, *supra*.

---

[6] *See* 1 Restatement (Third) of the Foreign Relations Law of the United States § 102(1) (1987).

[7] For instance, Switzerland is not a member of the U.N. and did not participate in drafting the Convention Against Torture and Other Cruel, Inhuman or Degrading Treatment or Punishment, G.A. res. 39/46, 39 U.N. GAOR Supp. (No.51) at 197, U.N. Doc. A/39/51 (1984), *entered into force* June 26, 1987, but nonetheless it was one of the first countries to become a party to the treaty.

The Vienna Treaty on Treaties sets a hierarchy of interpretive sources. The first is "the ordinary meaning to be given to the terms of the treaty in their context and in the light of their object and purpose." The context includes the treaty itself, any agreements among the parties in connection with the treaty, any subsequent practice that evidences the parties' agreement regarding the treaty's interpretation, any instrument made by one or more parties accepted by the other parties as an instrument related to the treaty, and relevant rules of international law. If the meaning so construed remains obscure or leads to a manifestly unreasonable result, recourse may be had to supplementary means of interpretation, including the preparatory work (*travaux préparatoires*) of the treaty and the circumstances of its conclusion. The expressed intent of a party is relevant only when it appears to have been accepted by the other parties. 1 Restatement (Third) of the Foreign Relations of the United States § 131, comment h, at 58 (1987).

A government may express its consent to be bound by a treaty by any means agreed upon by the parties, including ratification, signature, approval, and accession. Vienna Convention, Art. 11.

The U.S. is party to only a few of the scores of multilateral treaties that contain human rights provisions. The most important are the U.N. Charter, the Charter of the Organization of American States as amended by the Protocol of Buenos Aires, the four Geneva Conventions of 1949, the U.N. Protocol Relating to the Status of Refugees, and the Genocide Convention. The U.S. also is party to three U.N. treaties on slavery and the Convention on the Political Rights of Women. U.S. ratification of human rights treaties and procedures for ratification are discussed in chapter 9, *supra*.

1. Treaties in U.S. Law

A treaty accepted by the U.S. is part of the supreme law of the land, of equal dignity with federal statutes. U.S. Const. Art. VI, para 2. Conflicts between treaty clauses and existing U.S. law are resolved according to three rules. *First*, a treaty may not infringe on certain provisions of the U.S. Constitution. *Kinsella v. United States ex rel. Singleton*, 361 U.S. 248 (1960); *Reid v. Covert*, 354 U.S. 1, 16-17 (1957). *Second*, if a treaty and a federal statute conflict, the more recent prevails. *Reid v. Covert, supra*, 354 U.S. at 18 n. 34. *Third*, if a treaty and state law conflict, the treaty controls.[8] A well-established rule is that courts should endeavor to construe a treaty and a statute on the same subject so as to give effect to both. *Whitney v. Robertson*, 124 U.S. 190, 194 (1888). In particular, courts should

---

[8] *Zschernig v. Miller*, 389 U.S. 429, 440-41 (1968); *Clark v Allen*, 331 U.S. 503, 508 (1947); *see also Missouri v. Holland*, 252 U.S. 416, 433-35 (1920) (validity of treaty not undermined by possible infringement on states' rights under Tenth Amendment).

construe a treaty "in a broad and liberal spirit, and when two constructions are possible, one restrictive of rights that may be claimed under it and the other favorable to them, the latter is to be preferred." *Asakura v. City of Seattle*, 265 U.S. 332, 342 (1924).

The following excerpt shows the lengths to which a court may go in order to construe a statute to be consistent with a treaty, even one ratified before enactment of the statute. *U.S. v. Palestine Liberation Organization*, 695 F. Supp. 1456, 1471 (S.D.N.Y. 1988), held that the PLO could maintain its observer mission at the U.N. in New York, as authorized by the U.N. Headquarters Agreement (a treaty in force between the U.S. and the U.N.) even though the Anti-Terrorism Act (ATA) of 1988 appeared to require the mission's closure. By its terms the ATA prohibits the maintenance of "an office, headquarters, premises, or other facilities or establishments within the jurisdiction of the United States at the behest or direction of, or with funds provided by" the PLO, if the aim is to further the PLO's interests. 22 U.S.C. § 5202(3).

U.S. v. Palestine Liberation Organization, 695 F. Supp. 1456, 1468-71 (S.D.N.Y. 1988): . . .

Reconciliation of the ATA and the Headquarters Agreement.

The lengths to which our courts have sometimes gone in construing domestic statutes so as to avoid conflict with international agreements are suggested by a passage from Justice Field's dissent in *Chew Heong* . . . 112 U.S. at 560, 560-61 . . . (1884), . . . [which] concerned the interplay of legislation regarding Chinese laborers with treaties on the same subject. During the passage of the statute at issue in *Chew Heong*, "it was objected to the legislation sought that the treaty of 1868 stood in the way, and that while it remained unmodified, such legislation would be a breach of faith to China. . . ." *Id.* at 569. . . . In spite of that, and over Justice Field's dissent, the Court, in Justice Field's words, "narrow[ed] the meaning of the act so as measurably to frustrate its intended operation." Four years after the decision in *Chew Heong*, Congress amended the act in question to nullify that decision. . . . . With the amended statute, there could be no question as to Congress' intent to supersede the treaties, and it was the later enacted statute which took precedence. *The Chinese Exclusion Case*, . . . 130 U.S. at 598-99 . . . (1889).

The principles enunciated and applied in *Chew Heong* and its progeny . . . require the clearest of expressions on the part of Congress. We are constrained by these decisions to stress the lack of clarity in Congress' action in this instance. Congress' failure to speak with one clear voice on this subject requires us to interpret the ATA as inapplicable to the Headquarters Agreement. This is so, in short, for the reasons which follow.

First, neither the Mission nor the Headquarters Agreement is mentioned in the ATA itself. Such an inclusion would have left no doubt as to Congress' intent on a matter which had been raised repeatedly with respect to this act, and its absence here reflects equivocation and avoidance, leaving the court without clear interpretive guidance in the language of the act. Second, while the section of the ATA prohibiting the maintenance of an office applies "notwithstanding any provision of law to the contrary," 22 U.S.C. § 5202(3), it does not purport to apply notwithstanding any *treaty*. The absence of that interpretive instruction is especially relevant because elsewhere in the same legislation Congress expressly referred to "United States law (including any treaty)." 101 Stat. 1343. Thus Congress failed, in the text of the ATA, to provide guidance for the interpretation of the act, where it became repeatedly apparent before its passage that the prospect of an interpretive problem was inevitable. Third, no member of Congress expressed a clear and unequivocal intent to supersede the Headquarters Agreement by passage of the ATA. In contrast, most who addressed the subject of conflict denied that there would be a conflict: in their view, the Headquarters Agreement did not provide the PLO with any right to maintain an office. Here again, Congress provided no guidance for the interpretation of the ATA in the event of a conflict which was clearly foreseeable. . . .

. . .The proponents of the ATA were, at an early stage and throughout its consideration, forewarned that the ATA would present a potential conflict with the Headquarters Agreement. It was especially important in those circumstances for Congress to give clear, indeed unequivocal guidance, as to how an interpreter of the ATA was to resolve the conflict. Yet there was no reference to the Mission in the text of the ATA, despite extensive discussion of the Mission in the floor debates. Nor was there reference to the Headquarters Agreement, or to any treaty, in the ATA or in its "notwithstanding" clause, despite the textual expression of intent to supersede treaty obligations in other sections of the Foreign Relations Authorization Act, of which the ATA formed a part. Thus Congress failed to provide unequivocal interpretive guidance in the text of the ATA, leaving open the possibility that the ATA could be viewed as a law of general application and enforced as such, without encroaching on the position of the Mission at the United Nations.

That interpretation would present no inconsistency with what little legislative history exists. There were conflicting voices both in Congress and in the executive branch before the enactment of the ATA. Indeed, there is only one matter with respect to which there was unanimity — the condemnation of terrorism. This, however, is extraneous to the legal issues involved here. At oral argument, the United States Attorney conceded that there was no evidence before the court that the Mission had misused its position at the United Nations or engaged in any covert actions in furtherance of terrorism. If the PLO is benefiting from operating in the United States, as the ATA implies, the enforcement of its provisions outside the context of the United Nations can effectively curtail that benefit.

The record contains voices of congressmen and senators forceful in their condemnation of terrorism and of the PLO and supporting the notion that the legislation would close the Mission. There are other voices, less certain of the validity of the proposed congressional action and preoccupied by problems of constitutional dimension. And there are voices of Congressmen uncertain of the legal issues presented but desirous nonetheless of making a "political statement." During the discussions which preceded and followed the passage of the ATA, the Secretary of State and the Legal Adviser to the Department of State, a former member of this Court, voiced their opinions to the effect that the ATA presented a conflict with the Headquarters Agreement.

Yet no member of Congress, at any point, explicitly stated that the ATA was intended to override any international obligation of the United States. . . .

In sum, the language of the Headquarters Agreement, the longstanding practice under it, and the interpretation given it by the parties to it leave no doubt that it places an obligation upon the United States to refrain from impairing the function of the PLO Observer Mission to the United Nations. The ATA and its legislative history do not manifest Congress' intent to abrogate this obligation. We are therefore constrained to interpret the ATA as failing to supersede the Headquarters Agreement and inapplicable to the Mission.

NOTES AND QUESTIONS

1. What language added to the Anti-Terrorism Act would suffice to supersede the Headquarters Agreement?

For other opinions construing a statute to be consistent with, rather than to supersede, a treaty clause see: *Trans World Airlines, Inc. v. Franklin Mint Corp.*, 466 U.S. 243, 252 (1984); *Weinberger v. Rossi*, 456 U.S. 25, 32 (1982); *Washington v. Washington State Commercial Passenger Fishing Vessel Association*, 443 U.S. 658, 690, *modified*, 444 U.S. 816 (1979); *Menominee Tribe of Indians v. United States*, 391 U.S. 404, 412-13 (1968); *Cook v. United States*, 288 U.S. 102 (1933).

For cases holding that a federal statute did supersede a treaty clause see: *The Chinese Exclusion Case*, 130 U.S. 581, 599-602 (1889); *The Head Money Cases*, 112 U.S. 580, 597-99 (1884); *South African Airways v. Dole*, 817 F.2d 119, 121 (D.C.Cir.) (Anti-Apartheid Act of 1986, requiring termination of treaty between U.S. and South Africa, held irreconcilable with that treaty), *cert. denied*, 484 U.S. 896 (1987).

2. For a survey of post-World War II civil rights cases invoking the human rights clauses of the U.N. Charter, see Lockwood, *The U.N. Charter and United States Civil Rights Litigation: 1946-1955*, 69 Iowa L. Rev. 901 (1984).

3. Professor Hannum has urged that courts should show greater deference to treaty clauses when the inconsistent law is a state, rather than a federal, statute. H. Hannum, Materials on International Human Rights and U.S. Criminal Law and Procedure 10-11 (1989); *see Zschernig v. Miller*, 389 U.S. 429 (1968).

2. Treaties Signed But Not Ratified

The U.S. has signed but not ratified six treaties that form much of the core of U.N. human rights law: the Covenant on Economic, Social and Cultural Rights; the Covenant on Civil and Political Rights (the U.S. has not signed its Optional Protocol); the Convention on the Elimination of All Forms of Racial Discrimination; the Convention on the Elimination of All Forms of Discrimination Against Women; the Convention Against Torture and Other Cruel, Inhuman or Degrading Treatment or Punishment; and the American Convention on Human Rights. *See* chapter 9, *supra*. The Treaty Against Torture is the only one to which the Senate is likely to give its advice and consent within the foreseeable future.

Article 18 of the Vienna Treaty on Treaties requires a government that has signed but not ratified "to refrain from acts which would defeat the object and purpose of [the] treaty... until it shall have made its intention clear not to become a party...." 1155 U.N.T.S. 331, *entered into force* January 27, 1980. *See* chapter 7, *supra*, for discussion of a country's international obligations under Article 18. U.S. courts have not applied Article 18 to treaties the U.S. has signed but not ratified. Rather, to the extent they have relied on those instruments, they have looked to them as evidence of customary law or as aids in interpreting provisions of U.S. law.

3. The Doctrine of Self-Executing Treaties

Though the Constitution states that treaties are supreme law of the land, courts have developed a doctrine that only self-executing clauses are judicially enforceable. Sometimes the rule is phrased in the alternative: treaty clauses are judicially enforceable if they either are self-executing or have been implemented by legislation. In the latter case it is the legislation and not the treaty that becomes enforceable.

The Supreme Court introduced the requirement of self-execution in *Foster v. Neilson*, 27 U.S. (2 Pet.) 253, 254 (1829). It declared that a treaty clause is self-executing and hence "equivalent to an act of the legislature, whenever it operates by itself without the aid of any legislative provision." Subsequent cases have focused on the intent of the parties. *See, e.g., Cook v. United States*, 288 U.S. 102, 119 (1933). In *Frolova v. U.S.S.R.*, 761 F.2d 370, 373 (7th Cir. 1985), the court compiled this list of factors to be consulted:

> 1) the language and purposes of the agreement as a whole; (2) the circumstance surrounding its execution; (3) the nature of the obligations imposed by the agreement; (4) the availability and feasibility of alternative enforcement mechanisms; (5) the implications of permitting a private right of action; and (6) the capability of the judiciary to resolve the dispute.

For a similar list see *People of Saipan v. U.S. Dep't of Interior*, 502 F.2d 90, 97 (9th Cir. 1974), *cert. denied*, 420 U.S. 1003 (1975).

The Restatement (Third) suggests that "the intention of the United States determines whether an agreement is to be self-executing in the United States or should await implementing legislation." 1 Restatement (Third) of the Foreign Relations of the United States § 131, comment h, at 58 (1987). If the intent is unclear, courts should look to "any statement by the President in concluding the agreement or in submitting it to the Senate for consent or to the Congress as a whole for approval, and of any expression by the Senate or by Congress in dealing with the agreement." *Id.*

In multilateral treaties parties rarely make clear the process by which they are expected to incorporate the treaty into national law. Countries have different methods of fulfilling international obligations, and few have incorporated treaties directly into national law or selectively incorporated them through the doctrine of self-execution.[9] Hence, the intent of the parties generally is neither a fruitful nor an appropriate inquiry.

The test that appears most relevant to multilateral human rights treaties is the three-step inquiry proposed by Professor Riesenfeld; namely that a treaty ought to be deemed self-executing if it "(a) involves the rights and duties of individuals; (b) does not cover a subject for which legislative action is required by the Constitution; and (c) does not leave discretion to the parties in the application of the particular provision." Riesenfeld, *The Doctrine of Self-Executing Treaties and Gatt: A Notable German Judgment*, 65 Am. J. Int'l L. 548, 550 (1970); *see also* Riesenfeld, *The Doctrine of Self-Executing Treaties and U.S. v. Postal: Win at Any Price?*, 74 Am. J. Int'l L. 892, 896 (1980). That approach was amplified in the following excerpt.

Burke et al., *Application of International Human Rights Law in State and Federal Courts*, 1983 Tex. Int'l L. J. 291, 302 (1983) (footnotes omitted):

> Whether or not a clause is self-executing depends, therefore, on what obligations the clause creates. If the obligation is merely to negotiate a supplementary contract or to seek legislative action, the clause is not self-executing. Examples of clauses that are not self-executing include articles 43(3) and 45 of the United Nations Charter, which create duties to negotiate supplementary contracts and seek legislative action. Simply because a provision requires future negotiation or legislative action does not, however, render it non-self-executing if the provision also creates specific obligations or proscribes certain acts. For example, articles 25, 100, and 105 of the United Nations Charter have been interpreted as self-executing because they require governments to perform or to refrain from certain acts, even though the same articles also require governments to negotiate supplementary contracts and seek legislative action. *See* Keeney v. United States, 218 F.2d 843 (D.C. Cir. 1954).

* * *

For example, Article 47 of the OAS Charter, excerpted in the accompanying handbook, has been held to be non-self-executing. It reads:

> The Member States will exert the greatest efforts, in accordance

---

[9] Countries that have a self-execution doctrine include Argentina, Austria, Belgium, Cyprus, Egypt, France, Federal Republic of Germany, Greece, Italy, Japan, Luxembourg, Malta, Mexico, the Netherlands, Spain, Switzerland, Turkey, and the European Communities. Lillich, *Invoking International Human Rights Law in Domestic Courts*, 54 Cin. L. Rev. 367, 373 n. 31 (1985).

with their constitutional processes, to ensure the effective exercise of the right to education, on the following bases:

(a) Elementary education, compulsory for children of school age, shall also be offered to all others who can benefit from it. When provided by the State it shall be without charge. . . .

That language, a trial court explained was

[n]ot the kind of promissory language which confers rights in the absence of implementing legislation. The parties have engaged to perform a particular act, that is, to exert the greatest efforts to advance the cause of education. They have not contracted to provide free public education to all children of school age within the country.[10]

Nonetheless, the court opined that, in the absence of the introductory paragraph, part (a) would "no doubt [be] sufficiently direct to imply the intention to create affirmative and judicially enforceable rights." *In re Alien Children Litigation, supra,* 501 F. Supp. at 590.

Diggs v. Shultz,[11] held that U.S. citizens denied entry to Rhodesia because of their race or who had suffered economic harm as a result of the government's racist policies were intended beneficiaries of a Security Council resolution directing all U.N. members to impose an embargo on trade with Rhodesia. Accordingly the citizens had standing to sue to enforce that resolution pursuant to Article 25 of the U.N. Charter, which reads: "The Members of the United Nations agree to accept and carry out the decisions of the Security Council."[12] Just as the U.N. resolution at issue in *Diggs* rendered Article 25 judicially enforceable, growing international

---

[10] *In re Alien Children Litigation,* 501 F. Supp. 544, 590 (S.D. Tex. 1980), *aff'd unreported mem.* (5th Cir. 1981), *aff'd sub nom. Plyler v. Doe,* 457 U.S. 202 (1982). The issue was the lawfulness of a Texas statute used to deny free elementary education to children of undocumented aliens. 501 F. Supp. at 549. Both the Supreme Court and the district court found that the statute violated equal protection. The Supreme Court, however, did not discuss the international law arguments. 501 F. Supp. at 583-84; 457 U.S. at 210-30.

[11] 470 F.2d 461 (D.C. Cir. 1972), *cert. denied,* 411 U.S. 931 (1973); *but see Diggs v. Richardson,* 555 F.2d 848, 850 (D.C. Cir. 1976), finding that a Security Council resolution prohibiting commerce with Namibia did not confer rights upon citizens.

[12] Ultimately, the court dismissed the claims on the separate ground that they presented a non-justiciable political question. Dismissal was based on the fact that, after adoption of the Security Council resolution, Congress passed legislation permitting importation of certain metals from Rhodesia under certain circumstances. The court decided that Congress intended to abrogate the U.S. treaty obligation and, accordingly, that plaintiffs' dispute was with Congress, not the Executive. 470 F.2d at 466.

recognition of various human rights should render relevant articles of the U.N. and OAS Charters self-executing.

Are courts likely to hold human rights clauses of the U.N. and OAS Charters to be self-executing? In *Sei Fujii v. California*, 38 Cal. 2d 718, 242 P.2d 617 (1952), the California Supreme Court declared that articles 55(c) and 56 of the U.N. Charter are not self-executing. Several commentators have urged that *Sei Fujii*'s analysis be rejected, and some courts have echoed that view.[13] Nonetheless, most federal and state courts continue to accept the *Sei Fujii* dictum uncritically. In particular, they explain that Articles 55 and 56 are phrased in general terms that are hortatory, not mandatory, and create obligations enforceable through political and diplomatic processes rather than by judicial intervention. *See Frolova, supra,* 761 F.2d at 374-75 and cases cited there.

Past decisions compel the conclusion that courts are unlikely to rule Articles 55 and 56 of the U.N. Charter to be self-executing. If courts did so rule, they likely would do so on the theory that various U.N. instruments, in particular the International Bill of Human Rights (the Universal Declaration of Human Rights, the Covenant on Civil and Political Rights, and the Covenant on Economic, Social and Cultural Rights), have become authoritative interpretations of Articles 55 and 56 and, accordingly, lend sufficient specificity to render those articles self-executing.[14] Judge Tanaka of the International Court of Justice endorsed this idea when he stated that "the Universal Declaration of Human Rights...although not binding

---

[13] *See, e.g.*, R. Lillich & F. Newman, *International Human Rights: Problems of Law and Policy* 76 (1979):

> [I]t would be most difficult to conclude that the Charter provisions on human rights cannot legitimately be given effect by the courts in appropriate cases. Indeed, it would be contrary to the letter and the spirit of the supremacy clause of the Constitution if the courts did not attempt to carry out a treaty provision to the fullest extent possible.

Quoted in Von Dardel v. U.S.S.R., 623 F. Supp. 246, 256 (D.D.C. 1985) *vacated on other grounds,* — F. Supp. —, 1990 WL 55813 (D.D.C. 1990); *see also People v. Mirmirani*, 30 Cal. 3d 375, 388 n. 1, 636 P.2d 1130, 1138 n. 1 (1981) (Newman, J., concurring) (statements in *Sei Fujii* concerning the non-self-executing character of U.N. Charter articles were dicta and thus of dubious precedential value even in California); Schluter, *The Domestic Status of the Human Rights Clauses of the United Nations Charter*, 61 Calif. L. Rev. 110, 162 n. 291 (1973). *But see People v. Ghent*, 43 Cal. 3d 739, 739 P.2d 1250, 1276 (1987) (affirming *Sei Fujii* in dictum, without analysis).

[14] The position, nicknamed the Newman-Berkeley thesis, has been urged by several human rights groups in amicus briefs. *See* Newman, *Interpreting the Human Rights Clauses of the U.N. Charter*, 1972 Revue des Droits de l'Homme 283; Lillich, *Invoking International Human Rights Law in Domestic Courts*, 54 Cin. L. Rev. 367, 373 n. 54 (1985); *see also* Burke et al, *Application of International Human Rights Law in State and Federal Courts*, 18 Tex. Int'l L. J. 291, 309-10 (1983).

in itself, constitutes evidence of the interpretation and application of the relevant Charter provisions...." South West Africa (Ethiopia v. South Africa, Liberia v. South Africa), 1966 I.C.J. 6, 293 (Tanaka, J., dissenting). The International Court of Justice declared in its 1971 Advisory Opinion on Namibia (formerly South West Africa) that South Africa had an obligation under the Charter of the United Nations to observe and respect human rights:

> Under the Charter of the United Nations, the former Mandatory [South Africa] had pledged itself to observe and respect, in a territory having an international status [that is, Namibia], human rights and fundamental freedoms for all without distinction as to race. To establish instead, and to enforce distinctions, exclusions, restrictions and limitations exclusively based on race, colour, descent or national or ethnic origin which constitute a denial of fundamental human rights is a flagrant violation of the purposes and principles of the Charter.[15]

Hence, the International Court of Justice recognized that the human rights provisions of the U.N. Charter establish binding obligations on all U.N. member states. In its judgment in the case of the U.S. Diplomatic Staff in Tehran, the International Court of Justice observed,

> Wrongfully to deprive human beings of their freedom and to subject them to physical constraint in conditions of hardship is in itself manifestly incompatible with the principles of the Charter of the United Nations, as well as with the fundamental principles enunciated in the Universal Declaration of Human Rights.[16]

Whether Articles 55 and 56 should be found to be self-executing as to a particular right would depend on whether language in the interpreting documents is sufficiently precise and generally accepted. For instance, Article 7 of the Covenant on Civil and Political Rights clearly is such an article. It provides:

> No one shall be subjected to torture or to cruel, inhuman or degrading treatment or punishment. In particular, no one shall be subjected without his free consent to medical or scientific experimentation.

That provision is both sufficiently precise and generally accepted. Yet no

---

[15] *Advisory Opinion on the Legal Consequences for States of the Continued Presence of South Africa in Namibia*, 1971 I.C.J. 16, 57. *See* Schwelb, *The International Court of Justice and the Human Rights Clauses of the Charter*, 66 Am. J. Int'l L. 337 (1972).

[16] *United States Diplomatic and Consular Staff in Tehran* (United States v. Iran), 1980 I.C.J. 3, 42; *see also* Memorial of the Government of the United States of America, *Case Concerning United States Diplomatic and Consular Staff in Tehran* (Jan. 1980), 1982 I.C.J. 121, 182 (Memorials, Pleadings, Documents).

U.S. court apparently has accepted the argument that the human rights clauses of the U.N. or OAS Charters are self-executing to any extent. Compare U.N. Charter Art. 2(4), which obliges all U.N. members to "refrain...from the threat or use of force against the territorial integrity... of any State." In *U.S. v. Toscanino*, 500 F.2d 267, 277 (2d Cir. 1974), the court found that Article 2(4) would be violated and dismissal of the indictment required if U.S. agents participated in the seizure and ill-treatment of an alien from Uruguay (with which the U.S. had an extradiction treaty) in order to bring him to the U.S. for prosecution. Article 2(4) was found to be sufficiently precise to impose judicially enforceable obligations owing to a Security Council resolution that had condemned as a violation of Article 2(4) the kidnapping in 1960 of Adolf Eichmann from Argentina by Israeli "volunteers." On remand, the trial court concluded that U.S. agents had not participated in the seizure and that the prosecution could proceed. *U.S. v. Toscanino*, 398 F. Supp. 916 (E.D.N.Y. 1975).

Several courts have considered provisions of the Geneva Convention Relative to the Protection of Civilian Persons in Time of War (Fourth Geneva Convention) of 1949 to be non-self-executing. *See, e.g., Tel-Oren v. Libyan Arab Republic*, 726 F.2d 774, 809 (Bork, J., concurring); *Huynh Thi Anh v. Levi*, 586 F.2d 625, 629 (9th Cir. 1978). Below are excerpts from a much-cited decision of the U.S. Board of Immigration Appeals in *Matter of Medina* rejecting the contention that aliens may not be deported to countries whose governments are unable or unwilling to safeguard rights guaranteed by the Geneva Conventions and from an amicus brief urging that relevant treaty clauses be ruled self-executing.

Matter of Medina, Interim Decision No. 3078 (Board of Immigration Appeals 1988):

BY: Milhollan, Chairman; Dunne, Morris, and Vacca, Board Members

On July 25, 1985, the immigration judge entered a decision that found the respondent deportable as charged, denied her applications for asylum and withholding of deportation and for relief under the Geneva Conventions of 1949, but granted her the privilege of voluntary departure. The immigration judge certified his decision in this case to the Board . . . in view of his findings regarding "unusually complex and novel questions of law." Along with the briefs of respondent and the Immigration and Naturalization Service on certification, the American Civil Liberties Union, the Lawyer's Committee for International Human Rights, and the Department of State submitted amicus curiae briefs. The decision of the immigration judge will be affirmed in part and reversed in part.

The respondent is a 26-year-old single female, a native and citizen of El Salvador, who entered the United States without inspection in November 1980, at Hildago, Texas. . . .

At her deportation hearing, the respondent applied for asylum and withholding of deportation under sections 208(a) and 243(h) of the Act, 8 U.S.C. §§ 1158(a) and 1253(h) (1982). She also sought relief from deportation under the provisions of the Geneva Convention Relative to the Protection of Civilian Persons in Time of War ("the Fourth Convention" or "the Convention").

...For the reasons set forth below, we find that the immigration judge erred in holding that the Fourth Convention creates a basis for relief from deportation that can be advanced by a respondent in deportation proceedings before an immigration judge.

I.   *The Fourth Convention*

(a)   *Scope of Articles 1 and 3*

The Fourth Convention was the first Geneva convention to address the protection of civilians in time of war....

Article 3 provides:

> In the case of armed conflict not of an international character occurring in the territory of one of the High Contracting Parties, each Party to the conflict shall be bound to apply, as a minimum, the following provisions:
>
> (1) Persons taking no active part in the hostilities, including members of armed forces who have laid down their arms and those placed *hors de combat* by sickness, wounds, detention, or any other cause, shall in all circumstances be treated humanely, without any adverse distinction founded on race, colour, religion or faith, sex, birth or wealth, or any other similar criteria.
>
> To this end, the following acts are and shall remain prohibited at any time and in any place whatsoever with respect to the above-mentioned persons:
>
> > (a) violence to life and person, in particular murder of all kinds, mutilation, cruel treatment and torture;
> >
> > (b) taking of hostages;
> >
> > (c) outrages upon personal dignity, in particular humiliating and degrading treatment;
> >
> > (d) the passing of sentences and the carrying out of executions without previous judgment pronounced by a regularly constituted court, affording all the judicial guarantees which are recognized as indispensable by civilized peoples.
>
> (2) The wounded and sick shall be collected and cared for....

From its plain language, it is apparent that Article 3, which does not refer to the repatriation of displaced persons, applies only to *each party* to a non-international conflict. Since it binds only the parties to the conflict (in this case the Government of El Salvador and the guerrillas), by its terms it does not apply to the United States, which the respondent does not assert is a party to the conflict.

...Article 1, one of the shortest articles of the Convention, provides:

> The High Contracting Parties undertake to respect and ensure respect for the present Convention in all circumstances....

...[W]ithin the context of the Convention itself, it is doubtful whether Article 1 was intended to impose an affirmative duty on States of the nature argued by the respondent with regard to possible violations of Article 3 by other States, particularly those not under their control.

(b)   *"Self-Execution" of Article 1*

In any event, however, we cannot conclude that Article 1 of the Convention is "self-executing," as that term has been used to refer to the creation by treaty of rights that are privately enforceable by individuals in the absence of implementing legislation. We agree with the Government that the language of Article 1 (*i.e.*, that parties "undertake to respect and ensure respect" for the Convention) does not evince an intent to create judicially enforceable rights in private persons. The Article addresses itself to the political rather than the judicial branch of government and uses language suggesting declarations of principle, rather than a code of privately enforceable legal rights. The language is akin to that in various provisions of the United Nations Charter long held not to be self-executing. . . . Moreover, the nature of the requirement to "ensure respect" for the Convention raises foreign policy issues committed to the political branch of government and not delegated to the immigration judges or this Board. It is "essentially the kind of standard that is rooted in diplomacy and its incidents, rather than in conventional adjudication." *Diggs v. Richardson*, 555 F.2d 848, 851 (D.C. Cir. 1976).

We further note that the Convention sets forth a specific mechanism for inquiries to be instituted into alleged violations of its provisions (Article 149) and reflects that signatory states will take measures through their own laws to enforce its provisions (Articles 145 and 146). Treaties that call for implementing legislation have been found by federal courts not to be "self-executing." *See In re Demjanjuk v. Meese*, 784 F.2d 1114, 1116 (D.C. Cir. 1986). . . .

* * *

The amicus brief submitted by the American Civil Liberties Union in *Medina* asserted that the treaty provisions of the Geneva Convention IV were self-executing. Pertinent arguments follow: . . .

Immigration Judges Must Refuse to Deport Salvadorans to El Salvador to Ensure Respect for Geneva Convention.

1.   *The Applicable Treaty Norms.*

Respondent's treaty-based arguments are founded upon Article 1 of Geneva Convention IV . . .

Common Article 3 of the Convention prescribes the protections which must be provided to civilians during non-international armed conflict. . . .

Article 147 of the Convention further provides:

Grave breaches to which the preceding Article relates shall be those involving any of the following acts, if committed against persons or property protected by the present Convention: . . . unlawful deportation or transfer or unlawful confinement of a protected person, compelling a protected person to serve in the forces of a hostile power. . . .

The United States has acknowledged that norms protected by Common Article 3 of the Geneva Conventions are not being respected in El Salvador. . . .

The United States' forcible repatriation of civilians fleeing internal armed conflict in El Salvador contributes to additional violations and violates the treaty obligation to "ensure respect" for humanitarian law. . . .

2. *Treaties Are Self-Executing When They Contain a Rule by Which the Rights of Individuals Can be Determined, Unless There is a Clear Intent to the Contrary.*

The United States Constitution proclaims treaties to be the "supreme law of the Land,": U.S. Const. Art. VI § 2, and it has long been recognized that private parties can enforce the provisions of a treaty to which the United States is a party. In 1884 the Supreme Court stated:

> A treaty may...contain provisions which confer certain rights upon the citizens or subjects of one of the Nations residing in the territorial limits of the other, which partake of the nature of municipal law, and which are capable of enforcement as between private parties in the courts of the country.

The *Head Money Cases*, 112 U.S. [580, 598] (1884).

The issue for the courts is one of intent. *Foster v. Neilson*, 27 U.S. (2 Pet.) 253, 314 (1829). Moreover, the issue is one of intent as reflected in the specific treaty provisions at issue. Certain provisions in a treaty can be self-executing while others in the same treaty are not. Compare, *Sei Fujii v. State*...(Arts. 55 and 56 of the United Nations Charter are not self-executing) and *Curran v. City of New York*, 191 Misc. 229, 77 N.Y.S.2d 206 (1947) (Arts. 104 and 105 of the Charter are self-executing). . . .

In determining whether the provisions of a treaty are intended to be self-executing, courts look first to the language of the treaty. If the treaty provisions establish rights and duties of individuals, then they should be held to be self-executing, unless the treaty expresses a clear intent to the contrary. As the Supreme Court has stated,

> A treaty...is a law of the land as an Act of Congress is, whenever its provisions prescribe a rule by which the rights of the private citizen or subject may be determined.

The *Head Money Cases*, [112 U.S. at 598-99]. The *Restatement (Revised) Foreign Relations Law of United States*, § 131, Reporters Vol. 5 (1980) expresses this same rule in a slightly more general fashion:

> In general, agreements which can be readily given effect by executive or judicial bodies, federal or state, without further federal legislation, are deemed self-executing, unless a contrary intention is manifest....
> This has been true from early in our history....

In some cases it may be difficult to determine that a treaty provision has "the mandatory quality and definiteness that would indicate the States' intent to create judiciable rights in private persons immediately upon ratification." *Sei Fujii, supra*, 242 P.2d at 622. Nevertheless, usually treaties are "self-executing." *Amaya v. Stanolind Oil & Gas*, 158 F.2d 554, 556 (5th Cir. 1946), *cert. denied*, 331 U.S. 808 (1947). For example, in *People of Saipan v. United States Department of Interior*, 502 F.2d 90 (9th Cir. 1974), [the U.S. Court of Appeals] considered whether Article VI of the Trusteeship Agreement for the Pacific Islands, 61 Stat. 3301, was self-executing. Article VI requires the United States to "promote the economic advancement and self-sufficiency of the inhabitants, and to this end...regulate the use of natural resources" and to "protect the inhabitants against the loss of the their lands and resources. . . ." The plaintiffs in *Saipan* had brought an action to enjoin the construction of operation of a hotel on public land in *Saipan* until the environmental impact had been studied and evaluated. In holding the treaty to be self-executing, [the] court enunciated the following test for self-execution:

> The extent to which an international agreement established affirmative and judicially enforceable obligations without implementing legislation must be determined in each case by reference to any contextual factors: the purposes of the treaty and the objectives of its creators, the existence of domestic procedures and institutions appropriate for direct implementation, the availability and feasibility of alternative enforcement methods, and the immediate and long-range social consequences of self- or non-self execution.

Saipan, supra, 502 F.2d at 97. [The Court of Appeals] held that though the substantive rights guaranteed through the Trusteeship Agreement were not precisely defined, the Agreement was capable of judicial enforcement.

> Its language is no more general than such terms as "due process of law," "seaworthiness," "equal protection of the law," "good faith," or "restraint," which courts interpret every day.

Thus, it is only in the exceptional case that a treaty provision will be found to be non-self-executing. . . .

Amicus submits that the obligation not to return people to countries in which "grave breaches" of the Geneva Convention IV are occurring is so clear and so central to the overwhelming purpose of the Convention that the treaty provisions must be found to be "self-executing," unless congressional intent to the contrary is clear.

3.   *There is no Clear Intent that Articles 1, 3 and 147 of Geneva Convention IV Are "Non-Self-Executing."*

The Government has adduced no clear evidence that Congress intended Geneva Convention IV to be entirely "non-self-executing." Instead the Government argues that the Refugee Act of 1980 provides the exclusive avenue for the rights of refugees in the United States. However, the Government has cited to no passage in the legislative history of the Refugee Act of 1980 in which Geneva Convention IV is considered. . . .

4. Reservations

Chapters 7 and 9, *supra*, discuss the reservations, understandings, and declarations the Carter administration proposed to the Senate for attachment to its advice and consent to ratification of various human rights treaties. *See Four Treaties Pertaining to Human Rights: Message from the President of the United States*, 95th Cong., 2d Sess. (1978). Several proposed limitations to the Covenant on Civil and Political Rights may be relevant to the case of youths in detention. For example, the Carter Administration proposed a statement about Article 10 of the Covenant on Civil and Political Rights that would permit the U.S. progressively, rather than immediately, to achieve the separation in prison of accused individuals from convicted persons, and the separation of adults from juveniles. *Id.* at VII.

In assessing the proposed limitations, the Vienna Convention on the Law of Treaties, Art. 2(1)(d), 1155 U.N.T.S. 331, T.S. No. 58 (1980), 8 I.L.M. 679 (1979), *entered into force* January 27, 1980, defines a reservation as a "unilateral statement, however phrased or named, made by a state, when signing, ratifying, accepting, approving or acceding to a treaty, whereby it purports to exclude or to modify the legal effect of certain provisons of the treaty in their application to that state...." 14 M. Whiteman, Digest of International Law § 17, at 137-38 (1970), provides basic definitions of the terms "understanding," "declaration," and "statement":

The term "understanding" is often used to designate a statement when it is not intended to modify or limit any of the provisions of the treaty in its international operation but is intended merely to clarify or explain or to deal with some matter incidental to the operation of the treaty in a manner other than as a substantive reservation....

The terms "declaration" and "statement" are used most often when it is considered essential or desirable to give notice of certain matters of policy or principle, without an intention of derogating from the substantive rights or obligations stipulated in the treaty.

The International Court of Justice has delineated, in its *Advisory Opinion on Reservations to the Genocide Convention*, 1951 I.C.J. 16, 24, an authoritative standard for the assertion of reservations to a multilateral human rights treaty:

Object and purpose of the Convention limit both the freedom of making reservations and that of objecting to them. It follows that it is the compatibility of a reservation with the object and purpose of the Convention that must furnish the criterion for the attitude of a State in making the reservation or accession as well as for the appraisal by a State in objecting to the reservation.

Article 19 of the Vienna Convention on Treaties has codified the principle by providing that "A state may, when signing, ratifying, accepting, approving or acceding to a treaty, formulate a reservation unless...the reservation is incompatible with the object and purpose of the treaty."

Article 20 of the Vienna Convention establishes the process for governments to make objections to reservations to treaties. Articles 20 and 21 indicate that objections by other governments to particular reservations will not preclude the entry into force of the treaty. Unless an objecting government otherwise specifies, the treaty can go into force between the reserving and the objecting governments but the provisions to which the reservation relates do not apply as between those governments.

The use of extensive limitations to minimize the effect of a treaty on domestic practices of parties may contravene established principles of international law. The Vienna Convention on Treaties restates in Article 27 the fundamental relationship between domestic and treaty law: "A party may not invoke the provisions of its domestic law as justification for its failure to perform a treaty." Although the U.S. government could formally evade this rule by incorporating domestic law into the treaty by way of reservation or other limitations, such an attempt would violate the spirit of Article 27.

In the *Belilos Case*, 132 Eur. Ct. H.R. (ser. A) (1988), the European Court of Human Rights held an "interpretive declaration" to the European Convention on Human Rights to constitute a reservation and then held that reservation invalid as a reservation of a "general character" not permitted by Article 64 of the European Convention. *See* Bourguignon, *The Belilos Case: New Light on Reservations to Multilateral Treaties*, 29 Virginia J. Int'l L. 347 (1989).

Here is an excerpt from a critique of two limitations proposed by the Carter administration.

Weissbrodt, *United States Ratification of the Human Rights Covenants*, 63 Minn. L. Rev. 35, 63-72 (1978) (footnotes omitted):

...FEDERALISM

Article 28 of the Civil and Political Covenant...state[s], "The provisions of the present Covenant shall extend to all parts of federal States without any limitations or exceptions." The February 23rd letter [of the Carter Administration] proposes reservations that directly conflict with the language of Article...28... and thus would substantially limit the impact of the Covenants on state governments within the United States:

> The United States shall...implement all the provisions of the Covenant over whose subject matter the Federal Government exercises legislative and judicial jurisdiction; with respect to the provisions over whose subject matter constituent units exercise jurisdiction, the Federal Government shall take appropriate measures, to the end that the competent authorities of the constituent units may take appropriate measures for the fulfillment of this Covenant.

This reservation might be found unacceptable under international law as vitiating an essential component of the treaty....

Beyond this potential problem, there is considerable question about the need for such a reservation. In the early negotiations leading to the drafting of the Human Rights Covenants and other international agreements relating to human rights, the United States at first insisted upon treaty language that would have exempted the states from the impact of these treaties. Later, as the force of states' rights positions in this country decreased, United States representatives dropped their insistence upon such a federal-state clause. The proposed reservation reasserted this anachronistic concern.

Although there may have been some doubt in the early 1950's as to the authority of the federal government to legislate in many of the areas covered by the Covenants, those doubts have been resolved largely in favor of federal power. In view of the civil rights legislation of the past twenty years, it is clear that the federal government has the power under the commerce clause, as well as the enforcement clauses of the thirteenth, fourteenth, and fifteenth amendments to legislate in the areas covered by the Covenants. Only where the federal government attempts to interfere in "integral governmental functions of [state] bodies," such as the relations between a state and its employees, would there now be any question of federal legislative authority.

Furthermore, if there remains any residual doubt about federal authority, the Supreme Court's decision in *Missouri v. Holland* [252 U.S. 416, 432-34 (1920)] would support the Human Rights Covenants as valid exercises of the treaty power, even without other basis for federal action. In *Missouri v. Holland*, the Court rejected the argument that "what an act of Congress could not do unaided, in derogation of the powers reserved to the States, a treaty cannot do." Instead, the Court noted that under the Constitution "Acts of Congress are the supreme law of the land only when made in pursuance of the Constitution, while treaties are declared to be so when made under the authority of the United States." The Court then concluded that since the treaty did not contravene any express prohibition of the Constitution, it was not invalid simply because it might infringe on rights otherwise reserved to the states under the tenth amendment....

SELF-EXECUTING NATURE OF THE COVENANTS

...Whether or not a treaty is self-executing — and, therefore, to be treated as law without the need for legislative action — is initially a question for the President, who is constitutionally obligated to "take Care that the Laws be faithfully executed." But, while the views of the Executive are given great weight, the issue has been considered as ultimately one for the courts, which must determine whether to give the treaty effect as law without legislative implementation.

The February 23rd letter, however, attempts to remove this difficult issue from the courts by asserting a declaration to both treaties that the Covenants are not self-executing. The effect of this declaration is to deprive American courts of their most potent technique for contributing meaningfully to the interpretation of the Human Rights Covenants. If the Covenants are self-executing, litigants may use these treaties to support their positions. In furthering their specific interests, litigants may discover many possible applications for the Covenants that might otherwise be overlooked by the slow moving and very rudimentary international enforcement procedures established by the Covenants. [Because human rights abuses are prevalent throughout the world, the international procedures can probably be expected to focus only on the most serious human rights problems.] If the Covenants are self-executing, however, every lawyer in the United States is potentially an advocate for human rights. The final result of making the Covenants not self-executing can only be to diminish substantially the impact of the treaties in the United States....

Because much of the language in the Covenants denotes self-execution, and because self-execution provides an effective means of enforcement, it is improper for the United States to assert a declaration that categorically denies that effect. Just as United States courts have examined each article of the United Nations Charter separately to determine its self-executing effect, so too should the courts be allowed to consider each Article of the Covenant on Civil and Political Rights.

5. Implementing Legislation: The U.S. Refugee Act of 1980

The U.N. Protocol Relating to the Status of Refugees, 606 U.N.T.S.

267, 19 U.S.T. 6223, T.I.A.S. No. 6577, *entered into force* Oct. 4, 1967, is a human rights treaty that the Supreme Court concluded did include a self-executing clause. In *INS v. Cardoza-Fonseca*, 480 U.S. 421 (1987), the Court discussed Article 33.1 of the U.N. Convention Relating to the Status of Refugees, which is binding on the U.S. via incorporation in the U.N. Protocol. The court noted that Article 33.1 precluded the Attorney General, between 1968 when the U.S. ratified the Protocol and 1980 when Congress passed implementing legislation, from deporting people who met the definition of "refugee" set forth in the Refugee Convention.

The main lesson of *Cardoza-Fonseca*, however, is that once implementing legislation is passed it is the statute and not the treaty that will be applied. Moreover, though the Refugee Act of 1980 was enacted to bring the U.S. into compliance with its obligations under the U.N. Protocol, in construing the Refugee Act courts have looked to the content of the Protocol as internationally recognized in 1980 rather than as recognized at the time of the acts they are asked to adjudicate. Limiting the Refugee Act to the understanding of the Protocol in 1980 may fly in the face of the principle that courts must interpret international law not as it was understood at the time it was incorporated into U.S. law but "as it has evolved and exists among the nations of the world today." *Filartiga v. Peña-Irala*, 630 F.2d 876, 881 (2d Cir. 1980), discussed *infra*.

NOTES AND QUESTIONS

1. See part I of this chapter *infra* for discussion of the rights of Salvadorans seeking asylum under customary law.

2. The Board of Immigration Appeal's conclusion that Article 1 of the Fourth Geneva Convention is not self-executing was endorsed by Judge Peckham, then Presiding Judge of the District Court for the Northern District of California, in *American Baptist Churches v. Meese*, 712 F. Supp. 756 (N.D. Cal. 1989). He further agreed that Article 3 did not apply to the U.S. in deportation cases regarding Salvadorans because it restrains only the parties to non-international armed conflicts.

3. Judge Peckham nonetheless did uphold one very significant cause of action based on the Refugee Act. He agreed to allow plaintiff aliens to try to establish at trial that their right to equal protection had been violated by the Attorney General's practice of considering nationality in making decisions concerning withholding of deportation and asylum. To establish impermissible discrimination the refugees will have to show that: (1) Congress has not authorized the Attorney General to consider an alien's nationality in applying withholding of deportation and asylum provisions and (2) the Attorney General did, in fact, apply those statutes in a manner that discriminated on the basis of nationality. The court expressly rejected the aliens' argument that in applying Fifth Amendment protections it should be guided by international law principles. *Id.* at 774 n. 12. Rather, the court will look primarily at what Congress intended in enacting the Refugee Act.

If the aliens succeed at trial, they could win landmark relief for most Salvadorans and Guatemalans currently in the U.S. In particular, the U.S. government could be required to propose and implement "a plan for the orderly, non-discriminatory and procedurally fair reprocessing of all denied political asylum applications of Salvadorans and Guatemalans filed subsequent to 1980." *Id.* at 773-74.

4. What factual circumstances would strengthen a Salvadoran's claim to asylum under Articles 1 and 3 of the Fourth Geneva Convention?

5. The courts in *INS v. Cardoza-Fonseca*, 480 U.S. 421 (1987), and *American Baptist Churches v. Meese*, 712 F. Supp. 756 (N.D. Cal. 1989), assumed that they are to construe the Refugee Act in light of the international understanding of the U.N. Protocol in 1980. Do you think that courts are compelled to do so? That they should do so? If courts are to limit construction of implementing legislation to international understanding at the time of the legislation's enactment, in what sense are they applying the treaty?

6. In *Canas-Segovia v. I.N.S.*, _____ F.2d _____ (9th Cir. 1990), the Ninth Circuit relied principally upon the UNHCR, Handbook on Procedures And Criteria for Determining Refugee Status (1979) in interpreting both the U.N. Protocol Relating to the Status of Refugees, *supra,* which entered into force in 1967 and to which the U.S. acceded in 1968, and the Refugee Act of 1980.

7. In *United States v. Aguilar*, 871 F.2d 1436 (9th Cir. 1989), amended August 14, 1989, a panel of the Ninth Circuit, relying on a Supreme Court footnote, pronounced that "[t]he Protocol was not intended to be self-executing." *Id.* at 1454. The panel continued: "As the Protocol is not a self-executing treaty having the force of law, it is only helpful as a guide to Congress's statutory intent in enacting the 1980 Refugee Act." The footnote on which the panel relied states merely that "the language of Article 34 was precatory and not self-executing." *INS v. Stevic*, 467 U.S. 407, 428 n. 22 (1984). Did the *Aguilar* panel properly conclude that therefore "[t]he Protocol was not intended to be self-executing"?

8. The following cases ruled human rights clauses of treaties to be self-executing: *Clark v. Allen*, 331 U.S. 503 (1947) (treaty gave aliens rights relating to inheritance of property in U.S.); *Asakura v. Seattle*, 225 U.S. 332 (1924) (treaty granted alien equal right to engage in trade); *People of Saipan v. U.S. Dep't of Interior*, 502 F.2d 90, 97 (9th Cir. 1974), *cert. denied*, 420 U.S. 1003 (1975); *Von Dardel v. U.S.S.R.*, 623 F. Supp. 246, 256 (D.D.C. 1985) *vacated on other grounds,* _____ F. _____ , 1990 WL 55813 (D.D.C. 1990); *Curran v. City of New York*, 191 Misc. 229, 77 N.Y.S.2d 206 (1947) (U.N. Charter Arts. 104 and 105).

9. Cases that have found human rights clauses of treaties to be non-self-executing include the following: *Demjanjuk v. Meese*, 784 F.2d 1114, 1116 (D.C. Cir. 1986); *Frolova v. U.S.S.R.*, 761 F.2d 370, 374-76 (7th Cir. 1985) (U.N. Charter Arts. 55 and 56); *Filartiga v. Peña-Irala*, 630 F.2d 876, 881-82 n. 9 (2d Cir. 1980) (U.N. Charter Arts. 55 and 56); *Anh v. Levi*, 586 F.2d 625, 629 (6th Cir. 1978) (treaty language relied on was "very general . . . and does not answer the custody question presented by this case"); *United States v. Postal*, 589 F.2d 862, 876-77 (5th Cir.), *cert. denied*, 444 U.S. 832 (1979); *Handel v. Artukovic*, 601 F. Supp. 1421, 1425 (C.D. Cal. 1985); *Haitian Refugee Center v. Gracey*, 600 F. Supp. 1396, 1406 (D.D.C. 1985), *aff'd on other grounds*, 809 F.2d 794 (D.C. Cir. 1987); *Bertrand v. Sava*, 684 F.2d 204, 218-19 (2d Cir. 1982).

10. See Weston, *The Place of Foreign Treaties in the Courts of the United States: A Reply to Louis Henkin*, 101 Harv. L. Rev. 511 (1987), and Henkin, *Lexical Priority or "Political Question: A Response*, 101 Harv. L. Rev. 524 (1987), for different views regarding the relation between treaties and U.S. law; *see also* Iwasawa, *The Doctrine of Self-Executing Treaties in the United States: A Critical Analysis*, 26 Va. J. Int'l L. 627 (1986); Paust, *Self-Executing Treaties*, 82 Am. J. Int'l L. 760 (1983).

11. For arguments that Articles 1 and 3 of the Fourth Geneva Convention are self-executing, see Kravitz, *Beyond Asylum and Witholding of Deportation: A Framework for Relief Under Geneva Convention IV of 1949*, 1 Temple Int'l & Comp. L.J. 263 (1987).

I. CUSTOMARY INTERNATIONAL LAW

In addition to treaty law federal and state courts are bound to apply customary international law, subject to restrictions created by statute and judicial precedent.

Customary norms often reflect a general practice of governments accepted as law.[17] Only widespread, rather than unanimous, acquiescence is needed; and acquiescence may occur in a short period of time. I. Brownlie, Principles of Public International Law 6-7 (3d ed. 1979); 1 Restatement (Third) of the Foreign Relations Law of the United States § 102, comment b (1987) ("there is no precise formula to indicate how widespread a practice must be, but it should reflect wide acceptance among the states particularly involved in the relevant activity"). Generally there are disagreements as to precisely when a practice has ripened into a norm.

Government practice in negotiating and approving international instru-

---

[17] *North Sea Continental Shelf Cases* (W. Ger. v. Den.; W. Ger. v. Neth.), 1969 I.C.J. 3, 44; *Asylum Case* (Colum. v. Peru), 1950 I.C.J. 266, 276-77; *see also* Perluss and Hartman, *Temporary Refuge: Emergence of a Customary Norm*, 26 Va. J. Int'l L. 551, 554-58 (1986).

ments has been accorded an increasingly important role in the development of customary law. In the human rights field wide acceptance of treaties, declarations, resolutions, and other instruments arguably has become more significant than traditional practice in creating law. 2 Restatement (Third) of the Foreign Relations Law of the United States § 702 (1987). Authority for that development inheres in Article 38(1)(c) of the International Court's Statute, which directs the Court to apply "the general principles of law recognized by civilized nations."

A customary norm binds all governments, including those that have not recognized it, so long as they have not expressly and persistently objected to its development. 1 Restatement (Third), § 102, comment d; *North Sea Continental Shelf Cases* (W. Ger. v. Den.; W. Ger. v. Neth.), 1969 I.C.J. 3, 41-44 (1969). Customary norms thus differ from treaty clauses, which bind only the parties to the treaties.

The Supreme Court has declared that customary law is "part of our law, and must be ascertained and administered by the courts of justice of appropriate jurisdiction, as often as questions of right depending upon it are duly presented for their determination." *The Paquete Habana*, 175 U.S. 677, 700 (1900). More recently the Court acknowledged the "frequently reiterated" principle that federal common law is necessarily informed by international law. *First National City Bank v. Banco Para el Comercio Exterior de Cuba*, 462 U.S. 611, 623 (1983).

A court faces several issues when confronted with the argument that it should apply a customary norm. It must decide first whether the asserted rule has indeed ripened into a norm. If it has, a second, separate inquiry is whether the norm is judicially enforceable. Although customary and treaty law are accorded the same status under international law, *see* Restatement (Third) of the Foreign Relations Law of the United States § 111 (1987), U.S. courts have treated them differently in certain important respects. Courts have upheld norms, as they have treaty clauses, in the face of inconsistent state and local laws, and have tried to construe customary norms and federal statutes so as to give effect to both. Nonetheless, when courts have found that a customary norm conflicts with a federal statute or executive act, they generally have given effect to the legislative or executive act even when the norm arguably crystallized after the act's adoption. *See Garcia-Mir v. Meese*, 788 F.2d 1446 (11th Cir.), *cert. denied sub nom. Ferrer-Mazorra v. Meese*, 479 U.S. 889 (1986); *United States v. Aguilar*, 871 F.2d 1436, 1454 (9th Cir. 1989), amended August 14, 1989; *American Baptist Churches v. Meese*, 712 F. Supp. 756, 771-73 (N.D. Cal. 1989). Commentators have criticized those decisions on the ground that judicially enforceable norms should be accorded the same status as self-executing treaty clauses, that the later-in-time rule should prevail, and that executive acts should preempt customary norms only when the President exercises constitutional powers, *i.e.*, as commander-in-chief or as chief diplomat. *See* Kirgis, *Federal Statutes, Executive Orders* and *"Self-Executing Custom" (Cont'd)*, 81 AM. J. Int'l L. 371 (1987), excerpted in Part J, *infra*.

If a person invokes the norm as a defense to detention, deportation, or criminal prosecution, as discussed in the *Echeverria* brief and the necessity-defense cases, *infra* in part J, he or she may not need to show that the norm meets the higher test required to establish an international tort. No court has adequately addressed that issue, however. In this context, courts will also consider whether any congressional, executive, or judicial act bars application of the norm.

If the norm is invoked in an action against a current or former foreign official, the court must decide whether the defendant is protected by the act of state doctrine, discussed in part J, below. If the norm is invoked against a foreign sovereign, the court must decide whether the Foreign Sovereign Immunities Act bars the claim.

If the norm is invoked in a case brought by or against the U.S. government, other questions must be addressed. If there are foreign policy issues, a court may abstain from asserting jurisdiction because of the political question doctrine. But judges increasingly have chosen not to dismiss claims of injury on political question grounds and instead have focused on sovereign immunity, failure to state a cause of action, or lack of standing.

1. Identification of Customary Norms

To determine whether a rule has achieved the status of a customary norm judges often begin with the Supreme Court's enumeration of sources of law set forth in *United States v. Smith*, 18 U.S. (5 Wheat.) 153 (1820): "The law of nations ... may be ascertained by consulting the works of jurists, writing professedly on public law; or by the general usage and practice of nations; or by judicial decisions recognizing and enforcing that law." *Id.* at 160-61. One of the most important principles is that new norms must be applied as they emerge. *E.g.*, *Filartiga*, 630 F.2d at 881; *Forti I*, 672 F. Supp. at 1539. Hence, a conclusion that a rule has not achieved the status of a customary norm should not discourage lawyers from relitigating the issue after a period of time, assuming subsequent state practice or other evidence of the norm's development.

Some courts have imposed the further requirement, where a norm is invoked as the basis of an international tort, that the norm must be "universal, definable, and obligatory." *Forti v. Suarez-Mason (Forti I)*, 672 F. Supp. 1531, 1540 (N.D. Cal. 1987), excerpted below. To meet that test, a plaintiff "need not establish unanimity among nations ... [but only] a general recognition among states that a specific practice is prohibited." *Forti v. Suarez-Mason (Forti II)*, 694 F. Supp. 707, 709 (N.D. Cal. 1988). Nonetheless, the test appears to require more than the widespread acquiescence needed to establish a customary norm.

While reading the following excerpts, consider the sources of international law courts discuss and the varying weight attached to different sources.

Filartiga v. Peña-Irala, 630 F.2d 876 (2d Cir. 1980) (footnotes omitted):

Before FEINBERG, Chief Judge, KAUFMAN and KEARSE, Circuit Judges.

IRVING R. KAUFMAN, Circuit Judge . . .

I

The appellants, plaintiffs below, are citizens of the Republic of Paraguay. Dr. Joel Filartiga, a physician, describes himself as a longstanding opponent of the government of President Alfredo Stroessner, which has held power in Paraguay since 1954. His daughter, Dolly Filartiga, arrived in the United States in 1978 under a visitor's visa, and has since applied for permanent political asylum. The Filartigas brought this action in the Eastern District of New York against Americo Norberto Peña-Irala (Peña), also a citizen of Paraguay, for wrongfully causing the death of Dr. Filartiga's seventeen-year old son, Joelito. Because the district court dismissed the action for want of subject matter jurisdiction, we must accept as true the allegations contained in the Filartigas' complaint and affidavits for purposes of this appeal.

The appellants contend that on March 29, 1976, Joelito Filartiga was kidnapped and tortured to death by Peña, who was then Inspector General of Police in Asuncion, Paraguay. Later that day, the police brought Dolly Filartiga to Peña's home where she was confronted with the body of her brother, which evidenced marks of severe torture. As she fled, horrified, from the house, Peña followed after her shouting, "Here you have what you have been looking for for so long and what you deserve. Now shut up." The Filartigas claim that Joelito was tortured and killed in retaliation for his father's political activities and beliefs.

Shortly thereafter, Dr. Filartiga commenced a criminal action in the Paraguayan courts against Peña and the police for the murder of his son. As a result, Dr. Filartiga's attorney was arrested and brought to police headquarters where, shackled to a wall, Peña threatened him with death. This attorney, it is alleged, has since been disbarred without just cause. . . .

In July of 1978, Peña sold his house in Paraguay and entered the United States under a visitor's visa. He was accompanied by Juana Bautista Fernandez Villalba, who had lived with him in Paraguay. The couple remained in the United States beyond the term of their visas, and were living in Brooklyn, New York, when Dolly Filartiga, who was then living in Washington, D.C., learned of their presence. Acting on information provided by Dolly the Immigration and Naturalization Service arrested Peña and his companion, both of whom were subsequently ordered deported on April 5, 1979, following a hearing. They had then resided in the United States for more than nine months.

Almost immediately, Dolly caused Peña to be served with a summons and civil complaint at the Brooklyn Navy Yard, where he was being held pending deportation. The complaint alleged that Peña had wrongfully caused Joelito's death by torture and sought compensatory and punitive damages of $10,000,000. The Filartigas also sought to enjoin Peña's deportation to ensure his availability for testimony at trial. The cause of action is stated as arising under "wrongful death statutes; the U.N. Charter; the Universal Declaration on Human Rights; the U.N. Declaration Against Torture; the American Declaration of the Rights and Duties of Man; and other pertinent declarations, documents and practices constituting the customary international law of human rights and the law of nations," as well as 28 U.S.C. § 1350, Article II, sec. 2 and the Supremacy Clause of the U.S. Constitution. Jurisdiction is claimed under the general federal question provision, 28 U.S.C. § 1331, and, principally on this appeal, under the Alien Tort Statute, 28 U.S.C. § 1350.

Judge Nickerson stayed the order of deportation, and Peña immediately moved to dismiss the complaint on the grounds that subject matter jurisdiction was absent and for *forum non conveniens. . . .*

Judge Nickerson heard argument on the motion to dismiss on May 14, 1979, and on May 15 dismissed the complaint on jurisdictional grounds. The district judge recognized the strength of appellants' argument that official torture violates an emerging norm of customary international law. Nonetheless, he felt constrained by dicta contained in two recent opinions of this Court. . . to construe narrowly "the law of nations," as employed in § 1350, as excluding that law which governs a state's treatment of its own citizens.

The district court continued the stay of deportation for forty-eight hours while appellants applied for further stays. These applications were denied by a panel of this Court on May 22, 1979, and by the Supreme Court two days later. Shortly thereafter, Peña and his companion returned to Paraguay.

II

Appellants rest their principal argument in support of federal jurisdiction upon the Alien Tort Statute, 28 U.S.C. § 1350, which provides: "The district courts shall have original jurisdiction of any civil action by an alien for a tort only, committed in violation of the law of nations or a treaty of the United States." Since appellants do not contend that their action arises directly under a treaty of the United States, a threshold question on the jurisdictional issue is whether the conduct alleged violates the law of nations. In light of the universal condemnation of torture in numerous international agreements, and the renunciation of torture as an instrument of official policy by virtually all of the nations of the world (in principle if not in practice), we find that an act of torture committed by a state official against one held in detention violates established norms of the international law of human rights, and hence the law of nations.

The Supreme Court has enumerated the appropriate sources of international law. The law of nations "may be ascertained by consulting the works of jurists, writing professedly on public law; or by the general usage and practice of nations; or by judicial decisions recognizing and enforcing that law." . . .

The Paquete Habana, 175 U.S. 677 . . . (1900), reaffirmed that

> where there is no treaty, and no controlling executive or legislative act or judicial decision, resort must be had to the customs and usages of civilized nations; and, as evidence of these, to the works of jurists and commentators, who by years of labor, research and experience, have made themselves peculiarly well acquainted with the subjects of which they treat. Such works are resorted to by judicial tribunals, not for the speculations of their authors concerning what the law ought to be, but for trustworthy evidence of what the law really is.

Id. at 700 . . . . Modern international sources confirm the propriety of this approach. *Habana* is particularly instructive for present purposes, for it held that the traditional prohibition against seizure of an enemy's coastal fishing vessels during wartime, a standard that began as one of comity only, had ripened over the preceding century into "a settled rule of international law" by "the general assent of civilized nations." *Id.* at 694 . . . . Thus it is clear that courts must interpret international law not as it was in 1789, but as it has evolved and exists among the nations of the world today. . . .

The requirement that a rule command the "general assent of civilized nations" to become binding upon them all is a stringent one. Were this not so, the courts of one nation might feel free to impose idiosyncratic legal rules upon others, in the name of applying international law. . . .

The United Nations Charter (a treaty of the United States, *see* 59 Stat. 1033 (1945)) makes it clear that in this modern age a state's treatment of its own citizens is a matter of international concern. It provides:

> With a view to the creation of conditions of stability and well-being which are necessary for peaceful and friendly relations among nations . . . the United Nations shall promote . . . universal respect for, and observance of, human rights and fundamental freedoms for all without distinctions as to race, sex, language or religion.

Id. Art. 55. And further:

> All members pledge themselves to take joint and separate action in cooperation with the Organization for the achievement of the purposes set forth in Article 55.

Id. Art. 56.

While this broad mandate has been held not to be wholly self-executing, *Hitai v. Immigration and Naturalization Service*, 343 F.2d 466, 468 (2d Cir. 1965), this observation alone does not end our inquiry. For although there is no universal agreement as to the precise extent of the "human rights and fundamental freedoms" guaranteed to all by the Charter, there is at present no dissent from the view that the guaranties include, at a bare minimum, the right to be free from torture. This prohibition has become part of customary international law, as evidenced and defined by the Universal Declaration of Human Rights, General Assembly Resolution 217 (III)(A) (Dec. 10, 1948) which states in the plainest of terms, "no one shall be subjected to torture." The General Assembly has declared that the Charter precepts embodied in this Universal Declaration "constitute basic principles of international law." G.A.Res. 2625 (XXV) (Oct. 24, 1970).

Particularly relevant is the Declaration on the Protection of All Persons from Being Subjected to Torture, General Assembly Resolution 3452, 30 U.N. GAOR Supp. (No. 34) 91, U.N. Doc. A/1034 (1975). . . . The Declaration expressly prohibits any state from permitting the dastardly and totally inhuman act of torture. . . .

Turning to the act of torture, we have little difficulty discerning its universal renunciation in the modern usage and practice of nations. . . . The international consensus surrounding torture has found expression in numerous international treaties and accords. . . . The substance of these international agreements is reflected in modern municipal — *i.e.* national — law as well. Although torture was once a routine concomitant of criminal interrogations in many nations, during the modern and hopefully more enlightened era it has been universally renounced. According to one survey, torture is prohibited, expressly or implicitly, by the constitutions of over fifty-five nations, including both the United States and Paraguay.... [18]

Having examined the sources from which customary international law is derived — the usage of nations, judicial opinions and the works of jurists — we conclude that official torture is now prohibited by the law of nations. The prohibition is clear and unambiguous, and admits of no distinction between treatment of aliens and citizens.... The treaties and accords cited above, as well as the express foreign policy of our own government, all make it clear that international law confers fundamental rights upon all people vis-a-vis their own governments. While the ultimate scope of those rights will be a subject for continuing refinement and elaboration, we hold that the right to be free from torture is now among them. We therefore turn to the question whether the other requirements for jurisdiction are met.

III

Appellee submits that even if the tort alleged is a violation of modern international law, federal jurisdiction may not be exercised consistent with the dictates of Article III of the Constitution. The claim is without merit. Common law courts of general jurisdiction regularly adjudicate transitory tort claims between individuals over whom they exercise personal jurisdiction, wherever the tort occurred. Moreover, as part of an articulated scheme of federal control over external affairs, Congress provided, in the first Judiciary Act, § 9(b), 1 Stat. 73, 77 (1789), for federal jurisdiction over suits by aliens where principles of international law are in issue. The constitutional basis for the Alien Tort Statute is the law of nations, which has always been part of the federal common law.

It is not extraordinary for a court to adjudicate a tort claim arising outside of its territorial jurisdiction. A state or nation has a legitimate interest in the orderly resolution of disputes among those within its borders, and where the *lex loci delicti commissi* is applied, it is an expression of comity to give effect to the laws of the state where the wrong occurred.

...A case properly "aris[es] under the...laws of the United States" for Article III purposes if grounded upon statutes enacted by Congress or upon the common law of the United States....

As ratified, the judiciary article contained no express reference to cases arising under the law of nations. Indeed, the only express reference to that body of law is contained in Article I, sec. 8, cl. 10, which grants to the Congress the power to "define and punish...offenses against the law of nations." Appellees seize upon this circumstance and advance the proposition that the law of nations forms a part of the laws of the United States only to the extent that Congress has acted to

---

[18] The fact that the prohibition of torture is often honored in the breach does not diminish its binding effect as a norm of international law. As one commentator has put it, "The best evidence for the existence of international law is that every actual State recognizes that it does exist and that it is itself under an obligation to observe it. States often violate international law, just as individuals often violate municipal law; but no more than individuals do States defend their violations by claiming that they are above the law." J. Brierly, *The Outlook for International Law* 4-5 (Oxford 1944).

define it. This extravagant claim is amply refuted by the numerous decisions applying rules of international law uncodified in any act of Congress. . . .

Thus, it was hardly a radical initiative for Chief Justice Marshall to state in *The Nereide*, 13 U.S. (9 Cranch) 388, 422. . .(1815), that in the absence of a congressional enactment,[19] United States courts are "bound by the law of nations, which is a part of the law of the land.". . .

Although the Alien Tort Statute has rarely been the basis for jurisdiction during its long history, in light of the foregoing discussion, there can be little doubt that this action is properly brought in federal court.[20]. . .

Since federal jurisdiction may properly be exercised over the Filartigas' claim, the action must be remanded for further proceedings. . . .

Forti v. Suarez-Mason, 672 F. Supp. 1531 (N.D. Cal. 1987) (*Forti I*) (footnotes omitted):

JENSEN, District Judge.

I.
FACTS

This is a civil action brought against a former Argentine general by two Argentine citizens currently residing in the United States. Plaintiffs Forti and Benchoam sue on their own behalf and on behalf of family members, seeking damages from defendant Suarez-Mason for actions which include, *inter alia*, torture, murder, and prolonged arbitrary detention, allegedly committed by military and police personnel under defendant's authority and control. As will be discussed more fully below, plaintiffs predicate federal jurisdiction on 28 U.S.C. §§ 1350 (the "Alien Tort Statute") and 1331. They claim jurisdiction for their various state-law claims under the doctrine of pendent and ancillary jurisdiction. A brief recitation of the procedural background and historical context of this action is useful for a complete understanding of the issues raised by defendant's motion to dismiss. The events described and discussed in this opinion are drawn from the allegations of the Complaint and representations in the parties' moving papers. The Court makes no findings of fact with respect to these events.

A. *Background*

Plaintiffs' action arises out of events alleged to have occurred in the mid- to late 1970s during Argentina's so-called "dirty war" against suspected subversives.

---

[19] The plainest evidence that international law has an existence in the federal courts independent of acts of Congress is the long-standing rule of construction first enunciated by Chief Justice Marshall: "an act of Congress ought never to be construed to violate the law of nations, if any other possible construction remains. . . ." *The Charming Betsy*, 6 U.S. (2 Cranch), 34, 67. . .(1804), *quoted in Lauritzen v. Larsen*, 345 U.S. 571, 578 . . . (1953).

[20] We recognize that our reasoning might also sustain jurisdiction under the general federal question provision, 28 U.S.C. § 1331. We prefer, however, to rest our decision upon the Alien Tort Statute, in light of that provision's close coincidence with the jurisdictional facts presented in this case. . . .

In 1975 the activities of terrorists representing the extremes of both ends of the political spectrum induced the constitutional government of President Peron to declare a "state of siege" under Article 23 of the Argentine Constitution. President Peron also decreed that the Argentine Armed Forces should assume responsibility for suppressing terrorism. The country was accordingly divided into defense zones, each assigned to an army corps. In each zone the military was authorized to detain suspects and hold them in prison or in military installations pursuant to the terms of the "state of siege." Zone One — which included most of the Province of Buenos Aires and encompassed the national capital — was assigned to the First Army Corps. From January 1976 until January 1979 defendant Suarez-Mason was Commander of the First Army Corps.

On March 24, 1976 the commanding officers of the Armed Forces seized the government from President Peron. The ruling military junta continued the "state of siege" and caused the enactment of legislation providing that civilians accused of crimes of subversion would be judged by military law. *See, e.g.,* Law 21.264. In the period from 1976 to 1979, tens of thousands of persons were detained without charges by the military, and it is estimated that more than 12,000 were "disappeared," never to be seen again. *See generally, Nunca Mas: The Report of the Argentine National Commission on the Disappeared* (1986).

In January 1984 the constitutionally elected government of President Raul Alfonsín assumed power. The Alfonsín government commenced investigations of alleged human rights abuses by the military, and the criminal prosecution of certain former military authorities followed. The government vested the Supreme Council of the Armed Forces with jurisdiction over the prosecution of military commanders. Summoned by the Supreme Council in March 1984, defendant failed to appear and in fact fled the country. In January of 1987 Suarez-Mason was arrested in Foster City, California pursuant to a provisional arrest warrant at the request of the Republic of Argentina. While defendant was in custody awaiting an extradition hearing he was served with the Complaint herein.

Because of their importance to the issues raised by the dismissal motion, the Court provides a detailed recitation of plaintiffs' allegations.

B. *Allegations of the Complaint*

The Complaint alleges claims for damages based on acts allegedly committed by personnel within the defense zone under General Suarez-Mason's command. According to the Complaint, police and military officials seized plaintiff Alfredo Forti, along with his mother and four brothers, from an airplane at Buenos Aires' Ezeiza International Airport on February 18, 1977. Compl. [paras.] 3, 10. The entire family was held at the "Pozo de Quillmes" detention center, located in a suburb of Buenos Aires in Buenos Aires Province. *Id.* [paras.] 3, 11. No charges were ever filed against the Fortis. After six days the five sons were released, dropped blindfolded on a street in the capital. The mother, Nelida Azucena Sosa de Forti, was not released, and remains "disappeared" to this day, despite efforts on behalf of the Forti family by the Interamerican Commission on Human Rights and several members of the United States Congress. *Id.* [paras.] 3, 11-12, 14. . . .

An Argentine court which adjudicated criminal liability of the nine former junta members has attributed direct responsibility for the February 18, 1977 seizure of the Forti family to the First Army Corps. *Id.* [para.] 16.

As to plaintiff Debora Benchoam, the Complaint alleges that Benchoam and her brother were abducted from their Buenos Aires bedroom before dawn on July 25, 1977 by military authorities in plain clothes. *Id.* [paras.] 4, 17. At the time Benchoam was sixteen years old and her brother, seventeen.

Benchoam was blindfolded and taken first to an unidentified house and later to a police station in Buenos Aires, where she was held incommunicado for a month. *Id.* [para.] 18. For the first week of detention Benchoam was kept blindfolded with her hands handcuffed behind her back, and was provided neither food nor clothing. A guard attempted to rape her. *Id.*

On August 28, 1977, allegedly at the direction of defendant Suarez-Mason, Benchoam was transferred to Devoto Prison in Buenos Aires. Here she was imprisoned, without charge, for more than four years. *Id.* [para.] 19. In 1979 or 1980 plaintiff obtained a writ of habeas corpus, but the writ was reversed on appeal. Finally, as a result of international and domestic appeals, plaintiff was granted the "right of option" and allowed to leave the country. She was released from prison on November 5, 1981 and came to the United States as a refugee. *Id.* [paras.] 8, 19.

The military personnel also abducted plaintiff's seventeen-year-old brother on July 25, 1977. *Id.* [paras.] 4, 20. The brother's body was returned to the Benchoam family the following day. He had died of internal bleeding from bullet wounds, and his face was "severely disfigured" from blows. . . .

Although the individual acts are alleged to have been committed by military and police officials, plaintiffs allege that these actors were all agents, employees, or representatives of defendant acting pursuant to a "policy, pattern and practice" of the First Army Corps under defendant's command. Plaintiffs assert that defendant "held the highest position of authority" in Buenos Aires Province; that defendant was responsible for maintaining the prisons and detention centers there, as well as the conduct of Army officers and agents; and that he "authorized, approved, directed and ratified" the acts complained of. *Id.* [paras.] 23-24.

Plaintiff Forti filed a criminal complaint against defendant and others in November 1983, shortly after the election of President Alfonsín. That complaint has not yet been adjudicated as against Suarez-Mason. *Id.* [para.] 15. Plaintiff Benchoam has apparently not filed criminal charges against defendant. Although both plaintiffs retain their Argentine citizenship, both reside currently in Virginia. *Id.* [paras.] 7-8. Plaintiffs predicate federal jurisdiction principally on the "Alien Tort Statute," 28 U.S.C. § 1350 and alternatively on federal question jurisdiction, 28 U.S.C. § 1331. Additionally, they assert jurisdiction for their common-law tort claims under principles of pendent and ancillary jurisdiction. *Id.* [para.] 5.

Based on these above allegations, plaintiffs seek compensatory and punitive damages for violations of customary international law and laws of the United States, Argentina, and California. They press eleven causes of action. Both alleged claims for torture; prolonged arbitrary detention without trial; cruel, inhuman and degrading treatment; false imprisonment; assault and battery; intentional infliction of emotional distress; and conversion. Additionally Forti claims damages for "causing the disappearance of individuals," and Benchoam asserts claims for "murder and summary execution," wrongful death, and a survival action.

In response to these allegations, defendant moves to dismiss the entire Complaint under Federal Rule of Civil Procedure 12(b), subsections (1) and (6). He argues that the Court lacks subject matter jurisdiction under 28 U.S.C. § 1350 to adjudicate tort claims arising out of "politically motivated acts of violence in other countries'' and, alternatively, that not all of the torts alleged constitute violations of the law of nations. Defendant also argues that adjudication of the plaintiffs' claims is barred by the act of state doctrine, which prohibits United States courts from adjudicating the legality of the actions of a foreign government official acting in his official capacity. Further, he contends that plaintiffs' claims are time-barred under the applicable Argentine statute of limitations; that plaintiffs have failed to join indispensable parties, and that plaintiff Benchoam lacks capacity to sue for her brother's death.

The Court will address in turn each of defendant's contentions.

II.
SUBJECT MATTER JURISDICTION

As a threshold matter, defendant argues that the Court lacks subject matter jurisdiction under 28 U.S.C. § 1350, the ''Alien Tort Statute.'' Defendant urges the Court to follow the interpretation of § 1350 as a purely jurisdictional statute which requires that plaintiffs invoking it establish the existence of an independent, private right of action in international law. Defendant argues that the law of nations provides no tort cause of action for the acts of ''politically motivated terrorism'' challenged by plaintiffs' Complaint. Alternatively, defendant argues that even if § 1350 provides a cause of action for violations of the law of nations, not all of the torts alleged by plaintiffs qualify as violations of the law of nations. For the reasons set out below, the Court rejects defendant's construction of § 1350 and finds that plaintiffs allege sufficient facts to establish subject matter jurisdiction under the Alien Tort Statute and 28 U.S.C. § 1331. . . .

A.   The Alien Tort Statute

The Alien Tort Statute provides that federal district courts shall have ''original jurisdiction of any civil action by an alien for a tort only, committed in violation of the law of nations or a treaty of the United States.'' 28 U.S.C. § 1350 (1982). The district courts' jurisdiction is concurrent with that of state courts. *See* Act of Sept. 24, 1789 (First Judiciary Act), ch. 20, § 9, 1 Stat. 73, 77. As the cases and commentaries recognize, the history of the Alien Tort Statute is obscure. *See, e.g., IIT v. Vencap, Ltd.*, 519 F.2d 1001, 1015 (2d Cir. 1975) (§ 1350 a ''kind of legal Lohengrin''). Nonetheless, the proper interpretation of the statute has been discussed at some length in the principal decisions upon which the parties rely: The unanimous decision in *Filartiga v. Peña-Irala*, 630 F.2d 876 (2d Cir. 1980) and the three concurring opinions in *Tel-Oren v. Libyan Arab Republic*, 726 F.2d 774 (D.C. Cir. 1984), *cert. denied*, 470 U.S. 1003. . .(1985).

Defendant urges the Court to adopt the reasoning of Judges Bork and Robb in *Tel-Oren, supra,* where the court affirmed the dismissal of a § 1350 tort action against various defendants based on a terrorist attack in Israel by members of the Palestine Liberation Organization. While the three judges concurred in the result, they were unable to agree on the rationale. Judge Bork found that § 1350 constitutes no more than a grant of jurisdiction; that plaintiffs seeking to invoke it must establish a private right of action under either a treaty or the law of nations; and that in the latter category the statute can support jurisdiction at most over only three international crimes recognized in 1789 — violation of safe-conducts, infringement of ambassadorial rights, and piracy. *Tel-Oren, supra,* 726 F.2d at 798-823 (Bork, J., concurring). Judge Robb, on the other hand, found that the dispute involved international political violence and so was ''nonjusticiable'' within the meaning of the political question doctrine. *Id.* at 823-27 (Robb, J., concurring).

The Court is persuaded, however, that the interpretation of § 1350 forwarded by the Second Circuit in *Filartiga, supra,* and largely adopted by Judge Edwards in *Tel-Oren,* is better reasoned and more consistent with principles of international law. There appears to be a growing consensus that § 1350 provides a cause of action for certain "international common law torts." *See, e.g., Filartiga, supra; Tel-Oren, supra* (Edwards, J., concurring); *Guinto v. Marcos,* 654 F. Supp. 276, 279-80 (S.D. Cal. 1986); *Von Dardel v. USSR,* 623 F. Supp. 246, 256-59 (D.D.C. 1985) (finding violation under any of the three *Tel-Oren* approaches); *Siderman v. Republic of Argentina,* No. CV 82-1772-RMT(MCx) (C.D. Cal. Sept. 28, 1984) (Lexis, Genfed library, Dist. file[; 1984 WL 9080]). It is unnecessary that plaintiffs establish the existence of an independent, express right of action, since the law of nations clearly does not create or define civil actions, and to require such an explicit grant under international law would effectively nullify that portion of the statute which confers jurisdiction over tort suits involving the law of nations. *See Tel-Oren,* 726 F.2d at 778 (Edwards, J., concurring). Rather, a plaintiff seeking to predicate jurisdiction on the Alien Tort Statute need only plead a "tort . . . in violation of the law of nations."

The contours of this requirement have been delineated by the *Filartiga* court and by Judge Edwards in *Tel-Oren.* Plaintiffs must plead a violation of the law of nations as it has evolved and exists in its contemporary form. *Filartiga,* 630 F.2d at 881; *Tel-Oren,* 726 F.2d at 777 (Edwards, J., concurring); *Amerada Hess Shipping Corp. v. Argentine Republic,* 830 F.2d 421, 424 (2d Cir. 1987). This "international tort" must be one which is definable, obligatory (rather than hortatory), and universally condemned. *Filartiga,* 630 F.2d at 881; *Tel-Oren,* 726 F.2d at 781 (Edwards, J., concurring); *Guinto, supra,* 654 F. Supp. at 279-80; . . . . The requirement of international consensus is of paramount importance, for it is that consensus which evinces the willingness of nations to be bound by the particular legal principle, and so can justify the court's exercise of jurisdiction over the international tort claim. . . .

The Court thus interprets 28 U.S.C. § 1350 to provide not merely jurisdiction but a cause of action, with the federal cause of action arising by recognition of certain "international torts" through the vehicle of § 1350. These international torts, violations of current customary international law, are characterized by universal consensus in the international community as to their binding status and their content. That is, they are universal, definable, and obligatory international norms. The Court now examines the allegations of the Complaint to determine whether plaintiffs have stated cognizable international torts for purposes of jurisdiction under § 1350.

B.   *Analysis Under 28 U.S.C. § 1350*

In determining whether plaintiffs have stated cognizable claims under Section 1350, the Court has recourse to "the works of jurists, writing professedly on public law; . . . the general usage and practice of nations; [and] judicial decisions recognizing and enforcing that law." *United States v. Smith,* 18 U.S. (5 Wheat.) 153, 160-61, . . . (1820). For purposes of defendant's motion to dismiss, the Court must accept as true all of plaintiffs' allegations, construing them in the light most favorable to plaintiffs. . . .

1.   *Official Torture*

In Count One, plaintiffs both allege torture conducted by military and police personnel under defendant's command. The Court has no doubt that official torture constitutes a cognizable violation of the law of nations under § 1350. This was the very question addressed by the Second Circuit in *Filartiga, supra*. There, after examining numerous sources of international law, *see Filartiga*, 630 F.2d at 880-84 & n. 16, the court concluded that the law of nations contains a "clear and unambiguous" prohibition of official torture. This proscription is universal, obligatory, and definable. Of course, purely private torture will not normally implicate the law of nations, since there is currently no international consensus regarding torture practiced by non-state actors. *See Tel-Oren*, 726 F.2d at 791-95 (Edwards, J., concurring). Here, however, plaintiffs allege torture by military and police personnel under the supervision and control of defendant while he served as Commander of the First Army Corps. The claim would thus allege torture committed by *state officials* and so fall within the international tort first recognized in *Filartiga*.

Plaintiffs allege official torture in conclusory terms. . . . Accordingly, the Court orders plaintiffs to amend Count One to state the specific acts on which they base their claim of official torture.

2. *Prolonged Arbitrary Detention*

In Count Four plaintiffs both allege a claim for prolonged arbitrary detention, stating that defendant "arbitrarily and without justification, cause or privilege, forcibly confined both plaintiff Benchoam and Nelida Azucena Sosa de Forti for a prolonged period." Complaint [para.] 43. Elsewhere plaintiffs allege that Benchoam was imprisoned for more than four years without ever being charged, while Forti's mother was arrested in 1977 but was never charged or released.

There is case law finding sufficient consensus to evince a customary international human rights norm against arbitrary detention. *Rodriguez-Fernandez v. Wilkinson*, 505 F. Supp. 787, 795-98 (D. Kan. 1980) (citing international treaties, cases, and commentaries), *aff'd*, 654 F.2d 1382 (10th Cir. 1981); *see also De Sanchez, supra*, 770 F.2d at 1397 (right "not to be arbitrarily detained" incorporated into law of nations); *Nguyen Da Yen v. Kissinger*, 528 F.2d 1194, 1201 n. 13 (9th Cir. 1975) (illegal detention may constitute international tort) *but see Jean v. Nelson*, 727 F.2d 957, 964 & n. 4 (11th Cir. 1984) (disagreed with *Rodriguez-Fernandez* in holding that detention of uninvited aliens under national sovereign's exclusion power is no violation of customary international law), *aff'd*, 472 U.S. 846 . . . (1985). The consensus is even clearer in the case of a state's *prolonged* arbitrary detention of its own citizens. *See, e.g., Restatement (Revised) of the Foreign Relations Law of the United States* § 702 (Tent. Draft No. 6, 1985) (prolonged arbitrary detention by state constitutes international law violation). The norm is obligatory, and is readily definable in terms of the arbitrary character of the detention. The Court finds that plaintiffs have alleged international tort claims for prolonged arbitrary detention.

3. *Summary Execution*

The Second Count alleges plaintiff Benchoam's claim for "murder and summary execution." Benchoam alleges that "[d]efendant's torture, murder, beating and cruel, inhuman and degrading treatment of Ruben Benchoam resulted in and proximately caused his death." Complaint [para.] 32. In support of this claim, plaintiff cites several international documents which proscribe summary execution. Universal Declaration of Human Rights, art. 3, G.A. Res. 217A, U.N. Doc. A/810 (1948); International Covenant on Civil and Political Rights, art. 6, G.A. Res. 2200,

21 U.N. GAOR Supp. (No. 16), U.N. Doc. A/6316 (1966); American Convention on Human Rights, art. 5, OAS Treaty Series No. 36, OAS Off. Rec. OEA/Ser.4 v/II 23, doc. 21, rev. 2 (English ed. 1975). Similarly, murder — where practiced, encouraged, or condoned by a state — is listed among the international law violations to which Judge Edwards looked for guidance in identifying possible violations of the law of nations. *See Tel-Oren*, 726 F.2d at 781 (quoting *Restatement (Revised) of the Foreign Relations Law of the United States* § 702 (Tent. Draft No. 3, 1982)); *see also Guinto*, *supra*, 654 F. Supp. at 280. Further, the Fifth Circuit has acknowledged the right not to be murdered [by the state] as among the "basic rights" which "have been generally accepted — and hence incorporated into the law of nations." *De Sanchez*, *supra*, 770 F.2d at 1397.

The proscription of summary execution or murder by the state appears to be universal, is readily definable, and is of course obligatory. The Court emphasizes that plaintiff's allegations raise no issue as to whether or not the execution was within the lawful exercise of state power; rather, she alleges murder by state officials with neither authorization nor recourse to any process of law. Under these circumstances, the Court finds that plaintiff Benchoam has stated a cognizable claim under § 1350 for the 1977 murder/summary execution of her brother by Argentine military personnel.

4.   *Causing Disappearance*

In Count Three plaintiff Forti alleges a claim for "causing the disappearance" of his mother, in that defendant "arbitrarily and without justification, cause or privilege, abducted Nelida Azucena Sosa de Forti, held her in secret captivity and caused her 'disappearance' to this day." Complaint [para.] 38.

Sadly, the practice of "disappearing" individuals — i.e., abduction, secret detention, and torture, followed generally by either secret execution or release — during Argentina's "dirty war" is now well documented in the official report of the Argentine National Commission on the Disappeared, *Nunca Mas*. Nor are such practices necessarily restricted to Argentina. With mounting publicity over the years, such conduct has begun to draw censure as a violation of the basic right to life. Plaintiff cites a 1978 United Nations resolution and a 1980 congressional resolution to this effect. U.N.G.A. Res./173 (1978); H.R. Con. Res. 285, 96th Cong., 2d Sess. The Court notes, too, that the proposed Restatement of the Law of Foreign Relations lists "the murder or causing the disappearance of individuals," where practiced, encouraged or condoned by the state, as a violation of international law. *Restatement (Revised) of the Foreign Relations Law of the United States*, § 702 (Tent. Draft No. 6, 1985). However, plaintiffs do not cite the Court to any case finding that causing the disappearance of an individual constitutes a violation of the law of nations.

Before this Court may adjudicate a tort claim under § 1350, it must be satisfied that the legal standard it is to apply is one with universal acceptance and definition; on no other basis may the Court exercise jurisdiction over a claimed violation of the law of nations. Unfortunately, the Court cannot say, on the basis of the evidence submitted, that there yet exists the requisite degree of international consensus which demonstrates a customary international norm. Even if there were greater evidence of universality, there remain definitional problems. It is not clear precisely what conduct falls within the proposed norm, or how this proscription would differ from that of summary execution. The other torts condemned by the international community and discussed above — official torture, prolonged arbitrary detention, and summary execution — involve two types of conduct by the official actor: (1) taking the individual into custody; and (2) committing a wrongful, tortious act in excess of his authority over that person. In the case of "causing disappearance," only the first of these two actions can be proven — the taking into custody. However, the sole act of taking an individual into custody does not suffice to prove conduct which the international community proscribes. The Court recognizes the very real problems of proof presented by the disappearance of an individual following such custody. Yet there is no apparent international consensus as to the additional elements needed to make out a claim for causing the disappearance of an individual. For instance, plaintiffs have now shown that customary international law creates a presumption of causing disappearance upon a showing of prolonged absence after initial custody.

For these reasons the Court must dismiss Count Four for failure to state a claim upon which relief may be grounded. . . .

5.   Cruel, Inhuman and Degrading Treatment

Finally, in Count Five plaintiffs both allege a claim for "cruel, inhuman and degrading treatment" based on the general allegations of the Complaint and consisting specifically of the alleged torture, murder, forcible disappearance and prolonged arbitrary detention. Complaint [paras.] 47-48.

This claim suffers the same defects as Count Four. Plaintiffs do not cite, and the Court is not aware of, such evidence of universal consensus regarding the right to be free from "cruel, inhuman and degrading treatment" as exists, for example, with respect to official torture. Further, any such right poses problems of definability. The difficulties for a district court in adjudicating such a claim are manifest. Because this right lacks readily ascertainable parameters, it is unclear what behavior falls within the proscription — beyond such obvious torts as are already encompassed by the proscriptions of torture, summary execution and prolonged arbitrary detention. Lacking the requisite elements of universality and definability, this proposed tort cannot qualify as a violation of the law of nations. Accordingly, the Court dismisses Count Five of the Complaint for failure to state a claim upon which relief may be granted.

In sum, the Court finds that plaintiffs have stated claims for prolonged arbitrary detention and summary execution. On the other hand, the Court dismisses with prejudice Counts Three ("causing disappearance") and Five ("cruel, inhuman and degrading treatment") for failure to state a claim — i.e., failure to allege a violation of the law of nations cognizable under the Alien Tort Statute. The Court orders plaintiffs to amend Count One; to make a more definite statement of the acts upon which they allege the claim for official torture. It follows from the above statements that this Court has federal subject matter jurisdiction, with respect to both plaintiffs, under 28 U.S.C. § 1350.

C.   Federal Question Jurisdiction

Alternatively, plaintiffs predicate jurisdiction on 28 U.S.C. § 1331, the federal question statute. Section 1331 provides that "[t]he district courts shall have jurisdiction of all civil actions arising under the Constitution, laws, or treaties of the United States." This statute provides jurisdiction over claims founded on federal common law. *Illinois v. City of Milwaukee*, 406 U.S. 91, 100 [1972]. . . .

It has long been settled that federal common law incorporates international law. *The Nereide*, 13 U.S. (9 Cranch) 388, 423...(1815); *The Paquete Habana*, 175 U.S. 677, 700...(1900). More recently, the Supreme Court has held that the interpretation of international law is a federal question. *Sabbatino*, [376 U.S. 398, 415 (1964)]. Thus, a case presenting claims arising under customary international law arises under the laws of the United States for purposes of federal question jurisdiction.

***

Forti v. Suarez-Mason, 694 F. Supp. 707 (N.D. Cal. 1988) (*Forti II*) (footnotes omitted):

...The Court's previous Order held that the Alien Tort Statute provides a cause of action for "international torts"....672 F. Supp. at 1541.

The Court went on to hold that "on the basis of the evidence submitted" plaintiff Forti had failed to establish "the requisite degree of international consensus which demonstrates a customary international norm" in regard to his claim for causing the disappearance of his mother. The Court also dismissed both plaintiffs' claims for "cruel, inhuman or degrading treatment," holding that plaintiffs had failed to bring forth sufficient evidence of international consensus, and moreover that the tort "lacks readily ascertainable parameters." *Id.* at 1542-43.

Plaintiffs subsequently filed this Motion, supported by numerous international legal authorities, as well as affidavits from eight renowned international law scholars. The Court has reviewed these materials and concludes that plaintiffs have met their burden of showing an international consensus as to the status and content of the international tort of "causing disappearance." Accordingly, the motion to reconsider is GRANTED in this regard and the claim is reinstated. The Court also concludes that plaintiffs have again failed to establish that there is any international consensus as to what conduct falls within the category of "cruel, inhuman or degrading treatment." Absent such consensus as to the content of this alleged tort, it is not cognizable under the Alien Tort Statute. Therefore, the Motion to Reconsider dismissal of this claim is DENIED.

II.

As stated above and in the October, 1987 Order, the Court interprets the Alien Tort Statute as providing a cause of action for "international torts." 672 F.2d at 1540. The plaintiff's burden in stating a claim is to establish the existence of a "universal, definable, and obligatory international norm[]." *Id.* To meet this burden plaintiffs need not establish unanimity among nations. Rather, they must show a general recognition among states that a specific practice is prohibited. It is with this standard in mind that the Court examines the evidence presented by plaintiffs.

A....

The legal scholars whose declarations have been submitted in connection with this Motion are in agreement that there is universal consensus as to the two essential elements of a claim for "disappearance." In Professor Franck's words:

> The international community has also reached a consensus on the defi-
> nition of a "disappearance." It has two essential elements; (a) abduction

by a state official or by persons acting under state approval or authority; and (b) refusal by the state to acknowledge the abduction and detention.

Franck Declaration, [para.] 7. *See also Falk Declaration*, at 3; *Henkin Declaration*, [para.] 9; *Steiner Declaration*, [para.] 3, 5; *Weissbrodt Declaration*, [para.] 8(b); *Weston Declaration*, [para.] 5.

Plaintiffs cite numerous international legal authorities which support the assertion that "disappearance" is a universally recognized wrong under the law of nations. For example, United Nations General Assembly Resolution 33/173 recognizes "disappearance" as violative of many of the rights recognized in the Universal Declaration of Human Rights, G.A. Res. 217 A (III), adopted by the U.N. General Assembly, Dec. 10, 1948, U.N. Doc. A/810 (1948) [*hereinafter* Universal Declaration of Human Rights]. These rights include: (1) the right to life; (2) the right to liberty and security of the person; (3) the right to freedom from torture; (4) the right to freedom from arbitrary arrest and detention; and (5) the right to a fair and public trial. *Id.*, articles 3, 5, 9, 10, 11. *See also* International Covenant on Political and Civil Rights, G.A. Res. 2200 (XXI), adopted by the United Nations General Assembly, December 16, 1966, U.N. Doc. A/6316 (1966), articles 6, 7, 9, 10, 14, 15, 17.

Other documents support this characterization of "disappearance" as violative of universally recognized human rights. The United States Congress has denounced "prolonged detention without charges and trial" along with other "flagrant denial[s] of the right to life, liberty, or the security of person." 22 U.S.C. § 2304(d)(1). The recently published Restatement (Third) of the Foreign Relations Law of the United States § 702 includes "disappearance" as a violation of the international law of human rights. The Organization of American States has also denounced "disappearance" as "an affront to the conscience of the hemisphere and...a crime against humanity." Organization of American States, Inter-American Commission on Human Rights, General Assembly Resolution 666 (November 18, 1983).

Of equal importance, plaintiffs' submissions support their assertion that there is a universally recognized legal definition of what constitutes the tort of "causing disappearance." The Court's earlier order expressed concern that "the sole act of taking an individual into custody does not suffice to prove conduct which the international community proscribes." 672 F. Supp. at 1543. Plaintiffs' submissions on this Motion, however, establish recognition of a second essential element — official refusal to acknowledge that the individual has been taken into custody. For example, the United Nations General Assembly has expressed concern

> at the difficulties in obtaining reliable information from competent authorities as to the circumstances of such persons, including reports of the persistent refusal of such authorities or organizations to acknowledge that they hold such persons in custody or otherwise to account for them.

U.N. General Assembly Resolution 33/173 (December 20, 1978).

Likewise, the Organization of American States has recognized the importance of this element, commenting on the

> numerous cases wherein the government systematically denies the detention of individuals, despite the convincing evidence that the claimants provide to verify their allegations that such persons have been detained by police or military authorities and, in some cases, that those persons are, or have been, confined in specified detention centers.

Organization of American States, Inter-American Commission on Human Rights, 1977 Annual Report, at 26. *See also* M. Berman & R. Clark, *State Terrorism: Disappearances*, 13 Rutgers L.J. 531, 533 (1982) ("The denial of accountability is the factor which makes disappearance unique among human rights violations.").

In the Court's view, the submitted materials are sufficient to establish the existence of a universal and obligatory international proscription of the tort of "causing disappearance." This tort is characterized by the following two essential elements: (1) abduction by state officials or their agents; followed by (2) official refusals to acknowledge the abduction or to disclose the detainee's fate. Upon review of the Second Amended Complaint it is clear that plaintiff Forti has sufficiently pled both these elements. *See Second Amended Complaint*, [paras.] 3, 18. Therefore, the Motion to Reconsider is GRANTED in part and plaintiff Forti's claim is reinstated.

B.

In its October, 1987 Order the Court found that plaintiffs had stated claims under the Alien Tort Statute for "official torture," 672 F. Supp. at 1541, but had failed to state claims for "cruel, inhuman and degrading treatment." *Id.* at 1543. Plaintiffs have now combined their two previous claims to allege "torture or other cruel, inhuman or degrading treatment or punishment." *Second Amended Complaint*, [paras.] 53-56. The Second Amended Complaint does not state precisely what alleged actions constitute the proposed tort. Rather, it merely incorporates *all* the factual allegations and alleges that these acts constitute "torture or other cruel, inhuman or degrading treatment or punishment in violation of customary international law." *Id.*, [para.] 54.

In dismissing plaintiffs' earlier "cruel, inhuman or degrading treatment" claim this Court found that the proposed tort lacked "the requisite elements of universality and definability." 672 F. Supp. at 1543. Plaintiffs now submit the aforementioned declarations . . . and several international legal authorities in support of their argument that "[t]he definition of cruel, inhuman or degrading treatment or punishment is inextricably related to that for torture." *Plaintiff's Memorandum*, at 20. Specifically, plaintiffs argue that the two are properly viewed on a continuum, and that "torture and cruel, inhuman or degrading treatment differ essentially in the degree of ill treatment suffered." *Id.* Thus while the latter treatment is not torture it is an analytically distinct tort which, in plaintiffs' view, is actionable under the Alien Tort Statute.

Plaintiffs emphasize that virtually all international legal authorities which prohibit torture also prohibit cruel, inhuman or degrading treatment. For example, § 702 of the Restatement (Third) of the Foreign Relations Law of the United States: "A state violates international law if, as a matter of state policy, it practices, encourages, or condones. . . torture or other cruel, inhuman or degrading treatment or punishment." Likewise, 22 U.S.C. § 2304(d)(1) lists "torture or cruel, inhuman or degrading treatment or punishment," among "gross violations of internationally recognized human rights." Article 5 of the Universal Declaration of Human Rights, *supra*, states that "[n]o one shall be subjected to torture or to cruel, inhuman or degrading treatment." *See also De Sanchez v. Banco Central De Nicaragua*, 770 F.2d 1385, 1397 (5th Cir. 1985) (recognizing "right not to be. . . tortured, or otherwise subjected to cruel, inhuman or degrading treatment").

While these and other materials establish a recognized proscription of "cruel, inhuman or degrading treatment," they offer no guidance as to what constitutes such treatment. The Restatement does not define the term. The cited statute (22 U.S.C. § 2304) and the Universal Declaration of Human rights also both fail to offer a definition. The scholars whose declarations have been submitted likewise decline to offer any definition of the proposed tort. In fact, one of the declarations appears to concede the lack of a universally recognized definition. *See Lillich Declaration*, at 8 ("only the contours of the prohibition, not its existence as a norm of customary international law, are the subject of legitimate debate.").

This problem of definability is evidenced by the Second Amended Complaint. Plaintiffs simply incorporate all the factual allegations and without elaboration, allege that these constitute the alleged cruel, inhuman or degrading treatment. *Second Amended Complaint*, [paras.] 53-56. However, the complaint alleges a wide range of discrete acts associated with the detentions. Some of the acts result in physical injury, some do not. Does the proposed tort require physical injury? If purely psychological harm is cognizable, as it would appear to be, is it actionable when caused by purely verbal conduct? Was it "cruel, inhuman and degrading treatment" for the military officials to threaten Mrs. Forti if she did not leave the airplane voluntarily? *Second Amended Complaint*, [para.] 11. Was it actionable conduct not to allow Mrs. Forti to talk to the commander of the detention center? *Id.* [para.] 13. Absent some definition of what constitutes "cruel, inhuman or degrading treatment" this Court has no way of determining what alleged treatment is actionable, and what is not.

Plaintiffs cite *The Greek Case*, 12 Y.B. Eur. Conv. on Human Rights 186 (1969), for a definition of "degrading treatment" as that which "grossly humiliates [the victim] before others or drives him to act against his will or conscience." *Plaintiffs' Memorandum*, at 22. But this definitional gloss is of no help. From our necessarily global perspective, conduct, particularly verbal conduct, which is humiliating or even grossly humiliating in one cultural context is of no moment in another. An international tort which appears and disappears as one travels around the world is clearly lacking in that level of common understanding necessary to create universal consensus. Likewise, the term "against his will or conscience" is too abstract to be of help. For example, a pacifist who is conscripted to serve in his country's military has arguably been forced to act "against his will or conscience." Would he thus have a claim for degrading treatment?

To be actionable under the Alien Tort Statute the proposed tort must be characterized by universal consensus in the international community as to its binding status *and its content*. In short, it must be a "universal, *definable*, and obligatory international norm[]." *Forti*, 672 F. Supp. at 1541 (emphasis added). Plaintiffs' submissions fail to establish that there is anything even remotely approaching universal consensus as to what constitutes "cruel, inhuman or degrading treatment." Absent this consensus in the international community as to the tort's content it is not actionable under the Alien Tort Statute. Therefore, the Motion to Reconsider the Dismissal of this claim is DENIED. . . .

NOTES AND QUESTIONS

1. In *Forti II* Judge Jensen noted that, to establish a "universal" norm, a plaintiff need demonstrate only "general [rather than unanimous] recognition that a specific practice is prohibited." 694 F. Supp. at 709. What persuaded him to add that clarification? One possibility is suggested by the following footnote from an amicus brief submitted by Frank Newman in a related case, *Matter of the Requested Extradition of Suarez-Mason*, 694 F. Supp. 676 (1988):

> This court in *Forti* [*I*] uses "universal"...to describe the requisite degree of consensus. "Universal" conceivably could create confusion if it suggests "unanimous". Less ambiguous terms include "international consensus", "internationally recognized", and "widely accepted". *See* U.S. Government's Filartiga memorandum, 19 I.L.M. at 604 (1980) (requiring "a consensus in the international community that there is a widely shared understanding of the scope of this protection"). *See too* Foreign Assistance Act of 1961, Sections 116 and 502B (providing for termination of assistance to governments that engage in consistent patterns of "gross violations of internationally recognized human rights").

That paragraph underscores the importance of using correct adjectives and the danger of using terms such as "universal" that may have a connotation in international discourse different from U.S. usage.

2. For a discussion of various issues involved in Suarez-Mason's efforts to avoid extradition, see *Matter of the Requested Extradition of Suarez-Mason*, 694 F. Supp. 707 (N.D. Cal. 1988).

3. *Filartiga* states that "courts must interpret international law as it has evolved and exists among the nations of the world today." Do you think that statement does, could, or should apply to treaty as well as customary law? Do you think courts should construe treaty clauses to impose obligations based on understandings at the time of drafting, at the time the U.S. became party to the treaty, at the time that the court is applying the treaty, or at the time that the relevant events occurred? While it may make sense that courts apply customary law at the time relevant events occurred, did the Second Circuit do that? Note that the event, the torture and murder of Joelito Filartiga, occurred on March 29, 1976. To the extent that a major document on which the court relied was the Declaration Against Torture, adopted in 1975, does that suggest that the Court accepted the proposition that certain international instruments may be declarative of custom at the time of adoption? How would you justify the Court's citation to the Department of State's Country Reports, published February 1980?

4. What persuaded Judge Jensen in *Forti II* to change his decision regarding the existence of an international proscription of "causing disappearance"?

5. What were the considerations in his decision not to find the proscription of "cruel, inhuman or degrading treatment" to be a customary norm? If the U.S. ratifies the Convention Against Torture and Other Cruel, Inhuman or Degrading Treatment or Punishment (see discussion in chapters 8 and 9, *supra*), do you think a court would be inclined to accept the argument that the proscription had ripened into a customary norm? Can those treaty provisions be considered as general principles of law? Which of the *Forti* court's concerns would be addressed by ratification and which would not?

6. The Bush administration was so concerned about the *Soering* decision of the European Court of Human Rights (chapter 10, *supra*) that it proposed a reservation to Article 16 of the Treaty Against Torture stating that the prohibition of "cruel, inhuman or degrading treatment" would provide no more protection than afforded by the Fifth, Eighth, and Fourteenth Amendments of the U.S. Constitution. *See* chapter 9, *supra*. Would that reservation have an impact on a U.S. judge who might be considering whether the proscription of "cruel, inhuman or degrading treatment" qualifies as a customary norm? What if the Senate accepts the Bush administration proposal as to the Treaty Against Torture?

7. Do you think lack of definable contours of concepts such as due process and equal protection has deterred Judge Jensen from applying those concepts in cases for which he has been responsible?

8. Assume you are the lawyer assigned to brief and argue on appeal the part of the *Forti II* decision concerning "cruel, inhuman or degrading treatment." What arguments would you make? Federal Rule of Evidence 44.1 provides that foreign law presents a question of law, not fact, and has been construed to permit appellate courts to consider sources of law not presented to the district court. *See United States v. Peterson*, 812 F.2d 486 (9th Cir. 1987). Would you move to submit a supplemental affidavit by Professor Lillich pursuant to Rule 44.1? If he asked you to supply him with a draft, what points would you make? Consider the complaint's allegations discussed in the opinions excerpted above and in 672 F. Supp. at 1537. Which allegations appear to present the most viable claims for cruel, inhuman, or degrading treatment not amounting to torture, causing disappearance, arbitrary detention, or summary execution? *See* 2 Restatement (Third) of the Foreign Relations Law of the United States § 702 (1987).

9. For further reading, see: Burley, *The Alien Tort Statute and the Judiciary Act of 1789: A Badge of Honor*, 83 Am. J. Int'l L. 463 (1989); Maier, *The Authoritative Sources of Customary International Law in the United States*, 10 Mich. J. Int'l L. 450 (1989); Randall, *Federal Questions and the Human Rights Paradigm*, 73 Minn. L. Rev. 349 (1988).

2. Judicial Enforceability of Customary Norms

In *Forti I* Judge Jensen addressed the source of the cause of action necessary to invoke customary norms in cases like *Filartiga. See Davis v. Passman*, 442 U.S. 228, 238 (1979) (a cause of action traditionally has meant nothing more than that a litigant has "recognized legal rights" whose invasion furnishes a basis for a claim to judicial relief). The debate flared in the mid-1980s following issuance of three concurring opinions, including one by Judge Bork, in *Tel-Oren v. Libyan Arab Republic*, 726 F.2d 774 (D.C.Cir. 1984), *cert. denied*, 470 U.S. 1003 (1985). The debate was fanned by the Justice Department's endorsement of Bork's view in its amicus brief in *Trajano v. Marcos*, 878 F.2d 1439 (9th Cir. 1989). While the issue remains alive, Judge Jensen's well-reasoned discussion in *Forti I* may presage resolution of the debate. The question of where to find the cause of action, though it consumed reams of scholarly analysis, may well be an issue primarily of historical interest.

Judge Jensen rejected Bork's reasoning and held that the Alien Tort Statute, 28 U.S.C. § 1350, did provide a right of action. The court noted that, "since the law of nations clearly does not create or define civil actions, . . . to require such an explicit grant under international law would effectively nullify that portion of the statute which confers jurisdiction over tort suits involving the law of nations." *Forti I*, 672 F. Supp. at 1539.

In an alternative holding of great significance, Judge Jensen further held that 28 U.S.C. § 1331, the statute that confers jurisdiction over federal questions, creates a private right of action for international torts given that their prohibition is part of federal common law. The significance of that holding is that it grants U.S. citizens, in addition to aliens, a right to sue for international torts, thus eliminating a distinction that had led to the anomalous result that aliens, but not U.S. citizens, could sue in U.S. courts for international torts.

Some commentators maintain that Jensen was wrong concerning one point made by Bork. They agree with Jensen that both the Alien Tort Statute and the federal question statute create a private right of action but also maintain that the equivalent of a cause of action must be found in the international tort itself. Professor Riesenfeld, who propounded that view in the amicus memo of the U.S. in *Filartiga*, there defined an international tort to be a customary norm that includes an international expectation that the norm may be invoked by individuals in domestic forums.

A slight variant of that view — namely, that international law may but need not supply a cause of action — has been endorsed by a dozen international law experts in an amicus memorandum submitted in *Trajano v. Marcos*.[21] An excerpt follows.

---

[21] On the brief were D'Amato, Days, Falk, Glennon, Grossman, Hartman (Fitzpatrick), Koh, Lichtenstein, Lillich, Lobel, McDougal, Newman, Schachter, Steiner, Weissbrodt, Weston, and Lake. The brief was published in Cole, Lobel, & Koh, *Interpreting the Alien Tort Statute: Amicus Curiae Memorandum of International Law Scholars and Practitioners in Trajano v. Marcos*, 12 Hastings Int'l & Comp. L. Rev. 1 (1988). For a discussion of the historical and juridical underpinnings of the right to an effective remedy, see Paust, *On Human Rights: the Use of Human Rights Precepts in U.S. History and the Right to an Effective Remedy in Domestic Courts*, 10 Mich. J. Int'l L. 543-652 (1989).

Brief on Behalf of International Experts, Drafted by Center for Constitutional Rights, in *Trajano v. Marcos*, 878 F.2d 1439 (9th Cir. 1989) (footnotes omitted):

Even accepting *arguendo* the Justice Department's position that section 1350 does not itself provide a cause of action, it does not follow that plaintiffs lack an enforceable right of action. This Court may find that plaintiffs can derive a cause of action . . . directly from international law. Since Nuremberg, the customary international law of human rights has developed to the point where it provides individuals with a right to invoke it directly in domestic courts. As the United States itself established in its Memorandum in *Filartiga*, a right of action can be located *in international law itself* for certain egregious customary international law violations. *See* [Memorandum of the United States As Amicus curiae submitted in *Filartiga v. Peña-Irala, reprinted in*] 19 I.L.M. [585,] 601-06 (1980).

Arguing that the law of nations "does not give plaintiffs a private right of action," J.D. Br. at 24, the Justice Department now effectively renounces the position it maintained in *Filartiga*. Its argument, however, rests on a profound misunderstanding of the relation between customary international law and U.S. law, one which attempts to resurrect a strictly "statist" view of international law that neither the Framers nor contemporary international law scholars accept.

The Justice Department maintains that "the traditional role of the 'law of nations' is not the creation of private rights." *Id.* at 27. But it is precisely this "traditional" view of international law that the Government's 1980 *Filartiga* Memorandum pointed out had long been rejected. Government *Filartiga* Memorandum, 19 I.L.M. at 601-602. In *Filartiga*, the United States explained that international law had evolved considerably since the days when states were viewed as absolutely sovereign with regard to treatment of their own citizens, and that international law was deemed part of municipal law only when municipal law expressly incorporated it. *Id.* The United States' *Filartiga* Memorandum carefully delineated the development of an international law of human rights, from "[e]arly in this century" to 1980. *Id.* at 589-95. The Memorandum demonstrated the obsolescence of the view that international law is wholly international, and established that customary international law guarantees individuals "certain fundamental human rights," including the right to be free from torture. *Id.* at 589, 595-601. This evolution, the United States explained, is also reflected in the international law of remedies:

> A corollary to the traditional view that the law of nations dealt primarily with the relationship among nations rather than individuals was the doctrine that generally only states, not individuals, could seek to enforce rules of international law. . . . Just as the traditional view no longer reflects the state of customary international law, neither does the latter doctrine. . . . The more recently evolved international law of human rights similarly endows individuals with the right to invoke international law, in a competent forum and under appropriate circumstances.

Government *Filartiga* Memorandum, . . . 19 I.L.M. at 602. The historical evolution portrayed by the United States' Government *Filartiga* Memorandum has been widely accepted among scholars.

Thus, modern international law recognizes that individuals may invoke domestic remedies for violations of certain fundamental norms of international human rights law, such as torture. The Universal Declaration of Human Rights, which is widely acknowledged as reflecting binding norms of customary international law, guarantees the following procedural right:

> Everyone has the right to an effective remedy by the competent national tribunals for acts violating the fundamental rights granted him by the constitution or by law.

Universal Declaration of Human Rights, Article 8. The International Covenant on Civil and Political Rights, also cited by the United States . . . by the *Filartiga* court as evidence of customary international law, . . . similarly obligates states to provide individuals with "an effective remedy" for violations of human rights. International Covenant on Civil and Political Rights, Article 2(3).

While nations have discretion regarding which "national tribunals" will provide the effective remedy required, once an individual seeks redress from one tribunal the burden rests on the respondent to show that another effective tribunal is more appropriate. Where, as here, there is no effective remedy other than the domestic judicial remedy, customary law requires that that judicial remedy be made available.

The practice of nations, like the United States, that recognize international law as part of domestic law further confirms the customary obligation of the United States to provide effective judicial remedies for violations of fundamental human rights. Precedents from the nineteenth century prize cases to the twentieth century expropriation cases make clear that the direct enforceability of customary international law by individuals in federal courts is well-accepted in United States jurisprudence. Most recently in *Martinez-Baca v. Suarez-Mason*, No. C-87-2057-SC, Slip Op. (N.D. Cal. Jan. 12, 1988), the court held that a United States citizen could invoke customary international human rights law in federal court directly under 28 U.S.C. § 1331 for acts of torture and prolonged arbitrary detention. *See also Forti*, 672 F. Supp. at 1543-44. . . .

Customary law does not recognize a right of judicial enforcement for *all* violations of the law of nations, or even for all rights set forth in the Universal Declaration of Human Rights. Article 8 expressly limits the right to an effective remedy to "fundamental" rights. The United States, in its *Filartiga* memorandum, stressed this important limitation, reflected in the Supreme Court's decision in *Sabbatino*, 376 U.S. at 428, 430 n.34:

> Indeed, it is likely that only a few rights have the degree of specificity and universality to permit private enforcement and that the protection of other asserted rights must be left to the political branches of government.

See Government *Filartiga* Memorandum, . . . 19 I.L.M. at 604. But where, as here, individuals allege that they have suffered violations of fundamental customary international law norms, such as torture or degrading treatment or punishment, genocide, summary execution, arbitrary detention, or disappearance, international law contemplates domestic judicial enforcement.

NOTES AND QUESTIONS

1. Judge Jensen appears to have been influenced, in concluding that international law could not be the source of a private right of action, by Professor Henkin's statement:

> "International law itself, finally, does not require any particular reaction to violations of international law. . . . Whether and how the United States wishes to react to such violations are domestic questions . . . ." L. Henkin, Foreign Affairs and the Constitution 224 (1972).

That statement appears to have reflected the prevailing view in 1972. *See also United States v. Altstoetter (The "Justice Case")*, 3 Trials of War Criminals 970 (1951): "This universality and superiority of international law does not necessarily imply universality of its enforcement. . . . [N]otwithstanding the paramount authority of the substantive rules of common international law, the doctrine of national sovereignty has been preserved through [states'] control of enforcement machinery." The fact that a strong, perhaps prevailing, view now has emerged to the contrary illustrates the importance of knowing the recent writings in constructing international law arguments.

2. Courts of many countries have recognized that international law does include the right to an effective remedy for violation of rights. For example in *Borovsky v. Commissioner of Immigration*, 90 Phil. Rpts. 107 (1951), the Supreme Court of the Philippines, whose jurisprudence draws heavily on that of the U.S., ordered an excludable alien released from indefinite detention on the ground that his detention violated customary law as reflected in the Universal Declaration of Human Rights. Similarly the Constitutional Court of Germany has declared that though "generally recognized principles of international law included only a few legal rules that directly create rights and duties of private individuals by virtue of the international law itself," they do create such rights and duties in "the sphere of the minimum standards for the protection of human rights." *In the Matter of Republic of the Philippines*, 46 BVerfGE 342, 362 (2BvM 1/76 December 13, 1977).

3. What arguments support the conclusion that international law includes the right to an effective remedy by a national tribunal? If a government were party to the Optional Protocol to the Covenant on Civil and Political Rights, do you think that the availability of the Protocol's complaint procedure would satisfy the requirement of an effective national remedy, or would the government in addition be obliged to recognize a right to seek redress before a national judicial or administrative body?

3. General Principles of Law Recognized by the Community of Nations

A third source of international law identified by Article 38(1) of the Statute of the International Court of Justice can be derived from "general principles of law recognized by civilized nations" (also called the "community of nations" in contemporary writings).[22] Courts in the U.S. seem not to have addressed the status of general principles in U.S. law. A compelling argument may be made that general principles, like practice, are part of customary law, as discussed in R. Lillich & F. Newman, International Human Rights: Problems of Law and Policy 54-55 (1979):

> With respect to content as opposed to sources, it is convenient to classify international law norms in two groups: the written and the unwritten. The latter category, which resembles the unwritten common law of the Anglo-American legal tradition, consists of the customary rules and general principles mentioned above. Together these concepts comprise customary international law.... [C]ustomary international law is binding upon all states, even though its content is uncodified and therefore often is more difficult to ascertain.

U.S. courts have neither accepted nor rejected that view though a few have discussed general principles in the course of discussing customary law. *See, e.g., United States v. Arlington, Va.*, 702 F.2d 485, 487-88 (4th Cir. 1983) (foreign government-owned property used for public non-commercial purposes is exempt from local real estate taxation); *Jeanneret v. Vichey*, 693 F.2d 259 (2d Cir. 1982) (illegal export of an art object does not render a good-faith importer liable for reduction in value of object); *Von Dardel v. U.S.S.R.*, 623 F. Supp. 246 (D.D.C. 1985) (unlawful imprisonment of a foreign diplomat) *vacated on other grounds*, ____ F. Supp. ____, 1990 WL 55813 (D.D.C. Cir. 1990); *Chiriboga v. International Bank for Reconstruction & Development*, 616 F. Supp. 963 (D.D.C. 1985) (international organizations are immune from suits by employees arising out of the employment relationship).

General principles may be "drawn from private law principles common to the world's major legal systems and have been invoked primarily to develop international law interstitially, to resolve issues not adequately addressed by treaty or practice."[23] General principles may also be derived

---

[22] *See, e.g.*, Covenant on Civil and Political Rights, Art. 15; *see also* Coliver & Newman, *Using International Human Rights Law to Influence United States Foreign Population Policy: Resort to Courts or Congress?*, 20 N.Y.U.J. Int'l. L. & Pol. 53, 65 (1987).

[23] Coliver & Newman, *supra*, at 65.

from the resolutions, decisions, and other instruments of intergovernmental organizations. Some commentators view general principles "as derived from natural law: they exist regardless of whether or not they are followed in fact by states."[24]

4. Peremptory Norms

Vienna Convention on the Law of Treaties, 115 U.N.T.S. 331, T.S. No. 58 (1980), 8 I.L.M. 679 (1979), *entered into force* January 27, 1980:

Article 53
Treaties conflicting with a peremptory norm
of general international law (jus cogens)

A treaty is void if, at the time of its conclusion, it conflicts with a peremptory norm of general international law. For the purposes of the present Convention, a peremptory norm of general international law is a norm accepted and recognised by the international community of States as a whole as a norm from which no derogation is permitted and which can be modified only by a subsequent norm of general international law having the same character. . . .

Article 64
Emergence of a new peremptory norm
of general international law (jus cogens)

If a new peremptory norm of general international law emerges, any existing treaty which is in conflict with that norm becames void and terminates.

1 Restatement (Third) of the Foreign Relations Law of the United States § 102, reporter's note 6 (1987):

. . .The Vienna Convention requires that the norm (and its peremptory character) must be "accepted and recognized by the international community of States as a whole" . . ., [which] apparently . . . means by "a very large majority" of states, even if over dissent by "a very small number" of states. . . .

Although the concept of *jus cogens* is not accepted, its content is not agreed. There is general agreement that the principles of the United Nations Charter prohibiting the use of force are *jus cogens*. . . . It has been suggested that norms that create "international crimes" and obligate all states to proceed against violations are also peremptory. . . . Such norms might include rules prohibiting genocide, slave-trading and slavery, apartheid and other gross violations of human rights, and perhaps attacks on diplomats. . . .

---

[24]*See* R. Lillich & F. Newman, International Human Rights: Problems of Law and Policy 54 (1979); *see also* van Boven, *Survey of the Positive International Law of Human Rights*, in The International Dimensions of Human Rights 107 (K. Vasak ed. 1982).

J. OBSTACLES TO APPLICATION OF INTERNATIONAL HUMAN RIGHTS LAW

There are other issues that arise in applying international human rights law, including political questions, sovereign immunity, standing, failure to state a claim, national policies that contradict customary norms, acts of state, foreign sovereign immunity, statute of limitations, damages, and choice of law. Most of those issues could not be asserted in regard to the hypothetical situation presented at the beginning of this chapter about the two youths. Nonetheless, the issues are discussed here because they are frequently raised in both international human rights litigation and other cases involving international law.

1. Challenges to U.S. Foreign Policy: Political Questions, Sovereign Immunity, Standing, and Failure to State a Cause of Action

Committee of U.S. Citizens Living in Nicaragua v. Reagan, 859 F.2d 929 (D.C. Cir. 1988):

Judge MIKVA, Circuit Judge: . . .
[Plaintiffs sought to stop the U.S. from continuing to provide assistance to the Nicaraguan Democratic Resistance Forces, known as the Contras and which was an armed force opposed the government of Nicaragua. The plaintiffs relied upon the judgment of the International Council of Justice in the *Case Concerning Military and Paramilitary Activities in and Against Nicaragua* (Nicaragua v. United States), 1986 I.C.J. 14, which found the U.S. support of the Contras to be a violation of its international law obligations.]

A.   The Political Question Doctrine

"No branch of the law of justiciability is in such disarray as the doctrine of the 'political question.'" C. Wright, *The Law of Federal Courts* 74 (4th ed. 1983). Professor Wright concludes that "there is no workable definition of characteristics that distinguish political questions from justiciable questions, and . . . the category of political questions is 'more amenable to description by infinite itemization than by generalization.'" *Id.* at 75 (footnote omitted). The Supreme Court has voiced a similar sentiment, warning us that "it is error to suppose that every case or controversy which touches foreign relations lies beyond judicial cognizance." *Baker v. Carr*, 369 U.S. 186, 211 . . . (1962). Given the care with which the political question doctrine should be applied and given the variety of claims encompassed by the present case, we find the trial court's blanket invocation of the political question doctrine to be inappropriate.

To the extent that political question cases contain factors that make them genuinely nonjusticiable, some of those elements can be found here. For example, judicial refusal to resolve political questions "is founded primarily on the doctrine of separation of powers." C. Wright, *supra*, at 75. Courts often underscore this factor by pointing to "a textually demonstrable constitutional commitment of the issue to a coordinate branch of government." *Baker v. Carr*, 369 U.S. at 217 . . . ;

see also L. Tribe, *American Constitutional Law* 96 (2d ed. 1988) (distinguishing the textual commitment rationale as the "classical" version of the political question doctrine). As the trial court noted in this case, foreign policy decisions are the subject of just such a textual commitment. "The conduct of the foreign relations of our Government is committed by the Constitution to the Executive and Legislative — 'the political' — Departments." *Oetjen v. Central Leather Co.*, 246 U.S. 297, 302...(1918). Together, those departments possess the sole power to enter into treaties and subsequently to alter them. *See Whitney v. Robertson*, 124 U.S. 190, 194...(1887) ("Congress may modify [treaty] provisions, so far as they bind the United States"). Similarly, only the political departments can submit our nation to an international court's jurisdiction or thereafter rescind that commitment.

This facet of the political question doctrine may well bar consideration of some appellants' claims. The first two groups of appellants comprise organizations seeking to strengthen the United Nations and to help the citizens of Nicaragua. These organizations' claims seem especially vulnerable to dismissal under a doctrine that "excludes from judicial review those controversies which revolve around policy choices and value determinations constitutionally committed for resolution to the [political branches]." *Japan Whaling Ass'n v. American Cetacean Soc'y*, 478 U.S. 221, 230...(1986). Indeed, to the extent that the organizational appellants in this case allege "purely ideological interests in the agency's action," *Action Alliance of Senior Citizens v. Heckler*, 789 F.2d 931, 937 (D.C. Cir. 1986), they may even lack standing.

... Neither individuals nor organizations have a cause of action in an American court to enforce ICJ judgments. The ICJ is a creation of national governments working through the U.N.; its decisions operate between and among such governments and are not enforceable by individuals having no relation to the claim that the ICJ has adjudicated — in this case, a claim brought by the government of Nicaragua. Appellants try to sidestep this difficulty by alleging that our government has violated international law rather than styling their suit as an enforcement action in support of the ICJ judgment. The United States' contravention of an ICJ judgment may well violate principles of international law. But, as we demonstrate below, those violations are no more subject to challenge by private parties in this court than is the underlying contravention of the ICJ judgment. For these reasons, we do not rest on the political question doctrine in rejecting the claims brought by these first two groups of appellants. *See Sanchez-Espinoza v. Reagan*, 770 F.2d 202, 206 (D.C. Cir. 1985). Rather, we dismiss these claims on the ground that private parties have no cause of action in this court to enforce an ICJ decision.

The third and final group of claims in this case is brought by those appellants who allege infringement of their personal liberty and property rights. The trial court's determination that these claims raise political questions is troubling. This court's recent warning about the political question doctrine applies to the case before us with special force: the doctrine's "shifting contours and uncertain underpinnings" make it "susceptible to indiscriminate and overbroad application to claims properly before the federal courts." *Ramirez de Arellano v. Weinberger*, 745 F.2d 1500, 1514 (D.C. Cir. 1984) (en banc), *vacated on other grounds*, 471 U.S. 1113...(1985).

To be sure, even those appellants who advance claims based on personal rights persist in mingling those claims with an attempt to enforce the ICJ judgment. Nonetheless, the core of this third set of claims lies in the fifth amendment.

Appellants contend that funding of the Contras deprives them of liberty and property "without due process of law" not only because they are generally threatened by the war in Nicaragua but also because they are intended targets of the Contra "resistance." These are serious allegations and not ones to be dismissed as nonjusticiable. As our court declared in rejecting a political question defense to a fifth amendment takings claim, "[t]he Executive's power to conduct foreign relations free from the unwarranted supervision of the Judiciary cannot give the Executive *carte blanche* to trample the most fundamental liberty and property rights of this country's citizenry." *Ramirez de Arellano*, 745 F.2d at 1515. As appellants point out, the Supreme Court has repeatedly found that claims based on such rights are justiciable, even if they implicate foreign policy decisions. *See, e.g., Regan v. Wald*, 468 U.S. 222 . . . (1984); *Dames & Moore v. Regan*, 453 U.S. 654 . . . (1981).

Notwithstanding the fact that appellants' claims of infringed rights are justiciable, however, we find the claims themselves to be insufficient as a matter of law. Examining the factual pleadings closely, we find no allegation that the United States itself has participated in or in any way sought to encourage injuries to Americans in Nicaragua. We therefore conclude that appellants' fifth amendment cause of action fails to state a claim on which relief can be granted. On that basis, we dismiss this final group of appellants' claims.

B.   Appellants Have No Basis in Domestic Law for Enforcing the ICJ Judgment

   1.   *The status of international law in the United States' domestic legal order*

Appellants argue that the United States' decision to disregard the ICJ judgment and to continue funding the Contras violates three types of international law. First, contravention of the ICJ judgment is said to violate part of a United States treaty, namely Article 94 of the U.N. Charter. That article provides that "[e]ach Member of the United Nations undertakes to comply with the decision of the International Court of Justice in any case to which it is a party." U.N. Charter, art. 94. Second, disregard of the ICJ judgment allegedly violates principles of customary international law. One such principle holds that treaties in force shall be observed. Appellants contend that another such principle requires parties to ICJ decisions to adhere to those decisions. Third, the United States may have violated peremptory norms of international law. Such norms, often referred to as *jus cogens* (or "compelling law"), enjoy the highest status in international law and prevail over both customary international law and treaties. Appellants' contention that the United States has violated *jus cogens* forms their primary argument before this court. They contend that the obligation of parties to an ICJ judgment to obey that judgment is not merely a customary rule but actually a peremptory norm of international law.

For purposes of the present lawsuit, the key question is not simply whether the United States has violated any of these three legal norms but whether such violations can be remedied by an American court or whether they can only be redressed on an international level. In short, do violations of international law have domestic legal consequences? The answer largely depends on what form the "violation" takes. Here, the alleged violation is the law that Congress enacted and that the President signed, appropriating funds for the Contras. When our government's two political branches, acting together, contravene an international legal norm, does this court have any authority to remedy the violation? The answer is "no" if the type of international obligation that Congress and the President violate is either a treaty or a rule of customary international law. If, on the other hand, Congress and the President violate a peremptory norm (or *jus cogens*), the domestic legal consequences are unclear. We need not resolve this uncertainty, however, for we find that the principles appellants characterize as peremptory norms of international law are not recognized as such by the community of nations. Thus, as we explain below in greater detail, none of the claims that appellants derive from violations of international law can succeed in this court.

2.   *The effect of subsequent statutes upon prior inconsistent treaties*

. . . [As stated by the Supreme Court:]

[S]o far as a treaty made by the United States with any foreign nation can become the subject of judicial cognizance in the courts of this country, it is subject to such acts as Congress may pass for its enforcement, modification or repeal.

[*Head Money Cases*, 112 U.S. 580,] at 598-99 [1884]. . .; *see also Whitney v. Robertson*, 124 U.S. 190, 194. . .(1888). No American court has wavered from this view in the subsequent century. Indeed, in a comparatively recent case, our court reaffirmed the principle that treaties and statutes enjoy equal status and therefore that inconsistencies between the two must be resolved in favor of the *lex posterior*. In *Diggs v. Shultz*, 470 F.2d 461 (D.C. Cir. 1972), *cert. denied*, 411 U.S. 931. . . (1973), this court reviewed a claim by citizens of what was then Southern Rhodesia, assailing the United States' failure to abide by U.N. Security Council Resolution 232. That resolution directed U.N. members to impose a trade embargo against Rhodesia. The court found that America's contravention of Resolution 232 was required by Congress' adoption of the so-called Byrd Amendment "whose purpose and effect. . . was to detach this country from the U.N. boycott of Southern Rhodesia in blatant disregard of our treaty undertakings." *Id*. at 466. "Under our constitutional scheme," the court concluded, "Congress can denounce treaties if it sees fit to do so, and there is nothing the other branches of government can do about it. . . [; thus] the complaint [states] no tenable claim in law." *Id*. at 466-67.

These precedents dispose of any claim by appellants that the United States has violated its treaty obligation under Article 94. It is true, of course, that the facts here differ somewhat from the situation in *Diggs*. Congress has not clearly repudiated the requirement in Article 94 that every nation comply with an ICJ decision "in any case to which it is a party." U.N. Charter, art. 94. Rather, our government asserts that it never consented to ICJ jurisdiction in cases like the Nicaragua dispute. Thus, Congress may well believe that its support for the Contras, while contravening the ICJ judgment, does not violate its treaty obligation under Article 94. And, unless Congress makes clear its intent to abrogate a treaty, a court will not lightly infer such intent but will strive to harmonize the conflicting enactments. *See Cook v. United States*, 288 U.S. 102. . .(1933).

At this stage of the present case, however, the key question is not whether Congress intended to abrogate Article 94. Since appellants *allege* that Congress has breached Article 94, we must determine whether such a claim could ever prevail. The claim could succeed only if appellants could prove that a prior treaty — the U.N. Charter — preempts a subsequent statute, namely the legislation that funds the Contras. It is precisely that argument that the precedents of the Supreme

Court and of this court foreclose. We therefore hold that appellants' claims based on treaty violations must fail.

Our conclusion, of course, speaks not at all to whether the United States has upheld its treaty obligations under international law. As the Supreme Court said in the *Head Money Cases*, a treaty "depends for the enforcement of its provisions on the interest and honor of the governments which are parties to it. If these fail, its infraction becomes the subject of international negotiations and reclamations... [but] with all this the judicial courts have nothing to do and can give no redress." 112 U.S. at 598.... This conclusion reflects the United States' adoption of a partly "dualist" — rather than strictly "monist" — view of international and domestic law. "[D]ualists view international law as a discrete legal system [which]...operates wholly on an inter-nation plane."

... Given that dualist jurisprudence, we cannot find — as a matter of *domestic* law — that congressional enactments violate prior treaties.

Finally, we note that even if Congress' breach of a treaty were cognizable in domestic court, appellants would lack standing to rectify the particular breach that they allege here. Article 94 of the U.N. Charter simply does not confer rights on private individuals. Treaty clauses must confer such rights in order for individuals to assert a claim "arising under" them. *See* U.S. Const. art. III, § 2, cl. 1; 28 U.S.C. § 1331 (1982). Whether a treaty clause does create such enforcement rights is often described as part of the larger question of whether that clause is "self-executing." *See, e.g.*, Riesenfeld, *The Doctrine of Self-Executing Treaties and U.S. v. Postal: Win At Any Price?*, 74 Am. J. Int'l L. 892, 896-97 (1980) (question whether a particular treaty requires implementing legislation is different from the international law question of whether treaty "aims at the immediate creation of rights and duties of private individuals which are enforceable," but both questions are part of the "concept of self-executing treaties"); *cf.* Restatement (Third) of Foreign Relations Law § 111 comment h (1987) (question of treaty's self-executing nature is "distinct from whether the treaty creates private rights or remedies")....

...We conclude that appellants' attempt to enjoin funding of the Contras based on a violation of Article 94 would fail even if Congress' abrogation of treaties were cognizable in domestic courts.

3.   *Customary international law and subsequent inconsistent statutes*

In addition to relying on Article 94 to challenge continued funding of the Contras, appellants also invoke the rule "of customary international law that nations must obey the rulings of an international court to whose jurisdiction they submit.".... We accept that some version of this rule describes a norm of customary international law. *See, e.g.*, S. Rosenne, *The Law and Practice of the International Court of Justice* 127 (2d ed. 1985). Even so, it is far from clear that this rule governs situations like the present one, in which a nation that has consented in advance to the Court's jurisdiction disputes whether the terms of that consent extend to a particular case. *Cf.* ICJ Statute art. 36, para. 6 ("dispute as to whether the [ICJ] has jurisdiction...shall be settled by decision of the Court")....For the moment, we assume *arguendo* that Congress' decision to disregard the ICJ judgment violates customary international law.

The question is whether such a violation is cognizable by domestic courts. Once again, the United States' rejection of a purely "monist" view of the international and domestic legal orders shapes our analysis. Statutes inconsistent with principles of customary international law may well lead to international law violations. But within the domestic legal realm, that inconsistent statute simply modifies or supersedes customary international law to the extent of the inconsistency. Although the Supreme Court has never articulated this principle as a firm holding, the Court's persuasive dictum in an important early case established the principle that this and other courts follow.

In *The Paquete Habana*, 175 U.S. 677...(1900), the owner of fishing vessels captured and condemned as prize during the Spanish-American War sought compensation from the United States on the ground that customary international law prohibited such seizures. After canvassing prior state practice and the opinions of commentators, the Court concluded that the prohibition against seizure of boats engaged in coastal fishing, which arose at first from considerations of comity between nations, had ripened into "an established rule of international law." *Id.* at 708.... The Court therefore held that the condemnation was improper because "international law is part of our law, and must be ascertained and administered by the courts of justice of appropriate jurisdiction." *Id.* at 700....

Justice Gray, writing for the Court, qualified this famous statement about the domestic effect of international law with dictum of no less significance: "[W]here there is no treaty, and no controlling executive *or legislative act* or judicial decision, resort must be had to the customs and usages of nations." *Id.* (emphasis added)... Thus, so far as concerned domestic law, the rule was laid down that subsequently enacted statutes would preempt existing principles of customary international law — just as they displaced prior inconsistent treaties....

Few other courts have had occasion to consider the principle that, under domestic law, statutes supersede customary international law. But the principle is implicit in decisions that uphold the statutory abrogation of treaties, "since violation of a treaty is essentially a violation of the principle of customary international law requiring that treaties be observed." L. Henkin, *Foreign Affairs and the Constitution* 460 n. 61 (1972).

As with their refusal to take notice of statutory abrogation of treaties, the courts' disregard of statutory breaches of customary international law is not necessarily required by the Constitution.... Nonetheless, the law in this court remains clear: no enactment of Congress can be challenged on the ground that it violates customary international law. Those of appellants' claims that are predicated on this theory of illegality cannot succeed....

4. *Peremptory norms of internaltional law (jus cogens)*

...[I]n order for...a customary norm of international law to become a peremptory norm, there must be a further recognition by "the international community...*as a whole* [that this is] a norm from which no derogation is permitted." Vienna Convention, art. 53[25]...

Such basic norms of international law as the proscription against murder and slavery may well have the domestic legal effect that appellants suggest. That is, they may well restrain our government in the same way that the Constitution restrains it. If Congress adopted a foreign policy that resulted in the enslavement

---

[25 Vienna Convention, Article 53 is reproduced *supra* in part H.]

of our citizens or other individuals, that policy might well be subject to challenge in domestic court under international law. . . .

We think it clear, however, that the harm that results when a government disregards or contravenes an ICJ judgement does not generate the level of universal disapprobation aroused by torture, slavery, summary execution, or genocide. Appellants try to bootstrap the ICJ's judgment against the United States into a form of *jus cogens* by pointing out that the judgment *relies* on a peremptory norm of international law — that is, that the ICJ invoked the norm proscribing aggressive use of force between nations when it rendered its decision in the Nicaragua case. This argument, however, confuses the judgment itself with the ICJ's rationale for that judgment. The gravamen of appellants' complaint is that compliance with an ICJ judgment is a nonderogable norm of international law, not that a particular judgment constitutes collateral estoppel against the United States as to its violation of a nonderogable norm. Were appellants to advance the latter contention, they would be applying nonmutual, offensive collateral estoppel against the federal government, which generally is not permitted even in domestic law cases. . . much less in international law cases where our government disputes the prior court's jurisdiction. In sum, appellants' attempt to enjoin funding of the Contras on the ground that it violates a peremptory norm of international law by contravening an ICJ judgment is unavailing. The ICJ judgment does not represent such a peremptory norm. . . .

[Case dismissed.]

NOTES AND QUESTIONS

1. In *Committee of U.S. Citizens, supra,* 859 F.2d at 937, the court notes that appellants alleged that Congress breached Article 94 of the U.N. Charter by appropriating money for the Contras in violation of the I.C.J. judgment. The court therefore finds the question of whether Congress intended to breach Article 94 irrelevant. If appellants instead had alleged that Congress had not intended to breach Article 94, would they have had a stronger case? Compare the court's conclusion in the *PLO* case, *supra* in part H, that Congress did not intend to breach the U.N. Headquarters Agreement in passing a statute requiring closure of the PLO observer mission.

2. The court notes that whether a treaty clause "confers rights on private individuals" is but one "part of the larger question of whether that clause is self-executing." What other issues must be analyzed in order to determine whether a treaty clause is self-executing?

3. The court concludes that even if Congress' breach of the U.N. Charter were cognizable in U.S. courts, plaintiffs' claims would fail because Article 94 does not confer rights on individuals. Putting aside other jurisdictional concerns, do you think Nicaragua would have had a cause of action in a

U.S. court to enforce the I.C.J. judgment? If Nicaragua did sue, what allegations should it have made regarding continued funding of the Contras?

4. The court concludes that no challenge can be made to a statute on the ground that it conflicts with a customary norm. 859 F.2d at 939. The court made no effort, however, to construe the customary norm and the statute to be consistent. If you were assigned to raise the issue in a petition for rehearing, what arguments would you make? *See Echeverria* brief, *infra.* Assume that the statute appropriated a certain lump sum of Contra aid and neither designated how much, if any, had to be applied to purely humanitarian uses nor attached any similar limitations.

5. The underlying situation in *Committee of U.S. Citizens, supra,* was significantly changed when the Frente Sandinista Liberacion Nacional was defeated in elections and a Nicaraguan government was installed in 1990 with much more friendly relations with the U.S. government.

6. The court's discussion of peremptory norms is intriguing, in particiular its statement that "they may well restrain our government in the same way that the Constitution restrains it." Can you think of a case in which an argument might be strengthened by invocation of one of the peremptory norms listed in the opinion? In most cases, perhaps, the challenged conduct would be proscribed by the U.S. Constitution. Nonetheless might there be good reasons for making a peremptory-norm argument as well?

Consider a hypothetical case in which indigenous peoples in the Amazon Region seek your help in stopping a U.S.-supported venture from constructing oil wells in, and a road into, their territory. They have statements from respected anthropologists showing that the planned construction will result in the death within 20 years of 50% of the indigenous people over five and 90% of those under five. The U.S. does not challenge that projection but asserts its right to proceed based on the constractor's having obtained a license from the Latin American government in whose territory the development is planned. If a lawsuit were filed in the Second Circuit, do you think the trial judge might find a cause of action based on genocide or international rules that constrain the U.S. "in the same way that the [U.S.] Constitution" does?

---

2. Challenges to U.S. Policies: Customary Norms and Executive, Legislative, and Judicial Acts

In *Matter of Medina*, Interim Decision No. 3078 (BIA 1988), the Bureau of Immigration Appeals not only rejected Medina's claim that her deportation was barred by the Fourth Geneva Convention of 1949 (see excerpts in part H, *supra*); it also rejected her claim that she was entitled to temporary refuge in the U.S. under customary law. The BIA concluded that the right to temporary refuge had not ripened into a norm and that, in any event, Congress had preempted the operation of any such norm by failing to include the relief in the 1980 Refugee Act. Those conclusions were accepted by Judge Peckham in *American Baptist Churches v. Meese*, 712 F. Supp. 756 (N.D. Cal. 1989), discussed in part H, *supra*.

At the time of this writing no court of appeals has squarely addressed those issues. The following excerpt is from a brief submitted by amici Human Rights Advocates, Frank Newman, and the A.C.L.U. of Southern California in a case before the Ninth Circuit, *Echeverria v. INS*, No. 89-70236 (accepted for filing, December 11, 1989; several footnotes and citations omitted):

CONGRESS INTENDED THAT CUSTOMARY INTERNATIONAL NORMS BE APPLIED IN MAKING DEPORTATION DECISIONS

The Board in *Medina* concluded that "most fundamentally," immigration judges are not authorized to apply customary international law in deportation proceedings. Int. Dec 3078 at 18. The Board decided that the Attorney General had not delegated such authority to immigration judges or the Board. *Id.* That decision is fundamentally flawed.

The Attorney General delegated to immigration judges the authority to make deportation decisions "and to take any other action consistent with applicable law and regulations as may be appropriate." 8 C.F.R. § 242.8(a). Congress directed the Attorney General to determine deportability on the basis of "the provisions of this Act, or of any other law or treaty...." ... 8 U.S.C. § 1252(b). Congress defined the laws to be applied by the Attorney General to include "all laws, conventions, and treaties of the United States relating to the immigration, exclusion, deportation, or expulsion of aliens." [Immigration and Nationality Act (INA)] § 101(a)(17), 8 U.S.C. § 1101(a)(17). The Board has not pointed to any pronouncement in which either Congress or the Attorney General limited the mandate of immigration judges to apply all "applicable law."

A. LONGSTANDING RULES OF STATUTORY CONSTRUCTION REQUIRE THAT THE IMMIGRATION AND NATIONALITY ACT BE CONSTRUED TO BE CONSISTENT WITH INTERNATIONAL NORMS

Well established rules of statutory construction require that statutes be construed to be consistent with norms of customary international law unless Congress has clearly indicated its intent to renounce these norms. Chief Justice Marshall proclaimed that "an Act of Congress ought never to be construed to violate the law of nations, if any other possible construction remains...." *Murray v. Schooner Charming Betsy*, 6 U.S. (2 Cranch) 64, 118 (1804). *See also Weinberger v. Rossi*, 456 U.S. 25, 32 (1981); *McCulloch v. Sociedad Nacional de Marineros de Honduras*, 372 U.S. 10, 21-22 (1963); *Lauritzen v. Larsen*, 345 U.S. 571, 578 (1953). That pronouncement has given rise to the presumption that:

> "An act of Congress supersedes an earlier rule of international law or a provision of an international agreement as law of the United States [only] if the purpose of the act to supersede the earlier rule or provision is clear or if the act and the earlier rule or provision cannot be fairly reconciled."

American Law Institute, *Restatement (Third) of the Foreign Relations Law of the United States*, § 115(1)(a) (1987) ("Restatement").

Courts in applying that principle, have interpreted acts of Congress so as not to conflict with norms of customary international law. *See McCulloch*, 372 U.S. at 20-21 (statute construed to be consistent with State Department regulations and "well-established rule of international law") (cited with approval in *Weinberger*, 456 U.S. at 32); *Lauritzen*, 345 U.S. at 578-79 (Jones Act not applicable because United States shipping laws should be applied only to areas and transactions in which United States law considered operative under prevalent doctrines of international law); *Charming Betsy*, 6 U.S. at 118-19 (statute barring commerce between Americans and French construed so as not to violate rights of neutral shippers protected by "law of nations").

Consideration of international law principles in exclusion and deportation proceedings is particularly appropriate because, "in upholding the plenary power of Congress over exclusion and deportation of aliens, the Supreme Court has sought support in international law principles." *Rodriguez-Fernandez v. Wilkinson*, 654 F.2d 1382, 1388 (10th Cir. 1981) ("accepted international law principles" considered in determining that excludable alien could not be detained indefinitely). *See also Fong Yue Ting v. United States*, 149 U.S. 698 (1893) (international legal principles inform Congress' power over aliens); *Palma v. Verdeyen*, 676 F.2d 100, 103 (4th Cir. 1982) ("to ascertain what Congress has authorized" the Attorney General must consider "the treaties, agreements, and customary international law to which the United States subscribes" in determining the extent of process due aliens in exclusion proceedings). In particular, immigration judges have been required to consider relevant treaties in making deportation decisions. *See McCandless v. United States*, 25 F.2d 71 (3d Cir. 1928) (American Indian born in Canada not deportable because of treaty); *Matter of Yellowquill*, 16 I&N Dec. 576 (BIA 1978) (same).

For all of the above reasons, this court must construe the INA to be consistent with relevant international norms.

B.   THE REFUGEE ACT OF 1980 IS NOT A CONTROLLING LEGISLATIVE ACT THAT BARS APPLICATION OF THE NORM OF TEMPORARY REFUGE

The Board in *Medina* and the court in *American Baptist Churches* concluded that the Refugee Act of 1980 supersedes any applicable customary international law norms. *See Medina*, Int. Dec. 3078 at 17; *American Baptist Churches v. Meese*, 712 F. Supp. 756, 771 (N.D. Cal. 1989). The Board and court based their conclusions on the Supreme Court's statement that "where there is no treaty and no controlling executive or legislative act or judicial decision, resort must be had to the customs and usages of civilized nations...." *Id., quoting The Paquete Habana*, 175 U.S. 677, 700 (1900). The Board and court construed that statement to mean that essentially any executive, legislative, or judicial action preempts a customary norm concerning a similar subject. The Board and court failed to recognize that the rule set forth in *The Paquete Habana* merely restates Justice Marshall's maxim, and failed to examine whether the Refugee Act could be construed to be consistent with customary international law. *See Medina* at 17-18; *American Baptist Churches*, 712 F. Supp. at 771.

The Refugee Act of 1980 and the customary norm of temporary refuge are entirely consistent. While the Refugee Act covers only persons who fall within the United Nations Convention Relating to the Status of Refugees' definition, i.e., persons who have a well-founded fear of persecution on account of race, religion, nationality, membership in a particular social group, or political opinion, the customary norm applies to a broader category of persons, and provides for an alternative, more limited form of relief. While refugees may qualify for the more durable remedy of asylum, the customary norm of temporary refuge provides temporary relief from deportation to individuals displaced by civil strife in their home countries, whose physical security will be at risk if they are forced to return. *See Note on International Protection*, Thirty-Third Sess. of the Ex. Com. of the High Commissioner's Programme, U.N. Doc. A/AC.96/609/Rev. 1 at 6 (1982) (distinguishing between the more generous protection accorded to "refugees" and that accorded to persons fleeing civil strife: "the protection extended to persons covered by the wider concept may be correspondingly limited in time, pending a change of circumstances in their country of origin").

Congress should not be assumed to have excluded customary humanitarian law as a basis for relief from deportation in the absence of conclusive, explicit evidence of congressional intent. Unless Congress manifests a clear expression to the contrary, courts must assume that Congress intended that international law be applied in the context of deportation proceedings.

The court in *American Baptist Churches* concluded that Congress specifically rejected the norm of temporary refuge by failing to incorporate it expressly into U.S. law via the Refugee Act. 712 F. Supp. at 771. Congress' failure to include "displaced persons" within the statutory definition of refugee does not indicate its rejection of the norm or temporary refuge. Although there was debate in Congress over whether to grant the relief of *asylum* to displaced persons, not one member of Congress expressed an intent to override the customary norm of temporary refuge, nor did any member of Congress express an intent to deny this broader category of persons an alternative form of relief. There is simply no language in the Act that specifically rejects the norm.

The district court in *American Baptist Churches* further declared that Congress specifically rejected the norm of temporary refuge by rejecting various proposals that would have granted Salvadorans extended voluntary departure (EVD). 712 F. Supp. at 773. Congress' failure to pass a statute granting EVD to Salvadorans should not be construed either as affirmative rejection of the norm of temporary refuge or as approval of the failure of immigration judges and courts to apply the norm in individual deportation proceedings. As Justice Rutledge observed,

> Notwithstanding recent tendency, the idea cannot always be accepted that Congress, by remaining silent and taking no affirmative action in repudiation, gives approval to judicial misconstruction of its enactments. ... [T]here are many reasons, other than to indicate approval of what the courts have done, why Congress may fail to take affirmative action to repudiate their misconstruction of its duly adopted laws. Among them may be the sheer pressure of other and more important business. [Citation omitted.] At times political considerations may work to forbid taking corrective action. And in such cases, as well as others, there may be a strong and proper tendency to trust to the court to correct their own errors [citation], as they ought to do when experience has confirmed or demonstrated the errors' existence. *Cleveland v. United States*, 329 U.S. 14, 22 (1946) (Rutledge, J., concurring).

Although Congressional action might be a more efficient way to implement the United States' obligation to provide temporary refuge, Congress' failure to grant nationality-based relief in no way indicates Congressional intent to preclude immigration judges from applying all "applicable law" in individual cases. The norm does not require that entire nationality groups be granted relief such as EVD, but only that individual applicants not be forcibly repatriated. Moreover, Congress and the Attorney General explain their failure to grant relief to Salvadorans on the grounds that (a) most Salvadorans are "economic" refugees who seek better economic conditions, or (b) that the conflict in El Salvador currently is not resulting in significant humanitarian law violations (a factual determination that must be determined by immigration judges). Congress and the Executive do not claim that they are entitled to return aliens to countries whose governments are unwilling or unable to protect their fundamental rights under international humanitarian law.

Even if this Court should find that Congress intended the Refugee Act to supersede preexisting norms of customary law, it nonetheless should rule that the norm of temporary refuge is applicable because the norm has gained significantly in weight and in breadth of acceptance since passage of the Refugee Act.... [T]he international community, individual states, intergovernmental organizations, and even the United States increasingly have invoked the norm of temporary refuge in recent years, and have further codified the norm as the problem of displacement caused by civil strife has intensified. The crystallization of the norm reached the point where in 1985, the United Nations High Commissioner for Refugees ("UNHCR") stated that it "has now come to be characterized as a peremptory norm of international law," from which no derogation is permitted. *Report of the United Nations High Commissioner for Refugees*, para. 22-23, U.N. Doc. E/1985/ 62 (1985)....

Courts must take account of the dynamic nature of customary international law and must apply new customary norms as they evolve over time. *See e.g., Filartiga v. Peña-Irala*, 630 F.2d 876, 881 (2d Cir. 1981). *See also* Henkin, *The President and International Law*, 80 Am. J. Int'l L. 930, 933 (1986) ("a supervening principle of customary law will not be denied domestic effect because of some earlier act of Congress"). Therefore, the Board of Immigration Appeals erred in finding that the Refugee Act of 1980 had superseded the norm of temporary refuge.

In sum, because the Refugee Act and the customary norm of temporary refuge may be construed consistently, they must be construed to give effect to both. *See Charming Betsy*, 6 U.S. at 118.

NOTES

For further reading, see:

G. Goodwin-Gill, The Refugee in International Law (1983);

A. Grahl-Madsen, The Status of Refugees in International Law (1966, 1972);

Perluss & Hartman, *Temporary Refuge: Emergence of a Customary Norm*, 26 Va. J. Int'l L. 551 (1986);

Steinhardt, *The United Nations and Refugees: 1945-1988*, AIUSA Legal Support Network Newsl., Fall 1988, at 103.

Kirgis, *Agora: May the President Violate Customary International Law? (Cont'd)*, 81 Am. J. Int. L. 371 (1987) (several footnotes and citations omitted):

FEDERAL STATUTES, EXECUTIVE ORDERS AND "SELF-EXECUTING CUSTOM"

A hotly debated issue raised...during the drafting of the *Restatement of Foreign Relations Law of the United States (Revised)* has to do with the relationship between customary international law and federal law in the United States. Most of the debate addressed whether a newly emerged custom would supersede an earlier federal statute or self-executing treaty. The reporters of the *Restatement* took a strong stand at first, placing custom on the same plane as federal statutes and self-executing treaties: in case of conflict, the latest in time should prevail. Criticism rolled in, and the reporters eventually retreated a bit. The final version says only that since custom and international agreements have equal authority in international law, and both are law of the United States, "arguably later customary law should be given effect as law of the United States, even in the face of an earlier law or agreement, just as a later international agreement of the United States is given effect in the face of an earlier law or agreement."

A related question is whether custom could ever supersede a federal executive act, as a matter of U.S. law. Put conversely, the question is whether a federal executive act would prevail over a contrary customary rule. A recent case, *Garcia-Mir v. Meese*,[26] has redirected the debate toward this question. Professor Henkin appears to have the best of the debate so far, but his position still needs some modification. To that end, one must focus on the President's "sole" powers and on what could be called "self-executing custom."

Garcia-Mir dealt with an executive act as well as a congressional enactment. Cuban refugees were being detained in the Atlanta Penitentiary, as excludable aliens. One group had committed crimes in Cuba before joining the "freedom flotilla" to the United States, and consequently was never paroled into this country. A second group had been paroled into the United States, but parole was subsequently revoked. In the trial court, both groups obtained an order directing the U.S. Government to provide a separate parole revocation hearing for each refugee. On appeal, one issue was whether customary international law prohibiting prolonged arbitrary detention[27] required that the refugees be given individual hearings or released.

The court quoted well-known language from *The Paquete Habana*: "Where there is no treaty, and no controlling executive or legislative act or judicial decision, resort must be had to the customs and usages of civilized nations."[28] Taking this to mean that any executive or legislative act would prevail over custom — apparently without regard to whichever is later in time — the court found that a 1980

---

[26] 788 F.2d 1446 (11th Cir.), *cert. denied sub nom. Ferrer-Mazorra v. Meese*, 107 S.Ct. 289 (1986).

[27] *See, e.g., Restatement [Third]*... § 702...; Universal Declaration of Human Rights...[Art. 9]; International Covenant on Civil and Political Rights,... Art. 9(1); *Fernandez v. Wilkinson*, 654 F.2d 1382 (10th Cir. 1981)....

[28] 175 U.S. 677, 700 (1900).

legislative act precluded the application of customary international law to the first group and an executive act (by the Attorney General) precluded its application to the second group.

It is questionable whether there was indeed a preclusive legislative act as to the first group. I do not propose to address that issue. If the court was correct as to Congress's intent, the later-in-time rule would be on the side of the congressional enactment. However, if the custom was later in time, there is a question not recognized by the revised *Restatement* that should be answered before the custom could "arguably" prevail.

To examine the question, it is necessary to begin with an elementary point about treaties. Only self-executing treaties have the effect of federal domestic law in the United States. Not all treaties are self-executing. The same principle clearly should apply to customary international law. Although it is not common parlance to speak of "self-executing custom" it is apparent that certain rules of custom are, in effect, self-executing and others are not. The most obvious and most important of the potentially self-executing rules are many of those protecting basic human rights. They benefit individuals directly, and they are specific enough to be enforced judicially.

At the non-self-executing end of the spectrum would be most norms dealing with highly political types of intergovernmental conduct. Professor Henkin has given some examples (overflying foreign territory without consent, bringing down a foreign aircraft, violating a diplomat's immunity), but he has not dubbed them "non-self-executing." In fact, he has said elsewhere, quite flatly, that customary international law is "self-executing."[29] His own examples show that such a flat statement cannot be justified.

The rule against prolonged arbitrary detention would be a "self-executing custom," though not at the level of a peremptory norm. Thus, if any nonperemptory rule of custom could supersede an earlier federal statute, this one could. As a self-executing norm, it could stand on its own entirely apart from whatever auxiliary role it might play as an aid in interpreting constitutional rights and liberties.

With due respect, however, to the view of the reporters of the revised *Restatement*, it is extremely doubtful whether any customary rule, qua custom, could prevail over a validly enacted earlier federal statute. Custom exists as an independent source of U.S. law only as federal common law. At least in fields other than foreign relations, common law — including federal common law — yields to enacted statutory law. Usually, that comes up in the context of a statute later in time than the common law rule, but in a democratic society that has placed rule-making power in the hands of elected representatives, the principle is the same whether the enacted law is earlier or later in time than the nonconstitutional common law rule. Thus, in *Garcia-Mir*, even if the custom were later in time, it should not prevail as a nonconstitutional common law rule in the case of the first group of refugees — provided, of course, that Congress actually intended to authorize indefinite detention.

The result should be different, however, for the second group of refugees. It certainly does not follow from what has been said above that any otherwise-valid

---

[29] Henkin, *International Law as Law in the United States*, 82 Mich. L. Rev. 1555, 1561, 1566 (1984).

federal executive act would prevail over an earlier or later customary rule. In *Garcia-Mir*, the parties and the court focused on the question whether an executive act would have to emanate from the President, himself, to override contrary custom. The court thought not, and held that a decision by the Attorney General (to incarcerate the refugees indefinitely, pending deportation) would suffice. This holding does not fully address the issue.

Even if the President had personally ordered the indefinite detention of the second group of refugees, the contrary rule of customary international law should prevail in a U.S. court. The President has broad constitutional power to conduct foreign affairs, but his power is not unlimited. In particular, his independent power to take action that has domestic lawmaking effect must necessarily be subject to some constraints emanating from the Article I, section 1 grant of all legislative powers to Congress. That grant should preclude the President from exercising independent legislative powers, except to the extent that domestic legislative effect is a necessary concomitant of an Article II power granted to the President alone.

There are three Article II grants that might qualify. They are the grant of authority as commander-in-chief of the armed forces; the authority to receive ambassadors and other public ministers (i.e., to be the chief diplomat); and the authority to execute faithfully the laws of the United States. The latter grant, though sometimes regarded as a source of independent presidential authority, obviously is not. To treat it as a source of independent authority would simply be to grant undefined and undefinable powers to the presidency. Neither the intent of the Framers nor the practice of the last 200 years supports any such untamed presidential authority.

Much more convincing is the argument that, in the absence of authorization from an act of Congress, the President's domestic lawmaking power emanates only from his constitutional authority as commander-in-chief and as chief diplomat. This would give him such legislative power as is necessary for the effective use of the armed forces against opposing armed forces (at least in the event of a congressionally declared war or a true necessity for immediate self-defense), as well as lawmaking authority in the contexts of the recognition of foreign governments,[30] the diplomatic representation of American nationals in their dealings with foreign governments, and other essentially diplomatic functions. These are rather narrow powers, as well they should be in a constitutional system that allocates "all legislative powers" to Congress.

In *Garcia-Mir*, this means that the refugee-detention decision of the executive branch should not have prevailed over a contrary "self-executing" rule of customary international law. This would be true whether the custom crystallized before or after the executive branch's decision, and whether the decision was made by the President himself or by someone else in the executive branch. The decision to detain refugees simply was not the type of decision entrusted to a commander-in-chief of the armed forces or to a diplomat carrying out normal diplomatic functions. It was made by the Attorney General, essentially to maintain law and order. It is immaterial that the Attorney General's authority to deal with refugees stems from a foreign relations statute, the Immigration and Nationality Act. There is no

---

[30] *See United States v. Belmont*, 301 U.S. 324 (1937); *United States v. Pink*, 315 U.S. 203 (1942).

indication of congressional intent in that Act to authorize a step that would violate international law.

If a decision of the executive branch is not made by the President himself, or by authority the President has clearly delegated to a high-ranking civilian Defense Department official (in the case of the commander-in-chief power) or to a high-ranking State Department official (in the case of diplomacy), the presumption should be that it is not within the powers of the commander-in-chief or of the chief diplomat. If the presumption is not convincingly rebutted, "self-executing custom" should prevail as a matter of federal common law. Even if the executive branch's act is by the President or his high-ranking civilian delegate, "self-executing custom" should prevail unless the act squarely comes within one of the two relevant Article II powers.[31]

NOTES AND QUESTIONS

In another part of their brief in *Echeverria* amici advanced the argument that the Immigration and Nationality Act (INA) not only is consistent with the customary norm of temporary refuge, it in fact directly incorporates that and other widely accepted norms of customary law. That argument is based on the Act's direction to the Attorney General to consider "all laws, conventions, and treaties of the United States" in making deportation decisions. "All laws" include customary norms, amici argued, given that those norms unquestionably are part of U.S. law. A panel of the Ninth Circuit rejected that argument in *U.S. v. Aguilar*, 871 F.2d 1436, 1454 (9th Cir. 1989), amended August 14, 1989, holding that the failure of the INA expressly to include customary norms in its definition of "all laws," particularly in light of its reference to treaties, reflects congressional intent to exclude customary norms. What arguments would you make to counter that argument? *See, e.g., Forti I,* excerpted in part I, *supra.* Do you think that the *Aguilar* holding is fatal to amici's argument that the INA should be read to be consistent with customary norms even if it does not expressly incorporate them?

3. Act of State and Foreign Sovereign Immunity

Republic of the Philippines v. Marcos, 806 F.2d 344 (2d Cir. 1986) (*Marcos I*):

Oakes, Circuit Judge.

[The Republic of the Philippines sued to recover five pieces of property, four in New York City and one in Long Island, from the Marcoses and associates. The trial

[31] ...*See* Lobel, *The Limits of Constitutional Power: Conflicts between Foreign Policy and International Law,* 71 Va. L. Rev. 1071, 1120 (1985). ...

court granted a preliminary injunction to enjoin the Marcoses and others from transferring or encumbering the property. The Marcoses and others appealed. The court of appeals affirmed, rejecting the claim that challenged acts were protected by the act of state doctrine.]

Restatement (Second) of Foreign Relations Law § 41 (1965) provides further definition of the doctrine: United States courts "will refrain from examining the validity of an act of a foreign *state* by which that state has exercised its jurisdiction to give effect to its *public* interests" (emphasis added). *See also . . . Restatement (Revised) of Foreign Relations Law* § . . . 469 (Tent. Draft No. 7, 1986). . . . That the acts must be *public* acts of the *sovereign* has been repeatedly affirmed. *See Alfred Dunhill of London, Inc. v. Republic of Cuba*, 425 U.S. 682, 694 & n. 10 (1976). . . ; *Jimenez v. Aristeguieta*, 311 F.2d 547, 557-58 (5th Cir. 1962) (doctrine applies only when an official having sovereign authority acts in an official capacity; a dictator is not the sovereign and his financial crimes committed in violation of his position and not in pursuance of it are not acts of a sovereign, but rather were for his own benefit and "as far from being an act of state as rape"), *cert. denied* 373 U.S. 914 . . . (1963); *see also Arango v. Guzman Travel Advisors Corp.*, 621 F.2d 1371, 1380 (5th Cir. 1980); *Sharon v. Time, Inc.*, 599 F. Supp. 538, 544 (S.D.N.Y. 1984).

Cases relied on by appellants to the effect that acts that are illegal in the foreign state may still be protected from judicial scrutiny under the act of state doctrine are not to the contrary. In *Banco de España*, 114 F.2d at 444, this court held that if the acts are those of a foreign sovereign — including acts of officials purportedly operating in their official capacity — then the act of state doctrine applies. *See also Bernstein*, 163 F.2d at 249; *French v. Banco National de Cuba*, 23 N.Y.2d 46, 52, 242 N.E.2d 704, 709, 295 N.Y.S.2d 433, 440 (1968) (so long as the act is the act of the foreign sovereign, it matters not that the sovereign has transgressed its own laws).

Appellants simply fail to make the crucial distinction between acts of Marcos as head of state, which may be protected from judicial scrutiny even if illegal under Philippine law, and his purely private acts. Although the distinction between public and private acts of a foreign official may be difficult to determine, our courts have repeatedly done so. *See Dunhill*, 425 U.S. at 695 . . . ("Distinguishing between the public and governmental acts of sovereign states on the one hand and their private and commercial acts on the other is not a novel approach.") . . . Since the burden of proof is on the party invoking the act of state defense, *Dunhill*, 425 U.S. at 694, . . . appellants must ultimately demonstrate that the challenged acts of Marcos were in fact public acts (the allegations of the complaint covering both public and private acts). In addition, *Dunhill* appears to require a certain amount of formality to indicate that the act is in fact the act of the sovereign, although probably not the degree of formality suggested by former Judge Sofaer in *Sharon*, 599 F. Supp. at 544-45.

Two other considerations may limit the applicability of the doctrine even to Marcos' public acts. First, the Marcos government is no longer in power. Thus, the danger of interference with the Executive's conduct of foreign policy is surely much less than the typical case where the act of state is that of the current foreign government. Neither of the two cases in our circuit that have applied the doctrine to the acts of former governments, *Banco de España, supra*, and *Bernstein, supra*, discuss the separation of powers issue, and both cases appear more strongly to rely on the earlier sovereign immunity rationale. In *Sabbatino* the Court explicitly questioned this aspect of *Bernstein* in light of the doctrine's recast separation of powers rationale: "The balance of relevant considerations may also be shifted if the government which perpetrated the challenged act of state is no longer in existence, as in the *Bernstein* case, for the political interest of this country may, as a result, be measurably altered." 376 U.S. at 428 . . . . Thus, before the doctrine is applied even to Marcos' public acts, the court must weigh in balance the foreign policy interests that favor or disfavor application of the act of state doctrine.

Moreover, the act of state doctrine reflects respect for foreign states, so that when a state comes into our courts and asks that our courts scrutinize its actions, the justification for application of the doctrine may well be significantly weaker. . . .

In short, the district court will necessarily scrutinize the acts that The Republic challenges. Defendants must present evidence that these acts were public (e.g., that Marcos' wealth was obtained through official expropriation decrees or public monopolies). The court then must decide whether to examine these public acts in light of the considerations discussed above. If it chooses not to do so — and the determination whether the Marcoses obtained their wealth illegally, and hence the determination of ownership of the property at issue in this case, is impossible without such scrutiny — the court should consider deferring to a Philippine adjudication that comports with due process. But in any event, at this stage we agree with the position of the United States quoted above that the defendants have not discharged their burden of proving an act of state. Only after that burden is met do other relevant factors need to be considered.

. . . *Sovereign Immunity*

Appellants also claim that the Marcoses are entitled to sovereign immunity. We agree that appellants have no standing to assert this claim. But even if appellants had standing, we are not at all certain that the immunity of a foreign state, though it extends to its head of state, *Restatement (Second) of Foreign Relations Law* §§ 65, 66(b) (1965), goes so far as to render a former head of state immune as regards his private acts. . . . The rationale underlying sovereign immunity — avoiding embarrassment to our government and showing respect for a foreign state — may well be absent when the individual is no longer head of state and the current government is suing him. In any event, the Foreign Sovereign Immunity Act may not support appellants' immunity claim in light of its "commercial activity" exception, 28 U.S.C. § 1603(d), (e) (1982), and as we said above, these appellants lack standing to raise the immunity issue on the Marcoses' behalf, *Restatement (Second) of Foreign Relations Law* § 71 (1965).

Republic of the Philippines v. Marcos, 862 F.2d 1355 (9th Cir. 1988) (en banc), *cert. denied*, ___ U.S. ___, 109 S.Ct. 1933 (1989) (*Marcos II*):

NOONAN, Circuit Judge.

[In 1986 the Republic of the Philippines filed suit against the Marcoses and several associates alleging civil liability under the Racketeer Influenced Corrupt Organization Act ("RICO") for mail fraud, wire fraud, and transporting stolen property in foreign or interstate commerce of the United States. The Philippines sought to recover property worldwide, including $13 million identified in the U.S. and more than $1.5 billion believed to be held in Swiss bank accounts. The Philippines also sued for $50 billion in punitive damages. The trial court entered a preliminary injunction enjoining the Marcoses from disposing of any assets except for the payment of attorney fees and "normal" living expenses. The Marcoses appealed. A divided panel of the Ninth Circuit reversed. 818 F.2d 1473 (9th Cir. 1987). The Ninth Circuit heard the case en banc (represented by 11 of its judges) and affirmed the district court. Its discussion and the discussion of a dissent concerning act of state issues follow.]

As a practical tool for keeping the judicial branch out of the conduct of foreign affairs, the classification of "act of state" is not a promise to the ruler of any foreign country that his conduct, if challenged by his own country after his fall, may not become the subject of scrutiny in our courts. No estoppel exists insulating a deposed dictator from accounting. No guarantee has been granted that immunity may be acquired by an ex-chief magistrate invoking the magic words "act of state" to cover his or her past performance.

The classification might, it may be supposed, be used to prevent judicial challenge in our courts to many deeds of a dictator in power, at least when it is apparent that sustaining such challenge would bring our country into a hostile confrontation with the dictator. Once deposed, the dictator will find it difficult to deploy the defense successfully. The "balance of considerations" is shifted. *Sabbatino*, 376 U.S. at 428. . . . A *fortiori*, when a ruler's former domain has turned against him and seeks the recovery of what it claims he has stolen, the classification has little or no applicability. The act of state doctrine is supple, flexible, ad hoc. The doctrine is meant to facilitate the foreign relations of the United States, not to furnish the equivalent of sovereign immunity to a deposed leader.

In the instant case the Marcoses offered no evidence whatsoever to support the classification of their acts as acts of state. The burden of proving acts of state rested upon them. *Alfred Dunhill of London, Inc. v. Republic of Cuba*, 425 U.S. 682, 695 . . . (1976). They did not even undertake the proof. The United States, invited by the court to address this matter as an amicus, assures us that the Executive does not at present see the applicability of this defense. . . . The act of state doctrine, the Executive declares, has "no bearing" on this case as it stands. As the doctrine is a pragmatic one, we cannot exclude the possibility that, at some later point in the development of this litigation, the Marcoses might produce evidence that would warrant its application. On the present record, the defense does not apply. . . .

SCHROEDER, Circuit Judge, with whom CANBY, Circuit Judge, joins concurring in part and dissenting in part.
DISSENT: ACT OF STATE DOCTRINE

The majority of our three-judge panel concluded that the act of state doctrine bars consideration of the plaintiffs' claims. I agree with the majority of this en banc court that such a holding is not appropriate on this record. I do not agree with the majority, however, that this injunction can be affirmed without any regard to the act of state doctrine.

The panel majority's use of the act of state doctrine as a threshold bar in the circumstances of this case is not consistent with the development of that doctrine under Supreme Court authority. . . . We have expressly stated that the act of state doctrine is not jurisdictional. . . . Rather, the doctrine involves the judiciary's prudential decision to refrain from adjudicating the legality of a foreign sovereign's public acts that were committed within its own territory. . . . The Supreme Court, in addressing the act of state doctrine, has stated:

> Every sovereign state is bound to respect the independence of every other sovereign state, and the courts of one country will not sit in judgment on the acts of the government of another, done within its own territory. Redress of grievances by reason of such acts must be obtained through the means open to be availed of by sovereign powers as between themselves.

Sabbatino, 376 U.S. at 416. . .(quoting *Underhill v. Hernandez*, 168 U.S. 250, 252. . .(1897)).

The act of state doctrine "expresses the strong sense of the Judicial Branch that its engagement in the task of passing on the validity of foreign acts of state may hinder rather than further this country's pursuit of goals both for itself and for the community of nations as a whole in the international sphere." *Sabbatino*, 376 U.S. at 423 . . . . The Court further elaborated that the doctrine involves separation of powers:

> [The doctrine's] continuing vitality depends on its capacity to reflect the proper distribution of functions between the judicial and political branches of the Government on matters bearing upon foreign affairs. . . . [S]ome aspects of international law touch much more sharply on national nerves than do others; the less important the implications of an issue are for our foreign relations, the weaker the justification for exclusivity in the political branches. . . . [W]e decide only that the Judicial Branch will not examine the validity of a taking of property within its own territory by a foreign sovereign government, extant and recognized by this country at the time of suit. *Id.* at 427-28. . . .

However, these considerations are less compelling in the situation before us, where the foreign government has itself invoked our jurisdiction, and the challenged actions involve a government no longer in power. . . .

At this point, no determinations have been made regarding the capacity in which the Marcoses were acting when the alleged unlawful conduct occurred. Accordingly, the original panel majority erred in finding that, at this stage of the litigation, the act of state doctrine bars adjudication of the bulk of the Philippine government's pendent claims.

The majority decision here, however, goes much further. It declares that the injunction can be affirmed without regard to the act of state doctrine. In my view, we should instead instruct the district court to consider to what extent, if any, the doctrine applies in the circumstances of this case, and on the basis of the record which has developed more fully during the pendency of this interlocutory appeal. Until such consideration can be given, an injunction of this breadth is not appropriate.

This en banc court requested the amicus views of the Department of State on the act of state issues. Its brief concludes that the application of the act of state doctrine at this stage is speculative and the injunction premature. The majority's reliance upon the position of the United States as support for its holding is wholly misplaced. The government urges that an injunction should not have been entered on the basis of this record. The government amicus curiae brief states in appropriate context as follows:

> [T]he record before the district court, which did not include any detailed specification of the factual basis for the bulk of the nonfederal claims, did not make it possible even to analyze the extent to which those claims are properly before the court. . . .

> Even assuming jurisdiction, it is not clear at this stage that the district court should, as a prudential matter, undertake to adjudicate the bulk of the nonfederal claims. The court's capacity to do so fairly and expeditiously and without offending the sensibility of other nations cannot be resolved on this record. Adjudication in this district court may turn out to be barred by considerations of international comity and *forum non conveniens*. . . .

[The opinion of FLETCHER, Circuit Judge, concurring specially in Judge Schroeder's concurring and dissenting opinion has been omitted.]

Liu v. Republic of China, 892 F.2d 1419 (9th Cir. 1989) (footnotes omitted):

[Helen Liu brought an action against the Republic of China (ROC) and Admiral Wong, its Director of the Defense Intelligence Bureau, for ordering two gunmen to kill her husband in California.]

. . . THE ACT OF STATE DOCTRINE . . .

First, we address whether Liu's suit against the ROC for damages for the assassination of her husband is barred by the doctrine. Although the ROC did not raise this argument, we are concerned with the potential for embarrassing the Executive Branch, and raise the issue *sua sponte*.

In *Letelier*, 488 F. Supp. [665,] at 673-74 [(D.D.C. 1989)], Chile argued that even if its officials ordered the assassination of Letelier, those acts would be immune from review under this doctrine because they occurred within Chile, although the assassination occurred in the United States. The court rejected this argument because:

> To hold otherwise would totally emasculate the purpose and effectiveness of the Foreign Sovereign Immunities Act by permitting a foreign state to reimpose the so recently supplanted framework of sovereign immunity as defined prior to the Act "'through the back door, under the guise of the act of state doctrine.'" *Id.* at 674. . . .

In *International Ass'n of Machinists & Aerospace Workers v. OPEC*, this court held that the OPEC nations' price fixing activities, although not entitled to sovereign immunity under the FSIA, were acts of state. We held that the FSIA did not supersede the act of state doctrine because the doctrine addressed different concerns than the doctrine of sovereign immunity. *OPEC*, 649 F.2d [1354, 1359-60 (9th Cir. 1981) *cert denied*, 454 U.S. 1163 (1982)]. "While the FSIA ignores the underlying purpose of a state's action, the act of state doctrine does not." *Id.* at 1360. Consequently, the mere fact that the FSIA confers jurisdiction on this court to hear this type of case does not end our inquiry. We must still determine whether the act of state doctrine mandates abstention in cases alleging that a foreign government ordered the assassination of an American citizen in the United States. We conclude that it does not.

One factor we must consider is whether the foreign state was acting in the public interest. "When the state *qua state* acts in the public interest, its sovereignty is asserted. The courts must proceed cautiously to avoid an affront to that sovereignty." *Id*. Thus, any injunctive relief "instructing a foreign sovereign to alter its chosen means of allocating and profiting from its own valuable natural resources" would affront the sovereignty of a state. *Id*. at 1361. Ordinarily, this type of concern will be generated only when courts are asked to judge the legality or propriety of public acts committed within a foreign state's own borders. *See Sabbatino*, 376 U.S. 398, 400-01 [1964] (act of state involved the Cuban government's act of expropriating the property of aliens located within Cuba); *see also Republic of Iraq v. First Nat'l City Bank*, 353 F.2d 47, 51 (2d Cir. 1965), *cert. denied*, 382 U.S. 1027 . . . (1966) ("when property confiscated is within the United States at the time of the attempted confiscation, our courts will give effect to acts of state 'only if they are consistent with the policy and law of the United States.'" . . .). In this case, however, we are asked to judge the legality and propriety of an act that occurred within the borders of the United States. Such an inquiry would hardly affront the sovereignty of a foreign nation.

Another factor to be considered is the degree of international consensus regarding an activity. In *Sabbatino*, the Supreme Court stated:

> It should be apparent that the greater the degree of codification or consensus concerning a particular area of international law, the more appropriate it is for the judiciary to render decisions regarding it, since the courts can then focus on the application of an agreed principle to circumstances of facts rather than on the sensitive task of establishing a principle not inconsistent with the national interest or with international justice. Sabbatino, 376 U.S. at 428. . . .

Last, this is not the sort of case that is likely to hinder the Executive Branch in its formulation of foreign policy, or result in differing pronouncements on the same subject. *See OPEC*, 649 F.2d at 1358 ("[T]he United States must speak with one voice. . . ."). Rather, this court would more likely embarrass the Executive Branch if we summarily invoked the act of state doctrine to bar an American citizen from litigating a wrongful death suit for a murder that occurred in the United States. "The decision to deny access to judicial relief is not one we make lightly." *OPEC*, 649 F.2d at 1360. We conclude that none of the factors present in OPEC that warranted the invocation of the act of state doctrine is present in this type of case. . . .

To the credit of the ROC, rather than attempting to hide the sordid circumstances involved in Liu's assassination, it made an investigation and publicly brought to trial individuals involved, even including one in such a high position as Wong. Our decision merely applies California law to the facts as ascertained by the ROC courts. While the result may involve the financial responsibility of the ROC, it does not affront its sovereignty and can cause no more embarrassment than the exposures already made by the ROC courts. Because of our respondeat superior decision we need not decide whether or to what extent further inquiries might be made of ROC officials. Under these circumstances the act of state doctrine is not a bar to Liu's suit.

CONCLUSION

We hold that the act of state doctrine does not automatically bar a suit against a foreign nation when it is alleged that the nation ordered the assassination of an American citizen within the United States. We reverse the district court's decision dismissing the ROC as a party defendant. We hold that the ROC can be liable for Henry Liu's death under California's law of respondeat superior and the case is remanded for such further proceedings as may be necessary.

REVERSED and REMANDED.

NOTES

The Foreign Sovereign Immunities Act (FSIA), 28 U.S.C. § 1602 *et seq.*, enacted in 1976, grants immunity to foreign sovereigns except as expressly provided in the Act. 28 U.S.C. § 1604. The major exception to immunity is for commercial activities, construed to mean activities that private parties may and normally do perform. *See* § 1605(a)(2). Other exceptions are for taking property in violation of international law, § 1605(a)(3); tortious actions committed in the U.S. that are not discretionary acts of state, § 1605(a)(5); and claims for property located in the U.S., § 1605(a)(4).

Argentine Republic v. Amerada Hess Shipping Corp., 488 U.S. 428, 102 L. Ed. 2d 818, 109. S. Ct. 683 (1989) (several footnoes omitted):

[Amerada, a Liberian corporation with significant U.S. ownership interests, sued Argentina for bombing one of its ships as it passed through waters between Argentina and the Malvinas/Falkland Islands. Argentina claimed those waters as part of its territorial sea and justified the bombing in light of the pendency of the Malvinas/Falkland war.]

A divided panel of the United States Court of Appeals for the Second Circuit reversed. 830 F.2d 421 (1987). The Court of Appeals held that the District Court had jurisdiction under the Alien Tort Statute because respondents' consolidated action was brought by Liberian corporations, it sounded in tort ("the bombing of a ship without justification"), and it asserted a violation of international law ("attacking a neutral ship in international waters, without proper cause for suspicion or investigation"). *Id.*, at 424-425. Viewing the Alien Tort Statute as "no more than a jurisdictional grant based on international law," the Court of Appeals said that "who is within" the scope of that grant is governed by "evolving standards of international law." *Id.*, at 425, citing *Filartiga v. Peña-Irala*, 630 F.2d 876, 880 (CA2 Cir. 1980). The Court of Appeals reasoned that Congress' enactment of the FSIA was not meant to eliminate "existing remedies in United States courts for violations of international law" by foreign states under the Alien Tort Statute. 830 F.2d, at 426. . . .

Justice REHNQUIST delivered the opinion of the Court. . . .

We think that the text and structure of the FSIA demonstrate Congress' intention that the FSIA be the sole basis for obtaining jurisdiction over a foreign state in our courts. Section 1604 and § 1330(a) work in tandem: § 1604 bars federal and state courts from exercising jurisdiction when a foreign state *is* entitled to immunity, and § 1330(a) confers jurisdiction on district courts to hear suits brought by United States citizens and by aliens when a foreign state is *not* entitled to immunity. . . .

. . . Congress had violations of international law by foreign states in mind when it enacted the FSIA. For example, the FSIA specifically denies foreign states immunity in suits "in which rights in property taken in violation of international law are in issue." 28 U.S.C. § 1605(a)(3).

. . . Congress' failure to enact a *pro tanto* repealer of the Alien Tort Statute when it passed the FSIA in 1976 may be explained at least in part by the lack of certainty as to whether the Alien Tort Statute conferred jurisdiction in suits against foreign states. Enacted by the First Congress in 1789, the Alien Tort Statute provides that "[t]he district courts shall have original jurisdiction of any civil action by an alien for a tort only, committed in violation of the law of nations or a treaty of the United States." 28 U.S.C. § 1350. The Court of Appeals did not cite any decision in which a United States court exercised jurisdiction over a foreign state under the Alien Tort Statute, and only one such case has come to our attention — one which was decided after the enactment of the FSIA.[32] . . .

We think that Congress' failure in the FSIA to enact an express *pro tanto* repealer of the Alien Tort Statute speaks only faintly, if at all, to the issue involved in this case. In light of the comprehensiveness of the statutory scheme in the FSIA, we doubt that even the most meticulous draftsman would have concluded that Congress also needed to amend *pro tanto* the Alien Tort Statute and presumably such other grants of subject-matter jurisdiction in Title 28 as § 1331 (federal question), § 1333 (admiralty), § 1335 (interpleader), § 1337 (commerce and antitrust), and § 1338 (patents, copyrights and trademarks). Congress provided in § 1602 of the FSIA that "[c]laims of foreign states to immunity should *henceforth* be decided by courts of the United States in conformity with the principles set forth in this chapter," and very likely it thought that should be sufficient. § 1602 (emphasis added); see also H.R. Rep., at 12; S.rep., at 11, U.S. Code Cong. & Admin. News 1976, p. 6610 (FSIA "intended to preempt any other State and Federal law (excluding applicable international agreements) for according immunity to foreign sovereigns"). . . .

Having determined that the FSIA provides the sole basis for obtaining jurisdiction over a foreign state in federal court, we turn to whether any of the exceptions enumerated in the Act apply here. . . .

Respondents assert that FSIA exception for noncommercial torts, § 1605(a)(5), is most in point. . . . Section 1605(a)(5) is limited by its terms, however to those

---

[32] *See Von Dardel v. Union of Soviet Socialist Republics*, 623 F. Supp. 246 (DC 1985) (alternatively holding). The Court of Appeals did cite its earlier decision in *Filartiga v. Peña-Irala*, 630 F.2d 876 (CA2 1980), which involved a suit under the Alien Tort Statute by a Paraguayan national against a Paraguayan police official for torture; the Paraguayan Government was not joined as a defendant.

cases in which the damage to or loss of property occurs *in the United States.* Congress' primary purpose in enacting § 1605(a)(5) was to eliminate a foreign state's immunity for traffic accidents and other torts committed in the United States, for which liability is imposed under domestic tort law....

In this case, the injury to respondents' ship occurred on the high seas some 5,000 miles off the nearest shores of the United States. Despite these telling facts, respondents nonetheless claim that the tortious attack on the Hercules occurred "in the United States." They point out that the FSIA defines "United States" as including all "territory and waters, continental and insular, subject to the jurisdiction of the United States," § 1603(c), and that their injury occurred on the high seas, which is within the admiralty jurisdiction of the United States, see *The Plymouth*, 70 U.S. (3 Wall) 20, 36...(1866). They reason, therefore, that "by statutory definition" petitioner's attack occurred in the United States....

We find this logic unpersuasive. We construe the modifying phrase "continental and insular" to restrict the definition of United States to the continental United States and those islands that are part of the United States or its possessions; any other reading would render this phrase nugatory....

The result in this case is not altered by the fact that petitioner's alleged tort may have had effects in the United States....

We also disagree with respondents' claim that certain international agreements entered into by petitioner and by the United States create an exception to the FSIA here.... As noted the FSIA was adopted "[s]ubject to international agreements to which the United States [was] a party at the time of [its] enactment." § 1604. This exception applies when international agreements "expressly conflic[t]" with the immunity provisions of the FSIA..., hardly the circumstances in this case. Respondents point to the Geneva Convention on the High Seas, Apr. 29, 1958,... and the Pan American Maritime Neutrality Convention, Feb. 20, 1928.... These conventions, however, only set forth substantive rules of conduct and state that compensation shall be paid for certain wrongs. They do not create private rights of action for foreign corporations to recover compensation from foreign states in United States courts. Cf. *Head Money Cases*, 112 U.S. 580, 598-99...(1884); *Foster v. Neilson*, 27 U.S. (2 Pet.) 253...(1829). Nor do we see how a foreign state can waive its immunity under § 1605(a)(1) by signing an international agreement that contains no mention of a waiver of immunity to suit in United States courts or even the availability of a cause of action in the United States....

We hold that the FSIA provides the sole basis for obtaining jurisdiction over a foreign state in the courts of this country, and that none of the enumerated exceptions to the Act applies to the facts of this case. The judgment of the Court of Appeals is therefore
REVERSED.

Letelier v. Republic of Chile, 748 F.2d 790 (2d Cir. 1984) (footnotes omitted):

CARDAMONE, Circuit Judge.

Orlando Letelier, the former Chilean Ambassador to the United States, his aid, Michael Moffitt, and Moffitt's wife, Ronni, were riding to work in Washington, D.C. in September 1976 when an explosive device planted under the driver's seat in their car was detonated killing both Letelier and Ronni Moffitt and seriously injuring Michael Moffitt. That assassination gives rise to the present appeal.

Investigation by agencies of the United States government into these murders revealed the identity of nine assassins and their alleged connection to the government of Chile. Of the nine only Michael Vernon Townley, an American citizen working for Chilean intelligence, was convicted of a criminal offense. Three of those indicted were members of the Cuban Nationalist Movement who, although found guilty in the trial court, had their convictions reversed on appeal. *See United States v. Sampol*, 636 F.2d 621, 684 (D.C. Cir. 1980). Of the other five individuals indicted, none were brought to trial: three were Chilean nationals that Chile refused to extradite, and two remain at large.

In August 1978 the personal representatives of Letelier and Moffitt instituted a civil tort action in the United States District Court for the District of Columbia against the indicted individuals and the Republic of Chile. . . . The complaint alleged that the noncommercial tort exception of § 1605(a)(5) of the FSIA applied and that Chile was not entitled to sovereign immunity in the tort action.

All defendants defaulted. . . .

The resulting judgment against the Republic of Chile was entered in the United States District Court for the District of Columbia. Plaintiffs subsequently filed the judgment in the United States District Court for the Southern District of New York, *see* 28 U.S.C. § 1963 (1982), for the purpose of executing on the property interests that The Republic of Chile has in the Chilean national airline, Linea Aerea Nacional-Chile or LAN, which is located in New York. . . . LAN moved to dismiss claiming that it should not be held to answer for Chilean debts and that its assets were immune from execution. . . .

The principal issue is whether LAN's assets may be executed upon to satisfy the judgment obtained in the District of Columbia against Chile. This discussion necessarily focuses on the Foreign Sovereign Immunities Act of 1976, which is the exclusive source of subject matter jurisdiction over all suits involving foreign states or their instrumentalities. *Rex v. CIA Pervana de Vapores, S.A.*, 660 F.2d 61, 62 (3d Cir. 1981), *cert. denied*, 456 U.S. 926. . .(1982). According to § 1604, foreign states are immune from suit in our courts unless the conduct complained of comes within the exceptions set forth in §§ 1605 to 1607 of the Act. Similarly, under § 1609 foreign states are immune from execution upon judgments obtained against them, unless an exception set forth in §§ 1610 or 1611 of the FSIA applies.

The judgment creditors claim that § 1610(a)(2) allows them to execute upon LAN's assets in this case. . . . We consider first whether LAN's separate juridical existence may be ignored, thereby making its assets "[t]he property in the United States of a foreign state."

I.   *Separate Juridical Existence* . . .

In [*First Nat'l City Bank v. Banco Para El Comercio Exterior de Cuba (Bancec)*, 426 U.S. 611 (1983)], the Cuban bank of the same name brought suit against Citibank to collect on a letter of credit issued in its favor in 1960. Citibank counterclaimed arguing that it was entitled to set-off amounts as compensation due it for the Cuban government's expropriation of Citibank's assets in Cuba.

. . . The Supreme Court concluded in *Bancec* that the presumption of separateness had been overcome. It reasoned that the real beneficiary of any recovery would be the Cuban government, and that Cuba should not be permitted to obtain relief in American courts without answering for its seizure of Citibank's assets. The Court commented that "Cuba cannot escape liability for acts in violation of international law simply by retransferring the assets to separate juridical entities."...

Thus, *Bancec* rests primarily on two propositions. First, Courts may use set-off as a unique, equitable remedy to prevent a foreign government from eluding liability for its own acts when it affirmatively seeks recovery in an American judicial proceeding. *See National City Bank v. Republic of China*, 348 U.S. 356... (1955). The broader message is that foreign states cannot avoid their obligations by engaging in abuses of corporate form. The *Bancec* Court held that a foreign state instrumentality is answerable just as its sovereign parent would be if the foreign state has abused the corporate form, or where recognizing the instrumentality's separate status works a fraud or an injustice....

The district judge "found" the following facts based "on the record" and "established" by evidentiary sanctions imposed pursuant to Rule 37(b)(2)(A): From January 1975 through January 1979 LAN's assets and facilities were under the direct control of Chile, which had the power to use them; Chile could have decreed LAN's dissolution and taken over property interests held in LAN's name; Chile, through its agencies, officers, and employees, intentionally used facilities and personnel of LAN to plan and carry out its conspiracy to assassinate Orlando Letelier by (a) transporting Michael Vernon Townley between Chile and the United States, (b) transporting explosives on several occasions, (c) assisting with currency transactions involved in paying off the co-conspirators in the assassination, (d) providing a meeting place for the co-conspirators, (e) arranging for Townley to exit the United States under an alias after the assassination. By using LAN in these endeavors, the district court found, Chile ignored LAN's separate existence and abused the corporate form.

In our view this is not the sort of "abuse" that overcomes the presumption of separateness established by *Bancec*. Joint participation in a tort is not the "classic" abuse of corporate form to which the Supreme Court referred....

... As both *Bancec* and the FSIA legislative history caution against too easily overcoming the presumption of separateness, we decline to extend the *Bancec* holding to do so in this case.

II. *Commercial Activity*

Even assuming the district court was correct in disregarding LAN's corporate form and finding that LAN's assets were Chile's property in the United States, § 1610(a)(2) also requires that the property be "used for the commercial activity upon which the claim is based." In permitting execution against LAN's assets the court below essentially concluded that LAN's activities aided Townley in the assassination and constituted the "commercial activities" that § 1610(a)(2) requires. We cannot agree because a consistent application of the Act, analysis of the background of its enactment, its language and legislative history, and the case law construing it compel the opposite conclusion.

We first note that the district court for the District of Columbia found that Chile lost its immunity from jurisdiction pursuant to § 1605(a)(5), the "tortious activity" exception to jurisdictional immunity. Section 1605(a)(5) specifically states that it applies to situations "not otherwise encompassed in paragraph (2)." Section 1605(a)(2) is the commercial activity exception.

. . . If LAN, as the trial court found, acted in complicity with the Chilean secret police in the assassination, its activities had nothing to do with its place in commerce. The nature of its course of conduct could not have been as a merchant in the marketplace. Its activities would have been those of the foreign state: governmental, not private or commercial.

Chief Justice Marshall with his decision in *The Schooner Exchange v. Mc-Faddon*, 11 U.S. (7 Cranch) 116 . . . (1812) upheld France's plea of sovereign immunity. In that case American citizens claimed ownership of a French vessel of war berthed in Philadelphia. The executive department recommended to the Supreme Court that it dismiss the claim and the Supreme Court complied with that suggestion. After *The Schooner Exchange* it became the rule that American courts would exercise jurisdiction over foreign states unless the matter was intimately connected with foreign policy and the executive department charged with the conduct of foreign policy asked for judicial abstention. In 1976 Congress, acting pursuant to its Article I powers, changed that practice by enacting the Foreign Sovereign Immunities Act. The Act assigns the task of deciding whether a foreign sovereign is immune solely to federal and state courts sitting without juries.

The FSIA adopts a restrictive view of sovereign immunity. The absolutist view, which found foreign sovereigns immune from suit for any activity, fell into disfavor in other countries and a more restrictive rule succeeded it. In 1952 the United States Department of State signalled with its Tate Letter, 26 Dep't of State Bull. 984, that it embraced the new rule. *See National City Bank of New York v. Republic of China*, 348 U.S. 356 . . . (1955). This restrictive view grants immunity for "governmental" acts of a foreign state and denies it for acts of a "private" nature. This translates into the "commercial activity" exceptions in the FSIA.

FSIA § 1602 contains the findings and declaration of purpose for the Act. That section states:

> Under international law, states are not immune from the jurisdiction of foreign courts insofar as their *commercial activities* are concerned, and their commercial property *may be levied upon for the satisfaction of judgments rendered against them in connection with their commercial activities.* (emphasis furnished). . . .

Congress intended the "essential nature" of given behavior to determine its status for purposes of the commercial activities exception, and gave the courts a "great deal of latitude" to decide this issue. . . . The legislative history makes clear that courts should not deem activity "commercial" as a whole simply because certain aspects of it are commercial. . . .

The district court correctly noted that under § 1603(d) the court must inquire into the nature of conduct, not its purpose, to determine if it is "commercial." *See Texas Trading & Milling Corp. v. Federal Republic of Nigeria*, 647 F.2d 300, 310 (2d Cir. 1981), *cert. denied*, 454 U.S. 1148 . . . (1982) (Nigerian government's purchase of cement was a commercial activity irrespective of its purposes for so doing). . . . Inquiry therefore ordinarily focuses on whether the specific acts are those that private persons normally perform. . . . The court must inquire whether the activity is of the type an individual would customarily carry on for profit. . . .

A case that involved facts analogous to those before us is *Arango v. Guzman*

Travel Advisors Corp., 621 F.2d 1371 (5th Cir. 1980), which was decided under § 1605, not § 1610. In *Arango*, the plaintiffs sued the wholly owned, national airline of the Dominican Republic after being expelled from a flight because that country's officials would not permit them entry. Although the Court dismissed the appeal because it was taken from a non-appealable order, it discussed (in dicta) whether the "commercial activity" exception of § 1605(a)(2) would allow plaintiffs to bring their tort action against the airline. The *Arango* court considered the airline's actions in rerouting plaintiffs noncommercial because it concluded that the airline acted merely as the agent of the Dominican government. *Id.* at 1379.

We agree with the *Arango* analysis. The *Arango* court found that alleged "kidnapping" by a foreign state is not "commercial activity" under the FSIA because a private person cannot lawfully engage in that activity. 567 F. Supp. at 1501. A private person cannot lawfully engage in murder any more than he can in kidnapping or criminal assault. Carriage of passengers and packages is an activity in which a private person could engage. But it is not for those activities that LAN's assets are being executed against. Rather, plaintiffs assert that LAN itself participated in the assassination and essentially accuse LAN of being a co-conspirator or joint tort feasor. In other words, LAN is accused of engaging in state-sponsored terrorism the purpose of which, irrelevant under the FSIA, was to assassinate an opponent of the Chilean government. Politically motivated assassinations are not traditionally the function of private individuals. They can scarcely be considered commercial activity. Viewed in this light, LAN's participation, if any, in the assassination is not commercial activity that falls within the § 1610(a)(2) exception and its assets therefore are not stripped of immunity.

III. *Right Without a Remedy*

The district court's principal concern with finding LAN immune from execution on its assets was that "[h]aving determined to grant jurisdiction in both commercial and tort claims, it appears out of joint to conclude that Congress intended the surprising result of allowing only commercial creditors to execute on their judgments," 567 F. Supp. at 1499-1500. Hence, it concluded that Congress would not create a right without a remedy. Few would take issue with the district judge's comment as an abstract principle of statutory interpretation. Nevertheless, when drafting the FSIA Congress took into account the international community's view of sovereign immunity. That makes a world of difference in the Act's interpretation. The Act's history and the contemporaneous passage of similar European legislation strongly support the conclusion that under the circumstances at issue in this case Congress did in fact create a right without a remedy. Congress wanted the execution provisions of the FSIA to "remedy, *in part*, the [pre-FSIA] predicament of a plaintiff who has obtained a judgment against a foreign state." *House Report, supra*, at 6605-06 (emphasis added). . . .

The FSIA distinguishes between execution against property of an agency or instrumentality of a foreign state, which may be executed against regardless of whether the property was used for the activity on which the claim is based under § 1610(b)(2), and the property of the foreign state itself, which may be executed against only when the property was used for the commercial activity on which the claim is based under § 1610(a)(2). In so distinguishing, Congress sharply restricted immunity from execution against agencies and instrumentalities, but was more cautious when lifting immunity from execution against property owned by the

State itself. Congress passed the FSIA on the background of the views of sovereignty expressed in the 1945 Charter of the United Nations and the 1972 enactment of the European Convention, which left the availability of execution totally up to the debtor state, and its own understanding as the legislative history demonstrates, that prior to 1976 property of foreign states was absolutely immune from execution. *House Report* at 6606. It is plain then that Congress planned to and did lift execution immunity "in part." Yet, since it was not Congress' purpose to lift execution immunity wholly and completely, a right without a remedy does exist in the circumstances here. Our task must be to read the Act as it is expressed, and apply it according to its expressions. *See Berger v. United States*, 255 U.S. 22, 35 . . . (1921). . . .

NOTES AND QUESTIONS

1. Seeking what property may a successful plaintiff under the FSIA satisfy his or her judgment? If a plaintiff successfully sues for tortious conduct committed in the U.S., is there any way to compel the foreign government to pay? *Letelier* suggests that Chile might decide as an act of good will to honor the court's judgment or the U.S. might be persuaded to bring the claim before an international tribunal. Were those two suggestions realistic at the time of the decision? What about after the government of Chile changed?

2. Would suing the Marcos estate for murder in the U.S. of his opponents committed while he was president be controlled by the FSIA or the act of state doctrine? *See Domingo v. Republic of Philippines*, 694 F. Supp. 782 (W.D. Wash. 1988) (claims brought by families of two slain opponents, dismissed in 1981 on "head of state" grounds, reinstated when Marcos left office).

3. The act of state doctrine applies to foreign sovereigns (including national, state, and local governments), foreign heads of state, and foreign officials. The FSIA applies only to sovereigns. If a sovereign is sued, the initial inquiry is whether the FSIA bars the suit. If it does not, the court should consider the applicability of the act of state doctrine. Are heads of state "sovereigns"? Might a dictator with absolute powers be a sovereign under the FSIA? *See Republic of Philippines v. Marcos*, 806 F.2d 344, 358, 360 (2d Cir. 1986) (Marcos I), excerpted *supra*.

4. In applying the act of state doctrine a court must decide whether the doctrine even applies. What does a court consider to resolve that inquiry? If the doctrine does apply, a court must decide whether the doctrine bars adjudication. What considerations do courts balance in addressing that question? *See Forti I*, excerpted in part I, *supra*.

The dissent in *Marcos II* disagreed with the majority because it declared that the "injunction can be affirmed without any regard to the act of state doctrine." 862 F.2d at 1368. Given that the majority did discuss the doctrine, what more did the dissenters want it to do? Is the dissent correct? Assuming the doctrine may apply to a former dictator, to which of Marcos' acts do you think the dissent would be most likely to find the doctrine applies? *See Marcos I*, 806 F.2d at 359. Over which acts, if any, do you think a trial court should not assert jurisdiction?

5. Is there a relation between proving the existence of an international tort and determining whether the act of state doctrine bars adjudication?

6. *Filartiga*, excerpted in part I, *supra*, did not address the act of state issue because the defense was raised for the first time on appeal. The court noted that it doubted "whether action by a state official in violation of the Constitution and laws of the Republic of Paraguay, and wholly unratified by the nation's government, could properly be characterized as an act of state." *Id.* at 889. May an act violating laws of the official's country nonetheless be an act of state? If a government asserts that wrongdoing by an official was not performed as part of his or her official duties, is that assertion dispositive of the act of state doctrine's applicability? Or relevant in determining whether the doctrine bars adjudication? Would the answer be different if the official were part of a government that had been deposed and would have ratified the actions had it remained in power?

7. Does the Supreme Court's decision in *Amerada Hess* support or undermine the precedential value of the *Filartiga* decision?

8. The Supreme Court cited *Von Dardel v. U.S.S.R.*, 623 F. Supp. 246 (D.D.C. 1985), as the only contrary authority. That decision was vacated after the Soviet government made its first appearance in the case. _____ F. Supp. _____, 1990 WL 55813 (D.D.C. 1990).

---

4. Questions as to Statute of Limitations, Damages, and Choice of Law

Filartiga v. Peña-Irala, 577 F. Supp. 860 (E.D. N.Y. 1984):

[This opinion was issued on remand from *Filartiga v. Peña-Irala*, 630 F.2d 876 (2d Cir. 1980), excerpted in part I, *supra*.]

NICKERSON, District Judge. . . .

Following remand Peña took no further part in the action. This court granted a default and referred the question of damages to Magistrate John L. Caden for a report. The Magistrate, after a hearing recommended damages of $200,000 for Dr. Joel Filartiga and $175,000 for Dolly Filartiga. Plaintiffs filed objections to the report, and the matter is now here for determination. . . .

[Before addressing issues relating to conflict of laws and damages, the court concluded that the act of state doctrine did not apply to the case because the alleged acts constitute a "clear and unambiguous violation" of the Law of Nations. In addition, Paraguay had not ratified Peña's acts. The court also found that it had jurisdiction under 28 U.S.C. § 1350 because the "tort" specified in the Alien Tort Statute means wrong in violation of the law of nations, not merely wrong actionable under the law of the appropriate sovereign.]

III

The common law of the United States includes, of course, the principles collected under the rubric of conflict of laws. For the most part in international matters those principles have been concerned with the relevant policies of the interested national states, and with "the needs" of the "international systems." Restatement (Second) of Conflict of Laws (1971) § 6(2). The chief function of international choice-of-law rules has been said to be to further harmonious relations and commercial intercourse between states. *Id.*, comment d.

However, where the nations of the world have adopted a norm in terms so formal and unambiguous as to make it international "law," the interests of the global community transcend those of any one state. That does not mean that traditional choice-of-law principles are irrelevant. Clearly the court should consider the interests of Paraguay to the extent they do not inhibit the appropriate enforcement of the applicable international law or conflict with the public policy of the United States.

In this case the torture and death of Joelito occurred in Paraguay. The plaintiffs and Peña are Paraguayan and lived in Paraguay when the torture took place, although Dolly Filartiga has applied for permanent asylum in the United States. It was in Paraguay that plaintiffs suffered the claimed injuries, with the exception of the emotional trauma which followed Dolly Filartiga to this country. The parties' relationships with each other and with Joelito were centered in Paraguay.

Moreover, the written Paraguayan law prohibits torture. The Constitution of Paraguay, art. 50. The Paraguayan Penal Code, art. 337, provides that homicide by torture is punishable by [an] imprisonment for 15 to 20 years. Affidavit of Alejandro Miguel Garro, December 9, 1982 (Garro Aff.), [para.] 31. Paraguay is a signatory to the American Convention on Human Rights, which proscribes the use of torture. Paraguayan law purports to allow recovery for wrongful death, including specific pecuniary damages, "moral damage," and court costs and attorney's fees. Thus, the pertinent formal Paraguayan law is ascertainable.

All these factors make it appropriate to look first to Paraguayan law in determining the remedy for the violation of international law. *See Lauritzen v. Larsen*, 345 U.S. 571...(1953); Restatement (Second) of Conflict of Laws (1971) § 145(2). It might be objected that, despite Paraguay's official ban on torture, the "law" of that country is what it does in fact, Holmes, *The Path of the Law*, 10 Harv. L. Rev. 457, 461 (1897), and torture persists throughout the country. Amnesty International Report on Torture (1975) 214-16; D. Helfield and W. Wipfler, Mbarete: The Higher Law of Paraguay (The International League for Human Rights, 1980).

Where a nation's pronouncements form part of the consensus establishing an international law, however, it does not lie in the mouth of a citizen of that nation, though it professes one thing and does another, to claim that his country did not mean what it said. In concert with the other nations of the world Paraguay prohibited torture and thereby reaped the benefits the condemnation brought with it. Paraguayan citizens may not pretend that no such condemnation exists. If there be hypocrisy, we can only say with La Rochefoucauld that "hypocrisy is the homage which vice pays to virtue." Reflections; or Sentences and Moral Maxims 218 (1678).

To the extent that Peña might have expected that Paraguay would not hold him responsible for his official acts, that was not a "justified" expectation, Restatement (Second) of Conflict of Laws (1971) § 6(2)(d) and comment g, so as to make unfair the application to him of the written law of Paraguay.

IV

Plaintiffs claim punitive damages, and the Magistrate recommended they be denied on the ground that they are not recoverable under the Paraguayan Civil Code. While compensable "moral" injuries under that code include emotional pain and suffering, loss of companionship and disruption of family life, Paraguayan Civil Code, arts. 1102, 1103, 1112, plaintiffs' expert agrees that the code does not provide for what United States courts would call punitive damages. Paraguayan law, in determining the intensity and duration of the suffering and the consequent "moral" damages, takes into account the heinous nature of the tort. However, such damages are not justified by the desire to punish the defendant. They are designed to compensate for the greater pain caused by the atrocious nature of the act. Garro Aff. [paras.] 33, 34.

Yet because, as the record establishes, Paraguay will not undertake to prosecute Peña for his acts, the objective of the international law making torture punishable as a crime can only be vindicated by imposing punitive damages. . . .

Moreover, there is some precedent for the award of punitive damages in tort even against a national government. . . .

Where the defendant is an individual, the same diplomatic considerations that prompt reluctance to impose punitive damages are not present. . . .

This court concludes that it is essential and proper to grant the remedy of punitive damages in order to give effect to the manifest objectives of the international prohibition against torture.

V

In concluding that the plaintiffs were entitled only to damages recoverable under Paraguayan law, the Magistrate recommended they be awarded $150,000 each as compensation for emotional pain and suffering, loss of companionship and disruption of family life. He also suggested that Dolly Filartiga receive $25,000 for her future medical expenses for treatment of her psychiatric impairment and that Dr. Filartiga receive $50,000 for past expenses related to funeral and medical expenses and to lost income. The Magistrate recommended against an award of punitive damages and of $10,364 in expenses incurred in connection with this action. Plaintiffs object only to these last recommendations. . . .

Chief among the considerations the court must weigh is the fact that this case concerns not a local tort but a wrong as to which the world has seen fit to speak. Punitive damages are designed not merely to teach a defendant not to repeat his conduct but to deter others from following his example. . . .

There are no binding precedents to guide the court in determining what amount lies within those respectable bounds that hedge the judiciary and yet may serve to come to the attention of those who think to practice torture. . . .

The record in this case shows that torture and death are bound to recur unless deterred. This court concludes that an award of punitive damages of no less that $5,000,000 to each plaintiff is appropriate to reflect adherence to the world community's proscription of torture and to attempt to deter its practice.

VI

Judgment may be entered for plaintiff Dolly M.E. Filartiga in the amount of $5,175,000 and for plaintiff Joel Filartiga in the amount of $5,210,364, a total judgment of $10,385,364. So ordered.

NOTES

1. The *Filartiga* plaintiffs have been unable to collect the final award of $10.4 million. Peña did not have assets in the United States; efforts to recover on the judgment in Paraguay have been unsuccessful.

2. In *Forti I*, excerpted in part I, *supra*, the court held that the statute of limitations could be borrowed from the forum state, California, and that defendant's hiding tolled the statute of limitations.

K. USING INTERNATIONAL LAW TO GUIDE INTERPRETATION OF U.S. LAW

1. Prison Conditions

Lareau v. Manson, 507 F. Supp. 1117 (D. Conn. 1980) (several footnotes omitted) *modified on other grounds,* 651 F.2d 96 (2d Cir. 1981):

JOSÉ CABRANES, District Judge.

The plaintiffs in these consolidated actions are the class of inmates at the Hartford Community Correctional Center ("HCCC"), including both persons being detained pending trials on criminal charges and convicted inmates serving sentences of imprisonment. They challenge a number of the conditions of their confinement — principally, the overcrowding of the HCCC, but also other conditions, including allegedly inadequate health care, sanitation, food and heating — on constitutional grounds. The defendants are John R. Manson, Commissioner of Correction of the State of Connecticut and Richard Wezowicz, Warden of the HCCC. . . .

Summary of Facts . . .

The HCCC was designed to hold 390 inmates — one in each cell. However, soon after it opened in July 1977, the HCCC's population swelled. Since January 7, 1980, the institution has had no fewer than 500 inmates on any night; the number of inmates incarcerated there — which fluctuates from day to day — was expected to reach the range of 580 to 630 by December 1980. . . .

In an effort to accommodate the increasing number of inmates assigned to the HCCC, the defendants have converted 120 cells which were designed for one inmate into "double-bunked" cells. . . . On occasion, the defendants have assigned two inmates to one cell in which there is no double bunk-bed; in such a cell, one inmate must sleep on a mattress on the floor, placed between the desk (at one end of the cell) and the toilet (at the other). Inmates so confined have no room at all to move about their cell. . . .

The overcrowding at the HCCC is manifested not only in its housing conditions, but in other aspects of life at the institution. Particularly noteworthy is the overcrowding of the "dayrooms." . . . There are regularly 15 to 20 inmates (and occasionally as many as 24) in the "dayrooms"; while eating meals, inmates have had to sit on the floor, a radiator or even the single toilet in the "dayroom." The crowding of the "dayrooms" increases the level of tensions, and the incidence of fighting, among inmates at the HCCC. More generally, the overcrowded conditions at the HCCC have had an adverse psychological impact — above and beyond that which is inevitably caused by incarceration — on the inmates, particularly the young inmates who make up much of the facility's population. . . .

Finally, overcrowding has jeopardized security at the HCCC. Tensions and fights among inmates have increased; correctional officers, each of whom is responsible for 48 to 60 inmates, have found it more difficult to police the institution. . . .

THE CONSTITUTIONAL ISSUES

A.   *Bell v. Wolfish*

The starting point for the court's analysis of the plaintiffs' claims must be the decision of the Supreme Court in *Bell v. Wolfish*, 441 U.S. 520 [1979]. . . .

Wolfish was a class action challenging the conditions of confinement at the Metropolitan Correctional Center ("MCC"), which the Supreme Court described as "a federally operated short-term custodial facility in New York City designed primarily to house pretrial detainees." *Bell v. Wolfish, supra*, 441 U.S. at 523. . . .

. . . In the absence of a claim that a more specific constitutional right has been infringed — *i.e.*, where the detainee alleges only that he has been denied "the protection against deprivation of liberty without due process of law" — the Court held that "the proper inquiry is whether [the] conditions [of detention] amount to punishment of the detainee." *Id.* at 535. . . . The rationale for this standard, the Court noted, was that "under the Due Process Clause, a detainee may not be punished prior to an adjudication of guilt in accordance with due process of law." *Id.* (footnote omitted).

. . . The Court gave the following guidance to lower courts faced with the task of distinguishing impermissible "punishment" from constitutionally acceptable "regulatory restraints":

> A court must decide whether the disability is imposed for the purpose of punishment or whether it is but an incident of some other legitimate governmental purpose. Absent a showing of an expressed intent to punish on the part of detention facility officials, that determination generally will turn on "whether an alternative purpose to which [the restriction] may rationally be connected is assignable for it, and whether it appears excessive in relation to the alternative purpose assigned [to it]." Thus, if a particular condition or restriction of pretrial detention is reasonably related to a legitimate governmental objective, it does not, without more, amount to "punishment." . . .

In *Wolfish*, the Court also addressed the question of the constitutionality of certain limitations and restrictions on both pretrial detainees and sentenced inmates at the MCC. The Court summarized four principles "that inform [its] evaluation of the constitutionality" of such restrictions. *Id.* at 545. . . . First, the Court reiterated that "convicted prisoners do not forfeit all constitutional protections by reason of their conviction and confinement in prison." *Id.* Second, the Court noted that the rights of prisoners are "subject to restrictions and limitations" imposed not only by the fact that they are confined, but also by "the legitimate goals and policies of the penal institution." *Id.* at 545-46. . . . Third, "maintaining institutional security and preserving internal order and discipline are essential goals that may require limitation or retraction of the retained constitutional rights of convicted prisoners and pretrial detainees." *Id.* at 546. . . . Finally prison officials "should be accorded wide-ranging deference in the adoption and execution of policies and practices that in their judgment are needed to preserve internal order and discipline and to maintain institutional security." *Id.* at 547. . . .

B.   The Application of *Bell v. Wolfish* to Conditions at the HCCC

Under *Bell v. Wolfish*, the court must determine: (1) whether the overcrowded living conditions of pretrial detainees at the HCCC constitute impermissible "punishment," as defined in *Wolfish*, and thus violate the Due Process Clause; (2) whether the overcrowded conditions in which "double-bunked" convicted prisoners live violate a specific constitutional provision — here, the prohibition of cruel and unusual punishment in the Eighth Amendment; and (3) whether conditions to which both pretrial detainees and convicted inmates are subjected, without regard to their status, violate the due process standard of *Wolfish*.

(1)   *Overcrowding of Pretrial Detainees*. . .

As previously noted, under *Wolfish*, "if a restriction or condition is not reasonably related to a legitimate goal — if it is arbitrary or purposeless — a court permissibly may infer that the purpose of the governmental action is punishment that may not constitutionally be inflicted upon detainees *qua* detainees," *id.* at 539. . . . The Court noted that "'[t]here is, of course, a *de minimis* level of imposition with which the Constitution is not concerned.'" *Id.* at 539 n.21. . ., *quoting Ingraham v. Wright*, 430 U.S. 651, 674. . .(1977).

On the record before this court, it is clear that the overcrowded conditions to which the defendants subject pretrial detainees at the HCCC represents a substantial, rather than a *de minimis*, imposition. The conditions at the HCCC impose on inmates greater hardship than did conditions at the MCC. Many of the pretrial detainees in the plaintiff class are forced to live in cells and dormitory accommodations which leave them with approximately one-half as much space as is described, as minimally acceptable, by experts (including administrators of correctional facilities) concerned with the architecture of jails and prisons and the establishment of generally recognized correctional standards.[33] . . .

Under *Bell v. Wolfish*, such a finding is not the end of the inquiry. Rather, the court must determine whether the privations endured by the pretrial detainees are justifiable on the facts of the case. *See Bell v. Wolfish*, *supra*, 441 U.S. at 538-39. . . .

The record of this case is devoid of any indication that placing two inmates in a 60- or 65-square foot cell, or fifteen to twenty inmates in a 200-square foot "dayroom" while they are not in their cells or dormitory, or confining inmates not suffering from any disease or disorder to a cell in the hospital area (which they must sometimes share with inmates who are ill) for 23 hours a day, furthers in the least any legitimate purpose of the defendants — whether it be "ensuring a detainee's presence at trial," *Bell v. Wolfish, supra,* 441 U.S. at 540..., "maintaining security and order," *id.,* or anything else which might have any tendency to promote "the effective management of the detention facility." *Id.*

...On the facts of this case, the court therefore draws the inference, expressly permitted by the Supreme Court's decision in *Bell v. Wolfish,* that the purpose of the defendants' overcrowding of the facility "is punishment that may not constitutionally be inflicted upon detainees *qua* detainees." *Id.* It necessarily follows, under the test of *Bell v. Wolfish,* that the defendants have violated the due process rights, guaranteed by the Fourteenth Amendment to the United States Constitution, of pretrial inmates at the HCCC....

(2) *Overcrowding of Sentenced Inmates*

A different constitutional standard applies to the defendants' treatment of sentenced inmates. For sentenced inmates the question posed by the allegation that overcrowding violates the Constitution is whether those conditions contravene the Eighth Amendment's prohibition of "cruel and unusual punishment."...

There is no need to belabor the effects of overcrowded conditions on inmates at the HCCC. As noted previously, inmates — including those who have been convicted and sentenced — are required to live in such close quarters that their physical and mental well-being is harmed. The "evolving standards of decency" with which the overcrowding of inmates at the HCCC are incompatible include the Standard Minimum Rules for the Treatment of Prisoners, which have been adopted by the United Nations Economic and Social Council (the members of which include some nations whose standards of decency and human rights are far less stringent than our own) and thus form part of the body of international human rights principles establishing standards for decent and humane conduct by all nations.[34]...

The defendants themselves have embraced these international standards. In 1974, the defendants adopted the Standard Minimum Rules as the preamble to the Administrative Directives of the Connecticut Department of Correction. This action was apparently taken pursuant to Commissioner Manson's statutory mandate to promulgate "rules for administrative practices...*in accordance with recognized correctional standards.*" Conn. Gen. Stat. § 18-81 (emphasis added).

...In these circumstances, the court cannot avoid holding that the defendants have violated their duty under the Eighth Amendment to provide adequate housing for convicted inmates at the HCCC.

(3) *Other Conditions of Confinement...*

There is, however, one practice of the defendants which, standing alone, violates the Due Process Clause of the Constitution. The defendants have failed adequately to screen newly arrived inmates in order to identify and segregate from other inmates persons carrying communicable diseases....

---

[33] As noted above, a "double-bunked" inmate at the HCCC has approximately 30 to 32½ square feet of space (including space occupied by fixtures and furniture),

while an inmate assigned to the "fishtank" has less than 23 square feet of space (calculated the same way, on the assumption of 9 inmates in the "fishtank"). By way of contrast the plaintiffs have called the court's attention to the following standards:

> (a) The United Nations Standard Minimum Rules for the Treatment of Prisoners, adopted by the First United Nations Congress on the Prevention of Crime and Treatment of Offenders in 1955, and approved by the Economic and Social Council of the United Nations by its Resolutions 663C (LLIV) on July 31, 1957 and 2076 (LXII) on May 13, 1977. The Standard Minimum Rules — which were explicitly adopted as the "preamble to the Administrative Directives of the Connecticut Department of Correction" by the Connecticut Department of Correction on November 8, 1974, . . . — prohibit double-bunking. In adopting the Standard Minimum Rules, the Department acted in accordance with Conn. Gen. Stat. § 18-81, which provides that the Commissioner of Correction "shall establish rules for the administrative practices. . . of [state correctional] institutions and facilities *in accordance with recognized correctional standards.*" (emphasis supplied).
>
> Article 9(1) of the Standard Minimum Rules provides that "each prisoner shall occupy by night a cell or room by himself." . . . Article 86 of the Standard Minimum Rules provides that pretrial detainees "shall sleep singly in separate rooms, with the reservation of different local custom in respect of the climate." The Department made no observation that, as of 1974, it was not in compliance with this rule. . . .

Apart from Connecticut's administrative adoption of the United Nations Standard Minimum Rules for the Treatment of Prisoners, those standards may be significant as expressions of the obligations to the international community of the member states of the United Nations, *cf. Filartiga v. Peña-Irala*, 630 F.2d 876, 883 (2d Cir. 1980), and as part of the body of international law (including customary international law) concerning human rights which has been built upon the foundation of the United Nations Charter. . . . It is well established that customary international law is part of the law of the United States. . . . The United Nations Charter is, of course, a treaty ratified by the United States. 59 Stat. 1031, T.S. No. 993 (1945). Although not self-executing, *see Hitai v. Immigration & Naturalization Service*, 343 F.2d 466, 468 (2d Cir. 1965), the Charter's provisions on human rights are evidence of principles of customary international law recognized as part of the law of the United States. . . . Article 55 of the Charter provides that the United Nations shall promote the observance of human rights; in Article 56 the member states pledge "to take joint and separate action in cooperation with the Organization for the achievement" of the goals of Article 55; and Article 62(2) of the Charter authorizes the Economic and Social Council of the United Nations to "make recommendations for the purpose of promoting respect for, and observance of, human rights and fundamental freedoms for all."

In adopting the Standard Minimum Rules for the Treatment of Prisoners, the Economic and Social Council acted in furtherance of this mandate to set international standards promoting the observance of human rights. . . .

The adoption of the Standard Minimum Rules by the First United Nations

Congress on the Prevention of Crime and Treatment of Offenders and its subsequent approval by the Economic and Social Council does not necessarily render them applicable here. However, these actions constitute an authoritative international statement of basic norms of human dignity and of certain practices which are repugnant to the conscience of mankind. The standards embodied in this statement are relevant to the "canons of decency and fairness which express the notions of justice" embodied in the Due Process Clause. . . . The due process guarantees in our Constitution are based on a concept which "is not final and fixed," but evolves on the basis of judgments "reconciling the needs both of continuity and of change in a progressive society." *Rochin v. California*, . . . 342 U.S. [165,] 170, 171 [1952]. . . . *Cf. Estelle v. Gamble*, 429 U.S. 97, 102 . . . (1976) (Eighth Amendment prohibits punishment transgressing "the evolving standards of decency that mark the progress of a maturing society"); *Rudolph v. Alabama*, 375 U.S. 889, 890 & n.1 . . . (1963) (Goldberg, J., dissenting from denial of *certiorari*) (citing Economic and Social Council resolution as relevant to question whether Eighth Amendment has been violated). In this regard, it is significant that federal courts — including the Supreme Court and the Court of Appeals for the Second Circuit — have invoked the Standard Minimum Rules for guidance in particular cases. *See, e.g., Estelle v. Gamble, supra*, 429 U.S. at 103-104 & n.8 . . . (citing the Standard Minimum Rules as evidence of "contemporary standards of decency" for purposes of the Eighth Amendment); *Detainees of Brooklyn House of Detention for Men v. Malcolm*, 520 F.2d 392, 396 (2d Cir. 1975) (referring to the single cell provision of the Standard Minimum Rules).

[34] . . . The relevance of international norms such as the Standard Minimum Rules to the determination of the "evolving standards of decency" which are basic to our Eighth Amendment jurisprudence is underscored by Article 7 of the International Covenant on Civil and Political Rights, which prohibits "cruel, inhuman or degrading treatment or punishment" of individuals. The Covenant (which, in Article 7, parallels the Eighth Amendment to the United States Constitution) is an international treaty; although it has not been ratified by the United States Senate, it is not necessarily without significance for this country (which signed it on October 5, 1977, *see U.S., Fulfilling Promise, Signs 11-Year Old Rights Pacts at U.N.*, N.Y. Times, Oct. 6, 1977, p. A2, col. 5), since "multilateral agreements designed for adherence by states generally . . . may come to be law for non-parties by virtue of state practice and *opinio juris* resulting in customary law." Comment f to *Restatement of the Foreign Relations Law of the United States (Revised)* § 102 (Tent. Draft No. 1, 1980). Similarly, Article 5 of the Universal Declaration of Human Rights prohibits "cruel, inhuman or degrading treatment or punishment." . . .

NOTES

1. On appeal, the Second Circuit affirmed the trial court's findings of liability in *Lareau*, but remanded the case for reconsideration of the remedy. The court of appeals stated that duration of confinement must also be considered under some of the challenged conditions. Because the trial court did not allow for that item in its remedy, the court of appeals remanded the case. The court also vacated the imposition of an absolute population ceiling because it was not feasible. *Lareau v. Manson*, 651 F.2d 96 (2d Cir. 1981).

2. In *Sterling v. Cupp*, 290 Or. 611, 625 P.2d 123 (1981), the court discussed international law, not cited by the parties, in construing the Oregon Constitution's prohibition of "unnecessarily rigorous" treatment to prohibit full patdowns of male prisoners by female guards.

3. In *Conservatorship of Hofferber*, 28 Cal. 3d 161, 167 Cal. Rptr. 854, 616 P.2d 836 (1980), the court cited international law in support of the conclusion that the state has compelling interests in preventing inhumane treatment of the mentally disturbed.

2. U.S. Supreme Court Opinions

The U.S. Supreme Court has issued two important rulings concerning the execution of juvenile offenders in which international standards are discussed. In *Thompson v. Oklahoma*, 487 U.S. 815, (1988), a four-judge plurality concluded that a death sentence for an offender who was 15 at the time of his crime constituted cruel and unusual punishment under the Eighth Amendment. In that opinion Justice Stevens cited views of the international community in reasoning that the death penalty would "offend civilized standards of decency." *Id.* at 2688. He noted that leading Western European countries, as well as the Soviet Union, prohibit juvenile executions. In addition he cited three treaties ratified or signed by the U.S. that explicitly prohibit juvenile death penalties: the Covenant on Civil and Political Rights, the American Convention on Human Rights, and the Geneva Convention Relative to the Protection of Civilian Persons in Time of War.

Article 6(5) of the Covenant on Civil and Political Rights states that "[s]entence of death shall not be imposed for crimes committed by persons below eighteen years of age...." Article 4(5) of the American Convention likewise provides that "[c]apital punishment shall not be imposed upon persons who, at the time the crime was committed, were under eighteen years of age...." Article 68 of the Fourth Geneva Convention of 1949 prohibits the execution of juveniles during wartime.

Justice Scalia argued in dissent that international standards should never be imposed via the U.S. Constitution. *Id.* at 2716-17 n. 4. Justice O'Connor, concurring in *Thompson*, also referred to U.S. ratification of the Fourth Geneva Convention. *Id.* at 2707. In providing the fifth vote, however, she opined that it was unnecessary to decide the broad constitutional issue and accordingly concluded that a 15-year-old could not be executed pursuant to a statute that did not expressly specify a minimum execution age of 15 years or less.

One year after *Thompson* the Supreme Court concluded that imposition of capital punishment on an individual for a crime committed at 16 or 17 years of age does not constitute cruel and unusual punishment. Moreover, Justice Scalia writing for a five-judge majority, rejected the relevance of international law and the practices of other countries in construing the Eighth Amendment.

Stanford v. Kentucky, _____ U.S. _____, 109 S.Ct. 2969 (1989) (footnotes and most citations omitted):

Justice SCALIA (writing for himself and three other justices): . . .

The thrust of both Wilkins' and Stanford's arguments is that imposition of the death penalty on those who were juveniles when they committed their crimes falls within the Eighth Amendment's prohibition against "cruel and unusual punishments." Wilkins would have us define juveniles as individuals 16 years of age and under; Stanford would draw the line at 17. . . .

Thus petitioners are left to argue that their punishment is contrary to the "evolving standards of decency that mark the progress of a maturing society," *Trop v. Dulles*, 356 U.S. 86, 101 . . . (1958) (plurality opinion). They are correct in asserting that this Court has "not confined the prohibition embodied in the Eighth Amendment to 'barbarous' methods that were generally outlawed in the 18th century," but instead has interpreted the Amendment "in a flexible and dynamic manner." *Gregg v. Georgia*, 428 U.S. 153, 171 . . . (1976). In determining what standards have "evolved," however, we have looked not to our own conceptions of decency, but to those of modern American society as a whole.[35] . . .

"[F]irst" among the "'objective indicia that reflect the public attitude toward a given sanction'" are statutes passed by society's elected representatives. *McCleskey v. Kemp*, 481 U.S. 279, 300 . . . (1987), quoting *Gregg v. Georgia*, *supra*, 428 U.S., at 173. . . . Of the 37 States whose laws permit capital punishment, 15 decline to impose it upon 16-year-old offenders and 12 decline to impose it on 17-year-old offenders. This does not establish the degree of national consensus this Court has previously thought sufficient to label a particular punishment cruel and unusual. . . .

Having failed to establish a consensus against capital punishment for 16- and

---

[35] We emphasize that it is *American* conceptions of decency that are dispositive, rejecting the contention of petitioners and their various *amici* (accepted by the dissent. . .) that the sentencing practices of other countries are relevant. While "the practices of other nations, particularly other democracies, can be relevant to determining whether a practice uniform among our people is not merely an historical accident but rather so 'implicit in the concept of ordered liberty' that it occupies a place not merely in our mores, but, text permitting, in our Constitution as well," *see Thompson*, 487 U.S. 815, . . . n.4, (Scalia, J., dissenting), quoting *Palko v. Connecticut*, 302 U.S. 319, 325 . . . (1937) (Cardozo, J.), they cannot serve to establish the first Eighth Amendment prerequisite, that the practice is accepted among our people.

17-year-old offenders through state and federal statutes and the behavior of prosecutors and juries, petitioners seek to demonstrate it through other indicia, including public opinion polls, the views of interest groups and the positions adopted by various professional associations. We decline the invitation to rest constitutional law upon such uncertain foundations. A revised national consensus so broad, so clear and so enduring as to justify a permanent prohibition upon all units of democratic government must appear in the operative acts (laws and the application of laws) that the people have approved. . . .

We discern neither a historical nor a modern societal consensus forbidding the imposition of capital punishment on any person who murders at 16 or 17 years of age. Accordingly, we conclude that such punishment does not offend the Eighth Amendment's prohibition against unusual punishment. . . .

Affirmed.

[Justice O'CONNOR, concurred in part and concurred in the judgment.

Justice BRENNAN, with whom Justice MARSHALL, Justice BLACKMUN, and Justice STEVENS join, dissenting:]

I believe that to take the life of a person as punishment for a crime committed when below the age of 18 is cruel and unusual and hence is prohibited by the Eighth Amendment. . . .

Our cases recognize that objective indicators of contemporary standards of decency in the form of legislation in other countries is also of relevance to Eighth Amendment analysis. . . . Many countries, of course — over 50, including nearly all in Western Europe — have formally abolished the death penalty, or have limited its use to exceptional crimes such as treason. App. to Brief for Amnesty International as *Amicus Curiae.* Twenty-seven others do not in practice impose the penalty. *Ibid.* Of the nations that retain capital punishment, a majority — 65 — prohibit the execution of juveniles. *Ibid.* Sixty-one countries retain capital punishment and have no statutory provision exempting juveniles, though some of these nations are ratifiers of international treaties that do prohibit the execution of juveniles. *Ibid.* Since 1979, Amnesty International has recorded only eight executions of offenders under 18 throughout the world, three of these in the United States. The other five executions were carried out in Pakistan, Bangladesh, Rwanda, and Barbados. In addition to national laws, three leading human rights treaties ratified or signed by the United States explicitly prohibit juvenile death penalties. Within the world community, the imposition of the death penalty for juvenile crimes appears to be overwhelmingly disapproved. . . .

There are strong indications that the execution of juvenile offenders violates contemporary standards of decency: a majority of States decline to permit juveniles to be sentenced to death; imposition of the sentence upon minors is very unusual even in those States that permit it; and respected organizations with expertise in relevant areas regard the execution of juveniles as unacceptable, as does international opinion. These indicators serve to confirm in my view my conclusion that the Eighth Amendment prohibits the execution of persons for offenses they committed while below the age of 18, because the death penalty is disproportionate when applied to such young offenders, and fails measurably to serve the goals of capital punishment. I dissent.

NOTE

In *Estelle v. Gamble*, 429 U.S. 97, 102 (1976), the Court cited U.N. declarations as evidence of "evolving standards of decency that mark the progress of a maturing society" for Eighth Amendment purposes.

---

3. Defending Nonviolent Protesters

Declaration of Frank C. Newman in Support of Defendants, filed June 12, 1989, in *People v. Wylie, et. al*, Santa Clara Municipal Court, California, No. E8849052 (several footnotes omitted):[36]

I am advised that on August 9, 1988, defendants joined in a nonviolent protest at the Sunnyvale facility of Lockheed Missiles and Space Company to oppose Lockheed's role in the production of U.S. nuclear weapons systems, including what defendants believed to be a first-strike system, the Trident II missile. Defendants then were arrested and charged with trespass, Cal. Pen. Code Sec. 602(n).

I am further advised that, in their brief, defendants argue the reasonableness of their belief that current U.S. nuclear-weapons policy is unlawful under international law. This declaration augments that brief in two ways: 1) it highlights the Nuremberg prohibition of crimes against humanity, and 2) it sets forth judicially manageable standards for lawful protest of threatened crimes against humanity proscribed by international law.

Initially I wish to stress that adjudication of an international law defense to allegedly unlawful protest should focus on the reasonableness of protesters' beliefs and actions. To be consistent with the rule of law — an ideal underlying both national and international systems — protest should be judged lawful only when nonviolent and only if protesters reasonably believed that grave violations of the law are occurring or threatened and that protest was likely to contribute to efforts to halt the violations.

For reasons set forth below in part I of this declaration, I maintain that it *is* reasonable to believe that current U.S. development of nuclear capability violates international law. In part II, I emphasize that adjudication of an international law defense does not require determination of the criminality of the actions protested. In part III, I suggest that international human rights law, including Nuremberg law, provides an appropriate source of guidance for interpreting California law....

II.

Adjudication of an international law defense does not require determination of whether development of nuclear capability is a crime. It is necessary only to determine that the policy of nuclear deterrence, including option of first use, poses

---

[36] This declaration war prepared with the assistance of John Burroughs, Western States Legal Foundation, Oakland, California.

a grave risk in violation of norms binding on the U.S. As I have explained in another context:

> *[A] main contribution of the relevant [international] criminal law is its proscribing of illegal conduct.* What does that mean? It means that nearly all conduct proscribed in terms of criminal responsibility, criminal liability, etc. is also proscribed in terms of civil responsibility, civil liability, etc.

> Why is that important? For many reasons. A crucial fact is that too many people, once the word "Nuremberg" is mentioned for example, immediately begin discussing criminal intent, proof beyond a reasonable doubt and related concepts of penal law. Because those topics are labyrinthine, we tend to forget that governments and government officials may well have committed illegal acts whether or not the acts also were criminal.

> That is exactly what happened, for example, in numerous discussions of "Nuremberg and Vietnam". The cost to human rights law was not that possibly guilty individuals escaped prosecution. The greater cost was that, too often, all the talk of criminality left undiscussed and unsettled the basic issues as to whether the new and brutal techniques of warfare that were used in Vietnam were illegal or not.

> When issues as momentous as those are left undiscussed and unsettled (and there are many parallels to Vietnam), progress in civil and political rights is not encouraged.[37]

III.

In construing California statutory and constitutional law, international human rights law provides an accepted source of guidance. Relevant provisions are found in the Universal Declaration of Human Rights. That Declaration is now widely accepted as an authoritative interpretation of the human rights clauses of the United Nations Charter, a treaty to which the United States is a party. In addition the Universal Declaration evidences customary international law.[38]
Preambular paragraph three of the Universal Declaration states:

> [I]t is essential, if man is not to be compelled to have recourse, as a last resort, to rebellion against tyranny and oppression, that human rights should be protected by the rule of law. . . .

Preambular paragraph eight states:

> [E]very individual and every organ of society, keeping this Declaration constantly in mind, shall strive by teaching and education to promote respect for these rights and freedoms and by progressive measures, national and international, to secure their universal and effective recognition and observance, both among the peoples of Member States themselves and among the people of territories under their jurisdiction.

---

[37]Newman and Vasak, *Civil and Political Rights*, 1 The International Dimensions of Human Rights 162 (K. Vasak & P. Alston eds. 1982).

[38] R. Lillich and F. Newman, International Human Rights: Problems of Law and Policy 65-67 (1979); *Filartiga v. Peña-Irala*, 630 F.2d 876, 882-83 (2d Cir. 1980).

Art. 28 states:

> Everyone is entitled to a social and international order in which the rights and freedoms set forth in this Declaration can be fully realized.

Those provisions support a right of protest under the circumstances of this case; namely, peaceful protest of threatened crimes against humanity. Destruction of civilian populations is inconsistent with the principle that "human rights should be protected by the rule of law...." Peaceful protest of threatened destruction vindicates the rule of law while avoiding the extreme step of "recourse...to rebellion against tyranny and oppression." Peaceful protest fulfills also the responsibility to strive for the "recognition and observance" of human rights and promotes the attainment of a "social and international order in which rights and freedoms set forth in this Declaration can be fully realized."

The Nuremberg rules supply an additional source of guidance for judges called upon to interpret California law in cases involving conduct reasonably believed necessary to help prevent Nuremberg offenses. Those rules reaffirm the principle of individual responsibility, that individuals — not only governments — are obliged to comply with international law. *See, e.g., U.S. v. Goering*, 6 F.R.D. 69, 110 (1946) ("individuals have international duties which transcend the national obligations of obedience").

It would go too far at present to say that law *requires* individuals to protest threatened crimes against humanity. But such protest — an assumption of individual responsibility to help promote compliance with law — is certainly consistent with Nuremberg rules.

Those rules also reaffirm that national and state laws are subordinate to the proscriptions of international law. Thus "inhumane acts committed against any civilian population" are crimes against humanity "whether or not in violation of domestic law of the country where perpetrated." [Nuremberg Charter, Art. 6(c), 58 Stat. at 1547.] That suggests a balancing of the relative evils of any threatened violation of international law and the alleged violation of state law (here, trespass)....

NOTES

1. In *State of Vermont v. McCann*, No. 2857-7-86CnCr (D. Ct. Vt., Chittenden Cir. 1987), the defendant alleged that his nonviolent obstruction of traffic at a General Electric plant was aimed at preventing the use of a rapid-fire cannon in random attacks against civilian populations in El Salvador. Judge Frank Mahady, since elevated to the Vermont Supreme Court, ruled that the defendant could present evidence at trial that his actions were privileged under international law as developed by Nuremberg tribunals. He cited *In Re Yamashita*, 327 U.S. 1, 16 (1945) for the proposition that individuals may be required to take appropriate measures to prevent international crimes.

2. In *State of Hawaii v. Marley*, 500 P.2d 1095 (Hawaii 1973), nonviolent protesters had entered the premises of Honeywell Corporation to publicize what they believed to be the war crimes of Honeywell in supplying weapons for the Vietnam War. The trial court, upheld by the Hawaii Supreme Court, instructed the jury as follows:

> The United States has entered into treaties which prohibit as war crimes the use of weapons which cause unnecessary and indiscriminate injuries or death to non-combatant civilians, whether done by persons singly or in cooperation with others. You are further instructed that under law, an individual citizen or citizens may use reasonable means to prevent, or seek the prevention of, the commission of a crime only if such crime is being committed, or is about to be committed in such citizen or citizens' presence. *Id.* at 1105-06, 1108.

The jury convicted despite the instruction; on appeal, defendants argued against the presence requirement, but lost.

3. *See also U.S. v. May*, 622 F.2d 1000 (9th Cir. 1980); *U.S. v. Montgomery*, 772 F.2d 733 (11th Cir. 1985); F. Boyle, Defending Civil Resistance Under International Law (1988).

---

4. Rights of Aliens

Rodriquez-Fernandez v. Wilkinson, 654 F.2d 1382 (10th Cir. 1981) (footnotes omitted):

LOGAN, Circuit Judge.

This is an appeal from a decision of the district court granting a writ of habeas corpus, ordering immediate release of Pedro Rodriguez-Fernandez to the custody of an American citizen upon such conditions as the Attorney General of the United States may impose. . . .

By an order dated December 31, 1980, the district court held that Rodriguez-Fernandez has no rights to avoid detention under either the Fifth or Eighth Amendments to the United States Constitution. However, it held that the Attorney General's actions under the circumstances were arbitrary and an abuse of his discretion. It found that although the Attorney General's actions did not offend any statute, they violated principles of customary international law which create a right to be free from such detention. . . .

We dispose of the appeal by construing the applicable statutes to require Rodriguez-Fernandez' release at this time.

. . . Due process is not a static concept, it undergoes evolutionary change to take into account accepted current notions of fairness. . . . [W]e note that in upholding the plenary power of Congress over exclusion and deportation of aliens, the Supreme Court has sought support in international law principles. *E.g., Fong Yue Ting v. United States*, 149 U.S. 698. . .(1893). It seems proper then to consider international law principles for notions of fairness as to propriety of holding aliens in detention. No principle of international law is more fundamental than the concept that human beings should be free from arbitrary imprisonment. *See*

Universal Declaration of Human Rights, Arts. 3 and 9, U.N. Doc. A/801 (1948); The American Convention on Human Rights, Part I, ch. II, Art. 7, 77 Dept. of State Bull. 28 (July 4, 1977). For these several reasons, we believe [*Shaughnessy v. U.S. ex rel Mezei*, 345 U.S. 206 (1953)] does not compel the conclusion that no constitutional problems inhere in petitioner's detention status.

When it passed the Internal Security Act of 1950 and its successor, the Immigration and Naturalization Act of 1952, 8 U.S.C. § 1101 *et seq.*, Congress was painfully aware of more than 3,000 warrants of deportation made unenforceable by the refusals of the countries of origin to grant passports for these persons' return. . . . Most were nationals of iron-curtain countries and aliens residing in the United States. Despite these facts, or perhaps because of them, the Act provides for detention no longer than six months in deportation cases. 8 U.S.C. § 1252(c). Further detention is permitted only after conviction for violation of restrictions imposed upon release on parole, *id.* § 1252(d), or after conviction for willfully refusing to depart or to cooperate in securing departure. *Id.* § 1252(e).

Provisions relating to excludable aliens seeking entry are not as specific. They provide for "temporary removal" from the transportation vehicle or vessel to a place of "detention, pending a decision on the aliens' eligibility to enter the United States and until they are either allowed to land or returned to the care of the transportation line or to the vessel or aircraft which brought them." 8 U.S.C. § 1223(b). *See also id.* §§ 1223(a) and (c), 1225(b), and 1227(a). Temporary parole into the United States is permitted in the discretion of the Attorney General, but is not to be regarded as admission of the alien into the country. 8 U.S.C. § 1182(d)(5).

Are we to read these provisions to permit indefinite detention as an alternative to exclusion, in view of the fact that Congress imposed a specific time limitation on holding resident aliens but none as to those "standing at the border"? We do not. There is no evidence to suggest that prior to the instant case a significant number of excludable aliens have been physically detained for periods of long duration. Justice Tom Clark, who was Attorney General during the formation of the presently effective immigration laws, stated in *Leng May Ma v. Barber*, 357 U.S. 185, 190 . . . (1958), "[p]hysical detention of aliens is now the exception, not the rule, and is generally employed only as to security risks or those likely to abscond."

Neither will we read into the statute a specific time limit for detention. Rather, since the statute contemplates temporary detention, we hold that detention is permissible during proceedings to determine eligibility to enter and, thereafter, during a reasonable period of negotiations for their return to the country of origin or to the transporter that brought them here. After such a time, upon application of the incarcerated alien willing to risk the possible alternatives to continued detention, the alien would be entitled to release. This construction is consistent with accepted international law principles that individuals are entitled to be free of arbitrary imprisonment. It is also consistent with the statutory treatment of deportable resident aliens and with the constitutional principles outlined above.

We do not construe the Act to require release within the United States. The statute appears to contemplate that parole is to be in the absolute discretion of the Attorney General, at least as to aliens in Rodriguez-Fernandez' position, convicted of crimes involving moral turpitude. *See* 8 U.S.C. § 1182(d)(6). Parole within the country is one option available to the government, and we note that, under procedures approved by the predecessor to the present Attorney General, this petitioner was found to be qualified for such parole. But other options exist. He can be returned to the transportation vessel which brought him to the American shore, if it exists. *Id.* § 1223. We would not read 8 U.S.C. § 1227 to preclude his being sent to a country other than Cuba, if Cuba will not take him.

When an excludable alien in custody tests the detention by writ of habeas corpus pursuant to 8 U.S.C. § 1105a(a)(9) or 28 U.S.C. § 2241, we hold that the burden is upon the government to show that the detention is still temporary pending expulsion, and not simply incarceration as an alternative to departure. Information on this issue is more readily available to the government. On the record before us, it appears there are no current negotiations with Cuba or any other country to take petitioner and there is no reason for his continued incarceration other than the fact that no country has agreed to take him. That is insufficient reason to hold him further.

Since our interpretation of the applicable law and the relief ordered differs somewhat from that of the district court, we give the government thirty days in which to effectuate his release in a manner consistent with this opinion. It is so ordered. . . .

NOTES

1. The U.S. Court of Appeals for the Eleventh Circuit has disagreed with the Tenth Circuit in *Rodriquez-Fernandez. See Fernandez-Roque v. Smith*, 734 F.2d 576 (11th Cir. 1984); *Garcia-Mir v. Meese*, 781 F.2d 1450 (11th Cir. 1986).

2. In *Cerillo-Perez v. INS*, 809 F.2d 1419, 1423 (9th Cir. 1987), the court cited international law in support of its holding that the immigration judge erred in failing to consider the impact of the deportation of a Mexican couple on their U.S. citizen children.

3. In *INS v. Cardoza-Fonseca*, 480 U.S. 421 (1986), the Supreme Court held that an alien, in order to qualify for the discretionary relief of asylum, need show only a "well-founded fear of persecution" rather than that it is more likely than not that he or she will be persecuted in his or her home country, which is the showing an alien must make in order to qualify for the mandatory relief of withholding deportation. The Court reached that conclusion after noting that the Refugee Act of 1980 was intended to bring U.S. refugee law into conformity with U.S. obligations under the U.N. Protocol Relating to the Status of Refugees, 606 U.N.T.S. 268, 19 U.S.T. 6223, T.I.A.S. No. 6577, *entered into force* Oct. 4, 1967, to which the U.S. acceded in 1968. In particular, the Refugee's Act's definition of an alien entitled to asylum was based directly on the Protocol's definition of "refugee" and Congress intended that the statutory provision be construed consistent with the Protocol.

4. See also the *Echeverria* Brief in part J, *supra*, and cases cited therein.

5. Other Rights

In *Lipscomb v. Simmons*, 884 F.2d 1242 (9th Cir. 1989) (per curiam), the court discussed international law, even though not cited by the parties, in concluding that the right to live with one's family is a fundamental right and, accordingly, that Oregon violated substantive due process rights by denying foster care funding to children who live with close relatives.

In *Santa Barbara v. Adamson*, 27 Cal. 3d 123, 130, 164 Cal. Rptr. 539, 542, 610 P.2d 436, 439 (1980), an ordinance prohibiting unrelated persons from living together in a family residence zone violated the right of privacy under the California Constitution. The court cited international law in support of its conclusion that the right of privacy exists in one's home as well as within the family. *See also People v. Privatera*, 23 Cal. 3d 697, 740, 153 Cal. Rptr. 431, 458, 591 P.2d 919, 946 (1980) (Newman, J. dissenting).

In *Boehm v. Superior Court*, 178 Cal. App. 3d 494, 223 Cal. Rptr. 716 (1986), the court cited international law in concluding that a county was required to include clothing, transportation, and medical care when dispensing minimum subsistence grants.

In *Pauley v. Kelly*, 255 S.E.2d 859 (W. Va. 1979), the West Virginia Supreme Court prominently cited the Universal Declaration of Human Rights in holding education to be a fundamental right under the West Virginia Constitution.

L. INCORPORATING INTERNATIONAL LAW IN U.S. STATUTES

Courts have been most receptive to arguments that they should apply international law when some reference to that law is made in a relevant statute or regulation or, at the least, in legislative history. In the following excerpt the authors expound on that observation and suggest, illustratively, how reference to international law in the Foreign Assistance Act would strengthen arguments that the administration may not cut off funds to foreign, nongovernmental, family planning agencies solely on the ground that they provide abortion information or use non-U.S. funds to perform abortions.

Coliver & Newman, *Using International Human Rights Law to Influence United States Foreign Population Policy: Resort to Courts or Congress?*, 20 N.Y.U.J. Int'l L. & Pol. 1, 53 (1987) (several footnotes omitted) : . . .

DIRECT INCORPORATION OF INTERNATIONAL LAW INTO U.S. LEGISLATION

International law can be used most effectively to promote U.S. policies consistent with that law when it is expressly incorporated into U.S. law. Thus a law that allows aliens to sue for torts "in violation of the law of nations" sustained a judgment by two Paraguayans against a Paraguayan official for the torture and killing of a family member in Paraguay. A clause of the Immigration and Nationality Act (INA) that required consideration of "the provisions of this chapter or any other law or treaty" in deportation decisions provided the basis for a sanctuary worker's belief that a Salvadoran was lawfully in the United States even though he had entered without papers.[39] Because the definition of refugee that Congress adopted in the Refugee Act of 1980 "is virtually identical" to the one in the U.N. Protocol Relating to the Status of Refugees, the Supreme Court interpreted the clause in accord with that treaty. Adoption by the Connecticut Department of Correction of the U.N. Standard Minimum Rules for the Treatment of Prisoners as the preamble to its "Administrative Directives" persuaded a federal court to accord precedence to those rules in adjudicating inmates' claims of substandard prison conditions.

Incorporation in foreign assistance and policy legislation of international human rights language has had a notable impact on statutory programs and has nurtured U.S. attention to human rights generally. For example, the Foreign Assistance Act of 1961 precludes the provision of economic and security assistance, except under specified circumstances, "to any country the government of which engages in a consistent pattern of gross violations of internationally recognized human rights." Section 502B declares that "a principal goal of the foreign policy of the United States shall be to promote the increased observance of internationally recognized human rights by all countries, in accordance with its obligations as set forth in the Charter of the United Nations." To assist Congress in evaluating the human rights records of proposed aid recipients the Secretary of State must submit annually "a full and complete report...with respect to practices regarding the observance of and respect for internationally recognized human rights in each country."...

Similarly, incorporation of international human rights language into statutes that affect funding of foreign family planning activities seems desirable....

...Inclusion of those and other instruments in the amendment's legislative history, though certainly not uncontroversial might be a more realistic lobbying goal. Similarly desirable would be legislative gloss suggesting that prohibited funding policies should not be limited to those that violate judicially enforceable international norms but in addition should reach those that are "inconsistent with" widely accepted international principles that may not yet have achieved customary status.

NOTES

For further reading about human rights legislation relating to foreign assistance, see chapter 11, *supra*.

M. STRATEGY ISSUES: WHEN TO INVOKE INTERNATIONAL LAW IN U.S. COURTS; WHEN TO SEEK RELIEF THROUGH ADMINISTRATIVE PROCESSES; WHEN TO SEEK INCORPORATION OF INTERNATIONAL LAW IN U.S. STATUTES?

Gerstel & Segall, Conference Report: Human Rights in American Courts, 1 Am. U.J. Int'l L. & Pol'y 137 (1986) (several footnotes omitted):...

---

[39] *United States v. Merkt*, 764 F.2d 266 (5th Cir. 1985)....

Turning from the barriers to litigation, participants launched into a debate on the propriety and effectiveness of bringing actions where the probability of a positive legal determination is doubtful. A wide range of views existed on this issue. One perspective was that a strategy of prolific litigation raises public awareness, forces recognition of international law, and serves to educate the judiciary. The competing viewpoint advocates a more selective strategy. Under this latter formulation, careful selection among cases would help weed out frivolous suits and concentrate limited legal resources.

There were several comments on the question of whether doubtful suits should be used to achieve effective publicity. One participant argued that the goal of introducing and establishing human rights norms in United States courts must be paramount. "Where the President is aiding in the torture of others, we want the judiciary to be able to come in against the President. The purpose of continuing lawsuits which may be frivolous, therefore, is to attempt to bring the action into a legal context. It is necessary to create a means for dialogue even if you know you are going to lose." As an example, this participant cited the *Greenham Women* case,[40] in which "it was understood that the case [seeking an injunction against the deployment of cruise missiles in a town in England] was unwinnable." Although held by the district court to present a non-justiciable political question, *Greenham Women* proved effective in focusing media attention in Europe and the United States on NATO's cruise missile deployment policy.

There were many responses to this line of reasoning. One participant stressed the need to adhere to Rule 11 of the Federal Rules of Civil Procedure, which bars attorneys from initiating proceedings with knowledge that the case is frivolous. A distinction was raised, however, between cases which lack a sufficient legal basis and those which merely appear "unwinnable" even though warranted by law. Another participant contended that there is often little or no time to decide whether to initiate an action. Therefore, consistent with ethical obligations, a practicing attorney has a duty to bring the suit if she holds the conviction that the case is not frivolous in the first instance.

Several individuals feared that the law ultimately produced by the initiation of doubtful cases could produce bad precedent. Confronted with borderline cases, judges may create new barriers resulting in "bad law" under which every human rights lawyer will then be obliged to work. Despite the positive benefits of increased legal awareness, many participants suggested that such "bad law" has a ripple effect extending to cases of all kinds brought before all adjudicatory bodies. Query, how successful is a highly publicized case if the legal result presents a new hurdle for future litigants? Under the *Sanchez*[41] analysis, for example, a broad range of questions formerly open for adjudication might now be considered non-justiciable under the broad "political question" doctrine. If the primary goal of those who brought the suit was simply to direct public and media attention to the situation in Nicaragua, one participant argued that Congressional trips to Nicaragua could have produced a positive dramatic effect without creating bad legal precedent.

Another participant recounted a discussion he had with attorneys for the

---

[40] *Greenham Women Against Cruise Missiles v. Reagan*, 591 F. Supp. 1332 (S.D.N.Y. 1984).

[41] *Sanchez-Espinoza v. Reagan*, 770 F.2d 202 (D.C. Cir. 1985).

plaintiffs in a suit which had yielded a significant set back for human rights case law. Most human rights activists regarded the particular case, *Tel-Oren v. Libyan Arab Republic*,[42] as a disaster from the outset. When asked why they intended to file for *certiorari* with the Supreme Court in light of the damaging opinion they had received below, the attorneys stated that their sole duty was to their clients. Had the petition been granted, negative review by the Supreme Court could have increased substantially the damage done. Upon reflection, this participant asserted that the ethical obligations of attorneys extend beyond their clients; they also owe a duty to the proper development of the law. If the possibility arises that a case may create a negative result in the body of law, participants suggested that attorneys should at least inform their clients of that consideration.

Discussion shifted next to a consideration of appropriate legal, political, administrative, and educational strategies to be employed in the future. Participants deemed publicity of human rights issues to be essential, but not at any cost. There was a general consensus that attorneys must consider the most efficient use of limited resources in deciding whether to litigate. (Conferees returned to this theme throughout the day.) Participants noted that in the 1940's and 1950's the National Association for the Advancement of Colored People was the "only show in town" deeply involved in civil rights litigation. As a consequence, the NAACP could carefully select cases to be litigated, with a coordinated long-term strategy in mind. By contrast, many groups and individual practitioners involved in human rights cases today simply do not agree on strategy. They respond to different constituencies and different concepts of legal ethics and moral obligations. It is essential, participants stressed, that these groups and individuals meet on a more regular basis to coordinate their legal efforts and to consider how their respective suits may affect one another.

An exchange between two conference participants, who were each involved at the time of the conference in immigration litigation in different parts of the country, brought this need for coordination into particularly sharp focus. Although one of the two cases could produce negative precedent for the other, the participant whose organization had taken the first case explained that a number of political and strategic reasons obliged his group to go forward with the suit.

To facilitate the proper selection and coordination of cases, many conference participants agreed on the need to establish operative criteria to distinguish between "hard" cases — those having a strong statutory jurisdictional basis, a meritorious claim, and solid popular support — and "soft" cases — those which are not necessarily frivolous but which have little chance of success and a high probability of an adverse ruling. In selecting such hard cases, one must look to the degree to which human rights practitioners can mobilize public opinion.

Participants discussed political options to expand access to the courts in human rights cases throughout the session. They generally agreed that an effective political strategy should take advantage of every public outcry against terrorism. One proposal called for legislation to facilitate action on behalf of the family of Leon Klinghoffer, victim of the *Achille Lauro* tragedy. The suggested legislation would create district court jurisdiction and provide tort remedies for victims of

---

[42] *Tel-Oren v. Libyan Arab Republic*, 726 F.2d 774 (D.C. Cir. 1984) *cert. denied*, 470 U.S. 1003 (1985).

foreign terrorist acts to sue their perpetrators, but would likely be broad enough to encompass a wide range of human rights violations.[43]

In lieu of dramatic legislative reform, another participant called for increasing the efforts aimed at recognition of existing international law. For example, one strategy would be to declare terrorists *hostes humani generis* and, therefore, subject them to universal criminal jurisdiction. This could be accomplished by ratifying conventions which provide for such jurisdiction and by more stringently enforcing extradition provisions in existing treaties. The same legislation implementing these conventions could provide the basis for legal action against violators, without the need for drastic new statutory developments.

Some participants believed that the Senate would not approve new jurisdictional legislation due to perceived judicial infringement on executive discretion in the conduct of United States foreign policy. There was concern, moreover, that a floor debate in Congress on these issues would produce adverse statements on international human rights law and thereby provide new grounds for judges to justify dismissal of future cases.

As an alternative to court actions, various participants urged greater concentration on administrative hearings as an effective means to influence foreign policy. They noted that customs and trade statutes have provided a particularly significant basis for successful administrative proceedings. In the *South African Coal Case*,[44] for example, petitioners attacked a South African law that effectively obliged black miners to work under contracts enforceable by penal sanctions. Petitioners argued that the importation of coal mined under these circumstances violated a statute that prohibits importing goods produced by indentured labor into the United States.

Although the Commissioner of Customs Services dismissed this complaint on the grounds that the plaintiffs did not satisfy a statutory proviso fixing a domestic consumptive demand, the South African government subsequently repealed all of its penal servitude laws. While the Commissioner of Customs Services found that the plaintiffs had not satisfied statutory provisions and therefore dismissed the complaint, the hearing did create favorable press, helped to define such terms as indentured labor, and may actually have induced South Africa to change its policy vis-á-vis the rights of workers. . . .

Beyond the customs and trade statutes, one participant suggested that attorneys in the human rights field should examine a broad array of administrative provisions and procedures. As an example, she noted one case in which an administrative

---

[43 This suggestion refers to the Torture Victim Protection Act, H.R. 1662, 101st Cong., 1st Sess. passed by House, 135 Cong. Rec. H-6423 (Oct. 2, 1989), S. 1629, 101st Cong., 1st Sess. (1989); the Torture Victim Protection Act, Hearing and Markup, House Comm. on Foreign Affairs, 100th Cong., 2d Sess. (1988).]

[44] Importation of Coal from The Republic of South Africa Case, Treasury Dep't, U.S. Cust. Serv., Res. 3-R:E:R 703971 T (1975). This was a 1975 proceeding brought by the United Mine Workers and the State of Alabama under § 307 of the Tariff Act of 1930, 19 U.S.C. § 1307 (1982), before the Commissioner of Customs to prevent the release of South African coal being imported by Gulf Power, a utility company. Butcher, *Southern African Issues in United States Courts*, 26 How. L.J. 601, 616 n.50 (1983).

action brought under the Marine Mammals Protection Act[45] reinforced United States policy towards Namibia. The conference participants concluded that increased concentration on administrative hearings is a significant means by which to influence national policy. This approach, they generally agreed, may also lay the foundation for later successful litigation.

Finally, participants reached a consensus on the fundamental role of legal scholarship in enhancing the opportunities for successful domestic litigation of international human rights questions. Such scholarship is essential in raising the consciousness of the judiciary, and may in fact be a more effective way to educate judges than expending legal resources and talent on numerous lawsuits. Participants suggested that legal scholarship can also help practitioners anticipate the kinds of cases likely to arise in the future, and appropriate responses to those cases. . . .

B. LITIGATION STRATEGIES

Conference participants attempted to look behind the restrictive judicial attitude vis-á-vis international law often encountered in immigration cases. In so doing, certain participants laid the blame for this situation not with the judiciary, but with the faulty strategy of practitioners who come before it. Attorneys involved in immigration cases, it was remarked, often refrain from citing international law in their arguments. Attorneys are often concerned that judges will not be familiar with international standards and will therefore be confused by and uncomfortable with their invocation. For that reason, attorneys frequently raise international norms almost as an afterthought, thereby contributing to a denigrating judicial attitude toward this body of law. Particularly when cases raise questions as to the self-executing nature of treaties, many attorneys automatically assume that arguments based on international law will fail. In essence, they engage in a self-censoring process before the arguments are even raised. One participant argued that by not forcefully asserting claims based on international law where applicable, these immigration lawyers may in fact be guilty of malpractice in the representation of their clients.

It was also noted, however, that some attorneys in immigration cases "throw in international law" on too casual a basis. These practitioners use references to international law simply as boilerplate language to supplement their other arguments without careful consideration of the substance of the asserted international claims and their relative merits in each individual case. These practitioners may be equally culpable in providing the basis for a skeptical judicial approach to international law claims in immigration and asylum cases.

C. ADMINISTRATIVE HEARINGS

Conference participants noted that questions of immigration law are commonly raised not before the courts, but before those administrative tribunals designated by Congress as having exclusive original jurisdiction over deportation and asylum cases. This fact has yielded both positive and negative consequences. To the

---

[45] In re Fouke Co. to Waive the Moratorium on the Importation of Cape Fur Seal Skins, Doc. MMPAH No. 1, National Marine Fisheries Serv., Dept. of Commerce (1975). . . .

detriment of practitioners and their clients, one participant reiterated, domestic administrative law offers no relief to those refugees who fear returning to face an armed conflict, but only to those who will confront individualized persecution. In addition, several participants pointed out that administrative law judges in immigration cases are given only narrow authority and are reluctant to look beyond the relevant statute and regulations to broader questions of international law. On the positive side, proceedings before an administrative tribunal generally offer the opportunity to raise issues from a defensive posture, easing the burden a petitioner would encounter in an affirmative suit. . . .

D. THE NEED FOR JUDICIAL EDUCATION

Conference participants generally perceived domestic courts to be reluctant to rule on customary international law questions because of their tendency toward judicial restraint reinforced by judicial concern over deciding issues relatively alien to the domestic jurisprudential experience. Consequently, participants focused on the need to educate judges as to the existence of and the vital role to be played by customary international law. It was agreed that practitioners must take the initiative to show judges where and how to define international customary norms. They must also support these arguments with substantial and convincing evidence. Despite general agreement on the scope and nature of the challenge, participants' views varied widely on the means to be employed to accomplish this task.

One participant suggested that decisions of various European courts should be invoked to define terms and demarcate specific customary norms. Decisions of international courts may also help to demonstrate the contours of customary norms. It was noted, however, that attorneys must proceed cautiously with this approach, because certain European countries take a rather restrictive view with regard to issues affecting human rights.

Other conference participants recommended increased use of briefs *amicus curiae* to educate the judiciary. This strategy makes efficient and effective use of legal resources while providing a broader base of support for the preferred outcome. One participant also suggested that *amicus* briefs present an opportunity to advocate broad developments in the law rather than limiting the focus to the specific grievances of one party. Alternatively, attorneys can use *amicus* briefs to concentrate judicial attention on certain narrowly targeted issues. A practical problem with increased use of *amicus* briefs, it was observed, is the difficulty of locating appropriate litigation in progress in order to submit a brief in a timely fashion.

Conference participants concluded with a brief review of certain evolving customary norms, and focused particularly on the question of basing claims in domestic suits on developing international norms in the area of economic and social rights. *Price v. Cohen,*[46] which raised the question of whether a right to subsistence existed under the Fourteenth Amendment, was cited as an example of a case in which evidence of such customary norms might have proven useful. In cases such as *Price*, it was urged, attorneys could use proof of international norms to persuade judges to employ higher standards of review, or to encourage an affirmative finding that the particular right is of a fundamental and absolute nature.

[46] *Price v. Cohen,* 715 F.2d 87 (3d Cir. 1983). . . .

Some participants cautioned, however, that economic and social rights are not as clearly recognized as civil and political rights. Very little customary international law on economic and social rights exists. Where customary norms do exist, they are often very narrowly construed.

In addition, when asking a judge to consider a customary social or economic norm, an attorney must prove both the existence of the norm and its relationship to the domestic right sought. By clearly defining the nexus between customary international norms and domestic legal rights, human rights practitioners will educate the judiciary and significantly increase the likelihood that such arguments will succeed in United States federal courts.

NOTES AND QUESTIONS

1. There are many contexts in which international human rights law might be used. For example, prisoners sentenced to death in the U.S. are separated from the general prison population and held for years in places known as death row. Research shows that prolonged waiting on death row produces severe mental suffering often coupled with physical deterioration. *See* R. Johnson, Condemned to Die — Life Under Sentence of Death (1981). In *Trop v. Dulles*, 356 U.S. 86 (1958), the Supreme Court held that imposing a condition on an individual, in which severe mental suffering is inherent, violates the Eighth Amendment's prohibition against cruel and unusual punishment. U.S. courts, however, have consistently disregarded the issue of mental suffering on death row by either refusing to consider whether the suffering has reached unconstitutional proportions or by failing to separate the issue of mental suffering from the issue of exaction of the death penalty. *See* Note, *Mental Suffering Under Sentence of Death: A Cruel and Unusual Punishment*, 57 Iowa L. Rev. 814, 821 (1972). In addition, some courts have justified the time spent on death row as necessary in order to guarantee a careful review of the issues in the case. *Richmond v. Ricketts*, 640 F. Supp. 767, 803 (D.Ariz. 1986), declared also that the time spent on death row was not completely harmful because the prisoner developed "better skills in communicating with others" as well as "religious beliefs that he did not have before he went to prison." *Id.*

Although U.S. courts generally have failed to recognize the mental anxiety suffered on death row, such suffering recently influenced a decision by the European Court of Human Rights. In the *Soering Case*, 161 Eur. Ct. Hum. Rts. (series A) (1989), reproduced in chapter 10, *supra*, the European Court of Human Rights considered "the ever present and mounting anguish of awaiting execution of the death penalty" and concluded that, if the United Kingdom were to extradite Soering, a national of the Federal Republic of Germany, to the U.S. to face trial for capital murder, the United Kingdom would violate its obligation under Article 3 of the European Convention on Human Rights: "No one shall be subjected to torture or to inhuman or degrading treatment or punishment." In arriving at its conclusion the Court also considered the severity of the conditions on death row, Soering's age at the time of the offense (eighteen), and his impaired mental responsibility. How could the decision in *Soering* be used to challenge the prolonged waiting on death row by prisoners in the U.S.?

2. In 1980 Congress passed the Civil Rights of Institutionalized Persons Act (CRIPA), which gave the Attorney General power to protect mentally handicapped persons in state facilities. 42 U.S.C.A. § 1997 (1982). CRIPA authorizes the Attorney General to file a civil suit against a state if the Attorney General reasonably believes that the state is engaged in a "pattern or practice" subjecting residents of public institutions to "egregious or flagrant conditions" in violation of the constitutional or statutory rights of mentally handicapped persons.

Constitutional rights of instutionalized retarded people were clarified by the Supreme Court in *Youngberg v. Romeo*, 457 U.S. 307 (1982). The Court held that the Due Process Clause of the Fourteenth Amendment provides persons with mental retardation, who are involuntarily committed to a state institution, with the following substantive rights: adequate food, clothing, shelter, and medical care; reasonable safety; freedom from unnecessary bodily restraint; and adequate training to ensure safety and freedom from bodily restraint. *Id.* at 324. The Court did not decide whether mentally retarded persons had a right to treatment that would help them reach a maximum level of functioning. *Id.* at 318 n.23.

In determining whether a state has met its obligations with respect to the standards, the Court declared that "decision[s], if made by a professional, [are] presumptively valid; liability may be imposed only when the decision by the professional is such a substantive departure from accepted professional judgment, practice, or standards as to demonstrate that the person responsible actually did not base the decision on such a judgment." *Id.* at 323. Federal intervention, therefore, is allowed only when the government has reason to question the presumption.

Following *Youngberg* the Justice Department relaxed CRIPA enforcement. Six days after the decision, the Assistant Attorney General of the Civil Rights Division issued an internal memo stating that investigations should no longer include "whether the institutions provide 'psychiatric care, psychological treatment or individualized therapeutic efforts designed to enhance capacity, capability and competence.'" *See* Note, *The Constitutional Right to Treatment in Light of Youngberg v. Rome*, 72 Geo. L.J. 785, 785 (1984) (citing Memorandum from William Bradford Reynolds, Assistant Attorney General, to Arthur E. Peabody, Jr., Acting Chief, Special Litigation Section 3 (June 24, 1982)). For further discussion on the reluctance to litigate, *see* Dinerstein, *Absence of Justice*, 63 Neb. L. Rev. 680, 699 (1984); Note, *CRIPA: The Failure of Federal Intervention for Mentally Retarded People*, 97 Yale L.J. 845 (1988).

Some federal courts also have limited their recognition of the rights of the mentally retarded in light of *Youngberg*. For example, the Fifth Circuit has held that no constitutional right exists for institutionalized mentally handicapped persons that would insure care or treatment "in a least restrictive alternative setting." *Lelsz v. Kavanagh*, 807 F.2d 1243, 1250 (5th Cir. 1987). The court stated that "[t]he constitutional minimum standard of habilitation" does not relate to "the qualitative betterment of a retarded person's life...." *Id.* The Second Circuit similarly limited the training rights of mentally retarded residents in state institutions by stating that such rights do "...not include a right to such training as will improve a resident's basic self-care skills beyond those with which he or she entered SDC [Suffolk Developmental Center] and does not encompass skills that are not basic to self-care...." *Society for Good Will to Retarded Children, Inc. v. Cuomo*, 737 F.2d 1239, 1250 (2d Cir. 1984).

The First Circuit Court in *Doe v. Gaughan*, 808 F.2d 871 (1st Cir. 1986) used *Youngberg* in reasoning that the conditions of a state hospital for the mentally ill did not violate the patients' due process rights. The trial court in *Gaughan* had found that overcrowding and understaffing in the facility had decreased the hospital's ability to deliver services and had caused some patients to become even more ill. Despite its findings the court held that the conditions of the hospital did not violate patients' rights. The court of appeals affirmed. Its opinion adopted the trial court's reasoning that under *Youngberg* "[t]he Constitution does not require a state to provide an ideal environment for each person in its mental institution. Rather, it must provide an environment in which professional judgment may be exercised. Because Bridgewater's facilities are not so lacking as to prevent this exercise of professional judgment, these shortcomings do not rise to the level of a constitutional deprivation." *Id.* at 886.

3. After *Youngberg* does national law provide an adequate basis for protecting the rights of institutionalized persons with mental retardation?

4. Article 10(1) of the U.N.'s Draft Body of Principles and Guarantees for the Protection of Mentally-Ill Persons and for the Improvement of Mental Health Care provides that "[e]very patient shall have the right to be treated in the least restrictive environment and with the least restrictive or intrusive treatment appropriate to the patient's needs and the need to protect the physical safety of others." Article 10(2) states that "[t]he treatment and care of every patient shall be based on an individually prescribed plan, discussed with the patient, reviewed regularly, revised as necessary and provided by qualified professional staff." The principles are under consideration by a working group of the U.N. Human Rights Commission. *See* Report of the Working Group on the Draft Body of Principles and guarantees for the Protection of Mentally-Ill Persons and for the improvement of mental health care, U.N. Doc. E/CN.4/1990/31 (1990).

Might those U.N. norms influence a federal or state court in a lawsuit challenging conditions of detention for the mentally handicapped in a state institution?

5. Might a litigant be assisted by Article 5 of the Universal Declaration and Article 7 of the Civil and Political Covenant, which both state that no one shall be subjected to cruel, inhuman, or degrading treatment?

6. H. Hannum, *Materials on International Human Rights and U.S. Criminal Law and Procedure* (1989) has identified a number of other areas where international norms might be useful in U.S. courts:

a. The European Commission of Human Rights or the European Court of Human Rights considers the following acts to constitute deprivations of liberty: "a requirement that vagrants report to the police, even with the former's 'voluntary' agreement; the placing of a recidivist 'at the Government's disposal' for a ten-year period after completion of a prison sentence; revocation of parole; the confinement of persons to private houses in territory occupied by the armed forces; and taking a person by force to a medical institution for a blood test." *Id.* at 20.

b. Under the Bail Reform Act of 1984, U.S. courts will not presume pretrial release in "capital cases, cases with a sentence of greater than ten years, repeat offenders, crimes of violence or certain drug offenses. At the international level, there is essentially a presumption that accused persons should be released pending trial." *Id.* at 31.

c. The international prohibition of torture and cruel, inhuman, or degrading treatment or punishment is broader than the cruel and unusual punishment standard of the Eighth Amendment. *Id.* at 59-63.

d. As indicated, there are several international standards relating to prison conditions. *Id.* at 64-65.

e. Although the Supreme Court and the European Commission on Human Rights both guarantee a right of defense which may not necessarily be personal to the defendant, the European Commission has suggested that international norms may be violated if there was "a real divergence of opinion which could have influenced the . . . defence." *Id.* at 86. In addition, the European Commission has found that a government must replace an appointed lawyer when the accused demonstrates that the interests of justice would be served by replacing counsel. The European Commission does not require the accused to demonstrate that actual prejudice resulted. The Supreme Court, however, requires an accused to "show how specific errors undermined the reliability of the finding of guilt." *Id.* at 88-89.

f. The European Court of Human Rights has held that pressure brought on an accused to pay a small fine rather than face the closure of his business violated the right to a fair trial. Plea bargaining is an essential element of the U.S. criminal justice system. *Id.* at 95.

g. Under international law, the U.S. "dual sovereignty" theory, which permits retrial if a person has been acquitted of the same crime in another "sovereign" jurisdiction (*i.e.*, by a state or federal government), would not be acceptable. *Id.* at 115.

7. de la Vega, *Using International Human Rights Law in Legal Services Cases*, 22 Clearinghouse Rev. 1242-54 (1989), suggests how legal services lawyers can use international human rights law to help represent clients.

8. Professor Lillich has observed that counsel in *Bowers v. Hardwick*, 478 U.S. 186 (1986) (upholding Georgia's sodomy statute), might have used *Dudgeon v. United Kingdom*, 45 Eur. Ct. H.R. (ser. A) (1982) (adult male homosexuals have right to privacy). Lillich, *The Constitution and International Human Rights*, 83 Am. J. Int'l L. 851, 861 (1989).

9. For further reading, *see*:

Coliver & Newman, *Using International Human Rights Law to Influence United States Foreign Population Policy: Resort to Courts or Congress?*, 20 N.Y.U. J. Int'l L. & Pol'y 53 (1987);

Gibney, *Human Rights and Human Consequences: A Critical Analysis of Sanchez-Espinoza v. Reagan*, 10 Loy. L.A. Int'l & Comp. L.J. 299 (1988);

Strossen, *Recent U.S. and International Judicial Protection of Individual Rights: A Comparative Legal Process Analysis and Proposed Synthesis*, 41 Hastings L.J. 805 (1990);

Tolley, *International Human Rights Law in U.S. Courts, Public Interest Groups and Private Attorneys*, 1987 Annual Meeting, American Political Science Association;

Weissbrodt, *Ethical Problems of an International Human Rights Law Practice*, 7 Mich. Y.B. Int'l L. Stud. 217 (1985);

Weissbrodt, *Strategies for Selection and Pursuit of International Human Rights Objectives*, 8 Yale J. World Pub. Ord. 62 (1981);

Whisman, *Selected Bibliography: Articles and Cases on International Human Rights Law in Domestic Courts*, 18 International Lawyer 83 (1984).

XIII *HOW MAY THE INTERNATIONAL COURT OF JUSTICE USE ITS ADVISORY JURISDICTION TO HELP ENFORCE HUMANITARIAN AND OTHER HUMAN RIGHTS LAWS?*

ISRAEL AND OCCUPIED TERRITORIES

A. INTRODUCTION

Previous chapters have shown how judicial and quasi-judicial bodies interpret and implement human rights law. This chapter introduces a new source of that law, the complex aggregate of "humanitarian law" that governs armed conflicts. The Geneva Conventions of 1949 and their 1977 Protocols comprise the principal sources of humanitarian law. To illustrate the operation of that law, this chapter focuses principally on the Fourth Geneva Convention Relative to the Protection of Civilian Persons in Time of War. This chapter also discusses the role of the International Committee of the Red Cross (ICRC) in implementing humanitarian law.

As a factual situation for illustrating the operation of the Fourth Convention, this chapter uses the situation of Israel and the Occupied Territories. A dispute exists as to whether the Geneva Conventions even apply to the Occupied Territories. The questions ask readers to consider whether the Conventions do apply and, if so, what their application would mean.

In addition to introducing a new source of law, this chapter presents a rarely used, but very visible forum for pursuing international human rights concerns, the International Court of Justice (I.C.J.). The I.C.J. is established under the U.N. Charter and has power to render advisory opinions as well as to decide contentious cases. The focus here is the I.C.J.'s advisory jurisdiction; the overall inquiry is whether the I.C.J. could or should resolve the dispute over applicability of human rights and humanitarian law to the Occupied Territories through an advisory opinion.

B. QUESTIONS

The U.N. General Assembly has adopted many resolutions stating that the Fourth Geneva Convention does apply to Israel's occupation of the West Bank, the Gaza Strip, the Golan Heights, and East Jerusalem. Israel has disputed that conclusion.

Suppose the General Assembly requests an I.C.J. advisory opinion as to "What international laws apply to Israel's treatment of civilians in the Occupied Territories and what are the legal consequences of the continued presence of Israel in the Occupied Territories?" What arguments should advocates for U.N., Israel, and other interested states present to the Court? In preparing arguments, consider these questions:

1. Which U.N. bodies have authority to seek an I.C.J. advisory opinion? What is the scope of the I.C.J.'s advisory jurisdiction? (See U.N. Charter, Article 96; see also Articles 65-68 of the I.C.J. statute.)

2. What is the potential usefulness of an advisory opinion? Consider the majority opinion filed in *Namibia*. What has been the opinion's long-term impact? Would you expect parallel developments regarding the Occupied Territories?

3. What legal objections would Israel interpose to the exercise of the I.C.J.'s advisory jurisdiction?

4. Assuming the I.C.J. accepts advisory jurisdiction over the question, should it rule that the Fourth Convention applies in the Occupied Territories? What is the significance of Israel's ratification of that treaty? Who in the territories are "protected persons" within the definition of Article 4?

5. The Territories have been under Israeli occupation since 1967. Suppose Israel argues that Article 6 of the Convention makes the Convention inapplicable to the situation. What argument could you make in response? Is Israel engaged in "military operations" there?

6. What has been Israel's position on applicability of the Convention? Is that position tenable in light of Article 4's definition of "protected persons"?

7. In November 1988 the Palestine National Council declared an independent Palestinian state in the West Bank and Gaza. In July 1988 King Hussein seemed to have renounced Jordanian authority over the West Bank. Would establishment of a Palestinian state alter applicability of the Convention? (See Articles 2-6 of the Convention.)

8. What is the ICRC position as to applicability of the Convention? Would the ICRC benefit from an I.C.J. opinion?

9. Assume the Convention does apply to the Territories. Given the facts presented, which clauses of the Convention may Israel have violated? Consider especially Articles 27, 31-34, 49, 55, 56, and 83. What arguments would you expect Israel to make in response?

10. If there is no "occupation" under the Fourth Geneva Convention, could Common Article 3 apply? Has Common Article 3 been violated?

11. If the Geneva Conventions do not apply, do the Hague Rules? Has Israel violated the Hague Rules?

12. Might the I.C.J. rule that Israel must also observe the Universal Declaration of Human Rights? Consider especially Articles 3, 5, 9, 10, 12, 13, 14, 19, 20, 29, and 30.

13. Would it be wise for the I.C.J. to apply clauses of the International Bill of Human Rights to an armed conflict situation? How might such an opinion affect the impact of the Geneva Conventions?

14. The Covenant on Civil and Political Rights prescribes non-derogable protections for individuals under Articles 4, 6, 7, 8, 11, 15, 16, and 18. Though Israel is not a party to the Covenant, might the I.C.J. use the Covenant to interpret the Universal Declaration's Article 29 and Israeli obligations?

15. Should the I.C.J. refer to both the Geneva Conventions and the International Bill of Human Rights?

16. How should the I.C.J. handle inconsistencies between the protections afforded by human rights and humanitarian law? Should the I.C.J. rely upon the instrument which is the most protective of individual rights?

17. Should the I.C.J. hold that the Israeli Defense Forces and other security/police agencies have violated international humanitarian law and/or human rights law?

18. Would you argue that Israel's actions constitute "war crimes" or "crimes against humanity" under the Nuremberg Charter and/or Control Council Law No. 10?

C. INTERNATIONAL HUMANITARIAN LAW

1. Introduction

International humanitarian law constitutes a basis for efforts to prevent human rights violations, particularly during periods of international armed conflict and civil war. International humanitarian law has developed separately from international human rights law, but the two domains have begun to converge.

The nineteenth century brought the codification of protections for the victims of war and the first restraints on the methods and means of warfare. The 1863 Geneva International Conference founded the International Committee of the Red Cross (ICRC) for the purpose of reducing the casualties of war.[1] The ICRC was instrumental in preparing the initial draft of what became the first multilateral treaty protecting the victims of armed conflict: the Geneva Convention of 1864 for the Amelioration of the Condition of the Wounded and Sick in Armies in the Field.[2] This international treaty protected military hospitals from attack and required governments to accord enemy combatants the same quality of medical care as provided to their own armed forces. The fifteen Hague Conventions of 1899 and 1907 emphasized limits on the methods and means of warfare.[3] For example, the Hague Conventions prohibited the use of poisonous gases and other weapons calculated to cause unnecessary suffering.[4]

---

[1] Documents on the Laws of War 8 (A. Roberts & R. Guelff eds. 1982).

[2] T.S. 377, 22 Stat. 940, *entered into force* June 22, 1865. The ICRC also participated in drafting the Geneva Conventions of 1906, 1929, and 1949, as well as the Additional Protocols of 1977.

[3] *See* Solf, *Protection of Civilians Against the Effects of Hostilities Under Customary International Law and Under Protocol I*, 1 Am. U. J. Int'l L. & Pol'y 117, 122 (1986).

[4] *See also* Geneva Protocol for the Prohibition of the Use in War of Asphyxiating, Poisonous or Other Gases, and of Bacteriological Methods of Warfare, 26 U.S.T. 571, T.I.A.S. 8061, 94 L.N.T.S. 65, *entered in force* Feb. 8, 1928.

Following World War II, the ICRC initiated efforts to improve the protection for victims of war afforded by the Geneva Convention of 1864. Those efforts resulted in the four Geneva Conventions of 1949. The first three of the Geneva Conventions of 1949 provide for the treatment of sick and wounded members of armed forces in the field and at sea, and the treatment of prisoners of war.[5] The Fourth Geneva Convention extends protection to civilians in time of war.[6]

In 1974 the ICRC convened a conference to draft protocols intended to update and clarify the Geneva Conventions and to modernize the rules limiting methods and means of warfare. Those efforts resulted in the adoption of the two Additional Protocols of 1977 to the Geneva Conventions of 1949.[7] The Protocols attempted to combine the Geneva Conventions' focus on the protection of war victims with the Hague Conventions' concern about rules for waging war. Together the Geneva Conventions and Protocols and the Hague Conventions compose the principal sources of international humanitarian law.[8]

International humanitarian law confers rights on individual combatants and civilians. The Geneva Conventions give combatants the right to prisoner-of-war status once they are placed outside of battle by becoming sick, wounded, shipwrecked, or by voluntarily laying down their arms. The Geneva Conventions also establish minimum international standards for securing the life, liberty, and property of civilians in occupied territories. Under the Conventions, cultural objects and places of worship are to be protected from destruction; and the taking of hostages is prohibited. Civilians are to be protected from torture or mutilation. The Hague Conventions

---

[5] Geneva Convention for the Amelioration of the Condition of the Wounded and Sick in Armed Forces in the Field, 6 U.S.T. 3114, T.I.A.S. No. 3362, 75 U.N.T.S. 31 [hereinafter cited as First Geneva Convention]; Geneva Convention for the Amelioration of the Condition of Wounded, Sick and Shipwrecked Members of the Armed Forces at Sea, 6 U.S.T. 3217, T.I.A.S. No. 3363, 75 U.N.T.S. 85 [Second Geneva Convention]; Geneva Convention Relative to the Treatment of Prisoners of War, 6 U.S.T. 3316, T.I.A.S. No. 3364, 75 U.N.T.S. 135 [Third Geneva Convention], *entered into force* Oct. 21, 1950.

[6] Geneva Convention for the Protection of Civilian Persons in Time of War, 6 U.S.T. 3516, T.I.A.S. No. 3365, 75 U.N.T.S. 287 [Fourth Geneva Convention], *entered into force* Oct. 21, 1950.

[7] Protocol Additional to the Geneva Conventions of 12 August 1949 Relating to the Protection of Victims of International Armed Conflicts (Protocol I), U.N. Doc. A/32/144, Annex I, 16 I.L.M. 1391 (1977), *entered into force* Dec. 7, 1978; Protocol Additional to the Geneva Conventions of 12 August 1949, and Relating to the Protection of Victims of Non-International Armed Conflicts (Protocol II), U.N. Doc. A/32/144, Annex II, 16 I.L.M. 1442 (1977), *entered into force* Dec. 7, 1978.

[8] *See* Erickson, *Protocol I: A Merging of the Hague and Geneva Law of Armed Conflict*, 19 Va. J. Int'l L. 557, 559 (1979).

give combatants the right not to be targets of biological, bacteriological or chemical weapons, poison, and certain types of bullets.[9]

In order to apply humanitarian law one must ordinarily determine which sort of armed conflict is occurring and therefore which set of rules are relevant. The decision as to the sort of armed conflict often involves tricky questions regarding issues that are politically sensitive and facts that may be beyond the normal research competence of human rights organizations. Occasionally the assessments of other organizations may conflict with the judgments of the ICRC — the organization long recognized as the expert in this area.

International humanitarian law was specifically designed to limit human rights violations during periods of armed conflict against protected persons, such as soldiers who are wounded or otherwise *hors de combat*, and against the civilian population. International humanitarian law distinguishes four types of armed conflicts with different legal principles and instruments applicable to each: (1) international armed conflict to which the four Geneva Conventions of 1949, the Additional Protocol I of 1977, the Hague rules, and other legal rules apply; (2) wars of liberation or self-determination principally defined by and made subject to Protocol I of 1977; (3) non-international armed conflicts subjected to the rules of Common Article 3 in the four Geneva Conventions and some customary norms; and (4) non-international armed conflicts as narrowly defined and regulated by Protocol II of 1977.

If there exist only sporadic violence, internal disturbances, and tensions, international human rights law would apply, rather than international humanitarian law.

2. Advantages of Using Human Rights and Humanitarian Law

Serious human rights violations, including arbitrary killings, detention, and ill-treatment, are likely to increase in times of armed conflict. In the context of armed conflicts, international humanitarian law may provide a stronger basis for the protection of human rights than the Universal Declaration of Human Rights, the two International Human Rights Covenants, and other human rights instruments.

The principal multilateral treaties that legislate international humanitarian law — the four Geneva Conventions of 1949 and the Protocols of 1977 — are more broadly applicable than the main human rights treaties. As of 1990, there were 166 states parties to the Geneva Conventions of

---

[9] *See also* Convention on the Prohibition of the Development, Production and Stockpiling of Bacteriological (Biological) and Toxin Weapons and on their Destruction, 26 U.S.T. 583, T.I.A.S. 8062, 1015 U.N.T.S. 163, *entered into force* March 26, 1975.

1949; the Protocol I of 1977 has been ratified[10] by 92 nations, while 82 nations have become party to Additional Protocol II of 1977. The Hague Conventions of 1899 and 1907 are broadly accepted as restating customary international humanitarian law applicable to all countries.[11] By way of comparison, the International Covenant on Civil and Political Rights of 1966 has been ratified by 88 nations, while the International Covenant on Economic, Social and Cultural Rights has been ratified by 93 countries.

Some principles of humanitarian law are more exacting than the provisions of international human rights law. Humanitarian law applies specifically to emergency situations; international human rights law permits significant derogations during these same periods.[12]

Article 4 of the Covenant on Civil and Political Rights provides that in situations threatening the life of the nation, a government may suspend most human rights protections so long as (1) such a suspension is strictly required by the exigencies of the situation, (2) the suspension does not conflict with the nation's other international obligations (such as the Geneva Conventions), and (3) the U.N. Secretary-General is immediately informed. No derogation is permitted from the right to be free from discrimination on the basis of race, color, sex, language, religion, or social origin. Also, no derogation is permitted from the rights to be free from arbitrary killing; torture, or cruel, inhuman or degrading treatment or punishment; slavery; imprisonment for debt; retroactive penalties; or the failure to recognize a person before the law.[13]

Hence, in the 88 countries which have ratified the Covenant on Civil and Political Rights some of the most important human rights would be protected as non-derogable rights — particularly those concerning torture, inhuman treatment, and extrajudicial executions. Other rights, such as the right to be free from arbitrary arrest or detention and the right to a prompt and fair trial, would be subject to derogation in times of public emergency.[14]

Furthermore, many governments are not parties to the International Covenant on Civil and Political Rights. Those governments do not even have to take the formal steps required of states parties to derogate from their

---

[10] The term "ratify" is used as a shorthand for the various ways by which a government may become a party to a treaty, including accession and succession.

[11] *See, e.g.*, S. Mallison & W. Mallison, Armed Conflict in Lebanon, 1982: Humanitarian Law in a Real World Setting 67-68 (1983).

[12] *See* Meron, *Towards a Humanitarian Declaration on Internal Strife*, 78 Am. J. Int'l L. 859 (1984).

[13] *See* Hartman, *Derogations from Human Rights Treaties in Public Emergencies*, 22 Harv. Int'l L. J. 1 (1981).

[14] *See* International Commission of Jurists, States of Emergency, Their Impact on Human Rights 426-27 (1983). Article 75 of Additional Protocol I provides extensive procedural protections for the accused during periods of international armed conflict.

obligations under that treaty and are arguably not bound to guarantee the non-derogable rights identified in the Covenant. They may still be bound by customary international law to respect certain non-derogable rights including freedom from torture, arbitrary killing, etc.

In addition, humanitarian law may provide a stronger basis for efforts to curb the abuses of armed opposition groups than most of human rights law. Governments are principally responsible for the implementation of international human rights in peacetime and humanitarian law during periods of armed conflict.[15] During non-international armed conflicts, governments and armed opposition groups may bear responsibility for their obedience to humanitarian law.[16]

Since there are inconsistencies and gaps between the protections afforded by various human rights and humanitarian law instruments, as well as by national and local laws, the individual should be entitled to the most protective provisions of applicable international, national, or local laws. Accordingly, if humanitarian law affords better rights protections than human rights law, humanitarian law should be used — and *vice versa*.[17]

NOTES

For further reading, see: M. Bothe, K. Partsch, & W. Solf, New Rules for Victims of Armed Conflicts (1982); A. Cassese, ed., The New Humanitarian Law of Armed Conflict (1979); Dinstein, *Human Rights in Armed Conflict: International Humanitarian Law*, in Human Rights in International Law, Legal and Policy Issues 345 (T. Meron ed. 1984); F. Kalshoven and Y. Sandoz eds., Implementation of International Humanitarian Law (1989); Marks, *Principles and Norms of Human Rights Applicable in Emergency Situations: Underdevelopment, Catastrophes and Armed Conflicts*, in 1 International Dimension of Human Rights 175 (K. Vasak & P. Alston eds. 1982); Nahlik, *A Brief Outline of International Humanitarian Law*, 24 Int'l Rev. Red Cross 187 (1984); Schindler, *Human Rights and Humanitarian Law: The Interrelationship of the Laws*, 31 Am. U.L. Rev. 935 (1982); Weissbrodt, *The Role of International Organizations in the Implementation of Human Rights and Humanitarian Law in Situations of Armed Conflict*, 21 Vanderbilt J. Trans. L. 313 (1988).

---

[15] *See* International Covenant on Civil and Political Rights, Art. 2; Geneva Conventions, Common Article 1.

[16] *See, e.g.*, Geneva Conventions, Common Article 3; Additional Protocol II.

[17] *See* Newman, *Civil and Political Rights*, in The International Dimensions of Human Rights 135, 161 (K. Vasak & P. Alston eds. 1982).

D. THE ISRAELI OCCUPIED TERRITORIES; HUMAN RIGHTS AND HUMANITARIAN LAW

Department of State, Country Reports on Human Rights Practices for 1988, Report Submitted to the Senate Committee on Foreign Relations and the House Committee on Foreign Affairs, 101st Cong., 1st Sess. 1376 (1989):

THE OCCUPIED TERRITORIES

The United States considers Israel's occupation to be governed by the Hague Regulations of 1907 and the 1949 Fourth Geneva Convention Relative to the Protection of Civilian Persons in Time of War. Israel denies the applicability of the Fourth Geneva Convention to the West Bank and Gaza, but states that it observes the Convention's humanitarian provisions in those areas. Israel applies Jordanian law in the West Bank and British mandate law in Gaza, as well as its own military orders which changed these laws significantly.

. . . [M]ost of the occupied territories remain after 21 years under military government, and are, therefore subject in part to military law. That circumstance, in turn, was one of the consequences of the 1967 war between Israel and its neighbors. Since 1948 only Egypt has concluded a peace treaty with Israel (1979). . . . Although the Chairman of the Palestine Liberation Organization (PLO), which most Palestinians support, has stated that his organization recognizes Israel's right to exist and renounces terrorism, there are Palestinian factions which have not done so. The PLO has called for the uprising in the West Bank and Gaza to continue, and the future status of the occupied territories is now the central issue in the Arab-Israeli conflict.

Civilian unrest, reflecting Palestinian opposition to the occupation, has resulted in a number of outbreaks of violence during the last 21 years, which in turn have led periodically to sharp crackdowns by Israeli military forces. Beginning in December 1987, the occupation entered a new phase, referred to as the *intifada*, when civilian unrest became far more widespread and intensive than at any time heretofore. The active participants in these civil disturbances were primarily young men and women motivated by Palestinian nationalism and a desire to bring the occupation to an end. They gathered in groups, called and enforced strikes, threw stones and firebombs at Israeli security forces and civilian vehicles, or erected barricades and burned tires so as to interfere with traffic. The Israeli Government has regarded the uprising as a new phase of the 40-year war against Israel and as a threat to the security of the State. The Israeli Defense Forces, caught by surprise and untrained and inexperienced in riot control, responded in a manner which led to a substantial increase in human rights violations.

The West Bank (including East Jerusalem) had been annexed by Jordan in 1950. Even after the occupation of these areas by Israel in 1967, Jordan considered them its territory, recognized Palestinian residents of these areas as citizens of Jordan, and continued to provide financial support to the West Bank. Israel tacitly accepted these arrangements. A marked change occurred, however, in July 1988, when King Hussein [of Jordan] announced a significant reduction in administrative and financial support for the West Bank and Gaza. . . .

Amnesty International, Report 1989, at 260-64 (1989):

ISRAEL AND THE OCCUPIED TERRITORIES

More than 25,000 Palestinians were arrested in connection with the *intifada* (uprising) which began in the Occupied Territories of the West Bank and Gaza in December 1987. More than 5,000 of those arrested were held in administrative detention without charge or trial; some were prisoners of conscience. Hundreds of other Palestinians were summarily tried and imprisoned. At least 40 Israelis were imprisoned as conscientious objectors for refusing military service in the Occupied Territories and others, possible prisoners of conscience, were brought to trial on political charges. Thousands of Palestinians were victims of beatings while in the hands of Israeli forces; at least nine were reported to have died as a result. There were also many incidents in which Palestinians were shot in circumstances suggesting that Israeli forces had deliberately used excessive force. In a number of cases Palestinians were reported to have died as a result of deliberate misuse of tear-gas. Several political detainees died in custody in suspicious circumstances. One death sentence was imposed but there were no executions.

Throughout the year Palestinians protested against the Israeli occupation of the West Bank and Gaza through demonstrations in which stones and other missiles were often thrown, and through strikes and tax boycotts. They also set up popular committees to coordinate activities and to create alternative structures to the Israeli Civil Administration. The Israeli authorities responded with measures such as widespread arrests and the use of force, which was often excessive and indiscriminate and resulted in the death or injury of thousands, including many children. The populations of entire towns and villages were often restricted by prolonged curfews, apparently as punishment. Monitoring human rights violations became increasingly difficult as journalists and human rights workers were detained, newspapers and press services were closed, and access to villages and towns was often restricted.

More than 25,000 Palestinians, including children, were arrested in connection with the *intifada*. In the first few months of the *intifada* hundreds of teenagers and young people were summarily tried, often without legal representation, and sentenced to several months' imprisonment for disturbing public order. Many others were detained for several days and then released without charge.

More than 5,000 Palestinians were administratively detained without charge or trial on the grounds that they posed a threat to state or public security. They included many prisoners of conscience and possible prisoners of conscience. In March military orders for the Occupied Territories extended the power to issue administrative detention orders and suspended existing automatic and periodic judicial review of such orders. In June, after further changes, detainees could challenge their detention by appealing to a single Military Court judge and thereafter by petitioning the High Court of Justice. Appeals were held after delays of weeks or months, and were often the first opportunity — sometimes the only opportunity — detainees had to learn about the reasons for their detention. In almost every case detainees and their lawyers received information about reasons for detention insufficient to enable them to exercise effectively the right to challenge a detention order.

The vast majority of administrative detainees, including prisoners of conscience, were held in Ketziot, a new detention centre in a remote area of the Negev desert. Conditions at Ketziot were harsh: accommodation was in crowded tents which provided little protection from desert temperatures; medical services were inadequate; there were no family visits; and access to lawyers was restricted. Detainees were reported to have been beaten on the way to the detention centre and during detention, and subjected to arbitrary punishment. A high level of tension in the camp often erupted into clashes between detainees and the Israeli military. In the context of one such clash in August two detainees were shot dead.

Those detained under administrative orders included Ghazi Shashtari, a field-worker for the West Bank human rights organization *al-Haq*, who was arrested. . . .

At least 40 Israelis were imprisoned as prisoners of conscience for periods of between 14 and 35 days for refusing to carry out military service in the Occupied Territories. Many others were said to have refused service in the Occupied Territories but to have been offered alternative postings by their commanding officers.

In July four Israelis were fined and sentenced to 18 months' imprisonment, of which 12 were suspended, for meeting officials of the Palestine Liberation Organization (PLO) at a conference in Romania in 1986. They were convicted by a Magistrates' Court under Article 4(h) of the Prevention of Terrorism Ordinance, which makes it an offence to have contact with an official of an organization declared to be "terrorist" by the Israeli authorities. The court decided that the six months of their sentences would take the form of community service. On appeal their sentence was upheld by a district court. A further appeal to the Supreme Court was scheduled for 1989. . . .

In January, in what appeared to be endorsement of indiscriminate beatings, the Minister of Defence announced that the Israeli Defence Force (IDF) would prevent violent demonstrations with "force, power and blows". At about the same time commanding officers were reported to have given orders to break hands and feet. Later the Minister of Defence said there were orders to avoid beatings as punishment or after arrest. The Attorney General wrote to him in February saying that he had received enough complaints about excessive use of force to convince him that the irregularities were not exceptional cases. He said that beating demonstrators in order to punish or humiliate them was illegal, and that it was illegal for soldiers to obey orders to do so. Also in February the Chief of Staff sent a letter to all IDF commanders in the Occupied Territories containing guidelines on the use of force. He said that these were not new but because there had been "aberrations" by soldiers it was necessary to "emphasize and clarify existing orders". He stated that force was not to be used as punishment or after people had been apprehended.

Despite these statements beatings of Palestinians while in the hands of Israeli forces continued on a large scale throughout the year. In many instances this was clearly intended to punish or intimidate. Victims were kicked and hit with fists, clubs and rifle-butts. They included children and elderly people, as well as wounded Palestinians forcibly removed from hospitals. Many suffered multiple fractures and other severe injuries and at least nine were reported to have died as a result. According to eye-witnesses, Khader Tarazi died in February after he was severely beaten by four soldiers in a house in which he had been apprehended. A doctor who examined the body said that Khader Tarazi had a fractured spine, right frontal skull fracture, fractures of each arm and right hand, and multiple lacerations of the back, stomach, face and limbs. Internal injuries could not be assessed.

Between December 1987 and the end of 1988 about 300 Palestinians were shot dead by Israeli forces. Thousands of others were shot and injured, many critically. Many of those who died were killed during violent disturbances but others were killed even though they appeared not to have been involved in any violent activities at the time they were shot. The IDF initially made extensive use of lethal high-velocity bullets which were supposed to be fired only in life-threatening situations after warning procedures had been followed. In August special types of plastic bullet were introduced with the stated aim of injuring more people but reducing fatalities. It was claimed that they were not lethal and therefore were usable in non-life-threatening situations within specific limits. However, several deaths were attributed to their use.

Palestinians in the Occupied Territories also died apparently as a result of deliberate misuse of tear-gas by Israeli forces, who were reported to have used it in excessive concentrations or to have thrown canisters into houses, clinics, schools and mosques despite manufacturer's instructions not to use the gas in confined spaces as it was potentially lethal. Between December 1987 and the end of the year over 40 people reportedly died following tear-gas inhalation. Among them were particularly vulnerable people such as babies and the elderly. In May Khaled al-Najjar, aged 55, was reported to have died after exposure to tear-gas from two canisters which landed in his house.

According to the authorities, investigations were to be carried out following every fatal shooting incident involving Israeli forces and could lead to disciplinary measures or courts-martial. Investigations of beatings were to be carried out apparently only upon complaint. By the end of the year official figures indicated that since the beginning of the *intifada* investigations into human rights abuses by the IDF had resulted in legal action against 45 officers and soldiers. With less than half of the cases completed 15 people had been found guilty. By the end of the year two soldiers were known to have been convicted of manslaughter for having shot dead two Palestinians; one soldier received a suspended sentence of one year's imprisonment and the other a sentence of 18 months' imprisonment. Seven soldiers were brought to trial in two separate cases of alleged beatings resulting in deaths; their trials were continuing at the end of the year. A few others were found guilty in cases of punitive beatings, the heaviest sentence reportedly being two and a half months' imprisonment. In cases of apparently deliberate misuse of tear-gas no action was known to have been taken.

A number of Palestinians held in detention centres were reportedly ill-treated and at least five died in suspicious circumstances. The official cause of their deaths was apparently suicide. In October Ibrahim al-Matur died in the Dhahiriya detention centre, allegedly by hanging himself. He was reported to have been ill-treated in the days before his death, including by exposing him to tear-gas from a canister thrown into his cell. . . .

NOTES AND QUESTIONS

1. On August 10, 1989, Israeli military authorities amended the regulations governing administrative detention in the Occupied Territories. The amended regulations provide that administrative detention orders may be issued for renewable periods of up to a year rather than for six months, as had previously been the case. Administrative detainees may appeal any detention order to a military judge, who can confirm, shorten, or cancel an order. Detainees may also appeal a judge's decision to the Israeli High Court of Justice. Amnesty International, Israel and Occupied Territories: Maximum Period of Administrative Detention Extended, AI Index: NWS 11/34/89 (1989). Do these changes indicate whether Israel is continuing to follow the requirements of the Fourth Geneva Convention?

2. For further reading, see: J. Paust, G. von Glahn, and G. Woratsch, Inquiry into the Israeli Military Court System in the Occupied West Bank and Gaza (1989); International Commission of Jurists & Law in the Service of Man, Twenty Years of Israeli Occupation of the West Bank and Gaza (1987); International Commission of Jurists & Law in the Service of Man, Justice? The Military Court System in the Israeli Occupied Territories (1987); Israel National Section of the International Commission of Jurists, The Rule of Law in the Areas Administered by Israel (1981); Lawyers Committee for Human Rights, Detention of Human Rights Workers and Lawyers from the West Bank and Gaza and Conditions of Detention in Ketziot (1988); Playfair, *Administrative Detention in the Israeli-Occupied West Bank*, 13 Studie-en Informatiecentrum Mensenrechten 5 (Feb. 1986).

A. Roberts, B. Joergensen, & F. Newman, Academic Freedom Under Israeli Military Occupation 26-27, 30-31, 80-82 (1984) (footnotes omitted):

THE LAW APPLICABLE IN THE WEST BANK AND THE GAZA STRIP

To assert clearly, as we do, that these are occupied territories does not solve at a blow the question of what law is applicable there. It does however serve as a guide. As far as the subject of our enquiry is concerned, the following bodies of law are relevant:

(1) International law on military occupations; (2) International human rights law; (3) The law of these territories prior to the Israeli take-over in 1967; and (4) The law imposed by the occupant in these territories. These are considered in turn.

As far as the first two categories are concerned, we do not except in passing discuss the justiciability of international legal provisions in Israeli courts; rather we discuss the obligations incumbent on the government of Israel in its formulation and execution of policy.

1. *International Law on Military Occupations*

This body of international law is basically a part of the laws of war. Like all international law, its sources include not only formal international conventions (i.e. treaties), but also international custom, judicial decisions (of which there have been a very large number dealing with military occupations), and the work of distinguished legal experts. So far as international conventions are concerned, the main expressions of this body of law are the following:

1. *1907 Hague Regulations*, annexed to 1907 Hague Convention IV on Land Warfare. Entry into force: 26 January 1910. Israel, Jordan and Egypt are not formal parties. However, the Convention was expressly recognised by the International Military Tribunal at Nuremberg as declaratory of customary international law, and it is widely accepted on this basis, including by the Israeli Supreme Court. Articles 42-56 of the Regulations relate specifically to military occupations.

2. *1948 Genocide Convention.* Entry into force: 12 January 1951. Israel signed on 17 August 1949 and ratified on 9 March 1950. Jordan acceded on 3 April 1950. Egypt signed on 12 December 1948 and ratified on 8 February 1952. This agreement applies equally in time of peace or war, and can also be viewed as part of the international law of human rights.

3. *1949 Geneva Convention IV on Protection of Civilian Persons in Time of War*. Entry into force: 21 October 1950. Israel signed on 8 December 1949 and ratified on 6 July 1951. Jordan acceded on 29 May 1951. Egypt signed on 8 December 1949 and ratified on 10 November 1952. The main provisions on occupations are in Section III (articles 47-78).

4. *1954 Hague Cultural Property Convention and Protocol.* Entry into force: 7 August 1956. Israel signed the Convention on 14 May 1954, ratified it on 3 October 1957, and acceded to the Protocol on 1 April 1958. Jordan signed both on 22 December 1954 and ratified both on 2 October 1957. Egypt signed both on 30 December 1954 and ratified both on 17 August 1955.

5. *1977 Geneva Protocol I Additional to the 1949 Geneva Conventions.* Entry into force: 7 December 1978. Israel is not a party. Jordan signed on 12 December 1977 and ratified on 1 May 1979. Egypt signed on 12 December 1977 but has not ratified. . . .

2.   *International Human Rights Law*

Apart from the laws of war, international human rights law is the other main body of international conventional law which is relevant to the situation in the occupied territories. Of course, the laws of war themselves deal quite extensively with human rights in armed conflicts and occupations. Indeed, the laws of war can be viewed as one particular part of human rights law. International human rights law, as discussed here, is distinct from the laws of war partly by virtue of the fact that it is much more widely applicable: it applies in peacetime, and it applies within states, affecting for example the relations between governments and their own subjects. It also goes into greater detail on certain matters, including matters relating to education.

The general principle of the applicability of international human rights law to occupied territories has been the subject of relatively little consideration, and is not specifically addressed in the conventions themselves. However, the modern movement for human rights law grew out of the almost universal reaction against Nazi practices in Germany and the occupied countries in the Second World War. A number of writers have asserted the applicability of human rights law in time of armed conflict and occupation. It may have been partly with human rights law in mind (as well as the humanitarian laws of war) that the International Court of Justice pointed to the applicability of 'certain general conventions such as those of a humanitarian character' in Namibia, illegally occupied by South Africa. The *Cyprus v. Turkey* cases before the European Commission of Human Rights have confirmed the general principle of the applicability of human rights law with regard to the Turkish-occupied areas of Cyprus.

. . . [T]he question of what international agreements are applicable to the occupied territories has several distinct aspects. Among other things there has been a need for clarification regarding those agreements falling broadly within the human rights stream of law. Therefore in the course of enquiry we several times, both orally and by letter, sought information from the Israeli authorities regarding the applicability of some or all of the . . . accords relating to human rights. . . . Eventually we received the following memorandum dated 12 September 1984, prepared by the Office of the Legal Adviser in the Israeli Foreign Ministry. . . .

Text of Memorandum [from the Israeli Foreign Ministry] . . .

The 1948 Universal Declaration of Human Rights
The 1966 International Covenant on Economic, Social and Cultural Rights
The 1966 International Covenant on Civil and Political Rights

a) The question of the applicability of these documents, and in fact, of "human rights law" in general in the administered areas requires some elucidation, in view of the nature of the circumstances prevailing in those areas. As has been stated officially, since 1967, the areas are being administered by Israel pending the final settlement of their status through a peace process between the Parties concerned. Pending the successful completion of that process, it has from the outset, been the declared policy of the State of Israel that its military and civil organs abide by the *humanitarian* provisions of the Hague Regulations and the Fourth Geneva Convention (without entering into the academic question of the legal applicability of those documents).

b) The unique political circumstances, as well as the emotional realities present in the areas concerned, which came under Israeli administration during the armed conflict in 1967, render the situation *sui generis*, and as such, clearly not a classical situation in which the normal components of "human rights law" may be applied, as are applied in any standard, democratic system in the relationship between the "citizen" and his government. Hence the criteria applied in the areas administered by Israel, in view of the *sui generis* situation, are those of "humanitarian law," which balances the needs of humanity with the requirements of international law to administer the area whilst maintaining public order, safety and security.

c) In this context, it is most relevant to refer to a memorandum prepared by the Government of Jordan, and presented to the Secretary-General of the United Nations and circulated on 30 October 1981, regarding a Jordanian proposal for inclusion of a new item in the agenda of the General Assembly, entitled "New International Humanitarian Order" (A/36/245). In the annex to its letter, the Jordanian Government, *inter alia*, drew a comparison between the law of human rights and the humanitarian law of armed conflicts:

This humanitarian law of armed conflicts must be distinguished from the law of human rights, whether international, as in the two United Nations Covenants of Human Rights of 1966, or the regional law of the European Convention of Human Rights of 1950. In the human rights regimes the purpose is to defend the individual human being from loss

of life and liberty and from cruel treatment and oppression at the hands
of the State to which he is subjected, whether as a citizen or as a
"person temporarily subject to its jurisdiction". Human rights are the
legal shield against the oppression of the Government of the State directed
at the human being and his development. In the humanitarian law of
armed conflicts the purpose is to balance the needs of humanity against
the nature of warfare: no easy task.

There has been a modern tendency to relate closely human rights
with the law of war, as exemplified in the accepted United Nations
parlance of "Respect for human rights in armed conflicts". This is, in
juridical terms, a fundamental confusion of distinct legal regimes. With
the law of war, one is dealing with States and their populations, or other
entities which are in the relation of hostility, one to another, to an extent
that those States have resorted to armed force against the enemy State.
In the realm of human rights the law is concerned with the relationship
between the citizens of a State and the State Government, that is,
ensuring a system of protection of the governed against the Government.
(A/36/245 Annex, pp. 4,5). . . .

NOTES

For further readings on the Israeli government views, see: B. Keimbach,
Israel's Administration of the Territories, The Position in Law (1990);
Shamgar, *The Observance of International Law in the Administrated Territories*, 1 Israel Y.B. Hum. Rts. 262 (1971); M. Shamgar, ed., Military
Government in the Territories Administered by Israel 1967-1980 (1982); *see
also* Meron, *West Bank and Gaza: Human Rights and Humanitarian Law
in a Period of Transition*, 9 Israel Y.B. Hum. Rts. 108 (1979).

Note, *Recent Israeli Security Measure Under the Fourth Geneva Convention*,
3 Conn. J. Int'l L. 485, 485-95, 489-500 (1988) (authored by Peter J. Morgan,
III) (footnotes omitted):

I.   APPLICABILITY OF THE FOURTH GENEVA CONVENTION TO THE OCCUPIED TERRITORIES

In 1951 Israel ratified the Fourth Geneva Convention, yet it has never
acknowledged the Convention's applicability to the occupied territories. In 1971
then Attorney General Meir Shamgar announced that the Labour government would
act in de facto accordance with the Convention, but that it preferred to leave
open the legal question of the Convention's applicability to the occupied territories.
Six years later the Likud government flatly denied the applicability of the Convention, while still maintaining that its administration of the territories was in de
facto accordance with the Convention.

In denying the applicability of the Fourth Geneva Convention to the occupied
territories, Israeli publicists and governmental authorities have adopted a "territory-

oriented" approach to the Convention's interpretation, under which the Fourth Geneva Convention does not always govern territory obtained through armed conflict. An Israeli publicist, Dr. Yehuda Blum, formulated the major premise upon which this proposition rests:

> [T]he traditional rules of international law governing belligerent occupation are based on a twofold assumption, namely (a) that it was the legitimate sovereign which was ousted from the territory under occupation; and (b) that the ousting side qualifies as a belligerent occupant with respect to the territory. According to [Dr. Gerhard von] Glahn, "[b]elligerent occupation...as regulated by customary and conventional international law, presupposes a state of affairs in which the sovereign, the legitimate government of the occupied territory, is at war with the government of the occupying forces." This assumption of the concurrent existence in respect of the same territory, of both an ousted legitimate sovereign and a belligerent occupant lies at the root of all those rules of international law, which while recognizing and sanctioning the occupant's rights to administer the occupied territory, aim at the same time to safeguard the reversionary rights of the ousted sovereign.

Israel claims that Egypt's and Jordan's occupation of the territories in question were illegal under international law. Thus, according to Israel neither Egypt nor Jordan can claim to be a "legitimate sovereign" of the territories, and therefore humanitarian law in general and the Fourth Geneva Convention in particular do not apply to these territories.

These publicists and governmental authorities find textual support for their reasoning in article 2, paragraph 2 of the Fourth Geneva Convention, which reads: "The Convention shall also apply to all cases of partial or total occupation of the territory of a High Contracting Party." The Israeli concern is that if they were to accept the applicability of the Fourth Geneva Convention, the phrase "territory of a High Contracting Party" would imply that Israel recognized Egypt's sovereignty in the Gaza Strip and Jordan's sovereignty in the West Bank and East Jerusalem. Since the Israeli government categorically denies any such possibility, it has preferred to leave the question of applicability open and simply apply the convention de facto.

The Israeli position has been widely criticized. W. Thomas and Sally Mallison have offered five reasons requiring the rejection of the narrow construction of the term "territory" as including only territory over which the displaced government has de jure title.

First, they argue that such a construction of the word "territory" has no basis in either the text of the convention or in its negotiating history. Second the Mallisons demonstrate that reliance on the concept of "legitimate sovereign" as set forth by von Glahn is mistaken, since the term is not found in the text or in the negotiating history of the Convention.

The Mallisons' third and fourth points address the danger of requiring the belligerent occupant to first accept the validity of the title of the displaced government before applying the law of belligerent occupation. Again, neither the text of the Convention nor its negotiating history supports such a proposition. Furthermore, such a proposition would be contrary to the well established customary law based upon state practice. If the application of humanitarian law depended on the acceptance of the validity of its opponent's title, the law would never be applied. Humanitarian law, the Mallisons argue, must apply without regard to the validity of title.

Finally, the Mallisons attack the "territory-oriented" view of Israeli publicists and governmental authorities. As stated in the official International Committee of the Red Cross Commentary upon the Fourth Geneva Convention, "it is the first time that a set of international regulations has been devoted not to State interests but solely to the protection of the individual." Had the framing states at the Diplomatic Conference in Geneva intended to protect governmental rights they would have so expressed. . . .

Under this approach the Fourth Geneva Convention entered into force with the outbreak of war between Israel and the Arab nations. Once the inhabitants fell under the authority of the Israeli Defense Forces, they became "protected persons" as set forth in article 4, paragraph 1: "Persons protected by the Convention are those who, at a given moment and in any manner whatsoever, find themselves, in case of a conflict or occupation, in the hands of a Party to the conflict or Occupying Power of which they are not nationals." Individuals fall under the protection of the Fourth Geneva Convention as soon "as they fall into the hands of the Occupying Power."

Article 4's negotiating history is consistent with this distinction between the first and second paragraphs of article 2. In the negotiating history of article 4, "[i]t was understood that the term 'occupation' meant occupation without war, as provided for in the second paragraph of Article 2." Likewise, the report of Committee III stated:

> The purpose of this Article [4] is to determine the beginning and end of application of the Convention. There was no difficulty with regard to the former: application begins at the outset of a conflict, or as soon as there is occupation. That is stated in the first paragraph of the draft. It was perfectly well understood that the word "occupation" referred not only to occupation during war itself, but also to sudden occupation without war, as provided in the second paragraph of Article 2.

Fundamentally, the resolution of this issue depends more on political factors than on legal factors. Regardless of the determination of this issue, however, the Fourth Geneva Convention does set the standards upon which the actions of an Occupying Power are to be judged. It is necessary, therefore, with regard to particular Israeli security measures to understand the humanitarian provisions of the Fourth Geneva Convention.

II.   LEGALITY OF RECENT ISRAELI SECURITY MEASURES UNDER THE FOURTH GENEVA CONVENTION

Even though Israel denies that the Fourth Geneva Convention binds them by the force of law in the occupied territories, it has asserted that it will apply the Convention de facto. . . .

The authority of Israel, as an occupying Power, to proscribe security offenses is limited by article 64 of the Fourth Geneva Convention requiring that "[t]he penal laws of the occupied territory shall remain in force, with the exception that they may be repealed or suspended by the Occupying Power in cases where they constitute a threat to its security or an obstacle to the application of the present

Convention.'' This provision thus creates two systems of law within the occupied territories: a local law system and a system composed of the orders and proclamations of the Israeli commander.

In the West Bank, local law is comprised of Old Ottoman Law, British Mandatory Law and Jordanian legislation; the Gaza Strip derives its local law from Old Ottoman Law, British Mandatory Law and Egyptian military orders and proclamations. With regard to security offenses, British Mandatory Law is the most important form of local law. In 1945 the British enacted the Defence (Emergency) Regulations 1945 for application in both Palestine and Jordan. These regulations are significant because many of the security measures so widely criticized are employed by Israel pursuant to these regulations.

A. *Deportations*

Regulation 112(1) of the Defence (Emergency) Regulations authorizes deportations: "The High Commissioner shall have power to make an order under his hand for the deportation of any person from Palestine. A person in respect of whom a Deportation Order has been made shall remain out of Palestine so long as the Order remains in force." The Minister of Defence has replaced the High Commissioner in ordering deportations pursuant to Regulation 112(1). According to the Regulations, the individual against whom the order has been made may appeal to an advisory committee whose decision the Regional commander must affirm or reject. An individual may then appeal to the High Court of Justice.

. . . Article 49, paragraph 1 of the Fourth Geneva Convention reads: "Individual or mass forcible transfers, as well as deportations of protected persons from occupied territory to the territory of the Occupying Power or that of any other country, occupied or not, are prohibited, regardless of their motive." Notwithstanding Israeli reservations regarding the applicability of the Fourth Geneva Convention, the Israeli government has consistently contended that article 49 of the Convention does not apply to its deportations of individuals from the occupied territories. In support of this claim, Israel relies on the Official Commentary to article 49 in asserting that the article only prohibits deportations of the character that occurred during the Second World War. The Official Commentary states:

> There is doubtless no need to give an account here of the painful recollections called forth by the "deportations" of the Second World War, for they are still present in everyone's memory. It will suffice to mention that millions of human beings were torn from their homes, separated from their families and deported from their country, usually under inhumane conditions. These mass transfers took place for the greatest possible variety of reasons, mainly as a consequence of the formation of a forced labour service.

Based on this description, the Israeli government concludes that article 49 was adopted particularly to prohibit the "specific and terrible experiences of World War II." The Israelis further assert that the deportations from the occupied territories in no way resemble those deportations that occurred during the Second World War. According to this theory, the actions of the Israeli government are more similar to banishment or expulsion for security reasons than to deportation.

Israel cites two other provisions of the Convention as support for this interpretation. The Israelis argue that article 147, declaring "unlawful deportation or transfer or unlawful confinement of a protected person" as a "grave breach," is evidence that the Convention does not absolutely prohibit deportation. Since provision is made for the lawful transfer and lawful confinement of individuals, they reason that the drafters recognized the existence of lawful deportation. The Israelis find implicit support for this position in article 78, allowing that "[i]f the Occupying Power considers it necessary, for imperative reasons of security, to take safety measures concerning protected persons, it may, at the most, subject them to assigned residence or to internment." Thus, it is submitted, deportation is permissible when such deportation is less severe than continued and indefinite detention.

Certainly the atrocities of World War II influenced the drafting of article 49 as they did most of the Convention's other provisions, but in no way can it be said that the explicit language of article 49 limits itself only to similar contexts. Article 49 absolutely prohibits deportations "regardless of their motive," the only exception being that of the second paragraph of article 49, permitting evacuations for reasons of security or safety.

Furthermore, the most recent instances of deportation from the occupied territories demonstrate that they are not far removed from the deportations of World War II with regard to the hardship imposed by displacement. On 13 January 1988, four Palestinians accused "of continuing protests against the Israeli occupation" were taken by Army helicopter and released in a mountain pass in Lebanon. All the deportees were denied a visit with their families and their Israeli lawyer. Since Lebanon, Syria, Egypt and Jordan have all declared that they would not accept Palestinians deported by Israel, Lebanese Army troops returned the four men to the Israeli-controlled "security zone" in southern Lebanon. Perhaps Israeli arguments were plausible while the individuals deported were individuals confronted with the option of deportation or long and indefinite internment, but this most recent deportation illustrates the rationale behind article 49's absolute prohibition on deportation. The process and effect of deportation is the same regardless of its intentions. Even though individuals are not deported for the same heinous purposes as during the Second World War, they are still "torn from their homes, separated from their families and deported from their country." At least while imprisoned, the individual remains in his homeland and is not usually deprived of the ability to visit with his family. The same is not true of deportation. . . .

D.   *"Force, Power, and Blows"*

On 19 January 1988, Defence Minister Yitzhak Rabin announced that the Israeli Defence Forces would implement a new policy of using beatings instead of firearms against Palestinian protestors. While the extent of the violence precipitated by this policy is too early to assess, its legality is worthy of examination.

In the first place, the arbitrary use of force clearly violates the prohibitions against "[c]ollective penalties and likewise all measures of intimidation or of terrorism." However, even if the Israeli authorities were able to limit the infliction of force to only guilty individuals, article 32 of the Fourth Geneva Convention would still make this an impermissible policy. Article 32 reads:

> The High Contracting Parties specifically agree that each of them is prohibited from taking any measure of such a character as to cause the physical suffering or extermination of protected persons in their hands.

This prohibition applies not only to murder, torture, corporal punishment, [and] mutilation. . . , but also to any other measures of brutality whether applied by civilian or military agents.

Even though article 27 allows "measures of control and security in regard to protected persons as may be necessary as a result of war," article 32 provides a specific prohibition against the use of such extreme measures. Article 27 itself states that:

> Protected persons are entitled, in all circumstances to respect for their persons, their honour, their family rights, their religious convictions and practices, and their manner and customs. They shall at all times be humanely treated, and shall be protected against all acts of violence or threats thereof and against insults and public curiosity.

Such measures of control called for by the recent Israeli policy are specifically and absolutely denied to them.

> The requirement of humane treatment and the prohibition of certain acts incompatible with it are general and absolute in character, like the obligation enjoining respect for essential rights and fundamental liberties. They are valid "in all circumstances" and "at all times", and apply, for example, to cases where a protected person is the legitimate object of strict measures, since the dictates of humanity and measures of security or repression, even where they are severe, are not necessarily incompatible.

While the security concerns of the Israelis in the occupied territories are certainly clear, the dictates of the Convention are equally clear.

NOTES

For further reading, see Commentary, IV Geneva Convention Relative to the Protection of Civilian Persons in Time of War (J. Pictet, ed. 1958); Roberts, *Prolonged Military Occupation: The Israeli-Occupied Territories*, 84 Am. J. Int'l L. 44 (1990); G. von Glahn, The Occupation of Enemy Territory (1957).

·Geneva Convention Relative to the Protection of Civilian Persons in Time of War of August 12, 1949, 6 U.S.T. 3516, T.I.A.S. No. 3364, 75 U.N.T.S. 287 (Fourth Geneva Convention), *entered into force* Oct. 21, 1950:

PART I — GENERAL PROVISIONS

Article 1

The High Contracting Parties undertake to respect and to ensure respect for the present Convention in all circumstances.

Article 2

In addition to the provisions which shall be implemented in peacetime, the present Convention shall apply to all cases of declared war or of any other armed conflict which may arise between two or more of the High Contracting Parties even if the state of war is not recognized by one of them.

The Convention shall also apply to all cases of partial or total occupation of the territory of a High Contracting Party, even if the said occupation meets with no armed resistance.

Although one of the Powers in conflict may not be a party to the present Convention, the Powers who are parties thereto shall remain bound by it in their mutual relations. They shall furthermore be bound by the Convention in relation to the said Power, if the latter accepts and applies the provisions thereof.

Article 3

In the case of armed conflict not of an international character occurring in the territory of one of the High Contracting Parties, each Party to the conflict shall be bound to apply, as a minimum, the following provisions:

(1) Persons taking no active part in the hostilities, including members of armed forces who have laid down their arms and those placed *hors de combat* by sickness, wounds, detention, or any other cause, shall in all circumstance be treated humanely, without any adverse distinction founded on race, colour, religion or faith, sex, birth or wealth, or any other similar criteria.

To this end, the following acts are and shall remain prohibited at any time and in any place whatsoever with respect to the above-mentioned persons:

(a) violence to life and person, in particular murder of all kinds, mutilation, cruel treatment and torture;

(b) taking of hostages;

(c) outrages upon personal dignity, in particular humiliating and degrading treatment;

(d) the passing of sentences and the carrying out of executions without previous judgment pronounced by a regularly constituted court, affording all the judicial guarantees which are recognized as indispensable by civilized peoples.

(2) The wounded and sick shall be collected and cared for.

An impartial humanitarian body, such as the International Committee of the Red Cross, may offer its services to the Parties to the conflict.

The Parties to the conflict should further endeavour to bring into force, by means of special agreements, all or part of the other provisions of the present Convention.

The application of the preceding provisions shall not affect the legal status of the Parties to the conflict.

Article 4

Persons protected by the Convention are those who, at a given moment and in any manner whatsoever, find themselves, in case of a conflict or occupation, in the hands of a Party to the conflict or Occupying Power of which they are not nationals.

Nationals of a State which is not bound by the Convention are not protected by it. Nationals of a neutral State who find themselves in the territory of a belligerent State, and nationals of a co-belligerent State, shall not be regarded as protected persons while the State of which they are nationals has normal diplomatic representation in the State in whose hands they are.

The provisions of Part II are, however, wider in application, as defined in Article 13. . . .

Article 5

Where, in the territory of a Party to the conflict, the latter is satisfied that an individual protected person is definitely suspected of or engaged in activities hostile to the security of the State, such individual person shall not be entitled to claim such rights and privileges under the present Convention as would, if exercised in the favour of such individual person, be prejudicial to the security of such State.

Where in occupied territory an individual protected person is detained as a spy or saboteur, or as a person under definite suspicion of activity hostile to the security of the Occupying Power, such person shall, in those cases where absolute military security so requires, be regarded as having forfeited rights of communication under the present Convention.

In each case, such persons shall nevertheless be treated with humanity, and in case of trial, shall not be deprived of the rights of fair and regular trial prescribed by the present Convention. They shall also be granted the full rights and privileges of a protected person under the present Convention at the earliest date consistent with the security of the State or Occupying Power, as the case may be.

Article 6

The present Convention shall apply from the outset of any conflict or occupation mentioned in Article 2.

In the territory of Parties to the conflict, the application of the present Convention shall cease on the general close of military operations.

In the case of occupied territory, the application of the present Convention shall cease one year after the general close of military operations; however, the Occupying Power shall be bound, for the duration of the occupation to the extent that such Power exercises the functions of government in such territory, by the provisions of the following Articles of the present Convention: 1 to 12, 27, 29 to 34, 47, 49, 51, 52, 53, 59, 61 to 77, 143. . . .

Article 10

The provisions of the present Convention constitute no obstacle to the humanitarian activities which the International Committee of the Red Cross or any other impartial humanitarian organization may, subject to the consent of the Parties to the conflict concerned, undertake for the protection of civilian persons and for their relief. . . .

PART II — GENERAL PROTECTION OF POPULATIONS AGAINST
CERTAIN CONSEQUENCES OF WAR

Article 13

The provisions of Part II cover the whole of the populations of the countries in conflict, without any adverse distinction based, in particular, on race, nationality, religion or political opinion, and are intended to alleviate the sufferings caused by war. . . .

Article 18

Civilian hospitals organized to give care to the wounded and sick, the infirm and maternity cases, may in no circumstances be the object of attack, but shall at all times be respected and protected by the Parties to the conflict. . . .

PART III — STATUS AND TREATMENT OF PROTECTED PERSONS. . . .

Article 27

Protected persons are entitled, in all circumstances, to respect for their persons, their honour, their family rights, their religious convictions and practices, and their manners and customs. They shall at all times be humanely treated, and shall be protected especially against all acts of violence or threats thereof and against insults and public curiosity.

Women shall be especially protected against any attack on their honour, in particular against rape, enforced prostitution, or any form of indecent assault.

Without prejudice to the provisions relating to their state of health, age and sex, all protected persons shall be treated with the same consideration by the Party to the conflict in whose power they are, without any adverse distinction, based, in particular, on race, religion or political opinion.

However, the Parties to the conflict may take such measures of control and security in regard to protected persons as may be necessary as a result of the war. . . .

Article 31

No physical or moral coercion shall be exercised against protected persons, in particular to obtain information from them or from third parties.

Article 32

The High Contracting Parties specifically agree that each of them is prohibited from taking any measure of such a character as to cause the physical suffering or extermination of protected persons in their hands. This prohibition applies not only to murder, torture, corporal punishment, mutilation and medical or scientific experiments not necessitated by the medical treatment of a protected person, but also to any other measures of brutality whether applied by civilian or military agents.

Article 33

No protected person may be punished for an offence he or she has not personally committed. Collective penalties and likewise all measures of intimidation or of terrorism are prohibited.

Pillage is prohibited.

Reprisals against protected persons and their property are prohibited.

Article 34

The taking of hostages is prohibited. . . .

Article 43

Any protected person who has been interned or placed in assigned residence shall be entitled to have such action reconsidered as soon as possible by an appropriate court or administrative board designated by the Detaining Power for that purpose. If the internment or placing in assigned residence is maintained, the court or administrative board shall periodically, and at least twice yearly, give consideration to his or her case, with a view to the favourable amendment of the initial decision, if circumstances permit. . . .

Article 49

Individual or mass forcible transfers as well as deportations of protected persons from occupied territory to the territory of the Occupying Power or to that of any other country, occupied or not, are prohibited, regardless of their motive.

Nevertheless, the Occupying Power may undertake total or partial evacuation of a given area if the security of the population or imperative military reasons so demand. Such evacuations may not involve the displacement of protected persons outside the bounds of the occupied territory except when for material reasons it is impossible to avoid such displacement. Persons thus evacuated shall be transferred back to their homes as soon as hostilities in the area in question have ceased.

The Occupying Power undertaking such transfers or evacuations shall ensure, to the greatest practicable extent, that proper accommodation is provided to receive the protected persons, that the removals are effected in satisfactory conditions of hygiene, health, safety and nutrition, and that members of the same family are not separated.

The Protecting Power shall be informed of any transfers and evacuations as soon as they have taken place.

The Occupying Power shall not detain protected persons in an area particularly exposed to the dangers of war unless the security of the population or imperative military reasons so demand.

The Occupying Power shall not deport or transfer parts of its own civilian population into the territory it occupies. . . .

Article 53

Any destruction by the Occupying Power of real or personal property belonging individually or collectively to private persons, or to the State, or to other public authorities, or to social or co-operative organizations, is prohibited, except where such destruction is rendered absolutely necessary by military operations.

Article 55

To the fullest extent of the means available to it, the Occupying Power has the duty of ensuring the food and medical supplies of the population; it should, in particular, bring in the necessary foodstuffs, medical stores and other articles if the resources of the occupied territory are inadequate.

The Occupying Power may not requisition foodstuffs, articles or medical supplies available in the occupied territory, except for use by the occupation forces and administration personnel, and then only if the requirements of the civilian population have been taken into account. Subject to the provisions of other international Conventions, the Occupying Power shall make arrangements to ensure that fair value is paid for any requisitioned goods. . . .

Article 56

To the fullest extent of the means available to it, the Occupying Power has the duty of ensuring and maintaining, with the co-operation of national and local authorities, the medical and hospital establishments and services, public health and hygiene in the occupied territory, with particular reference to the adoption and application of the prophylactic and preventive measures necessary to combat the spread of contagious diseases and epidemics. Medical personnel of all categories shall be allowed to carry out their duties. . . .

Article 68

Protected persons who commit an offence which is solely intended to harm the Occupying Power, but which does not constitute an attempt on the life or limb of members of the occupying forces or administration, nor a grave collective danger, nor seriously damage the property of the occupying forces or administration or the installations used by them, shall be liable to internment or simple imprisonment, provided the duration of such internment or imprisonment is proportionate to the offence committed. Furthermore, internment or imprisonment shall, for such offences, be the only measure adopted for depriving protected persons of liberty. . . .

Article 83

The Detaining Power shall not set up places of internment in areas particularly exposed to the dangers of war.

The Detaining Power shall give the enemy Powers through the intermediary of the Protecting Powers, all useful information regarding the geographical location of places of internment. . . .

RATIFICATIONS BY ISRAEL AND ITS NEIGHBORS

Egypt, Iraq, Israel, Jordan, and Lebanon are member states of the United Nations, have ratified the Four Geneva Conventions of 1949, and have ratified the Convention on the Prevention and Punishment of the Crime of Genocide. When Israel ratified the Four Geneva Conventions on July 14, 1951, it reserved the right to use the Red Shield of David rather than the Red Cross as the distinctive emblem for the medical services of its armed forces. On December 19, 1966, Israel signed the Covenant on Economic, Social and Cultural Rights and the Covenant on Civil and Political Rights, but Israel has never ratified those treaties. Egypt, Iraq, Jordan, and Lebanon have ratified both Covenants.

Additional Protocol I of 1977 to the Geneva Conventions of 1949, 16 I.L.M. 1391 (1977), *entered into force* Dec. 7, 1978, broadens the definition of international armed conflicts to which the Four Geneva Conventions would apply and strengthens some protections for victims of such conflicts. Article 1 of Protocol I applies the Geneva Conventions to ''armed conflicts in which peoples are fighting against colonial domination and alien occu-

pation and against racist regimes in the exercise of their right of self-
determination...." Egypt, Iraq, Israel, and Lebanon have not, however,
ratified Protocol I; Jordan has ratified Protocol I. For further reading, see
Commentary on the Additional Protocols of 8 June 1977 to the Geneva
Conventions of 12 August 1949 (Y. Sandoz, C. Swinarski, & B. Zimmerman
eds. 1987).

DEVELOPMENTS TOWARD AN INDEPENDENT PALESTINE

On November 15, 1988, Palestine Liberation Organization (P.L.O.) chairman Yasser Arafat declared at the Palestine National Council meeting in
Algiers the establishment of an independent Palestine in the West Bank
and Gaza Strip. East Jerusalem would serve as the capitol. Palestine received
recognition as a state from most Arab and Eastern European states.

One month later the U.S. Government ended a 13-year moratorium on
dialogue with the P.L.O., citing the organization's denunciation of terrorism
and recognition of Israel's right to exist as fulfilling preconditions for
renewed talks. The U.S. has not, however, formally recognized the new
state.

Concurrent with the re-establishment of U.S.-P.L.O. talks, the U.N.
General Assembly in 1988 adopted two pertinent resolutions. The first
resolution called for a Middle East Peace Conference that includes participation by the five permanent members of the U.N. Security Council. It also
called for Israeli withdrawal of settlers from the Occupied Territories and
establishment of a U.N. peacekeeping force for the Territories. The second
resolution changed the name of the Palestinian U.N. mission from "PLO
Observer Mission" to "Palestine Observer Mission," a symbolic recognition
of progress toward statehood.

In fall 1989 the U.N. General Assembly considered, but did not adopt
a resolution which would have accorded Palestine the status of an observer
nation, similar to the status presently accorded the Democratic People's
Republic of Korea, the Republic of Korea, and the Vatican. Such a resolution
would have recognized Palestine as a sovereign nation. The U.S. and several
of its allies objected to this move on the ground that Palestine did not
possess several of the requisites for recognition as a state, such as control
over territory and a governmental structure. The U.S. also threatened to
withdraw financial support from the U.N., if the General Assembly adopted
a resolution recognizing Palestine as a nation. The General Assembly did
not act on the resolution.

Palestine has not ratified the Geneva Conventions of 1949 or any of
the other human rights instruments discussed in this chapter. There have
been indications that the P.L.O. was willing to be bound by the provisions
of the Geneva Conventions.

INTERNATIONAL COMMITTEE OF THE RED CROSS (ICRC)

The International Red Cross has three principal components: the International Conference, the League of Red Cross Societies, and the ICRC.

The International Conference functions as "supreme deliberative body" for the entire Red Cross movement. The national societies, such as the American Red Cross in the U.S., are responsible for disaster relief and other activities within their respective nations. The League of Red Cross and Red Crescent Societies coordinates the work of the national societies.

The ICRC, comprised solely of Swiss nationals, is responsible for carrying out humanitarian work regarding victims of armed conflict. Article 4(1) of the ICRC Statutes provide that its role is:

(c) to undertake the tasks incumbent on it under the Geneva Conventions, to work for the faithful application of these Conventions and to take cognizance of any complaints regarding alleged breaches of the humanitarian Conventions;

(d) to take action in its capacity as a neutral institution, especially in case of war, civil war or internal strife; to endeavour to ensure at all times that the military and civilian victims of such conflicts and of their direct results receive protection and assistance, and to serve, in humanitarian matters as an intermediary between the parties; . . .

(f) to contribute, in view of such conflicts, to the preparation and development of medical personnel and medical equipment, in cooperation with the Red Cross organizations, the medical services of the armed forces, and other competent authorities;

(g) to work for the continual improvement of humanitarian international law and for the better understanding and dissemination of the Geneva Conventions and to prepare for their possible extension. . . . International Red Cross Handbook 422 (12th ed. 1983).

2. The ICRC may also take any humanitarian initiative which comes within its role as a specifically neutral and independent institution. . . .

NOTES

For further reading, see C. Swinarski, ed., Studies and Essays on International Humanitarian Law and Red Cross Principles (1984); ICRC, The Red Cross and Human Rights (1983); Forsythe, *Present Role of the Red Cross in Protection* in Final Report: An Agenda for the Red Cross (1975).

International Committee of the Red Cross, *Israel and the Occupied Territories*, Annual Report 80-82 (1988):

[Ed.: The following excerpt provides both information about the situation in the Occupied Territories and an excellent insight into the work of the ICRC. In reviewing this material, readers might consider whether a ruling by the International Court of Justice would assist or hinder the ICRC in its humanitarian efforts.]

The continuing unrest in the Israeli-occupied territories since 9 December 1987, the dimension it assumed and the means adopted by the Israeli authorities to repress it left their mark on the year 1988. The ICRC delegation found itself compelled to adapt its operational capacity accordingly, for the changed situation in the West Bank and Gaza Strip rendered the question as to the Fourth Geneva Convention's applicability even more acute and called for the delegation's presence to be much more sustained both in the field and in the places of detention, where the number of people in custody increased considerably over the year.

The Israeli authorities maintain that "in view of the *sui generis* status of Judea, Samaria and the Gaza District, the *de jure* applicability of the Fourth Geneva Convention to these areas is doubtful, Israel prefers to leave aside the legal question of the status of these areas and has decided, since 1967, to act *de facto* in accordance with the humanitarian provisions of that Convention". The ICRC, however, considers that the conditions for application of the Fourth Convention are fulfilled in all of the occupied territories, namely the Western Bank, the Gaza Strip, Golan and East Jerusalem. In 1988 the ICRC intervened many times to remind the civilian and military authorities of the obligations this Convention entails for the protection of the civilian population.

The ICRC was in regular contact with the Israeli authorities throughout the year, in particular with those responsible for the places of detention. Discussions were also held with the authorities concerning protected persons in the "security zone" in southern Lebanon.... On 19 May the delegation sent a report to the Israeli Minister of Defence about the behaviour of the Israeli army (IDF) towards the civilian population in the occupied territories. This report included a series of recommendations designed to end the violations of international humanitarian law observed by ICRC delegates.

Several ICRC representatives visited Israel and the occupied territories for high-level meetings to back up approaches, both oral and written, made by ICRC headquarters and by its delegation in Tel Aviv to express the institution's concern over the prevailing situation in the occupied territories and in places of detention. The Director of Operations and the Delegate General for the Middle East went to Israel three times during 1988. These missions allowed the ICRC to take up questions linked to the *intifada*, along with matters related to detention that had been left pending for some time but had now become more acute due to the sudden increase in the prison population.

The turn of events in the occupied territories, with violent demonstrations continuing to break out almost every day, required a sustained ICRC presence: the delegation had to act rapidly, taking all necessary measures to face increased needs. As a result, the number of delegates more than doubled, from 18 to 37 (including one doctor and two nurses), and the number of local employees rose from 46 to 77. The ICRC furthermore decided to base three delegates in Nablus as from June to handle its activities in the northern districts of the West Bank. Sub-delegations were maintained in Jerusalem and in Gaza, and offices in Bethlehem, Hebron, Jericho, Ramallah, Jenin, Tulkarem, Rafah and Khan Yunis.

Activities for detainees

As several thousand residents of the occupied territories were arrested in connection with the *intifada*, the Israeli authorities enlarged the three existing *military detention centres* (Fara'a, Tulkarem and Katiba) and opened new temporary or permanent centres (Atlit, Meggido, Dahariye, Hebron II Ofer, Anatot, Qziot). The sudden increase in the number of detainees created problems: even more often than in the past, notifications took too long and were incomplete, whether they concerned people newly imprisoned, transferred from one place of detention to another, from one section to another, or subject to a change of legal status. Some progress as regards notifications was recorded, however, in the course of the year. ICRC delegates rapidly obtained access to all military detention centres and were able to register all detainees held in general sections, most of whom were awaiting trial, sentenced, or under administrative detention. The delegation was able to inform the families concerned and above all to monitor the material, medical and psychological conditions of detention. The delegates' observations were passed on to the relevant authorities either in official written reports or during the final interview that followed each visit. According to the figures compiled by the ICRC, there were 6,333 people held in military detention centres at the end of 1988.

On the basis of the existing agreement between the ICRC and the Israeli authorities, delegates continued to visit persons arrested and placed *under interrogation*: 239 of these detainees were seen by an ICRC delegate during the year. Major problems arose concerning notification and thus access to this category of detainees as well. In addition, many people remained under interrogation far longer than the maximum length of time, in principle not more than four weeks, except where imperative or absolute military security or necessity so requires. The 1979 agreement (confirmed in 1986) between the Israeli government and the ICRC stipulates that the ICRC must be informed of arrests within twelve days and have access, within 14 days of their arrest, to security detainees under interrogation.

Among persons detained in connection with the *intifada*, besides those who have been sentenced or are awaiting trial, particular mention must be made of those held in *administrative detention*. The Israeli authorities resorted to this form of preventive detention, which is based on administrative warrants generally issued for a renewable period of six months, much more systematically than in the past. There were 1,356 detainees of this category at the end of 1988, compared with 50 at the end of the previous year. Most of them were being held in Qziot camp, situated in the Negev desert on Israeli soil and therefore outside the occupied territories, contrary to the provisions of the Fourth Geneva Convention, which also stipulates that these detainees should benefit from special conditions of detention.

Alongside these visits to military detention centres, ICRC delegates continued to make regular visits to the thirteen *police stations* and seventeen *prisons under the jurisdiction of the Israeli Prison Service*. The annual series of visits to these places of detention will end with the presentation of complete reports to the authorities concerned, covering visits to some 4,400 detainees.

The ICRC also visited 87 *people arrested in southern Lebanon or on the high seas*, who had been transferred to Israel contrary to the provisions of the Fourth Geneva Convention, and repatriated 17 people released from Israeli prisons.

Throughout the year, the ICRC carried on with its *assistance programmes* for persons detained in prisons, police stations and military detention centres, as well as for their families. The ICRC delegation continued to organize and finance *family visits* for detainees. Problems arose concerning family visits for detainees in Qziot prison, because Qziot is situated near the Egyptian border, on Israeli territory, inside a closed military zone. Consequently, the ICRC approached the relevant authorities several times in this connection.

Protection for the civilian population

ICRC activities to protect the civilian population also had to be completely readjusted. From the outset, the Israeli authorities have given their agreement in principle for ICRC delegates to have access to all areas in the occupied territories placed under curfew or declared closed military areas. The consistent presence of ICRC delegates in the territories was meant to contribute to the passive protection of civilians living in the camps, districts and villages concerned. Delegates were able to observe the effects of measures taken by the Israeli authorities such as prolonged curfews, the use of force that led to brutality, collective punishment carried out more and more frequently (destruction of houses and crops, confiscation of identity cards), the consequences of the excessive use of firearms, expulsions from the occupied territories. Systematic representations were made in writing to the relevant authorities about these violations of international humanitarian law. The ICRC also appealed publicly to the State of Israel to put an end to violations of the Fourth Convention.

Material assistance

The delegation regularly evaluated living conditions among the civilian population in the occupied territories. No urgent needs were observed during 1988, as other organizations were at work on the spot. The ICRC nevertheless provided tents and relief supplies for families whose houses were demolished, in particular after several dozen houses were demolished in the village of Jiftlik in November, leaving over 700 people homeless.

Medical assistance

Tension in the occupied territories and frequent clashes between residents and the Israeli army made it necessary to conduct regular evaluations of existing medical facilities. These proved satisfactory and no urgent needs were observed. ICRC nurses made numerous visits to injured people taken to hospital after demonstrations or repressive measures, to monitor their state of health and enquire about the circumstances that had led to their hospitalization. Finally, very frequent interventions were made at all levels to ensure that casualties were quickly evacuated during clashes and that ambulances could enter camps, villages and areas placed under curfew and leave again without hindrance. Unfortunately several incidents were noted in this connection, and armed soldiers entered hospitals in the occupied territories more than once during the year.

Considerable efforts were made to assist local "Red Crescent" societies in the occupied territories; in particular, the ICRC provided them with seven ambulances. For the first time and with the participation of the "Magen David Adom" [Red Shield of David], a training course was organized for ambulance attendants working for these local Red Crescent branches. The ICRC also financed the fitting out of a dispensary and a blood bank for the West Bank "Red Crescent" Society.

Tracing Agency

In order to keep track of developments as regards detention (the considerable increase in the number of people in custody and the state of flux created by frequent transfers and sentences for short terms of imprisonment), the ICRC delegation had additional staff assigned to it who were specially trained in taking a census of detainees. At the same time, tracing delegates continued to search for persons missing in connection with the Arab-Israeli conflict and to forward Red Cross messages (over 20,000 in 1988). The ICRC also organized a family reunification and a number of repatriations across demarcation lines and issued 26,600 certificates of detention. . . .

International Committee of the Red Cross, *ICRC reacts to Israeli violations of Geneva Convention*, ICRC Bulletin No. 152, at 1 (September 1988):

. . .

The ICRC also protested in August against the expulsion to Lebanon by the Israeli authorities of a total of 12 residents of the occupied territories and the issuing of expulsion orders to an additional 25 people. The Fourth Geneva Convention clearly stipulates that individual or mass forcible transfers, as well as deportations of protected persons from occupied territory, are forbidden, regardless of their motive.

The ICRC office in Ksara provided the deportees with blankets and family parcels, and gave them the opportunity of writing Red Cross messages to be distributed to their families.

A total of 32 residents of the occupied territories have been expelled to Lebanon by the Israeli authorities since the beginning of the year, without counting the 25 expulsion orders issued recently. . . .

In its latest public statement, the ICRC made a solemn appeal to Israel to put an end to the use of all measures that breach the Fourth Geneva Convention causing unnecessary suffering and hardship. Such measures include the disproportionate use of violence, and collective punishments such as the wilful destruction or walling-up of houses, bans on travel and the growing of crops, and restrictions on economic activity.

HAGUE RULES

On the initiative of President Theodore Roosevelt, 44 governments met at the Hague, Netherlands, in 1907 to continue the work they had begun during the First Hague Peace Conference of 1899. The 1907 conference adopted 13 treaties and one declaration. One of those treaties was the Convention Respecting the Laws and Customs of War on Land (Hague Convention No. IV), 36 Stat. 2277, T.S. 539, *entered into force* Jan. 26, 1910. Hague Convention No. IV annexes Regulations Respecting the Laws and Customs of War on Land, which states parties are required to apply as between each other. The Hague Regulations cover many aspects of land warfare and include the following provisions:

SECTION II - HOSTILITIES

CHAPTER I - *Means of Injuring the Enemy, Sieges, and Bombardments*

Article 22

The right of belligerents to adopt means of injuring the enemy is not unlimited.

Article 23

In addition to the prohibitions provided by special Conventions, it is especially forbidden — . . .

(*c*) To kill or wound an enemy who, having laid down his arms, or having no longer means of defence, has surrendered at discretion;

(*d*) To declare that no quarter will be given;

(*e*) To employ arms, projectiles, or material calculated to cause unnecessary suffering. . . .

Article 25

The attack or bombardment, by whatever means, of towns, villages, dwellings, or buildings which are undefended is prohibited. . . .

Article 27

In sieges and bombardments all necessary steps must be taken to spare, as far as possible, buildings dedicated to religion, art, science, or charitable purposes, historic monuments, hospitals, and places where the sick and wounded are collected, provided they are not being used at the time for military purposes.

It is the duty of the besieged to indicate the presence of such buildings or places by distinctive and visible signs, which shall be notified to the enemy beforehand. . . .

SECTION III - MILITARY AUTHORITY OVER THE TERRITORY OF THE HOSTILE STATE

Article 42

Territory is considered occupied when it is actually placed under the authority of the hostile army.

The occupation extends only to the territory where such authority has been established and can be exercised.

Article 43

The authority of the legitimate power having in fact passed into the hands of the occupant, the latter shall take all the measures in his power to restore, and ensure, as far as possible, public order and safety, while respecting, unless absolutely prevented, the laws in force in the country.

Article 44

A belligerent is forbidden to force the inhabitants of territory occupied by it to furnish information about the army of the other belligerent, or about its means of defence.

Article 45

It is forbidden to compel the inhabitants of occupied territory to swear allegiance to the hostile Power.

Article 46

Family honor and rights, the lives of persons, and private property, as well as religious convictions and practice, must be respected.

Private property can not be confiscated.

Article 47

Pillage is formally forbidden.

Article 48

If, in the territory occupied, the occupant collects the taxes, dues, and tolls imposed for the benefit of the State, he shall do so, as far as is possible, in accordance with the rules of assessment and incidence in force, and shall in consequence be bound to defray the expenses of the administration of the occupied territory to the same extent as the legitimate Government was so bound. . . .

Article 50

No general penalty, pecuniary or otherwise, shall be inflicted upon the population on account of the acts of individuals for which they can not be regarded as jointly and severally responsible. . . .

Article 56

The property of municipalities, that of institutions dedicated to religion, charity and education, the arts and sciences, even when State property, shall be treated as private property.

All seizure of, destruction or wilful damage done to institutions of this character, historic monuments, works of art and science, is forbidden, and should be made the subject of legal proceedings.

NOTES

The Hague Convention No. IV of 1907 has been accepted by 37 nations, including the U.S. and the U.S.S.R., but not Egypt, Iraq, Israel, Jordan, or Lebanon. Nevertheless, in 1946 the International Military Tribunal recognized the Hague Convention No. IV as declaratory of customary international law.

NUREMBERG RULES

Prosecuting the perpetrators of war-time abuses was one approach to the enforcement of the guarantee of international human rights emphasized during World War II and the immediate post-war period. Throughout 1942 the Allied governments received numerous reports of Nazi atrocities involving civilians. In response, the Allies vowed to punish the responsible individuals. The International Military Tribunal that sat at Nuremberg was created on August 8, 1945, when representatives of the Soviet Union, the United Kingdom, the United States, and the provisional government of the French Republic signed the "Agreement for the Prosecution and Punishment of the Major War Criminals of the European Axis," otherwise known as the London Agreement. 58 Stat. 1544, E.A.S. No. 472, 82 U.N.T.S. 280. The London Agreement contained the Charter of the International Military Tribunal, Article 6 of which set forth crimes within the jurisdiction of the Tribunal for which there was individual responsibility: crimes against peace, war crimes, and crimes against humanity:

> The following acts, or any of them, are crimes coming within the jurisdiction of the Tribunal for which there shall be individual responsibility:
>
> (a) Crimes against Peace: namely, planning, preparation, initiation, or waging of a war of aggression, or a war in violation of international treaties, agreements, or assurances, or participation in a common plan or conspiracy for the accomplishment of any of the foregoing:
>
> (b) War Crimes: namely, violations of the laws or customs of war. Such violations shall include, but not be limited to, murder, ill-treatment, or deportation to slave labor or for any other purpose of civilian population of or in occupied territory, murder or ill-treatment of prisoners of war or persons on the seas, killing of hostages, plunder of public or private property, wanton destruction of cities, towns, or villages, or devastation not justified by military necessity:
>
> (c) Crimes against Humanity: namely, murder, extermination, enslavement, deportation, and other inhumane acts committed against any civilian population, before or during the war, or persecutions on political, racial or religious grounds in execution of or in connection with any crime within the jurisdiction of the Tribunal, whether or not in violation of the domestic law of the country where perpetrated. . . .

The trials of the twenty-two Nazi military and political leaders indicted under Article 6 of the London Agreement commenced on November 20, 1945, and judgments were announced on September 30 and October 1, 1946. Nineteen of the accused were convicted; three were acquitted. Twelve of the nineteen convicted were sentenced to death.

The Judgment of the Tribunal declared, "The rules of land warfare expressed in the [Hague No. IV] convention undoubtedly represented an advance over existing international law at the time of their adoption. But the convention expressly stated that it was an attempt 'to revise the general laws and customs of war,' which it thus recognized to be then existing, but by 1939 these rules laid down in the convention were recognized by all civilized nations, and were regarded as being declaratory of the laws and customs of war which are referred to in Article 6(b) of the Charter." Trial of German Major War Criminals, Cmd. 6964, Misc. No. 12, at 65 (1946).

The Control Council of Germany issued a law to implement the London Agreement and to define triable offenses for the numerous cases not pursued by the International Military Tribunal. Control Council Law No. 10, Punishment of Persons Guilty of War Crimes, Crimes Against Peace and Against Humanity, 3 Official Gazette Control Council for Germany 50-55 (1946), stated:

> In order to give effect to the terms of the. . . London Agreement of 8 August 1945, and the Charter issued pursuant thereto and in order to establish a uniform legal basis in Germany for the prosecution of war criminals and other similar offenders, other than those dealt with by the International Military Tribunal,
>
> the Control Council enacts as follows: . . .

Article II

1. Each of the following acts is recognized as a crime:

a)   *Crimes against Peace.* . . .

b)   *War Crimes.* . . .

c)   *Crimes against Humanity.* Atrocities and offenses, including but not limited to murder, extermination, enslavement, deportation, imprisonment, torture, rape, or other inhumane acts committed against any civilian population, or persecutions on political, racial or religious grounds whether or not in violation of the domestic laws of the country where perpetrated.

2. [Persons responsible for offenses.]

3. [Punishments.]

4.a) The official position of any person, whether as Head of State or as a responsible official in a Government Department, does not free him from responsibility for a crime or entitle him to mitigation of punishment.

b)   The fact that any person acted pursuant to the order of his government or of a superior does not free him from responsibility for a crime, but may be considered in mitigation. . . .

Does Control Council Law No. 10 define crimes against humanity more broadly than the London Agreement?

In 1947 the U.N. General Assembly adopted a resolution affirming "the principles of international law recognized by the Charter of the Nürnberg Tribunal and the judgment of the Tribunal." G.A. res. 95(I), U.N. Doc. A/64/Add.1, at 188 (1947). Proscription of the Nuremberg crimes has been broadly recognized as international customary law, which is one of the sources of international law identified by Article 38(1)(b) of the International Court of Justice. *See also* U.S. Army Field Manual 27-10, The Law of Land Warfare § 498 (1956). The Nuremberg rules also reaffirm the principle of individual responsibility, that individuals — not only governments — are obliged to comply with international law. *See, e.g., U.S. v. Goering*, 6 F.R.D. 69, 110 (1946) ("individuals have international duties which transcend the national obligations of obedience"). In addition, the Nuremberg rules reaffirm that national laws are subordinate to the proscriptions of international law. Accordingly, as Article 6(c) of the Nuremberg Charter commands, "inhumane acts committed against any civilian population" are crimes against humanity "whether or not in violation of domestic law of the country where perpetrated."

Once the International Law Commission had been established, the General Assembly in 1947 directed the Commission to "Formulate the principles of international law recognized by the Charter of the Nürnberg Tribunal and in the judgment of the Tribunal, and . . . [p]repare a draft code of offences against the peace and security of mankind, indicating clearly the place to be accorded to the principles mentioned . . . above." G.A. res. 177(II), U.N. Doc. A/519, at 111-12 (1948). The International Law Commission at its second session, in 1950, adopted a formulation of the principles of international law including acknowledgement, as suggested by Control Council Law No. 10, that crimes against humanity may be committed during peacetime as well as during war. The International Law Commission submitted those principles, together with commentaries, to the General Assembly. 2 Y.B. Int'l L. Comm., U.N. Doc. A/CN.4/SER.A/1950/Add.1, at 374-78 (1950). The International Law Commission did not express any "appreciation of these principles as principles of international law," because "the Nürnberg principles had been affirmed by the General Assembly." The General Assembly never acted upon the Commission's formulation of the principles.

The International Law Commission continued its drafting of a Code of Offences Against the Peace and Security of Mankind, which it submitted to the General Assembly in 1954. 2 Y.B. Int'l L. Comm., U.N. Doc. A/2673, at 150-52 (1954). The General Assembly did not approve that draft code in 1954. In 1981 the General Assembly asked the International Law Commission to resume its work on the draft Code. The drafting effort continues. *See* Report Int'l L. Comm., 43 U.N. GAOR Supp. No. 10, U.N. Doc. A/43/10, at 140 (1988); U.N. Doc. A/CN.4/L.436 (1989).

NOTES

For further reading, see T. Meron, Human Rights and Humanitarian

Norms as Customary Law (1989); Taylor, *Nuremberg Trials, War Crimes and International Law,* International Conciliation 242 (No. 450, April 1949); Note, *The Nuremberg Principles: A Defense for Political Protesters,* 40 Hastings L.J. 397 (1989).

Interrelationship Between Human Rights and International Peace, U.N. Doc. E/CN.4/Sub. 2/1988/2, at 4-10 (1988) (footnotes omitted): . . .

7. There is a complex interrelationship between the promotion and protection of human rights and fundamental freedoms, the maintenance of international peace and security, and the achievement of international economic, social and cultural development. The United Nations has repeatedly stressed that if mankind wishes to restore and develop human rights, to promote social and economic progress, it must secure peace on earth. Both gross violations of human rights and economic inequities between the developed and the developing countries adversely affect the promotion of international peace and security. The full achievement of human rights and fundamental freedoms and the overall achievement of international development goals are clearly facilitated by conditions of peace and security and friendly relations and co-operation among nations large and small. As long as there is hunger, disease and a lack of opportunities for education, shelter and employment, as long as there is oppression in the world, there can be neither lasting peace nor significant development.

8. This complex interrelationship has been reflected in a number of international documents adopted by the organs of the United Nations, since their inception. It has been underlined that the enjoyment of human rights could not be generated under conditions of war, nor could the development of individuals, countries or regions be achieved in the absence of peace. The right of peoples and of each individual separately to a peaceful, untroubled life lies at the very heart of their existence and is a prerequisite for the enjoyment of all other rights and freedoms contained in United Nations instruments.

A. INTERNATIONAL PROVISIONS AND STANDARDS

9. The link between human rights and peace is expressed in the Charter of the United Nations. The Preamble and Article 1 of the Charter, which set out the purposes of the United Nations, emphasize the interrelationship that exists between the maintenance of international peace and security, on the one hand, and the promotion and encouragement of respect for human rights and fundamental freedoms on the other by declaring that "the peoples of the United Nations determined to save succeeding generations from the scourge of war, which twice in our lifetime has brought untold sorrow to mankind, and to reaffirm faith in fundamental human rights, in the dignity and worth of the human person, in the equal rights of men and women and of nations large and small...".

10. The interdependence between peace, social progress and human rights is also affirmed in other provisions of the Charter, notably in Articles 55 and 56, which refer to the creation of conditions of stability and well-being which are necessary for peaceful and friendly relations among nations. . . .

13. The Universal Declaration of Human Rights and the two International Covenants on Human Rights declare in their first preambular paragraph that the recognition of the inherent dignity and of the equal and inalienable rights of all members of the human family is the foundation of freedom, justice and peace in the world, and that it is essential, if man is not to be compelled to have recourse, as a last resort, to rebellion against tyranny and oppression, that human rights should be protected by the rule of law.

14. In its article 3, the Universal Declaration of Human Rights stipulates that "everyone has the right to life, liberty and security of person", and in its article 28 it provides that "everyone is entitled to a social and international order in which the rights and freedoms set forth in this Declaration can be fully realized". . . .

B. DECLARATIONS AND RESOLUTIONS ADOPTED BY THE UNITED NATIONS AND OTHER ORGANS OF THE UNITED NATIONS SYSTEM . . .

24. In the Declaration on the Granting of Independence to Colonial Countries and Peoples, adopted and proclaimed in General Assembly resolution 1514 (XV) of 14 December 1960, the Assembly expresses, in the fourth preambular paragraph, its awareness "of the increasing conflicts resulting from the denial of or impediments in the way of freedom of [dependent] peoples, which constitute a serious threat to world peace". Principle 1 of the Declaration states that "the subjection of peoples to alien subjugation, domination and exploitation constitutes a denial of fundamental human rights" and is "an impediment to the promotion of world peace and co-operation". . . .

26. Both the Declaration on Principles of International Law concerning Friendly Relations and Co-operation among States in accordance with the Charter of the United Nations of 24 October 1970, and the Declaration on the Strengthening of International Security of 16 December 1970, make reference to the link between human rights and peace. . . .

30. In the Declaration on the Preparation of Societies for Life in Peace, of 15 December 1978, the Assembly reaffirms the right of individuals, States and all mankind to life in peace. Principle 1, set out in the Declaration, provides that: "Every nation and every human being, regardless of race, conscience, language or sex, has the inherent right to life in peace. Respect for that right, as well as for other human rights, is in the common interests of all mankind and an indispensable condition of advancement of all nations, large and small, in all fields." . . .

42. Since that time, the General Assembly has considered the relationship between peace, development and human rights under various items of its agenda and condemned, *inter alia*, nuclear war as being contrary to human conscience and reason, a crime against peoples and a violation of the right to life (resolution 38/75). . . .

REMEDIES FOR VICTIMS OF HUMAN RIGHTS VIOLATIONS IN THE OCCUPIED TERRITORIES

Several channels for relief may be accessible to individuals in the

Occupied Territories who seek the protection of international human rights law.

Residents of the Occupied Territories may file complaints in Israeli courts for wrongs committed by the occupying forces. The legal system of the Occupied Territories has been a hybrid of old Ottoman, British mandatory, and Jordanian law, subject to a 1967 military proclamation that granted the Israeli commander legislative and administrative powers. Residents of the Occupied Territories may challenge the validity of actions taken under the 1967 military proclamation by appeal to the Israel Supreme Court.

Historically, occupying powers have not given occupied populations access to review by a civilian supreme court. Shamgar, *The Observance of International Law in the Administered Territories*, 1 Israel Y.B. Hum. Rts. 262, 273 (1971). That procedure, though, has seldom been used by residents of the Occupied Territories. In many cases the Supreme Court has upheld the military's acts with little scrutiny. Further, residents may view resort to the Israeli judicial system as legitimizing the Israeli presence in the Occupied Territories. In one 1989 case, however, the Supreme Court ruled that the Israeli army must give Palestinians accused of wrongdoing time to appeal through military and civilian courts before the army destroys their homes. N.Y. Times, July 31, 1989, at p. A1.

Residents of the Occupied Territories may also voice grievances to a U.N. Special Committee to Investigate Israeli Practices Affecting the Human Rights of the Occupied Territories, established by General Assembly resolution 2443 (XXIII), 23 U.N. GAOR Supp. (No. 18) at 50, U.N. Doc. A/7218 (1968).

The Israeli government objected to the establishment of the Special Committee and has refused to allow the Committee to pursue on-site investigations of alleged human rights violations, including the ill-treatment of individuals detained inside the Occupied Territories. In carrying out its mandate to investigate Israeli human rights practices, the Special Committee has thus met in Geneva and in countries bordering Israel where there are concentrations of Palestinian refugees in order to hear the testimony of persons with first-hand knowledge of the situation in the Occupied Territories. The Committee also relies on Israeli press reports, pronouncements by responsible Israeli government officials, and other reports appearing in news media, including the international press and the Arab-language newspapers published in the Occupied Territories.

In addition, the Special Committee has received the cooperation of the governments of Egypt, Jordan, and the Syrian Arab Republic, as well as the Palestine Liberation Organization. They provide written statements and other reports on the situation in the Occupied Territories. The Committee also receives written information from individuals and various intergovernmental and nongovernmental organizations.

The Special Committee compiles this information and presents a yearly report to the General Assembly. *See, e.g.*, Report(s) of the Special Committee to Investigate Israeli Practices Affecting the Human Rights of the Occupied Territories, U.N. Docs. A/45/84 (1990), A/44/599 (1989), A/43/694 (1988), A/42/650 (1987), A/41/680 (1986). On the basis of those reports, the General Assembly has regularly adopted resolutions reaffirming that the Fourth Geneva Convention applies to the Occupied Territories and condemning Israeli policies and practices that give rise to human rights violations. *See, e.g.*, G.A. res. 42/160B, 42 U.N. GAOR Supp. (No. 49) at 113, U.N. Doc. A/42/49 (1988).

For further reading, see A. Gerson, Israel, the West Bank and International Law (1978); Reicin, *Preventive Detention, Curfews, Demolition of Houses and Deportations: An Analysis of Measures Employed by Israel in the Administered Territories*, 8 Cardozo L. Rev. 515 (1987).

E. THE ADVISORY JURISDICTION OF THE INTERNATIONAL COURT OF JUSTICE

The International Court of Justice (I.C.J.) is the principal judicial organ of the United Nations. Established in 1945, the I.C.J. is the successor to the Permanent Court of International Justice, which was created by the League of Nations in 1920. The I.C.J. operates in accordance with its Statute, which is part of the United Nations Charter. *See* U.N. Charter Arts. 92, 93(1).

The I.C.J. consists of fifteen judges, no two of whom may be nationals of the same state. Article 2 of its Statute provides that the I.C.J. is "composed of a body of independent judges, elected regardless of their nationality from among persons of high moral character, who possess the qualifications required in their respective countries for appointment to the highest judicial offices, or are...of recognized competence in international law." The judges are elected by the General Assembly and the Security Council for a term of nine years and may be re-elected.

The I.C.J. has both contentious (adversary) and advisory jurisdiction. Article 96 of the Charter provides that "the General Assembly or the Security Council may request the International Court of Justice to give an advisory opinion on any legal question. Other organs of the United Nations and specialized agencies, which may at any time be so authorized by the General Assembly, may also request advisory opinions of the Court on legal questions arising within the scope of their activities." States and individuals cannot request an advisory opinion but may ask an authorized body to request the opinion.

An advisory opinion is not binding, unlike a decision rendered in a contentious case; but agreements may provide that disputes related to the agreement will be submitted to the I.C.J. and that the advisory opinion will be binding on the disputing parties. For example, Article IX of the Convention on the Prevention and Punishment of the Crime of Genocide provides: "Disputes between the Contracting Parties relating to the interpretation, application or fulfillment of the present Convention...shall be submitted to the International Court of Justice at the request of any of the parties to the dispute." Convention on the Prevention and Punishment of the Crime of Genocide, 78 U.N.T.S. 277, *entered into force* Jan. 12, 1951; *see* chapter 9, *supra*.

The competence of the I.C.J. to render an advisory opinion does not depend on the consent of parties to a dispute, even if the case concerns a legal question actually pending between the parties. Lack of consent, however, might constitute a ground for denial by the I.C.J. of a request for an opinion "if, in the circumstances of a given case, considerations of judicial propriety should oblige the Court to refuse an opinion." *See Western Sahara* (Spain v. Morocco), 1975 I.C.J. 12, 24-26. As an example, the *Western Sahara* judgment involved a situation where giving a reply "would have the effect of circumventing the principle that a State is not obliged to allow its disputes to be submitted to judicial settlement without its consent." *See also Eastern Carelia*, 1923 P.C.I.J. ser. B, No. 9.

Article 38(1) of the I.C.J. Statute, reprinted below, specifies the sources of law which the Court is to apply in addressing disputes and is generally considered to be an authoritative list of the sources of international law. Article 38(1)(d) of the I.C.J. Statute provides that, subject to Article 59, judicial decisions are to be used as a means of determining international law. The Reporters' Notes to Restatement § 102 explain that judicial decisions themselves are not sources of international law since they are not "ways in which law is made or accepted. But an opinion may provide evidence as to whether some rule has in fact become or been accepted as international law." 1 Restatement (Third) of the Foreign Relations Law of the United States § 102 Reporters' Note 1 (1987).

This interpretation is consistent with Article 59 of the I.C.J. Statute which provides that "[t]he decision of the Court has no binding force except between the parties and in respect of that particular case." In other words, the doctrine of *stare decisis* does not apply to I.C.J. decisions in contentious cases or advisory opinions. It appears that the I.C.J. is not intended to have the authority to create international law but instead must find the law in international agreements, customs, and general principles of law. Nevertheless, I.C.J. decisions are widely relied upon as statements of international law and the Court itself often cites its earlier opinions. Hence, the I.C.J. plays a significant role in shaping international law.

NOTES

For further reading, see Butcher, *The Consonance of U.S. Positions with the International Court's Advisory Opinions*, in The International Court of Justice at a Crossroads 423 (L. Damrosch ed. 1987); M. Pomerance, The Advisory Function of the International Court in the League and U.N.

Eras (1973); D. Pratap, The Advisory Jurisdiction of the International Court (1972); Rodley, *Human Rights and Humanitarian Intervention: The Case Law of the World Court*, 38 Int'l & Comp. L.Q. 321 (1989); S. Rosenne, The Law and Practice of the International Court (1965).

Statute of the International Court of Justice, 59 Stat. 1031, *entered into force* Oct. 24, 1945:

Article 38

1. The Court whose function is to decide in accordance with international law such disputes as are submitted to it, shall apply:

    a.   international conventions, whether general or particular, establishing rules expressly recognized by the contesting states;

    b.   international custom, as evidence of a general practice accepted as law;

    c.   the general principles of law recognized by civilized nations;

    d.   subject to the provisions of Article 59, judicial decisions and the teachings of the most highly qualified publicists of the various nations, as subsidiary means for the determination of rules of law.

2. This provision shall not prejudice the power of the Court to decide a case *ex aequo et bono*, if the parties agree thereto. . . .

Article 65

1. The Court may give an advisory opinion on any legal question at the request of whatever body may be authorized by or in accordance with the Charter of the United Nations to make such a request.

2. Questions upon which the advisory opinion of the Court is asked shall be laid before the Court by means of a written request containing an exact statement of the question upon which an opinion is required, and accompanied by all documents likely to throw light upon the question.

Article 66

1. The Registrar shall forthwith give notice of the request for an advisory opinion to all states entitled to appear before the Court.

2. The Registrar shall also, by means of a special and direct communication, notify any state entitled to appear before the Court or international organization considered by the Court, or, should it not be sitting, by the President, as likely to be able to furnish information on the question, that the Court will be prepared to receive, within a time limit to be fixed by the President, written statements, or to hear, at a public sitting to be held for the purpose, oral statements relating to the question. . . .

Article 67

The Court shall deliver its advisory opinions in open Court, notice having been given to the Secretary-General and to the representatives of

Members of the United Nations, of other states and of international organizations immediately concerned.

Article 68

In the exercise of its advisory functions the Court shall further be guided by the provisions of the present Statute which apply in contentious cases to the extent to which it recognizes them to be applicable.

Legal Consequences for States of the Continued Presence of South Africa in Namibia (South West Africa) Notwithstanding Security Council Resolution 276 (1970), 1971 I.C.J. 15:

[Ed.: In 1920 the League of Nations gave South Africa an international mandate to administer the former German colony of South West Africa, which is now Namibia. After the formation of the U.N. and the dissolution of the League of Nations, the U.N. General Assembly invited states administering territories under the League mandates to submit trusteeship agreements for the General Assembly's approval. South Africa asked the General Assembly if it could annex the territory of South West Africa. The General Assembly refused and requested that South West Africa be placed under the international trusteeship system. In response, South Africa refused to comply with the reporting requirement of the trusteeship system, whose goal is to end colonialism and allow new nations to achieve independence.

In 1949, the General Assembly asked the I.C.J. to render an advisory opinion on the status of South West Africa and on the obligations of South Africa in regard to the territory. In 1950 the I.C.J. decided that South Africa's obligations under the mandate were still in force and that the General Assembly was competent to discharge the supervisory functions previously exercised by the League of Nations. 1950 I.C.J. 128.

Nevertheless, South Africa refused to submit to U.N. supervision in its administration of South West Africa; it continued to practice *apartheid* in the region. Ethiopia and Liberia then instituted proceedings in the I.C.J. against South Africa for its failure to fulfill its obligations under the mandate it had received from the League and assumed from the U.N. The I.C.J. found that the League of Nations Covenant had made no provision for state versus state actions. Hence, Ethiopia and Liberia were held to have no standing. 1966 I.C.J. 5.

On July 19, 1950, the U.N. Security Council asked the I.C.J. for an advisory opinion on the following question:

"What are the legal consequences for States of the continued presence of South Africa in Namibia...?"

Before examining the merits, the Court considered two procedural arguments presented by South Africa:

First, due to perceived procedural flaws in the filing of the matter,

South Africa asserted that the I.C.J. was not competent to deliver an opinion.

Second, even if the I.C.J. was competent, it should, as a matter of judicial propriety, refuse to exercise its competence because (a) political pressures prevented the I.C.J. from performing as a court of law and (b) the I.C.J. will be forced to decide a legal issue pending between states (rather than render a strictly advisory opinion).

The Court disposed of those objections and proceeded to examine the substantive issues.]

125. In general, the nonrecognition of South Africa's administration of the Territory should not result in depriving the people of Namibia of any advantages derived from international co-operation. In particular, while official acts performed by the Government of South Africa on behalf of or concerning Namibia after the termination of the Mandate are illegal and invalid, this invalidity cannot be extended to those acts, such as, for instance, the registration of births, deaths and marriages, the effects of which can be ignored only to the detriment of the inhabitants of the Territory.

126. As to non-member States, although not bound by Articles 24 and 25 of the Charter, they have been called upon in paragraphs 2 and 5 of resolution 276 (1970) to give assistance in the action which has been taken by the United Nations with regard to Namibia. In the view of the Court, the termination of the Mandate and the declaration of the illegality of South Africa's presence in Namibia are opposable to all States in the sense of barring *erga omnes* the legality of a situation which is maintained in violation of international law: in particular, no State which enters into relations with South Africa concerning Namibia may expect the United Nations or its Members to recognize the validity or effects of such relationship, or of the consequences thereof. The Mandate having been terminated by decision of the international organization in which the supervisory authority over its administration was vested, and South Africa's continued presence in Namibia having been declared illegal, it is for non-member States to act in accordance with those decisions.

127. As to the general consequences resulting from the illegal presence of South Africa in Namibia, all States should bear in mind that the injured entity is a people which must look to the international community for assistance in its progress towards the goals for which the sacred trust was instituted. . . .

128. In its oral statement and in written communications to the Court, the Government of South Africa expressed the desire to supply the Court with further factual information concerning the purposes and objectives of South Africa's policy of separate development or *apartheid*, contending that to establish a breach of South Africa's substantive international obligations under the Mandate it would be necessary to prove that a particular exercise of South Africa's legislative or administrative powers was not directed in good faith towards the purpose of promoting to the utmost the well-being and progress of the inhabitants. It is claimed by the Government of South Africa that no act or omission on its part would constitute a violation of its international obligations unless it is shown that such

act or omission was actuated by a motive, or directed towards a purpose other than one to promote the interests of the inhabitants of the Territory.

129. The Government of South Africa having made this request the Court finds that no factual evidence is needed for the purpose of determining whether the policy of *apartheid* as applied by South Africa in Namibia is in conformity with the international obligations assumed by South Africa under the Charter of the United Nations. In order to determine whether the laws and decrees applied by South Africa in Namibia, which are a matter of public record, constitute a violation of the purposes and principles of the Charter of the United Nations, the question of intent or governmental discretion is not relevant; nor is it necessary to investigate or determine the effects of those measures upon the welfare of the inhabitants.

130. It is undisputed, and is amply supported by documents annexed to South Africa's written statement in these proceedings, that the official governmental policy pursued by South Africa in Namibia is to achieve a complete physical separation of races and ethnic groups in separate areas within the Territory. The application of this policy has required, as has been conceded by South Africa, restrictive measures of control officially adopted and enforced in the Territory by the coercive power of the former Mandatory. These measures establish limitations, exclusions or restrictions for the members of the indigenous population groups in respect of their participation in certain types of activities, fields of study or of training, labour or employment and also submit them to restrictions or exclusions of residence and movement in large parts of the Territory.

131. Under the Charter of the United Nations, the former Mandatory had pledged itself to observe and respect, in a territory having an international status, human rights and fundamental freedoms for all without distinction as to race. To establish instead, and to enforce, distinctions, exclusions, restrictions and limitations exclusively based on grounds of race, colour, descent or national or ethnic origin which constitute a denial of fundamental human rights is a flagrant violation of the purposes and principles of the Charter. . . .

132. The Government of South Africa also submitted a request that a plebiscite should be held in the Territory of Namibia under the joint supervision of the Court and the Government of South Africa. . . . This proposal was presented in connection with the request to submit additional factual evidence and as a means of bringing evidence before the Court. The Court having concluded that no further evidence was required, that the Mandate was validly terminated and that in consequence South Africa's presence in Namibia is illegal and its acts on behalf of or concerning Namibia are illegal and invalid, it follows that it cannot entertain this proposal. . . .

133. For these reasons,

THE COURT IS OF OPINION,

in reply to the question:

> "What are the legal consequences for States of the continued presence of South Africa in Namibia, notwithstanding Security Council resolution 276 (1970)?"

by 13 votes to 2,

(1)   that the continued presence of South Africa in Namibia being illegal, South

Africa is under obligation to withdraw its administration from Namibia immediately and thus put an end to its occupation of the Territory:

by 11 votes to 4,

(2)   that States Members of the United Nations are under obligation to recognize the illegality of South Africa's presence in Namibia and the invalidity of its acts on behalf of or concerning Namibia, and to refrain from any acts and in particular any dealings with the Government of South Africa implying recognition of the legality of, or lending support or assistance to, such presence and administration;

(3)   that it is incumbent upon States which are not Members of the United Nations to give assistance, within the scope of subparagraph (2) above, in the action which has been taken by the United Nations with regard to Namibia.

NOTES AND QUESTIONS

1. Does paragraph 131 of the *Namibia* opinion above indicate that the human rights provisions in the U.N. Charter establish binding obligations on all U.N. member states?

2. The International Court of Justice in 1980 made another observation on the effect of the human rights provisions of the U.N. Charter in its Judgment in the *Case Concerning United States Diplomatic and Consular Staff in Tehran:*

> Wrongfully to deprive human beings of their freedom and to subject them to physical constraint in conditions of hardship is in itself manifestly incompatible with the principles of the Charter of the United Nations, as well as with the fundamental principles enunciated in the Universal Declaration of Human Rights. 1980 I.C.J. 3, 42.

What is the effect of the court's reference to both the U.N. Charter and the Universal Declaration of Human Rights?

3. The 1971 advisory opinion helped strengthen world consensus against South Africa's continued presence in Namibia and enforcement of the *apartheid* system. For example, the U.N. Security Council in 1972 declared that the situation in Namibia constituted a "breach of the peace," thereby allowing action under Chapter VII of the U.N. Charter. For further reading, see: *Human Rights in the Post-Apartheid South African Constitution*, 21 Columbia Hum. Rts. L. Rev. 1 *et seq.* (1989); Lachs, *Some Reflections on the Contribution of the International Court of Justice to the Development of International Law*, 10 Syracuse J. Int'l L. & Com. 239 (1983); McDougal, *International Law, Human Rights, and Namibian Independence*, 8 Hum. Rts. Q. 443 (1986); Schwelb, *The International Court of Justice and the Human Rights Clauses of the Charter*, 66 Am. J. Int'l, L. 337 (1972);

Weissbrodt and Mahoney, *International Legal Action Against Apartheid*, 4 Law & Ineq. J. 485, 497 (1986).

4. On November 14, 1989, the South West Africa People's Organization (SWAPO) won Namibia's first free election, enabling that organization to initiate the drafting of Namibia's constitution and form of government. U.N. security forces and international civilian observers monitored the elections and related steps toward independence. U.N. representatives certified the election as free and fair. Namibia's independence was finally realized on March 21, 1990, and it became the 160th member of the U.N.

Case Concerning Military and Paramilitary Activities in and Against Nicaragua (Nicaragua v. United States of America), 1986 I.C.J. 14, 129-30:

254. The Court now turns to the question of the application of humanitarian law to the activities of the United States complained of in this case. Mention has already been made . . . of the violations of customary international law by reason of the failure to give notice of the mining of the Nicaraguan ports, for which the Court has found the United States directly responsible. Except as regards the mines, Nicaragua has not however attributed any breach of humanitarian law to . . . United States personnel . . . , as distinct from the *contras*. The Applicant has claimed that acts perpetrated by the *contras* constitute breaches of the "fundamental norms protecting human rights"; it has not raised the question of the law applicable in the event of conflict such as that between the *contras* and the established Government. In effect, Nicaragua is accusing the *contras* of violations both of the law of human rights and humanitarian law, and is attributing responsibility for these acts to the United States. The Court has however found . . . that this submission of Nicaragua cannot be upheld; but it has also found the United States responsible for the publication and dissemination of the manual on "Psychological Operations in guerrilla Warfare" . . . .

255. The Court has also found . . . that general principles of humanitarian law include a particular prohibition, accepted by States, and extending to activities which occur in the context of armed conflicts, whether international in character or not. By virtue of such general principles, the United States is bound to refrain from encouragement of persons or groups engaged in the conflict in Nicaragua to commit violations of Article 3 which is common to all four Geneva Conventions of 12 August 1949. The question here does not of course relate to the definition of the circumstances in which one State may be regarded as responsible for acts carried out by another State, which probably do not include the possibility of incitement. The Court takes note of the advice given in the manual on psychological operations to "neutralize" certain "carefully selected and planned targets," including judges, police officers, State Security officials, etc., after the local population have been gathered in order to "take part in the act and formulate accusations against the oppressor." In the view of the Court, this must be regarded as contrary to the prohibition in Article 3 of the Geneva Conventions, with respect to non-combatants, of

"the passing of sentences and the carrying out of executions without previous judgment pronounced by a regularly constituted court, affording all the judicial guarantees which are recognized as indispensable by civilized peoples"

and probably also of the prohibition of "violence to life and person, in particular murder to all kinds, ...".

256. It is also appropriate to recall the circumstances in which the manual of psychological operations was issued. When considering whether the publication of such a manual, encouraging the commission of acts contrary to general principles of humanitarian law, is unlawful, it is material to consider whether that encouragement was offered to persons in circumstances where the commission of such acts was likely or foreseeable. The Court has however found...that at the relevant time those responsible for the issue of the manual were aware of, at the least, allegations that the behaviour of the *contras* in the field was not consistent with humanitarian law; it was in fact even claimed by the CIA that the purpose of the manual was to "moderate" such behaviour. The publication and dissemination of a manual in fact containing the advice quoted above must therefore be regarded as an encouragement, which was likely to be effective, to commit acts contrary to general principles of international humanitarian law reflected in treaties. ...

NOTES

The Economic and Social Council (ECOSOC) is one of the U.N. organs authorized by the General Assembly to request advisory opinions from the International Court of Justice. G.A. res. 89(I), U.N. Doc. A/64/Add.1, at 176 (1947). In 1989 ECOSOC used its authority to request an opinion regarding a human rights issue.

At the opening of the 1988 session of the U.N. Sub-Commission on Prevention of Discrimination and Protection of Minorities, it was learned that Dimitru Mazilu, former member of the Sub-Commission from Romania and the special rapporteur on human rights and youth, would not be coming to Geneva to present his draft report. Mazilu had also not attended the 1987 session of the Sub-Commission. There was widespread speculation that the Romanian government had prevented him from attending. This speculation was confirmed by a handwritten letter sent in April 1987 by Mazilu to the chairman of the 1987 session.

Mazilu stated in his letter that his government was strongly against his report on human rights and youth, and that when he sought approval to travel to the U.N. Centre for Human Rights in Geneva, the government used pressure tactics to encourage him to abandon the study. Those tactics included withdrawing his candidature for the International Law Commission, revoking his passport, interrupting his foreign correspondence, stopping telephone calls, and deploying police officers to follow Mazilu and his family.

The Romanian authorities went to considerable lengths to convince the Sub-Commission that Mazilu was simply ill and unable to travel to Geneva. Copies of medical transcripts "verified" by physicians were sent to the Centre for Human Rights to prove that Mazilu was suffering from a cardiac condition and was in a health resort attempting to recuperate from a heart attack. Both the Romanian government observer and the newly elected expert from Romania told the Sub-Commission that they were present at the time of Mazilu's heart attacks. The Romanian expert even distributed a report on human rights and youth that was apparently intended to supplant the Mazilu report.

The Sub-Commission attempted to contact Mazilu by a series of telexes sent to the U.N. Information Center in Bucharest. Having failed, the Sub-Commission asked the U.N. Secretary-General to request that the Romanian government assist in finding Mazilu and facilitate a visit by a member of the Sub-Commission to help Mazilu finish his study. The Romanian government refused to offer such assistance.

Finally, the Sub-Commission called on the Secretary-General to attempt once again to obtain the Romanian government's cooperation in finding Mazilu by invoking the Convention on the Privileges and Immunities of the United Nations, which provides that "United Nations officials are to be accorded the privileges and immunities necessary for the independent exercise of their functions." Convention on the Privileges and Immunities of the United Nations, 1 U.N.T.S. 15, 21 U.S.T. 1418, T.I.A.S. 6900, *entered into force* Sept. 17, 1946. In case of denial, the Sub-Commission requested that the Commission on Human Rights be informed if the Romanian government denied the applicability of the Convention in the case of Mazilu. If so, the Sub-Commission determined to call upon the Commission, through its parent body, the Economic and Social Council, to seek an advisory opinion from the International Court of Justice to determine the applicability of the Convention. Sub-Comm'n res. 1988/37, U.N. Doc. E/CN.4/Sub.2/1988/45, at 64 (1988). The decision of the Sub-Commission to seek an advisory opinion indicated its belief in Mazilu's claims that the Romanian government was violating his human rights. In May 1989 the Economic and Social Council concluded that a difference had arisen between the U.N. and the government of Romania as to the applicability of the Convention to Mazilu as special rapporteur of the Sub-Commission and requested an advisory opinion on this issue from the International Court of Justice. ECOSOC res. 1989/75, U.N. Doc. E/1989/INF/7, at 153 (1989). The International Court of Justice rendered its opinion on December 15, 1989, that the Convention does protect Mazilu. *Applicability of Article VI, Section 22, of the Convention on the Privileges and Immunities of the United Nations*, 1989 I.C.J. 9; I.C.J. Communique No. 89/24 (Dec. 15, 1989).

In January 1989 Dimitru Mazilu was released from prison, served briefly as Vice-President of Romania, and was able to visit the U.N. in Geneva.

Use of Advisory Opinions in International Human Rights Law

The International Court of Justice is not the only international tribunal that makes use of advisory opinions. Chapter 7, for example, examined an advisory opinion of the Inter-American Court of Human Rights (Inter-American Court), established under the American Convention on Human Rights. The Inter-American Court has power to render advisory opinions on request by a member or organ of the Organization of American States (OAS). American Convention on Human Rights, art. 64(1), Appendix A-81. The Inter-American Court has authority to interpret not only the American Convention but also "other treaties concerning the protection of human rights in the American states." Moreover, the Convention allows OAS member states to request that the Inter-American Court provide advisory opinions as to the compatibility of national laws with the Convention or other human rights treaties. *E.g.*, *Proposed Amendments to the Naturalization Provisions of the Political Constitution of Costa Rica*, Advisory Opinion No. OC-4/84, 4 Inter-Am. Ct. H.R. (Ser. A) (1984), in which the government of Costa Rica asked the Inter-American Court to determine if proposed constitutional amendments were compatible with the Convention. Hence, it seems probable that an O.A.S. member could ask the Inter-American Court for an advisory opinion on such matters as the applicability of the 1949 Geneva Conventions to hostilities in Central America.

The Inter-American Court has defined "advisory opinion" in ways that might be useful to the I.C.J. In the *Restrictions to the Death Penalty* case, the Inter-American Commission sought an opinion from the Inter-American Court while conducting an investigation of human rights practices in Guatemala. *Restrictions to the Death Penalty (Arts. 4(2) and 4(4) American Convention on Human Rights)*, Advisory Opinion No. OC-2/82, 2 Inter-Am. Ct. H.R. (Ser. A) (1982), 22 I.L.M. 37 (1983). Guatemala argued that the matter involved a contentious case masquerading as an advisory proceeding. The argument resembled South Africa's jurisdictional challenge in *Namibia*. The Inter-American court disposed of the argument by reasoning that the existence of a dispute between Guatemala and the Commission does not diminish the Court's power to interpret the Convention. For further discussion of the Inter-American Court's advisory jurisdiction, see chapter 7.

The advisory opinion can be especially useful to tribunals interested in developing international law but lacking a supply of contentious cases, or to governments unwilling to accept contentious jurisdiction. Professor Thomas Buergenthal, a member of the Inter-American Court, has stated that "to be useful and effective, the advisory process has to be expeditious and capable of providing...legally sound judicial rulings conceived in an atmosphere that inspires trust in the deliberative and interpretive process." Buergenthal, *The Advisory Practice of the Inter-American Human Rights Court*, 79 Am. J. Int'l L. 1, 25 (1985).

BIBLIOGRAPHY FOR RESEARCH ON INTERNATIONAL HUMAN RIGHTS LAW

A. Compilations of Human Rights Instruments
   1. United Nations (UN)
   2. International Labour Organisation (ILO)
   3. UN Educational, Scientific and Cultural Organization (UNESCO)
   4. UN High Commissioner for Refugees (UNHCR)
   5. Council of Europe
   6. Organization of African Unity (OAU)
   7. Organization of American States (OAS)
   8. Helsinki Conference
   9. Humanitarian Law
   10. United States
   11. Other Collections

B. Status of Human Rights Instruments

C. Legislative History of Human Rights Instruments

D. Human Rights Case Law, Jurisprudence, Decisions, and Digests
   1. UN
   2. ILO
   3. Council of Europe and European Community
   4. OAS
   5. Other

E. Texts

F. Research Guides and Bibliographies

G. Periodicals

H. Book and Periodical Indices
   1. Print Indices
   2. Computer Indices

I. Practice Guides

J. Congressional Material

K. Factfinding Methodology

L. Country Situations
   1. Legal System Information Sources
   2. Country Reports
   3. Constitutions
   4. Criminal Codes and Criminal Procedure Codes
   5. Other Legislation
   6. Directories
   7. Nongovernmental Organization (NGO) Reports
   8. UN Documents
   9. Inter-American Commission on Human Rights
   10. Media Services

A. COMPILATIONS OF HUMAN RIGHTS INSTRUMENTS

1. United Nations (UN)

Human Rights: A Compilation of International Instruments (New York: Centre for Human Rights, UN, 1988) (ST/HR/1/Rev. 3) (paperback). 416p.

> Texts of 67 conventions, declarations, recommendations, resolutions, and other instruments adopted by the UN, the ILO, and UNESCO concerning human rights. Included are the International Bill of Human Rights, dates of the conventions' entry into force and a chronological list of instruments in the order of their adoption.

International Human Rights Instruments of the United Nations, 1948-1982 (Pleasantville, NY: UNIFO Publishers, 1983). 175p.

2. International Labour Organisation (ILO)

Constitution of the International Labour Organisation and Standing Orders of the International Labour Conference (Geneva: ILO, 1989). 88p.

International Labour Office, International Labour Conventions and Recommendations, 1919-1981 (Geneva: ILO, 1982). 1167p.

International Labour Office, Chart of Ratifications of International Labour Conventions (Geneva: ILO, 1990). 1p.

3. UN Educational, Scientific and Cultural Organization (UNESCO)

UNESCO'S Standard-Setting Instruments (Paris: UNESCO, 1981-) (looseleaf).

UNESCO, Executive Board, *Decisions Adopted By the Executive Board at Its 104th Session*, 104 EX/Decision 3.3 (Paris: UNESCO, 1978) (sets forth UNESCO procedures in human rights cases). 6 p.

4. UN High Commissioner for Refugees (UNHCR)

Collection of International Conventions, Agreements and Other Texts Concerning Refugees (Geneva: UNHCR, 1979). 333p.

Conclusions on the International Protection of Refugees Adopted by the Executive Committee of the UNHCR Programme (HCR/IP/2/Eng/REV.1986) (Geneva: UNHCR, 1986). 103p.

Handbook on Procedures and Criteria for Determining Refugee Status Under the 1951 Convention and the 1967 Protocol Relating to the Status of Refugees (HCR/ID/4/Eng.) (Geneva: UNHCR, 1979). 93p.

Status of Accessions to and Ratifications of Multilateral Treaties Concerning Refugees (A/AC.96/INF.172/Rev.2) (Geneva: UN, 1989).

United Nations Resolutions and Decisions Relating to the Office of the United Nations High Commissioner for Refugees (HCR/INF.49/Rev.3) (Geneva: UNHCR, 1989-) (looseleaf).

5. Council of Europe

J. Alderson, Human Rights and the Police (Strasbourg: Council of Europe, 1984) (Council of Europe guidelines for police). 207p.

Collection of Recommendations, Resolutions and Declarations of the Committee of Ministers Concerning Human Rights, 1949-87 (Strasbourg: Council of Europe, 1989). 214p.

Council of Europe, European Convention on Human Rights: Collected Texts = Convention européenne des droits de l'homme: recueil des textes (Dordrecht, the Netherlands: Martinus Nijhoff Pub., 1987). 236p.

> Texts of the European Convention on Human Rights and its Protocols, rules of procedure of the European Commission and Court of Human Rights and the Committee of Ministers, and selected other human rights instruments from other organs of the Council of Europe. Included are signatures, ratifications, declarations, and reservations concerning the European Convention and its Protocols.

Human Rights in International Law: Basic Texts (Strasbourg: Council of Europe, Directorate of Human Rights, 1985) (European Convention, eight Protocols, and other principal human rights instruments). 261p.

European Convention on Human Rights: Texts and Documents (H. Miehsler & H. Petzold eds., Köln: Carl Heymanns Verlag, 1982) (collection in the official languages) (2v.).

Yearbook of the European Convention on Human Rights (The Hague: Martinus Nijhoff Pub., v. 1- , 1955/1957-) (the first volume contains the Convention; later volumes contain the Protocols as promulgated).

6. Organization of African Unity (OAU)

Rules of Procedure of the African Commission on Human and Peoples' Rights, 9 Human Rights L.J. 326 (1988), 40 Int'l Comm'n Juriste Rev. 26 (1988).

M. Hamalengwa, C. Flinterman & E. Dankwa, The International Law of Human Rights in Africa: Basic Documents and Annotated Bibliography (Dordrecht: Martinus Nijhoff Pub., 1988). 427p.

7. Organization of American States (OAS)

Basic Documents Pertaining to Human Rights in the Inter-American System

(Washington, D.C.: General Secretariat, Organization of American States, 1988) (OEA/ser.L/V/II.71, doc. 6 rev. 1). 160p.

> Texts of the American Declaration of the Rights and Duties of Man, American Convention on Human Rights with information on its status, the statute and regulations of the Inter-American Commission on Human Rights, the statute and rules of procedure of the Inter-American Court of Human Rights, Agreement between Costa Rica and the Court, list of publications of the Commission and Court, and a model complaint. It is a revision of *Handbook of Existing Rules Pertaining to Human Rights in the Inter-American System* (1985).

Human Rights: The Inter-American System (T. Buergenthal & R. Norris eds., Dobbs Ferry, NY: Oceana Publications, Inc., 1984-) (looseleaf).

> Texts of basic documents: OAS Charter, American Convention on Human Rights and its legislative history, related inter-American conventions, statutes, rules, decisions, advisory opinions and resolutions of the Inter-American Commission and Court of Human Rights, OAS General Assembly resolutions, selected findings of country reports and annual reports. Included are status information for instruments, bibliographies, and indexes by case number, country, right, article of instrument, topic and victim's name.

T. Buergenthal, R. Norris, & D. Shelton eds., Protecting Human Rights in the Americas: Selected Problems 323-86 (2d ed., Kehl (Germany); Arlington, VA: Engel, 1986). 389p.

8. Helsinki Conference

Conference on Security and Cooperation in Europe: Final Act, 73 Dept. St. Bull. 323-50; 14 I.L.M. 1292-1325 (1975).

Human Rights, European Politics, and the Helsinki Accord: The Documentary Evolution of the Conference on Security and Co-operation in Europe, 1973-75 (I. Kavass, J. Granier & M. Dominick eds., Buffalo, NY: Hein, 1981) (6v.).

Human Rights, the Helsinki Accords, and the United States: Selected Executive and Congressional Documents (I. Kavass & J. Granier eds., Buffalo, NY: Hein, 1982) (9 v., reprint ed.).

9. Humanitarian Law

Documents on the Laws of War (A. Roberts & R. Guelff 2d ed., Oxford: Clarendon Press, 1989) (comprehensive and annotated). 509p.

International Committee of the Red Cross, International Red Cross Handbook (12th ed., Geneva: ICRC, 1983). 744p.

The Laws of Armed Conflicts: A Collection of Conventions, Resolutions and Other Documents (D. Schindler & J. Toman 3d rev. ed., Dordrecht: Martinus Nijhoff Pub., 1988). 1033p.

10. United States

Human Rights Documents: Compilation of Documents Pertaining to Human Rights (Washington, D.C.: U.S. Congress, Staff of House Committee on Foreign Affairs, 1983) (98th Cong., 1st Sess., Committee Print) (documents of particular interest to the U.S.). 774p.

International Human Rights Instruments: A Compilation of Treaties, Agreements and Declarations of Especial Interest to the United States (R. Lillich ed., Buffalo, NY: W.S. Hein, 1983-) (looseleaf).

> Texts of over 40 key human rights treaties and agreements concluded through the UN, OAS, ILO, and other international bodies. Included are related reservations, declarations, U.S. action, case citations to the instruments, and a bibliography.

International Human Rights Law Group, U.S. Legislation Relating Human Rights to U.S. Foreign Policy (4th ed., Washington, D.C. Law Group, 1989) (forthcoming).

Lawyers Committee for Human Rights, Human Rights and U.S. Foreign Policy: Report and Recommendations 58-60 (New York: Lawyers Committee, 1988) (citations to primary statutes and programs). 68p.

11. Other Collections

Amnesty International, Ethical Codes and Declarations Relevant to the Health Professions (AI Index: ACT 75/01/85) (2d ed. London: AI, 1985). 59p.

Human Rights Sourcebook (A. Blaustein, R. Clark, & J. Sigler eds., New York: Paragon House Publishers, 1987) ("A Washington Institute Book"). 970p.

> Texts of major human rights instruments and related documents such as procedural rules for enforcement, national constitutional provisions, statutes, and cases.

Basic Documents on Human Rights (I. Brownlie 2d ed., Oxford: Clarendon Press, 1981). 505p.

> Texts of instruments including UN, ILO, Council of Europe, OAS, and OAU.

M. Tardu, Human Rights: The International Petition System (Dobbs Ferry, NY: Oceana Publications, Inc., 1979-) (3v. looseleaf).

B. STATUS OF HUMAN RIGHTS INSTRUMENTS

The principal compilations of human rights instruments listed above often include the status of the instruments.

Human Rights: Status of International Instruments (New York: UN, 1987) (ST/HR/5). 336p.

> Revision of *Human Rights — International Instruments: Signatures, Ratifications, Accessions, etc.* previously published by the Centre for Human Rights. Listed for each instrument are parties; dates of signature, ratification, accession, succession, and entry into force; texts of declarations and reservations; and notes. Information derived from *Multilateral Treaties, infra.* A pocket insert updates the information.

Multilateral Treaties Deposited with the Secretary-General: Status as at 31 December 1988 (New York: UN, 1989) (ST/LEG/SER.E/7). 907p.

Reservations, Declarations, Notifications and Objections Relating to the International Covenant on Civil and Political Rights and the Optional Protocol Thereto (Geneva: UN, 1989) (CCPR/C/Rev. 2). 93p.

Status of the Convention Against Torture and Other Cruel, Inhuman or Degrading Treatment or Punishment and Reservations, Declarations and Objections Under the Convention (Geneva: UN, 1989) (CAT/C/Add.1). 15p.

C. LEGISLATIVE HISTORY OF HUMAN RIGHTS INSTRUMENTS

Collected Edition of the "Travaux Préparatoires" of the European Convention on Human Rights = Recueil des travaux préparatoires de la Convention européenne des droits de l'homme (The Hague: Martinus Nijhoff Pub., 1975-1985) (8v.).

M. Bossuyt, Guide to the "Travaux Préparatoires" of the International Covenant on Civil and Political Rights (Dordrecht: Martinus Nijhoff Pub., 1987). 851p.

A. Verdoodt, Naissance et Signification de la Déclaration Universelle des Droits de L'Homme (Louvain-Paris: Editions Nauwelaerts, 1964). 356p.

D. HUMAN RIGHTS CASE LAW, JURISPRUDENCE, DECISIONS, AND DIGESTS

1. UN

Commission on Human Rights, *Report on the...Session* (New York: UN, 1946-).

> Covers the Commission's resolutions and decisions. Another significant document is the Annotated Agenda, issued several weeks before each

session listing issues and documents to be considered; ordinarily identified by the symbol: E/CN.4/year of the session/1/Add.1.

Human Rights Committee, *General Comments* (New York: UN, 1989) (CCPR/C/21/Rev.1). 25p.

Human Rights Committee, *Selected Decisions Under the Optional Protocol (Second to Sixteenth Sessions)*(New York: UN, 1985) (CCPR/C/OP/1) (a second compilation is forthcoming). 167p.

Report of the Committee on Economic, Social and Cultural Rights (New York: UN, 1987-) (ESC/).

Reflects consideration given to reports of governments submitted pursuant to the Covenant on Economic, Social and Cultural Rights.

Report of the Committee on the Elimination of Discrimination Against Women (New York: UN, 1981-) (CEDAW/).

Reflects consideration given to reports of governments submitted pursuant to the Convention on the Elimination of All Forms of Discrimination Against Women.

Report of the Committee on the Elimination of Racial Discrimination (New York: UN, 1970-) (CERD/).

Reflects consideration given to reports of governments under the Convention on the Elimination of All Forms of Racial Discrimination.

Report of the Human Rights Committee (New York: UN, 1977-) (CCPA/).

Decisions of the Human Rights Committee on cases submitted under the Optional Protocol to the Civil and Political Covenant. Also includes the general comments of the Committee on the meaning of various Covenant provisions.

Report of the Sub-Commission on Prevention of Discrimination and Protection of Minorities on its...Session (Geneva: UN, 1946-).

Reports of the Sub-Commission's resolutions and decisions. Another significant document is the Annotated Agenda, issued several weeks before each session listing issues and documents to be considered; ordinarily identified by the symbol: E/CN.4/Sub.2/year of the session/1/Add.1.

Resolutions and Decisions Adopted by the General Assembly During the First Part of its...Session (New York: UN).

A massive press release of each mid-January containing resolutions and decisions of the General Assembly for the session just concluded in December. The press release is not an official UN record, but it is the most comprehensive account of the General Assembly's actions until the official records are issued many months later. One volume of the official records contains the resolutions and decisions. That volume ordinarily has the same title as indicated above with the following document symbol: A/number of the session/number of the supplement.

Yearbook on Human Rights (New York: UN, 1946-) (annual 1946-72, biennial 1973-).

Extracts of selected reports on national human rights developments, texts of relevant decisions, and descriptions of human rights activities including the specialized agencies of the UN (Food and Agriculture Organization (FAO), ILO, UNESCO, and World Health Organization (WHO)). The most recent *Yearbook*, published in 1989, covers 1985.

2. ILO

International Labour Office, Freedom of Association: A Workers' Education Manual (2d rev. ed., Geneva: ILO, 1987) (Digest of decisions of the ILO Freedom of Association Committee). 149p.

Report of the Committee of Experts on the Application of Conventions and Recommendations (Geneva: International Labour Conference, 1936-).

Observations on reports submitted by governments indicating their compliance with ILO conventions and recommendations. The Committee of Experts, established each year by the International Labour Conference, held its 76th session in June 1989.

3. Council of Europe and European Community

V. Berger, The Case Law of the European Court of Human Rights: A Practical Guide (Sarasota, FL: UNIFO Publishers, Inc., v. 1- , 1989-). 478p.

Volume one summarizes facts and law of 117 cases (1960-1987) and includes brief bibliographies and notes on domestic changes influenced by the cases. Appendices include a bibliography, text of the European Convention on Human Rights, and ratification information.

Collection of Recommendations, Resolutions and Declarations of the Committee of Ministers Concerning Human Rights, 1949-87 (Strasbourg: Council of Europe, 1989). 214p.

Collection of Resolutions Adopted by the Committee of Ministers in Application of Articles 32 and 54 of the European Convention for the Protection of Human Rights and Fundamental Freedoms, 1959-1983 (Strasbourg: Council of Europe, 1984). 148p.

Digest of Strasbourg Case-Law Relating to the European Convention on Human Rights (Köln: C. Heymanns Verlag, 1984-1985) (6v. and supplemental updating volumes).

European Commission of Human Rights, Decisions and Reports = Décisions et rapports (Strasbourg: European Commission, v. 1- , 1975-) (continues *Collection of Decisions* with indices, but about four years behind; 1989 volume covers 1985).

European Human Rights Reports (London: European Law Centre Ltd., v. 1- , 1979-) (unofficial).

> Decisions of the European Court of Human Rights (1960-), selected decisions of the Commission of Human Rights, and resolutions of the Committee of Ministers. Beginning with volume five, part 18, included are summaries and extracts of resolutions of the Committee of Ministers and decisions of the Commission with headnotes and cross-references to European Commission cases. Also included are decisions of the Inter-American Court of Human Rights (OAS). The *Reports* are available in the LEXIS EURCOM library and CASES file.

Publications of the European Court of Human Rights = Publications de la Cour européenne des droits de l'homme (Strasbourg: Council of Europe).

> In Series A are the official texts of judgments and decisions of the European Court of Human Rights; each decision is numbered and separately published, but with no index. In Series B are oral arguments, pleadings, and documents. The *Yearbook of the European Convention on Human Rights* often includes summaries of decisions of the Court of Human Rights. A bi-monthly unofficial periodical, *European Law Review*, also contains summaries of European Court of Human Rights decisions.

Reports of Cases Before the Court (Luxembourg: Court of Justice of the European Communities, 1959-) (available in the LEXIS EURCOM Library and CASES file).

Stock-Taking on the European Convention on Human Rights: A Periodic Note on the Concrete Results Achieved Under the Convention: The First Thirty Years: 1954 Until 1984 (Strasbourg: European Commission of Human Rights, 1984) (updated by yearly supplements). 333p.

> Brief information on the procedures of the European Commission and Court of Human Rights and the Committee of Ministers, a summary of decisions of those bodies between 1954 and 1984 relating to construction of the European Human Rights Convention, statistics on the disposition of cases, and an index by principal Convention article with a listing of cases.

Yearbook of the European Convention on Human Rights (The Hague: Martinus Nijhoff Pub., v. 1- , 1955/1957-).

> In Part One are texts of new Protocols to the European Convention, instruments, ratifications, reservations, procedures of the European Commission and Court of Human Rights, and descriptions of related activities of the Council of Europe. Part Two contains the text of selected European Commission decisions, statistical charts, summaries of judgments of the European Court, and related resolutions of the Committee of Ministers. Part Three covers measures implementing the European Convention by governments, the Council of Europe, and the European Communities. It contains a bibliography on the Convention and an alphabetical index.

4. OAS

Annual Report of the Inter-American Commission on Human Rights (Washington, D.C.: OAS, 1960-).

> Covers activities of the Commission, resolutions on the cases decided by the Commission during the year, updates on human rights situations in several countries, and new instruments in the Inter-American human rights system.

Human Rights: The Inter-American System (T. Buergenthal & R. Norris eds., Dobbs Ferry: Oceana Pub., Inc., 1982-) (looseleaf).

Inter-American Commission on Human Rights, Ten Years of Activities, 1971 -1981 (Washington, D.C.: OAS, 1982). 403p.

> Collection of decisions and activities of the Inter-American Commission providing easy access to the jurisprudence of the Commission.

Inter-American Court of Human Rights, Annual Report (Washington, D.C.: OAS, 1976-) (OEA/ser.L/).

Inter-American Court of Human Rights, Judgments and Opinions (San Jose, Costa Rica: Court Secretariat, 1982-)

> A separate paperback pamphlet contains each judgment and opinion of the Court: Series A (Advisory Opinions); Series B (Pleadings, oral arguments, documents); Series C (contentious cases).

Inter-American Yearbook on Human Rights = Anuario inter-americano de derechos humanos (Dordrecht: Martinus Nijhoff Pub., 1985-) (1968-84 issued by the Secretariat of the Inter-American Commission on Human Rights).

> Background information on the Inter-American system for the protection of human rights, bodies involved, and key instruments. Included are texts of instruments, status information, statutes and procedural rules,

relevant resolutions, and discussion of human rights practices in selected OAS countries.

5. Other

The International Court of Justice (3d ed., The Hague: I.C.J., 1986). 168p.

> Summaries of the court's decisions between 1946 and 1986, the court's history, its operation, advisory and contentious jurisdiction, and sources of law it applies.

International Law Reports (London: Butterworth, 1919/22-).

International Legal Materials (Washington, D.C.: American Society of International Law, v.1- , 1962-).

> Significant decisions and instruments on many issues, including human rights, with annual indices; also indexed by LEGALTRAC.

NOTES

Researchers should also consult references in chapter 12 of this book for U.S. cases relating to international human rights.

E. TEXTS

T. Buergenthal, International Human Rights in a Nutshell (St. Paul, MN: West Publishing Co., 1988). 283p.

> An overview of the doctrinal and institutional framework of international human rights.

T. Buergenthal & H. Maier, Public International Law in a Nutshell (2d ed., St. Paul, MN: West Publishing Co., 1990). 275p.

> An introduction to the basic principles of public international law including human rights. Research guide at 243-57 includes the key sources of and about public international law.

T. Buergenthal, R. Norris & D. Shelton eds., Protecting Human Rights in the Americas (2d ed., Kehl (Germany); Arlington, VA: Engel, 1986). 389p.

J. Donnelly, Universal Human Rights in Theory and Practice (Ithaca, N.Y.: Cornell Univ. Press, 1989). 245p.

R. Drinan, Cry of the Oppressed: The History and Hope of the Human Rights Revolution (San Francisco: Harper & Row, 1987). 210p.

A. Eide, Pocket Guide to the Development of Human Rights Institutions and Mechanisms (Strasbourg: Council of Europe, 1989). 31p.

8 Encyclopedia of Public International Law (R. Bernhardt ed., Amsterdam: North-Holland, 1985). 551p.

> Covers human rights, the individual in international law, and international economic relations. Separately-authored articles include titles such as "Indigenous Populations, Protection," "African Charter on Human and People's Rights," and "International Commission of Jurists."

The European Convention on Human Rights: Cases and Materials (H. Petzold, 5th ed., Köln: Carl Heymanns Verlag, 1984). 529p.

D. Forsythe, Human Rights and World Politics (2d rev. ed., Lincoln, NE: University of Nebraska Press, 1989). 316p.

Human Rights in International Law: Legal and Policy Issues (T. Meron ed., Oxford: Clarendon Press, 1984). 566p.

Human Rights in the World Community: Issues and Action (R. Claude & B. Weston eds., Philadelphia: University of Pennsylvania Press, 1989). 376p.

The International Dimensions of Human Rights (K. Vasak & P. Alston eds., Westport, CT: Greenwood Press; Paris: UNESCO, 1982) (2v.). 755 p.

> Volume I on Principles and Norms of Human Rights includes chapters on self-determination and non-discrimination; sources of human rights law; economic, social, and cultural rights; civil and political rights; and human rights in armed conflict. Volume II on International Institutions includes chapters on the UN, ILO, UNESCO, the International Committee of the Red Cross, the Council of Europe, the Organization of African Unity, and possibilities for cooperation among Asian states. Authors include Alston, Gross Espiell, Kartashkin, Marks, Newman, Schwelb, van Boven, and Vasak.

International Human Rights: Problems of Law and Policy (R. Lillich & F. Newman eds., Boston: Little, Brown, 1979). 1030p.

International Human Rights: Problems of Law, Policy and Practice (R. Lillich ed., Boston: Little, Brown, 1990) (forthcoming).

International Protection of Human Rights (L. Sohn & T. Buergenthal eds., Indianapolis, IN: Bobbs-Merrill, 1973). 1402p.

7A Modern Legal Systems Cyclopedia (K. Redden ed., Buffalo, NY: William S. Hein & Co., 1984-).

> Articles on the Inter-American Commission and Court of Human Rights; humanitarian law (including the role of the International Committee of the Red Cross); and the Western/U.S. and Socialist approaches to human rights. Texts of several human rights instruments and status information are also included.

E. Osmanczyk, The Encyclopedia of the United Nations and International Agreements (Philadelphia: Taylor and Francis, 1985) (translation from Polish original). 1059p.

B. Ramcharan, *The Concept and Present Status of International Protection of Human Rights: Forty Years After the Universal Declaration* (Dordrecht: Martinus Nijhoff Pub., 1988). 611p.

Restatement of the Law (Third) The Foreign Relations Law of the United States (St. Paul, MN: American Law Institute Pub., 1987 & Supp. 1988) (2v. and annual supplements).

> Rules that restate generally accepted principles of law, including international human rights law. *See* 2 Restatement §§ 701–03, 711–13; *see also* 1 Restatement at 144–51. Rules are followed by comments, notes, and references.

A. Robertson & J. Merrills, Human Rights in the World: An Introduction to the Study of the International Protection of Human Rights (3d ed., New York: St. Martin's Press, 1989). 300p.

N. Rodley, The Treatment of Prisoners under International Law (Paris & Oxford: UNESCO & Clarendon Press, 1987). 374p.

P. Sieghart, The International Law of Human Rights (Oxford: Clarendon Press, 1983). 569p.

United Nations Action in the Field of Human Rights (New York: UN, 1988) (ST/HR/2/Rev.3). 359p.

> Detailed description of UN actions for the promotion and protection of human rights, 1945 through 1987.

The Universal Declaration of Human Rights, 1948-1988: Human Rights, The United Nations, and Amnesty International (New York: Amnesty International USA, 1988). 180p.

F. RESEARCH GUIDES AND BIBLIOGRAPHIES

J. Andrews & W. Hines, Keyguide to Information Sources on the International Protection of Human Rights (New York: Facts on File Publications, 1987). 169p.

> Part I: background information on human rights and literature. Part II: annotated list of sources. Part III: addresses of selected intergovernmental and nongovernmental organizations.

Bibliography of International Humanitarian Law Applicable in Armed Conflicts (2d ed., rev. & updated, Geneva: ICRC & Henry Dunant Institute, 1987). 605p.

T. Buergenthal, R. Norris, & D. Shelton eds., Protecting Human Rights in the Americas 315-22 (2d ed., Kehl (Germany); Arlington, VA: Engel, 1986). 389p.

Cobbah & Hamalengua, *The Human Rights Literature on Africa: A Bibliography*, 8 Hum. Rts. Q. 115-25 (1986).

M. Cohen, R. Berring & K. Olson, *How to Find the Law* 450-513 (9th ed., St. Paul, MN: West Publishing Co., 1989). 716p.

> Includes sources for texts of treaties, UN resolutions, other documents, and decisions of international tribunals.

Dissertation Abstracts Online (listing by subject, title, and author of U.S. dissertations since 1861; available in File 35 of the DIALOG database).

Documentation Sources on Human Rights (Strasbourg: Council of Europe, 1990) (H(90)1). 52p.

J. Friedman & M. Sherman, Human Rights: An International and Comparative Law Bibliography (Westport, CN: Greenwood Press, 1985) (Bibliographies and Indexes in Law and Political Science; no. 4). 868p.

> Unannotated listing of sources by type of human right, instrument, court, organization, and subject.

Greenfield, *The Human Rights Literature of Eastern Europe*, 3 Hum. Rts. Q. 136-48 (1981).

Greenfield, *The Human Rights Literature of Latin America*, 4 Hum. Rts. Q. 275-98, 508-21 (1982).

Greenfield, *The Human Rights Literature of South Asia*, 3 Hum. Rts. Q. 129-39 (1981).

Greenfield, *The Human Rights Literature of the Soviet Union*, 4 Hum. Rts. Q. 124-36 (1982).

Guide to International Legal Research, 20 Geo. Wash. J. Int'l L. & Econ. 1-413 (1986) (a comprehensive research guide to foreign and international legal materials, arranged by type of source).

Human Rights: A Directory of Resources (T. Fenton & M. Heffron comps. & eds., Maryknoll, NY: Orbis Books, 1989). 156p.

> Mostly-annotated lists of organizations, books, directories, guides, periodicals, pamphlets, articles, and audiovisual materials related to Third World issues. It contains an ''information sources'' section for finding other materials.
>
> Human Rights: A Topical Bibliography (Boulder, CO: Westview Press, 1983). 299p.

L. Louis-Jacques & S. Nevin, Human Rights in the Soviet Union and Eastern Europe: A Research Guide and Bibliography (Littleton, CO: Fred B. Rothman & Co., 1990) (forthcoming).

Reynolds, *Highest Aspirations or Barbarous Acts...The Explosion in Human Rights Documentation: A Bibliographic Survey*, 71 Law Library J. 1-48 (1978).

RLIN (Research Libraries Information Network).

A bibliographic database containing holdings of major academic research libraries nationwide such as the Library of Congress, Harvard Law School Library, and Columbia University Law Library. It provides for searches by subject as well as author, title, and keyword in context. Searches can also be limited by date and by language. Another database, OCLC, contains the holdings of smaller, largely public libraries and is useful for verification of a title or for determining if another library has a book or periodical.

S. Rosenne, Practice and Methods of International Law (Dobbs Ferry, NY: Oceana Publications, Inc., 1984) (reference guide to international legal materials). 169p.

C. Szladits, A Bibliography on Foreign and Comparative Law: Books and Articles in English (Dobbs Ferry, NY: Oceana Publications, Inc., 1955-) (Parker School Studies in Foreign and Comparative Law) (v. 1- , 1790-Apr. 1, 1953-).

Lists books and articles by subject, country, and author, on a variety of topics including human rights.

J. Tobin, Guide to Human Rights Research (Cambridge, MA: Human Rights Program, Harvard Law School, 1985). 15p.

Vincent-Daviss, *Human Rights Law: A Research Guide to the Literature — Part I: International Law and the United Nations*, 14 N.Y.U.J. Int'l L. & Pol. 209-319 (1981).

Vincent-Daviss, *Human Rights Law: A Research Guide to the Literature — Part II: International Protection of Refugees and Humanitarian Law*, 14 N.Y.U.J. Int'l L. & Pol. 487-573 (1982).

Vincent-Daviss, *Human Rights Law: A Research Guide to the Literature — Part III: The International Labor Organization and Human Rights*, 15 N.Y.U.J. Int'l L. & Pol. 211-87 (1982).

L. Whalen, Human Rights: A Referral Handbook (Santa Barbara, CA: ABC-CL10, 1989). 218p.

T. Young, *International Human Rights: A Selected Bibliography* (Los Angeles, CA: Center for the Study of Armament & Disarmament, California State University Los Angeles, 1978) (Political Issues Series; v. 5, no. 4). 58p.

G. PERIODICALS

American Journal of International Law (Washington, D.C.: American Society of International Law, v.1- , 1907-) (quarterly).

> The leading scholarly journal on contemporary concerns in public international law, featuring discussions on such issues as status of custom vis-a-vis executive acts, International Court of Justice decision in *Nicaragua v. United States*, pros and cons regarding U.S. ratification of the 1977 protocols to the Geneva Conventions, and the rights of refugees.

Amnesty International, *Newsletter* (London: Amnesty International, v. 1- , 1971-) (monthly) (brief articles relating to AI's current human rights concerns).

Amnesty International USA Legal Support Network Newsletter (New York: Amnesty International USA, v. 1- , 1984-) (about 3/year) (articles on human rights activities at the UN, notes on current litigation, and other material of interest to lawyers).

Bulletin of Human Rights (Geneva: UN Centre for Human Rights, v. 1- , no. 1- , 1969-) (quarterly).

Columbia Human Rights Law Review (New York: Columbia Law School, v. 1- , 1970-) (twice/year).

Department of State Bulletin (Washington, D.C.: Office of Public Communications, Bureau of Public Affairs, v. 1- , 1939-) (monthly).

> Articles on activities of the President and Secretary of State, treaty information, articles, excerpts of speeches, and an annual index; available on LEXIS.

Dissemination (Geneva: ICRC, v. 1- , 1985-) (three/year) (information regarding ratification of the Geneva Conventions and Protocols).

Harvard Human Rights Journal (Cambridge, MA: Harvard Law School, v. 1- , 1988-) (a student-edited publication continuing *Harvard Human Rights Yearbook*).

Human Rights (Chicago: American Bar Association, v. 1- , no. 1- , 1970-) (magazine issued by the Individual Rights and Responsibilities Section; available on WESTLAW in the HUMRT database).

Human Rights Internet Reporter (Cambridge, MA: Human Rights Internet, Harvard Law School, v. 1- , 1976-) (quarterly).

Articles on human rights; calendar of upcoming conferences and seminars; international and national developments such as NGO activities, IGO decisions and actions, national measures related to human rights, and news of attacks on human rights activists; and an annotated bibliography of new literature.

Human Rights Law Journal (Kehl: Engel, v. 1- , 1980-) (quarterly; continuation of *Human Rights Review*).

Articles, decisions, reports, and documentation including texts of resolutions, declarations, case reports (*e.g.*, European Parliament's annual report, *Human Rights in the World and Community Policy on Human Rights for the Year...*). Issued in association with the International Institute of Human Rights, Strasbourg, France.

Human Rights Newsletter (Geneva: UN Centre for Human Rights, v. 1- , no. 1- , 1988-) (current information about the activities of the Centre).

Human Rights Quarterly: A Comparative and International Journal of the Social Sciences, Humanities, and Law (Baltimore, MD: Johns Hopkins University Press, v. 3- , 1981-) (formerly *Universal Human Rights*) (quarterly).

Interdisciplinary articles and book reviews related to all aspects of human rights. Sponsored by the Urban Morgan Institute for Human Rights, University of Cincinnati College of Law.

International Commission of Jurists, *Review* (Geneva: The Commission, no. 1- , 1969-).

Typically contains a "Human Rights in the World" section with a brief report on human rights developments in selected countries, commentaries, articles, and text of key documents.

International Committee of the Red Cross, *Bulletin* (Geneva: ICRC, no. 1- , 1976-) (current highlights of ICRC activities).

International Journal of Refugee Law (Oxford: Oxford Univ. Press, v. 1- , 1989-).

International Labour Office, *Official Bulletin* (Geneva: ILO, v. 1- , 1928-) (information about the activities of the ILO, including inquiries into conditions of workers in various countries).

International Review of the Red Cross (Geneva: International Committee of the Red Cross, no. 1- , 1961-).

Israel Yearbook on Human Rights (Tel Aviv: Faculty of Law, Tel Aviv University, v.1- , 1971-).

Minority Rights Group, *Report* (London: Minority Rights Group, no. 1- , 1970-) (covers problems facing minorities around the world).

New York Law School Journal of Human Rights (New York: New York Law School, v. 5, pt. 1- , 1987-) (formerly *New York Law School Human Rights Annual*) (book reviews and articles on current issues).

Netherlands Quarterly of Human Rights (Utrecht: Netherlands Institute of Human Rights, v. 7, no. 1- , 1989-) (formerly *SIM Newsletter*).

Nordic Journal on Human Rights = Mennesker og Rettigheter (Oslo: Norwegian Institute of Human Rights, v.1-, no. 1-, 1983-) (quarterly).

South African Journal on Human Rights (Johannesburg: Centre for Applied Legal Studies, University of Witwatersrand, v. 1- , 1985-).

H. BOOK AND PERIODICAL INDICES

Library catalogs and periodical indices contain listings under the Library of Congress Subject Headings: "HUMAN RIGHTS," "CIVIL RIGHTS (INTERNATIONAL LAW)," and "CIVIL RIGHTS." The online catalog provides access to keywords in the bibliographic record of a book or title of an article.

1. Print Indices

Current Bibliographical Information = Information bibliographique courante (New York: Dag Hammarskjöld Library, UN, v. 1- , Jan. 1971-) (ST/LIB/Ser.K) (monthly).

> Lists authors and subjects of books published by the UN, specialized agencies, and non-UN organizations. Also covered are related articles from over 700 periodicals. (*UNDOC: A Current Index*, principally a list of new acquisitions of the Dag Hammarskjöld Library, covers strictly UN materials.) Human Rights materials are listed under item 141.

Index to Foreign Legal Periodicals: A Subject Index to Selected International and Comparative Law Periodicals and Collections of Essays (Chicago: American Association of Law Libraries, v. 1- , no. 1- , 1960-) (updated quarterly).

> Covers selected legal periodicals on public and private international, comparative, and domestic law of countries other than the U.S., the British Isles, and the British Commonwealth. "Human Rights (International Law)" is the search term for articles on human rights.

Index to Legal Periodicals (New York: H.W. Wilson, Co., 1929-).

Public International Law: A Current Bibliography of Articles (Berlin: Springer-Verlag, v. 1- , 1975-) (twice/year).

> List of articles in some 1,000 journals and collected works, prepared by the Max Planck Institute; human rights articles are listed under the classification number "12."

UNDOC: Current Index (New York: UN, Dag Hammarskjöld Library, v. 1- , no. 1- , Jan./Feb. 1979-) (became a quarterly in 1984) (ST/LIB/Ser.M).

> Titles and document series of UN documents and publications by subject, organization, and title. Also contains a list of mimeographed documents republished in the official records of the main UN organs. A helpful "User's Guide" appears in each issue.

2. Computer Indices

CONGRESSIONAL MASTERFILE (CD-ROM access to Congressional Information Service indices for all congressional publications issued since the first Congress in 1789, by subject, witness, committee, etc.; see CIS, *infra.*).

LEGALTRAC (CD-ROM version of *Current Law Index* and *Legal Resource Index*; extensive coverage of international law journals published in English; indexes over 750 legal periodicals).

LEXIS (LAWREV contains full text of general U.S. law reviews plus LEGALTRAC index in the LGLIND file. NEXIS, the non-legal counterpart of LEXIS, contains full text of news wires, newspapers, and magazines; sample sources include *Current Digest of the Soviet Press, Reuters Library Report,* and *UN Chronicle*).

PAIS INTERNATIONAL (online version of paper indices, *PAIS Bulletin* and *PAIS Foreign Language Index,* available in DIALOG File 49; 1976- *Bulletin,* 1972- *Foreign Language*; covers legal periodicals in various languages).

SOC SCISEARCH (multidisciplinary index corresponding to the print index, *Social Science Citation Index,* available in DIALOG File 7; 1972- ; indexes many foreign and international law journals in the major European languages).

WESTLAW (full text of selected articles from hundreds of law reviews including many international law journals in the TP database; INT-TP is limited to international law journals; contains LEGALTRAC in LRI database; ABA *Human Rights* periodical in HUMRT database).

I. PRACTICE GUIDES

Amnesty International, Summary of Selected International Procedures and Bodies Dealing with Human Rights Matters (London: AI, 1989) (AI Index: IOR 30/01/89). 75 p.

> Short descriptions, addresses, references to books and articles, and other relevant material for using principal human rights procedures of IGOs and some NGOs.

Guide to International Human Rights Practice (H. Hannum ed., Philadelphia: University of Pennsylvania Press, 1984). 310p.

> General information on human rights law, the petition and reporting procedures, NGO activities, and domestic remedies for human rights violations, followed with references to reports, decisions, instruments, books, and articles. Appendices contain a handy bibliographic note, a checklist for selecting an appropriate forum, a model communication, IGO addresses, ratification information on selected instruments, and membership of expert bodies. A new edition is expected.

International Women's Rights Action Watch, Assessing the Status of Women (New York: Columbia University, 1988). 44p.

> A guide to preparing government reports under and using the Convention on the Elimination of All Forms of Discrimination Against Women.

> D. O'Donnell, Proteccion Internacional de los Derechos Humanos (Lima: Andean Commission of Jurists, 1989). 752p.

Symposium: International Human Rights, 20 Santa Clara L. Rev. 559-772 (1980).

> The symposium contains introductory articles on the ECOSOC resolution 1503 procedure, procedures for the protection of detainees, the ILO, UNESCO, the European Convention, and the Inter-American Commission on Human Rights.

UN Centre for Human Rights, *Fact Sheets* (Geneva: UN, 1987-).

> Cover various aspects of human rights: No. 1 (Human Rights Machinery), No. 2 (The International Bill of Human Rights), No. 3 (Advisory Services and Technical Assistance in the Field of Human Rights), No. 4 (Methods of Combatting Torture), No. 5 (Programme of Action for the Second Decade to Combat Racism and Racial Discrimination), No. 6 (Enforced or Involuntary Disappearances), No. 7 (Communications Procedures), and No. 8 (World Public Information Campaign for Human Rights).

UNITAR/Centre for Human Rights, *Manual on Human Rights Reporting* (1990) (forthcoming).

> Guidance on the preparation and consideration of governmental reports under the major international human rights instruments.

D. Weissbrodt & P. Parker, The U.N. Commission on Human Rights: An Orientation Manual for Non-Governmental Organizations (Geneva: 1988) (Human Rights Series, v. 1) (joint publication of the International Service for Human Rights in Geneva and the Minnesota Lawyers International Human Rights Committee in Minneapolis). 86p.

An introductory guide to NGO work in international human rights bodies with advice on how to gather and report information; give speeches; and make contacts with the press, Commission members, and NGOs.

M. Tardu, Human Rights: The International Petition System (Dobbs Ferry, NY: Oceana Publications, Inc., 1979-) (3v. looseleaf).

Detailed discussion of procedures for individuals and NGOs in filing complaints of human rights violations before international bodies. Focuses mainly on the UN petition system including the ILO and UNESCO with an overview of the European and Inter-American petition systems.

World Organisation Against Torture, Practical Guide to the International Procedures Relative to Complaint and Appeals Against Acts of Torture, Disappearances and Other Inhuman or Degrading Treatment (Geneva: S.O.S. Torture, 1988). 92p.

J. CONGRESSIONAL MATERIAL

The Subcommittee on International Organizations of the House Committee on Foreign Affairs began a series of hearings in 1973 on human rights matters. The hearings led to several statutes linking human rights to U.S. foreign policy and assistance. The Subcommittee was later renamed Subcommittee on Human Rights and International Organizations and continues to hold hearings on human rights topics. Other subcommittees of the House Committee on Foreign Affairs (*e.g.*, the Africa Subcommittee), the full Committee, the Senate Committee on Foreign Relations, and its subcommittees have also held hearings and considered legislation related to human rights. For example, the Senate Foreign Relations Committee regularly holds hearings on the confirmation of ambassadors at which human rights questions may be asked and has occasionally considered the ratification of human rights treaties. The Judiciary Committees of both Senate and House have considered immigration legislation, the Torture Victim Protection Act, and other relevant statutes.

Hearings, reports, and prints of congressional committees may be located in *CIS* (Washington, D.C.: Congressional Information Service, 1970-) (predecessor indices start with the first Congress of 1789). They may be accessed by subject, witness, committee or subcommittee, etc. CIS *Congressional Masterfile* provides online access.

K. FACTFINDING METHODOLOGY

Franck & Fairley, *Procedural Due Process in Human Rights Fact-Finding by International Agencies*, 74 Am. J. Int'l L. 308-45 (1980).

Guidelines for International Election Observing (L. Garber ed., Washington, D.C.: International Human Rights Law Group, 1984). 101p.

International Law and Fact-Finding in the Field of Human Rights (B. Ramcharan ed., The Hague: Martinus Nijhoff Pub., 1982) (International Studies in Human Rights; v. 1). 259p.

> Articles on substantive and procedural law applicable to factfinding by human rights bodies. Annexes include model procedural rules.

Orentlicher, *Bearing Witness: The Art and Science of Human Rights Fact-finding*, 3 Harv. Hum. Rts. J. 83-135 (1990).

H. Thoolen & B. Verstappen, *Human Rights Missions: A Study of the Fact-Finding Practice of Non-Governmental Organizations* (Dordrecht: Martinus Nijhoff Pub., 1986) (International Studies in Human Rights). 184p.

Weissbrodt, *International Trial Observers*, 18 Stanford J. Int'l L. 27-121 (1982).

Weissbrodt & McCarthy, *Fact-Finding by International Human Rights Organizations*, 22 Va. J. Int'l L. 1-89 (1981).

L. COUNTRY SITUATIONS

1. Legal System Information Sources

International Encyclopedia of Comparative Law (Tübingen: J.C.B. Mohr (Paul Siebeck)).

> Contains alphabetically-arranged "National Reports" updated by installments. A report for a country typically provides information on formation of the government, constitutional system (including legislative and judicial structure), sources of law (decrees, orders, court decisions, custom, etc.), and brief history of the development of law, private law (contracts, torts, etc.), commercial law, intellectual property law, civil procedure, and private international law. Each report concludes with a short bibliography of books, articles, and/or periodicals to consult for additional information. The entries are up to date through the early 1970's.

Legal Traditions and Systems: An International Handbook (A. Katz ed., Westport, CT: Greenwood Press, 1986) (discussion of the legal system of several countries with notes and a selective bibliography). 450p.

Modern Legal Systems Cyclopedia (K. Redden ed., Buffalo, NY: Hein, 1984-) (looseleaf).

> Description of the political organization, sources of law, legislature, judiciary, and administrative structure of each country.

2. Country Reports

Amnesty International, Report (London: Amnesty International Publications, 1962-) (annual).

> Documents AI's work for the year prior to the date of issue (usually July). Substantial information on work in many countries, for prisoners of conscience and against torture, the death penalty, extrajudicial executions, disappearances, and unfair trials for political prisoners.

Country Reports on Human Rights Practices (Washington, D.C.: U.S. Government Printing Office, 1977-) (annual).

> Covers human rights practices of nations that receive assistance from the U.S. or which are members of the UN. Other nations are also included. It includes relevant political, social, and economic information on a country and an evaluation of each country's respect for human rights (mainly civil and political, plus fair conditions of labor) based on its own constitution, legislative measures, and actions towards its citizens. Prepared by the U.S. Department of State for the House Committee on Foreign Affairs and the Senate Committee on Foreign Relations; issued as a congressional committee print.

Critique: Review of the Department of State's Country Reports on Human Rights Practices for ... (New York: Lawyers Committee for Human Rights & Human Rights Watch, 1983–) (annual is also called *Critique of DOS Country Reports*; beginning in 1990 the *Critique* became the project of the Lawyers Committee alone).

Freedom in the World (New York: Freedom House, 1978-) (Freedom House Book) (annual).

Human Rights in Developing Countries (M. Nowak & T. Swinehart eds., Oslo: Norwegian University Press, 1985-) (Publications from the Danish Center for Human Rights) (annual).

> Covers the human rights situation in such countries as Bangladesh, Botswana, India, Kenya, Mozambique, Nicaragua, Pakistan, the Philippines, Sri Lanka, Suriname, Tanzania, Zambia, and Zimbabwe. Reports are prepared in cooperation with several human rights centers in Europe and Canada.

International Committee of the Red Cross, Annual Report (Geneva: ICRC, 1952-).

> Covers the work of the ICRC in each country where the ICRC has made representations or undertaken activities on behalf of prisoners of war, civilians in armed conflict, or detainees; has supplied medical and other material relief; or has performed other services. The annual reports are ordinarily issued late in the year following the date of the report.

International Handbook of Human Rights (J. Donnelly & R. Howard eds., Westport, CN: Greenwood Press, 1987). 495p.

> Alphabetically-arranged studies of human rights practices in 19 countries (Canada, Chile, China, Cuba, El Salvador, India, Israel, Jamaica, Japan, Lebanon, Nicaragua, the Philippines, Poland, Senegal, South Africa, Spain, Uganda, the USSR, and the U.S.). Each separately-authored study discusses the historical background of the country as well as civil, political, economic, social, and cultural rights. The introduction provides background information about human rights in general. The appendices contain the Universal Declaration of Human Rights, a ratification chart for human rights instruments, basic economic and social indicators, a selected bibliography, and an index.

The Reagan/Bush Administration's Record on Human Rights in...(New York: Human Rights Watch & Lawyers Committee for Human Rights, 1986-) (beginning in 1990 the *Bush Administration Record* became the project of Human Rights Watch alone).

> Reviews implementation of human rights legislation; ratification of human rights treaties; voting record and human rights activities in the UN; refugee, asylum, and immigration policy; and policy toward over 20 countries where human rights issues have arisen.

3. Constitutions

Constitutions of Dependencies & Special Sovereignties (A. Blaustein ed., Dobbs Ferry, NY: Oceana Publications, Inc., 1975-).

Constitutions of the Countries of the World (A. Blaustein & G. Flanz eds., Dobbs Ferry, NY: Oceana Publications, Inc., 1971-).

4. Criminal Codes and Criminal Procedure Codes

American Series of Foreign Penal Codes (South Hackensack, NJ: Fred B. Rothman & Co., 1960-).

> English-language translations of penal codes of Argentina, Austria, China, Colombia, Finland, France, Federal Republic of Germany (West), Greece, Greenland, Japan, Republic of Korea (South), Norway, Poland, Sweden, and Turkey; criminal procedure codes of France, Federal Republic of Germany, Israel, and Turkey.

5. Other Legislation

C. Szladits, Bibliography on Foreign and Comparative Law: Books and Articles in English (Dobbs Ferry, NY: Oceana Publications, Inc., 1955-) (codes and statutes available in books and periodicals through 1983).

6. Directories

Africa: Human Rights Directory and Bibliography, 12 Hum. Rts. Internet Reporter 1-308 (1988/89) (special issue, no. 4).

Describes organizations concerned with human rights in Africa and lists relevant books, articles, and periodicals.

Encyclopedia of Associations: International Organizations (Detroit, MI: Gale Research Co., 1989-) (annual).

Human Rights Directory: Latin America, Africa, Asia (L. Wiseberg & H. Scoble eds., Washington, D.C.: Human Rights Internet, 1981) (similar to the Africa directory described above). 243p.

Human Rights Directory: Western Europe (L. Wiseberg & H. Sirett eds., Washington, D.C.: Human Rights Internet, 1982). 335p.

Human Rights Internet Directory: Eastern Europe & the USSR (L. Wiseberg ed., Cambridge, MA: Human Rights Internet, Harvard Law School, 1987). 304p.

Master List of Human Rights Organizations & Serial Publications (3d ed., Cambridge, MA: Human Rights Internet, Harvard Law School, 1989-90).

Supplements *Human Rights Internet Reporter* with lists of organizations named in the *Reporter*.

North American Human Rights Directory (L. Wiseberg & H. Sirett 3d ed., Washington, D.C.: Human Rights Internet, 1984). 264p.

Yearbook of International Organizations (Munich: K.G. Saur, 1967-).

7. Nongovernmental Organization (NGO) Reports

Several of the numerous NGOs working in the area of human rights produce excellent country reports on a range of rights and regions. Among those organizations are:

Amnesty International, 1 Easton Street, London WC1 8DJ, U.K.
Article 19, 90 Borough High Street, London SE1, 1LL, U.K.
Human Rights Advocates, P.O. Box 5675, Berkeley, CA 94705
Human Rights Watch, 485 Fifth Ave., New York, NY 10017
    Africa Watch
    Americas Watch
    Asia Watch
    Helsinki Watch
    Middle East Watch
International Alert, 29 Craven Street, London WC2N 5NT, U.K.
International Commission of Jurists, 109 route de Chëne, CH-1223
    Geneva, Switzerland

> International Committee of the Red Cross, Information Department, 19
>   avenue de la Paix, CH-1202 Geneva, Switzerland
> International Human Rights Law Group, 1601 Connecticut Ave. N.W.,
>   Washington, D.C. 20009
> International League for Human Rights, 432 Park Ave., New York, NY
>   10016
> Inter-Parliamentary Union, Place du Petit-Saconnex, C.P. 438, CH-1211
>   Geneva 19, Switzerland
> Lawyers Committee for Human Rights, 330 Seventh Ave., 10th Floor,
>   New York, NY 10001
> Minnesota Lawyers International Human Rights Committee, 514 Nicollet
>   Mall, Minneapolis, MN 55402
> Minority Rights Group, 29 Craven St., London, WC2N 5NT, U.K.
> Physicians for Human Rights, 58 Day Street, Somerville, MA 02144

The *Human Rights Internet Reporter* and the human rights directories include entries by the above organizations and others.

8. UN Documents

The UN publishes many reports submitted by UN organs and member states detailing countries' adherence to international human rights standards. The Commission on Human Rights, for example, authorizes working groups, special rapporteurs, representatives, experts, Commission members, the Secretary-General, and other envoys to monitor violations or make direct contacts in particular countries: Afghanistan (1984-present), Bolivia (1981-1982), Chile (1979-1990), Cuba (1988), Democratic Kampuchea (1980-1983), El Salvador (1981-present), Equatorial Guinea (1979-1980, 1984), Guatemala (1983-1987), Iran (1984-present), Poland (1982), and Romania (1989).

In addition, the Commission on Human Rights has established special rapporteurs and a working group on thematic topics: Working Group on Enforced or Involuntary Disappearances (1980-present), Special Rapporteur on summary or arbitrary executions (1982-present), Special Rapporteur on torture (1985-present), Special Rapporteur on religious intolerance (1986-present), and Special Rapporteur on mercenaries (1987-present). The special rapporteurs and working groups produce annual reports discussing human rights violations in many countries and detailing country visits.

The Commission on Human Rights has authorized experts on advisory services for the restoration of human rights in countries such as Equatorial Guinea, Guatemala, and Haiti. The reports of those experts provide information on countries receiving advisory services.

The *ad hoc* Working Group of Experts on Southern Africa, the Special Committee Against *Apartheid*, and the UN Council for Namibia have also issued specialized reports.

Within the framework of the Human Rights Committee, Committee on Economic, Social and Cultural Rights, Committee on the Elimination of

Discrimination against Women (CEDAW), and the Committee on the Elimi-nation of All Forms of Racial Discrimination (CERD), states parties are required to submit periodic reports on domestic developments. Those reports, along with the published questions, responses, and decisions taken by the committees, provide indispensable information about the countries.

The Special Committee on Decolonization receives reports from its delegations to dependent territories: American Samoa, Anguilla, Bermuda, British Virgin Islands, Cayman Islands, East Timor, Falkland Islands (Mal-vinas), Gibraltar, Guam, Montserrat, New Caledonia, Pitcairn, St. Helena, Tokelau, Trust Territory of the Pacific Islands, Turks and Caicos Islands, U.S. Virgin Islands, and Western Samoa.

UN documents, listed in *UNDOC: Current Index* (1979-) and prede-cessor indices, are organized by document symbols referring to the UN organ, type of document, session number, and document number. Document symbols relevant to human rights include:

General Assembly

A/	Document for plenary
A/INF	Information paper for the General Assembly
A/RES	General Assembly Resolution
A/C.1 through C.6, A/SEC, A/ BLR	Main committees of the General Assembly, *e.g.*, the Third Committee (A/C.3) considers social, humanitarian, and cultural matters; the Sixth Committee deals with legal matters. Documents issued only during Assembly sessions.
A/AC.109	Special Committee on Decolonization
A/AC.115	Special Committee on *Apartheid*
A/AC.131	Council for Namibia
A/AC.160	Committee on International Terrorism

Economic and Social Council (ECOSOC)

E/	Document for ECOSOC plenary
E/INF	Information papers for ECOSOC
E/RES	ECOSOC resolution
E/C.2	Committee on Non-Governmental Organizations
E/CN.4	Commission on Human Rights
E/CN.4/Sub.2	Sub-Commission on Prevention of Discrimination and Protection of Minorities
E/CN.5	Commission for Social Development
E/CN.6	Commission on Status of Women

Other Major Organs

DC/	Disarmament Commission
S/	Security Council

ST/	Secretariat
T/	Trusteeship Council

International Covenant on Civil and Political Rights

CCPR/	Human Rights Committee
CCPR/SP	Meetings of the states parties

International Covenant on Economic, Social and Cultural Rights

ESC/	Committee on Economic, Social and Cultural Rights

International Convention on the Elimination of All Forms of Racial Discrimination

CERD/	Committee on the Elimination of Racial Discrimination

International Convention on the Elimination of All Forms of Discrimination Against Women

CEDAW/	Committee on the Elimination of Discrimination Against Women

International Convention on Torture and Cruel, Inhuman or Degrading Treatment or Punishment

CAT	Committee Against Torture

Functional symbols

___/Add.	Addendum
___/CONF.	Conference
___/Corr.	Corrigendum
___/L.	Document with limited distribution (often draft resolutions or reports, generally available only at the time of issue)
___/NGO	Document submitted by a nongovernmental organization
___/PR.	Press release
___/R.	Document with restricted distribution (not generally available to NGOs or individuals)
___/Rev.	Revision
___/SR.	Summary records
___/WG.	Working group

9. Inter-American Commission on Human Rights (OAS)

The Inter-American Commission on Human Rights publishes periodic reports on its visits to investigate allegations of human rights violations in

OAS member states. Annual reports of the Commission contain updates on the country visit reports or summaries of reports not separately issued. Reports have been prepared on Argentina (1980), Bolivia (1981), Chile (1974, 1976, 1977, 1985), Colombia (1981), Cuba (1962, 1963, 1967, 1970, 1976, 1979, 1983), El Salvador (1978, 1986), Guatemala (1981, 1983, 1986, 1988), Haiti (1979, 1988), Nicaragua (1981, 1984, 1988), Panama (1978, 1989), Paraguay (1978), Suriname (1983, 1985), and Uruguay (1978).

10. Media Services

Foreign Broadcast Information Service (FBIS) (New Canaan, CT: NewsBank).

> The *FBIS Daily Report* contains current news and information on eight countries/regions of the world: China, East Europe, Soviet Union, East Asia, Near East & South Asia, Africa (Sub-Sahara), Latin America, and West Europe. Most of the information derives from U.S. government monitoring of international radio services and other media. Joint Publications Research Service (JPRS) publications issued periodically by the National Technical Information Service (Springfield, VA) contain less timely information. FBIS and JPRS are available in microfiche and hardcopy.

NEXIS (online service containing the full text of news wires, newspapers, and magazines; see Computer Indices, *supra*).

TABLE OF AUTHORITIES

References are to pages in the Preface and Chapters 1–13; excerpts are noted in **bold print**.

BOOKS AND ARTICLES

Abbott, *Linking Trade to Political Goals: Foreign Policy Export Controls in the 1970s and 1980s*, 65 Minn. L. Rev. 739 (1981), *552*

Adams, *U.S. Protests Reporter's Ouster*, San Francisco Chron., Dec. 1, 1988, at A25, *41*

Africa Watch, Forcible Return of Somali Refugees, Government Repression of Kenyan Somalis, November 17, 1989, *500*

Africa Watch, Kenya: Harassment of Ethnic Somalis, December 6, 1989, *500*

Africa Watch, Kenya: Suppression of Press Freedom, Banning of Critical Papers and Intolerance of Dissent, December 6, 1989, *500*

Amnesty International, Report 1989 (1989), *32*, ***105–08***, *458*, *500*, ***690–92***

Amnesty International, Report on Torture (1975), *652*

Amnesty International, Romania: Human Rights Violations in the Eighties (1987), *461*

Amnesty International, Summary of Selected International Procedures and Bodies Dealing with Human Rights Measures, AI Index: IOR 30/01/89 (1989), *141*

Amnesty International, Suriname: Violations of Human Rights, AI Index: AMR 84/02/87 (1987), *229*

Amnesty International, Torture in Greece: The First Torturers' Trial 1975 (1977), *479*

Amnesty International, United States of America: The Death Penalty, AI Index: AMR 51/01/87 (1987), *255*

Amnesty International, USSR: Four Long-Term Prisoners Still Awaiting a Review, AI Index: 46/10/90 (1990), *458*

Amnesty International, Yugoslavia: Prisoners of Conscience (1985), *461*

An-Na'im, *Religious Minorities Under Islamic Law and the Limits of Cultural Relativism*, 9 Hum. Rts. Q. 1 (1987), *357*

Andean Commission of Jurists, Andean Newsletter, Nos. 30–35 (1989), *32*

Andean Commission of Jurists, Perú y Chile: Poder Judicial y Derechos Humanos (1988), *32*

N. Andren & K. Birnbaum, eds., Belgrade and Beyond: The CSCE Process in Perspective (1980), *418*

Argentine National Commission on the Disappeared, Nunca Más (1986), *252*

Arrangio-Ruiz, *Human Rights and Non-Intervention in the Helsinki Final Act*, 157 Recueil des Cours 195 (1977), *428*

Asia Watch, Burma (Myanmar): Worsening Repression (1990), *109*

Asia Watch & Minnesota Lawyers International Human Rights Committee, Human Rights in the Democratic People's Republic of Korea (North Korea) (1988), ***233–39***

R. Atkins & R. Pisani, The Hassle of Your Life: A Handbook For the Friends and Families of Americans Imprisoned Abroad (1982), ***32–34***

Baker, *The International Agenda and FY 1990 Budget Request*, State Dept. Bureau of Public Affairs, Current Policy No. 1147 (1989), ***507, 508***

Baker, *U.S.-Soviet Relations: A Discussion of Perestroika and Economic Reform*, State Dept. Bureau of Public Affairs, Current Policy No. 1209 (1989), *461*

Barsh, *Indigenous Peoples: An Emerging Object of International Law*, 80 Am. J. Int'l L. 369 (1986), ***88–90***

M. Bartolomei, Gross and Massive Violations of Human Rights in Argentina, 1976–1983, draft LL.D. thesis in International Law, University of Lund, Sweden (1990), *244*

M. Bartolomei & D. Weissbrodt, The Impact of Factfinding and International Pressures on the Human Rights Situation in Argentina, 1976–1983, ***244–52***

Bassiouni, *Perspectives on the Transfer of Prisoners Between the United States and Other Countries*, in V. Nanda & M. Bassiouni, International Criminal Law 271 (1987), *34*

Bayefsky, *The Human Rights Committee and the Case of Sandra Lovelace*, 20 Canadian Y.B. Int'l L. Ann. 244 (1982), *84*

Becket, *The Greek Case Before the European Human Rights Commission*, 1 Hum. Rts. J. 91 (1970), *479*

Bedau, *Human Rights and Foreign Assistance Programs*, in Human Rights and U.S. Foreign Policy 29 (P. Brown & D. MacLean eds. 1979), *521*

R. Beddard, Human Rights and Europe: A Study of the Machinery of Human Rights Protection of the Council of Europe (1980), *465*

The Belgrade Minimum Rules of Procedure for International Human Rights Fact-finding Visits, 75 Am. J. Int'l L. 163 (1981), *209*

D. Bennett and K. Sharpe, Transnational Corporations Versus the State: The Political Economy of the Mexican Auto Industry (1985), *56*

Berenstein, *Economic and Social Rights: Their Inclusion in the European Convention on Human Rights Problems of Formulation and Interpretation*, 2 Human Rights L.J. 257 (1981), *465*

Berman, *ILO and Indigenous Peoples: Revision of ILO Convention 107*, 41 Rev. Int'l Comm. Jurists 48 (1988), *91*

Berman & Clark, *State Terrorism: Disappearances*, 13 Rutgers L.J. 531 (1982), *174*, *611*

T. Biersteker, Distortion of Development: Contending Perspectives on the Multinational Corporation (1978), *56*

Bilder, *Integrating International Human Rights Law into Domestic Law — U.S. Experience*, 4 Hous. J. Int'l L. (1981), *573*

Cerna & Young, *The Inter-American Commission on Human Rights and the Death Penalty*, 34 Fed. B. News & J. 398 (1987), *271*

Chalidze, *The Humanitarian Provisions of the Helsinki Accord: A Critique of their Significance*, 13 Vanderbilt J. Trans. L. 429 (1980), *428*

E. Chossudovsky, The Helsinki Final Act Viewed in the United Nations Perspective (1980), *430*

Christenson, *The Uses of Human Rights Norms to Inform Constitutional Interpretation*, 4 Hous. J. Int'l L. 39 (1981), *573*

Christopher, *The Diplomacy of Human Rights: The First Year*, in Human Rights and U.S. Foreign Policy 257 B. Rubin & E. Spiro eds. (1979), *544*

Christopher, *Human Rights and the National Interest*, State Dept. Bureau of Public Affairs, Current Policy No. 206 (1980), ***503–07***

Clarizio, Clements, & Geetter, *United States Policy Toward South Africa*, 11 Hum. Rts. Q. 249 (1989), *552*

E. Cleary, Crisis and Change: The Church in Latin America Today (1986), *57*

Clinebell & Thompson, *Sovereignty and Self-Determination: The Rights of Native Americans Under International Law*, 27 Buffalo L. Rev. 669 (1978), *81*

Cobbah, *African Values and the Human Rights Debate: An African Perspective*, 9 Human Rts. Q. 309 (1987), *356*

Cohen, *Conditioning U.S. Security Assistance on Human Rights Practices*, 76 Am. J. Int'l L. 246 (1982), *519*, ***533–39***

Cohn, *International Fact-Finding Processes*, 18 Rev. Int'l Commission Jurists 40 (1977), *239*

Cole, Lobel, & Koh, *Interpreting the Alien Tort Statute: Amicus Curiae Memorandum of International Law Scholars and Practitioners in Trajano v. Marcos*, 12 Hastings Int'l & Comp. L. Rev. 1 (1988), *615*

Coliver, *European Court of Human Rights Condemns Conditions on Virginia's Death Row*, 13 Hum. Rts. Advocates News. 23 (November 1989), *477*

Coliver, *United Nations Machineries on Women's Rights: How Might They Better Help Women Whose Rights are Being Violated?*, in New Directions in Human Rights 25 (E. Lutz, H. Hannum, & K. Burke eds. 1989), *100*, *129*

Coliver & Newman, *Using International Human Rights Law to Influence United States Foreign Population Policy: Resort to Courts or Congress?*, 20 N.Y.U.J. Int'l. L. & Pol. 53 (1987), *619*, *669–70*, *680*

Comm'n on Security and Cooperation in Europe, Human Rights in Czechoslovakia: The Documents of Charter '77, 1977–1982 (1982), *440*

Comm'n on Security and Cooperation in Europe, Human Rights in Czechoslovakia: The Documents of Charter 77, 1982–1987 (1988), *440*

Comment, *Human Rights and United States Security Assistance: El Salvador and the Case for Country-Specific Legislation*, 24 Harv. Int'l L.J. 75 (1983), *520*

Comment, *International Convention on the Prevention and Punishment of the Crime of Genocide: United States Senate Grant of Advice and Consent to Ratification*, 1 Harv. Hum. Rts. Y.B. 227 (1988), *403*

Comment, *Monitoring Mechanisms for International Agreements Respecting Economic and Social Human Rights*, 12 Yale J. Int'l L. 390 (1987), *385*

Comment, *The Use of Nonviolent Coercion: A Study in Legality Under Article 2(4) of the Charter of the United Nations*, 122 Univ. Pa. L. Rev. 983 (1974), *552*

Commentary, IV Geneva Convention Relative to the Protection of Civilian Persons in Time of War (J. Pictet ed. 1958), *701*

Commentary on the Additional Protocols of 8 June 1977 to the Geneva Conventions of 12 August 1949 (Y. Sandoz, C. Swinarski, & B. Zimmerman eds. 1987), *707*

Commission on Security and Cooperation in Europe, A Thematic Survey of the Documents of the Moscow Helsinki Group, May 12, 1981, ***433, 434***

Conferences on Moslem Doctrine and Human Rights in Islam (1974), *337*

Costello and Worthington, *Incarcerating Status Offenders: Attempts to Circumvent the Juvenile Justice & Delinquency Prevention Act*, 16 Harv. C.R.-C.L. L. Rev. 40 (1981), *564*

Council of Europe, *Committee of Experts for the Improvement of Procedures for the Protection of Human Rights*, 11 Eur. Hum. Rts. Rep. 421 (1989), *464*

Council of Europe, Stock-Taking on the European Convention on Human Rights (1954–1984) (1984), *479*

J. Crawford, The Rights of Peoples (1988), *81*

Eagleburger, *The Challenge of the European Landscape in the 1990s*, 89 State Dept. Bull. 37 (1989), *461*

J. Egeland, Humanitarian Initiatives Against Political "Disappearances" (1982), ***181, 182***

A. Ehrenzweig, Law: A Personal View (1977), *340*

Eide, *Making Human Rights Universal: Unfinished Business*, 6 Nordic J. Hum. Rts. 51 (No. 4, 1988), *356*

S. Ercman, European Convention on Human Rights: Guide to Case Law (1981), *466*

Erickson, *Protocol I: A Merging of the Hague and Geneva Law of Armed Conflict*, 19 Va. J. Int'l L. 557 (1979), *685*

W. Eskridge & Frickey, Cases and Materials on Legislation: Statutes and the Creation of Public Policy (1988), *293*

European Comm'n Hum. Rts., Organisation, procedures and activities (1990), *466*

The Evian Assembly 1970: Resolution on Human Rights, in A Lutheran Reader on Human Rights 1 (J. Lissner & A. Sovik eds. 1978), *57*

Farer, *The Inter-American Commission on Human Rights: Operations and Doctrine*, 9 Int'l J.L. Libr. 251 (1981), *288*

Farer, *The United States as Guarantor of Democracy in the Caribbean Basin: Is There a Legal Way?*, 10 Human Rts. Q. 157 (1988), *510*

Farer & Rowles, *The Inter-American Commission on Human Rights*, in International Human Rights Law and Practice 47 (J. Tuttle ed. 1978), *46*

Farraq, Human Rights in a Pluralistic World (J. Berting et al. eds. 1990), *337*

W. Feld, Nongovernmental Forces and World Politics: A Study of Business, Labor, and Political Groups (1972), *48*

Ferguson, *Comments* in U.S. Ratification of the Human Rights Treaties: With or Without Reservation? 41 (R. Lillich ed. 1981), *396*

Fischer, *Reporting Under the Covenant on Civil and Political Rights: The First Five Years of the Women Rights Committee*, 76 Am. J. Int'l L. 142 (1982), *70, 318*

Fitzpatrick, *UN Action With Respect to "Disappearances" and Summary or Arbitrary Executions*, 5 AIUSA Legal Support Network Newsl. 35 (Fall 1988), *160, 171,* ***180, 181***

Foroohar, *Liberation Theology: The Response of Latin American Catholics to Socioeconomic Problems*, 13 Latin American Perspectives 37 (No. 3, 1986), *57*

Forsythe, *Congress and Human Rights in U.S. Foreign Policy: The Fate of General Legislation*, 9 Hum. Rts. Q. 382 (1987), *515*

D. Forsythe, Human Rights and Foreign Policy: Congress Reconsidered (1988), *521*

D. Forsythe, Human Rights and World Politics (1983), *510*

Forsythe, *Present Role of the Red Cross in Protection*, in Final Report: An Agenda for the Red Cross (1975), *708*

Foster, *The European Court of Justice and the European Convention for the Protection of Human Rights*, 8 Hum. Rts. L.J. 245 (1987), *438*

Franck & Fairley, *Procedural Due Process in Human Rights Fact-Finding by International Agencies*, 74 Am. J. Int'l L. 308 (1980), *239*

Fraser, *Congress's Role in the Making of International Human Rights Policy*, in Human Rights and American Foreign Policy 247 (D. Kommers & G. Loescher eds. 1979), ***517–19***

Freeman, *Racism, Rights and the Quest for Equality of Opportunity: A Critical Legal Essay*, 23 Harv. C.R.-C.L. L. Rev. 295 (1988), ***340–43***

L. Fritz, Native Law Bibliography (1984), *90*

Frowein, *The Interrelationship between the Helsinki Final Act, the International Covenants on Human Rights, and the European Convention on Human Rights*, in Human Rights, International Law and the Helsinki Accord 71 (T. Buergenthal ed. 1977), *430*

Gabel, *The Phenomenology of Rights-Consciousness and the Pact of the Withdrawn Selves*, 62 Tex. L. Rev. 1563 (1984), *344*

W. Galenson, The International Labour Organisation: An American View 284 (1981), *48*

Galey, *Congress, Foreign Policy and Human Rights Ten Years After Helsinki*, 7 Hum. Rts. Q. 334 (1985), *432, 521*

L. Garber, Guidelines for International Election Observing (1984), *239*

A. Gerson, Israel, the West Bank and International Law (1978), *721*

Gerstel & Segall, *Conference Report: Human Rights in American Courts*, Am. U.J. Int'l L. & Pol'y 137 (1986), ***670–76***

Gibney, *Human Rights and Human Consequences: A Critical Analysis of Sanchez-Espinoza v. Reagan*, 10 Loy. L.A. Int'l & Comp. L.J. 299 (1988), *680*

L. Hinds, Illusions of Justice: Human Rights Violations in the United States (1978), *254*

Hoffman, *The Application of International Human Rights in State Courts: A View From California*, 18 Int'l Lawyer 61 (1984), *570*

Hoffman, *Universities and Human Rights*, 6 Human Rights Q. 5 (1984), *58*

Holmes, *The Path of the Law*, 10 Harv. L. Rev. 457 (1897), *652*

Horton & Sellier, *The Utility of Presidential Certifications of Compliance with United States Human Rights Policy: The Case of El Salvador*, 1982 Wis. L. Rev. 825, *520*

Howard, *Monitoring Human Rights: Problems of Consistency*, 4 Ethics & Int'l Affairs 33 (1990), *527*

Howard, *The Full Belly Thesis: Should Economic Rights Take Priority Over Civil and Political Rights?*, 5 Hum. Rts. Q. 467 (1983), *390*

Human Rights Advisory Committee, Human Rights in Suriname (1984), *229*

Human Rights in Islam: Report of a Seminar Held in Kuwait, December 1980 (1982), *337*

Human Rights in the Post-Apartheid South African Constitution, 21 Columbia Hum. Rts. L. Rev. 1 *et seq.* (1989), *727*

Human Rights Internet, Directory: Eastern Europe and the USSR (1987), *432*

Human Rights Watch, The Bush Administration's Record on Human Rights in 1989 (1990), *458*, ***527–33***

Human Rights Watch & Lawyers Committee for Human Rights, Critique: A Review of the Department of State's Country Reports on Human Rights Practices for 1987 (1988), *211, 500*

Human Rights Watch & Lawyers Committee for Human Rights, Critique: Review of the Department of State's Country Reports on Human Rights Practices for 1988 (1989), ***495–99, 523–26***

Implementation of the Helsinki Accords, Hearings Before Commission on Security and Cooperation in Europe, 99th Cong., 1st Sess. 5–9 (1985) (testimony of Ambassador Richard Schifter), ***434–37***

Industrial Research Unit, The Wharton School, Multinational Union Organizations in the Manufacturing Industries (1980), *48*

Inter-American Commission on Human Rights, 25 Years of Struggle for Human Rights in the Americas (1984), *288*

Inter-American Commission on Human Rights (IACHR), *Washington: Application of Death Penalty on Juveniles in the U.S./Violation of Human Rights Obligation Within the Inter-American System*, 8 Hum. Rts. L.J. 345 (1987), *272*

International Alert, Suriname (1988), *229*

International Commission of Jurists, The Events in East Pakistan 70 (1972), *81*

International Commission of Jurists, Human and Peoples' Rights in Africa and the African Charter (1986), *305*

International Commission of Jurists, Human Rights in Islam (1982), *357*

International Commission of Jurists, The Return of Democracy in Sudan 72–73 (1986), *333*

International Commission of Jurists, States of Emergency, Their Impact on Human Rights 426–27 (1983), *687*

International Commission of Jurists & Law in the Service of Man, Justice? The Military Court System in the Israeli Occupied Territories (1987), *693*

International Commission of Jurists & Law in the Service of Man, Twenty Years of Israeli Occupation of the West Bank and Gaza (1987), *693*

International Committee of the Red Cross, Annual Report 1985 (1986), *59*

International Committee of the Red Cross, *ICRC reacts to Israeli violations of Geneva Convention*, ICRC Bulletin No. 152, at 1 (September 1988), ***712***

International Committee of the Red Cross, *Israel and the Occupied Territories*, Annual Report (1988), ***708–12***

International Committee of the Red Cross, The Red Cross and Human Rights (1983), *708*

International Committee of the Red Cross and League of Red Cross Societies, International Red Cross Handbook (12th ed. 1983), *59*

International Institute of Higher Studies in Criminal Sciences, Draft Charter of Human and People's Rights in the Arab World (1987), *337*

International Institute of Human Rights, Pour une Commission d'etude sur la protection des droits de l'homme dans le context musulman (1971), *337*

International Institute of Human Rights, Sélection bibliographique des ouvrages concernant de droit en général et les droits de l'homme dans les pays islamiques (1971), *337*

International Labour Office, International Labour Standards (1982), *48*

Lachs, *Some Reflections on the Contribution of the International Court of Justice to the Development of International Law*, 10 Syracuse J. Int'l L. & Com. 239 (1983), *727*

E. Landy, The Effectiveness of International Supervision: Thirty Years of ILO Experience (1966), *253*

Lawyers Committee for Human Rights, The Detention of Asylum Seekers in the United States: A Cruel and Questionable Policy (1990), *255*

Lawyers Committee for Human Rights, Detention of Human Rights Workers and Lawyers from the West Bank and Gaza and Conditions of Detention in Ketziot (1988), *693*

Lawyers Committee for Human Rights, Human Rights and U.S. Foreign Policy: Bureaucracy and Diplomacy (1989), ***540, 541***

Lawyers Committee for Human Rights, Human Rights and U.S. Foreign Policy: Report and Recommendations (1988), *541*

Lawyers Committee for Human Rights, Linking Security Assistance and Human Rights (1989), *541*

Lawyers Committee for Human Rights, United States Policy Toward South Africa (1989), *541, 552*

Lawyers Committee for Human Rights, Worker Rights under the U.S. Trade Laws (1989), *516, 541*

V. Leary, International Labor Conventions and National Law: The Effectiveness of the Automatic Incorporation of Treaties in National Legal Systems (1982), *253*

Leary, *A New Role for Non-governmental Organizations in Human Rights: A Case Study of Non-governmental Participation in the Development of International Norms on Torture*, in UN Law/Fundamental Rights: Two Topics in International Law 197 (A. Cassese ed. 1979), *54*

Leblanc, *The ICJ, the Genocide Convention, and the United States*, Wisc. I.L.J. 43 (1987), *403*

Leblanc, *The Intent to Destroy Groups in the Genocide Convention: the Proposed U.S. Understanding*, 78 Am. J. Int'l L. 369 (1984), *403*

L. LeBlanc, The OAS and the Promotion and Protection of Human Rights (1977), *288*

Leckie, *The Inter-State Complaint Procedure in International Human Rights Law: Hopeful Prospects or Wishful Thinking?*, 10 Hum. Rts. Q. 249 (1988), *480*

Legal Reform in the Soviet Union, 28 Colum. J. Transnat'l L. 1 (1990), *462*

P. Leuprecht & P. van Dijk eds., Digest of Strasbourg Case-Law Relating to the European Convention on Human Rights (1984), *466*

Lillich, *The Constitution and International Human Rights*, 83 Am. J. Int'l L. 851 (1989), *680*

R. Lillich ed., International Human Rights Instruments (1986), *403*

R. Lillich, International Law of State Responsibility for Injuries to Aliens (1983), *49*

Lillich, *Invoking International Human Rights Law in Domestic Courts*, 54 Cin. L. Rev. 367 (1985), *573, 580, 582*

Lillich, *The United States Constitution and International Human Rights Law*, 3 Harv. Hum. Rts. J. 53 (1990), *573*

Lillich, *A United States Policy of Humanitarian Intervention and Intercession*, in Human Rights and American Foreign Policy 278, 287–90 (D. Kommers & G. Loescher eds. 1979), ***545–47***

R. Lillich & F. Newman, International Human Rights: Problems of Law & Policy (1979), *479, 582, 619, 620, 664*

Linde, *Comments*, 18 Int'l Lawyer 77 (1984), ***570–73***

Lippman, *Human Rights Revisited: The Protection of Human Rights under the International Covenant on Civil and Political Rights*, 10 Cal. W. Int'l L.J. 450 (1980), *70*

D. Little, J. Kelsay, & A. Sachedina, Human Rights and the Conflict of Cultures: Western and Islamic Perspectives on Religious Liberty (1988), *357*

L. Livezey, Nongovernmental Organizations and the Ideas of Human Rights (1988), *54*

Livezey, *US Religious Organizations and the International Human Rights Movement*, 11 Hum. Rts. Q. 14 (1989), *58*

Lobel, *The Limits of Constitutional Power: Conflicts between Foreign Policy and International Law*, 71 Va. L. Rev. 1071 (1985), *636*

Lockwood, *The U.N. Charter and United States Civil Rights Litigation: 1946–1955*, 69 Iowa L. Rev. 901 (1984), *578*

L. Louis-Jacques & S. Nevin, Human Rights in the Soviet Union and Eastern Europe, A Research Guide and Bibliography (1990), *419*

G. Lundestad, The Relationship Between Justice and Stability in Eastern Europe, Feb. 16, 1990, *462*

MacDonald, *Economic Sanctions in the International System*, (1969) Can. Y.B. Int'l L. 61, *253*

Mullerson, *Sources of International Law: New Tendencies in Soviet Thinking*, 83 Am. J. Int'l L. 494 (1989), *340*

J. Muravchik, The Uncertain Crusade: Jimmy Carter and the Dilemmas of Human Rights Policy (1986), *389, 510*

Nagan, *Economic Sanctions, U.S. Foreign Policy, International Law and the Anti-Apartheid Act of 1986*, 4 Florida Int'l L.J. 85 (1988), *56, 552*

Nahlik, *A Brief Outline of International Humanitarian Law*, 24 Int'l Rev. Red Cross 187 (1984), *688*

Nash, *Contemporary Practice of the United States Relating to International Law*, 75 Am. J. Int'l L. 142 (1981), *290*

Nasr, *The Concept and Reality of Freedom in Islam and Islamic Civilization*, in The Philosophy of Human Rights: International Perspectives 95 (Rosenbaum ed. 1980), *337*

NATO At 40, Senate Comm. on Foreign Relations, 101st Cong., 1st Sess. (1989), *439*

Newman, *Interpreting the Human Rights Clauses of the U.N. Charter*, 1972 Revue des Droits de l'Homme 283, *294, 582*

Newman, *Natural Justice, Due Process, and the New International Covenants on Human Rights: Prospectus*, 1967 Pub. L. 274, *294*

Newman, *The New United Nations Procedure for Human Rights Complaints: Reform, Status Quo, or Chamber of Horrors?*, 34 Annales des Droit 129 (1974), *140*

F. Newman & S. Surrey, Legislation: Cases and Materials (1955), *293*

Newman & Vasak, *Civil and Political Rights*, 1 The International Dimensions of Human Rights 135 (K. Vasak & P. Alston eds. 1982), *664, 688*

Newsom, *The Diplomacy of Human Rights: A Diplomat's View*, in The Diplomacy of Human Rights 3 (D. Newsom, ed. 1987), **541–44**

J. Nickel, Making Sense of Human Rights: Philosophical Reflections on the Universal Declaration of Human Rights (1987), *353*

Norris, *The Individual Petition Procedure of the Inter-American System for the Protection of Human Rights*, in Guide to International Human Rights Practice 108 (H. Hannum ed. 1984), *46, 288*

Norris, *Observations In Loco: Practice and Procedure of the Inter-American Commission on Human Rights, 1979–1983*, 19 Tex. Int'l L.J. 285 (1984), *239*

Note, *Constitutional Law: Equal Protection: Martinez v. Santa Clara Pueblo — Sexual Equality Under the Indian Civil Rights Act*, 6 Am. Indian L. Rev. 187 (1978), *68*

Note, *The Constitutional Right to Treatment in Light of Youngberg v. Rome*, 72 Geo. L.J. 785 (1984), *677*

Note, *CRIPA: The Failure of Federal Intervention for Mentally Retarded People*, 97 Yale L.J. 845 (1988), *677*

Note, *Economic Sanctions Against South Africa: Problems and Prospects for Enforcement of Human Rights Norms*, 22 Va. J. Int'l L. 345 (1982), *552*

Note, *Examination of the United States Prisoner Transfer Treaties*, 6 N.Y.L. Sch. J. Int'l & Comp. L. 709 (1986), *34*

Note, *Human Rights Practices in the Arab States: The Modern Impact of Shari'a Values*, 12 Ga. J. Int'l & Comp. L. 55 (1982), *337*

Note, *Mental Suffering Under Sentence of Death: A Cruel and Unusual Punishment*, 57 Iowa L. Rev. 814 (1972), *676*

Note, *The Nuremburg Principles: A Defense for Political Protesters*, 40 Hastings L.J. 397 (1989), *718*

Note, *Recent Israeli Security Measures Under the Fourth Geneva Convention*, 3 Conn. J. Int'l L. 485 (1988), **696–701**

Note, *The United States-Iran Hostage Agreement: A Study in Presidential Powers*, 15 Cornell Int'l L.J. 149 (1982), *45*

Nowak, *The Strained Human Rights Situation in Peru: Interview with Francisco Soberon Garrido, Coordinator of the Peruvian Human Rights Association APRODEH*, 6 Netherlands Q. Hum. Rts. 28 (No. 3, 1988), *190*

Nowak, *UN-Human Rights Committee: Survey of Decisions Given Up Till July 1986*, 7 Hum. Rts. L.J. 287 (1986), *70*

R. Nozick, Anarchy, State and Utopia (1974), *340*

D. O'Donnell, Protección Internacional de los Derechos Humanos (1989), *288*

Oliver, *Problems of Cognition and Interpretation in Applying Norms of Customary International Law of Human Rights in United States Courts*, 4 Hous. J. Int'l L. 59 (1981), *573*

Opekokew, *International Law, International Institutions, and Indigenous Issues*, in The Rights of Indigenous Peoples in International Law: Selected Essays on Self-Determination 1 (R. Thompson ed. 1987), *81*

Opekokew, *Self-Identification and Cultural Preservation: A Commentary On Recent Indian Act Amendments*, 2 Canadian Native L. Rep. 1 (1986), *81, 82*

Opsahl & de Zayas, *The Uncertain Scope of Article 15(1) of the International Covenant on Civil and Political Rights*, 1983 Canadian Hum. Rts. Y.B. 237, *70*

Orentlicher, *Bearing Witness: The Art and Science of Human Rights Fact-Finding*, 3 Harv. Hum. Rts. J. 83 (1990), *239*

Organization of American States, Inter-American Commission on Human Rights, 1977 Annual Report (1977), *611*

Palau: Islands' Quest for Autonomy Making Headway on Hill, Congressional Quarterly, August 19, 1989, at 2184, *200*

Paust, *Litigating Human Rights: A Commentary on the Comments*, 4 Hous. J. Int'l L. 81 (1981), *573*

Paust, *On Human Rights: the Use of Human Rights Precepts in U.S. History and the Right to an Effective Remedy in Domestic Courts*, 10 Mich. J. Int'l L. 543 (1989), *615*

Paust, *Self-Executing Treaties*, 82 Am. J. Int'l L. 760 (1983), *594*

Paust, *Transnational Freedom of Speech: Legal Aspects of the Helsinki Final Act*, 45 Law & Contemporary Prob. 53 (1982), *429*

J. Paust, G. Von Glahn, & G. Woratsch, Inquiry into the Israeli Military Court System in the Occupied West Bank and Gaza (1989), *693*

Pechota, *East European Perceptions of the Helsinki Final Act and the Role of Citizen Initiatives*, 13 Vanderbilt J. Trans. L. 467 (1980), *432*

C. Pei-heng, Nongovernmental Organizations at the United Nations: Identity, Role and Function (1981), *54*

Pentney, *Lovelace v. Canada: A Case Comment*, 5 Canadian Legal Aid Bulletin 259 (1982), *83*

Perkovich, *Soviet Jews and American Foreign Policy*, 5 World Policy J. 435 (1988), *57*

Perlez, *Nairobi Orders Closing of 2d Magazine in a Year*, N.Y. Times, May 10, 1989, at A7, cols. 2–7, *500*

Perluss & Hartman, *Temporary Refuge: Emergence of a Customary Norm*, 26 Va. J. Int'l L. 551 (1986), *594, 632*

Playfair, *Administrative Detention in the Israeli-Occupied West Bank*, 13 Studie-en Informatie-centrum Mensenrechten 5 (Feb. 1986), *693*

L. Polakiewicz & N. Davies, Solidarity Lives (1990), *432*

Pollis, *Liberal, Socialist, and Third World Perspectives of Human Rights*, in Toward a Human Rights Framework 1 (P. Schwab & A. Pollis eds. 1982), *339*

M. Pomerance, The Advisory Function of the International Court in the League and U.N. Eras (1973), *722*

D. Poneman, Argentina: Democracy on Trial (1987), *252*

Posner & Zavis, *Human Rights Priorities for a New Administration and Congress*, 28 Va. J. Int'l L. 893 (1988), *522*

D. Pratap, The Advisory Jurisdiction of the International Court (1972), *722*

Ptacek, *U.S. Protestants and Liberation Theology*, 30th Orbis 433 (1986), *58*

Puryear, *Higher Education, Development Assistance and Repressive Regimes*, 17 Stud. Int'l Development 1 (1982), *58*

B. Ramcharan, The Concept and Present Status of the International Protection of Human Rights (1989), *140*

B. Ramcharan ed., International Law and Fact-finding in the Field of Human Rights (1982), *239*

Randall, *Federal Questions and the Human Rights Paradigm*, 73 Minn. L. Rev. 349 (1988), *614*

J. Rawls, A Theory of Justice (1971), *340*

Reicin, *Preventive Detention, Curfews, Demolition of Houses and Deportations: An Analysis of Measures Employed by Israel in the Administered Territories*, 8 Cardozo L. Rev. 515 (1987), *721*

Reinke, *Treaty and Non-Treaty Human Rights Agreements: A Case Study of Freedom of Movement in East Germany*, 24 Columbia J. Trans. L. 647 (1986), *429*

Reisman, *American Human Rights Diplomacy: The Next Phase*, 28 Va. J. Int'l L. 899 (1988), *527*

Renteln, *The Unanswered Challenge of Relativism and the Consequences for Human Rights*, 7 Human Rts. Q. 514 (1985), *356*

Reoch, *"Disappearances" and the International Protection of Human Rights*, 36 Y.B. World Aff. 166 (1982), *174*

Report of the Argentine National Commission on the Disappeared, *Nunca Más*, (1986), *602, 606*

Riesenfeld, *The Doctrine of Self-Executing Treaties and Gatt: A Notable German Judgment*, 65 Am. J. Int'l L. 548 (1970), *580*

Riesenfeld, *The Doctrine of Self-Executing Treaties and U.S. v. Postal: Win at Any Price?*, 74 Am. J. Int'l L. 892 (1980), *580, 625*

Roberts, *Prolonged Military Occupation: The Israeli-Occupied Territories*, 84 Am. J. Int'l L. 44 (1990), *701*

A. Roberts, B. Joergensen, & F. Newman, Academic Freedom Under Israeli Military Occupation (1984), **693–96**

Robertson, *The Implementation System: International Measures*, in the International Bill of Rights: The Covenant on Civil and Political Rights 332 (L. Henkin ed. 1981), *70*

Rodley, *Human Rights and Humanitarian Intervention: The Case Law of the World Court*, 38 Int'l & Comp. L.Q. 321 (1989), *722*

Rodley, *On the Necessity of United States Ratification of the International Human Rights Conventions*, in U.S. Ratification of the Human Rights Treaties: With or Without Reservations? 3 (R. Lillich ed. 1981), **397–99**

N. Rodley, The Treatment of Prisoners Under International Law (1987), *160, 174, 189, 327, 333*

Rodley, *United Nations Action Procedures Against "Disappearances," Summary or Arbitrary Executions, and Torture*, 8 Hum. Rts. Q. 700 (1986), *160*

N. Ronzitti, Rescuing Nationals Abroad Through Military Coercion and Intervention on Grounds of Humanity (1985), *41, 547*

S. Rosenne, The Law and Practice of the International Court of Justice (2d ed. 1985), *625*

Rossiter & Smith, *Human Rights: The Carter Record, The Reagan Reaction*, Int'l Pol'y Rep., Sept. 1984, *510*

Rothberg, *Sections 402 and 403 of the Comprehensive Anti-Apartheid Act of 1986*, 22 George Washington J. Int'l L. & Econ. 117 (1988), *552*

Rovine, *Comments* in U.S. Ratification of the Human Rights Treaties: With or Without Reservations? 54 (R. Lillich ed. 1981), *396*

Roy & Alfredsson, *Indigenous Rights: the Literature Explosion*, 13 Transnat'l Persp. 19 (1987), *91*

B. Roy & D. Miller, The Rights of Indigenous Peoples in International Law: An Annotated Bibliography (1985), *90, 91*

B. Rudden, Basic Community Cases (1987), *438*

S. Rushdie, The Satanic Verses (1989), *356*

Said, *Human Rights in Islamic Perspectives*, in Human Rights: Culture and Ideological Perspectives 86 (A. Pollis & P. Schwab eds. 1979), *337*

Salzberg, *The Carter Administration and Human Rights*, in The Diplomacy of Human Rights 61 (D. Newsom ed. 1986), *544*

Sanders, *The UN Working Group on Indigenous Populations*, 11 Hum. Rts. Q. 406 (1989), *91, 253*

Sanford, *U.S. Policy Toward the Multilateral Development Banks: The Role of Congress*, 22 George Washington J. Int'l L. & Econ. 1 (1988), *545*

Schachter, *The Human Rights Provisions of the Helsinki Final Act: A Report on a Conference Convened by the Committee on International Human Rights*, 33 The Record 105 (1978), *429*

Schachter, *International Law in Theory and Practice: General Course in Public International Law*, 178 Collected Courses of the Hague Academy of International Law 1 (1982), *350*

Scharansky, Bonner, & Alekseyeva, *The Tenth Year of the Watch*, N.Y. Rev. Books, June 26, 1986, at 5, *430*

H. Schermers, Judicial Protection in the European Communities (3d ed. 1983), *438*

Schifter, *Building Firm Foundations: The Institutionalization of United States Human Rights Policy in the Reagan Years*, 2 Harv. Hum. Rts. Y.B. 3 (1989), *510*

R. Schifter, The Helsinki Process: Then and Now, January 29, 1990, *462*

Schifter, *U.S.-Soviet Quality of Life: A Comparison*, State Dept. Bureau of Public Affairs, Current Policy No. 713 (1985), **388, 389**

Schindler, *Human Rights and Humanitarian Law: The Interrelationship of the Laws*, 31 Am. U.L. Rev. 935 (1982), *688*

Schluter, *The Domestic Status of the Human Rights Clauses of the United Nations Charter*, 61 Calif. L. Rev. 110 (1973), *582*

C. Swinarski ed., Studies and essays on international humanitarian law and Red Cross principles (1984), *708*

Symposium on Human Rights: An Agenda For the New Administration, 28 Va. J. Int'l L. 827 (1988), *540*

Szabó, *Historical Foundations of Human Rights and Subsequent Developments*, in The International Dimensions of Human Rights 11 (K. Vasak & P. Alston eds. 1982), *340*

Szabó, *The Theoretical Foundations of Human Rights*, in International Protection of Human Rights (A. Eide & A. Schou eds. 1967), *337–39*

Szasz, *The International Legal Aspects of the Human Rights Program of the United States*, 12 Cornell Int'l L. J. 161 (1979), *552*

A. Szymanski, Human Rights in the Soviet Union (1984), *458*

M. Tardu, *The "Gross Violations" Procedure under Council Resolution 1503 (LVII)* in 1 Human Rights: International Petition System 25 (1985), *140*

Tardu, *United Nations Response to Gross Violations of Human Rights: The 1503 Procedure*, 20 Santa Clara L. Rev. 567 (1980), *140*

Taubenfield & Taubenfield, *The Economic Weapon: the League and the United Nations*, 58 Am. Soc. Int'l L. Proc. 183 (1964), *253*

Taylor, *Nuremberg Trials, War Crimes and International Law*, International Conciliation 242 (No. 450, April 1949), *718*

F. Tesón, Humanitarian Intervention: An Inquiry into Law and Morality (1988), *547*

Tesón, *International Human Rights and Cultural Relativism*, 25 Va. J. Int'l L. 869 (1985), *357*

Thyden, *An Inside View of United States Foreign Policy Under the Reagan Administration*, 7 Whittier L. Rev. 705 (1985), *544*

H. Thoolen & B. Verstappen, Human Rights Missions: A Study of the Fact-finding Practice of Non-governmental Organizations (1986), *239*

Tolley, *The Concealed Crack in the Citadel: The United Nations Commission on Human Rights' Response to Confidential Communications*, 6 Hum. Rts. Q. 420 (1984), *121, 140*

Tolley, *International Human Rights Law in U.S. Courts, Public Interest Groups and Private Attorneys*, 1987 Annual Meeting, American Political Science Association, *680*

H. Tolley, The U.N. Commission on Human Rights (1987), *140, 319*

K. Tomashevski, Development Aid and Human Rights (1989), *516*

K. Tomashevski, Foreign Aid and Human Rights: Case Studies of Bangladesh and Kenya (1988), *517*

K. Tomashevski, The Right to Food (1987), *408*

R. Toscano, Soviet Human Rights Policy and Perestroika (1989), *458*

L. Tribe, American Constitutional Law (2d ed. 1988), *621*

Trubek, *Economic, Social, and Cultural Rights in The Third World: Human Rights Law and Human Needs Programs*, in Human Rights in International Law: Legal and Policy Issues 205 (T. Meron ed. 1984), *363–65*

Trusteeship Council told 'overwhelming majority' in Palau wants 'free association' status, UN Chronicle, September 1989, at 28–30, *200*

Tushnet, *An Essay on Rights*, 62 Tex. L. Rev. 1363 (1984), *344*

U.S., Congressional Presentation for Security Assistance Programs, Fiscal Year 1990 (1989), *31*

U.S. Army Field Manual 27–10, The Law of Land Warfare 498 (1956), *717*

U.S., Fulfilling Promise, Signs 11-Year Old Rights Pacts at U.N., N.Y. Times, Oct. 6, 1977, at A2, col. 5, *659*

U.S. Helsinki Watch Committee, The Moscow Helsinki Monitors: Their Vision, Their Achievement, the Price They Paid (1986), *432*

U.S. Helsinki Watch Committee, Soviet Abuse of Psychiatry for Political Purposes: A Helsinki Watch Report Update (1988), *458*

U.S. Helsinki Watch Committee, Ten Years Later: Violations of the Helsinki Accords (1985), *458*

U.S. Helsinki Watch Committee, Violations of the Helsinki Accords, Romania: A Report Prepared for the Helsinki Review Conference (1986), *462*

United Movement for Democracy in Kenya, Moi's Reign of Terror (1989), *500*

United Nations Action in the Field of Human Rights, U.N. Doc. ST/HR/2/Rev.3 (1988), *140*

United Nations Centre for Human Rights, Communications Procedures, Fact Sheet No. 7 (1989), *118, 130, 140*

United Nations Centre for Human Rights, Enforced or Involuntary Disappearances, Fact Sheet No. 6 (1989), *174*

United Nations Centre for Human Rights, Human Rights Machinery, Fact Sheet No. 1 (1988) (updated to February 1990), *4-17, 99, 100, 326*

G. Urban, Social and Economic Rights in the Soviet Bloc: A Documentary Review Seventy Years after the Bolshevik Revolution (1988), *434*

van Boven, *Creative and Dynamic Strategies for Using United Nations Institutions and Procedures: The Frank Newman File* in New Directions in Human Rights 215 (E. Lutz, H. Hannum, & K. Burke eds. 1989), *141*

van Boven, *Survey of the Positive International Law of Human Rights*, in The International Dimensions of Human Rights 107 (K. Vasak & P. Alston eds. 1982), *620*

P. van Dijk & G. van Hoof, Theory and Practice of the European Convention of Human Rights (1984), *466*

van Dyke, *Prospects for the Development of Intergovernmental Human Rights Bodies in Asia and the Pacific*, in New Directions in Human Rights 51 (E. Lutz, H. Hannum, & K. Burke eds. 1989), *303*

Vance, *Human Rights and Foreign Policy*, 7 Ga. J. Int'l & Comp. L.J. 223 (1977), *389*

Vance, *The Human Rights Imperative*, 63 Foreign Policy 3 (1986), *509*

Vargas, *Individual Access to the Inter-American Court of Human Rights*, 1 Int'l L. & Pol. 601 (1984), *297*

Vargas, *Visits on the Spot: The Experience of the Inter-American Commission on Human Rights*, in International Law and Fact-Finding in the Field of Human Rights 137–50 (B. Ramcharan ed. 1982), ***229–33***

B. Verstappen, Human Rights Reports: An Annotated Bibliography of Fact-Finding Missions (1987), *240*

G. von Glahn, Law Among Nations: An Introduction to Public International Law (5th ed. 1986), *49*

G. von Glahn, The Occupation of Enemy Territory (1957), *701*

von Potobsky, *On-the-Spot Visits: An Important Cog in the ILO's Supervisory Machinery*, 120 Int'l Labour Rev. 581 (1981), *240*

Washington Post, July 28, 1987, at A-27, *499*

Watch Committees & Lawyers Committee for Human Rights, Critique: Review of the Department of State's Country Reports on Human Rights Practices for 1985 (1986), *211*

Watson, *Normativity and Reality in International Human Rights Law*, 13 Stetson L. Rev. 221 (1984), *350*

Weissbrodt, *The Contribution of International Nongovernmental Organizations to the Protection of Human Rights*, in Human Rights in International Law: Legal and Policy Issues 403 (T. Meron ed. 1984), *54*

Weissbrodt, *Ethical Problems of an International Human Rights Law Practice*, 7 Mich. Y.B. Int'l Legal Stud. 217 (1985), *267, 680*

Weissbrodt, *Execution of Juvenile Offenders by the United States Violates International Human Rights Law*, 3 Am. U. J. Int'l L. & Pol'y 339 (1987), *272*

Weissbrodt, *Human Rights Legislation and U.S. Foreign Policy*, 7 Ga. J. Int'l & Comp. L. 231 (1977), *209, 521*

Weissbrodt, *International Factfinding in Regard to Torture*, 57 Nordic J. Int'l L. 151 (1988), *240*

Weissbrodt, *International Legal Action Against Apartheid*, 4 Law & Inequality J. 485 (1986), *552*

Weissbrodt, *International Trial Observers*, 18 Stan. J. Int'l L. 27 (1982), *240, 253*

Weissbrodt, *The Role of International Nongovernmental Organizations in the Implementation of Human Rights*, 12 Texas J. Int'l L. 293 (1977), *54*

Weissbrodt, *The Role of International Organizations in the Implementation of Human Rights and Humanitarian Law in Situations of Armed Conflict*, 21 Vand. J. Transnat'l L. 313 (1988), *182, 688*

Weissbrodt, *Strategies for Selection and Pursuit of International Human Rights Objectives*, 8 Yale J. World Pub. Ord. 62 (1981), *680*

Weissbrodt, *The Three "Theme" Special Rapporteurs of the UN Commission on Human Rights*, 80 Am. J. Int'l L. 685 (1986), ***156–60, 480***

Weissbrodt, *United States Ratification of the Human Rights Covenants*, 63 Minn. L. Rev. 35 (1978), 402, ***590, 591***

Weissbrodt & Andrus, *The Right to Life During Armed Conflict: Disabled Peoples' International v. United States*, 29 Harv. Int'l L.J. 59 (1988), *272*

Weissbrodt & Mahoney, *International Legal Action Against Apartheid*, 4 Law & Ineq. J. 485 (1986), *728*

Weissbrodt & McCarthy, *Fact-Finding by International Nongovernmental Human Rights Organizations*, 22 Va. J. Int'l L. 7 (1981), *202–08, 211, 233*

Weston, *The Place of Foreign Treaties in the Courts of the United States: A Reply to Louis Henkin*, 101 Harv. L. Rev. 511 (1987), *594*

Weston, *U.S. Ratification of the International Covenant on Economic, Social and Cultural Rights: With or Without Qualifications*, in U.S. Ratification of the Human Rights Treaties: With or Without Reservations? 27 (R. Lillich ed. 1981), *392–96*

Weston, Lukes, & Hnatt, *Regional Human Rights Regimes: A Comparison and Appraisal*, 20 Vand. J. Transnat'l L. 585 (1987), *288, 305, 466*

R. Wetzel, *Introduction*, The Vienna Convention of the Law of Treaties, Travaux Préparatoires 12 (1978), *291*

Whisman, *Selected Bibliography: Articles and Cases on International Human Rights Law in Domestic Courts*, 18 International Lawyer 83 (1984), *680*

M. Whiteman, Digest of International Law (1970), *589*

G. Willemin & R. Heacock, The International Committee of the Red Cross (1984), *59*

M. Winston, The Philosophy of Human Rights (1989), *340*

Wiseberg & Scoble, *Monitoring Human Rights Violations: The Role of NGOs*, in Human Rights and American Foreign Policy 179 (D. Kommers & G. Loescher eds. 1979), *54*

C. Wright, The Law of Federal Courts (4th ed. 1983), *621*

Yamane, *Approaches to Human Rights in Asia*, in International Enforcement of Human Rights 99 (R. Bernhardt & J. Jolowicz eds. 1987), *303*

E. Yambrusic, Treaty Interpretation: Theory and Reality (1987), *294*

Zalaquett, *Confronting Human Rights Violations Committed by Former Governments: Principles Applicable and Political Constraints*, in State Crimes: Punishment or Pardon 23 (A. Henkin ed. 1989), *252*

T. Zuidwijk, Petitioning the United Nations (1982), *141*

TREATIES

African [Banjul] Charter on Human and Peoples' Rights, OAU Doc. CAB/LEG/67/3 rev. 5, 21 I.L.M. 58 (1982), *entered into force* Oct. 21, 1986, *304*

Agreement for the Prosecution and Punishment of the Major War Criminals of the European Axis, Aug. 8, 1945, 58 Stat. 1544, E.A.S. No. 472, 82 U.N.T.S. 280, **715**

American Convention on Human Rights, O.A.S. Off. Rec. OEA/Ser.L./V/II.23, doc. 21, rev. 6 (1979), *entered into force* July 18, 1978, *360, 402, 731*

Charter of the Organization of African Unity, 479 U.N.T.S. 39, *entered into force* Sept. 13, 1963, *304*

Convention Against Torture and Other Cruel, Inhuman and Degrading Treatment or Punishment, G.A. res. 39/46, 39 U.N. GAOR Supp. (No. 51) at 197, U.N. Doc. A/39/51 (1984), *entered into force* June 26, 1987, *325, 401, 574, 613*

Convention on the Abolition of Forced Labour (ILO No. 105), 320 U.N.T.S. 291, *entered into force* Jan. 17, 1959, *401*

Convention on the Consent to Marriage, Minimum Age for Marriage and Registration of Marriages, 521 U.N.T.S. 231, *entered into force* Dec. 9, 1964, *401*

Convention on the Elimination of All Forms of Discrimination against Women, *entered in force* Sept. 3, 1981, G.A. res. 34/180, U.N. GAOR Supp. (No. 46) at 193, U.N. Doc. A/34/46 (1980), *reprinted in* 19 I.L.M. 33 (1980), **97–98**, *99, 401*

Convention on the Political Rights of Women, 193 U.N.T.S. 135, *entered into force* July 7, 1954, *401*

Convention on the Prevention and Punishment of the Crime of Genocide, 78 U.N.T.S. 277, *entered into force* Jan. 12, 1951, *401, 722*

Convention on the Privileges and Immunities of the United Nations, 1 U.N.T.S. 15, 21 U.S.T. 1418, T.I.A.S. 6900, *entered into force* Sept. 17, 1946, *730*

Convention on the Rights of the Child, G.A. res. 44/25, 28 I.L.M. 1448 (1989), *569*

Convention Respecting the Laws and Customs of War on Land (Hague Convention No. IV), 36 Stat. 2277, T.S. 539, *entered into force* Jan. 26, 1910, **712–14**

European Convention for the Prevention of Torture and Inhuman or Degrading Treatment or Punishment, Doc. No. H(87)4 (1987), *entered into force* Feb. 1, 1989, *463*

[European] Convention for the Protection of Human Rights and Fundamental Freedoms, 213 U.N.T.S. 222 (1950), *entered into force* Sept. 3, 1953, *463*

European Social Charter, E.T.S. 35, *entered into force* Feb. 26, 1965, *463*

Geneva Convention for the Amelioration of the Condition of the Wounded and Sick in Armed Forces in the Field, 6 U.S.T. 3114, T.I.A.S. No. 3362, 75 U.N.T.S. 31 [hereinafter cited as First Geneva Convention], *332, 401, 684, 688*

Geneva Convention for the Amelioration of the Condition of Wounded, Sick and Shipwrecked Members of the Armed Forces at Sea, 6 U.S.T. 3217, T.I.A.S. No. 3363, 75 U.N.T.S. 85 [Second Geneva Convention], *332, 401, 684*

Geneva Convention Relative to the Treatment of Prisoners of War, 6 U.S.T. 3316, T.I.A.S. No. 3364, 75 U.N.T.S. 135 [Third Geneva Convention], *entered into force* Oct. 21, 1950, *332, 684, 688, **701–06***

Geneva Convention for the Protection of Civilian Persons in Time of War, 6 U.S.T. 3516, T.I.A.S. No. 3365, 75 U.N.T.S. 287 [Fourth Geneva Convention], *entered into force* Oct. 21, 1950, *332, 401, 584, 585, 684, 688, **701–06***

Geneva Convention of 1864 for the Amelioration of the Condition of the Wounded and Sick in Armies in the Field, T.S. 377, 22 Stat. 940, *entered into force* June 22, 1865, *684*

Geneva Protocol for the Prohibition of the Use in War of Asphyxiating, Poisonous or Other Gases, and of Bacteriological Methods of Warfare, 26 U.S.T. 571, T.I.A.S. 8061, 94 L.N.T.S. 65, *entered in force* Feb. 8, 1928, *684*

Hague Convention for the Pacific Settlement of Disputes of 1907, 36 Stat. 2199, T.S. No. 536, *208*

Inter-American Convention on the Granting of Political Rights to Women, 27 U.S.T. 3301, *entered into force* Apr. 22, 1949, *401*

International Convention on the Elimination of All Forms of Racial Discrimination, 660 U.N.T.S. 195, *entered into force* Jan. 4, 1969, *70, 401*

International Covenant on Civil and Political Rights, G.A. res. 2200A (XXI), 21 U.N. GAOR Supp. (No.16) at 52, U.N. Doc. A/6316 (1966), 999 U.N.T.S. 717, *entered into force* Mar. 23, 1976, *2, 69, 308, 401, **568, 583**, 590, 606, 610, 617, 619, 633, 688, passim*

International Covenant on Economic, Social and Cultural Rights, Dec. 16, 1966, G.A. res. 2200A (XXI), 21 U.N. GAOR Supp. (No. 16), U.N. Doc. A/6316 (1966), 993 U.N.T.S. 3, *entered into force* Jan. 3, 1976., *2, 3, 360, 401, passim*

International Labour Organisation, Convention Concerning Indigenous and Tribal Peoples in Independent Countries (No. 169), *91*

North Atlantic Treaty, 34 U.N.T.S. 243 (1949), *entered into force* August 24, 1949, *411, 438*

O.A.S. Charter, 119 U.N.T.S. 3, *entered into force* Dec. 13, 1951, *amended* 721 U.N.T.S. 324, *entered into force* Feb. 27, 1970, *360, 401, 575, **580–81***

Optional Protocol to the International Covenant on Civil and Political Rights, Dec. 16, 1966, G.A. res. 2200A (XXI), 21 U.N. GAOR Supp. (No. 16), U.N. Doc. A/6316 (1966), 999 U.N.T.S. 302, *entered into force* Mar. 23, 1976, *2, 70, **73–75**, 172*

Protocol Additional to the Geneva Conventions of 12 August 1949 Relating to the Protection of Victims of International Armed Conflicts (Protocol I), U.N. Doc. A/32/144, Annex I, 16 I.L.M. 1391 (1977), *entered into force* Dec. 7, 1978, *402, 685, 706*

Protocol Additional to the Geneva Conventions of 12 August 1949, and Relating to the Protection of Victims of Non-International Armed Conflicts (Protocol II), U.N. Doc. A/32/144, Annex II, 16 I.L.M. 1442 (1977), *entered into force* Dec. 7, 1978, *402, 685, 688*

Protocol Amending the Slavery Convention, 182 U.N.T.S. 51, *entered into force* Dec. 7, 1953, *400*

Protocol Relating to the Status of Refugees, 606 U.N.T.S. 268, 19 U.S.T. 6223, T.I.A.S. No. 6577, *entered into force* Oct. 4, 1967, *401, 591–92, 668*

Slavery Convention, 46 Stat. 2183, *entered into force* Dec. 7, 1927, *400*

Statute of the International Court of Justice, 59 Stat. 1031, *entered into force* Oct. 24, 1945, *574, 619, **723–24***

Supplementary Convention on the Abolition of Slavery, the Slave Trade and Institutions and Practices Similar to Slavery, 226 U.N.T.S. 3, *entered into force* April 30, 1957, *401*

U.N. Charter, June 26, 1945, 59 Stat. 1031, T.S. 993, *entered into force* Oct. 24, 1945, *2, 109, 360, 575, 599, 721, passim*

U.S. Prisoner Transfer Treaties with Bolivia, Canada, France, Republic of Korea, Mexico, Panama, Turkey, Western Europe (multilateral treaty), *34*

Vienna Convention on Consular Relations, 21 U.S.T. 77, T.I.A.S. No. 6820, 596 U.N.T.S. 261,

SUBJECT INDEX

References are to Pages in the Preface and Chapters 1-13

Central Intelligence Agency (CIA), 729
CENTRE FOR HUMAN RIGHTS, U.N., 3, 12–13, 118, 729–30
See U.N.
Chemical weapons, 137
Child, rights of, 3, 4, 270, 385, 390
See Beijing Rules; Convention on the Rights of the Child; Minimum Rules for the Administration
    of Juvenile Justice
Chile, 6, 32, 113, 124–26, 131, 133, 139, 151–52, 158–59, 240, 250, 319, 523, 549, 550, 641,
    645–50
China, People's Republic of, 89, 104, 137, 237, 524–25, 528, 576
China, Republic of (See Republic of China)
Civil rights actions, 561, 564. 578
Civil Rights of Institutionalized Persons Act (CRIPA), 677
Clothing, right to, 3, 378, 669
Code of Conduct for Law Enforcement Officials, 447
Colombia, 37, 131, 136, 172, 190, 231–32, 248, 523, 531
Colville, Lord, 240–42
COMMISSION OF THE CHURCHES ON INTERNATIONAL AFFAIRS, 51
See World Council of Churches
COMMISSION ON HUMAN RIGHTS, U.N.
  In general, 3, 5–6, 12, 53, 109, 113, 121, 125–40, 147–53, 240–43, 249–52, 254, 368, 376, 532–
    33, 730
Working Group on the Draft Body of Principles and Guarantees for the Protection of Mentally-
    Ill Persons and for the Improvement of Mental Health Care, 678
Commission on the Status of Women, 3, 5, 7–8, 99–100, 130
COMMITTEE AGAINST TORTURE
  In general, 3, 11–12, 13, 325–26
Rules, 209
See Convention against Torture and Other Cruel, Inhuman or Degrading Treatment or Punishment
Committee on Crime Prevention and Control, 160
COMMITTEE ON ECONOMIC, SOCIAL AND CULTURAL RIGHTS
  In general, 3, 10–11, 13, 16, 360, 375–85
Committee on the Elimination of All Forms of Racial Discrimination (CERD), 3, 8–9, 13, 70–71
Committee on the Elimination of Discrimination against Women (CEDAW), 3, 11, 99
COMMUNICATIONS
  In general, 13, 110–11, 113–25, 130, 172, 249–52
Human Rights Committee, 70–74
Inter-American Commission on Human Rights, 272–79, 281–88
Sub-Commission Working Group on Communications, 7, 118–19, 249–50
UNESCO, 15
See Committee against Torture; Confidentiality; ECOSOC resolution 728F; ECOSOC resolution
    1235; ECOSOC resolution 1503; Human Rights Committee
Comoros, 159
Compensation, 277, 317
CONFERENCE ON SECURITY AND COOPERATION IN EUROPE (CSCE; Helsinki process),
  In general, 388, 411–56, 480, 481, 483, 517
Role of nongovernmental organizations, 451
See Helsinki Final Act
CONFIDENTIALITY, 118–21, 123–25, 142–43, 171, 249, 325
See ECOSOC resolution 1503; Communicatins
CONFLICT OF LAWS
Choice of law, 651–54
Damages, 651–54
Congress on the Prevention of Crime and the Treatment of Offenders, 14, 657